P9-AQL-468

黒鷺死体宅配便

the KUROSAGI corpse delivery service

黒鷺死体宅配便
the KUROSAGI corpse delivery service

DARK HORSE MANGA

story
EIJI OTSUKA

art
HOUSUI YAMAZAKI

original cover design
BUNPEI YORIFUJI

translation
TOSHIFUMI YOSHIDA
AND **TAYLOR ENGEL**

editor and english adaptation
CARL GUSTAV HORN

lettering and touchup
IHL

OMNIBUS EDITION

SPECIAL NOTE

This omnibus collects **the KUROSAGI corpse delivery service** volumes 7–9. Because each individual volume has a numbered sound FX glossary and story notes section at its end, the original page numbers have been kept for this omnibus, so the page numbers start over again at the beginning of each volume.

黒鷺死体宅配便
the KUROSAGI corpse delivery service

7

story
EIJI OTSUKA

art
HOUSUI YAMAZAKI

original cover design
BUNPEI YORIFUJI

translation
TAYLOR ENGEL and TOSHIFUMI YOSHIDA

editor and english adaptation
CARL GUSTAV HORN

lettering and touch-up
IHL

DARK HORSE MANGA

contents

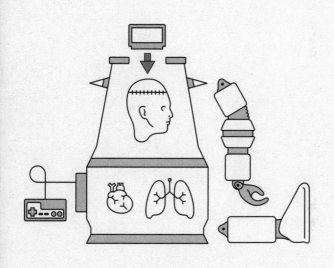

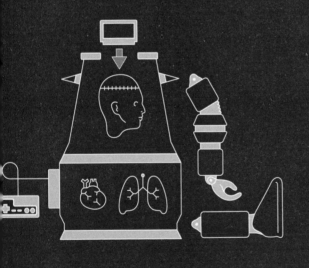

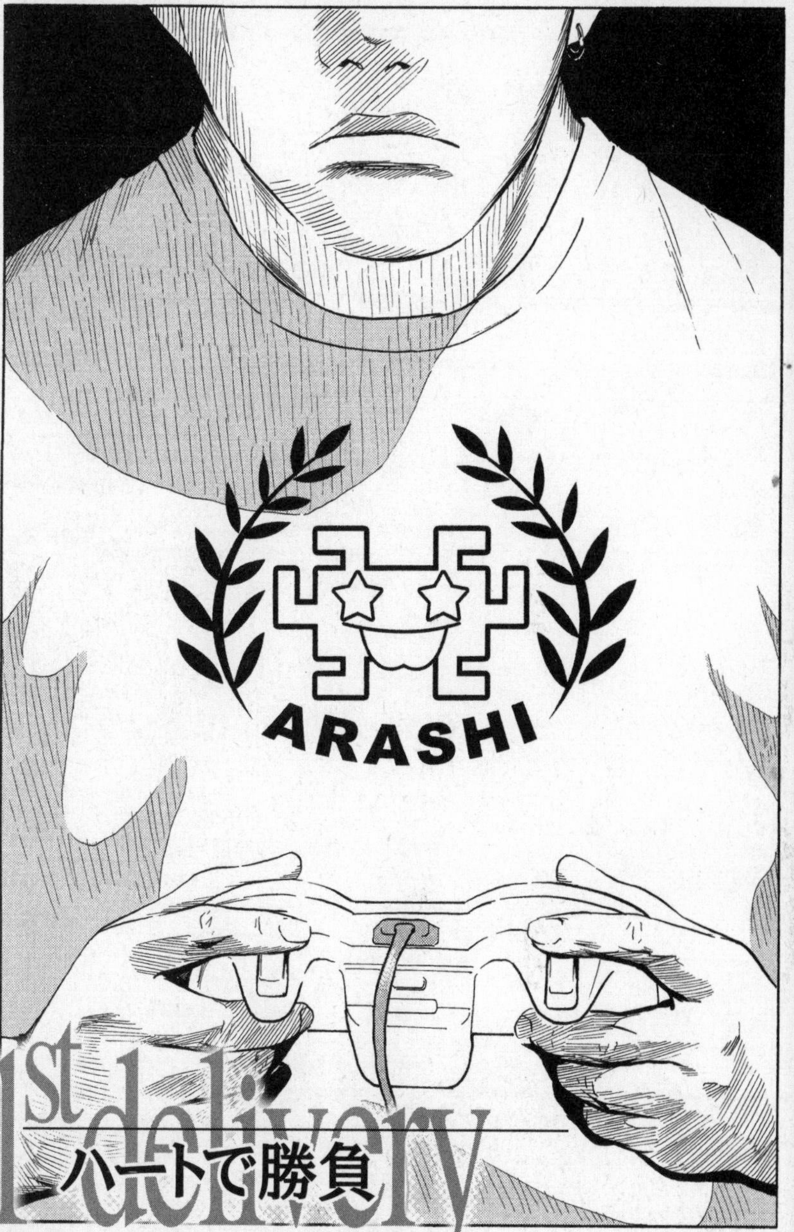
ARASHI

1st delivery ハートで勝負

fight with my heart

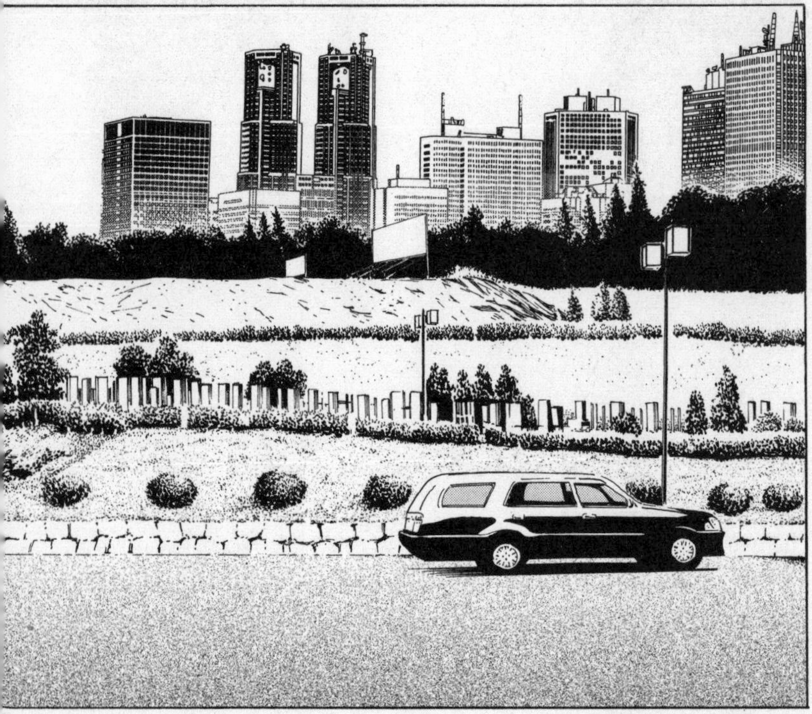

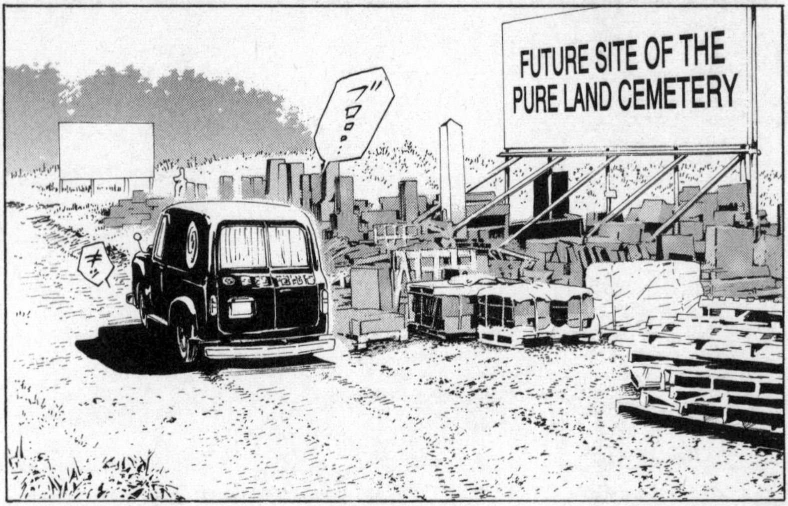
FUTURE SITE OF THE
PURE LAND CEMETERY
ブロロ…
キッ

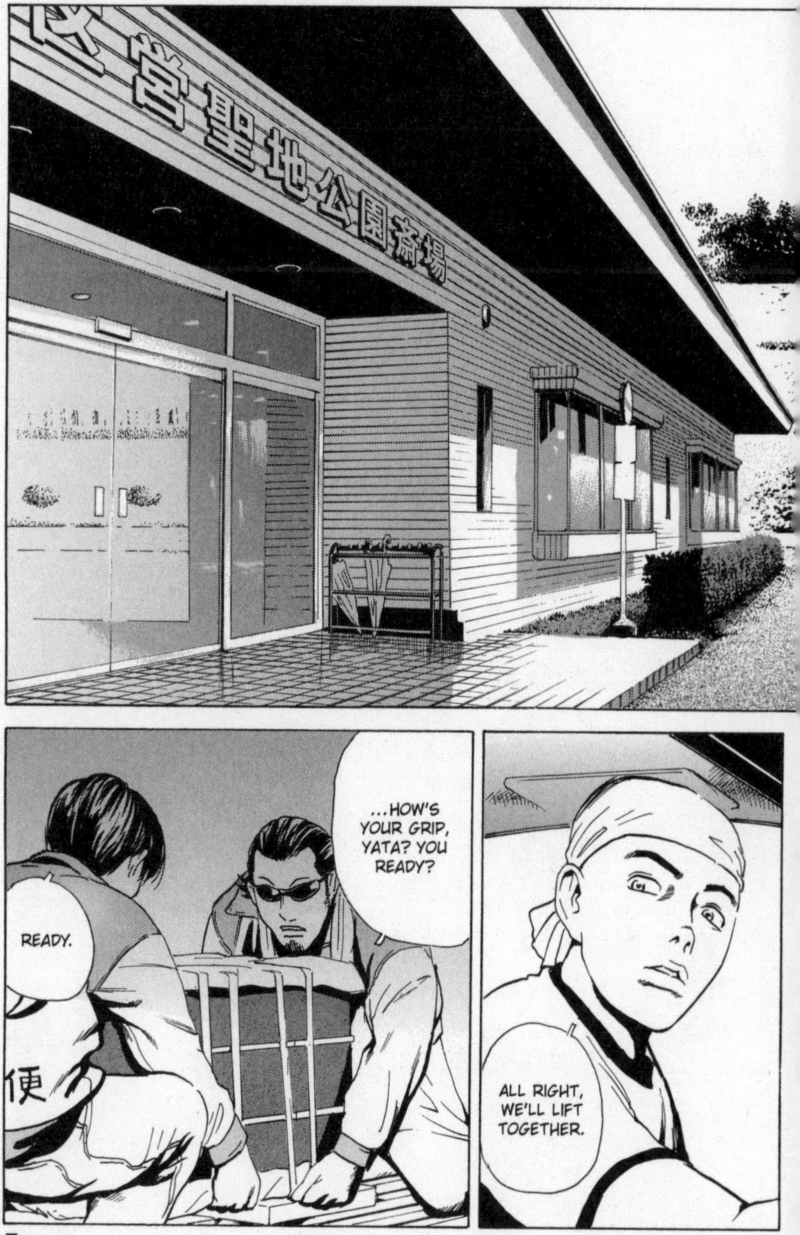
営聖地公園斎場
ALL RIGHT, WE'LL LIFT TOGETHER.
...HOW'S YOUR GRIP, YATA? YOU READY?
READY.
便

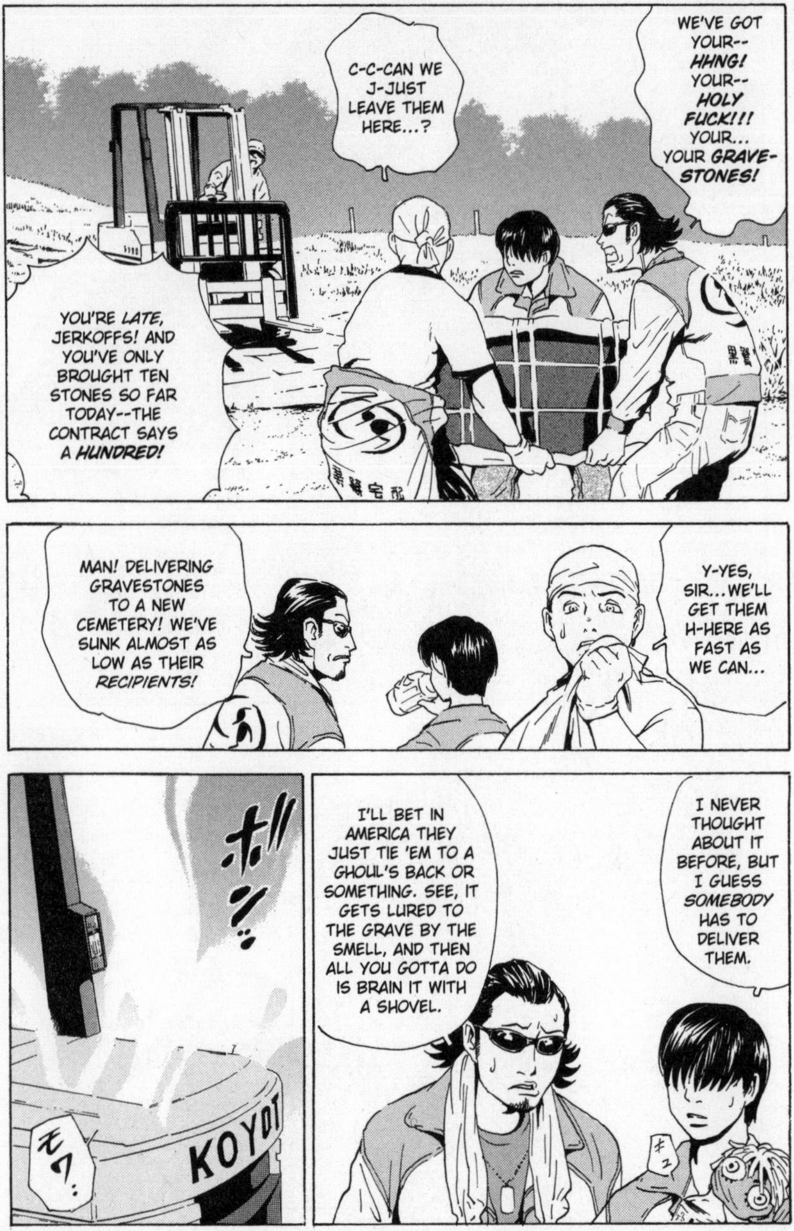
WE'VE GOT YOUR-- HHNG! YOUR-- HOLY FUCK!!! YOUR... YOUR GRAVESTONES!
C-C-CAN WE J-JUST LEAVE THEM HERE...?
YOU'RE LATE, JERKOFFS! AND YOU'VE ONLY BROUGHT TEN STONES SO FAR TODAY--THE CONTRACT SAYS A HUNDRED!
Y-YES, SIR...WE'LL GET THEM H-HERE AS FAST AS WE CAN...
MAN! DELIVERING GRAVESTONES TO A NEW CEMETERY! WE'VE SUNK ALMOST AS LOW AS THEIR RECIPIENTS!
I NEVER THOUGHT ABOUT IT BEFORE, BUT I GUESS SOMEBODY HAS TO DELIVER THEM.
I'LL BET IN AMERICA THEY JUST TIE 'EM TO A GHOUL'S BACK OR SOMETHING. SEE, IT GETS LURED TO THE GRAVE BY THE SMELL, AND THEN ALL YOU GOTTA DO IS BRAIN IT WITH A SHOVEL.
KOYOT

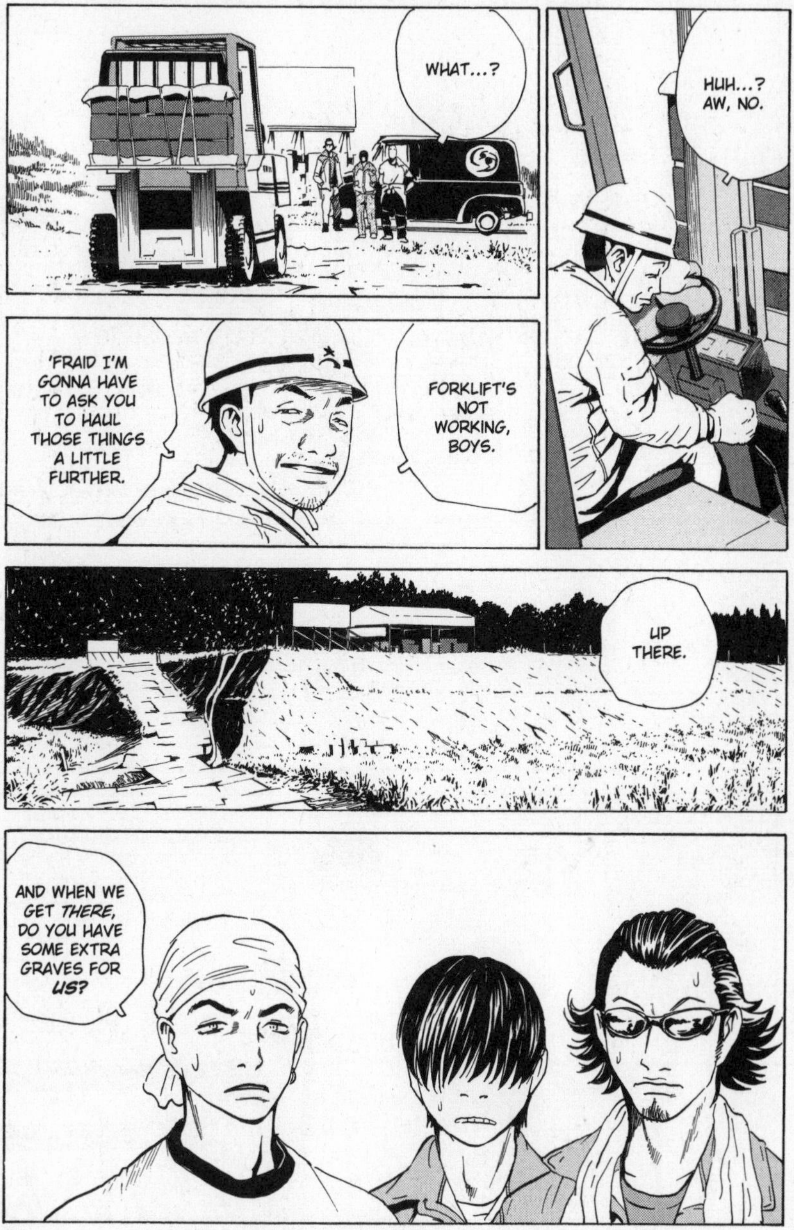
HUH...? AW, NO.
WHAT...?
FORKLIFT'S NOT WORKING, BOYS.
'FRAID I'M GONNA HAVE TO ASK YOU TO HAUL THOSE THINGS A LITTLE FURTHER.
UP THERE.
AND WHEN WE GET *THERE*, DO YOU HAVE SOME EXTRA GRAVES FOR *US?*

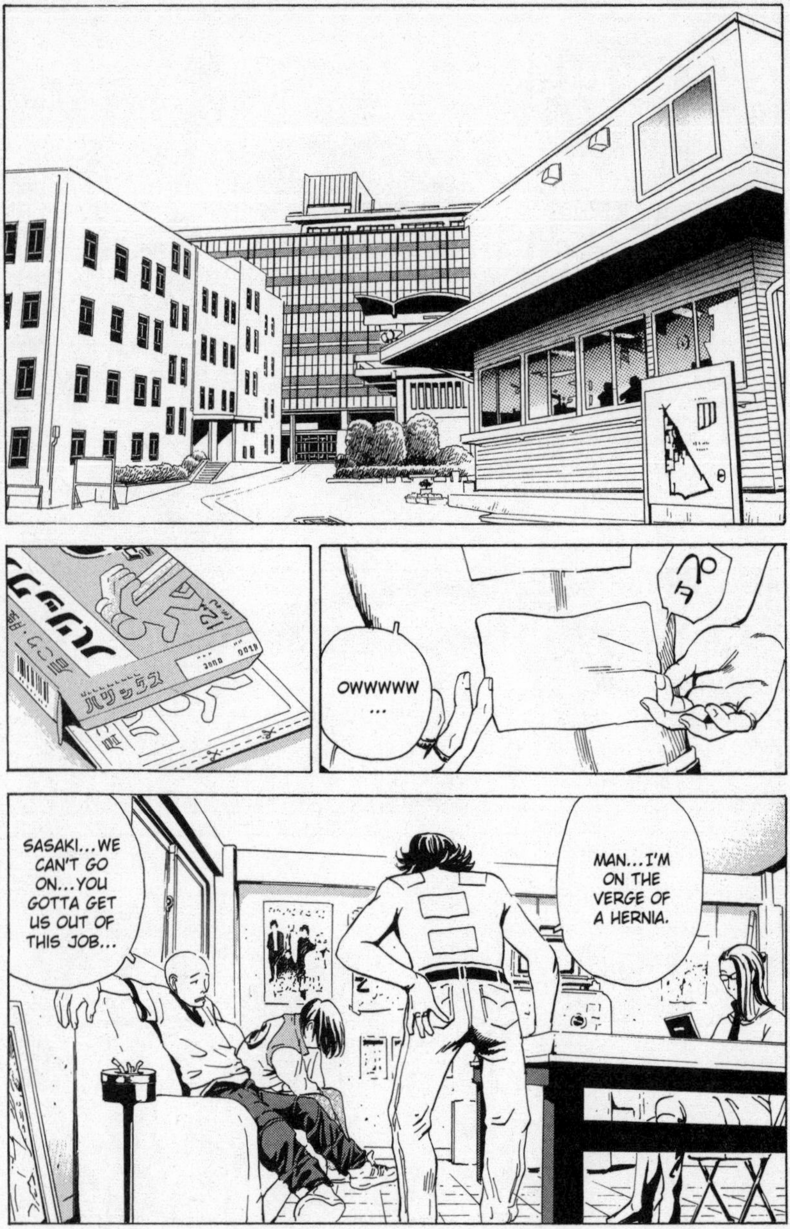
ペタ
OWWWWW ...
MAN...I'M ON THE VERGE OF A HERNIA.
SASAKI...WE CAN'T GO ON...YOU GOTTA GET US OUT OF THIS JOB...

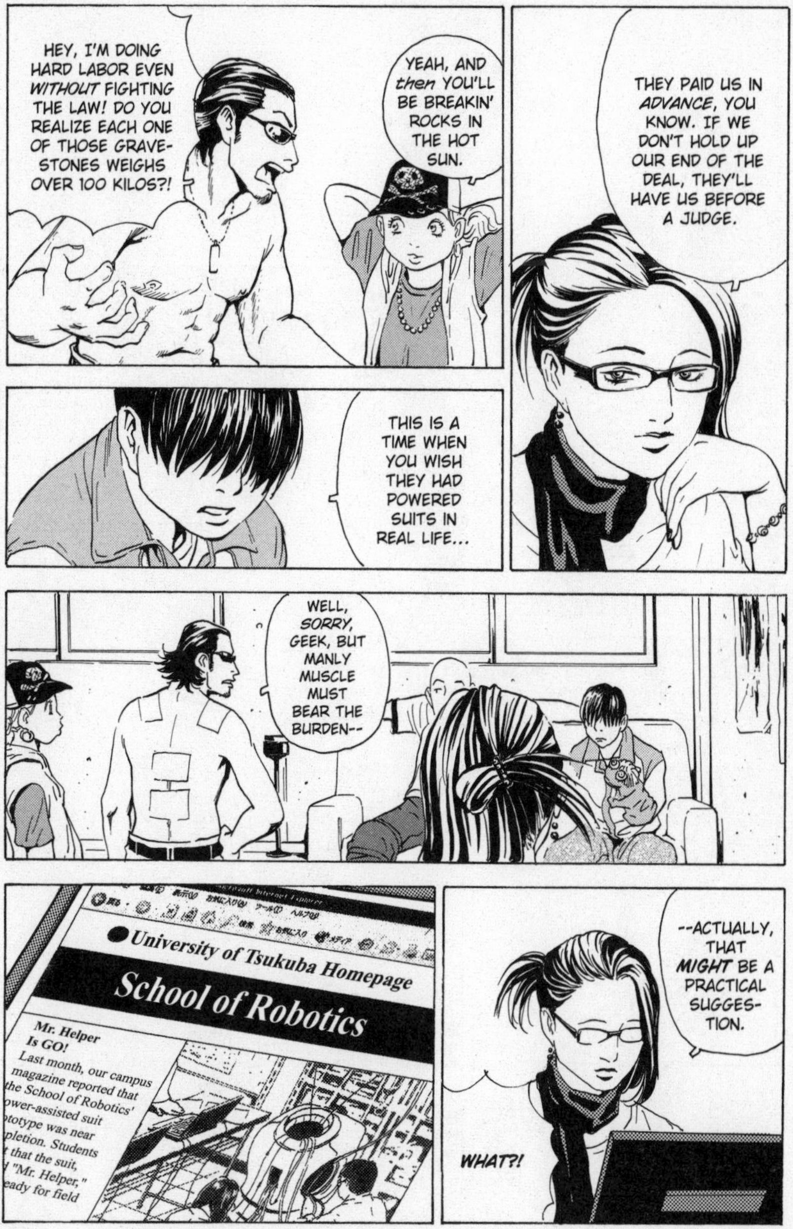
THEY PAID US IN *ADVANCE*, YOU KNOW. IF WE DON'T HOLD UP OUR END OF THE DEAL, THEY'LL HAVE US BEFORE A JUDGE.
HEY, I'M DOING HARD LABOR EVEN *WITHOUT* FIGHTING THE LAW! DO YOU REALIZE EACH ONE OF THOSE GRAVE-STONES WEIGHS OVER 100 KILOS?!
YEAH, AND *then* YOU'LL BE BREAKIN' ROCKS IN THE HOT SUN.
THIS IS A TIME WHEN YOU WISH THEY HAD POWERED SUITS IN REAL LIFE...
WELL, *SORRY*, GEEK, BUT MANLY MUSCLE MUST BEAR THE BURDEN--
--ACTUALLY, THAT ***MIGHT*** BE A PRACTICAL SUGGES-TION.
WHAT?!
University of Tsukuba Homepage
School of Robotics
Mr. Helper Is GO!
Last month, our campus magazine reported that the School of Robotics' ower-assisted suit ototype was near pletion. Students t that the suit, l "Mr. Helper," eady for field

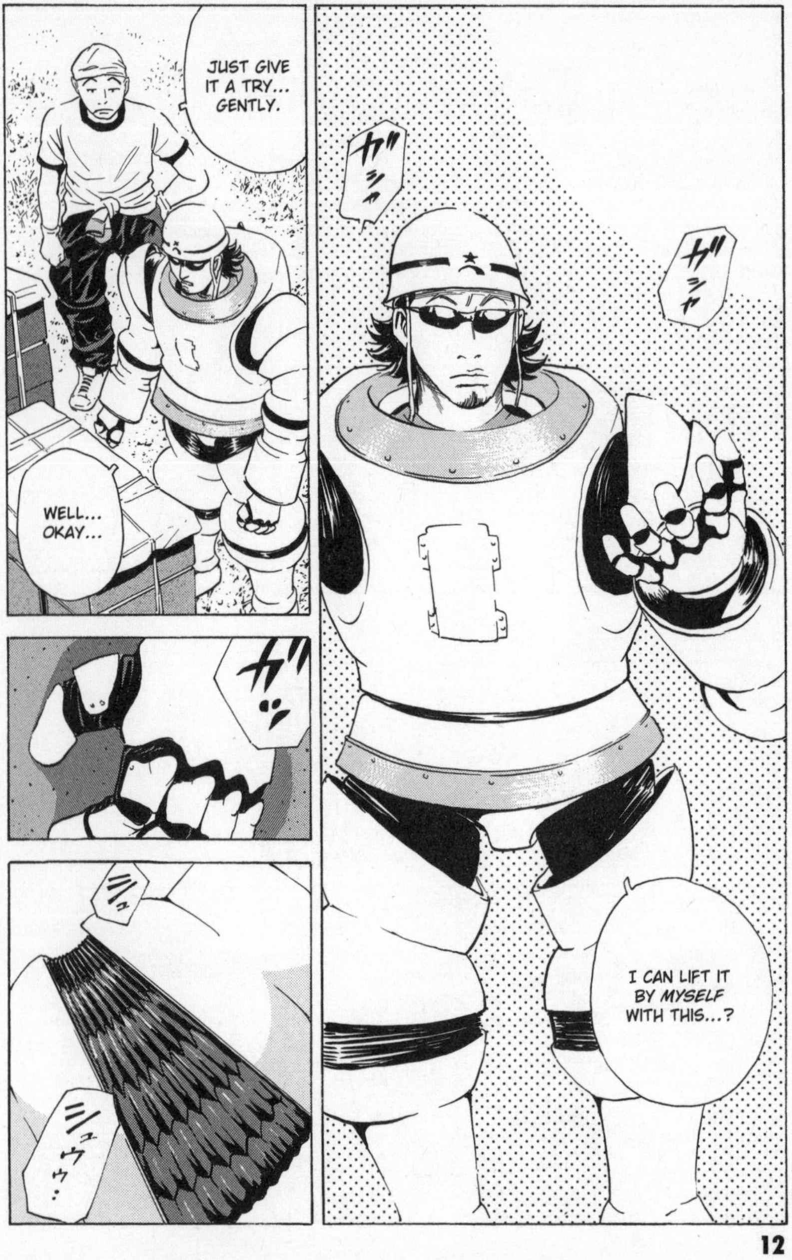
ガシャ
ガシャ
I CAN LIFT IT BY *MYSELF* WITH THIS...?
JUST GIVE IT A TRY... GENTLY.
WELL... OKAY...
ガッ
シュ
シュウウ・・

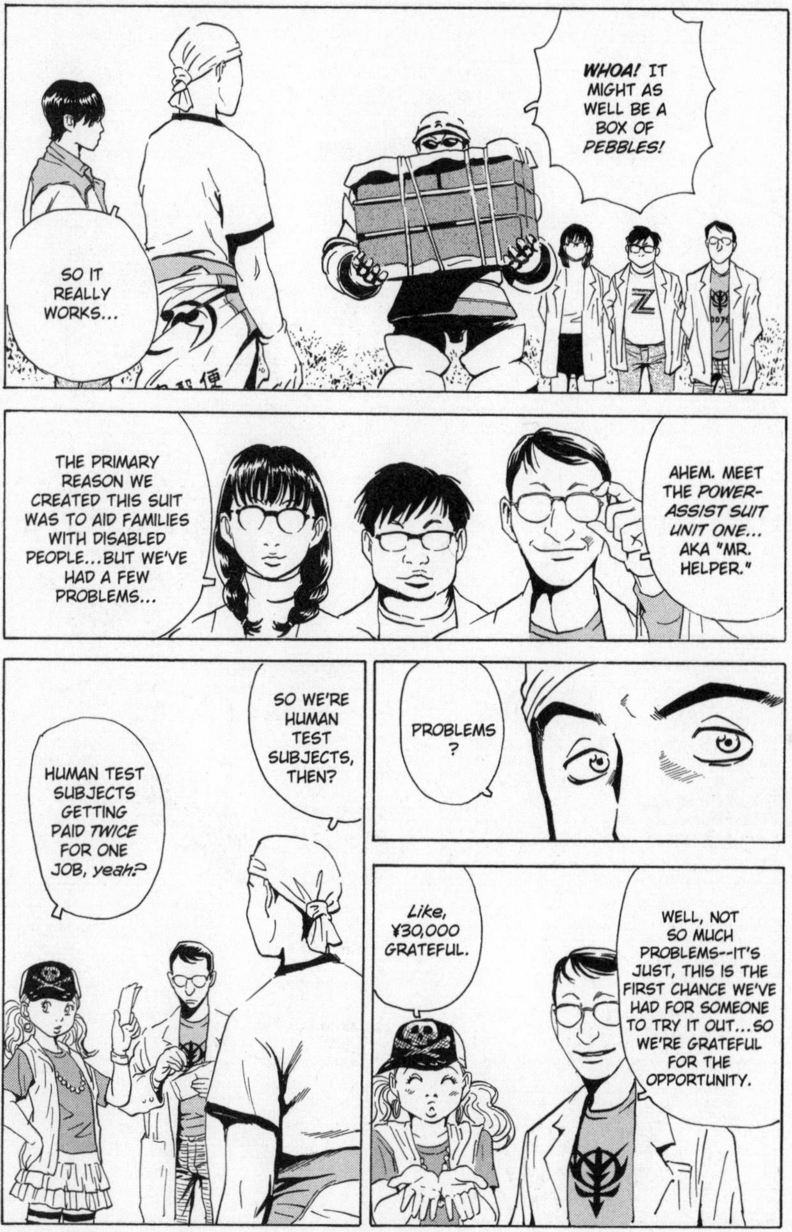
WHOA! IT MIGHT AS WELL BE A BOX OF PEBBLES!
SO IT REALLY WORKS...
AHEM. MEET THE POWER-ASSIST SUIT UNIT ONE... AKA "MR. HELPER."
THE PRIMARY REASON WE CREATED THIS SUIT WAS TO AID FAMILIES WITH DISABLED PEOPLE...BUT WE'VE HAD A FEW PROBLEMS...
PROBLEMS?
WELL, NOT SO MUCH PROBLEMS--IT'S JUST, THIS IS THE FIRST CHANCE WE'VE HAD FOR SOMEONE TO TRY IT OUT...SO WE'RE GRATEFUL FOR THE OPPORTUNITY.
Like, ¥30,000 GRATEFUL.
SO WE'RE HUMAN TEST SUBJECTS, THEN?
HUMAN TEST SUBJECTS GETTING PAID TWICE FOR ONE JOB, yeah?

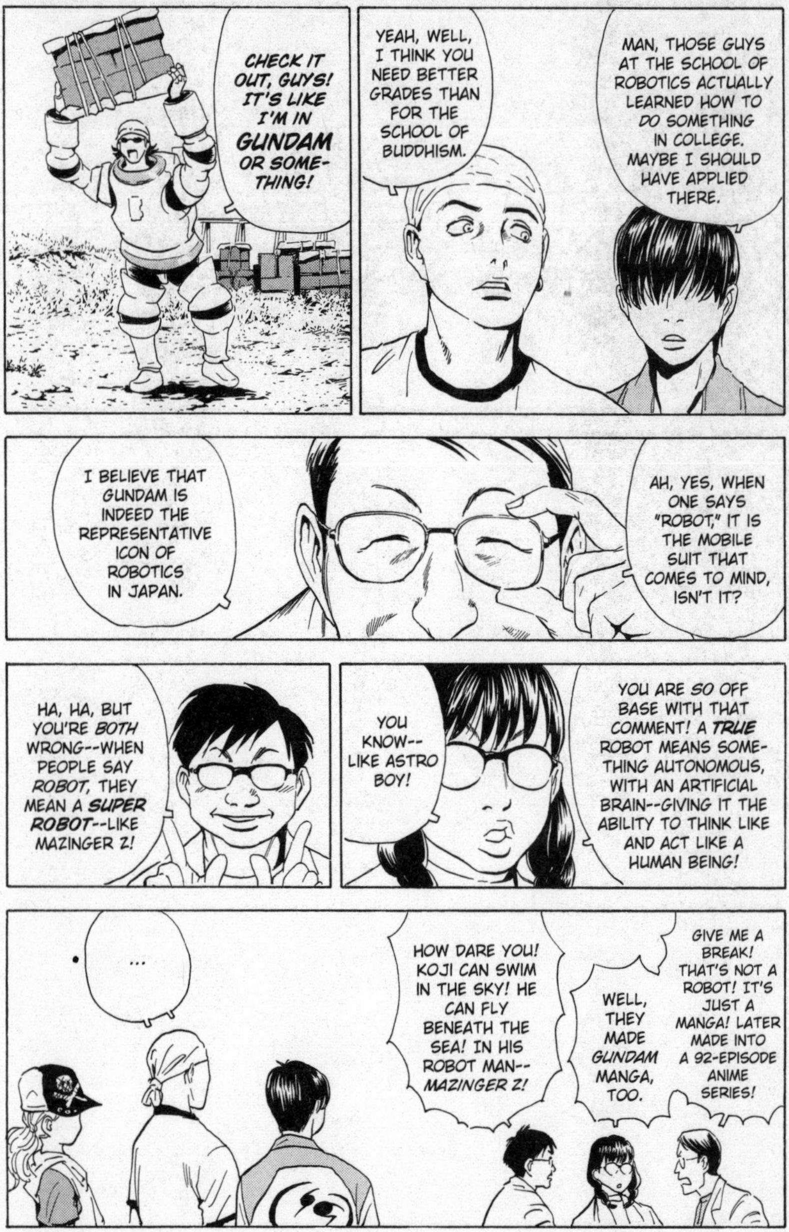
MAN, THOSE GUYS AT THE SCHOOL OF ROBOTICS ACTUALLY LEARNED HOW TO DO SOMETHING IN COLLEGE. MAYBE I SHOULD HAVE APPLIED THERE.
YEAH, WELL, I THINK YOU NEED BETTER GRADES THAN FOR THE SCHOOL OF BUDDHISM.
CHECK IT OUT, GUYS! IT'S LIKE I'M IN GUNDAM OR SOME-THING!
AH, YES, WHEN ONE SAYS "ROBOT," IT IS THE MOBILE SUIT THAT COMES TO MIND, ISN'T IT?
I BELIEVE THAT GUNDAM IS INDEED THE REPRESENTATIVE ICON OF ROBOTICS IN JAPAN.
YOU ARE SO OFF BASE WITH THAT COMMENT! A TRUE ROBOT MEANS SOME-THING AUTONOMOUS, WITH AN ARTIFICIAL BRAIN--GIVING IT THE ABILITY TO THINK LIKE AND ACT LIKE A HUMAN BEING!
YOU KNOW--LIKE ASTRO BOY!
HA, HA, BUT YOU'RE BOTH WRONG--WHEN PEOPLE SAY ROBOT, THEY MEAN A SUPER ROBOT--LIKE MAZINGER Z!
GIVE ME A BREAK! THAT'S NOT A ROBOT! IT'S JUST A MANGA! LATER MADE INTO A 92-EPISODE ANIME SERIES!
WELL, THEY MADE GUNDAM MANGA, TOO.
HOW DARE YOU! KOJI CAN SWIM IN THE SKY! HE CAN FLY BENEATH THE SEA! IN HIS ROBOT MAN--MAZINGER Z!
...

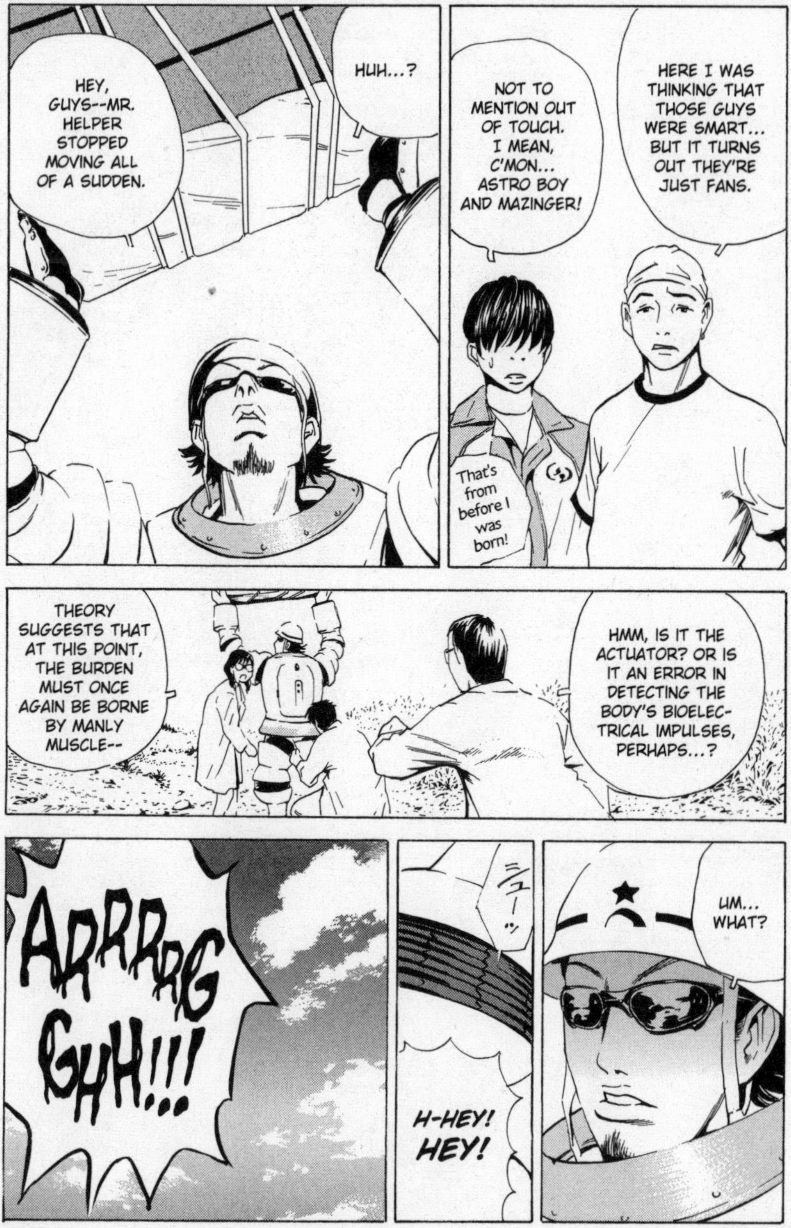
HERE I WAS THINKING THAT THOSE GUYS WERE SMART... BUT IT TURNS OUT THEY'RE JUST FANS.
NOT TO MENTION OUT OF TOUCH. I MEAN, C'MON... ASTRO BOY AND MAZINGER!
That's from before I was born!
HUH...?
HEY, GUYS--MR. HELPER STOPPED MOVING ALL OF A SUDDEN.
HMM, IS IT THE ACTUATOR? OR IS IT AN ERROR IN DETECTING THE BODY'S BIOELEC-TRICAL IMPULSES, PERHAPS...?
THEORY SUGGESTS THAT AT THIS POINT, THE BURDEN MUST ONCE AGAIN BE BORNE BY MANLY MUSCLE--
UM... WHAT?
ミュー ッ
H-HEY! HEY!
ARRRRG GHH!!!

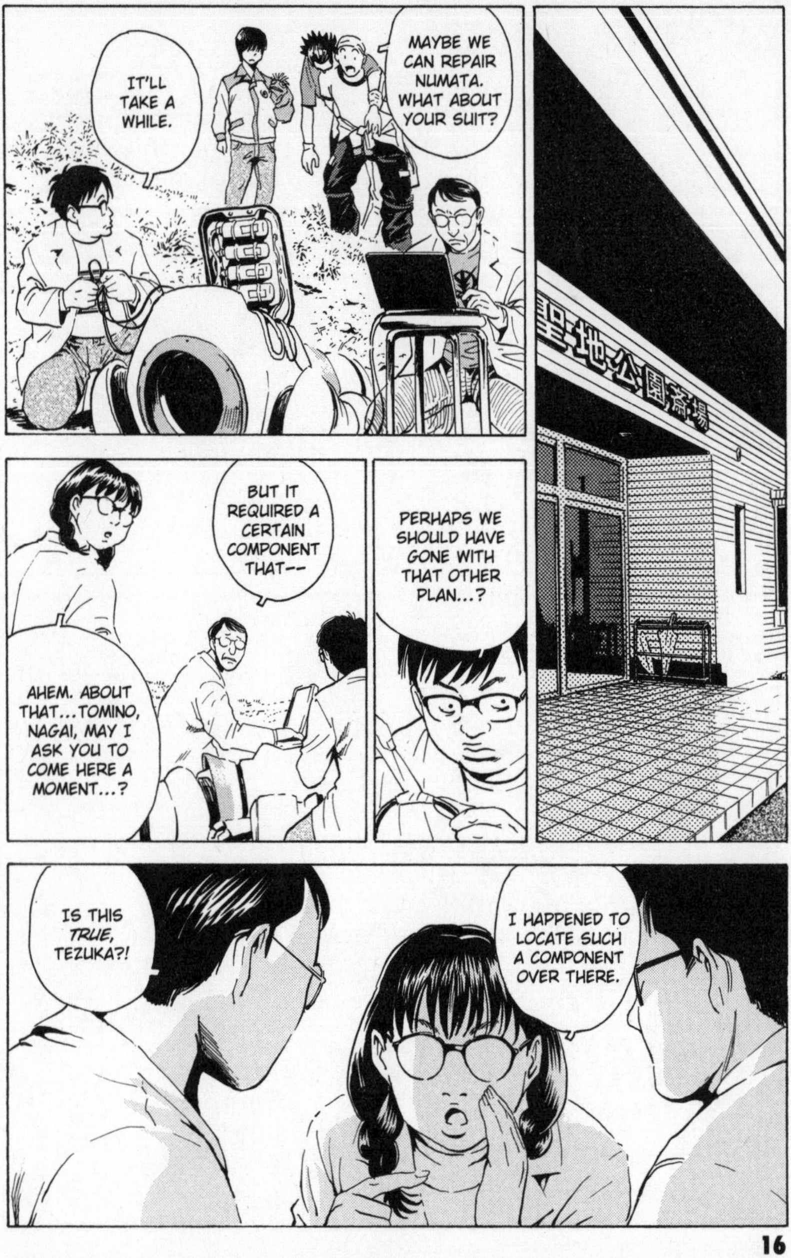
聖地公園斎場
MAYBE WE CAN REPAIR NUMATA. WHAT ABOUT YOUR SUIT?
IT'LL TAKE A WHILE.
PERHAPS WE SHOULD HAVE GONE WITH THAT OTHER PLAN...?
BUT IT REQUIRED A CERTAIN COMPONENT THAT--
AHEM. ABOUT THAT...TOMINO, NAGAI, MAY I ASK YOU TO COME HERE A MOMENT...?
I HAPPENED TO LOCATE SUCH A COMPONENT OVER THERE.
IS THIS *TRUE*, TEZUKA?!

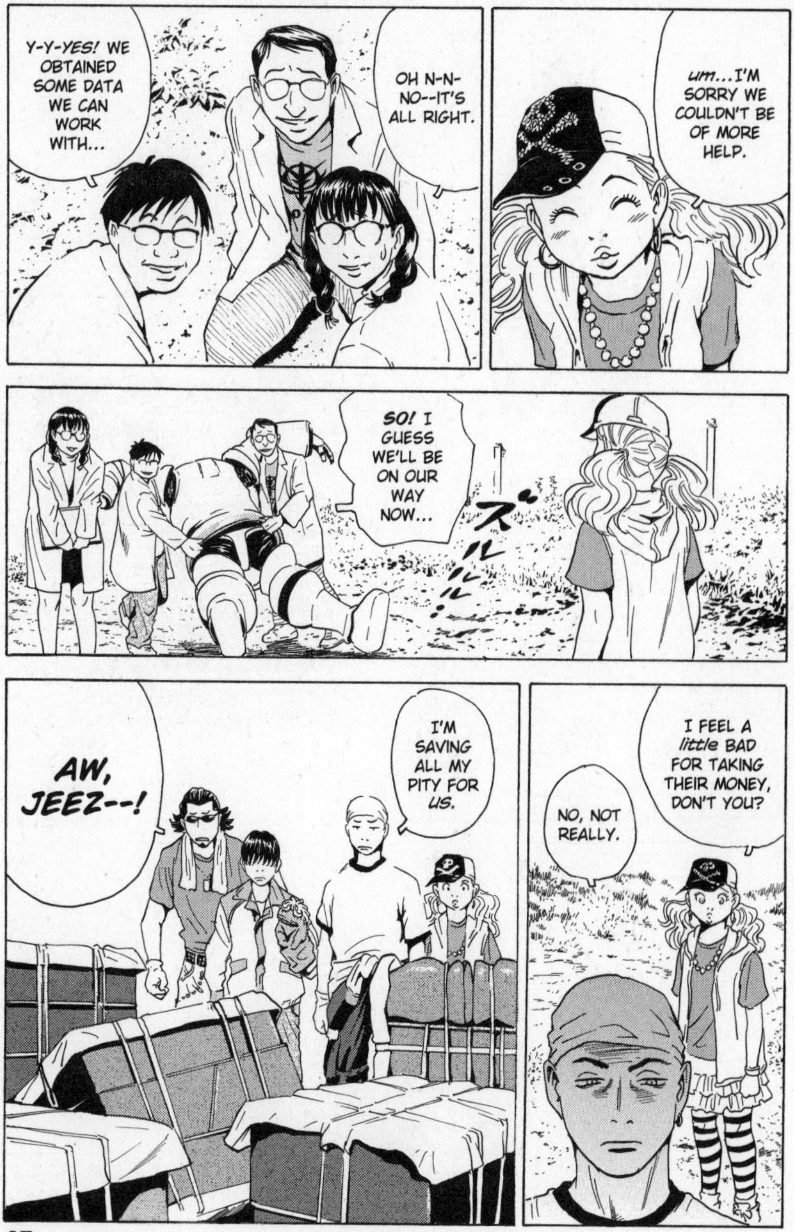
um...I'M SORRY WE COULDN'T BE OF MORE HELP.
OH N-N-NO--IT'S ALL RIGHT.
Y-Y-YES! WE OBTAINED SOME DATA WE CAN WORK WITH...
SO! I GUESS WE'LL BE ON OUR WAY NOW...
ズルルル!
I FEEL A little BAD FOR TAKING THEIR MONEY, DON'T YOU?
NO, NOT REALLY.
I'M SAVING ALL MY PITY FOR us.
AW, JEEZ--!

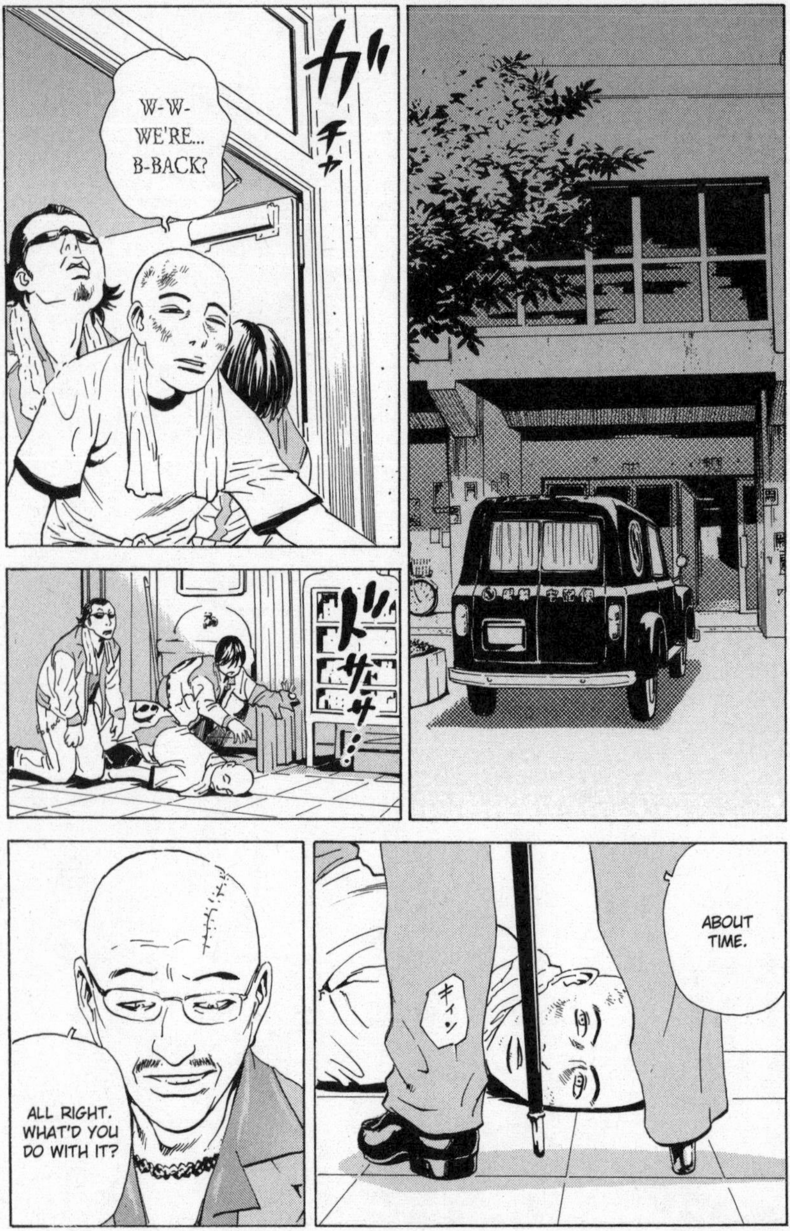
W-W-
WE'RE...
B-BACK?
ガチャ
ABOUT TIME.
キィン
ALL RIGHT. WHAT'D YOU DO WITH IT?

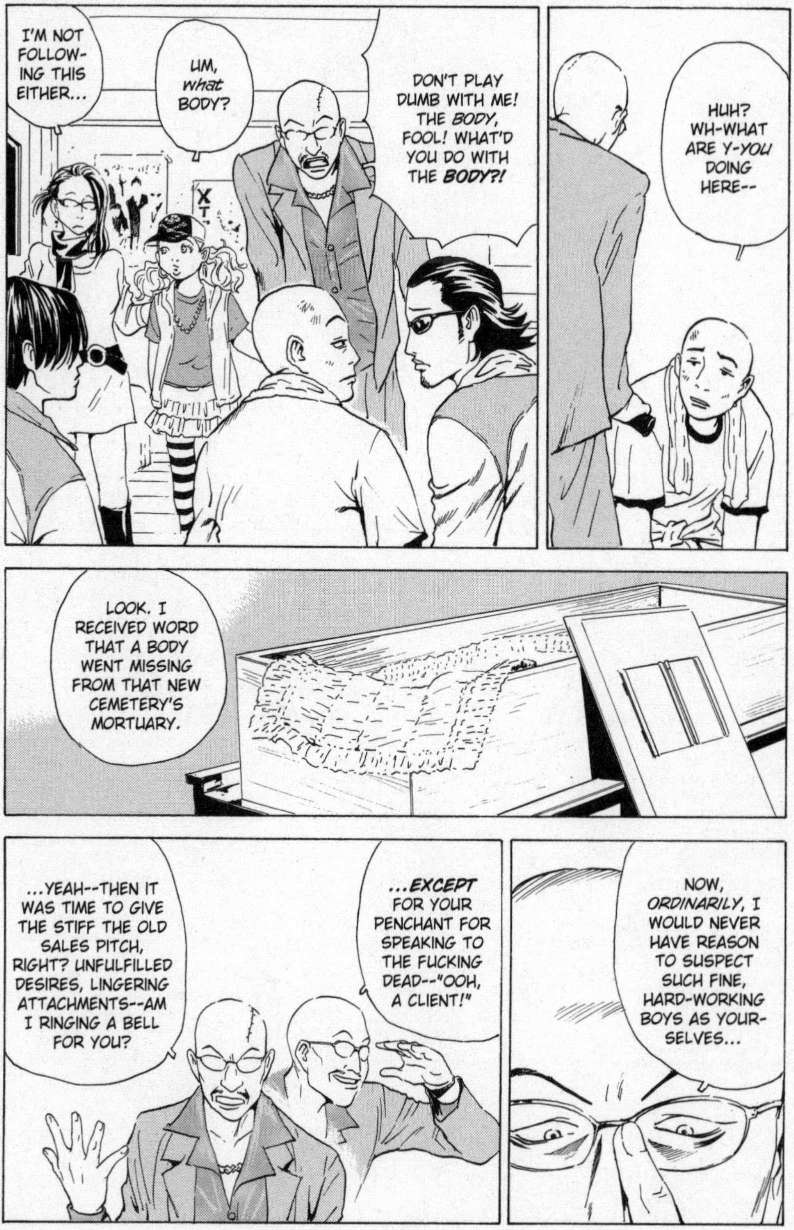
HUH? WH-WHAT ARE Y-YOU DOING HERE--
DON'T PLAY DUMB WITH ME! THE BODY, FOOL! WHAT'D YOU DO WITH THE BODY?!
UM, what BODY?
I'M NOT FOLLOWING THIS EITHER...
LOOK. I RECEIVED WORD THAT A BODY WENT MISSING FROM THAT NEW CEMETERY'S MORTUARY.
NOW, ORDINARILY, I WOULD NEVER HAVE REASON TO SUSPECT SUCH FINE, HARD-WORKING BOYS AS YOURSELVES...
...EXCEPT FOR YOUR PENCHANT FOR SPEAKING TO THE FUCKING DEAD--"OOH, A CLIENT!"
...YEAH--THEN IT WAS TIME TO GIVE THE STIFF THE OLD SALES PITCH, RIGHT? UNFULFILLED DESIRES, LINGERING ATTACHMENTS--AM I RINGING A BELL FOR YOU?

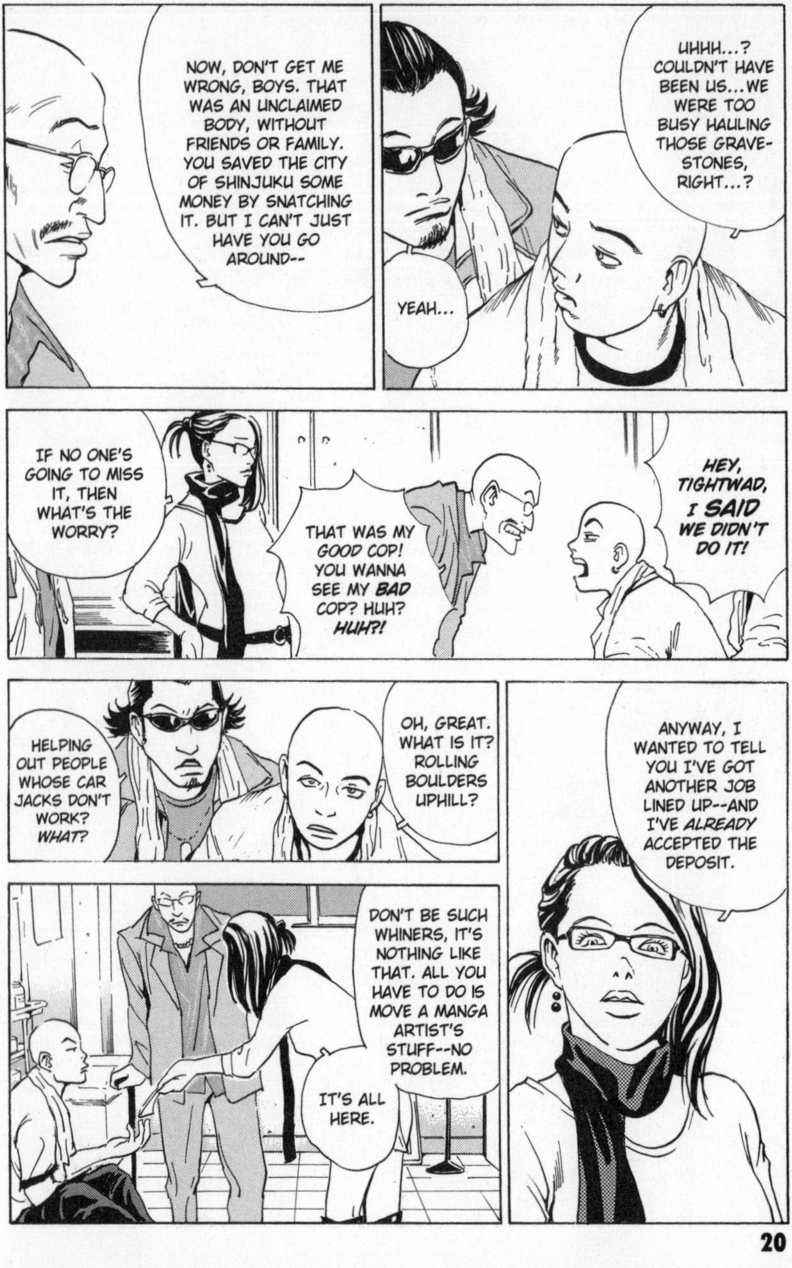
UHHH...? COULDN'T HAVE BEEN US...WE WERE TOO BUSY HAULING THOSE GRAVE-STONES, RIGHT...?
YEAH...
NOW, DON'T GET ME WRONG, BOYS. THAT WAS AN UNCLAIMED BODY, WITHOUT FRIENDS OR FAMILY. YOU SAVED THE CITY OF SHINJUKU SOME MONEY BY SNATCHING IT. BUT I CAN'T JUST HAVE YOU GO AROUND--
HEY, TIGHTWAD, I SAID WE DIDN'T DO IT!
THAT WAS MY GOOD COP! YOU WANNA SEE MY BAD COP? HUH? HUH?!
IF NO ONE'S GOING TO MISS IT, THEN WHAT'S THE WORRY?
ANYWAY, I WANTED TO TELL YOU I'VE GOT ANOTHER JOB LINED UP--AND I'VE ALREADY ACCEPTED THE DEPOSIT.
OH, GREAT. WHAT IS IT? ROLLING BOULDERS UPHILL?
HELPING OUT PEOPLE WHOSE CAR JACKS DON'T WORK? WHAT?
DON'T BE SUCH WHINERS, IT'S NOTHING LIKE THAT. ALL YOU HAVE TO DO IS MOVE A MANGA ARTIST'S STUFF--NO PROBLEM.
IT'S ALL HERE.

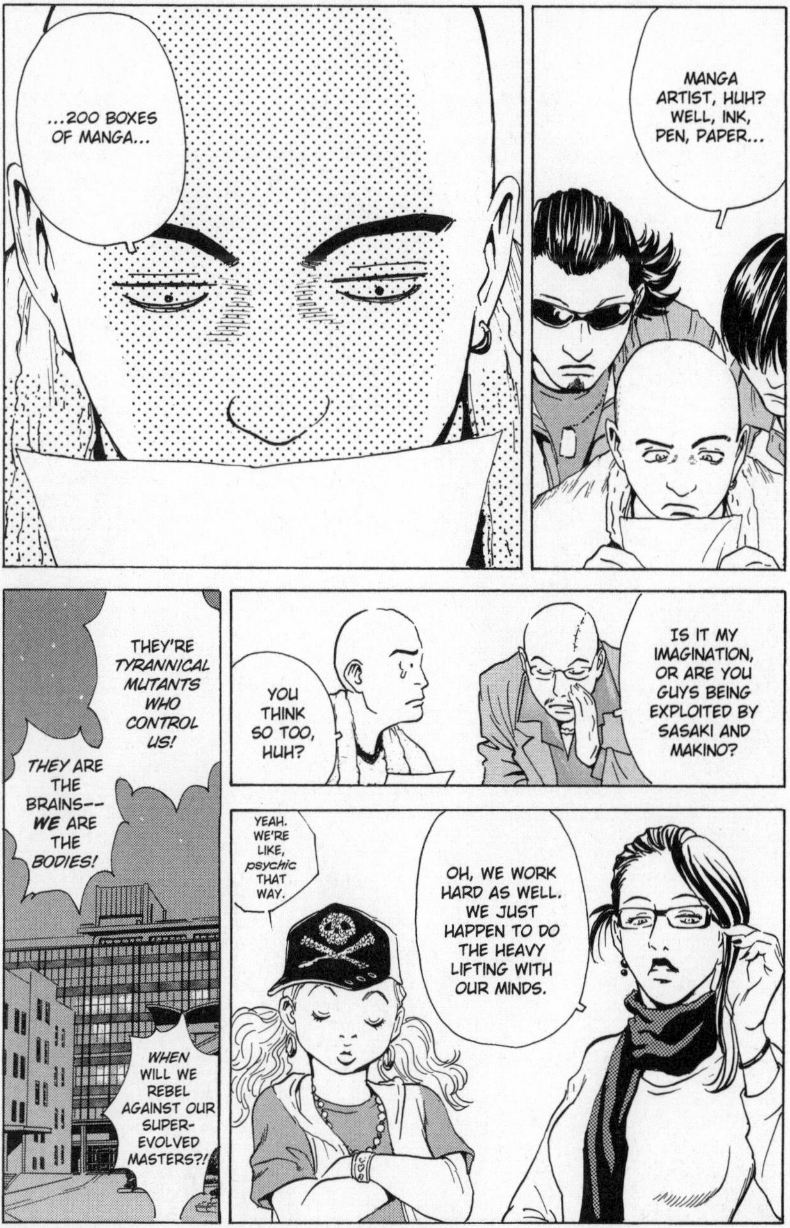
MANGA ARTIST, HUH? WELL, INK, PEN, PAPER...
...200 BOXES OF MANGA...
IS IT MY IMAGINATION, OR ARE YOU GUYS BEING EXPLOITED BY SASAKI AND MAKINO?
YOU THINK SO TOO, HUH?
OH, WE WORK HARD AS WELL. WE JUST HAPPEN TO DO THE HEAVY LIFTING WITH OUR MINDS.
YEAH. WE'RE LIKE, *psychic* THAT WAY.
THEY'RE *TYRANNICAL MUTANTS WHO CONTROL US!*
THEY ARE THE BRAINS-- ***WE*** ARE THE *BODIES!*
WHEN WILL WE REBEL AGAINST OUR SUPER-EVOLVED MASTERS?!

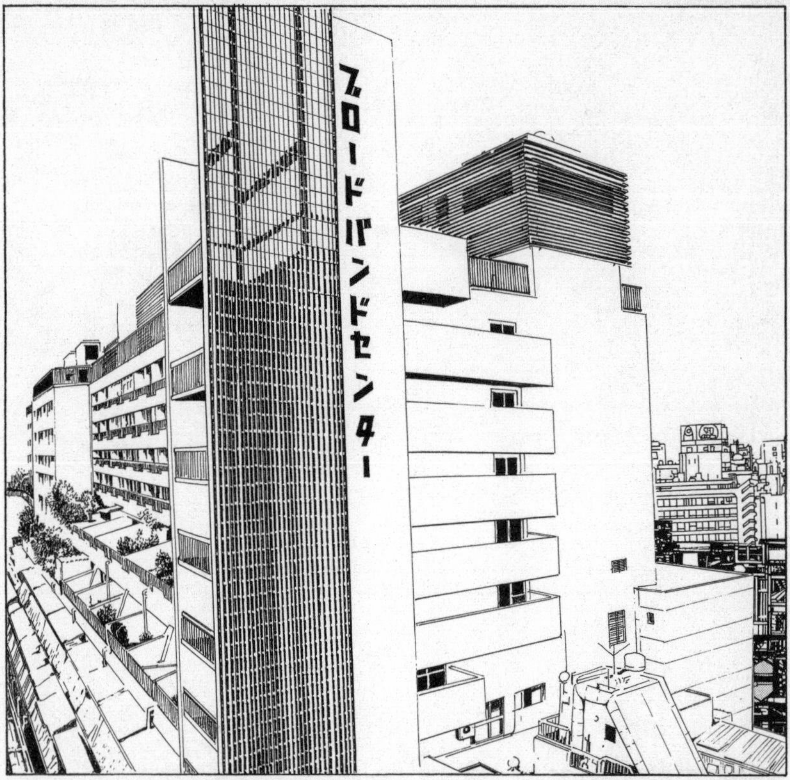
ブロードバンドセンター

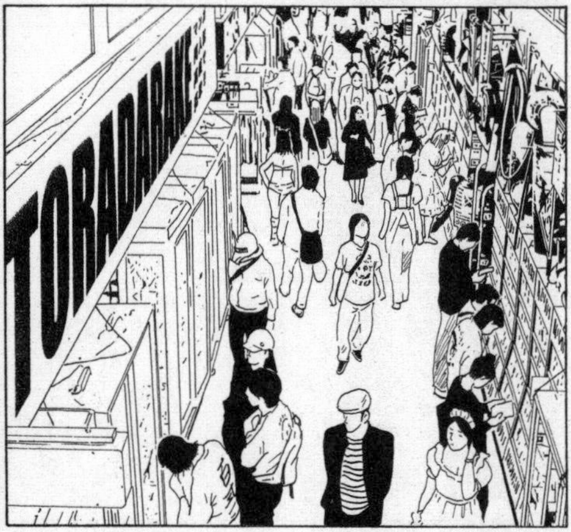
TORADARAKE

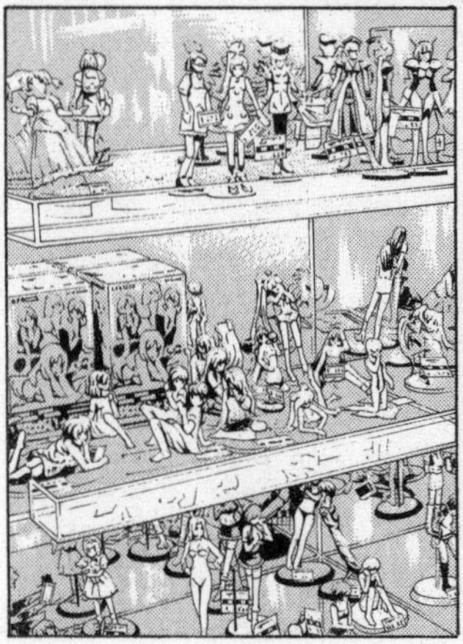

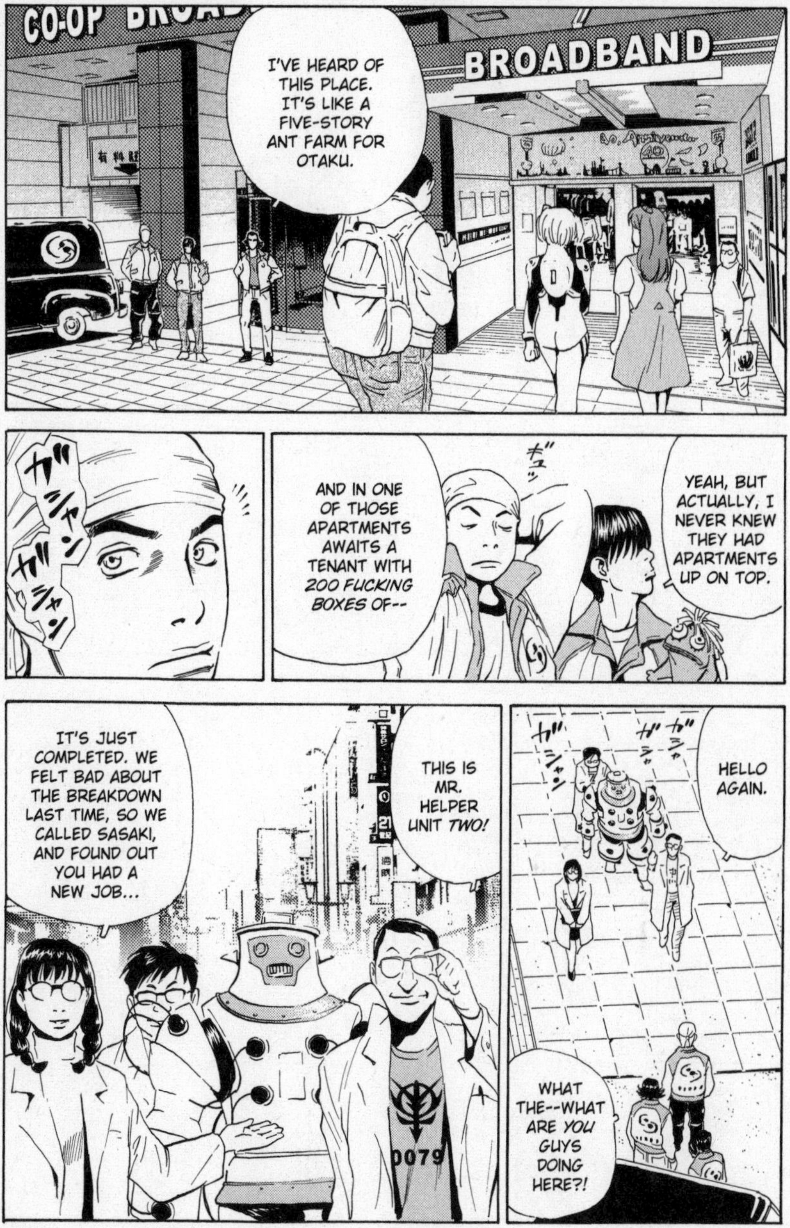
CO-OP BROAD
BROADBAND
I'VE HEARD OF THIS PLACE. IT'S LIKE A FIVE-STORY ANT FARM FOR OTAKU.
YEAH, BUT ACTUALLY, I NEVER KNEW THEY HAD APARTMENTS UP ON TOP.
AND IN ONE OF THOSE APARTMENTS AWAITS A TENANT WITH *200 FUCKING BOXES OF--*
ガシャン
ガシャン
HELLO AGAIN.
WHAT THE--WHAT ARE *YOU* GUYS DOING HERE?!
THIS IS MR. HELPER UNIT *TWO!*
IT'S JUST COMPLETED. WE FELT BAD ABOUT THE BREAKDOWN LAST TIME, SO WE CALLED SASAKI, AND FOUND OUT YOU HAD A NEW JOB...

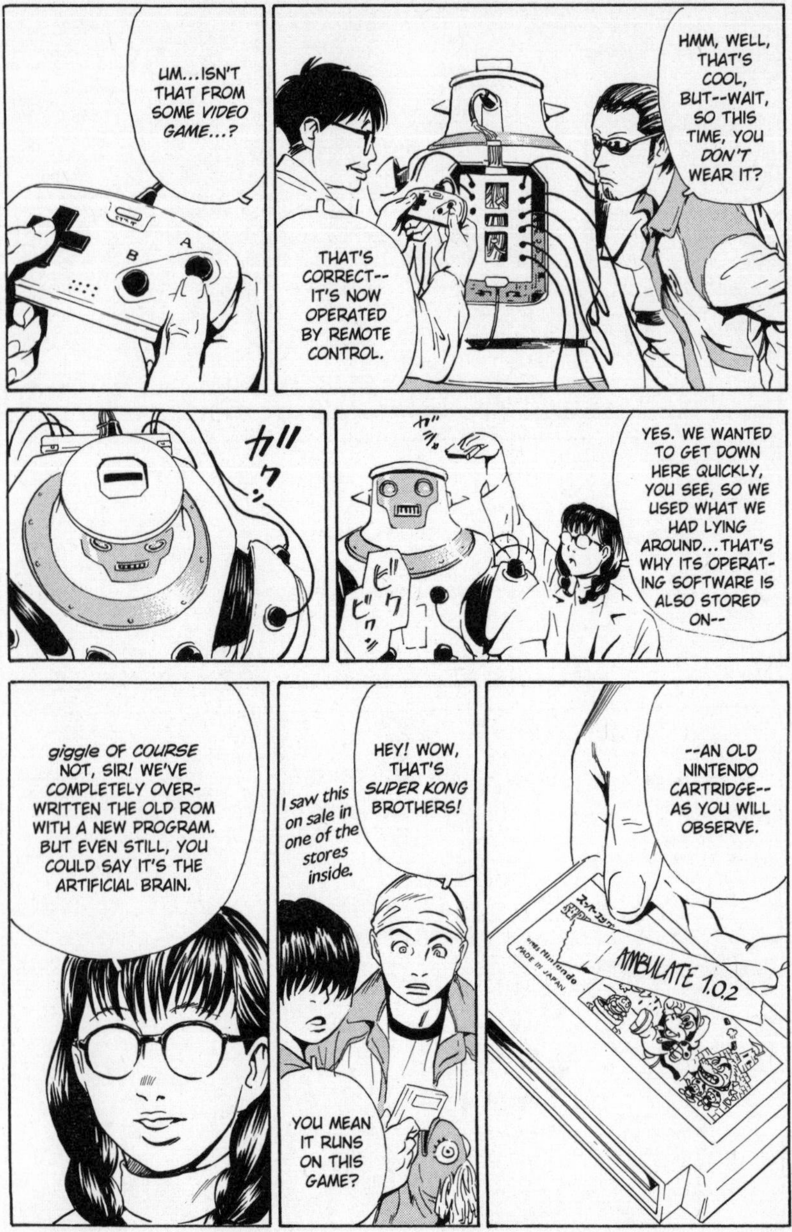
HMM, WELL, THAT'S COOL, BUT--WAIT, SO THIS TIME, YOU DON'T WEAR IT?
THAT'S CORRECT-- IT'S NOW OPERATED BY REMOTE CONTROL.
UM...ISN'T THAT FROM SOME VIDEO GAME...?
YES. WE WANTED TO GET DOWN HERE QUICKLY, YOU SEE, SO WE USED WHAT WE HAD LYING AROUND...THAT'S WHY ITS OPERATING SOFTWARE IS ALSO STORED ON--
--AN OLD NINTENDO CARTRIDGE-- AS YOU WILL OBSERVE.
AMBULATE 1.0.2
MADE IN JAPAN
HEY! WOW, THAT'S SUPER KONG BROTHERS!
I saw this on sale in one of the stores inside.
YOU MEAN IT RUNS ON THIS GAME?
giggle OF COURSE NOT, SIR! WE'VE COMPLETELY OVER-WRITTEN THE OLD ROM WITH A NEW PROGRAM. BUT EVEN STILL, YOU COULD SAY IT'S THE ARTIFICIAL BRAIN.

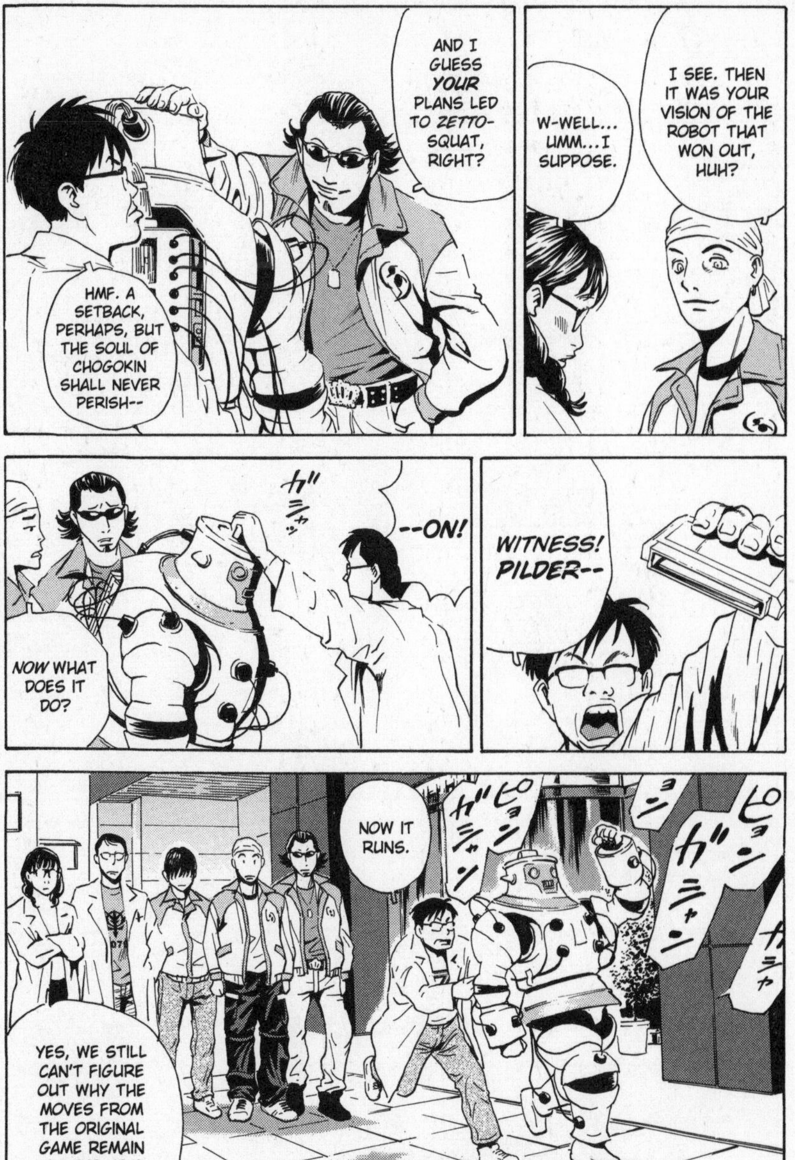
I SEE. THEN IT WAS YOUR VISION OF THE ROBOT THAT WON OUT, HUH?
W-WELL... UMM...I SUPPOSE.
AND I GUESS *YOUR* PLANS LED TO *ZETTO*-SQUAT, RIGHT?
HMF. A SETBACK, PERHAPS, BUT THE SOUL OF CHOGOKIN SHALL NEVER PERISH--
WITNESS! PILDER--
--ON!
NOW WHAT DOES IT DO?
ピョン
ガシャン
NOW IT RUNS.
ピョン
ガシャン
カシャ
YES, WE STILL CAN'T FIGURE OUT WHY THE MOVES FROM THE ORIGINAL GAME REMAIN ON THE NEW PROGRAM...

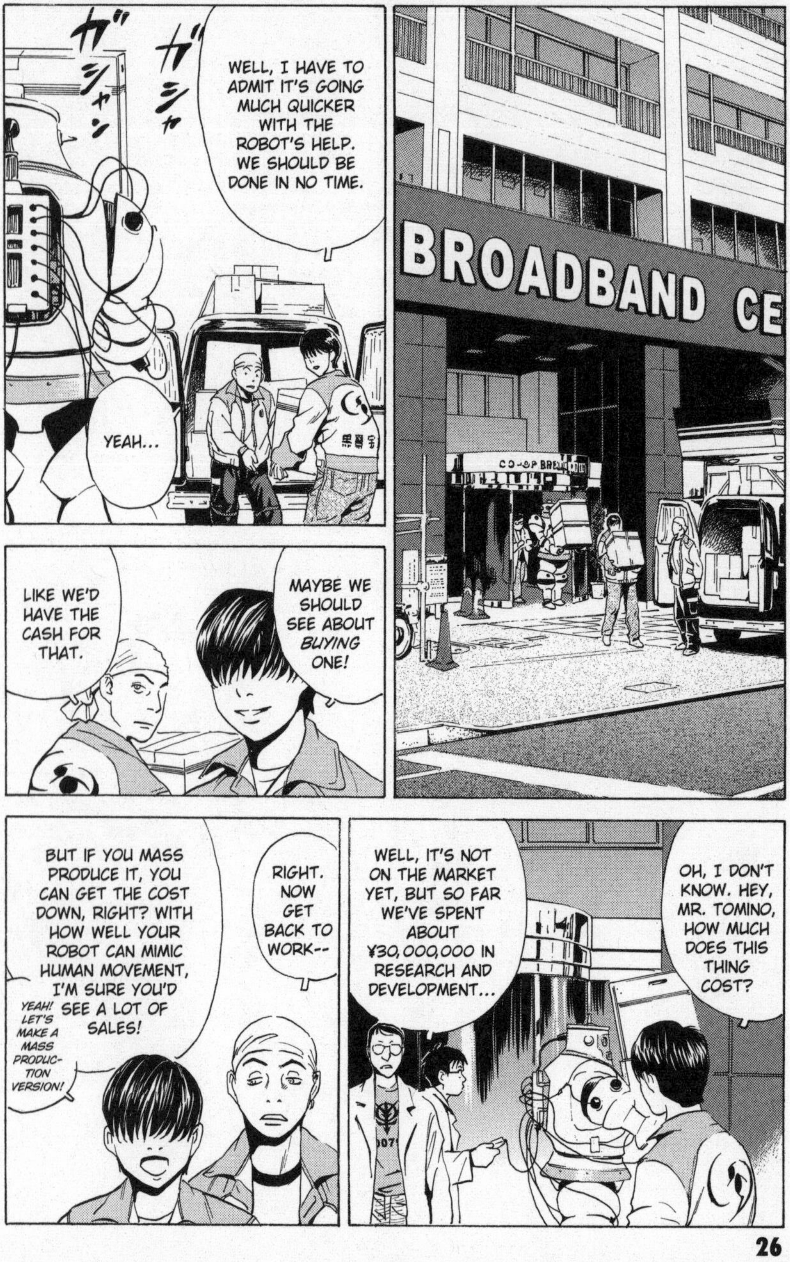
BROADBAND CE
ガシャ
ガシャン
WELL, I HAVE TO ADMIT IT'S GOING MUCH QUICKER WITH THE ROBOT'S HELP. WE SHOULD BE DONE IN NO TIME.
YEAH...
MAYBE WE SHOULD SEE ABOUT *BUYING* ONE!
LIKE WE'D HAVE THE CASH FOR THAT.
OH, I DON'T KNOW. HEY, MR. TOMINO, HOW MUCH DOES THIS THING COST?
WELL, IT'S NOT ON THE MARKET YET, BUT SO FAR WE'VE SPENT ABOUT ¥30,000,000 IN RESEARCH AND DEVELOPMENT...
RIGHT. NOW GET BACK TO WORK--
BUT IF YOU MASS PRODUCE IT, YOU CAN GET THE COST DOWN, RIGHT? WITH HOW WELL YOUR ROBOT CAN MIMIC HUMAN MOVEMENT, I'M SURE YOU'D SEE A LOT OF SALES!
YEAH! LET'S MAKE A MASS PRODUCTION VERSION!

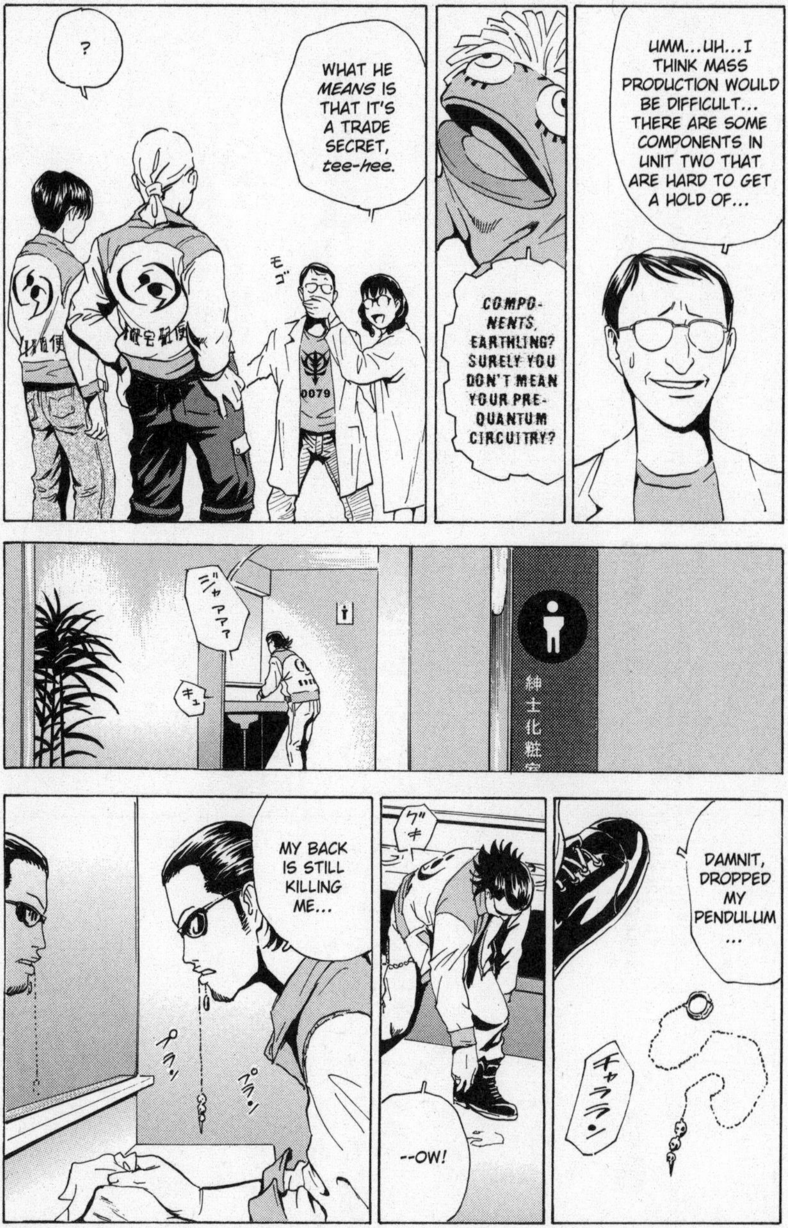
UMM...UH...I THINK MASS PRODUCTION WOULD BE DIFFICULT... THERE ARE SOME COMPONENTS IN UNIT TWO THAT ARE HARD TO GET A HOLD OF...
COMPONENTS, EARTHLING? SURELY YOU DON'T MEAN YOUR PRE-QUANTUM CIRCUITRY?
WHAT HE *MEANS* IS THAT IT'S A TRADE SECRET, *tee-hee*.
?
モゴ
0079
ジャアァァ
キュ
紳士化粧
DAMNIT, DROPPED MY PENDULUM ...
チャララン
グキ
--OW!
MY BACK IS STILL KILLING ME...
プラン
プラン

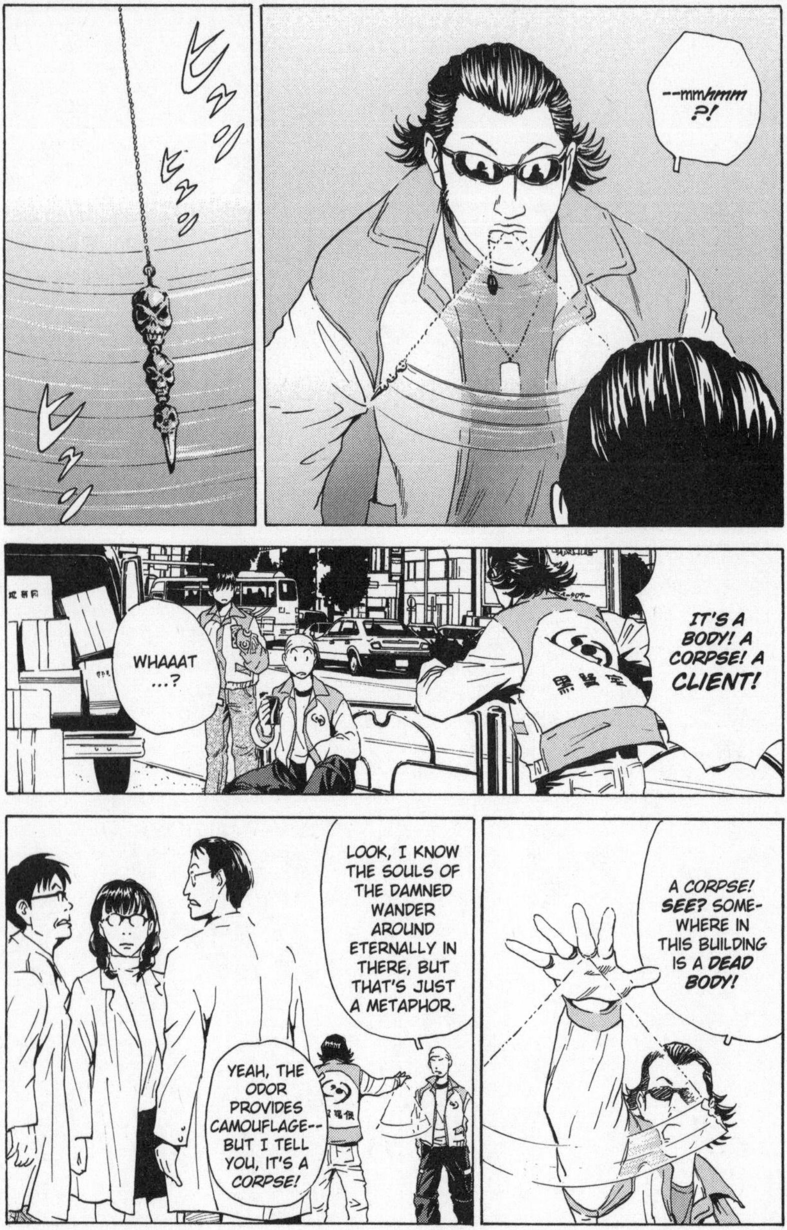
--mmhmm ?!
IT'S A BODY! A CORPSE! A CLIENT!
WHAAAT ...?
A CORPSE! SEE? SOME-WHERE IN THIS BUILDING IS A DEAD BODY!
LOOK, I KNOW THE SOULS OF THE DAMNED WANDER AROUND ETERNALLY IN THERE, BUT THAT'S JUST A METAPHOR.
YEAH, THE ODOR PROVIDES CAMOUFLAGE-- BUT I TELL YOU, IT'S A CORPSE!

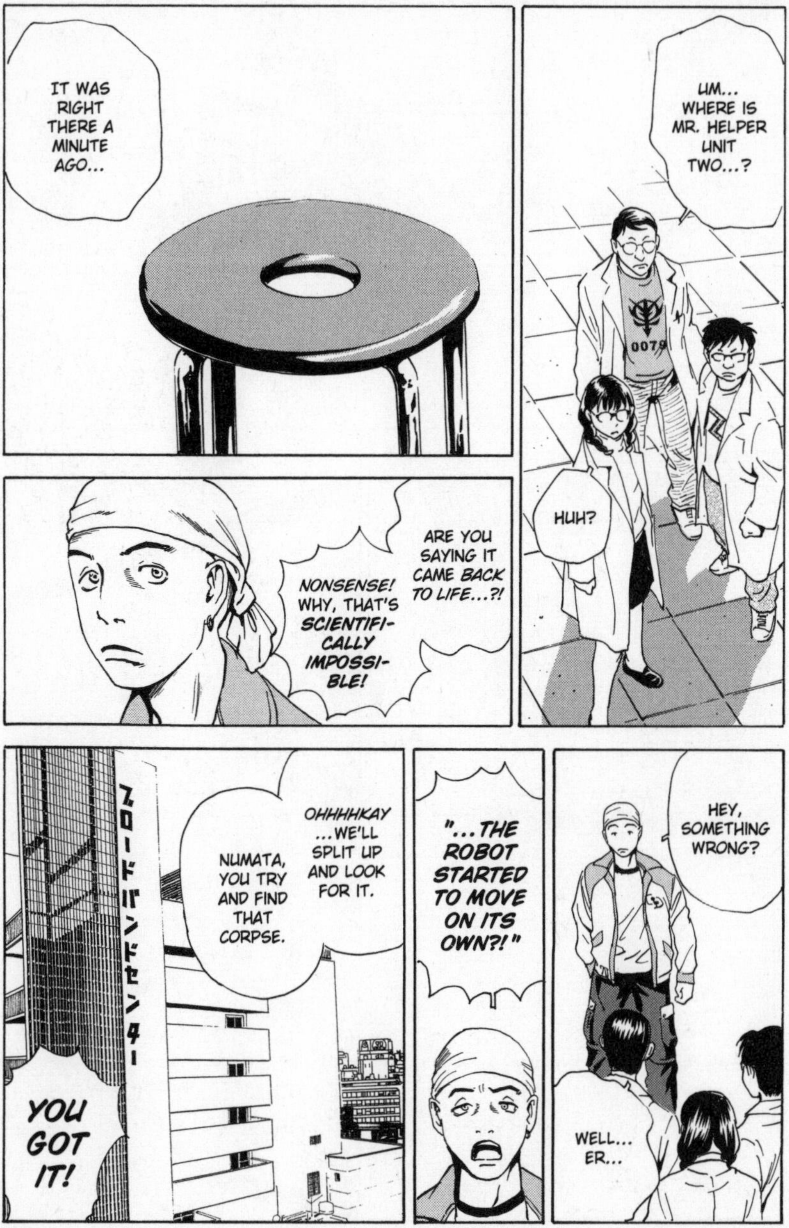
UM... WHERE IS MR. HELPER UNIT TWO...?
HUH?
IT WAS RIGHT THERE A MINUTE AGO...
ARE YOU SAYING IT CAME BACK TO LIFE...?!
NONSENSE! WHY, THAT'S SCIENTIFICALLY IMPOSSIBLE!
HEY, SOMETHING WRONG?
WELL... ER...
"...THE ROBOT STARTED TO MOVE ON ITS OWN?!"
OHHHHKAY ...WE'LL SPLIT UP AND LOOK FOR IT.
NUMATA, YOU TRY AND FIND THAT CORPSE.
ブロードバンドセンター
YOU GOT IT!

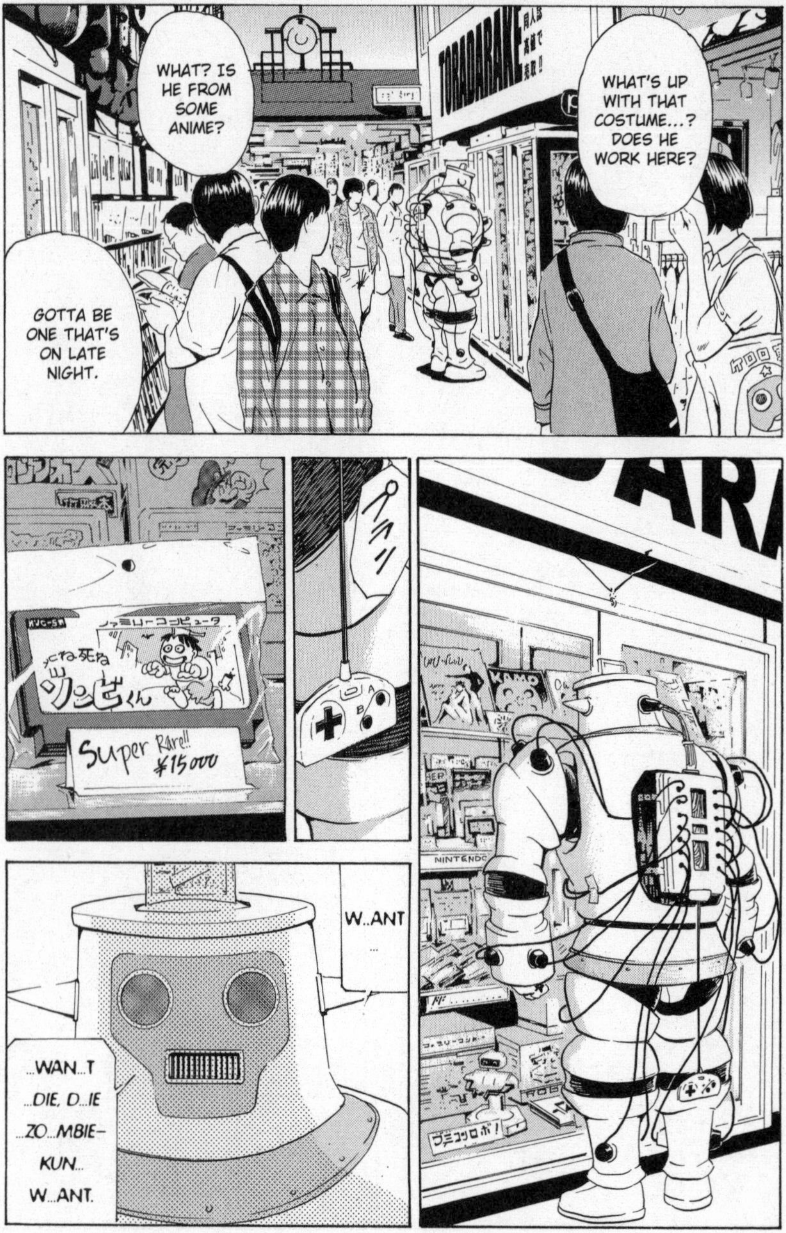
TORADARAKE
WHAT'S UP WITH THAT COSTUME...? DOES HE WORK HERE?
WHAT? IS HE FROM SOME ANIME?
GOTTA BE ONE THAT'S ON LATE NIGHT.
NINTENDO
ファミリーコンピュータ
Super Rare!! ¥15000
W..ANT ...
...WAN...T ...DIE, D...IE ...ZO...MBIE-KUN... W...ANT.

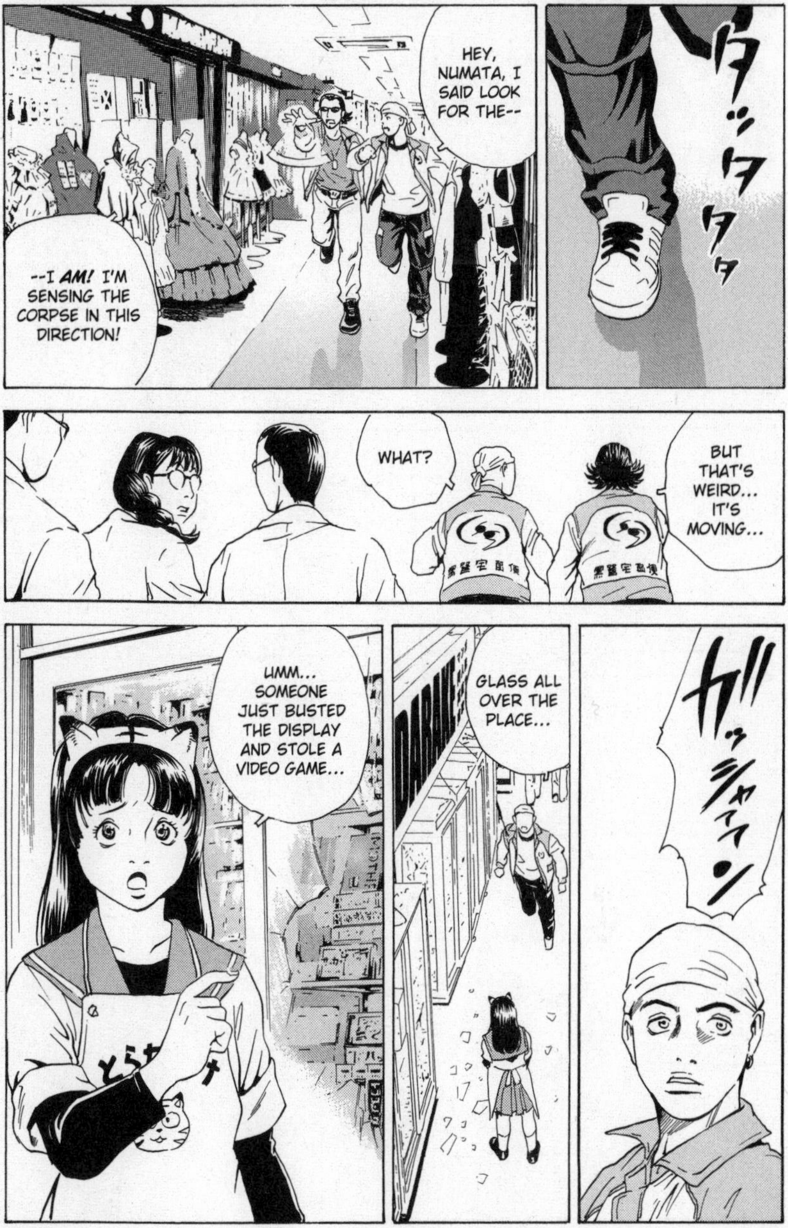
タッタタタ
HEY, NUMATA, I SAID LOOK FOR THE--
--I *AM!* I'M SENSING THE CORPSE IN THIS DIRECTION!
BUT THAT'S WEIRD... IT'S MOVING...
WHAT?
ガッシャァァン
GLASS ALL OVER THE PLACE...
UMM... SOMEONE JUST BUSTED THE DISPLAY AND STOLE A VIDEO GAME...

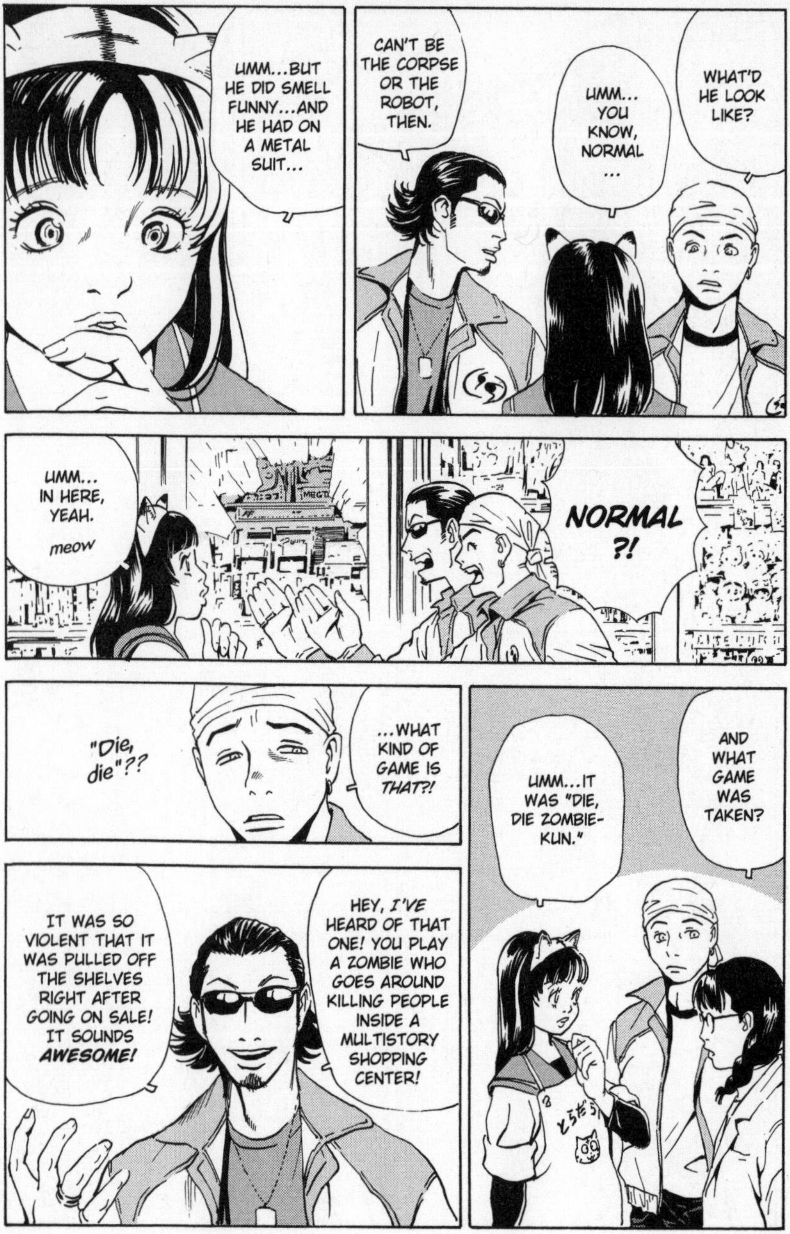
WHAT'D HE LOOK LIKE?
UMM... YOU KNOW, NORMAL ...
CAN'T BE THE CORPSE OR THE ROBOT, THEN.
UMM...BUT HE DID SMELL FUNNY...AND HE HAD ON A METAL SUIT...
NORMAL ?!
UMM... IN HERE, YEAH.
meow
AND WHAT GAME WAS TAKEN?
UMM...IT WAS "DIE, DIE ZOMBIE-KUN."
...WHAT KIND OF GAME IS THAT?!
"Die, die"??
HEY, I'VE HEARD OF THAT ONE! YOU PLAY A ZOMBIE WHO GOES AROUND KILLING PEOPLE INSIDE A MULTISTORY SHOPPING CENTER!
IT WAS SO VIOLENT THAT IT WAS PULLED OFF THE SHELVES RIGHT AFTER GOING ON SALE! IT SOUNDS AWESOME!

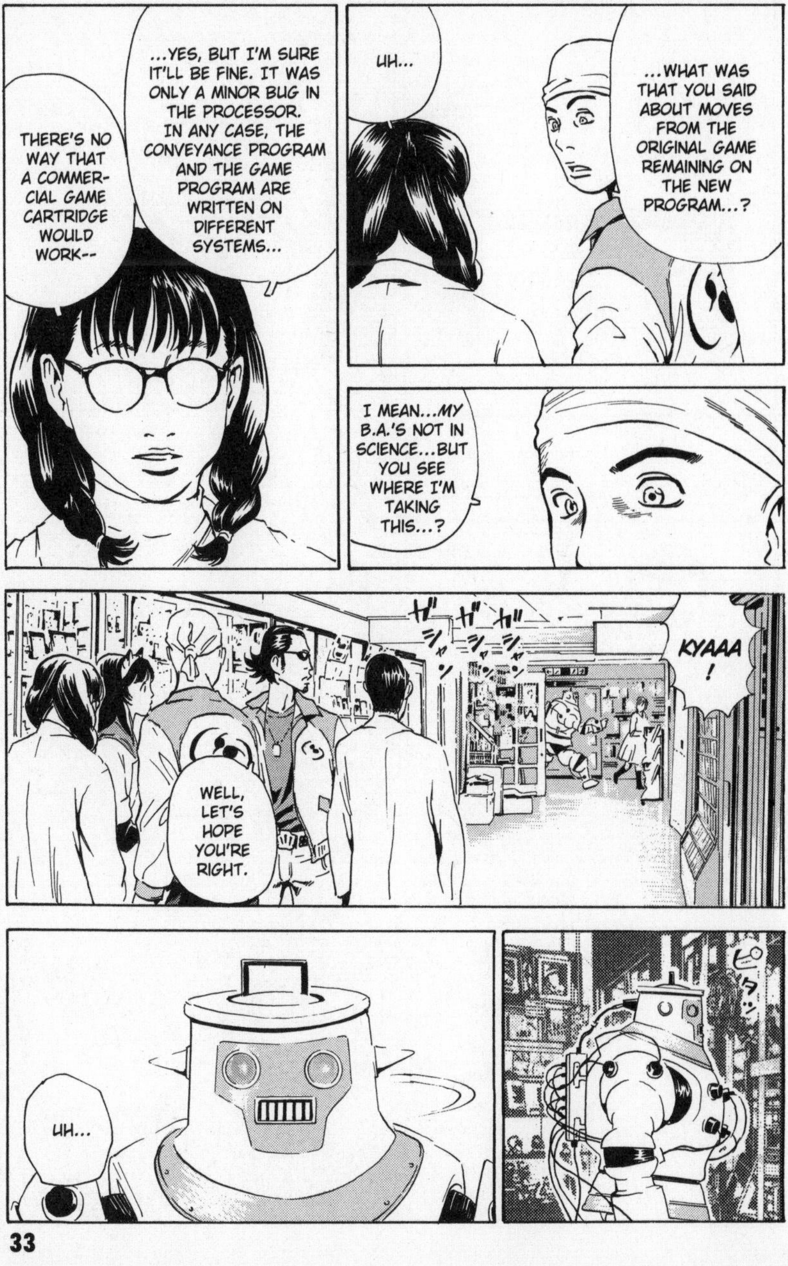
...WHAT WAS THAT YOU SAID ABOUT MOVES FROM THE ORIGINAL GAME REMAINING ON THE NEW PROGRAM...?
UH...
I MEAN...*MY* B.A.'S NOT IN SCIENCE...BUT YOU SEE WHERE I'M TAKING THIS...?
...YES, BUT I'M SURE IT'LL BE FINE. IT WAS ONLY A MINOR BUG IN THE PROCESSOR. IN ANY CASE, THE CONVEYANCE PROGRAM AND THE GAME PROGRAM ARE WRITTEN ON DIFFERENT SYSTEMS...
THERE'S NO WAY THAT A COMMERCIAL GAME CARTRIDGE WOULD WORK--
KYAAA!
WELL, LET'S HOPE YOU'RE RIGHT.
UH...

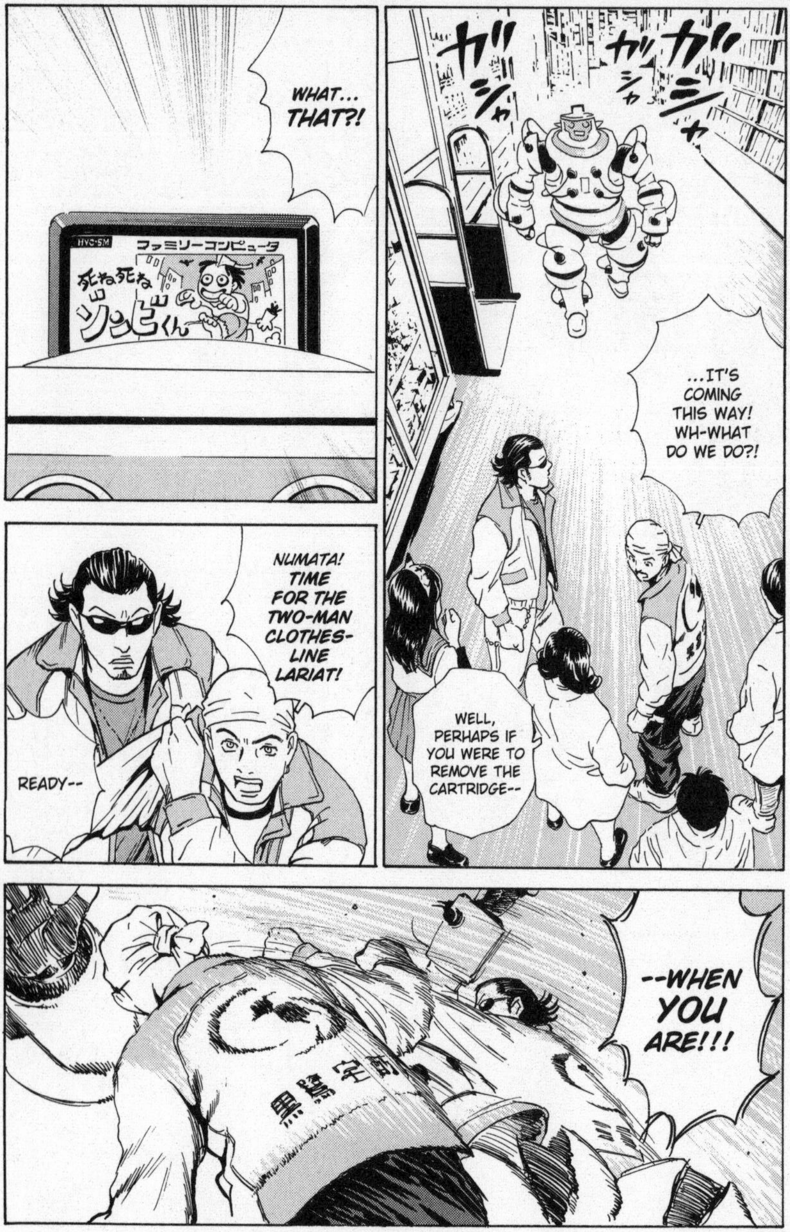
ガシャ
ガシャ ガシャ
...IT'S COMING THIS WAY! WH-WHAT DO WE DO?!
WELL, PERHAPS IF YOU WERE TO REMOVE THE CARTRIDGE--
WHAT... THAT?!
HVC-SM
ファミリーコンピュータ
死ね死ねゾンビくん
NUMATA! TIME FOR THE TWO-MAN CLOTHES-LINE LARIAT!
READY--
--WHEN YOU ARE!!!

THE ROBOT'S DOWN...

...UM...

ALL RIGHT!

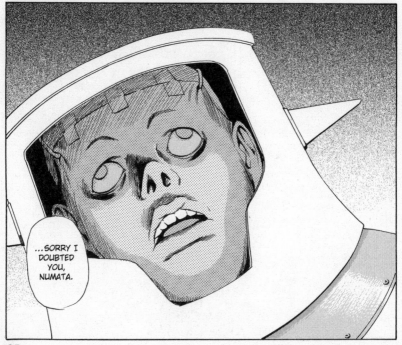

...SORRY I DOUBTED YOU, NUMATA.

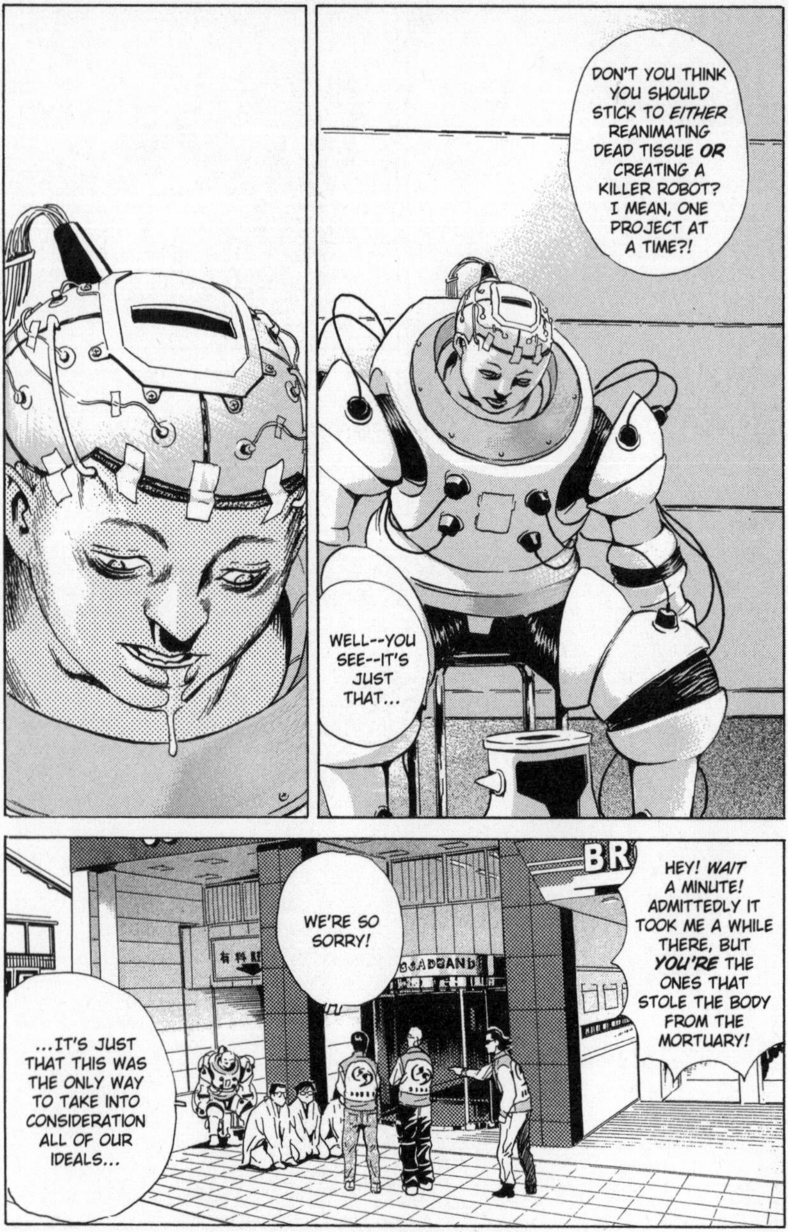

DON'T YOU THINK YOU SHOULD STICK TO *EITHER* REANIMATING DEAD TISSUE ***OR*** CREATING A KILLER ROBOT? I MEAN, ONE PROJECT AT A TIME?!
WELL--YOU SEE--IT'S JUST THAT...
HEY! *WAIT* A MINUTE! ADMITTEDLY IT TOOK ME A WHILE THERE, BUT ***YOU'RE*** THE ONES THAT STOLE THE BODY FROM THE MORTUARY!
WE'RE SO SORRY!
...IT'S JUST THAT THIS WAS THE ONLY WAY TO TAKE INTO CONSIDERATION ALL OF OUR IDEALS...

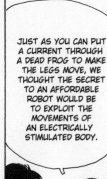

WHAT DO YOU MEAN?
ahem. WELL, IN ORDER FOR THE ROBOT TO HAVE A.) AN ELECTRONIC BRAIN, B.), A "PILDER ON"-STYLE START-UP, AND C.) THE CONCEPTS OF A MOBILE SUIT--
...HOW ABOUT A.) STEALING DEAD BODIES, B.) *STEALING DEAD BODIES...*
WELL, IT'S KIND OF LIKE BEING FREEGAN, BUT WITH CORPSES.
JUST AS YOU CAN PUT A CURRENT THROUGH A DEAD FROG TO MAKE THE LEGS MOVE, WE THOUGHT THE SECRET TO AN AFFORDABLE ROBOT WOULD BE TO EXPLOIT THE MOVEMENTS OF AN ELECTRICALLY STIMULATED BODY.
LATER MODELS WERE GOING TO INCORPORATE REFRIGERATION, OF COURSE.
ピク
PERSONALLY, *I* WANTED TO STICK TO THE MOBILE SUIT CONCEPT, BUT ***THOSE*** TWO...
キラッ
WHAT ARE YOU SAYING?! I WANTED AN AUTONOMOUS UNIT LIKE ASTRO TO BEGIN WITH!
AND ALL I EVER ASKED FOR WAS A "PILDER ON!" ***THAT'S ALL I EVER ASKED FOR!***
FOOLS! WE COULD HAVE KIDNAPPED A *LIVING* TEST SUBJECT NO ONE WOULD MISS--I HAD IN MIND THAT CERAMICS MAJOR...

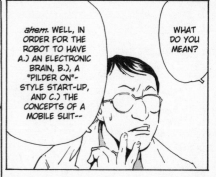

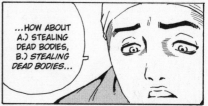

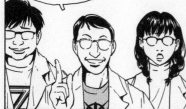

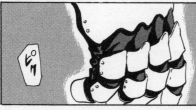

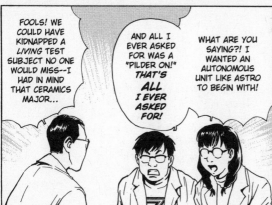

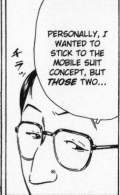

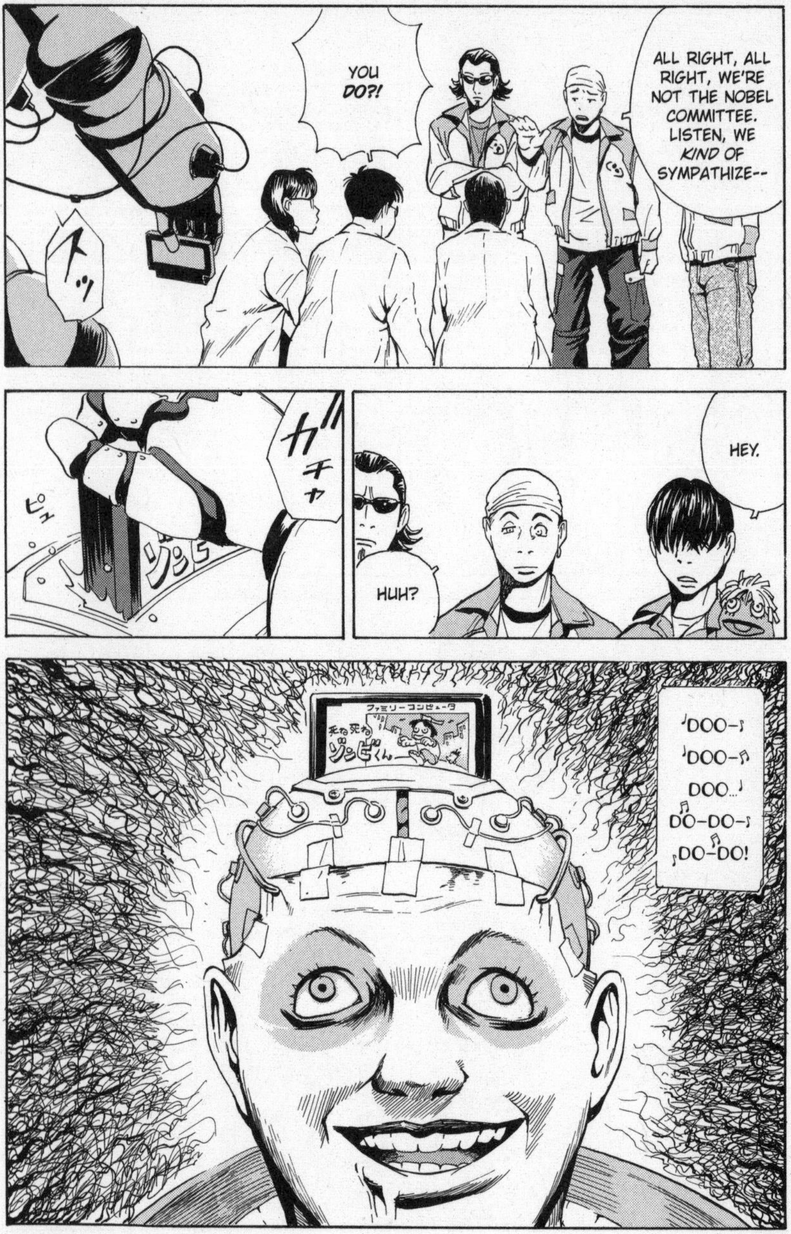
ALL RIGHT, ALL RIGHT, WE'RE NOT THE NOBEL COMMITTEE. LISTEN, WE *KIND* OF SYMPATHIZE--
YOU *DO*?!
スッ
HEY.
HUH?
カチャ
ピュ
♩DOO-♪
♩DOO-♫
DOO...♩
♫DO-DO-♪
♪DO-DO!
ファミリーコンピュータ
死ね死ね
ゾンビくん

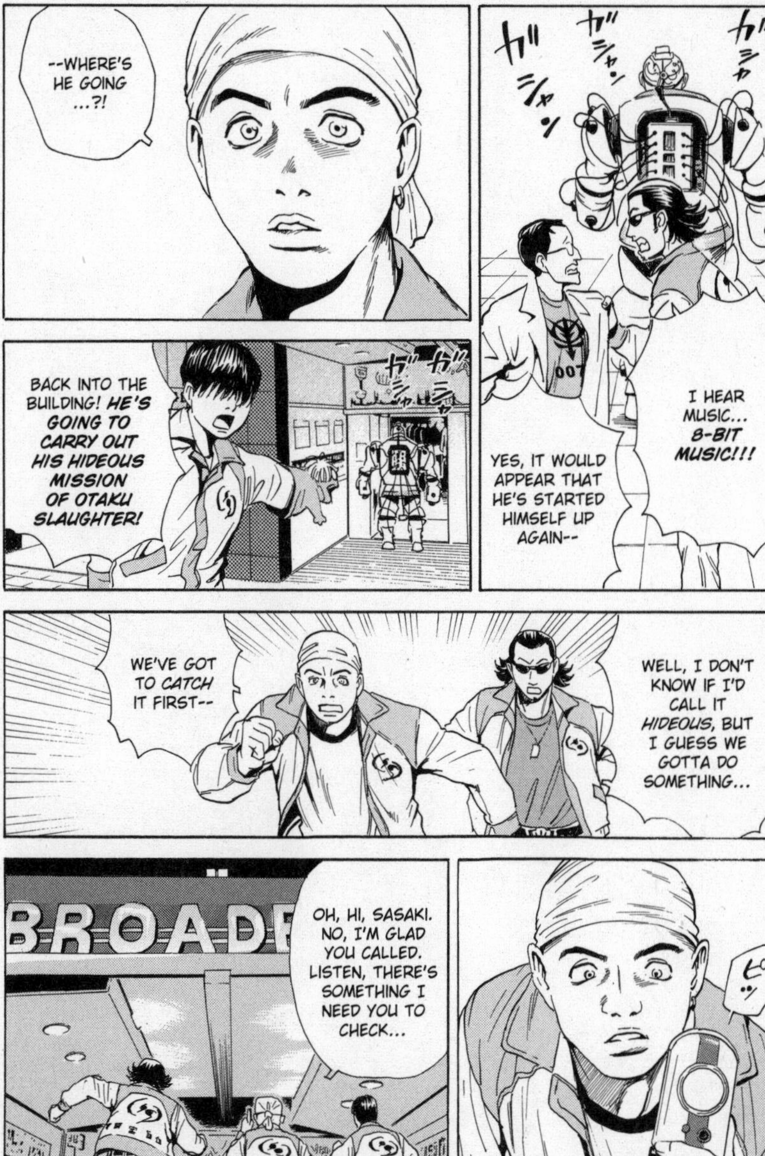
ガシャ
ガシャン
ガシャン
I HEAR MUSIC... 8-BIT MUSIC!!!
YES, IT WOULD APPEAR THAT HE'S STARTED HIMSELF UP AGAIN--
--WHERE'S HE GOING ...?!
BACK INTO THE BUILDING! HE'S GOING TO CARRY OUT HIS HIDEOUS MISSION OF OTAKU SLAUGHTER!
ガシャ
ガシャ
WELL, I DON'T KNOW IF I'D CALL IT HIDEOUS, BUT I GUESS WE GOTTA DO SOMETHING...
WE'VE GOT TO CATCH IT FIRST--
ピッ
OH, HI, SASAKI. NO, I'M GLAD YOU CALLED. LISTEN, THERE'S SOMETHING I NEED YOU TO CHECK...
BROADE

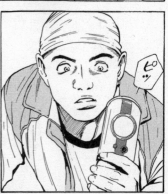

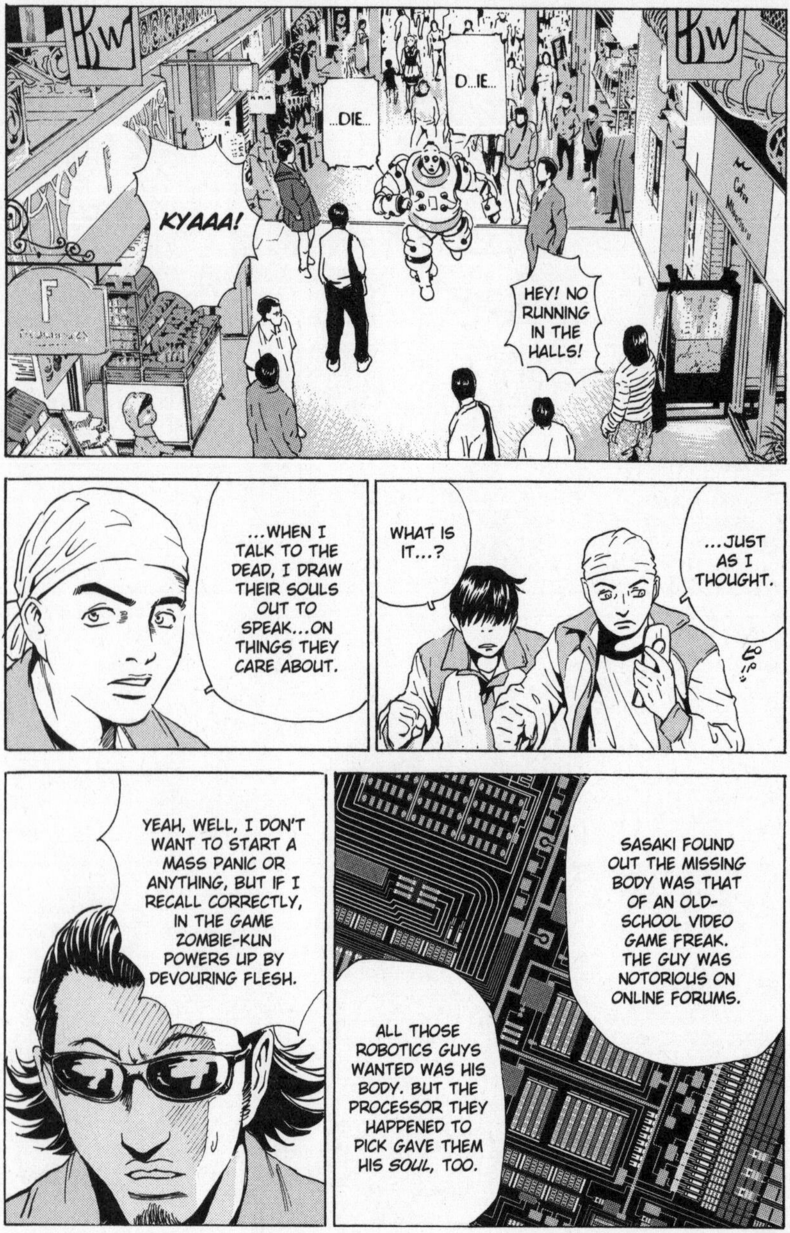
D...IE...
...DIE...
KYAAA!
HEY! NO RUNNING IN THE HALLS!
...JUST AS I THOUGHT.
WHAT IS IT...?
...WHEN I TALK TO THE DEAD, I DRAW THEIR SOULS OUT TO SPEAK...ON THINGS THEY CARE ABOUT.
SASAKI FOUND OUT THE MISSING BODY WAS THAT OF AN OLD-SCHOOL VIDEO GAME FREAK. THE GUY WAS NOTORIOUS ON ONLINE FORUMS.
ALL THOSE ROBOTICS GUYS WANTED WAS HIS BODY. BUT THE PROCESSOR THEY HAPPENED TO PICK GAVE THEM HIS *SOUL*, TOO.
YEAH, WELL, I DON'T WANT TO START A MASS PANIC OR ANYTHING, BUT IF I RECALL CORRECTLY, IN THE GAME ZOMBIE-KUN POWERS UP BY DEVOURING FLESH.

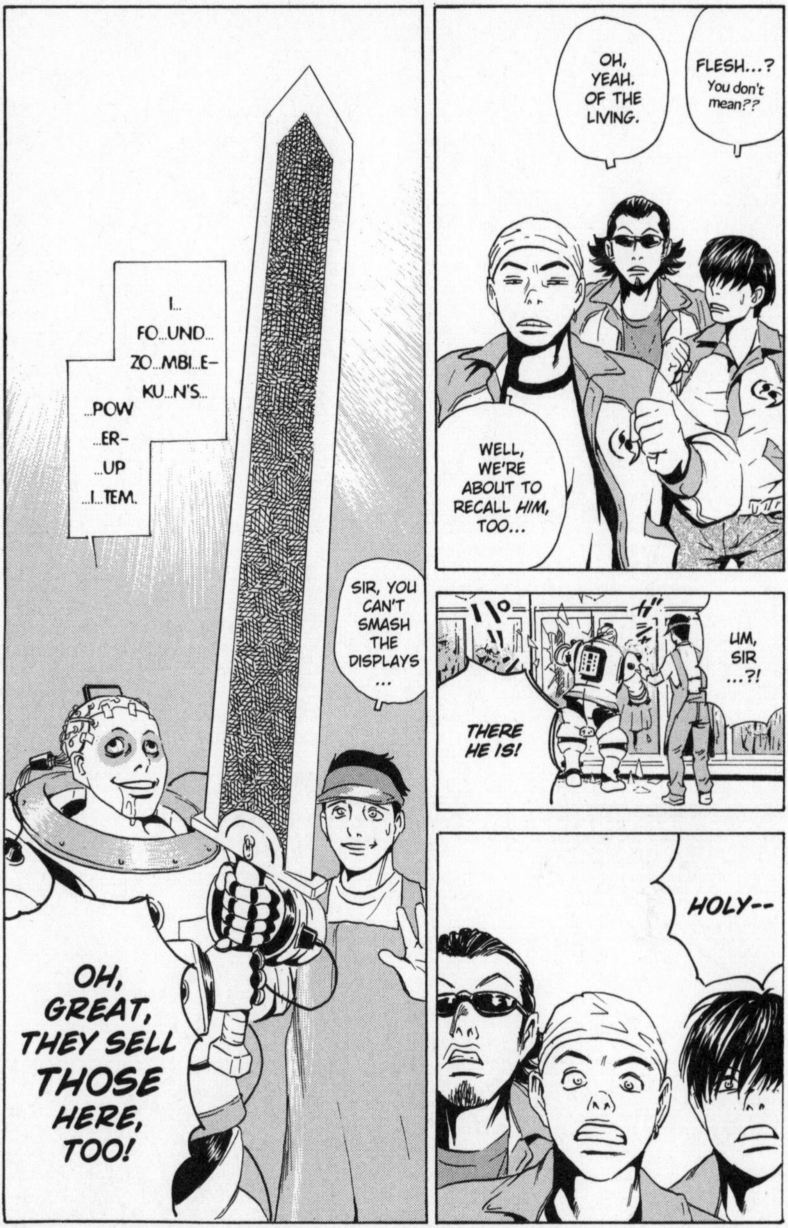

FLESH...? You don't mean??
OH, YEAH. OF THE LIVING.
WELL, WE'RE ABOUT TO RECALL HIM, TOO...
UM, SIR ...?!
THERE HE IS!
HOLY--
SIR, YOU CAN'T SMASH THE DISPLAYS ...
I... FO...UND... ZO...MBI...E-KU...N'S... ...POW ...ER- ...UP ...I...TEM.
OH, GREAT, THEY SELL THOSE HERE, TOO!

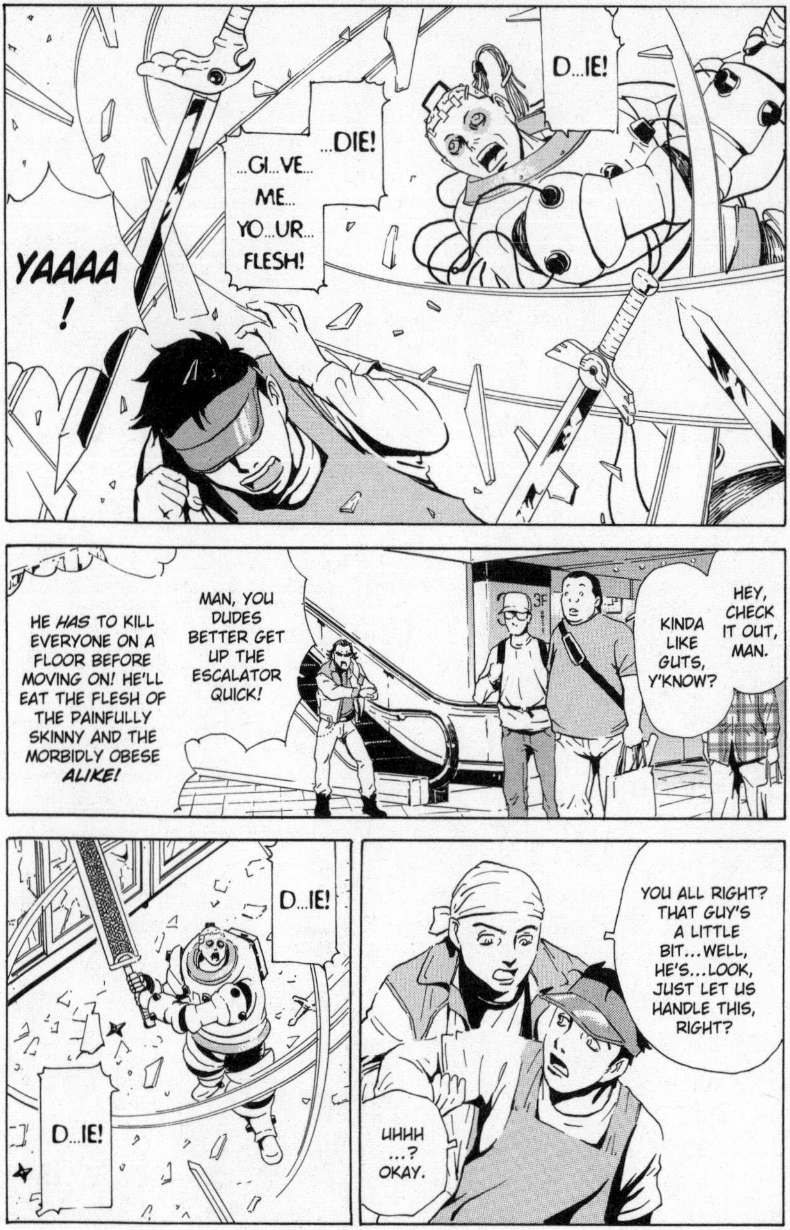
D...IE!
...DIE!
...GI...VE... ME... YO...UR... FLESH!
YAAAA !
HEY, CHECK IT OUT, MAN.
KINDA LIKE GUTS, Y'KNOW?
MAN, YOU DUDES BETTER GET UP THE ESCALATOR QUICK!
HE *HAS* TO KILL EVERYONE ON A FLOOR BEFORE MOVING ON! HE'LL EAT THE FLESH OF THE PAINFULLY SKINNY AND THE MORBIDLY OBESE *ALIKE!*
YOU ALL RIGHT? THAT GUY'S A LITTLE BIT...WELL, HE'S...LOOK, JUST LET US HANDLE THIS, RIGHT?
UHHH ...? OKAY.
D...IE!
D...IE!

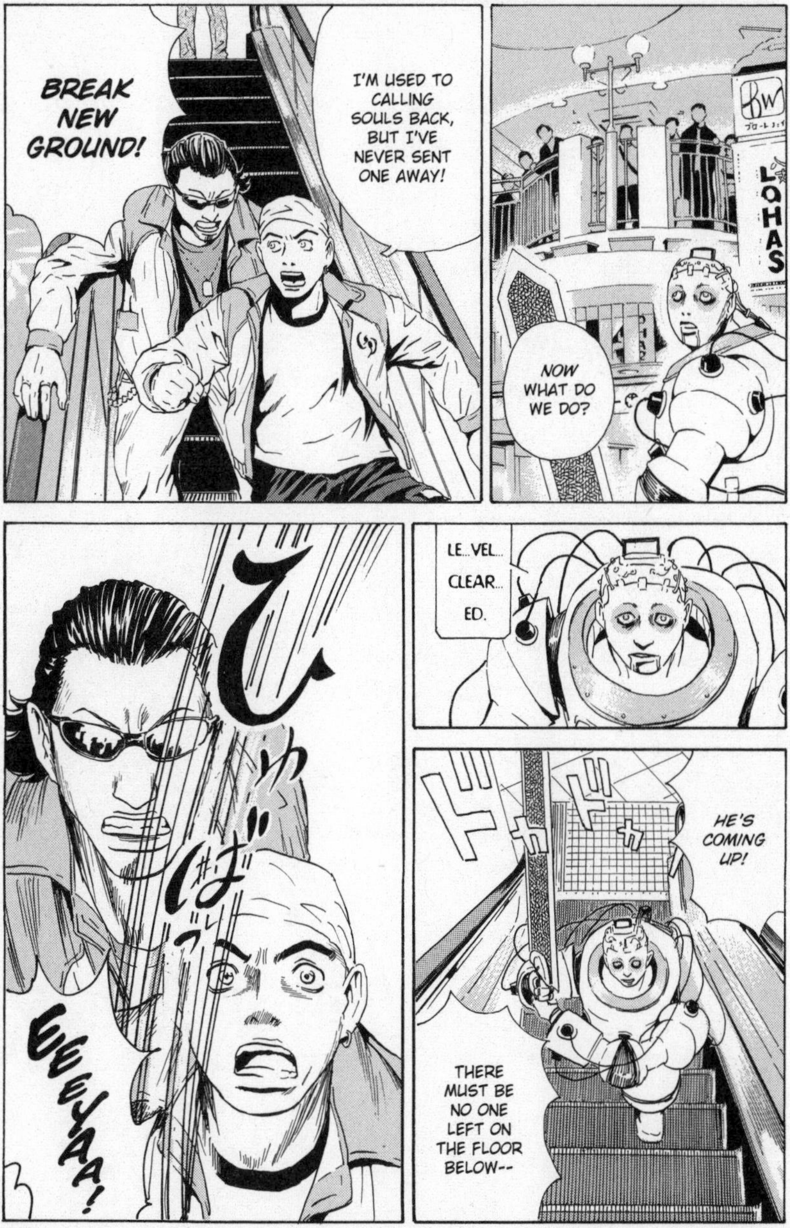
LOHAS
NOW WHAT DO WE DO?
I'M USED TO CALLING SOULS BACK, BUT I'VE NEVER SENT ONE AWAY!
BREAK NEW GROUND!
LE...VEL... CLEAR... ED.
HE'S COMING UP!
THERE MUST BE NO ONE LEFT ON THE FLOOR BELOW--
EEEJYAA!

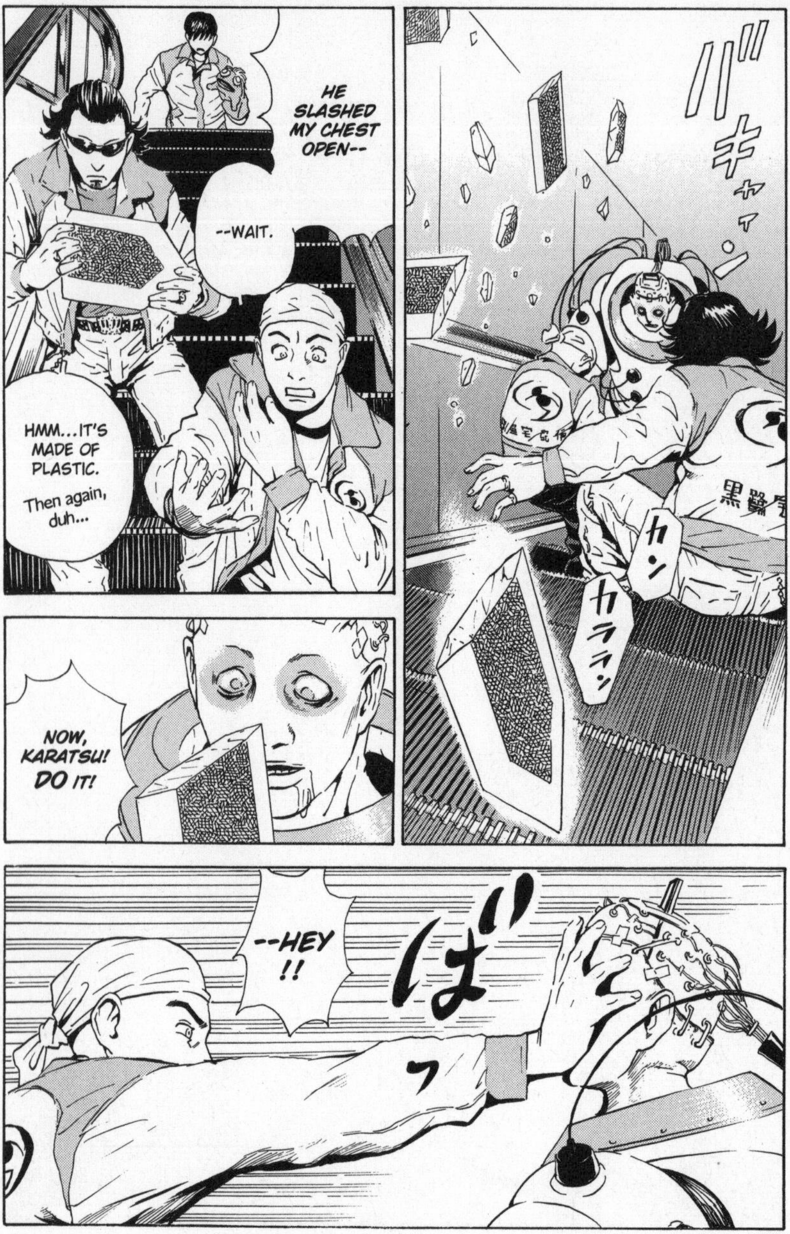
バキャィン
カン
カララン
HE SLASHED MY CHEST OPEN--
--WAIT.
HMM...IT'S MADE OF PLASTIC.
Then again, duh...
NOW, KARATSU! DO IT!
--HEY !!
ばッ

YOU'RE ALREADY DEAD...

...SO LEAVE THAT BODY NOW.

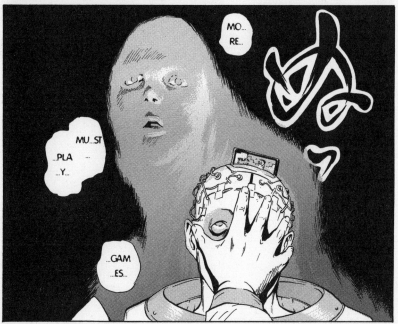

MO... RE...

MU...ST ...PLA ...Y...

...GAM ...ES...

45

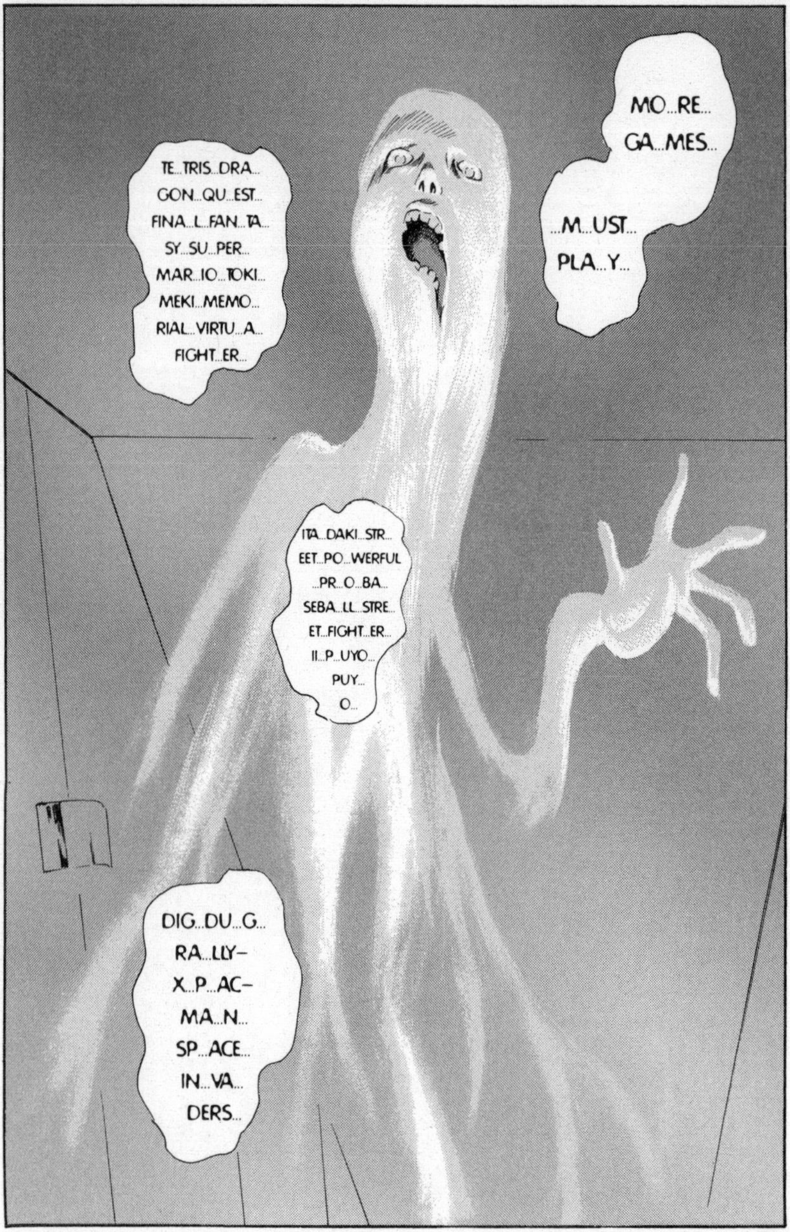
MO...RE... GA...MES...
...M...UST... PLA...Y...
TE...TRIS...DRA... GON...QU...EST... FINA...L...FAN...TA... SY...SU...PER... MAR...IO...TOKI... MEKI...MEMO... RIAL...VIRTU...A... FIGHT...ER...
ITA...DAKI...STR... EET...PO...WERFUL ...PR...O...BA... SEBA...LL...STRE... ET...FIGHT...ER... II...P...UYO... PUY... O...
DIG...DU...G... RA...LLY– X...P...AC– MA...N... SP...ACE... IN...VA... DERS...

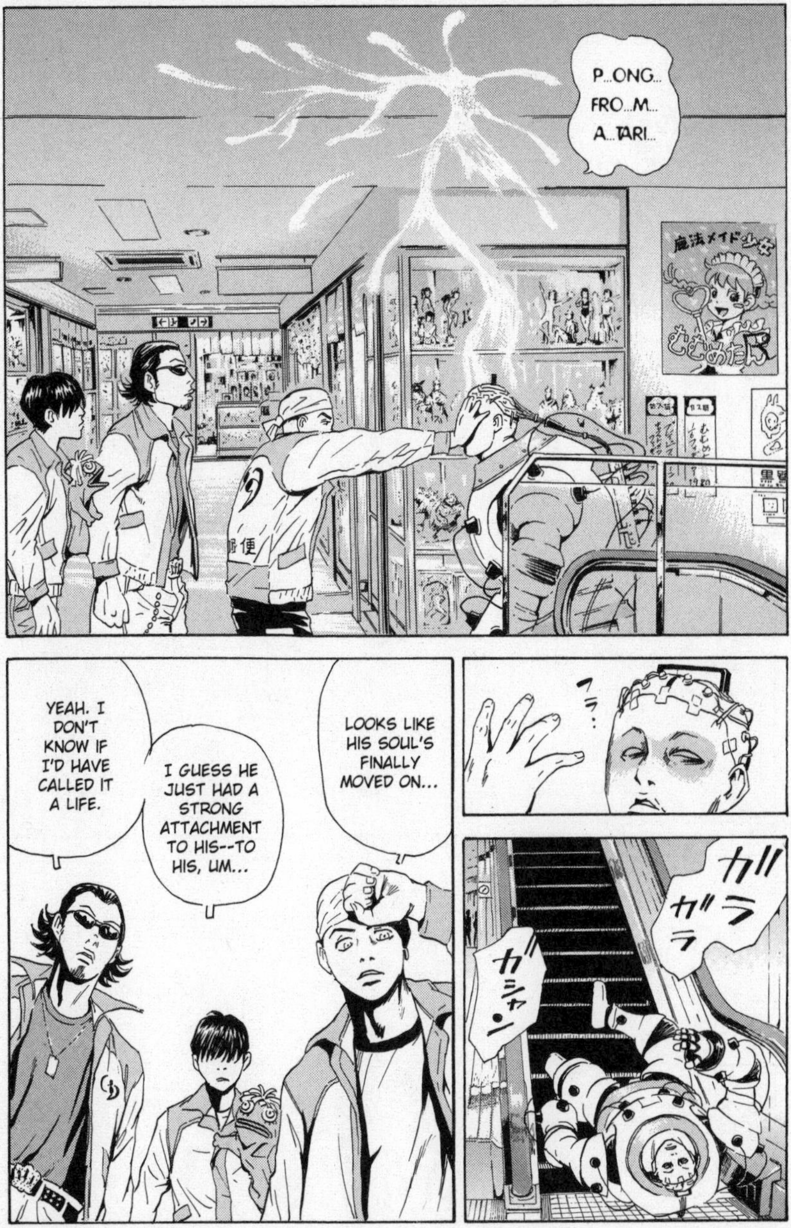
P...ONG...
FRO...M...
A...TARI...
魔法メイド少女
フラ...
ガラガラ
ガシャン
LOOKS LIKE HIS SOUL'S FINALLY MOVED ON...
I GUESS HE JUST HAD A STRONG ATTACHMENT TO HIS--TO HIS, UM...
YEAH. I DON'T KNOW IF I'D HAVE CALLED IT A LIFE.

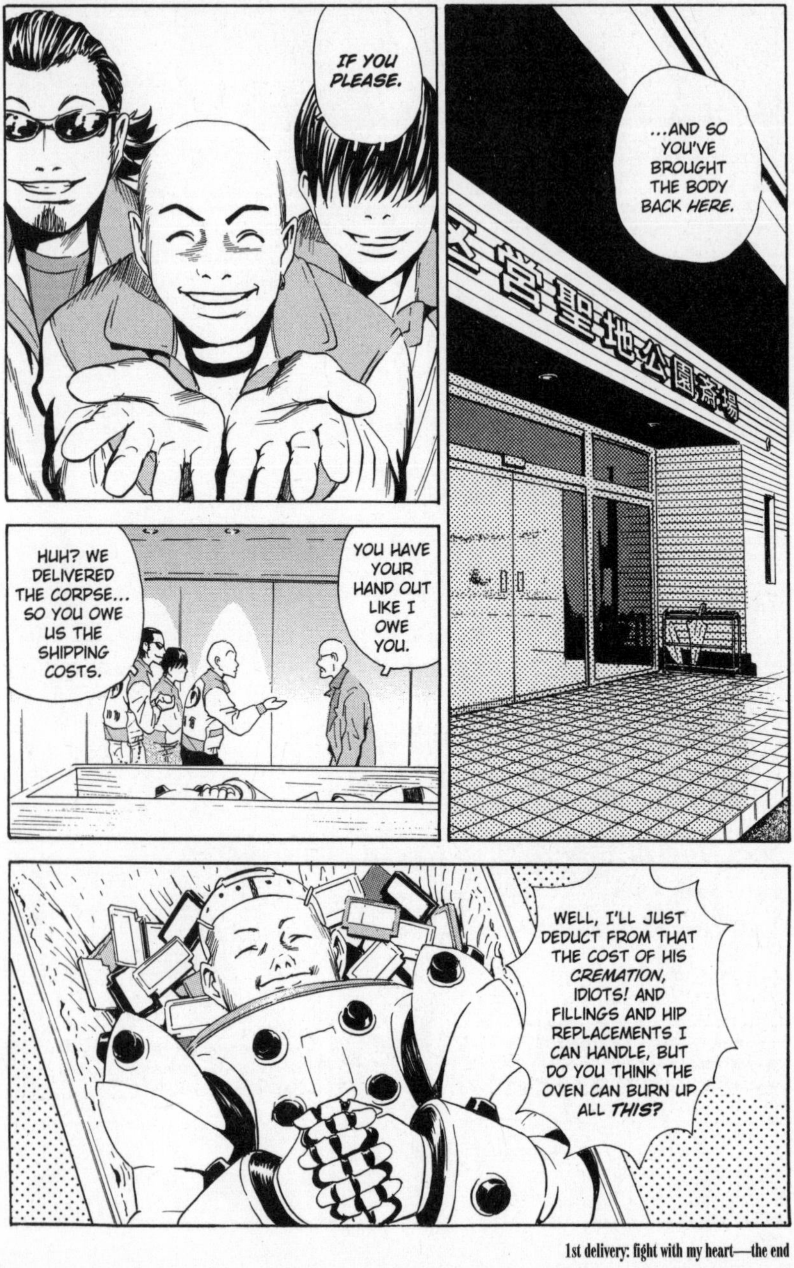
...AND SO YOU'VE BROUGHT THE BODY BACK *HERE.*
営聖地公園斎場
IF YOU PLEASE.
YOU HAVE YOUR HAND OUT LIKE I OWE YOU.
HUH? WE DELIVERED THE CORPSE... SO YOU OWE US THE SHIPPING COSTS.
WELL, I'LL JUST DEDUCT FROM THAT THE COST OF HIS *CREMATION,* IDIOTS! AND FILLINGS AND HIP REPLACEMENTS I CAN HANDLE, BUT DO YOU THINK THE OVEN CAN BURN UP ALL *THIS?*

1st delivery: fight with my heart—the end

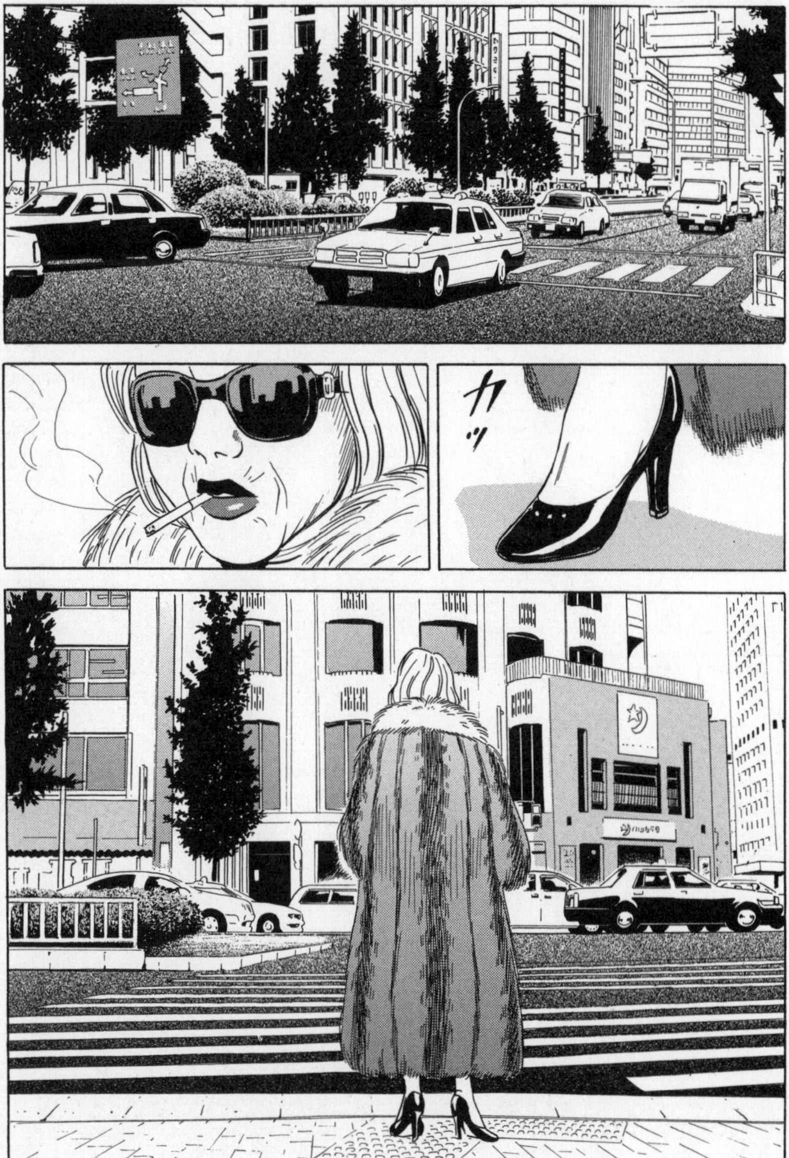
カッ

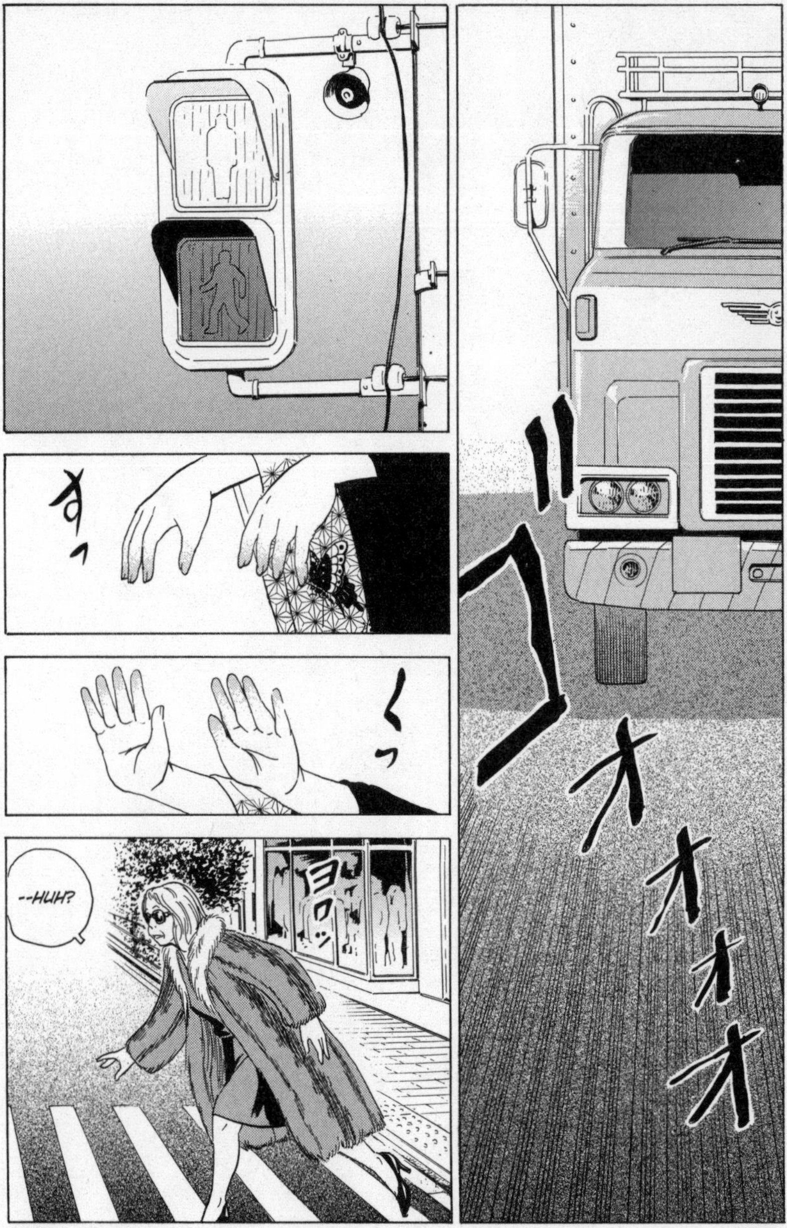
ゴオオオオ
すっ
くっ
--HUH?
ヨロッ

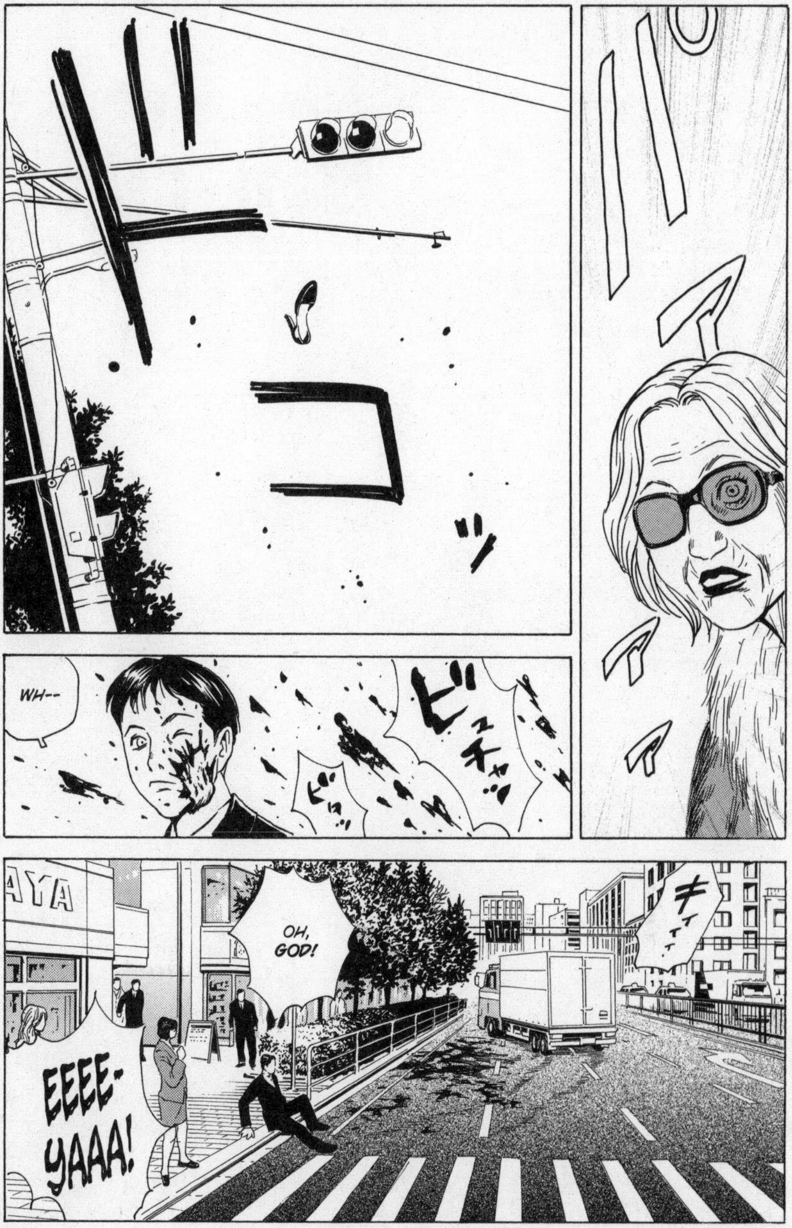
WH--
OH, GOD!
EEEE-YAAA!

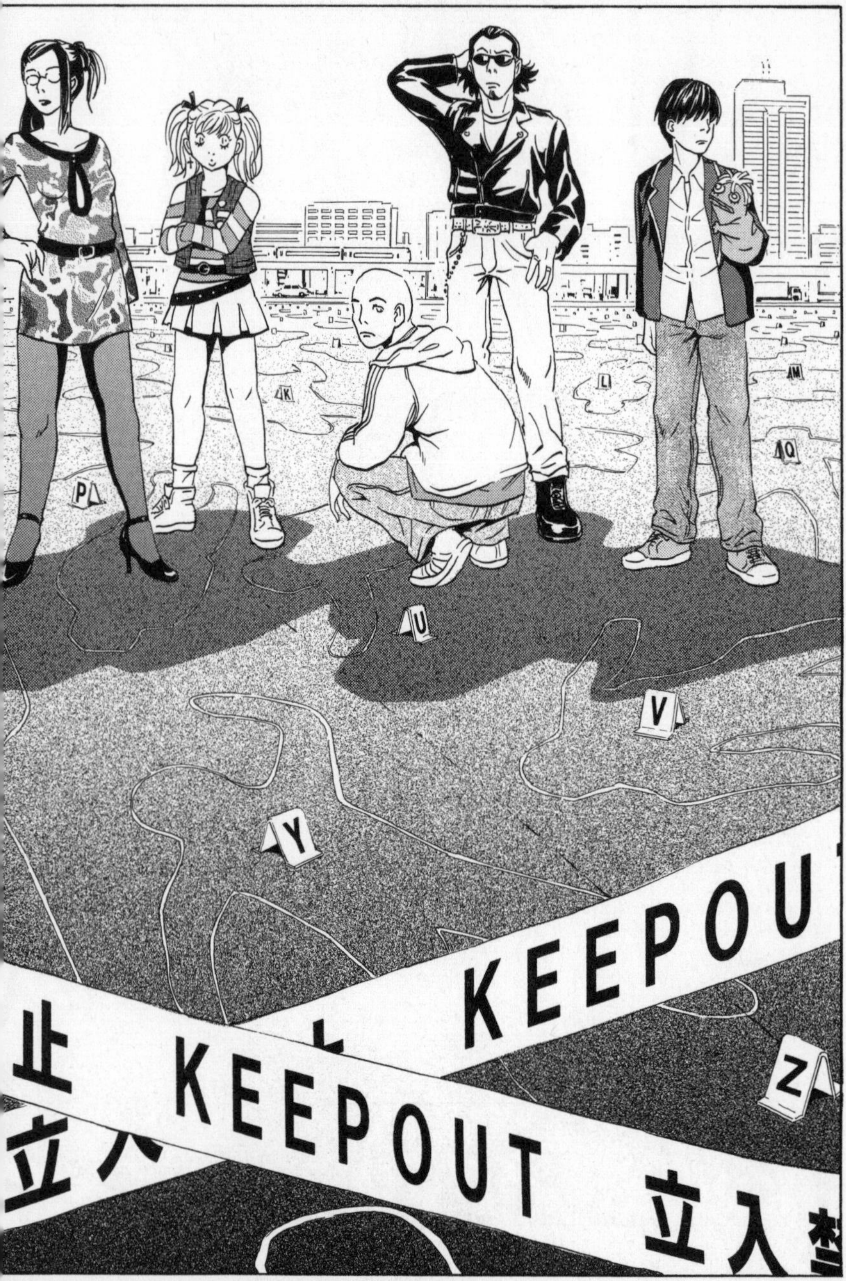
KEEPOU
止
KEEPOUT
立入

2nd delivery プリティー・プリティ

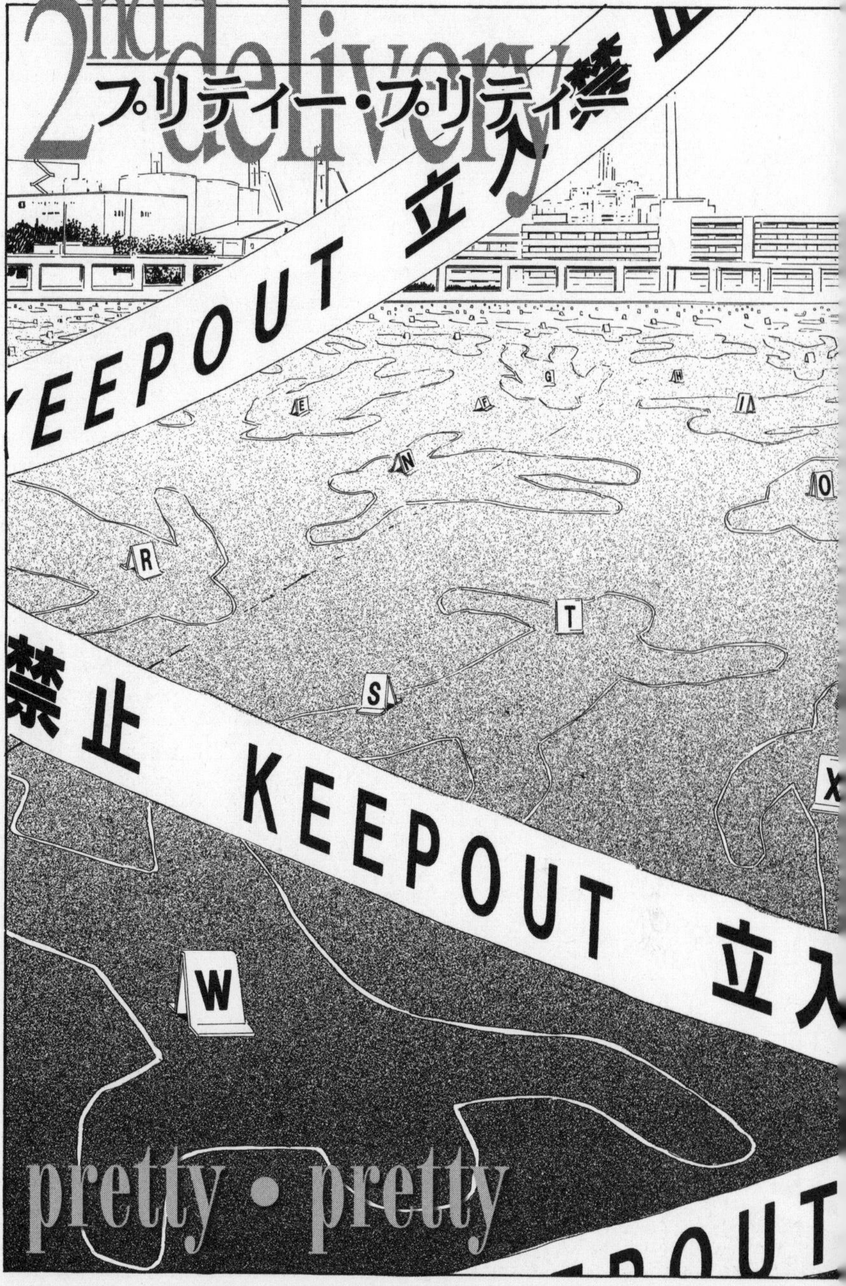
KEEPOUT 立入
禁止 KEEPOUT 立入

pretty • pretty

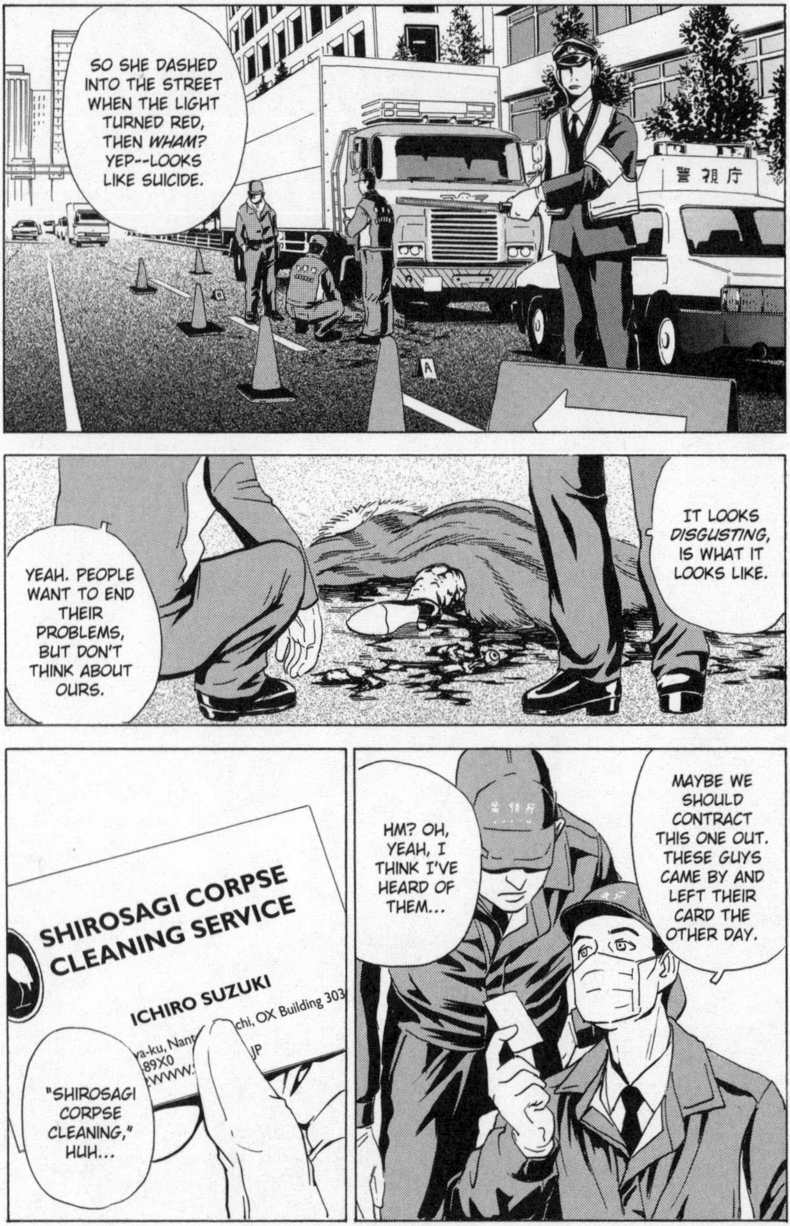
SO SHE DASHED INTO THE STREET WHEN THE LIGHT TURNED RED, THEN *WHAM*? YEP--LOOKS LIKE SUICIDE.
警視庁
IT LOOKS *DISGUSTING*, IS WHAT IT LOOKS LIKE.
YEAH. PEOPLE WANT TO END THEIR PROBLEMS, BUT DON'T THINK ABOUT OURS.
MAYBE WE SHOULD CONTRACT THIS ONE OUT. THESE GUYS CAME BY AND LEFT THEIR CARD THE OTHER DAY.
HM? OH, YEAH, I THINK I'VE HEARD OF THEM...
SHIROSAGI CORPSE CLEANING SERVICE
ICHIRO SUZUKI
"SHIROSAGI CORPSE CLEANING," HUH...

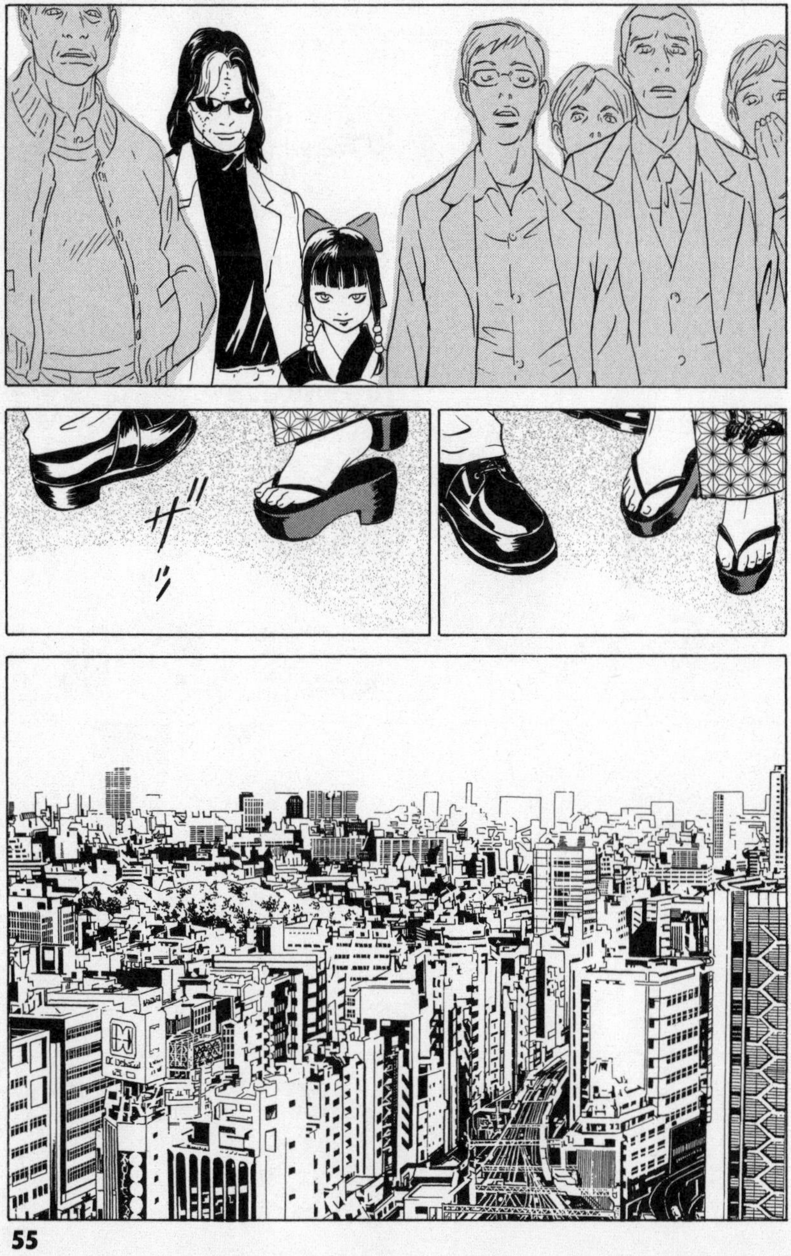
ザッ

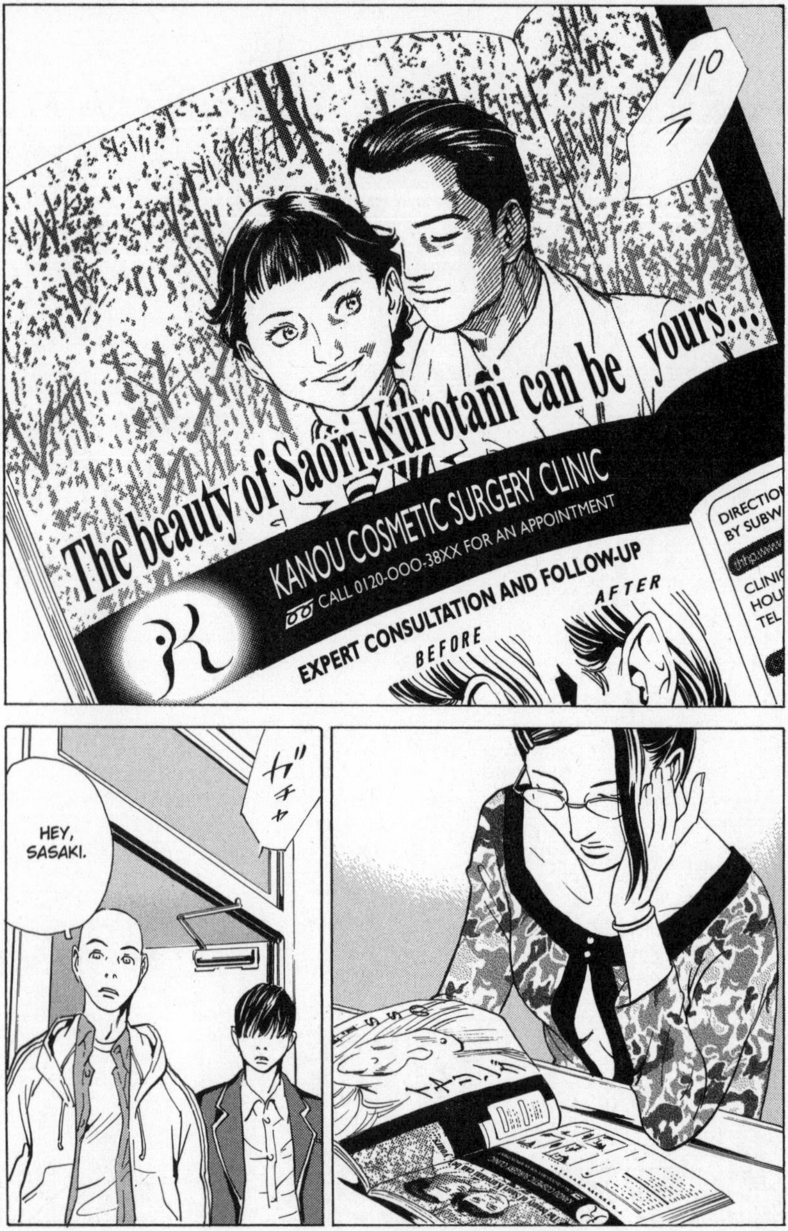
パラ
The beauty of Saori Kurotani can be yours...
KANOU COSMETIC SURGERY CLINIC
CALL 0120-000-38XX FOR AN APPOINTMENT
EXPERT CONSULTATION AND FOLLOW-UP
BEFORE
AFTER
ガチャ
HEY, SASAKI.

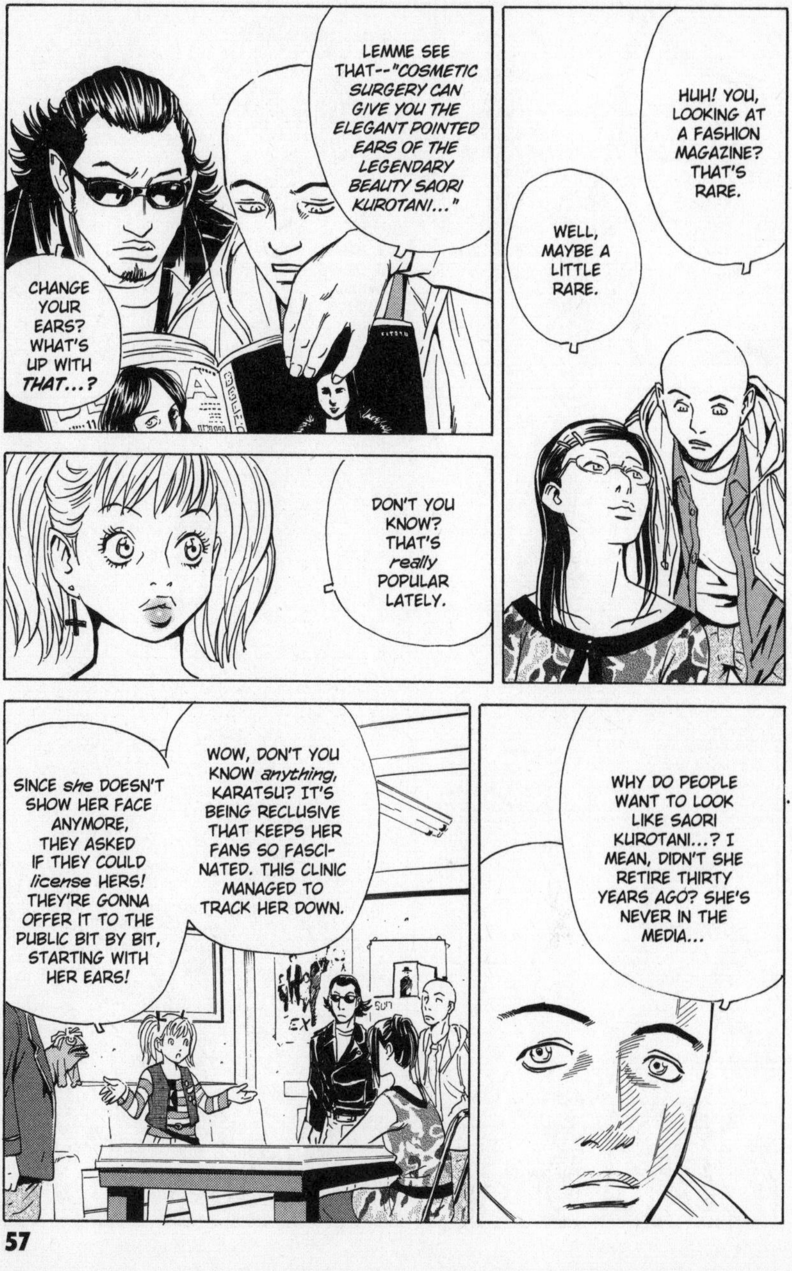
HUH! YOU, LOOKING AT A FASHION MAGAZINE? THAT'S RARE.
WELL, MAYBE A LITTLE RARE.
LEMME SEE THAT--"COSMETIC SURGERY CAN GIVE YOU THE ELEGANT POINTED EARS OF THE LEGENDARY BEAUTY SAORI KUROTANI..."
CHANGE YOUR EARS? WHAT'S UP WITH *THAT...?*
DON'T YOU KNOW? THAT'S *really* POPULAR LATELY.
WHY DO PEOPLE WANT TO LOOK LIKE SAORI KUROTANI...? I MEAN, DIDN'T SHE RETIRE THIRTY YEARS AGO? SHE'S NEVER IN THE MEDIA...
WOW, DON'T YOU KNOW *anything,* KARATSU? IT'S BEING RECLUSIVE THAT KEEPS HER FANS SO FASCI-NATED. THIS CLINIC MANAGED TO TRACK HER DOWN.
SINCE *she* DOESN'T SHOW HER FACE ANYMORE, THEY ASKED IF THEY COULD *license* HERS! THEY'RE GONNA OFFER IT TO THE PUBLIC BIT BY BIT, STARTING WITH HER EARS!

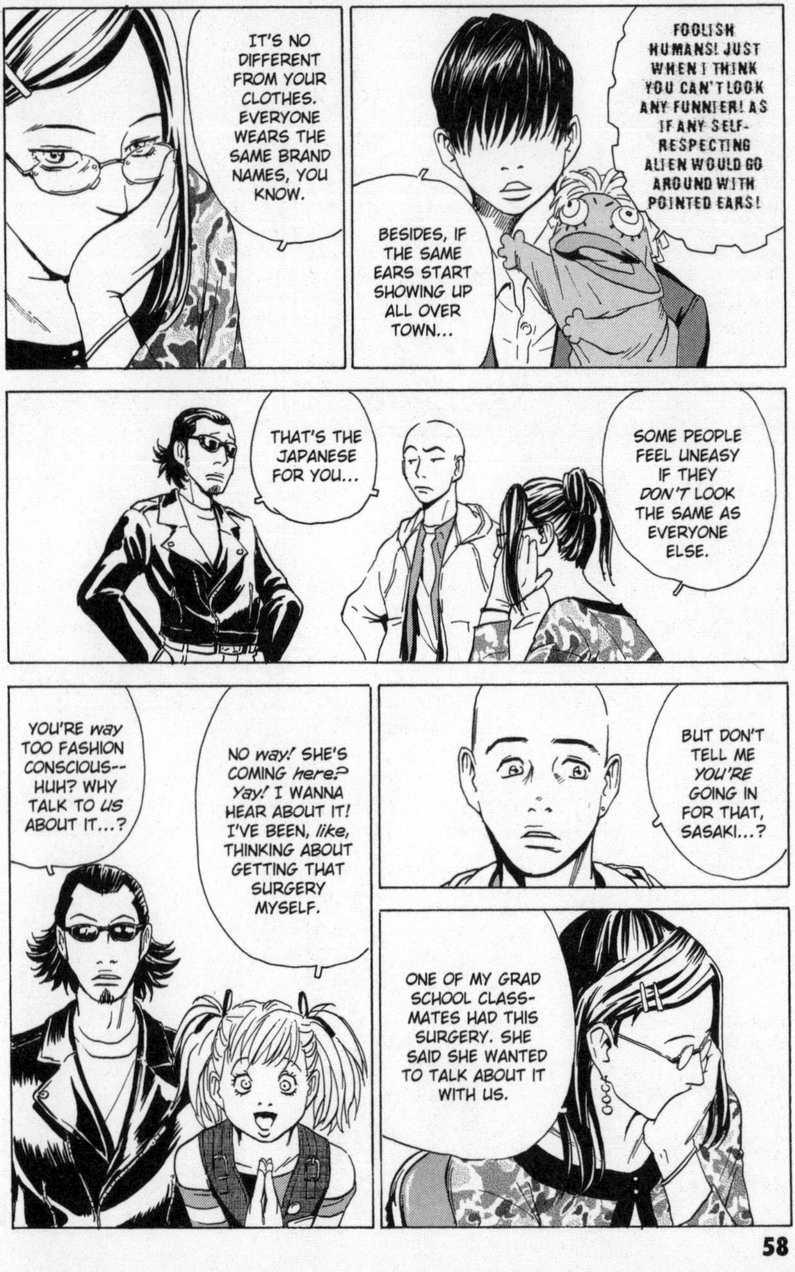
FOOLISH HUMANS! JUST WHEN I THINK YOU CAN'T LOOK ANY FUNNIER! AS IF ANY SELF-RESPECTING ALIEN WOULD GO AROUND WITH POINTED EARS!
BESIDES, IF THE SAME EARS START SHOWING UP ALL OVER TOWN...
IT'S NO DIFFERENT FROM YOUR CLOTHES. EVERYONE WEARS THE SAME BRAND NAMES, YOU KNOW.
SOME PEOPLE FEEL UNEASY IF THEY *DON'T* LOOK THE SAME AS EVERYONE ELSE.
THAT'S THE JAPANESE FOR YOU...
BUT DON'T TELL ME *YOU'RE* GOING IN FOR THAT, SASAKI...?
ONE OF MY GRAD SCHOOL CLASSMATES HAD THIS SURGERY. SHE SAID SHE WANTED TO TALK ABOUT IT WITH US.
NO *way!* SHE'S COMING *here? Yay!* I WANNA HEAR ABOUT IT! I'VE BEEN, *like,* THINKING ABOUT GETTING THAT SURGERY MYSELF.
YOU'RE *way* TOO FASHION CONSCIOUS-- HUH? WHY TALK TO *US* ABOUT IT...?

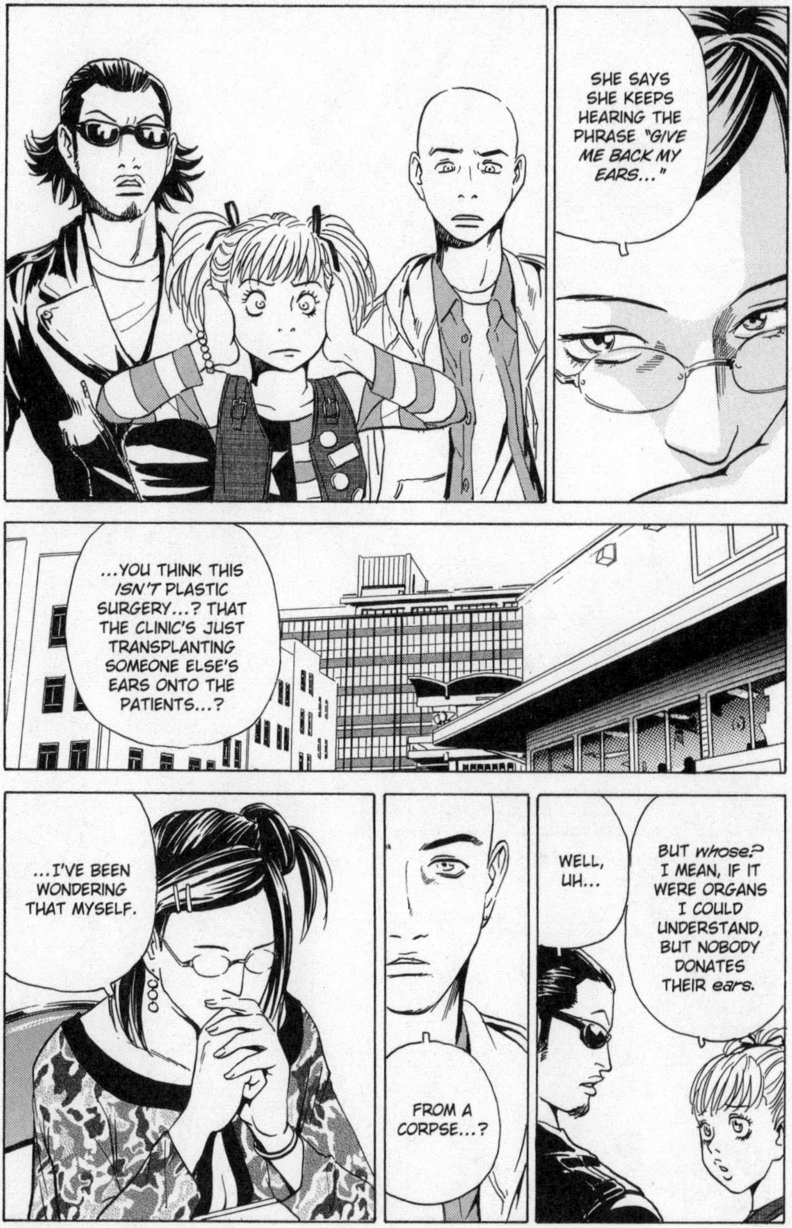
SHE SAYS SHE KEEPS HEARING THE PHRASE *"GIVE ME BACK MY EARS..."*
...YOU THINK THIS *ISN'T* PLASTIC SURGERY...? THAT THE CLINIC'S JUST TRANSPLANTING SOMEONE ELSE'S EARS ONTO THE PATIENTS...?
BUT *whose?* I MEAN, IF IT WERE ORGANS I COULD UNDERSTAND, BUT NOBODY DONATES THEIR *ears.*
WELL, UH...
FROM A CORPSE...?
...I'VE BEEN WONDERING THAT MYSELF.

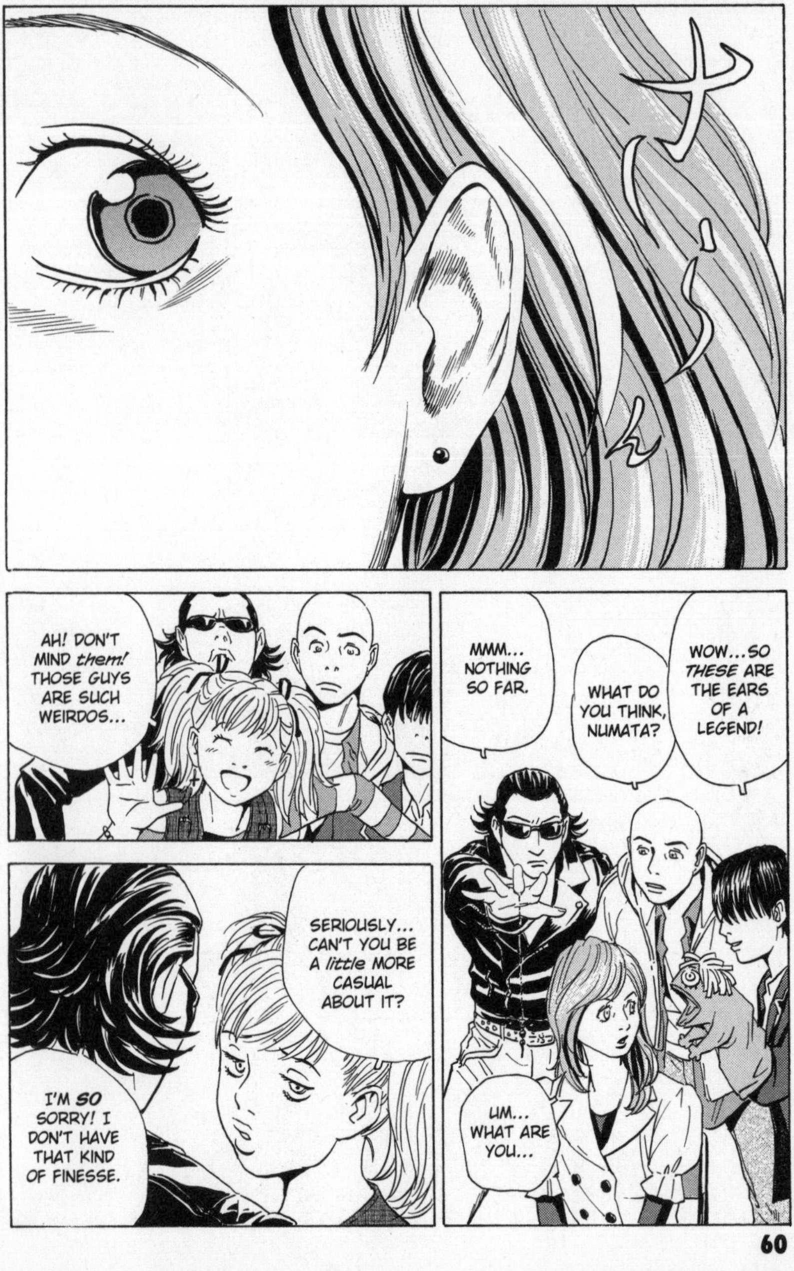
WOW...SO *THESE* ARE THE EARS OF A LEGEND!
WHAT DO YOU THINK, NUMATA?
MMM... NOTHING SO FAR.
UM... WHAT ARE YOU...
AH! DON'T MIND *them!* THOSE GUYS ARE SUCH WEIRDOS...
SERIOUSLY... CAN'T YOU BE A *little* MORE CASUAL ABOUT IT?
I'M *SO* SORRY! I DON'T HAVE THAT KIND OF FINESSE.

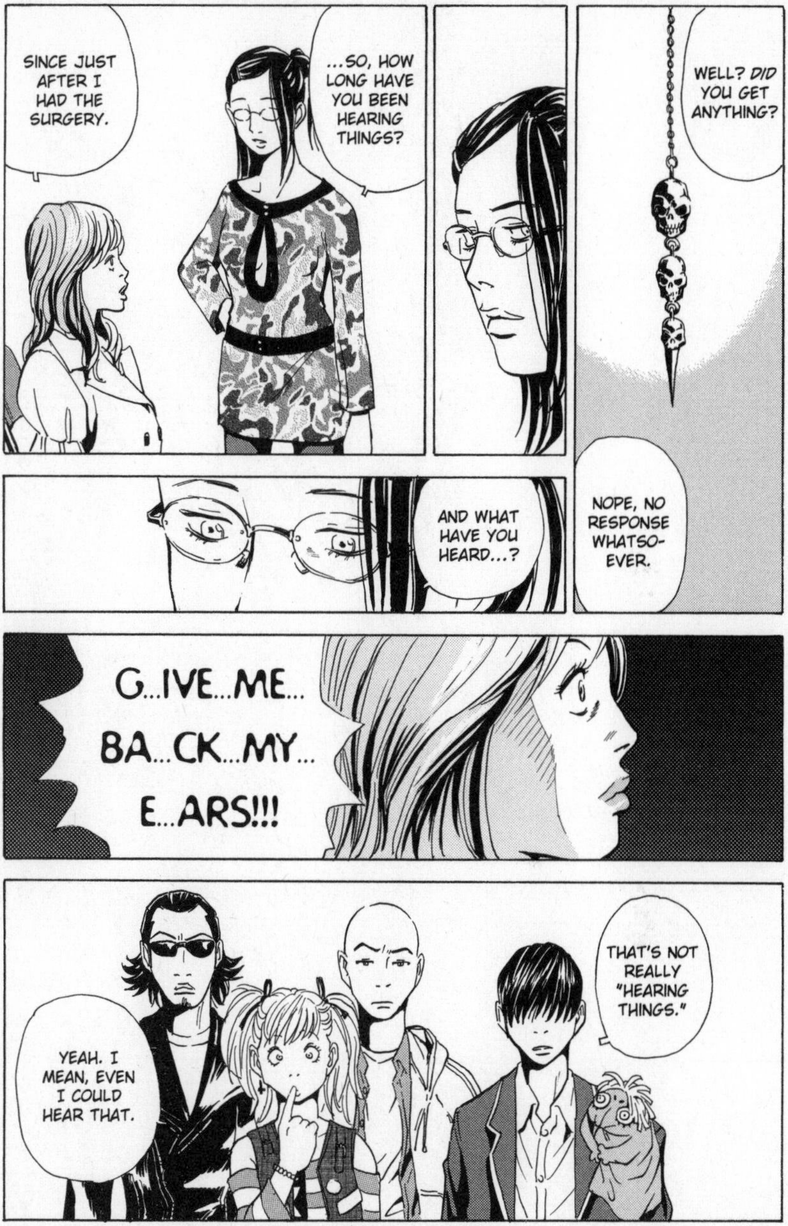
WELL? *DID* YOU GET ANYTHING?
NOPE, NO RESPONSE WHATSO-EVER.
...SO, HOW LONG HAVE YOU BEEN HEARING THINGS?
SINCE JUST AFTER I HAD THE SURGERY.
AND WHAT HAVE YOU HEARD...?
G...IVE...ME... BA...CK...MY... E...ARS!!!
THAT'S NOT REALLY "HEARING THINGS."
YEAH. I MEAN, EVEN I COULD HEAR THAT.

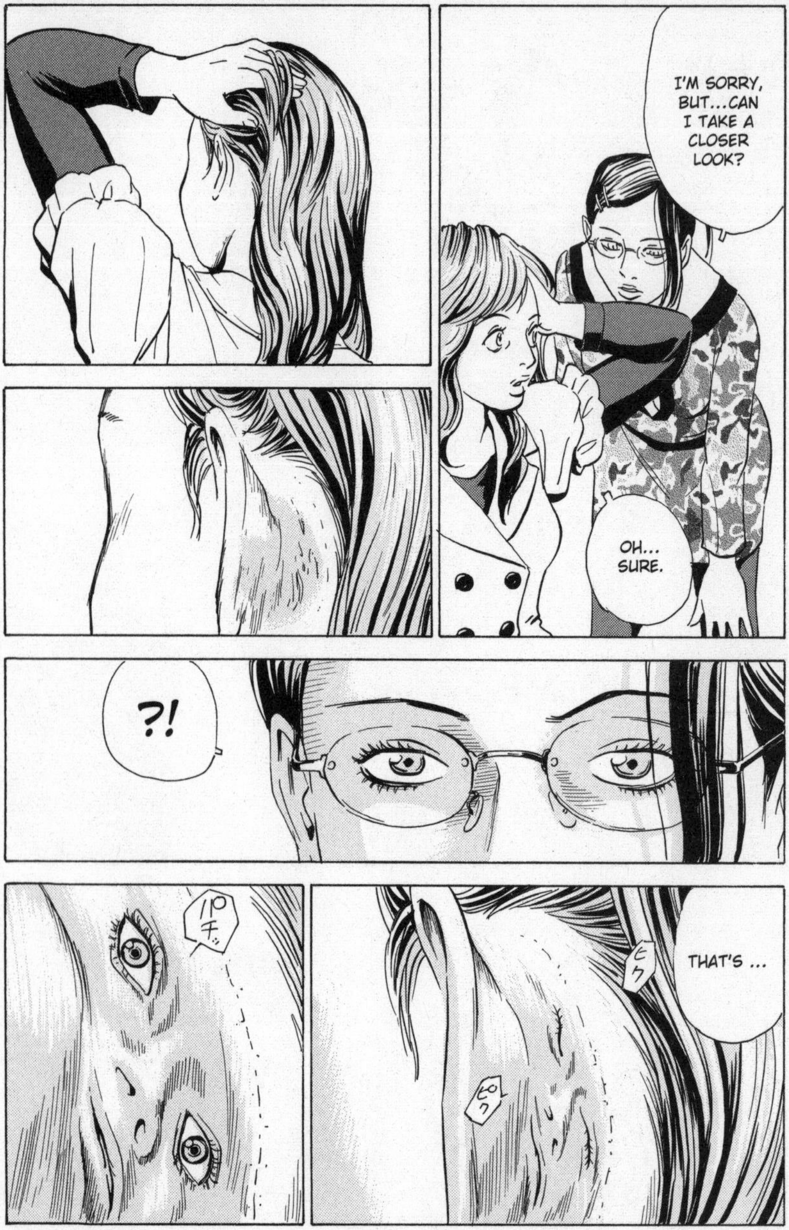
I'M SORRY, BUT...CAN I TAKE A CLOSER LOOK?
OH... SURE.
?!
THAT'S ...

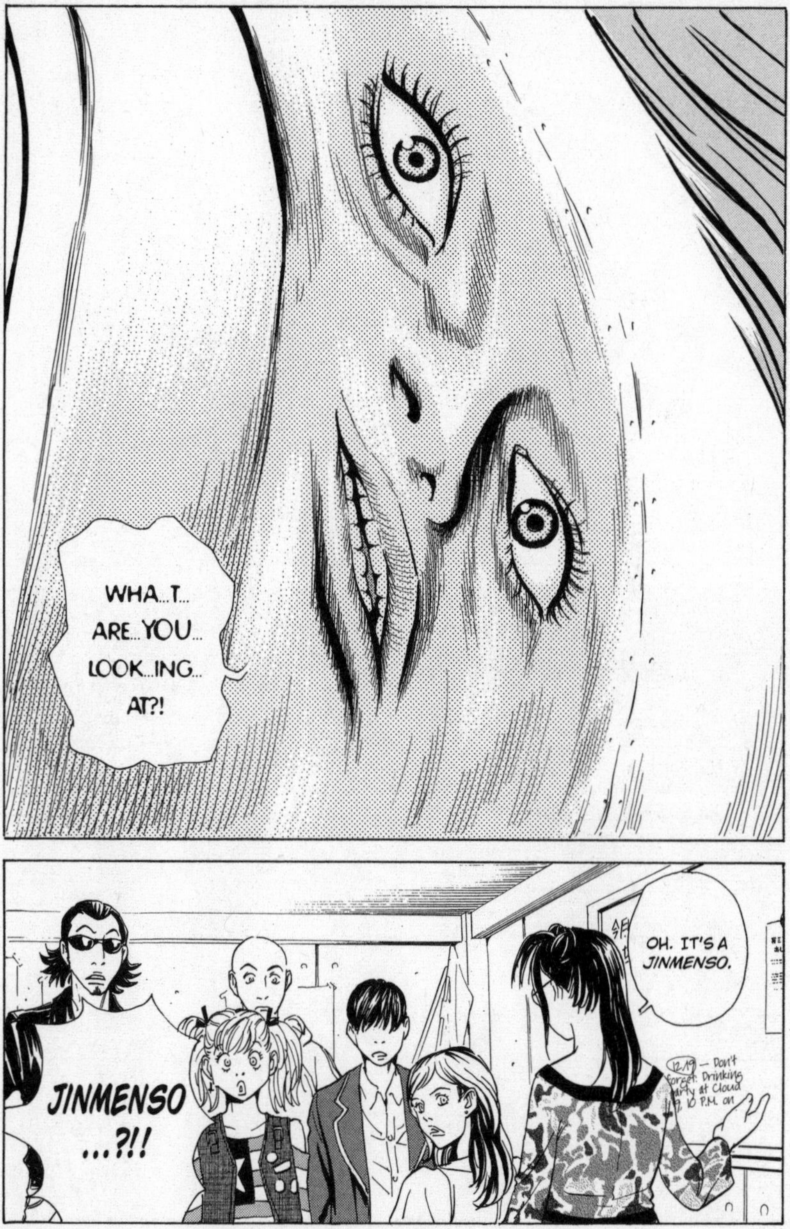
WHA...T... ARE...YOU... LOOK...ING... AT?!
OH. IT'S A JINMENSO.
12.19 — Don't forget: Drinking party at Cloud 10 P.M. on
JINMENSO ...?!!

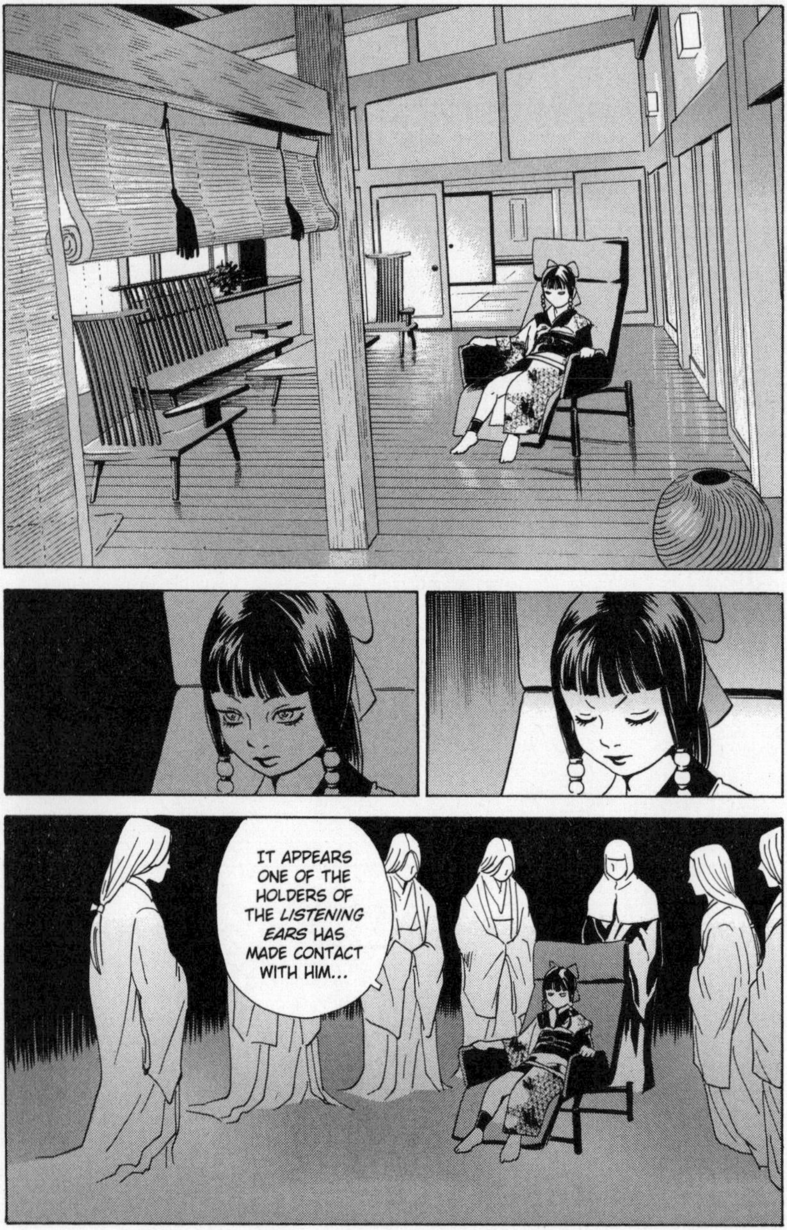
IT APPEARS ONE OF THE HOLDERS OF THE *LISTENING EARS* HAS MADE CONTACT WITH HIM...

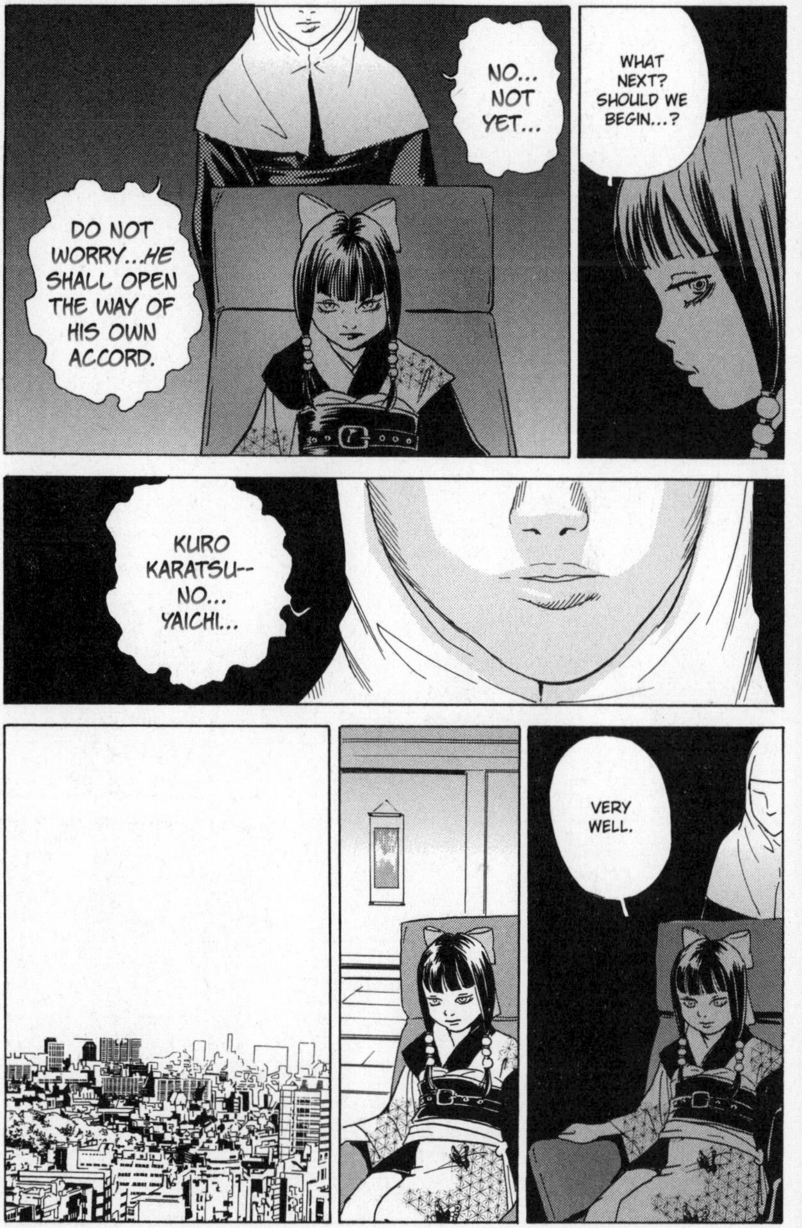
WHAT NEXT? SHOULD WE BEGIN...?
NO... NOT YET...
DO NOT WORRY...*HE* SHALL OPEN THE WAY OF HIS OWN ACCORD.
KURO KARATSU--NO... YAICHI...
VERY WELL.

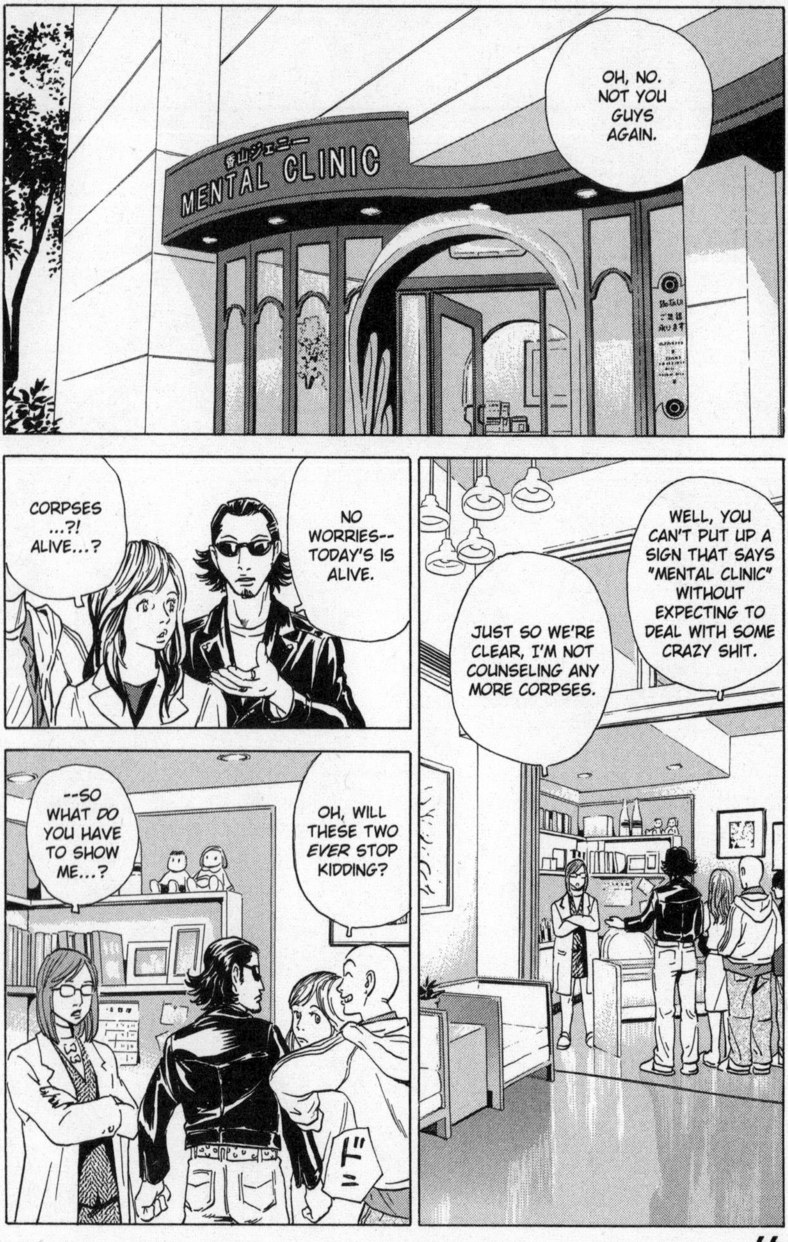
香山ジェニー
MENTAL CLINIC
OH, NO. NOT YOU GUYS AGAIN.
WELL, YOU CAN'T PUT UP A SIGN THAT SAYS "MENTAL CLINIC" WITHOUT EXPECTING TO DEAL WITH SOME CRAZY SHIT.
JUST SO WE'RE CLEAR, I'M NOT COUNSELING ANY MORE CORPSES.
NO WORRIES-- TODAY'S IS ALIVE.
CORPSES ...?! ALIVE...?
OH, WILL THESE TWO *EVER* STOP KIDDING?
--SO WHAT *DO* YOU HAVE TO SHOW ME...?
ドン

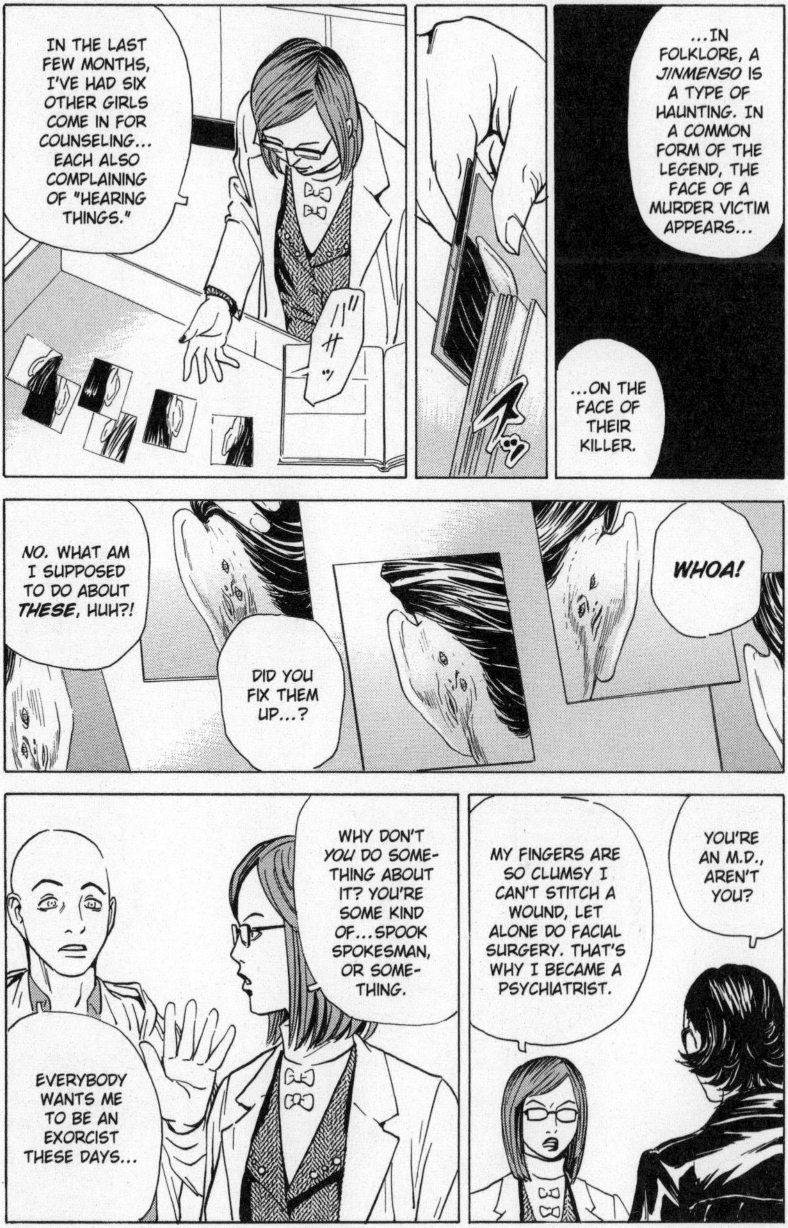
...IN FOLKLORE, A *JINMENSO* IS A TYPE OF HAUNTING. IN A COMMON FORM OF THE LEGEND, THE FACE OF A MURDER VICTIM APPEARS...
...ON THE FACE OF THEIR KILLER.
IN THE LAST FEW MONTHS, I'VE HAD SIX OTHER GIRLS COME IN FOR COUNSELING... EACH ALSO COMPLAINING OF "HEARING THINGS."
WHOA!
DID YOU FIX THEM UP...?
NO. WHAT AM I SUPPOSED TO DO ABOUT ***THESE***, HUH?!
YOU'RE AN M.D., AREN'T YOU?
MY FINGERS ARE SO CLUMSY I CAN'T STITCH A WOUND, LET ALONE DO FACIAL SURGERY. THAT'S WHY I BECAME A PSYCHIATRIST.
WHY DON'T *YOU* DO SOMETHING ABOUT IT? YOU'RE SOME KIND OF...SPOOK SPOKESMAN, OR SOMETHING.
EVERYBODY WANTS ME TO BE AN EXORCIST THESE DAYS...

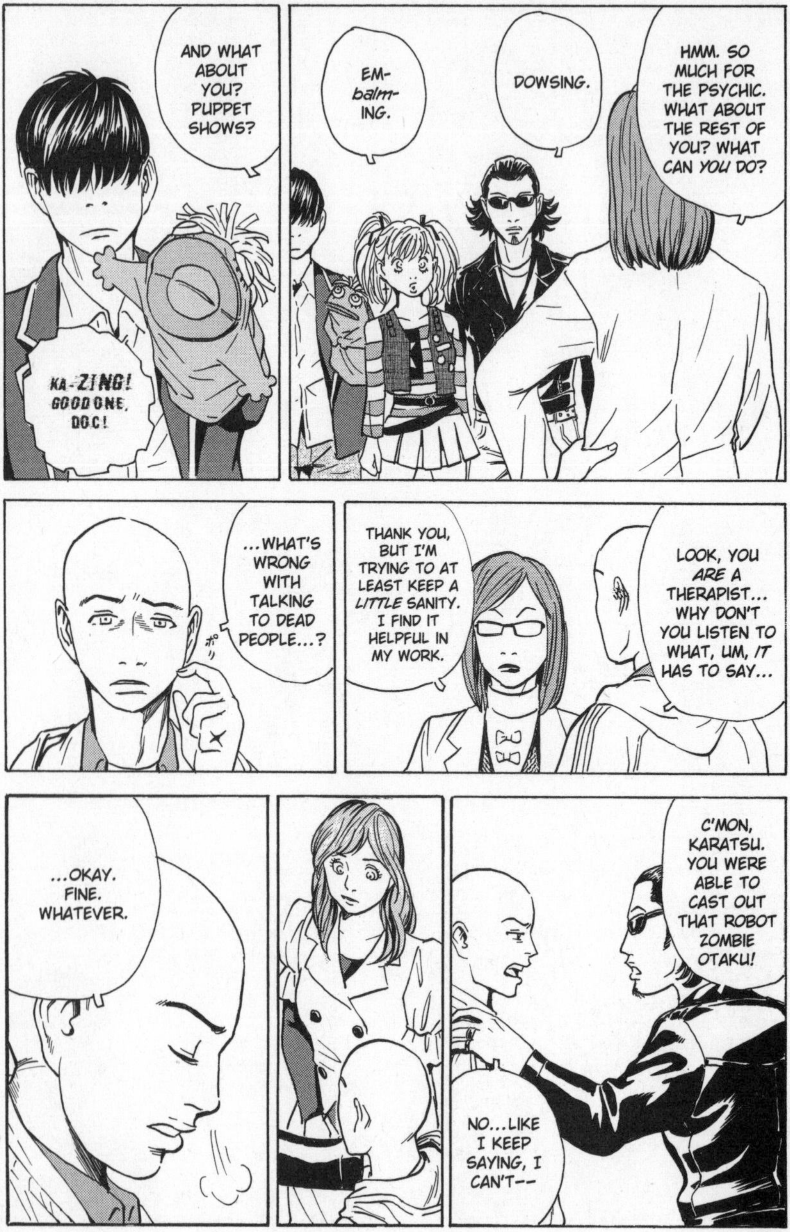
HMM. SO MUCH FOR THE PSYCHIC. WHAT ABOUT THE REST OF YOU? WHAT CAN *YOU* DO?
DOWSING.
EM-*balm*-ING.
AND WHAT ABOUT YOU? PUPPET SHOWS?
KA-ZING! GOOD ONE, DOC!
LOOK, YOU *ARE* A THERAPIST... WHY DON'T YOU LISTEN TO WHAT, UM, *IT* HAS TO SAY...
THANK YOU, BUT I'M TRYING TO AT LEAST KEEP A *LITTLE* SANITY. I FIND IT HELPFUL IN MY WORK.
...WHAT'S WRONG WITH TALKING TO DEAD PEOPLE...?
C'MON, KARATSU. YOU WERE ABLE TO CAST OUT THAT ROBOT ZOMBIE OTAKU!
NO...LIKE I KEEP SAYING, I CAN'T--
...OKAY. FINE. WHATEVER.

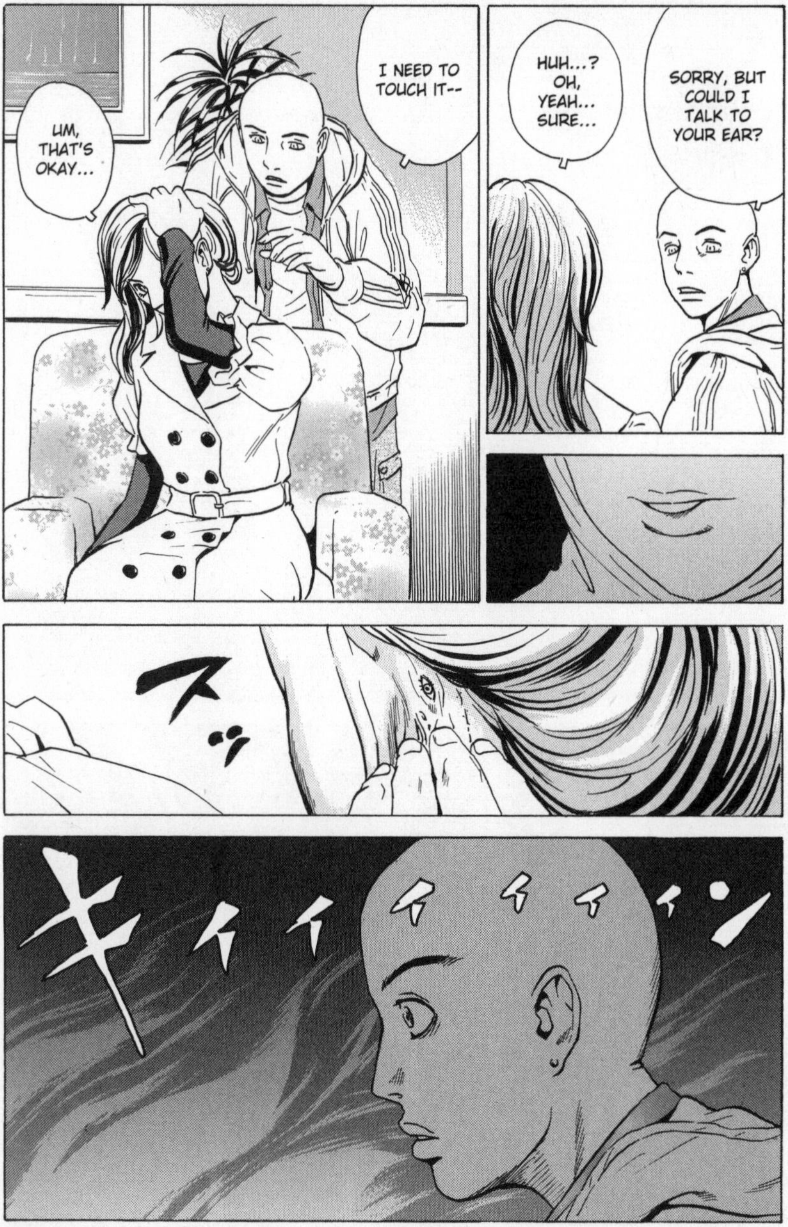
SORRY, BUT COULD I TALK TO YOUR EAR?
HUH...? OH, YEAH... SURE...
I NEED TO TOUCH IT--
UM, THAT'S OKAY...
スッ
キィィィィン

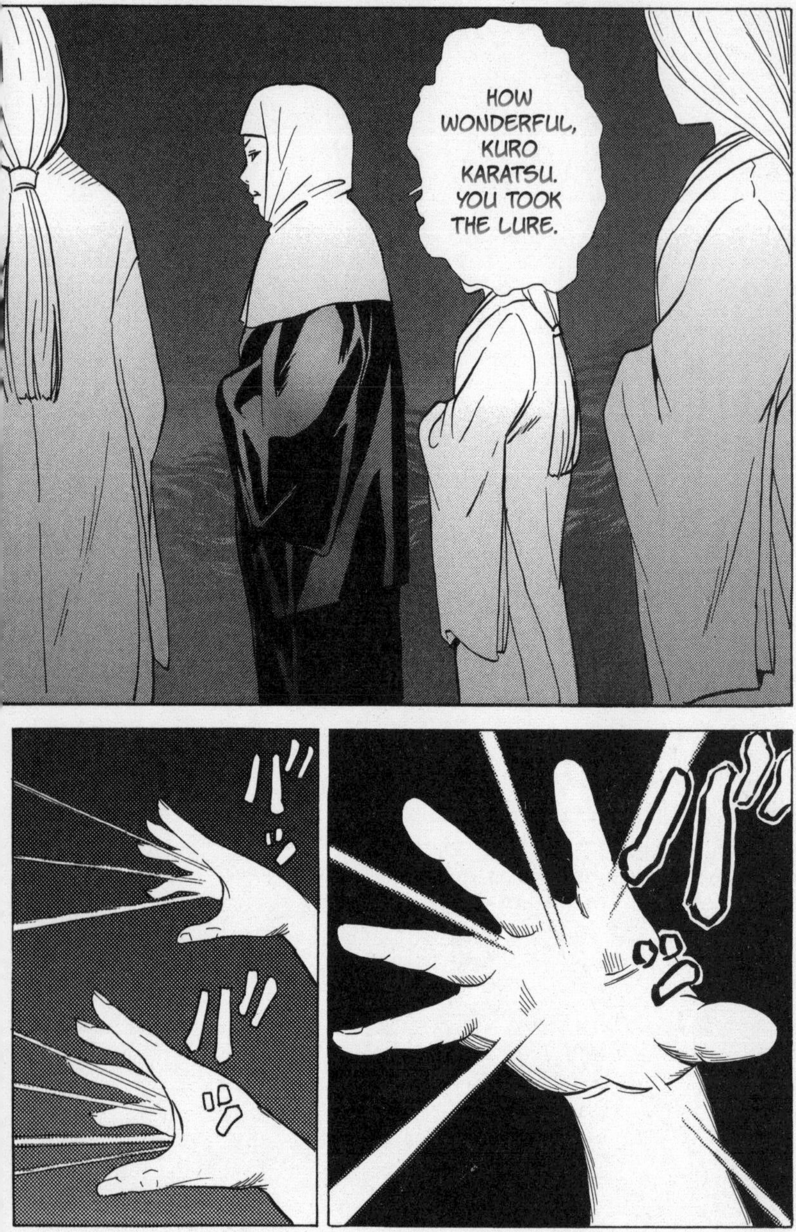
HOW WONDERFUL, KURO KARATSU. YOU TOOK THE LURE.

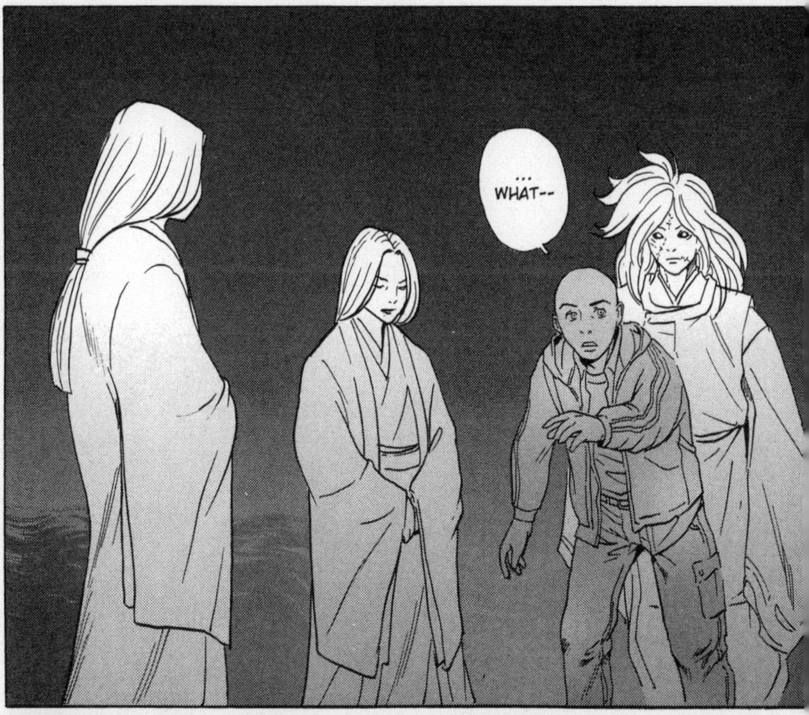
...
WHAT--
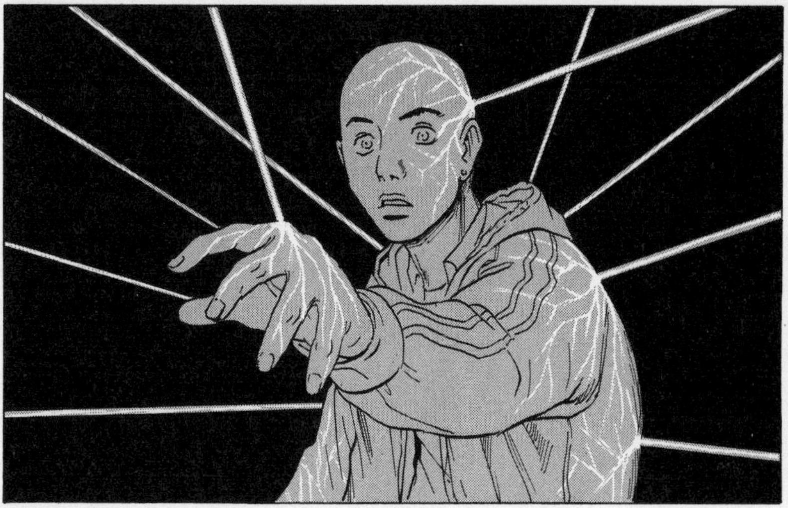

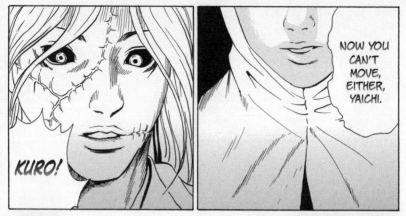

KURO!

NOW YOU CAN'T MOVE, EITHER, YAICHI.

ズブブ

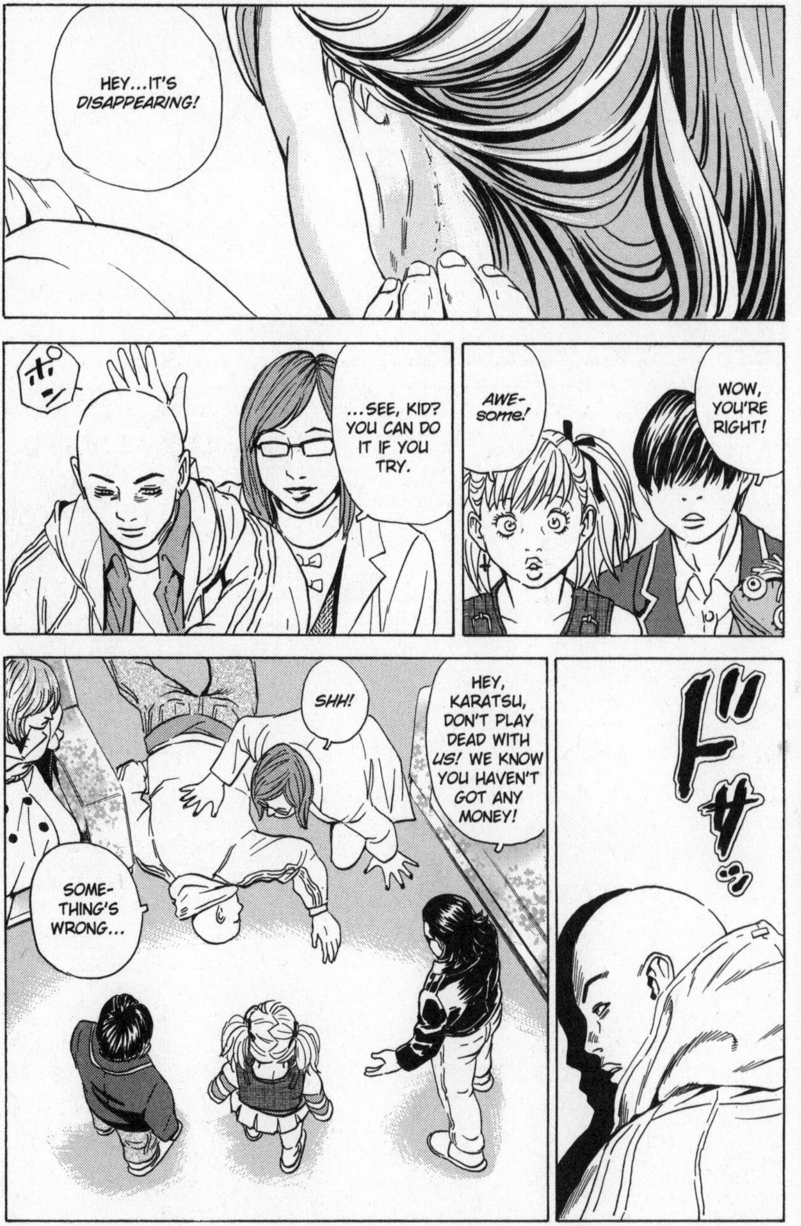
HEY...IT'S *DISAPPEARING!*
WOW, YOU'RE RIGHT!
AWE-some!
ポン
...SEE, KID? YOU CAN DO IT IF YOU TRY.
ドサッ
HEY, KARATSU, DON'T PLAY DEAD WITH *US!* WE KNOW YOU HAVEN'T GOT ANY MONEY!
SHH!
SOME-THING'S WRONG...

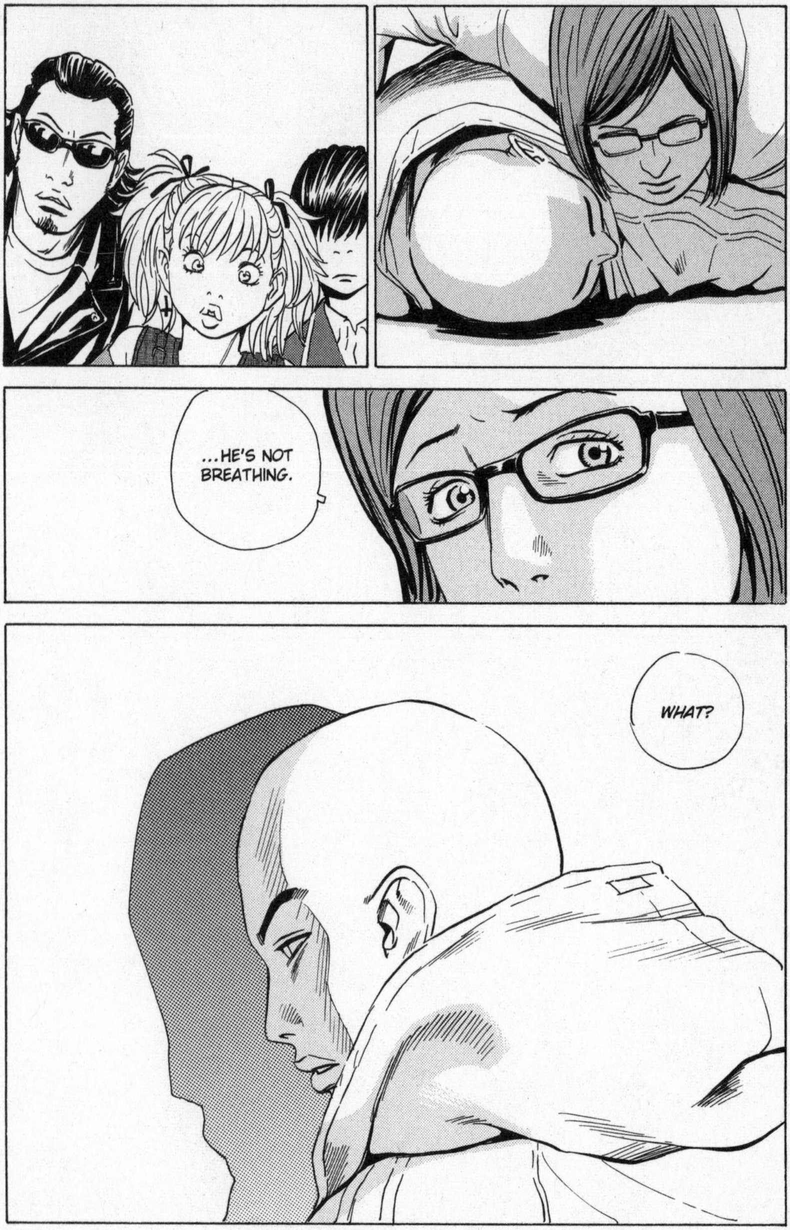
...HE'S NOT BREATHING.
WHAT?

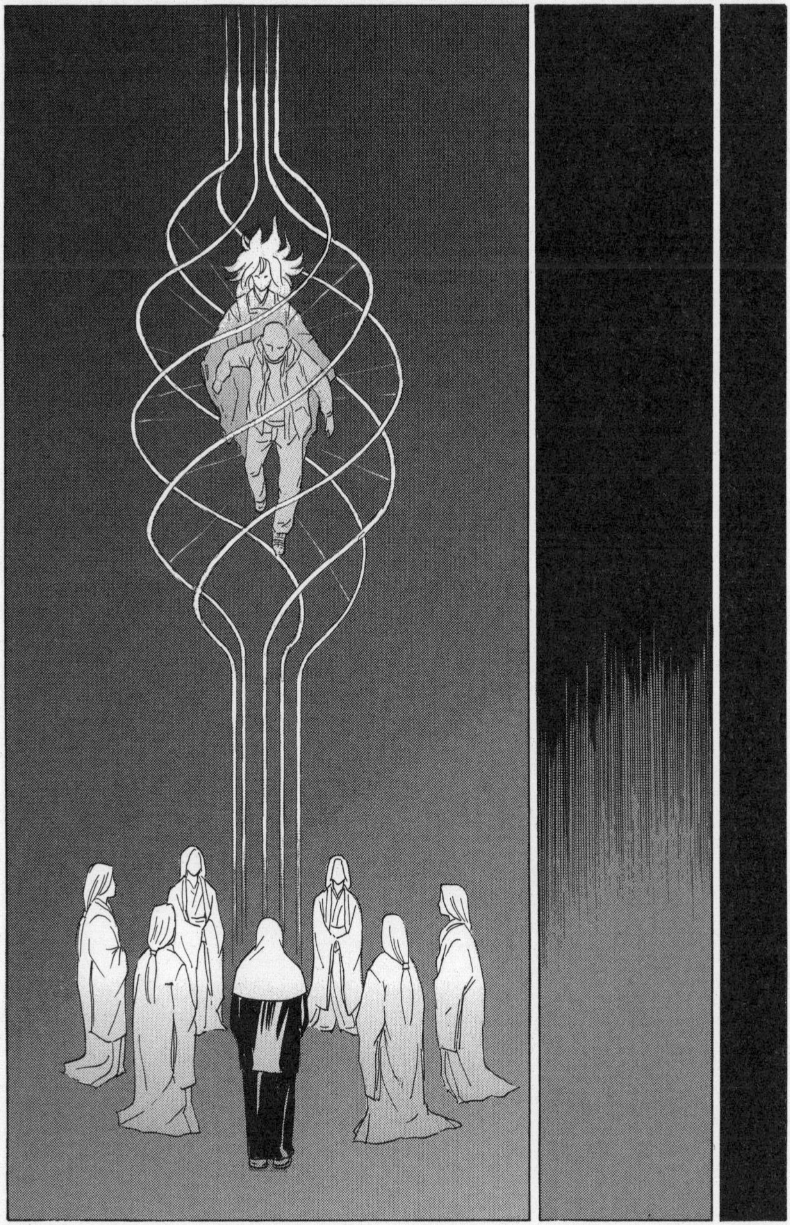

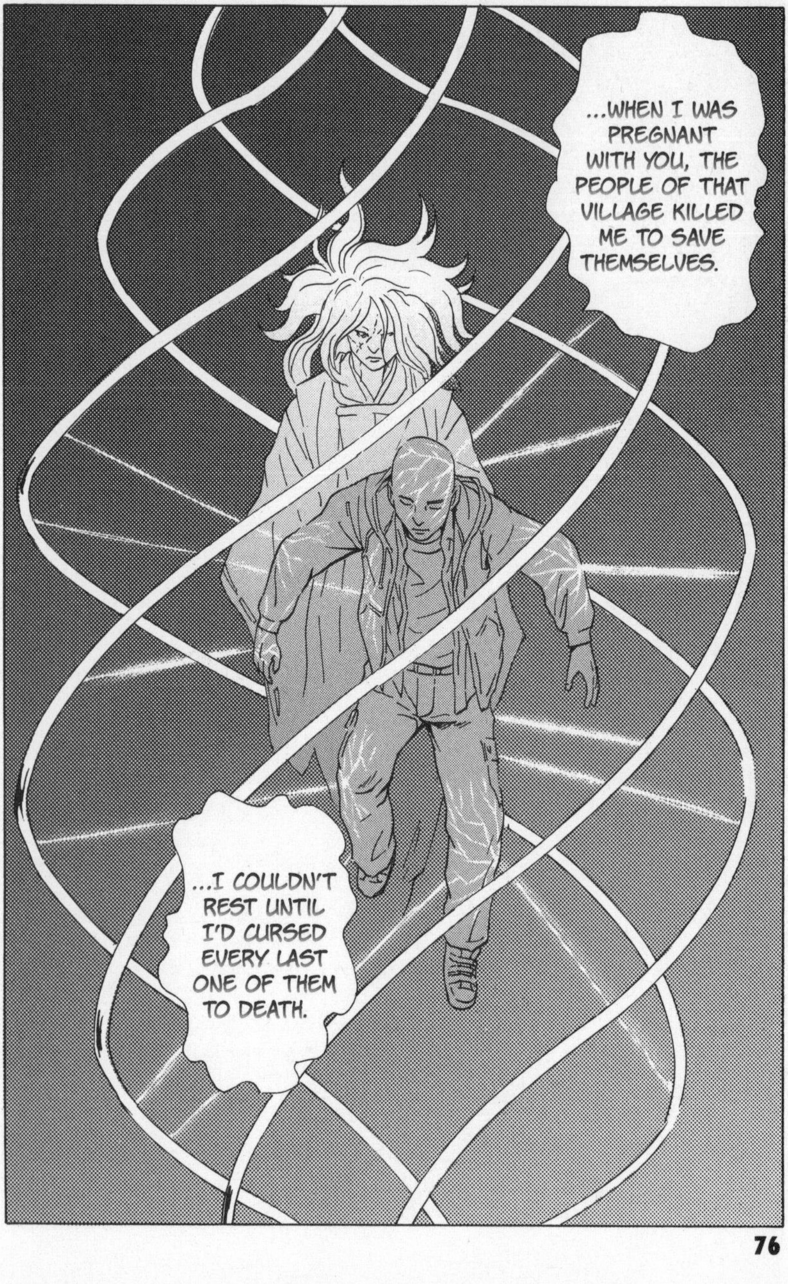
...WHEN I WAS PREGNANT WITH YOU, THE PEOPLE OF THAT VILLAGE KILLED ME TO SAVE THEMSELVES.
...I COULDN'T REST UNTIL I'D CURSED EVERY LAST ONE OF THEM TO DEATH.

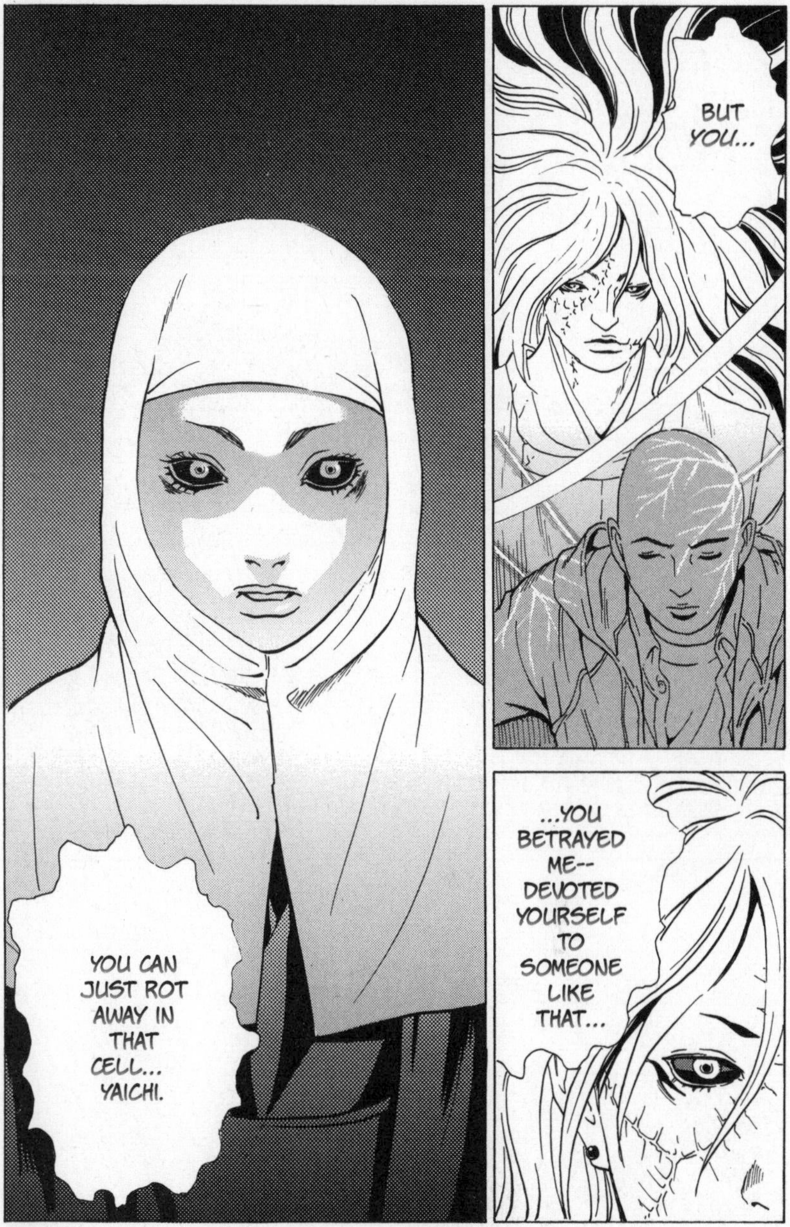
BUT YOU...
...YOU BETRAYED ME-- DEVOTED YOURSELF TO SOMEONE LIKE THAT...
YOU CAN JUST ROT AWAY IN THAT CELL... YAICHI.

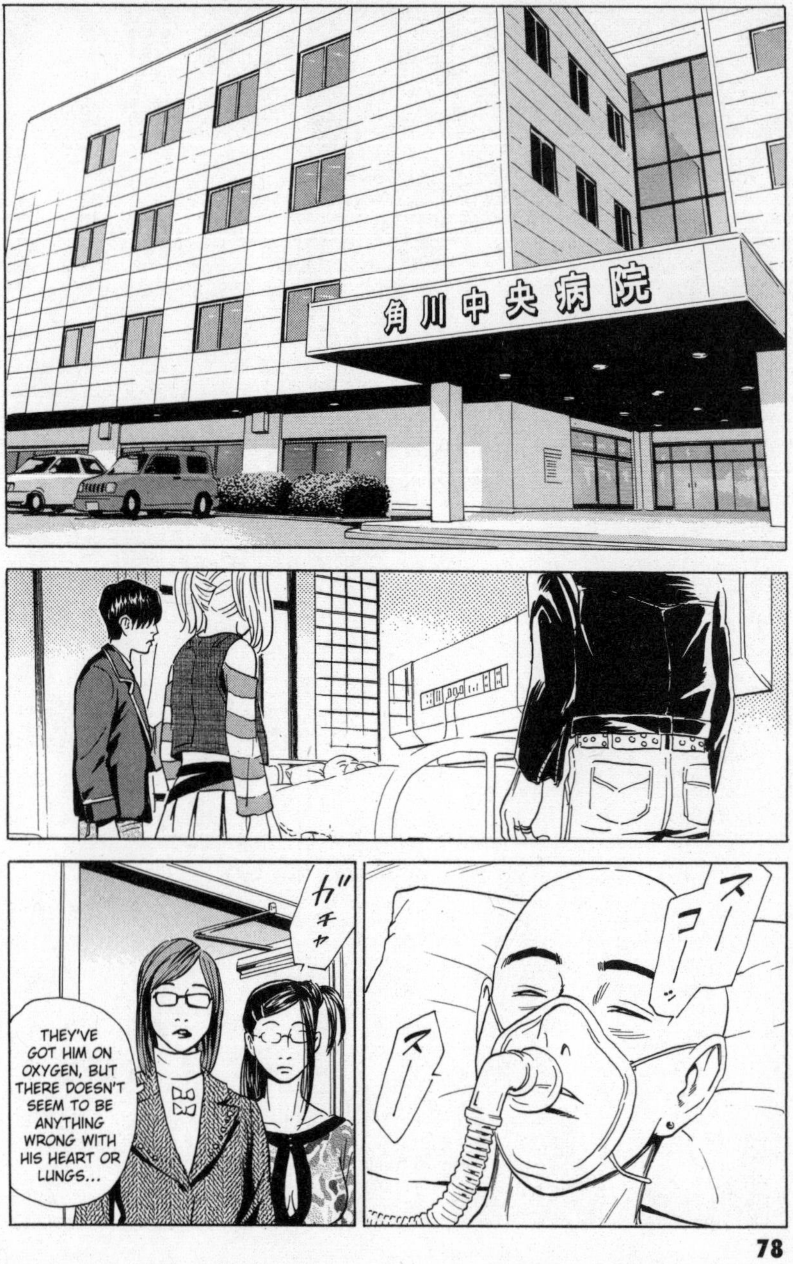

角川中央病院
スー
スー
ガチャ
THEY'VE GOT HIM ON OXYGEN, BUT THERE DOESN'T SEEM TO BE ANYTHING WRONG WITH HIS HEART OR LUNGS...

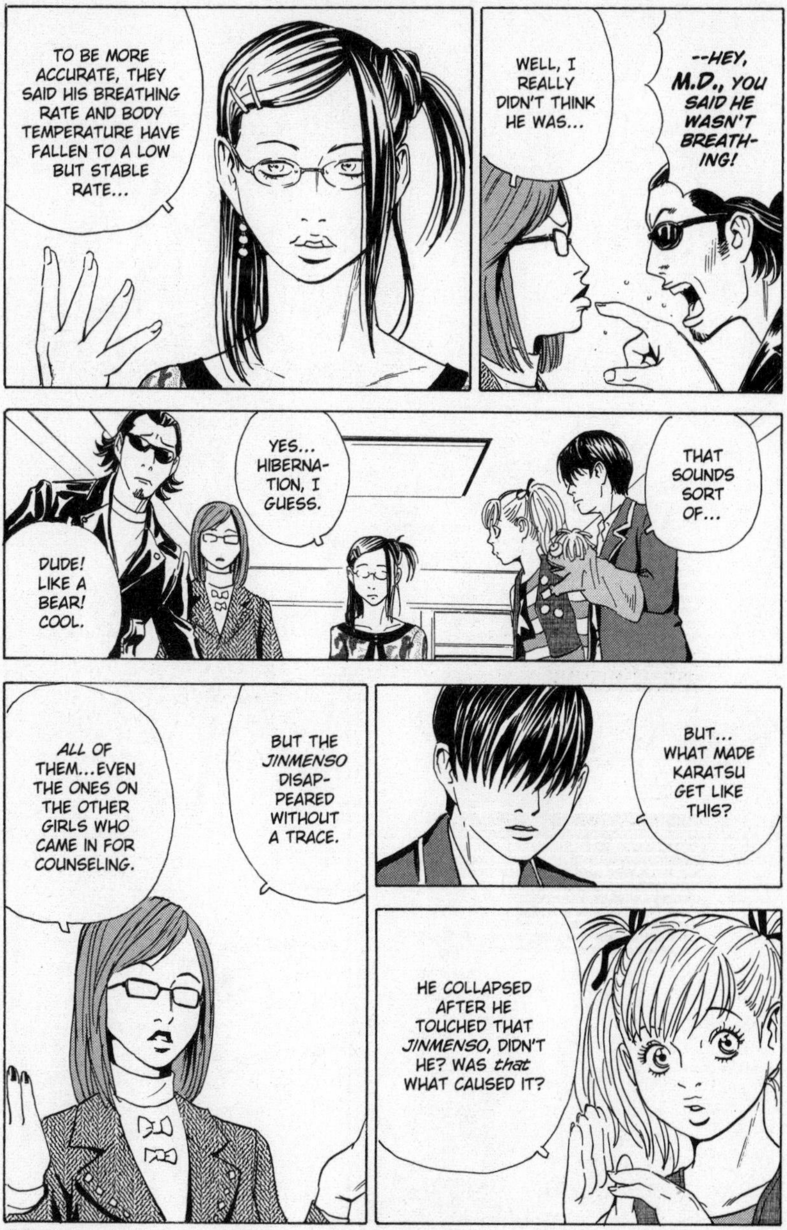
--HEY, M.D., YOU SAID HE WASN'T BREATHING!
WELL, I REALLY DIDN'T THINK HE WAS...
TO BE MORE ACCURATE, THEY SAID HIS BREATHING RATE AND BODY TEMPERATURE HAVE FALLEN TO A LOW BUT STABLE RATE...
THAT SOUNDS SORT OF...
YES... HIBERNATION, I GUESS.
DUDE! LIKE A BEAR! COOL.
BUT... WHAT MADE KARATSU GET LIKE THIS?
HE COLLAPSED AFTER HE TOUCHED THAT *JINMENSO*, DIDN'T HE? WAS *that* WHAT CAUSED IT?
BUT THE *JINMENSO* DISAPPEARED WITHOUT A TRACE.
ALL OF THEM...EVEN THE ONES ON THE OTHER GIRLS WHO CAME IN FOR COUNSELING.

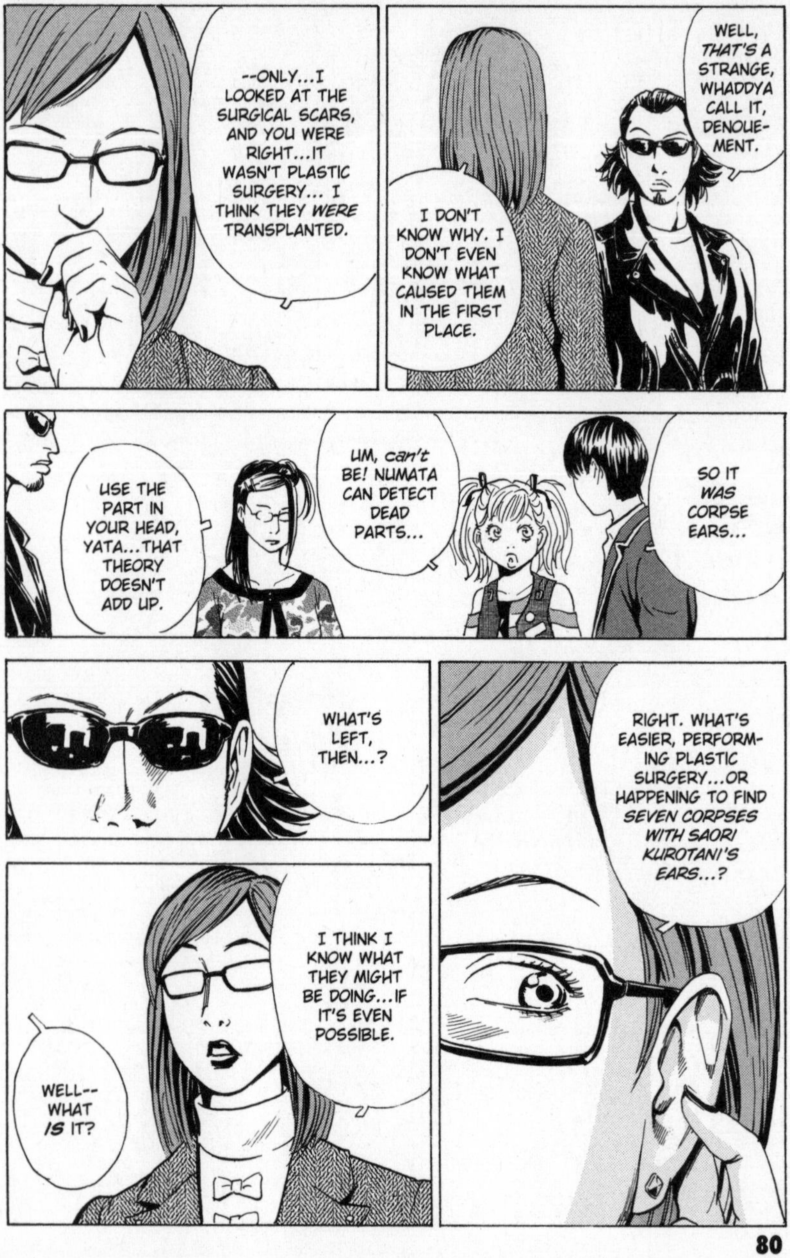
WELL, *THAT'S* A STRANGE, WHADDYA CALL IT, DENOUEMENT.
I DON'T KNOW WHY. I DON'T EVEN KNOW WHAT CAUSED THEM IN THE FIRST PLACE.
--ONLY...I LOOKED AT THE SURGICAL SCARS, AND YOU WERE RIGHT...IT WASN'T PLASTIC SURGERY... I THINK THEY *WERE* TRANSPLANTED.
SO IT *WAS* CORPSE EARS...
UM, *can't* BE! NUMATA CAN DETECT DEAD PARTS...
USE THE PART IN YOUR HEAD, YATA...THAT THEORY DOESN'T ADD UP.
RIGHT. WHAT'S EASIER, PERFORMING PLASTIC SURGERY...OR HAPPENING TO FIND *SEVEN CORPSES WITH SAORI KUROTANI'S EARS...?*
WHAT'S LEFT, THEN...?
I THINK I KNOW WHAT THEY MIGHT BE DOING...IF IT'S EVEN POSSIBLE.
WELL--WHAT *IS* IT?

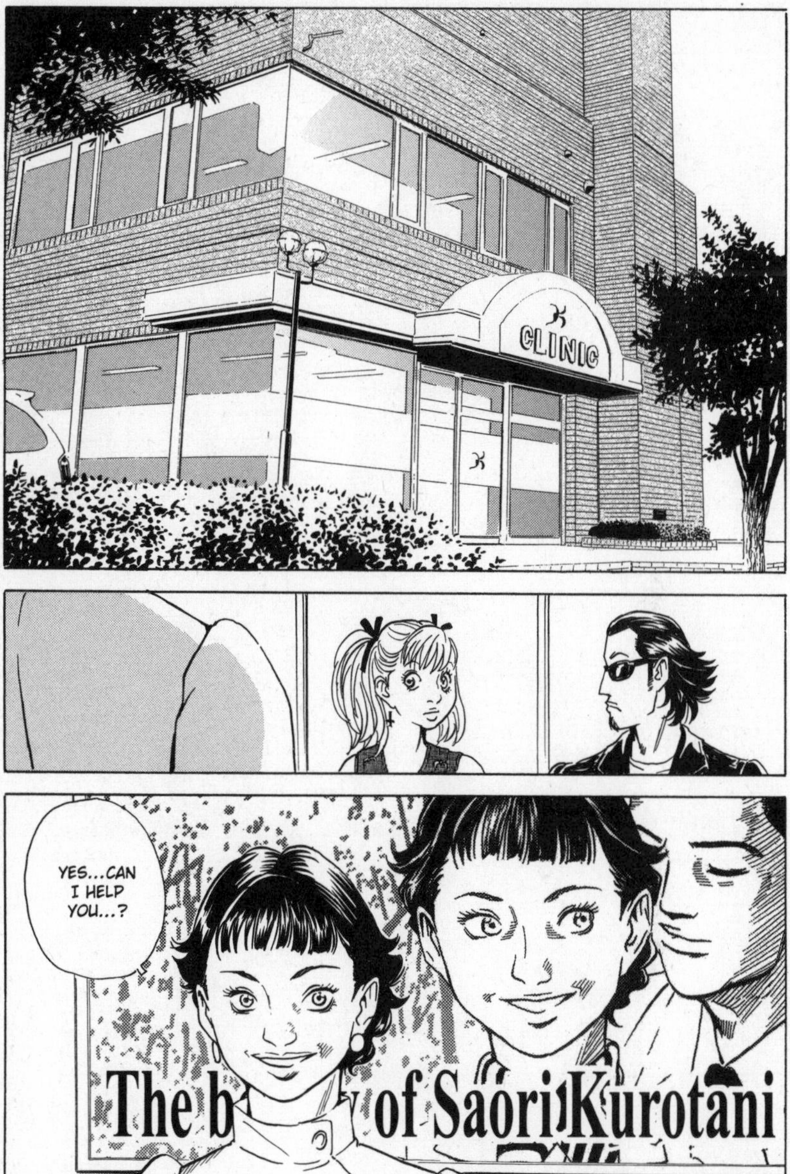
CLINIC
YES...CAN I HELP YOU...?
of Saori Kurotani

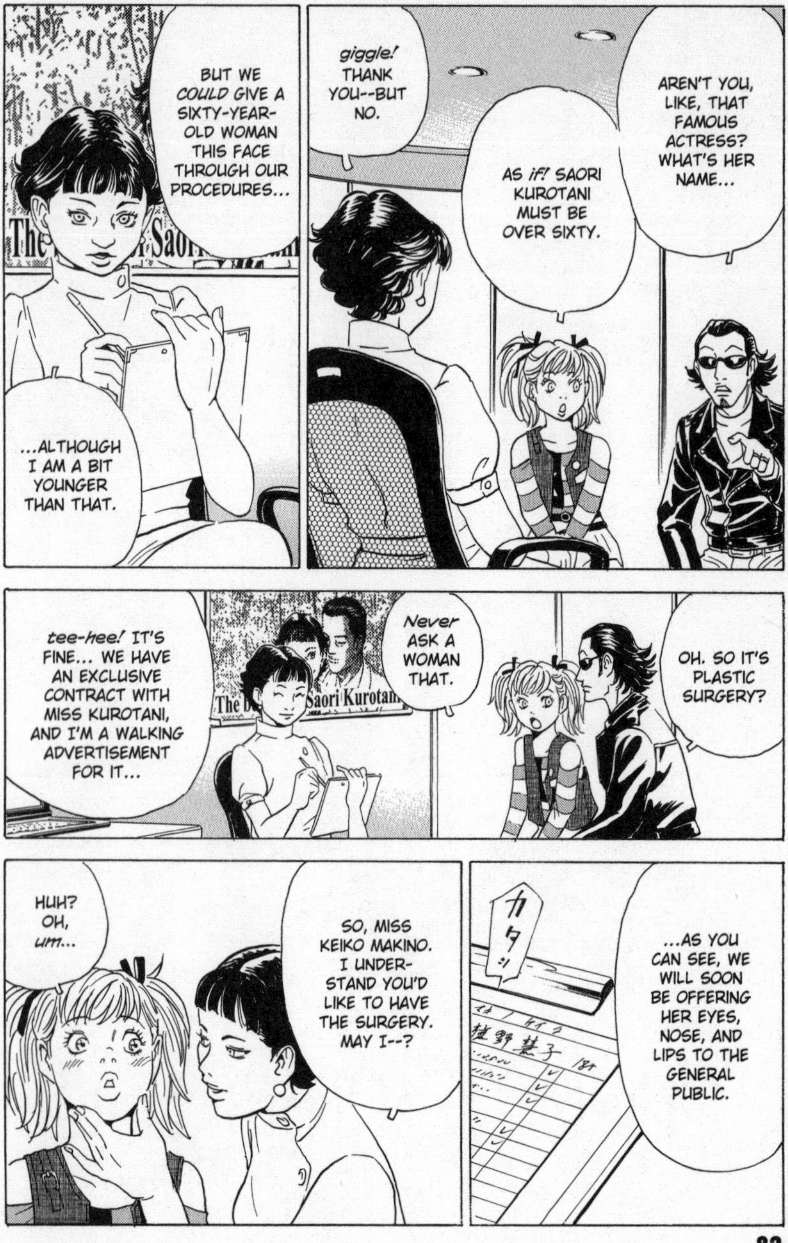
AREN'T YOU, LIKE, THAT FAMOUS ACTRESS? WHAT'S HER NAME...
AS *if!* SAORI KUROTANI MUST BE OVER SIXTY.
giggle! THANK YOU--BUT NO.
BUT WE *COULD* GIVE A SIXTY-YEAR-OLD WOMAN THIS FACE THROUGH OUR PROCEDURES...
...ALTHOUGH I AM A BIT YOUNGER THAN THAT.
OH. SO IT'S PLASTIC SURGERY?
Never ASK A WOMAN THAT.
tee-hee! IT'S FINE... WE HAVE AN EXCLUSIVE CONTRACT WITH MISS KUROTANI, AND I'M A WALKING ADVERTISEMENT FOR IT...
カタッ
...AS YOU CAN SEE, WE WILL SOON BE OFFERING HER EYES, NOSE, AND LIPS TO THE GENERAL PUBLIC.
SO, MISS KEIKO MAKINO. I UNDER-STAND YOU'D LIKE TO HAVE THE SURGERY. MAY I--?
HUH? OH, *um...*

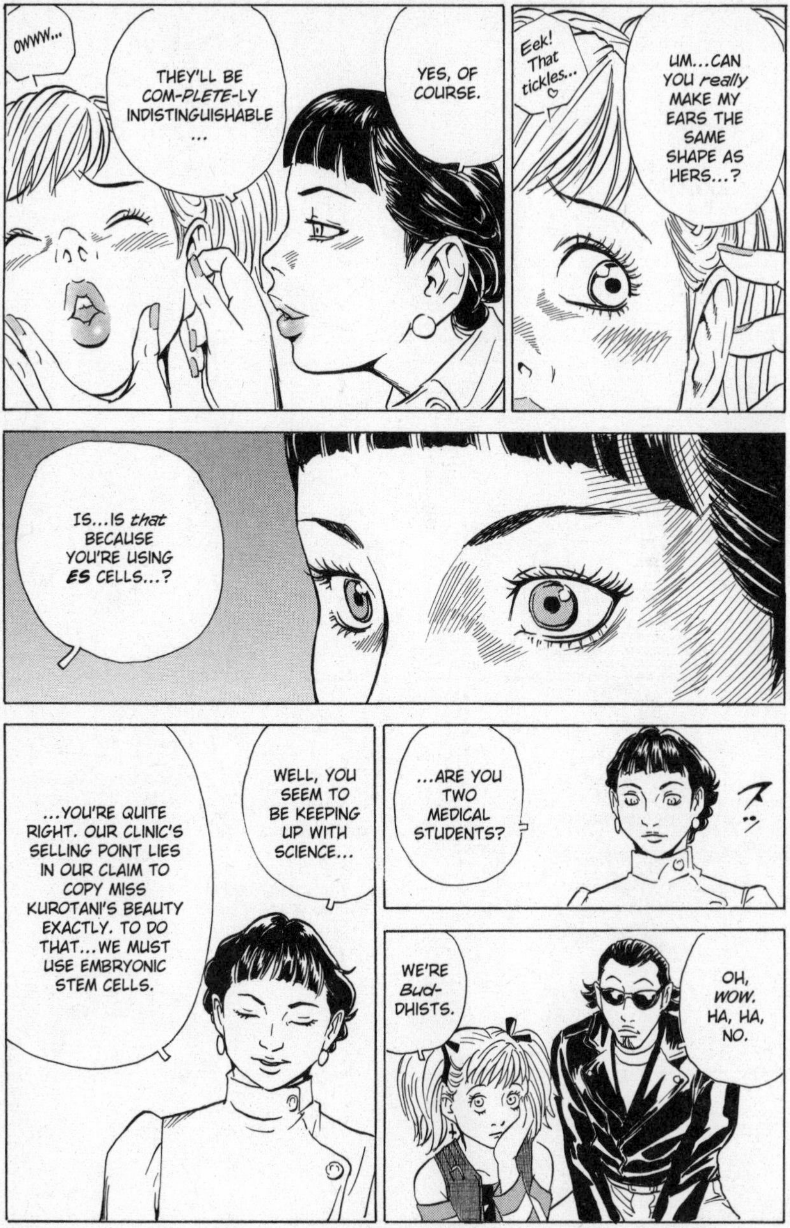
UM...CAN YOU *really* MAKE MY EARS THE SAME SHAPE AS HERS...?
Eek! That tickles... ♡
YES, OF COURSE.
THEY'LL BE COM-*PLETE*-LY INDISTINGUISHABLE ...
OWWW...
IS...IS *that* BECAUSE YOU'RE USING ES CELLS...?
...ARE YOU TWO MEDICAL STUDENTS?
OH, WOW. HA, HA, NO.
WE'RE *Bud*-DHISTS.
WELL, YOU SEEM TO BE KEEPING UP WITH SCIENCE...
...YOU'RE QUITE RIGHT. OUR CLINIC'S SELLING POINT LIES IN OUR CLAIM TO COPY MISS KUROTANI'S BEAUTY EXACTLY. TO DO THAT...WE MUST USE EMBRYONIC STEM CELLS.

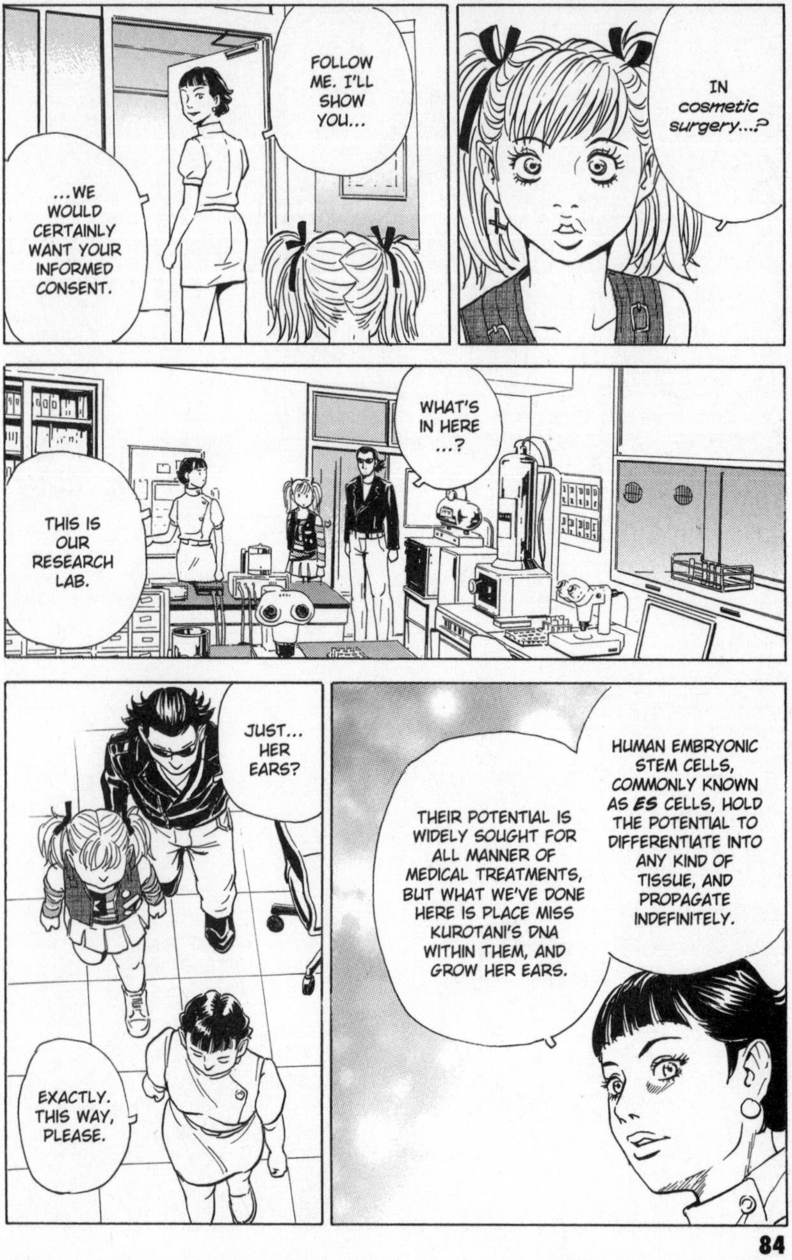
IN cosmetic surgery...?
FOLLOW ME. I'LL SHOW YOU...
...WE WOULD CERTAINLY WANT YOUR INFORMED CONSENT.
WHAT'S IN HERE ...?
THIS IS OUR RESEARCH LAB.
HUMAN EMBRYONIC STEM CELLS, COMMONLY KNOWN AS ES CELLS, HOLD THE POTENTIAL TO DIFFERENTIATE INTO ANY KIND OF TISSUE, AND PROPAGATE INDEFINITELY.
THEIR POTENTIAL IS WIDELY SOUGHT FOR ALL MANNER OF MEDICAL TREATMENTS, BUT WHAT WE'VE DONE HERE IS PLACE MISS KUROTANI'S DNA WITHIN THEM, AND GROW HER EARS.
JUST... HER EARS?
EXACTLY. THIS WAY, PLEASE.

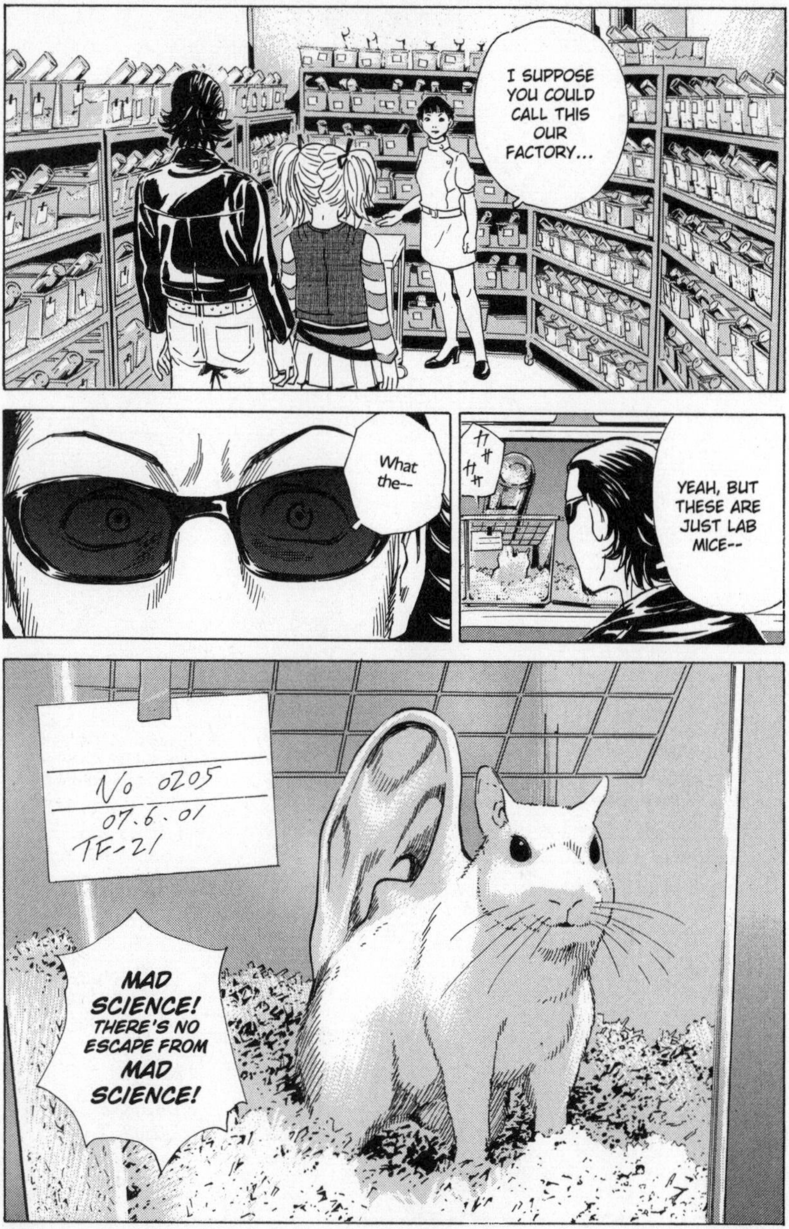
I SUPPOSE YOU COULD CALL THIS OUR FACTORY...
YEAH, BUT THESE ARE JUST LAB MICE--
What the--
No 0205
07.6.01
TF-21
MAD SCIENCE! THERE'S NO ESCAPE FROM MAD SCIENCE!

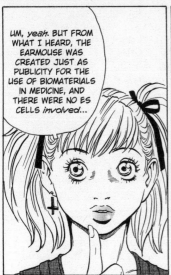

CALM *down*, NUMATA-- IT'S JUST AN EARMOUSE.
Oh, right... huh?
I'M... SURPRISED YOU KNEW ABOUT THAT.
UM, *yeah*. BUT FROM WHAT I HEARD, THE EARMOUSE WAS CREATED JUST AS PUBLICITY FOR THE USE OF BIOMATERIALS IN MEDICINE, AND THERE WERE NO ES CELLS *involved*...
RIGHT AGAIN. WHAT THREE DOCTORS AND A BIOMATERIALS ENGINEER PUBLISHED IN 1997 WERE ONLY THE RESULTS OF CARTILAGE CELLS, CULTIVATED ON A SCAFFOLD OF MACRO-MOLECULAR FIBERS.
THIS IS AN ADVANCED FORM OF THE PROCEDURE. HUMAN ES CELLS ARE INJECTED INTO THE MOUSE'S BACK, AND THE EAR IS GROWN UPON IT.
THIS WAY, NOT ONLY EARMICE, BUT NOSEMICE AND EYEMICE ARE THEORETICALLY POSSIBLE.
I KNOW YOU GOT A STERILE ENVIRONMENT HERE, BUT EXCUSE ME WHILE I PUKE.
...YEAH, *theoretically*. BUT HOW ARE YOU ABLE TO ACHIEVE THIS IN THE BACK OF A *plastic surgery clinic*...?

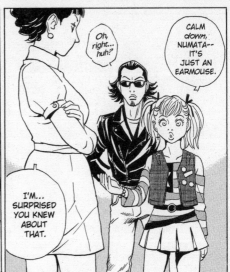

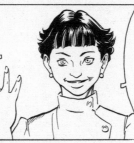

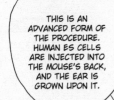

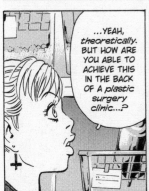

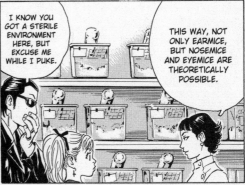

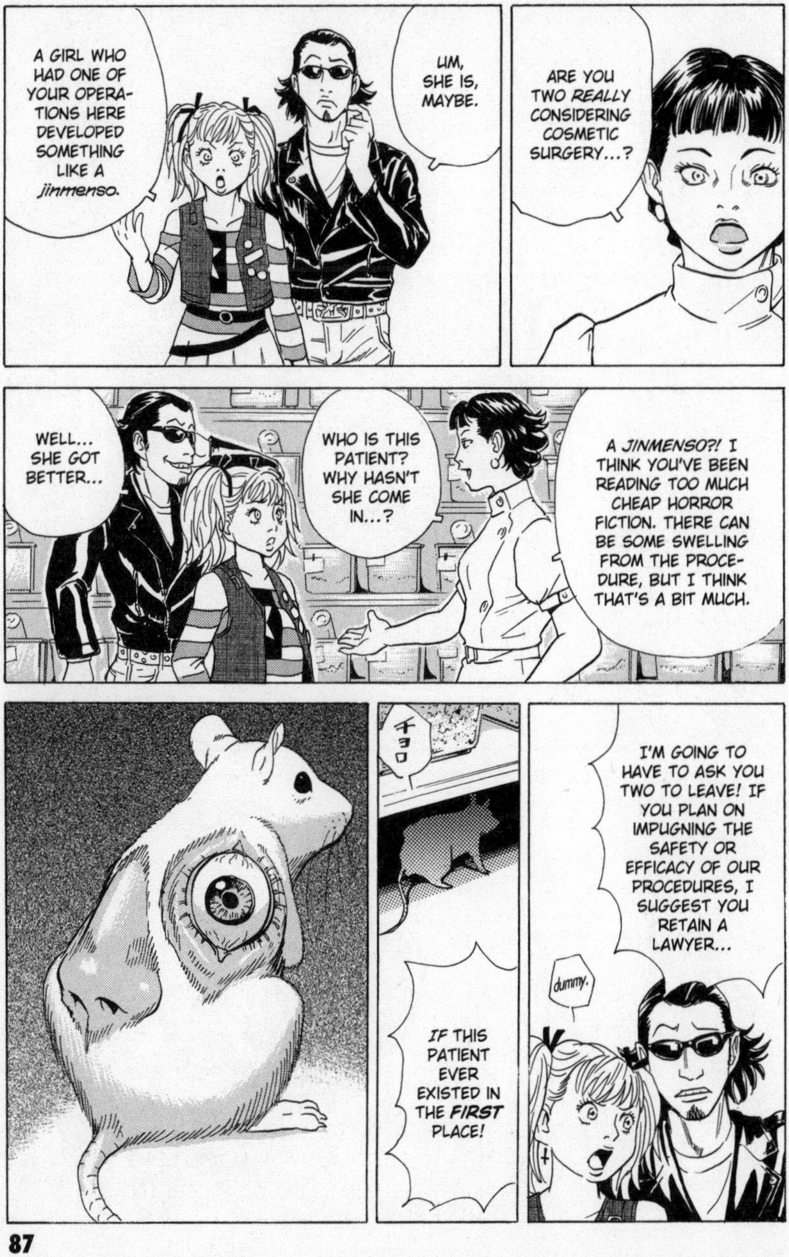
ARE YOU TWO *REALLY* CONSIDERING COSMETIC SURGERY...?
UM, SHE IS, MAYBE.
A GIRL WHO HAD ONE OF YOUR OPERATIONS HERE DEVELOPED SOMETHING LIKE A *jinmenso*.
A *JINMENSO?!* I THINK YOU'VE BEEN READING TOO MUCH CHEAP HORROR FICTION. THERE CAN BE SOME SWELLING FROM THE PROCEDURE, BUT I THINK THAT'S A BIT MUCH.
WHO IS THIS PATIENT? WHY HASN'T SHE COME IN...?
WELL... SHE GOT BETTER...
I'M GOING TO HAVE TO ASK YOU TWO TO LEAVE! IF YOU PLAN ON IMPUGNING THE SAFETY OR EFFICACY OF OUR PROCEDURES, I SUGGEST YOU RETAIN A LAWYER...
dummy.
チョロ
IF THIS PATIENT EVER EXISTED IN THE *FIRST* PLACE!

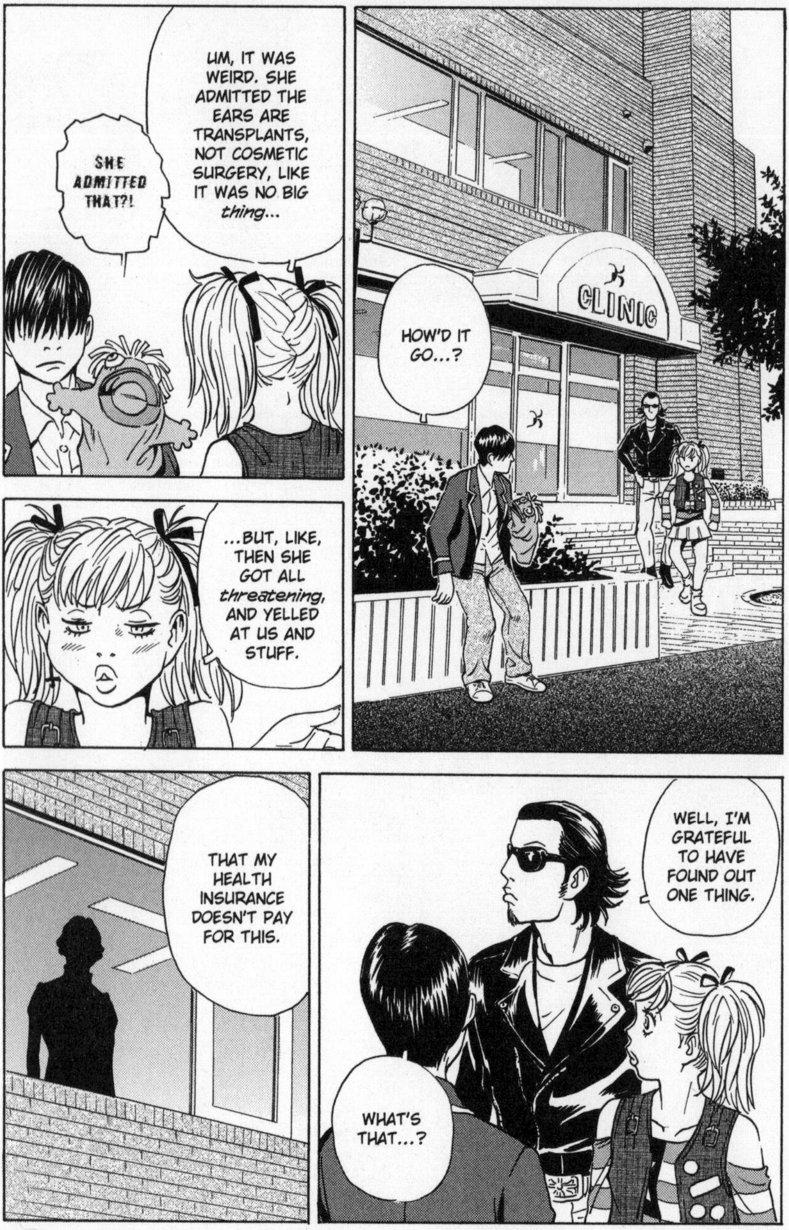
HOW'D IT GO...?
UM, IT WAS WEIRD. SHE ADMITTED THE EARS ARE TRANSPLANTS, NOT COSMETIC SURGERY, LIKE IT WAS NO BIG *thing*...
SHE ADMITTED THAT?!
...BUT, LIKE, THEN SHE GOT ALL *threatening*, AND YELLED AT US AND STUFF.
CLINIC
WELL, I'M GRATEFUL TO HAVE FOUND OUT ONE THING.
WHAT'S THAT...?
THAT MY HEALTH INSURANCE DOESN'T PAY FOR THIS.

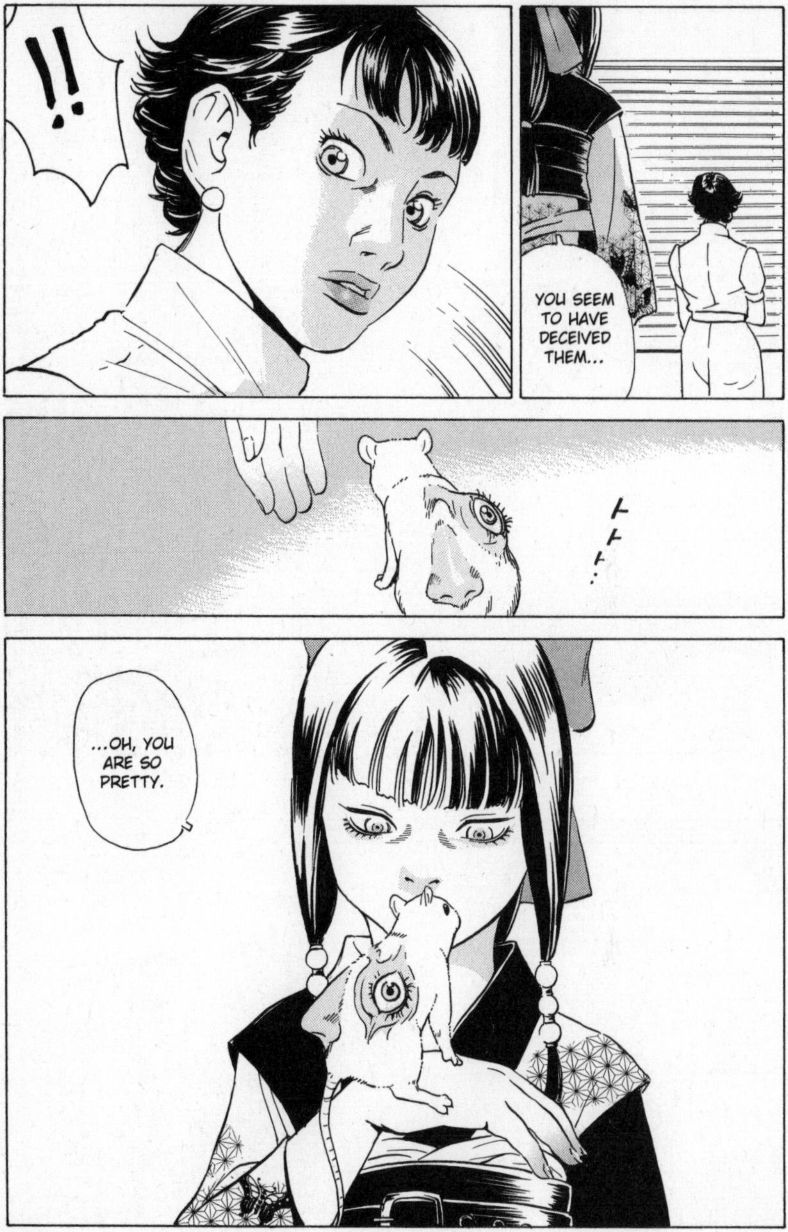
YOU SEEM TO HAVE DECEIVED THEM...
!!
トトト…
...OH, YOU ARE SO PRETTY.

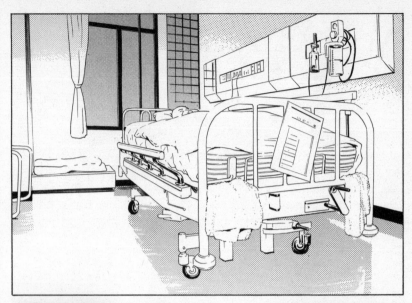

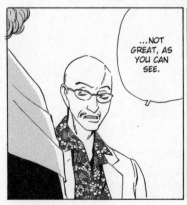

ガチャッ
SORRY TO SUMMON YOU FOR THIS.
OH, IT'S NO TROUBLE. HOW'S THE BOY?
スコー
スーッ
...NOT GREAT, AS YOU CAN SEE.

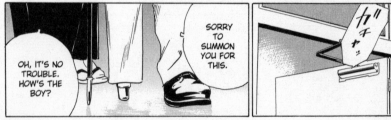

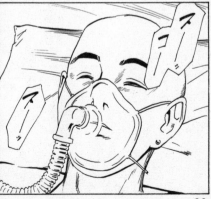

...NO, NOT AT ALL. HIS SPIRIT HAS BEEN STOLEN.

CAN YOU HELP HIM...?

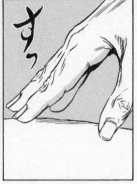

NO... THERE'S NOTHING I CAN DO.

BUT I KNOW THERE IS ONLY ONE WHO COULD HAVE SEALED THIS BOY'S SOUL AWAY--THAT WOMAN.

2nd delivery: pretty • pretty—the end

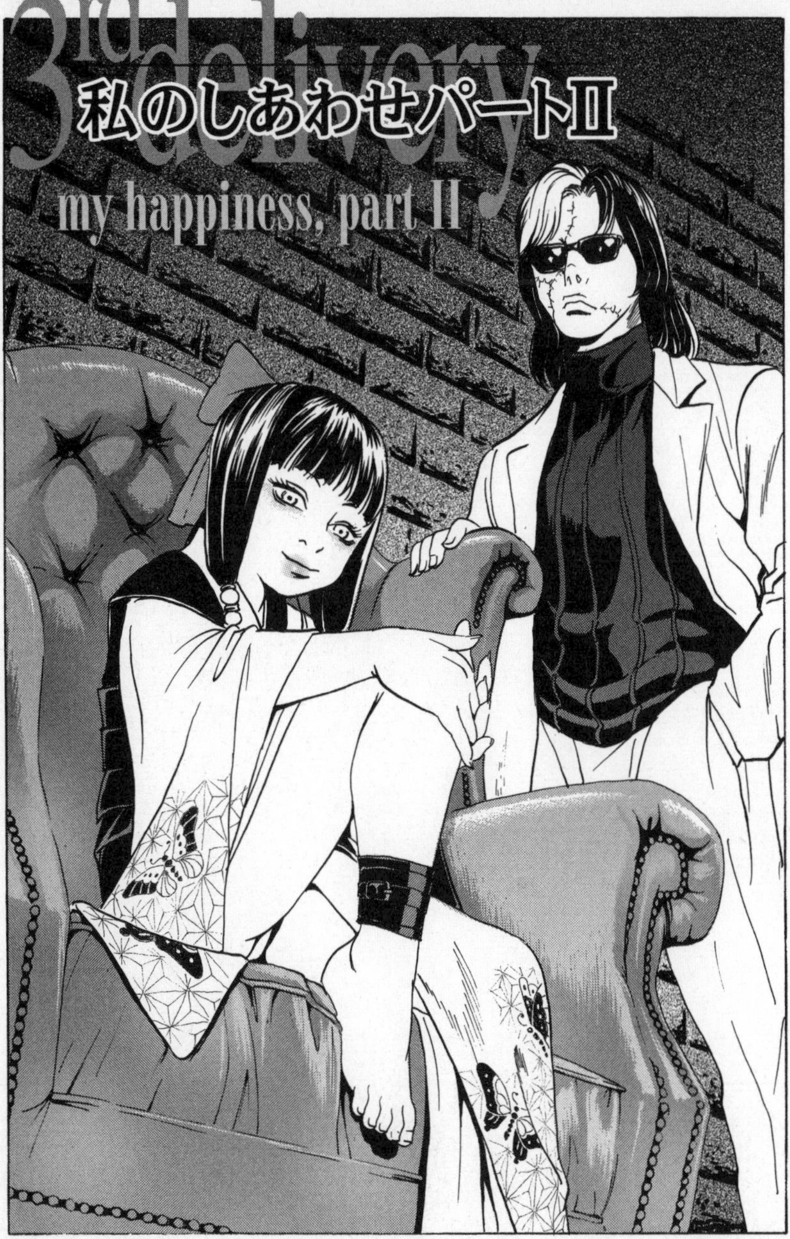
3rd delivery
私のしあわせパートII
my happiness, part II

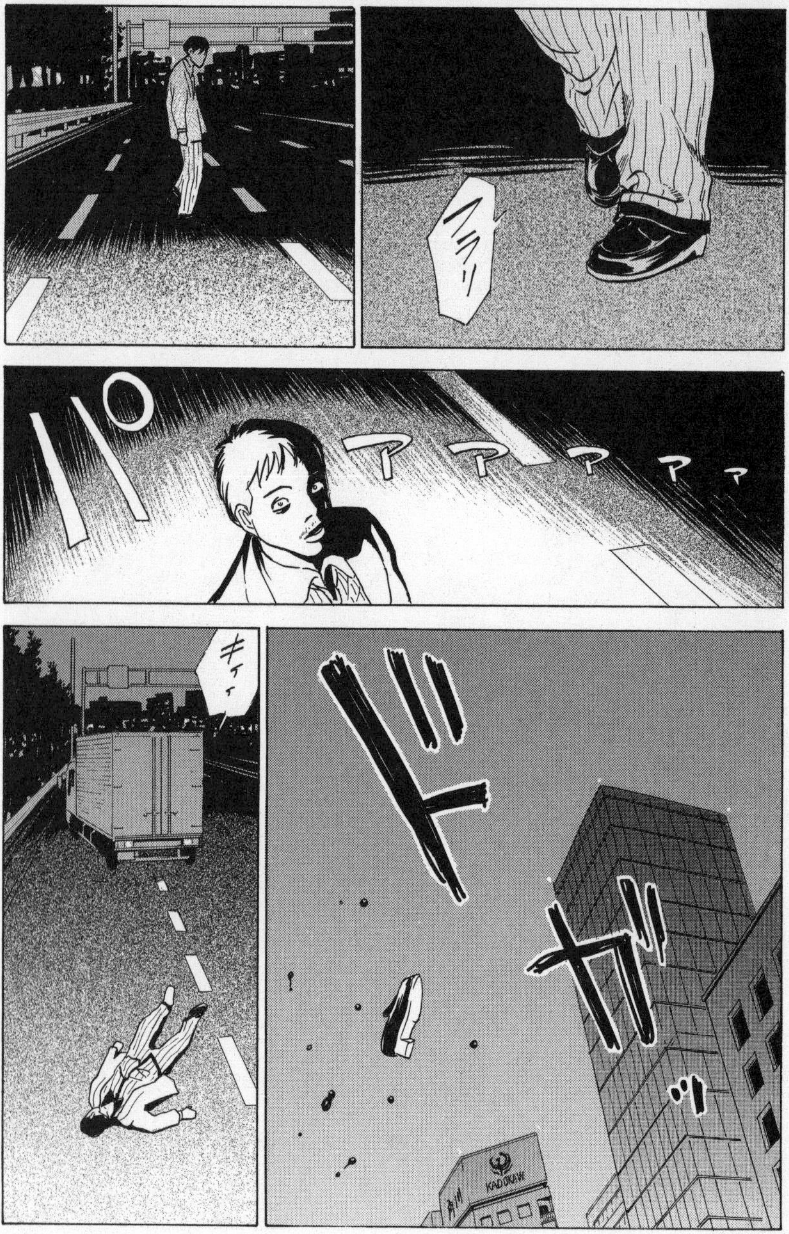
フラッ
パアアアアァ
ドガッ
キィィ

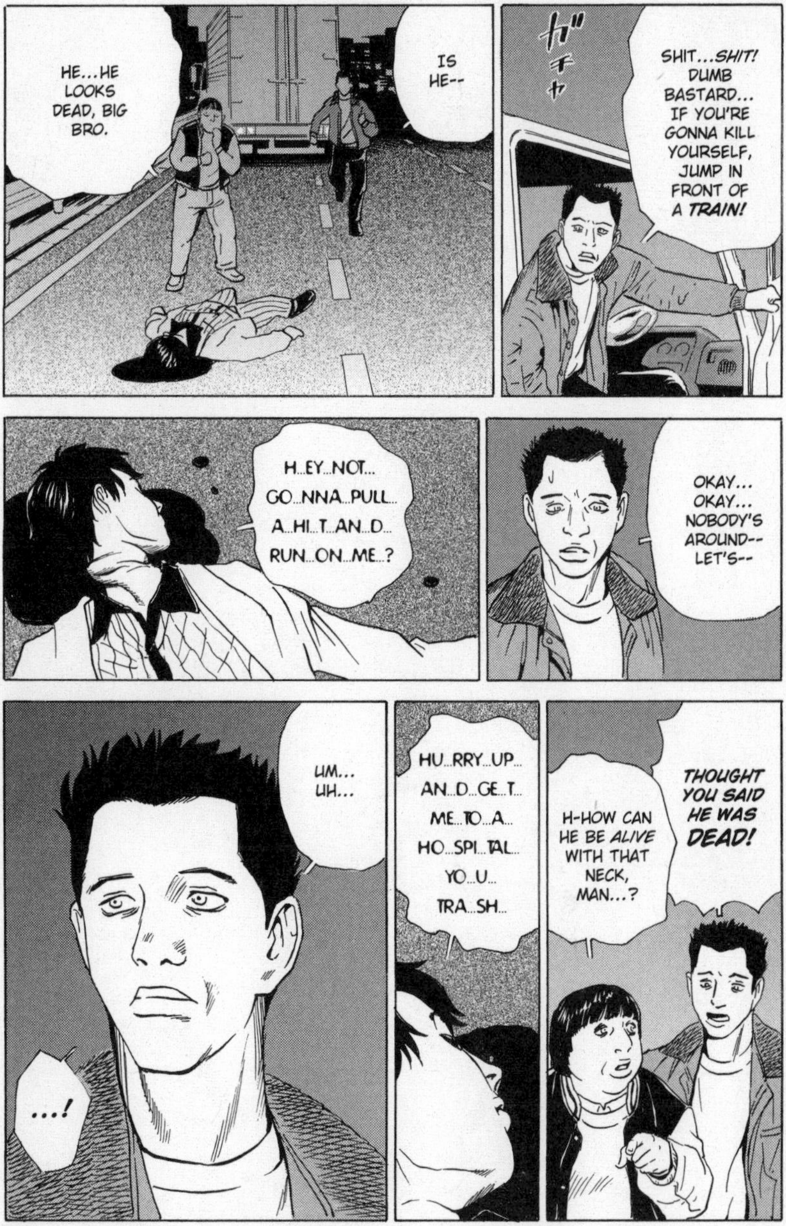
ガチャ
SHIT...SHIT! DUMB BASTARD... IF YOU'RE GONNA KILL YOURSELF, JUMP IN FRONT OF A TRAIN!
IS HE--
HE...HE LOOKS DEAD, BIG BRO.
OKAY... OKAY... NOBODY'S AROUND-- LET'S--
H...EY...NOT... GO...NNA...PULL... A...HI...T...AN...D... RUN...ON...ME...?
THOUGHT YOU SAID HE WAS DEAD!
H-HOW CAN HE BE ALIVE WITH THAT NECK, MAN...?
HU...RRY...UP... AN...D...GE...T... ME...TO...A... HO...SPI...TAL... YO...U... TRA...SH...
UM... UH...
...!

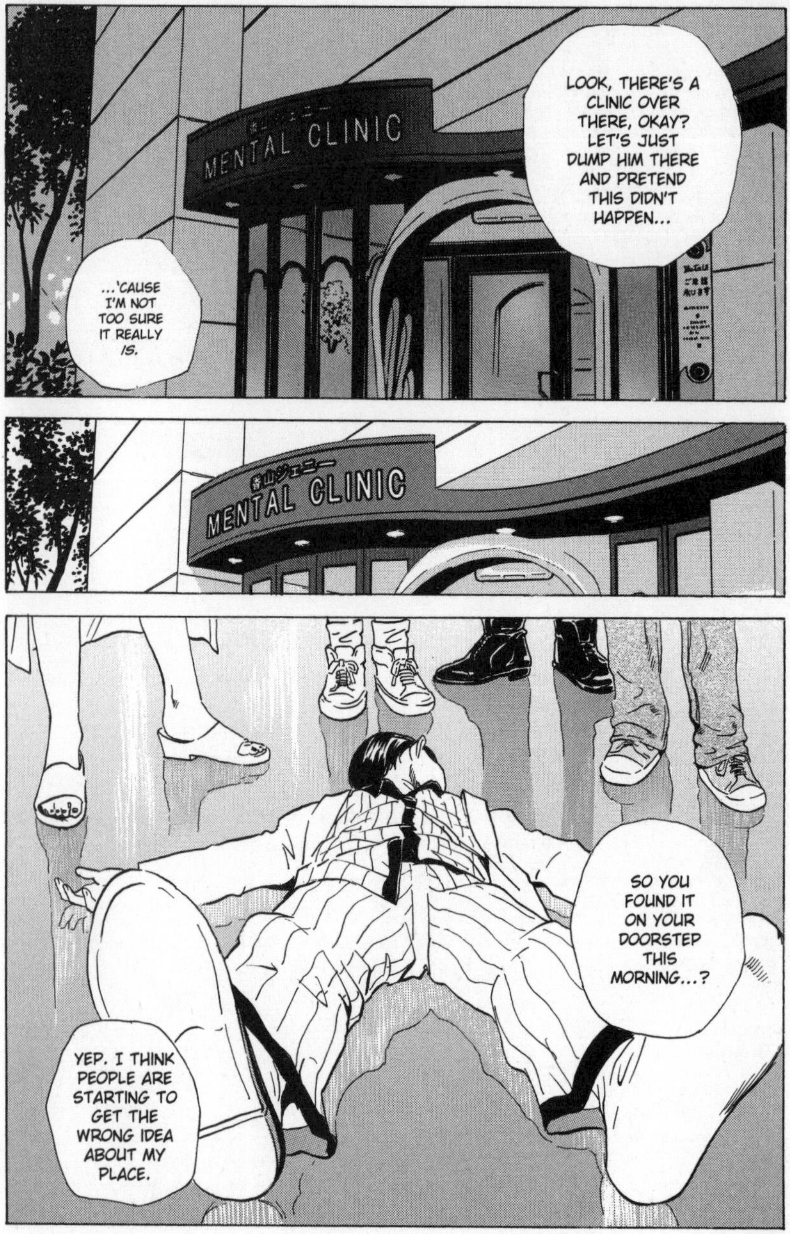
MENTAL CLINIC
LOOK, THERE'S A CLINIC OVER THERE, OKAY? LET'S JUST DUMP HIM THERE AND PRETEND THIS DIDN'T HAPPEN...
...'CAUSE I'M NOT TOO SURE IT REALLY IS.
MENTAL CLINIC
SO YOU FOUND IT ON YOUR DOORSTEP THIS MORNING...?
YEP. I THINK PEOPLE ARE STARTING TO GET THE WRONG IDEA ABOUT MY PLACE.

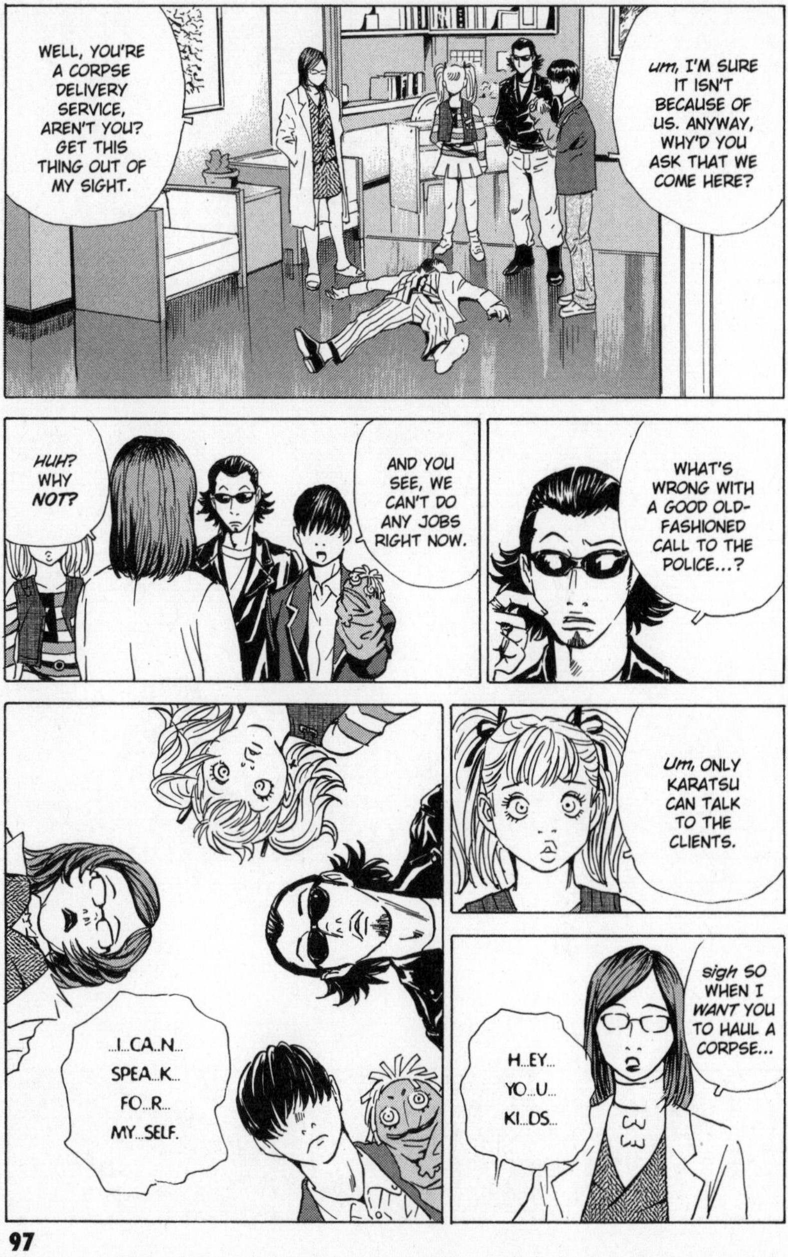

um, I'M SURE IT ISN'T BECAUSE OF US. ANYWAY, WHY'D YOU ASK THAT WE COME HERE?
WELL, YOU'RE A CORPSE DELIVERY SERVICE, AREN'T YOU? GET THIS THING OUT OF MY SIGHT.
WHAT'S WRONG WITH A GOOD OLD-FASHIONED CALL TO THE POLICE...?
AND YOU SEE, WE CAN'T DO ANY JOBS RIGHT NOW.
HUH? WHY NOT?
Um, ONLY KARATSU CAN TALK TO THE CLIENTS.
sigh SO WHEN I WANT YOU TO HAUL A CORPSE...
H...EY... YO...U... KI...DS...
...I...CA...N... SPEA...K... FO...R... MY...SELF.

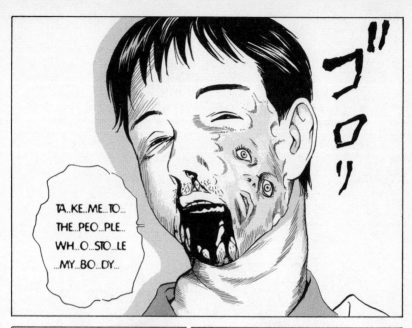

ゴロリ
TA..KE..ME...TO... THE...PEO...PLE... WH...O...STO...LE ...MY...BO...DY...
ANOTHER JINMENSO ....?!
IT WOULD APPEAR SO...LOOK, CAN WE *PLEASE* GET THIS OUT OF MY OFFICE?

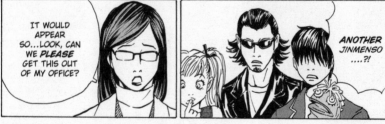

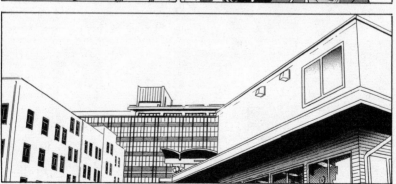

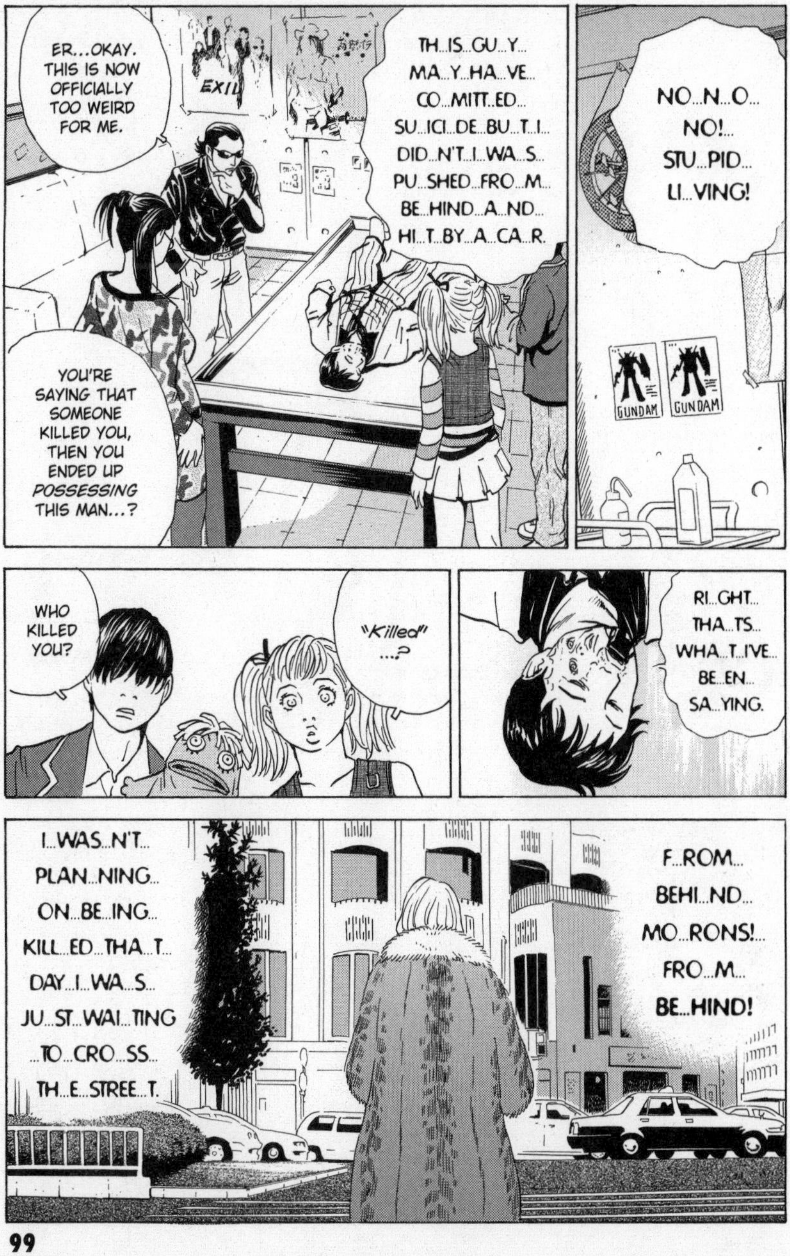
NO...N...O... NO!... STU...PID... LI...VING!
TH...IS...GU...Y... MA...Y...HA...VE... CO...MITT...ED... SU...ICI...DE...BU...T...I... DID...N'T...I...WA...S... PU...SHED...FRO...M... BE...HIND...A...ND... HI...T...BY...A...CA...R.
ER...OKAY. THIS IS NOW OFFICIALLY TOO WEIRD FOR ME.
EXIL
YOU'RE SAYING THAT SOMEONE KILLED YOU, THEN YOU ENDED UP *POSSESSING* THIS MAN...?
GUNDAM
GUNDAM
RI...GHT... THA...TS... WHA...T...I'VE... BE...EN... SA...YING.
"*Killed*" ...?
WHO KILLED YOU?
I...WAS...N'T... PLAN...NING... ON...BE...ING... KILL...ED...THA...T... DAY...I...WA...S... JU...ST...WAI...TING ...TO...CRO...SS... TH...E...STREE...T.
F...ROM... BEHI...ND... MO...RONS!... FRO...M... BE...HIND!

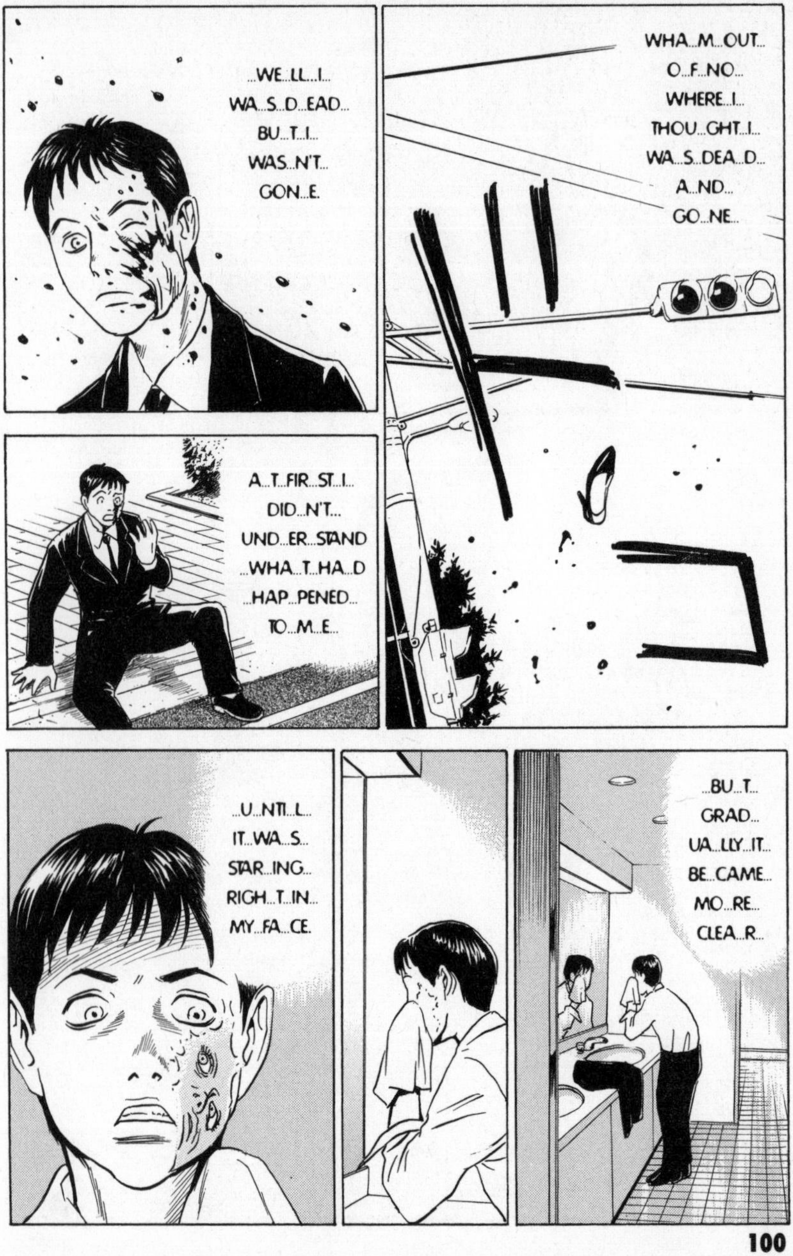
WHA...M...OUT... O...F...NO... WHERE...I... THOU...GHT...I... WA...S...DEA...D... A...ND... GO...NE...
...WE...LL...I... WA...S...D...EAD... BU...T...I... WAS...N'T... GON...E.
A...T...FIR...ST...I... DID...N'T... UND...ER...STAND ...WHA...T...HA...D ...HAP...PENED... TO...M...E...
...BU...T... GRAD... UA...LLY...IT... BE...CAME... MO...RE... CLEA...R...
...U...NTI...L... IT...WA...S... STAR...ING... RIGH...T...IN... MY...FA...CE.

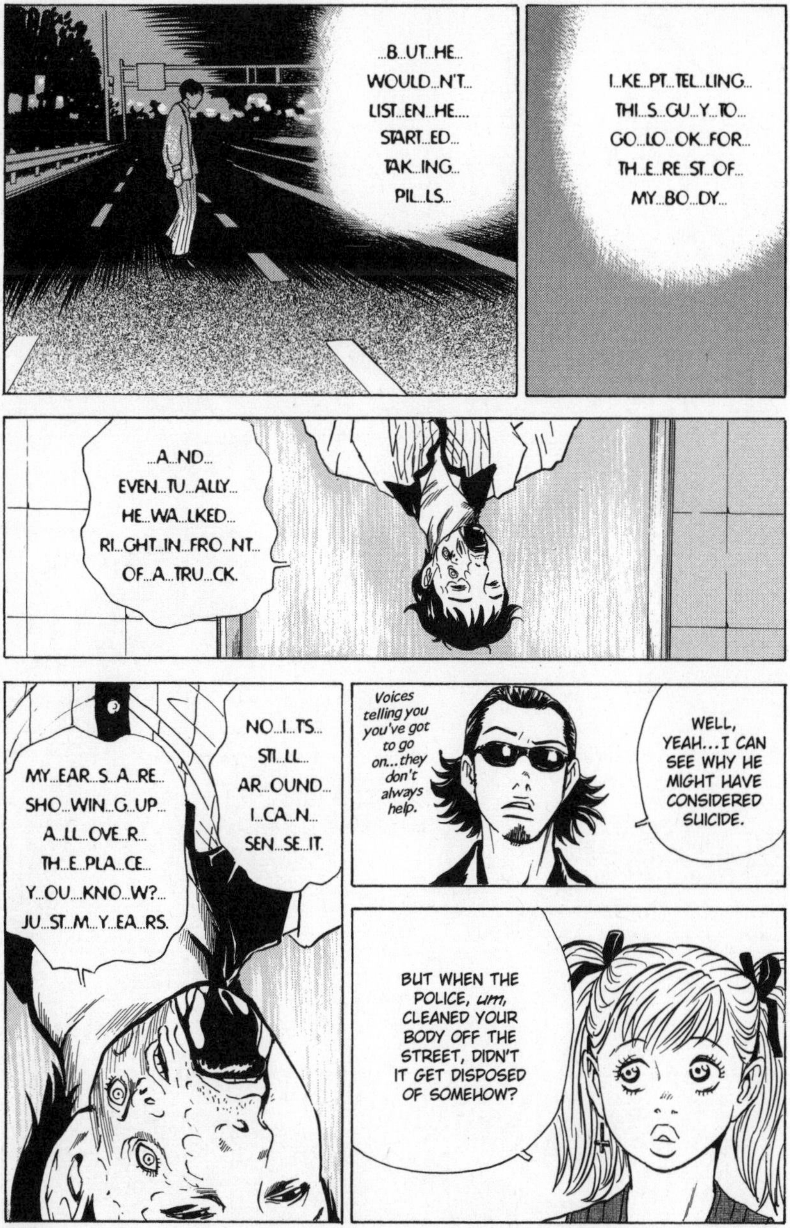
I..KE..PT..TEL..LING.. THI..S..GU..Y..TO.. GO..LO..OK..FOR.. TH..E..RE..ST..OF.. MY..BO..DY..
..B..UT..HE.. WOULD..N'T.. LIST..EN..HE.... START..ED.. TAK..ING.. PIL..LS..
..A..ND.. EVEN..TU..ALLY.. HE..WA..LKED.. RI..GHT..IN..FRO..NT.. OF..A..TRU..CK.
WELL, YEAH...I CAN SEE WHY HE MIGHT HAVE CONSIDERED SUICIDE.
Voices telling you you've got to go on...they don't always help.
BUT WHEN THE POLICE, *um*, CLEANED YOUR BODY OFF THE STREET, DIDN'T IT GET DISPOSED OF SOMEHOW?
NO..I..TS.. STI..LL.. AR..OUND.. I..CA..N.. SEN..SE..IT.
MY..EAR..S..A..RE.. SHO..WIN..G..UP.. A..LL..OVE..R.. TH..E..PLA..CE.. Y..OU..KNO..W?.. JU..ST..M..Y..EA..RS.

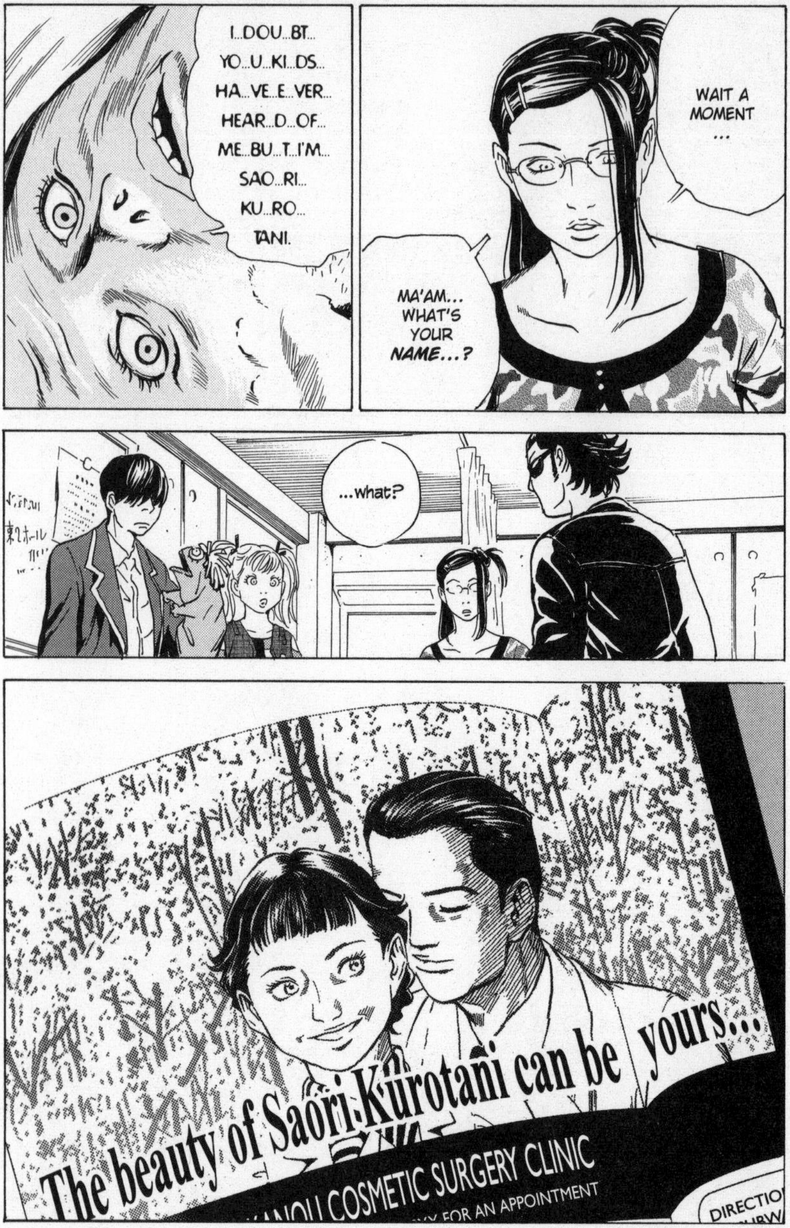
WAIT A MOMENT ...
MA'AM... WHAT'S YOUR *NAME...?*
I...DOU...BT... YO...U...KI...DS... HA...VE...E...VER... HEAR...D...OF... ME...BU...T...I'M... SAO...RI... KU...RO... TANI.
...what?
The beauty of Saori Kurotani can be yours...
COSMETIC SURGERY CLINIC
FOR AN APPOINTMENT

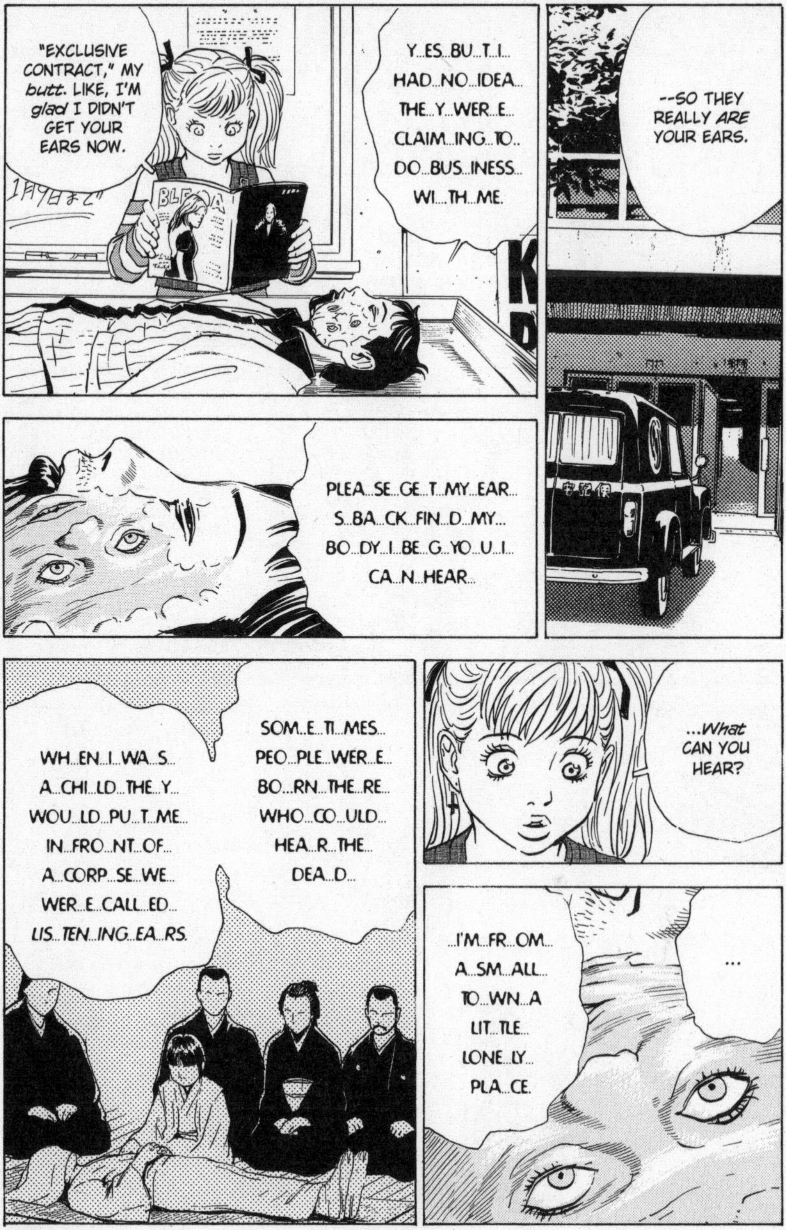
--SO THEY REALLY *ARE* YOUR EARS.
Y..ES..BU..T..I.. HAD..NO..IDEA.. THE..Y..WER..E.. CLAIM..ING..TO.. DO..BUS..INESS.. WI..TH..ME.
"EXCLUSIVE CONTRACT," MY *butt*. LIKE, I'M *glad* I DIDN'T GET YOUR EARS NOW.
PLEA..SE..GE..T..MY..EAR.. S..BA..CK..FIN..D..MY.. BO..DY..I..BE..G..YO..U..I.. CA..N..HEAR..
...*What* CAN YOU HEAR?
...
..I'M..FR..OM.. A..SM..ALL.. TO..WN..A LIT..TLE.. LONE..LY.. PLA..CE.
SOM..E..TI..MES.. PEO..PLE..WER..E.. BO..RN..THE..RE.. WHO..CO..ULD.. HEA..R..THE.. DEA..D..
WH..EN..I..WA..S.. A..CHI..LD..THE..Y.. WOU..LD..PU..T..ME.. IN..FRO..NT..OF.. A..CORP..SE..WE.. WER..E..CALL..ED.. *LIS..TEN..ING..EA..RS.*

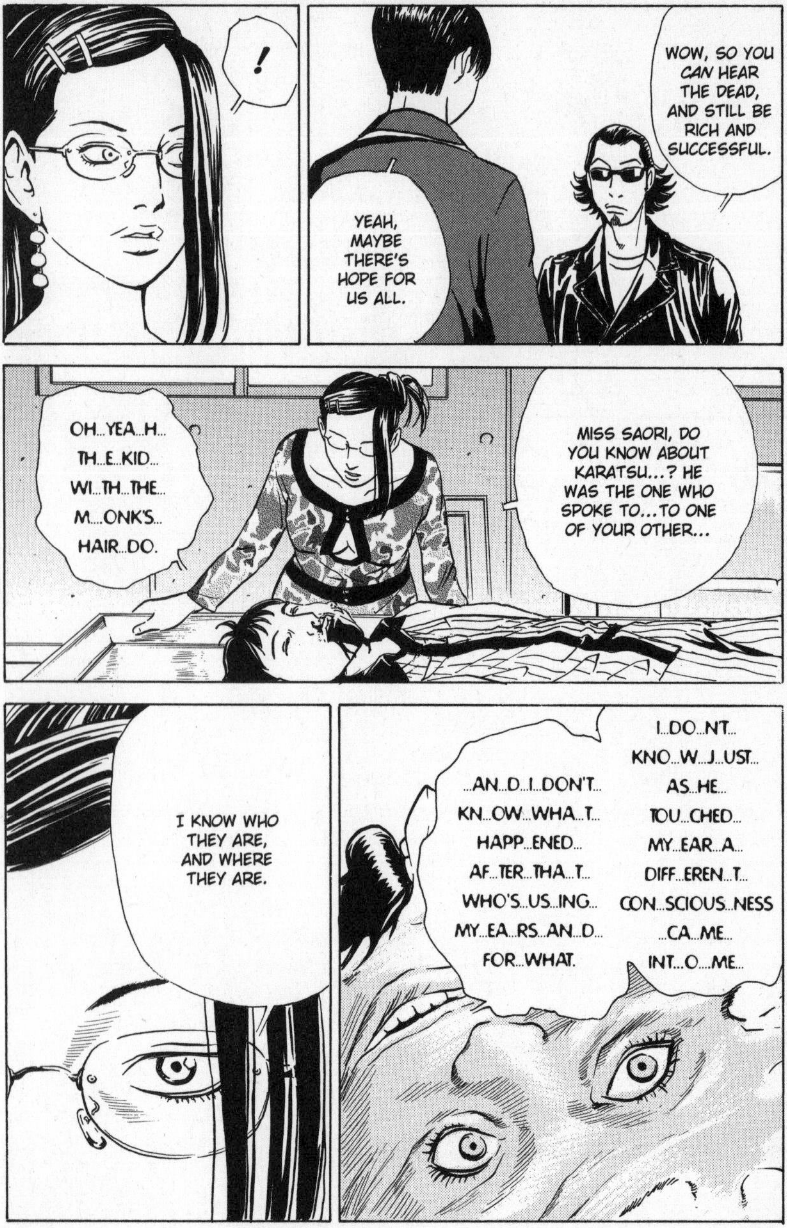
WOW, SO YOU CAN HEAR THE DEAD, AND STILL BE RICH AND SUCCESSFUL.
YEAH, MAYBE THERE'S HOPE FOR US ALL.
!
MISS SAORI, DO YOU KNOW ABOUT KARATSU...? HE WAS THE ONE WHO SPOKE TO...TO ONE OF YOUR OTHER...
OH...YEA...H... TH...E...KID... WI...TH...THE... M...ONK'S... HAIR...DO.
I...DO...NT... KNO...W...J...UST... AS...HE... TOU...CHED... MY...EAR...A... DIFF...EREN...T... CON...SCIOUS...NESS ...CA...ME... INT...O...ME...
...AN...D...I...DON'T... KN...OW...WHA...T... HAPP...ENED... AF...TER...THA...T... WHO'S...US...ING... MY...EA...RS...AN...D... FOR...WHAT.
I KNOW WHO THEY ARE, AND WHERE THEY ARE.

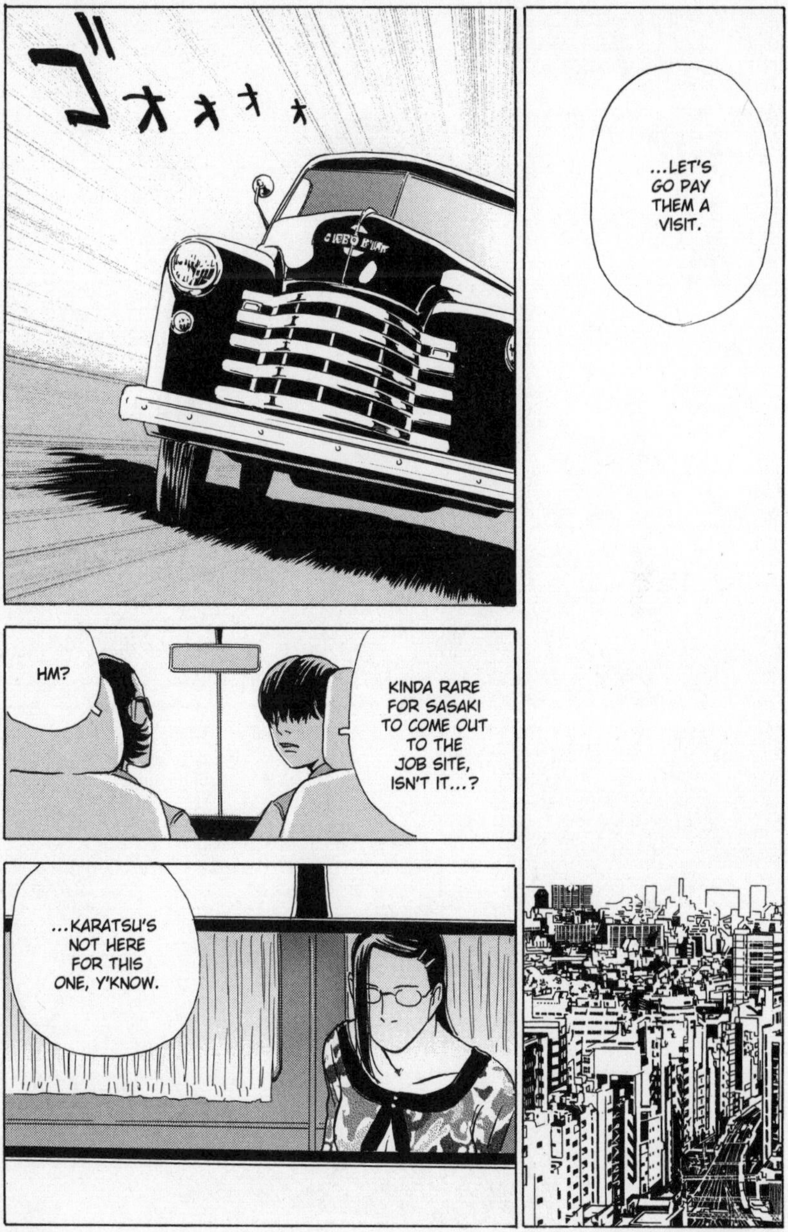
...LET'S GO PAY THEM A VISIT.
ゴオォォォ
KINDA RARE FOR SASAKI TO COME OUT TO THE JOB SITE, ISN'T IT...?
HM?
...KARATSU'S NOT HERE FOR THIS ONE, Y'KNOW.

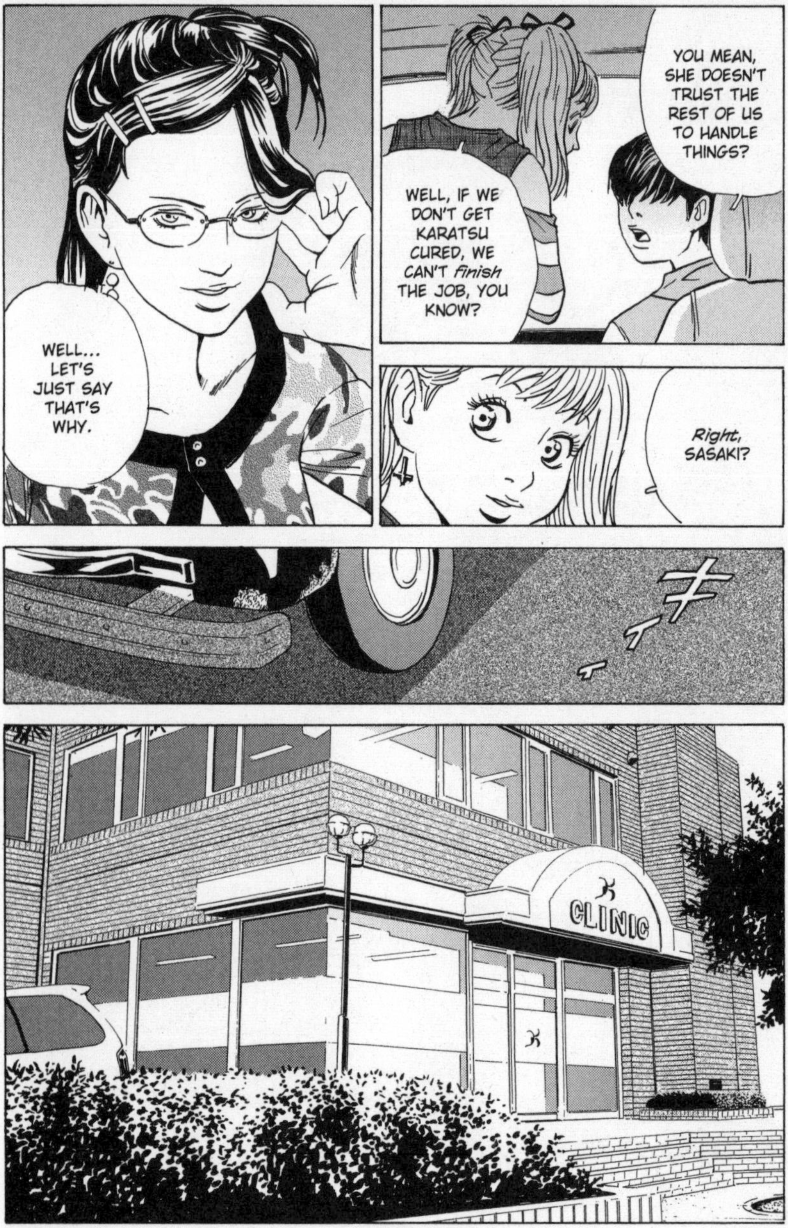
YOU MEAN, SHE DOESN'T TRUST THE REST OF US TO HANDLE THINGS?
WELL, IF WE DON'T GET KARATSU CURED, WE CAN'T *finish* THE JOB, YOU KNOW?
Right, SASAKI?
WELL... LET'S JUST SAY THAT'S WHY.
キィィ
CLINIC

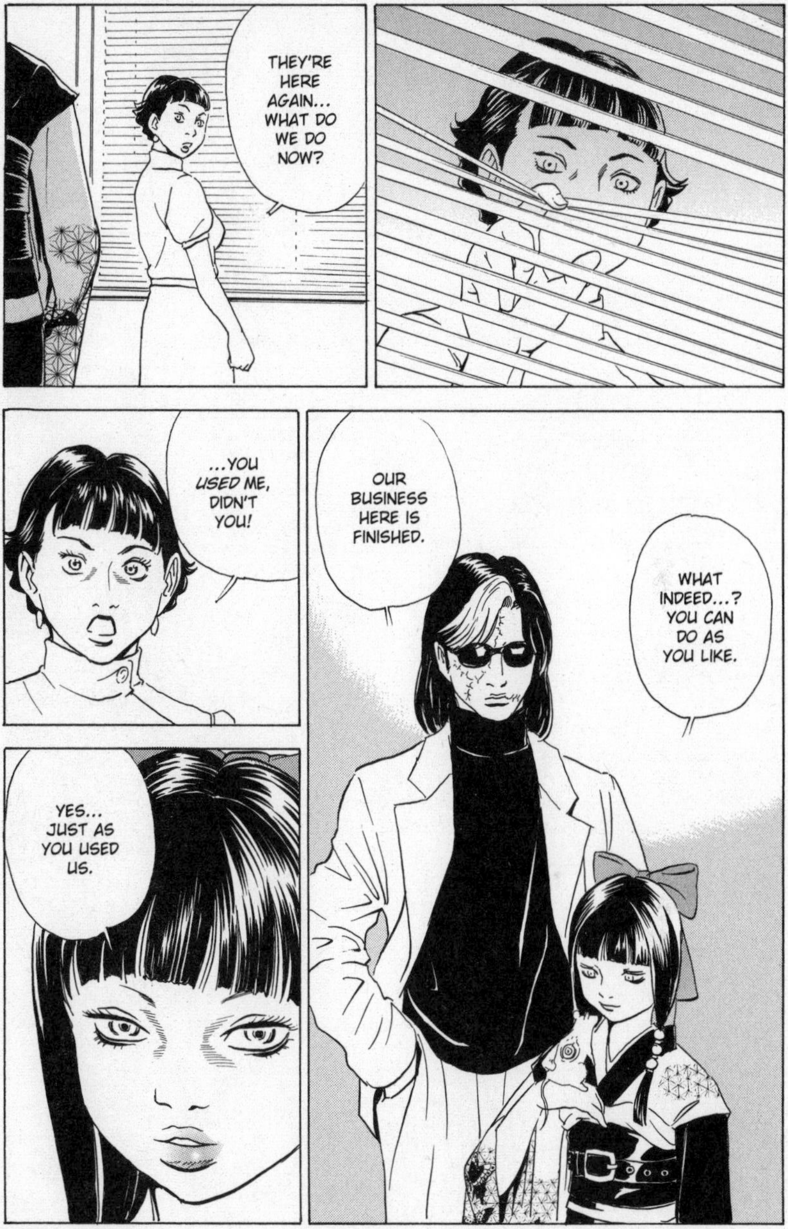
THEY'RE HERE AGAIN... WHAT DO WE DO NOW?
WHAT INDEED...? YOU CAN DO AS YOU LIKE.
OUR BUSINESS HERE IS FINISHED.
...YOU USED ME, DIDN'T YOU!
YES... JUST AS YOU USED US.

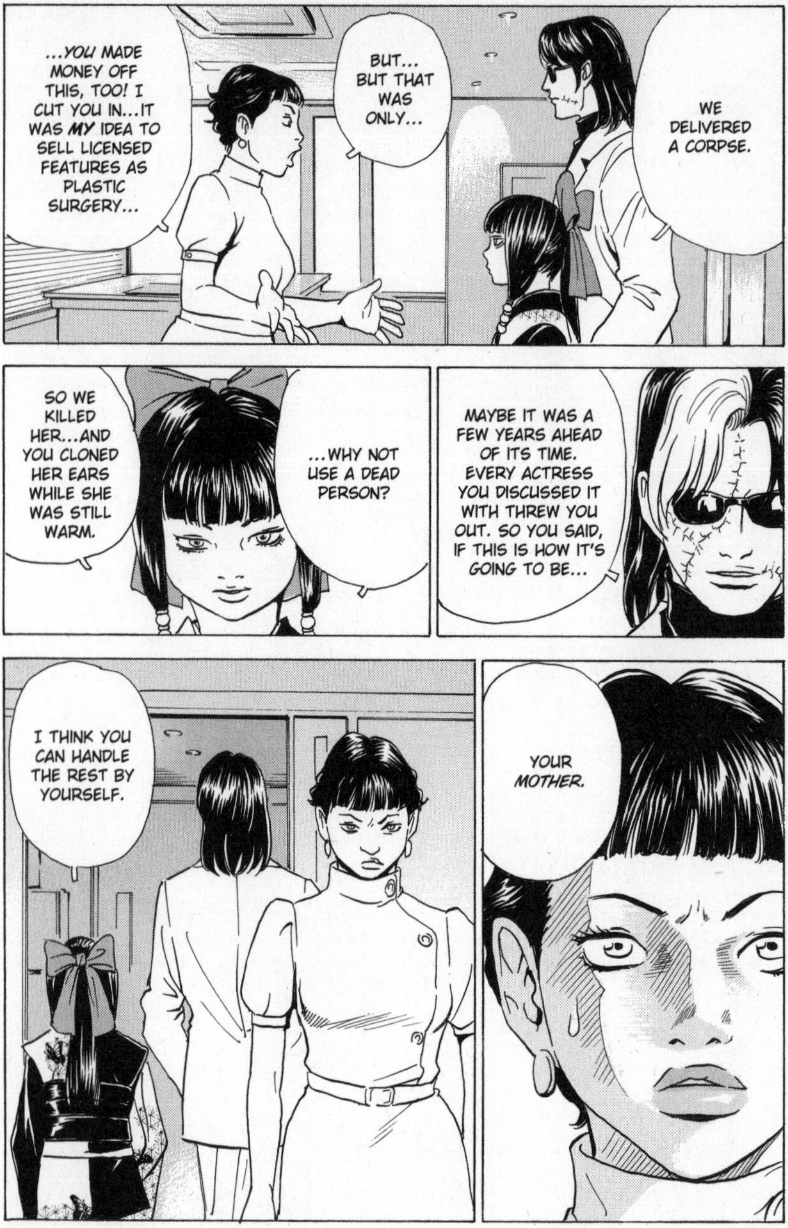
WE DELIVERED A CORPSE.
BUT... BUT THAT WAS ONLY...
...YOU MADE MONEY OFF THIS, TOO! I CUT YOU IN...IT WAS *MY* IDEA TO SELL LICENSED FEATURES AS PLASTIC SURGERY...
MAYBE IT WAS A FEW YEARS AHEAD OF ITS TIME. EVERY ACTRESS YOU DISCUSSED IT WITH THREW YOU OUT. SO YOU SAID, IF THIS IS HOW IT'S GOING TO BE...
...WHY NOT USE A DEAD PERSON?
SO WE KILLED HER...AND YOU CLONED HER EARS WHILE SHE WAS STILL WARM.
YOUR *MOTHER.*
I THINK YOU CAN HANDLE THE REST BY YOURSELF.

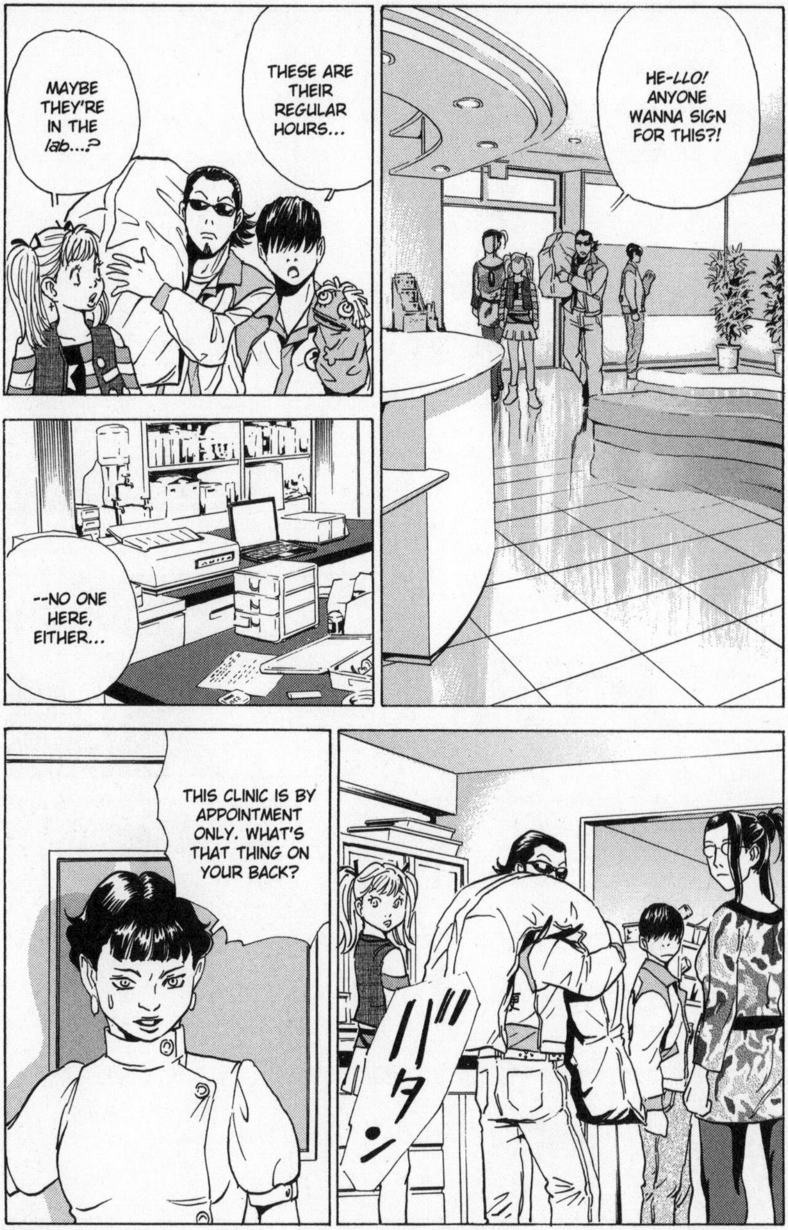
HE-*LLO!* ANYONE WANNA SIGN FOR THIS?!
THESE ARE THEIR REGULAR HOURS...
MAYBE THEY'RE IN THE *lab*...?
--NO ONE HERE, EITHER...
バタン
THIS CLINIC IS BY APPOINTMENT ONLY. WHAT'S THAT THING ON YOUR BACK?

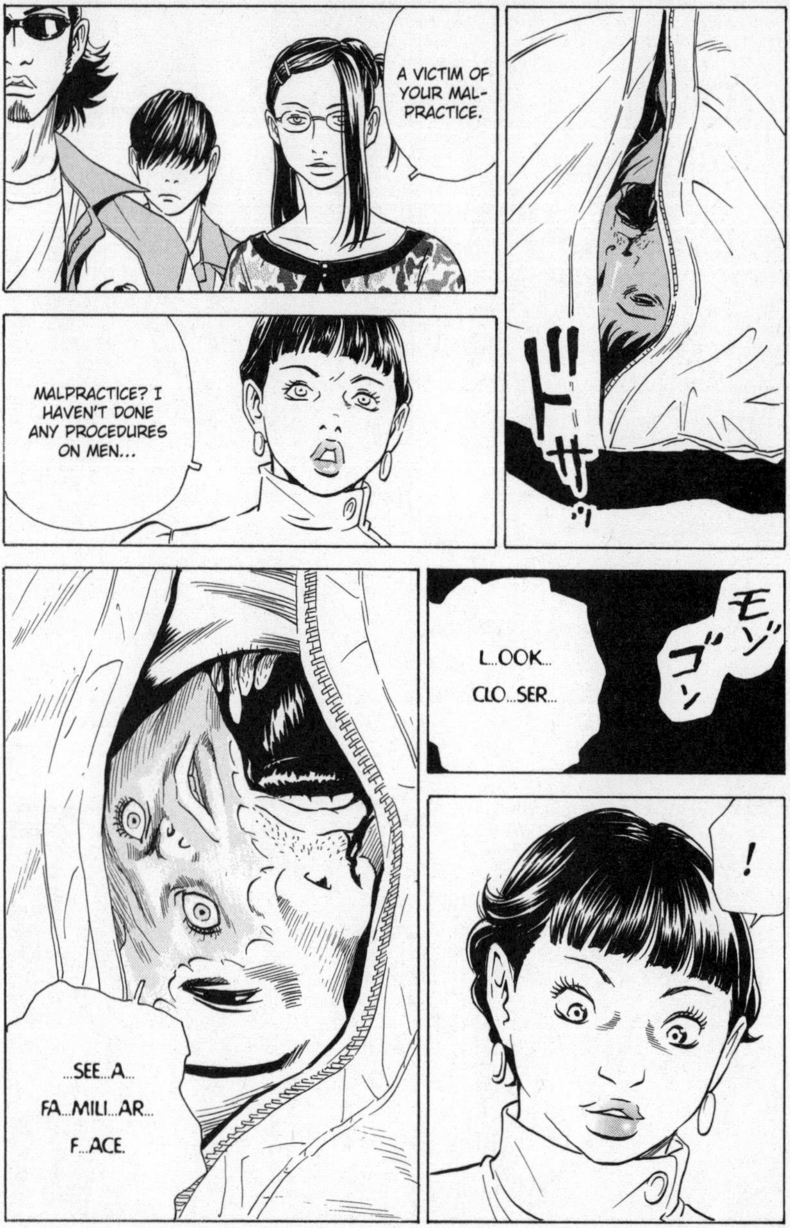
ドサッ
A VICTIM OF YOUR MAL-PRACTICE.
MALPRACTICE? I HAVEN'T DONE ANY PROCEDURES ON MEN...
L...OOK... CLO...SER...
モゾゴン
!
...SEE...A... FA...MILI...AR... F...ACE.

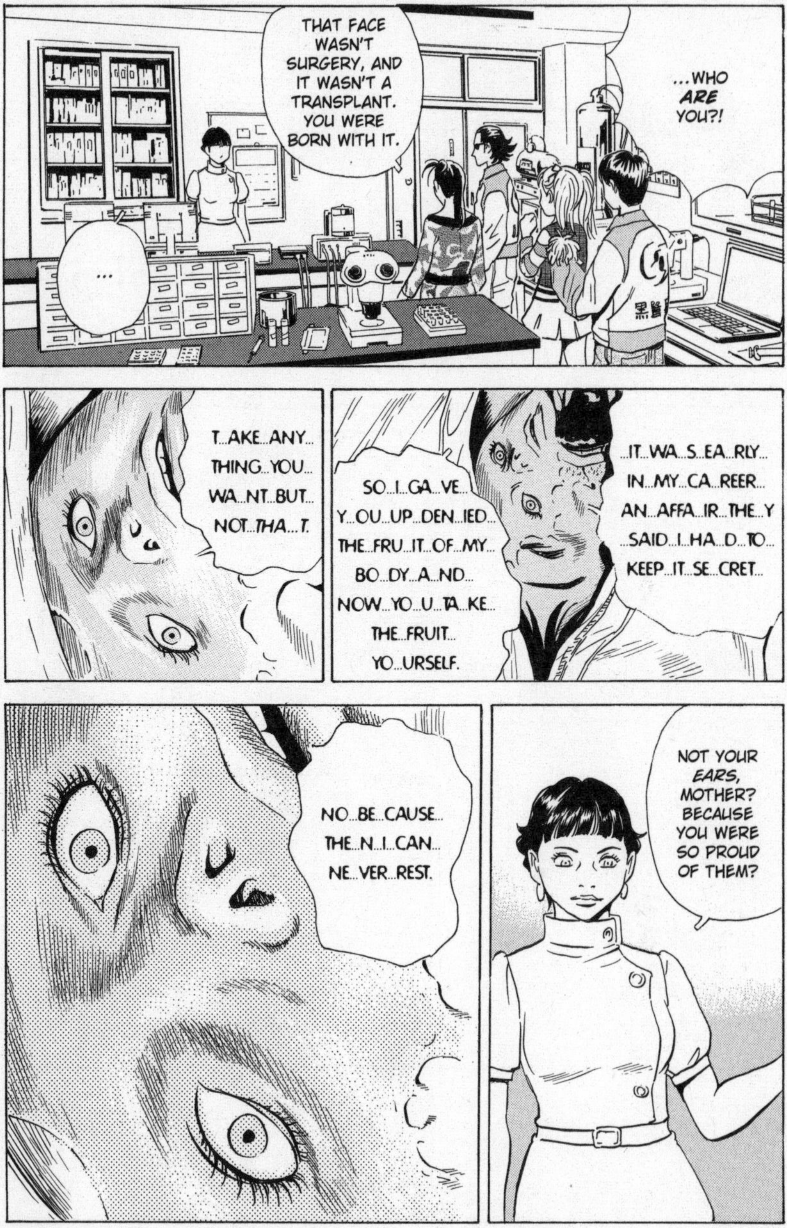
THAT FACE WASN'T SURGERY, AND IT WASN'T A TRANSPLANT. YOU WERE BORN WITH IT.
...WHO *ARE* YOU?!
...
...IT...WA...S...EA...RLY... IN...MY...CA...REER... AN...AFFA...IR...THE...Y ...SAID...I...HA...D...TO... KEEP...IT...SE...CRET...
SO...I...GA...VE... Y...OU...UP...DEN...IED... THE...FRU...IT...OF...MY... BO...DY...A...ND... NOW...YO...U...TA...KE... THE...FRUIT... YO...URSELF.
T...AKE...ANY... THING...YOU... WA...NT...BUT... NOT...*THA*...T.
NOT YOUR *EARS*, MOTHER? BECAUSE YOU WERE SO PROUD OF THEM?
NO...BE...CAUSE... THE...N...I...CAN... NE...VER...REST.

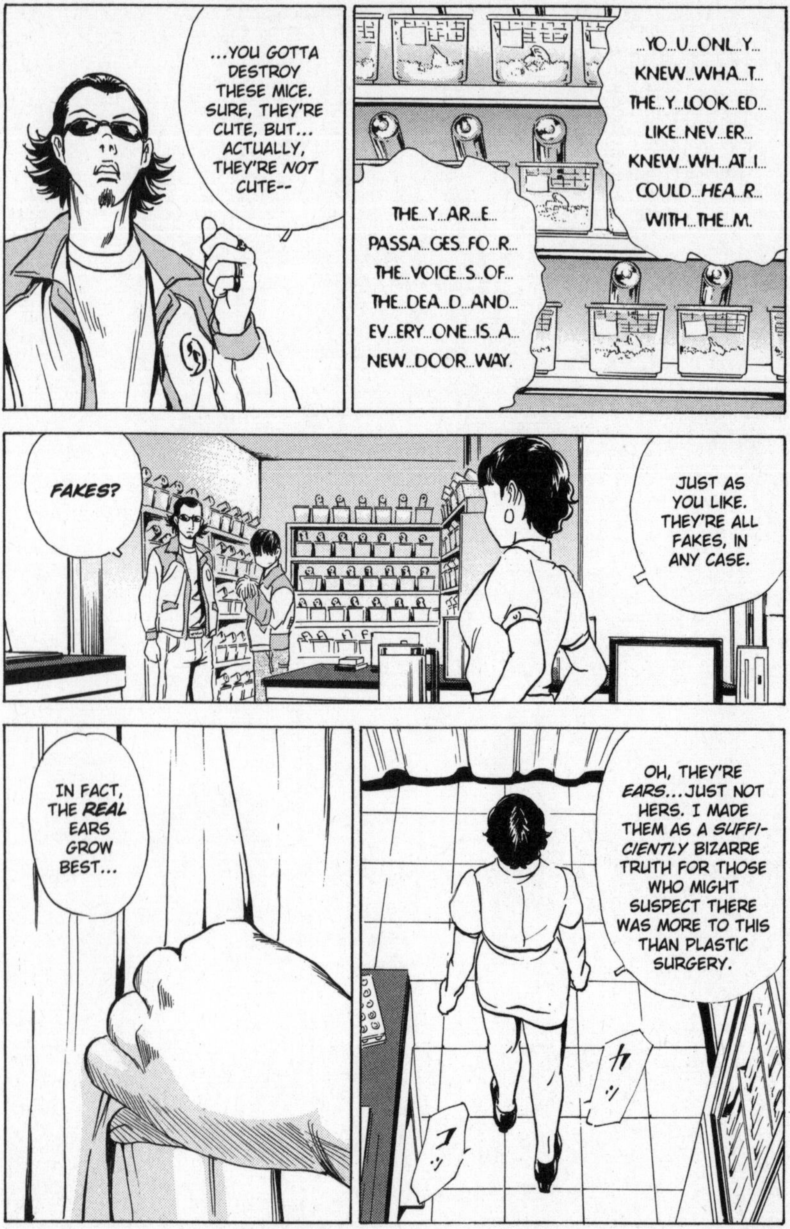
...YO...U...ONL...Y... KNEW...WHA...T... THE...Y...LOOK...ED... LIKE...NEV...ER... KNEW...WH...AT...I... COULD...HEA...R... WITH...THE...M.
THE...Y...AR...E... PASSA...GES...FO...R... THE...VOICE...S...OF... THE...DEA...D...AND... EV...ERY...ONE...IS...A... NEW...DOOR...WAY.
...YOU GOTTA DESTROY THESE MICE. SURE, THEY'RE CUTE, BUT... ACTUALLY, THEY'RE *NOT* CUTE--
JUST AS YOU LIKE. THEY'RE ALL FAKES, IN ANY CASE.
FAKES?
OH, THEY'RE *EARS*... JUST NOT HERS. I MADE THEM AS A *SUFFICIENTLY* BIZARRE TRUTH FOR THOSE WHO MIGHT SUSPECT THERE WAS MORE TO THIS THAN PLASTIC SURGERY.
カッ
コッ
IN FACT, THE *REAL* EARS GROW BEST...

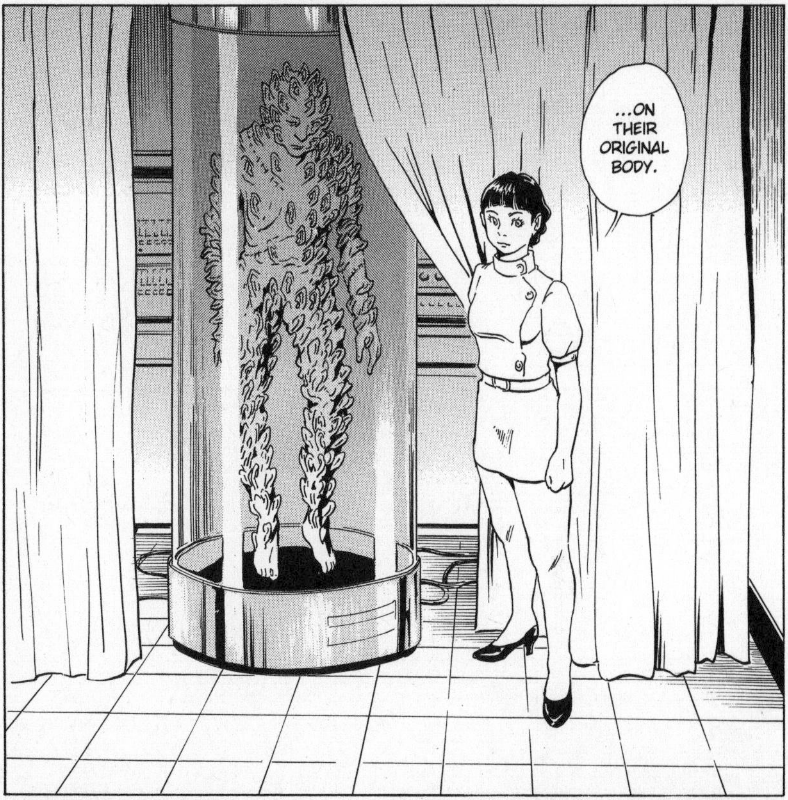
...ON THEIR ORIGINAL BODY.
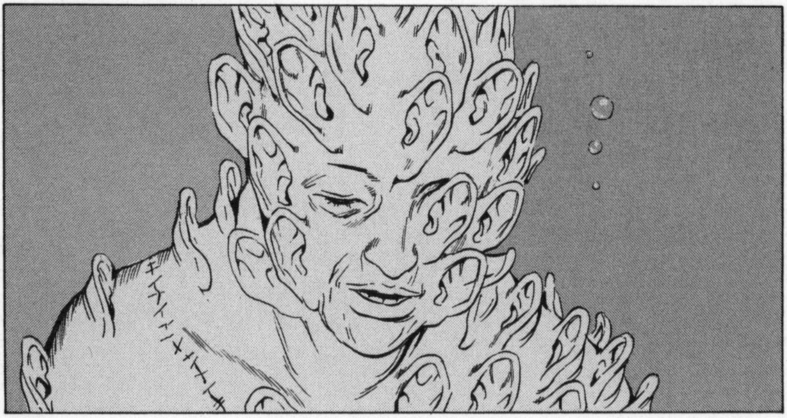

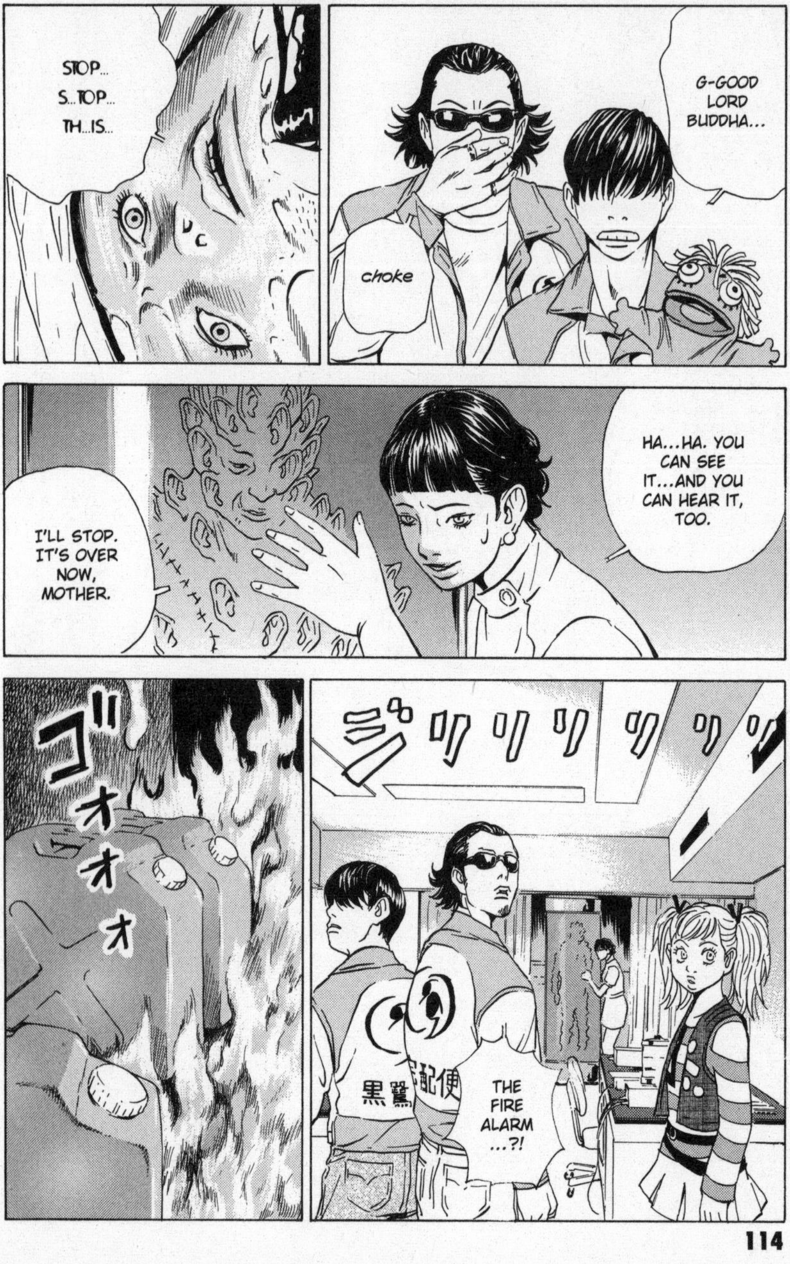
G-GOOD LORD BUDDHA...
choke
STOP... S...TOP... TH...IS...
HA...HA. YOU CAN SEE IT...AND YOU CAN HEAR IT, TOO.
I'LL STOP. IT'S OVER NOW, MOTHER.
ジリリリリリ
黒鷺
配便
THE FIRE ALARM ...?!
ゴオオオ

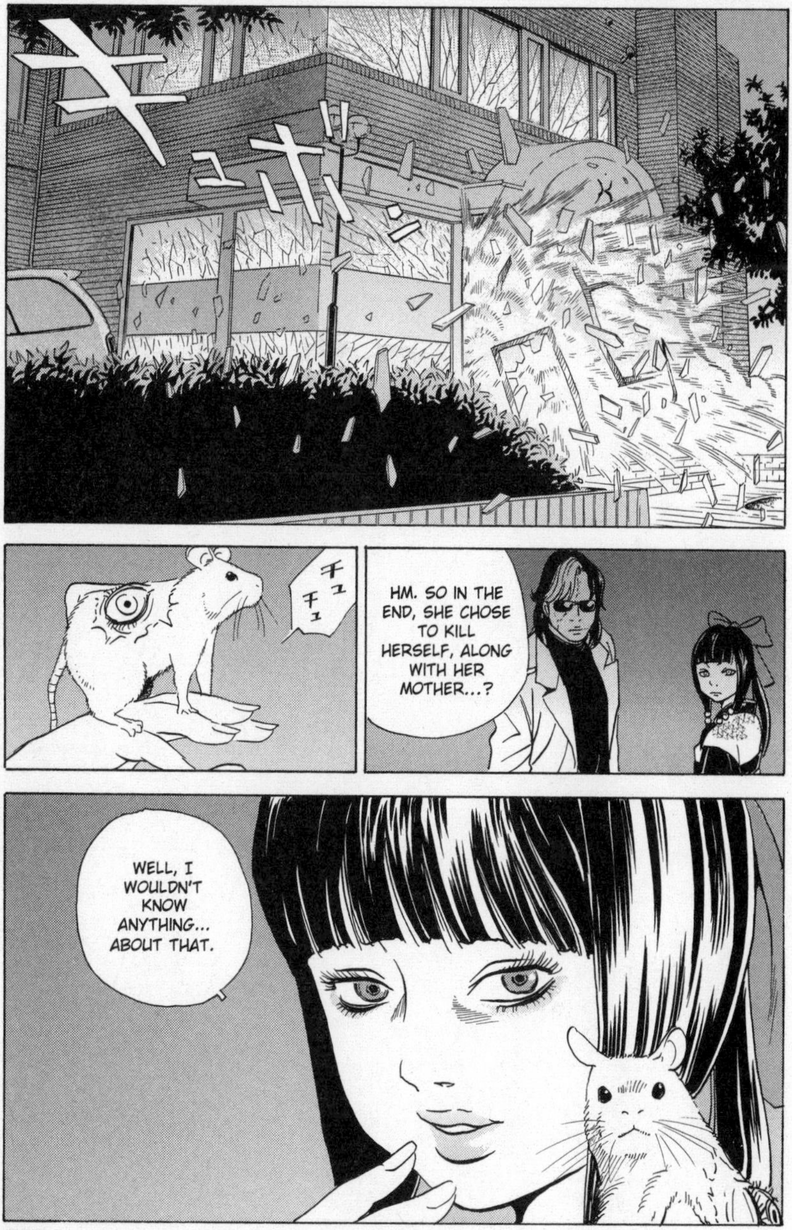
HM. SO IN THE END, SHE CHOSE TO KILL HERSELF, ALONG WITH HER MOTHER...?
チュ チュ
WELL, I WOULDN'T KNOW ANYTHING... ABOUT THAT.

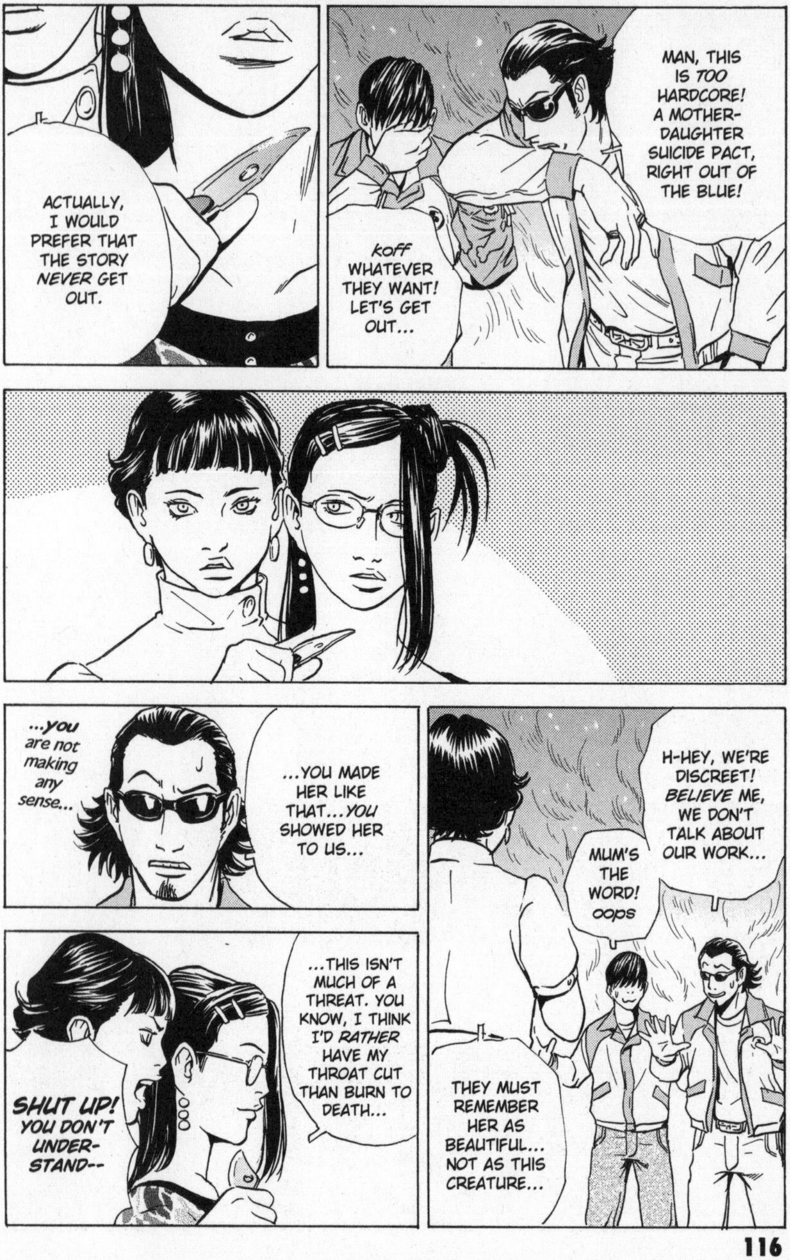
MAN, THIS IS *TOO* HARDCORE! A MOTHER-DAUGHTER SUICIDE PACT, RIGHT OUT OF THE BLUE!
koff WHATEVER THEY WANT! LET'S GET OUT...
ACTUALLY, I WOULD PREFER THAT THE STORY *NEVER* GET OUT.
H-HEY, WE'RE DISCREET! *BELIEVE ME,* WE DON'T TALK ABOUT OUR WORK...
MUM'S THE WORD! *oops*
THEY MUST REMEMBER HER AS BEAUTIFUL... NOT AS THIS CREATURE...
...YOU MADE HER LIKE THAT... *YOU* SHOWED HER TO US...
...*you* are not making any sense...
...THIS ISN'T MUCH OF A THREAT. YOU KNOW, I THINK I'D *RATHER* HAVE MY THROAT CUT THAN BURN TO DEATH...
SHUT UP! YOU DON'T UNDER-STAND--

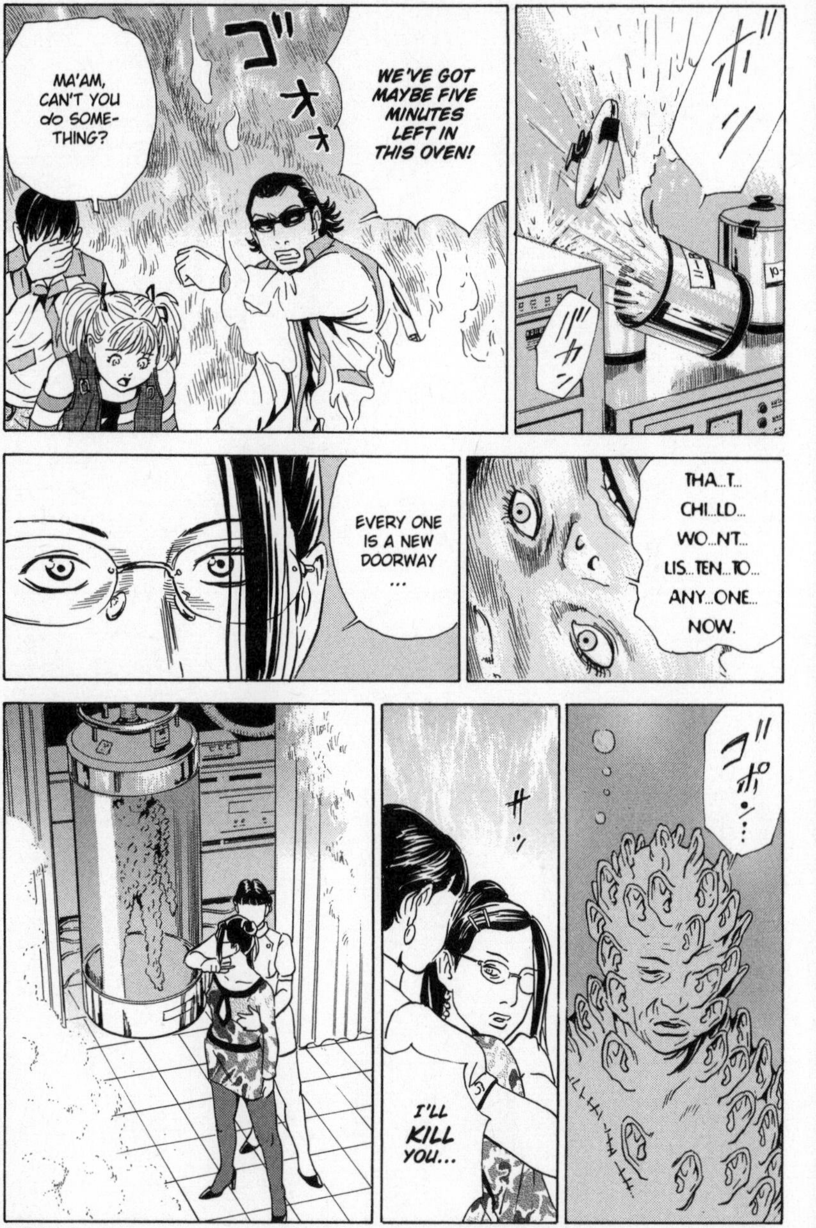
WE'VE GOT MAYBE FIVE MINUTES LEFT IN THIS OVEN!
MA'AM, CAN'T YOU do SOME-THING?
THA...T... CHI...LD... WO...NT... LIS...TEN...TO... ANY...ONE... NOW.
EVERY ONE IS A NEW DOORWAY ...
I'LL KILL YOU...

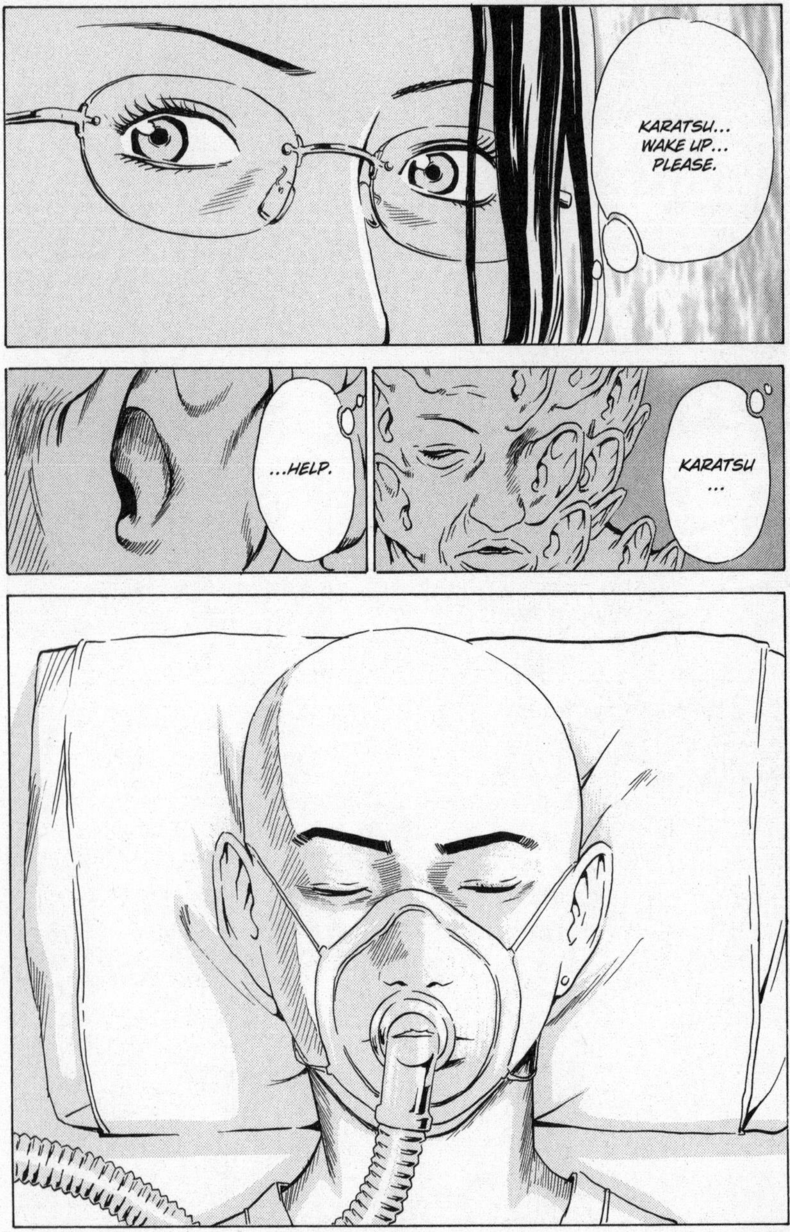
KARATSU... WAKE UP... PLEASE.
KARATSU ...
...HELP.

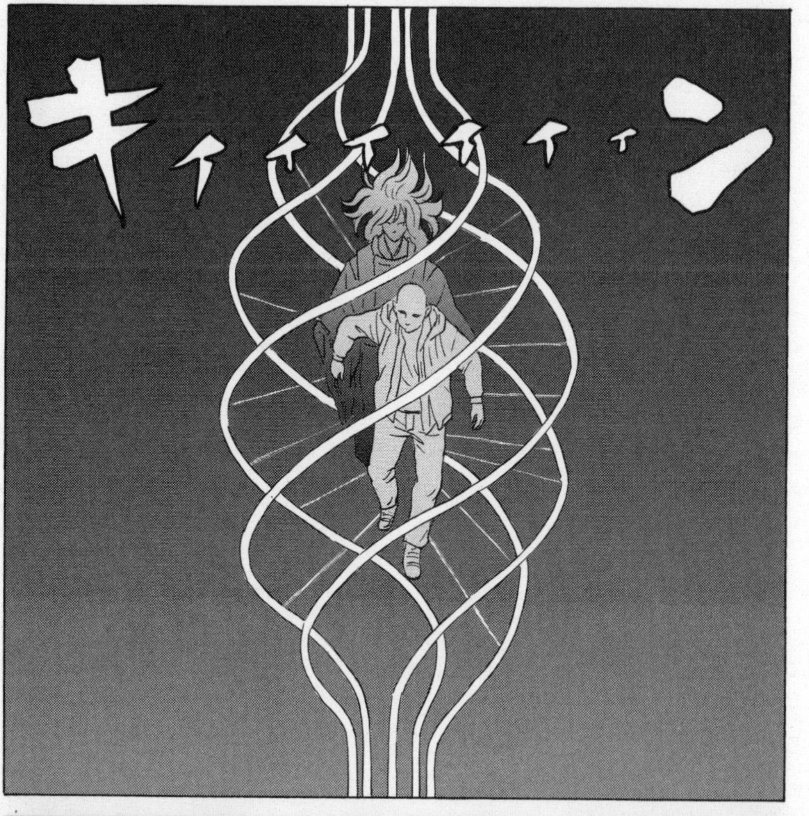
キィィィィィィン
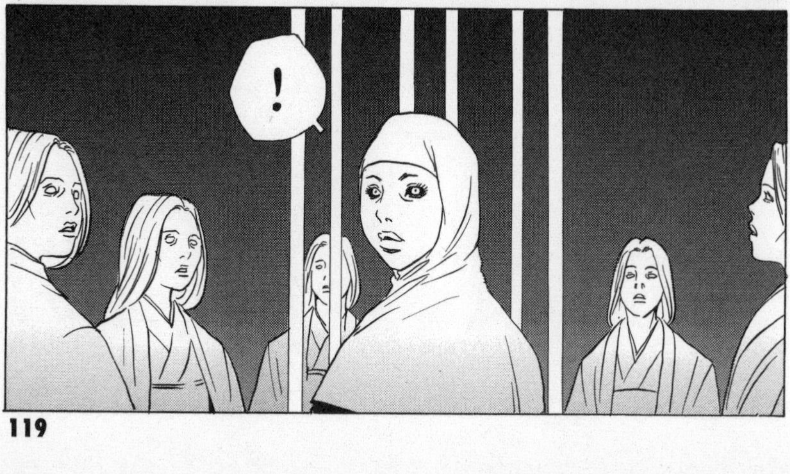
!

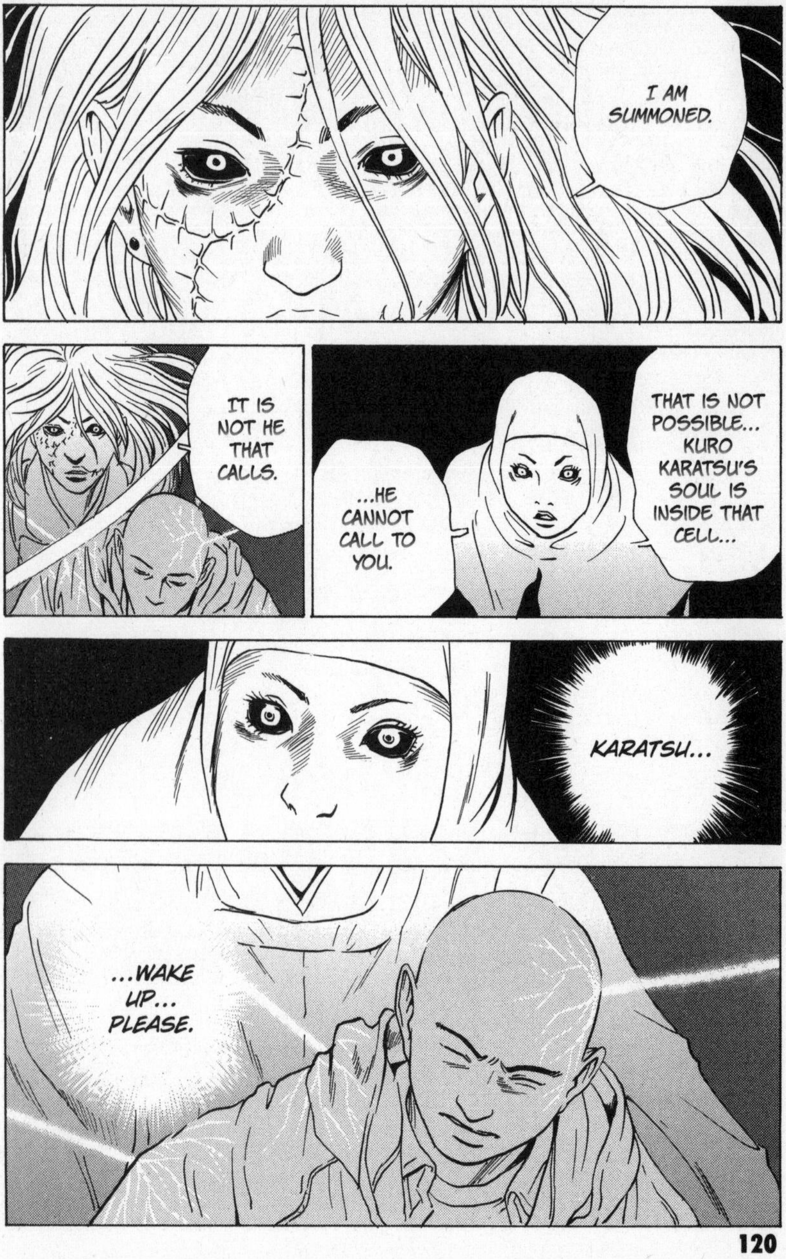
I AM SUMMONED.
THAT IS NOT POSSIBLE... KURO KARATSU'S SOUL IS INSIDE THAT CELL...
...HE CANNOT CALL TO YOU.
IT IS NOT HE THAT CALLS.
KARATSU...
...WAKE UP... PLEASE.

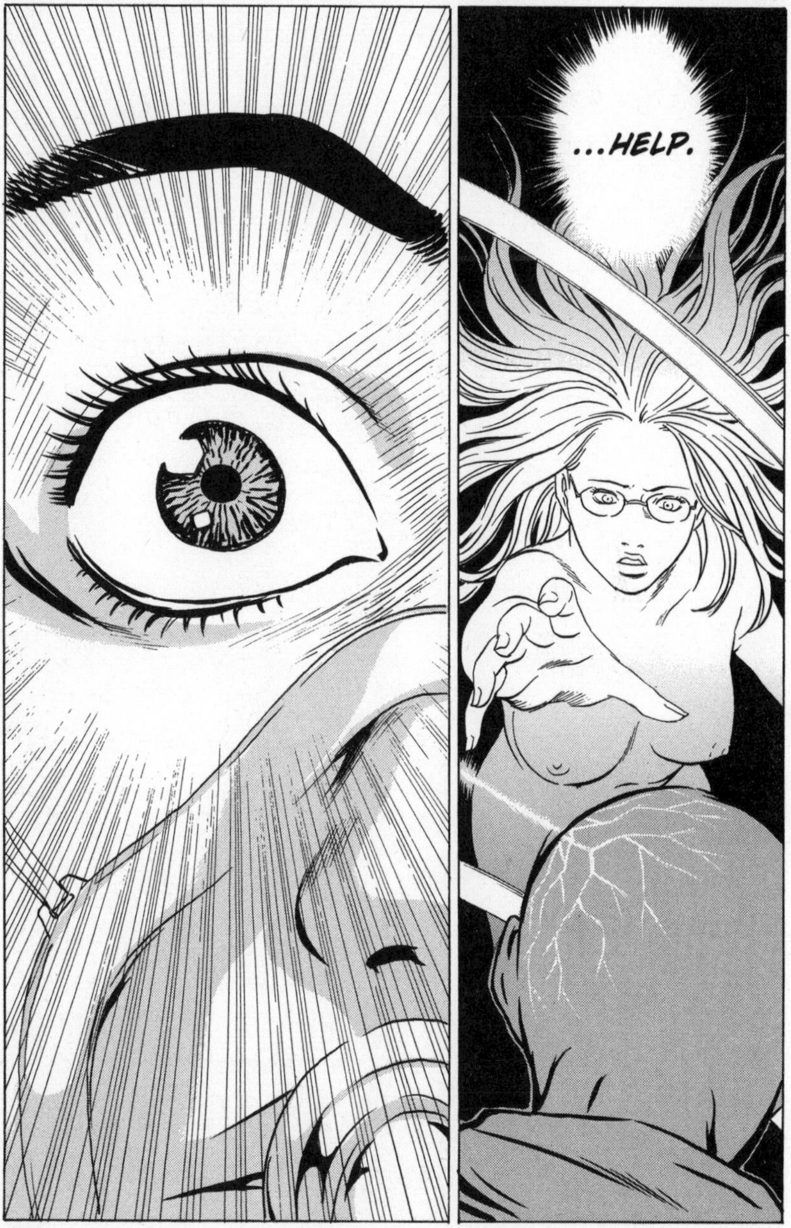
...HELP.

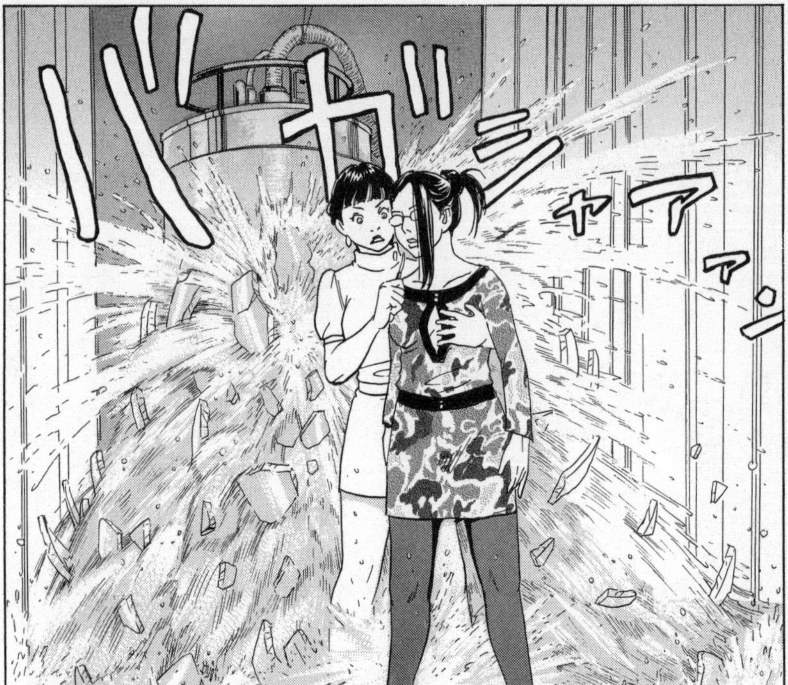
バッシャアアン
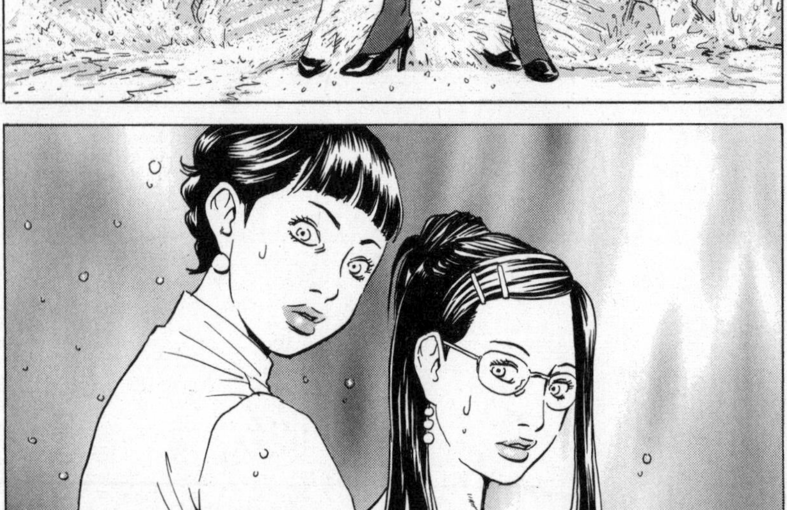

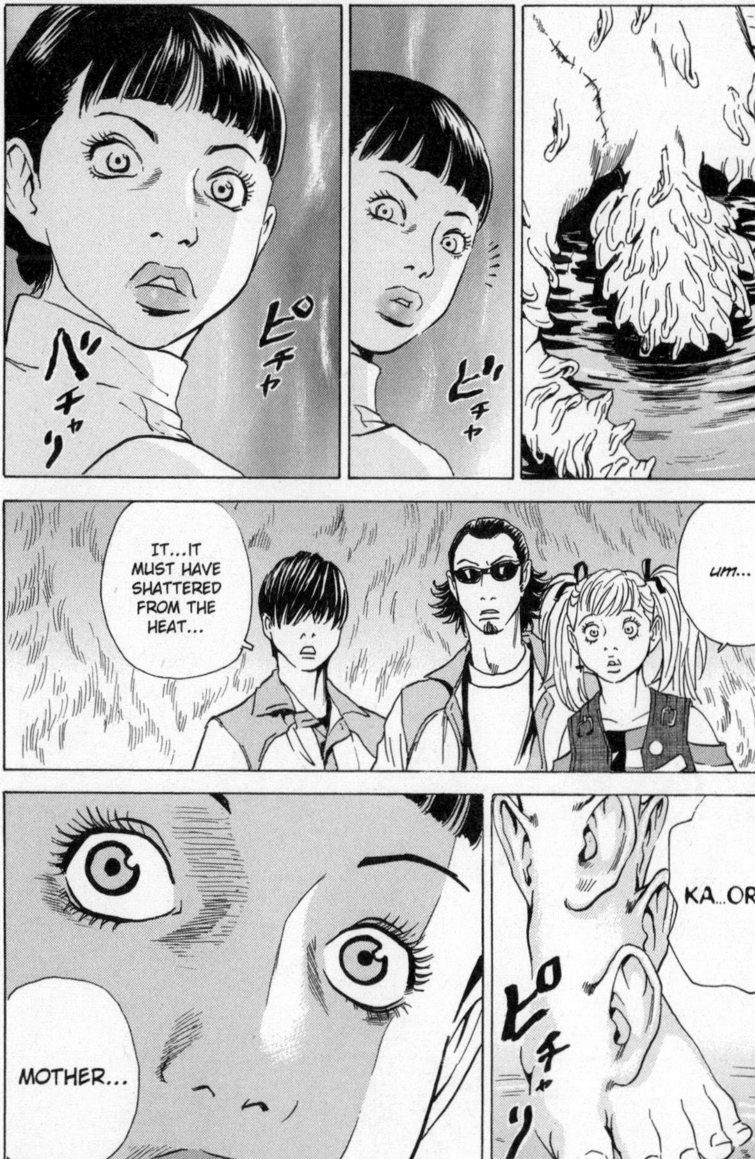
ビチャ
ピチャ
バチャリ
um...
IT...IT MUST HAVE SHATTERED FROM THE HEAT...
KA...ORI...
ピチャリ
MOTHER...

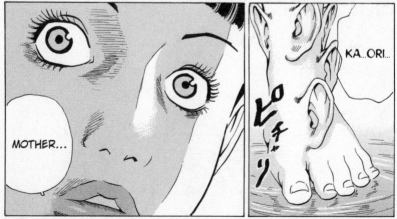

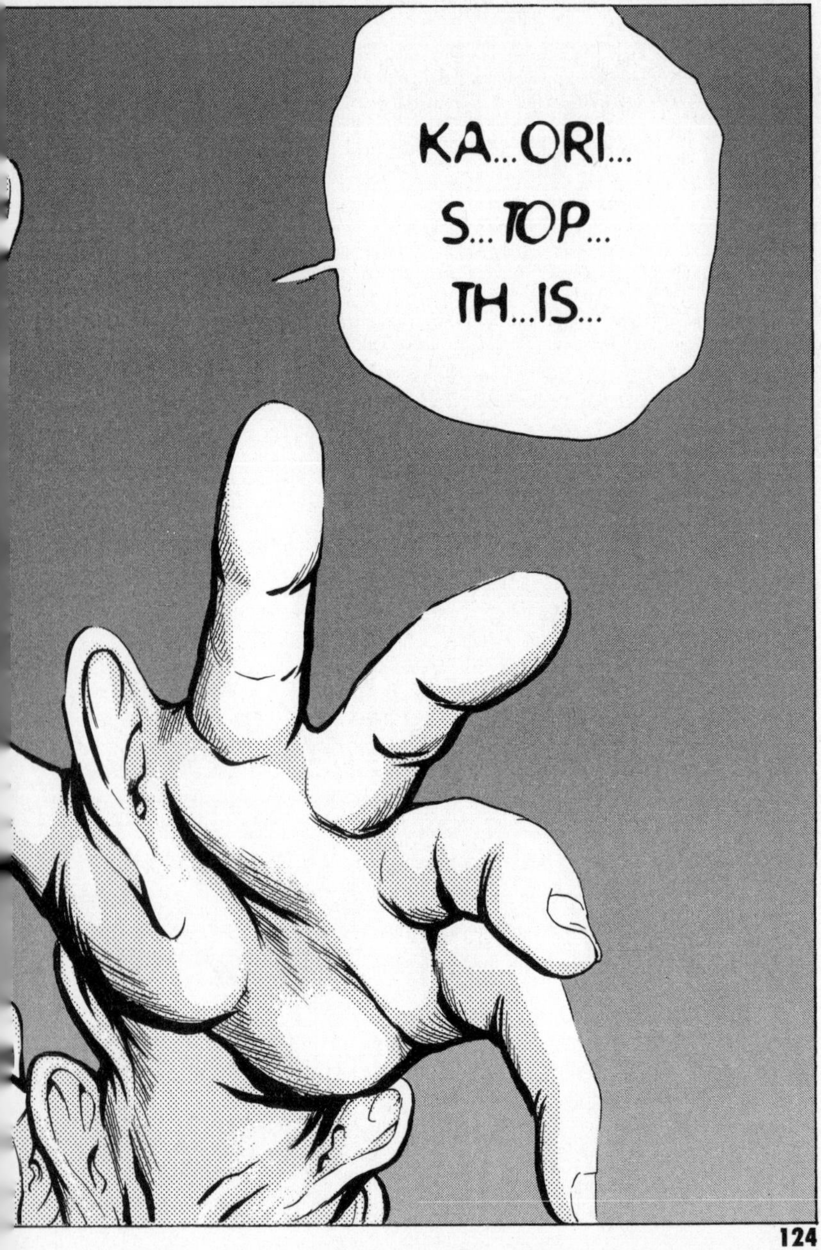
KA...ORI...
S...TOP...
TH...IS...

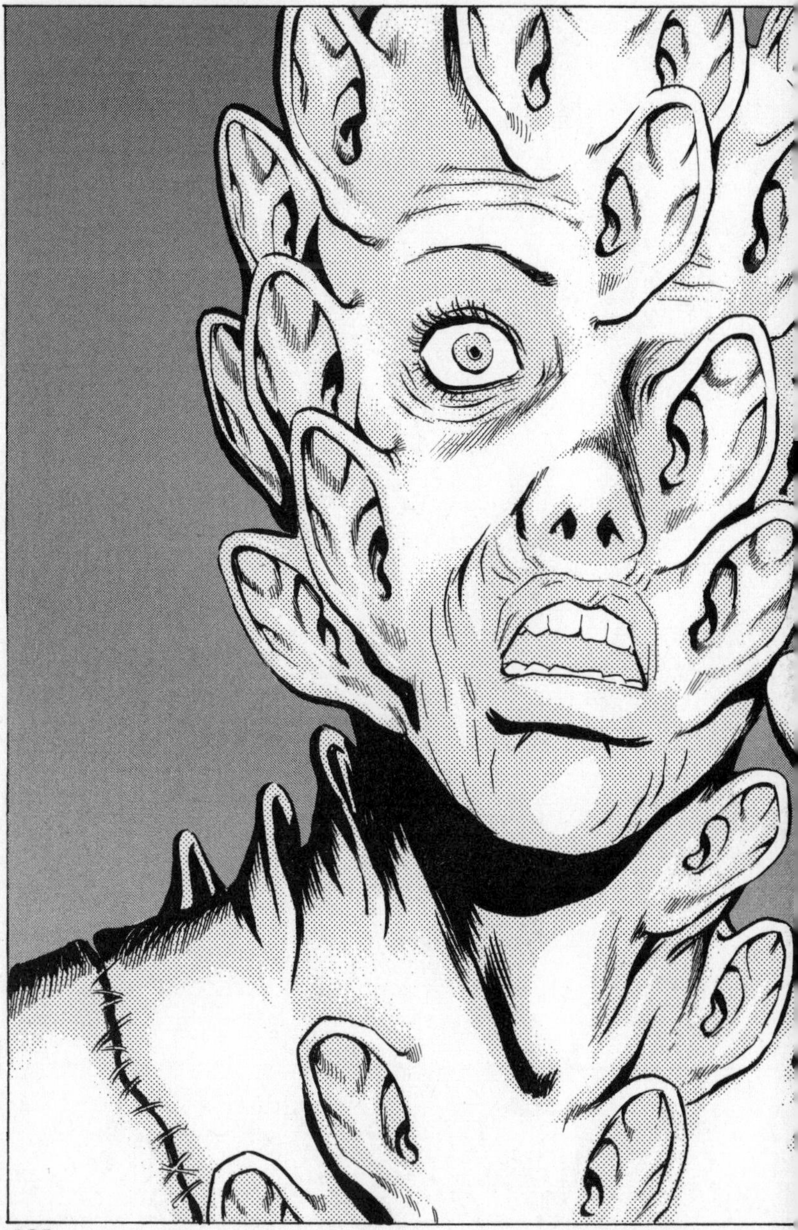

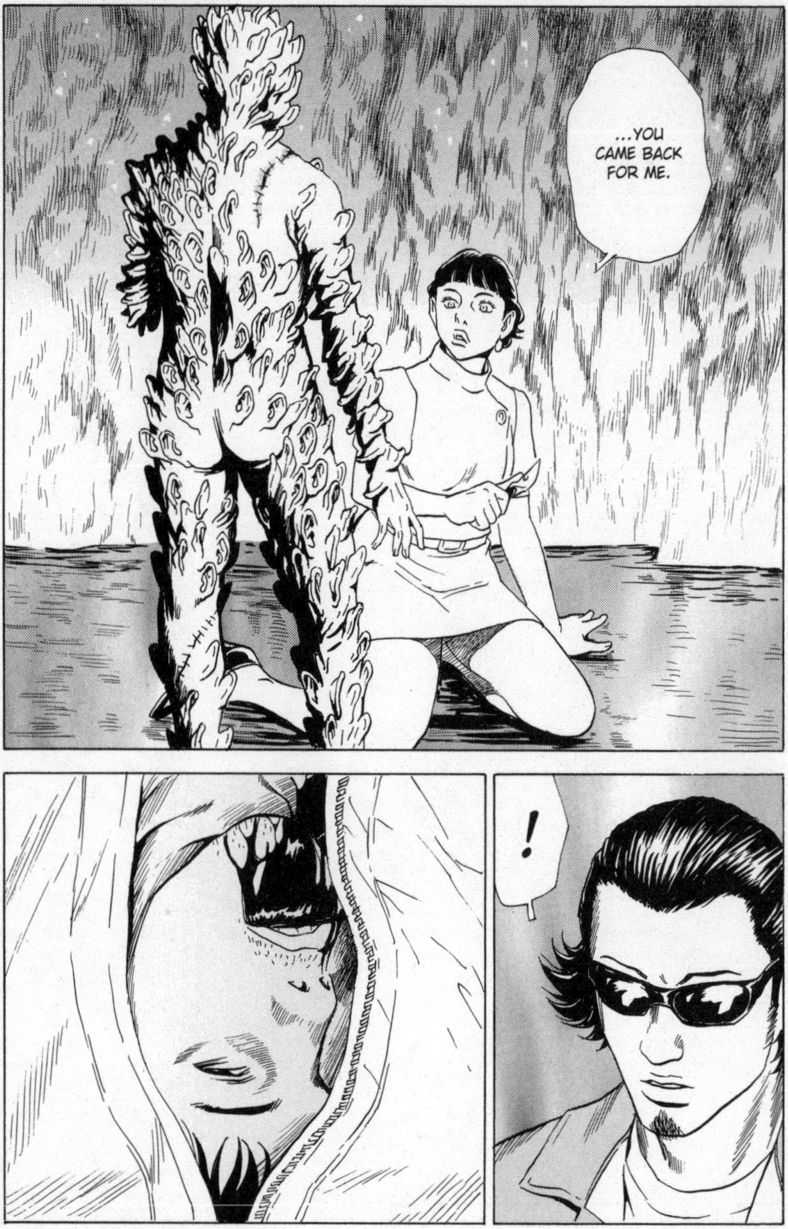
...YOU CAME BACK FOR ME.
!

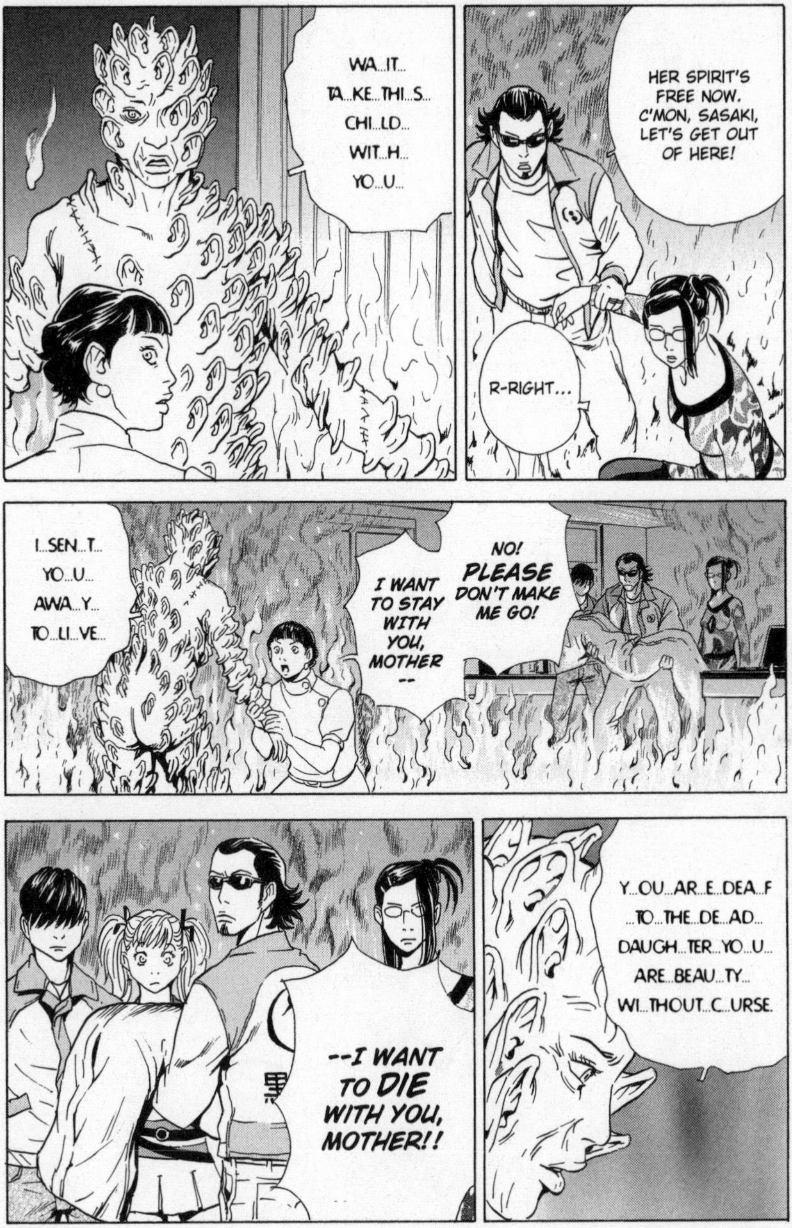
HER SPIRIT'S FREE NOW. C'MON, SASAKI, LET'S GET OUT OF HERE!
R-RIGHT...
WA...IT... TA...KE...THI...S... CHI...LD... WIT...H... YO...U...
NO! PLEASE DON'T MAKE ME GO!
I WANT TO STAY WITH YOU, MOTHER --
I...SEN...T... YO...U... AWA...Y... TO...LI...VE...
Y...OU...AR...E...DEA...F ...TO...THE...DE...AD... DAUGH...TER...YO...U... ARE...BEAU...TY... WI...THOUT...C...URSE.
--I WANT TO DIE WITH YOU, MOTHER!!

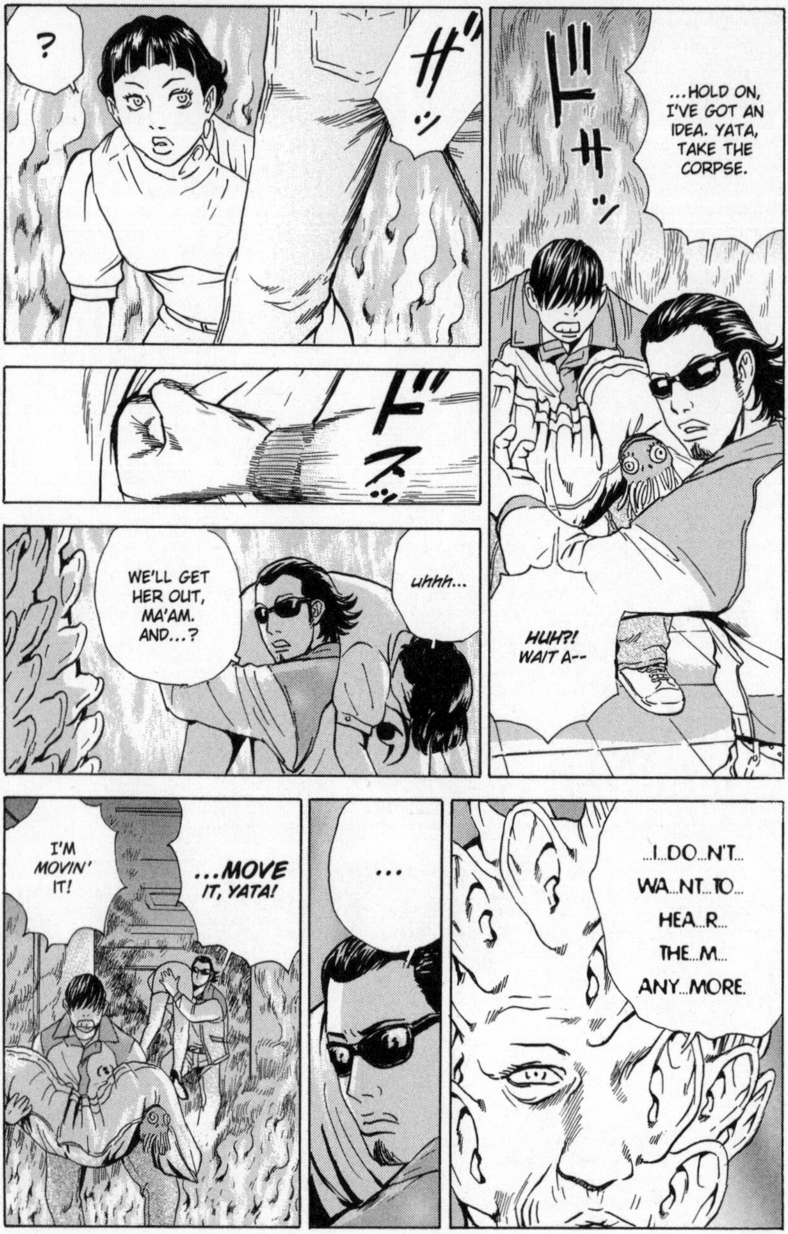
...HOLD ON, I'VE GOT AN IDEA. YATA, TAKE THE CORPSE.
HUH?! WAIT A--
?
ザッ
ドスッ
uhhh...
WE'LL GET HER OUT, MA'AM. AND...?
...I...DO...N'T... WA...NT...TO... HEA...R... THE...M... ANY...MORE.
...
...MOVE IT, YATA!
I'M MOVIN' IT!

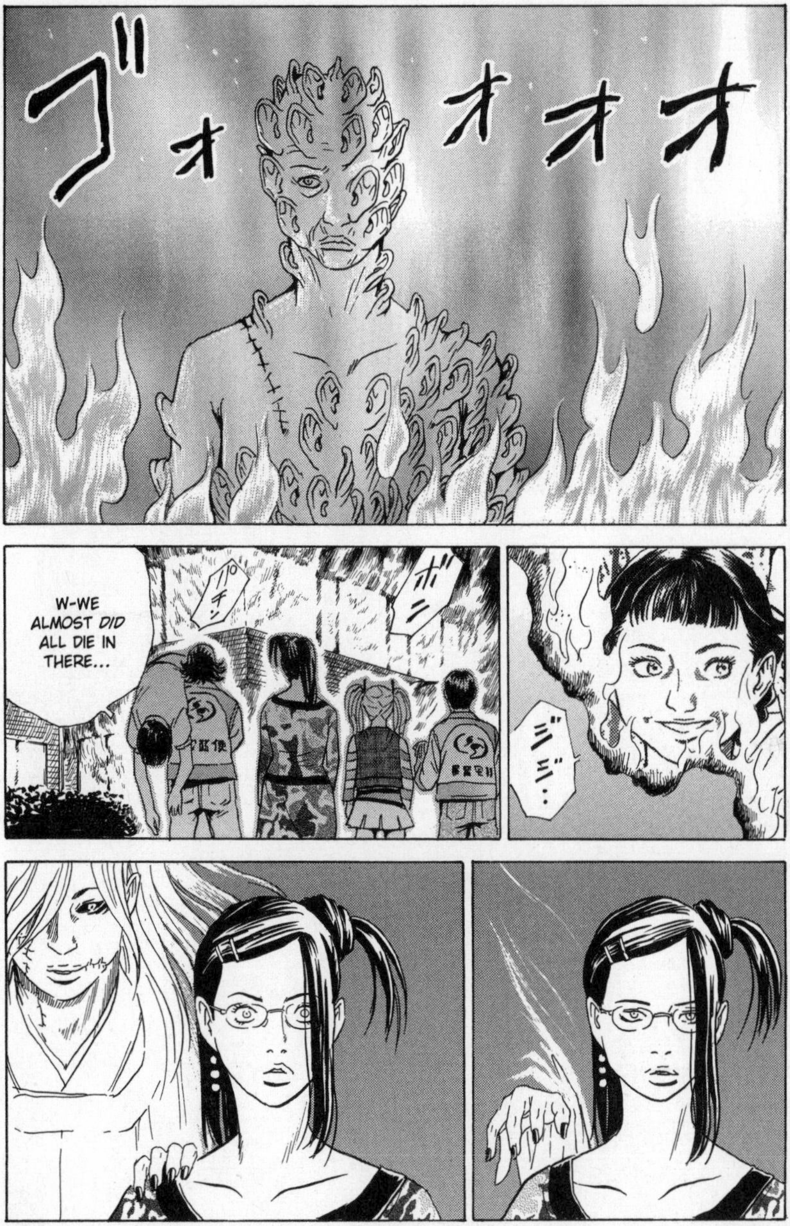
ゴォオオオ
ジジ…
ボン
パチン
W-WE ALMOST DID ALL DIE IN THERE...

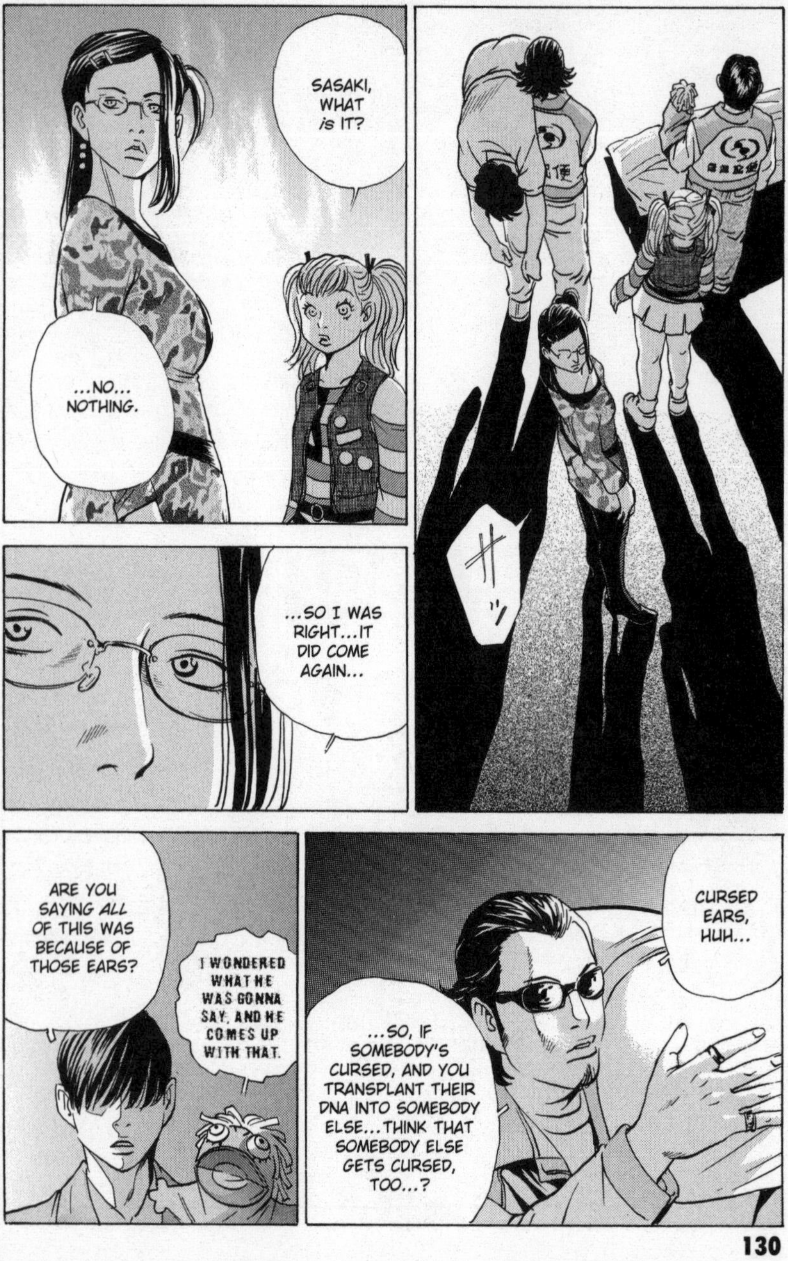
ザッ
SASAKI, WHAT *is* IT?
...NO... NOTHING.
...SO I WAS RIGHT...IT DID COME AGAIN...
CURSED EARS, HUH...
...SO, IF SOMEBODY'S CURSED, AND YOU TRANSPLANT THEIR DNA INTO SOMEBODY ELSE...THINK THAT SOMEBODY ELSE GETS CURSED, TOO...?
ARE YOU SAYING *ALL* OF THIS WAS BECAUSE OF THOSE EARS?
I WONDERED WHAT HE WAS GONNA SAY, AND HE COMES UP WITH THAT.

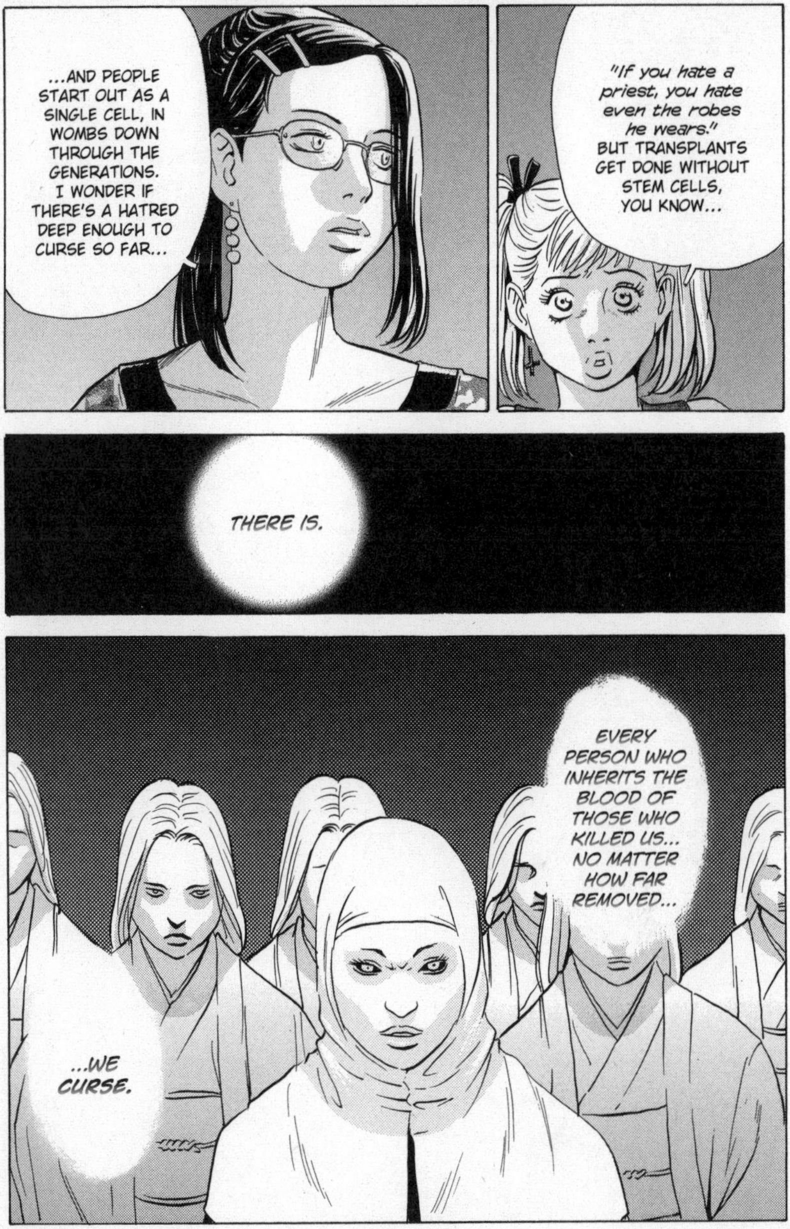
"If you hate a priest, you hate even the robes he wears." BUT TRANSPLANTS GET DONE WITHOUT STEM CELLS, YOU KNOW...
...AND PEOPLE START OUT AS A SINGLE CELL, IN WOMBS DOWN THROUGH THE GENERATIONS. I WONDER IF THERE'S A HATRED DEEP ENOUGH TO CURSE SO FAR...
THERE IS.
EVERY PERSON WHO INHERITS THE BLOOD OF THOSE WHO KILLED US... NO MATTER HOW FAR REMOVED...
...WE CURSE.

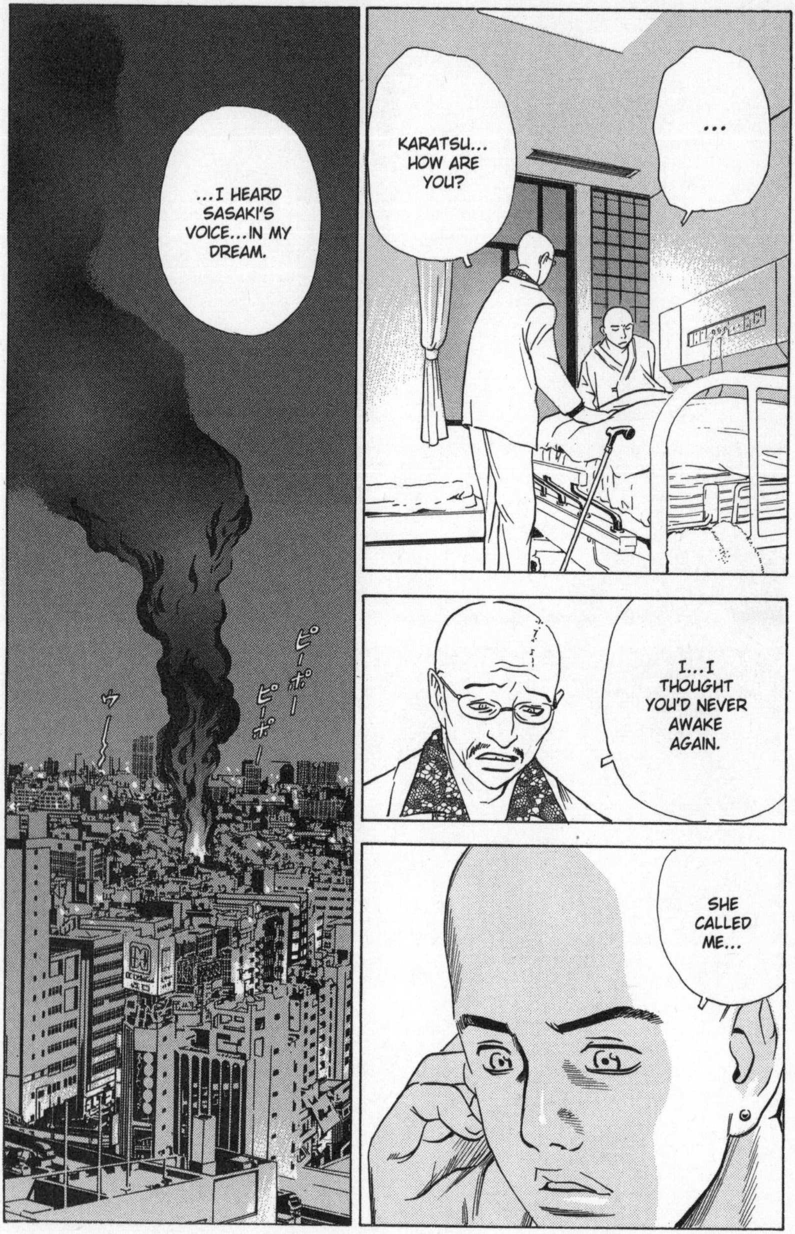
...
KARATSU... HOW ARE YOU?
I...I THOUGHT YOU'D NEVER AWAKE AGAIN.
SHE CALLED ME...
...I HEARD SASAKI'S VOICE...IN MY DREAM.
ピーポー ピーポー
ウー

3rd delivery: my happiness, part II—the end

4th delivery
わたしの首領（ドン）
my don

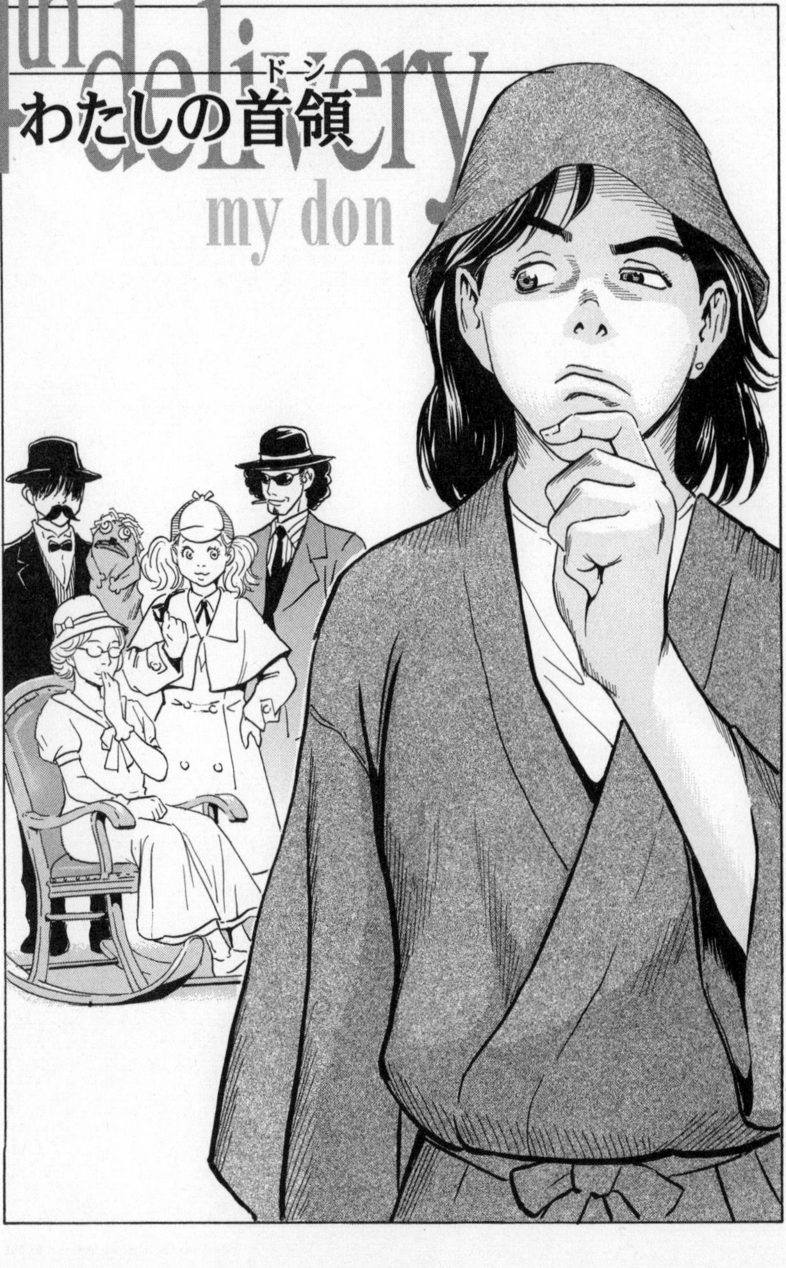

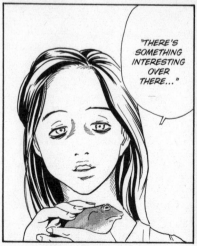

"THERE'S SOMETHING INTERESTING OVER THERE..."

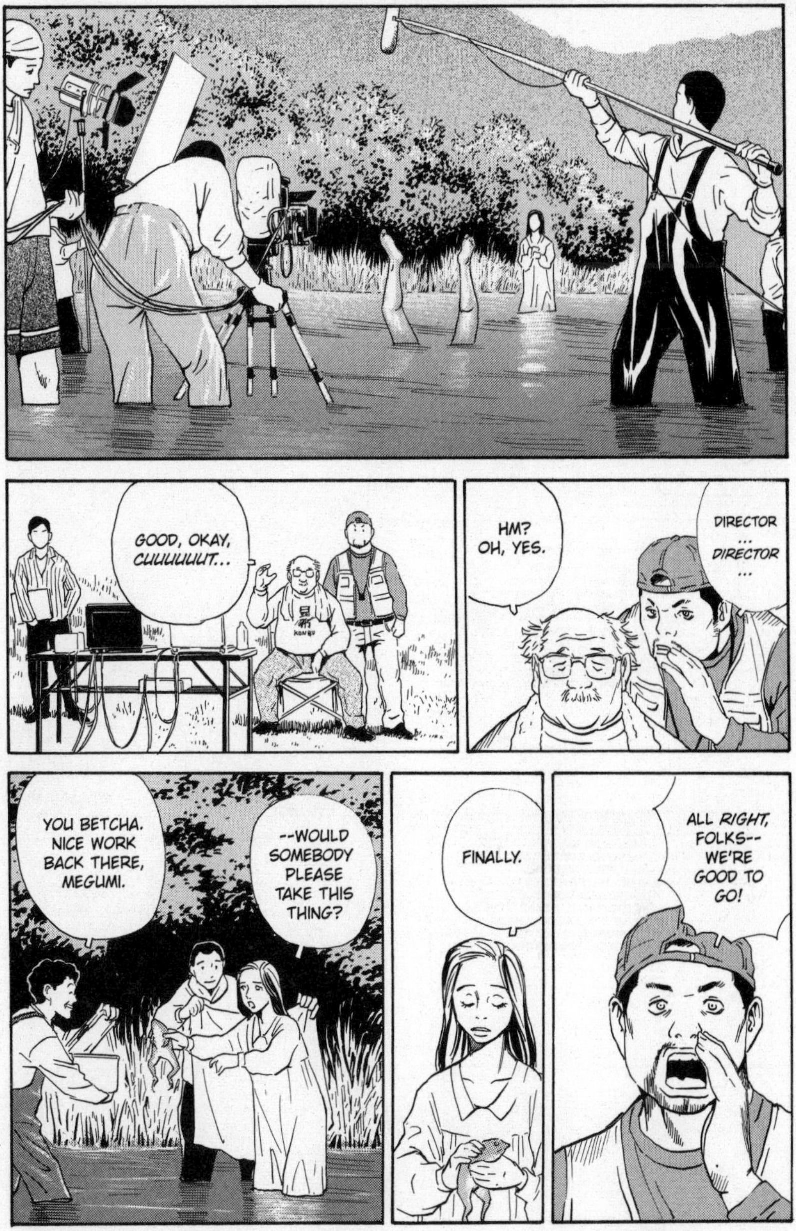
DIRECTOR ... DIRECTOR ...
HM? OH, YES.
GOOD, OKAY, CUUUUUUT...
ALL RIGHT, FOLKS-- WE'RE GOOD TO GO!
FINALLY.
--WOULD SOMEBODY PLEASE TAKE THIS THING?
YOU BETCHA. NICE WORK BACK THERE, MEGUMI.

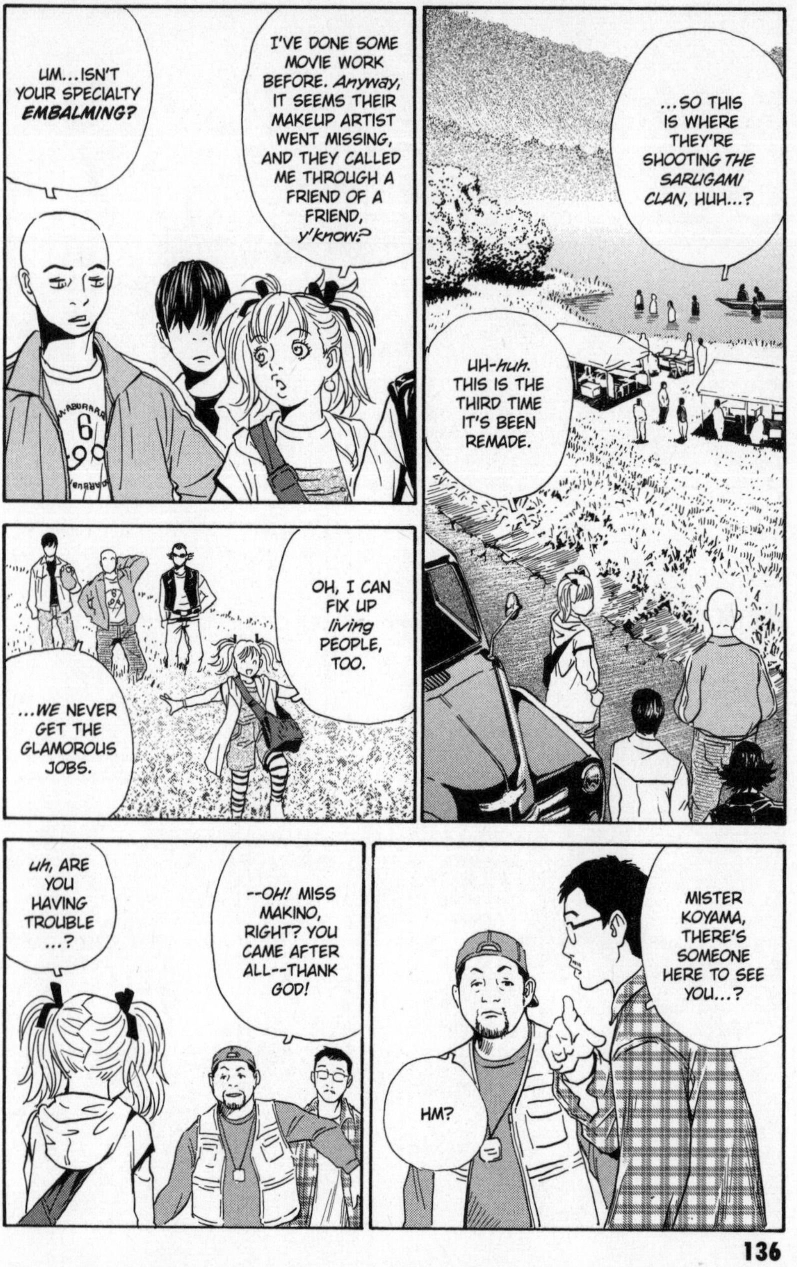
...SO THIS IS WHERE THEY'RE SHOOTING *THE SARUGAMI CLAN*, HUH...?
UH-*huh*. THIS IS THE THIRD TIME IT'S BEEN REMADE.
I'VE DONE SOME MOVIE WORK BEFORE. *Anyway*, IT SEEMS THEIR MAKEUP ARTIST WENT MISSING, AND THEY CALLED ME THROUGH A FRIEND OF A FRIEND, *y'know*?
UM...ISN'T YOUR SPECIALTY ***EMBALMING?***
OH, I CAN FIX UP *living* PEOPLE, TOO.
...*WE* NEVER GET THE GLAMOROUS JOBS.
MISTER KOYAMA, THERE'S SOMEONE HERE TO SEE YOU...?
HM?
--*OH!* MISS MAKINO, RIGHT? YOU CAME AFTER ALL--THANK GOD!
uh, ARE YOU HAVING TROUBLE ...?

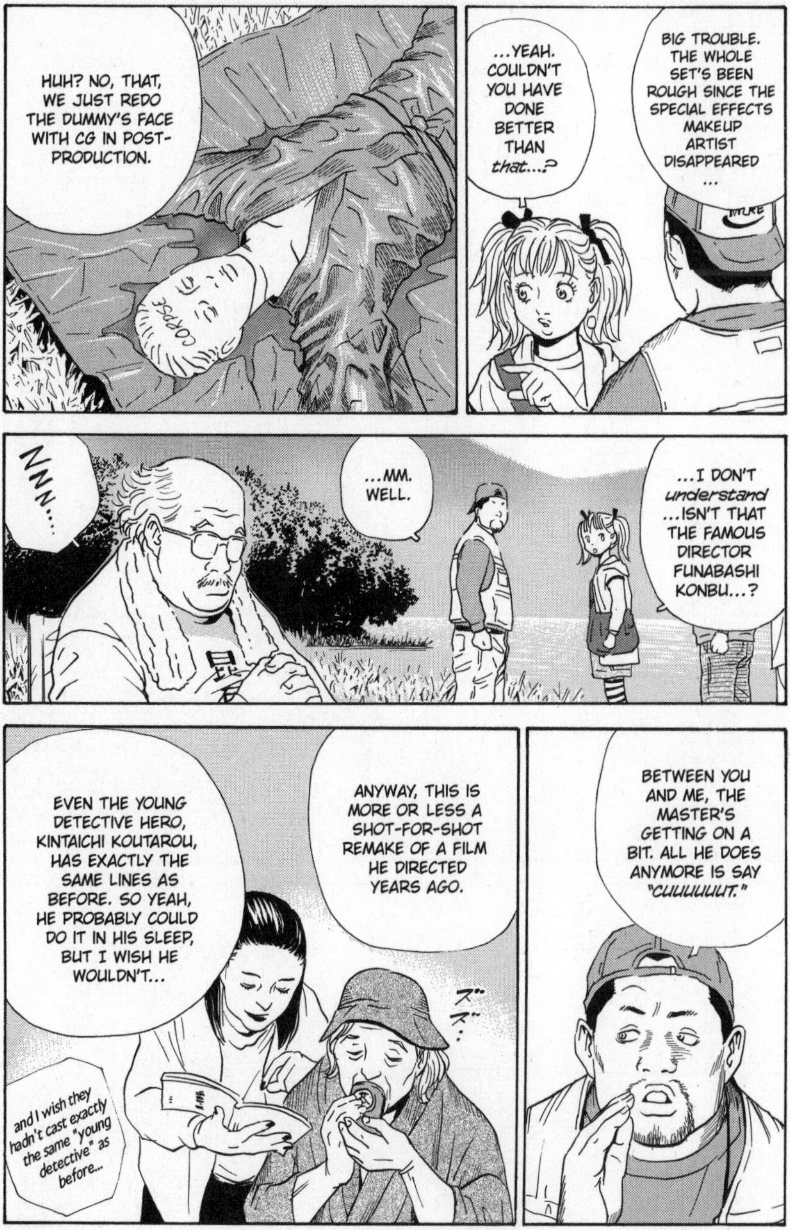
BIG TROUBLE. THE WHOLE SET'S BEEN ROUGH SINCE THE SPECIAL EFFECTS MAKEUP ARTIST DISAPPEARED ...
...YEAH. COULDN'T YOU HAVE DONE BETTER THAN *that*...?
HUH? NO, THAT, WE JUST REDO THE DUMMY'S FACE WITH CG IN POST-PRODUCTION.
CORPSE
...I DON'T *understand* ...ISN'T THAT THE FAMOUS DIRECTOR FUNABASHI KONBU...?
...MM. WELL.
NNN...
BETWEEN YOU AND ME, THE MASTER'S GETTING ON A BIT. ALL HE DOES ANYMORE IS SAY *"CUUUUUUT."*
ANYWAY, THIS IS MORE OR LESS A SHOT-FOR-SHOT REMAKE OF A FILM HE DIRECTED YEARS AGO.
EVEN THE YOUNG DETECTIVE HERO, KINTAICHI KOUTAROU, HAS EXACTLY THE SAME LINES AS BEFORE. SO YEAH, HE PROBABLY COULD DO IT IN HIS SLEEP, BUT I WISH HE WOULDN'T...
ズズ…
and I wish they hadn't cast exactly the same "young detective" as before...

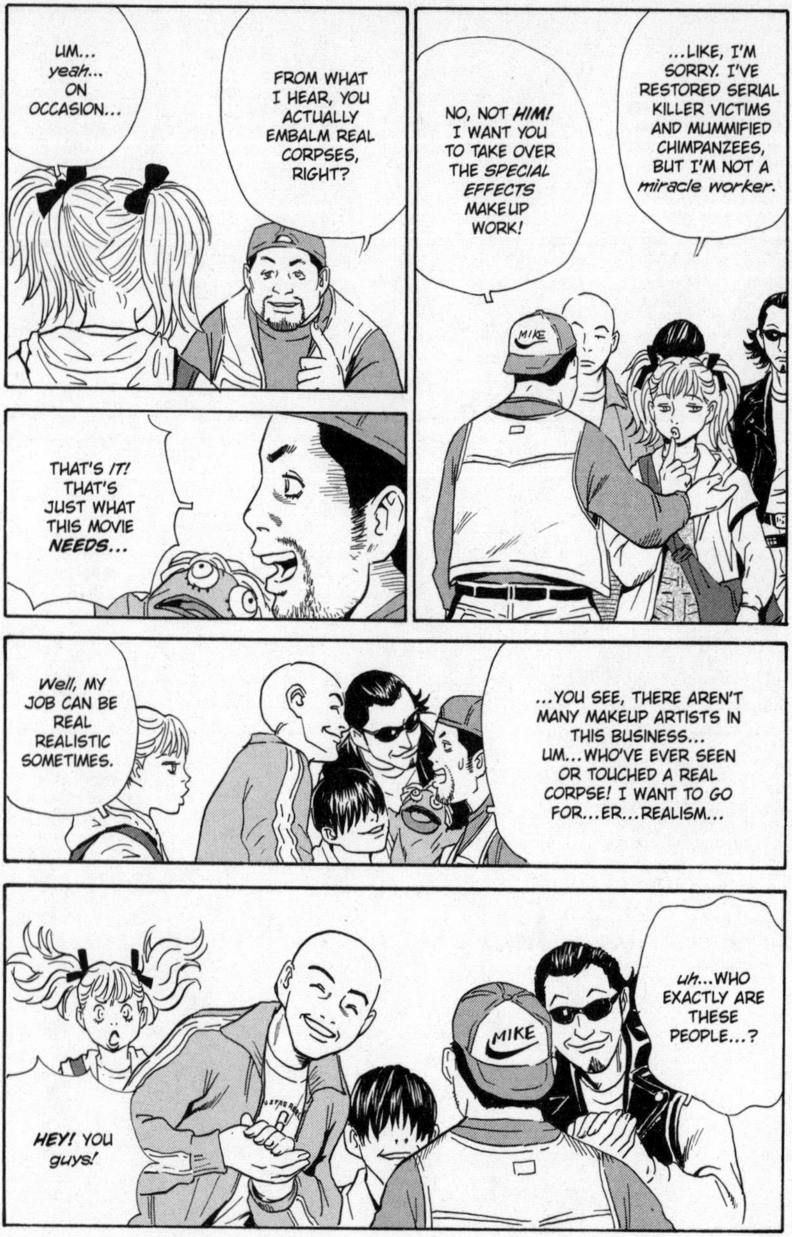
...LIKE, I'M SORRY. I'VE RESTORED SERIAL KILLER VICTIMS AND MUMMIFIED CHIMPANZEES, BUT I'M NOT A *miracle worker*.
NO, NOT ***HIM!*** I WANT YOU TO TAKE OVER THE *SPECIAL EFFECTS* MAKEUP WORK!
MIKE
FROM WHAT I HEAR, YOU ACTUALLY EMBALM REAL CORPSES, RIGHT?
UM... *yeah*... ON OCCASION...
THAT'S *IT!* THAT'S JUST WHAT THIS MOVIE ***NEEDS...***
...YOU SEE, THERE AREN'T MANY MAKEUP ARTISTS IN THIS BUSINESS... UM...WHO'VE EVER SEEN OR TOUCHED A REAL CORPSE! I WANT TO GO FOR...ER...REALISM...
Well, MY JOB CAN BE REAL REALISTIC SOMETIMES.
uh...WHO EXACTLY ARE THESE PEOPLE...?
MIKE
HEY! YOU *guys!*

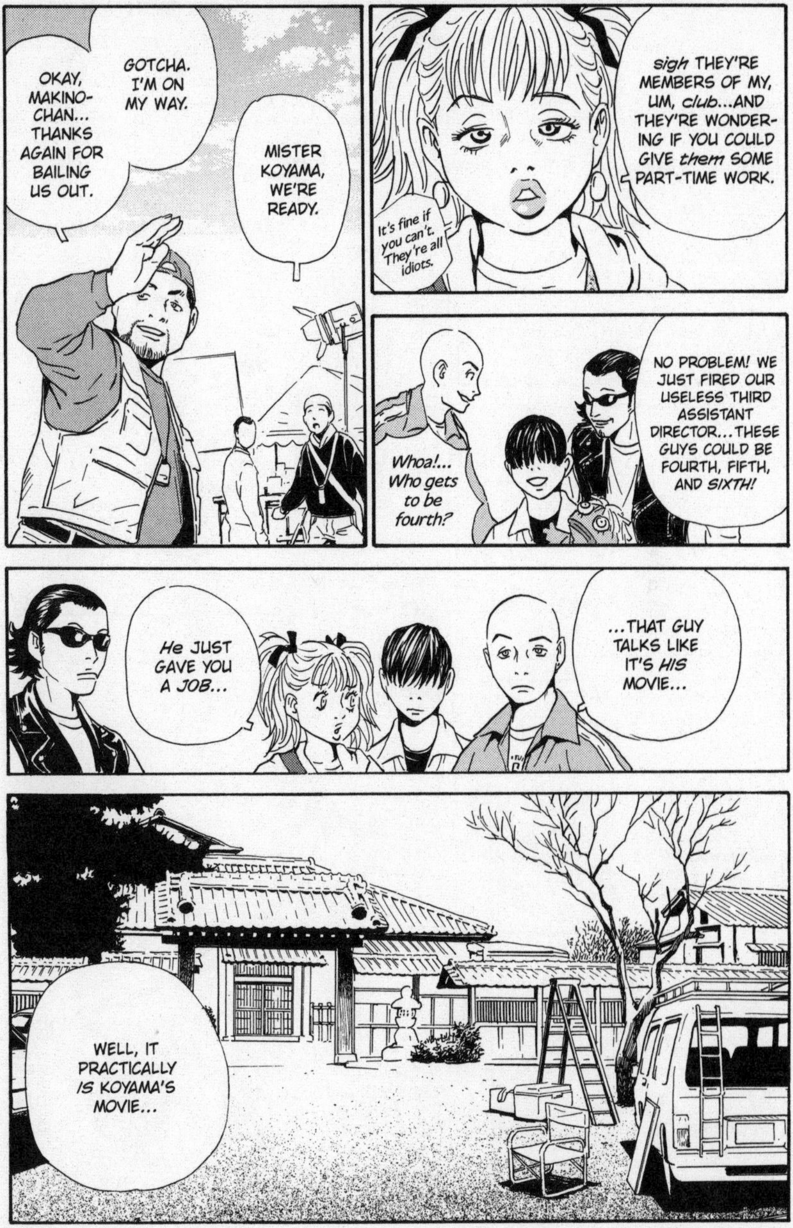
sigh THEY'RE MEMBERS OF MY, UM, *club*...AND THEY'RE WONDERING IF YOU COULD GIVE *them* SOME PART-TIME WORK.
It's fine if you can't. They're all idiots.
NO PROBLEM! WE JUST FIRED OUR USELESS THIRD ASSISTANT DIRECTOR...THESE GUYS COULD BE FOURTH, FIFTH, AND *SIXTH!*
Whoa!... Who gets to be fourth?
MISTER KOYAMA, WE'RE READY.
GOTCHA. I'M ON MY WAY.
OKAY, MAKINO-CHAN... THANKS AGAIN FOR BAILING US OUT.
...THAT GUY TALKS LIKE IT'S *HIS* MOVIE...
He JUST GAVE YOU A *JOB*...
WELL, IT PRACTICALLY *IS* KOYAMA'S MOVIE...

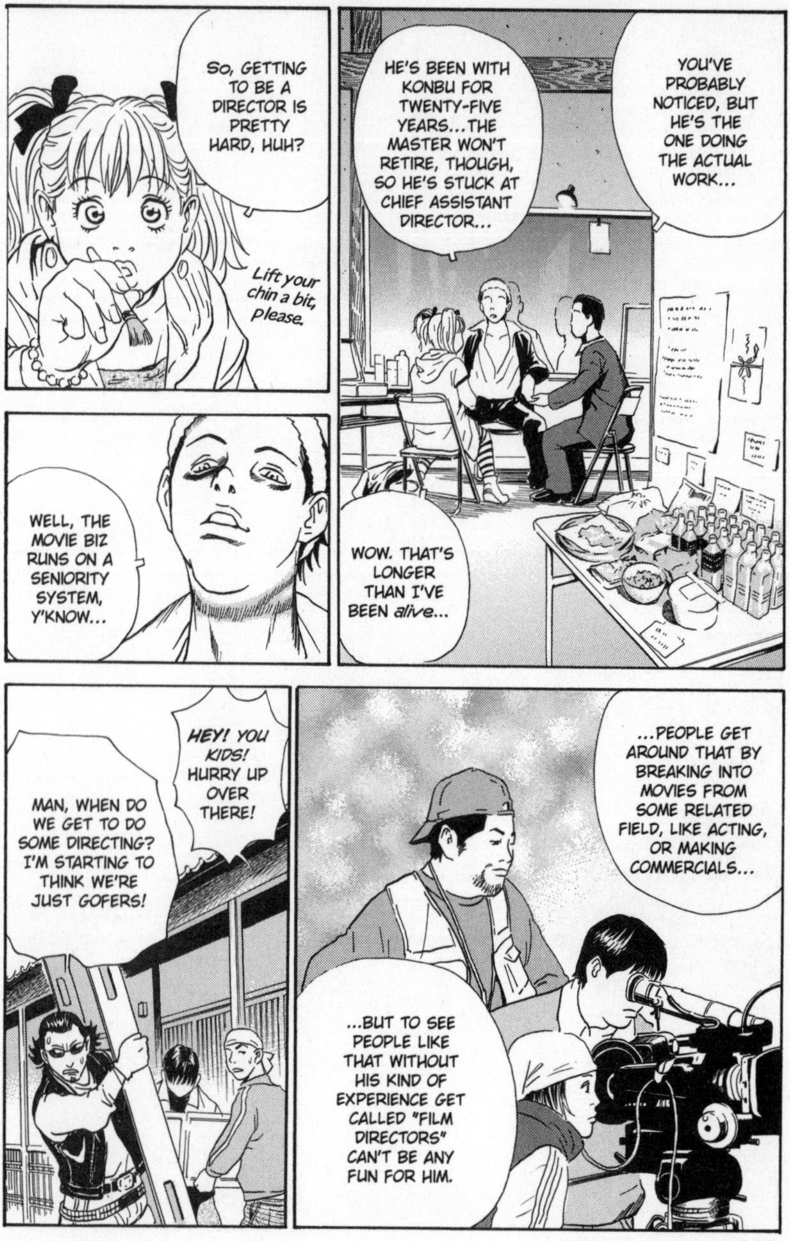
YOU'VE PROBABLY NOTICED, BUT HE'S THE ONE DOING THE ACTUAL WORK...
HE'S BEEN WITH KONBU FOR TWENTY-FIVE YEARS...THE MASTER WON'T RETIRE, THOUGH, SO HE'S STUCK AT CHIEF ASSISTANT DIRECTOR...
WOW. THAT'S LONGER THAN I'VE BEEN *alive*...
So, GETTING TO BE A DIRECTOR IS PRETTY HARD, HUH?
Lift your chin a bit, please.
WELL, THE MOVIE BIZ RUNS ON A SENIORITY SYSTEM, Y'KNOW...
...PEOPLE GET AROUND THAT BY BREAKING INTO MOVIES FROM SOME RELATED FIELD, LIKE ACTING, OR MAKING COMMERCIALS...
...BUT TO SEE PEOPLE LIKE THAT WITHOUT HIS KIND OF EXPERIENCE GET CALLED "FILM DIRECTORS" CAN'T BE ANY FUN FOR HIM.
HEY! YOU KIDS! HURRY UP OVER THERE!
MAN, WHEN DO WE GET TO DO SOME DIRECTING? I'M STARTING TO THINK WE'RE JUST GOFERS!

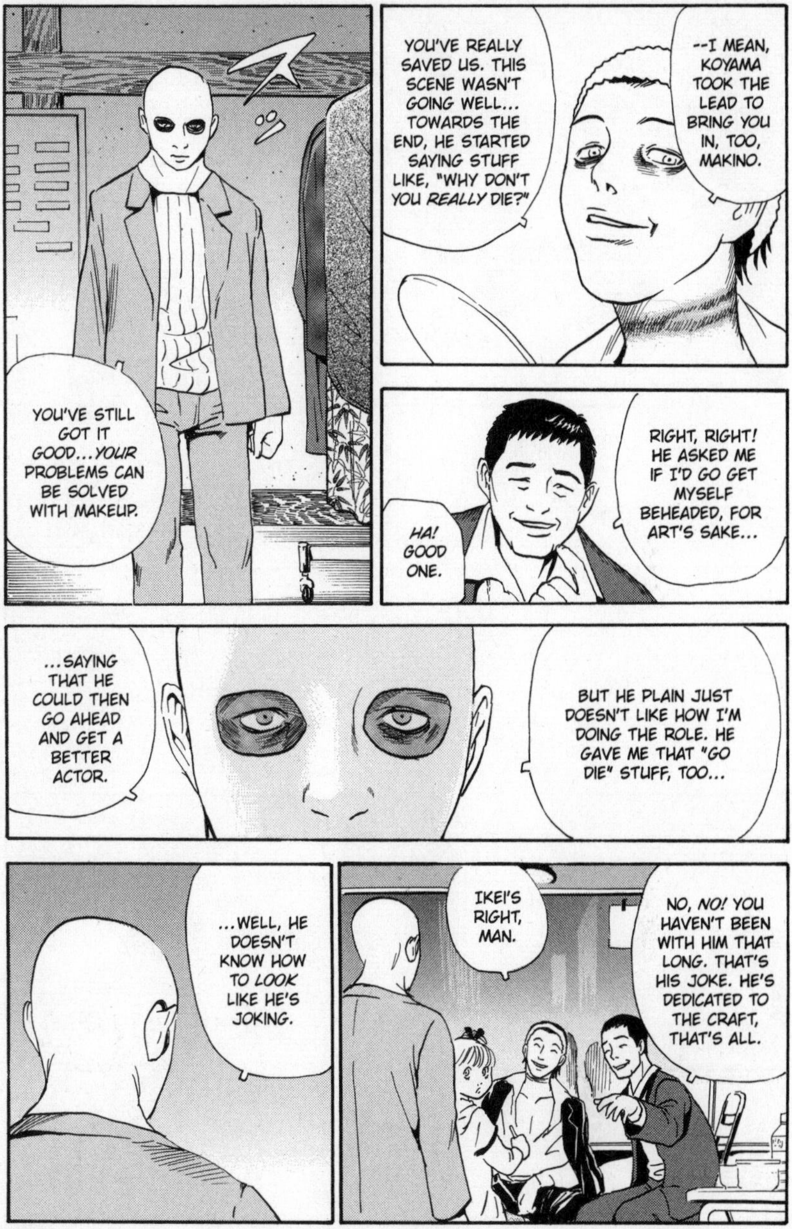
--I MEAN, KOYAMA TOOK THE LEAD TO BRING YOU IN, TOO, MAKINO.
YOU'VE REALLY SAVED US. THIS SCENE WASN'T GOING WELL... TOWARDS THE END, HE STARTED SAYING STUFF LIKE, "WHY DON'T YOU *REALLY* DIE?"
RIGHT, RIGHT! HE ASKED ME IF I'D GO GET MYSELF BEHEADED, FOR ART'S SAKE...
HA! GOOD ONE.
YOU'VE STILL GOT IT GOOD... *YOUR* PROBLEMS CAN BE SOLVED WITH MAKEUP.
BUT HE PLAIN JUST DOESN'T LIKE HOW I'M DOING THE ROLE. HE GAVE ME THAT "GO DIE" STUFF, TOO...
...SAYING THAT HE COULD THEN GO AHEAD AND GET A BETTER ACTOR.
NO, *NO!* YOU HAVEN'T BEEN WITH HIM THAT LONG. THAT'S HIS JOKE. HE'S DEDICATED TO THE CRAFT, THAT'S ALL.
IKEI'S RIGHT, MAN.
...WELL, HE DOESN'T KNOW HOW TO *LOOK* LIKE HE'S JOKING.

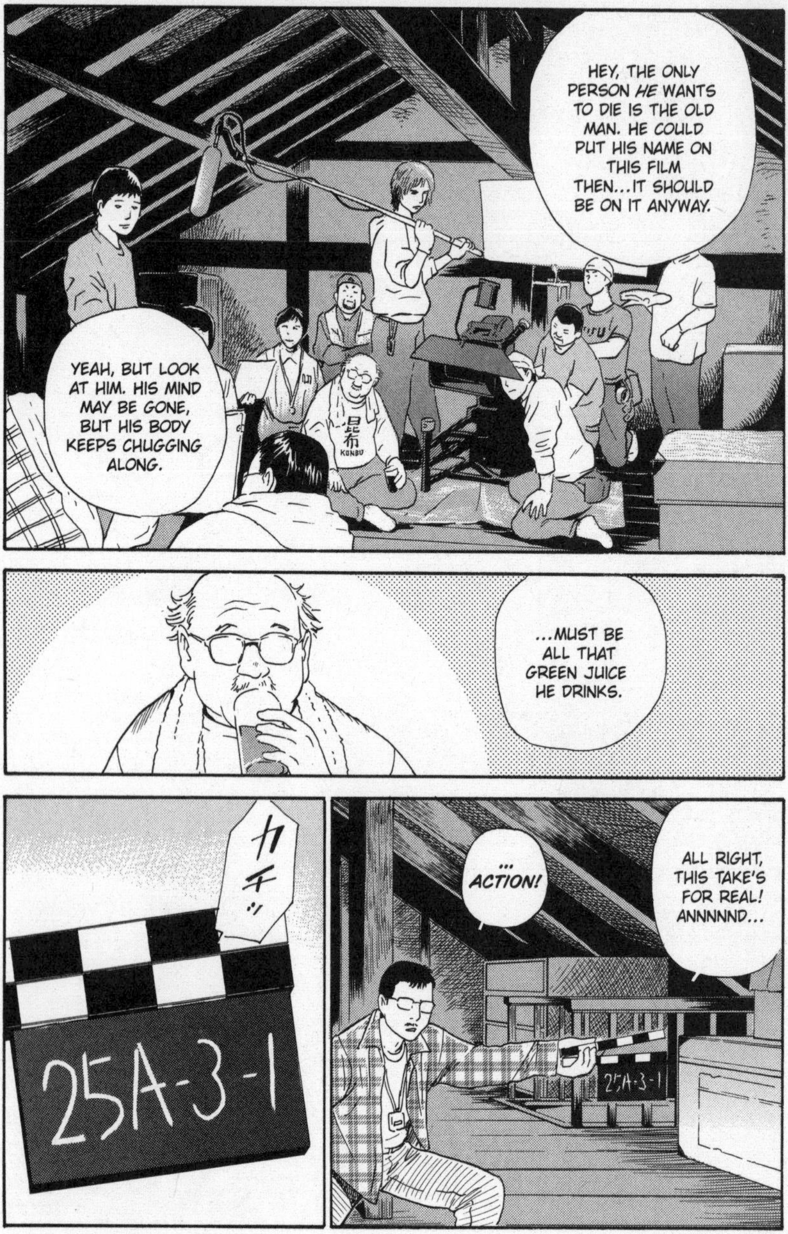
HEY, THE ONLY PERSON *HE* WANTS TO DIE IS THE OLD MAN. HE COULD PUT HIS NAME ON THIS FILM THEN...IT SHOULD BE ON IT ANYWAY.
YEAH, BUT LOOK AT HIM. HIS MIND MAY BE GONE, BUT HIS BODY KEEPS CHUGGING ALONG.
...MUST BE ALL THAT GREEN JUICE HE DRINKS.
ALL RIGHT, THIS TAKE'S FOR REAL! ANNNNND...
... ACTION!
カチッ
25A-3-1

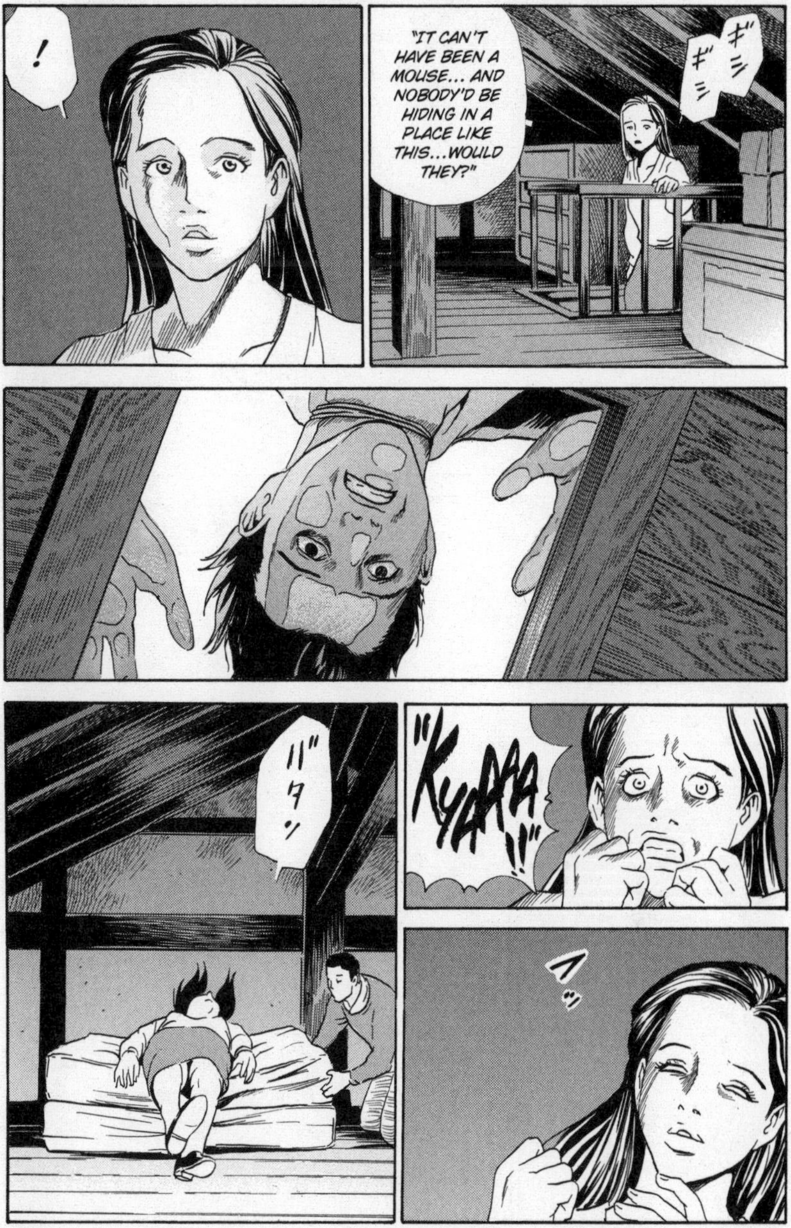
ギシ ギシ
"IT CAN'T HAVE BEEN A MOUSE... AND NOBODY'D BE HIDING IN A PLACE LIKE THIS...WOULD THEY?"
!
"KYAAAA!!"
ハッ
バタッ

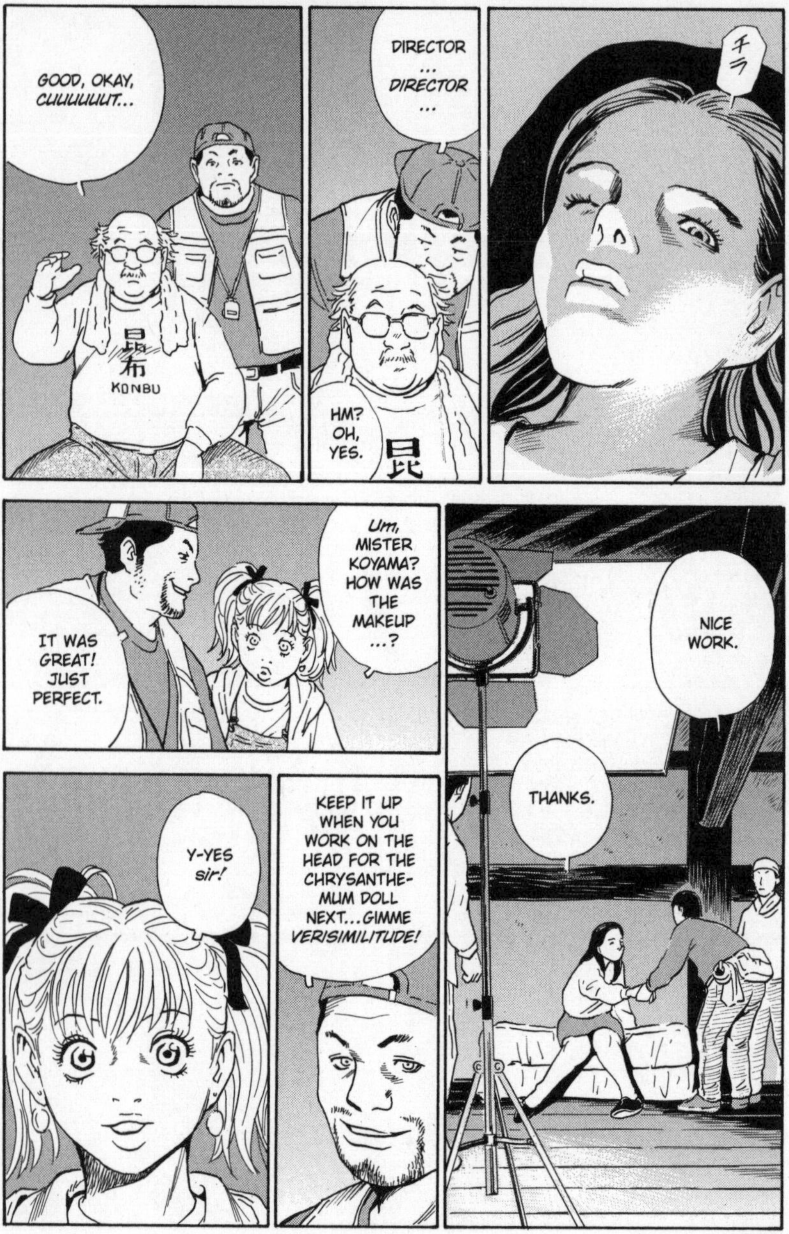
チラ
DIRECTOR ... DIRECTOR ...
HM? OH, YES.
GOOD, OKAY, CUUUUUUT...
NICE WORK.
THANKS.
Um, MISTER KOYAMA? HOW WAS THE MAKEUP ...?
IT WAS GREAT! JUST PERFECT.
KEEP IT UP WHEN YOU WORK ON THE HEAD FOR THE CHRYSANTHEMUM DOLL NEXT...GIMME *VERISIMILITUDE!*
Y-YES *sir!*

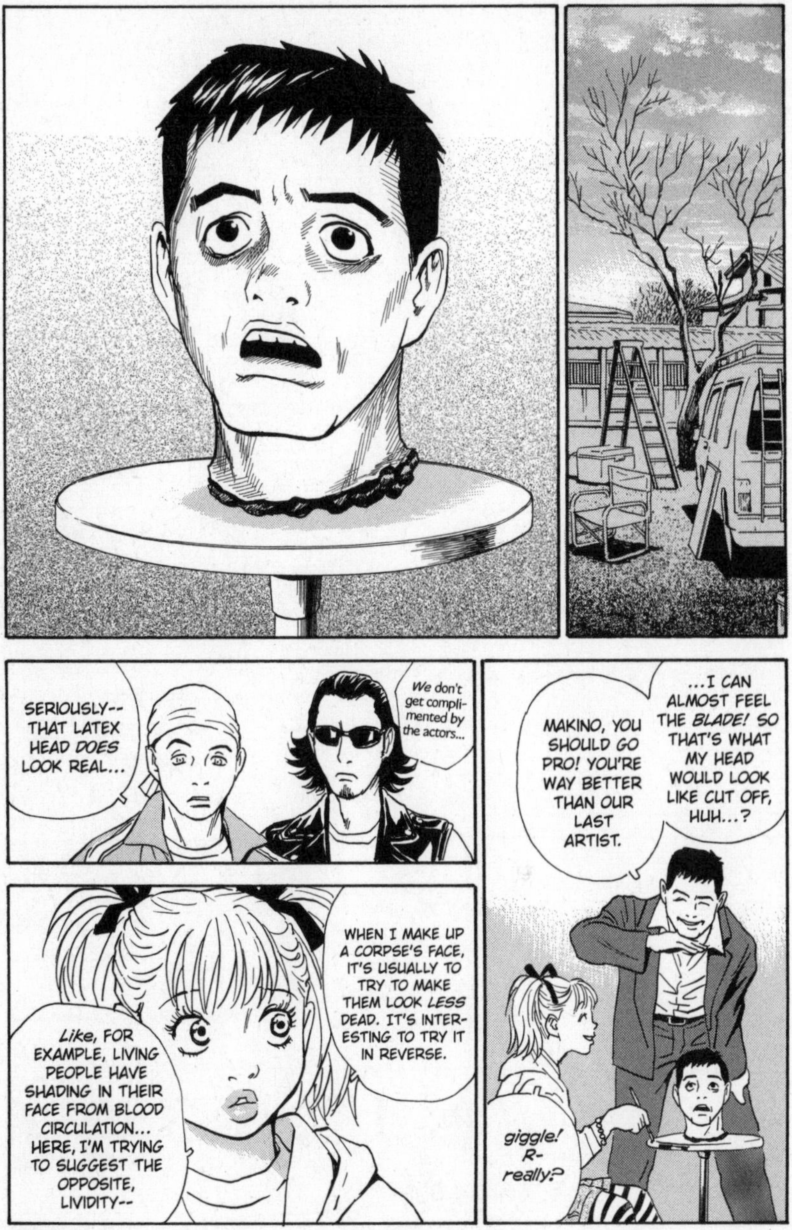
...I CAN ALMOST FEEL THE *BLADE!* SO THAT'S WHAT MY HEAD WOULD LOOK LIKE CUT OFF, HUH...?
MAKINO, YOU SHOULD GO PRO! YOU'RE WAY BETTER THAN OUR LAST ARTIST.
giggle! R-really?
We don't get complimented by the actors...
SERIOUSLY-- THAT LATEX HEAD *DOES* LOOK REAL...
WHEN I MAKE UP A CORPSE'S FACE, IT'S USUALLY TO TRY TO MAKE THEM LOOK *LESS* DEAD. IT'S INTERESTING TO TRY IT IN REVERSE.
Like, FOR EXAMPLE, LIVING PEOPLE HAVE SHADING IN THEIR FACE FROM BLOOD CIRCULATION... HERE, I'M TRYING TO SUGGEST THE OPPOSITE, LIVIDITY--

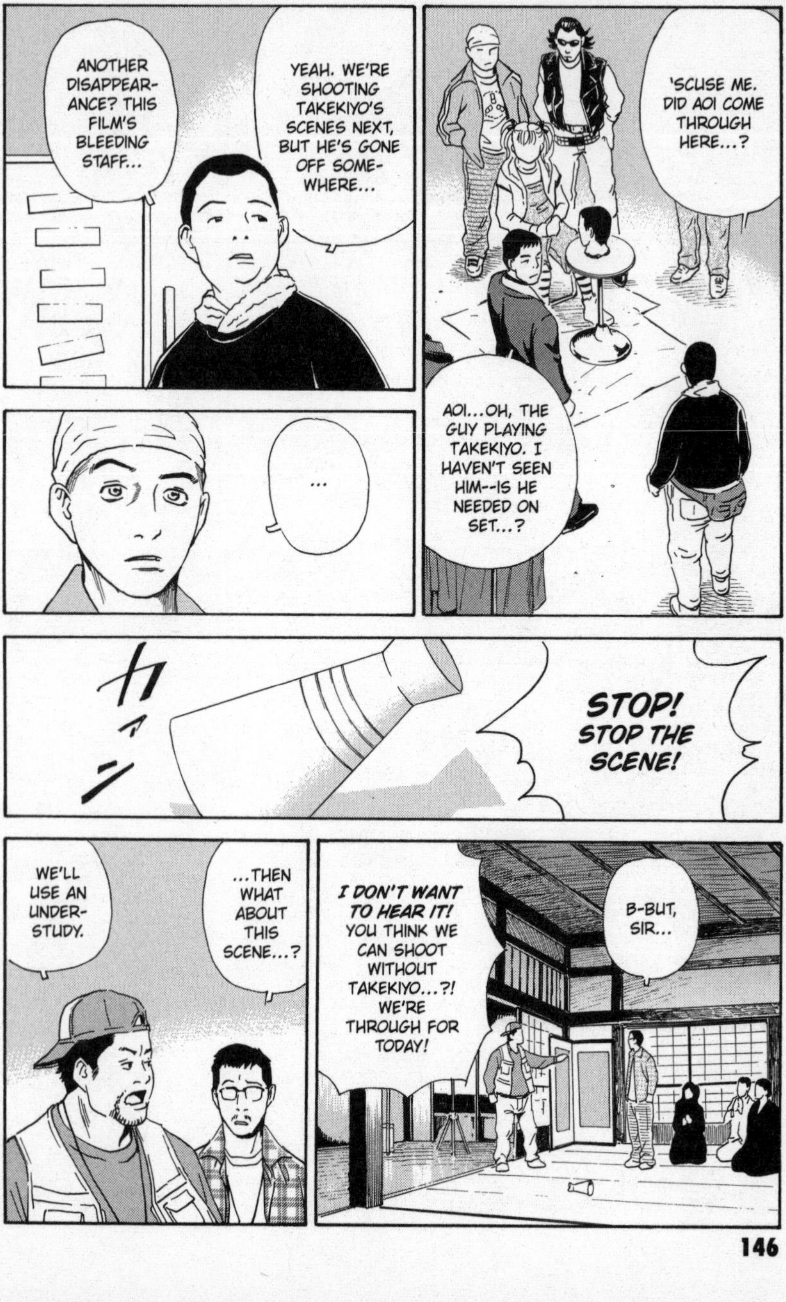
'SCUSE ME. DID AOI COME THROUGH HERE...?
AOI...OH, THE GUY PLAYING TAKEKIYO. I HAVEN'T SEEN HIM--IS HE NEEDED ON SET...?
YEAH. WE'RE SHOOTING TAKEKIYO'S SCENES NEXT, BUT HE'S GONE OFF SOME-WHERE...
ANOTHER DISAPPEAR-ANCE? THIS FILM'S BLEEDING STAFF...
...
STOP! STOP THE SCENE!
カァン
B-BUT, SIR...
I DON'T WANT TO HEAR IT! YOU THINK WE CAN SHOOT WITHOUT TAKEKIYO...?! WE'RE THROUGH FOR TODAY!
...THEN WHAT ABOUT THIS SCENE...?
WE'LL USE AN UNDER-STUDY.

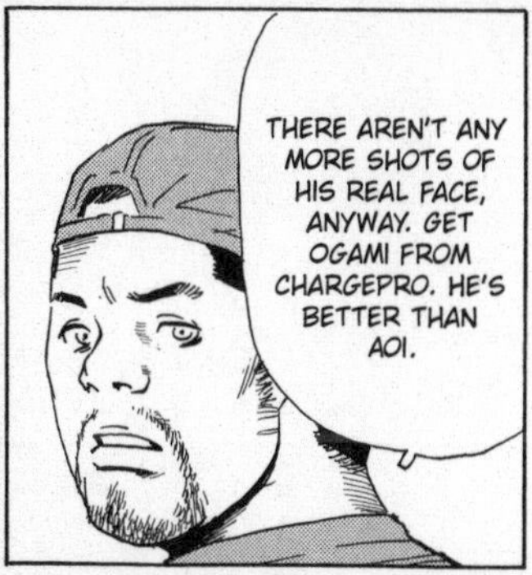
THERE AREN'T ANY MORE SHOTS OF HIS REAL FACE, ANYWAY. GET OGAMI FROM CHARGEPRO. HE'S BETTER THAN AOI.
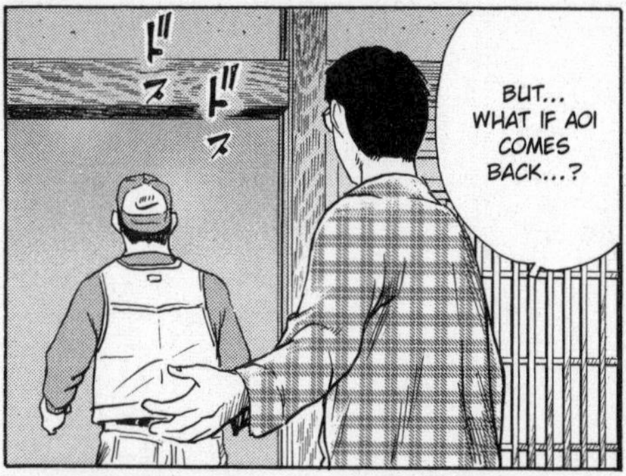
BUT... WHAT IF AOI COMES BACK...?
ドス ドス
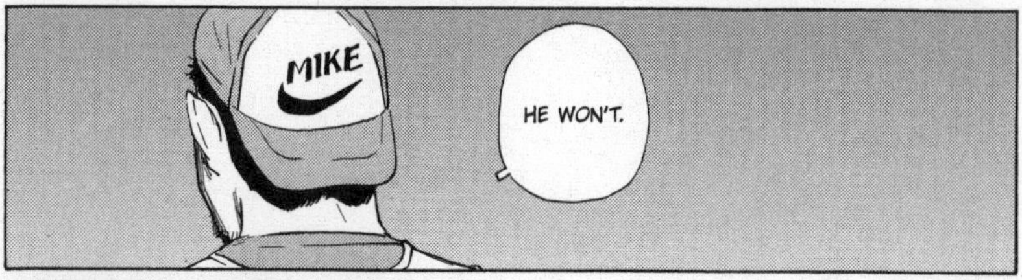
MIKE
HE WON'T.
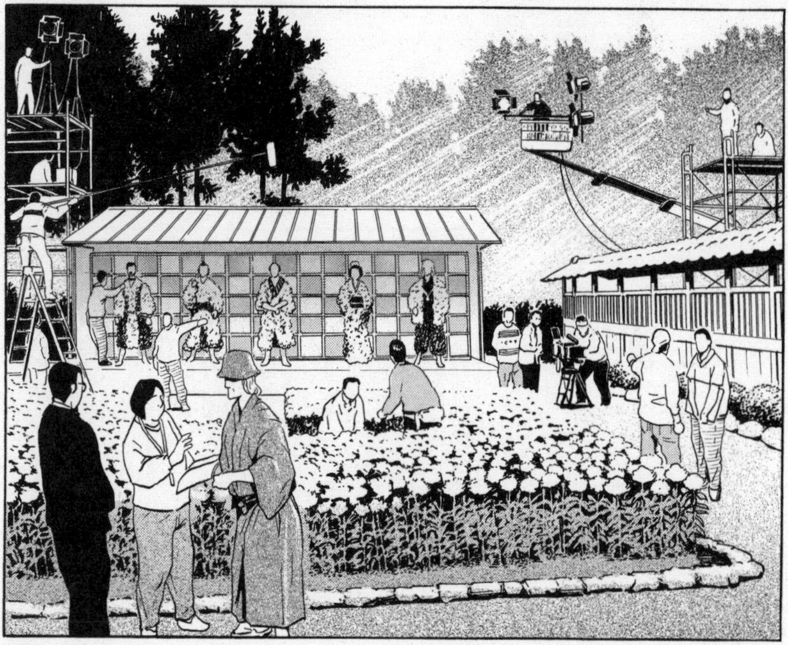

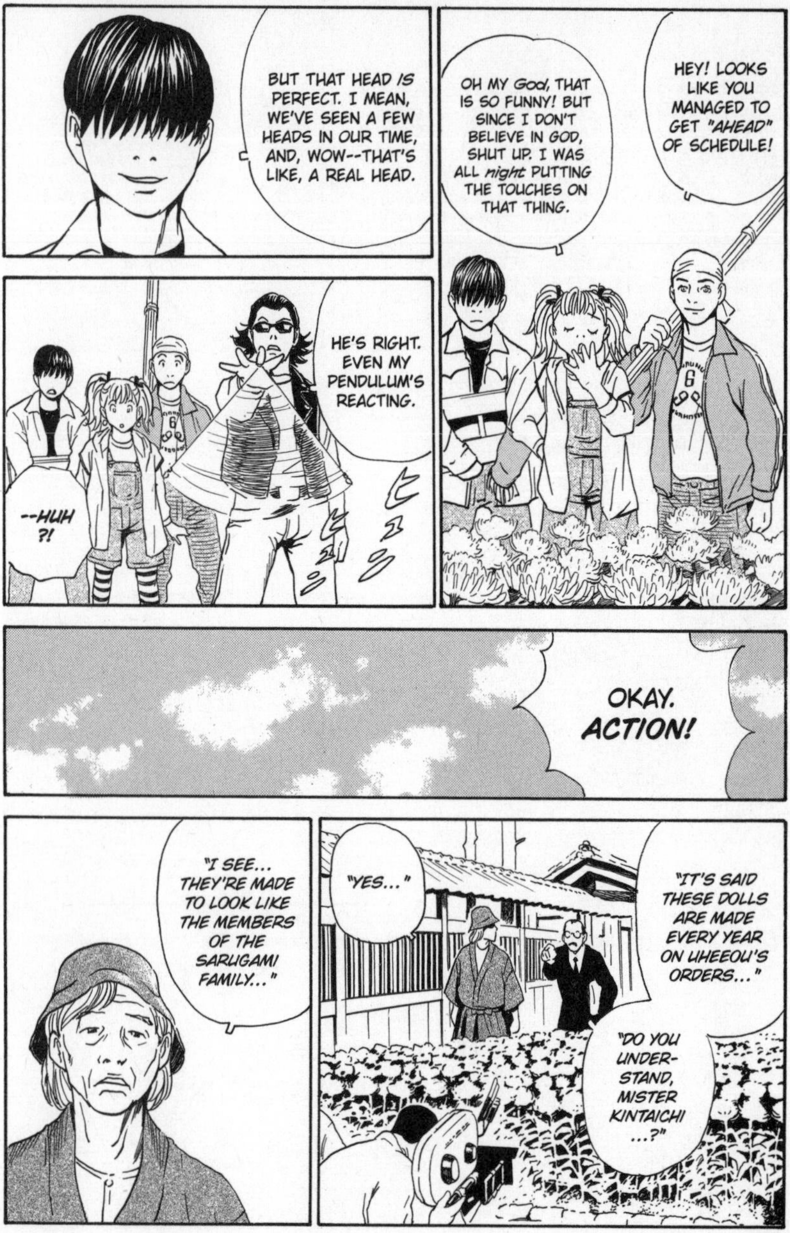
HEY! LOOKS LIKE YOU MANAGED TO GET "AHEAD" OF SCHEDULE!
OH MY God, THAT IS SO FUNNY! BUT SINCE I DON'T BELIEVE IN GOD, SHUT UP. I WAS ALL night PUTTING THE TOUCHES ON THAT THING.
BUT THAT HEAD IS PERFECT. I MEAN, WE'VE SEEN A FEW HEADS IN OUR TIME, AND, WOW--THAT'S LIKE, A REAL HEAD.
HE'S RIGHT. EVEN MY PENDULUM'S REACTING.
--HUH ?!
OKAY. ACTION!
"IT'S SAID THESE DOLLS ARE MADE EVERY YEAR ON UHEEOU'S ORDERS..."
"YES..."
"DO YOU UNDER-STAND, MISTER KINTAICHI ...?"
"I SEE... THEY'RE MADE TO LOOK LIKE THE MEMBERS OF THE SARUGAMI FAMILY..."

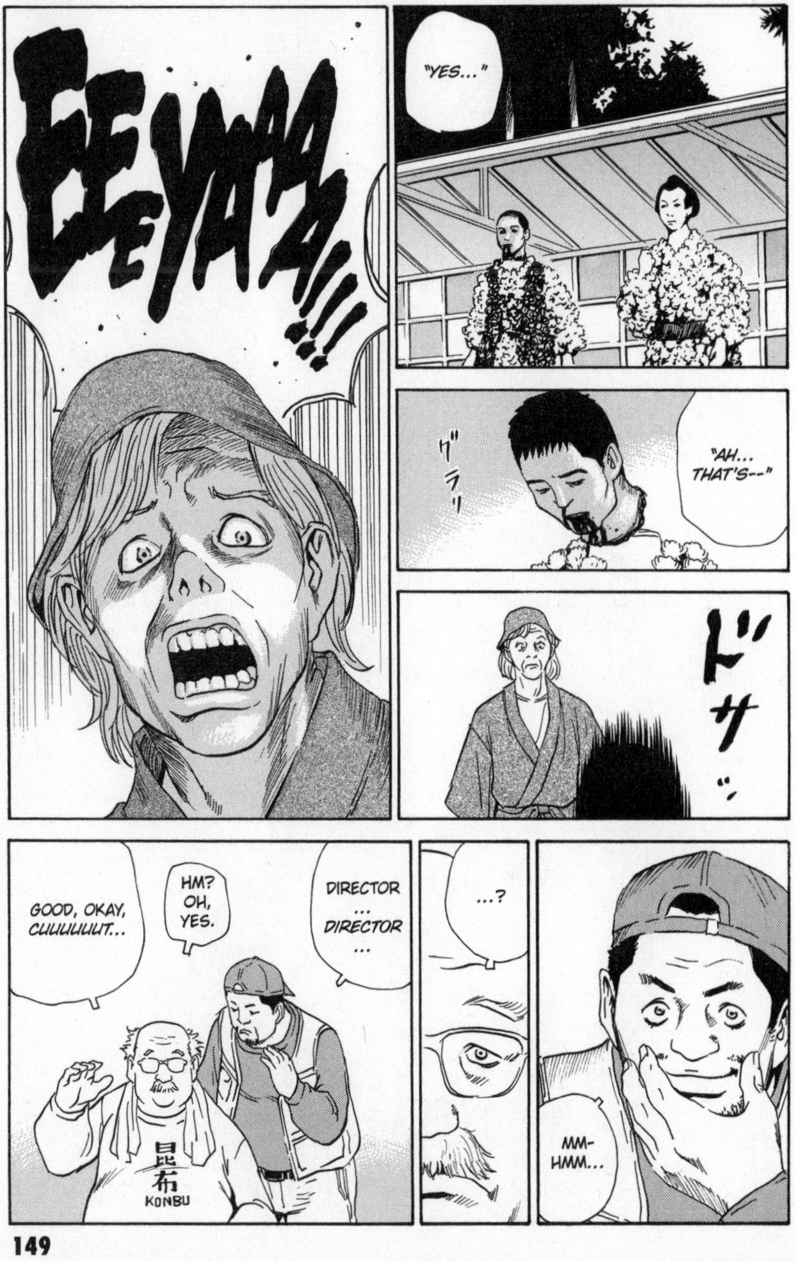

"YES..."
"AH...
THAT'S--"
グラリ
ドサッ
EEEYAAA!!!
MM-HMM...
...?
DIRECTOR ... DIRECTOR ...
HM? OH, YES.
GOOD, OKAY, CUUUUUUT...
昆布
KONBU

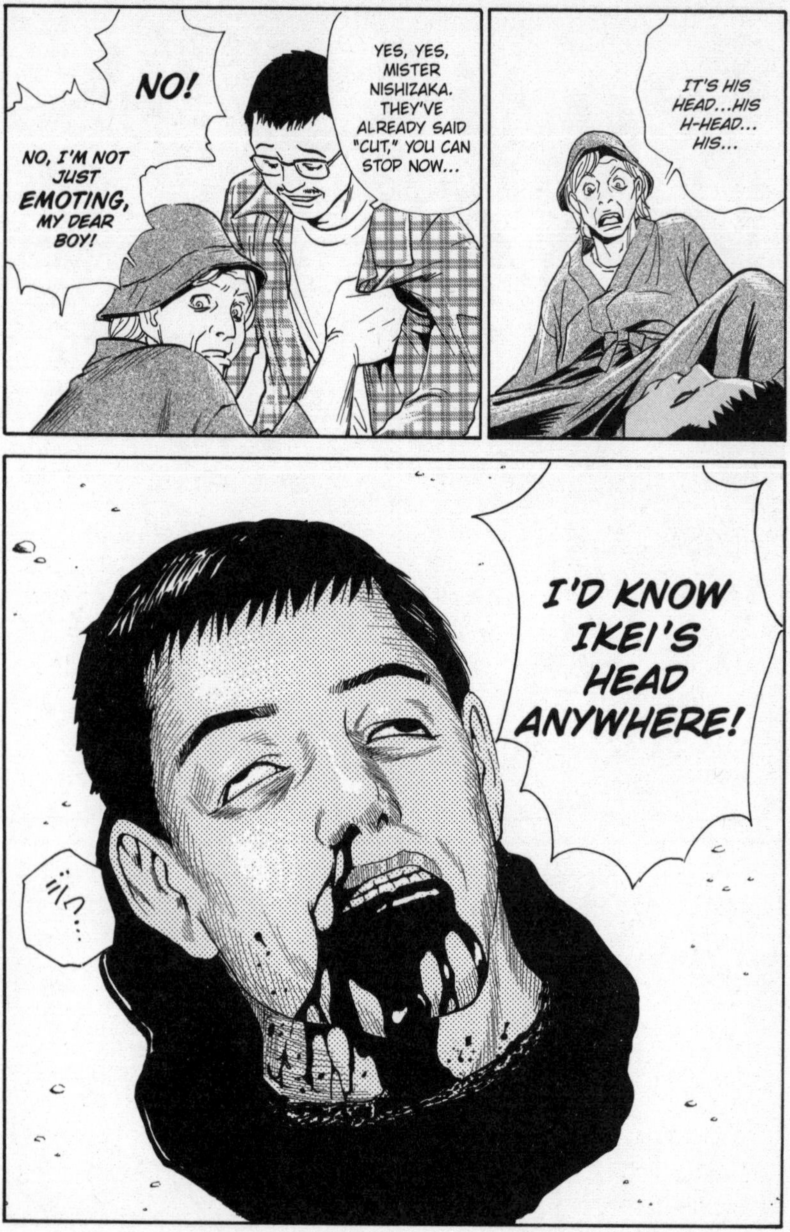
IT'S HIS HEAD...HIS H-HEAD... HIS...
YES, YES, MISTER NISHIZAKA. THEY'VE ALREADY SAID "CUT," YOU CAN STOP NOW...
NO!
NO, I'M NOT JUST EMOTING, MY DEAR BOY!
I'D KNOW IKEI'S HEAD ANYWHERE!

4th delivery: my don—the end

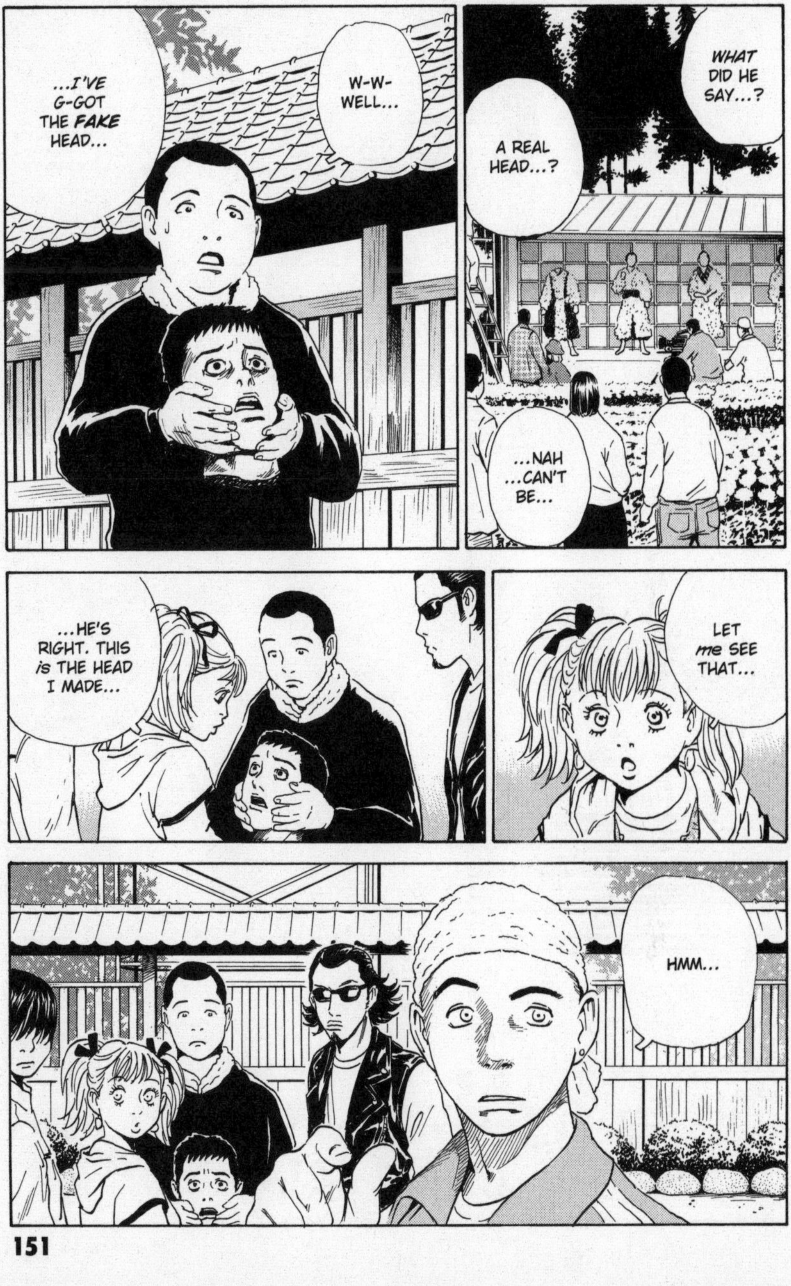
WHAT DID HE SAY...?
A REAL HEAD...?
...NAH ...CAN'T BE...
W-W-WELL...
...I'VE G-GOT THE FAKE HEAD...
LET me SEE THAT...
...HE'S RIGHT. THIS is THE HEAD I MADE...
HMM...

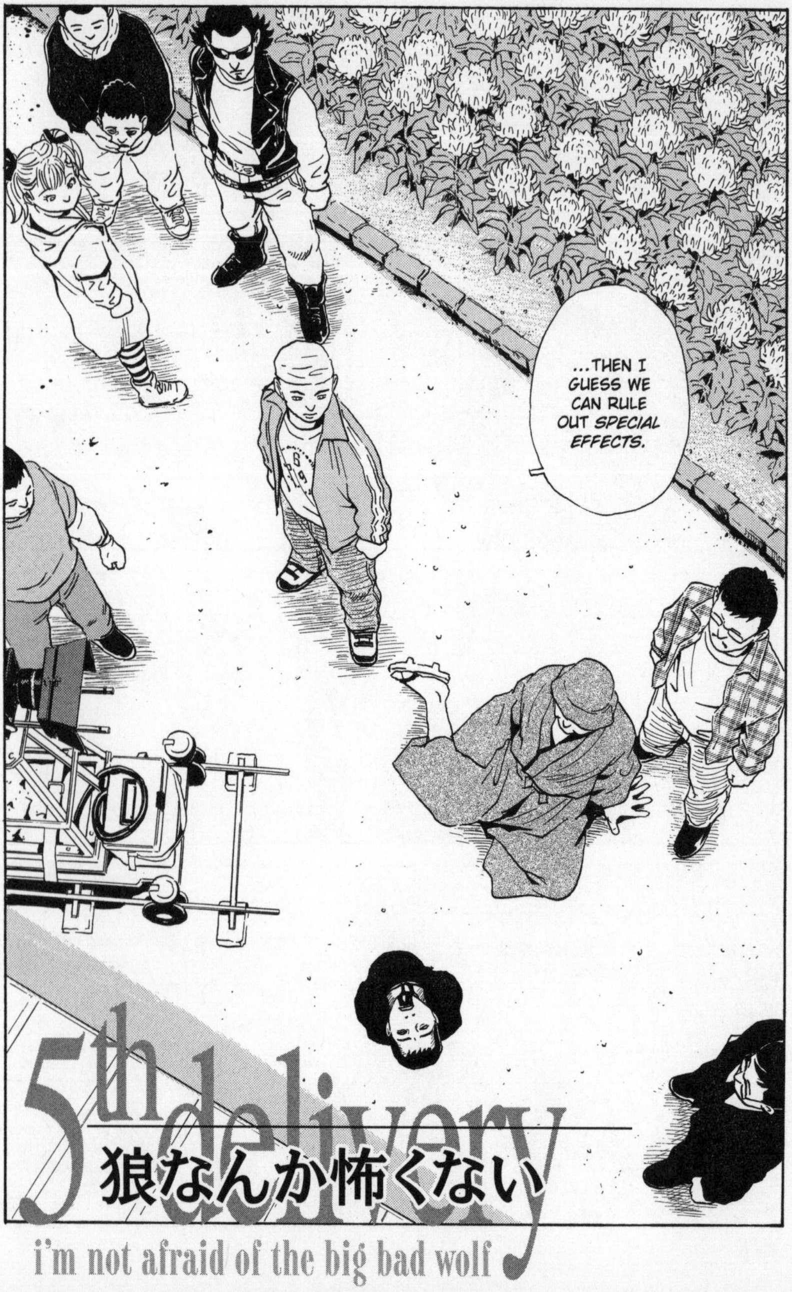
...THEN I GUESS WE CAN RULE OUT SPECIAL EFFECTS.

5th delivery

狼なんか怖くない

i'm not afraid of the big bad wolf

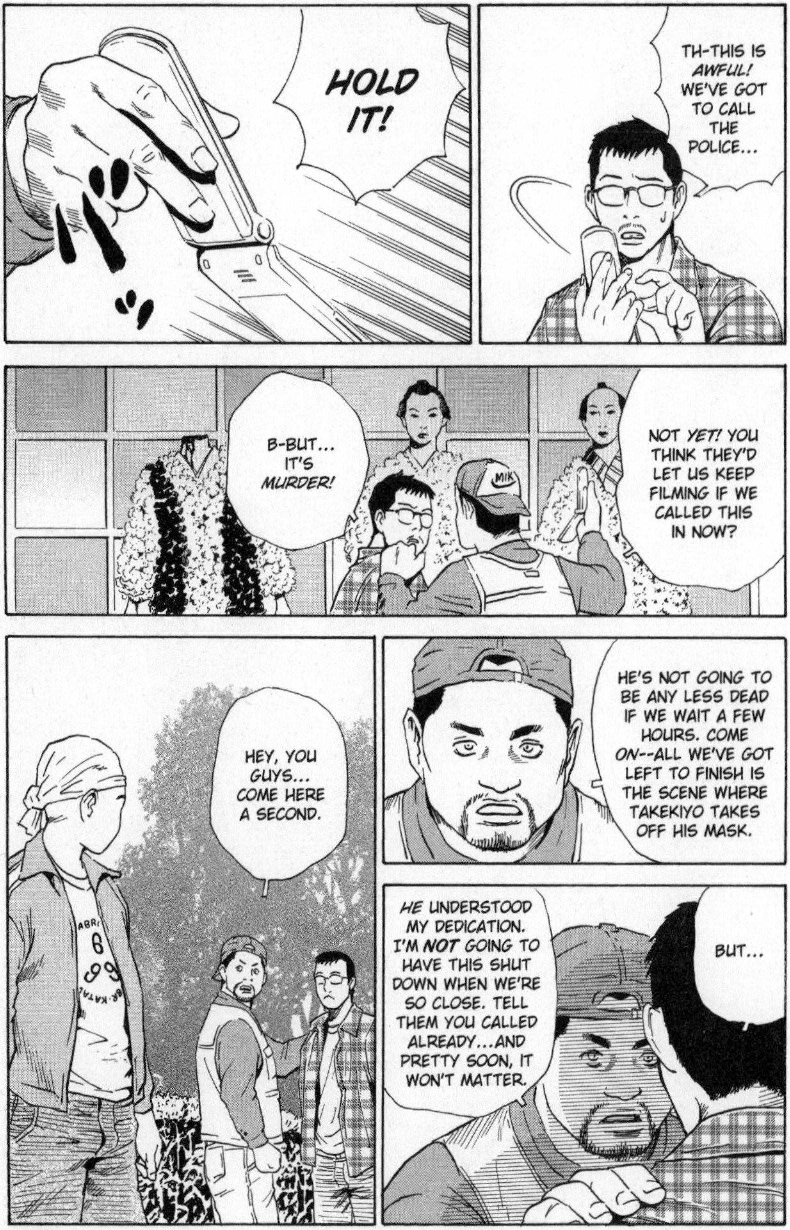
TH-THIS IS *AWFUL!* WE'VE GOT TO CALL THE POLICE...
HOLD IT!
NOT *YET!* YOU THINK THEY'D LET US KEEP FILMING IF WE CALLED THIS IN NOW?
B-BUT... IT'S *MURDER!*
HE'S NOT GOING TO BE ANY LESS DEAD IF WE WAIT A FEW HOURS. COME *ON*--ALL WE'VE GOT LEFT TO FINISH IS THE SCENE WHERE TAKEKIYO TAKES OFF HIS MASK.
BUT...
HE UNDERSTOOD MY DEDICATION. I'M ***NOT*** GOING TO HAVE THIS SHUT DOWN WHEN WE'RE SO CLOSE. TELL THEM YOU CALLED ALREADY...AND PRETTY SOON, IT WON'T MATTER.
HEY, YOU GUYS... COME HERE A SECOND.

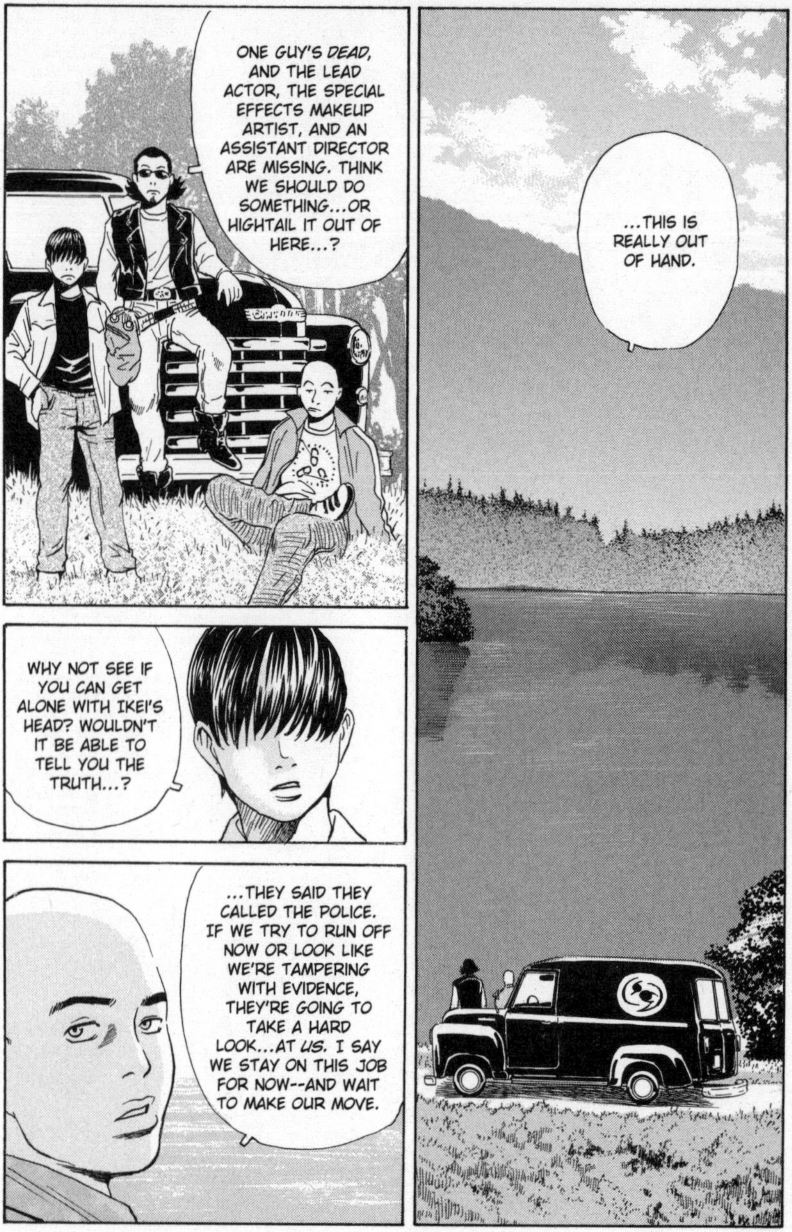
...THIS IS REALLY OUT OF HAND.
ONE GUY'S *DEAD*, AND THE LEAD ACTOR, THE SPECIAL EFFECTS MAKEUP ARTIST, AND AN ASSISTANT DIRECTOR ARE MISSING. THINK WE SHOULD DO SOMETHING...OR HIGHTAIL IT OUT OF HERE...?
WHY NOT SEE IF YOU CAN GET ALONE WITH IKEI'S HEAD? WOULDN'T IT BE ABLE TO TELL YOU THE TRUTH...?
...THEY SAID THEY CALLED THE POLICE. IF WE TRY TO RUN OFF NOW OR LOOK LIKE WE'RE TAMPERING WITH EVIDENCE, THEY'RE GOING TO TAKE A HARD LOOK...AT *US*. I SAY WE STAY ON THIS JOB FOR NOW--AND WAIT TO MAKE OUR MOVE.

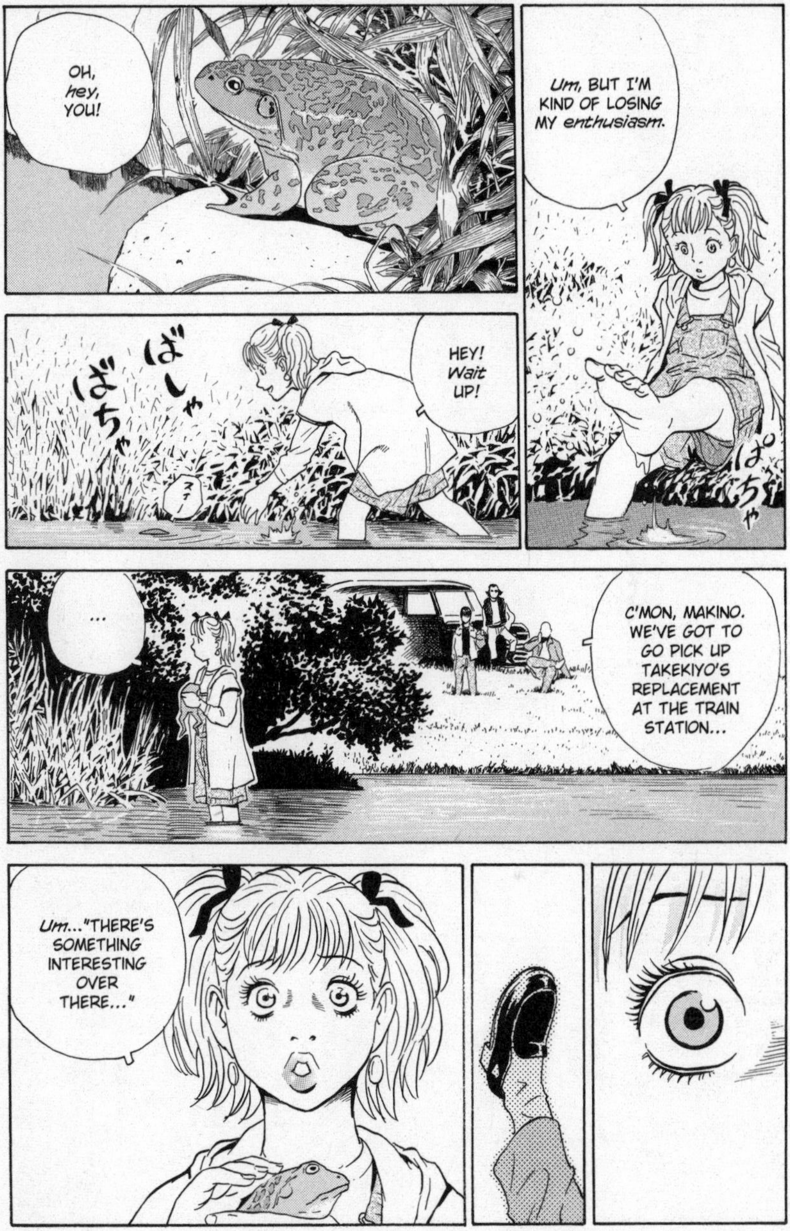

Um, BUT I'M KIND OF LOSING MY enthusiasm.
ぱちゃ
OH, hey, YOU!
HEY! Wait UP!
ばしゃ
ばちゃ
C'MON, MAKINO. WE'VE GOT TO GO PICK UP TAKEKIYO'S REPLACEMENT AT THE TRAIN STATION...
...
Um..."THERE'S SOMETHING INTERESTING OVER THERE..."

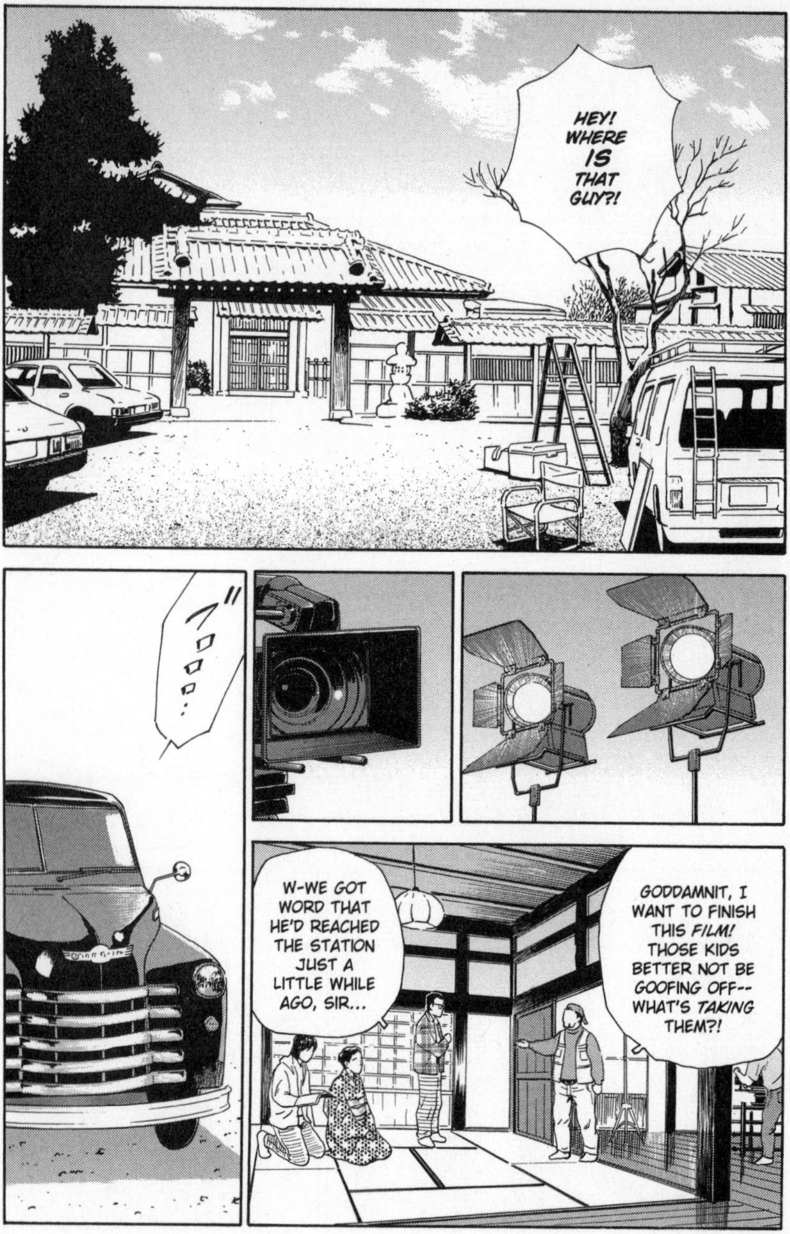
HEY! WHERE IS THAT GUY?!
GODDAMNIT, I WANT TO FINISH THIS FILM! THOSE KIDS BETTER NOT BE GOOFING OFF-- WHAT'S TAKING THEM?!
W-WE GOT WORD THAT HE'D REACHED THE STATION JUST A LITTLE WHILE AGO, SIR...
ブロロロ...

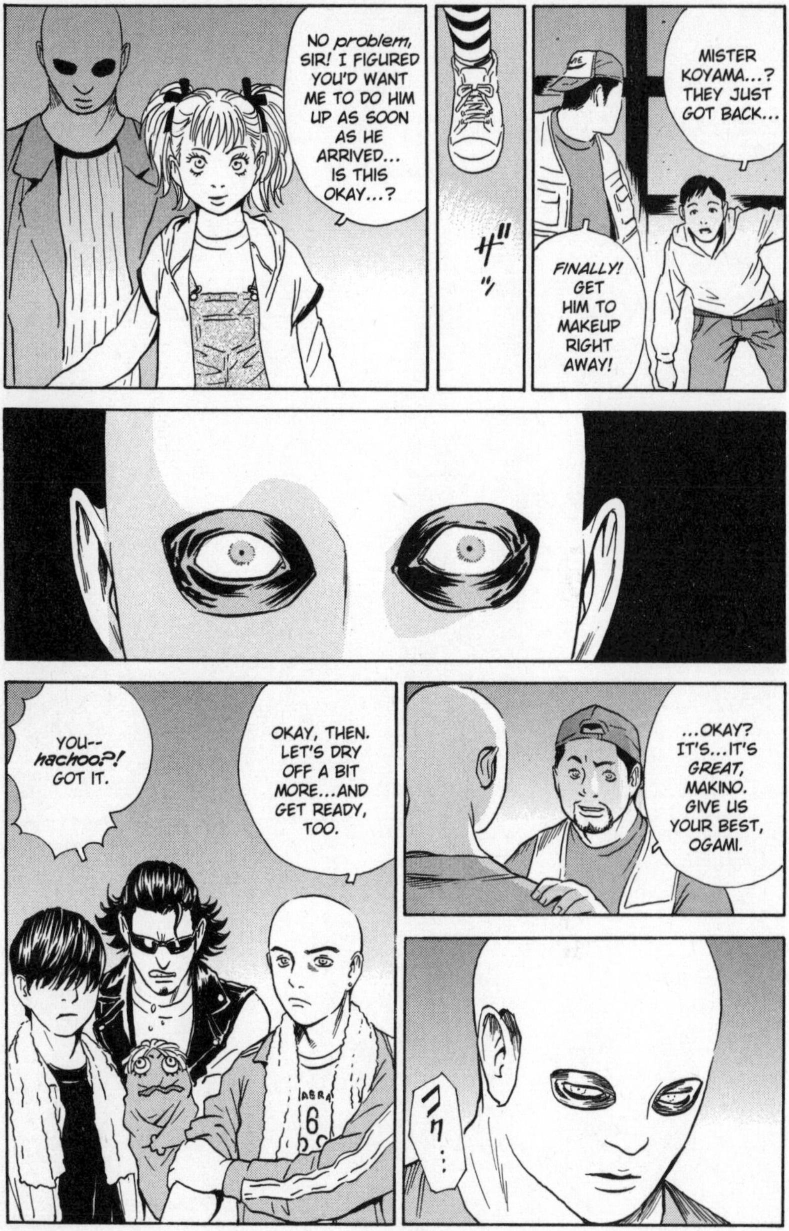
MISTER KOYAMA...? THEY JUST GOT BACK...
FINALLY! GET HIM TO MAKEUP RIGHT AWAY!
ザッ
NO *problem,* SIR! I FIGURED YOU'D WANT ME TO DO HIM UP AS SOON AS HE ARRIVED... IS THIS OKAY...?
...OKAY? IT'S...IT'S *GREAT,* MAKINO. GIVE US YOUR BEST, OGAMI.
ゴク...
OKAY, THEN. LET'S DRY OFF A BIT MORE...AND GET READY, TOO.
YOU-- *hachoo?!* GOT IT.

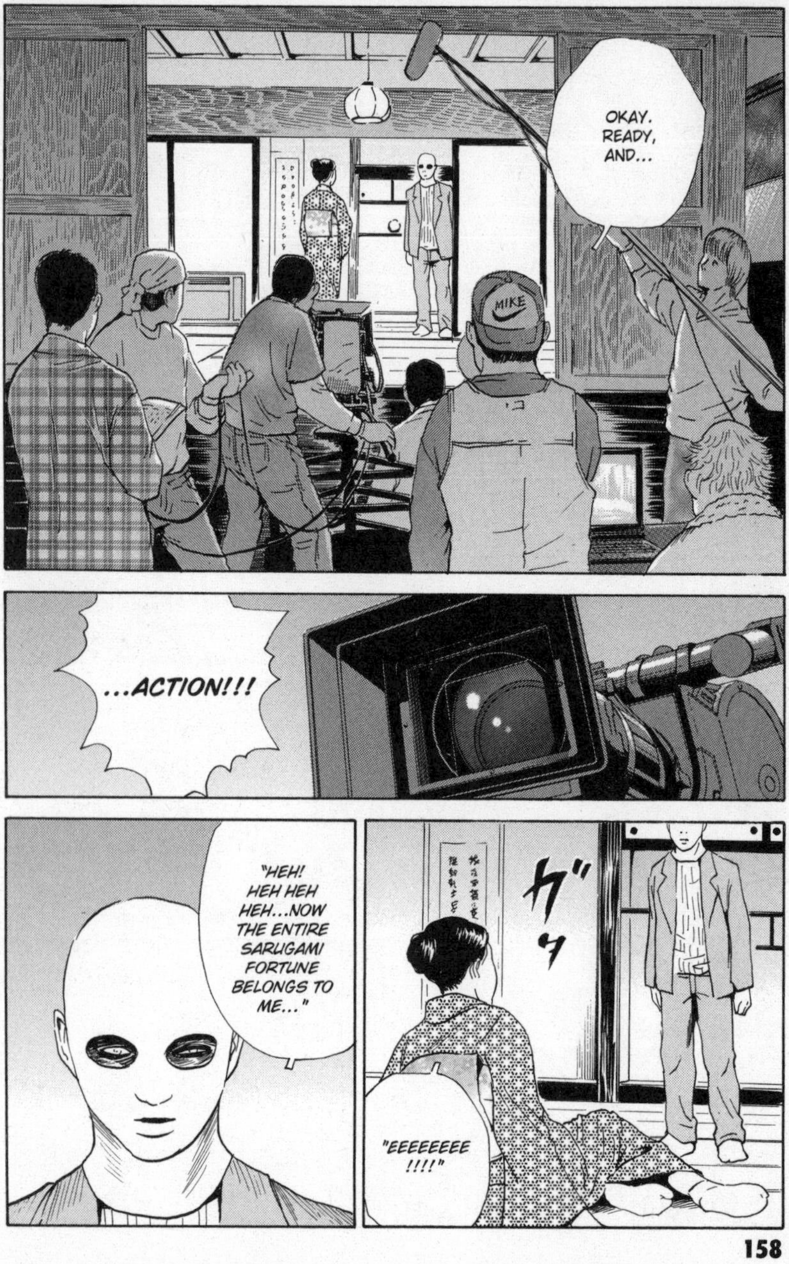
OKAY. READY, AND...
...ACTION!!!
ガッ
"EEEEEEEE !!!!"
"HEH! HEH HEH HEH...NOW THE ENTIRE SARUGAMI FORTUNE BELONGS TO ME..."

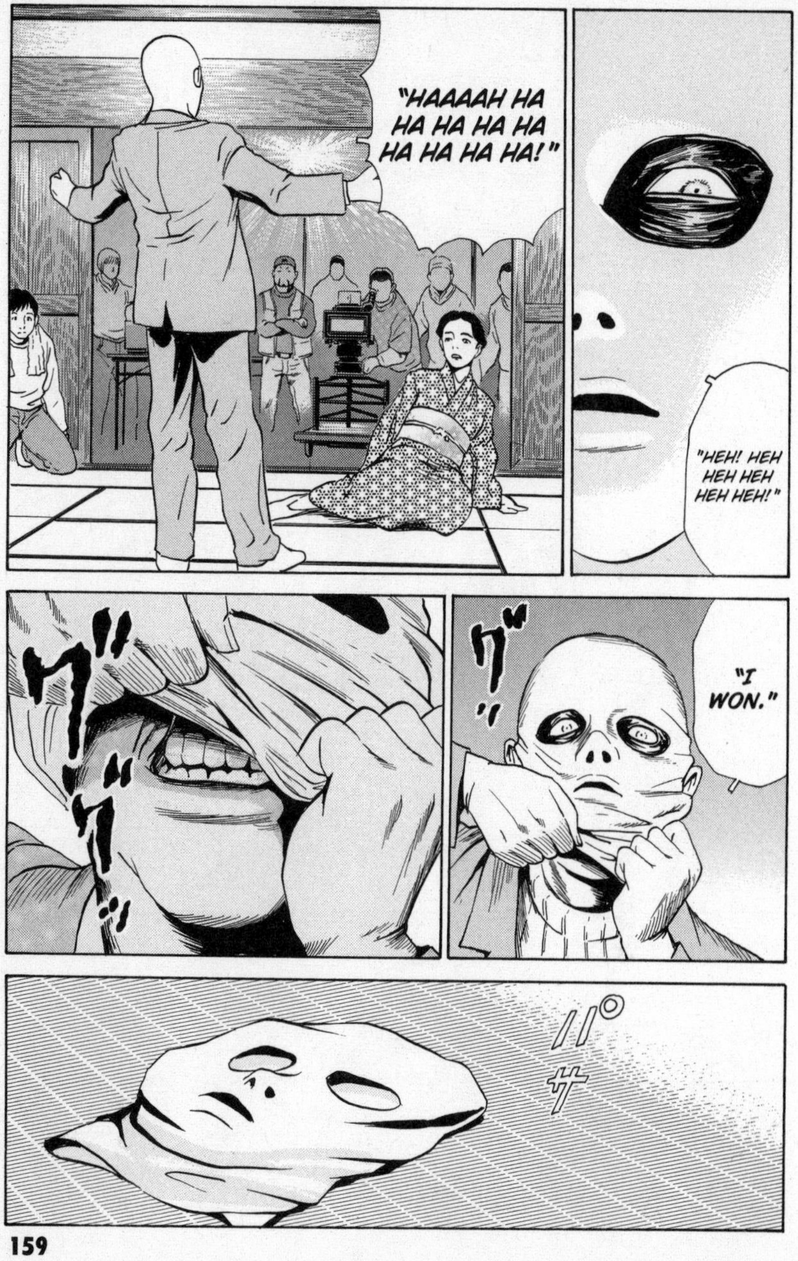
"HEH! HEH
HEH HEH
HEH HEH!"
"HAAAAH HA
HA HA HA HA
HA HA HA HA!"
"I
WON."
パサ

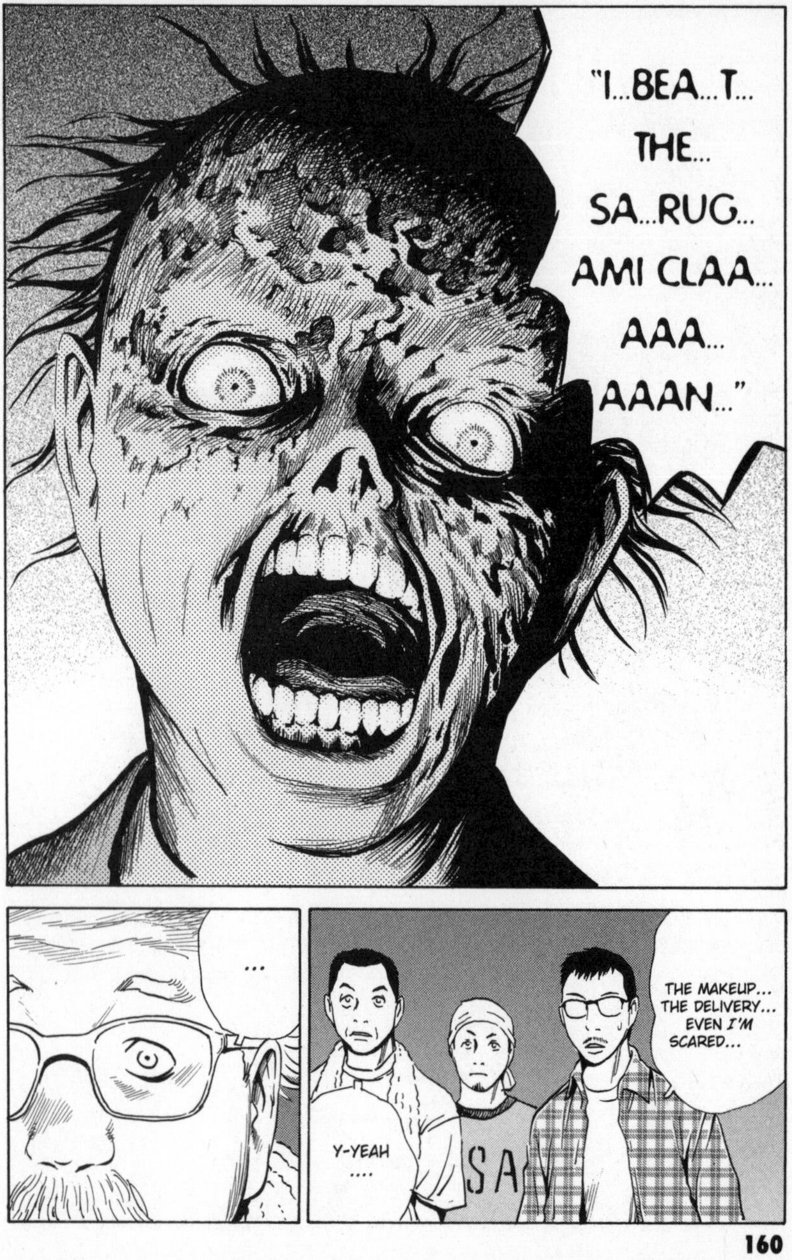
"I...BEA...T... THE... SA...RUG... AMI CLAA... AAA... AAAN..."
THE MAKEUP... THE DELIVERY... EVEN *I'M* SCARED...
Y-YEAH ....
...

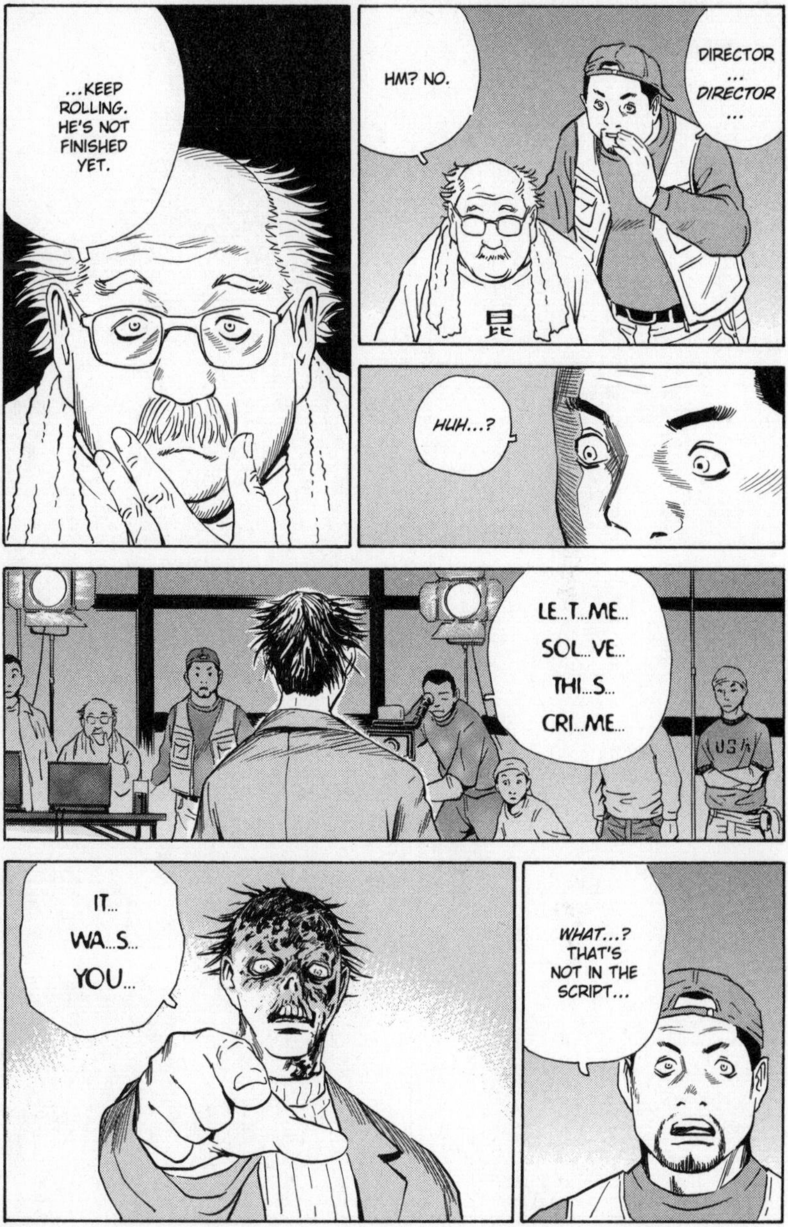
DIRECTOR ... DIRECTOR ...
HM? NO.
HUH...?
...KEEP ROLLING. HE'S NOT FINISHED YET.
LE...T...ME... SOL...VE... THI...S... CRI...ME...
WHAT...? THAT'S NOT IN THE SCRIPT...
IT... WA...S... YOU...

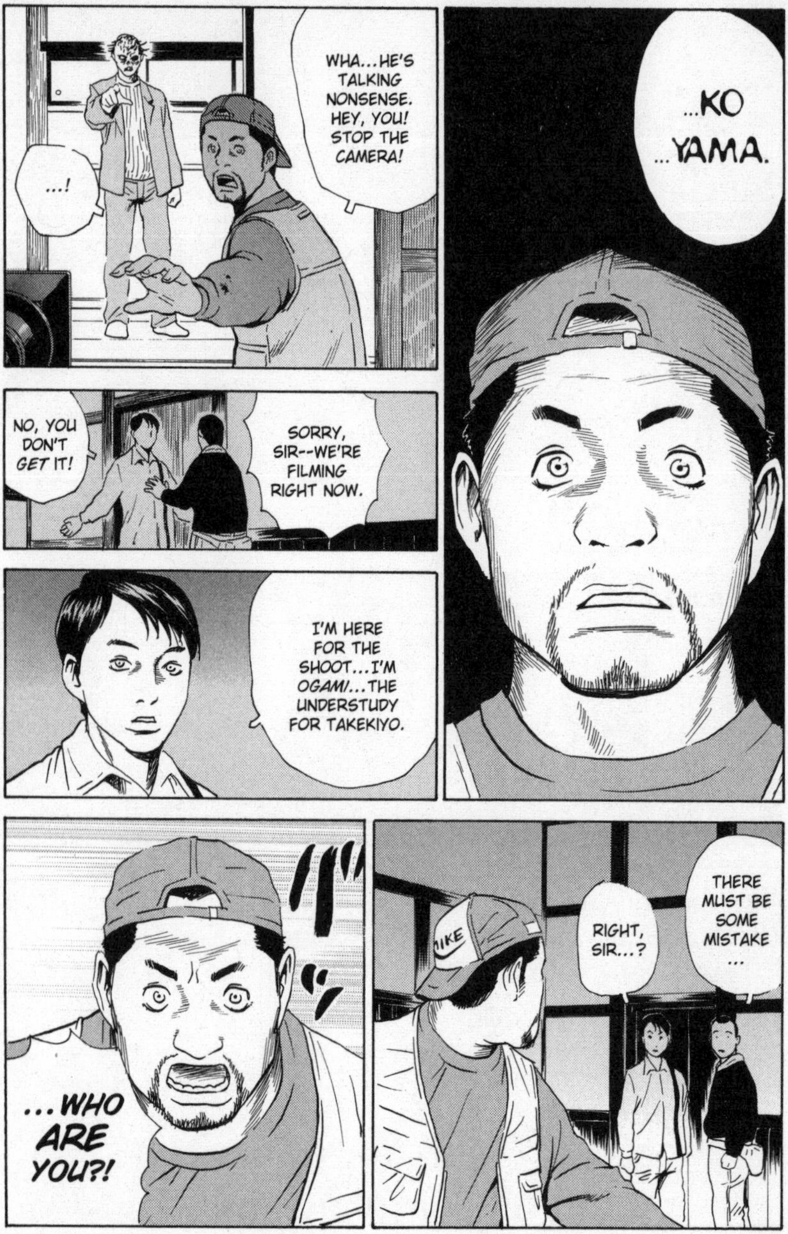

...KO
...YAMA.
WHA...HE'S TALKING NONSENSE. HEY, YOU! STOP THE CAMERA!
...!
SORRY, SIR--WE'RE FILMING RIGHT NOW.
NO, YOU DON'T *GET* IT!
I'M HERE FOR THE SHOOT...I'M *OGAMI*...THE UNDERSTUDY FOR TAKEKIYO.
THERE MUST BE SOME MISTAKE ...
RIGHT, SIR...?
...WHO ARE YOU?!

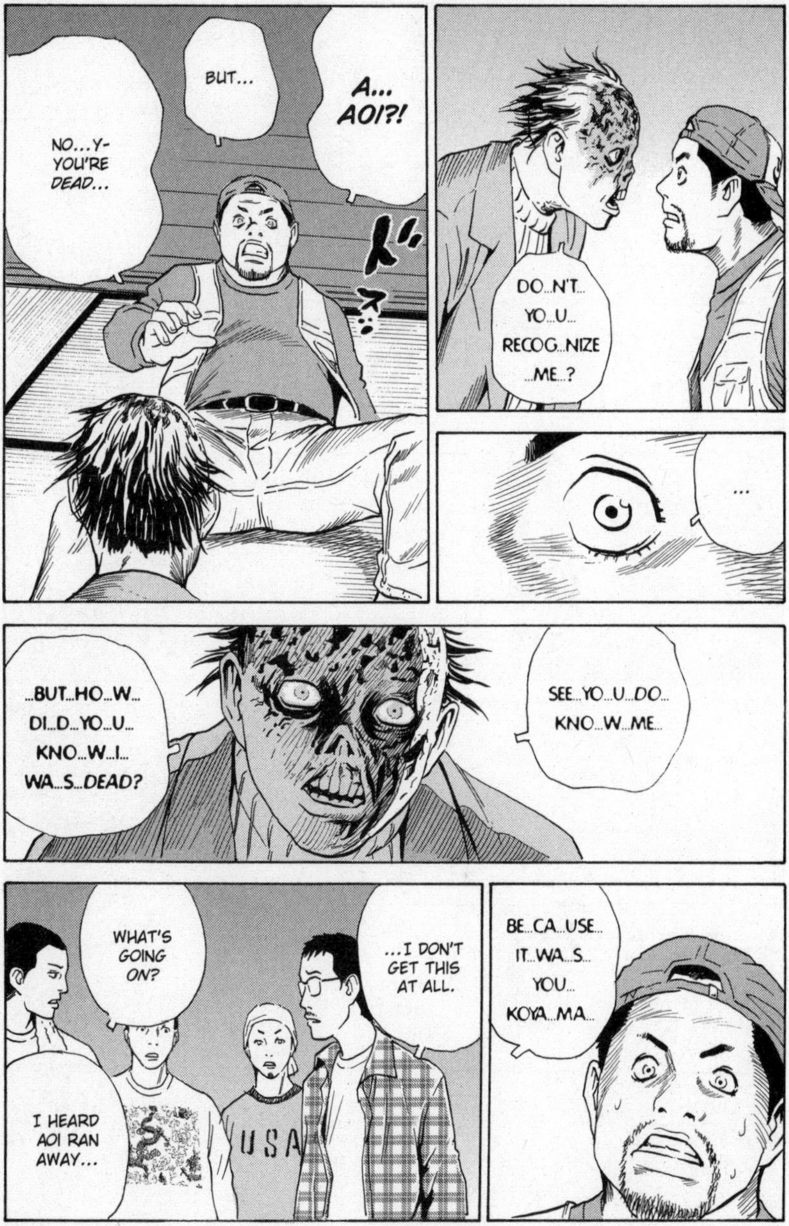
DO...N'T... YO...U... RECOG...NIZE ...ME...?
...
A... AOI?!
BUT...
NO... Y-YOU'RE DEAD...
SEE...YO...U...DO... KNO...W...ME...
...BUT...HO...W... DI...D...YO...U... KNO...W...I... WA...S...DEAD?
BE...CA...USE... IT...WA...S... YOU... KOYA...MA...
...I DON'T GET THIS AT ALL.
WHAT'S GOING ON?
I HEARD AOI RAN AWAY...

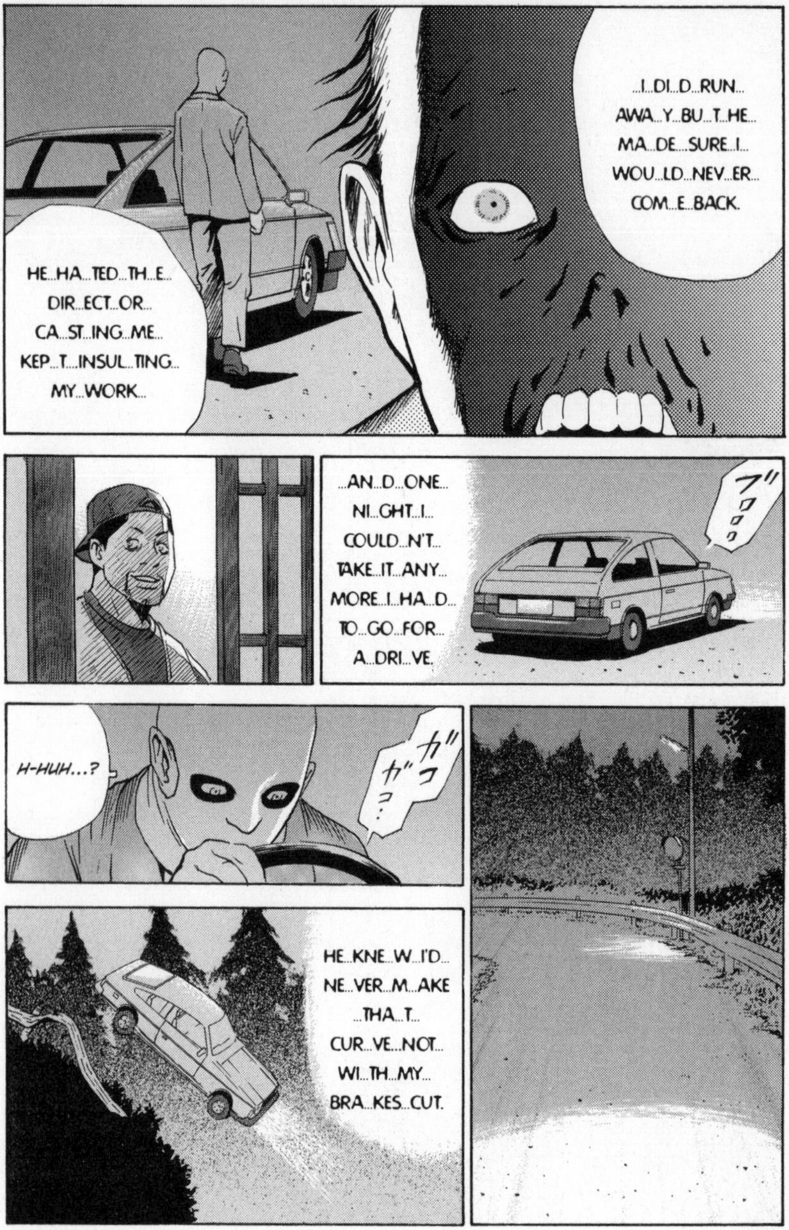
..I..DI..D..RUN.. AWA..Y..BU..T..HE.. MA..DE..SURE..I.. WOU..LD..NEV..ER.. COM..E..BACK.
HE..HA..TED..TH..E.. DIR..ECT..OR.. CA..ST..ING..ME.. KEP..T...INSUL..TING.. MY..WORK..
..AN..D..ONE.. NI..GHT..I.. COULD..N'T.. TAKE..IT..ANY.. MORE..I..HA..D.. TO..GO..FOR.. A..DRI..VE.
ブロロロ
H-HUH...?
ガコ
ガコ…
HE..KNE..W..I'D.. NE..VER..M..AKE ..THA..T.. CUR..VE..NOT.. WI..TH..MY.. BRA..KES..CUT.

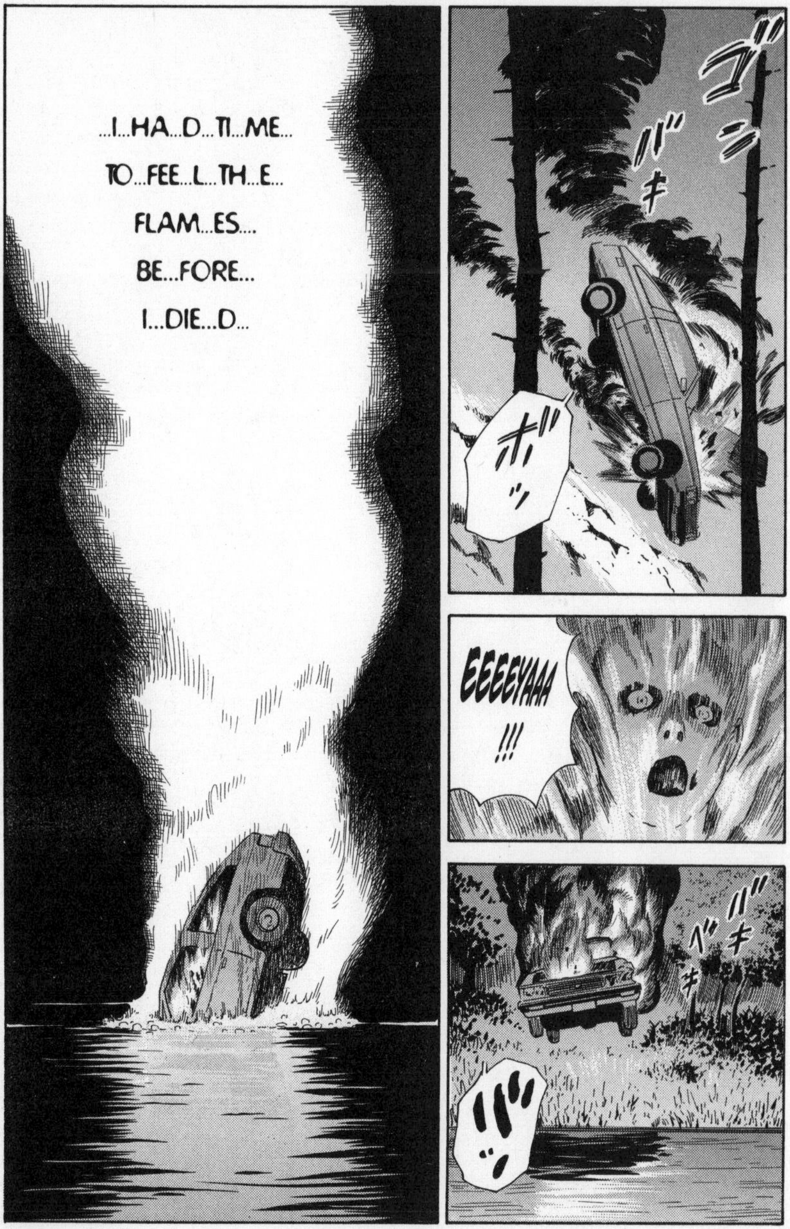

ゴン
バキ
ボッ
EEEEYAAA !!!
バキ
ベキ
バッ
...I...HA...D...TI...ME... TO...FEE...L...TH...E... FLAM...ES... BE...FORE... I...DIE...D...

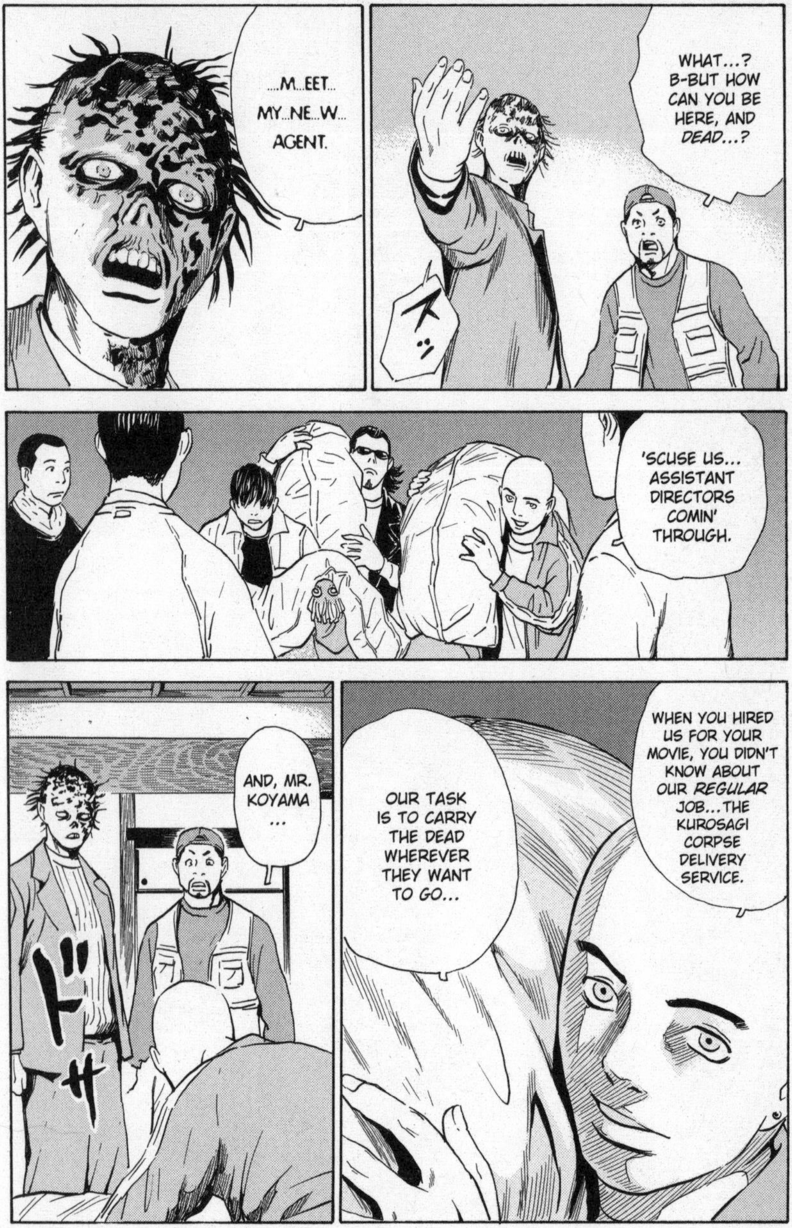
WHAT...? B-BUT HOW CAN YOU BE HERE, AND *DEAD*...?
...M...EET... MY...NE...W... AGENT.
'SCUSE US... ASSISTANT DIRECTORS COMIN' THROUGH.
WHEN YOU HIRED US FOR YOUR MOVIE, YOU DIDN'T KNOW ABOUT OUR *REGULAR* JOB...THE KUROSAGI CORPSE DELIVERY SERVICE.
OUR TASK IS TO CARRY THE DEAD WHEREVER THEY WANT TO GO...
AND, MR. KOYAMA ...

...THANKS AGAIN FOR ALL THE WORK YOU'VE GIVEN US.

5th delivery: i'm not afraid of the big bad wolf—the end

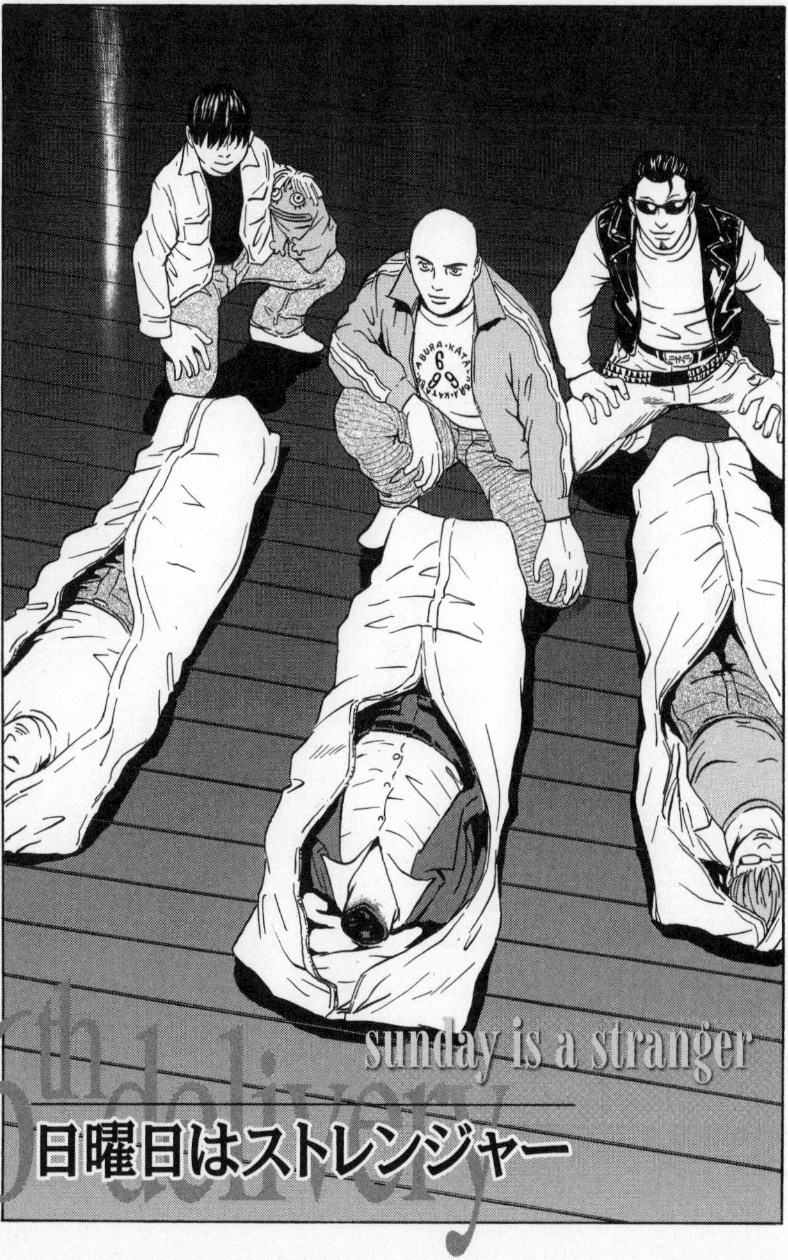
6th delivery
sunday is a stranger
日曜日はストレンジャー

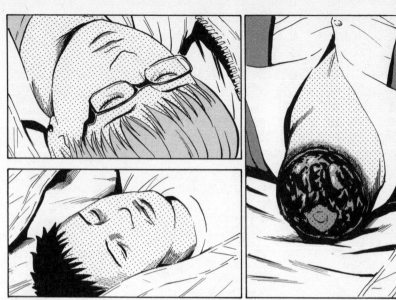

YOU...
FOUND
THESE
BODIES...?

I-IS...
THAT...
IKEI...?

THE MISSING
SPECIAL EFFECTS
MAKEUP ARTIST
AND THE THIRD
ASSISTANT
DIRECTOR, TOO. IF
THIS IS A JOKE--

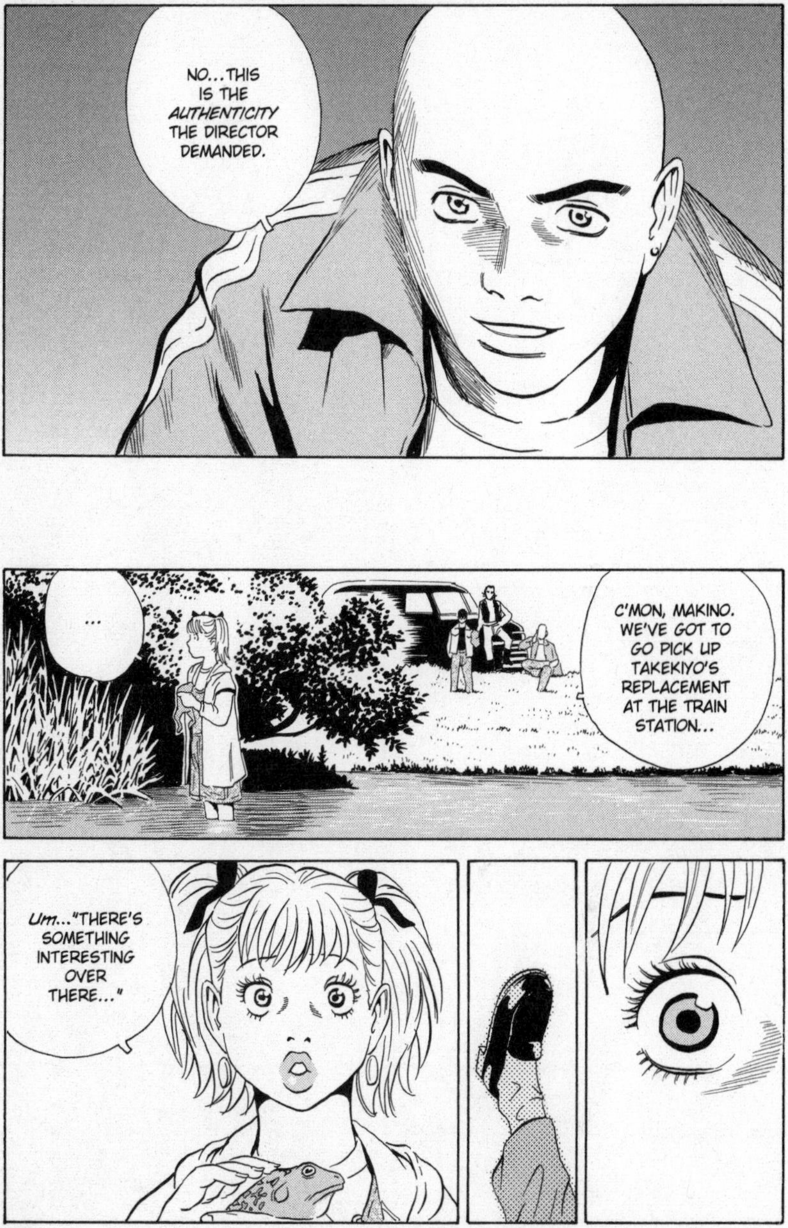
NO...THIS IS THE *AUTHENTICITY* THE DIRECTOR DEMANDED.
C'MON, MAKINO. WE'VE GOT TO GO PICK UP TAKEKIYO'S REPLACEMENT AT THE TRAIN STATION...
...
Um..."THERE'S SOMETHING INTERESTING OVER THERE..."

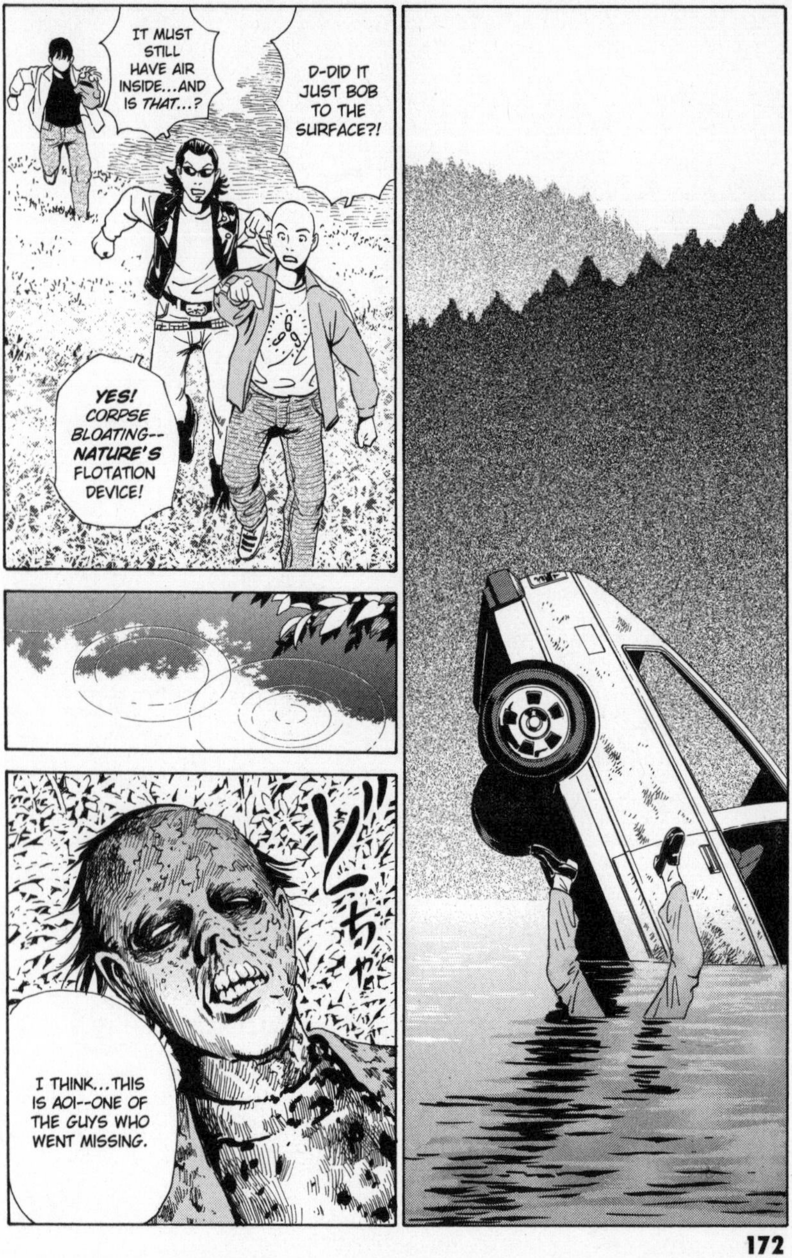
D-DID IT JUST BOB TO THE SURFACE?!
IT MUST STILL HAVE AIR INSIDE...AND IS *THAT*...?
YES! CORPSE BLOATING-- ***NATURE'S*** FLOTATION DEVICE!
I THINK...THIS IS AOI--ONE OF THE GUYS WHO WENT MISSING.

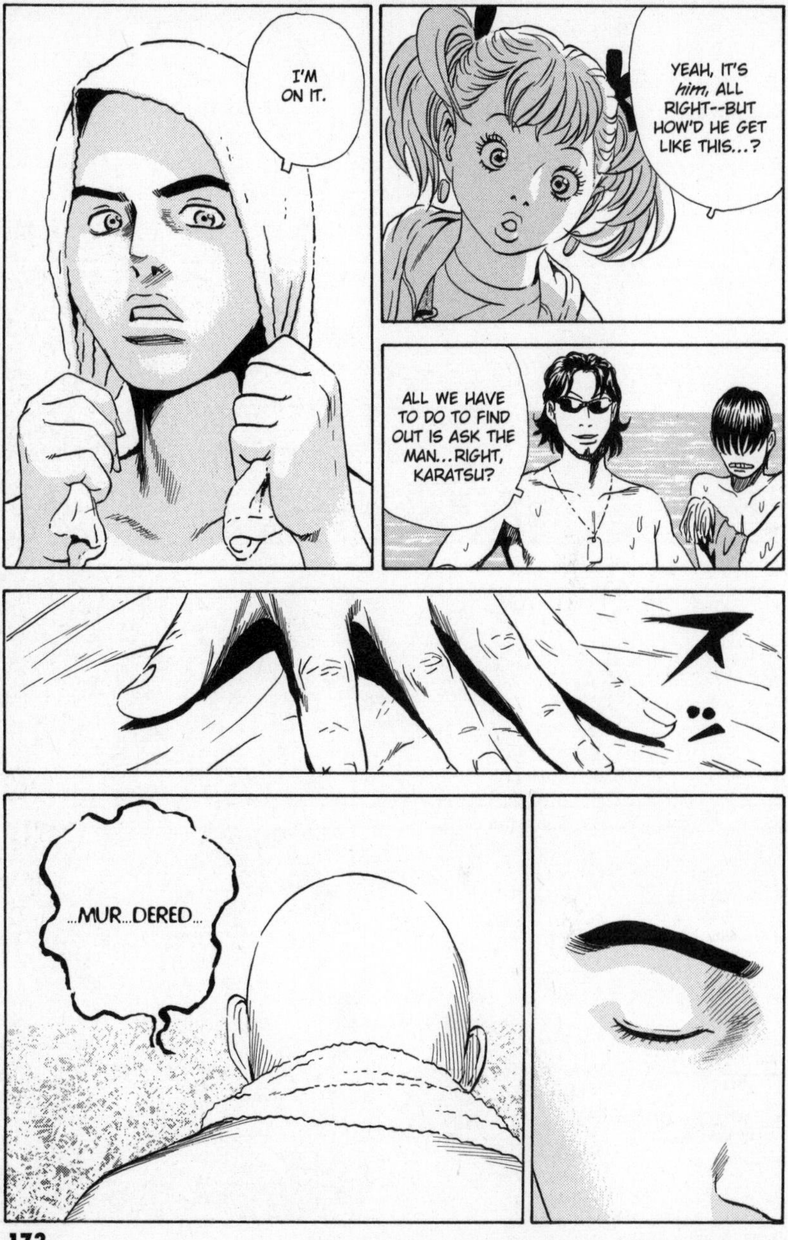
YEAH, IT'S *him*, ALL RIGHT--BUT HOW'D HE GET LIKE THIS...?
ALL WE HAVE TO DO TO FIND OUT IS ASK THE MAN...RIGHT, KARATSU?
I'M ON IT.
...MUR...DERED...

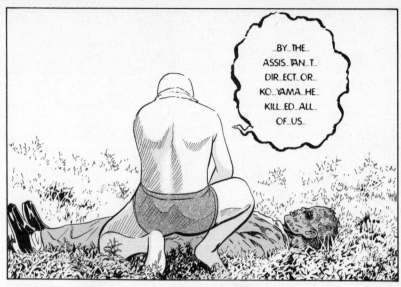

...BY...THE... ASSIS...TAN...T... DIR...ECT...OR... KO...YAMA...HE... KILL...ED...ALL... OF...US...
LIKE, NO *WAY!* WHY WOULD KOYAMA...
AND WH-WHAT DID HE MEAN BY "ALL OF US"...?
ユラ…
THERE'RE MORE CORPSES IN THIS LAKE...
...I'D SAY, AT LEAST ONE OR TWO.
OH, YOU GOTTA BE KIDDING ME.
ヒュン
ヒュン

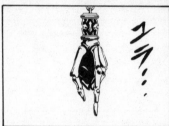

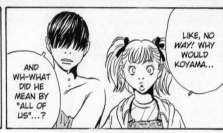

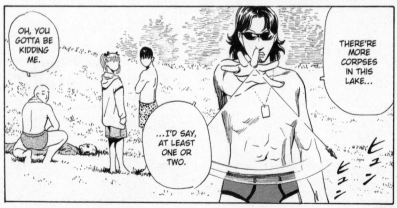

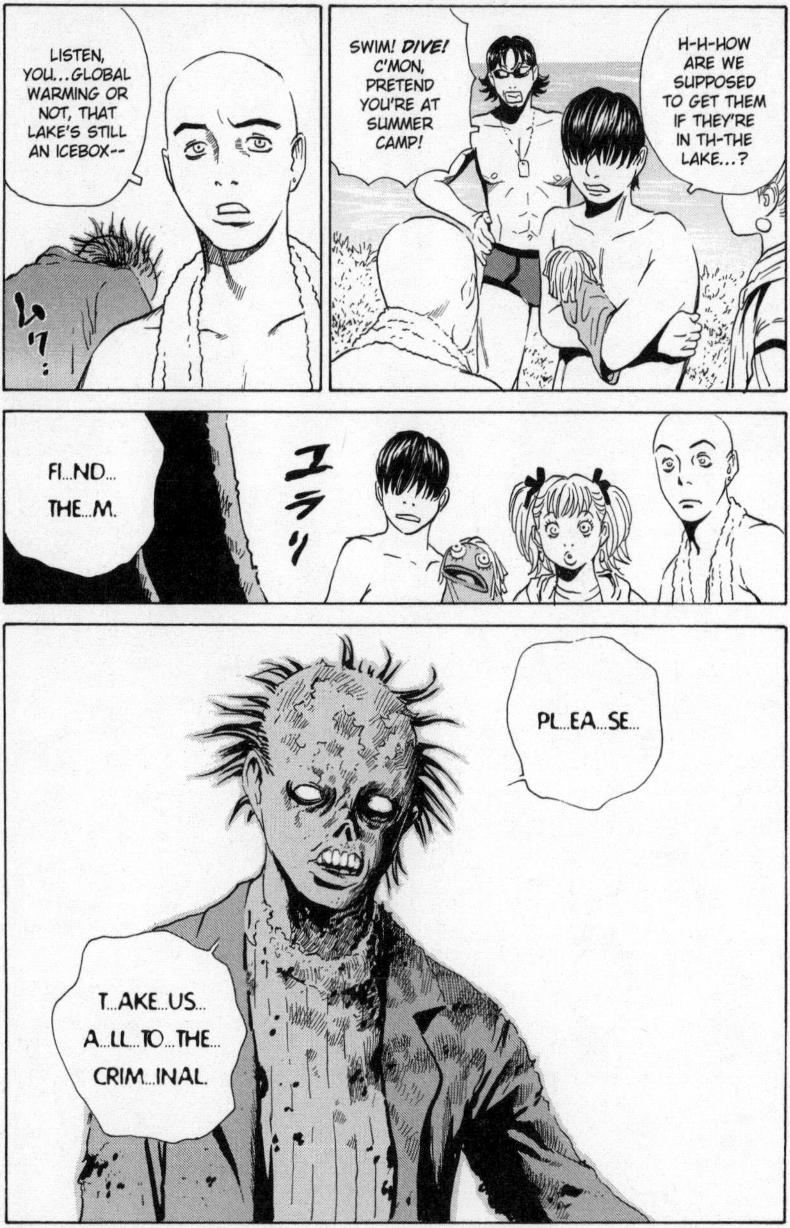
H-H-HOW ARE WE SUPPOSED TO GET THEM IF THEY'RE IN TH-THE LAKE...?
SWIM! *DIVE!* C'MON, PRETEND YOU'RE AT SUMMER CAMP!
LISTEN, YOU...GLOBAL WARMING OR NOT, THAT LAKE'S STILL AN ICEBOX--
ムッ
ユラリ
FI...ND... THE...M.
PL...EA...SE...
T...AKE...US... A...LL...TO...THE... CRIM...INAL.

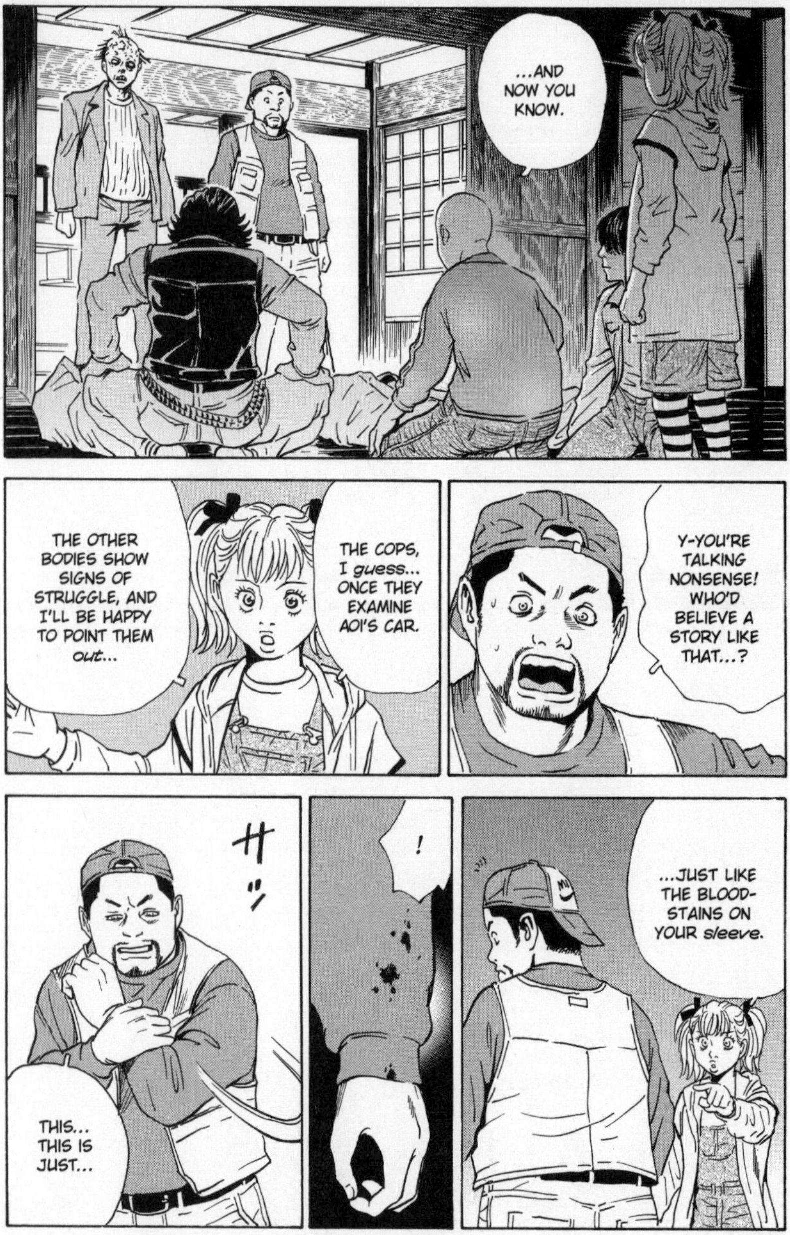
...AND NOW YOU KNOW.
Y-YOU'RE TALKING NONSENSE! WHO'D BELIEVE A STORY LIKE THAT...?
THE COPS, I *guess*... ONCE THEY EXAMINE AOI'S CAR.
THE OTHER BODIES SHOW SIGNS OF STRUGGLE, AND I'LL BE HAPPY TO POINT THEM *out*...
...JUST LIKE THE BLOOD-STAINS ON YOUR *sleeve*.
!
ザッ
THIS... THIS IS JUST...

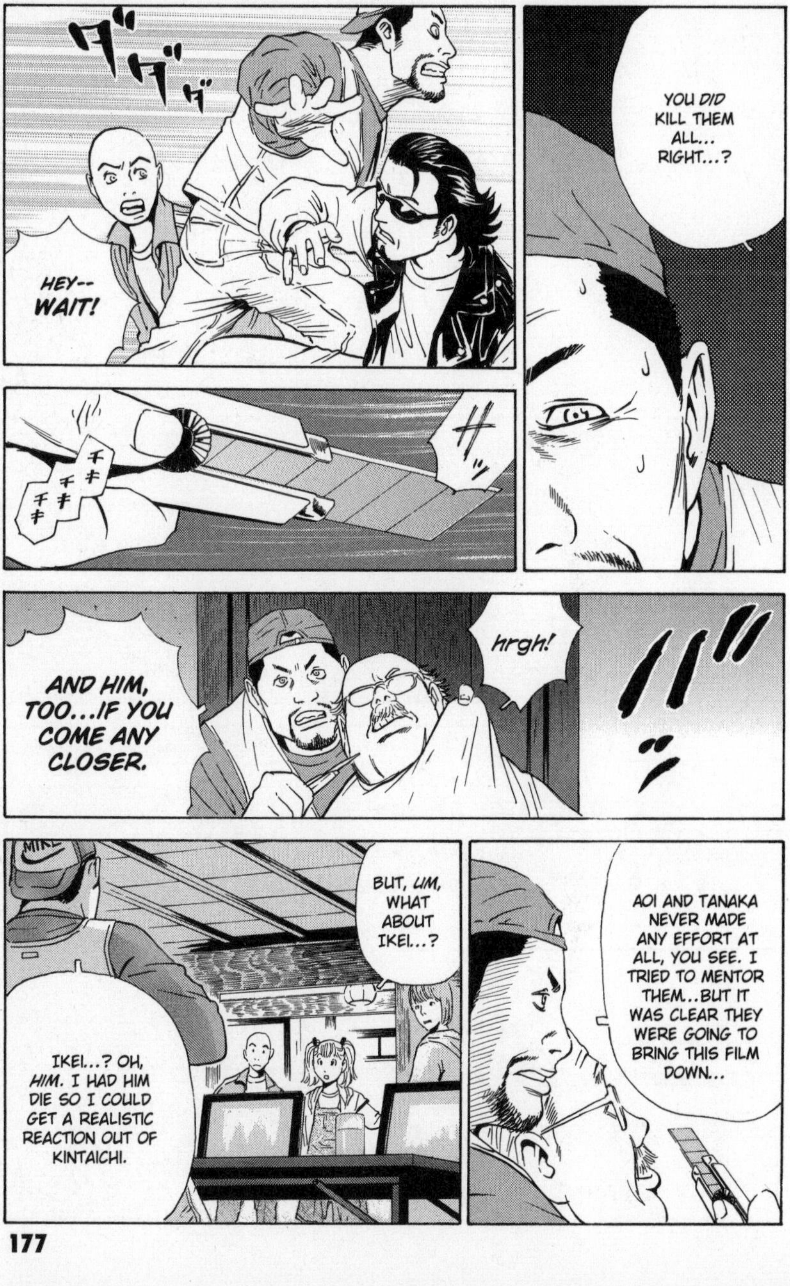

YOU *DID* KILL THEM ALL... RIGHT...?
ダダダ
HEY-- WAIT!
チチチチチチ
AND HIM, TOO...IF YOU COME ANY CLOSER.
hrgh!
AOI AND TANAKA NEVER MADE ANY EFFORT AT ALL, YOU SEE. I TRIED TO MENTOR THEM...BUT IT WAS CLEAR THEY WERE GOING TO BRING THIS FILM DOWN...
BUT, *UM*, WHAT ABOUT IKEI...?
IKEI...? OH, *HIM*. I HAD HIM DIE SO I COULD GET A REALISTIC REACTION OUT OF KINTAICHI.

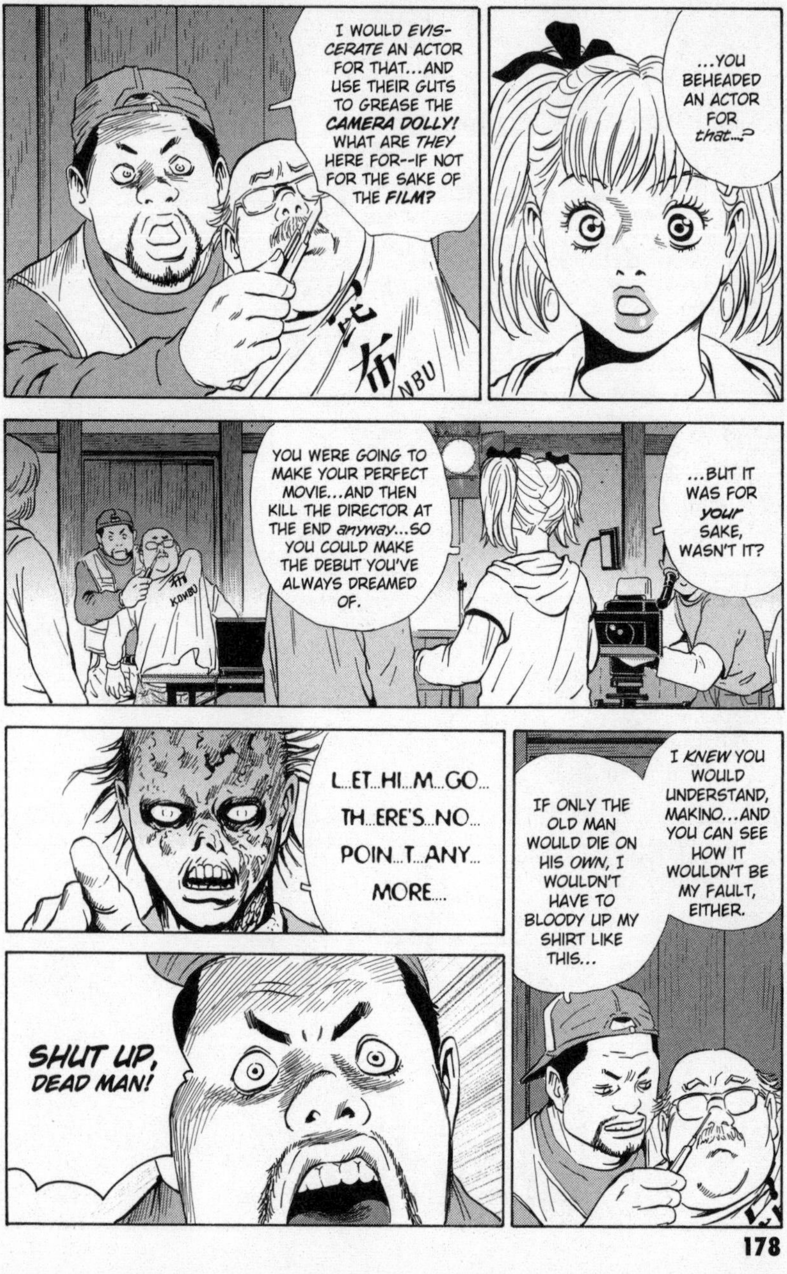
...YOU BEHEADED AN ACTOR FOR *that*...?
I WOULD *EVIS-CERATE* AN ACTOR FOR THAT...AND USE THEIR GUTS TO GREASE THE ***CAMERA DOLLY!*** WHAT ARE *THEY* HERE FOR--IF NOT FOR THE SAKE OF THE ***FILM?***
NBU
...BUT IT WAS FOR ***your*** SAKE, WASN'T IT?
YOU WERE GOING TO MAKE YOUR PERFECT MOVIE...AND THEN KILL THE DIRECTOR AT THE END *anyway*...SO YOU COULD MAKE THE DEBUT YOU'VE ALWAYS DREAMED OF.
KONBU
I *KNEW* YOU WOULD UNDERSTAND, MAKINO...AND YOU CAN SEE HOW IT WOULDN'T BE MY FAULT, EITHER.
IF ONLY THE OLD MAN WOULD DIE ON HIS *OWN*, I WOULDN'T HAVE TO BLOODY UP MY SHIRT LIKE THIS...
L...ET...HI...M...GO... TH...ERE'S...NO... POIN...T...ANY... MORE....
SHUT UP, DEAD MAN!

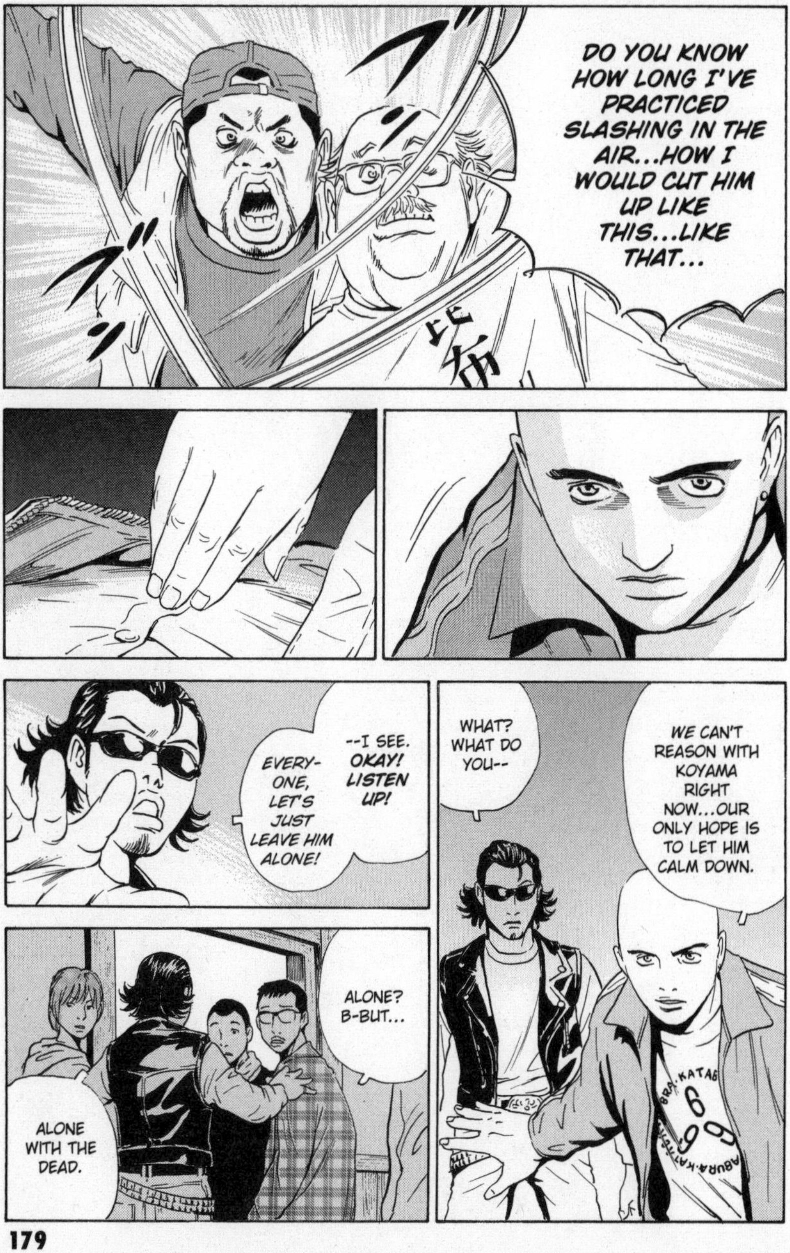
DO YOU KNOW HOW LONG I'VE PRACTICED SLASHING IN THE AIR...HOW I WOULD CUT HIM UP LIKE THIS...LIKE THAT...
WE CAN'T REASON WITH KOYAMA RIGHT NOW...OUR ONLY HOPE IS TO LET HIM CALM DOWN.
WHAT? WHAT DO YOU--
--I SEE. OKAY! LISTEN UP!
EVERY-ONE, LET'S JUST LEAVE HIM ALONE!
ALONE? B-BUT...
ALONE WITH THE DEAD.

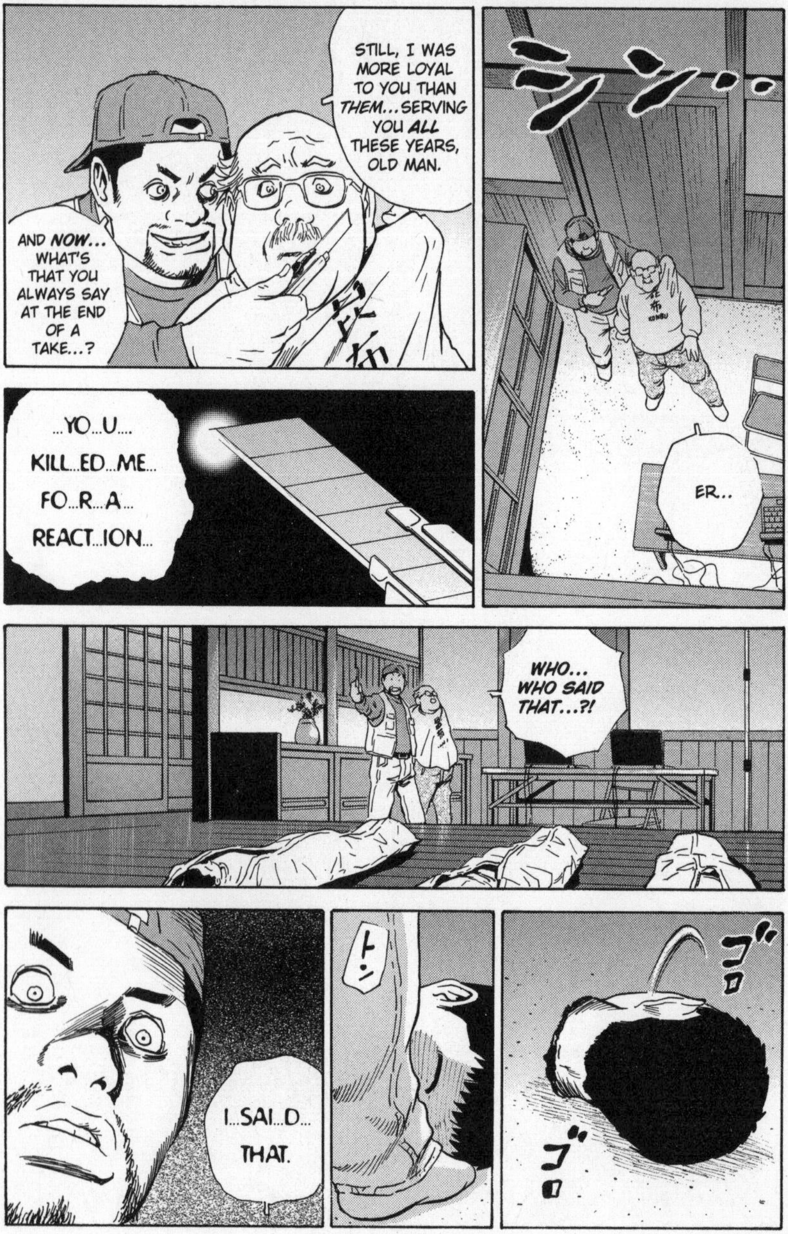
シン…
ER...
STILL, I WAS MORE LOYAL TO YOU THAN *THEM*... SERVING YOU ***ALL*** THESE YEARS, OLD MAN.
AND ***NOW***... WHAT'S THAT YOU ALWAYS SAY AT THE END OF A TAKE...?
...YO...U.... KILL...ED...ME... FO...R...A... REACT...ION...
WHO... WHO SAID THAT...?!
ゴロ
ゴロ
トン
I...SAI...D... THAT.

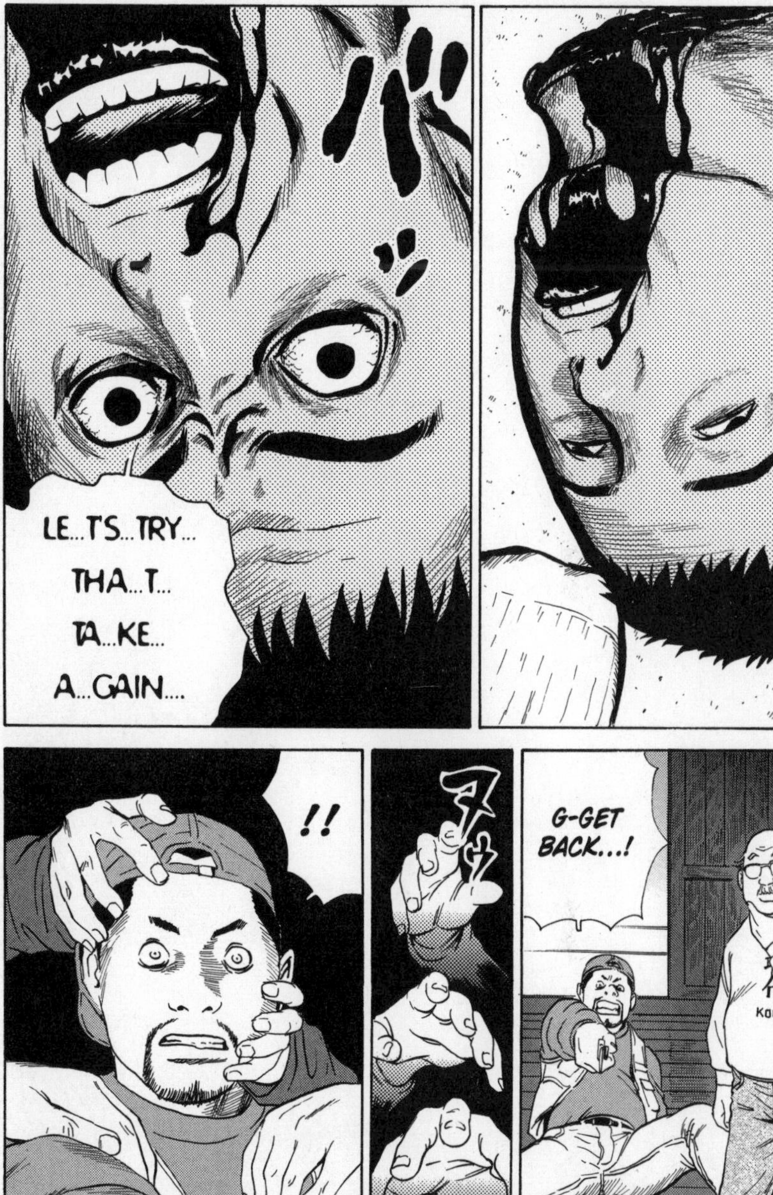
LE...T'S...TRY...
THA...T...
TA...KE...
A...GAIN....
G-GET BACK...!
KON
!!

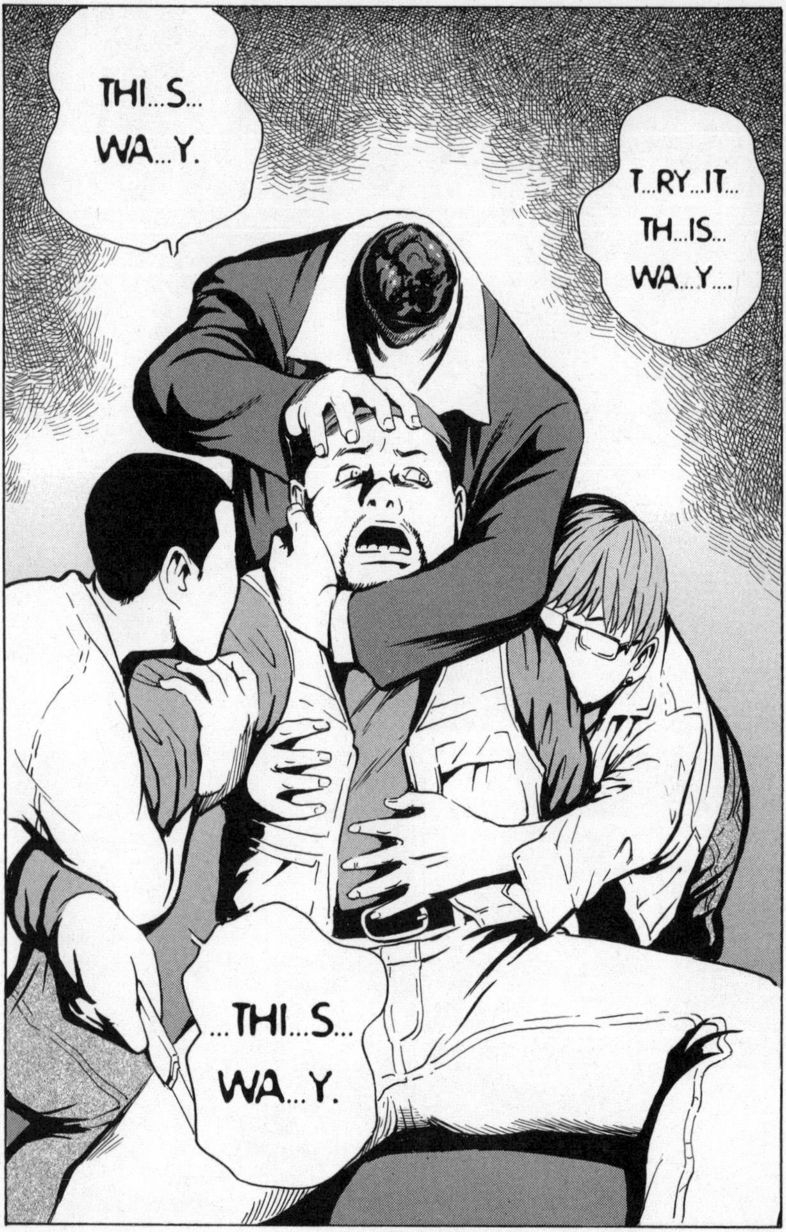
T...RY...IT... TH...IS... WA...Y....
THI...S... WA...Y.
...THI...S... WA...Y.

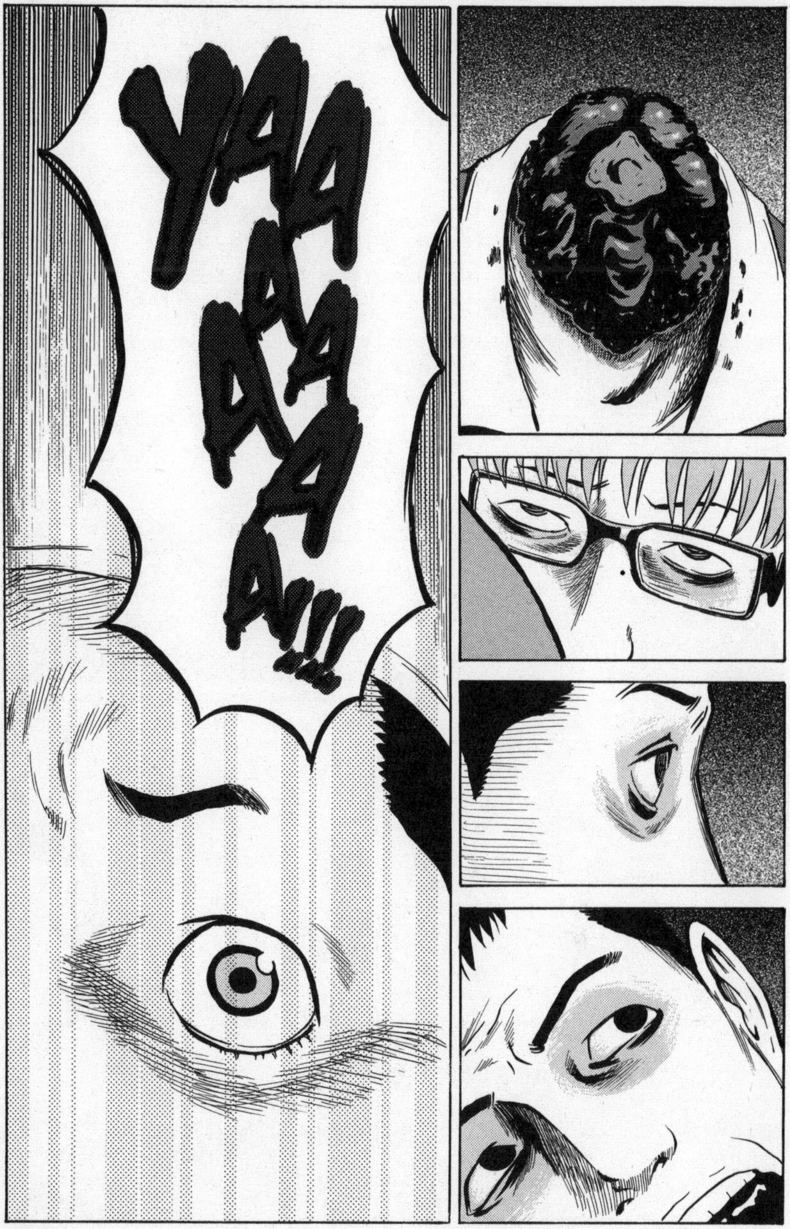
YAAAAAAAA!!!

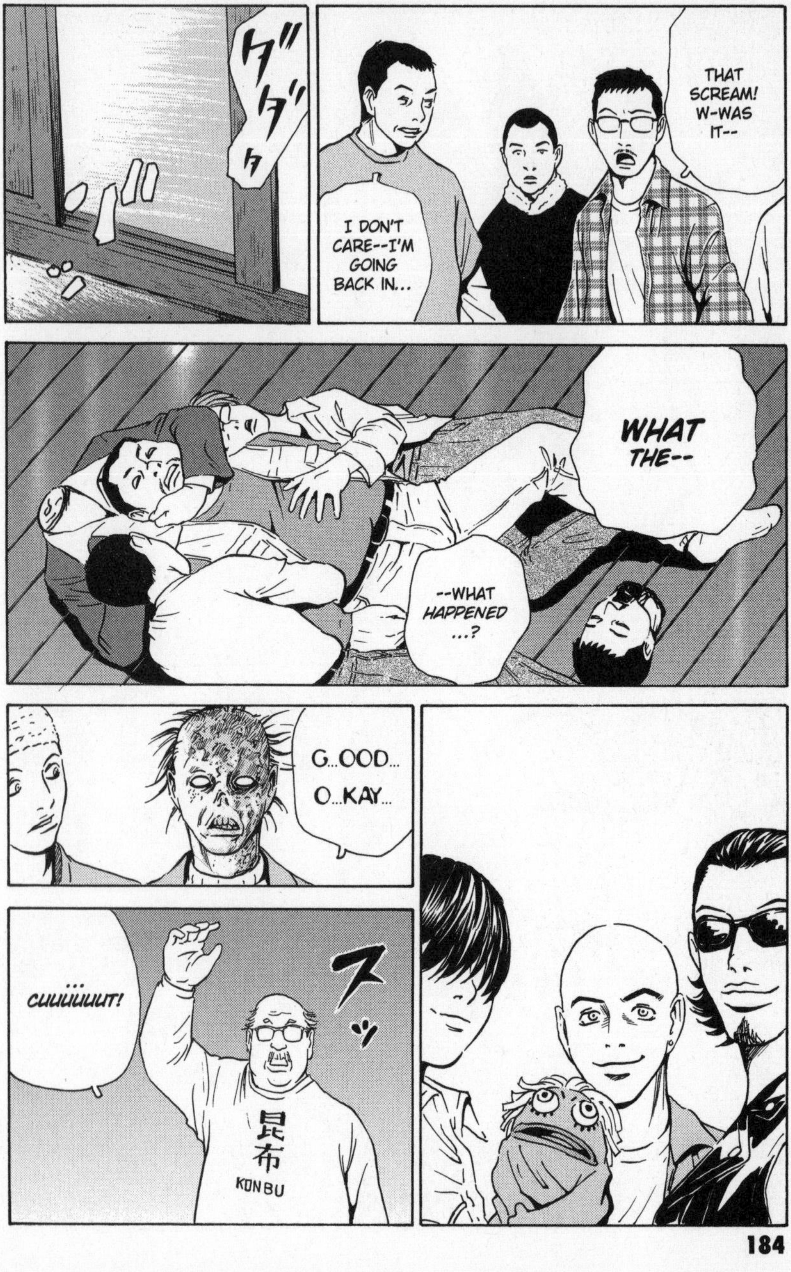
THAT SCREAM! W-WAS IT--
I DON'T CARE--I'M GOING BACK IN...
ダダダ
WHAT THE--
--WHAT HAPPENED ...?
G...OOD... O...KAY...
...CUUUUUUT!
スッ
昆布
KONBU

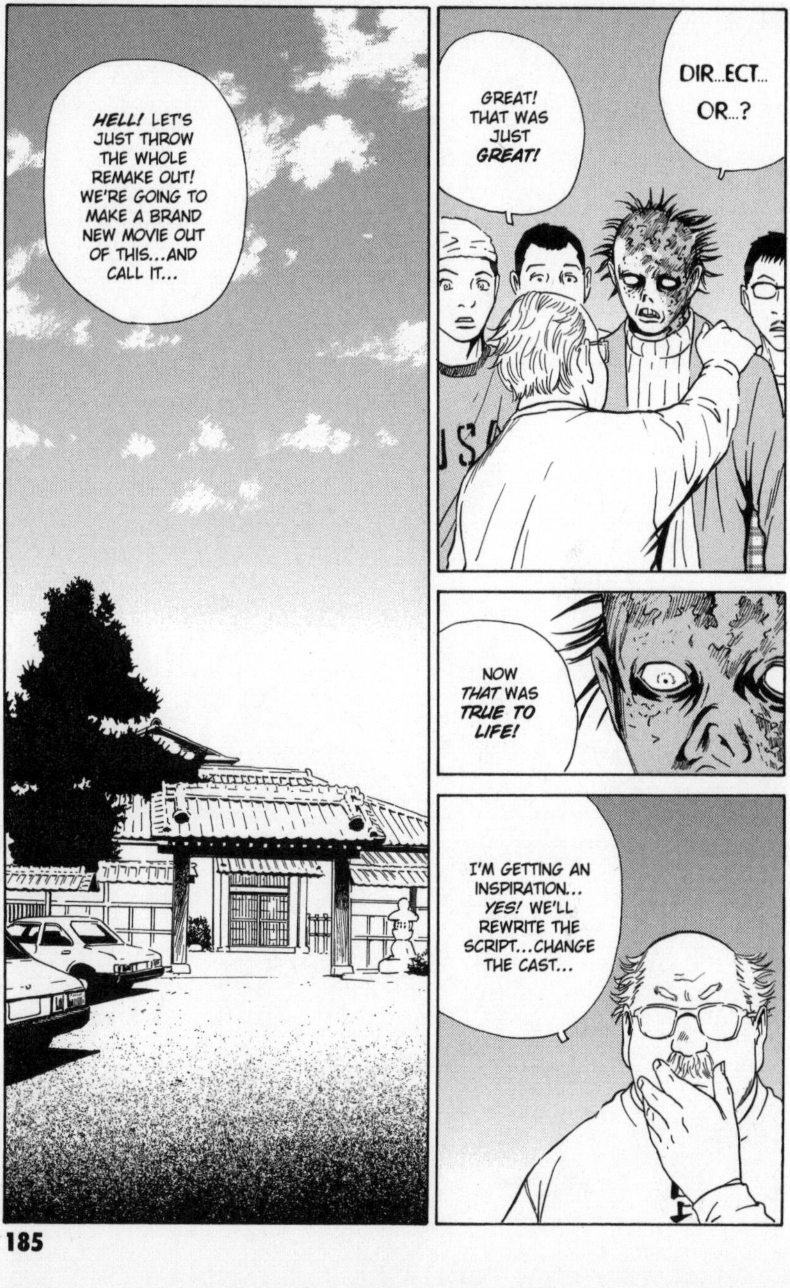
DIR...ECT... OR...?
GREAT! THAT WAS JUST *GREAT!*
NOW *THAT* WAS *TRUE TO LIFE!*
I'M GETTING AN INSPIRATION... *YES!* WE'LL REWRITE THE SCRIPT...CHANGE THE CAST...
HELL! LET'S JUST THROW THE WHOLE REMAKE OUT! WE'RE GOING TO MAKE A BRAND NEW MOVIE OUT OF THIS...AND CALL IT...

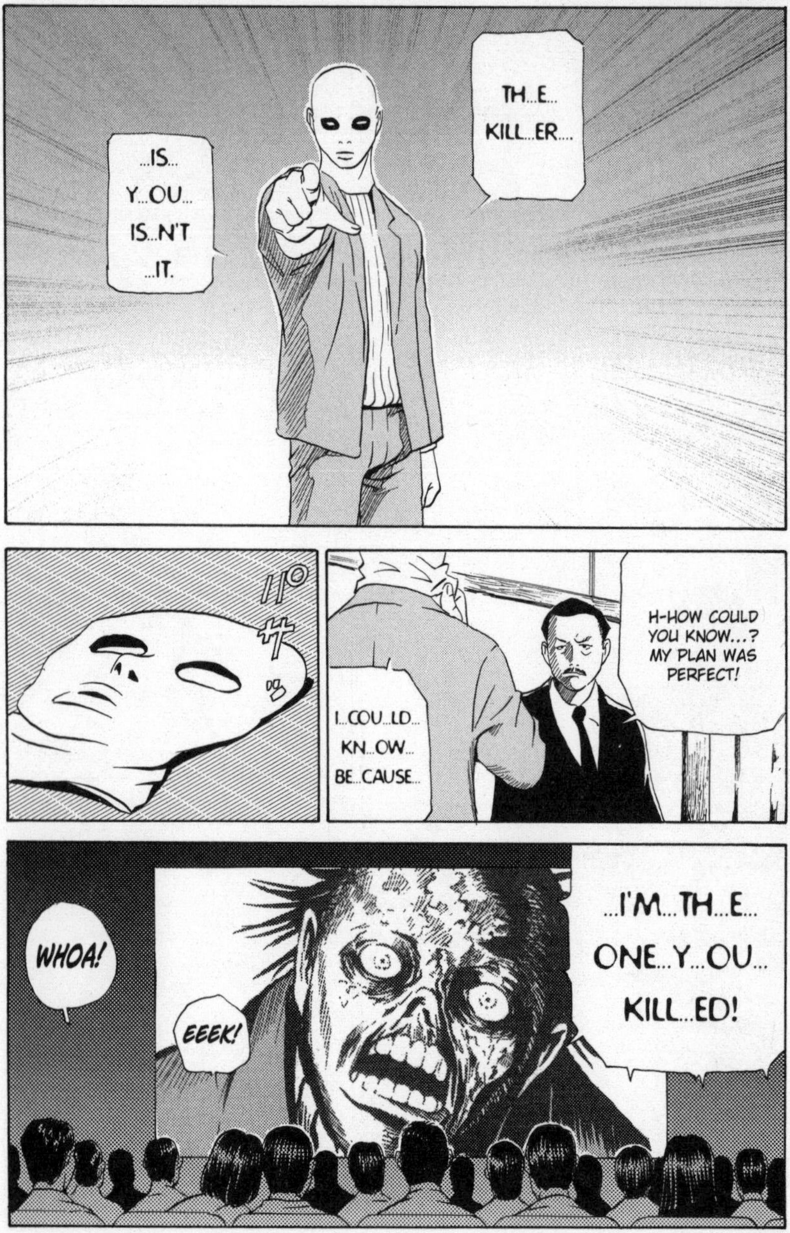
TH...E... KILL...ER....
...IS... Y...OU... IS...N'T ...IT.
H-HOW COULD YOU KNOW...? MY PLAN WAS PERFECT!
I...COU...LD... KN...OW... BE...CAUSE...
パサ
...I'M...TH...E... ONE...Y...OU... KILL...ED!
EEEK!
WHOA!

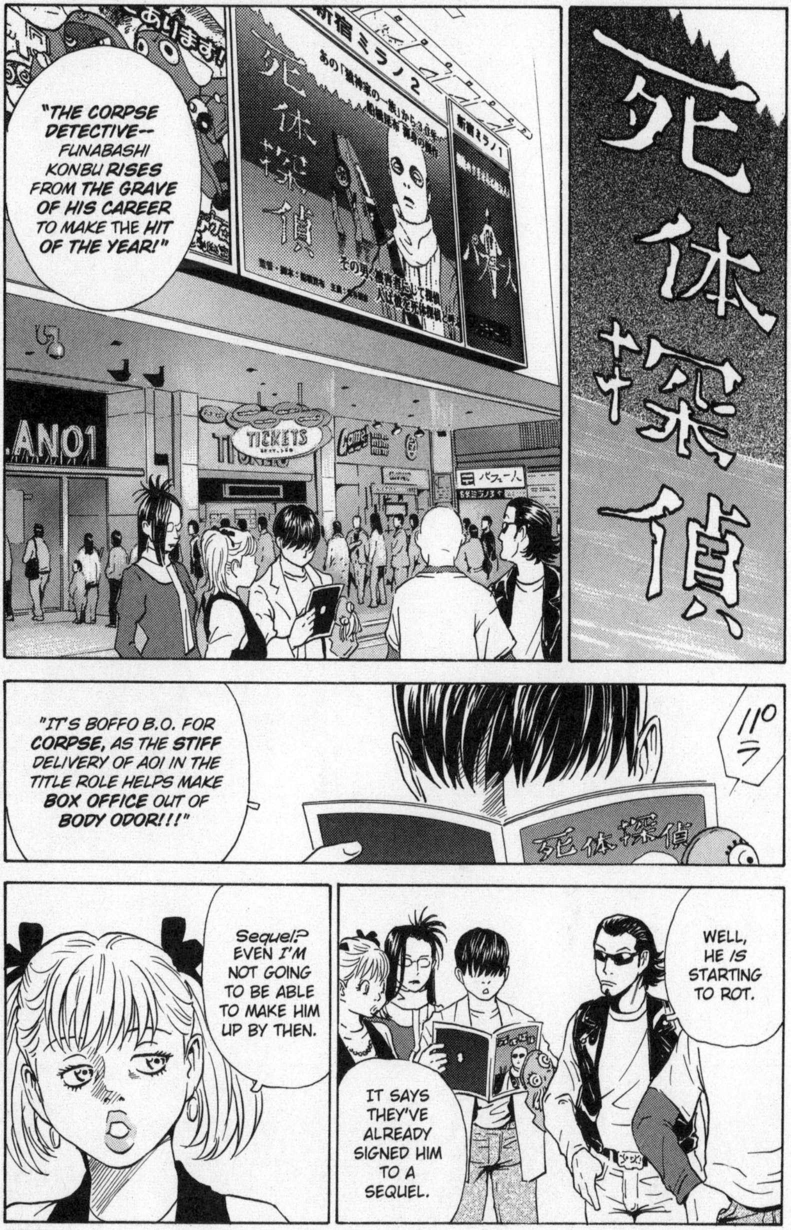
死体探偵
新宿ミラノ2
新宿ミラノ1
"THE CORPSE DETECTIVE-- FUNABASHI KONBU RISES FROM THE GRAVE OF HIS CAREER TO MAKE THE HIT OF THE YEAR!"
.ANO1
TICKETS
パラ
"IT'S BOFFO B.O. FOR CORPSE, AS THE STIFF DELIVERY OF AOI IN THE TITLE ROLE HELPS MAKE BOX OFFICE OUT OF BODY ODOR!!!"
死体探偵
IT SAYS THEY'VE ALREADY SIGNED HIM TO A SEQUEL.
Sequel? EVEN I'M NOT GOING TO BE ABLE TO MAKE HIM UP BY THEN.
WELL, HE IS STARTING TO ROT.

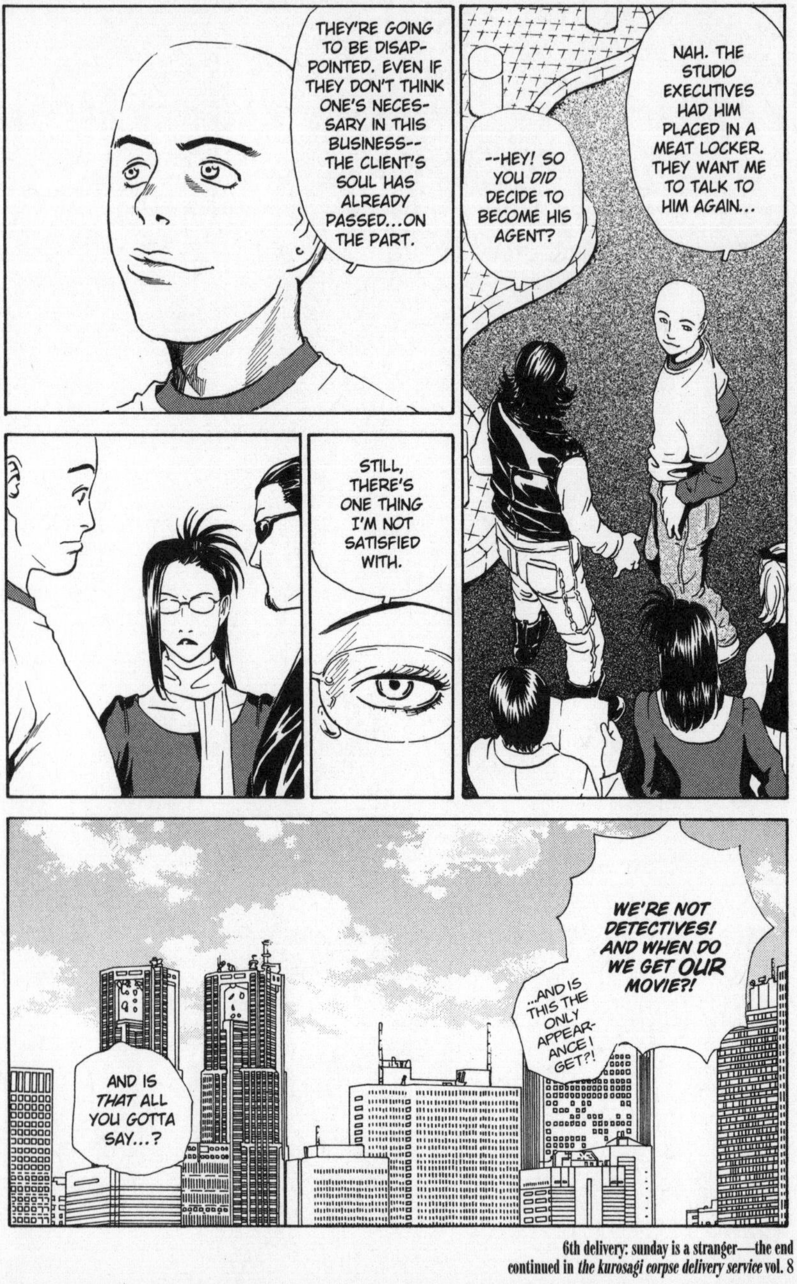
NAH. THE STUDIO EXECUTIVES HAD HIM PLACED IN A MEAT LOCKER. THEY WANT ME TO TALK TO HIM AGAIN...
--HEY! SO YOU *DID* DECIDE TO BECOME HIS AGENT?
THEY'RE GOING TO BE DISAPPOINTED. EVEN IF THEY DON'T THINK ONE'S NECESSARY IN THIS BUSINESS-- THE CLIENT'S SOUL HAS ALREADY PASSED...ON THE PART.
STILL, THERE'S ONE THING I'M NOT SATISFIED WITH.
WE'RE NOT DETECTIVES! AND WHEN DO WE GET OUR MOVIE?!
...AND IS THIS THE ONLY APPEARANCE I GET?!
AND IS *THAT* ALL YOU GOTTA SAY...?

6th delivery: sunday is a stranger—the end
continued in *the kurosagi corpse delivery service* vol. 8

DISJECTA MEMBRA

SOUND FX GLOSSARY AND NOTES ON *KUROSAGI* VOL. 7 BY TAYLOR ENGEL AND TOSHIFUMI YOSHIDA

introduction and additional comments by the editor

TO INCREASE YOUR ENJOYMENT of the distinctive Japanese visual style of this manga, we've included a guide to the sound effects (or "FX") used in this manga. It is suggested the reader *not* constantly consult this glossary as they read through, but regard it as supplemental information, in the manner of footnotes. If you want to imagine it being read aloud by Osaka, after the manner of her lecture to Sakaki on hemorrhoids in episode five of *Azumanga Daioh*, please go right ahead. In either Yuki Matsuoka or Kira Vincent-Davis's voice— I like them both.

Japanese, like English, did not independently invent its own writing system, but instead borrowed and modified the system used by then-dominant cultural power in their part of the world. We still call the letters we use to write English today the "Roman" alphabet, for the simple reason that about 1600 years ago the earliest English speakers, living on the frontier of the Roman Empire, began to use the same letters the Romans used for their Latin language to write out English.

Around that very same time, on the other side of the planet, Japan, like England, was another example of an island civilization lying across the sea from a great empire, in this case, that of China. Likewise the Japanese borrowed from the Chinese writing system, which then, as now, consisted of thousands of complex symbols— today in China officially referred to in the Roman alphabet as *hanzi*, but which the Japanese pronounce as *kanji*. For example,

all the Japanese characters you see on the front cover of *The Kurosagi Corpse Delivery Service*—the seven which make up the original title and the four each which make up the creators' names—are examples of kanji. Of course, all of them were hanzi first—although the Japanese did also invent some original kanji of their own, just as new hanzi have been created over the centuries as Chinese evolved.

(Note that whereas both *kanji* and *hanzi* are examples of writing foreign words in Roman letters, "kanji" gives English speakers a fairly good idea of how the Japanese word is really pronounced— *khan-gee*—whereas "hanzi" does not—in Mandarin Chinese it sounds something like *n-tsuh*. The reason is fairly simple: whereas the most commonly used method of writing Japanese in Roman letters, called the Hepburn system, was developed by a native English speaker, the most commonly used method of writing Chinese in Roman letters, called the Pinyin system, was developed by native Mandarin speakers. In fact, Pinyin was developed to help teach Mandarin pronunciation to speakers of other Chinese dialects; unlike Hepburn, it was not intended as a learning tool for English speakers per se, and hence has no particular obligation to "make sense" to English speakers or, indeed, users of the many other languages spelled with the Roman alphabet.)

Whereas the various dialects of Chinese are written entirely in hanzi, it is impractical to render the Japanese language entirely in them. To compare once more, English is a notoriously difficult language in which to spell properly, and this is in part because it uses an alphabet designed for another language, Latin, whose sounds are different (this is, of course, putting aside the fact the sounds of both languages experienced change over time). The challenges the Japanese faced in using the Chinese writing system for their own language were even greater, for whereas spoken English and Latin are at least from a common language family, spoken Japanese is unrelated to any of the various dialects of spoken Chinese. The complicated writing system that Japanese evolved represents an adjustment to these great differences.

When the Japanese borrowed hanzi to become kanji, what they were getting was a way to write out (remember, they already had ways to *say*) their vocabulary. Nouns, verbs, many adjectives, the names of places and people—that's what kanji are used for, the fundamental data of the written language. The practical use and processing of that "data"—its grammar and pronunciation—is another matter entirely. Because spoken Japanese neither sounds nor functions like Chinese, the first work-around tried was a system called *manyogana*, where individual kanji were picked to represent certain syllables in Japanese. A similar method is still used in Chinese today to spell out foreign names; companies and individuals often try to choose hanzi for this purpose that have an auspicious, or at least not insulting, meaning. As you will also observe in *Kurosagi* and elsewhere, the meaning behind the characters that make up a personal name are an important literary element of Japanese as well.

The commentary in *Katsuya Terada's The Monkey King* (also available from Dark Horse, and also translated by Toshifumi Yoshida) notes the importance that not only Chinese, but also Indian culture had on Japan at this time in history—particularly through Buddhism. Similarly, in Western history at this time, religious communities in Asia were associated with learning, since priests and monks were more likely to be literate than other groups in society. It is believed the Northeast Indian *Siddham* script studied by Kukai (died 835 AD), founder of the Shingon sect of Japanese Buddhism, inspired him to create the solution for writing Japanese still used today. Kukai is credited with the idea of taking the manyogana and making shorthand versions of them—which are now known simply as *kana*. The improvement in efficiency was dramatic: a kanji, used previously to represent a sound, that might have taken a dozen strokes to draw, was now reduced to three or four.

Unlike the original kanji they were based on, the new kana had *only* a sound meaning. And unlike the thousands of kanji, there are only forty-six kana, which can be used to spell out any word in the Japanese language, including the many ordinarily written with kanji (Japanese keyboards work on this principle). The same set of forty-six kana is written two different ways depending on their intended use: cursive style, *hiragana*, and block style, *katakana*. Naturally, sound FX in manga are almost always written out using kana.

Kana work somewhat differently than the Roman alphabet. For example, while there are separate kana for each of the five vowels (the Japanese order is not A-E-I-O-U as in English, but A-I-U-E-O), there are, except for "n," no separate kana for consonants (the middle "n" in the word *ninja* illustrates this exception). Instead, kana work by grouping together consonants with vowels: for example, there are five kana for sounds starting with "k," depending on which vowel follows it—in Japanese vowel order, they go KA, KI, KU, KE, KO. The next set of kana begins with "s" sounds, so SA, SHI, SU, SE, SO, and so on. You will observe this kind of consonant-vowel pattern in the FX listings for *Kurosagi* Vol. 7 below.

Katakana are almost always the kind that get used for manga sound FX, but on occasion hiragana are used instead. This is commonly done when the sound is one associated with a human body, but can be a subtler aesthetic choice by the artist as well. In *Kurosagi* Vol. 7 you can see an example on 43.5, with the HYUBA swish-strike of the sword, which in hiragana style is written ひゅばつ. Note its more cursive appearance compared to the other FX. If it had been written in katakana style, it would look like ヒュバツ.

To see how to use this glossary, take an example from page 8: "8.4 FX: BON—sound of something exploding under hood." 8.4 means the FX is the one on page 8, in panel 4. BON is the sound these kana—ボンツ—literally stand for. After the dash comes an explanation of what the sound represents (in some cases, it will be less obvious than others). Note that in cases where there are two or more different sounds in a single panel, an extra number is used to differentiate them from right to left; or, in cases where right and left are less clear, in clockwise order.

The use of kana in these FX also illustrates another aspect of written Japanese—its flexible reading order. For example, the way you're reading the pages and panels of this book in general: going from right to left, and from top to bottom—is similar to the order in which Japanese is also written in most forms of print: books, magazines, and newspapers. However, many of the FX in *Kurosagi* (and manga in general) read left to right. This kind of flexibility is also to be found on Japanese web pages, which usually also read left to right. In other words, Japanese doesn't simply read "the other way" from English; the Japanese themselves are used to reading it in several different directions.

As might be expected, some FX "sound" short, and others "sound" long. Manga represent this in different ways. One of many instances of "short sounds" in *Kurosagi* Vol. 7 is to be found in the example from 43.5 given above: HYUBA. See the small つ mark it has at the end—note again that this is the hiragana "tsu," and you will far more often see it in its katakana form, ツ, as (for example) in the other above example, 8.4's BON. This mark ordinarily represents the sound "tsu," but its half-size use at the end of FX like this means the sound is the kind which stops or cuts off suddenly; that's why the sound is written as BON and not BONTSU—you don't "pronounce" the TSU in such cases. Note the small "tsu" has another occasional use *inside*, rather than at the end, of a particular FX, where it indicates a doubling of the consonant sound that follows it.

There are three different ways you may see "long sounds"—where a vowel sound is extended—written out as FX. One is with an ellipsis, as in 6.2.1's BURORORO. Another is with an extended line, as in 78.3's SUU KOO. Still another is by simply repeating a vowel several times, as in 69.5's KIIIIIIIIN. You will note that the KOO in 78.3's SUU KOO has a "tsu" at its end, suggesting an elongated sound that's suddenly cut off; the methods may be combined within a single FX. As a visual element in manga, FX are an art rather than a science, and are used in a less rigorous fashion than kana are in standard written Japanese.

The explanation of what the sound represents may sometimes be surprising, but every culture "hears" sounds differently. Note that manga FX do not even necessarily represent literal sounds. Such "mimetic" words, which represent an imagined sound, or even a state of mind, are called *gitaigo* in Japanese. Like the onomatopoeic *giseigo* (the words used to represent literal sounds—i.e., most FX in this glossary are classed as giseigo), they are also used in colloquial speech and writing. A Japanese, for example, might say that something bounced by saying PURIN, or talk about eating by saying MUGU MUGU. It's something like describing chatter in English by saying "yadda yadda yadda" instead.

One important last note: all these spelled-out kana vowels should be pronounced as they are in Japanese: "A" as *ah*, "I" as *eee*, "U" as *ooh*, "E" as *eh*, and "O" as *oh*.

2.1   We're back to once again having song titles for this volume. This time around, they're all singles from Mako Ishino between 1978 and 1981. Although she began her career as an idol singer, Ishino has moved on to become an actor since her last single was released in 1987. She's appeared in TV series and movies, including a number based off manga, such as *Ping Pong* (as Player A's mom), *Boys Over Flowers* (as Tsukushi's mom) and *Dance Till Tomorrow* (as Shimo-mura). The translator notes, by the way, that the title of "1st Delivery"

could be alternately rendered as "Challenge of My Heart," and "6th Delivery"'s as "A Stranger Called Sunday."

6.2.1   **FX/balloon: BURORORO—** engine sound

6.2.2   **FX/balloon: KI—**car brake sound. "Pure Land," *joodo* in Japanese, is a reference to a popular form of Buddhism as practiced in East Asia (in Southeast Asia and Sri Lanka the doctrine is less common) that stresses salvation through faith and prayer to the incarnation of the Buddha named Amitabha. This is in contrast to the "classic" practice of Buddhism, in which salvation depends on the individual's own effort toward proper works and mindfulness. Pure Land Buddhists believe that Amitabha perceived that worldly existence is so corrupt as to stand in the way of most beings' personal enlightenment, so he created a pure land as a sanctuary that souls might reach after death by having faith in Amitabha, known as *Amida* in Japanese. To reach the pure land after death is not the same thing as achieving final enlightenment, but it is believed to be a place where all souls can and will receive enlightenment, as opposed to the uncertainty and suffering of being reborn into the ordinary world.

7.2   No, you're not imagining things—Karatsu is back to more or less normal after Vol. 6's cliffhanger, with no explanation as to what happened to him between then and now. We are assured Eiji

Otsuka will explain this . . . in good time, reader, in good time.

8.2 In case you're wondering *what was therein inhum'd* (to quote H. P. Lovecraft) in a Japanese cemetery such as this one, the answer is, of course, the ashes of the dead, which take up much less space than an actual body.

8.4.1 FX: BON—sound of something exploding under hood

8.4.2 FX/balloon: MOWA—sound of smoke starting to come out

10.2 FX/balloon: PETA—applying heating/cooling patch

10.3 As you might guess, these are heating/cooling patches for shoulder aches and back pain. Harix brand company homepage, yo: http://www.harix.jp/.

12.1.1 FX/balloon: GASHA—sound of shifting metal

12.1.2 FX/balloon: GASHA—sound of shifting metal

12.3 FX/balloon: GA—grabbing sound

12.4.1 FX/balloon: SHU—sound of pneumatics activating

12.4.2 FX/balloon: SHUU—sound of pneumatics

14.6 Each of the robotics students is, of course, named after the inventor of the (imaginary) robot whose paradigm they champion: Tomino, from Yoshiyuki Tomino, creator of *Gundam* (he's also wearing the Zeon symbol from *Gundam* on his T-shirt); Nagai, from Go Nagai, creator of *Mazinger Z* (he likewise wears a "Z" on his own shirt); and Tezuka, from—wait for

it—Osamu Tezuka, creator of *Astro Boy* (she, showing somewhat better taste, sports a white turtleneck). As you can see from their conversation, they represent three different images anime has given pop culture in Japan of what a "robot" is. *Gundam*, which premiered in 1979, epitomizes the so-called "real robot," where a robot is a mass-produced weapon, just like a plane or tank, made for future wars driven by politics, ideology, or economics, just like today's wars. *Mazinger Z*, which premiered in 1972, exemplified the "super robot," where a robot is a rare or unique machine that typically fights the "monster of the week" unleashed by the flamboyant forces of evil. The distinction is valid, yet is also understandably often lost on people who aren't otaku, seeing as how both kinds of shows involve young pilots commanding giant, humanoid robots; moreover, popular shows such as 1995's *Evangelion* combined elements of the "super" and "real" robot, to the extent that fans now speak of "hybrid robot" shows. If you haven't fallen asleep by now, the larger distinction would seem to be between both "super" and "real" robots and the kind exemplified by *Astro Boy*. Some would say that, properly speaking, those former two categories aren't robots at all, and when you think "robot," you really mean something like the eponymous Astro Boy—not a machine with a human inside controlling it, but a human-sized machine that independently moves and thinks on its own. Of course, Americans might be more likely to think of the Terminator, rather than Astro Boy . . . In Brian Winston's fascinating book *Media Technology and Society*, the author shows that inventions are developed not only because they become technically possible, but because society shows a need for them; conversely, if society doesn't desire an invention, its progress might be slowed or abandoned. Japan seems to be the world leader in robotics in part because their society seems simply to like the idea of robots more than ours, and it's fair to say that *is* in part due to the influence of manga such as *Astro Boy*.

15.1 Yata's remark makes me think about the *Akira* movie. It's one of the greatest anime films ever made, and in fact made such a strong impression in the late '80s and early '90s, that fans sometimes had trouble explaining to newcomers that not all anime had to be like *Akira*. But, to many of today's anime fans, *Akira* isn't something that's overexposed—*Akira* is something that came out before they were *born*.

15.5 **FX: SHUU**—air leaking sound

17.3 **FX: ZURURURU**—dragging sound

18.2 **FX: GACHA**—door opening

18.3 **FX: DOSASA**—group falling down exhausted

18.4 **FX/balloon: KIIN**—sound of metal tip of cane striking floor

19.2 I can't help but notice that, although Ao and Sasayama presumably also wear glasses to correct vision, theirs are more stylish than Nagai, Tezuka, and Tomino's. At Fanime-Con '08, it seemed half the Gainax contingent was wearing the kind of narrow, Chanel-style frames that Ao sports. Of course, from a *meganekko* perspective, it's frequently the case that the bigger and more unstylish the glasses, the *more* erotic, as seen with Nagai, Koyomi Mizuhara, Yomiko Readman, or Morrissey when he did "Heaven Knows I'm Miserable Now" on *Top of the Pops*. I'm sorry to sexualize everything, but when I became an otaku, I gave up my moral rights, much like a Shining Stars contract.

22.1 The "Broadband Center" in which the rest of this story takes place is a play on the actual Nakano Broadway building, a multistory shopping center in the Nakano district of Tokyo. Akihabara is the neighborhood that gets international attention for its otaku scene (even in Japan, ordinary folk have been known to gawk at the ~~beautiful~~ freaks, the same way they used to have bus tours of Haight-Ashbury in the 1960s). But Nakano is the older hardcore fan hangout, for in 1987, Mandarake was established in the Broadway Building—and Mandarake was basically the first collector's store for anime and manga goods (it is a sign, perhaps, of how mainstream comics are in Japan, that it took so long to develop a specialized collectors' market). The Kurosagi gang drove there, but you'll probably take the JR Chuo Line. Getting off at Nakano Station, you'll take the north exit and enter a long, broad hallway that looks more or less like an American shopping mall—but this is only the Sun Mall Shopping Center, and the Broadway, attached to it, is at the end. The Broadway itself, being a forty-year-old building, is narrower in its walkways and is divided into small, swap-meet-sized partitions, of which some stores take up only one, while others (such as Mandarake) take up many. Not only does Broadway have the goods (there are *nineteen* different Mandarake substores inside, each specializing in such wares as doujinshi, toys, old videocassettes, LDs, and even 8mm reels), it has character: the vegetarian restaurant, mysterious flyers posted about, and Taco Ché, the world's greatest postcard and T-shirt store, give parts of it a vaguely student-union air. The nicest thing about both Mandarake and the Broadway Building is that they're genuinely interested in foreign customers; Mandarake has staff that speak English, Spanish, French, Korean, and Mandarin. The English-language homepage of Mandarake's store in the Broadway is http://www.mandarake.co.jp/en/shop/nkn.html, whereas the English-language page of the Broadway Building itself is at www.bwy.jp, although, mysteriously, it plays Paris Hilton's "Stars Are Blind" upon opening. As much as I feel she betrayed the proud legacy of Conrad Hilton (growing up in hotel rooms with their Gideons, I thought *Be My Guest* was the Apocrypha), it's a perfectly good song. Let us separate the creator from their art.

22.2 *Toradarake* is a portmanteau—if that's the word I'm looking for, Jeeves—of Mandarake with the name of another real-life store, Toranoana. There is, in fact, no Toranoana in the Broadway Building (there are five of the stores in other parts of Tokyo, however, including Akihabara), but the zombie robot is probably artistic license, too. Toranoana (which, unlike Mandarake, does not make foreign sales) specializes in selling doujinshi—self-published zines, usually consisting of manga content—and as you may have heard, most doujinshi are unauthorized parodies of licensed characters (there are so many "doujin" published, however, that there are thousands of original ones each year as well). But, being a brick-and-mortar store chain, it represents just how un-underground doujinshi are in Japan; in fact, Toranoana habitually takes out the back-cover ad on the monthly *Shonen Ace* magazine, the original home of *Kurosagi*—and of many manga parodied in the doujinshi Toranoana sells. Now, this utterly cavalier treatment of intellectual property by both rights-holder and fan may seem horrific by American legal standards, but tell me: if it's so detrimental, then how come the Japanese comics industry is much bigger than ours? How come it's better *mon-e-tized?* And don't tell me it's because "the Japanese are different"; that's the same simple excuse that was used in the 1970s and '80s in our auto and electronics industries. Businesses and legal practices reflect a larger culture, but they are also things that are changed by people and companies, through new decisions, theories, and initiatives. History doesn't have to run in a straight line; consider that in the 1980s, the trendsetting portable music player was Japanese, the Sony Walkman; today, it is American, Apple's iPod. Speaking of turning things around, perhaps you're wondering if anyone's made a *Kurosagi Corpse Delivery Service* doujinshi in Japan. No, not that I know of. Show the world the true spirit of Yankee innovation, and be the first! I heard there's a Yata/Karatsu shipper out there.

22.3 There actually *is* a swap-meet element to the Nakano Broadway; some of its myriad glass display cases are the wares of its resident stores, but some are available for a monthly rent to individual collectors, who can use them to show off and sell their personal stuff on consignment. Now, having just sung a long paragraph of praise about the Mandarake in Nakano, Patrick Macias and Matt Alt have reported on the recent opening of the *new* Mandarake store in the T-shirt-stretched belly of the beast, Akihabara, saying that it appears to have better stock than the one in Nakano. Hear the scoop on episode #4 of the official podcast of *Otaku USA*, the magazine that's putting the man into the manga, and the fu fu into the fujoshi (http://patrickmacias.blogs.com/er/files/otaku_usa_podcast_4.mp3).

22.3.1 All right, back to the sound effects.

23.2 **FX: GYU**—tightening his bandanna

23.3 **FX/balloon: GASHAN GASHAN**—sound of metallic footsteps

23.4 **FX: GASHA GASHA GASHAN**—metallic footsteps

24.3.1 **FX: GASHA**—pulling out cartridge sound

24.3.2 **FX/balloon: BIKU BIKUN**—robot shuddering/twitching when the cart is pulled

24.4 **FX: GAKUN**—robot slumping over

24.5 In the original Japanese, she said a Famicom cartridge—which was what Nintendo was called in Japan (it was a contraction of *Family Computer*).

24.6 Made up, from combining the genuine games *Super Mario Brothers* and *Donkey Kong*.

25.2 Whereas Americans pronounce the letter "Z" as *zee*, the Japanese use the traditional British *zed*, pronounced as *zetto*; hence *Mazinger Z* is sometimes spoken out as *Mazinger Zetto*. "Soul of Chogokin" is the name of Bandai's line of high-end adult collector's toys based on classic robot series such as *Mazinger Z*; in the anime, the robot itself was said to be made of *chogokin*, or "super alloy." This is the same Mazinger, by the way, that was part of the dope Shogun Warriors toy line, if you were lucky enough to have one in the 1970s. The editor was not lucky enough. Had things worked out differently for him in the Carter years, he would have arranged a fitting showdown between Mazinger and his Marx Navarone Giant Play Set.

25.3 *Pilder on!* is what hot-blooded young hero Koji Kabuto calls out when he docks his Hover Pilder craft with Mazinger Z's head, which then becomes the cockpit where he controls the robot. You're thinking I know why it's called "Pilder," but I don't.

25.4 **FX: GASHU**—sound of the cartridge being put in

25.5.1 **FX/balloon: SHAN**—sound of a robot landing

25.5.2 **FX/balloon: PYON GASHAN**—jumping sound, then a robot landing sound

25.5.3 **FX: YON**—jumping sound

25.5.4 **FX/balloon: PYON GASHAN**—jumping sound, then a robot landing sound

26.2 **FX: GASHA GASHAN**—mechanical footsteps

26.5 It's a cliché in giant robot anime that you start off with such robots being few: rare technological artifacts, or advanced prototypes, and then sooner or later, someone figures out how to make a "mass production version."

27.3 **FX: MOGO**—muffled sound

27.4.1 **FX/balloon: JAAA**—sound of running water

27.4.2 **FX/balloon: KYU**—sound of a tap being closed

27.5 **FX/balloon: CHARARAN**—sound of pendulum falling on the floor

27.6 **FX/balloon: GUKI**—sound of lower back straining

27.7 **FX: PURAN PURAN**—sound of the pendulum dangling

28.2 **FX: HYUN HYUN**—sound of the pendulum swinging

30.1 The last ten years have seen a lot of new anime shows assigned to late-night time slots on cable—generally, this happens to shows that are considered to have appeal mainly to hardcore fans, as opposed to an anime directed at the mass market such as *Naruto*, which would air at better hours. *Neon Genesis Evangelion* was on broadcast TV at 7 PM on Sundays; but I suspect that were the show to have aired for the first time today, it might have been assigned to late-night cable instead—where it might never reach the nationwide audience among whom it became a phenomenon in 1995.

30.3 **FX/balloon: PURAN**—sound of the controller dangling

31.1 **FX: TA TA TA**—running sound

31.4 **FX/balloon: GASHAAN**—sound of breaking glass

31.5 The cat ears, or *nekomimi*, are part of the real Toranoana staff style, as their mascot is a tiger cub (*tora* means tiger), and the store name itself is said to come from writer Ikki Kajiwara (cocreator also of the famous sports manga *Ashita no Joe* and *Star of the Giants*) and artist Naoki Tsuji's wrestling epic *Tiger Mask*. Fred Schodt had a genius in his 1983 book *Manga! Manga!* for picking panels that seemed to sum up an entire series, and I vividly remember (this was in the late Rory Root's onetime store on Telegraph Ave., Best of Both Worlds) the image Schodt chose for *Tiger Mask*, showing the eponymously vizarded hero launching himself feet first at his hooded foe Golgotha Cross—who takes his stance in the ring next to a giant, nail-studded cross, for he is Golgotha Cross by name, and Golgotha Cross by nature. You can see why I spent the twenty bucks

I had planned for *X-Men* #121 on *Manga! Manga!* instead—even Claremont, Byrne, and Austin put together couldn't compete with *that*.

33.4 **FX: GASHAN GASHAN GASHAN**—running robot sound

33.5 **FX: PITA**—robot stopping

34.1 **FX: GASHA GASHA GASHA**—robot footsteps

35.1.1 **FX: GORORO**—rolling sound

35.1.2 **FX/balloon: GASHAN**—sound of robot hitting the ground

35.2 **FX/balloon: KARAN**—faceplate clanking on ground

37.3 Tomino is referring to the famous 1783 observation by Luigi Galvani, who was dissecting a frog when his assistant touched a scalpel to the frog's sciatic nerve. The scalpel, having built up an electrical charge earlier, transferred it to the nerve, causing the frog's leg to kick. This was the first evidence that electricity had a role to play in animating life, and, as you might guess, helped to inspire Mary Shelley's 1818 novel *Frankenstein*.

37.4 **FX/balloon: PIKU**—robot twitching

37.5 **FX: CHIRA**—glancing over sound

38.1 **FX/balloon: SU**—picking up game

38.3 **FX/balloon: GACHA**—sound of a game cart being pushed in

38.4 **FX/box: PIRO RIRO RIROOON**—8-bit game music starting. This is the editor's attempt to express the *Donkey Kong* theme, the only 8-bit theme he knows.

39.1 **FX: GASHA GASHAN GASHAN**—robot footsteps

39.5 **FX/balloon: PI**—pressing a button on the cell phone

40.2 **FX: PIPA**—hanging-up sound

41.2.1 **FX: GASHAN**—breaking glass

41.2.2 **FX: PARIN**—falling glass shattering

41.4 **FX/robot: PIRORIROON**—video-game sound

42.1 The translator suggests Zombie-kun is swinging Guts's sword from *Berserk*, whereas the blade to the right looks like the Master Sword from the *Zelda* video-game series, and the sword to the left seems to come from *Card Captor Sakura*.

43.4 **FX: DOKA DOKA**—running up stairs sound

43.5 **FX: HYUBA**—giant sword coming down

44.1.1 **FX: BAKYAAAN**—plastic sword shattering

44.1.2 **FX/balloon: KAN**—piece of sword hitting escalator

44.1.3 **FX/balloon: KARARAN**—piece of sword hitting escalator

44.4 **FX: BA**—putting hand on head

45.4 **FX: NU**—sound of the soul coming out

47.1 Even at this critical moment in the plot, please note the *Magical Maid Girl Mumume-Tan R* poster—the character Makino was forced to cosplay in Vol. 5. The "R" implies that a sequel has now been made, as the second season of *Sailor Moon* was called *Sailor Moon R* (for "Return"). You have not, by the way, seen the last of Mumume-tan in this manga.

47.2 FX: FURA—body starting to fall over

47.3.1 FX/balloon: GARA GARA—sound of robot sliding down escalator

47.3.2 FX/balloon: GASHAN—robot coming to a stop at the bottom

49.1 As you may have noticed, there are two translation credits in Vol.7; right after Toshifumi Yoshida did "1st Delivery," he had to take a hiatus from the book—but for a good cause, as he was hired by Bandai as an anime dub producer, his first assignment being the English version of *Tengen Toppa Gurren Lagann*, which should have been on the Sci-Fi Channel's Ani-Monday block for several weeks by the time you read this (as mentioned previously in "Disjecta Membra," Toshi was the producer of the English dubs of *Inu-Yasha*, *Ranma 1/2*, *Maison Ikkoku*, and *Jin-Roh*). I am grateful to Taylor Engel who was able to pinch-hit for the rest of the volume; many of the notes in this volume's "Disjecta Membra" are therefore also hers.

49.2 FX: KA—high heel clicking on pavement

50.1 FX: GOOOOO—sound of speeding truck

50.3 FX: SU—hands being stealthily raised

50.4 FX: KU—pushing

50.5 FX: YORO—woman stumbling forward

51.1 FX: PAAAA—truck's horn blaring

51.2 FX: DOKO—whud!

51.3.1 FX/balloon: BYUCHA—wet splatter

51.3.2 FX/balloon: BITA—something splattering and sticking

51.4 FX/balloon: KIIII—squealing brakes

55.3 FX: ZA—turning to leave

56.1 FX/balloon: PARA—page turning

56.3 FX/balloon: GACHA—Door opening

57.5 Sydney-based Japanese media scholar and artist Zen Yipu has written in a 2004 issue of the journal *Humanities Research* on "generations of Japanese female audiences who have idolized and imitated Audrey Hepburn . . . She is popular not only among middle-aged women who have grown up watching her movies, and therefore might have nostalgic memories of her, but also among young women in their mid-20s who would have no such recollections of her. This latter group has learnt about her either through watching old films or through seeing her 'reincarnations' [as a number of dead actors have in America, Hepburn has been CG-reanimated for commercials in Japan—ed.] in the marketplace. There is no other western idol who enjoys the same level of popularity in Japan, a popularity which endures even today, in 2004, more than a decade after her death." Zen goes on to quote Japan's trend-tracking magazine *Dime*'s explanation that "[Hepburn] has black hair, black eyes and a slender physique just like the Japanese. Unlike the blonde glamour of a [Marilyn] Monroe type, her appearance has a feeling of familiarity with that of the Japanese female."

58.3 See 19.2. Or read *Dime*, which, by the way, is published by Shogakukan, better known in the U.S. for their manga. It's good to remember that manga publishers large and small in Japan are often part of larger book- and magazine-publishing entities. *The Kurosagi Corpse Delivery Service*, for example, appears in Kadokawa's *Comic Charge* magazine, but Kadokawa's best-selling magazine isn't a manga one, but rather the weekly what's-happening-in-town *Tokyo Walker*. Complicating the issue a bit more in the best "Disjecta Membra" manner, non-manga magazines in Japan are known to sometimes have a regular manga feature. Yoshinori Kobayashi's controversial (*"How would you feel about playing a controversial manga-ka?"* *"Yeah, I'm with it!"*) *Gomanism Sengen* ("The Arrogance Manifesto") runs in the contemporary biweekly affairs newsmagazine *Sapio*, whereas Kazuo Koike and Hideki Mori's *New Lone Wolf and Cub* ran in the weekly (middle-aged) men's magazine *Shukan Post*. Such a slot in a nonmanga magazine might be advantageous for an individual manga, since it doesn't have to compete for attention with other stories, may connect with people who ordinarily wouldn't follow manga (there are plenty of these in Japan; comics readership isn't universal in Japan,

it's just wider and more accepted than in the U.S.), and, as mentioned, may find itself having a wider circulation than in an actual manga magazine.

60.1 **FX: SARAN**—hair being swept out of the way, model-style.

62.5.1 **FX/balloon: HIKU**—twitching

62.5.2 **FX/balloon: PIKU**—quiver

62.6 **FX/balloon: PACHI**—eyes opening

65.2 The woman in back is wearing the habit of a Buddhist nun, or *bhikkhuni*. It is the editor's impression that even though neither Asian nor European culture has had any shortage of sexism, nevertheless it was historically more accepted and respectable for women to take holy orders in Catholicism than Buddhism—perhaps because of the prominence given to a figure such as the Virgin Mary. Even though Buddhism has the longer tradition in Japan, it seems more common to find Catholic nuns as heroines in manga, such as Rosette Christopher of *Chrono Crusade* and Yumie Takagi from *Hellsing*. Now, these nuns are admittedly portrayed with a smidgen of poetic license, but at least Japan still thinks nuns are cute, an attitude that hasn't been seen in the West since the youth of Sally Field.

66.4 **FX/balloon: DON**—jabbing with elbow

67.1 The translator notes a *jinmenso* is usually seen as able to talk and even eat, and can therefore be killed by feeding it medicine or poison. It is possibly inspired by the rare congenital abnormality of a parasitic twin.

67.2 FX: SU—drawing photos out of file

67.3 FX/balloon: BASA—scattering photos across table

68.2 In the original Japanese, Kereellis said *Nande ya nen!* which the translator points out means "What was *that* for?" in a Kansai accent (usually associated with the city of Osaka, which bears a cultural relationship to Tokyo *somewhat* comparable to that which Brooklyn or New Jersey does to Manhattan). It's a stock phrase in traditional Kansai *manzai*, or double act comedy. The internationally known actor and director Takeshi Kitano (*Battle Royale*, *HANA-BI*) got his start in manzai; although well known in Japan as a comedian, perhaps the closest Americans have gotten to that side of him is on Spike TV's *MXC*, a facetiously dubbed version of his late-'80s game show *Takeshi's Castle* (like *Iron Chef*, it has been one of the more internationally popular Japanese live-action series).

68.4 FX: PORI—scritch

69.4 FX: SU—soft touch

69.5 FX: KIIIIIIIIIN—high-pitched ringing in the ears

70-71.2 FX: BA—energy (?) shooting from hand

70-71.3 FX: BA BA—energy (?) shooting from hand

72.3 FX: ZUZU—Karatsu's soul getting pulled out of his body

73.3 FX/balloon: PON—slapping on the shoulder

73.4 FX: DOSA—Karatsu's body falling to the floor

77.2 It is assumed "someone like that" refers to Karatsu, but the pronoun she uses isn't gendered, so there's a possibility that she means someone else.

78.1 You can set your watch by the Kadokawa references in *Kurosagi*, and here it turns out they run the "Kadokawa Central Hospital," too.

78.3.1 FX/balloon: SUU KOO—breathing on a respirator

78.3.2 FX/balloon: SUU—breathing on a respirator

78.4 FX/balloon: GACHYA—door opening

82.1 The translator notes that her chuckling in the original has the sound *u fu fu*, a sort of "weird, close-mouthed" sound for which it's hard to find an exact equivalent in American English.

82.4 FX/balloon: KATA—Clipboard clicking against the desk. Note the chart claims Makino is only *18!* Although that would make her elderly by the standards of many manga, it seems perhaps too young for someone who's presumably been in college a while. Of course, she might have either a.) started college early, or b.) be lying on the form. Sasaya-ma's transition in appearance between *MPD-Psycho* and *Kurosagi* certainly establishes a precedent for uncertainty in an Eiji Otsuka manga.

83.4 FX: SU—standing up

85.2 FX/balloon: KASA KASA—sawdust rustling

86.1 In Japanese, "ear" is mimi (see 31.5), but in the original manga, Numata heard it as "*mini*," and thought Makino was referring to Minnie Mouse. It's interesting to observe his thought processes.

86.3 In the August 1997 issue of the journal *Plastic and Reconstructive Surgery*. The doctors were Joseph P. Vacanti, Keith T. Paige, and Joseph Upton; the biomaterials engineer was Yilin Cao—although he in fact holds a medical degree as well. Incidentally, the editor started working professionally in the U.S. anime and manga industry while a medical librarian in Houston (it was more *Slacker* than *Reality Bites*), a job that could have inspired any number of *Corpse Delivery Service* stories. The library was eliminated from the Texas Medical Center's budget (and much of its holdings simply thrown away; I made off with a 16mm film in French about onchocerciasis) in part, I was told, because of the massive subscription fees charged at the time to institutions—as much as $15,000 a year per journal. It looked to me back then as if the *real* money was in publishing.

87.5 FX/balloon: CHORO—skitter

89.3 FX: TO TO TO—mouse scampering over

90.2 FX/balloon: GACHYA—door opening

90.4.1 FX/balloon: SUU KOO—breathing on a respirator

90.4.2 FX/balloon: SUU—breathing on a respirator

91.1 FX: SU—soft touch

94.1 FX/balloon: FURARI—unsteady, faltering walk

94.3 FX: PAAAAA—car horn honking

94.4 FX: DOGA—whud! Did you spot the Kadokawa building? The real Kadokawa building, by the way, has their phoenix logo rendered on its front in a pattern of raised bricks.

94.5 FX/balloon: KII—Squealing brakes

95.1 FX: GACHYA—door opening

95.2 In the original Japanese, "big bro" (as said by a man) is *aniki*. Its use in this context suggests the two are involved in organized crime—as small-timers, from the look of it.

96.2 By the way, the Japanese above "MENTAL CLINIC" says "Jenny Kayama," the name of the proprietor.

98.1 FX: GORORI—head rolling over lazily

100.1 FX: DOKO—whump!

105.2 FX: GOOOO—speeding car

106.4 FX: KII—car braking

109.4 FX/balloon: BATAN—door closing sharply

110.1 FX: DOSA—body bag being dumped on the ground

110.4.1 FX/balloon: MOZO GOSO—something rustling inside thick fabric

110.4.2 FX/balloon: KATSU KOTSU—heels clicking on tile

113.1 The letterer notes that this image puts him in mind of the 1999 Korean horror film *Tell Me Something*.

114.4 FX: JIRIRIRIRIRIRI—fire alarm

114.5 **FX: GOOOOO**—fire roaring

115.1 **FX: KYUBON**—the sound of a glass-fronted building exploding

115.2 **FX/balloon: CHU CHU**—mouse squeaking

117.1.1 **FX/balloon: BON**—container clanging over onto its side

117.1.2 **FX/balloon: BAKAN**—lid popping off from the heat

117.2 **FX: GOOO**—fire roaring

117.5 **FX/balloon: GOPON**—underwater burbling

117.6 **FX: SA**—Sasaki shifting position, quickly

119.1 **FX: KIIIIN**—high-pitched ringing in the ears

121.1 The translator notes that Sasaki's spirit form has kept her glasses on, even though she's lost her clothes. But that's the power of a *meganekko*.

122.1 **FX: BAGASHAAAN**—tank shattering

123.2 **FX: DOCHA**—splish

123.3.1 FX: PICHA—drip

123.3.2 FX: BECHARI—wet squishing

123.4 **FX: PICHIRI**—wet bare footstep

128.1 **FX: DOSA**—Numata dumping the corpse on Yata

128.2 **FX/balloon: ZA**—quick movement

128.3 **FX: DOSU**—whump!

129.1 **FX: GOOOOOO**—roaring fire

129.2 **FX/balloon: JIJI**—paper sizzling away

129.3.1 FX/balloon: BON—muffled explosion

129.3.2 FX/balloon: PACHIN—glass shattering

130.1 **FX/balloon: SA**—Sasaki turning quickly

132.4.1 FX: PIIIPOOOPIIIPOOO—fire engine sirens

132.4.2 FX: UUUUUU—alarm

133.1 They are all cosplaying literary detectives: Karatsu as Kousuke Kindaichi—also the "real" protagonist of the movie being parodied in this episode—a fictional Japanese sleuth made famous in the postwar novels of Seishi Yokomizo. The manga series *The Kindaichi Case Files*, released in the U.S. by Tokyopop ("Disjecta Membra"'s cracks taketh away, and "Disjecta Membra"'s cracks giveth) stars Hajime, the supposed grandson of Yokomizo's character, although it is said, much as with *Lupin III*, this is an unauthorized tribute. Makino is doing . . . oh, who could that be. Numata, not surprisingly, is playing private eye Shunsaku Kudo, from the 1979–90 TV series *Tantei Monogatari* ("Detective Story"), portrayed by the late Yusaku Matsuda, an actor still the epitome of cool to many Japanese men—his appearance is said to have inspired that of Spike Spiegel in *Cowboy Bebop*. Anyway, Yata is dressed as Agatha Christie's Belgian, not French, detective Hercule Poirot, whereas Sasaki (rather charmingly) portrays Christie's Miss Marple. The appearance of these last two is possibly inspired by the recent 2004–2005 anime series on NHK,

Agatha Christie's Great Detectives Poirot and Marple (homepage http://www3.nhk.or.jp/anime/agatha/).

134.2.1 FX: JYABU JYABU—splash splash

134.2.2 FX: CHAPU—splish

135.3 The director's shirt has the kanji for *konbu*, seaweed, which is also the character's last name. He is a parody of the late Ichikawa Kon, who died on February 13 of this year at the age of 92, the last surviving representative of a group of directors (including Akira Kurosawa and Hiroshi Inagaki) who brought Japanese cinema to world attention in the 1950s.

136.1 The film being shot here is a parody of Ichikawa Kon's *Inugamike no ichizoku*, or *The Inugami Clan*. Written in 1950, this is one of Seishi Yokomizo's famous Kousuke Kindaichi mysteries—the story of the death of silk tycoon Sahei Inugami at his lakeside villa, and the string of gruesome murders over his inheritance that ensue. It has in fact been adapted as a movie three times to date in Japan, in 1954, 1976, and 2006. The last two versions were done by Kon, and the 1976 one, in particular, was one of the biggest domestic box-office successes in Japanese history. It was produced by Haruki Kadokawa—former president of the itself formidable Kadokawa clan. Despite its fame inside Japan, there is no U.S. release on home video, although a Hong Kong (Region 3) DVD under the title *The Inugami Family* is available with English subtitles. An English-language

version of the original novel of *The Inugami Clan* is available from my stromies, my homies, Stone Bridge Press (www.stonebridge.com).

137.5 FX: ZUZU—slurping tea. The detective in the parody is named Koutarou Kintaichi rather than Kousuke Kindaichi; "suke" and "tarou" are both common endings for boys' names.

139.3 Koyama has switched from saying "Makino-san" at the beginning of this conversation to saying "Makino-chan" here; indicating he's gone from formal to familiar.

141.3 FX: SU—appearing abruptly

142.3 FX/balloon: KACHI—clapper board clicking

143.1 FX/balloon: GISHI GISHI—old stair treads creaking

143.4 FX: FU—fainting

143.5 FX/balloon: BATAN—fwump

144.1 FX/balloon: CHIRA—peek

146.4 FX: KAAN—megaphone hitting floor

147.2 FX: DOSU DOSU—stomp stomp

148.3 FX: HYUN HYUN—pendulum swinging vigorously

148.5 The translator notes that this is a remarkably awkward name to try to pronounce in English: "ooh-heh-eh-ohh."

149.2 FX: GURARI—teeter

149.3 FX: DOSA—thump

150.3 FX/balloon: JIWA—seep

153.2 FX: BA!—snatching cell phone away

155.1   **FX: PACHA**—splish

155.3.1 FX: BASHA BASHA—splash splash

155.3.2 FX/balloon: SUI—frog sliding into water

155.7   Makino is, of course, quoting the actress's line from 134.1.

156.5   **FX/balloon: BURORORO**—vrooooom

157.2   **FX: ZA**—footstep

157.6   **FX/balloon: KOKU**—nod

157.7   Judging by Kereellis's expression, that lake must have been mighty chilly, even by the standards of the interstellar void. As the late Sullivan Carew pointed out, "space is one cold motherfucker."

158.3   **FX: GATA**—clatter

158.4   The original Japanese laugh went *hu hu hu hu*, and the translator suggests that English isn't very good at expressing the changing nuance of the laughter here; the first time he laughs, it's a deep-throated chuckle, the second time, it's sort of a menacing snigger, and the last time is full-out maniacal laughter.

159.3   **FX: GU**—tug

159.4   **FX: GU GU**—pulling the mask off

159.5   **FX: PASA**—mask hitting the floor

162.6   **FX: BA**—Koyama turning back quickly

163.3   **FX: DOSU**—heavy thump

164.2   **FX/balloon: BURORORO**—vrooooom

164.4   **FX/balloon: GAKO GAKO**—empty clunking

165.1.1 FX: GON—muted explosion

165.1.2 FX: BAKI—snap

165.1.3 FX/balloon: BO—bursting into flames

165.3.1 FX: BAKI BEKI—snapping underbrush noises

165.3.2 FX/balloon: BA—car becoming airborne

166.1   **FX/balloon: SU**—hand being raised

166.5   **FX: DOSA**—heavy thud

167.1   **FX/balloon: JI JI JI**—body bag zipper being unzipped

172.4   **FX: DOCHA**—wet squelch

173.4   **FX: SU**—placing fingers on corpse

174.3   **FX: YURA**—pendulum beginning to swing

174.4   **FX: HYUN HYUN**—pendulum swinging violently

175.2   **FX: MUKU**—corpse getting up

175.3   **FX: YURARI**—corpse swaying on its feet

176.3   In the original, Makino uses the technical term *kaeri chi*, meant specifically to refer to blood that splashes back onto the killer from their victim; it is also used when discussing this phenomenon in close combat. This might be a good time to note that I've been seeing a lot of Spartans at anime and manga cons lately. As a purist I should object, but as a Dark Horse employee, I just pretend they're from *Arion*. Now, every once in a while you'll have an Akiba moment in Portland. Today, about 11 AM, I saw an individual in full Stormtrooper kit walking across Burnside at

21st. Burnside is one of our main streets, four lanes, supermarkets, gas stations, what have you. It was an odd hour for a costume party, and if it was for a graduation, there weren't any schools for several blocks. But to paraphrase LL Cool J, I love it when an otaku ain't scared to do his thing.

176.6 FX: SA!—Koyama hastily covering the stain

177.2 FX: DA DA DA—heavy running footsteps

177.3.1 FX/balloon: SA!—brandishing box cutter

177.3.2 FX/balloon: CHIKI CHIKI CHIKI—box cutter blade being extended

177.4 FX: BA!—Koyama yanking the director to him

179.1 FX: BUN BUN—swinging the box cutter around

180.1 FX: SHIN—silence

180.5 FX: GORO GORO—roll roll

180.6 FX/balloon: TON—light tap

181.2 FX: BA!—eyes and mouth flying open

181.4 FX: NUU—loom

184.2.1 FX/balloon: DA DA TA—running feet

184.2.2 FX: BA!—door being yanked open

184.6 FX: SU!—director raising his hand

186.2 FX: PASA—mask falling to floor

187.2 The close-up on the billboard in panel 1 and the film program Yata is reading in panel 3 (while rare in America, theater-style film program books are a common marketing tool in Japan; in the 1980s and '90s, the program books for anime films were much-sought-after import items by American fans hungry for images and info) says *The Corpse Detective*, naturally. It's playing on screen 2 of the Shinjuku Milano, a real movie house that as of this writing (June 2008) was screening *Shoot 'Em Up, Prince Caspian*, and *Rambo*—the last of which, as Patrick Macias has detailed, had a much better promo campaign in Japan, where you could get the Rambo Hot Dog (deployed on camouflage cardboard for "sneaking snacking"), the Rambo coffee-based energy drink, and the Rambo crocodile burger, served on an eco-friendly palm leaf. Gory pictures on the May 18 posting at patrickmacias.blogs.com, which you really should be reading every day anyway. Playing next door appears to be the *Keroro Gunso* (known as *Sgt. Frog* in the U.S.) movie *The Deep Sea Princess*. Movie tickets for an adult in Tokyo, by the way, average 1800 yen; one reason manga are so successful is that they're one of the few entertainment *values* in Japan— they pay more than Americans for DVDs, CDs, and even songs on iTunes.

187.3 FX/balloon: PARA—page turning

188.4 We're working on it! Seriously, we are. You know Dark Horse doesn't give up when it comes to making titles into movies (or TV shows). It took forty-five years between *Iron Man* the comic and the movie—I bet you we do better than that. And thanks to everyone who's supporting *The Kurosagi Corpse Delivery Service*—see you in January 2009 for Volume 8!

STAFF D

Embalming
［エンバーミング］：死体修復

STAFF E

Channeling
［チャネリング］：宇宙人と交信

STAFF E'

Puppet
［マペット］：宇宙人が憑依

お届け物は死体です。

黒鷺死体宅配便
the KUROSAGI corpse delivery service

story
EIJI OTSUKA

art
HOUSUI YAMAZAKI

original cover design
BUNPEI YORIFUJI

translation
TOSHIFUMI YOSHIDA

editor and english adaptation
CARL GUSTAV HORN

lettering and touch-up
IHL

DARK
HORSE
MANGA

contents

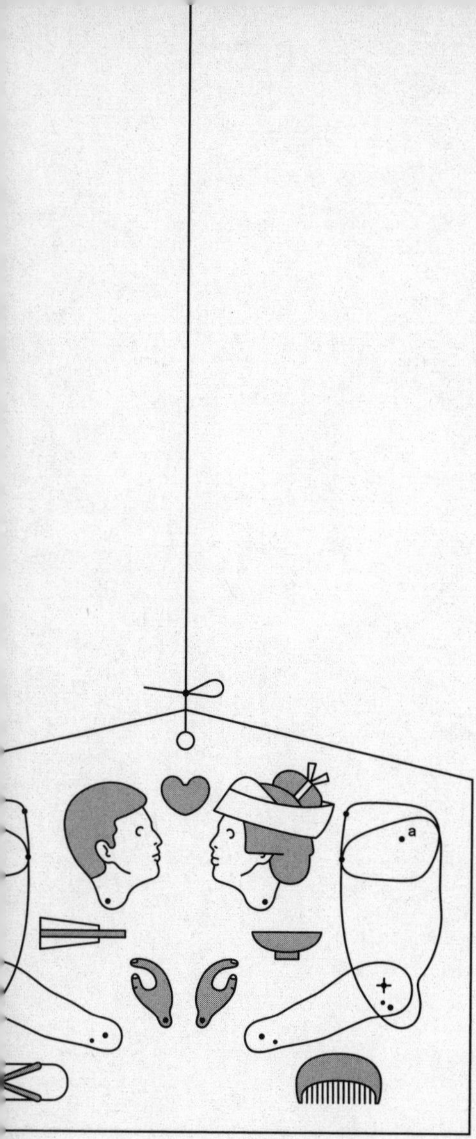
a

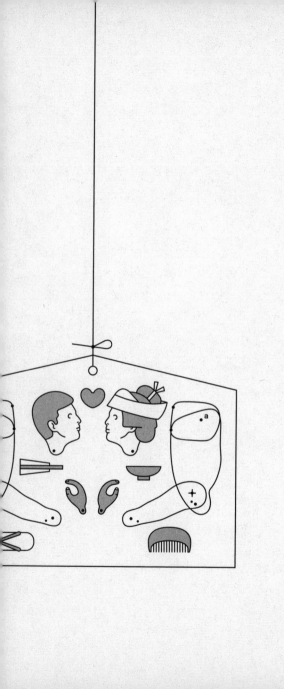

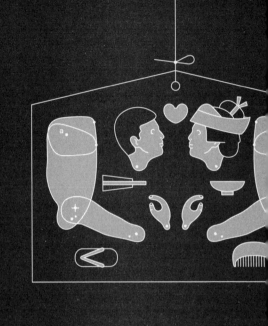

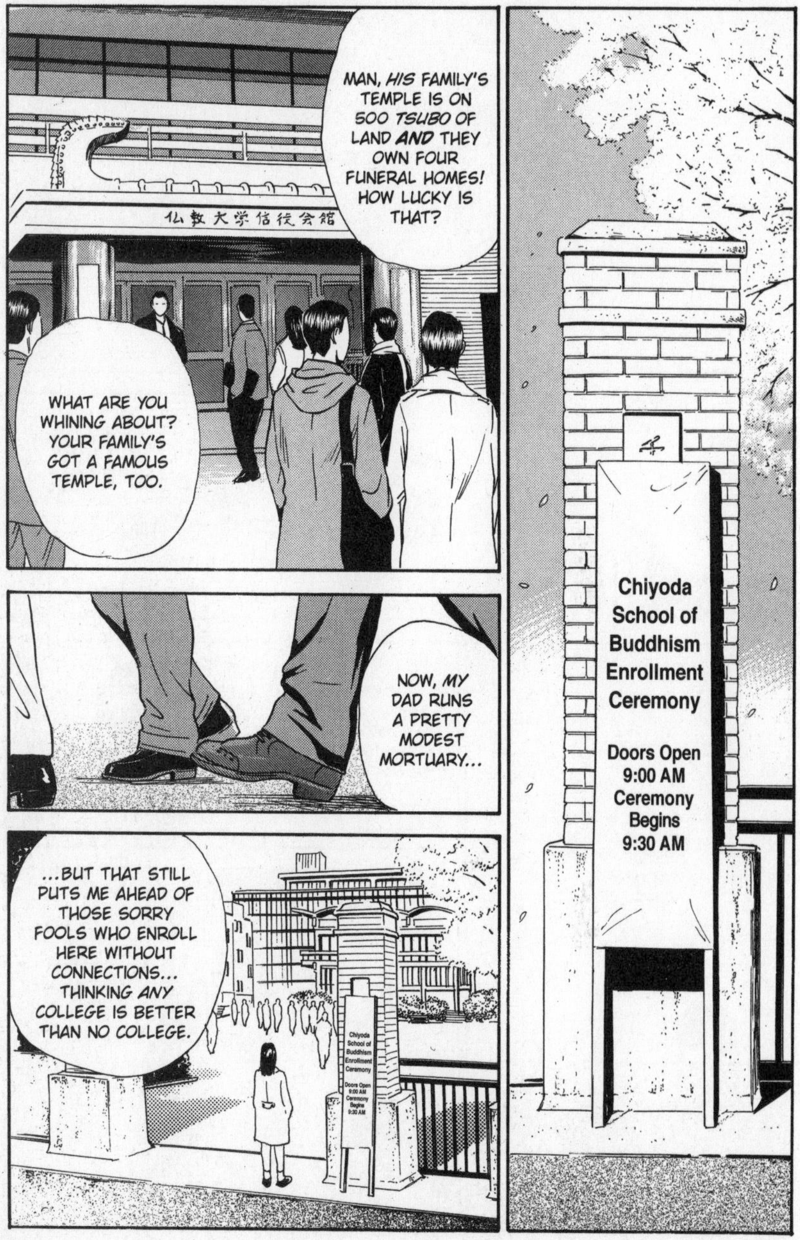
Chiyoda School of Buddhism Enrollment Ceremony
Doors Open 9:00 AM Ceremony Begins 9:30 AM
MAN, *HIS* FAMILY'S TEMPLE IS ON 500 *TSUBO* OF LAND **AND** THEY OWN FOUR FUNERAL HOMES! HOW LUCKY IS THAT?
仏教大学信徒会館
WHAT ARE YOU WHINING ABOUT? YOUR FAMILY'S GOT A FAMOUS TEMPLE, TOO.
NOW, *MY* DAD RUNS A PRETTY MODEST MORTUARY...
...BUT THAT STILL PUTS ME AHEAD OF THOSE SORRY FOOLS WHO ENROLL HERE WITHOUT CONNECTIONS... THINKING *ANY* COLLEGE IS BETTER THAN NO COLLEGE.

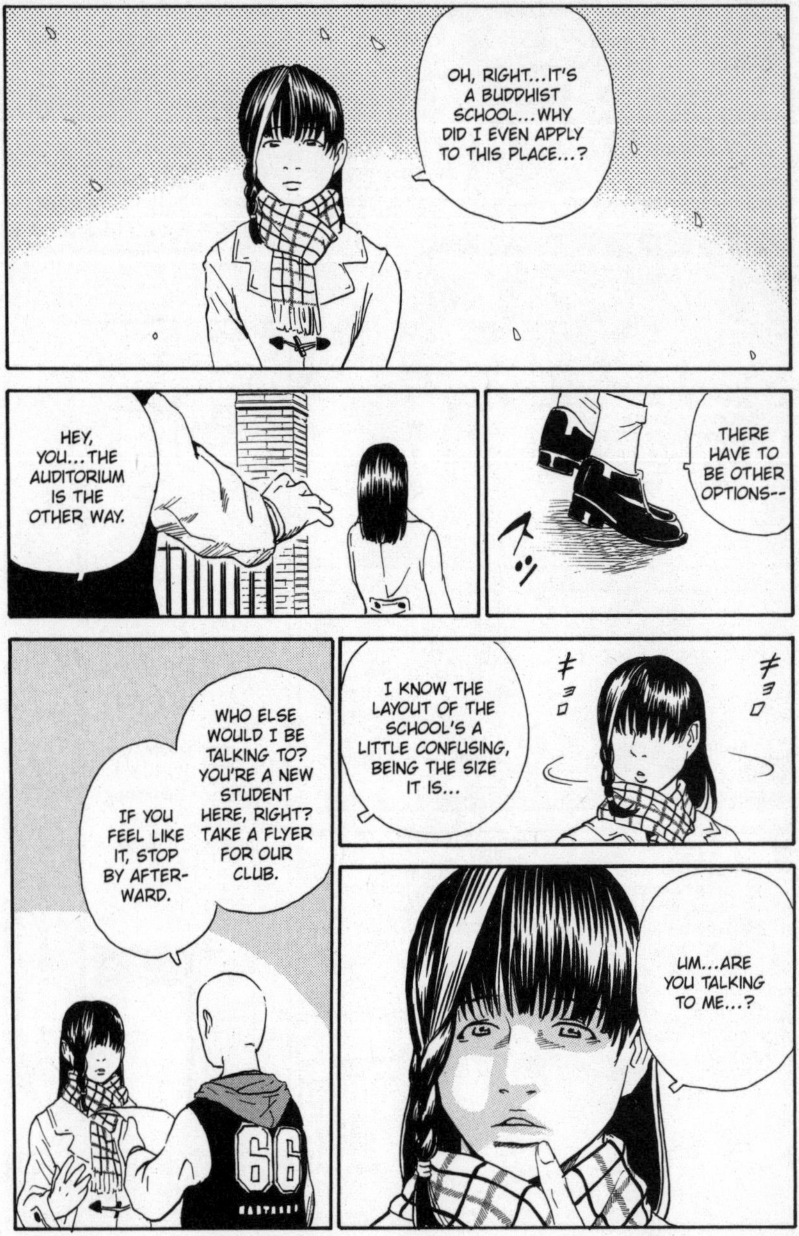
OH, RIGHT...IT'S A BUDDHIST SCHOOL...WHY DID I EVEN APPLY TO THIS PLACE...?
THERE HAVE TO BE OTHER OPTIONS--
スッ
HEY, YOU...THE AUDITORIUM IS THE OTHER WAY.
キョロ
キョロ
I KNOW THE LAYOUT OF THE SCHOOL'S A LITTLE CONFUSING, BEING THE SIZE IT IS...
UM...ARE YOU TALKING TO ME...?
WHO ELSE WOULD I BE TALKING TO? YOU'RE A NEW STUDENT HERE, RIGHT? TAKE A FLYER FOR OUR CLUB.
IF YOU FEEL LIKE IT, STOP BY AFTER-WARD.
66

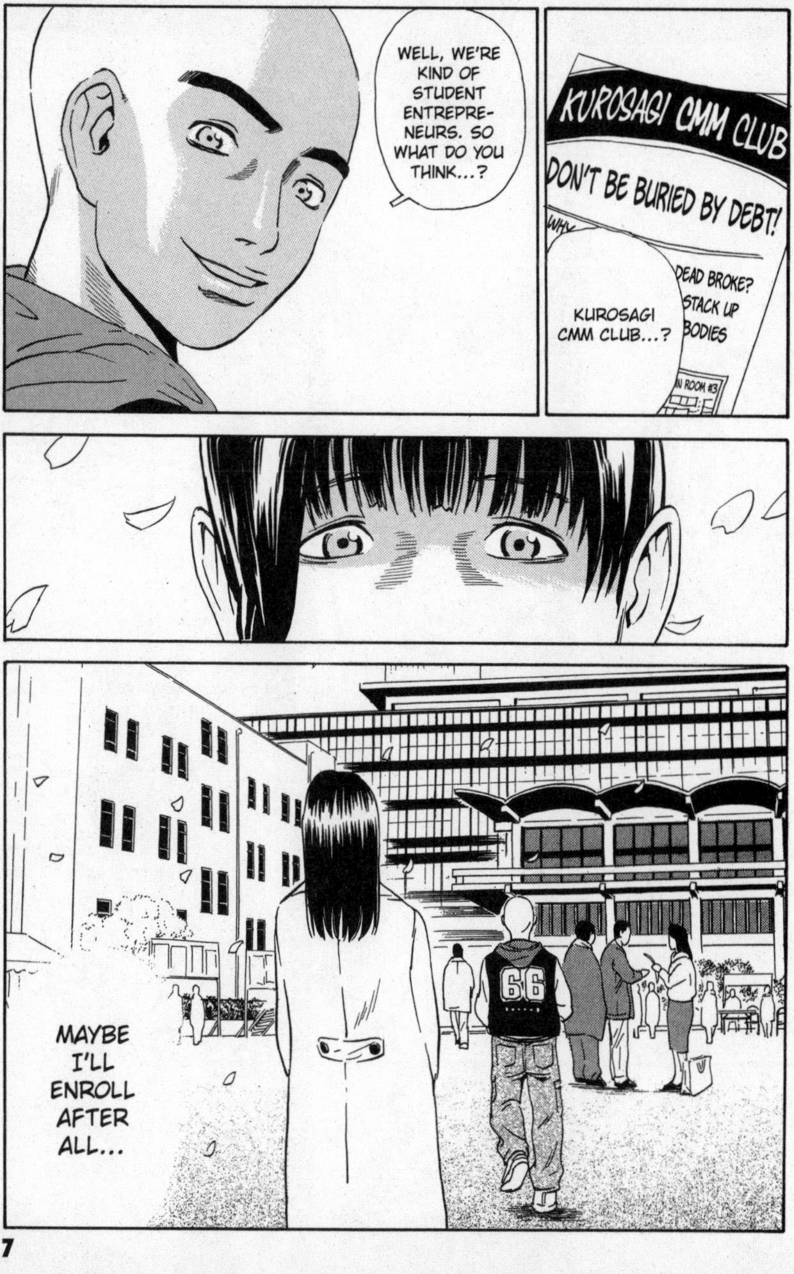
KUROSAGI CMM CLUB
DON'T BE BURIED BY DEBT!
DEAD BROKE? STACK UP BODIES
KUROSAGI CMM CLUB...?
WELL, WE'RE KIND OF STUDENT ENTREPRENEURS. SO WHAT DO YOU THINK...?
MAYBE I'LL ENROLL AFTER ALL...

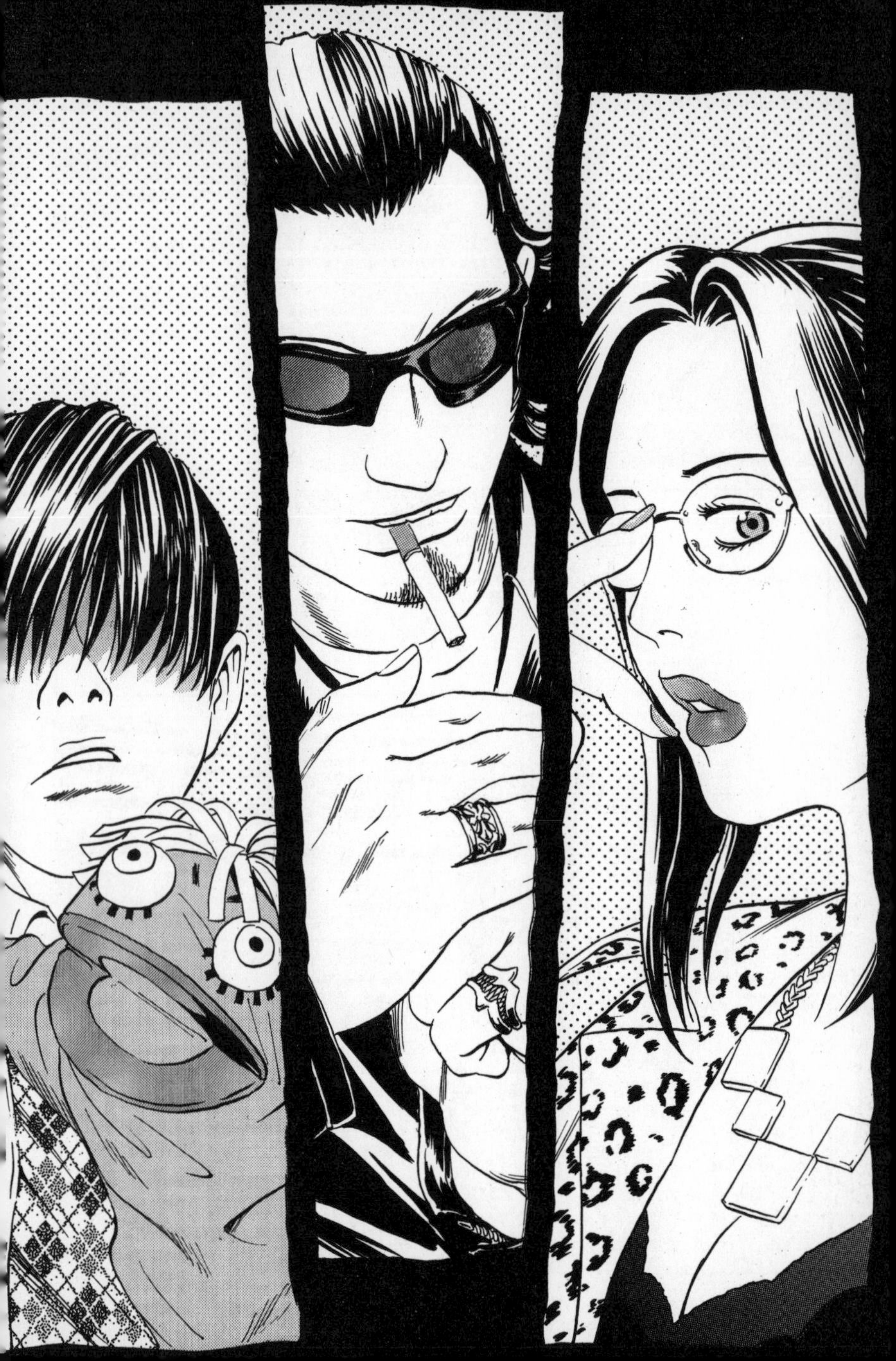

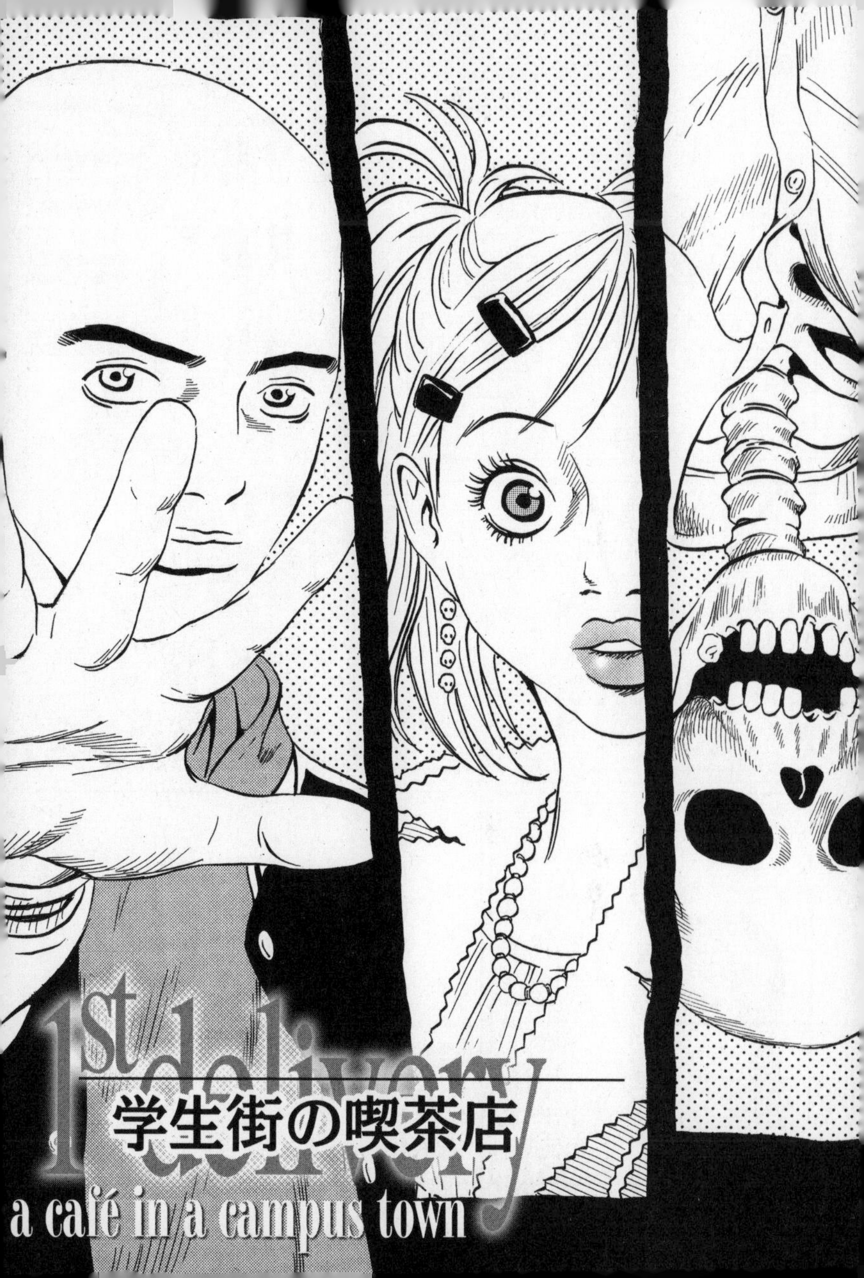
1st delivery
学生街の喫茶店
a café in a campus town

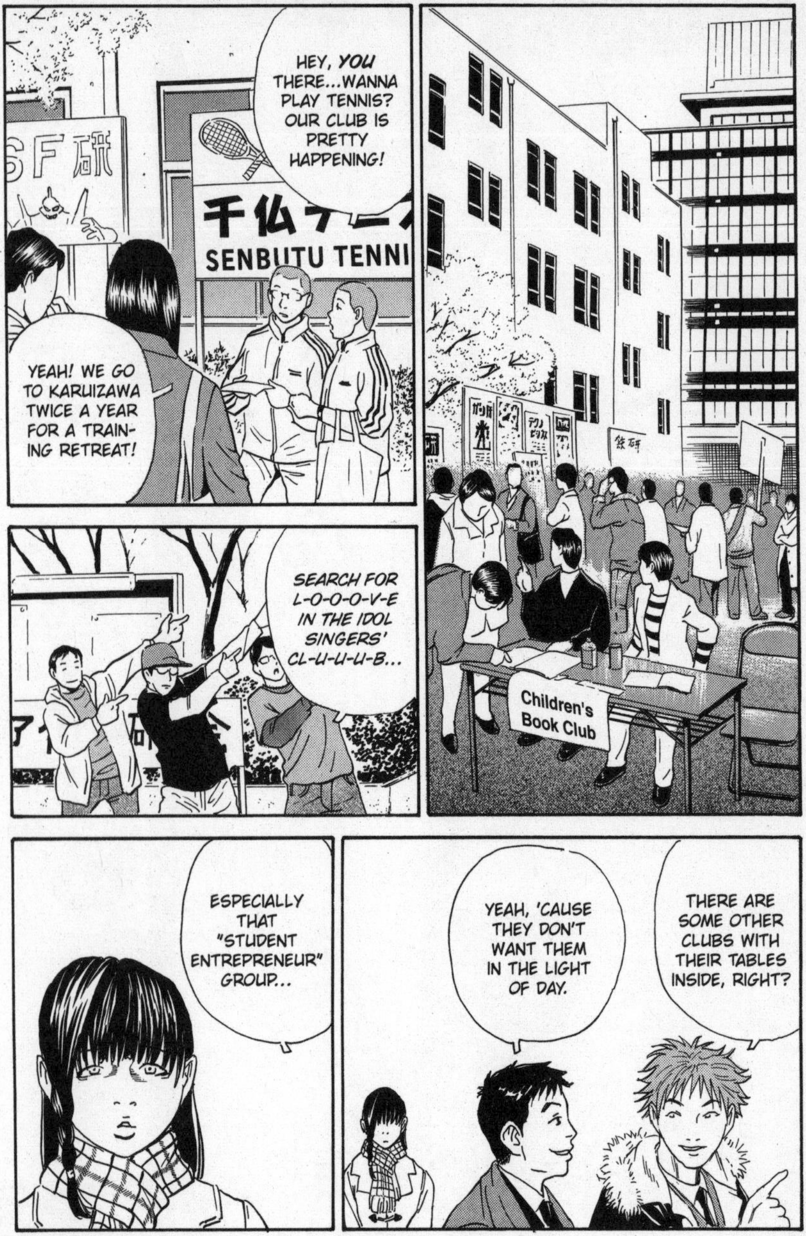
Children's Book Club
SF研
千仏テニ
SENBUTU TENNI
HEY, *YOU* THERE...WANNA PLAY TENNIS? OUR CLUB IS PRETTY HAPPENING!
YEAH! WE GO TO KARUIZAWA TWICE A YEAR FOR A TRAINING RETREAT!
SEARCH FOR L-O-O-O-V-E IN THE IDOL SINGERS' CL-U-U-U-B...
THERE ARE SOME OTHER CLUBS WITH THEIR TABLES INSIDE, RIGHT?
YEAH, 'CAUSE THEY DON'T WANT THEM IN THE LIGHT OF DAY.
ESPECIALLY THAT "STUDENT ENTREPRENEUR" GROUP...

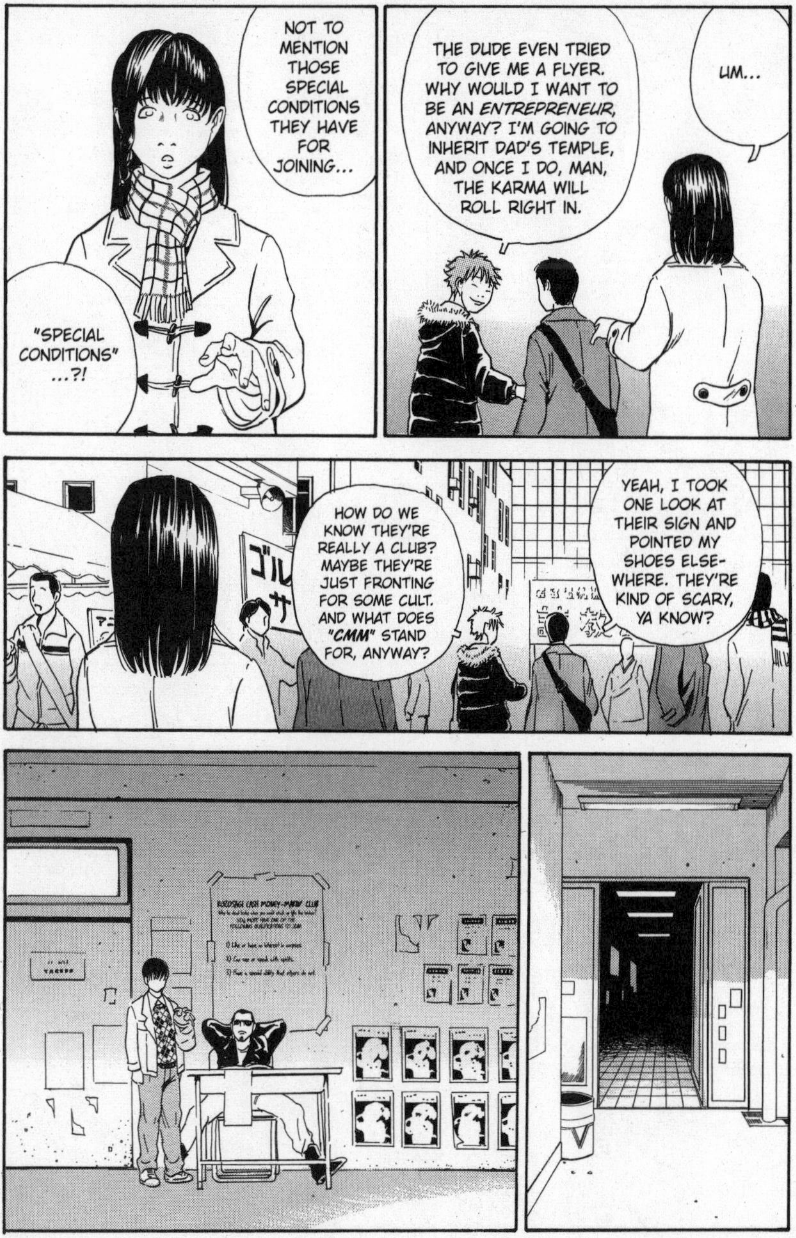
UM...
THE DUDE EVEN TRIED TO GIVE ME A FLYER. WHY WOULD I WANT TO BE AN *ENTREPRENEUR*, ANYWAY? I'M GOING TO INHERIT DAD'S TEMPLE, AND ONCE I DO, MAN, THE KARMA WILL ROLL RIGHT IN.
NOT TO MENTION THOSE SPECIAL CONDITIONS THEY HAVE FOR JOINING...
"SPECIAL CONDITIONS" ...?!
YEAH, I TOOK ONE LOOK AT THEIR SIGN AND POINTED MY SHOES ELSE-WHERE. THEY'RE KIND OF SCARY, YA KNOW?
HOW DO WE KNOW THEY'RE REALLY A CLUB? MAYBE THEY'RE JUST FRONTING FOR SOME CULT. AND WHAT DOES "***CMM***" STAND FOR, ANYWAY?

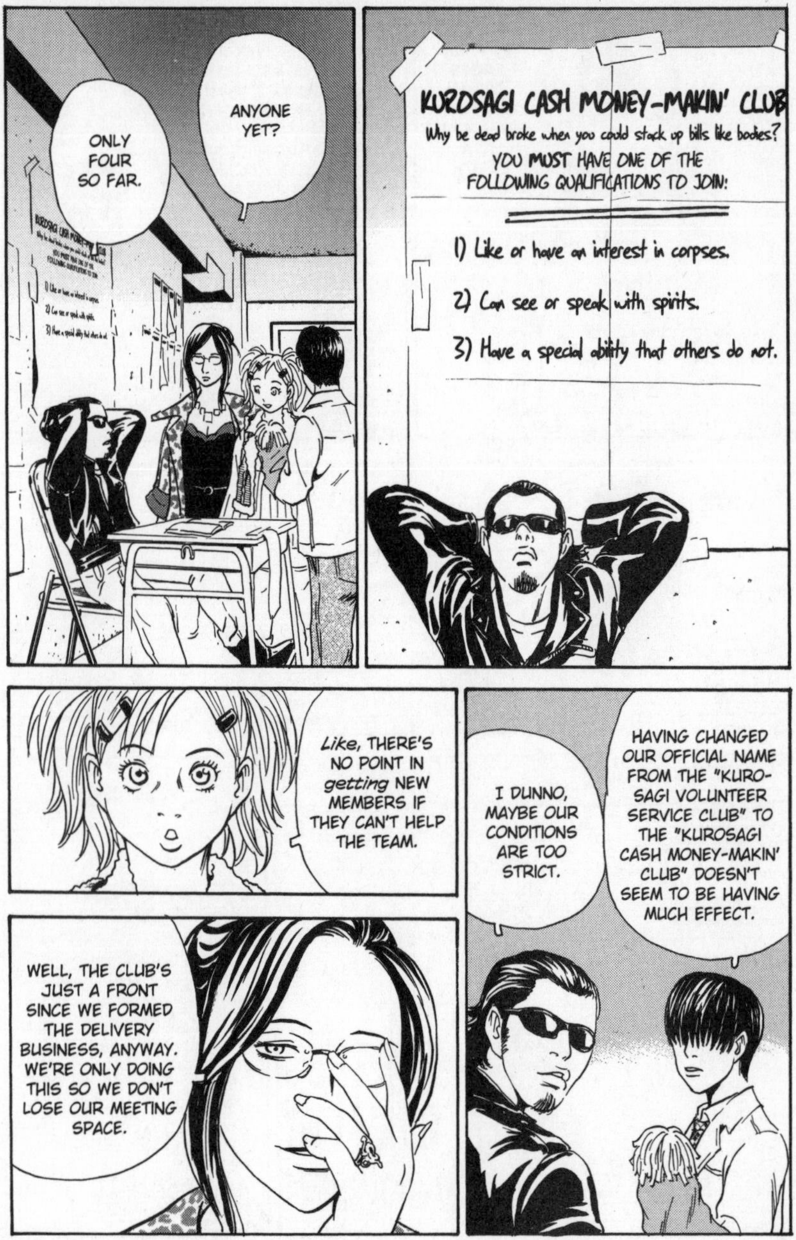
KUROSAGI CASH MONEY-MAKIN' CLUB
Why be dead broke when you could stack up bills like bodies?
YOU MUST HAVE ONE OF THE FOLLOWING QUALIFICATIONS TO JOIN:
1) Like or have an interest in corpses.
2) Can see or speak with spirits.
3) Have a special ability that others do not.
ANYONE YET?
ONLY FOUR SO FAR.
HAVING CHANGED OUR OFFICIAL NAME FROM THE "KUROSAGI VOLUNTEER SERVICE CLUB" TO THE "KUROSAGI CASH MONEY-MAKIN' CLUB" DOESN'T SEEM TO BE HAVING MUCH EFFECT.
I DUNNO, MAYBE OUR CONDITIONS ARE TOO STRICT.
Like, THERE'S NO POINT IN *getting* NEW MEMBERS IF THEY CAN'T HELP THE TEAM.
WELL, THE CLUB'S JUST A FRONT SINCE WE FORMED THE DELIVERY BUSINESS, ANYWAY. WE'RE ONLY DOING THIS SO WE DON'T LOSE OUR MEETING SPACE.

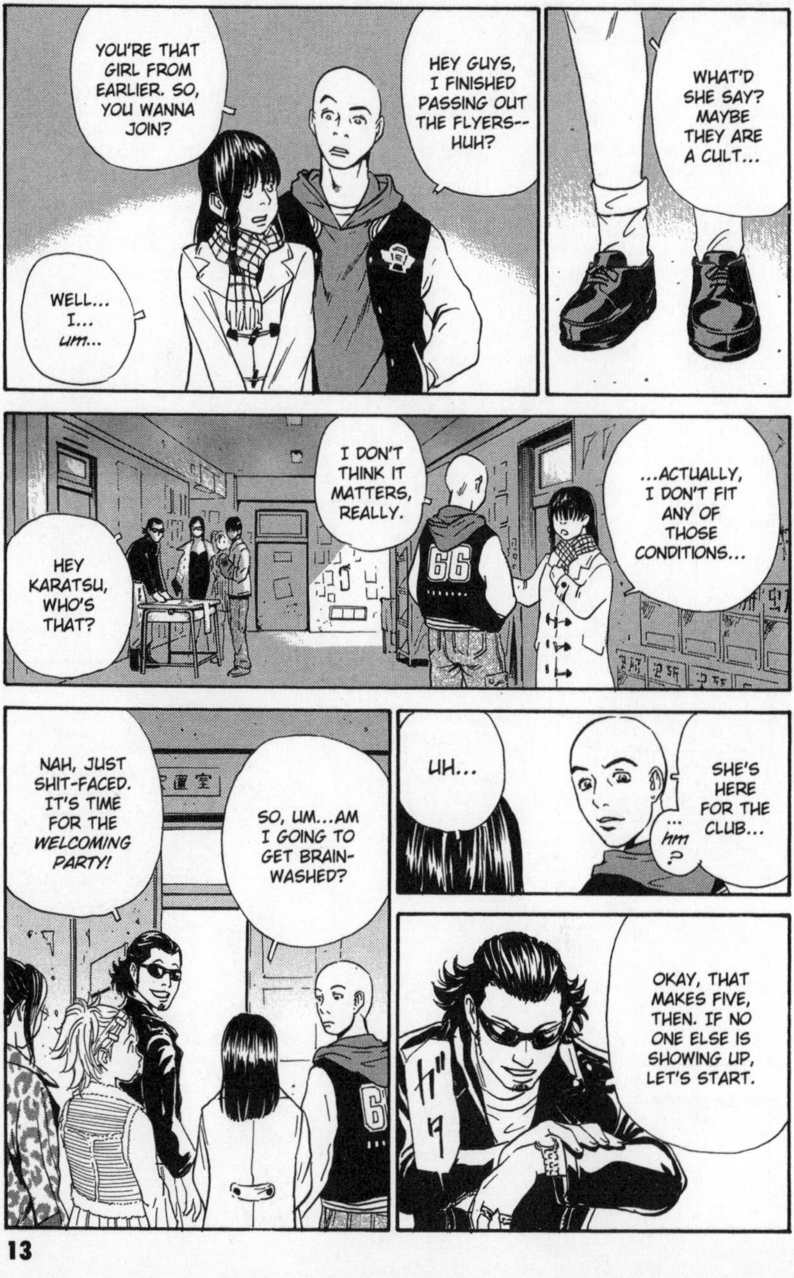
WHAT'D SHE SAY? MAYBE THEY ARE A CULT...
HEY GUYS, I FINISHED PASSING OUT THE FLYERS--HUH?
YOU'RE THAT GIRL FROM EARLIER. SO, YOU WANNA JOIN?
WELL... I... *um...*
...ACTUALLY, I DON'T FIT ANY OF THOSE CONDITIONS...
I DON'T THINK IT MATTERS, REALLY.
HEY KARATSU, WHO'S THAT?
SHE'S HERE FOR THE CLUB...
...*hm*?
UH...
OKAY, THAT MAKES FIVE, THEN. IF NO ONE ELSE IS SHOWING UP, LET'S START.
ガッ
SO, UM...AM I GOING TO GET BRAIN-WASHED?
NAH, JUST SHIT-FACED. IT'S TIME FOR THE *WELCOMING PARTY!*

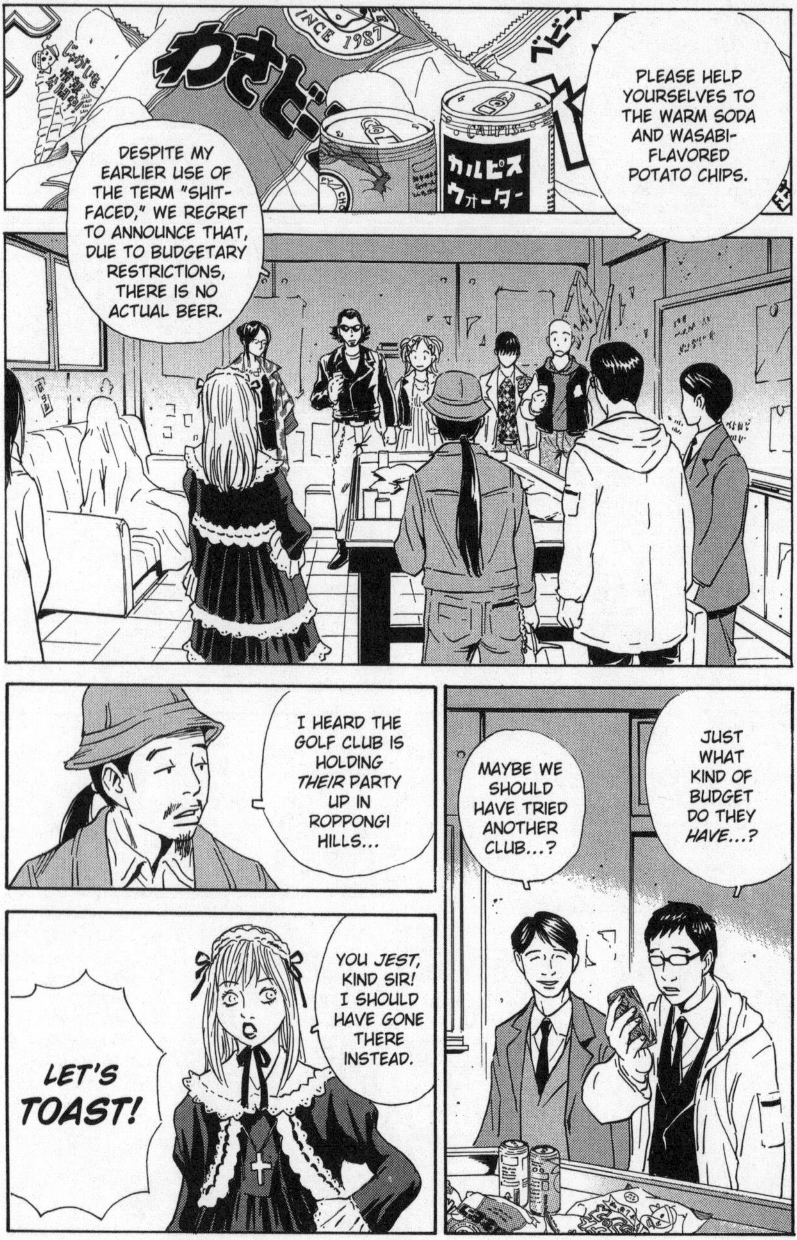

PLEASE HELP YOURSELVES TO THE WARM SODA AND WASABI-FLAVORED POTATO CHIPS.
DESPITE MY EARLIER USE OF THE TERM "SHIT-FACED," WE REGRET TO ANNOUNCE THAT, DUE TO BUDGETARY RESTRICTIONS, THERE IS NO ACTUAL BEER.
カルピス ウォーター
JUST WHAT KIND OF BUDGET DO THEY *HAVE*...?
MAYBE WE SHOULD HAVE TRIED ANOTHER CLUB...?
I HEARD THE GOLF CLUB IS HOLDING *THEIR* PARTY UP IN ROPPONGI HILLS...
YOU *JEST*, KIND SIR! I SHOULD HAVE GONE THERE INSTEAD.
LET'S TOAST!

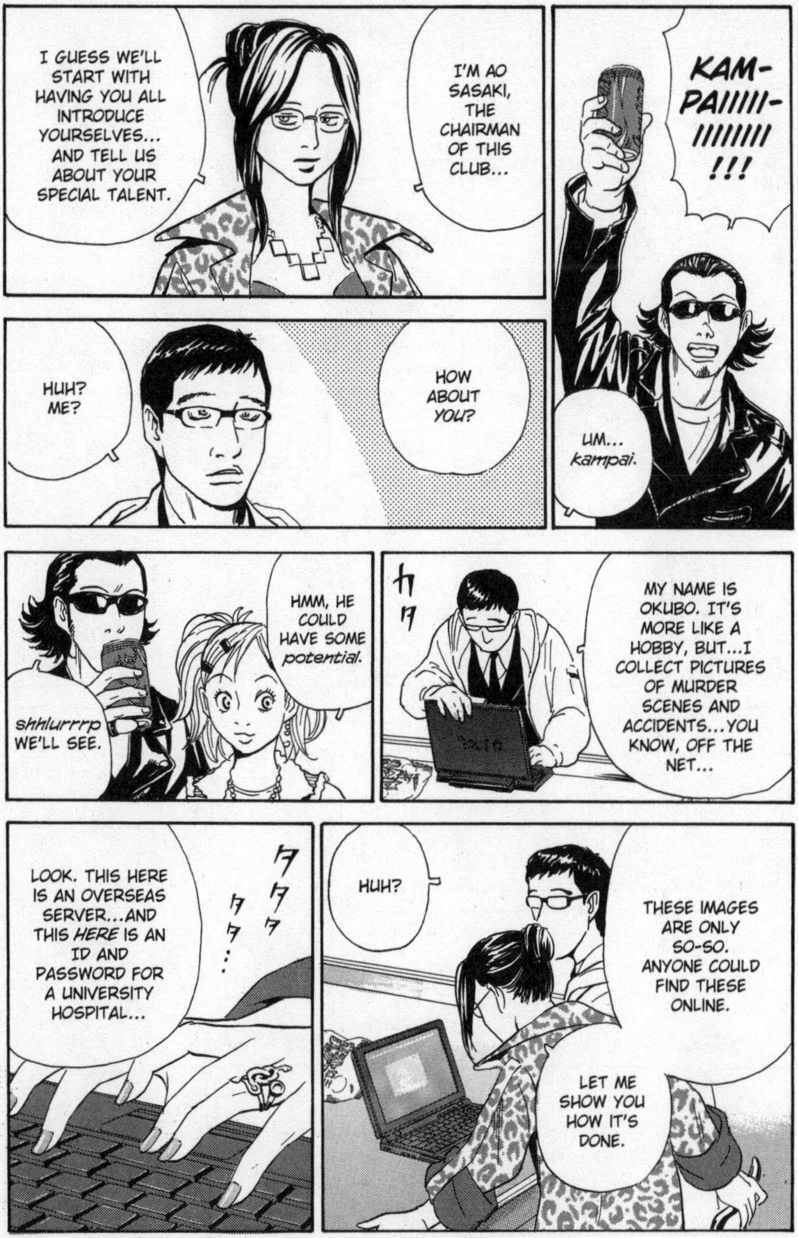
KAM-PAI!!!!!-!!!!!!!!!!!
UM... *kampai.*
I'M AO SASAKI, THE CHAIRMAN OF THIS CLUB...
I GUESS WE'LL START WITH HAVING YOU ALL INTRODUCE YOURSELVES... AND TELL US ABOUT YOUR SPECIAL TALENT.
HOW ABOUT *YOU?*
HUH? ME?
カタ
MY NAME IS OKUBO. IT'S MORE LIKE A HOBBY, BUT...I COLLECT PICTURES OF MURDER SCENES AND ACCIDENTS...YOU KNOW, OFF THE NET...
HMM, HE COULD HAVE SOME *potential.*
shhlurrrp WE'LL SEE.
THESE IMAGES ARE ONLY SO-SO. ANYONE COULD FIND THESE ONLINE.
HUH?
LET ME SHOW YOU HOW IT'S DONE.
タタタタタ...
LOOK. THIS HERE IS AN OVERSEAS SERVER...AND THIS *HERE* IS AN ID AND PASSWORD FOR A UNIVERSITY HOSPITAL...

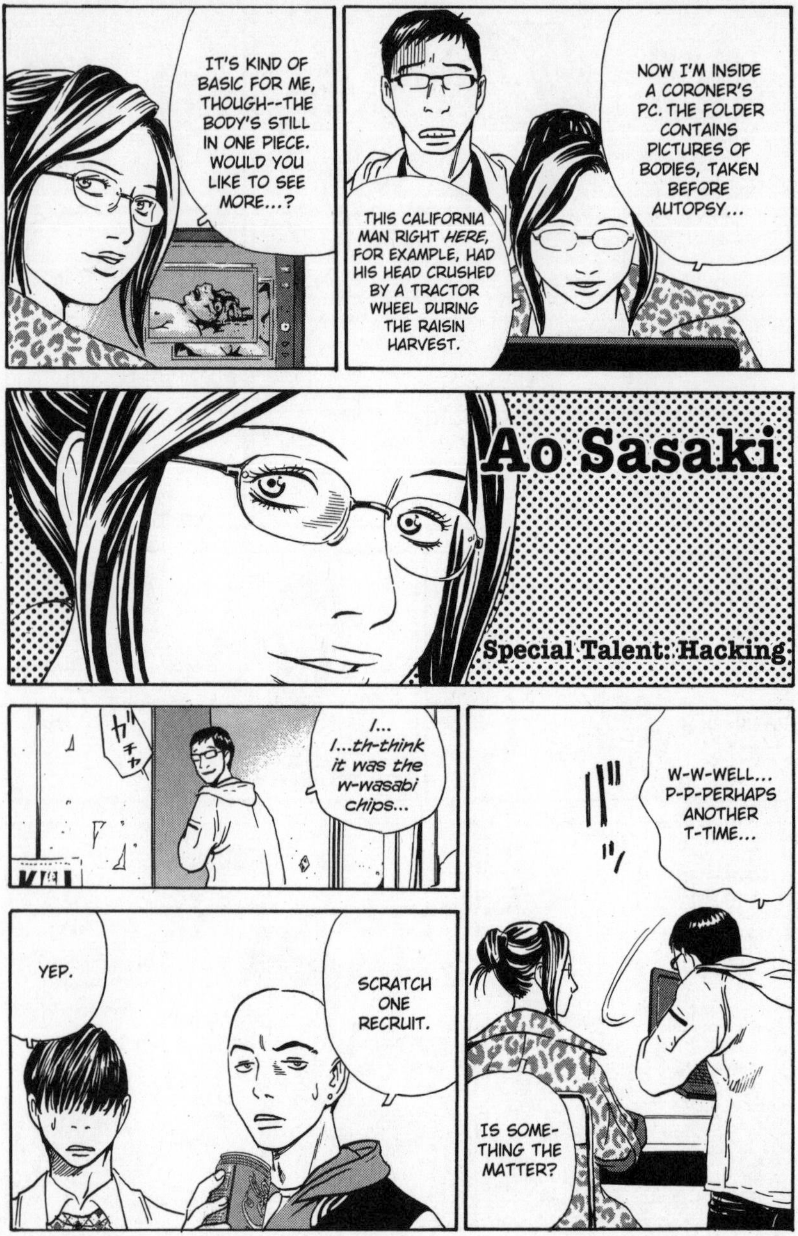
NOW I'M INSIDE A CORONER'S PC. THE FOLDER CONTAINS PICTURES OF BODIES, TAKEN BEFORE AUTOPSY...
THIS CALIFORNIA MAN RIGHT *HERE*, FOR EXAMPLE, HAD HIS HEAD CRUSHED BY A TRACTOR WHEEL DURING THE RAISIN HARVEST.
IT'S KIND OF BASIC FOR ME, THOUGH--THE BODY'S STILL IN ONE PIECE. WOULD YOU LIKE TO SEE MORE...?
Ao Sasaki
Special Talent: Hacking
W-W-WELL... P-P-PERHAPS ANOTHER T-TIME...
IS SOME-THING THE MATTER?
ガチャ
I... I...th-think it was the w-wasabi chips...
SCRATCH ONE RECRUIT.
YEP.

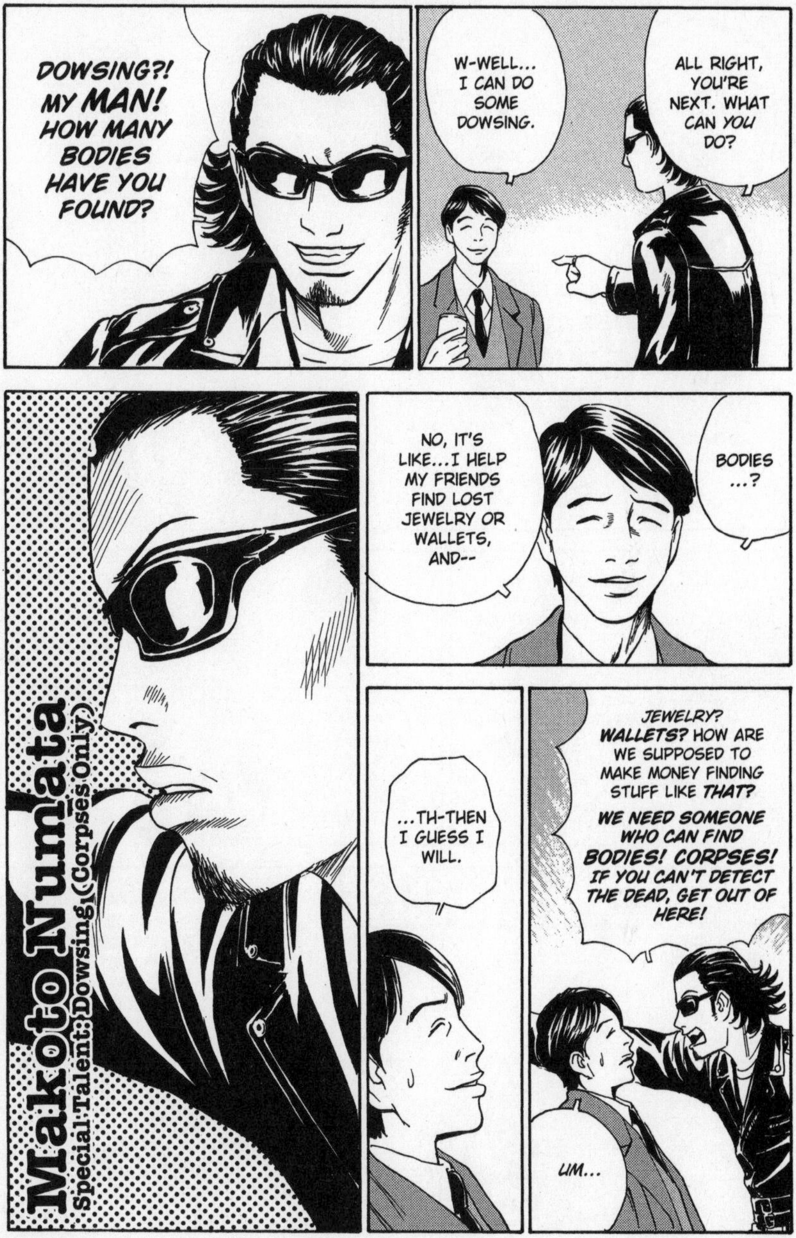

ALL RIGHT, YOU'RE NEXT. WHAT CAN YOU DO?
W-WELL... I CAN DO SOME DOWSING.
DOWSING?! MY MAN! HOW MANY BODIES HAVE YOU FOUND?
BODIES ...?
NO, IT'S LIKE...I HELP MY FRIENDS FIND LOST JEWELRY OR WALLETS, AND--
JEWELRY? WALLETS? HOW ARE WE SUPPOSED TO MAKE MONEY FINDING STUFF LIKE THAT? WE NEED SOMEONE WHO CAN FIND BODIES! CORPSES! IF YOU CAN'T DETECT THE DEAD, GET OUT OF HERE!
UM...
...TH-THEN I GUESS I WILL.
Makoto Numata
Special Talent: Dowsing (Corpses Only)

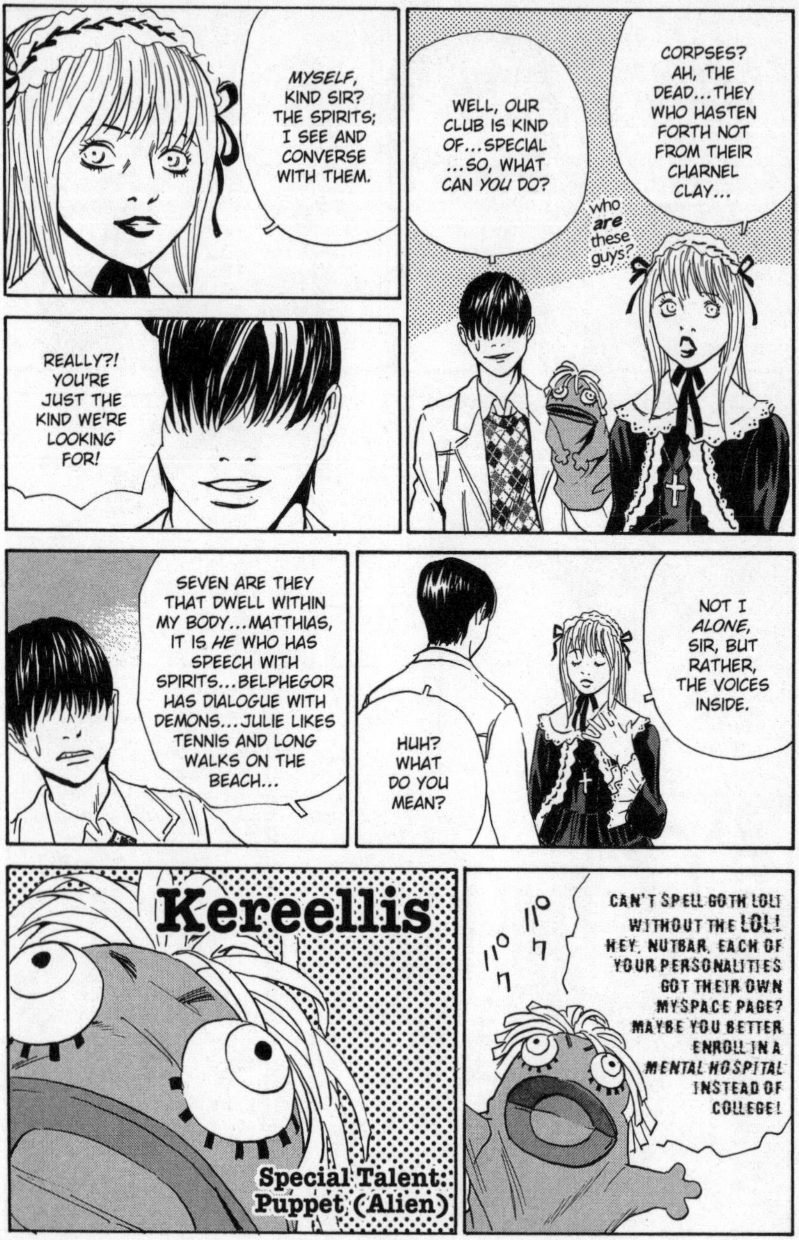

CORPSES? AH, THE DEAD...THEY WHO HASTEN FORTH NOT FROM THEIR CHARNEL CLAY...
WELL, OUR CLUB IS KIND OF...SPECIAL ...SO, WHAT CAN *YOU* DO?
who **are** these guys?
MYSELF, KIND SIR? THE SPIRITS; I SEE AND CONVERSE WITH THEM.
REALLY?! YOU'RE JUST THE KIND WE'RE LOOKING FOR!
NOT I *ALONE*, SIR, BUT RATHER, THE VOICES INSIDE.
HUH? WHAT DO YOU MEAN?
SEVEN ARE THEY THAT DWELL WITHIN MY BODY...MATTHIAS, IT IS *HE* WHO HAS SPEECH WITH SPIRITS...BELPHEGOR HAS DIALOGUE WITH DEMONS...JULIE LIKES TENNIS AND LONG WALKS ON THE BEACH...
パク パク
CAN'T SPELL GOTH LOLI WITHOUT THE LOL! HEY, NUTBAR, EACH OF YOUR PERSONALITIES GOT THEIR OWN MYSPACE PAGE? MAYBE YOU BETTER ENROLL IN A *MENTAL HOSPITAL* INSTEAD OF COLLEGE!
Kereellis
Special Talent: Puppet (Alien)

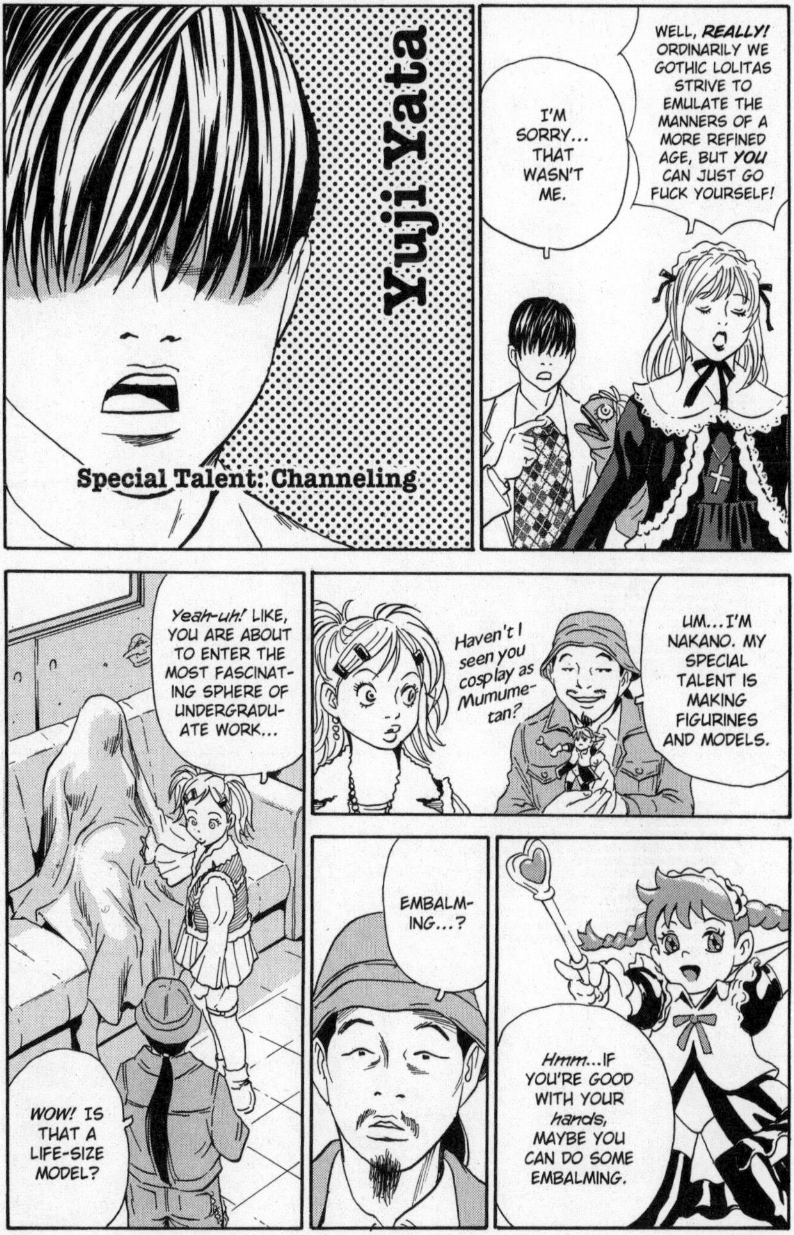
WELL, REALLY! ORDINARILY WE GOTHIC LOLITAS STRIVE TO EMULATE THE MANNERS OF A MORE REFINED AGE, BUT YOU CAN JUST GO FUCK YOURSELF!
I'M SORRY... THAT WASN'T ME.
Yuji Yata
Special Talent: Channeling
UM...I'M NAKANO. MY SPECIAL TALENT IS MAKING FIGURINES AND MODELS.
Haven't I seen you cosplay as Mumume-tan?
Hmmm...IF YOU'RE GOOD WITH YOUR hands, MAYBE YOU CAN DO SOME EMBALMING.
EMBALMING...?
Yeah-uh! LIKE, YOU ARE ABOUT TO ENTER THE MOST FASCINATING SPHERE OF UNDERGRADUATE WORK...
WOW! IS THAT A LIFE-SIZE MODEL?

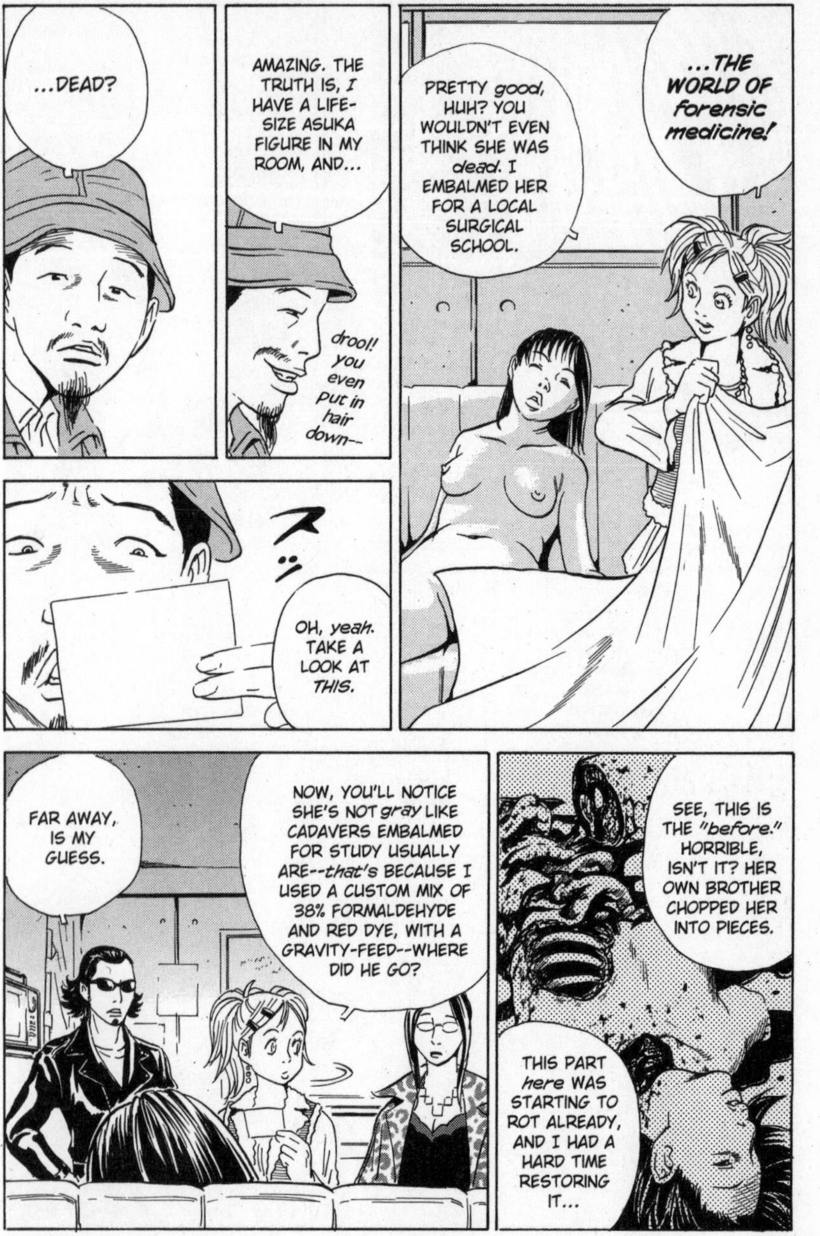
...THE WORLD OF *forensic medicine!*
PRETTY *good*, HUH? YOU WOULDN'T EVEN THINK SHE WAS *dead*. I EMBALMED HER FOR A LOCAL SURGICAL SCHOOL.
AMAZING. THE TRUTH IS, *I* HAVE A LIFE-SIZE ASUKA FIGURE IN MY ROOM, AND...
drool! you even put in hair down--
...DEAD?
ス
OH, *yeah*. TAKE A LOOK AT *THIS*.
SEE, THIS IS THE *"before."* HORRIBLE, ISN'T IT? HER OWN BROTHER CHOPPED HER INTO PIECES.
THIS PART *here* WAS STARTING TO ROT ALREADY, AND I HAD A HARD TIME RESTORING IT...
NOW, YOU'LL NOTICE SHE'S NOT *gray* LIKE CADAVERS EMBALMED FOR STUDY USUALLY ARE--*that's* BECAUSE I USED A CUSTOM MIX OF 38% FORMALDEHYDE AND RED DYE, WITH A GRAVITY-FEED--WHERE DID HE GO?
FAR AWAY, IS MY GUESS.

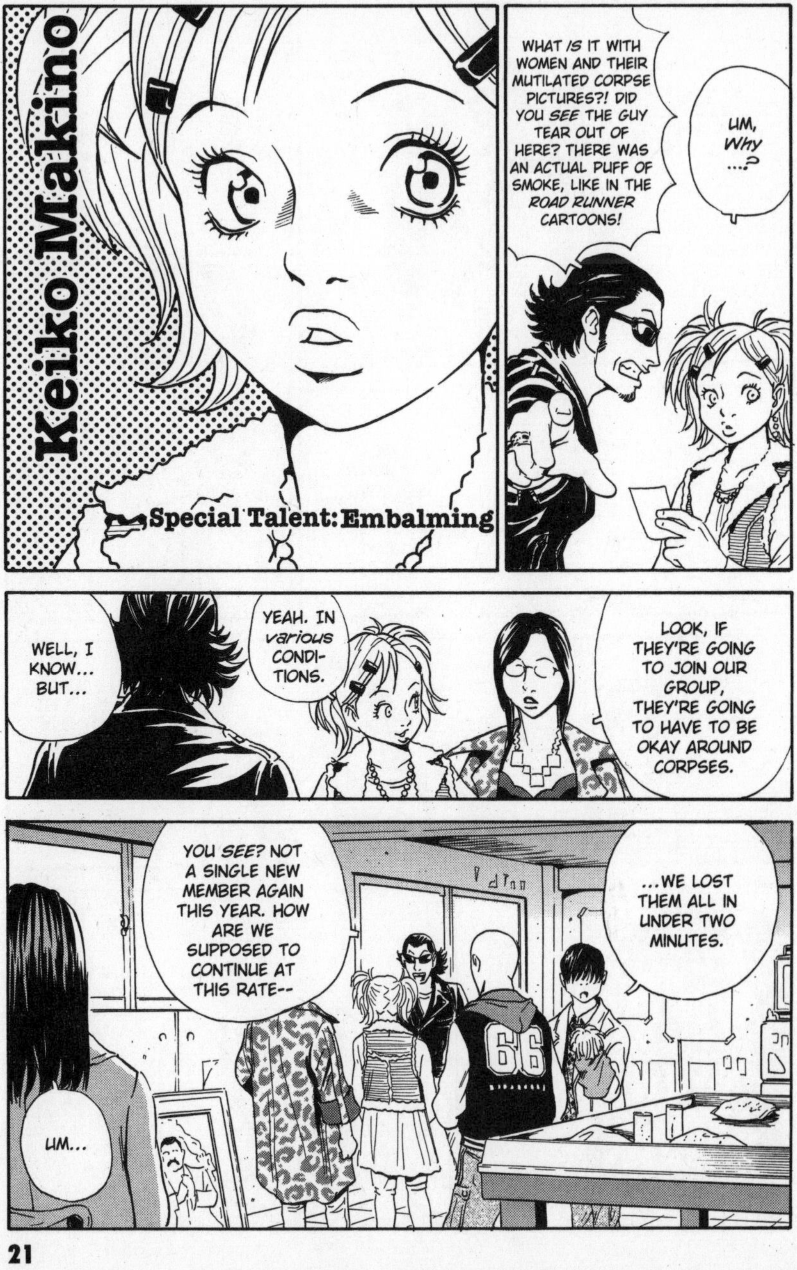
WHAT IS IT WITH WOMEN AND THEIR MUTILATED CORPSE PICTURES?! DID YOU SEE THE GUY TEAR OUT OF HERE? THERE WAS AN ACTUAL PUFF OF SMOKE, LIKE IN THE ROAD RUNNER CARTOONS!
UM, WHY ...?
Keiko Makino
Special Talent: Embalming
LOOK, IF THEY'RE GOING TO JOIN OUR GROUP, THEY'RE GOING TO HAVE TO BE OKAY AROUND CORPSES.
YEAH. IN various CONDITIONS.
WELL, I KNOW... BUT...
...WE LOST THEM ALL IN UNDER TWO MINUTES.
YOU SEE? NOT A SINGLE NEW MEMBER AGAIN THIS YEAR. HOW ARE WE SUPPOSED TO CONTINUE AT THIS RATE--
UM...

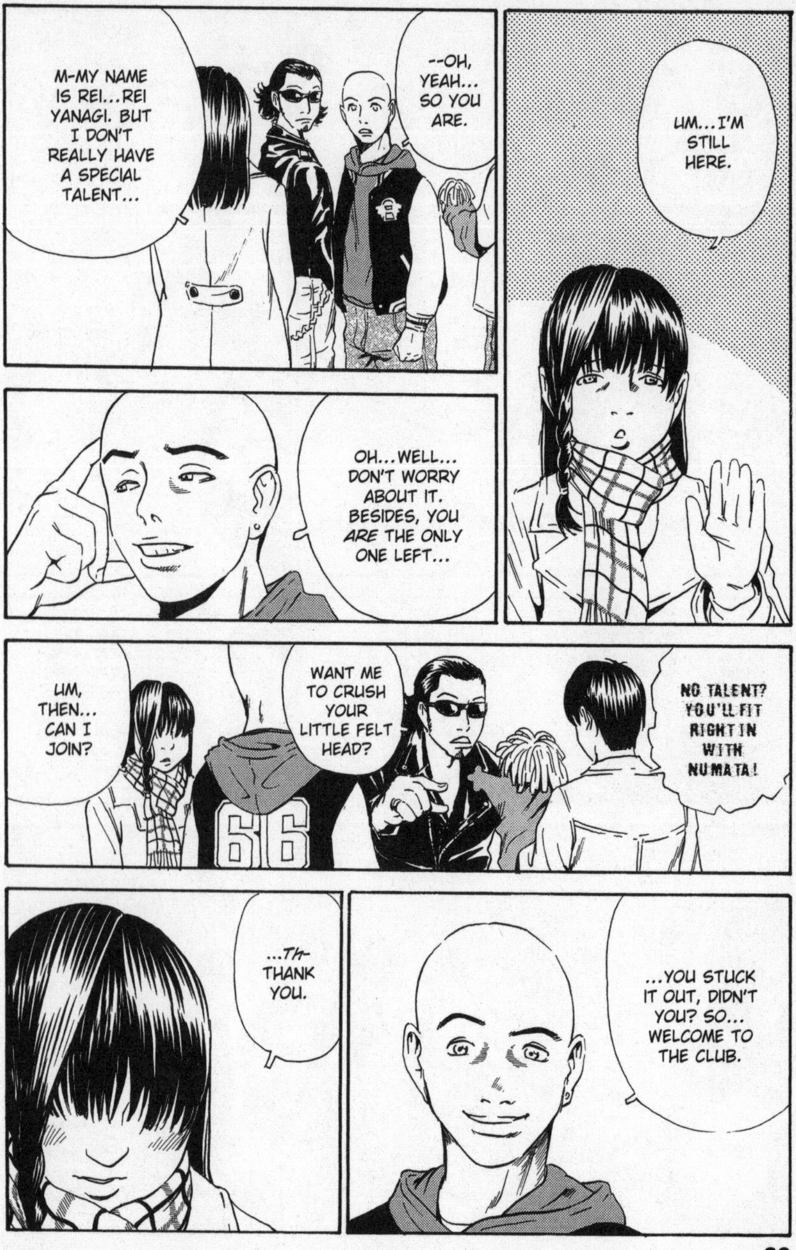
UM...I'M STILL HERE.
--OH, YEAH... SO YOU ARE.
M-MY NAME IS REI...REI YANAGI. BUT I DON'T REALLY HAVE A SPECIAL TALENT...
OH...WELL... DON'T WORRY ABOUT IT. BESIDES, YOU *ARE* THE ONLY ONE LEFT...
NO TALENT? YOU'LL FIT RIGHT IN WITH NUMATA!
WANT ME TO CRUSH YOUR LITTLE FELT HEAD?
UM, THEN... CAN I JOIN?
66
...YOU STUCK IT OUT, DIDN'T YOU? SO... WELCOME TO THE CLUB.
...Th- THANK YOU.

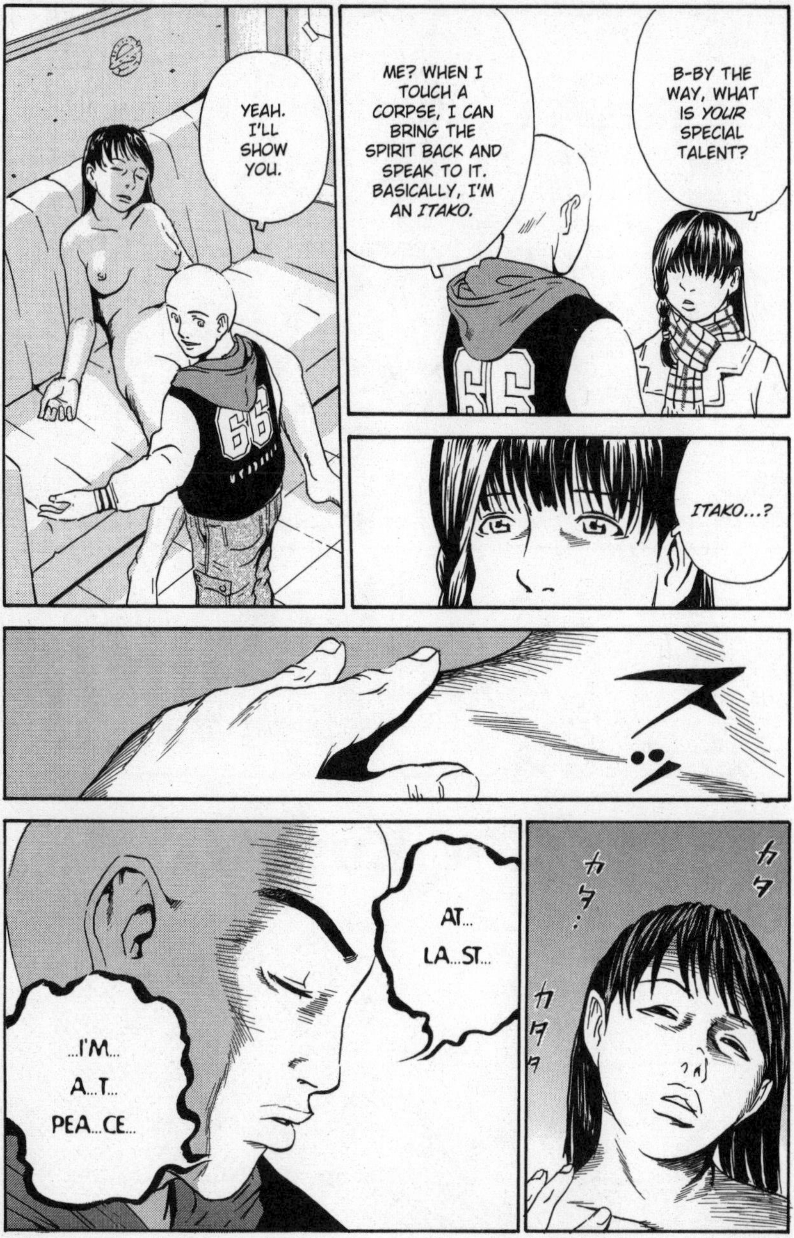
B-BY THE WAY, WHAT IS *YOUR* SPECIAL TALENT?
ME? WHEN I TOUCH A CORPSE, I CAN BRING THE SPIRIT BACK AND SPEAK TO IT. BASICALLY, I'M AN *ITAKO.*
ITAKO...?
YEAH. I'LL SHOW YOU.
スッ
カタ
カタ…
カタタ
AT... LA...ST...
...I'M... A...T... PEA...CE...

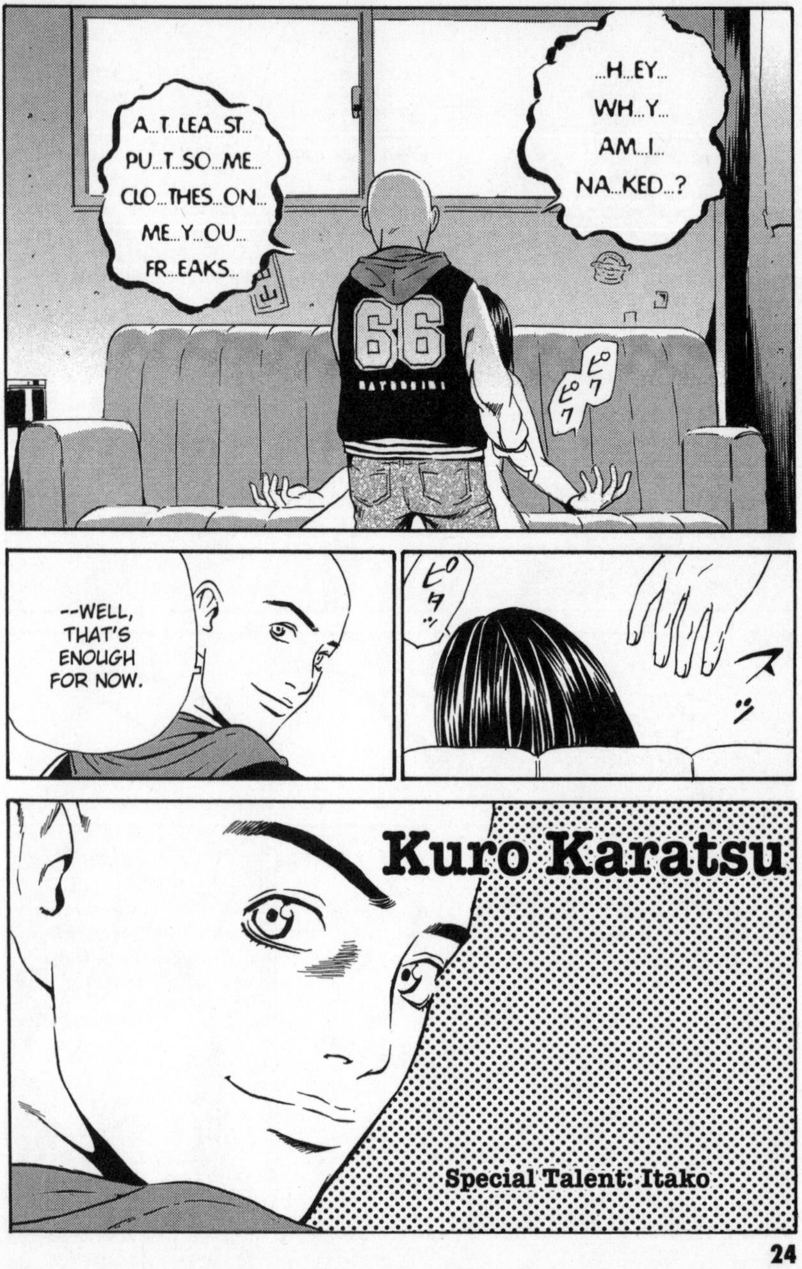

...H...EY... WH...Y... AM...I... NA...KED...?
A...T...LEA...ST... PU...T...SO...ME... CLO...THES...ON... ME...Y...OU... FR...EAKS...
ピクピク
ピタッ
スッ
--WELL, THAT'S ENOUGH FOR NOW.
Kuro Karatsu
Special Talent: Itako

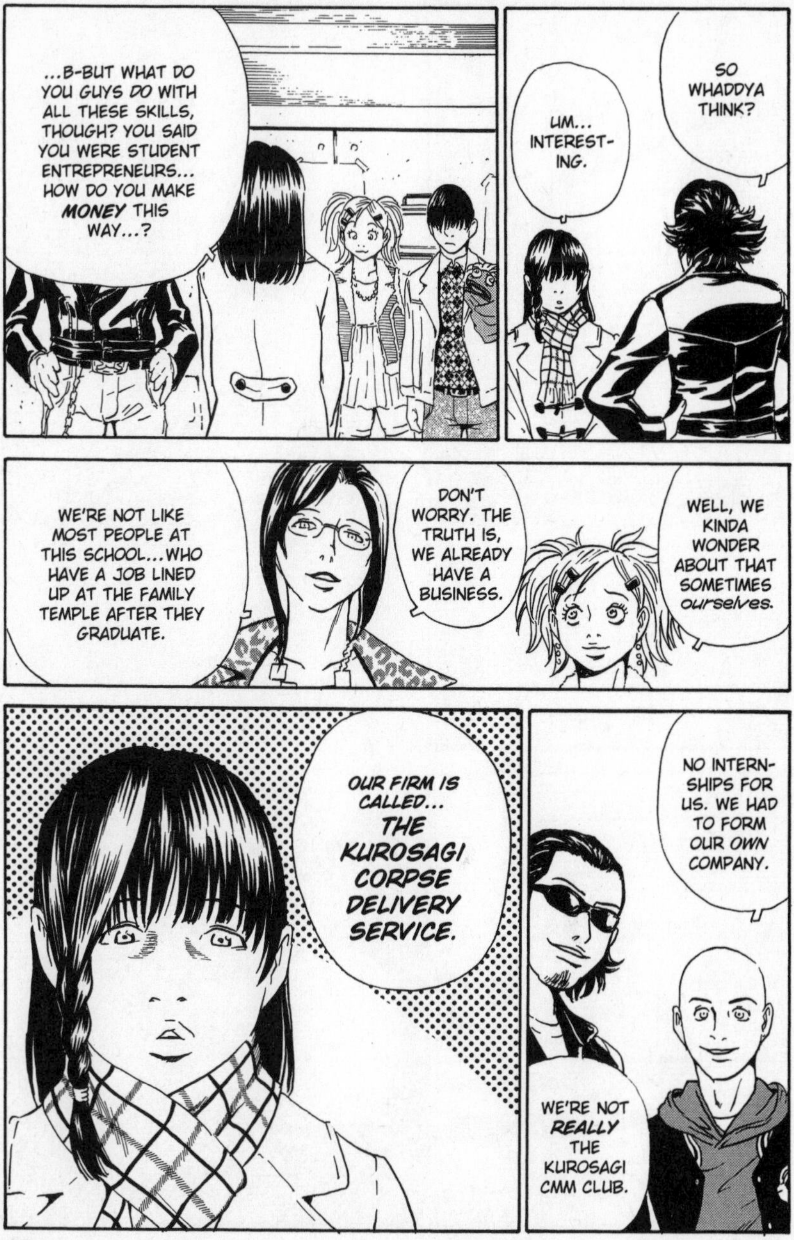
SO WHADDYA THINK?
UM... INTEREST-ING.
...B-BUT WHAT DO YOU GUYS DO WITH ALL THESE SKILLS, THOUGH? YOU SAID YOU WERE STUDENT ENTREPRENEURS... HOW DO YOU MAKE MONEY THIS WAY...?
WELL, WE KINDA WONDER ABOUT THAT SOMETIMES ourselves.
DON'T WORRY. THE TRUTH IS, WE ALREADY HAVE A BUSINESS.
WE'RE NOT LIKE MOST PEOPLE AT THIS SCHOOL...WHO HAVE A JOB LINED UP AT THE FAMILY TEMPLE AFTER THEY GRADUATE.
NO INTERN-SHIPS FOR US. WE HAD TO FORM OUR OWN COMPANY.
WE'RE NOT REALLY THE KUROSAGI CMM CLUB.
OUR FIRM IS CALLED... THE KUROSAGI CORPSE DELIVERY SERVICE.

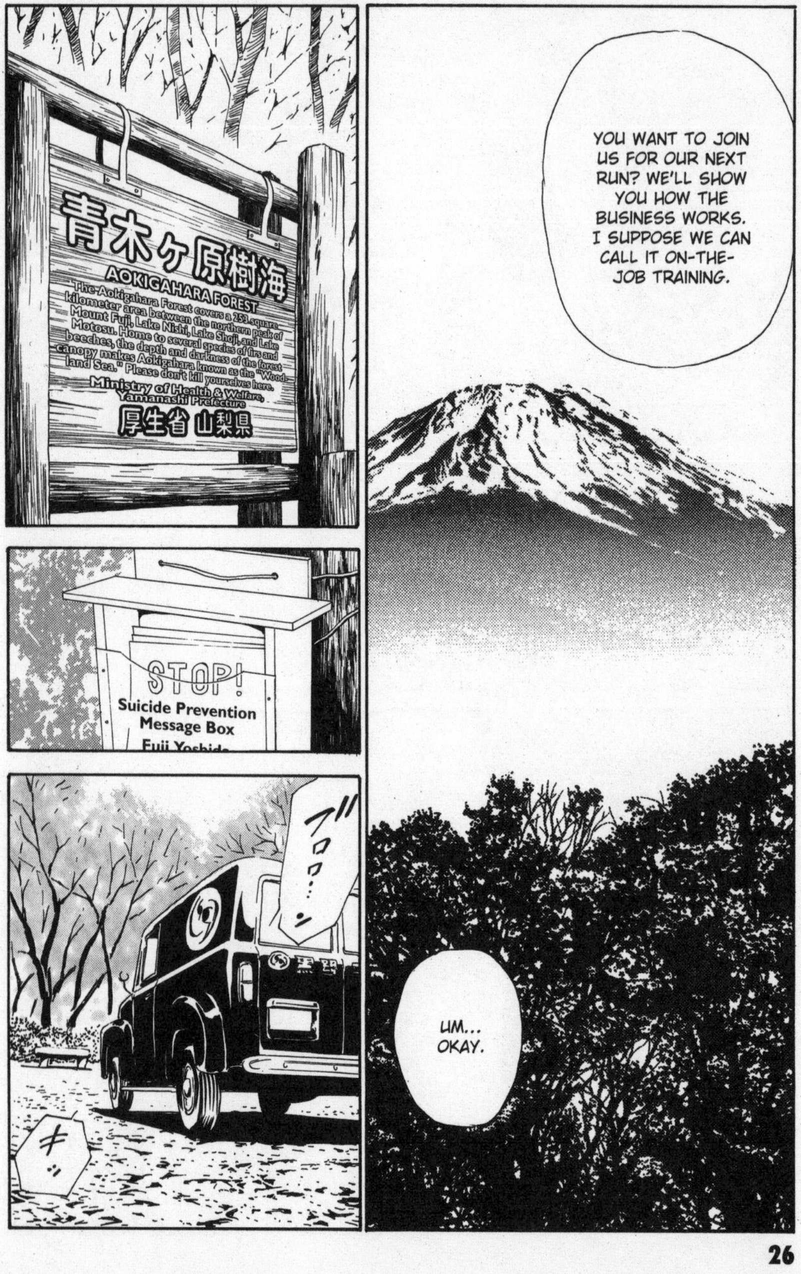
YOU WANT TO JOIN US FOR OUR NEXT RUN? WE'LL SHOW YOU HOW THE BUSINESS WORKS. I SUPPOSE WE CAN CALL IT ON-THE-JOB TRAINING.
UM... OKAY.
青木ヶ原樹海
AOKIGAHARA FOREST
The Aokigahara Forest covers a 253-square-kilometer area between the northern peak of Mount Fuji, Lake Nishi, Lake Shoji, and Lake Motosu. Home to several species of firs and beeches, the depth and darkness of the forest canopy makes Aokigahara known as the "Wood-land Sea." Please don't kill yourselves here.
Ministry of Health & Welfare, Yamanashi Prefecture
厚生省 山梨県
STOP!
Suicide Prevention Message Box
ブロロ…ン
キッ

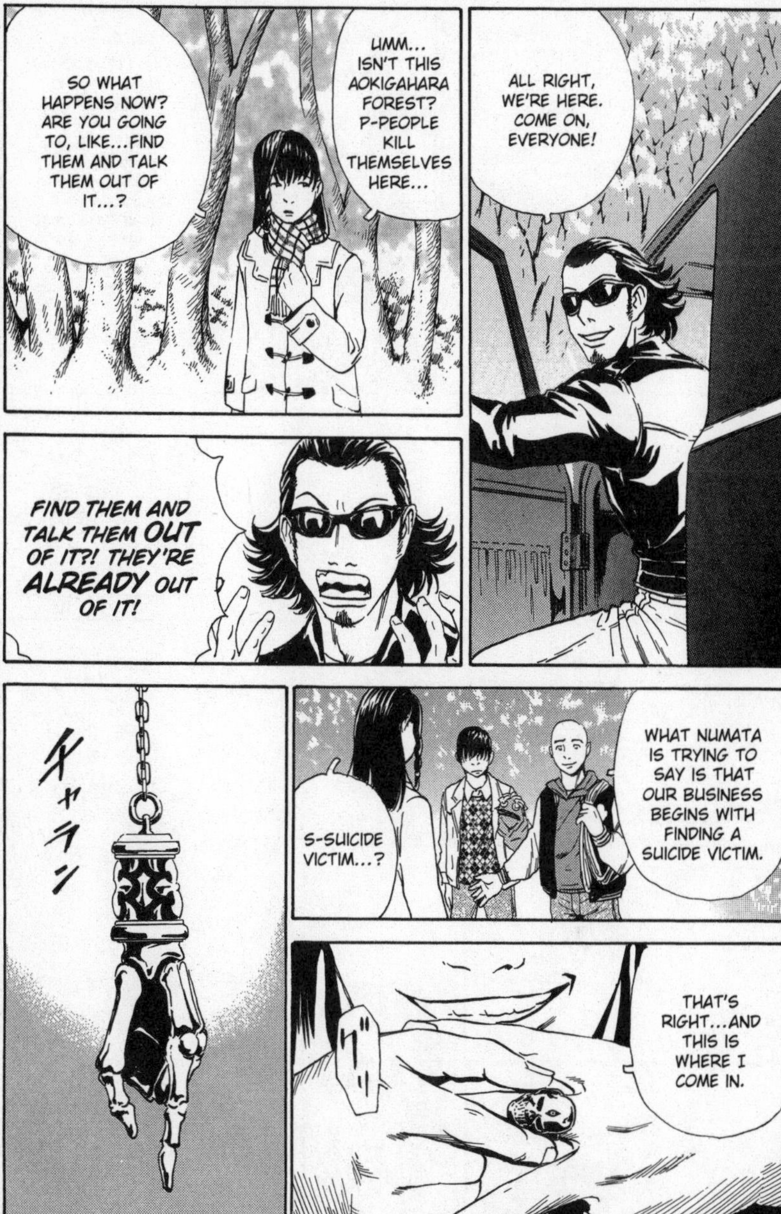
ALL RIGHT, WE'RE HERE. COME ON, EVERYONE!
UMM... ISN'T THIS AOKIGAHARA FOREST? P-PEOPLE KILL THEMSELVES HERE...
SO WHAT HAPPENS NOW? ARE YOU GOING TO, LIKE...FIND THEM AND TALK THEM OUT OF IT...?
FIND THEM AND TALK THEM OUT OF IT?! THEY'RE ALREADY OUT OF IT!
WHAT NUMATA IS TRYING TO SAY IS THAT OUR BUSINESS BEGINS WITH FINDING A SUICIDE VICTIM.
S-SUICIDE VICTIM...?
THAT'S RIGHT...AND THIS IS WHERE I COME IN.
ジャラン

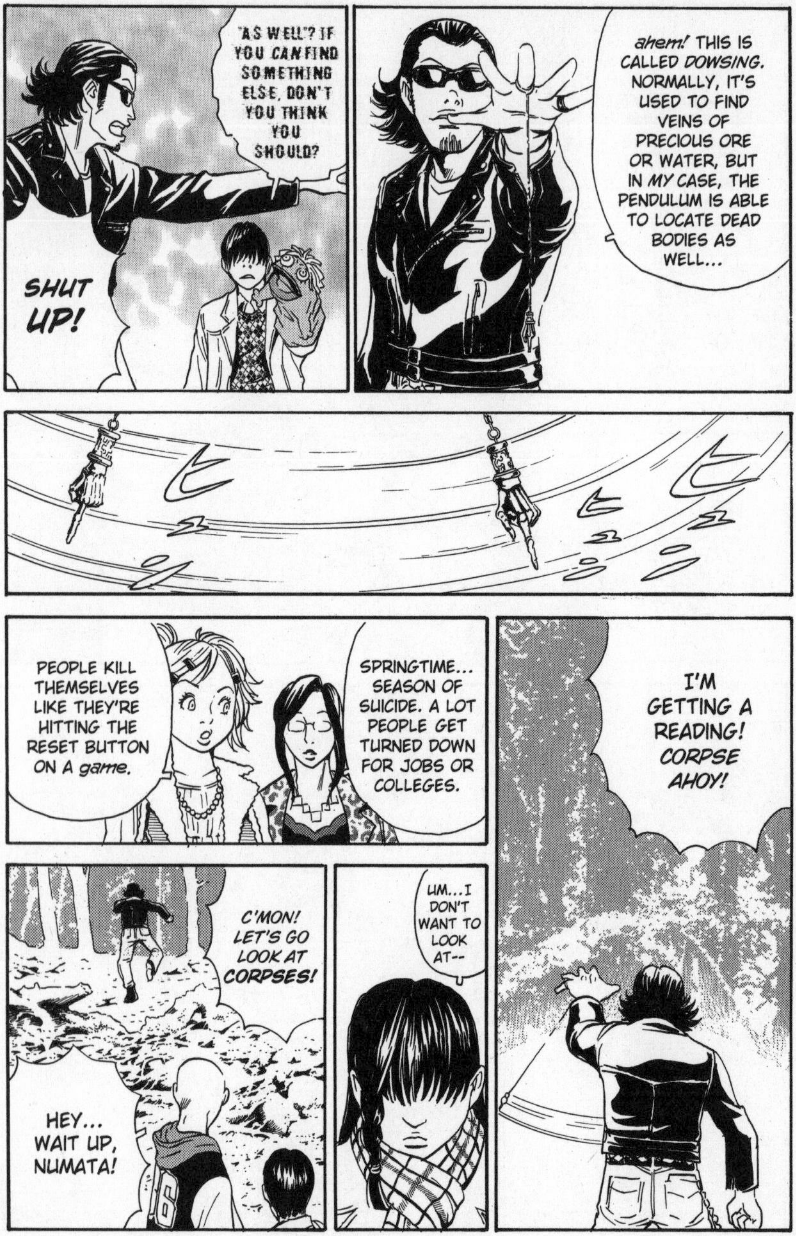
ahem! THIS IS CALLED DOWSING. NORMALLY, IT'S USED TO FIND VEINS OF PRECIOUS ORE OR WATER, BUT IN MY CASE, THE PENDULUM IS ABLE TO LOCATE DEAD BODIES AS WELL...
"AS WELL"? IF YOU CAN FIND SOMETHING ELSE, DON'T YOU THINK YOU SHOULD?
SHUT UP!
I'M GETTING A READING! CORPSE AHOY!
SPRINGTIME... SEASON OF SUICIDE. A LOT PEOPLE GET TURNED DOWN FOR JOBS OR COLLEGES.
PEOPLE KILL THEMSELVES LIKE THEY'RE HITTING THE RESET BUTTON ON A game.
UM...I DON'T WANT TO LOOK AT--
C'MON! LET'S GO LOOK AT CORPSES!
HEY... WAIT UP, NUMATA!

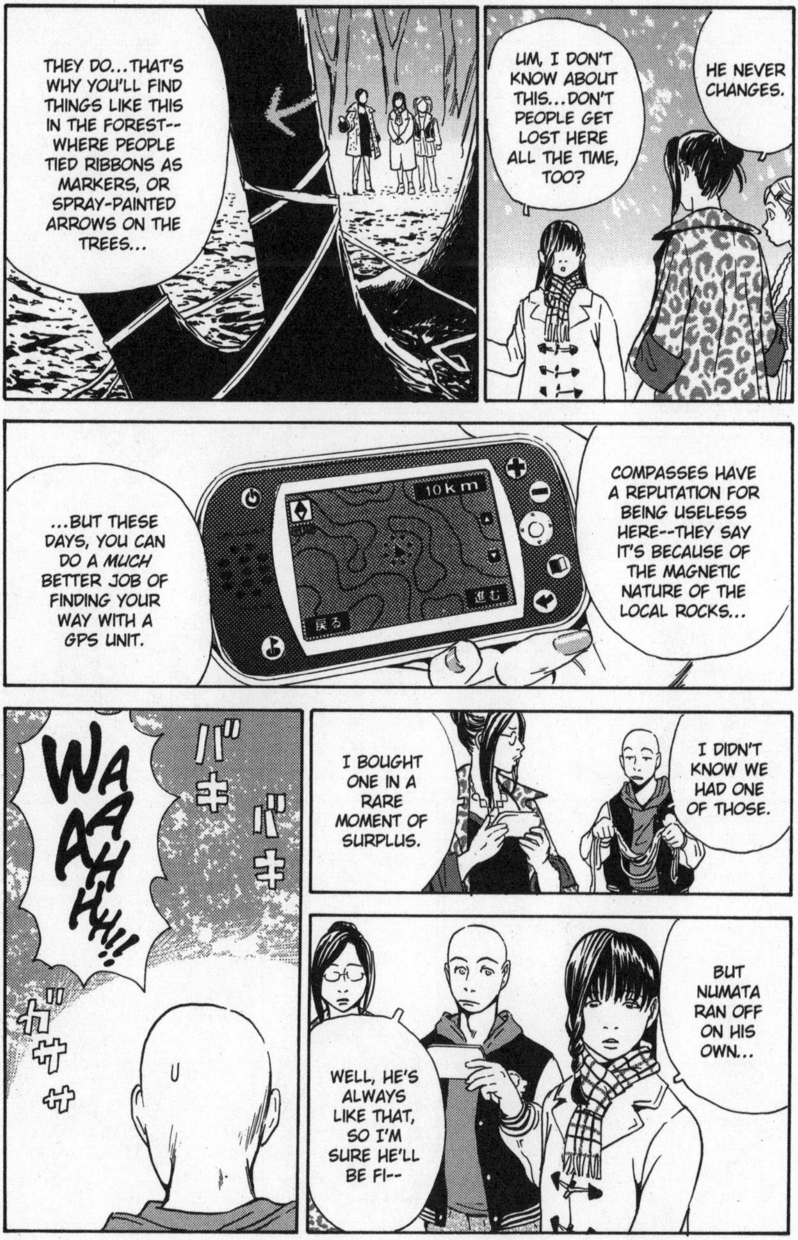
HE NEVER CHANGES.
UM, I DON'T KNOW ABOUT THIS...DON'T PEOPLE GET LOST HERE ALL THE TIME, TOO?
THEY DO...THAT'S WHY YOU'LL FIND THINGS LIKE THIS IN THE FOREST--WHERE PEOPLE TIED RIBBONS AS MARKERS, OR SPRAY-PAINTED ARROWS ON THE TREES...
COMPASSES HAVE A REPUTATION FOR BEING USELESS HERE--THEY SAY IT'S BECAUSE OF THE MAGNETIC NATURE OF THE LOCAL ROCKS...
10km
進む
戻る
...BUT THESE DAYS, YOU CAN DO A *MUCH* BETTER JOB OF FINDING YOUR WAY WITH A GPS UNIT.
I DIDN'T KNOW WE HAD ONE OF THOSE.
I BOUGHT ONE IN A RARE MOMENT OF SURPLUS.
BUT NUMATA RAN OFF ON HIS OWN...
WELL, HE'S ALWAYS LIKE THAT, SO I'M SURE HE'LL BE FI--
バキ
バキ
WAAAHH!!
ガサササ

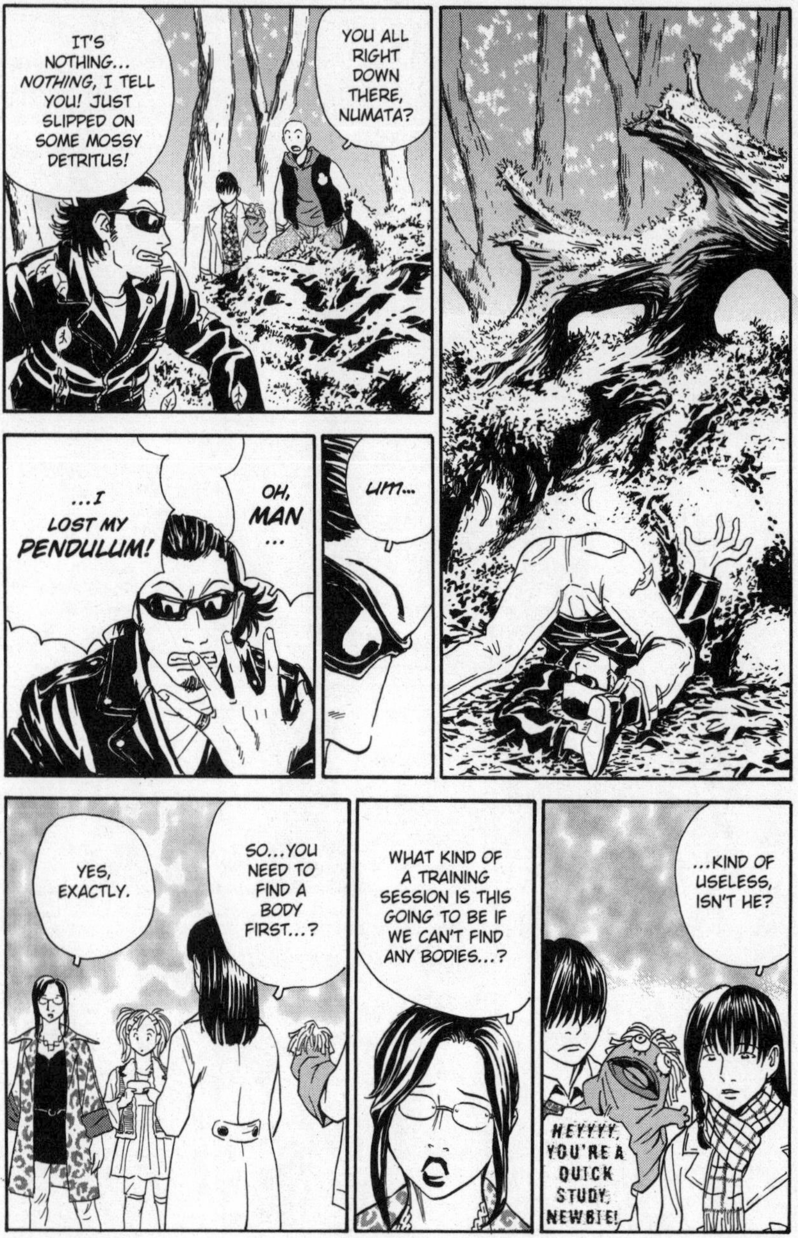
YOU ALL RIGHT DOWN THERE, NUMATA?
IT'S NOTHING... *NOTHING*, I TELL YOU! JUST SLIPPED ON SOME MOSSY DETRITUS!
UM...
OH, MAN ...
...I LOST MY PENDULUM!
...KIND OF USELESS, ISN'T HE?
HEYYYY, YOU'RE A QUICK STUDY, NEWBIE!
WHAT KIND OF A TRAINING SESSION IS THIS GOING TO BE IF WE CAN'T FIND ANY BODIES...?
SO...YOU NEED TO FIND A BODY FIRST...?
YES, EXACTLY.

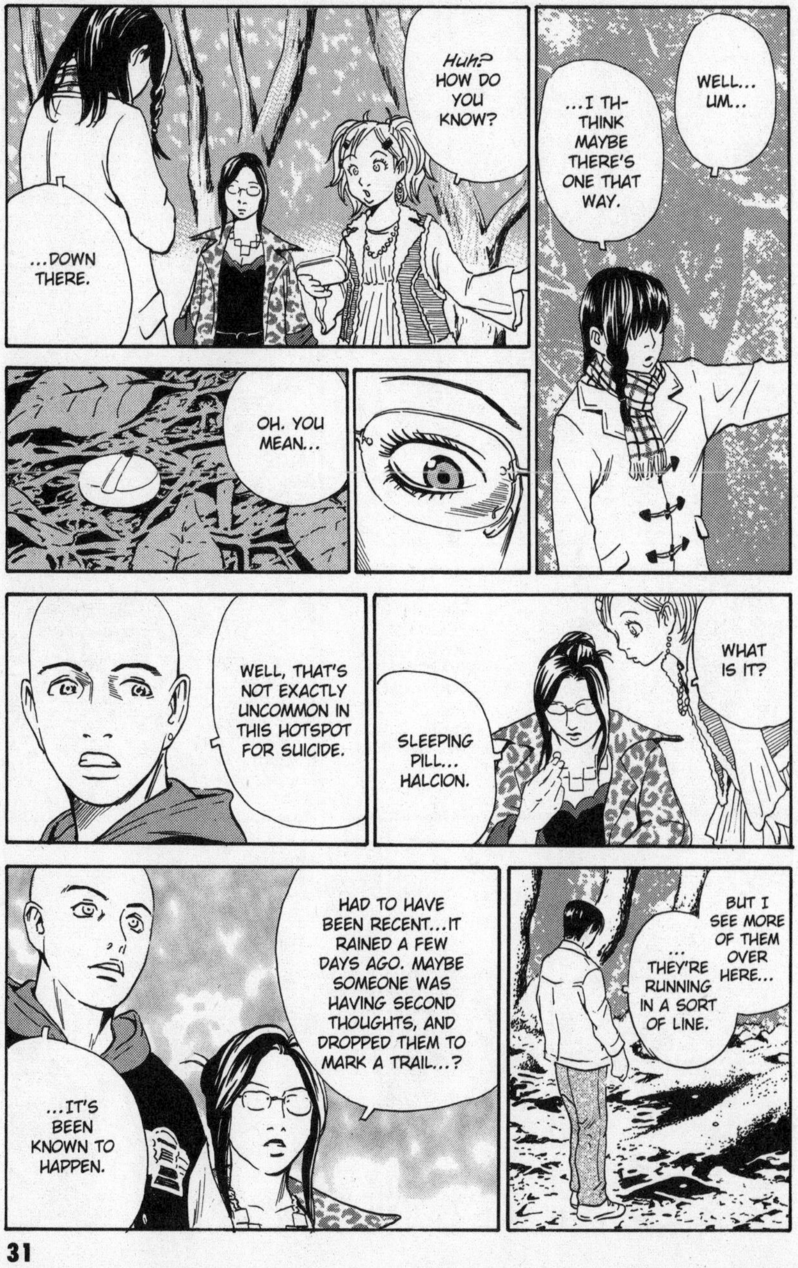
WELL... UM...
...I TH-THINK MAYBE THERE'S ONE THAT WAY.
Huh? HOW DO YOU KNOW?
...DOWN THERE.
OH. YOU MEAN...
WHAT IS IT?
SLEEPING PILL... HALCION.
WELL, THAT'S NOT EXACTLY UNCOMMON IN THIS HOTSPOT FOR SUICIDE.
BUT I SEE MORE OF THEM OVER HERE...
...THEY'RE RUNNING IN A SORT OF LINE.
HAD TO HAVE BEEN RECENT...IT RAINED A FEW DAYS AGO. MAYBE SOMEONE WAS HAVING SECOND THOUGHTS, AND DROPPED THEM TO MARK A TRAIL...?
...IT'S BEEN KNOWN TO HAPPEN.

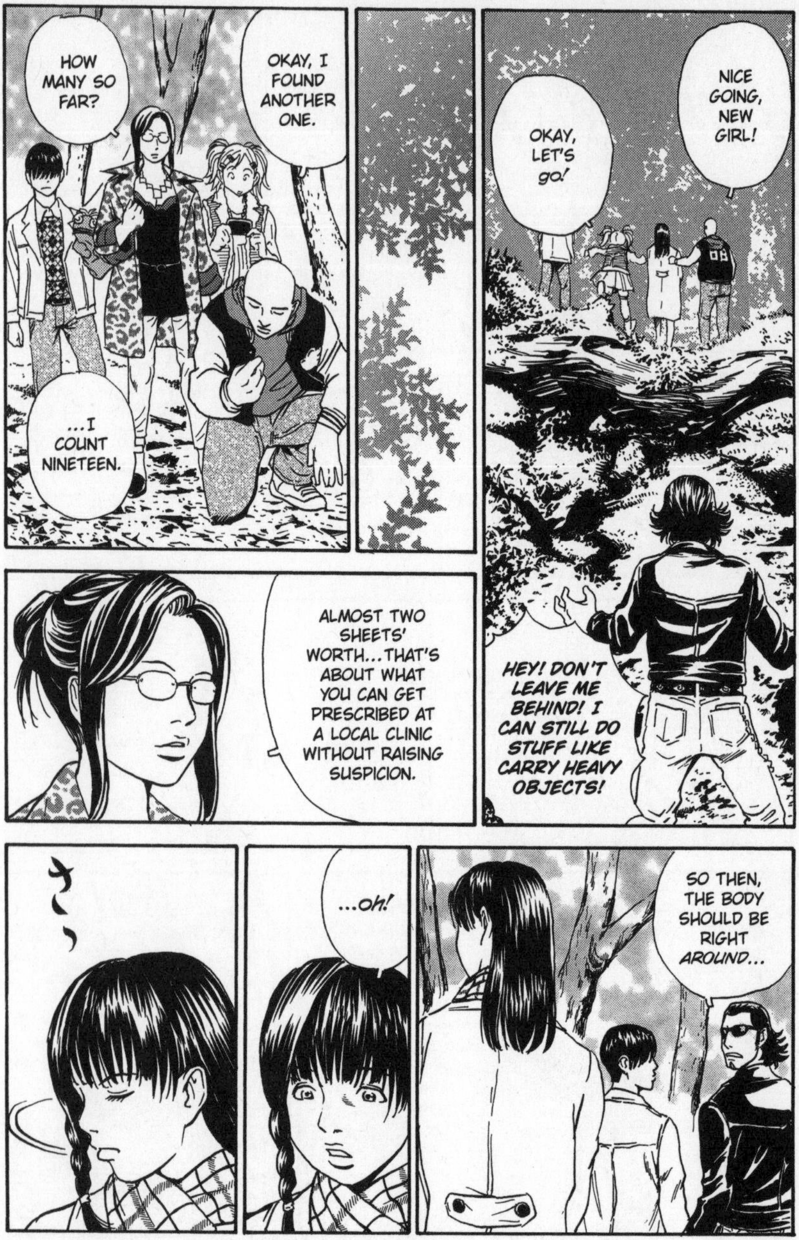
NICE GOING, NEW GIRL!
OKAY, LET'S go!
HEY! DON'T LEAVE ME BEHIND! I CAN STILL DO STUFF LIKE CARRY HEAVY OBJECTS!
OKAY, I FOUND ANOTHER ONE.
HOW MANY SO FAR?
...I COUNT NINETEEN.
ALMOST TWO SHEETS' WORTH...THAT'S ABOUT WHAT YOU CAN GET PRESCRIBED AT A LOCAL CLINIC WITHOUT RAISING SUSPICION.
SO THEN, THE BODY SHOULD BE RIGHT AROUND...
...oh!

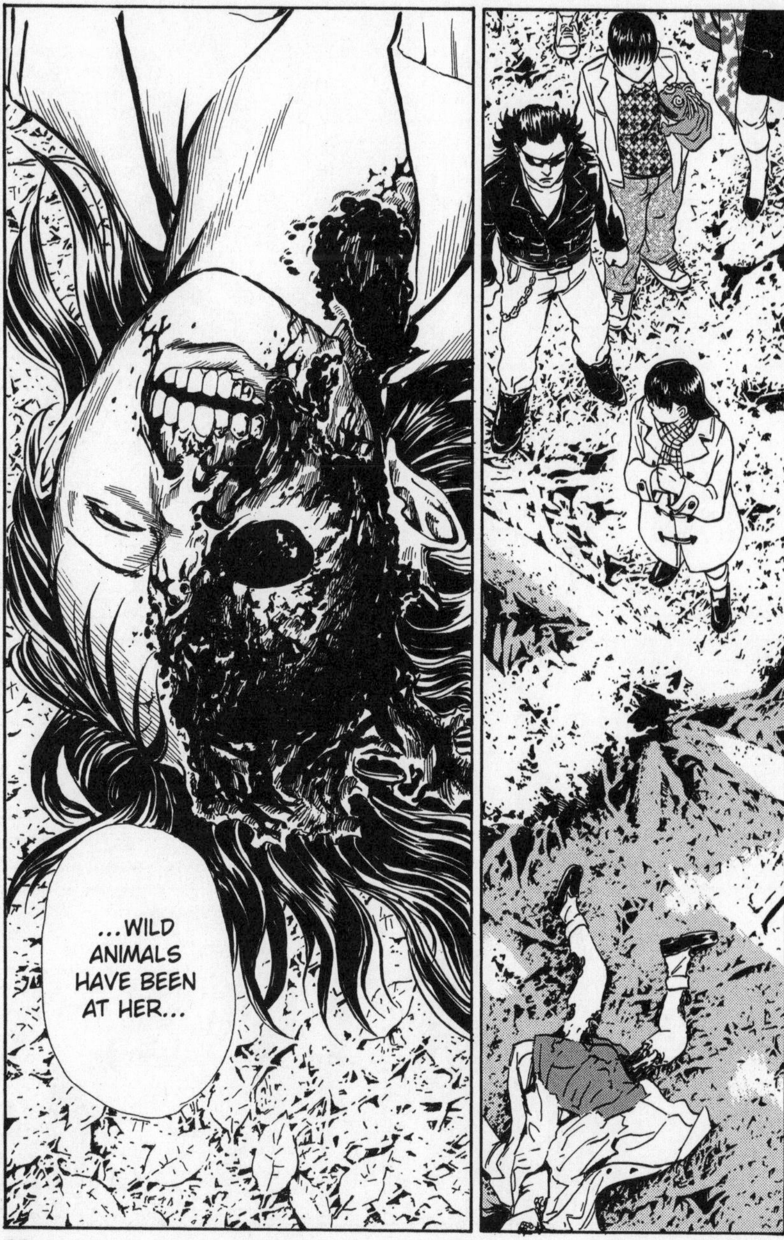
...WILD ANIMALS HAVE BEEN AT HER...

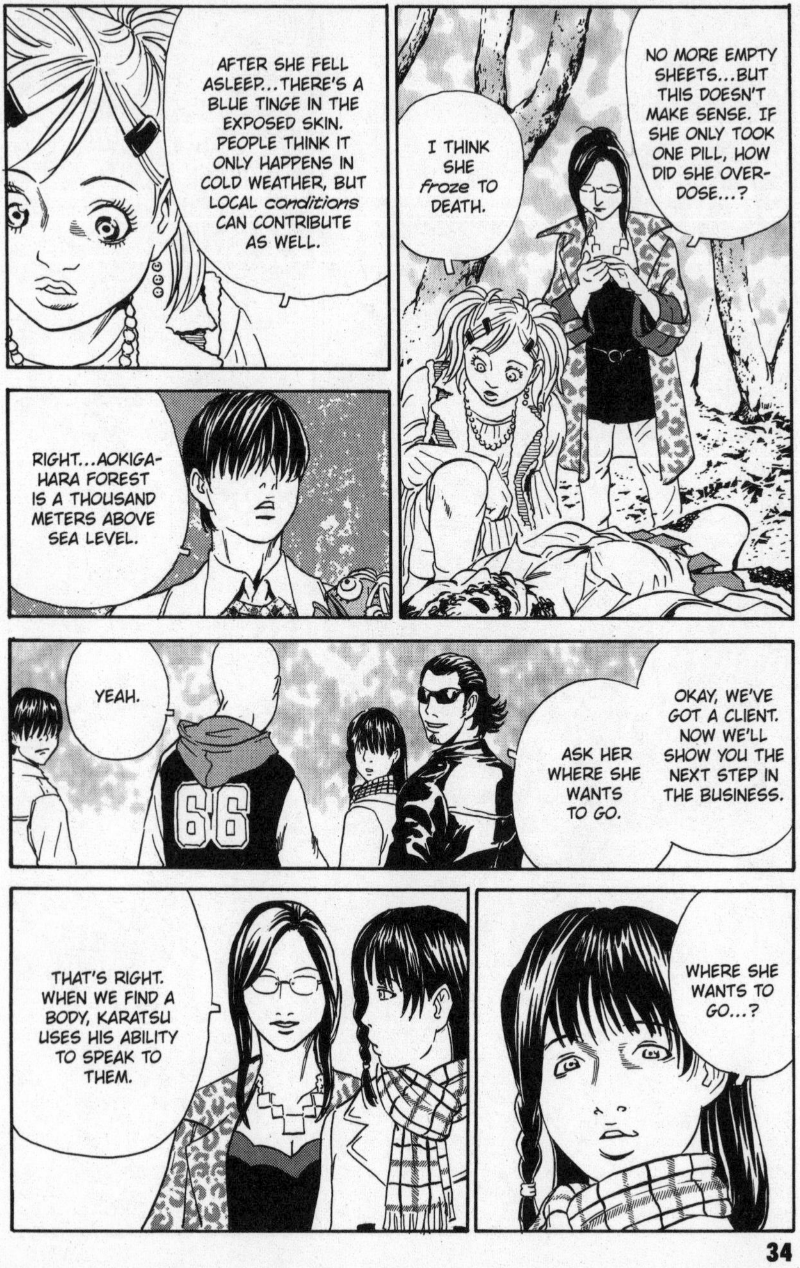
NO MORE EMPTY SHEETS...BUT THIS DOESN'T MAKE SENSE. IF SHE ONLY TOOK ONE PILL, HOW DID SHE OVER-DOSE...?
I THINK SHE *froze* TO DEATH.
AFTER SHE FELL ASLEEP...THERE'S A BLUE TINGE IN THE EXPOSED SKIN. PEOPLE THINK IT ONLY HAPPENS IN COLD WEATHER, BUT LOCAL *conditions* CAN CONTRIBUTE AS WELL.
RIGHT...AOKIGA-HARA FOREST IS A THOUSAND METERS ABOVE SEA LEVEL.
OKAY, WE'VE GOT A CLIENT. NOW WE'LL SHOW YOU THE NEXT STEP IN THE BUSINESS.
ASK HER WHERE SHE WANTS TO GO.
YEAH.
WHERE SHE WANTS TO GO...?
THAT'S RIGHT. WHEN WE FIND A BODY, KARATSU USES HIS ABILITY TO SPEAK TO THEM.

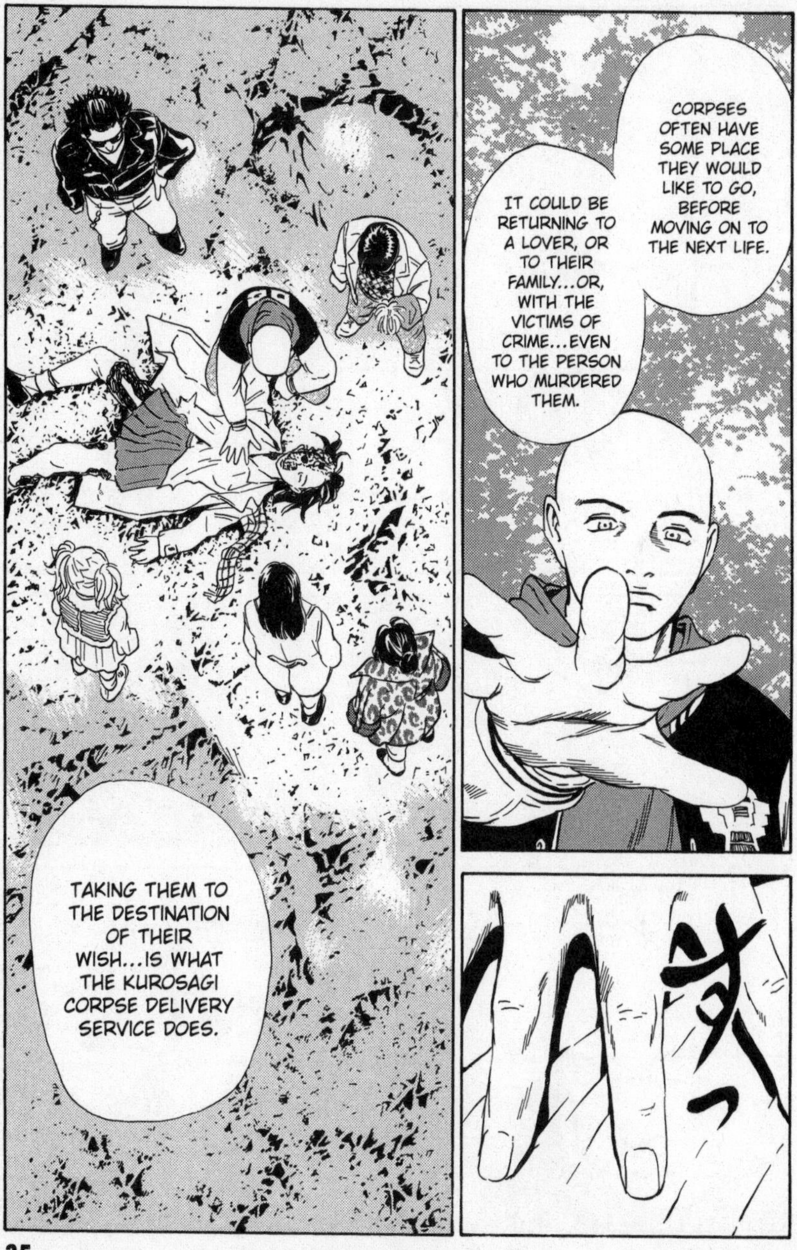
CORPSES OFTEN HAVE SOME PLACE THEY WOULD LIKE TO GO, BEFORE MOVING ON TO THE NEXT LIFE.
IT COULD BE RETURNING TO A LOVER, OR TO THEIR FAMILY...OR, WITH THE VICTIMS OF CRIME...EVEN TO THE PERSON WHO MURDERED THEM.
TAKING THEM TO THE DESTINATION OF THEIR WISH...IS WHAT THE KUROSAGI CORPSE DELIVERY SERVICE DOES.

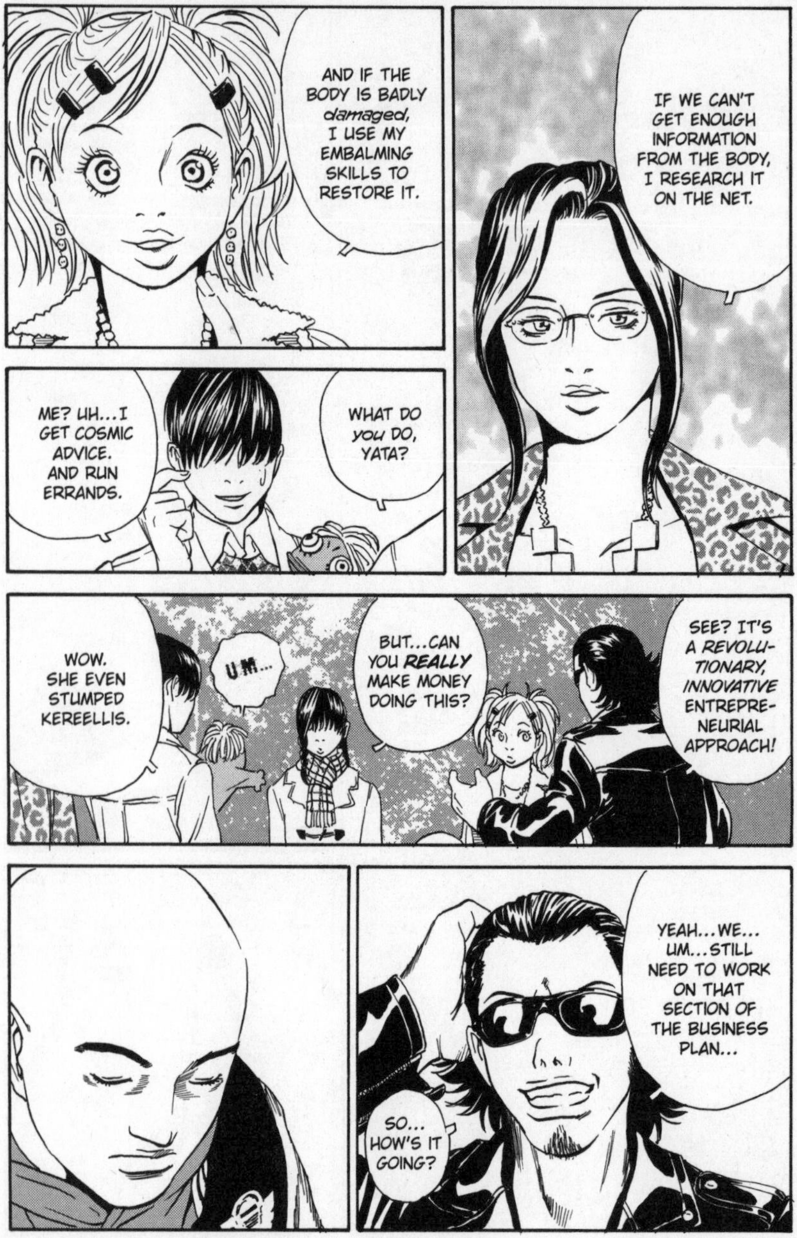
IF WE CAN'T GET ENOUGH INFORMATION FROM THE BODY, I RESEARCH IT ON THE NET.
AND IF THE BODY IS BADLY *damaged,* I USE MY EMBALMING SKILLS TO RESTORE IT.
WHAT DO *you* DO, YATA?
ME? UH...I GET COSMIC ADVICE. AND RUN ERRANDS.
SEE? IT'S A *REVOLUTIONARY, INNOVATIVE* ENTREPRENEURIAL APPROACH!
BUT...CAN YOU ***REALLY*** MAKE MONEY DOING THIS?
UM...
WOW. SHE EVEN STUMPED KEREELLIS.
YEAH...WE... UM...STILL NEED TO WORK ON THAT SECTION OF THE BUSINESS PLAN...
SO... HOW'S IT GOING?

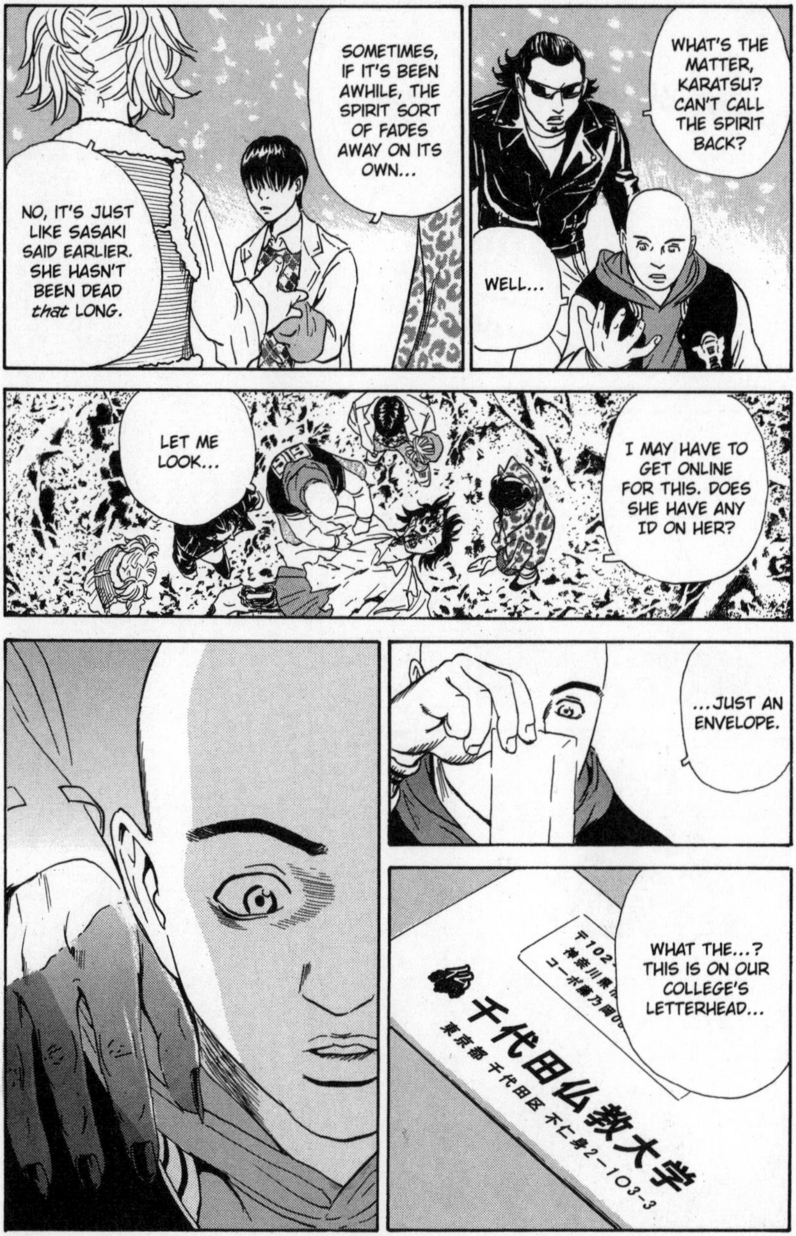
WHAT'S THE MATTER, KARATSU? CAN'T CALL THE SPIRIT BACK?
WELL...
SOMETIMES, IF IT'S BEEN AWHILE, THE SPIRIT SORT OF FADES AWAY ON ITS OWN...
NO, IT'S JUST LIKE SASAKI SAID EARLIER. SHE HASN'T BEEN DEAD *that* LONG.
I MAY HAVE TO GET ONLINE FOR THIS. DOES SHE HAVE ANY ID ON HER?
LET ME LOOK...
...JUST AN ENVELOPE.
WHAT THE...? THIS IS ON OUR COLLEGE'S LETTERHEAD...
千代田仏教大学
東京都 千代田区 不仁身2−103−3

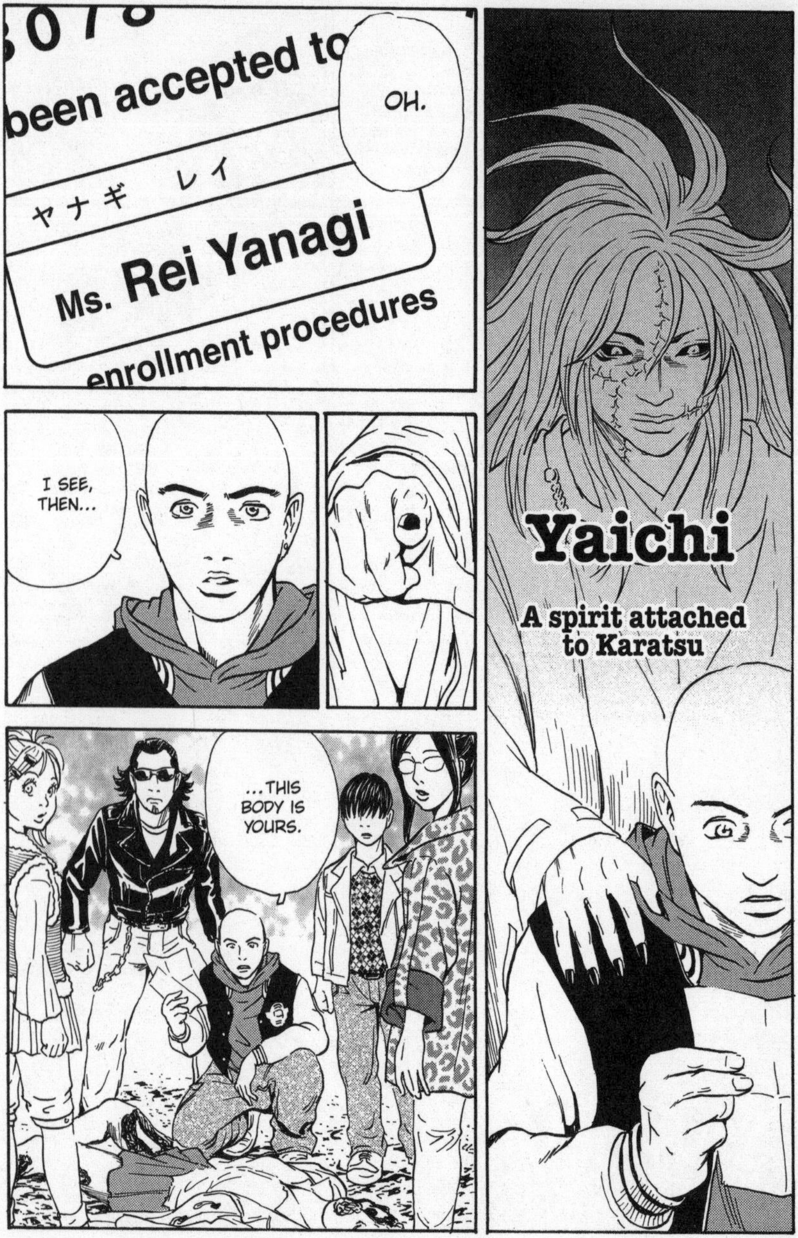
Yaichi
A spirit attached to Karatsu
3078
been accepted to
ヤナギ レイ
Ms. Rei Yanagi
enrollment procedures
OH.
I SEE, THEN...
...THIS BODY IS YOURS.

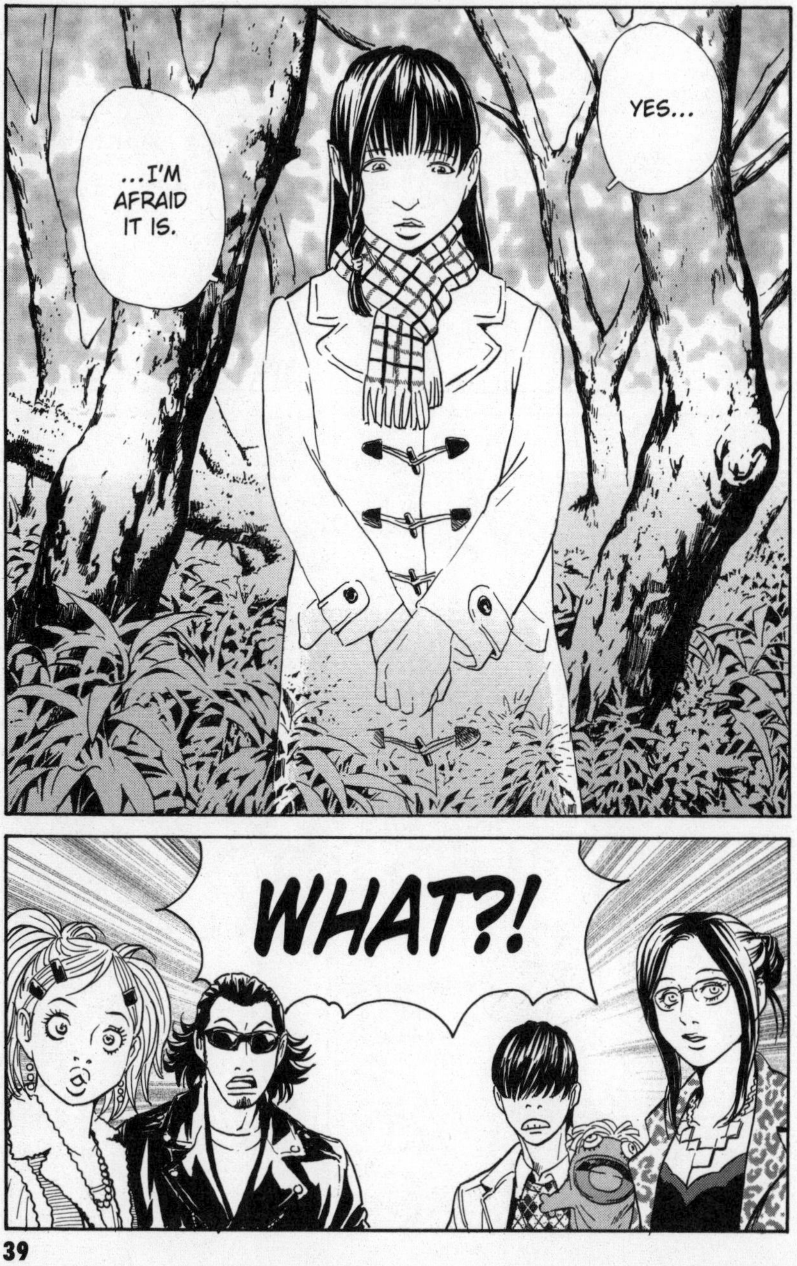
YES...
...I'M AFRAID IT IS.
WHAT?!

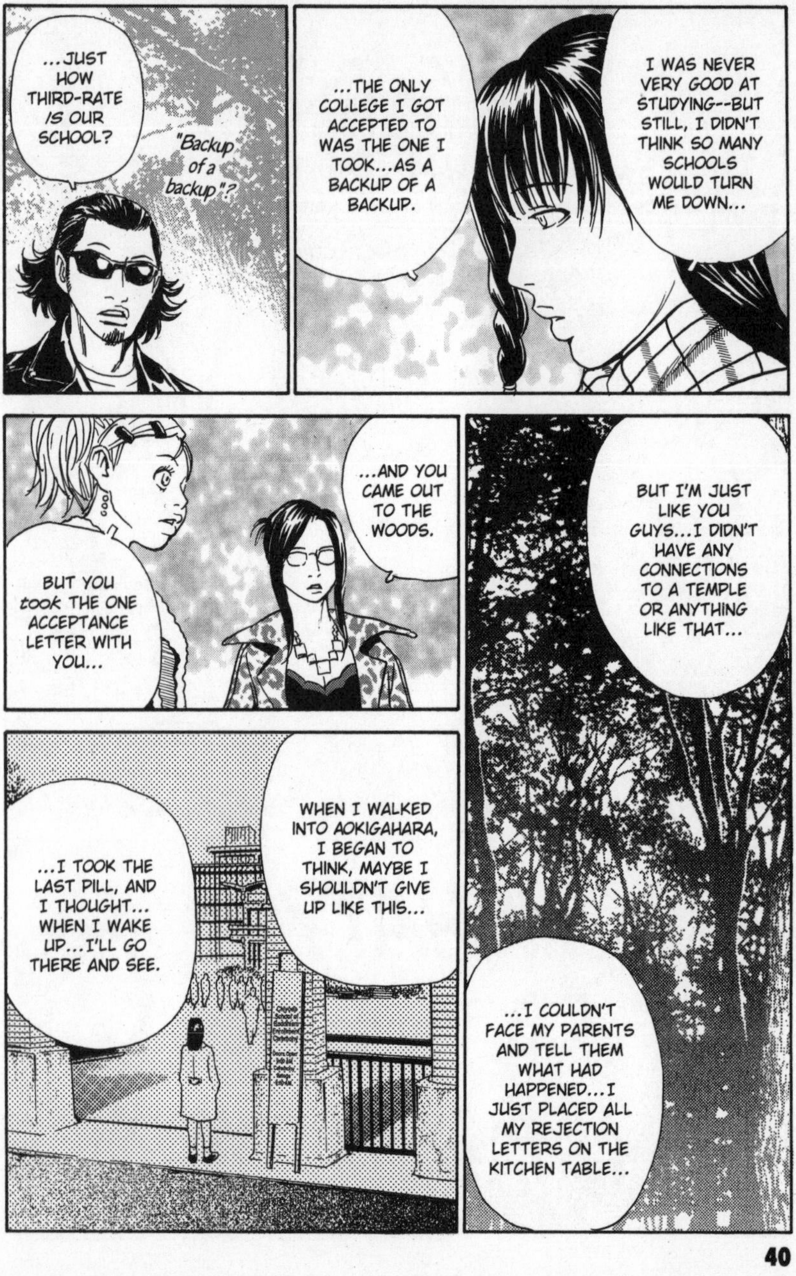
I WAS NEVER VERY GOOD AT STUDYING--BUT STILL, I DIDN'T THINK SO MANY SCHOOLS WOULD TURN ME DOWN...
...THE ONLY COLLEGE I GOT ACCEPTED TO WAS THE ONE I TOOK...AS A BACKUP OF A BACKUP.
"Backup of a backup"?
...JUST HOW THIRD-RATE *IS* OUR SCHOOL?
BUT I'M JUST LIKE YOU GUYS...I DIDN'T HAVE ANY CONNECTIONS TO A TEMPLE OR ANYTHING LIKE THAT...
...I COULDN'T FACE MY PARENTS AND TELL THEM WHAT HAD HAPPENED...I JUST PLACED ALL MY REJECTION LETTERS ON THE KITCHEN TABLE...
...AND YOU CAME OUT TO THE WOODS.
BUT YOU *took* THE ONE ACCEPTANCE LETTER WITH YOU...
WHEN I WALKED INTO AOKIGAHARA, I BEGAN TO THINK, MAYBE I SHOULDN'T GIVE UP LIKE THIS...
...I TOOK THE LAST PILL, AND I THOUGHT... WHEN I WAKE UP...I'LL GO THERE AND SEE.

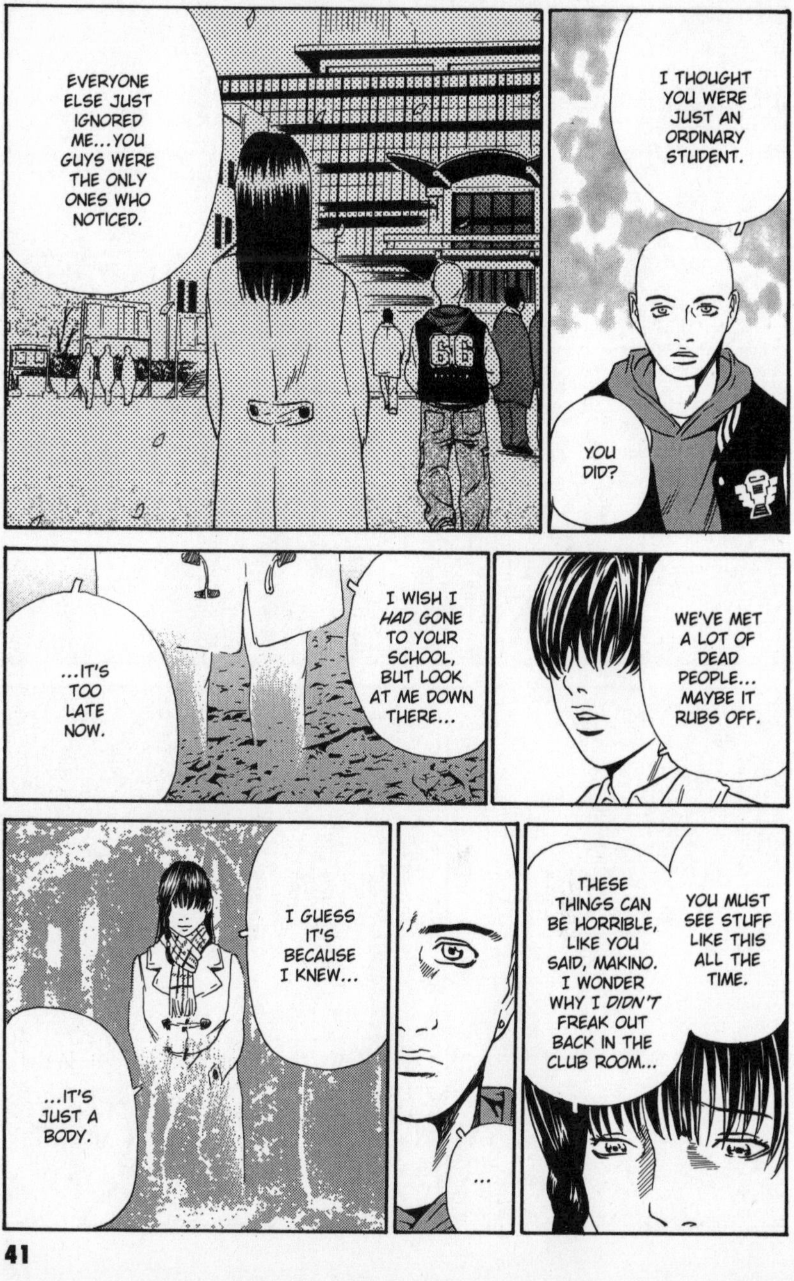
I THOUGHT YOU WERE JUST AN ORDINARY STUDENT.
YOU DID?
EVERYONE ELSE JUST IGNORED ME...YOU GUYS WERE THE ONLY ONES WHO NOTICED.
WE'VE MET A LOT OF DEAD PEOPLE... MAYBE IT RUBS OFF.
I WISH I *HAD* GONE TO YOUR SCHOOL, BUT LOOK AT ME DOWN THERE...
...IT'S TOO LATE NOW.
YOU MUST SEE STUFF LIKE THIS ALL THE TIME.
THESE THINGS CAN BE HORRIBLE, LIKE YOU SAID, MAKINO. I WONDER WHY I *DIDN'T* FREAK OUT BACK IN THE CLUB ROOM...
...
I GUESS IT'S BECAUSE I KNEW...
...IT'S JUST A BODY.

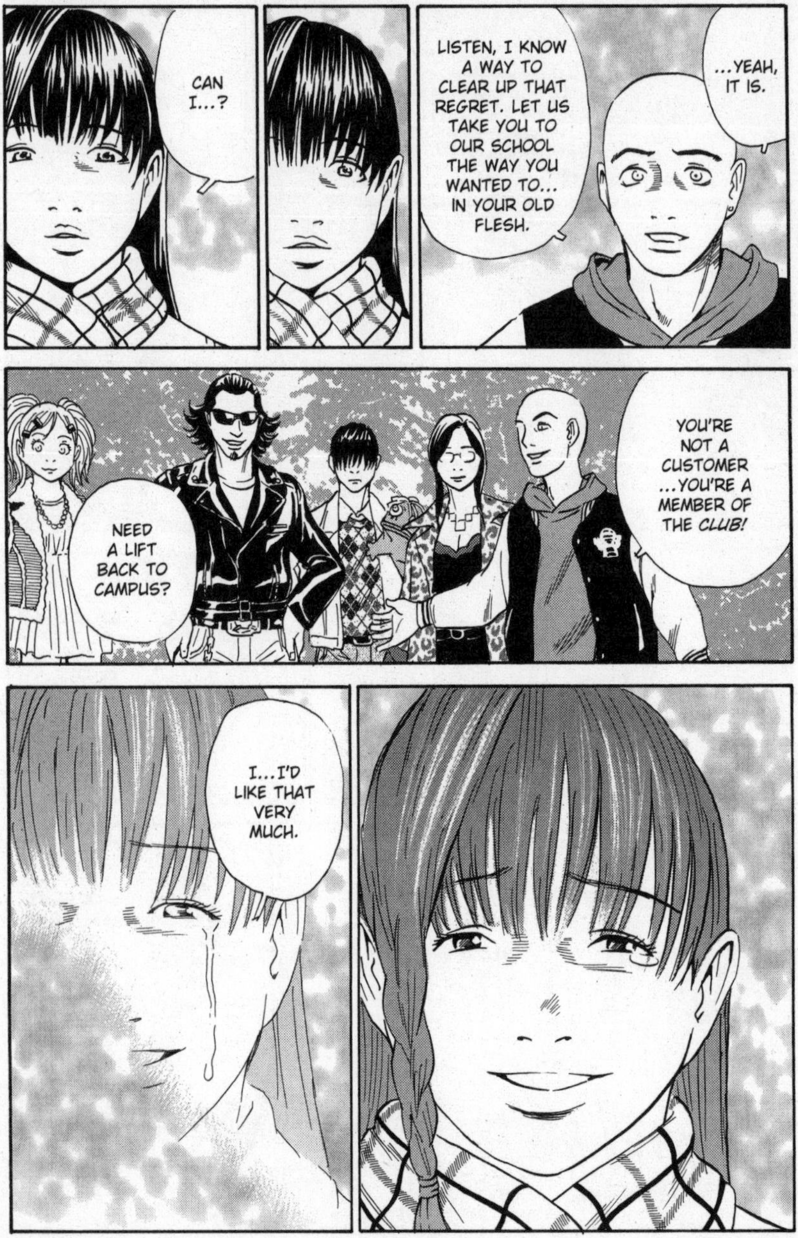
...YEAH, IT IS.
LISTEN, I KNOW A WAY TO CLEAR UP THAT REGRET. LET US TAKE YOU TO OUR SCHOOL THE WAY YOU WANTED TO... IN YOUR OLD FLESH.
CAN I...?
YOU'RE NOT A CUSTOMER ...YOU'RE A MEMBER OF THE *CLUB!*
NEED A LIFT BACK TO CAMPUS?
I...I'D LIKE THAT VERY MUCH.

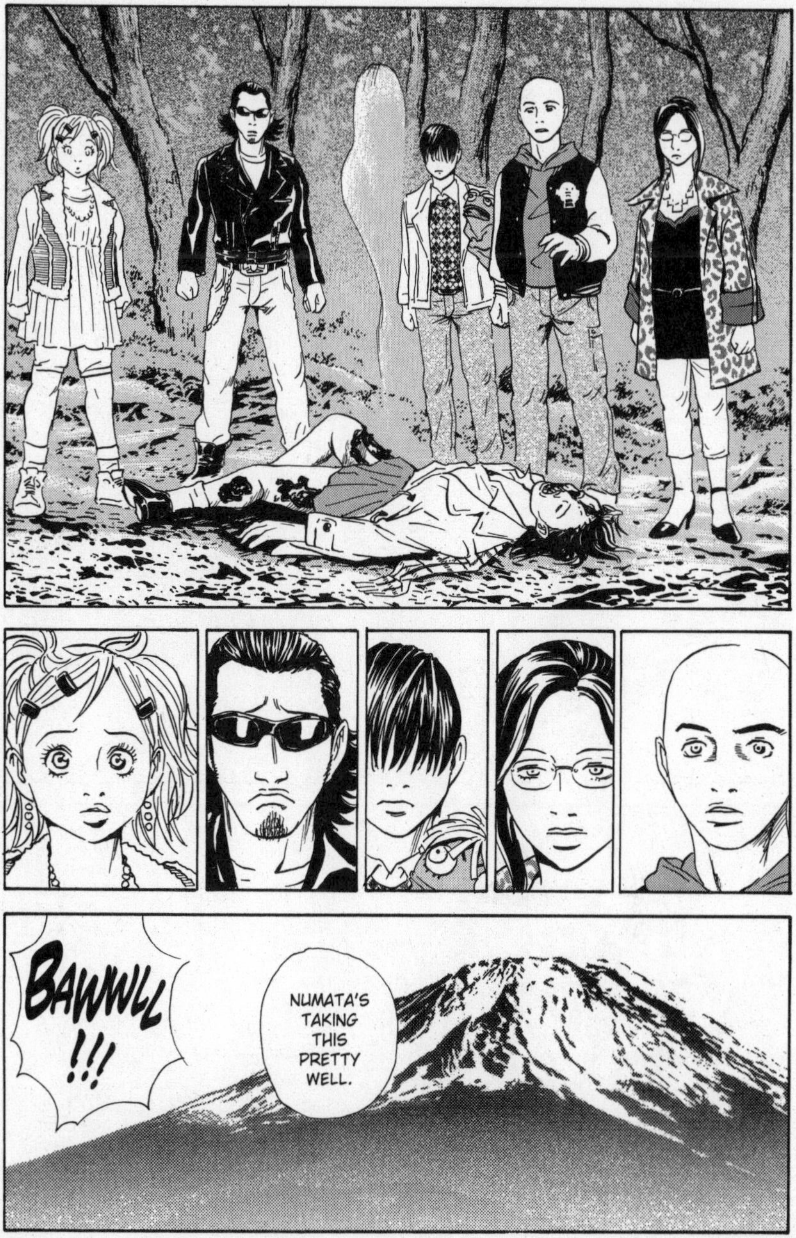
NUMATA'S TAKING THIS PRETTY WELL.
BAWWLL !!!

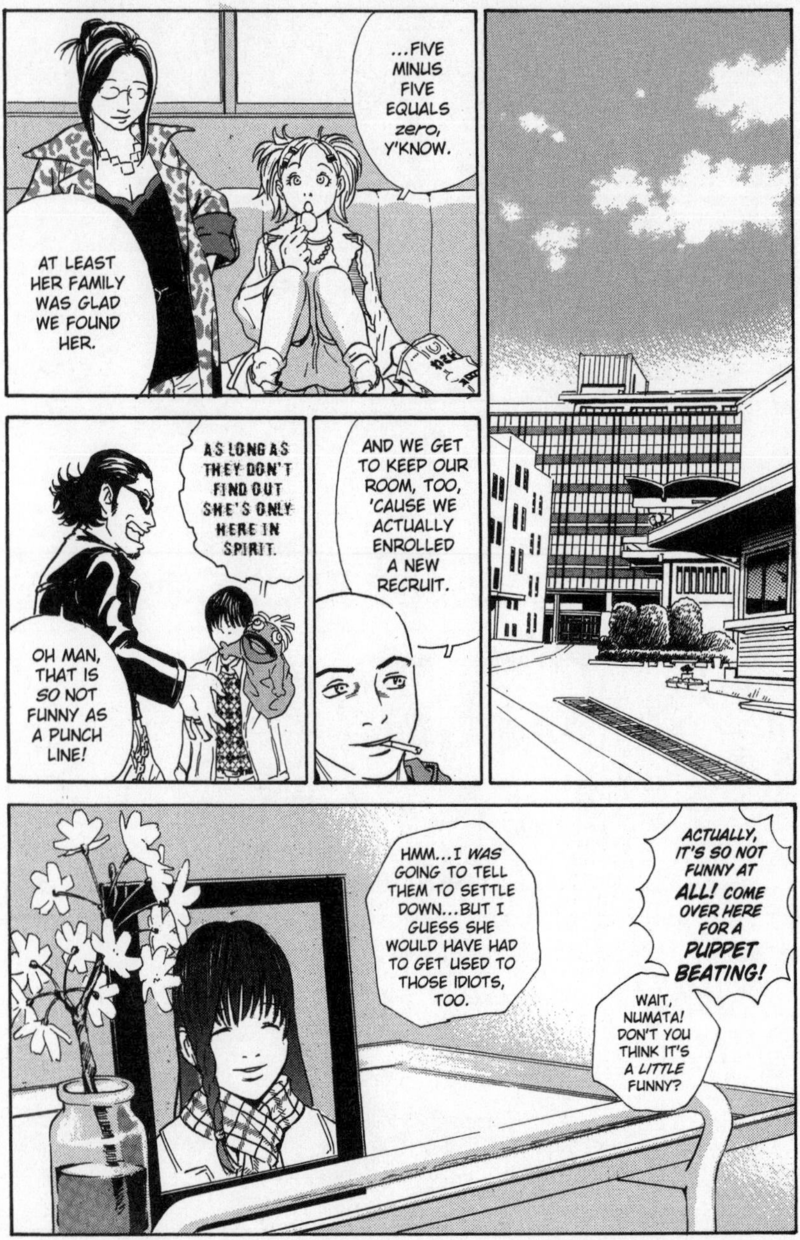
...FIVE MINUS FIVE EQUALS zero, Y'KNOW.
AT LEAST HER FAMILY WAS GLAD WE FOUND HER.
AND WE GET TO KEEP OUR ROOM, TOO, 'CAUSE WE ACTUALLY ENROLLED A NEW RECRUIT.
AS LONG AS THEY DON'T FIND OUT SHE'S ONLY HERE IN SPIRIT.
OH MAN, THAT IS SO NOT FUNNY AS A PUNCH LINE!
ACTUALLY, IT'S SO NOT FUNNY AT ALL! COME OVER HERE FOR A PUPPET BEATING!
HMM...I WAS GOING TO TELL THEM TO SETTLE DOWN...BUT I GUESS SHE WOULD HAVE HAD TO GET USED TO THOSE IDIOTS, TOO.
WAIT, NUMATA! DON'T YOU THINK IT'S A LITTLE FUNNY?

1st delivery: a café in a campus town—the end

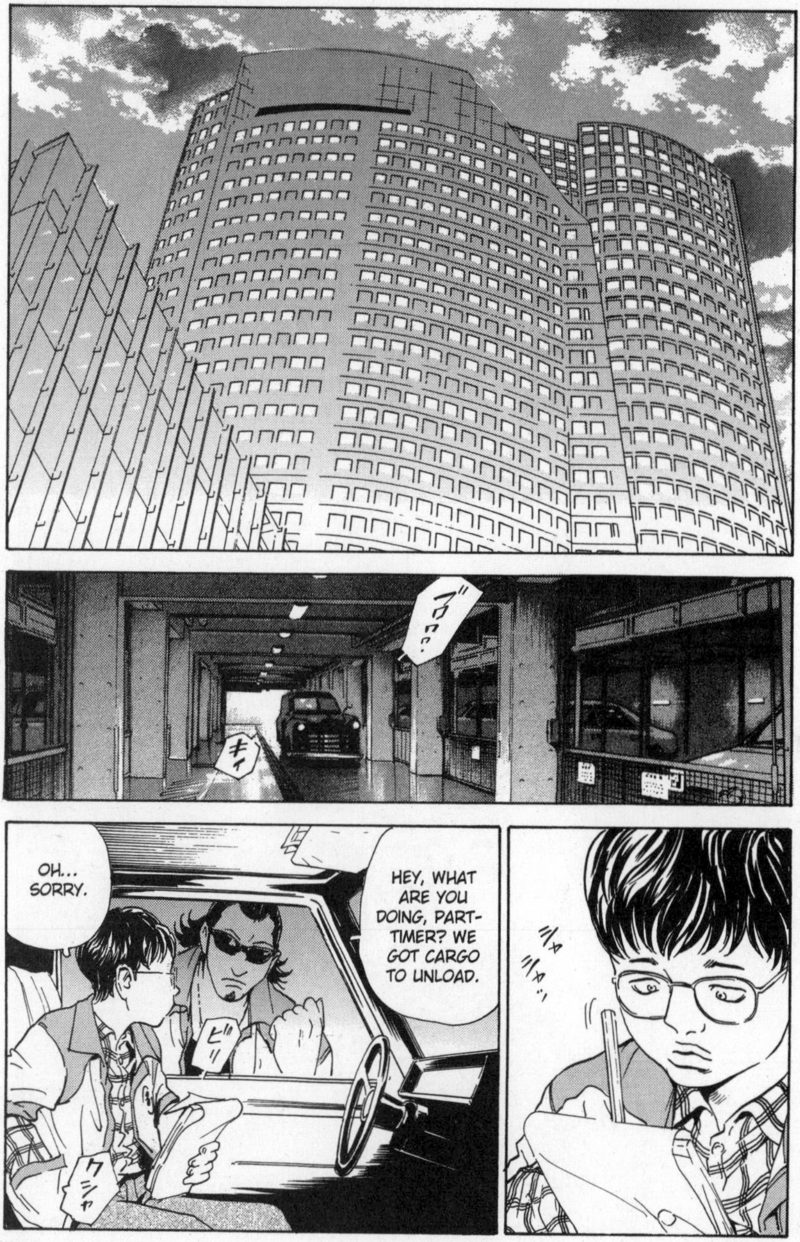
HEY, WHAT ARE YOU DOING, PART-TIMER? WE GOT CARGO TO UNLOAD.
OH... SORRY.

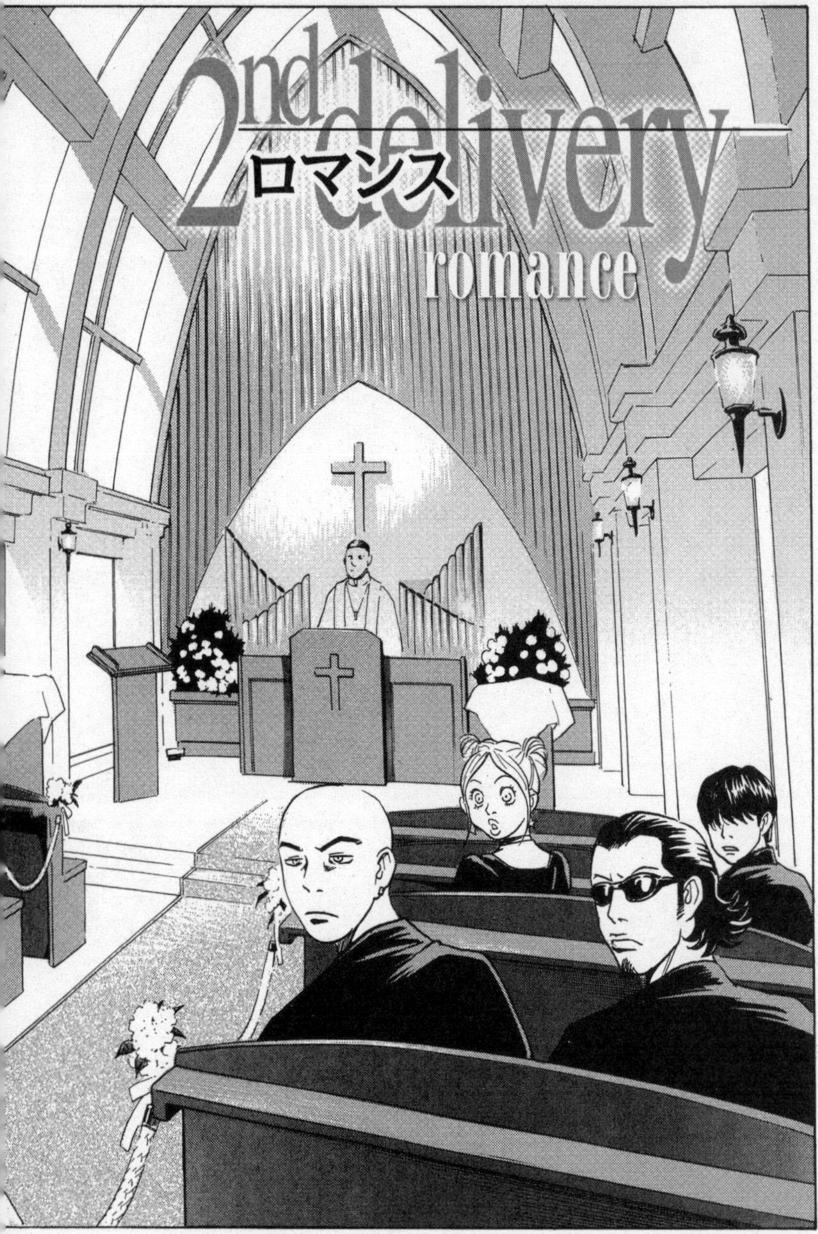
2nd delivery
ロマンス
romance

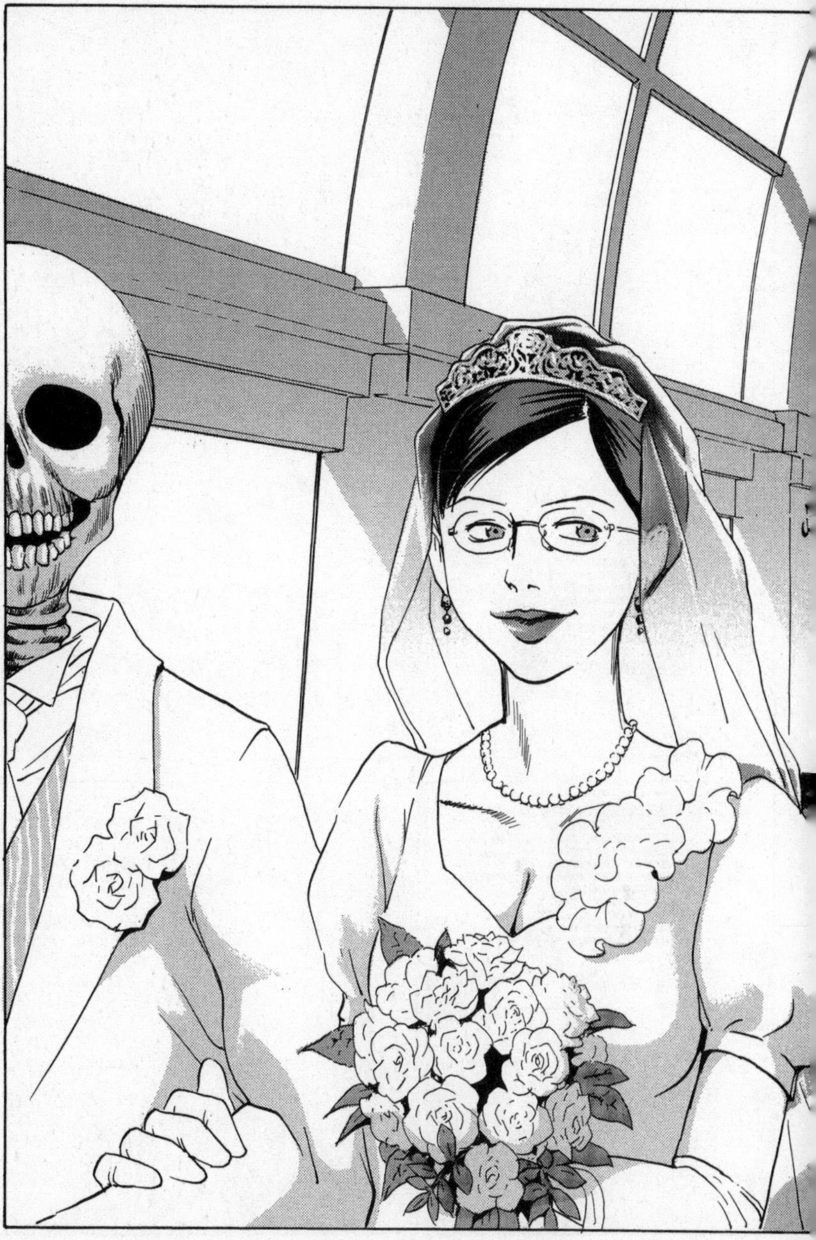

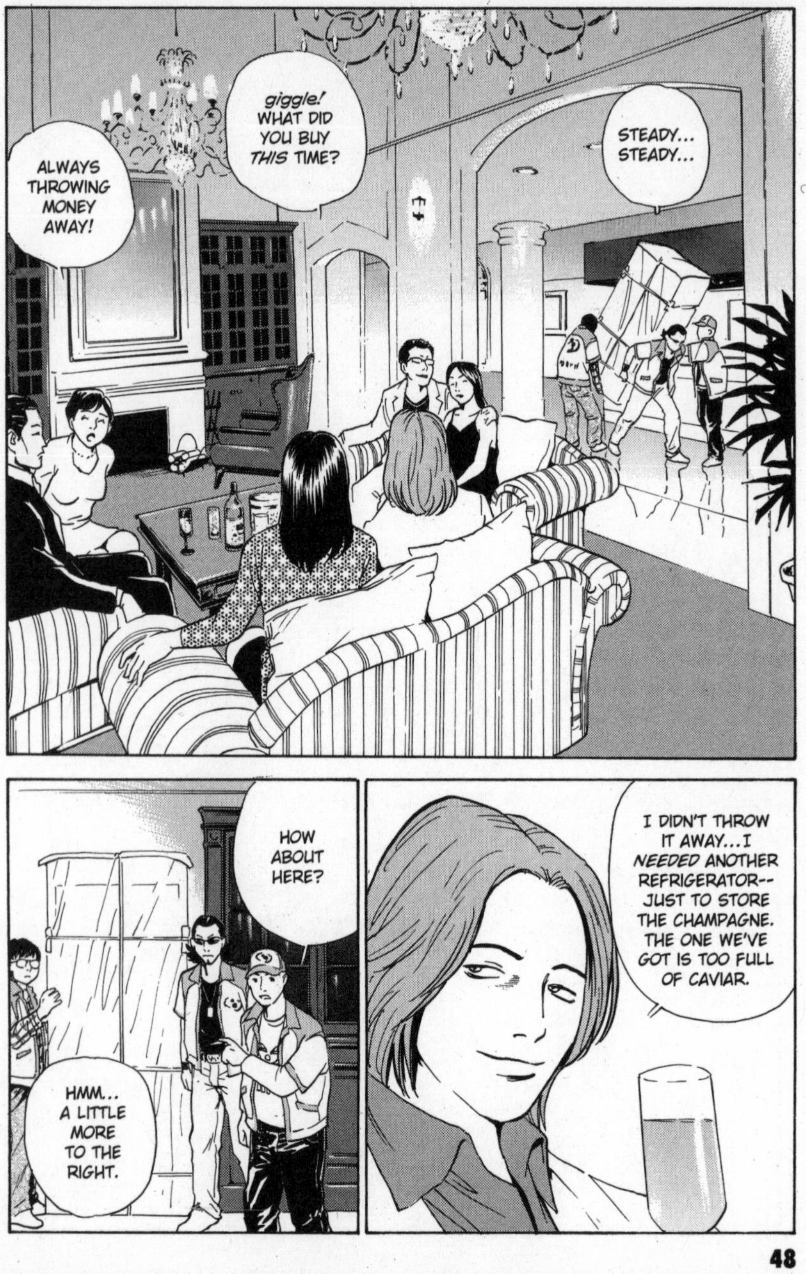
STEADY... STEADY...
giggle! WHAT DID YOU BUY THIS TIME?
ALWAYS THROWING MONEY AWAY!
I DIDN'T THROW IT AWAY...I NEEDED ANOTHER REFRIGERATOR-- JUST TO STORE THE CHAMPAGNE. THE ONE WE'VE GOT IS TOO FULL OF CAVIAR.
HOW ABOUT HERE?
HMM... A LITTLE MORE TO THE RIGHT.

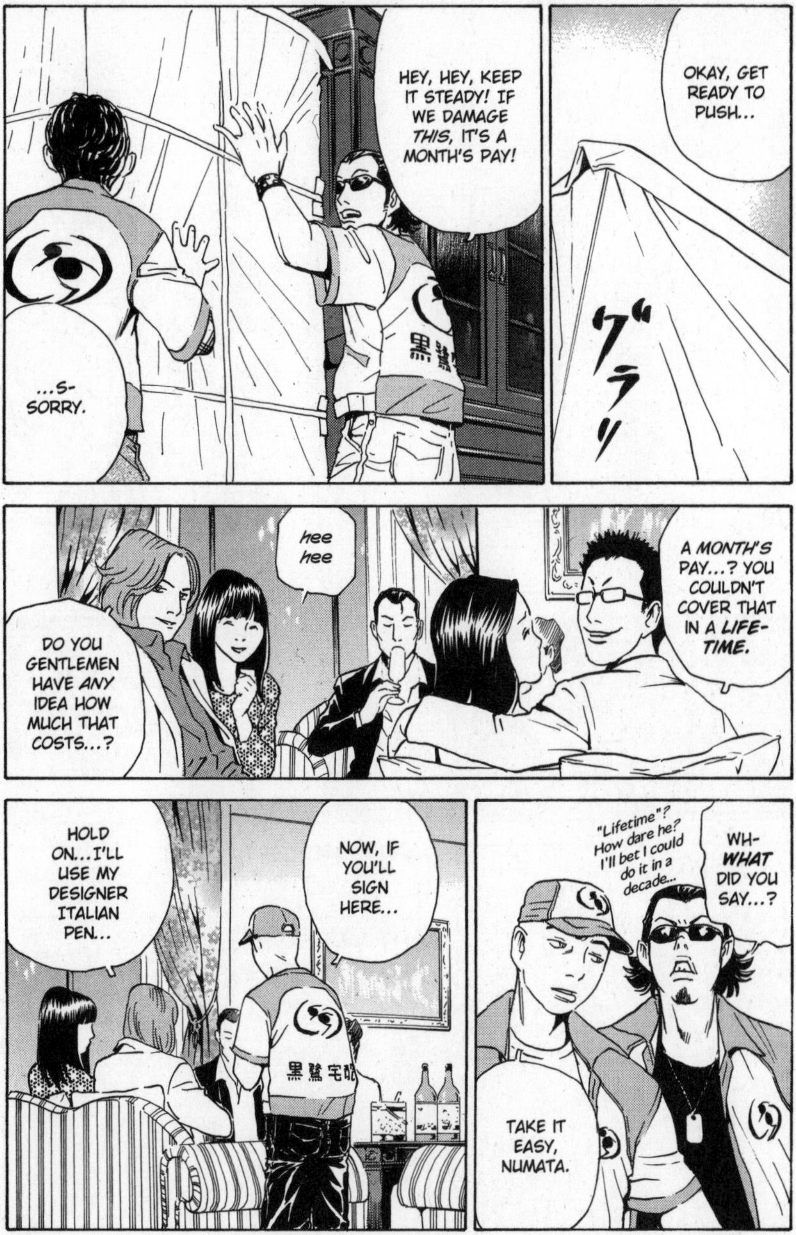
OKAY, GET READY TO PUSH...
グラッ
HEY, HEY, KEEP IT STEADY! IF WE DAMAGE *THIS*, IT'S A MONTH'S PAY!
...S- SORRY.
A *MONTH'S* PAY...? YOU COULDN'T COVER THAT IN A *LIFE-TIME.*
hee hee
DO YOU GENTLEMEN HAVE *ANY* IDEA HOW MUCH THAT COSTS...?
WH- *WHAT* DID YOU SAY...?
"Lifetime"? How dare he? I'll bet I could do it in a decade...
TAKE IT EASY, NUMATA.
NOW, IF YOU'LL SIGN HERE...
HOLD ON...I'LL USE MY DESIGNER ITALIAN PEN...
黒鷺宅配

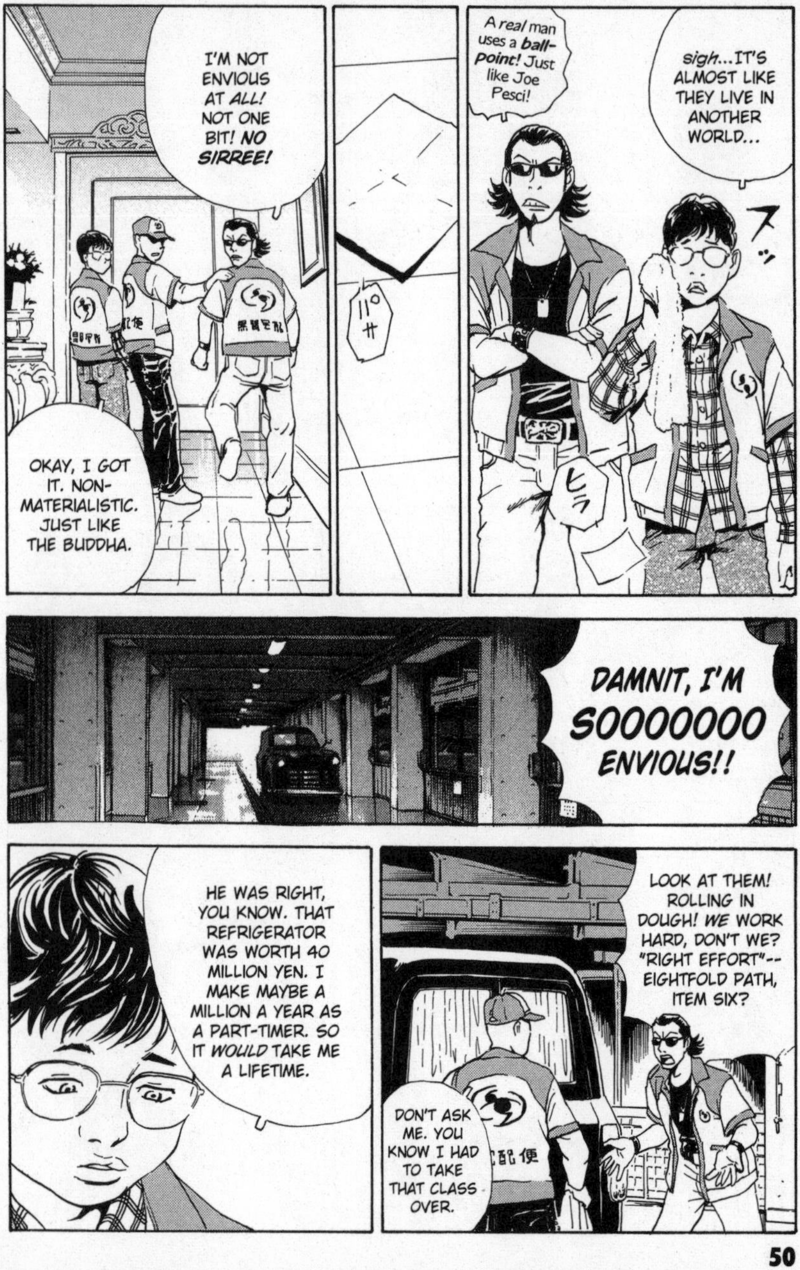

sigh...IT'S ALMOST LIKE THEY LIVE IN ANOTHER WORLD...
A *real* man uses a **ball-point!** Just like Joe Pesci!
I'M NOT ENVIOUS AT *ALL!* NOT ONE BIT! ***NO SIRREE!***
OKAY, I GOT IT. NON-MATERIALISTIC. JUST LIKE THE BUDDHA.
DAMNIT, I'M SOOOOOOO ENVIOUS!!
LOOK AT THEM! ROLLING IN DOUGH! *WE* WORK HARD, DON'T WE? "RIGHT EFFORT"-- EIGHTFOLD PATH, ITEM SIX?
DON'T ASK ME. YOU KNOW I HAD TO TAKE THAT CLASS OVER.
HE WAS RIGHT, YOU KNOW. THAT REFRIGERATOR WAS WORTH 40 MILLION YEN. I MAKE MAYBE A MILLION A YEAR AS A PART-TIMER. SO IT *WOULD* TAKE ME A LIFETIME.

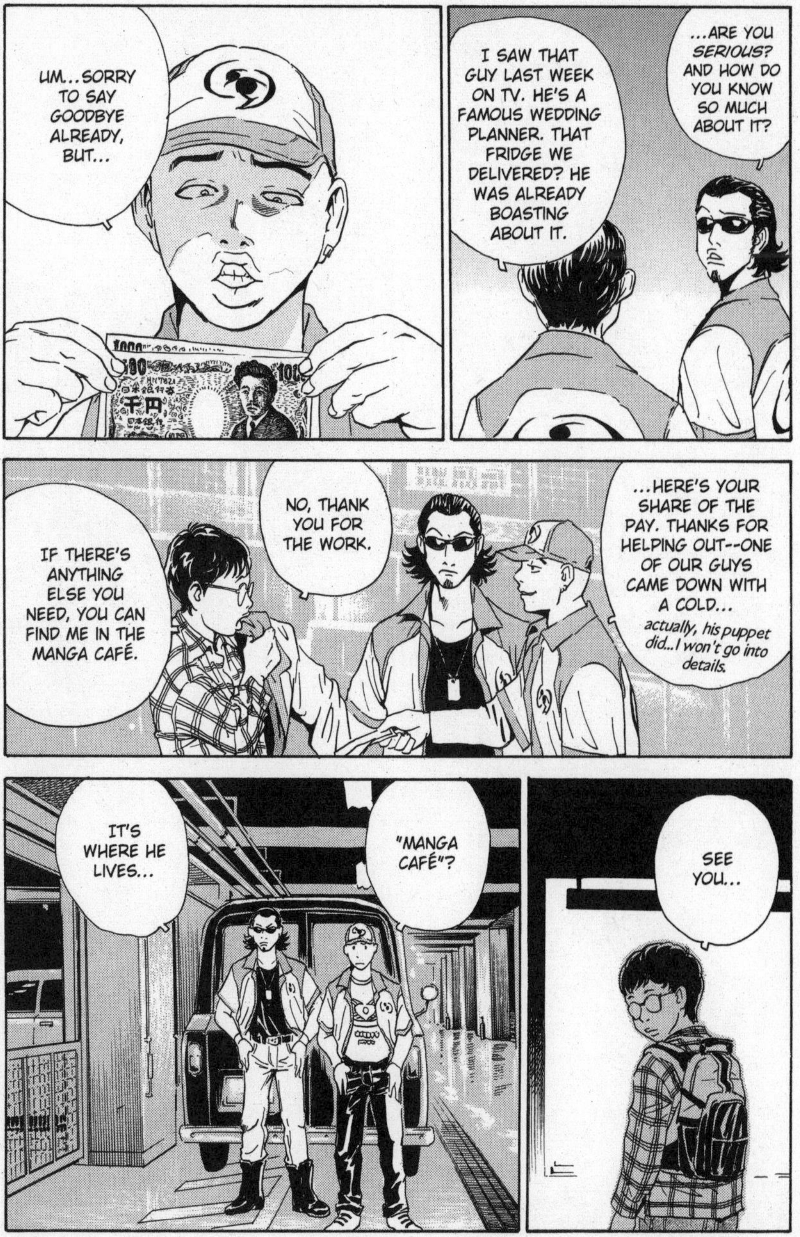
...ARE YOU SERIOUS? AND HOW DO YOU KNOW SO MUCH ABOUT IT?
I SAW THAT GUY LAST WEEK ON TV. HE'S A FAMOUS WEDDING PLANNER. THAT FRIDGE WE DELIVERED? HE WAS ALREADY BOASTING ABOUT IT.
UM...SORRY TO SAY GOODBYE ALREADY, BUT...
...HERE'S YOUR SHARE OF THE PAY. THANKS FOR HELPING OUT--ONE OF OUR GUYS CAME DOWN WITH A COLD...
actually, his puppet did...I won't go into details.
NO, THANK YOU FOR THE WORK.
IF THERE'S ANYTHING ELSE YOU NEED, YOU CAN FIND ME IN THE MANGA CAFÉ.
SEE YOU...
"MANGA CAFÉ"?
IT'S WHERE HE LIVES...

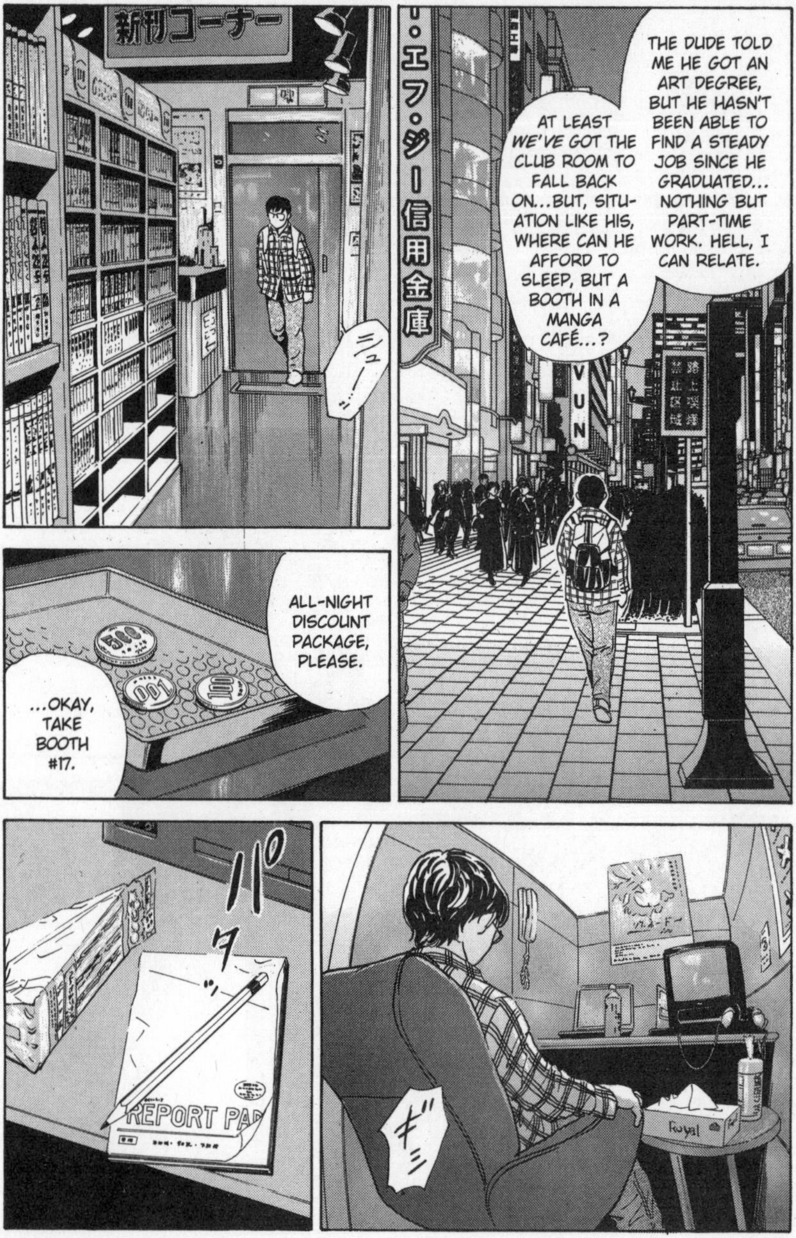
THE DUDE TOLD ME HE GOT AN ART DEGREE, BUT HE HASN'T BEEN ABLE TO FIND A STEADY JOB SINCE HE GRADUATED... NOTHING BUT PART-TIME WORK. HELL, I CAN RELATE.
AT LEAST *WE'VE* GOT THE CLUB ROOM TO FALL BACK ON...BUT, SITUATION LIKE HIS, WHERE CAN HE AFFORD TO SLEEP, BUT A BOOTH IN A MANGA CAFÉ...?
・エフ・ジー信用金庫
VUN
新刊コーナー
ニュー…
ALL-NIGHT DISCOUNT PACKAGE, PLEASE.
...OKAY, TAKE BOOTH #17.
ギシ
パタ
ツ
REPORT PAD

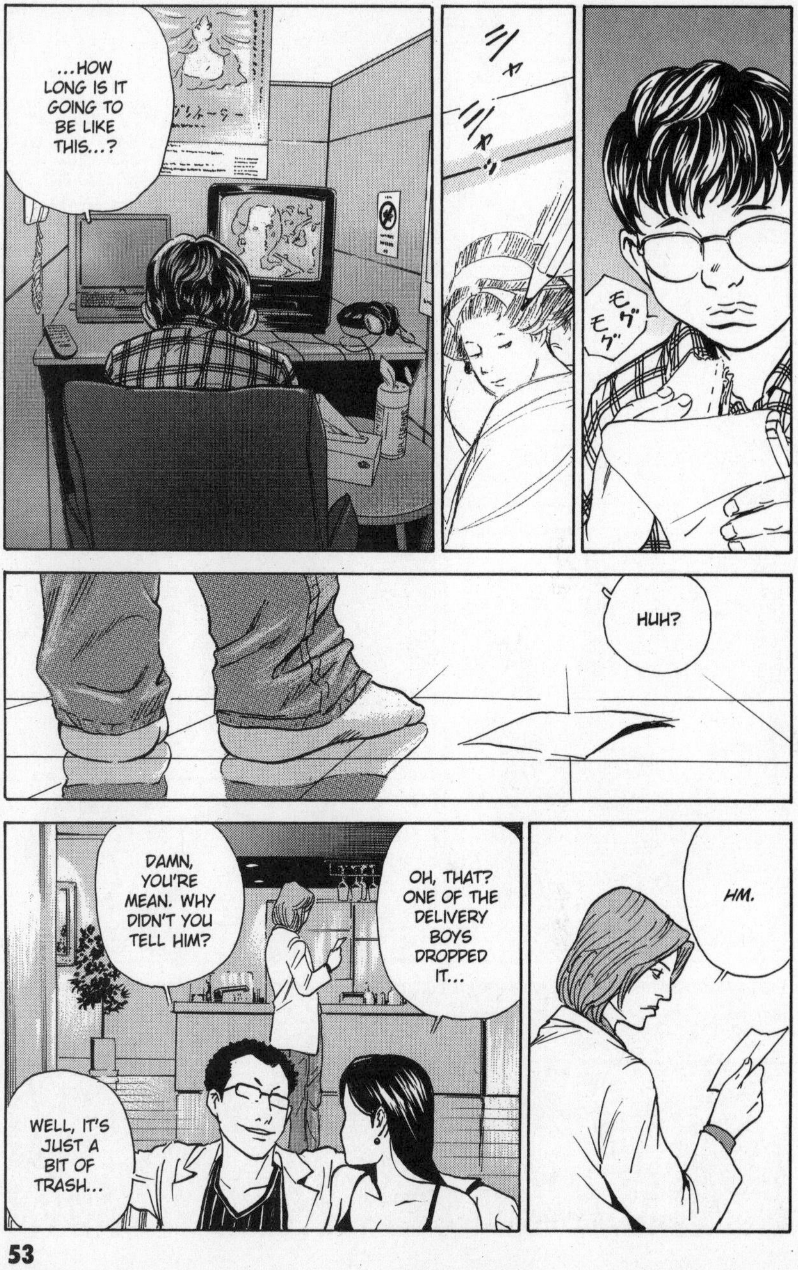
モグモグ
シャシャッ
...HOW LONG IS IT GOING TO BE LIKE THIS...?
HUH?
HM.
OH, THAT? ONE OF THE DELIVERY BOYS DROPPED IT...
DAMN, YOU'RE MEAN. WHY DIDN'T YOU TELL HIM?
WELL, IT'S JUST A BIT OF TRASH...

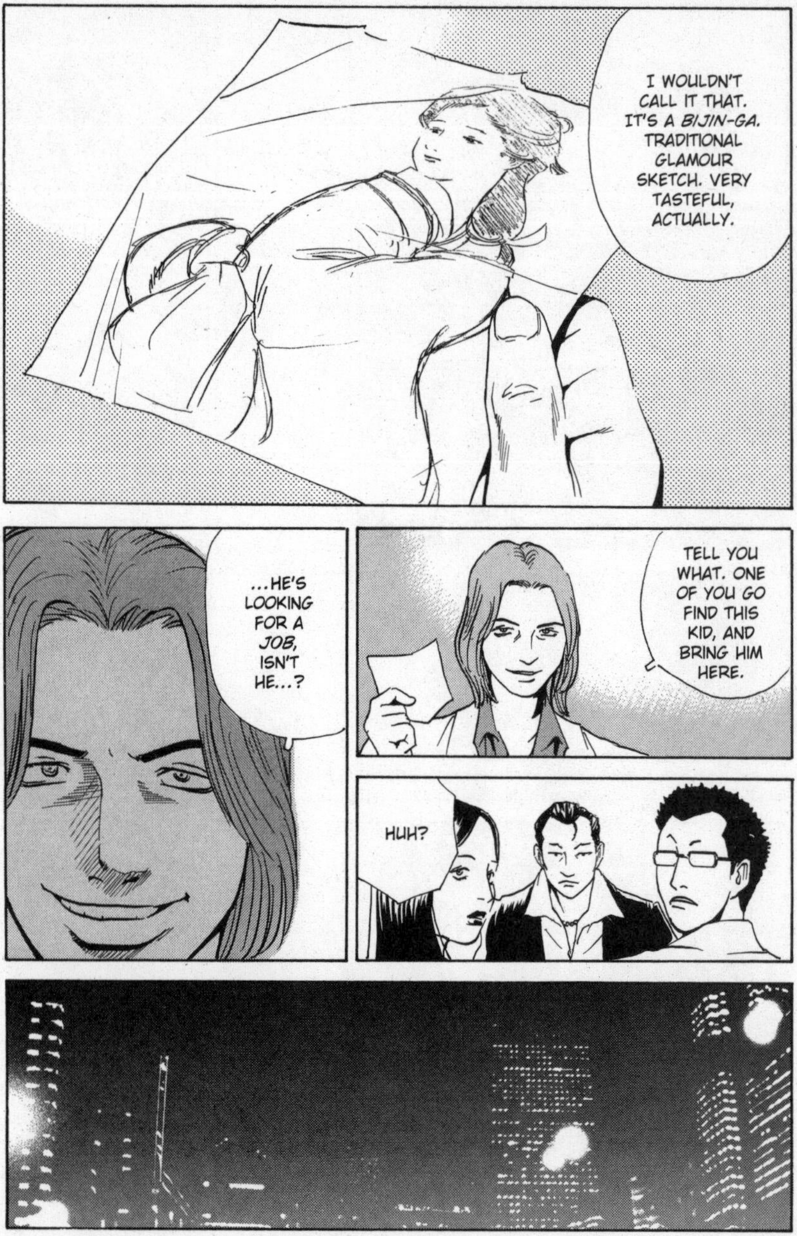
I WOULDN'T CALL IT THAT. IT'S A *BIJIN-GA.* TRADITIONAL GLAMOUR SKETCH. VERY TASTEFUL, ACTUALLY.
TELL YOU WHAT. ONE OF YOU GO FIND THIS KID, AND BRING HIM HERE.
HUH?
...HE'S LOOKING FOR A *JOB,* ISN'T HE...?

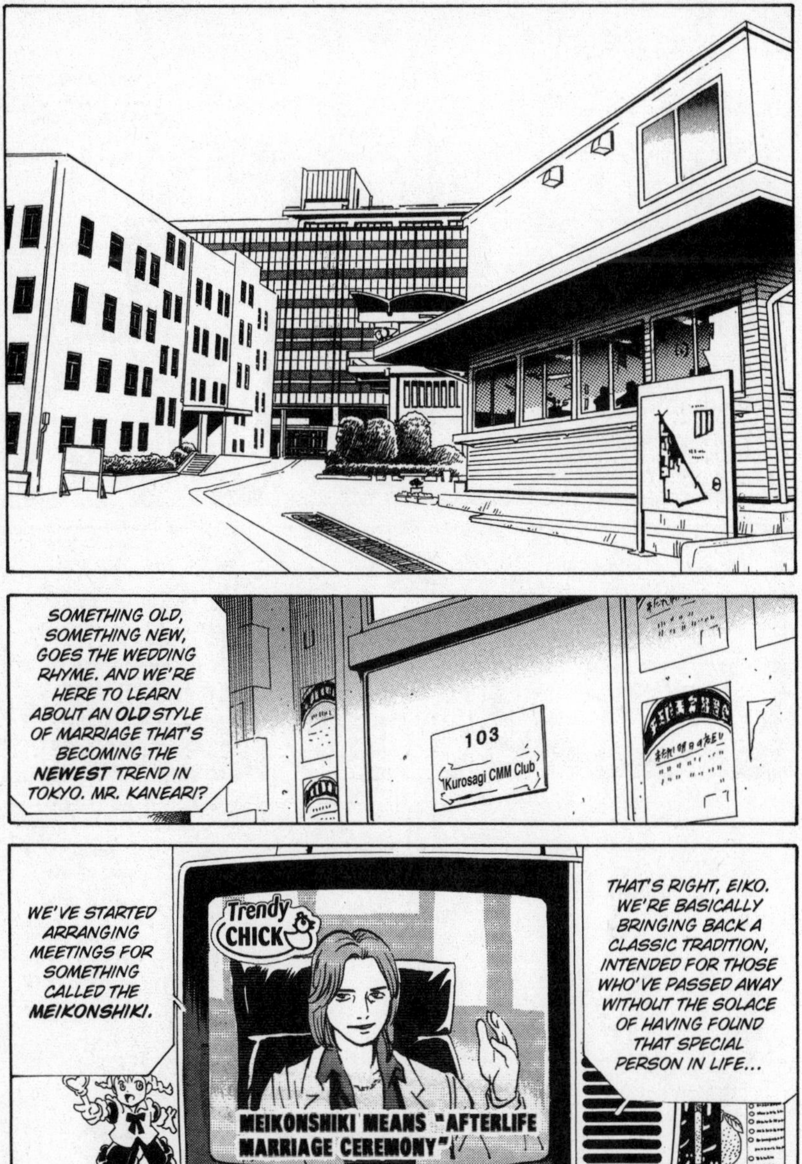
SOMETHING OLD, SOMETHING NEW, GOES THE WEDDING RHYME. AND WE'RE HERE TO LEARN ABOUT AN **OLD** STYLE OF MARRIAGE THAT'S BECOMING THE **NEWEST** TREND IN TOKYO. MR. KANEARI?
103
Kurosagi CMM Club
THAT'S RIGHT, EIKO. WE'RE BASICALLY BRINGING BACK A CLASSIC TRADITION, INTENDED FOR THOSE WHO'VE PASSED AWAY WITHOUT THE SOLACE OF HAVING FOUND THAT SPECIAL PERSON IN LIFE...
Trendy CHICK
MEIKONSHIKI MEANS "AFTERLIFE MARRIAGE CEREMONY"
WE'VE STARTED ARRANGING MEETINGS FOR SOMETHING CALLED THE **MEIKONSHIKI**.

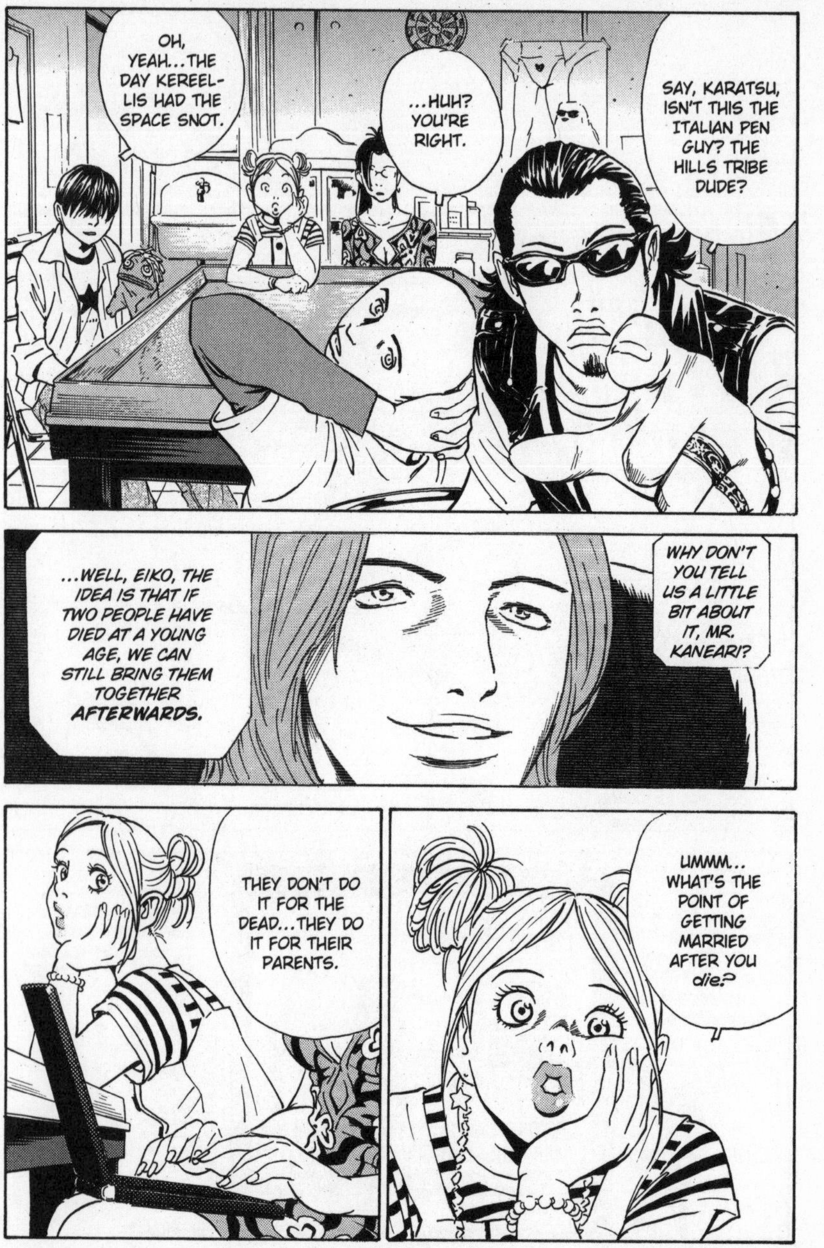
SAY, KARATSU, ISN'T THIS THE ITALIAN PEN GUY? THE HILLS TRIBE DUDE?
...HUH? YOU'RE RIGHT.
OH, YEAH...THE DAY KEREEL-LIS HAD THE SPACE SNOT.
WHY DON'T YOU TELL US A LITTLE BIT ABOUT IT, MR. KANEARI?
...WELL, EIKO, THE IDEA IS THAT IF TWO PEOPLE HAVE DIED AT A YOUNG AGE, WE CAN STILL BRING THEM TOGETHER **AFTERWARDS.**
UMMM... WHAT'S THE POINT OF GETTING MARRIED AFTER YOU *die?*
THEY DON'T DO IT FOR THE DEAD...THEY DO IT FOR THEIR PARENTS.

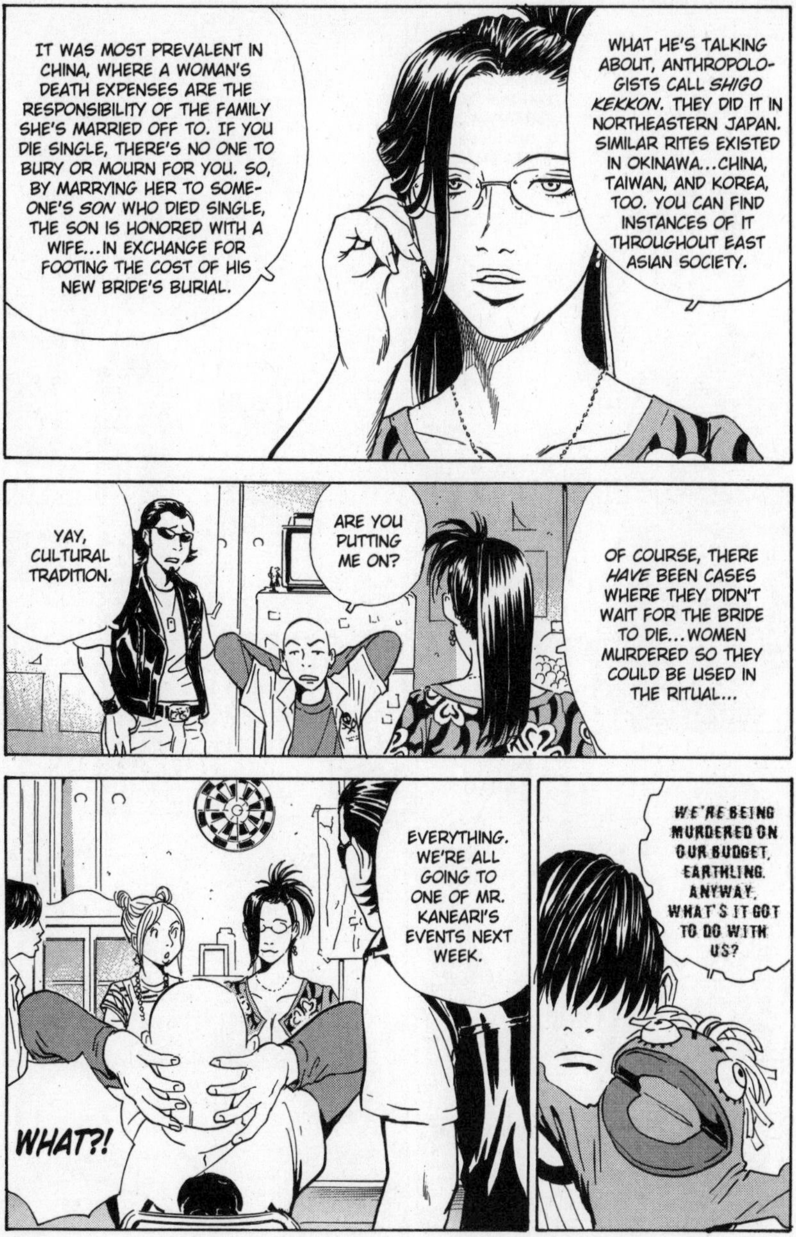
WHAT HE'S TALKING ABOUT, ANTHROPOLOGISTS CALL *SHIGO KEKKON*. THEY DID IT IN NORTHEASTERN JAPAN. SIMILAR RITES EXISTED IN OKINAWA...CHINA, TAIWAN, AND KOREA, TOO. YOU CAN FIND INSTANCES OF IT THROUGHOUT EAST ASIAN SOCIETY.
IT WAS MOST PREVALENT IN CHINA, WHERE A WOMAN'S DEATH EXPENSES ARE THE RESPONSIBILITY OF THE FAMILY SHE'S MARRIED OFF TO. IF YOU DIE SINGLE, THERE'S NO ONE TO BURY OR MOURN FOR YOU. SO, BY MARRYING HER TO SOMEONE'S *SON* WHO DIED SINGLE, THE SON IS HONORED WITH A WIFE...IN EXCHANGE FOR FOOTING THE COST OF HIS NEW BRIDE'S BURIAL.
OF COURSE, THERE *HAVE* BEEN CASES WHERE THEY DIDN'T WAIT FOR THE BRIDE TO DIE...WOMEN MURDERED SO THEY COULD BE USED IN THE RITUAL...
ARE YOU PUTTING ME ON?
YAY, CULTURAL TRADITION.
WE'RE BEING MURDERED ON OUR BUDGET, EARTHLING. ANYWAY, WHAT'S IT GOT TO DO WITH US?
EVERYTHING. WE'RE ALL GOING TO ONE OF MR. KANEARI'S EVENTS NEXT WEEK.
WHAT?!

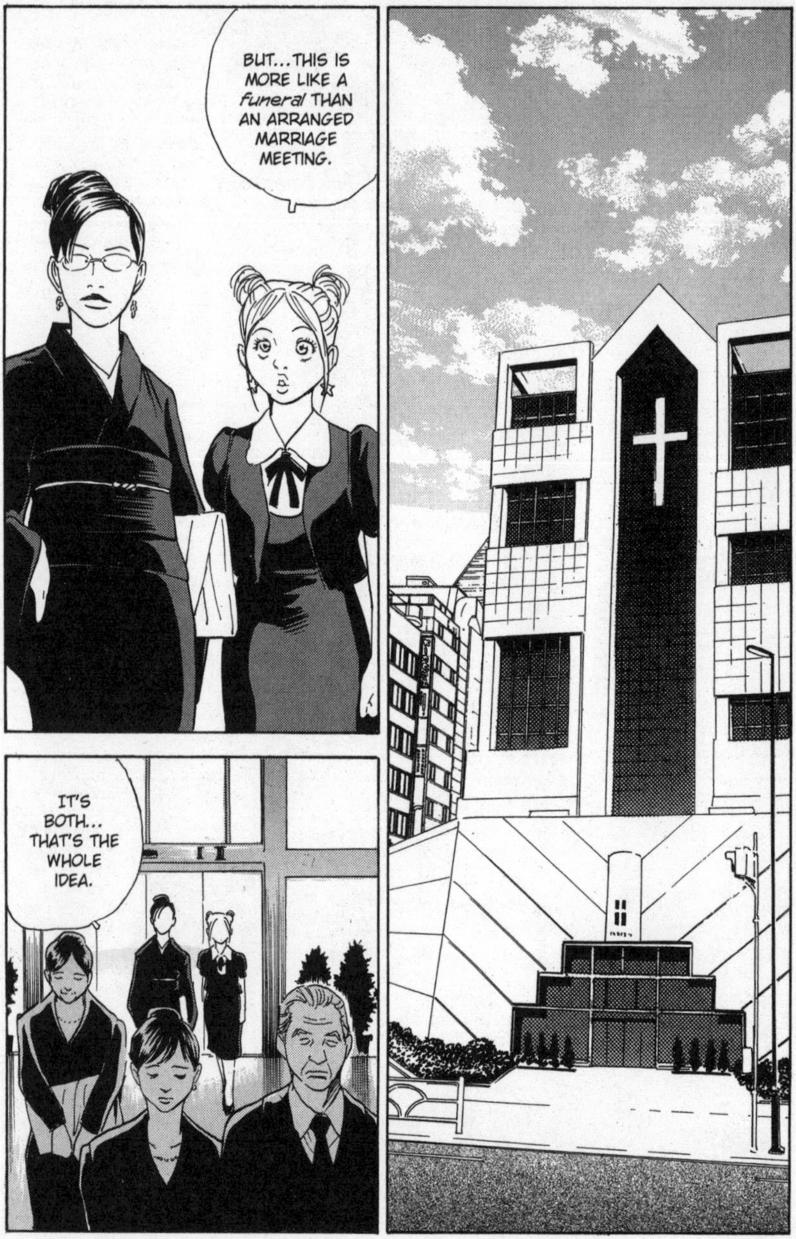
BUT...THIS IS MORE LIKE A *funeral* THAN AN ARRANGED MARRIAGE MEETING.
IT'S BOTH... THAT'S THE WHOLE IDEA.

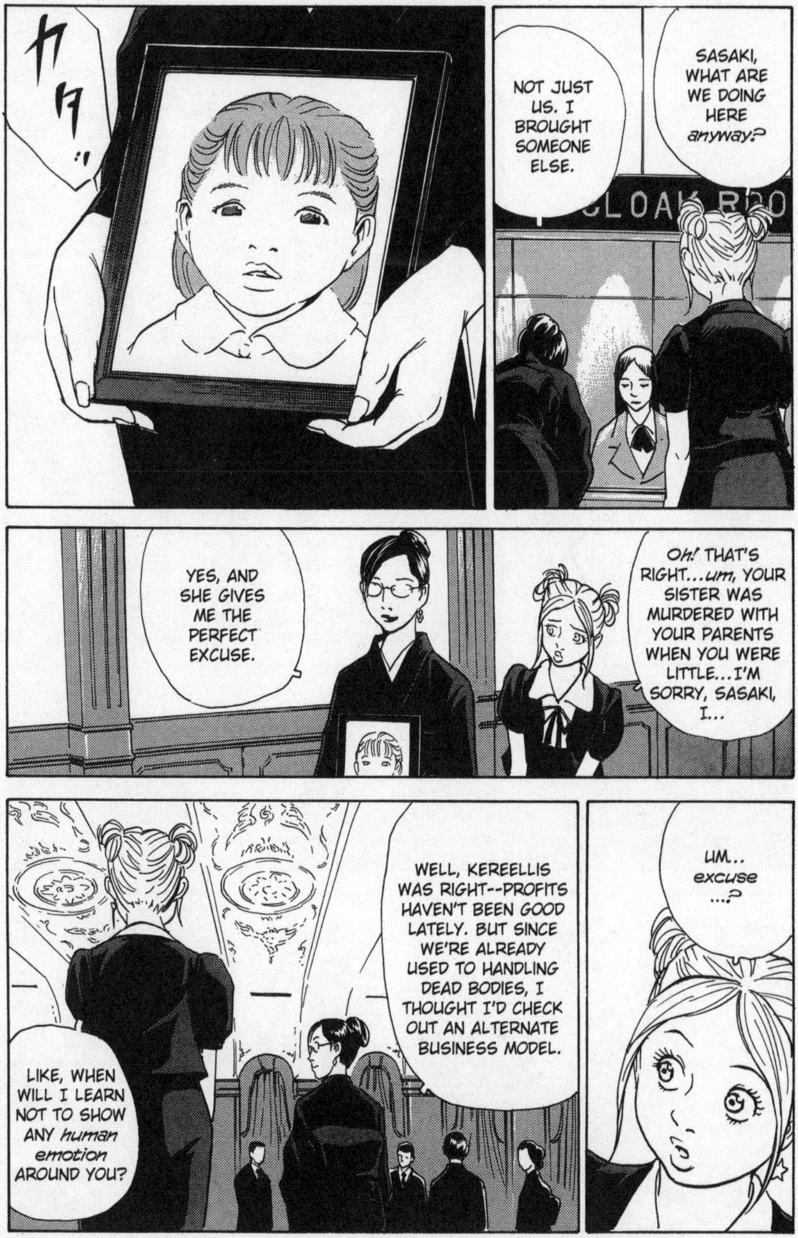
SASAKI, WHAT ARE WE DOING HERE *anyway?*
NOT JUST US. I BROUGHT SOMEONE ELSE.
CLOAK ROO
Oh! THAT'S RIGHT...*um,* YOUR SISTER WAS MURDERED WITH YOUR PARENTS WHEN YOU WERE LITTLE...I'M SORRY, SASAKI, I...
YES, AND SHE GIVES ME THE PERFECT EXCUSE.
UM.. *excuse* ...?
WELL, KEREELLIS WAS RIGHT--PROFITS HAVEN'T BEEN GOOD LATELY. BUT SINCE WE'RE ALREADY USED TO HANDLING DEAD BODIES, I THOUGHT I'D CHECK OUT AN ALTERNATE BUSINESS MODEL.
LIKE, WHEN WILL I LEARN NOT TO SHOW ANY *human emotion* AROUND YOU?

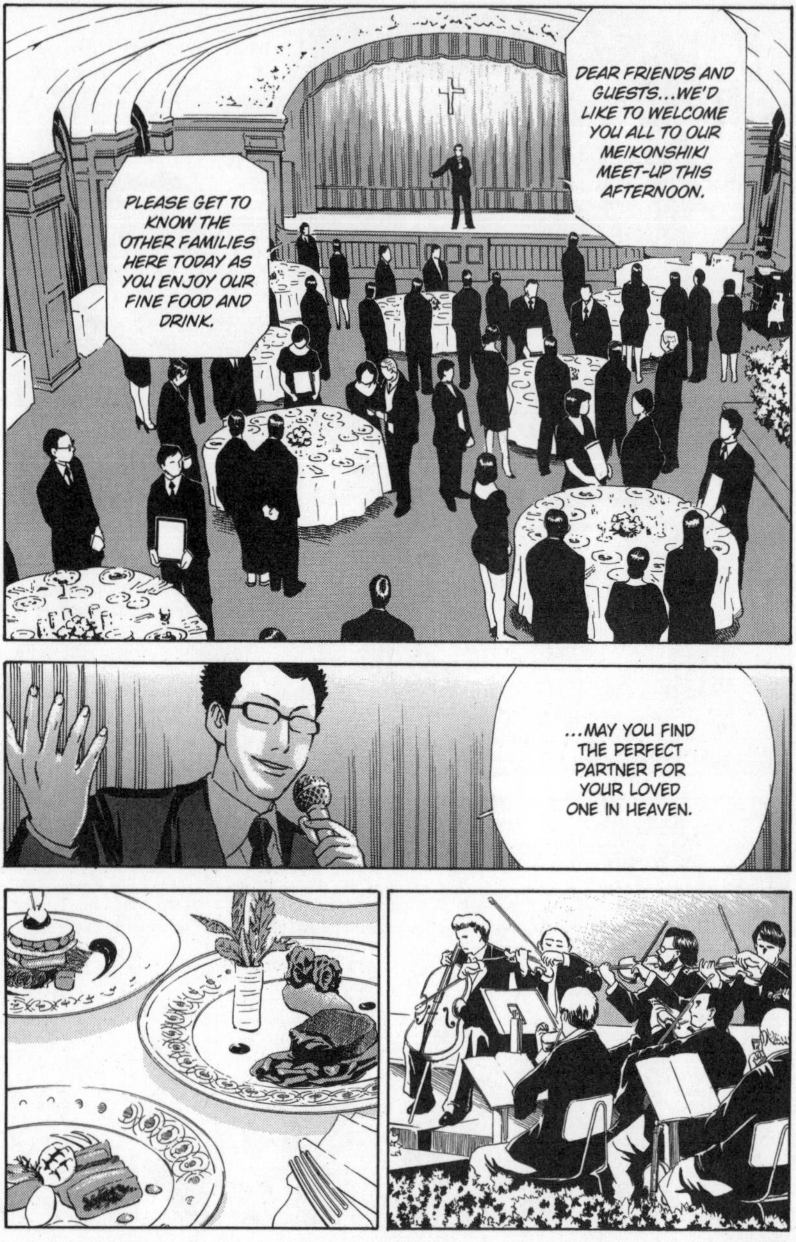
DEAR FRIENDS AND GUESTS...WE'D LIKE TO WELCOME YOU ALL TO OUR MEIKONSHIKI MEET-UP THIS AFTERNOON.
PLEASE GET TO KNOW THE OTHER FAMILIES HERE TODAY AS YOU ENJOY OUR FINE FOOD AND DRINK.
...MAY YOU FIND THE PERFECT PARTNER FOR YOUR LOVED ONE IN HEAVEN.

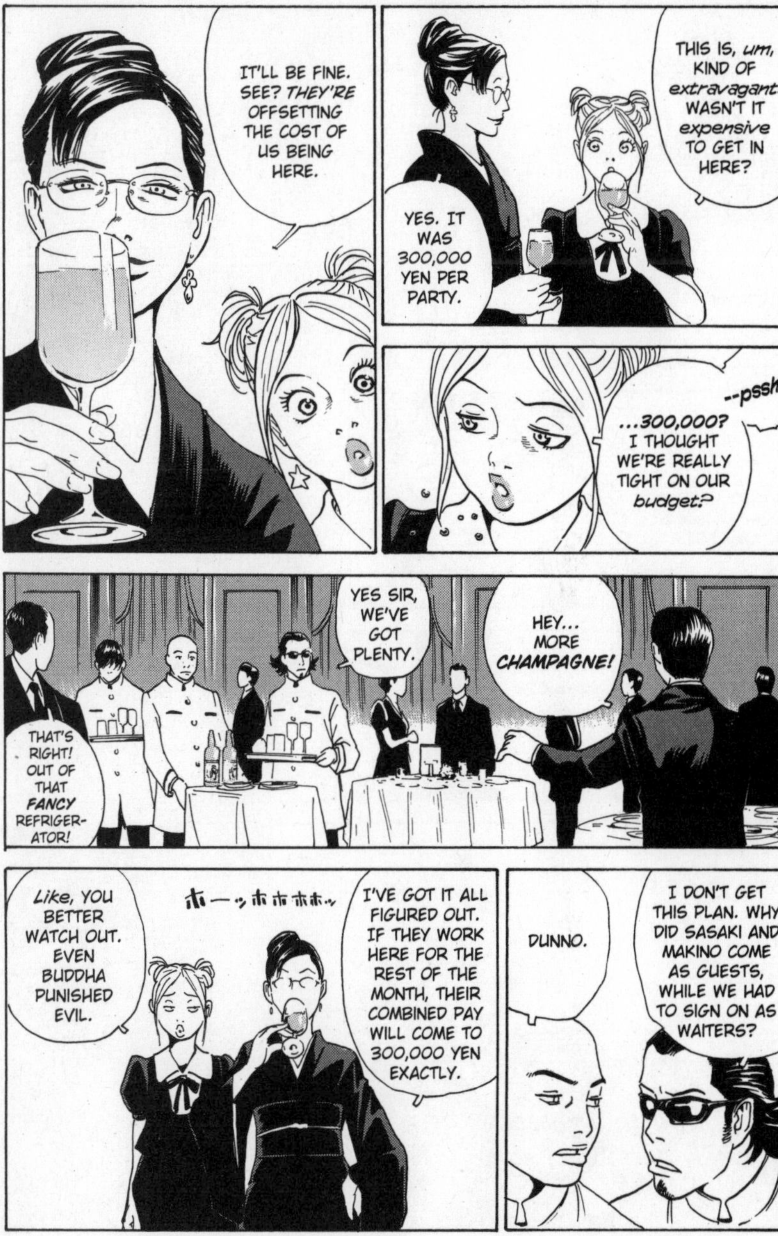
THIS IS, *um*, KIND OF *extravagant*. WASN'T IT *expensive* TO GET IN HERE?
YES. IT WAS 300,000 YEN PER PARTY.
--pssh!
...300,000? I THOUGHT WE'RE REALLY TIGHT ON OUR *budget?*
IT'LL BE FINE. SEE? *THEY'RE* OFFSETTING THE COST OF US BEING HERE.
HEY... MORE *CHAMPAGNE!*
YES SIR, WE'VE GOT PLENTY.
THAT'S RIGHT! OUT OF THAT *FANCY* REFRIGER-ATOR!
I DON'T GET THIS PLAN. WHY DID SASAKI AND MAKINO COME AS GUESTS, WHILE WE HAD TO SIGN ON AS WAITERS?
DUNNO.
I'VE GOT IT ALL FIGURED OUT. IF THEY WORK HERE FOR THE REST OF THE MONTH, THEIR COMBINED PAY WILL COME TO 300,000 YEN EXACTLY.
ホーッホホホホッ
Like, YOU BETTER WATCH OUT. EVEN BUDDHA PUNISHED EVIL.

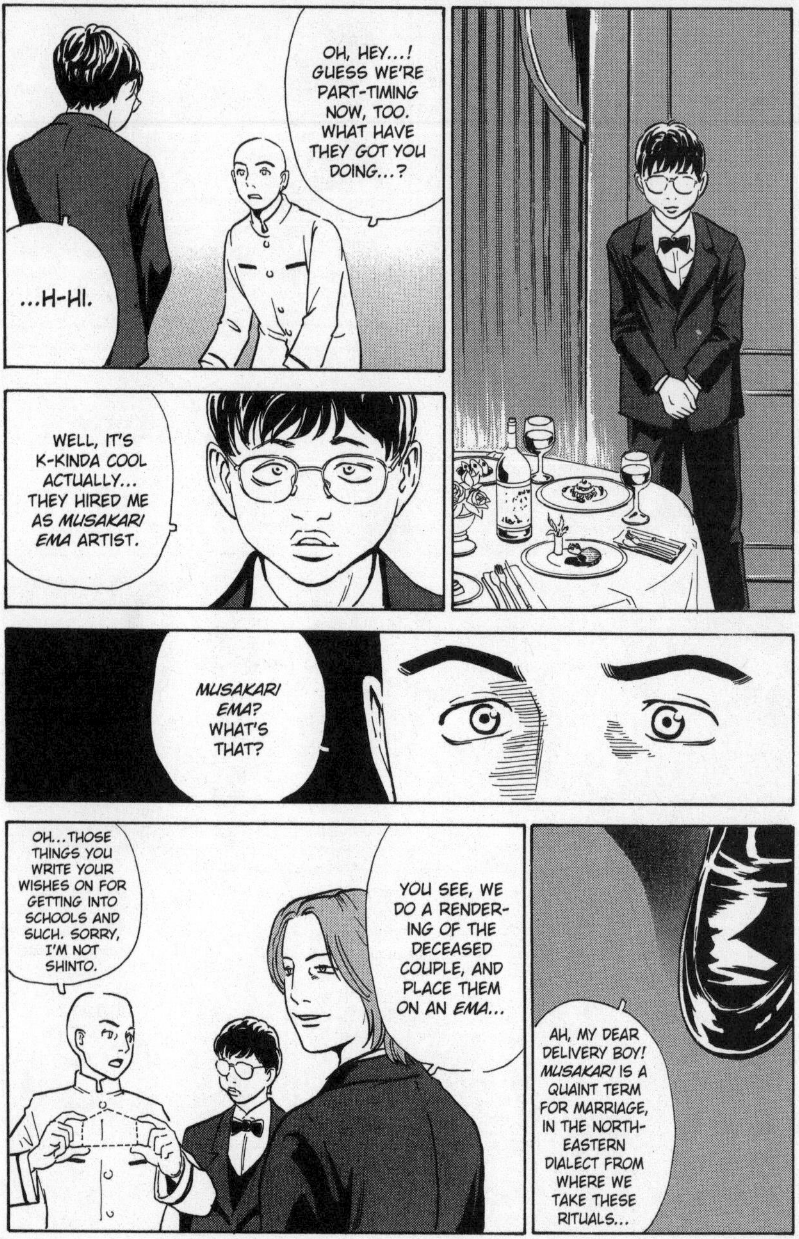
OH, HEY...! GUESS WE'RE PART-TIMING NOW, TOO. WHAT HAVE THEY GOT YOU DOING...?
...H-HI.
WELL, IT'S K-KINDA COOL ACTUALLY... THEY HIRED ME AS *MUSAKARI EMA* ARTIST.
MUSAKARI EMA? WHAT'S THAT?
AH, MY DEAR DELIVERY BOY! *MUSAKARI* IS A QUAINT TERM FOR MARRIAGE, IN THE NORTH-EASTERN DIALECT FROM WHERE WE TAKE THESE RITUALS...
YOU SEE, WE DO A RENDER-ING OF THE DECEASED COUPLE, AND PLACE THEM ON AN *EMA*...
OH...THOSE THINGS YOU WRITE YOUR WISHES ON FOR GETTING INTO SCHOOLS AND SUCH. SORRY, I'M NOT SHINTO.

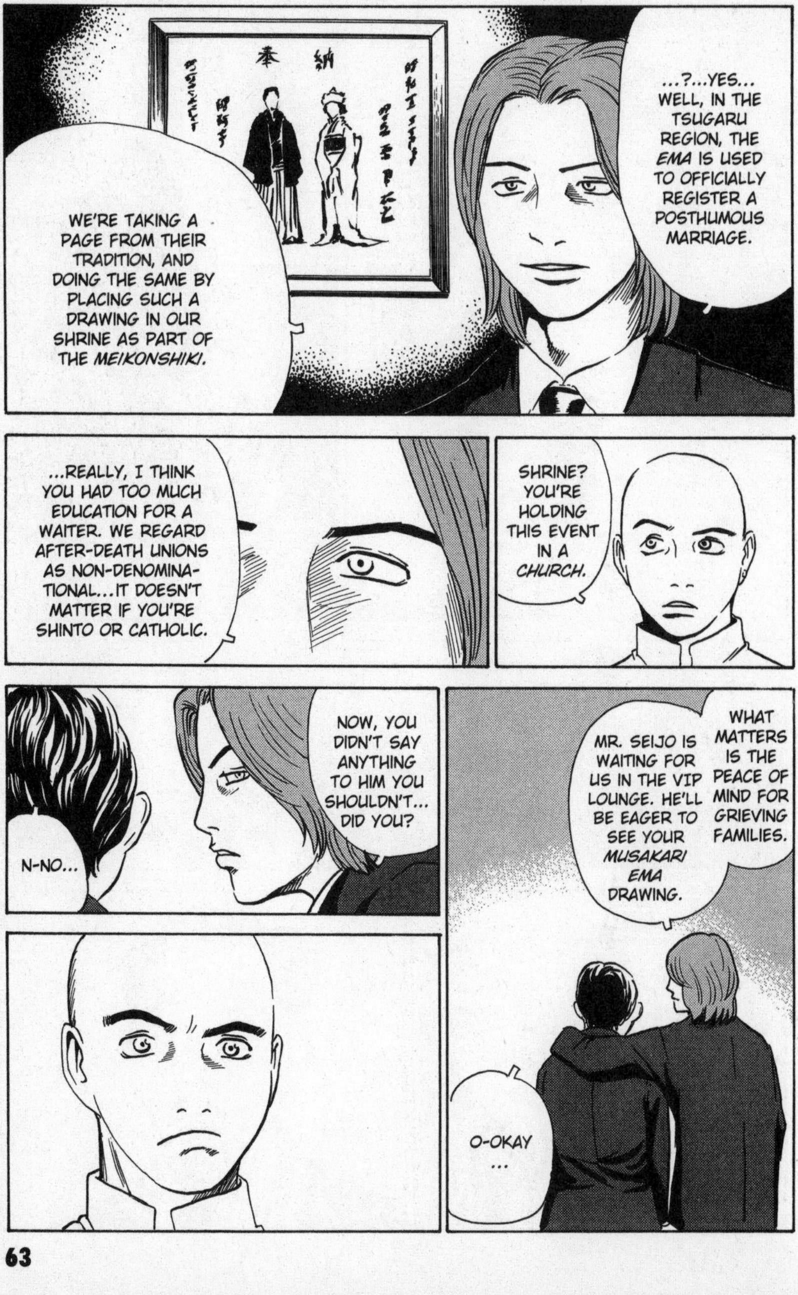
...?...YES... WELL, IN THE TSUGARU REGION, THE *EMA* IS USED TO OFFICIALLY REGISTER A POSTHUMOUS MARRIAGE.
WE'RE TAKING A PAGE FROM THEIR TRADITION, AND DOING THE SAME BY PLACING SUCH A DRAWING IN OUR SHRINE AS PART OF THE *MEIKONSHIKI*.
SHRINE? YOU'RE HOLDING THIS EVENT IN A *CHURCH*.
...REALLY, I THINK YOU HAD TOO MUCH EDUCATION FOR A WAITER. WE REGARD AFTER-DEATH UNIONS AS NON-DENOMINATIONAL...IT DOESN'T MATTER IF YOU'RE SHINTO OR CATHOLIC.
WHAT MATTERS IS THE PEACE OF MIND FOR GRIEVING FAMILIES.
MR. SEIJO IS WAITING FOR US IN THE VIP LOUNGE. HE'LL BE EAGER TO SEE YOUR *MUSAKARI EMA* DRAWING.
O-OKAY ...
NOW, YOU DIDN'T SAY ANYTHING TO HIM YOU SHOULDN'T... DID YOU?
N-NO...

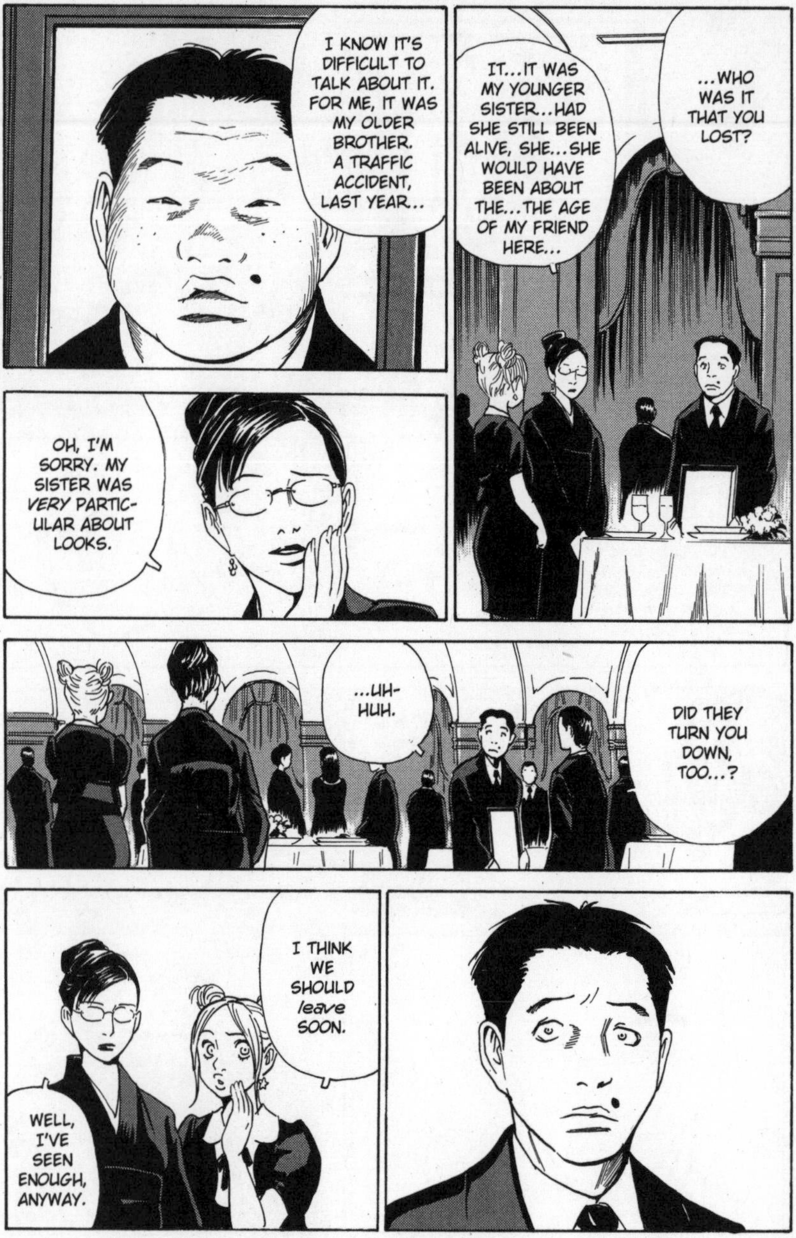
...WHO WAS IT THAT YOU LOST?
IT...IT WAS MY YOUNGER SISTER...HAD SHE STILL BEEN ALIVE, SHE...SHE WOULD HAVE BEEN ABOUT THE...THE AGE OF MY FRIEND HERE...
I KNOW IT'S DIFFICULT TO TALK ABOUT IT. FOR ME, IT WAS MY OLDER BROTHER. A TRAFFIC ACCIDENT, LAST YEAR...
OH, I'M SORRY. MY SISTER WAS *VERY* PARTIC-ULAR ABOUT LOOKS.
DID THEY TURN YOU DOWN, TOO...?
...UH-HUH.
I THINK WE SHOULD *leave* SOON.
WELL, I'VE SEEN ENOUGH, ANYWAY.

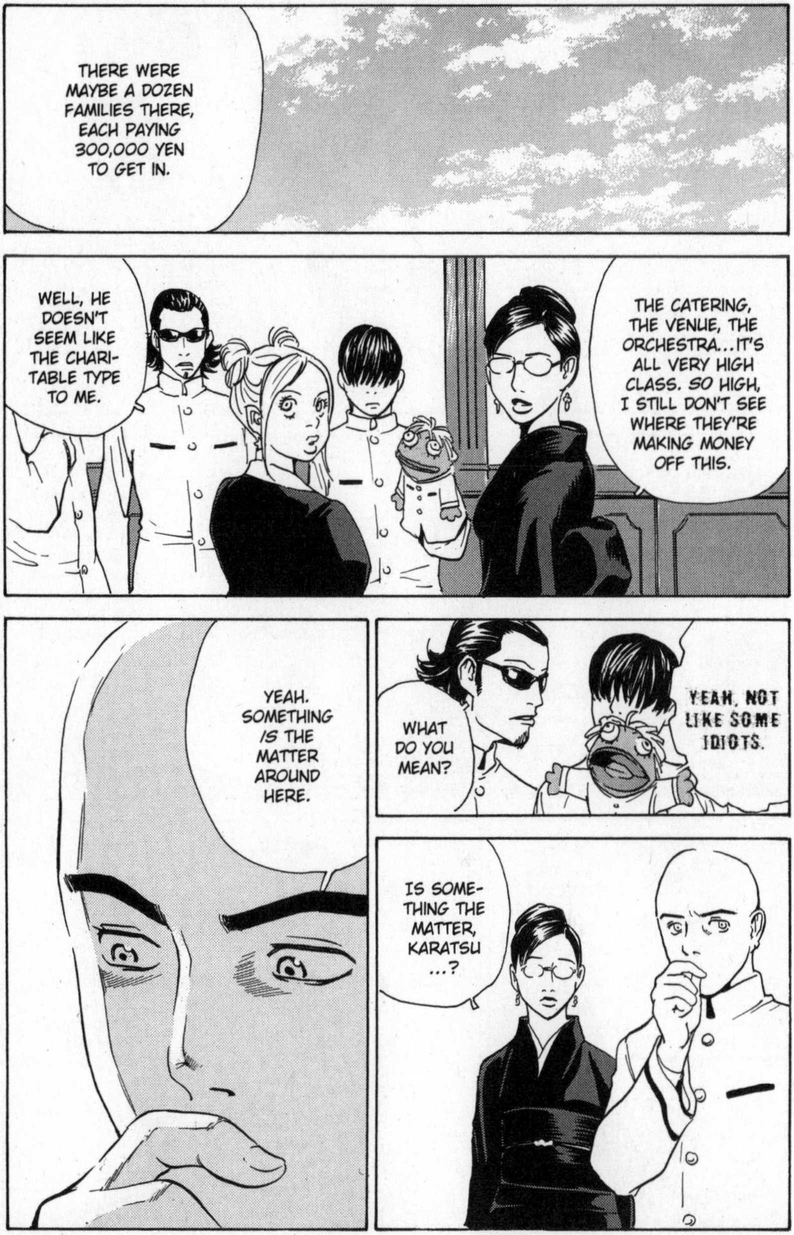
THERE WERE MAYBE A DOZEN FAMILIES THERE, EACH PAYING 300,000 YEN TO GET IN.
THE CATERING, THE VENUE, THE ORCHESTRA...IT'S ALL VERY HIGH CLASS. SO HIGH, I STILL DON'T SEE WHERE THEY'RE MAKING MONEY OFF THIS.
WELL, HE DOESN'T SEEM LIKE THE CHARI-TABLE TYPE TO ME.
YEAH, NOT LIKE SOME IDIOTS.
WHAT DO YOU MEAN?
IS SOME-THING THE MATTER, KARATSU ...?
YEAH. SOMETHING IS THE MATTER AROUND HERE.

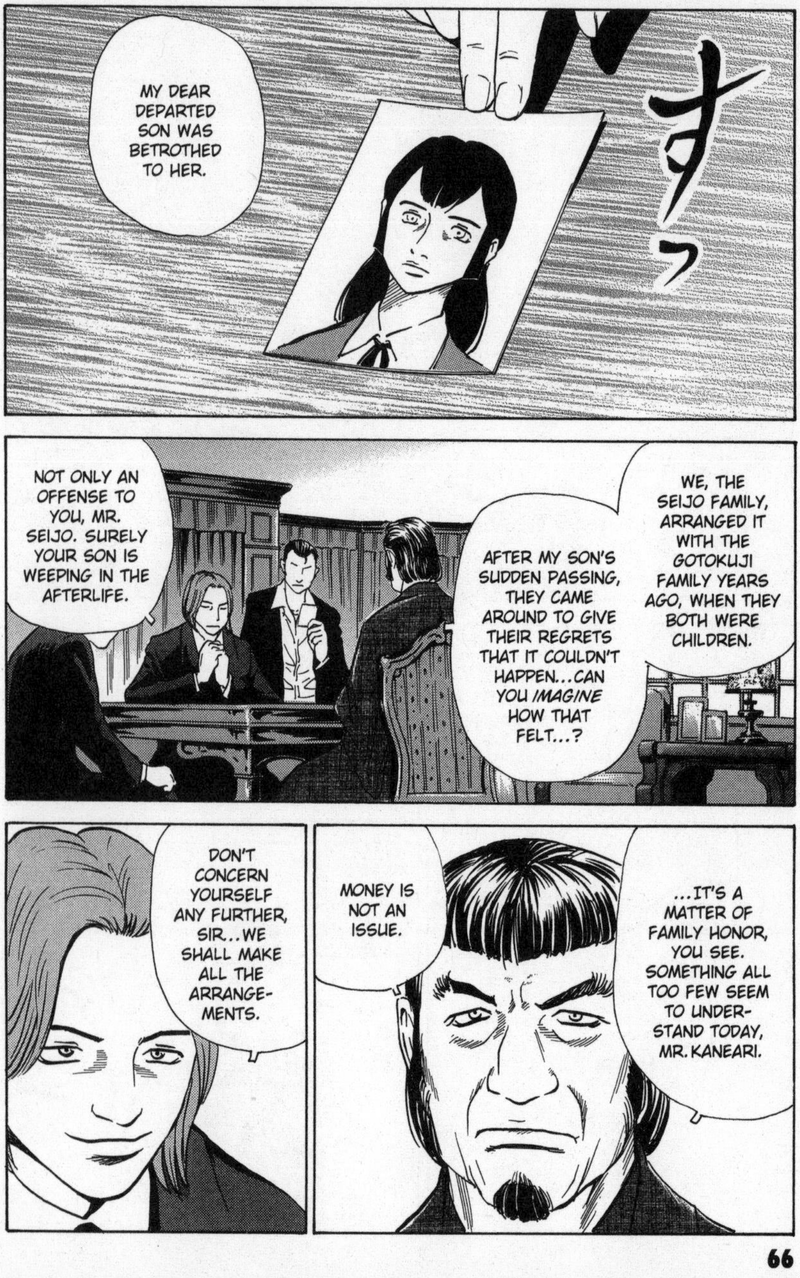
すッ
MY DEAR DEPARTED SON WAS BETROTHED TO HER.
WE, THE SEIJO FAMILY, ARRANGED IT WITH THE GOTOKUJI FAMILY YEARS AGO, WHEN THEY BOTH WERE CHILDREN.
AFTER MY SON'S SUDDEN PASSING, THEY CAME AROUND TO GIVE THEIR REGRETS THAT IT COULDN'T HAPPEN...CAN YOU *IMAGINE* HOW THAT FELT...?
NOT ONLY AN OFFENSE TO YOU, MR. SEIJO. SURELY YOUR SON IS WEEPING IN THE AFTERLIFE.
...IT'S A MATTER OF FAMILY HONOR, YOU SEE. SOMETHING ALL TOO FEW SEEM TO UNDERSTAND TODAY, MR. KANEARI.
MONEY IS NOT AN ISSUE.
DON'T CONCERN YOURSELF ANY FURTHER, SIR...WE SHALL MAKE ALL THE ARRANGEMENTS.

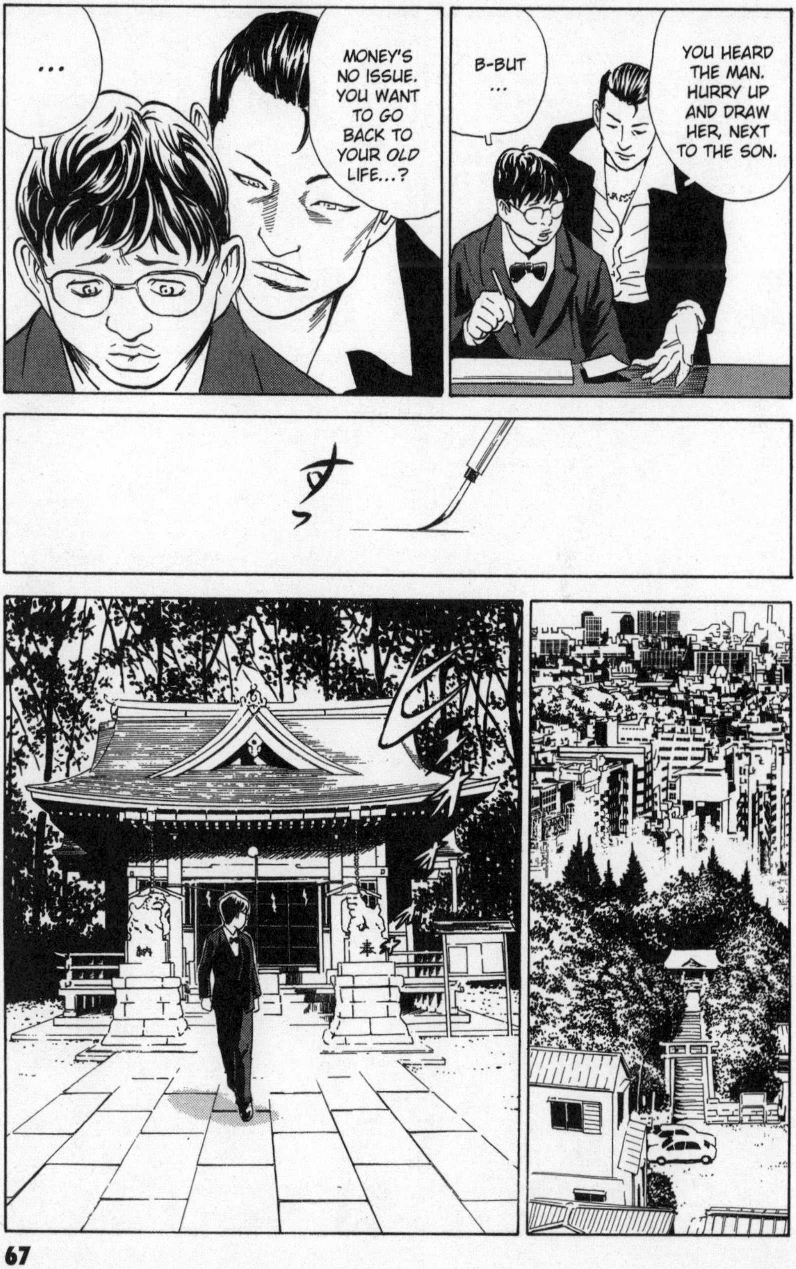
YOU HEARD THE MAN. HURRY UP AND DRAW HER, NEXT TO THE SON.
B-BUT ...
MONEY'S NO ISSUE. YOU WANT TO GO BACK TO YOUR *OLD* LIFE...?
...
すっ

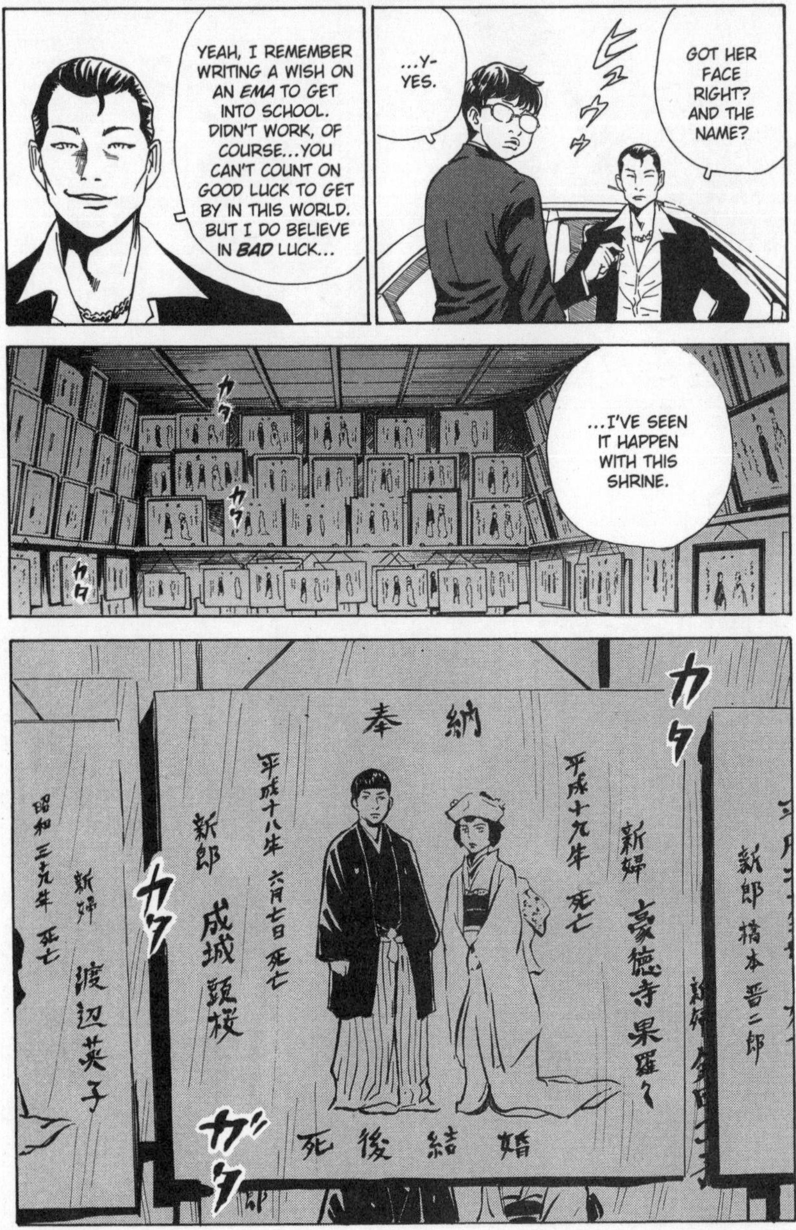
GOT HER FACE RIGHT? AND THE NAME?
ヒュウウ
...Y-YES.
YEAH, I REMEMBER WRITING A WISH ON AN *EMA* TO GET INTO SCHOOL. DIDN'T WORK, OF COURSE...YOU CAN'T COUNT ON GOOD LUCK TO GET BY IN THIS WORLD. BUT I DO BELIEVE IN ***BAD*** LUCK...
...I'VE SEEN IT HAPPEN WITH THIS SHRINE.
カタ
カタ
カタ
カタ
新郎 橋本晋二郎
奉納
平成十九年 死亡
新婦 豪徳寺果羅々
平成十八年 六月七日 死亡
新郎 成城頚桜
昭和三十九年 死亡
新婦 渡辺英子
死後結婚
カタ
ガタ

2nd delivery: romance—the end

3rd delivery

僕は死なないだろう

i probably won't die

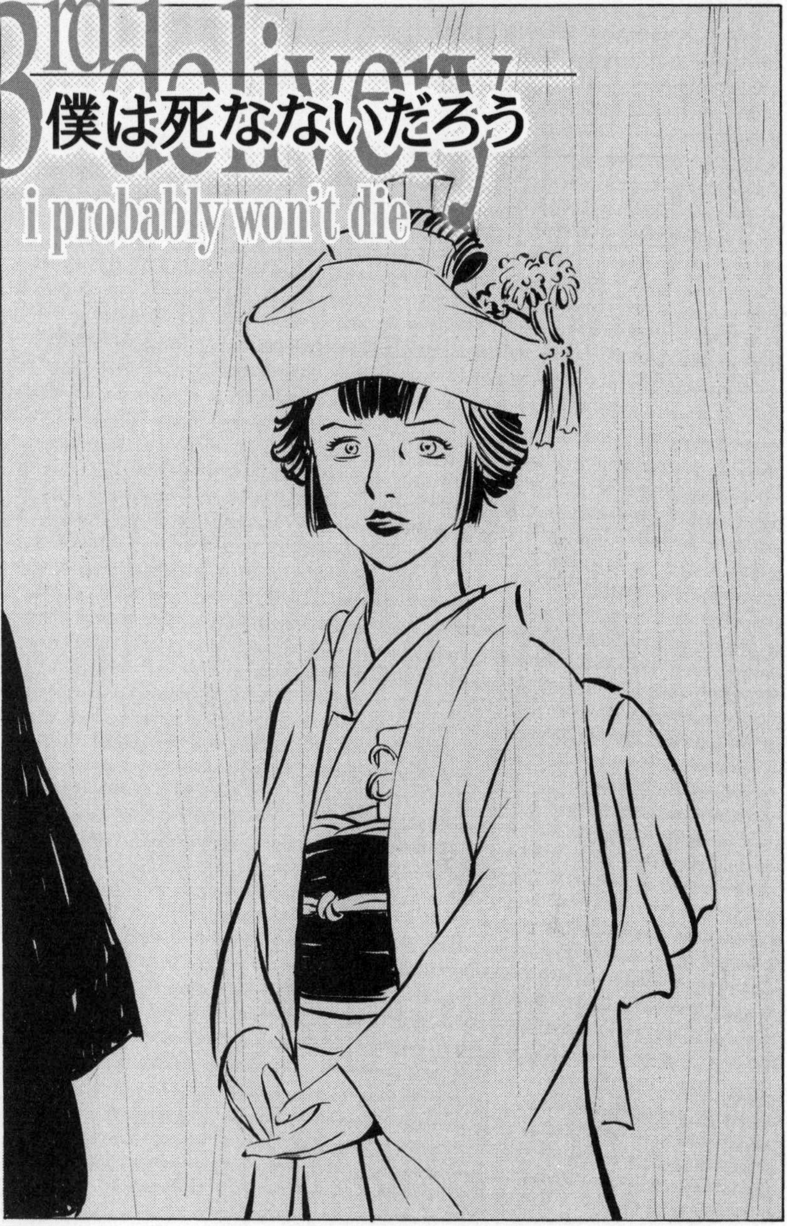

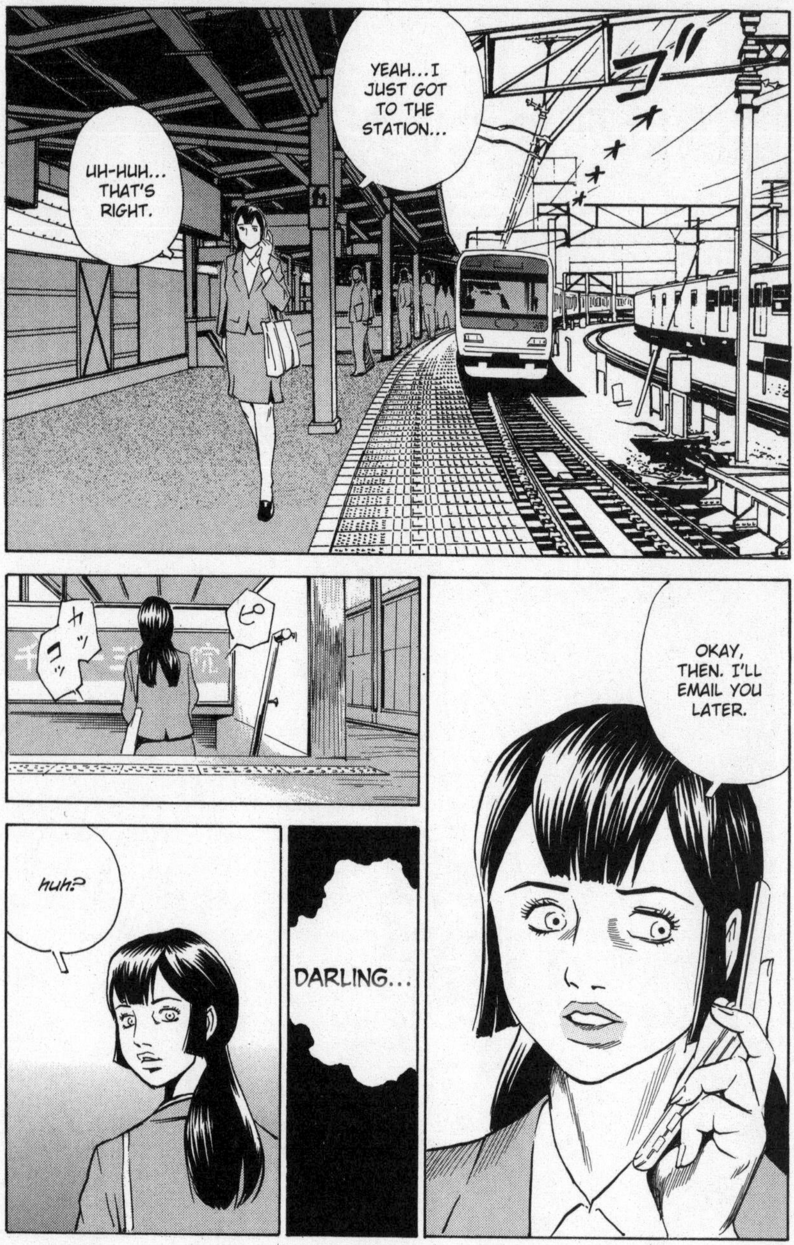
YEAH...I JUST GOT TO THE STATION...
ゴォォォォ
UH-HUH... THAT'S RIGHT.
OKAY, THEN. I'LL EMAIL YOU LATER.
ピ
カッコッ
DARLING...
huh?

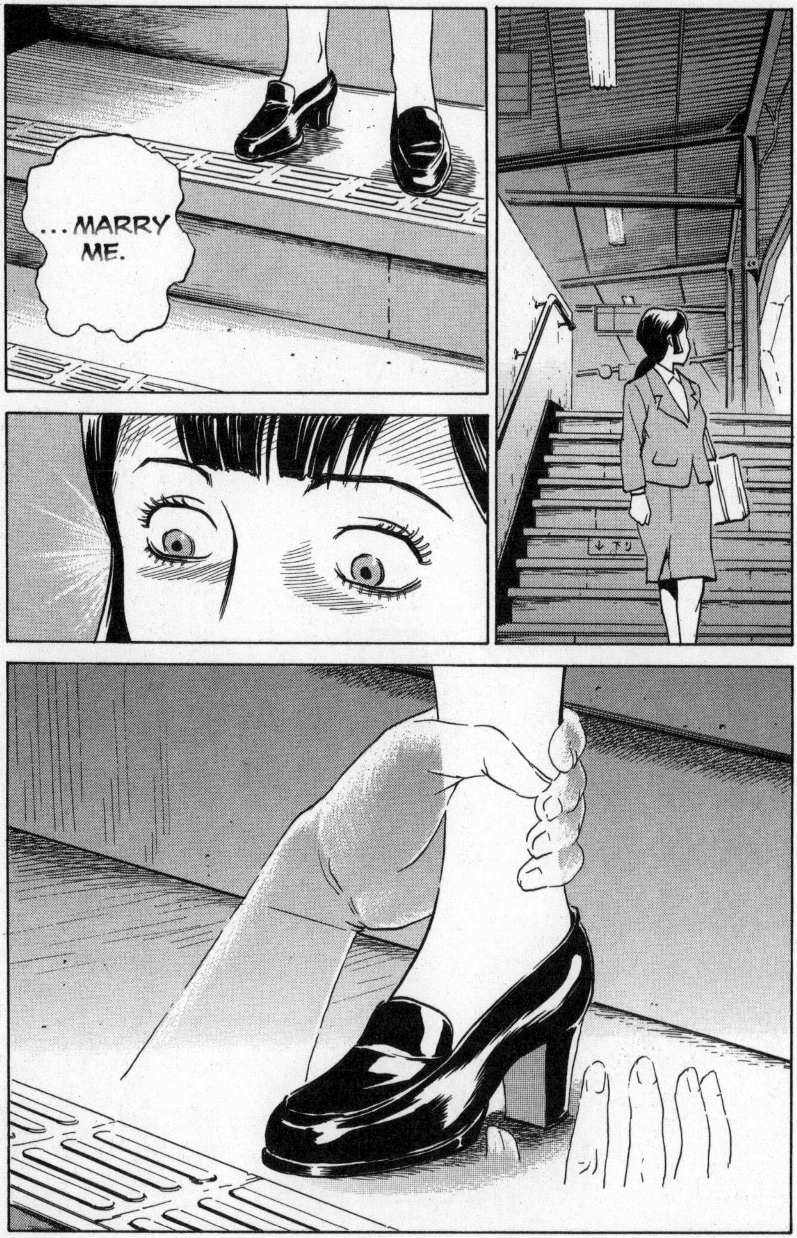
...MARRY ME.
↓下り

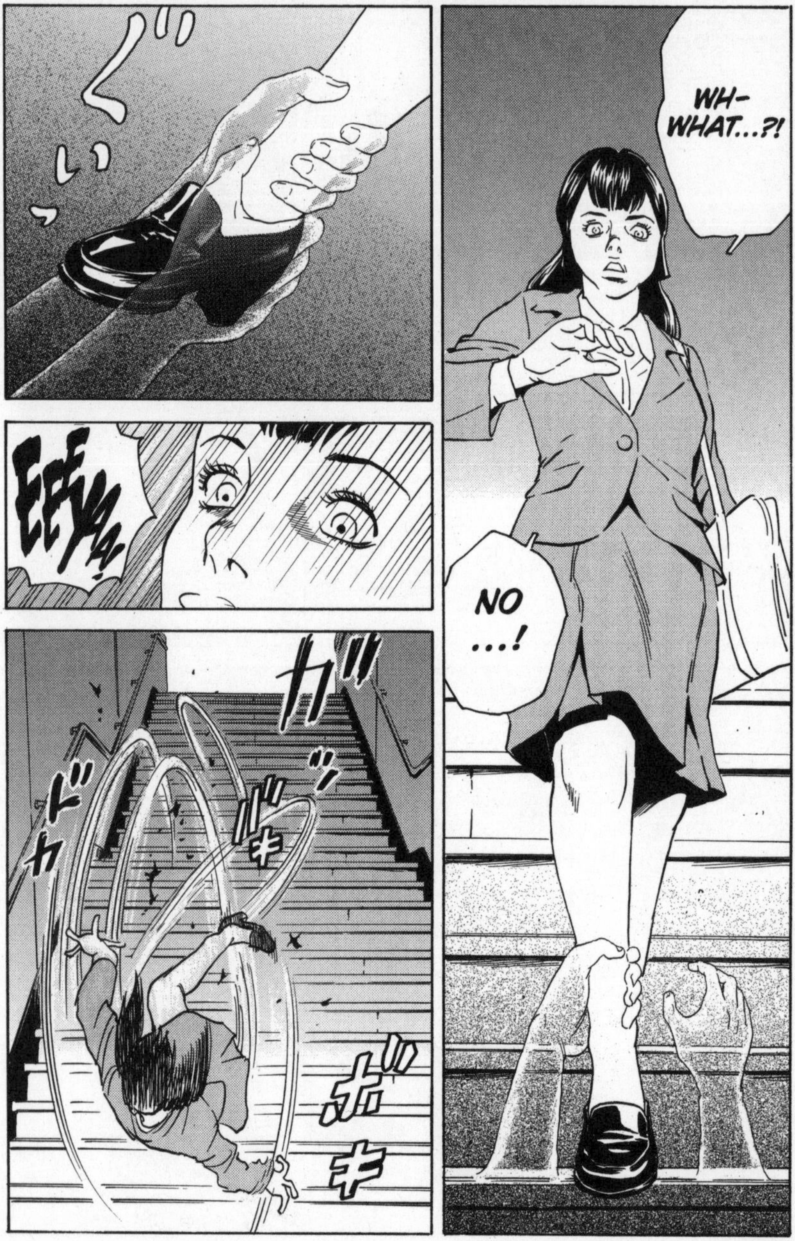
WH-
WHAT...?!
NO
...!
ぐい
EEYAA!

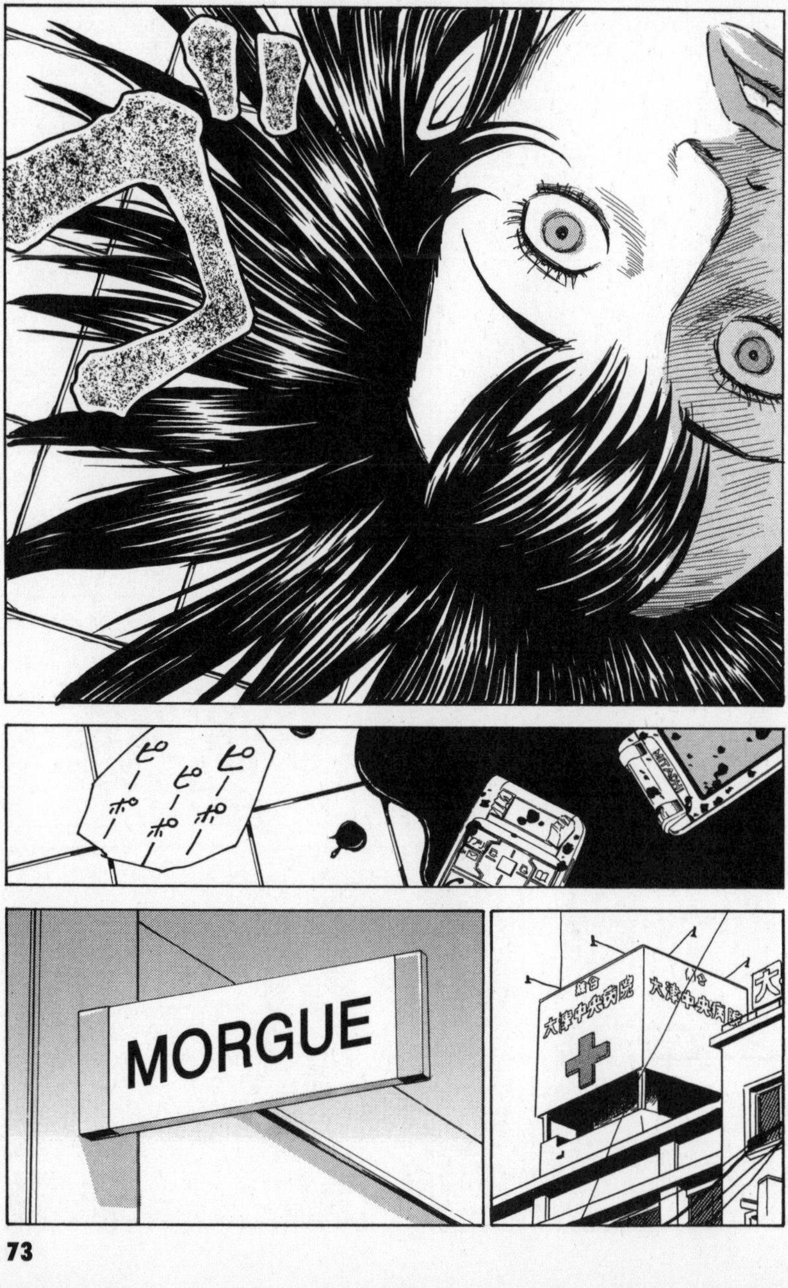
ピーポー
ピーポー
ピーポー
MITACHI
総合
大津中央病院
大津中央病院
大
MORGUE

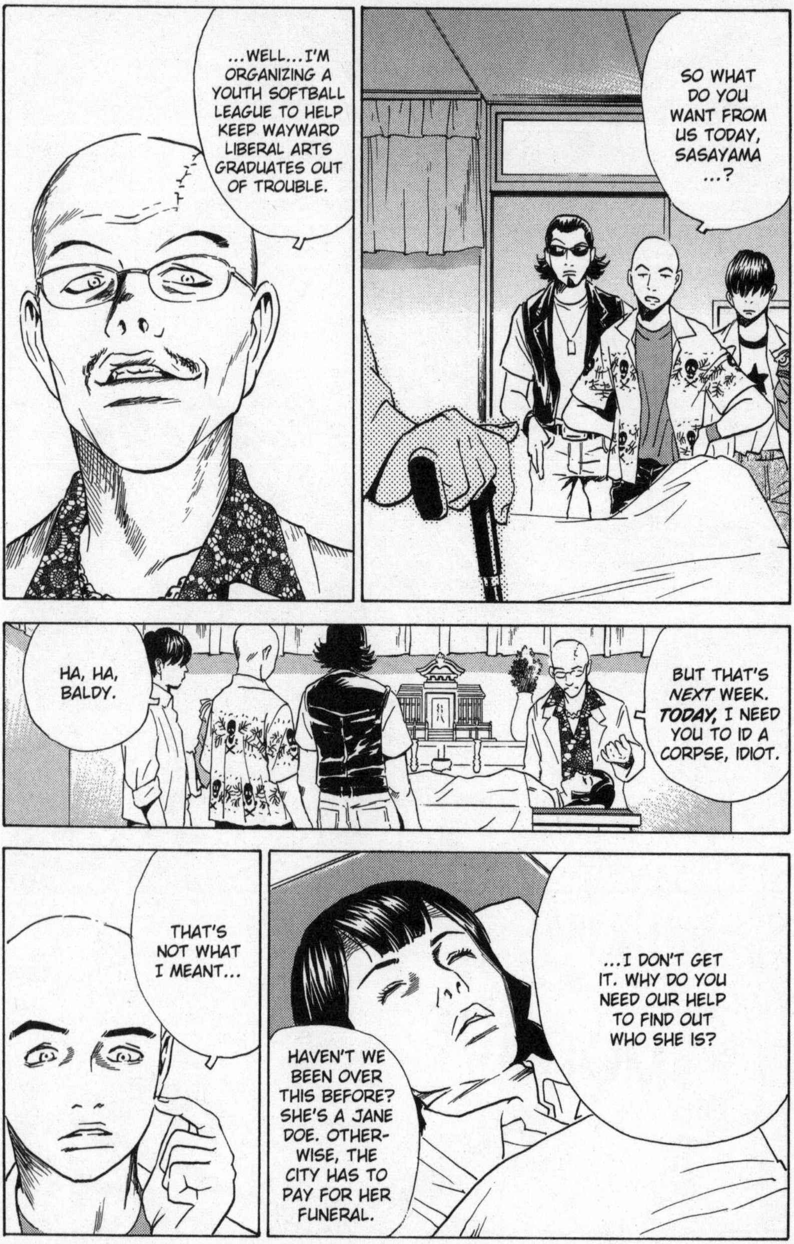
SO WHAT DO YOU WANT FROM US TODAY, SASAYAMA ...?
...WELL...I'M ORGANIZING A YOUTH SOFTBALL LEAGUE TO HELP KEEP WAYWARD LIBERAL ARTS GRADUATES OUT OF TROUBLE.
BUT THAT'S *NEXT* WEEK. ***TODAY,*** I NEED YOU TO ID A CORPSE, IDIOT.
HA, HA, BALDY.
...I DON'T GET IT. WHY DO YOU NEED OUR HELP TO FIND OUT WHO SHE IS?
HAVEN'T WE BEEN OVER THIS BEFORE? SHE'S A JANE DOE. OTHER-WISE, THE CITY HAS TO PAY FOR HER FUNERAL.
THAT'S NOT WHAT I MEANT...

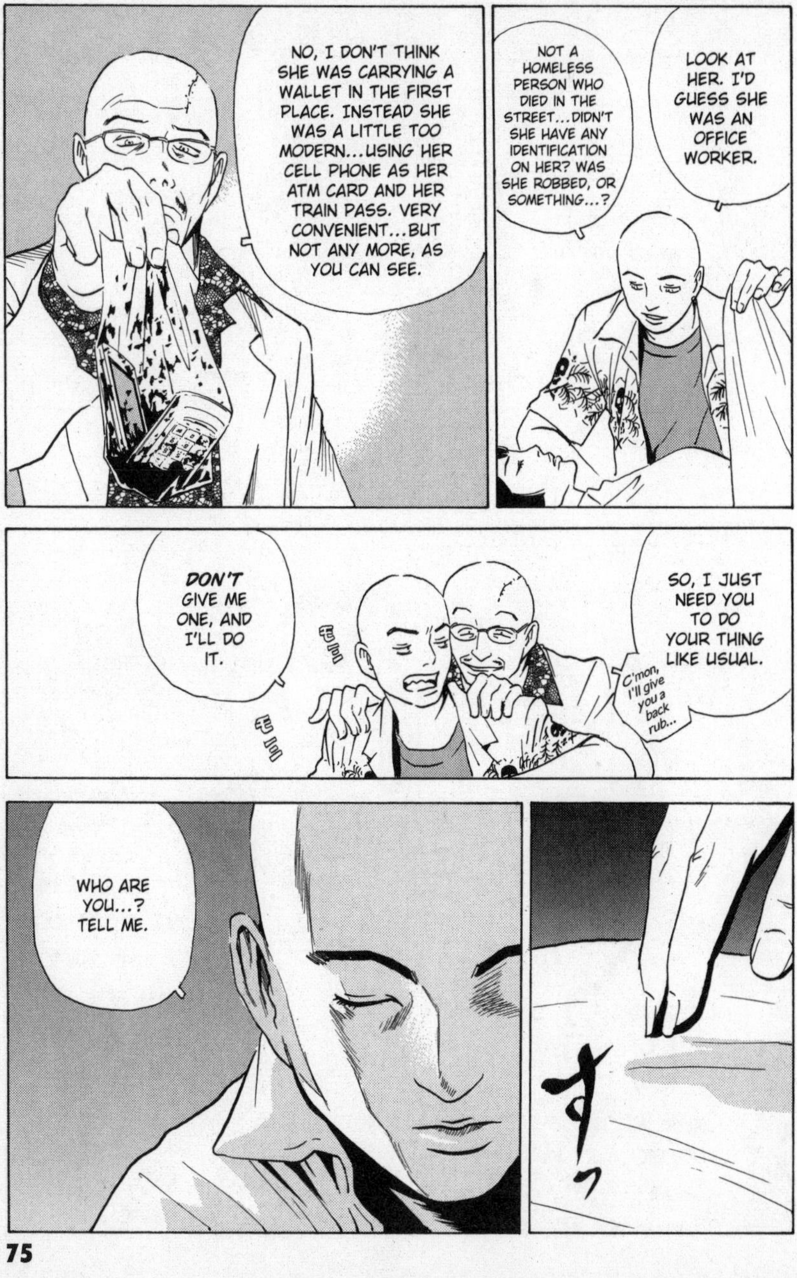
LOOK AT HER. I'D GUESS SHE WAS AN OFFICE WORKER.
NOT A HOMELESS PERSON WHO DIED IN THE STREET...DIDN'T SHE HAVE ANY IDENTIFICATION ON HER? WAS SHE ROBBED, OR SOMETHING...?
NO, I DON'T THINK SHE WAS CARRYING A WALLET IN THE FIRST PLACE. INSTEAD SHE WAS A LITTLE TOO MODERN...USING HER CELL PHONE AS HER ATM CARD AND HER TRAIN PASS. VERY CONVENIENT...BUT NOT ANY MORE, AS YOU CAN SEE.
SO, I JUST NEED YOU TO DO YOUR THING LIKE USUAL.
C'mon, I'll give you a back rub...
モミ
モミ
DON'T GIVE ME ONE, AND I'LL DO IT.
すっ
WHO ARE YOU...? TELL ME.

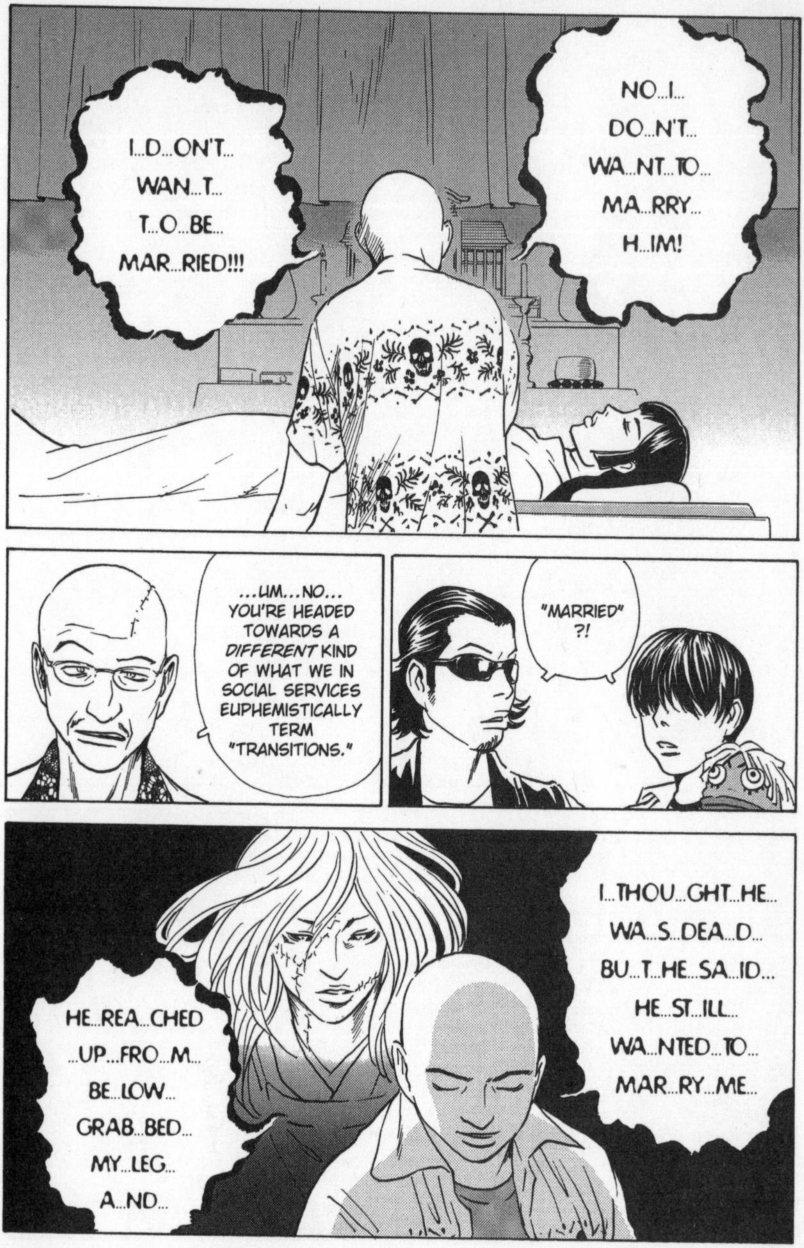
NO...I... DO...N'T... WA...NT...TO... MA...RRY... H...IM!
I...D...ON'T... WAN...T... T...O...BE... MAR...RIED!!!
"MARRIED" ?!
...UM...NO... YOU'RE HEADED TOWARDS A *DIFFERENT* KIND OF WHAT WE IN SOCIAL SERVICES EUPHEMISTICALLY TERM "TRANSITIONS."
I...THOU...GHT...HE... WA...S...DEA...D... BU...T...HE...SA...ID... HE...ST...ILL... WA...NTED...TO... MAR...RY...ME...
HE...REA...CHED ...UP...FRO...M... BE...LOW... GRAB...BED... MY...LEG... A...ND...

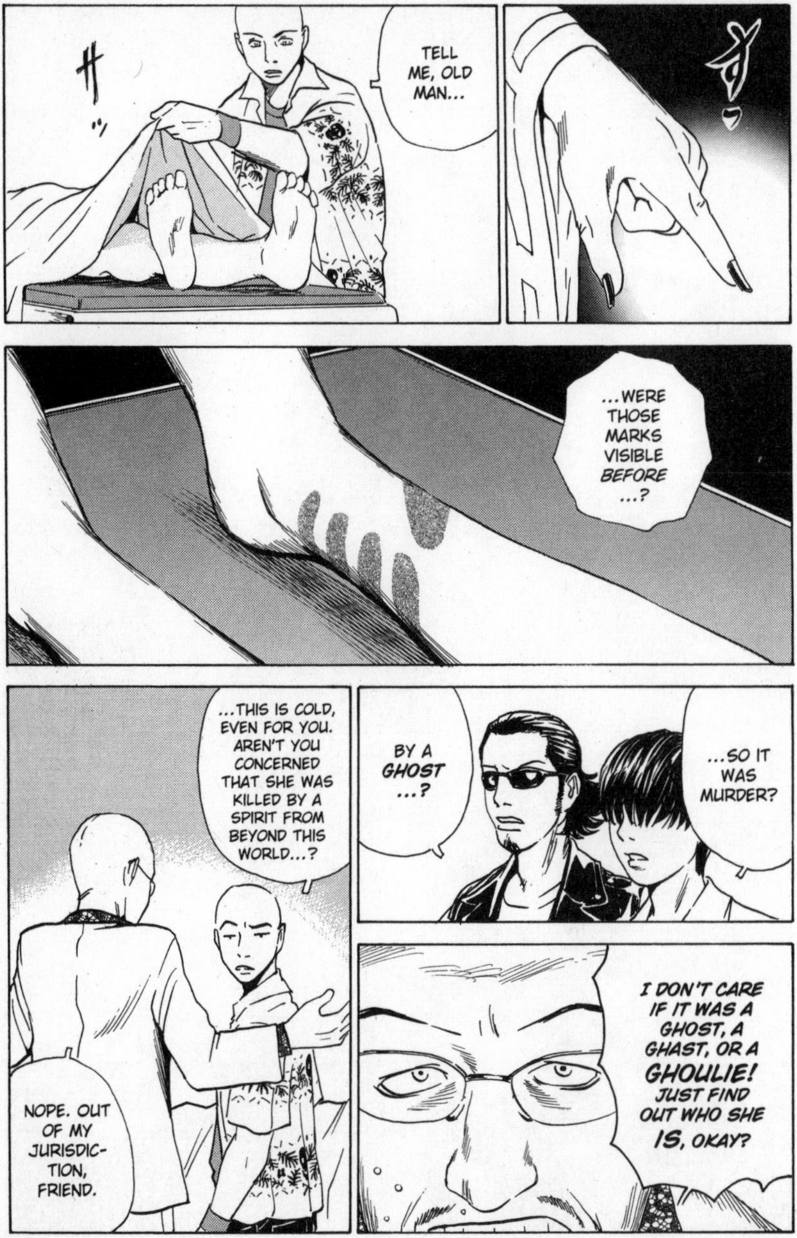
TELL ME, OLD MAN...
...WERE THOSE MARKS VISIBLE *BEFORE* ...?
...SO IT WAS MURDER?
BY A *GHOST* ...?
I DON'T CARE IF IT WAS A GHOST, A GHAST, OR A GHOULIE! JUST FIND OUT WHO SHE *IS*, OKAY?
...THIS IS COLD, EVEN FOR YOU. AREN'T YOU CONCERNED THAT SHE WAS KILLED BY A SPIRIT FROM BEYOND THIS WORLD...?
NOPE. OUT OF MY JURISDIC-TION, FRIEND.

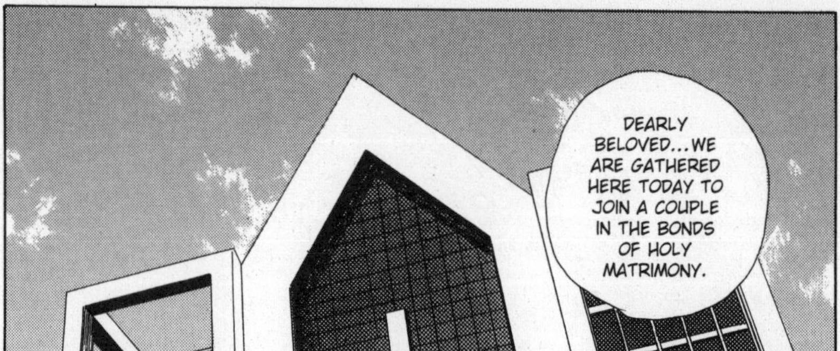
DEARLY BELOVED...WE ARE GATHERED HERE TODAY TO JOIN A COUPLE IN THE BONDS OF HOLY MATRIMONY.
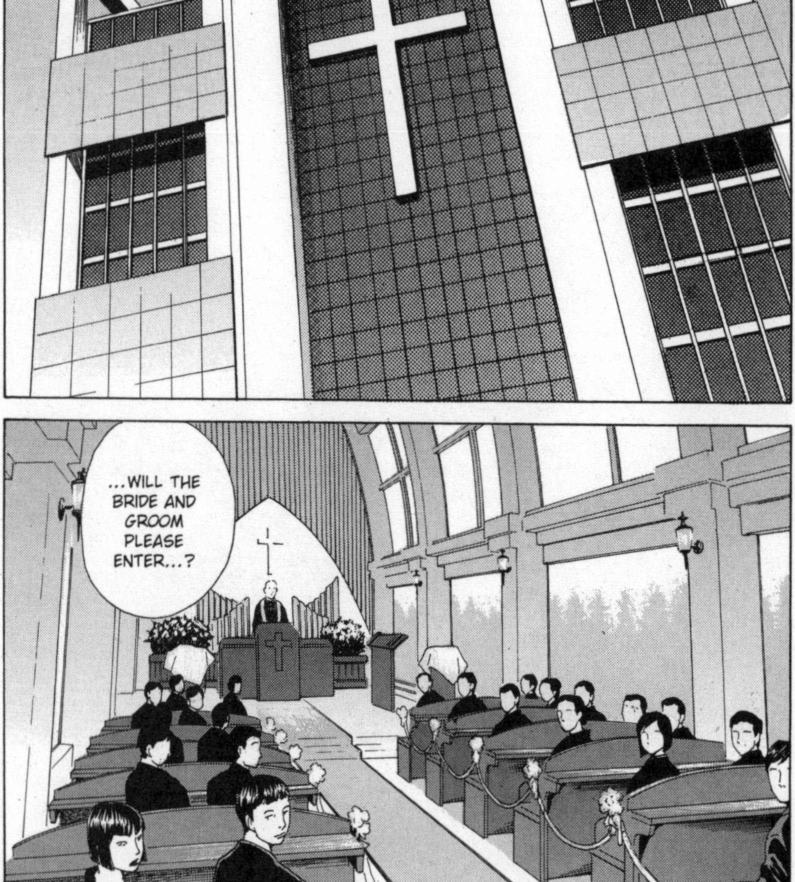
...WILL THE BRIDE AND GROOM PLEASE ENTER...?

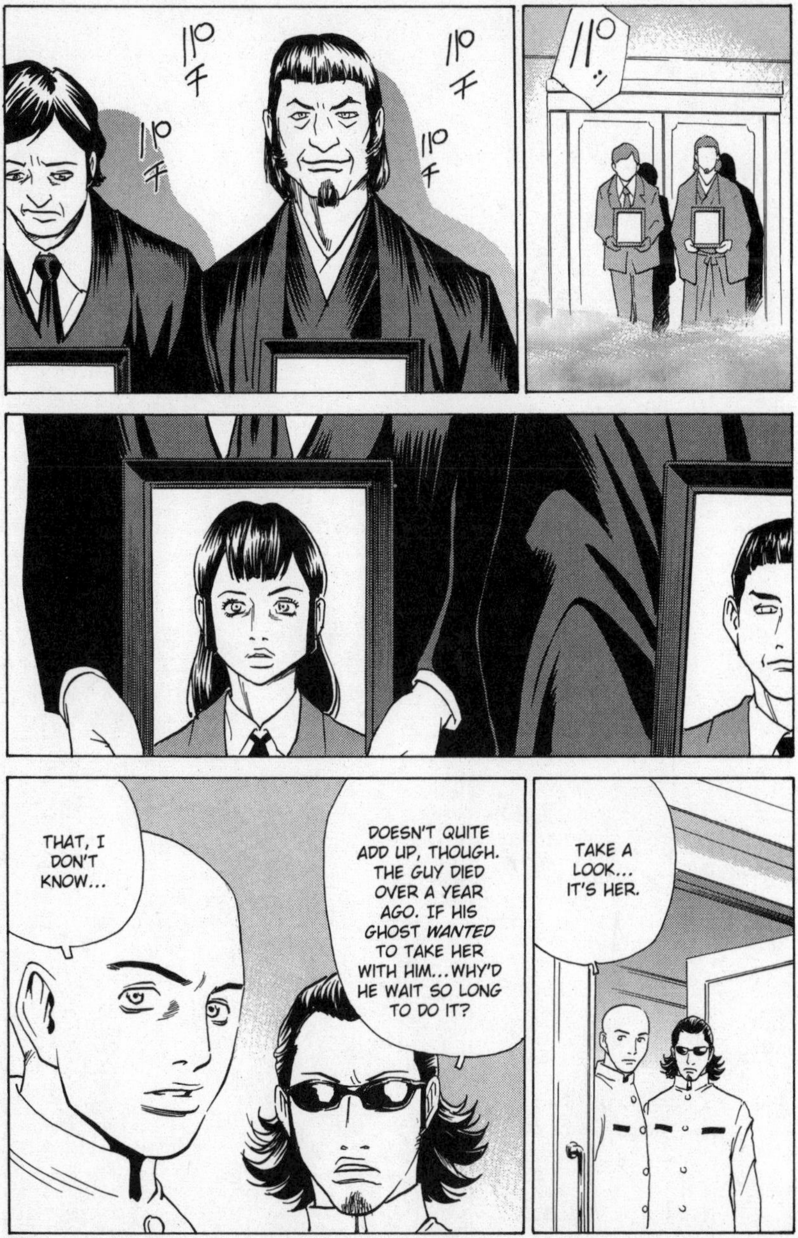
パ
パチ
パチ
パチ
パチ
TAKE A LOOK... IT'S HER.
DOESN'T QUITE ADD UP, THOUGH. THE GUY DIED OVER A YEAR AGO. IF HIS GHOST *WANTED* TO TAKE HER WITH HIM...WHY'D HE WAIT SO LONG TO DO IT?
THAT, I DON'T KNOW...

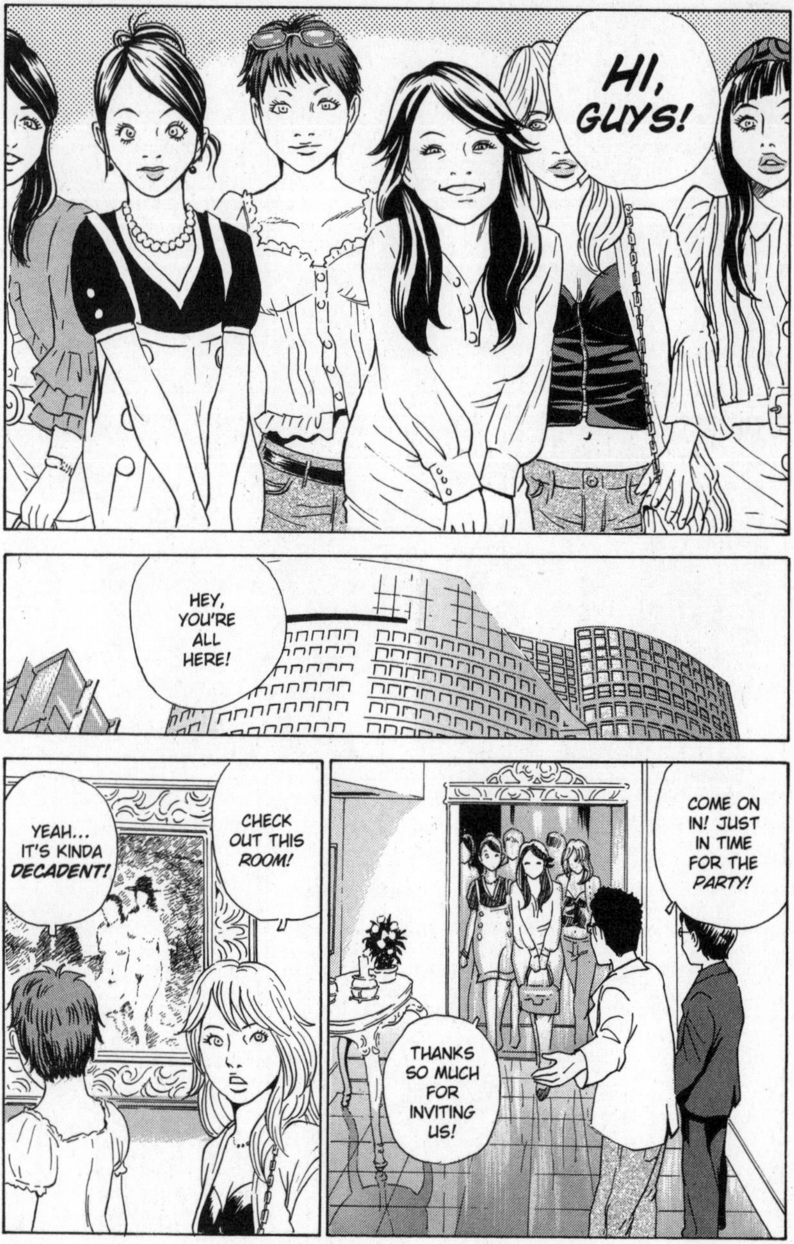
HI, GUYS!
HEY, YOU'RE ALL HERE!
COME ON IN! JUST IN TIME FOR THE *PARTY!*
THANKS SO MUCH FOR INVITING US!
CHECK OUT THIS *ROOM!*
YEAH... IT'S KINDA *DECADENT!*

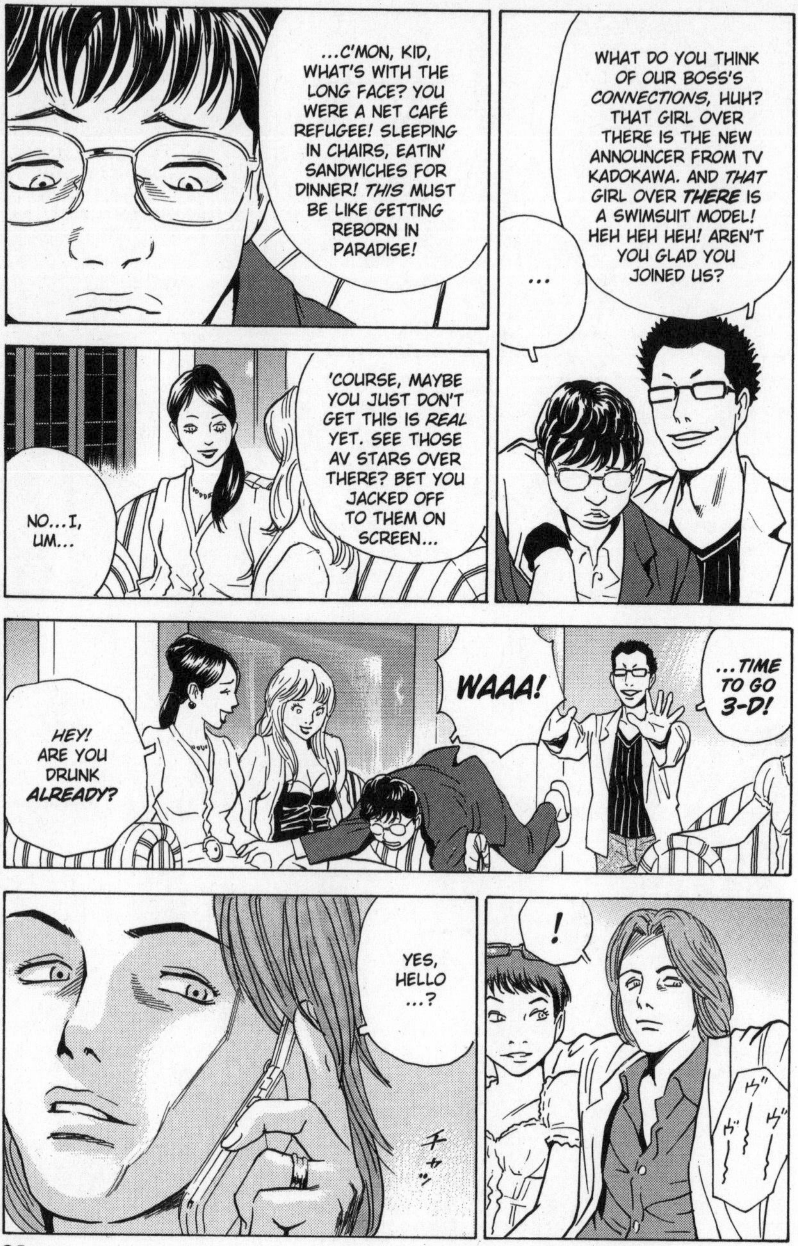

WHAT DO YOU THINK OF OUR BOSS'S *CONNECTIONS*, HUH? THAT GIRL OVER THERE IS THE NEW ANNOUNCER FROM TV KADOKAWA. AND *THAT* GIRL OVER ***THERE*** IS A SWIMSUIT MODEL! HEH HEH HEH! AREN'T YOU GLAD YOU JOINED US?
...
...C'MON, KID, WHAT'S WITH THE LONG FACE? YOU WERE A NET CAFÉ REFUGEE! SLEEPING IN CHAIRS, EATIN' SANDWICHES FOR DINNER! *THIS* MUST BE LIKE GETTING REBORN IN PARADISE!
'COURSE, MAYBE YOU JUST DON'T GET THIS IS *REAL* YET. SEE THOSE AV STARS OVER THERE? BET YOU JACKED OFF TO THEM ON SCREEN...
NO...I, UM...
...TIME TO GO **3-D!**
WAAA!
HEY! ARE YOU DRUNK ***ALREADY?***
!
YES, HELLO ...?

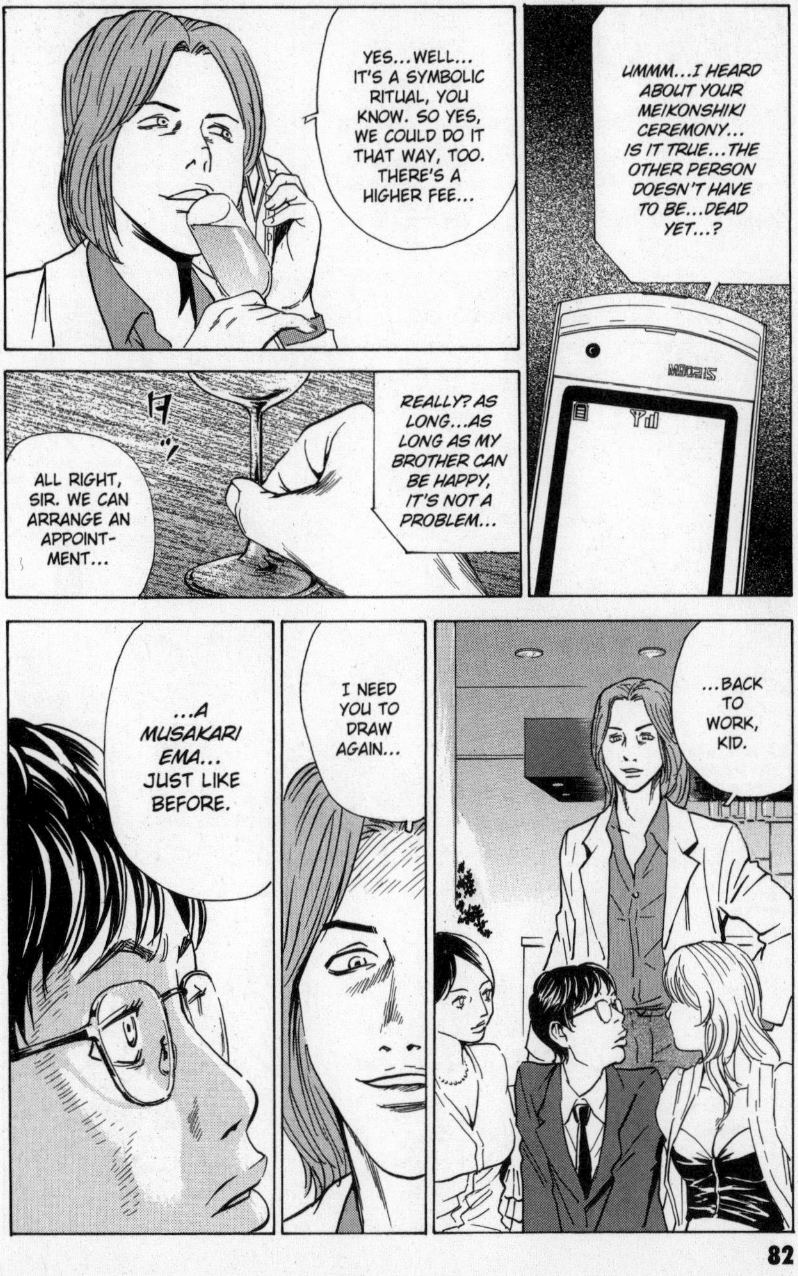
UMMM...I HEARD ABOUT YOUR MEIKONSHIKI CEREMONY... IS IT TRUE...THE OTHER PERSON DOESN'T HAVE TO BE...DEAD YET...?
YES...WELL... IT'S A SYMBOLIC RITUAL, YOU KNOW. SO YES, WE COULD DO IT THAT WAY, TOO. THERE'S A HIGHER FEE...
REALLY? AS LONG...AS LONG AS MY BROTHER CAN BE HAPPY, IT'S NOT A PROBLEM...
ALL RIGHT, SIR. WE CAN ARRANGE AN APPOINTMENT...
...BACK TO WORK, KID.
I NEED YOU TO DRAW AGAIN...
...A MUSAKARI EMA... JUST LIKE BEFORE.

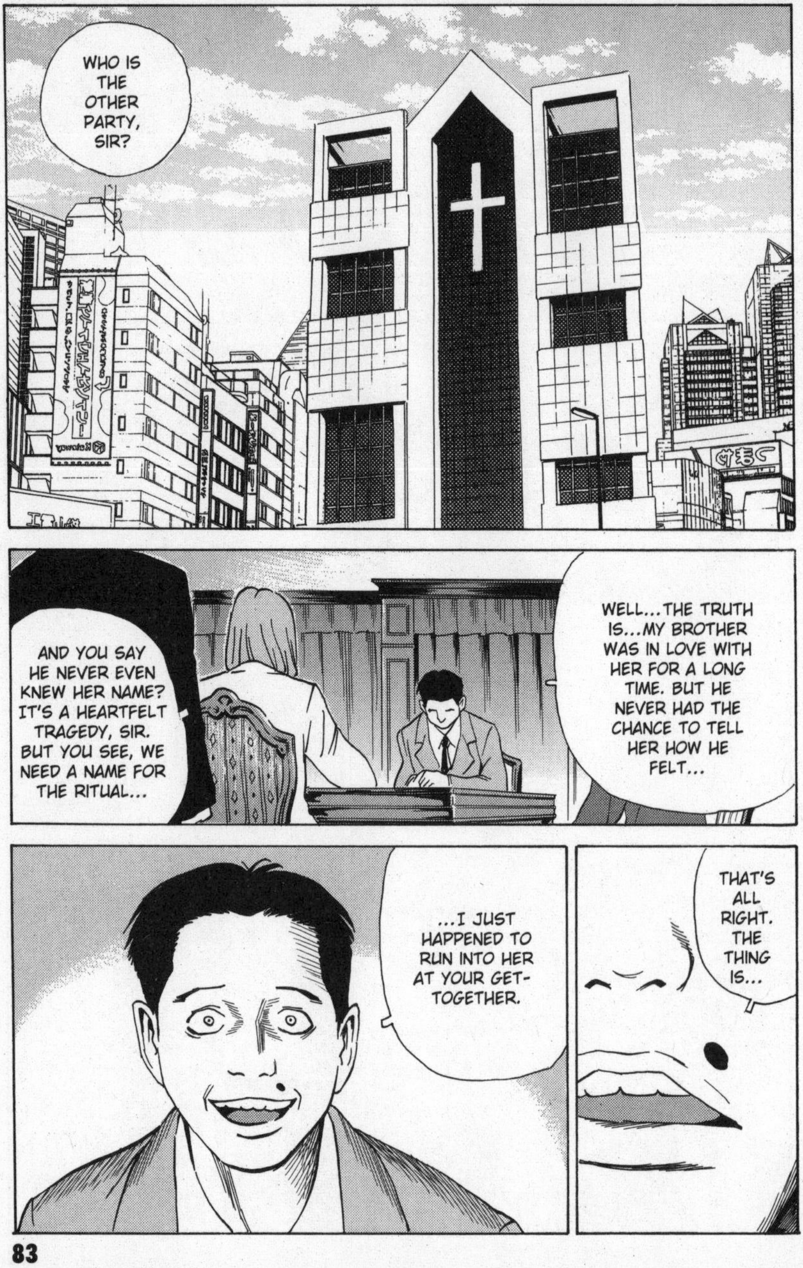
WHO IS THE OTHER PARTY, SIR?
WELL...THE TRUTH IS...MY BROTHER WAS IN LOVE WITH HER FOR A LONG TIME. BUT HE NEVER HAD THE CHANCE TO TELL HER HOW HE FELT...
AND YOU SAY HE NEVER EVEN KNEW HER NAME? IT'S A HEARTFELT TRAGEDY, SIR. BUT YOU SEE, WE NEED A NAME FOR THE RITUAL...
THAT'S ALL RIGHT. THE THING IS...
...I JUST HAPPENED TO RUN INTO HER AT YOUR GET-TOGETHER.

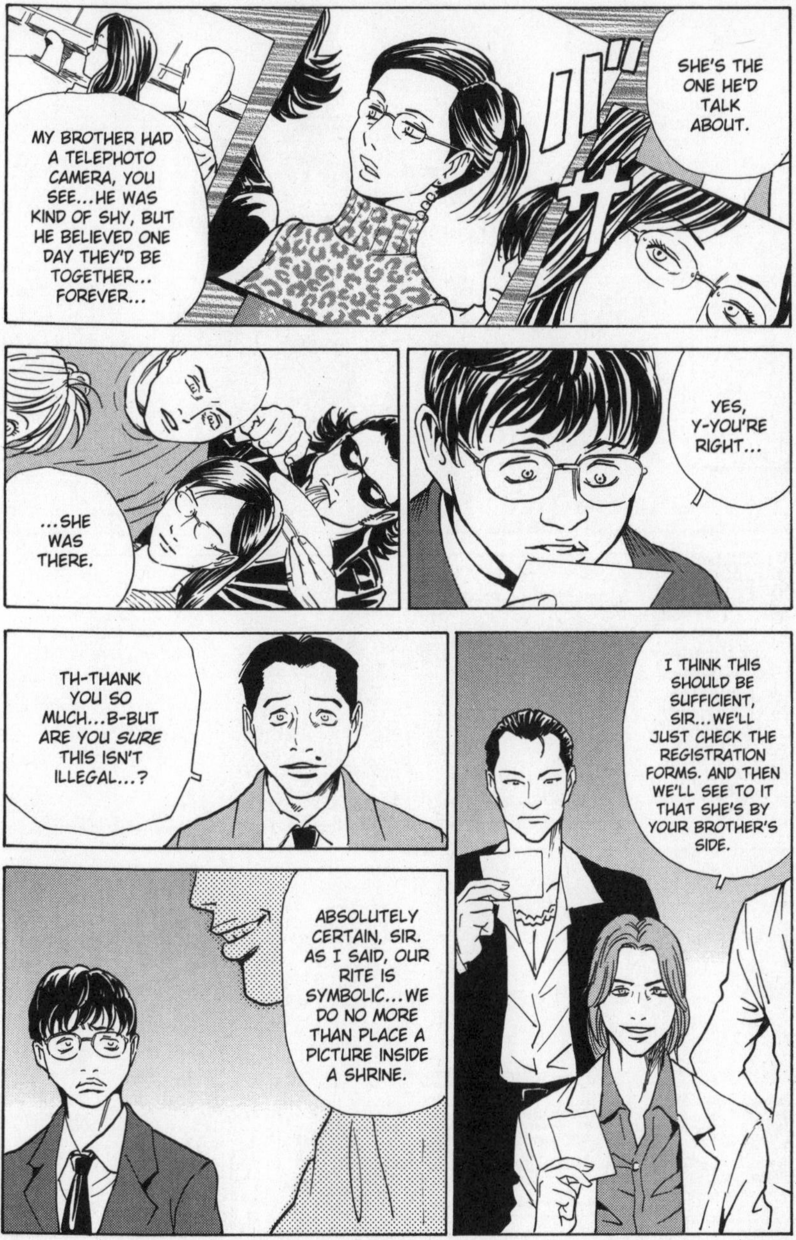
SHE'S THE ONE HE'D TALK ABOUT.
MY BROTHER HAD A TELEPHOTO CAMERA, YOU SEE...HE WAS KIND OF SHY, BUT HE BELIEVED ONE DAY THEY'D BE TOGETHER... FOREVER...
YES, Y-YOU'RE RIGHT...
...SHE WAS THERE.
I THINK THIS SHOULD BE SUFFICIENT, SIR...WE'LL JUST CHECK THE REGISTRATION FORMS. AND THEN WE'LL SEE TO IT THAT SHE'S BY YOUR BROTHER'S SIDE.
TH-THANK YOU SO MUCH...B-BUT ARE YOU *SURE* THIS ISN'T ILLEGAL...?
ABSOLUTELY CERTAIN, SIR. AS I SAID, OUR RITE IS SYMBOLIC...WE DO NO MORE THAN PLACE A PICTURE INSIDE A SHRINE.

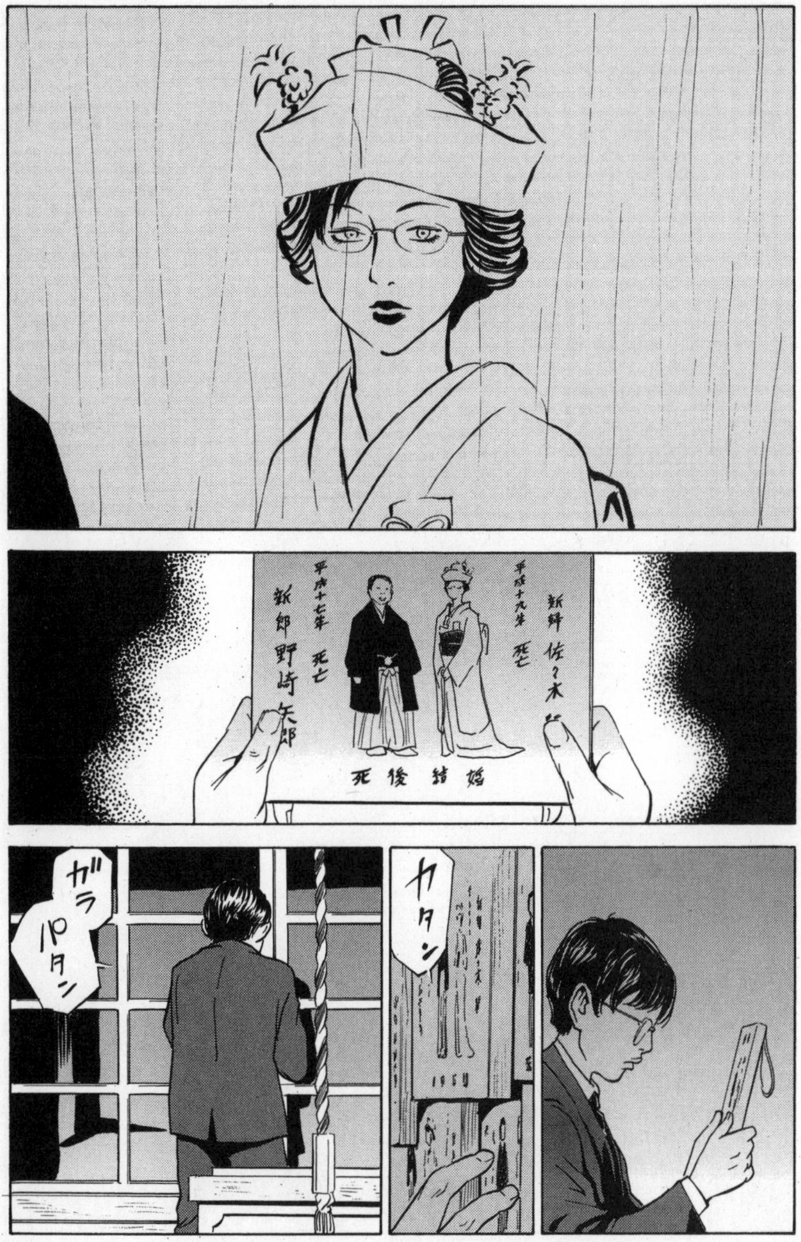
新婦 佐々木
平成十九年 死亡
平成十七年 死亡
新郎 野崎矢郎
死後結婚
カタン
ガラ
パタン

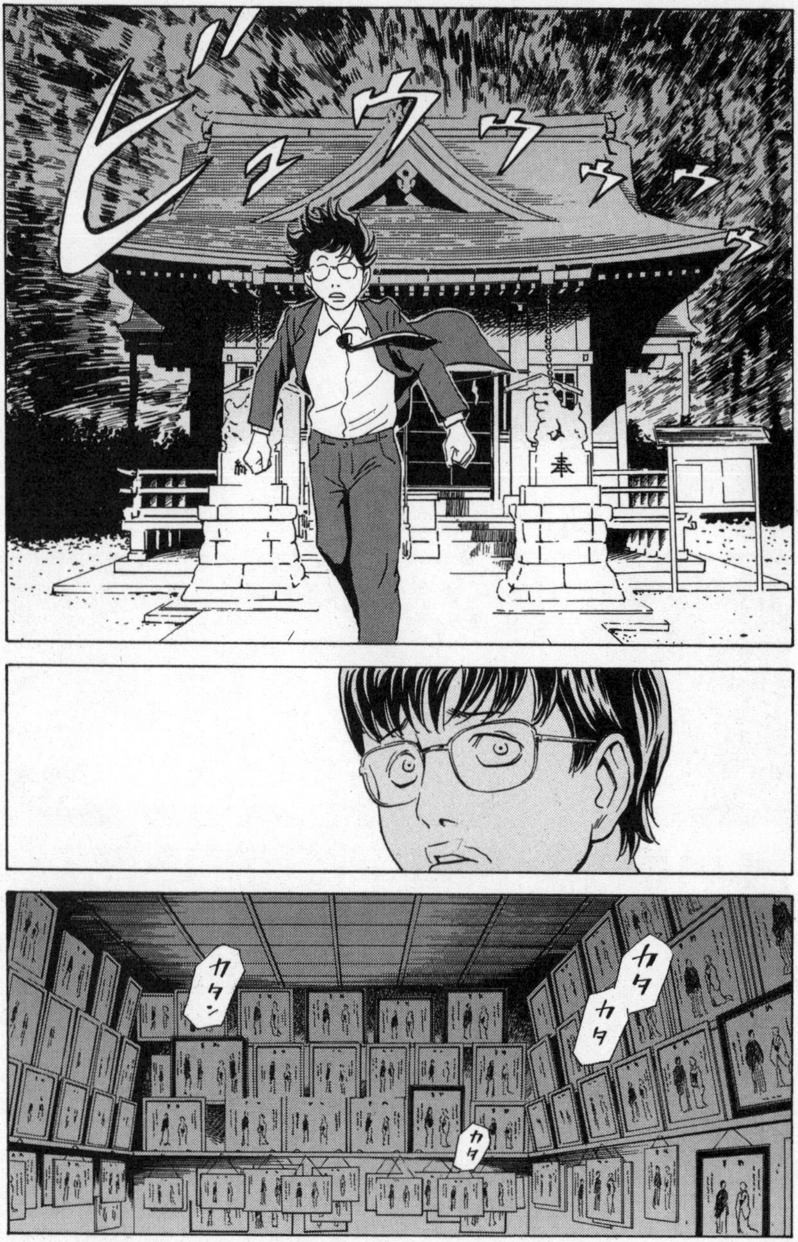
ビュウウウウウ
奉
カタ
カタ
カタン
カタ

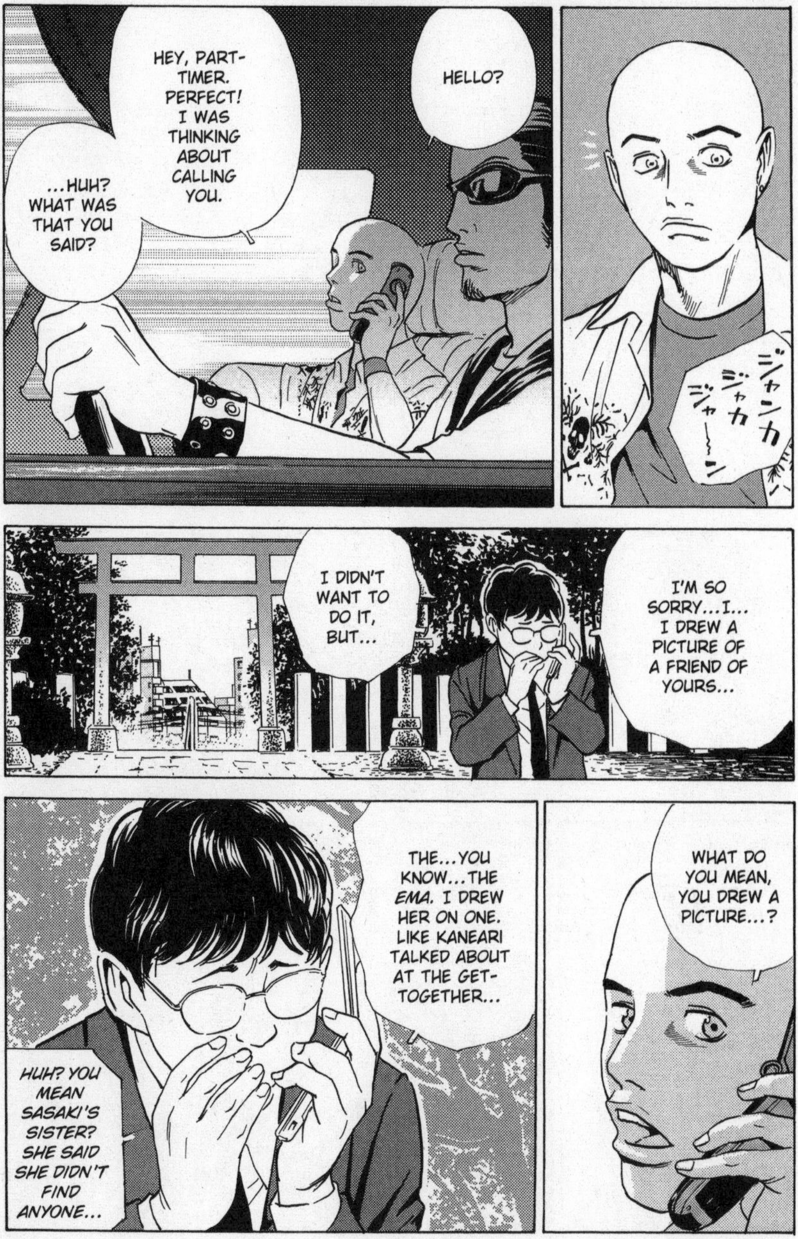
ジャンカジャカジャ〜ン
HELLO?
HEY, PART-TIMER. PERFECT! I WAS THINKING ABOUT CALLING YOU.
...HUH? WHAT WAS THAT YOU SAID?
I'M SO SORRY...I... I DREW A PICTURE OF A FRIEND OF YOURS...
I DIDN'T WANT TO DO IT, BUT...
WHAT DO YOU MEAN, YOU DREW A PICTURE...?
THE...YOU KNOW...THE *EMA.* I DREW HER ON ONE. LIKE KANEARI TALKED ABOUT AT THE GET-TOGETHER...
HUH? YOU MEAN SASAKI'S SISTER? SHE SAID SHE DIDN'T FIND ANYONE...

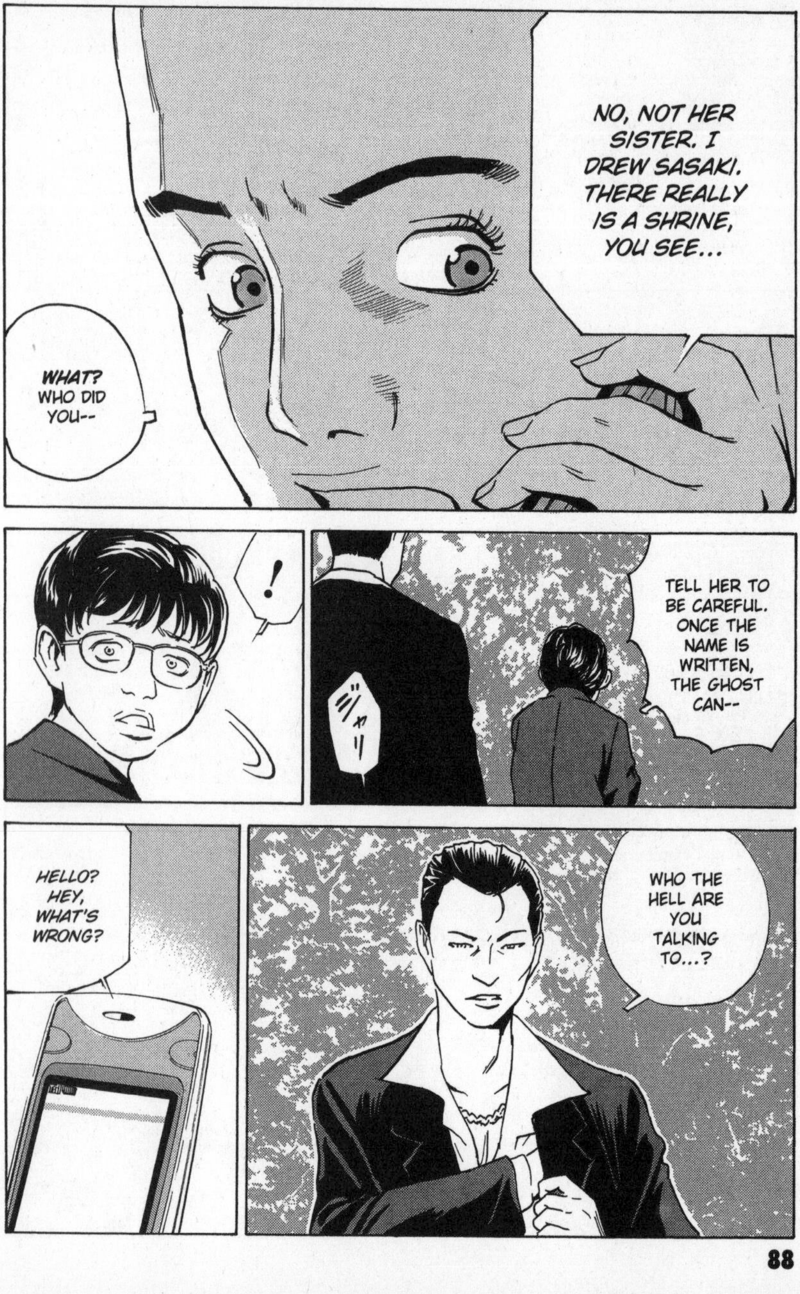
NO, NOT HER SISTER. I DREW SASAKI. THERE REALLY IS A SHRINE, YOU SEE...
WHAT? WHO DID YOU--
TELL HER TO BE CAREFUL. ONCE THE NAME IS WRITTEN, THE GHOST CAN--
ジャリ
!
WHO THE HELL ARE YOU TALKING TO...?
HELLO? HEY, WHAT'S WRONG?

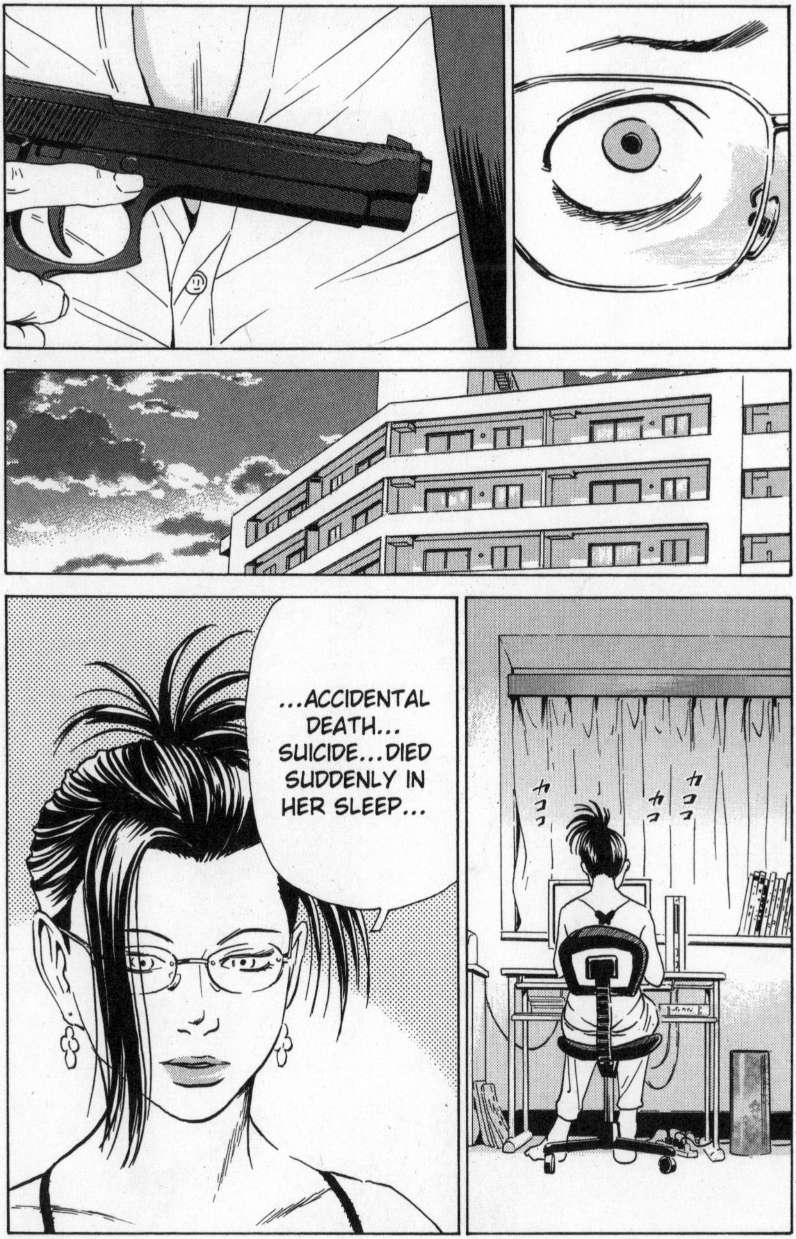
カココ
カコ
カココ
...ACCIDENTAL DEATH... SUICIDE...DIED SUDDENLY IN HER SLEEP...

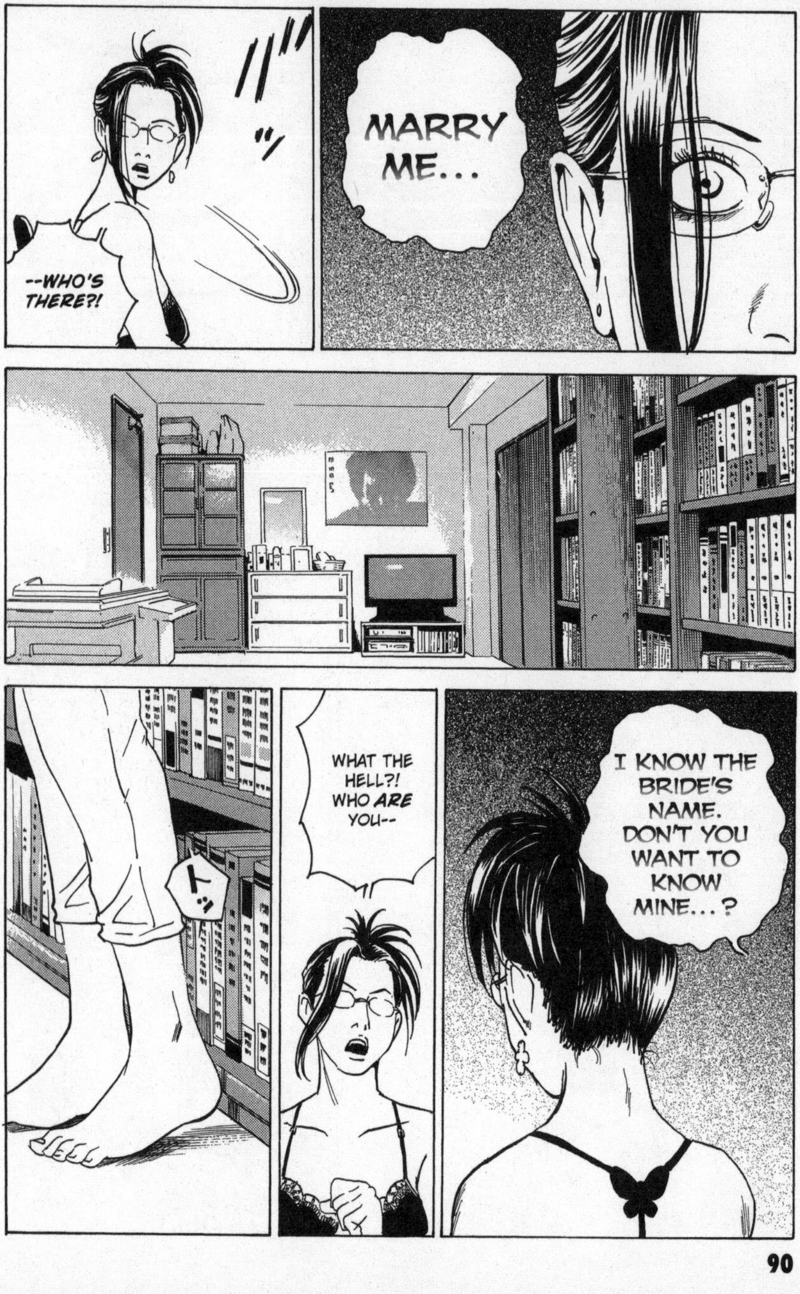
MARRY ME...
--WHO'S THERE?!
I KNOW THE BRIDE'S NAME. DON'T YOU WANT TO KNOW MINE...?
WHAT THE HELL?! WHO *ARE* YOU--

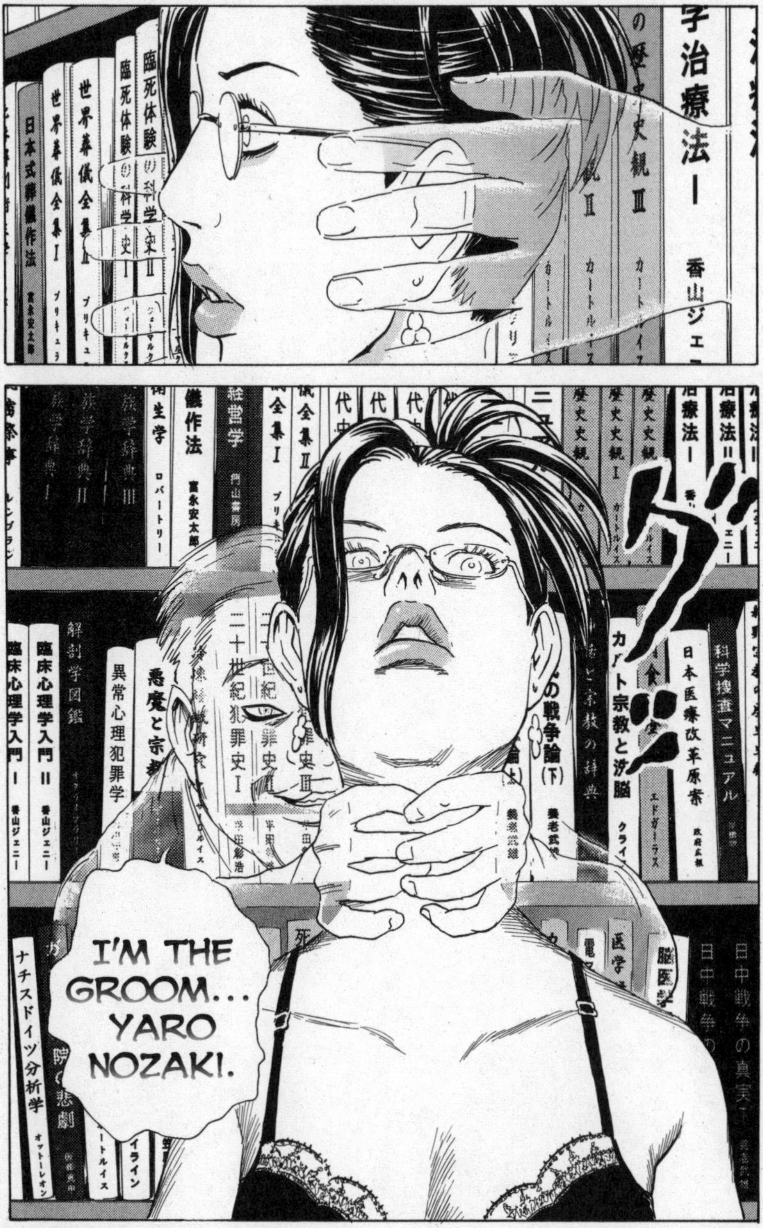
グッ
I'M THE GROOM... YARO NOZAKI.

3rd delivery: i probably won't die—the end

4th delivery
ラブソングはいらない
no need for a love song

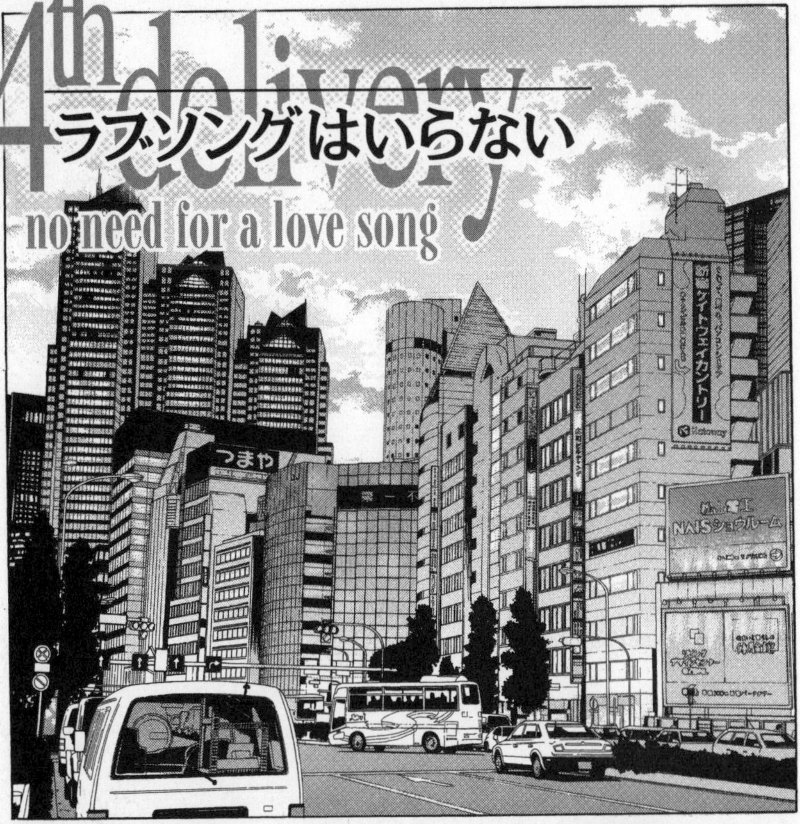
つまや
NAISショウルーム

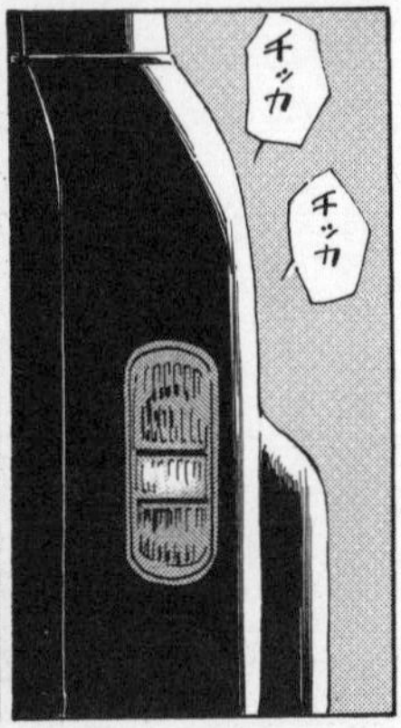
チッカ
チッカ

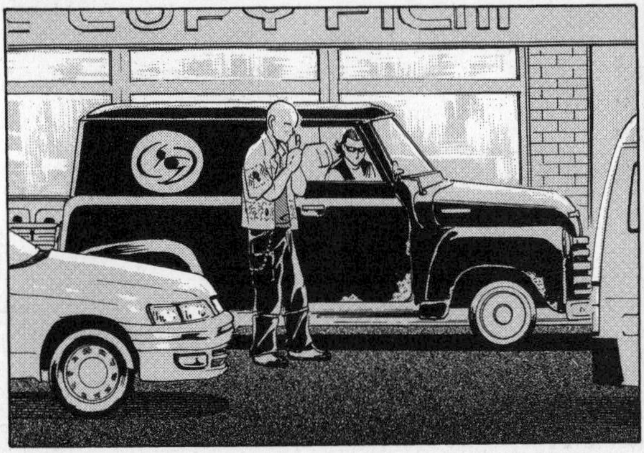

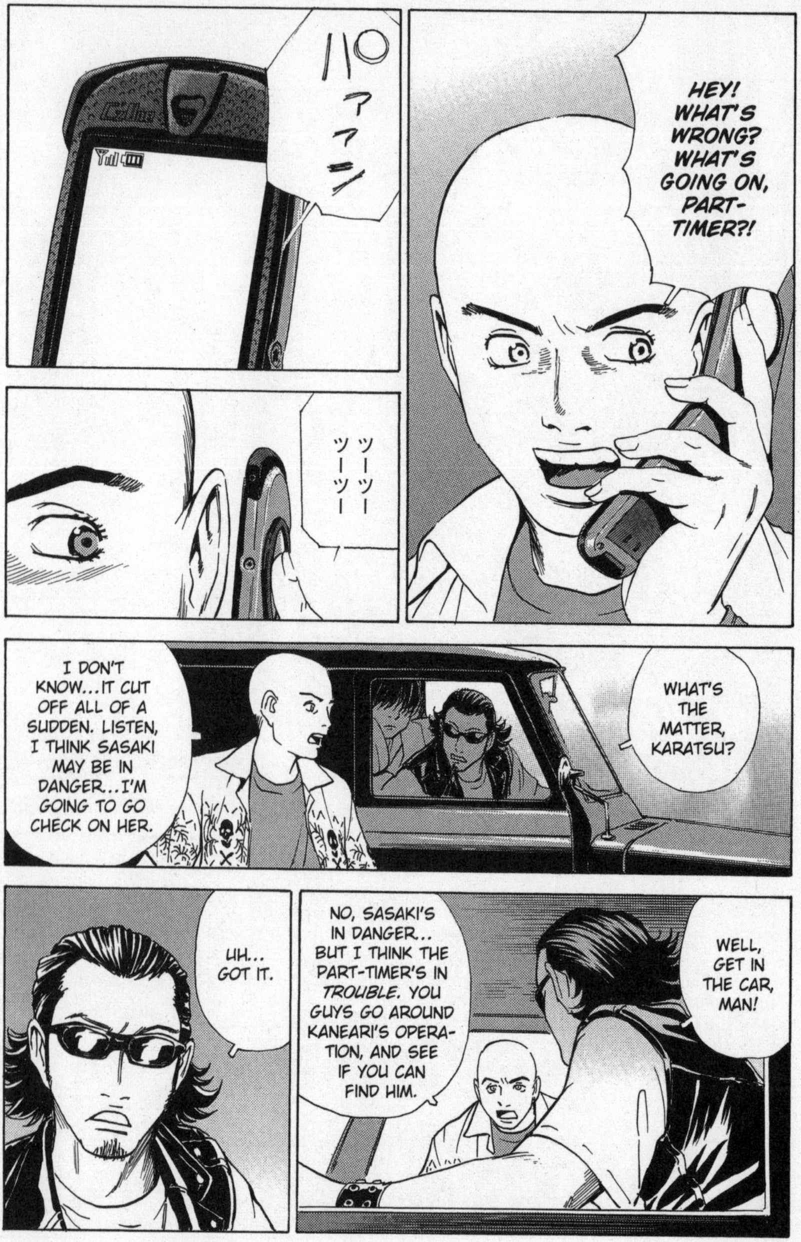

HEY! WHAT'S WRONG? WHAT'S GOING ON, PART-TIMER?!
パアアン
ツーツー ツーツー
WHAT'S THE MATTER, KARATSU?
I DON'T KNOW...IT CUT OFF ALL OF A SUDDEN. LISTEN, I THINK SASAKI MAY BE IN DANGER...I'M GOING TO GO CHECK ON HER.
WELL, GET IN THE CAR, MAN!
NO, SASAKI'S IN DANGER... BUT I THINK THE PART-TIMER'S IN *TROUBLE*. YOU GUYS GO AROUND KANEARI'S OPERATION, AND SEE IF YOU CAN FIND HIM.
UH... GOT IT.

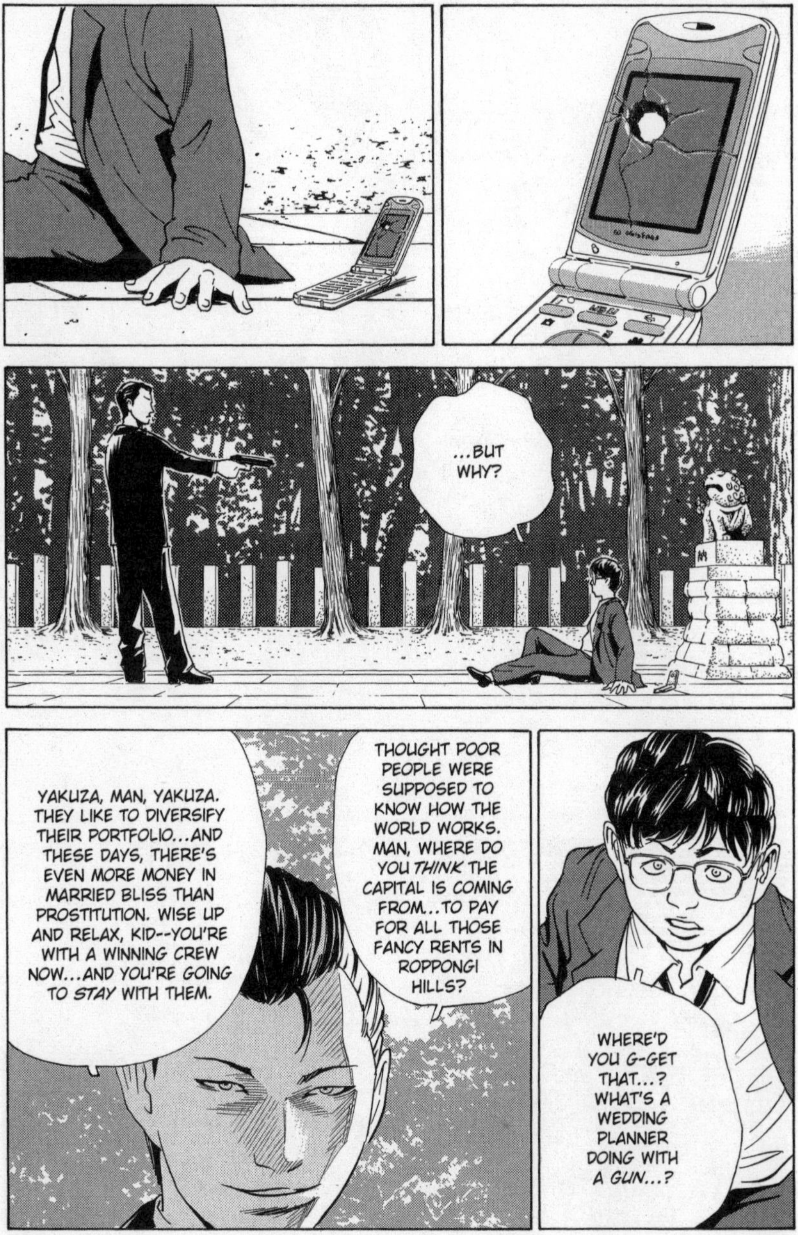
...BUT WHY?
WHERE'D YOU G-GET THAT...? WHAT'S A WEDDING PLANNER DOING WITH A *GUN*...?
THOUGHT POOR PEOPLE WERE SUPPOSED TO KNOW HOW THE WORLD WORKS. MAN, WHERE DO YOU *THINK* THE CAPITAL IS COMING FROM...TO PAY FOR ALL THOSE FANCY RENTS IN ROPPONGI HILLS?
YAKUZA, MAN, YAKUZA. THEY LIKE TO DIVERSIFY THEIR PORTFOLIO...AND THESE DAYS, THERE'S EVEN MORE MONEY IN MARRIED BLISS THAN PROSTITUTION. WISE UP AND RELAX, KID--YOU'RE WITH A WINNING CREW NOW...AND YOU'RE GOING TO *STAY* WITH THEM.

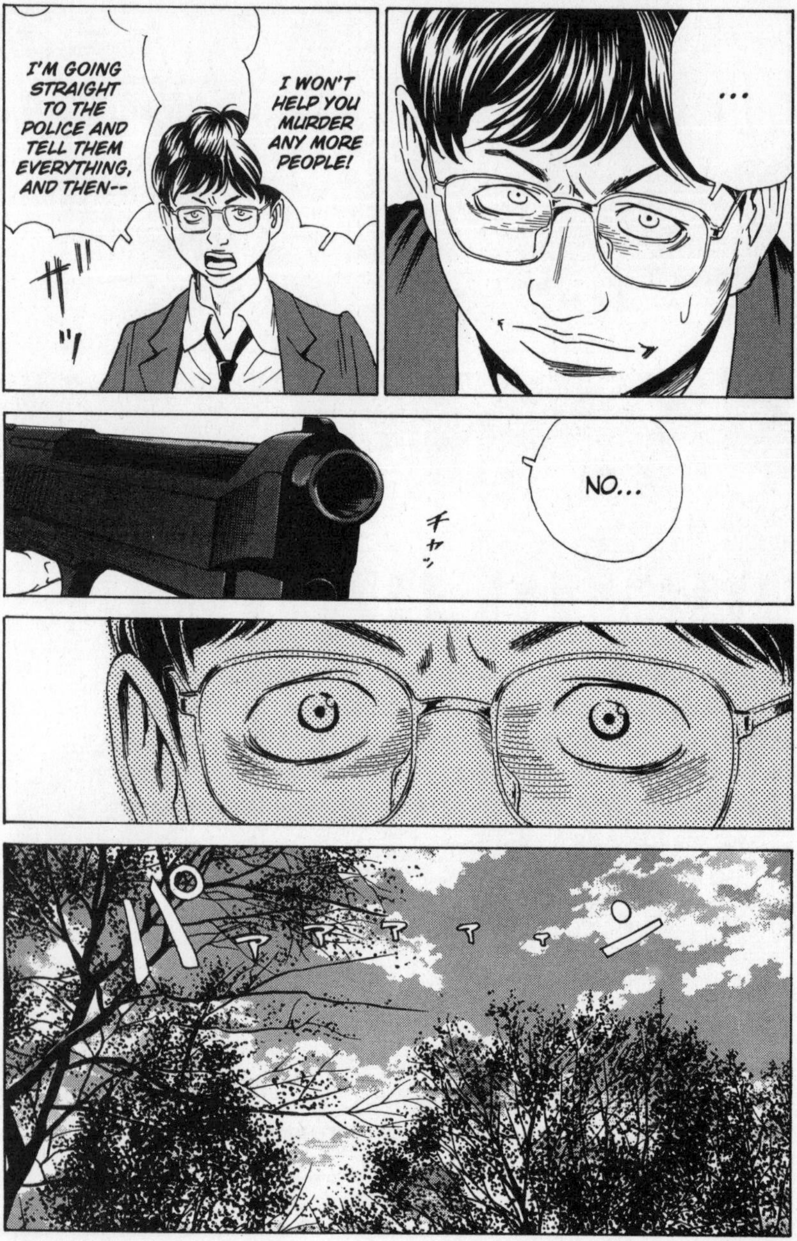
...
ザッ
I WON'T HELP YOU MURDER ANY MORE PEOPLE!
I'M GOING STRAIGHT TO THE POLICE AND TELL THEM EVERYTHING, AND THEN--
NO...
チャッ

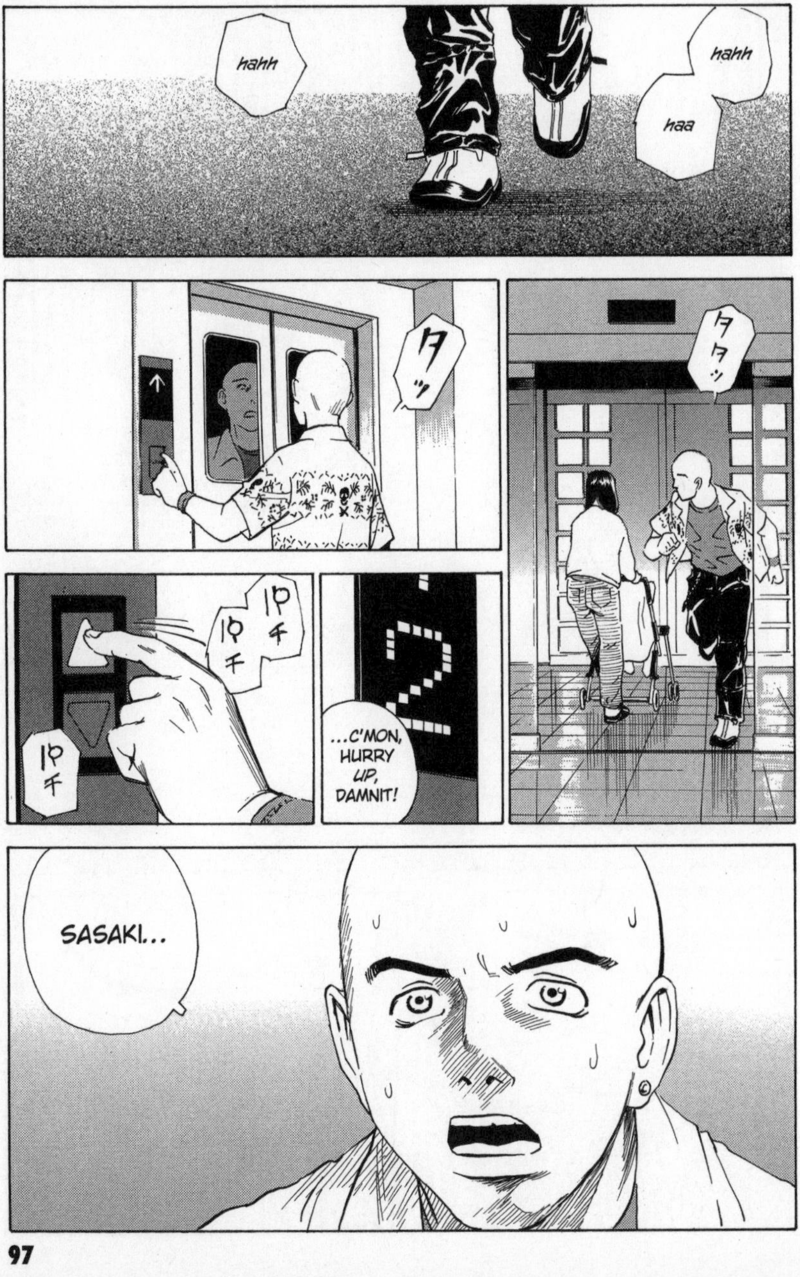
hahh
haa
hahh
タタッ
タッ
...C'MON, HURRY UP, DAMNIT!
ポチ
ポチ
ポチ
SASAKI...

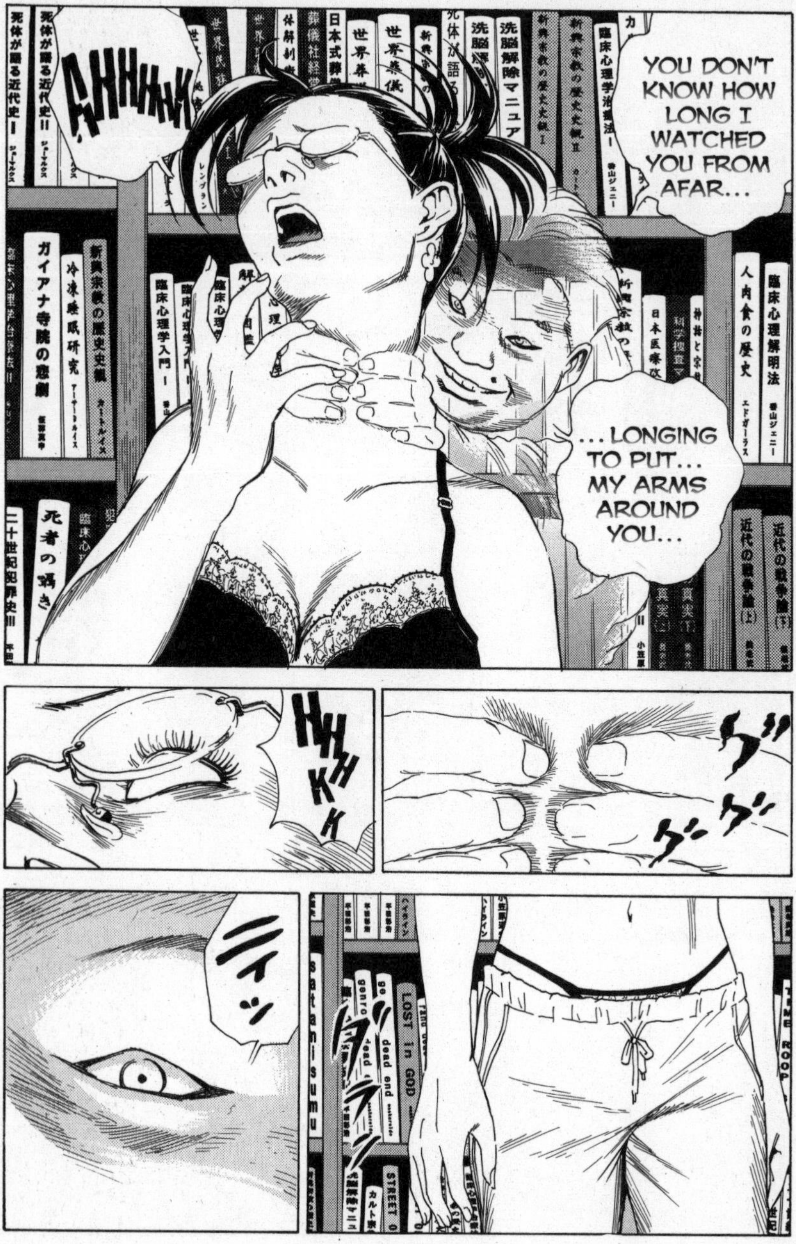
YOU DON'T KNOW HOW LONG I WATCHED YOU FROM AFAR...
AHHHHK
...LONGING TO PUT... MY ARMS AROUND YOU...
HHHHKK
ニイッ

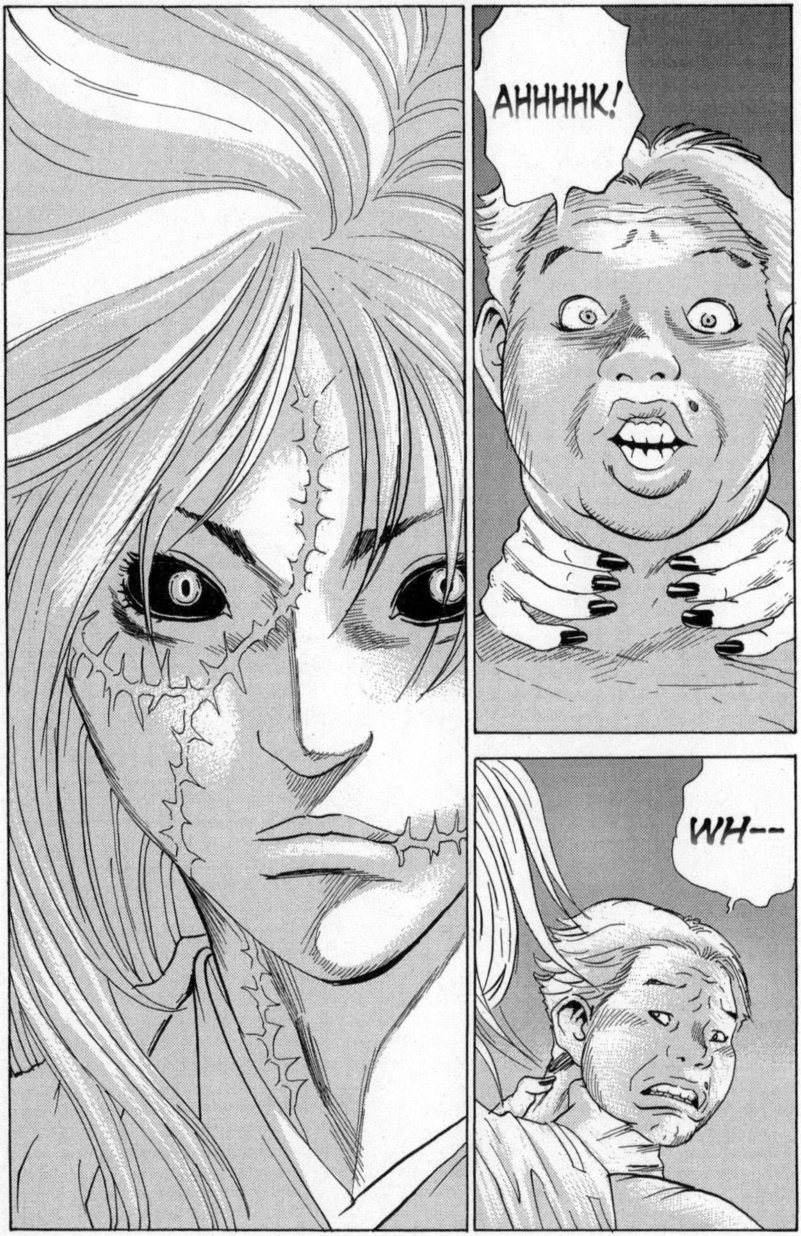
AHHHHK!
WH--

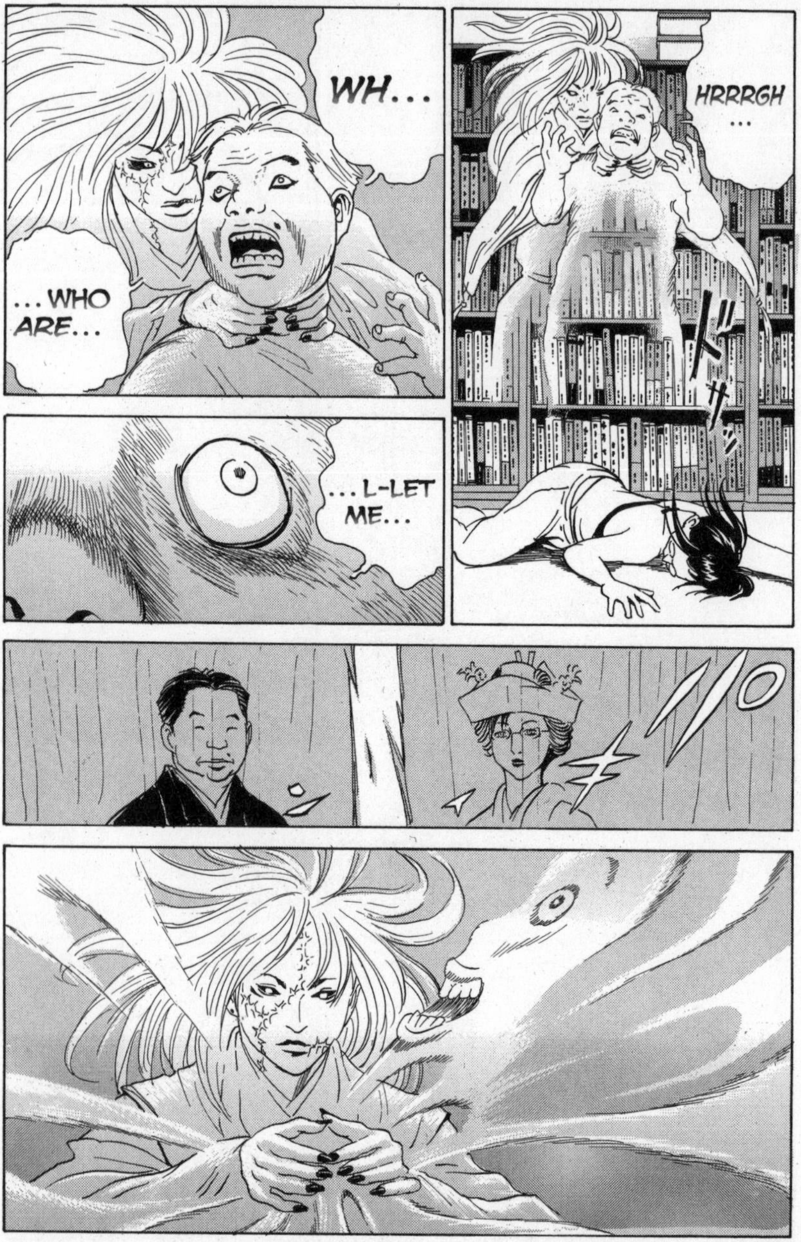
HRRRGH ...
ドザッ
WH...
...WHO ARE...
...L-LET ME...
パキ

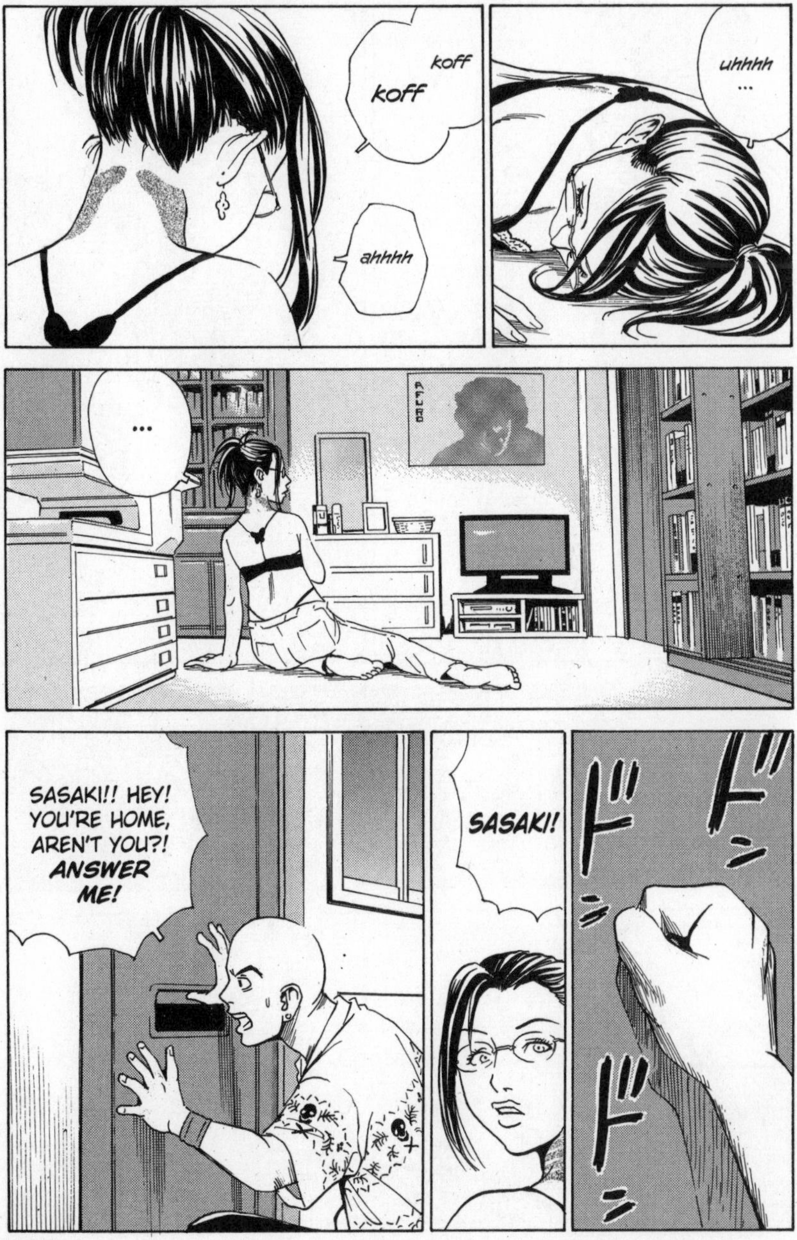
uhhhh ...
koff koff
ahhhh
...
ドン
ドン
SASAKI!
SASAKI!! HEY! YOU'RE HOME, AREN'T YOU?! **ANSWER ME!**

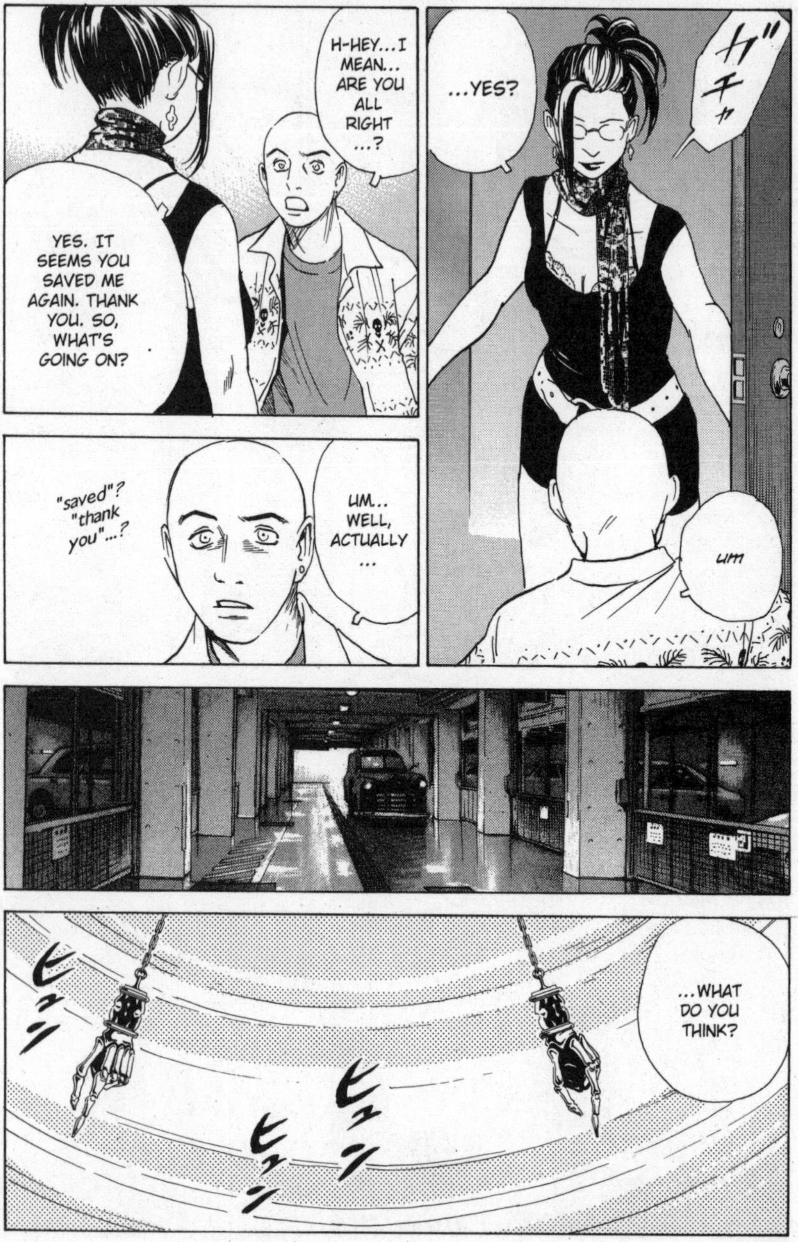

ガチャ
...YES?
um
H-HEY...I MEAN... ARE YOU ALL RIGHT ...?
YES. IT SEEMS YOU SAVED ME AGAIN. THANK YOU. SO, WHAT'S GOING ON?
UM... WELL, ACTUALLY ...
"saved"? "thank you"...?
...WHAT DO YOU THINK?
ヒュン
ヒュン
ヒュン

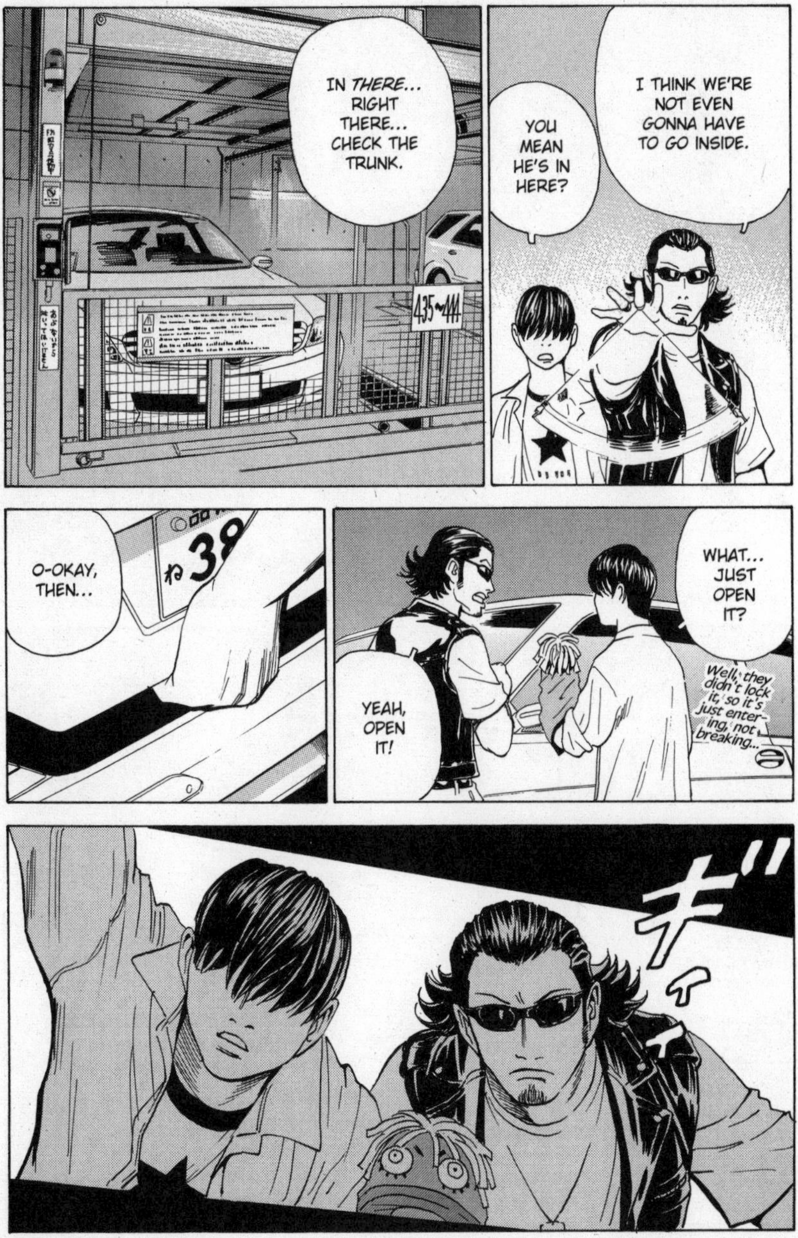
I THINK WE'RE NOT EVEN GONNA HAVE TO GO INSIDE.
YOU MEAN HE'S IN HERE?
IN *THERE*... RIGHT THERE... CHECK THE TRUNK.
WHAT... JUST OPEN IT?
Well, they didn't lock it, so it's just entering, not breaking...
YEAH, OPEN IT!
O-OKAY, THEN...
ギィ

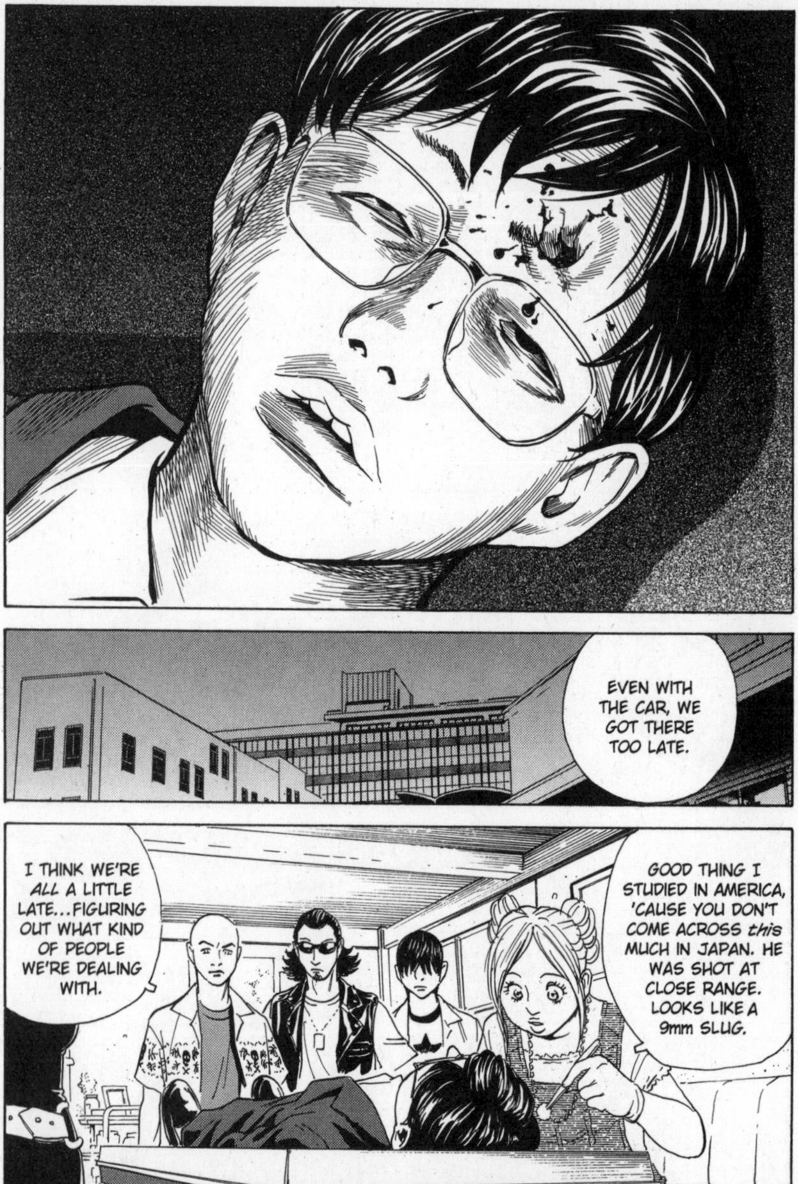
EVEN WITH THE CAR, WE GOT THERE TOO LATE.
GOOD THING I STUDIED IN AMERICA, 'CAUSE YOU DON'T COME ACROSS *this* MUCH IN JAPAN. HE WAS SHOT AT CLOSE RANGE. LOOKS LIKE A 9mm SLUG.
I THINK WE'RE *ALL* A LITTLE LATE...FIGURING OUT WHAT KIND OF PEOPLE WE'RE DEALING WITH.

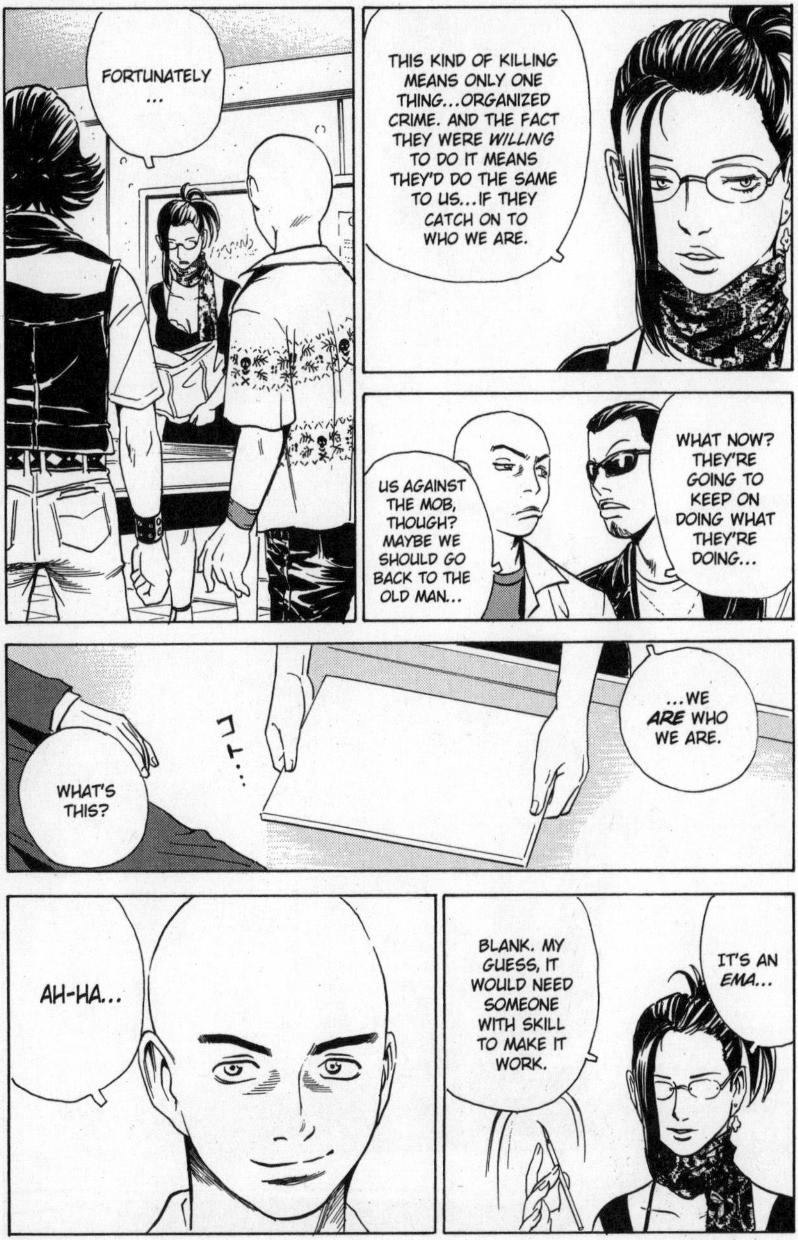
THIS KIND OF KILLING MEANS ONLY ONE THING...ORGANIZED CRIME. AND THE FACT THEY WERE *WILLING* TO DO IT MEANS THEY'D DO THE SAME TO US...IF THEY CATCH ON TO WHO WE ARE.
WHAT NOW? THEY'RE GOING TO KEEP ON DOING WHAT THEY'RE DOING...
US AGAINST THE MOB, THOUGH? MAYBE WE SHOULD GO BACK TO THE OLD MAN...
FORTUNATELY ...
...WE ***ARE*** WHO WE ARE.
コト...
WHAT'S THIS?
IT'S AN *EMA*...
BLANK. MY GUESS, IT WOULD NEED SOMEONE WITH SKILL TO MAKE IT WORK.
AH-HA...

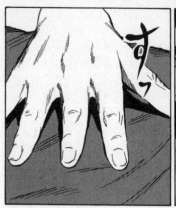

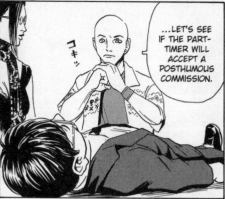

...LET'S SEE IF THE PART-TIMER WILL ACCEPT A POSTHUMOUS COMMISSION.

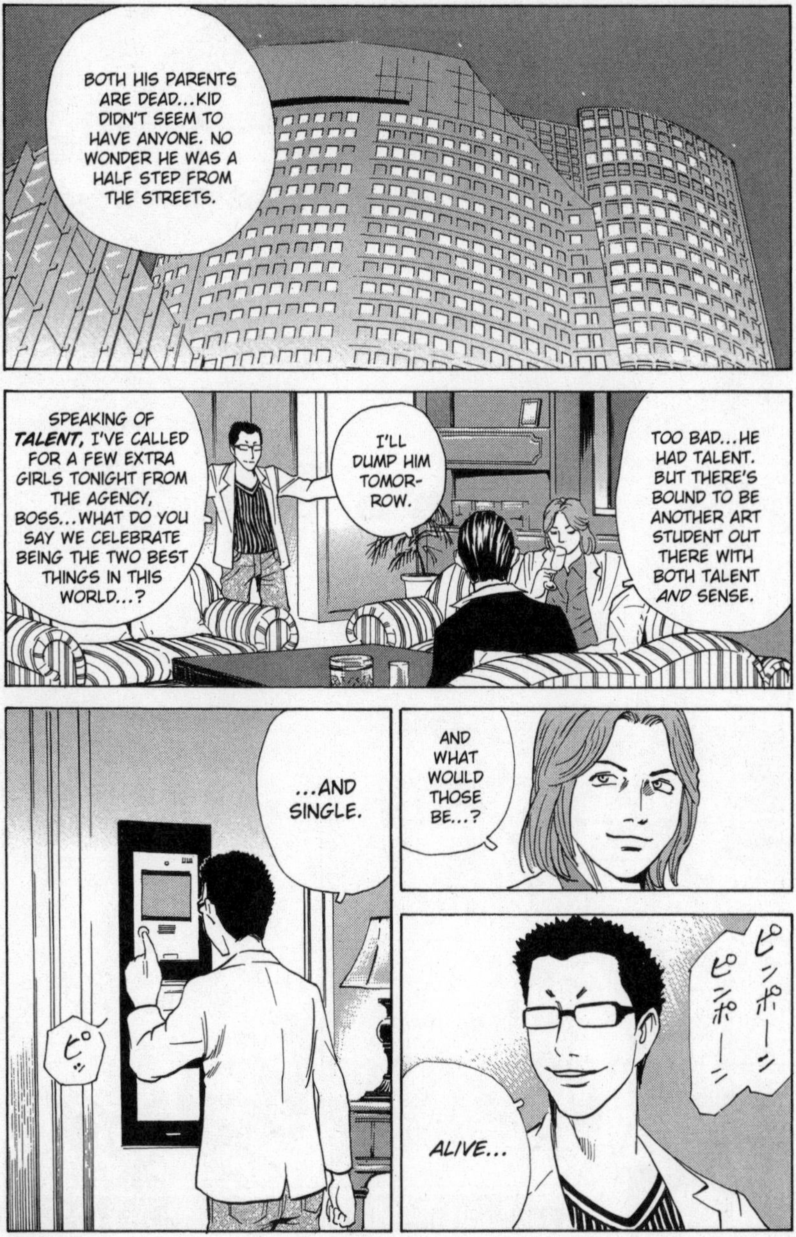
BOTH HIS PARENTS ARE DEAD...KID DIDN'T SEEM TO HAVE ANYONE. NO WONDER HE WAS A HALF STEP FROM THE STREETS.
TOO BAD...HE HAD TALENT. BUT THERE'S BOUND TO BE ANOTHER ART STUDENT OUT THERE WITH BOTH TALENT *AND* SENSE.
I'LL DUMP HIM TOMORROW.
SPEAKING OF ***TALENT,*** I'VE CALLED FOR A FEW EXTRA GIRLS TONIGHT FROM THE AGENCY, BOSS...WHAT DO YOU SAY WE CELEBRATE BEING THE TWO BEST THINGS IN THIS WORLD...?
AND WHAT WOULD THOSE BE...?
ピンポーン
ピンポーン
ALIVE...
...AND SINGLE.
ピッ

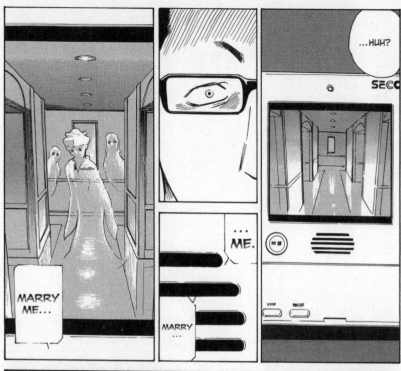

...HUH?

SECO

...
ME.

MARRY
ME...

MARRY
...

HUH?
WHAT'S
THE
MATTER?

TH-THE
W-WOMEN
...TH-TH-
THEY...

GEEYAAA!!!

108

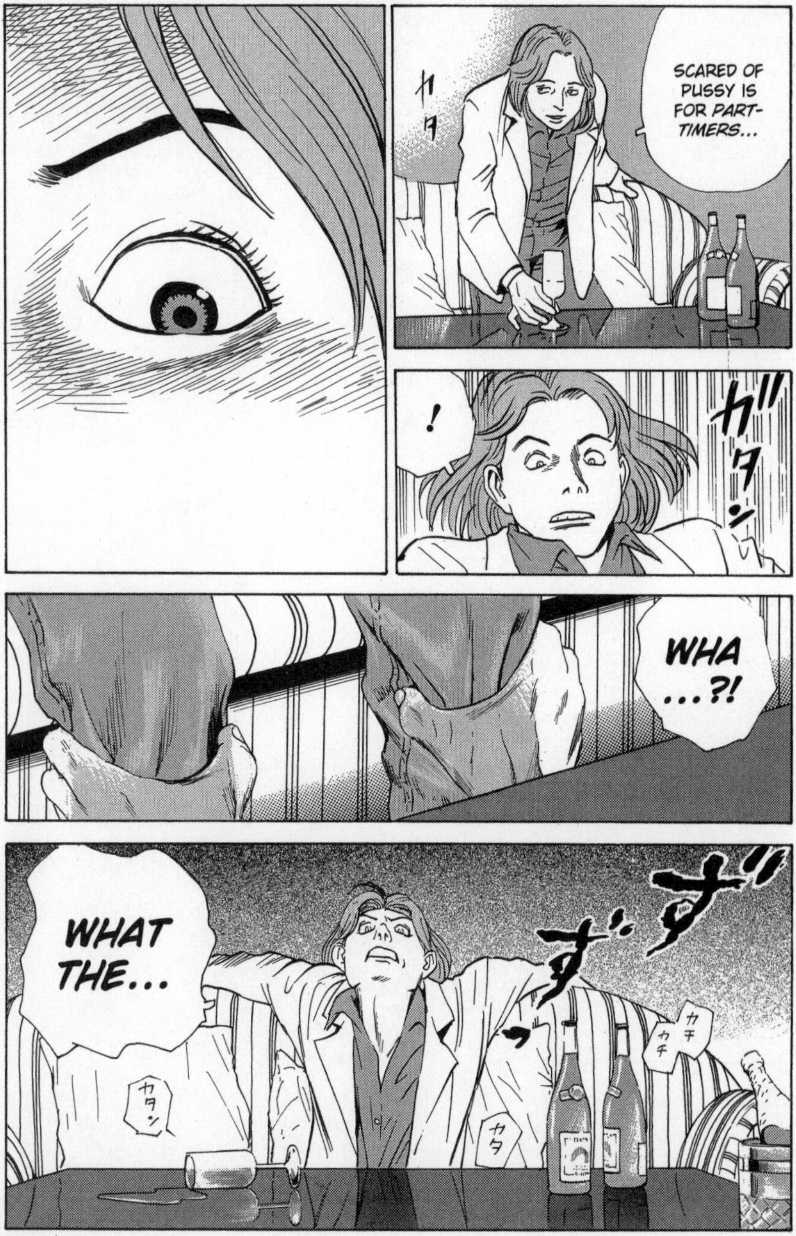
SCARED OF PUSSY IS FOR PART-TIMERS...
カタ
!
ガタン
WHA...?!
WHAT THE...
カチ
カチ
カタ
カタン

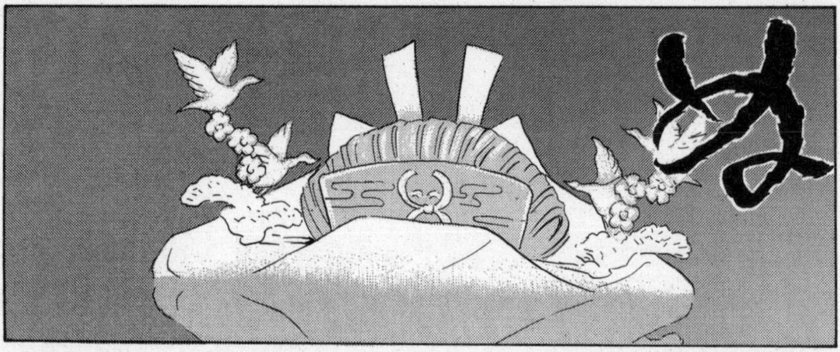
ぬ

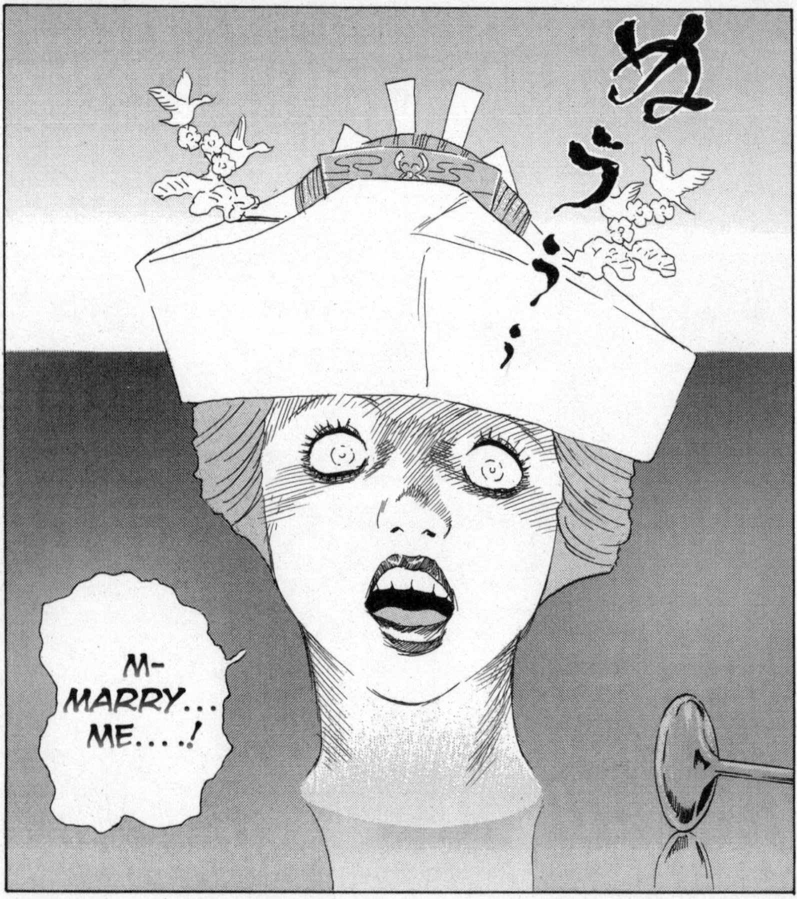
ぬう
M- MARRY... ME....!

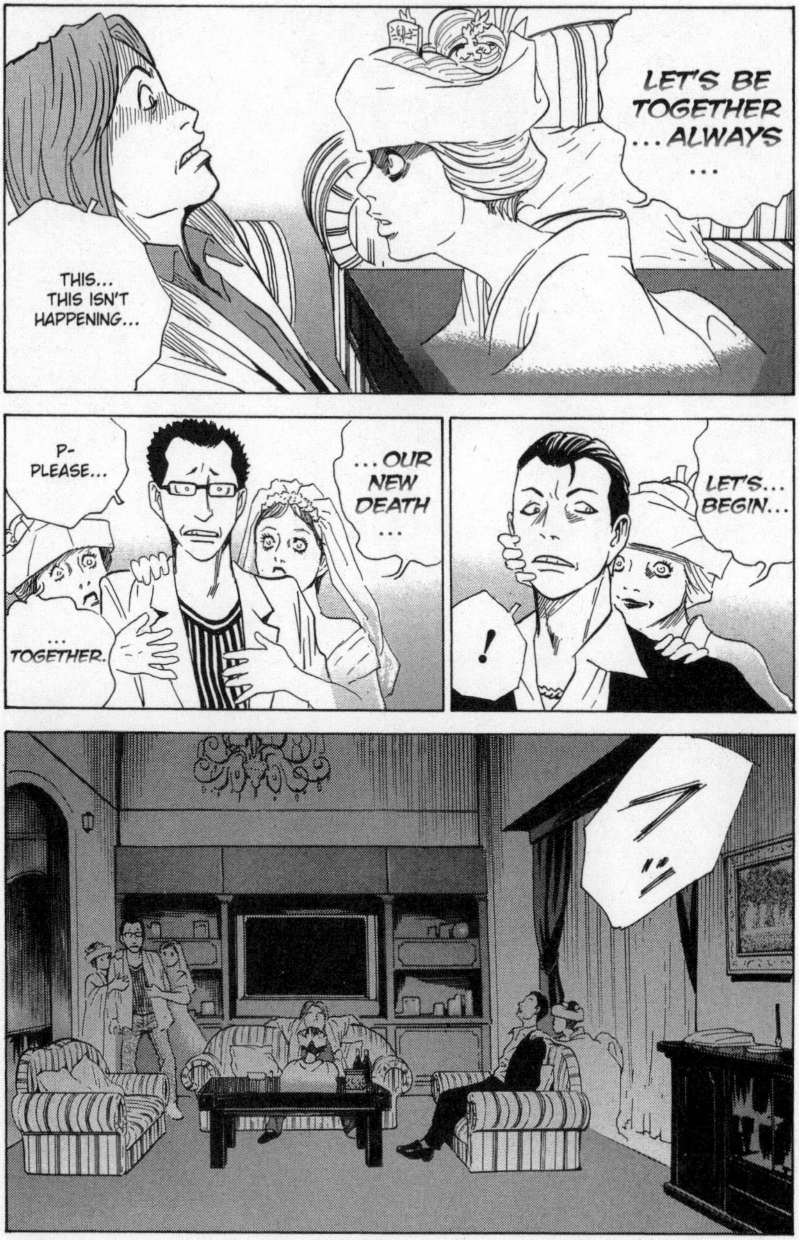
LET'S BE TOGETHER ...ALWAYS ...
THIS... THIS ISN'T HAPPENING...
LET'S... BEGIN...
!
...OUR NEW DEATH ...
P- PLEASE...
... TOGETHER.

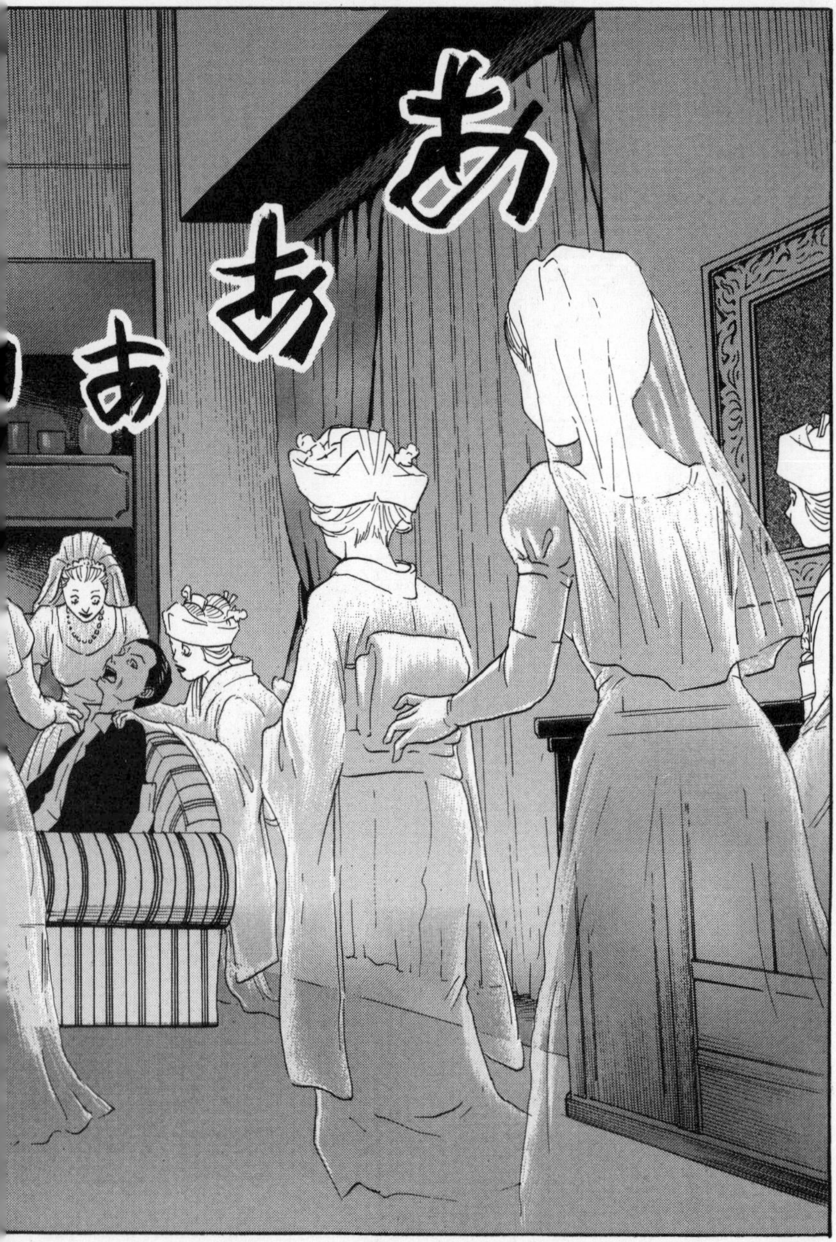
あああ

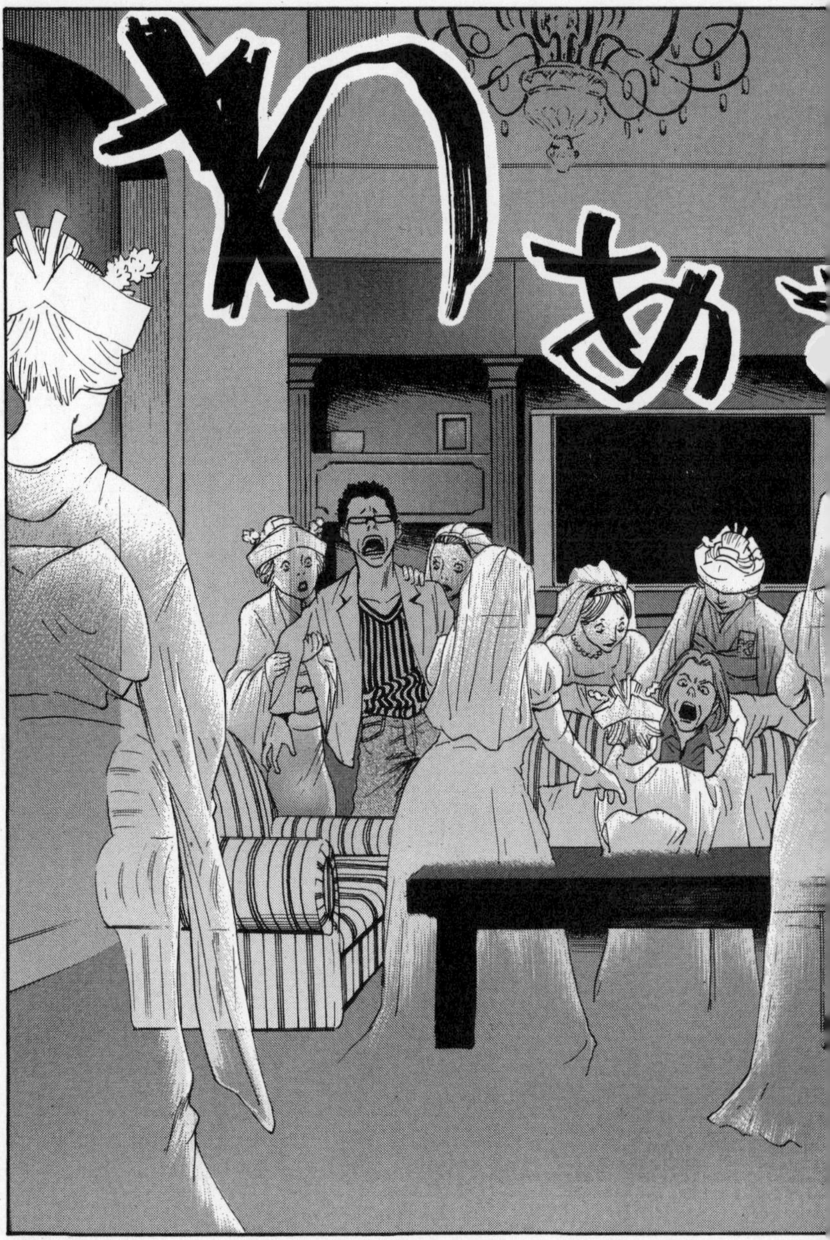

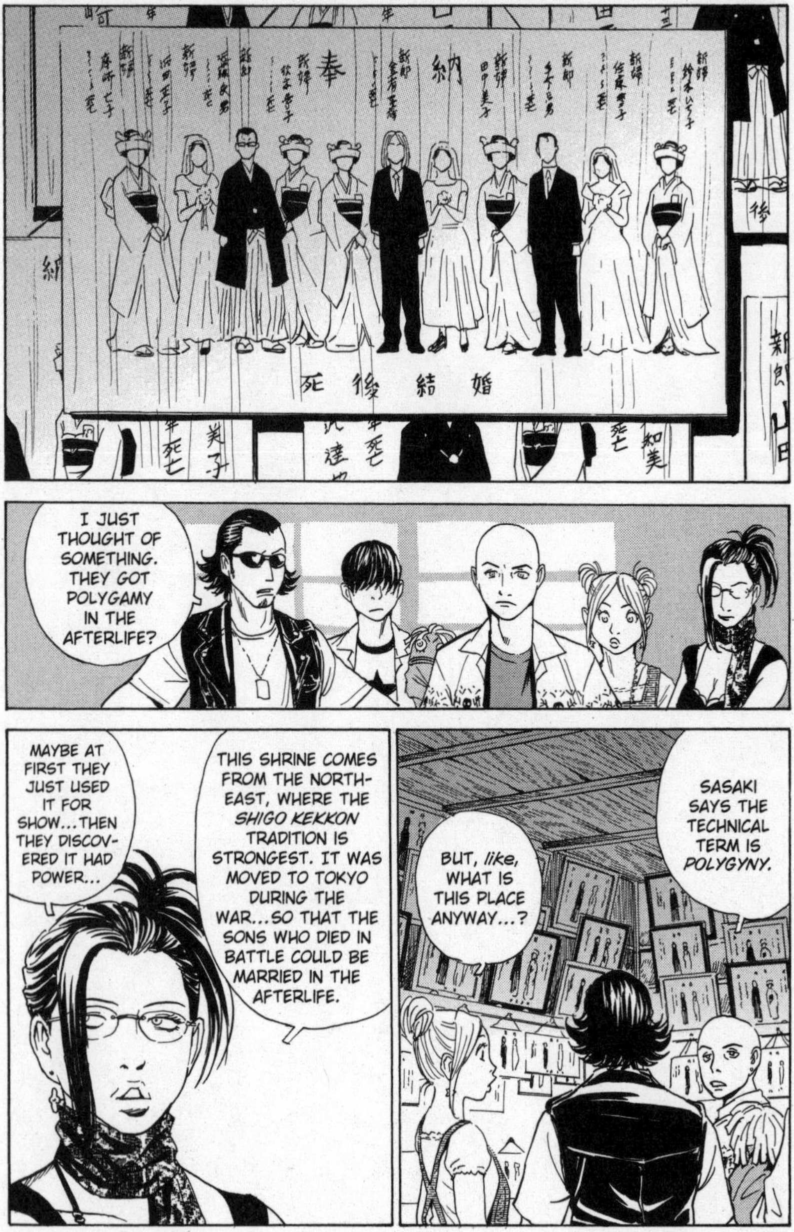
奉納
死後結婚
I JUST THOUGHT OF SOMETHING. THEY GOT POLYGAMY IN THE AFTERLIFE?
SASAKI SAYS THE TECHNICAL TERM IS *POLYGYNY.*
BUT, *like,* WHAT IS THIS PLACE ANYWAY...?
THIS SHRINE COMES FROM THE NORTH-EAST, WHERE THE *SHIGO KEKKON* TRADITION IS STRONGEST. IT WAS MOVED TO TOKYO DURING THE WAR...SO THAT THE SONS WHO DIED IN BATTLE COULD BE MARRIED IN THE AFTERLIFE.
MAYBE AT FIRST THEY JUST USED IT FOR SHOW...THEN THEY DISCOVERED IT HAD POWER...

...HUH? WHAT'S THIS?
カタッ
THIS IS SASAKI'S *EMA*...WHAT'S IT DOING BROKEN...?
ボッ
WHOA! HOT! HOT!
パチ
パチ…
WHAT THE *HELL*?
I GUESS IT MEANS...IT'S NOT TIME FOR SASAKI TO DIE YET.

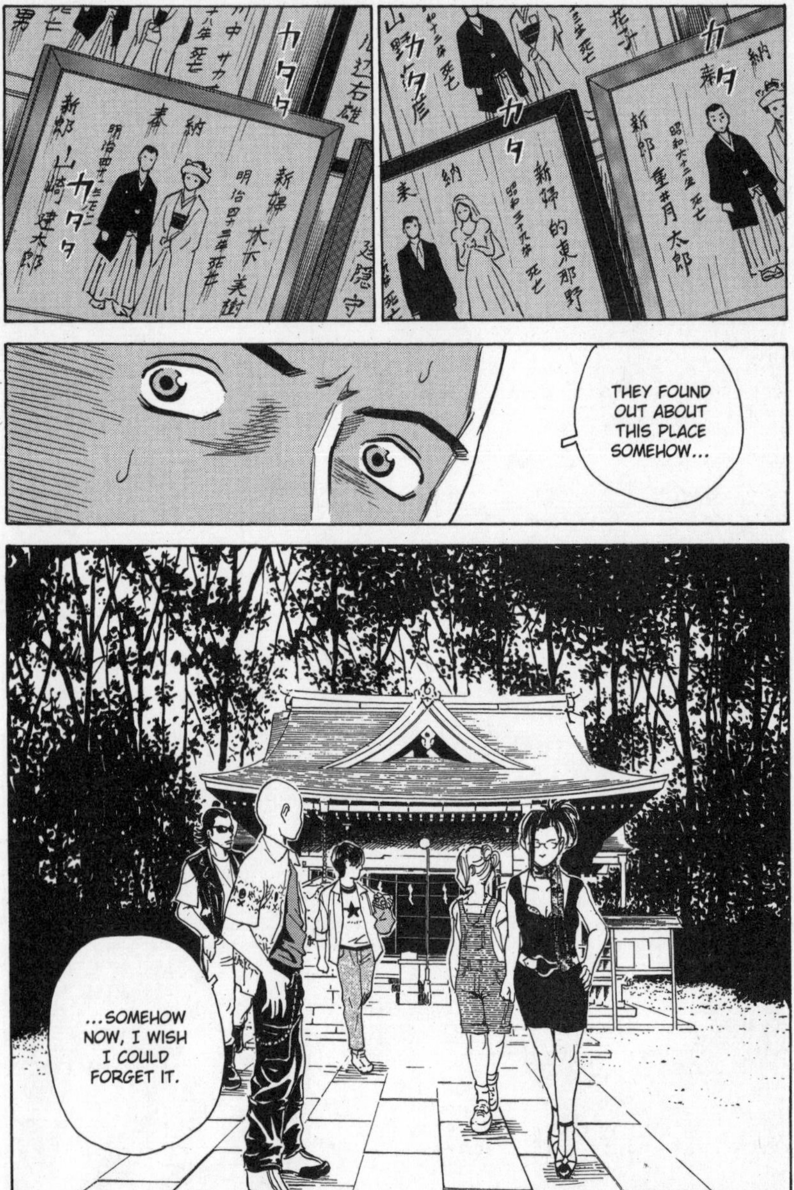
カタ
カタ
カタタ
カタタ
THEY FOUND OUT ABOUT THIS PLACE SOMEHOW...
...SOMEHOW NOW, I WISH I COULD FORGET IT.

4th delivery: no need for a love song—the end

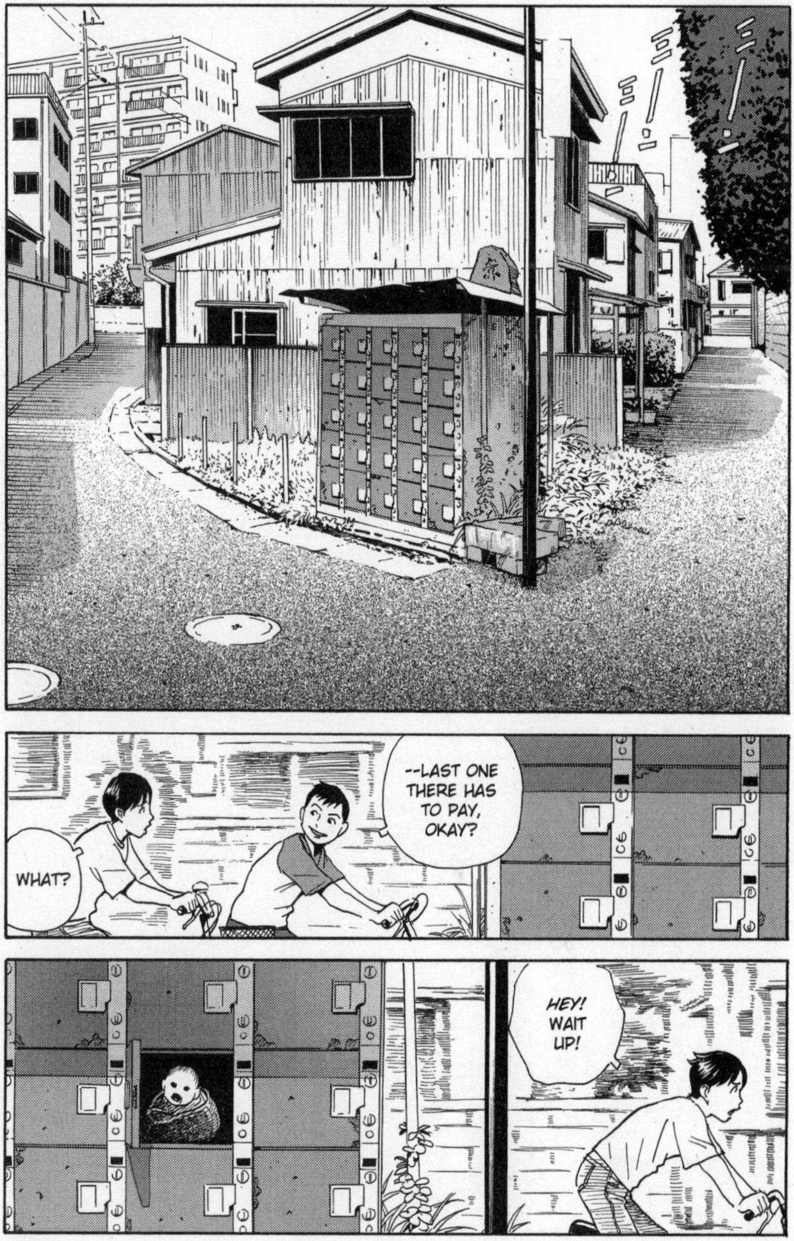
--LAST ONE THERE HAS TO PAY, OKAY?
WHAT?
HEY! WAIT UP!

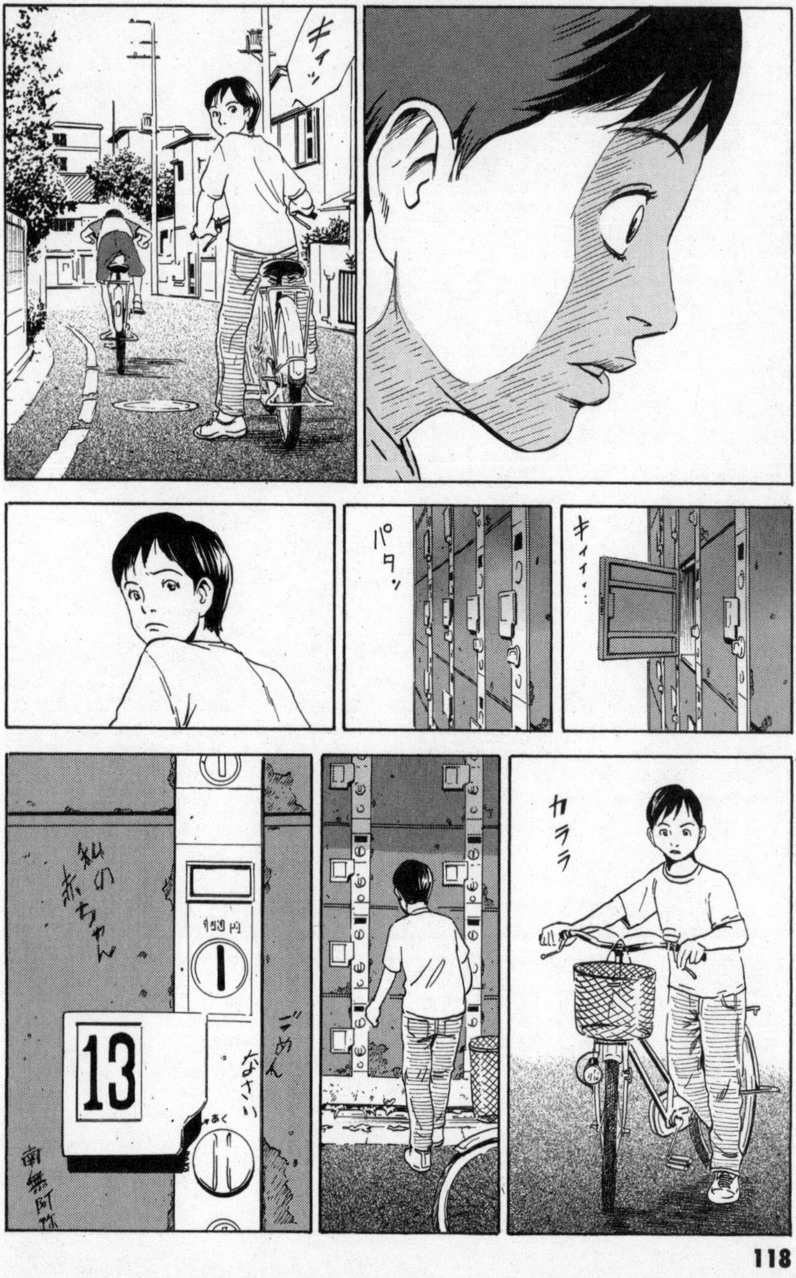
キィッ
キィィ…
パタッ
カララ
ごめんなさい
100円
あく
13
私の赤ちゃん
南無阿弥

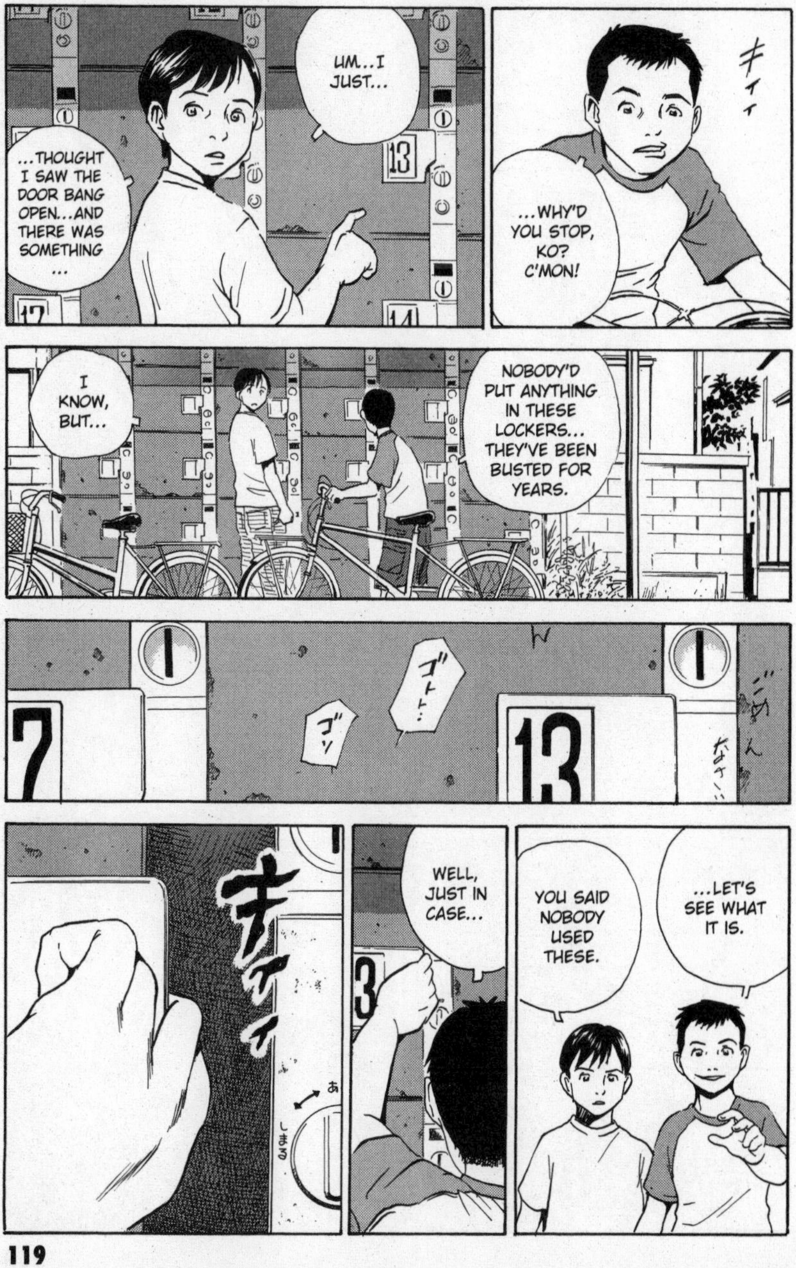
キイイ
...WHY'D YOU STOP, KO? C'MON!
UM...I JUST...
...THOUGHT I SAW THE DOOR BANG OPEN...AND THERE WAS SOMETHING ...
NOBODY'D PUT ANYTHING IN THESE LOCKERS... THEY'VE BEEN BUSTED FOR YEARS.
I KNOW, BUT...
ごめん
ゴトト‥
ゴツ
...LET'S SEE WHAT IT IS.
YOU SAID NOBODY USED THESE.
WELL, JUST IN CASE...
キイイ

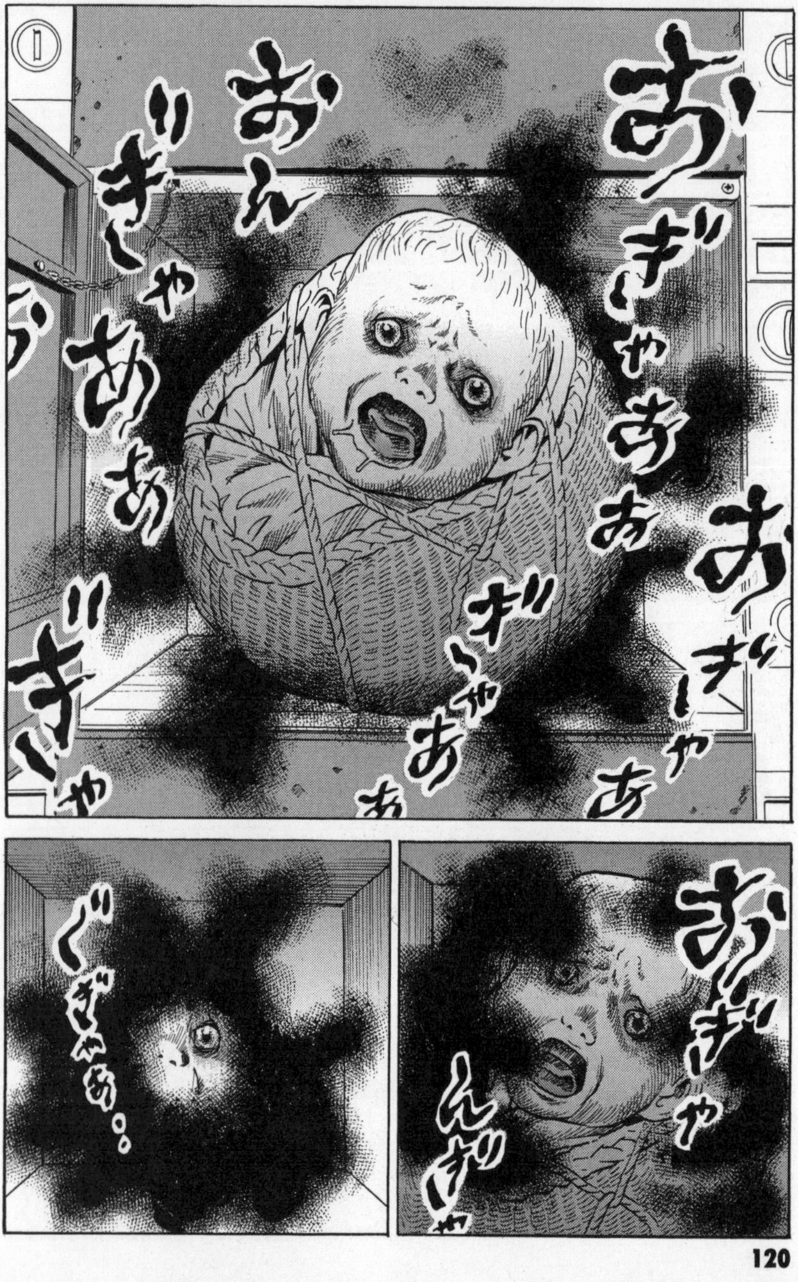
おぎゃああ
おぎゃあ
ぎゃああ
おん
ぎゃあああ
ぎゃ
おぎゃ
んぎゃ
ぐぎゃあ。。

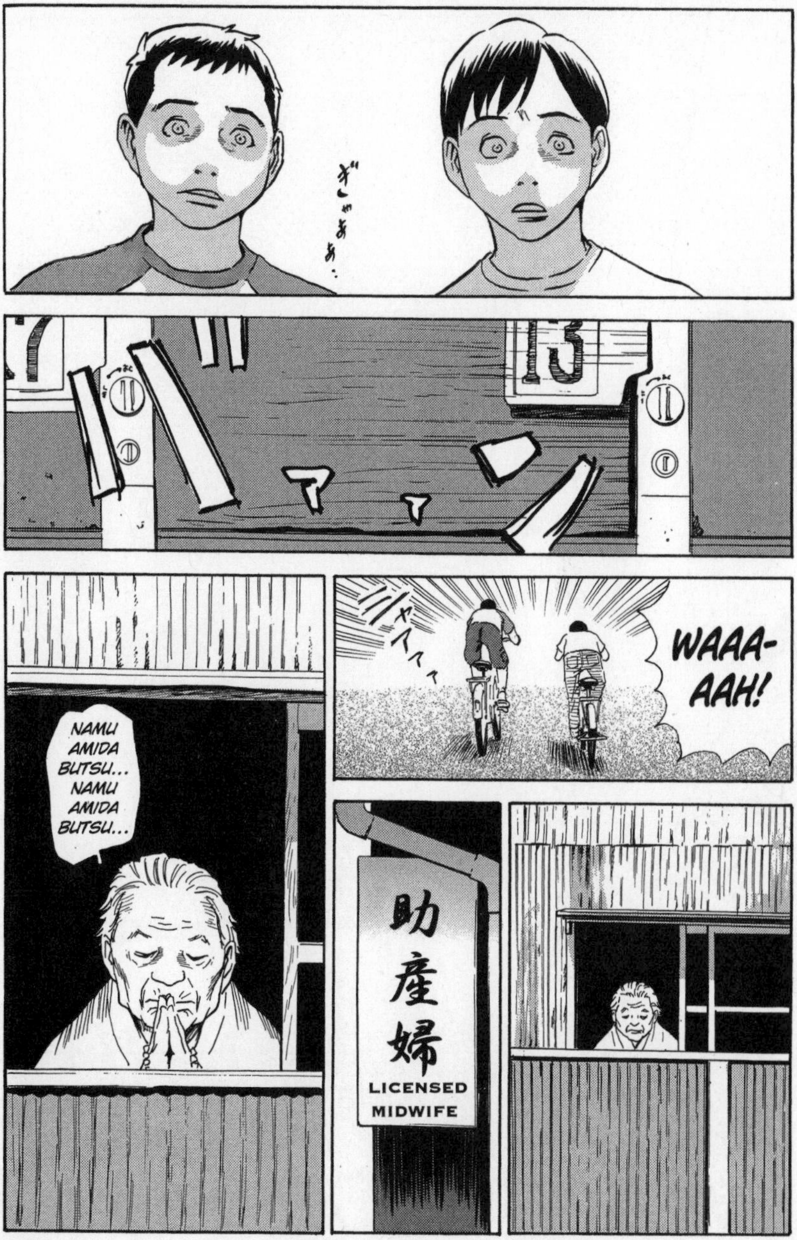
WAAAA-
AAH!
助産婦
LICENSED
MIDWIFE
NAMU AMIDA BUTSU... NAMU AMIDA BUTSU...

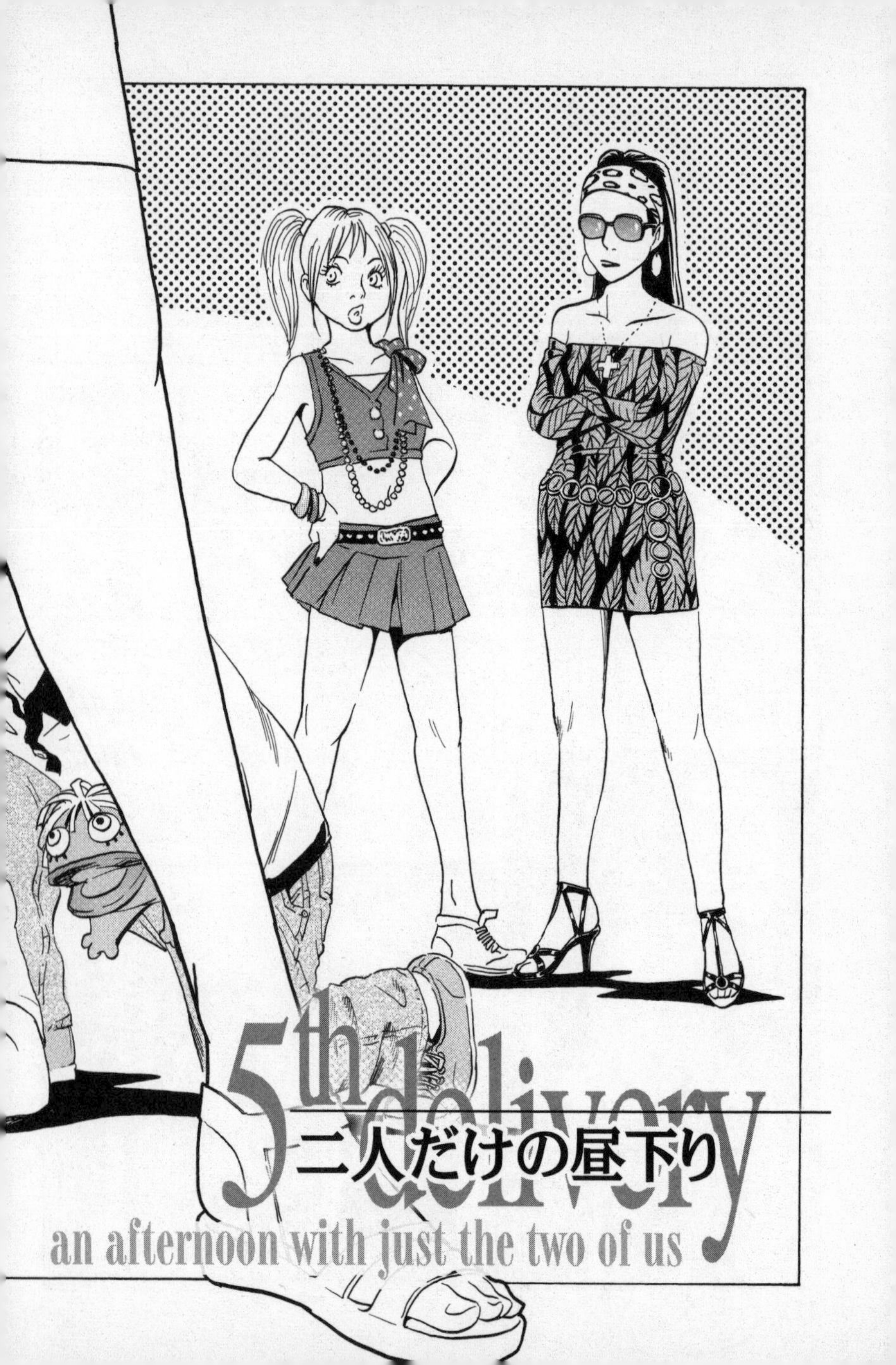
5th delivery
二人だけの昼下り
an afternoon with just the two of us

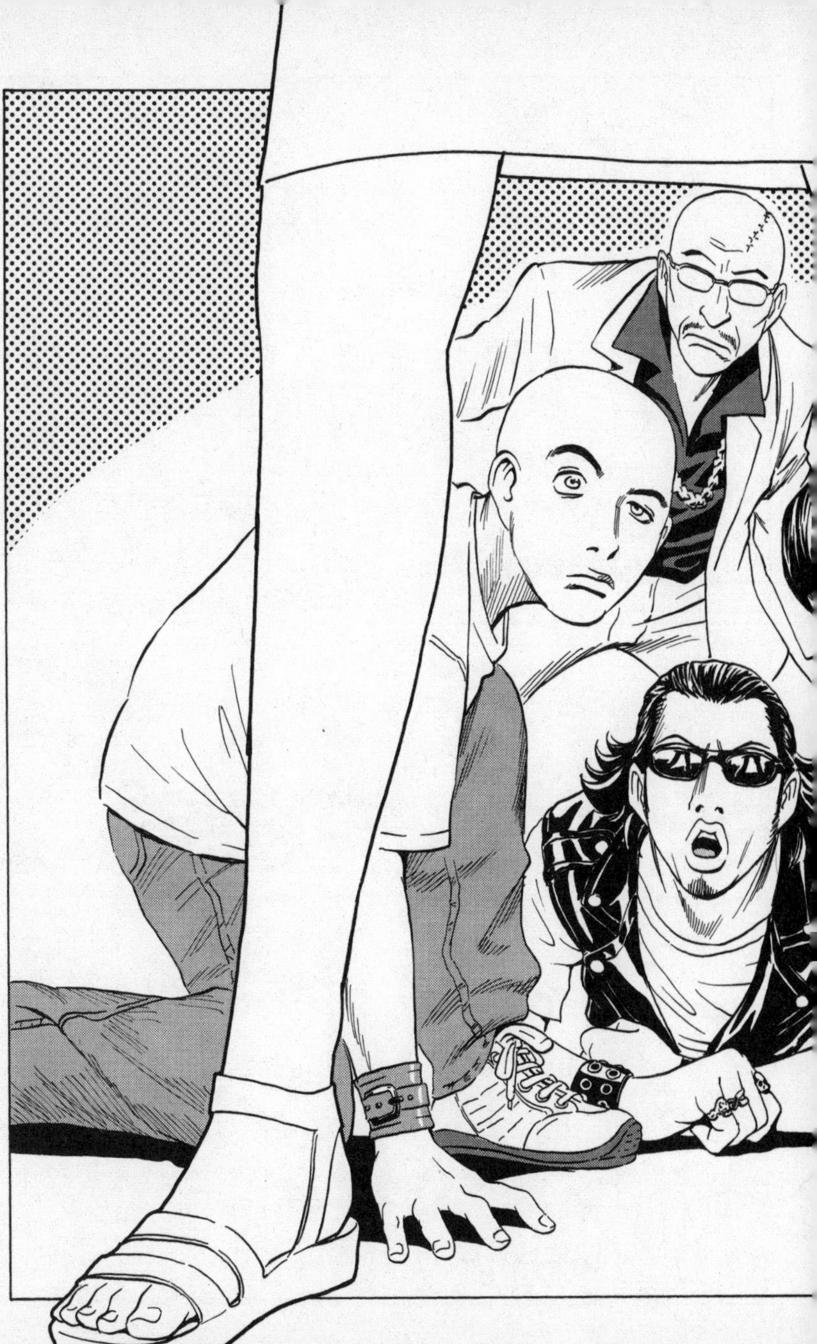

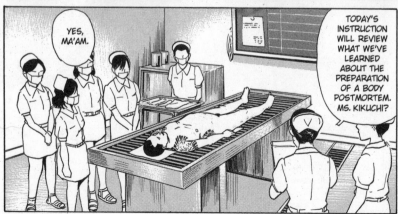

YES, MA'AM.

TODAY'S INSTRUCTION WILL REVIEW WHAT WE'VE LEARNED ABOUT THE PREPARATION OF A BODY POSTMORTEM. MS. KIKUCHI?

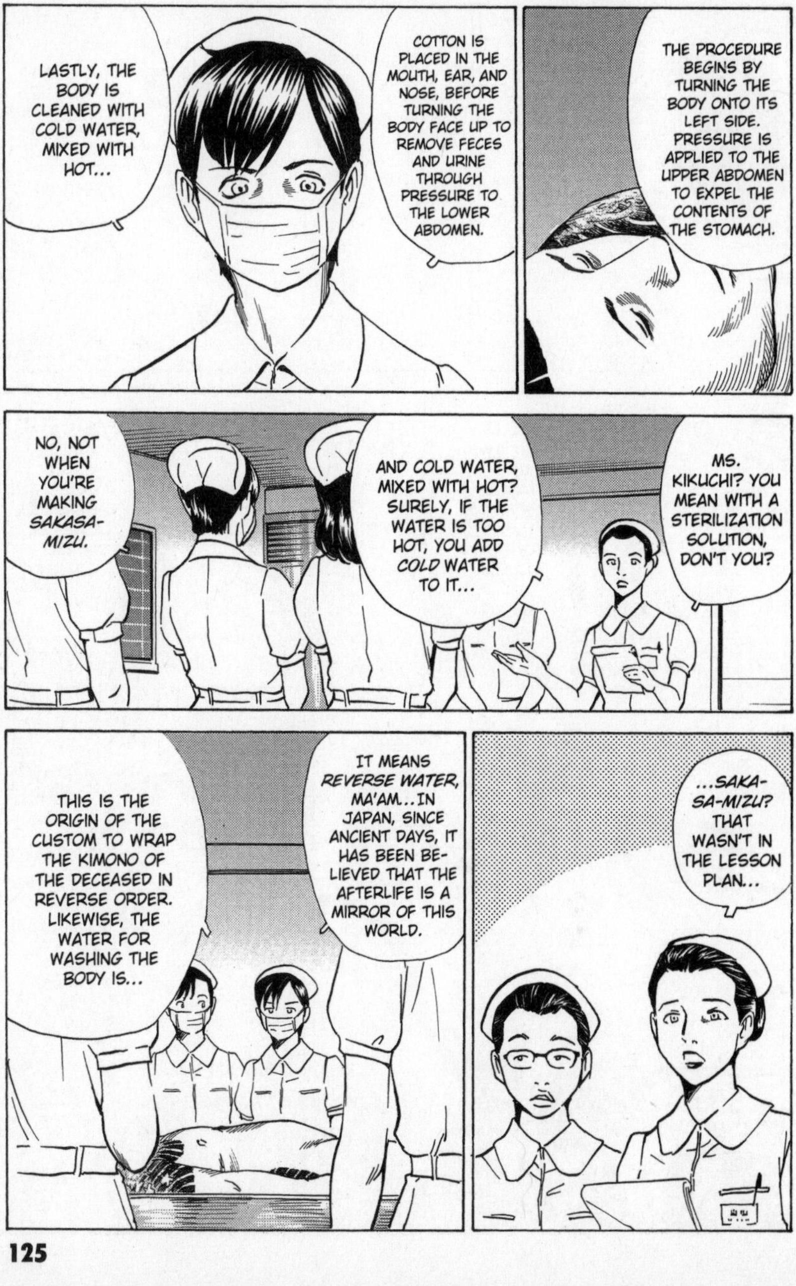
THE PROCEDURE BEGINS BY TURNING THE BODY ONTO ITS LEFT SIDE. PRESSURE IS APPLIED TO THE UPPER ABDOMEN TO EXPEL THE CONTENTS OF THE STOMACH.
COTTON IS PLACED IN THE MOUTH, EAR, AND NOSE, BEFORE TURNING THE BODY FACE UP TO REMOVE FECES AND URINE THROUGH PRESSURE TO THE LOWER ABDOMEN.
LASTLY, THE BODY IS CLEANED WITH COLD WATER, MIXED WITH HOT...
MS. KIKUCHI? YOU MEAN WITH A STERILIZATION SOLUTION, DON'T YOU?
AND COLD WATER, MIXED WITH HOT? SURELY, IF THE WATER IS TOO HOT, YOU ADD *COLD* WATER TO IT...
NO, NOT WHEN YOU'RE MAKING *SAKASA-MIZU*.
...*SAKA-SA-MIZU*? THAT WASN'T IN THE LESSON PLAN...
IT MEANS *REVERSE WATER*, MA'AM...IN JAPAN, SINCE ANCIENT DAYS, IT HAS BEEN BE-LIEVED THAT THE AFTERLIFE IS A MIRROR OF THIS WORLD.
THIS IS THE ORIGIN OF THE CUSTOM TO WRAP THE KIMONO OF THE DECEASED IN REVERSE ORDER. LIKEWISE, THE WATER FOR WASHING THE BODY IS...

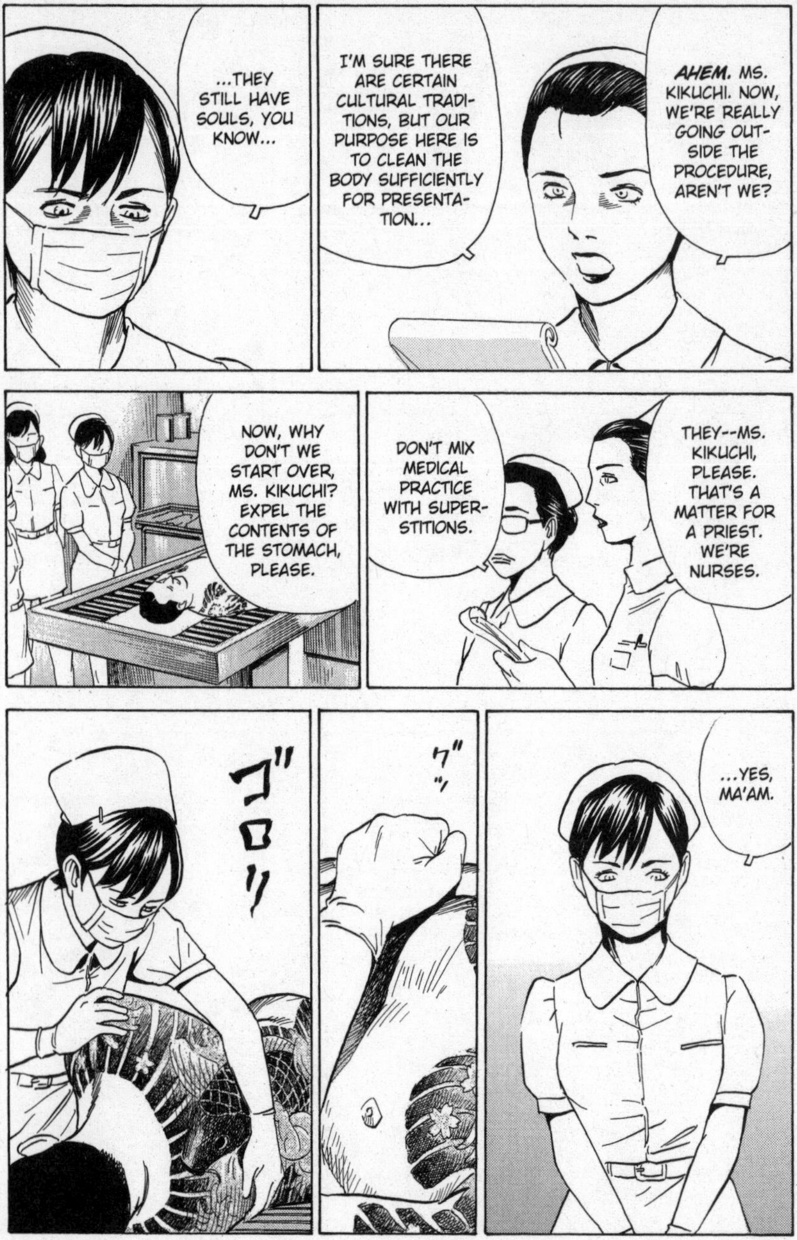
AHEM. MS. KIKUCHI. NOW, WE'RE REALLY GOING OUTSIDE THE PROCEDURE, AREN'T WE?
I'M SURE THERE ARE CERTAIN CULTURAL TRADITIONS, BUT OUR PURPOSE HERE IS TO CLEAN THE BODY SUFFICIENTLY FOR PRESENTATION...
...THEY STILL HAVE SOULS, YOU KNOW...
THEY--MS. KIKUCHI, PLEASE. THAT'S A MATTER FOR A PRIEST. WE'RE NURSES.
DON'T MIX MEDICAL PRACTICE WITH SUPERSTITIONS.
NOW, WHY DON'T WE START OVER, MS. KIKUCHI? EXPEL THE CONTENTS OF THE STOMACH, PLEASE.
...YES, MA'AM.
グッ
ゴロリ

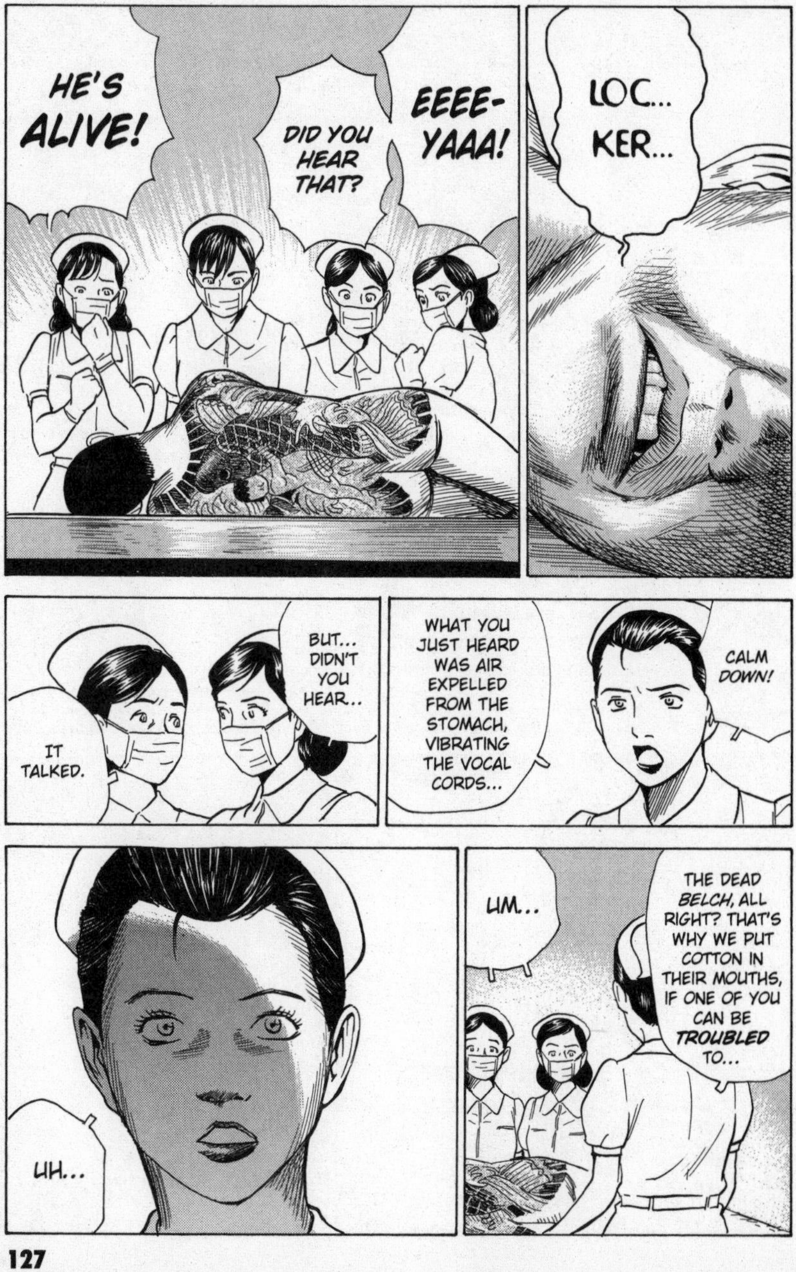
LOC... KER...
EEEE-YAAA!
DID YOU HEAR THAT?
HE'S ALIVE!
CALM DOWN!
WHAT YOU JUST HEARD WAS AIR EXPELLED FROM THE STOMACH, VIBRATING THE VOCAL CORDS...
BUT... DIDN'T YOU HEAR...
IT TALKED.
THE DEAD BELCH, ALL RIGHT? THAT'S WHY WE PUT COTTON IN THEIR MOUTHS, IF ONE OF YOU CAN BE TROUBLED TO...
UM...
UH...

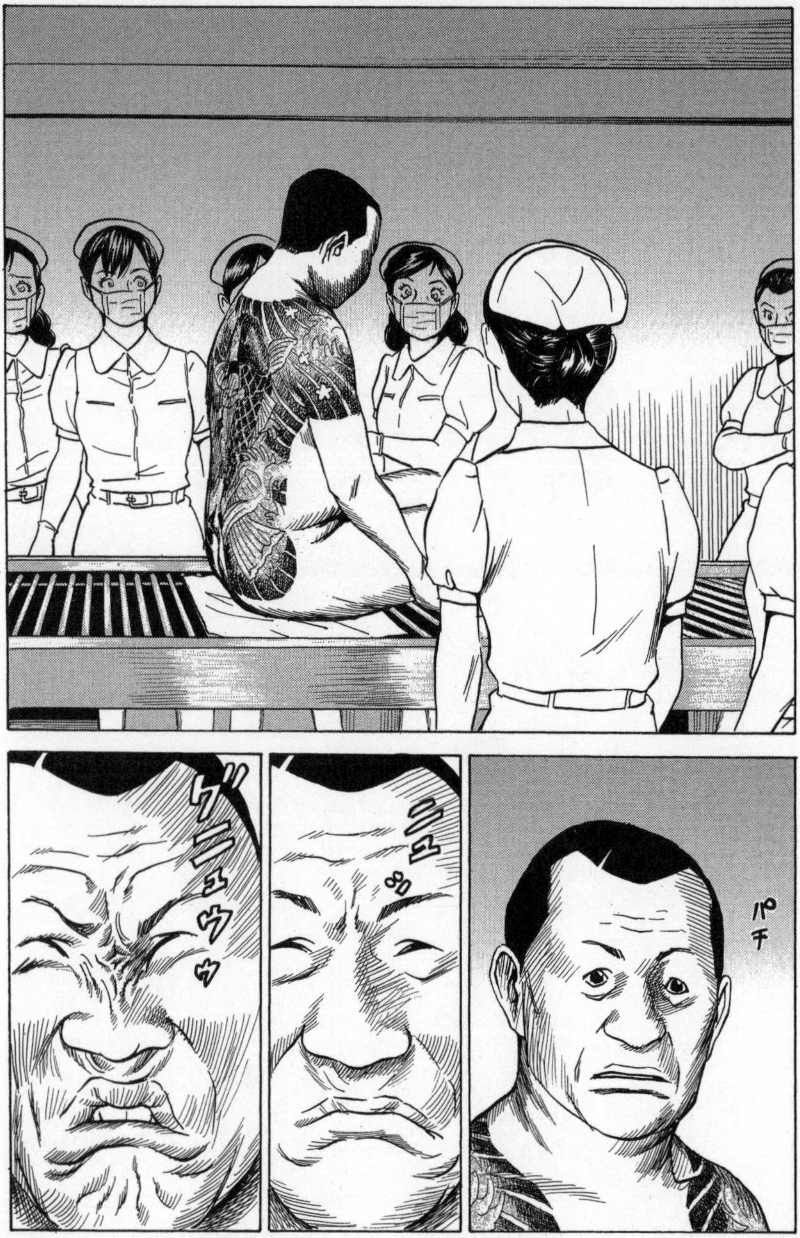
パチ
ニュ
グニュウウ

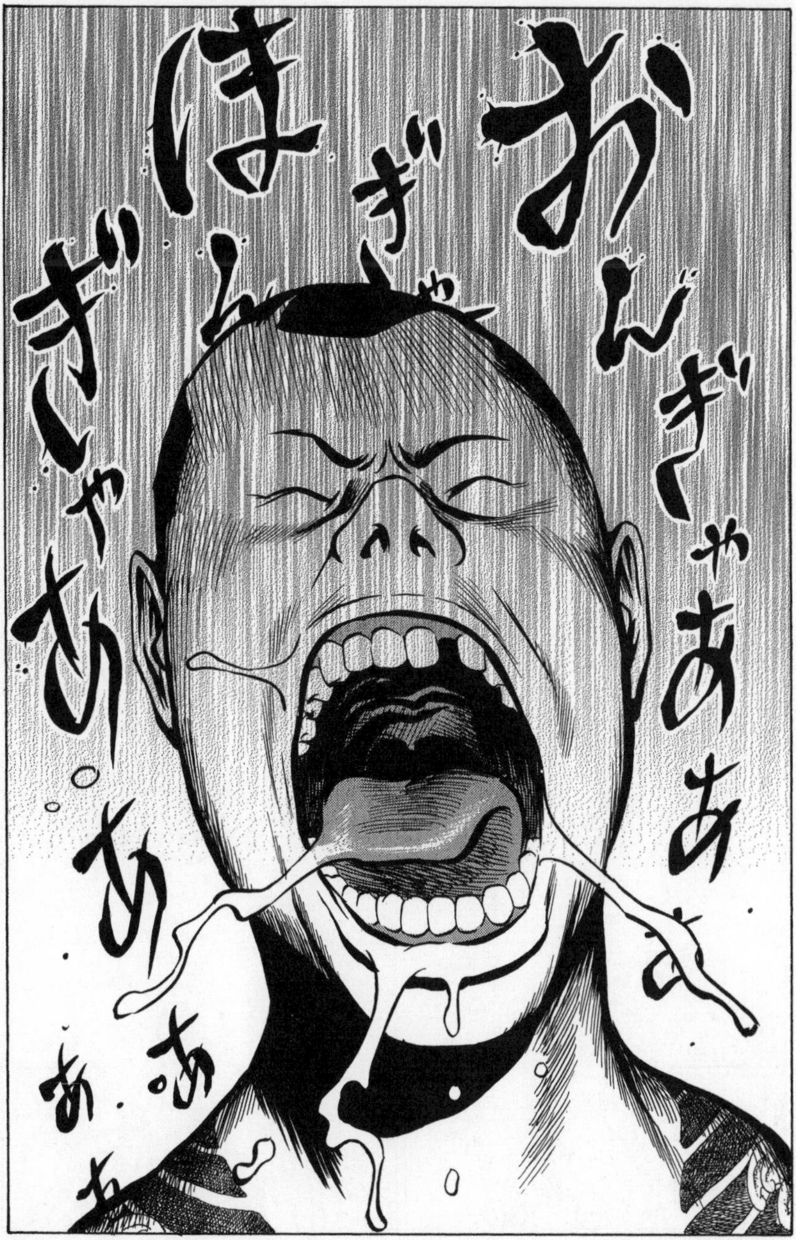

おんぎゃあああ
ぎゃ
ほんぎゃあああああ

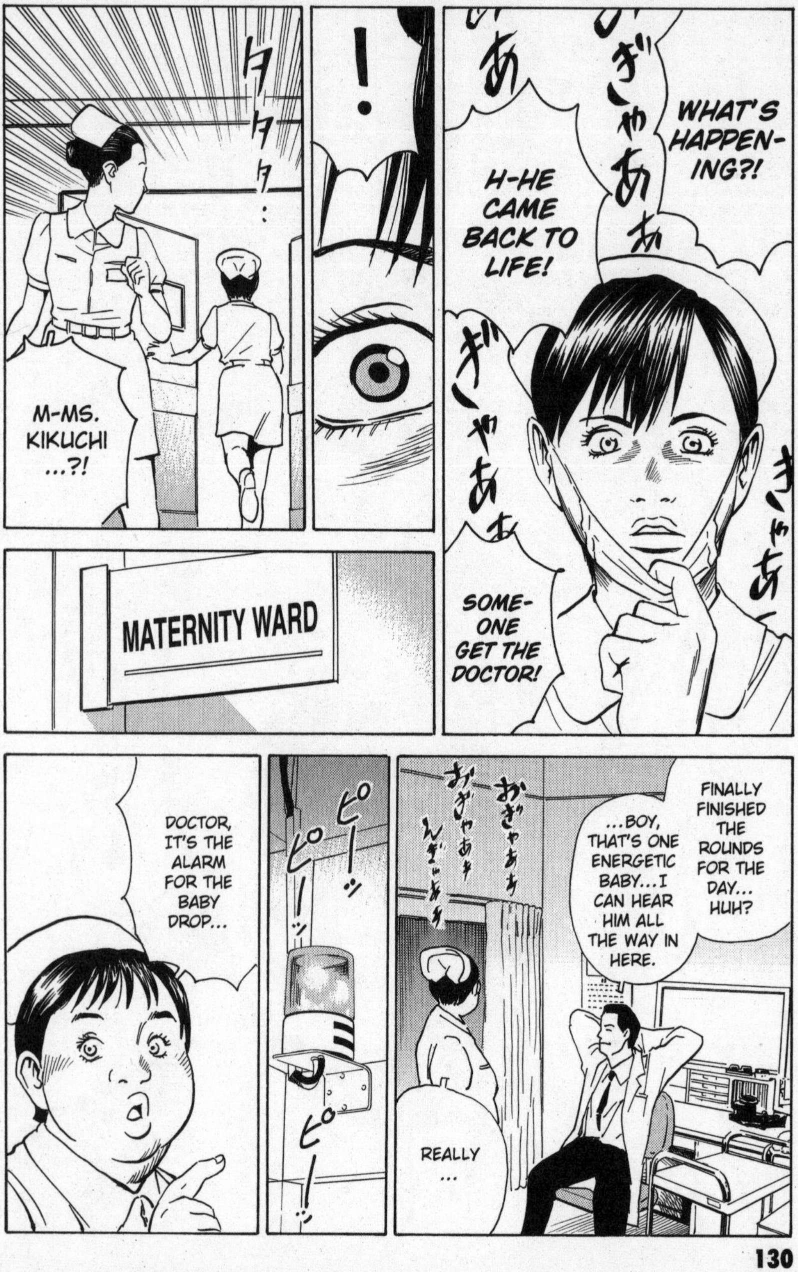
WHAT'S HAPPEN-ING?!
H-HE CAME BACK TO LIFE!
SOME-ONE GET THE DOCTOR!
!
M-MS. KIKUCHI ...?!
MATERNITY WARD
FINALLY FINISHED THE ROUNDS FOR THE DAY... HUH?
...BOY, THAT'S ONE ENERGETIC BABY...I CAN HEAR HIM ALL THE WAY IN HERE.
REALLY ...
DOCTOR, IT'S THE ALARM FOR THE BABY DROP...

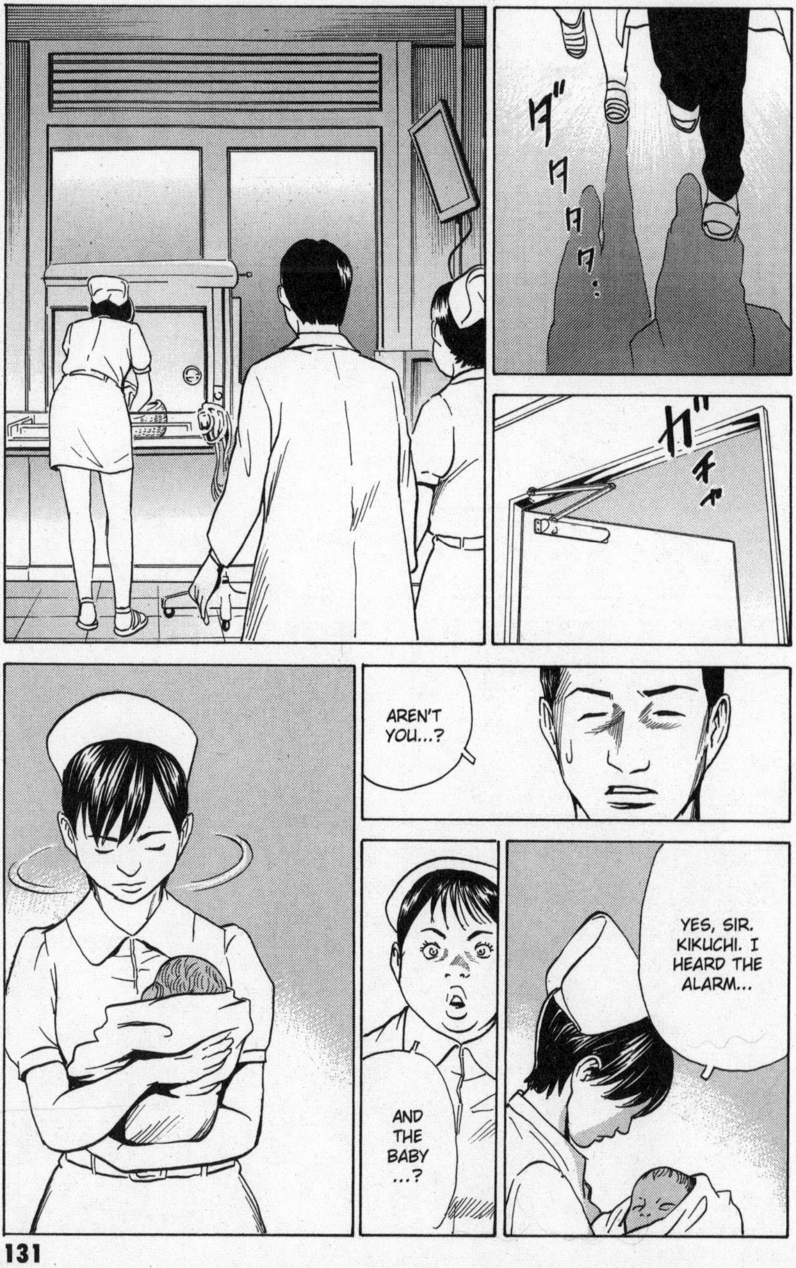
ダタタッ..
ガチャ
AREN'T YOU...?
YES, SIR. KIKUCHI. I HEARD THE ALARM...
AND THE BABY ...?

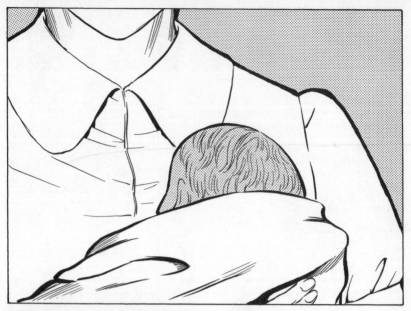

...AGAIN.

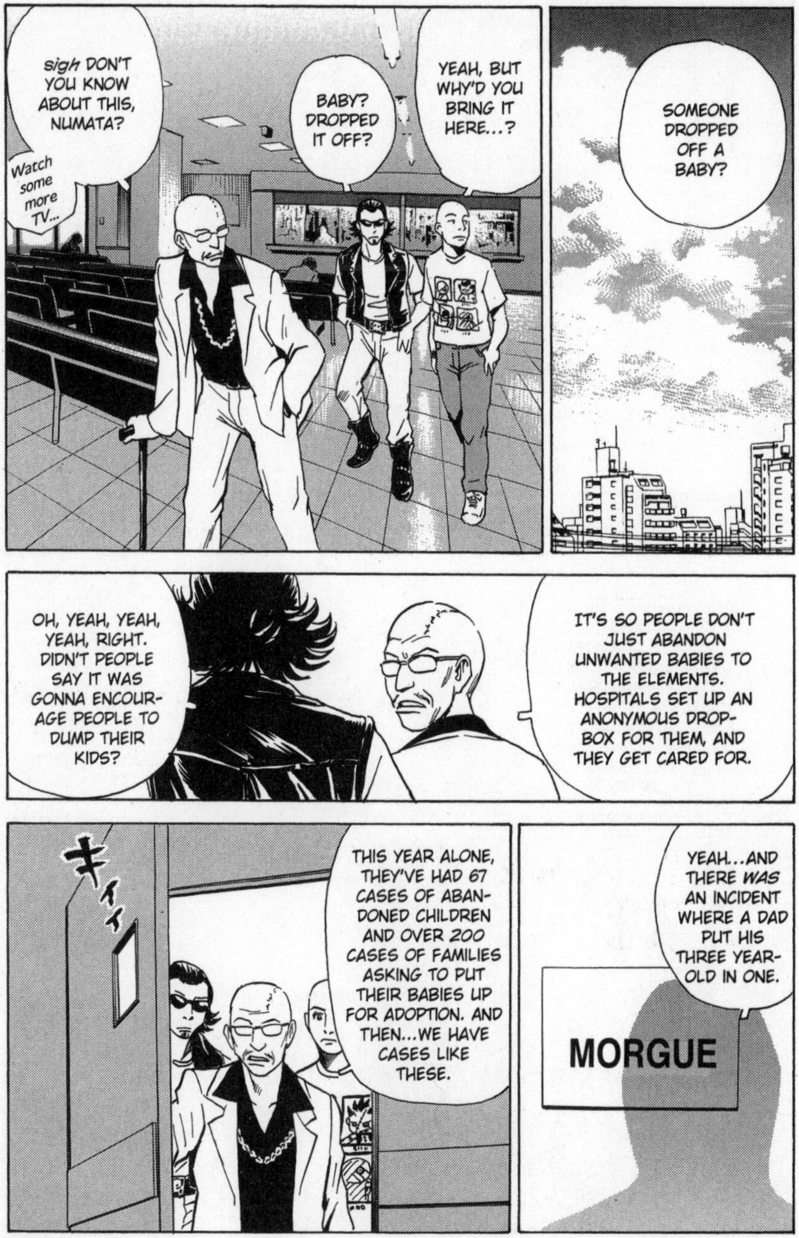
SOMEONE DROPPED OFF A BABY?
YEAH, BUT WHY'D YOU BRING IT HERE...?
BABY? DROPPED IT OFF?
sigh DON'T YOU KNOW ABOUT THIS, NUMATA?
Watch some more TV...
IT'S SO PEOPLE DON'T JUST ABANDON UNWANTED BABIES TO THE ELEMENTS. HOSPITALS SET UP AN ANONYMOUS DROP-BOX FOR THEM, AND THEY GET CARED FOR.
OH, YEAH, YEAH, YEAH, RIGHT. DIDN'T PEOPLE SAY IT WAS GONNA ENCOURAGE PEOPLE TO DUMP THEIR KIDS?
YEAH...AND THERE *WAS* AN INCIDENT WHERE A DAD PUT HIS THREE YEAR-OLD IN ONE.
MORGUE
THIS YEAR ALONE, THEY'VE HAD 67 CASES OF ABANDONED CHILDREN AND OVER 200 CASES OF FAMILIES ASKING TO PUT THEIR BABIES UP FOR ADOPTION. AND THEN...WE HAVE CASES LIKE THESE.
キィィ

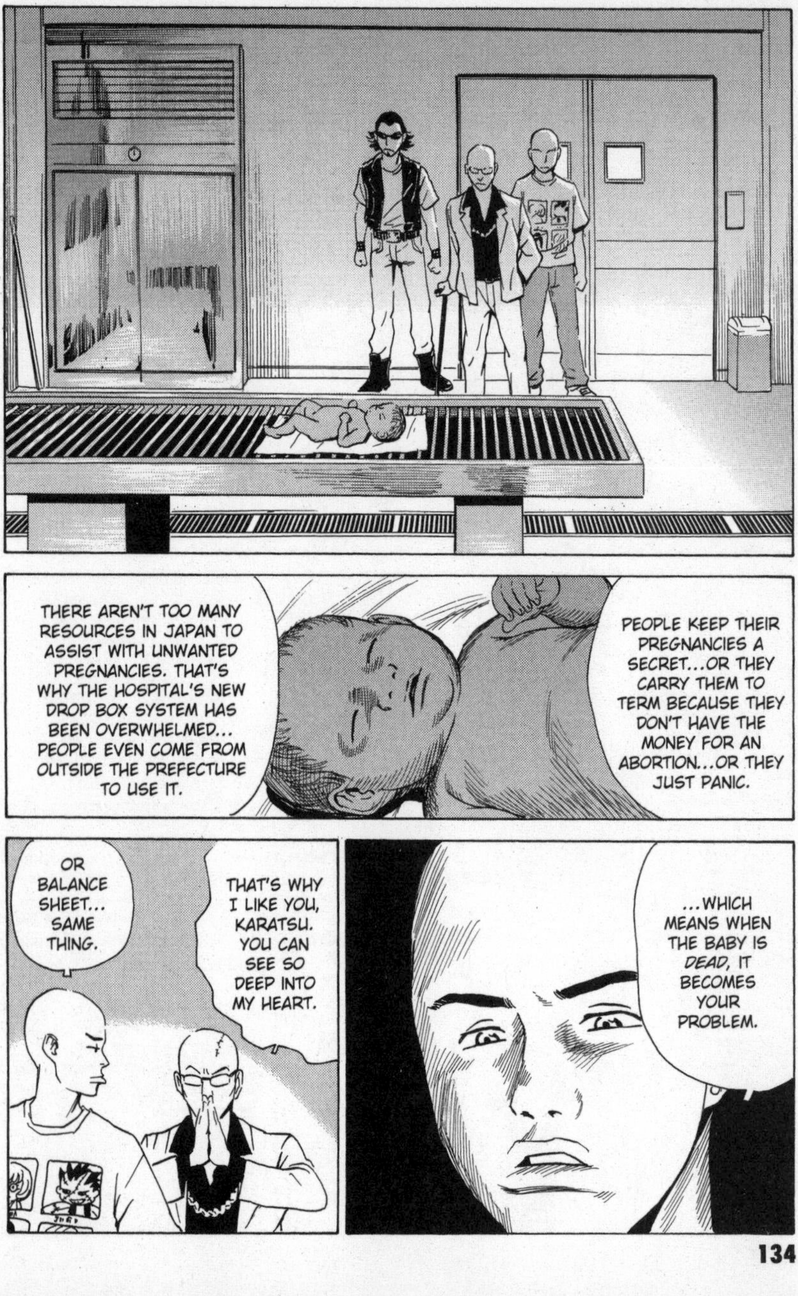
PEOPLE KEEP THEIR PREGNANCIES A SECRET...OR THEY CARRY THEM TO TERM BECAUSE THEY DON'T HAVE THE MONEY FOR AN ABORTION...OR THEY JUST PANIC.
THERE AREN'T TOO MANY RESOURCES IN JAPAN TO ASSIST WITH UNWANTED PREGNANCIES. THAT'S WHY THE HOSPITAL'S NEW DROP BOX SYSTEM HAS BEEN OVERWHELMED... PEOPLE EVEN COME FROM OUTSIDE THE PREFECTURE TO USE IT.
...WHICH MEANS WHEN THE BABY IS *DEAD*, IT BECOMES YOUR PROBLEM.
OR BALANCE SHEET... SAME THING.
THAT'S WHY I LIKE YOU, KARATSU. YOU CAN SEE SO DEEP INTO MY HEART.

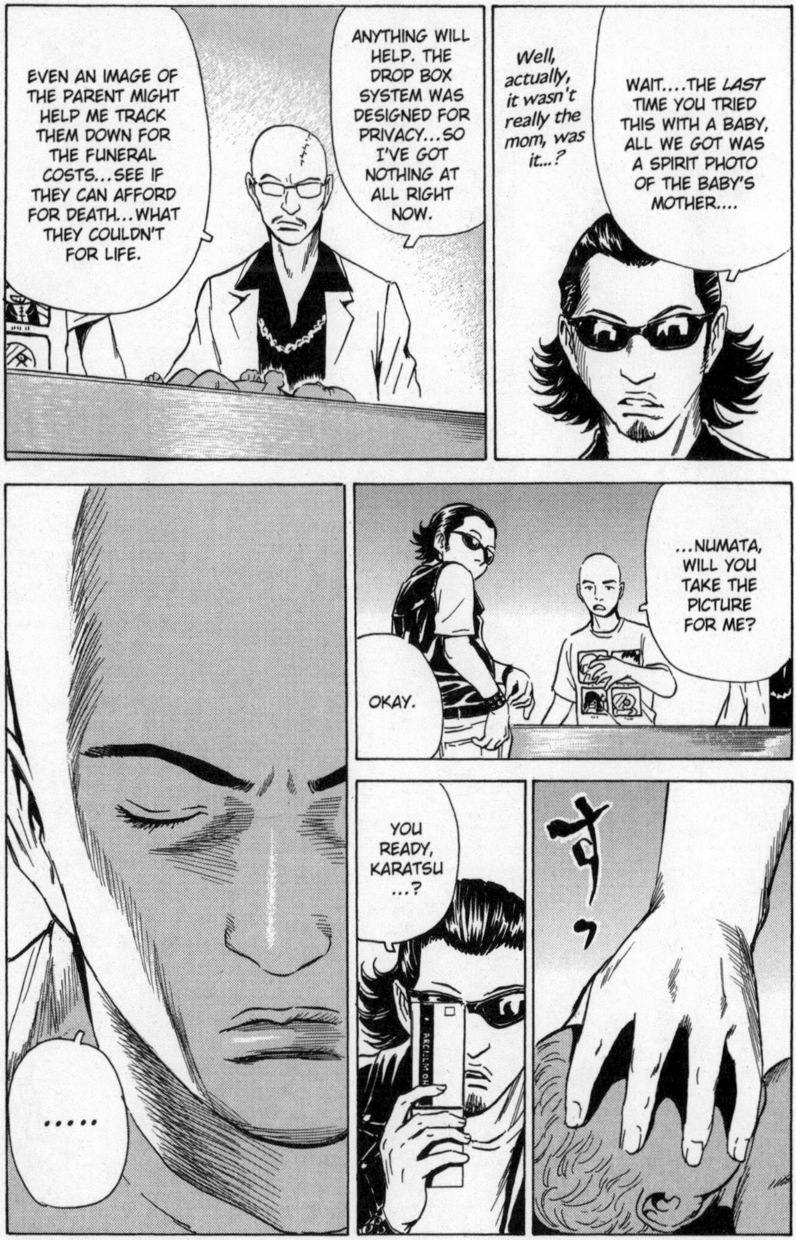

WAIT....THE *LAST* TIME YOU TRIED THIS WITH A BABY, ALL WE GOT WAS A SPIRIT PHOTO OF THE BABY'S MOTHER....
Well, actually, it wasn't really the mom, was it...?
ANYTHING WILL HELP. THE DROP BOX SYSTEM WAS DESIGNED FOR PRIVACY...SO I'VE GOT NOTHING AT ALL RIGHT NOW.
EVEN AN IMAGE OF THE PARENT MIGHT HELP ME TRACK THEM DOWN FOR THE FUNERAL COSTS...SEE IF THEY CAN AFFORD FOR DEATH...WHAT THEY COULDN'T FOR LIFE.
...NUMATA, WILL YOU TAKE THE PICTURE FOR ME?
OKAY.
YOU READY, KARATSU ...?
.....

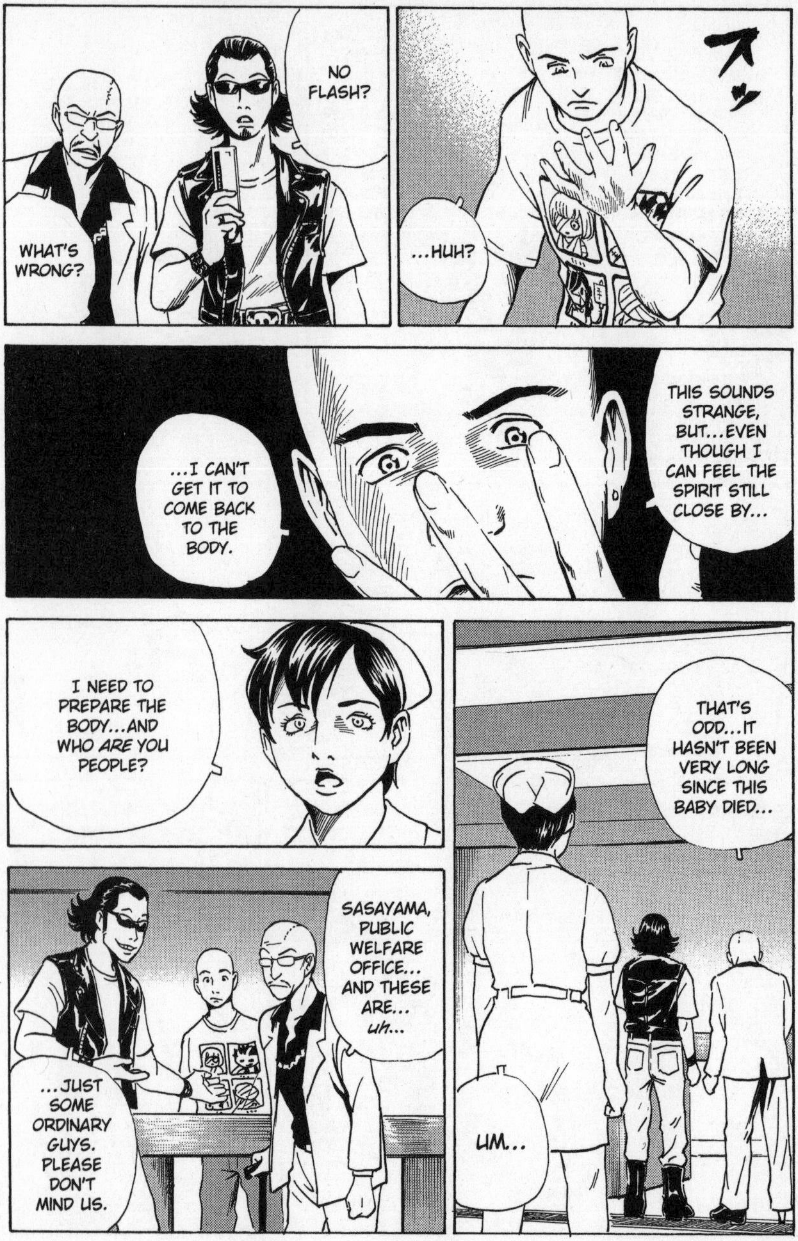
スッ
...HUH?
NO FLASH?
WHAT'S WRONG?
THIS SOUNDS STRANGE, BUT...EVEN THOUGH I CAN FEEL THE SPIRIT STILL CLOSE BY...
...I CAN'T GET IT TO COME BACK TO THE BODY.
THAT'S ODD...IT HASN'T BEEN VERY LONG SINCE THIS BABY DIED...
UM...
I NEED TO PREPARE THE BODY...AND WHO *ARE* YOU PEOPLE?
SASAYAMA, PUBLIC WELFARE OFFICE... AND THESE ARE... *uh*...
...JUST SOME ORDINARY GUYS. PLEASE DON'T MIND US.

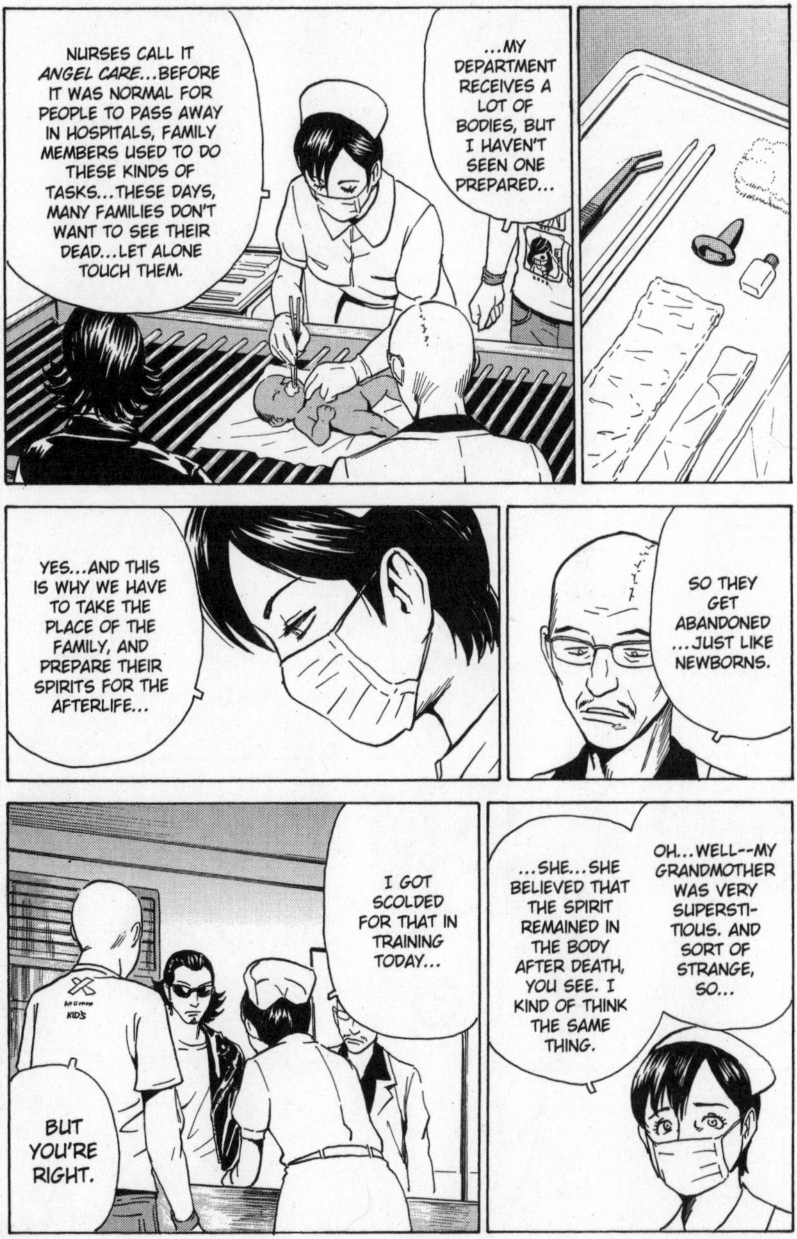
...MY DEPARTMENT RECEIVES A LOT OF BODIES, BUT I HAVEN'T SEEN ONE PREPARED...
NURSES CALL IT *ANGEL CARE*...BEFORE IT WAS NORMAL FOR PEOPLE TO PASS AWAY IN HOSPITALS, FAMILY MEMBERS USED TO DO THESE KINDS OF TASKS...THESE DAYS, MANY FAMILIES DON'T WANT TO SEE THEIR DEAD...LET ALONE TOUCH THEM.
SO THEY GET ABANDONED ...JUST LIKE NEWBORNS.
YES...AND THIS IS WHY WE HAVE TO TAKE THE PLACE OF THE FAMILY, AND PREPARE THEIR SPIRITS FOR THE AFTERLIFE...
OH...WELL--MY GRANDMOTHER WAS VERY SUPERSTI-TIOUS. AND SORT OF STRANGE, SO...
...SHE...SHE BELIEVED THAT THE SPIRIT REMAINED IN THE BODY AFTER DEATH, YOU SEE. I KIND OF THINK THE SAME THING.
I GOT SCOLDED FOR THAT IN TRAINING TODAY...
BUT YOU'RE RIGHT.

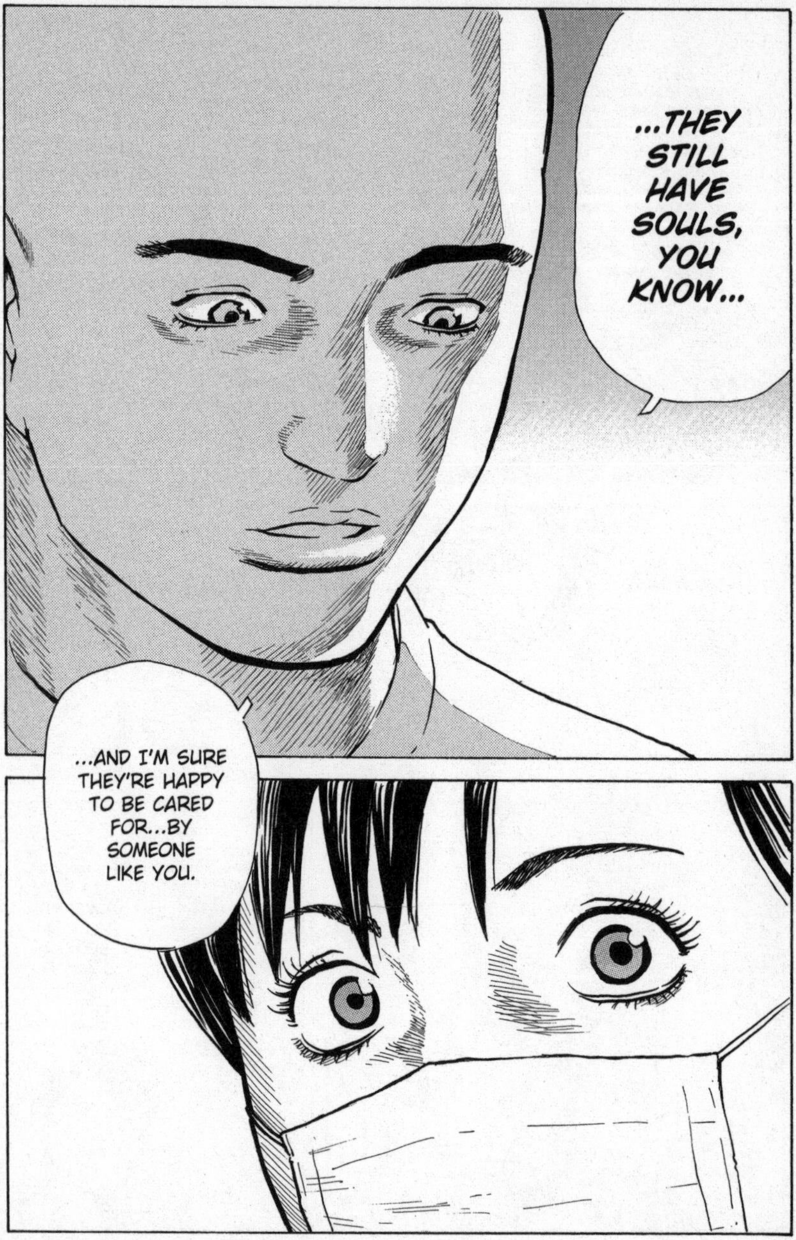
...THEY STILL HAVE SOULS, YOU KNOW...
...AND I'M SURE THEY'RE HAPPY TO BE CARED FOR...BY SOMEONE LIKE YOU.

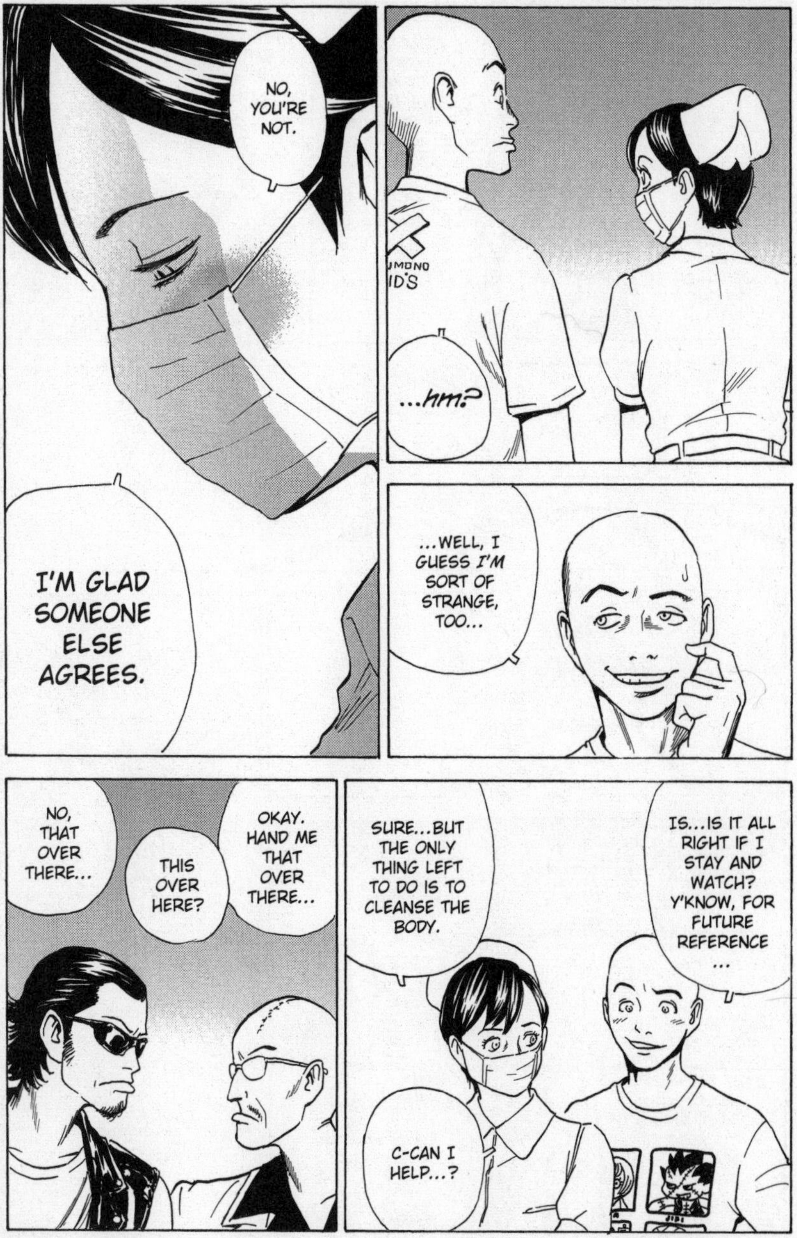
...hm?
...WELL, I GUESS I'M SORT OF STRANGE, TOO...
NO, YOU'RE NOT.
I'M GLAD SOMEONE ELSE AGREES.
IS...IS IT ALL RIGHT IF I STAY AND WATCH? Y'KNOW, FOR FUTURE REFERENCE...
SURE...BUT THE ONLY THING LEFT TO DO IS TO CLEANSE THE BODY.
C-CAN I HELP...?
OKAY. HAND ME THAT OVER THERE...
THIS OVER HERE?
NO, THAT OVER THERE...

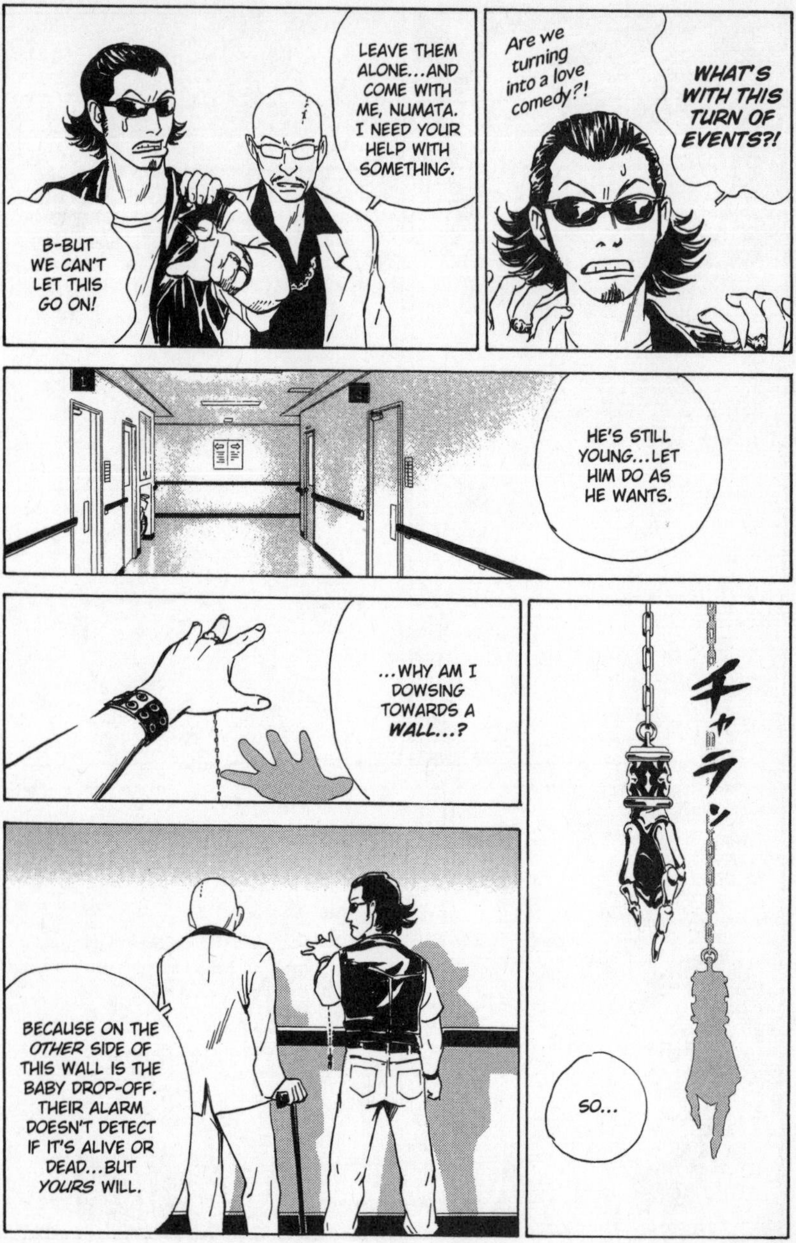
WHAT'S WITH THIS TURN OF EVENTS?!
Are we turning into a love comedy?!
LEAVE THEM ALONE...AND COME WITH ME, NUMATA. I NEED YOUR HELP WITH SOMETHING.
B-BUT WE CAN'T LET THIS GO ON!
HE'S STILL YOUNG...LET HIM DO AS HE WANTS.
チャラン
SO...
...WHY AM I DOWSING TOWARDS A WALL...?
BECAUSE ON THE OTHER SIDE OF THIS WALL IS THE BABY DROP-OFF. THEIR ALARM DOESN'T DETECT IF IT'S ALIVE OR DEAD...BUT YOURS WILL.

HUH? WHY DON'T WE JUST WATCH IT FROM THE OUTSIDE?

AND IT'S NOT LIKE PEOPLE DROP OFF DEAD BABIES EVERY DAY, RIGHT?

WHACK OF THE CANE, *ONE*--IF WE KEEP WATCH OUTSIDE, NOBODY'S GOING TO GO NEAR THAT DROP BOX...

OW...

WHACK OF THE CANE, *TWO*-- OLD STITCH- DOME HERE... YEAH, I *KNOW* YOU CALL ME THAT...

...SUSPECTS THEY'RE BEING LEFT INTENTION- ALLY.

OW...! INTENTION- ALLY? WHAT DO YOU MEAN?

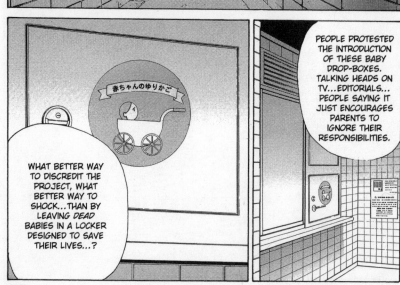

赤ちゃんのゆりかご

PEOPLE PROTESTED THE INTRODUCTION OF THESE BABY DROP-BOXES. TALKING HEADS ON TV...EDITORIALS... PEOPLE SAYING IT JUST ENCOURAGES PARENTS TO IGNORE THEIR RESPONSIBILITIES.

WHAT BETTER WAY TO DISCREDIT THE PROJECT, WHAT BETTER WAY TO SHOCK...THAN BY LEAVING *DEAD* BABIES IN A LOCKER DESIGNED TO SAVE THEIR LIVES...?

I DON'T KNOW...

YOU... REALLY THINK SOMEONE'S DOING THAT...?

...BUT I INTEND TO FIND OUT.

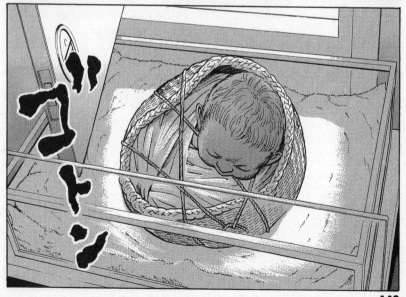

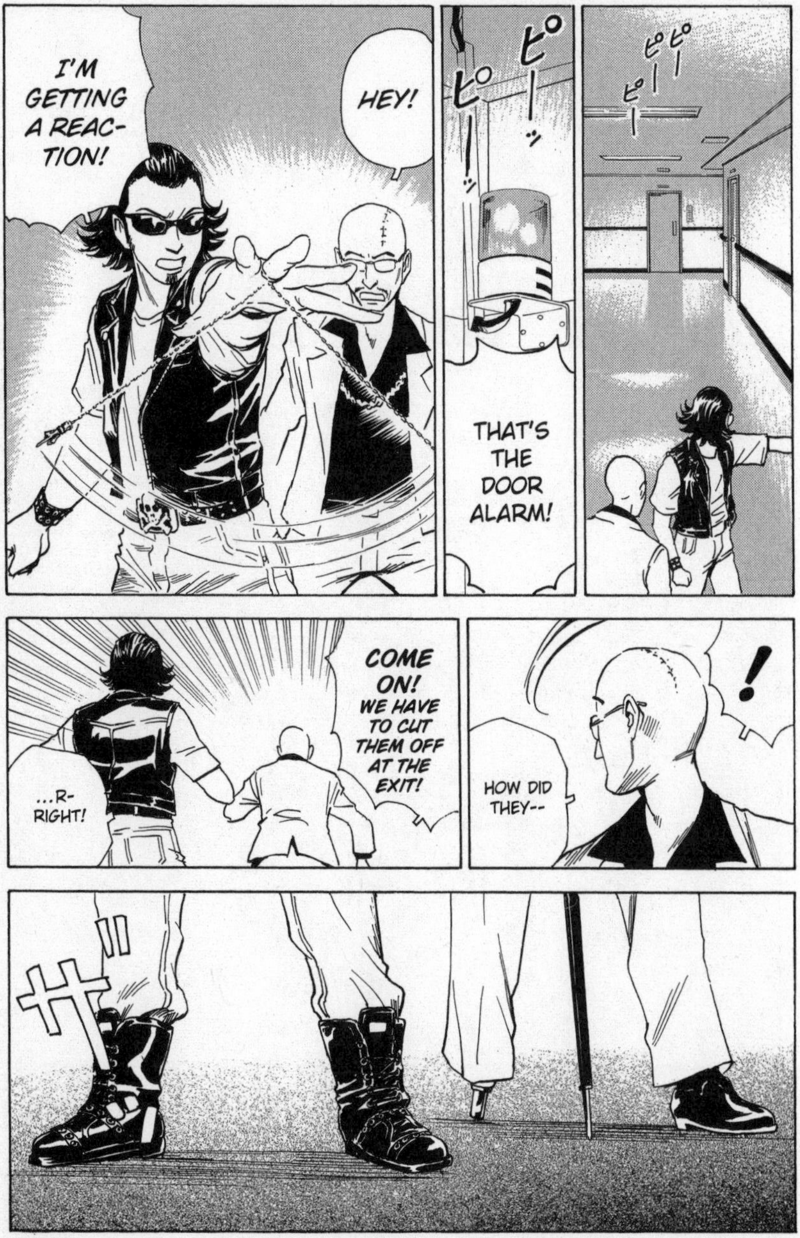
ピーピー
ピーッ
ピーッ
THAT'S THE DOOR ALARM!
HEY!
I'M GETTING A REACTION!
!
HOW DID THEY--
COME ON! WE HAVE TO CUT THEM OFF AT THE EXIT!
...R-RIGHT!
ザッ

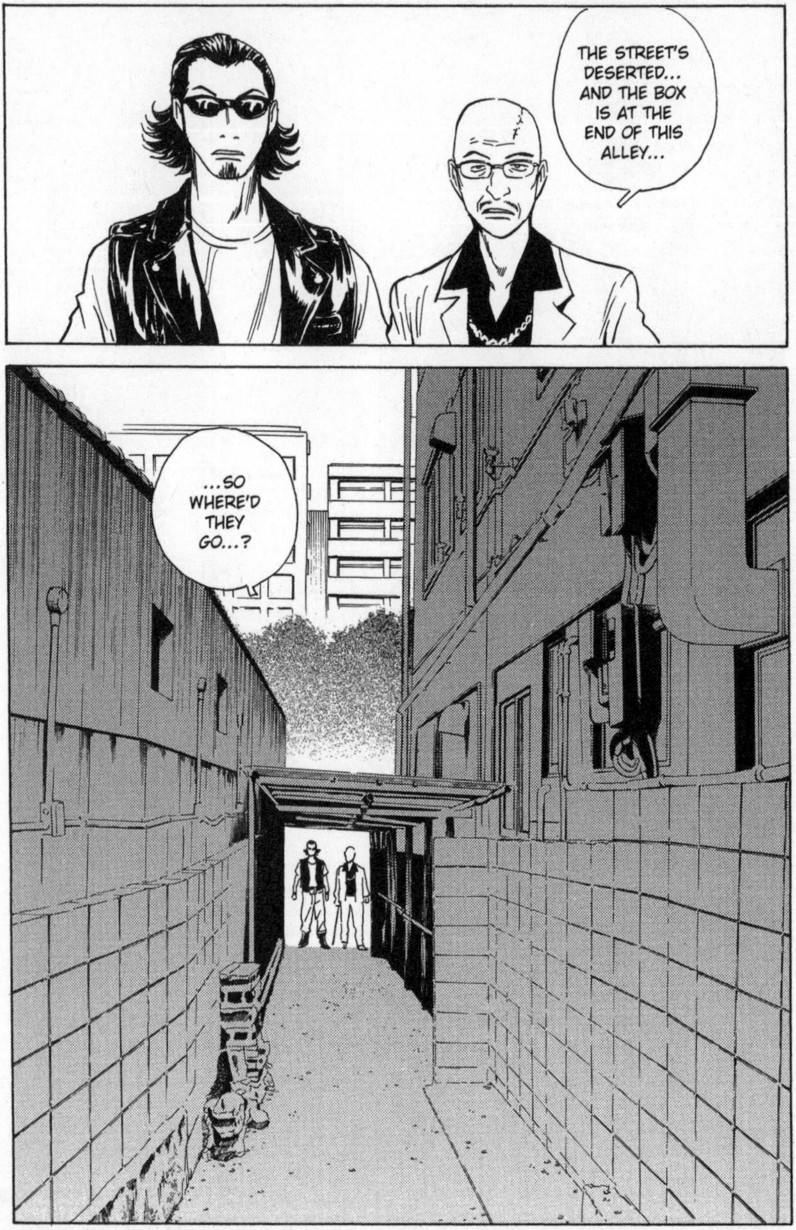
THE STREET'S DESERTED... AND THE BOX IS AT THE END OF THIS ALLEY...
...SO WHERE'D THEY GO...?

5th delivery: an afternoon with just the two of us—the end

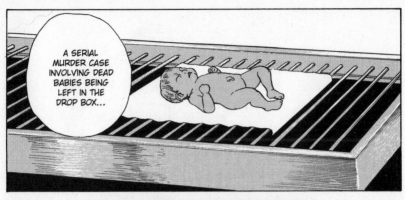

A SERIAL MURDER CASE INVOLVING DEAD BABIES BEING LEFT IN THE DROP BOX...
...IN THE ALLEY THAT LEADS TO THE BOX, THERE ARE NO CAMERAS OR MONITORS.
THE ALLEY ITSELF HAS HIGH WALLS, BLOCKING THE SIGHT OF ANY WITNESSES...
AND THERE WAS NO ONE ON THE STREET OUTSIDE, SO...NOTHING TO GO ON.
角川中央病院
NOTHING, THAT IS, EXCEPT THIS WICKER BASKET.

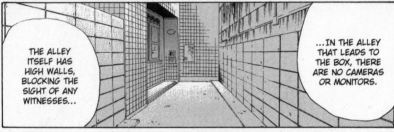

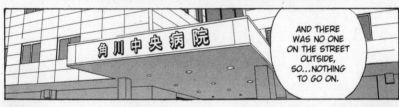

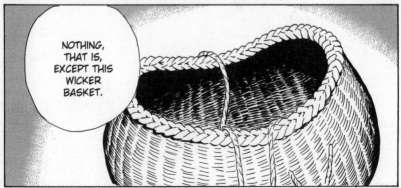

6th delivery 姫鏡台 princess's mirror

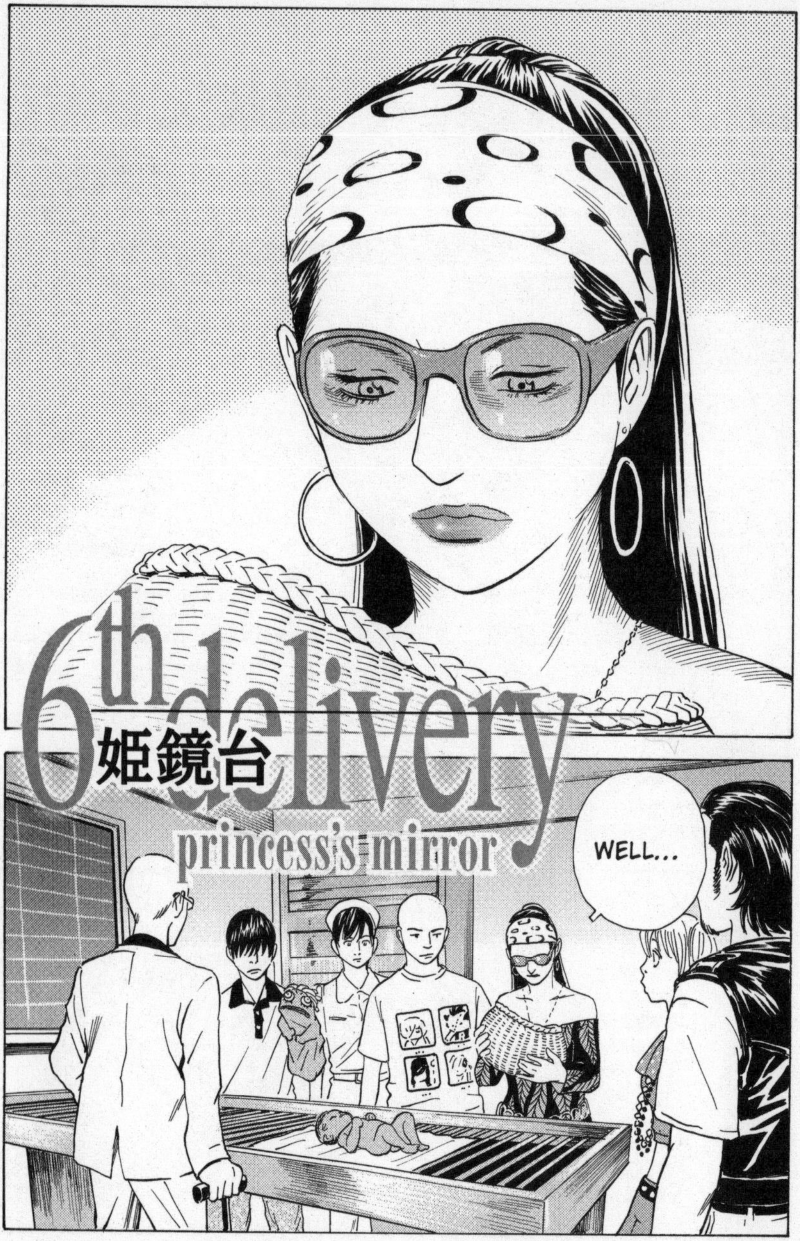
WELL...

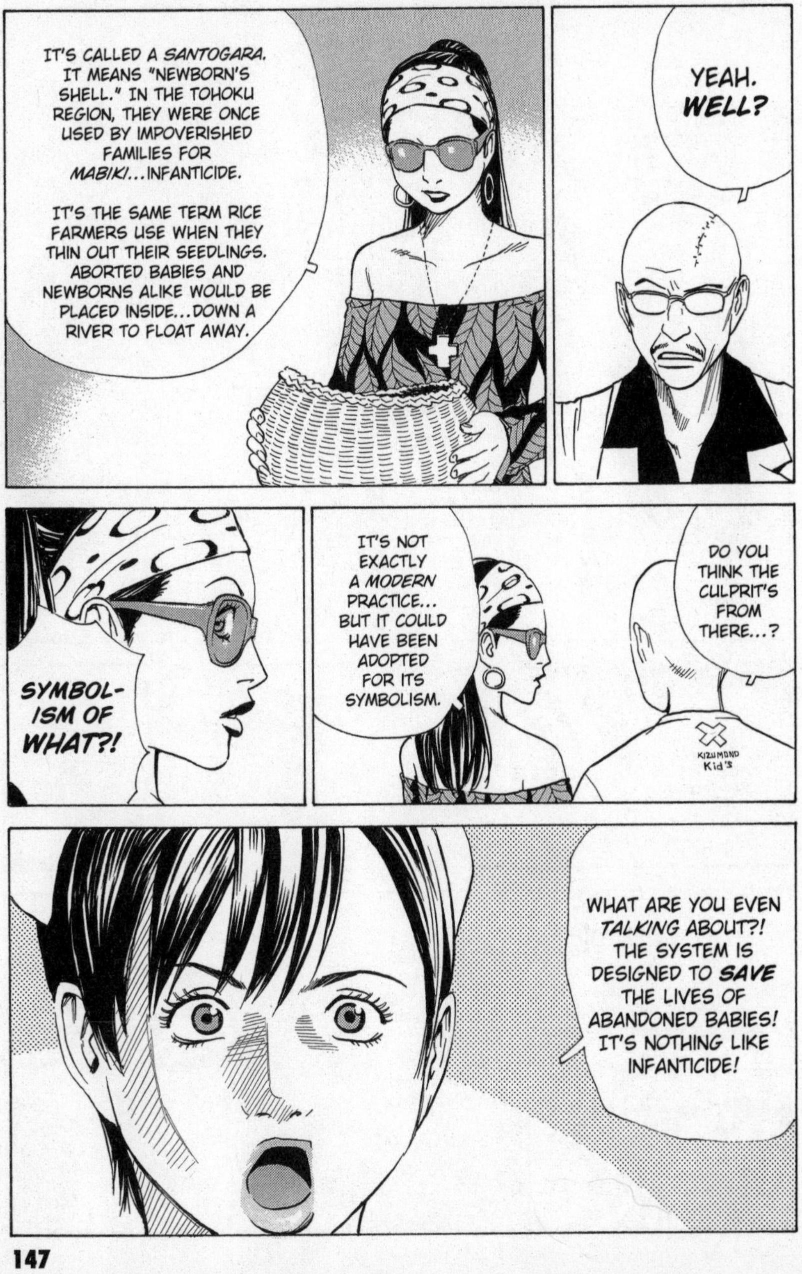
YEAH. **WELL?**
IT'S CALLED A *SANTOGARA*. IT MEANS "NEWBORN'S SHELL." IN THE TOHOKU REGION, THEY WERE ONCE USED BY IMPOVERISHED FAMILIES FOR *MABIKI*...INFANTICIDE.
IT'S THE SAME TERM RICE FARMERS USE WHEN THEY THIN OUT THEIR SEEDLINGS. ABORTED BABIES AND NEWBORNS ALIKE WOULD BE PLACED INSIDE...DOWN A RIVER TO FLOAT AWAY.
DO YOU THINK THE CULPRIT'S FROM THERE...?
KIZUMONO Kid's
IT'S NOT EXACTLY A *MODERN* PRACTICE... BUT IT COULD HAVE BEEN ADOPTED FOR ITS SYMBOLISM.
SYMBOLISM OF WHAT?!
WHAT ARE YOU EVEN *TALKING* ABOUT?! THE SYSTEM IS DESIGNED TO ***SAVE*** THE LIVES OF ABANDONED BABIES! IT'S NOTHING LIKE INFANTICIDE!

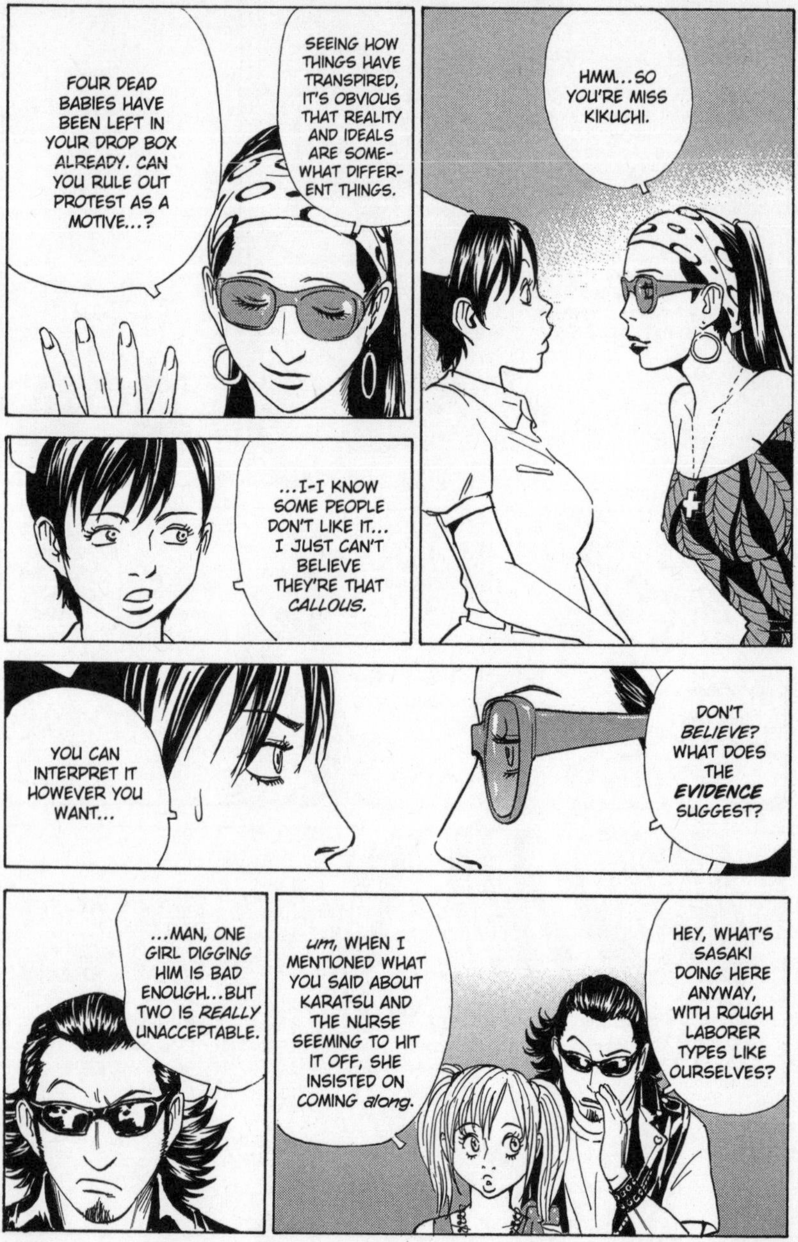
HMM...SO YOU'RE MISS KIKUCHI.
SEEING HOW THINGS HAVE TRANSPIRED, IT'S OBVIOUS THAT REALITY AND IDEALS ARE SOME-WHAT DIFFER-ENT THINGS.
FOUR DEAD BABIES HAVE BEEN LEFT IN YOUR DROP BOX ALREADY. CAN YOU RULE OUT PROTEST AS A MOTIVE...?
...I-I KNOW SOME PEOPLE DON'T LIKE IT... I JUST CAN'T BELIEVE THEY'RE THAT *CALLOUS.*
DON'T *BELIEVE?* WHAT DOES THE ***EVIDENCE*** SUGGEST?
YOU CAN INTERPRET IT HOWEVER YOU WANT...
HEY, WHAT'S SASAKI DOING HERE ANYWAY, WITH ROUGH LABORER TYPES LIKE OURSELVES?
um, WHEN I MENTIONED WHAT YOU SAID ABOUT KARATSU AND THE NURSE SEEMING TO HIT IT OFF, SHE INSISTED ON COMING *along.*
...MAN, ONE GIRL DIGGING HIM IS BAD ENOUGH...BUT TWO IS *REALLY* UNACCEPTABLE.

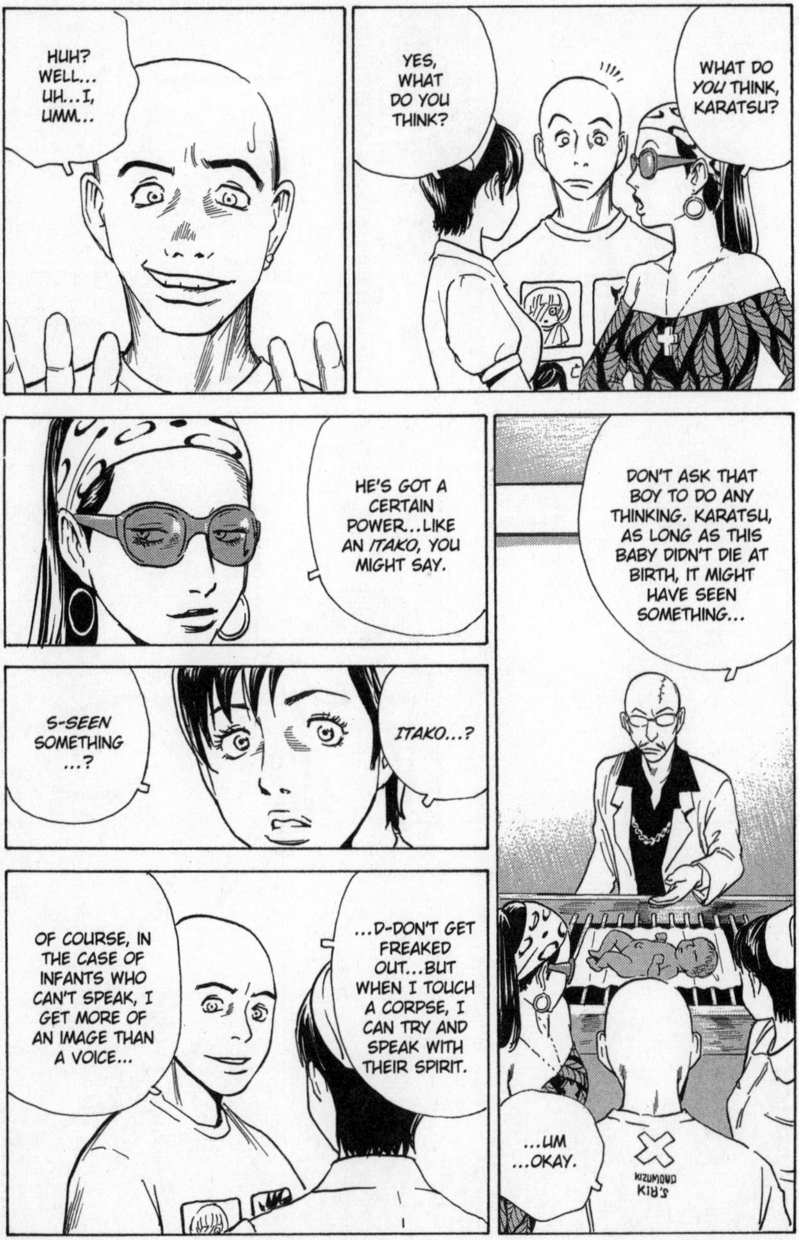

WHAT DO *YOU* THINK, KARATSU?
YES, WHAT DO YOU THINK?
HUH? WELL... UH...I, UMM...
DON'T ASK THAT BOY TO DO ANY THINKING. KARATSU, AS LONG AS THIS BABY DIDN'T DIE AT BIRTH, IT MIGHT HAVE SEEN SOMETHING...
KIZUMONO
...UM ...OKAY.
HE'S GOT A CERTAIN POWER...LIKE AN *ITAKO*, YOU MIGHT SAY.
ITAKO...?
S-SEEN SOMETHING ...?
...D-DON'T GET FREAKED OUT...BUT WHEN I TOUCH A CORPSE, I CAN TRY AND SPEAK WITH THEIR SPIRIT.
OF COURSE, IN THE CASE OF INFANTS WHO CAN'T SPEAK, I GET MORE OF AN IMAGE THAN A VOICE...

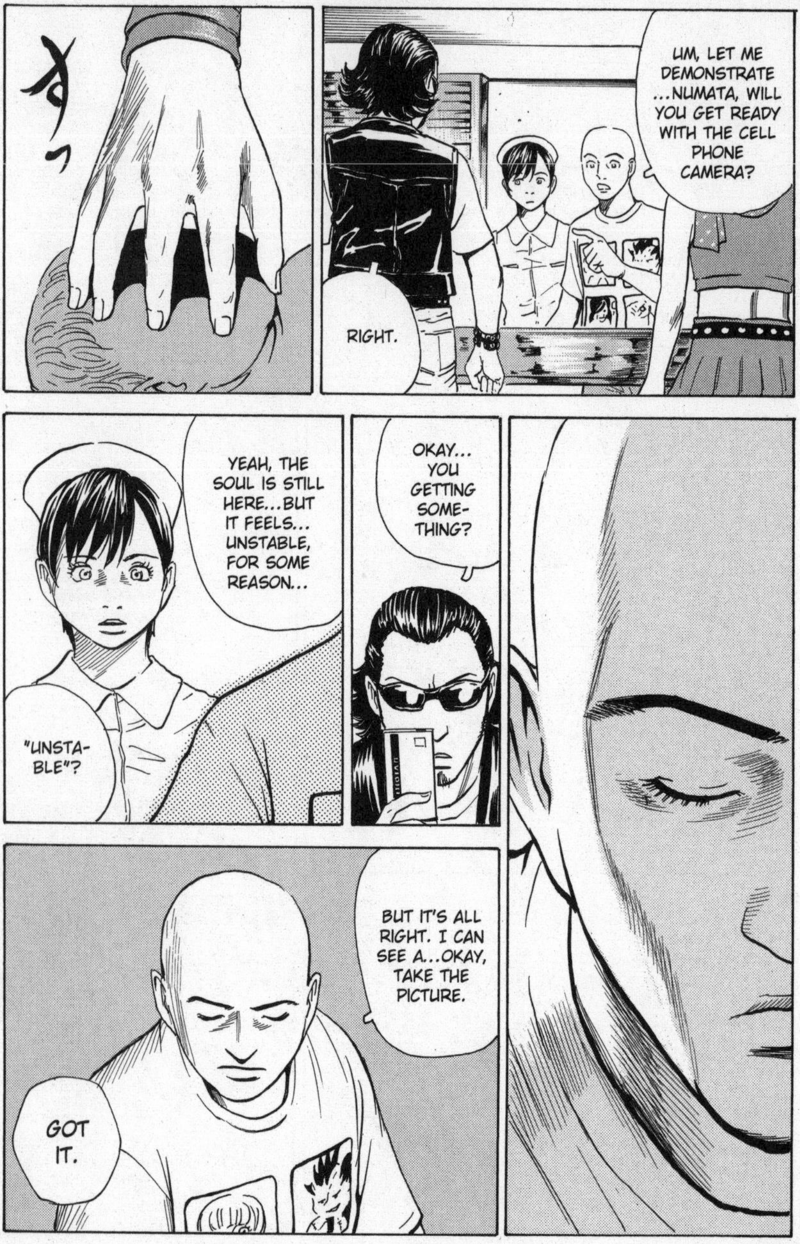
UM, LET ME DEMONSTRATE ...NUMATA, WILL YOU GET READY WITH THE CELL PHONE CAMERA?
RIGHT.
すっ
OKAY... YOU GETTING SOME-THING?
YEAH, THE SOUL IS STILL HERE...BUT IT FEELS... UNSTABLE, FOR SOME REASON...
"UNSTA-BLE"?
BUT IT'S ALL RIGHT. I CAN SEE A...OKAY, TAKE THE PICTURE.
GOT IT.

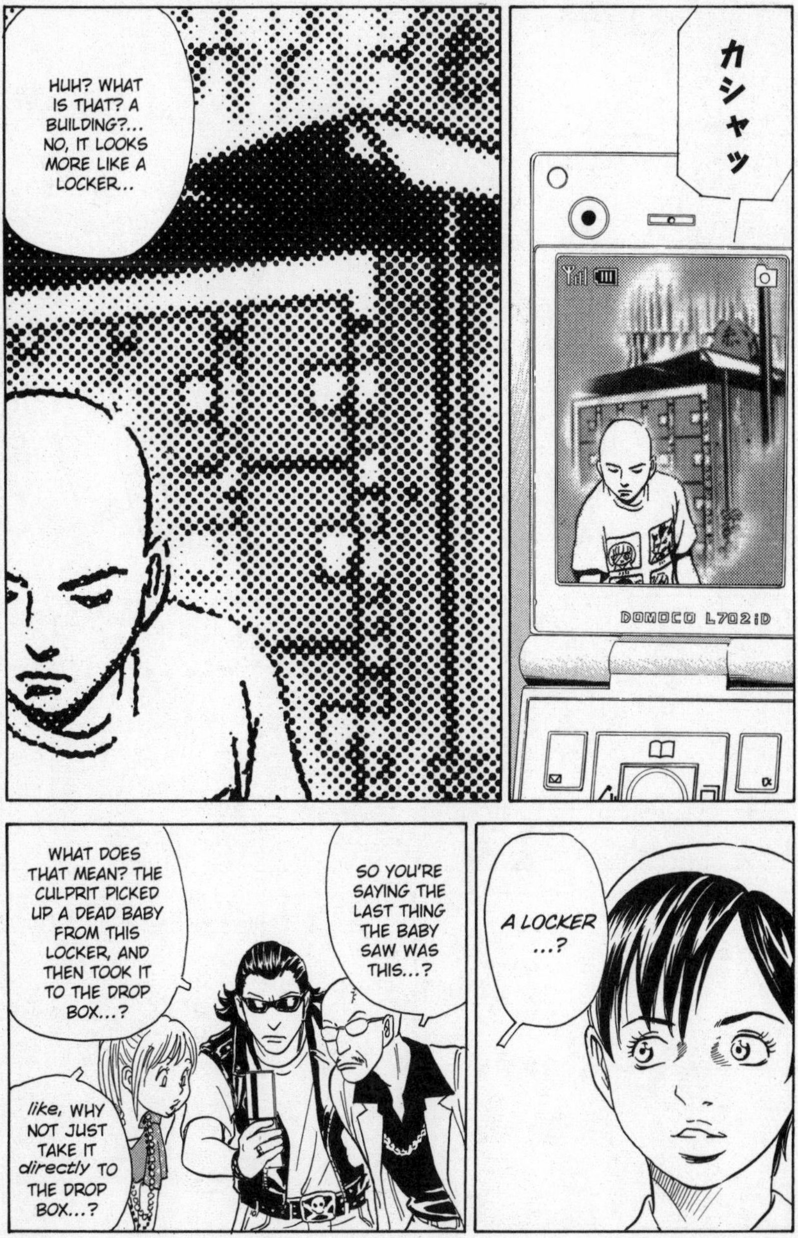
カシャッ
DOMOCO L702iD
HUH? WHAT IS THAT? A BUILDING?... NO, IT LOOKS MORE LIKE A LOCKER...
A LOCKER ...?
SO YOU'RE SAYING THE LAST THING THE BABY SAW WAS THIS...?
WHAT DOES THAT MEAN? THE CULPRIT PICKED UP A DEAD BABY FROM THIS LOCKER, AND THEN TOOK IT TO THE DROP BOX...?
like, WHY NOT JUST TAKE IT *directly* TO THE DROP BOX...?

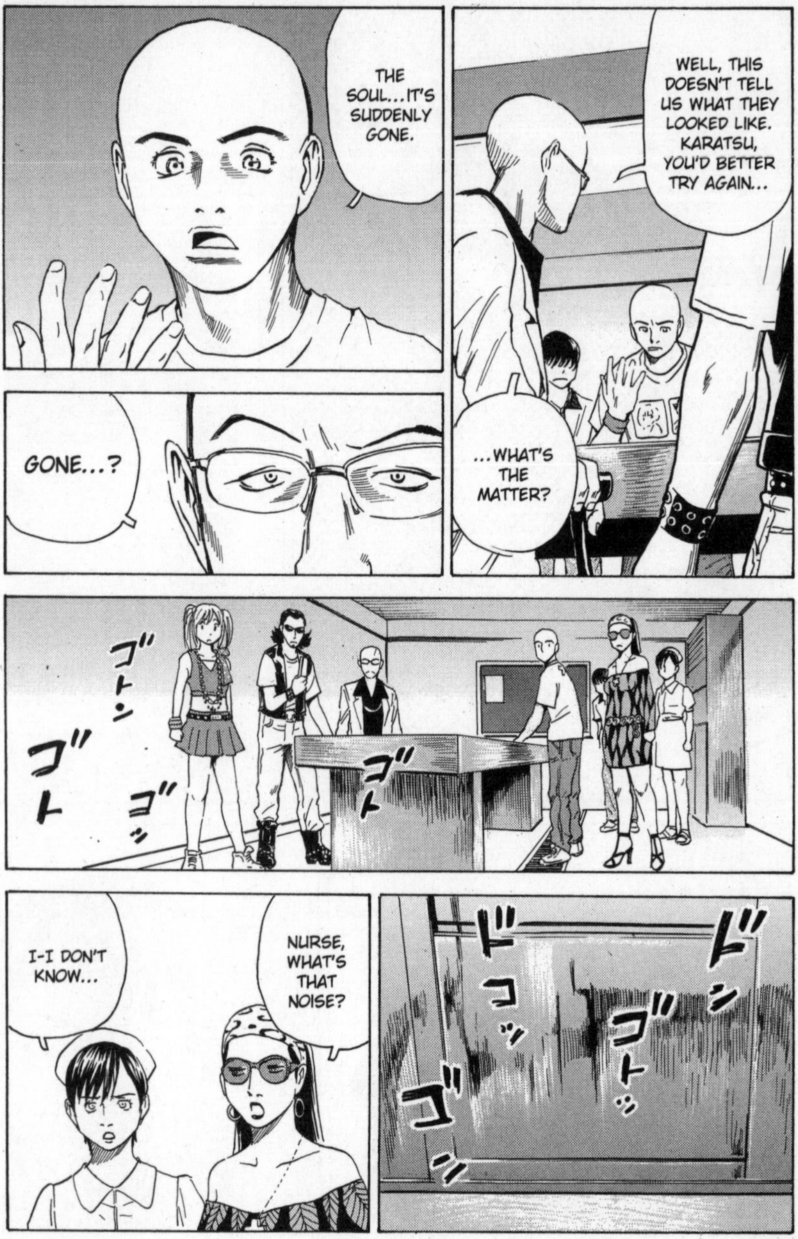
WELL, THIS DOESN'T TELL US WHAT THEY LOOKED LIKE. KARATSU, YOU'D BETTER TRY AGAIN...
...WHAT'S THE MATTER?
THE SOUL...IT'S SUDDENLY GONE.
GONE...?
ゴトン
ゴト
ゴッ
ゴト
ドン
ゴトッ
ドコッ
ゴッ
NURSE, WHAT'S THAT NOISE?
I-I DON'T KNOW...

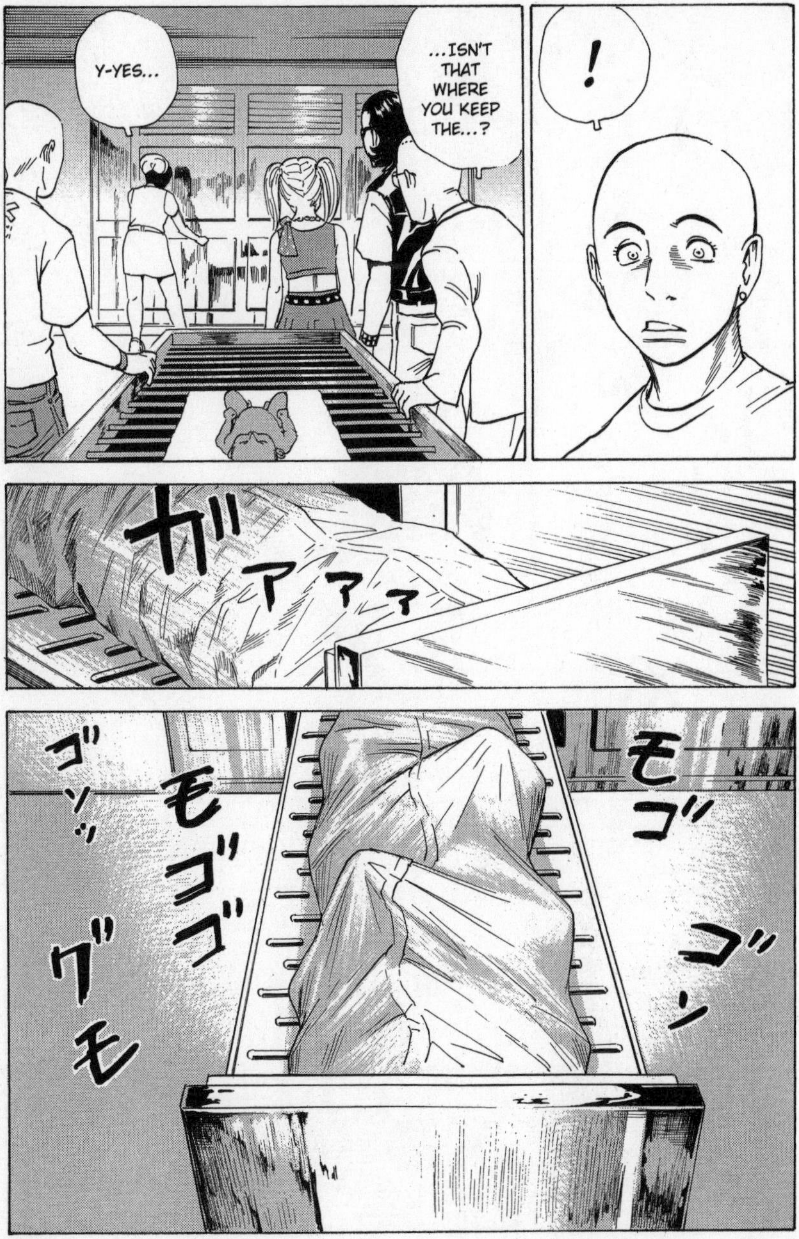
!
...ISN'T THAT WHERE YOU KEEP THE...?
Y-YES...
ガアァァ
モゴ
ゴン
ゴッ
モゴゴ
グモ

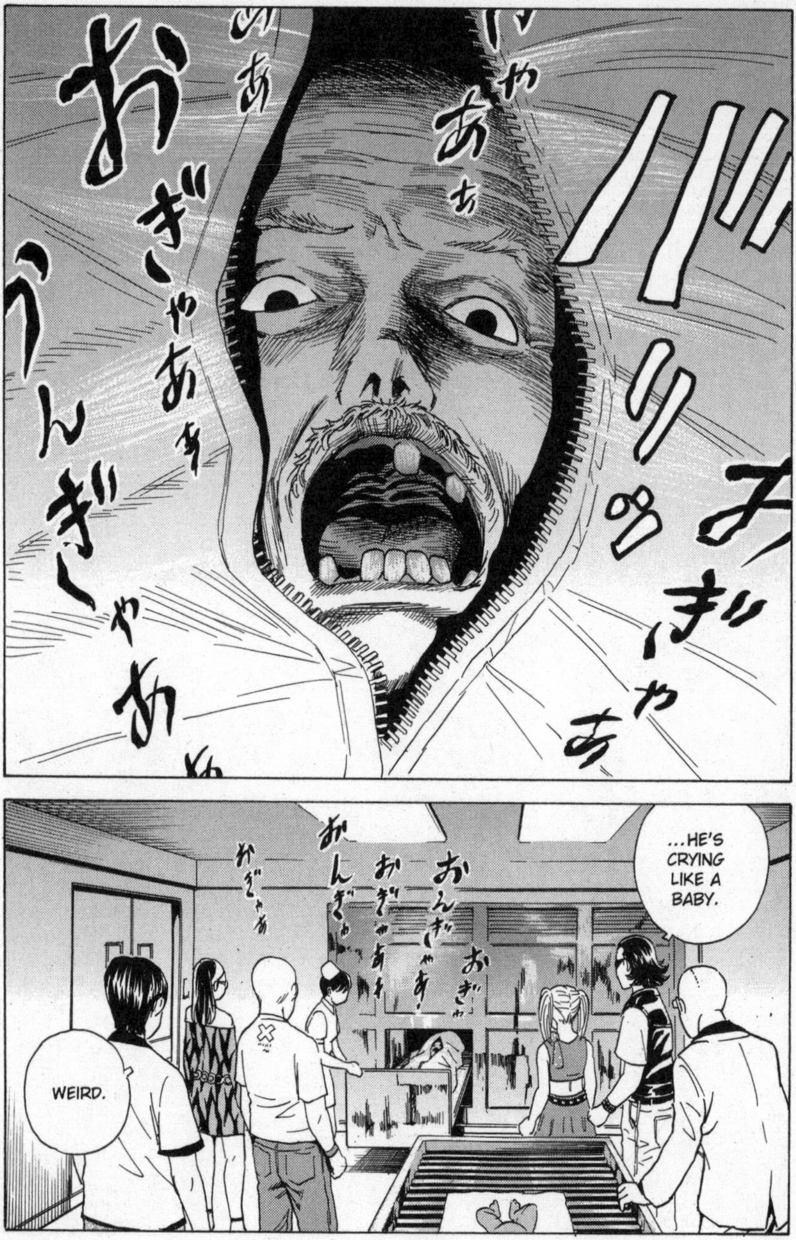
...HE'S CRYING LIKE A BABY.
WEIRD.

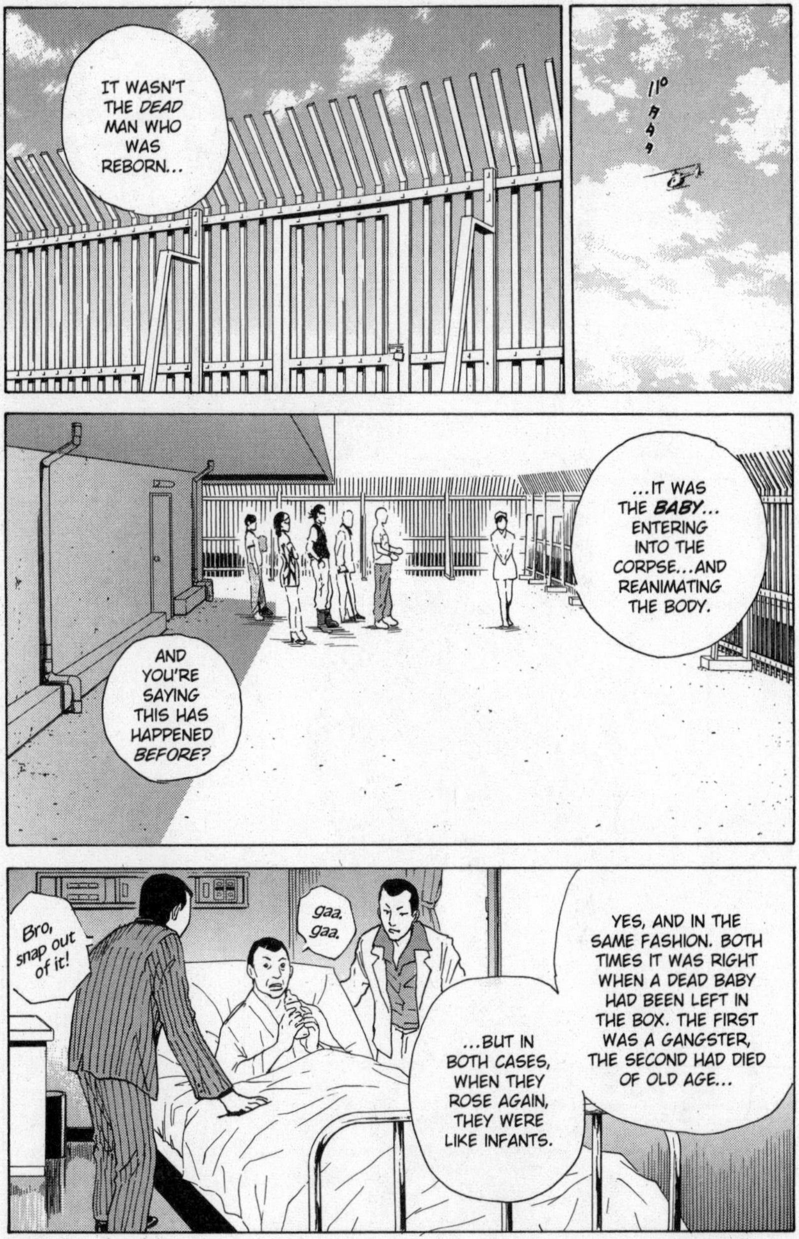
IT WASN'T THE *DEAD* MAN WHO WAS REBORN...
...IT WAS THE ***BABY***... ENTERING INTO THE CORPSE...AND REANIMATING THE BODY.
AND YOU'RE SAYING THIS HAS HAPPENED *BEFORE?*
YES, AND IN THE SAME FASHION. BOTH TIMES IT WAS RIGHT WHEN A DEAD BABY HAD BEEN LEFT IN THE BOX. THE FIRST WAS A GANGSTER, THE SECOND HAD DIED OF OLD AGE...
...BUT IN BOTH CASES, WHEN THEY ROSE AGAIN, THEY WERE LIKE INFANTS.
gaa. gaa.
Bro, snap out of it!

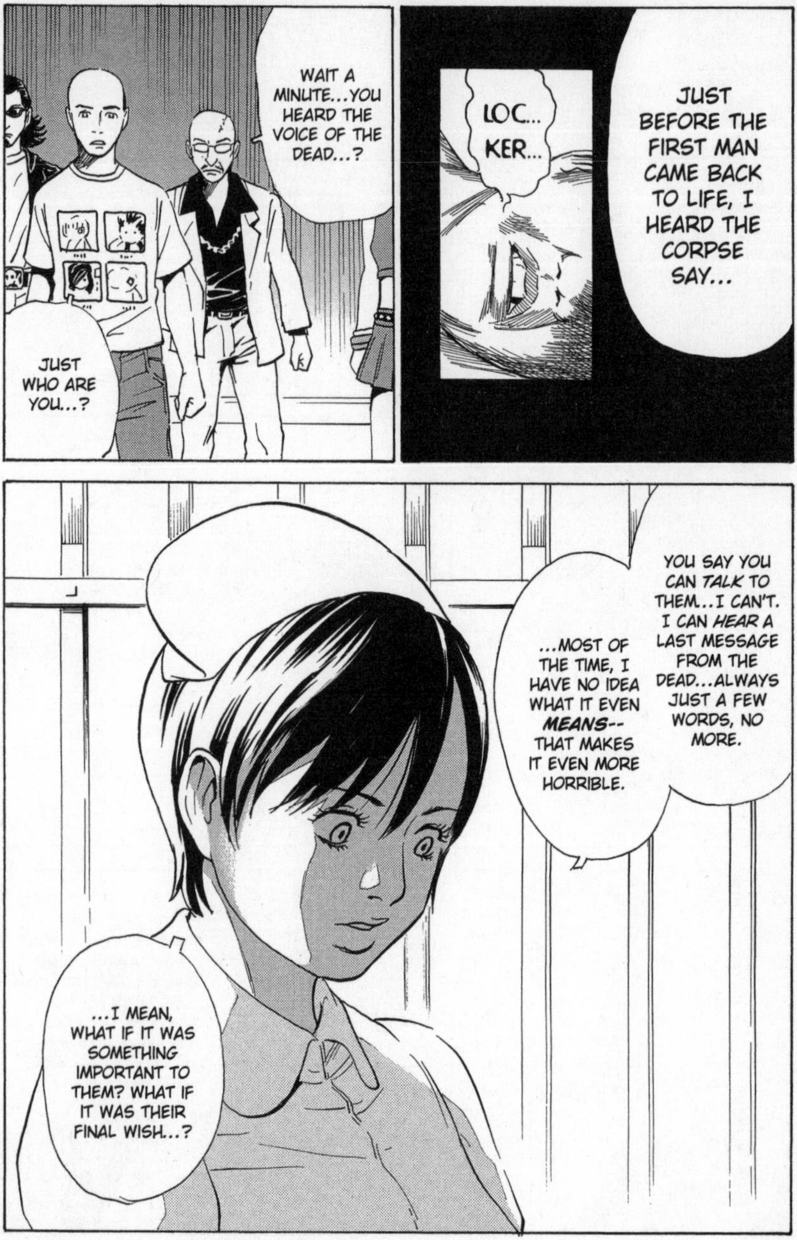
JUST BEFORE THE FIRST MAN CAME BACK TO LIFE, I HEARD THE CORPSE SAY...
LOC... KER...
WAIT A MINUTE...YOU HEARD THE VOICE OF THE DEAD...?
JUST WHO ARE YOU...?
YOU SAY YOU CAN *TALK* TO THEM...I CAN'T. I CAN *HEAR* A LAST MESSAGE FROM THE DEAD...ALWAYS JUST A FEW WORDS, NO MORE.
...MOST OF THE TIME, I HAVE NO IDEA WHAT IT EVEN *MEANS*-- THAT MAKES IT EVEN MORE HORRIBLE.
...I MEAN, WHAT IF IT WAS SOMETHING IMPORTANT TO THEM? WHAT IF IT WAS THEIR FINAL WISH...?

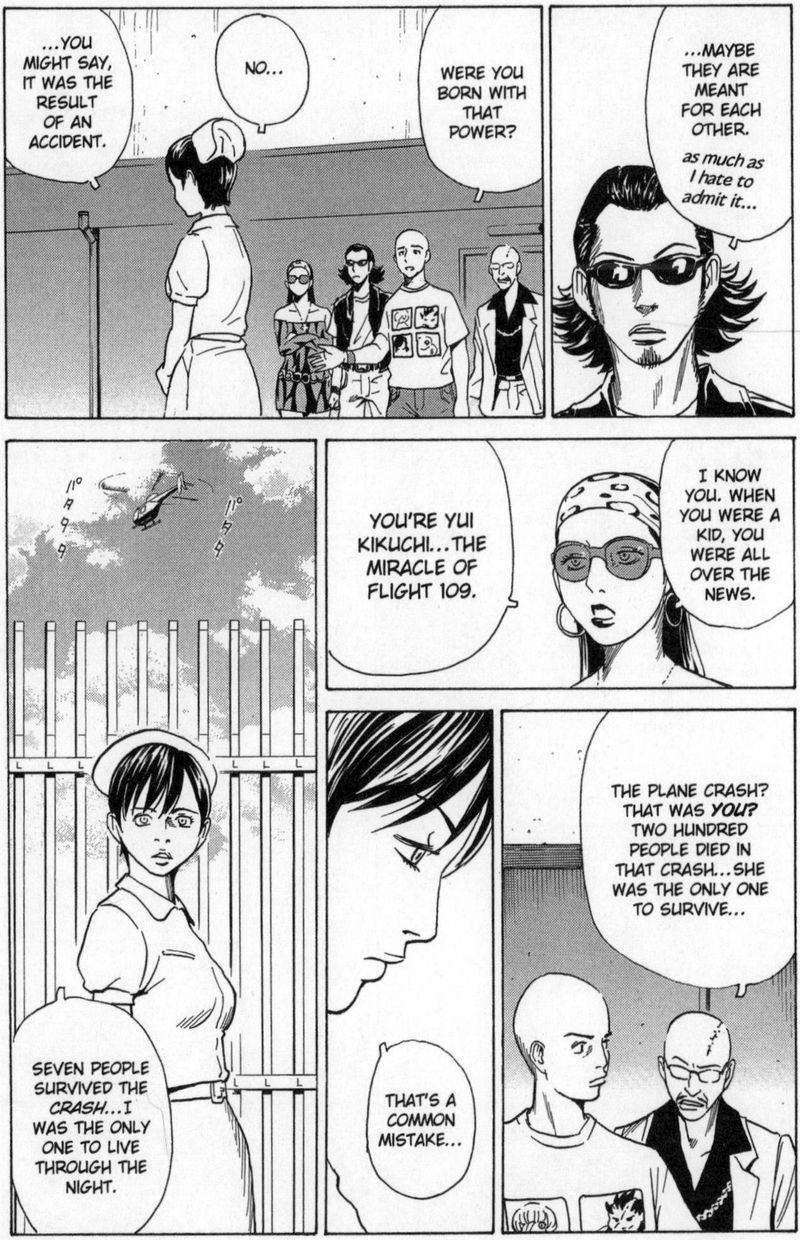

...MAYBE THEY ARE MEANT FOR EACH OTHER.
as much as I hate to admit it...
WERE YOU BORN WITH THAT POWER?
NO...
...YOU MIGHT SAY, IT WAS THE RESULT OF AN ACCIDENT.
I KNOW YOU. WHEN YOU WERE A KID, YOU WERE ALL OVER THE NEWS.
YOU'RE YUI KIKUCHI...THE MIRACLE OF FLIGHT 109.
THE PLANE CRASH? THAT WAS ***YOU?*** TWO HUNDRED PEOPLE DIED IN THAT CRASH...SHE WAS THE ONLY ONE TO SURVIVE...
THAT'S A COMMON MISTAKE...
パタタ
パタタタ
SEVEN PEOPLE SURVIVED THE *CRASH*...I WAS THE ONLY ONE TO LIVE THROUGH THE NIGHT.

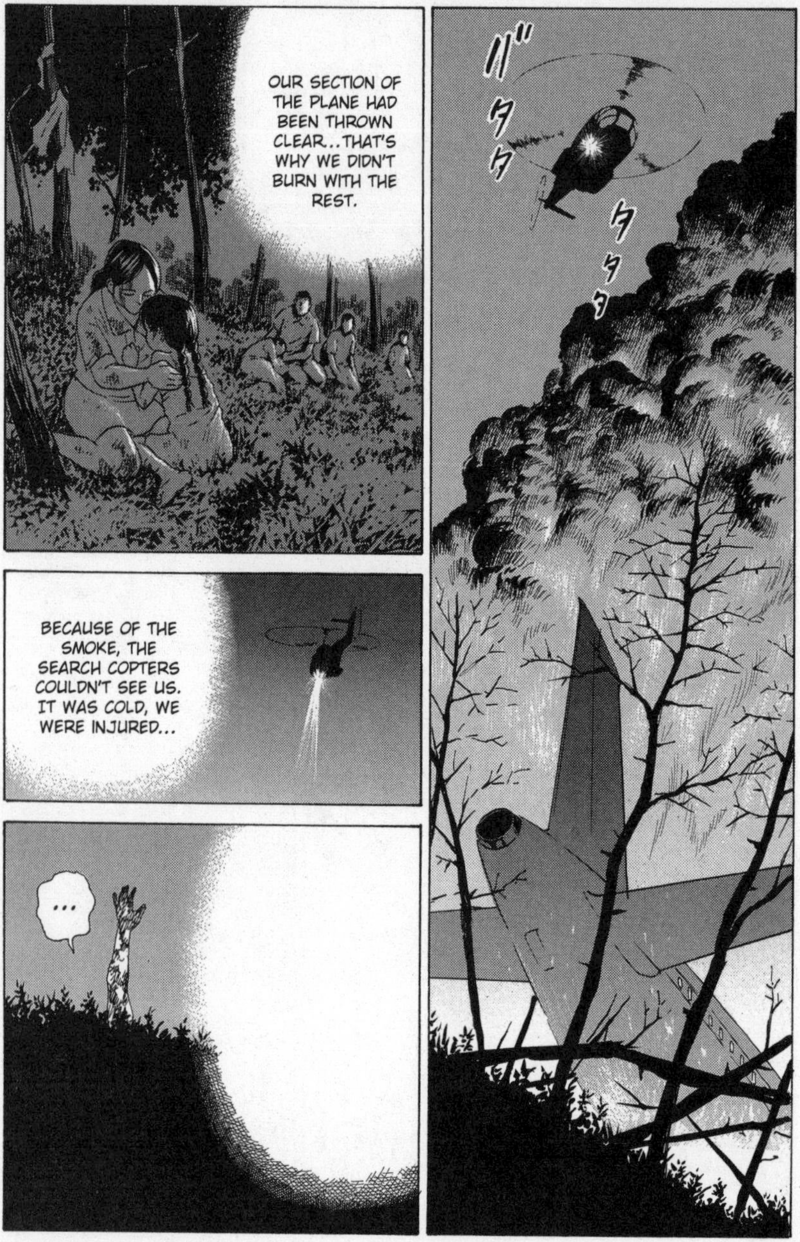
バタタ
タタタ
OUR SECTION OF THE PLANE HAD BEEN THROWN CLEAR...THAT'S WHY WE DIDN'T BURN WITH THE REST.
BECAUSE OF THE SMOKE, THE SEARCH COPTERS COULDN'T SEE US. IT WAS COLD, WE WERE INJURED...
...

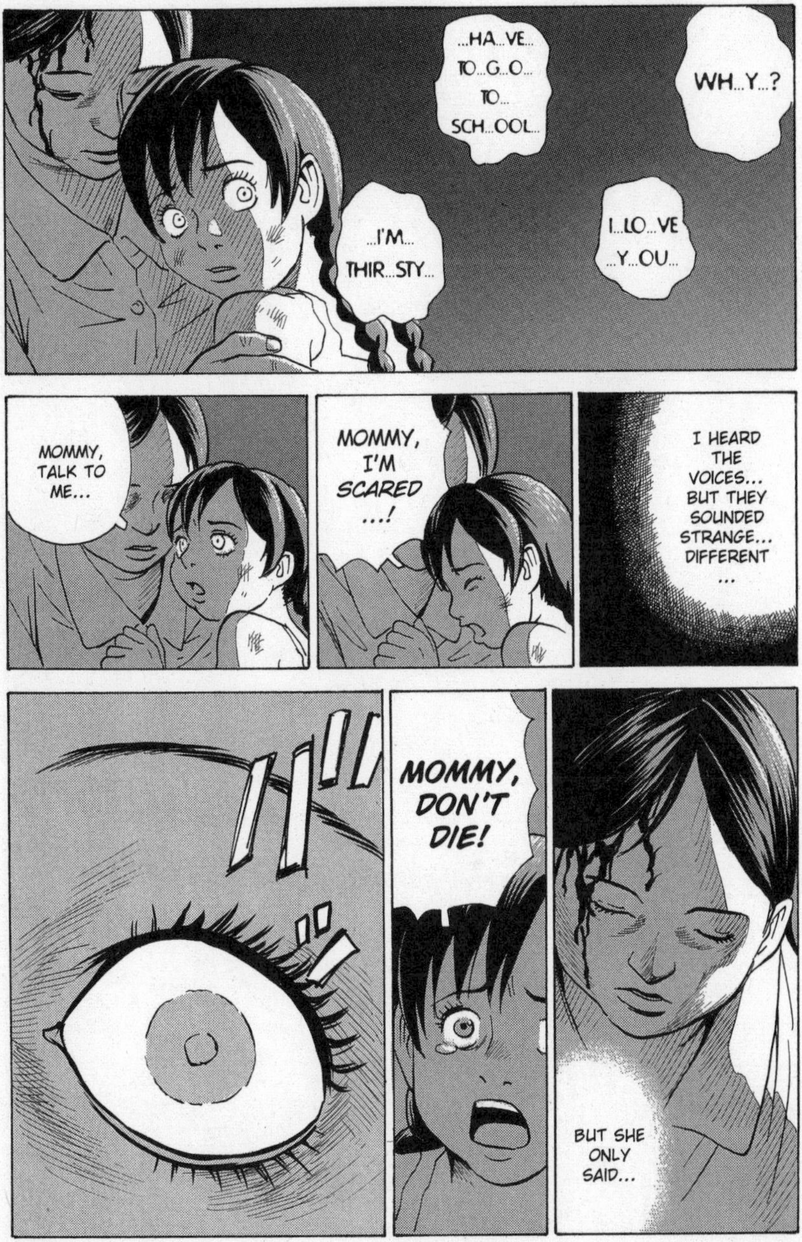
WH...Y...?
...HA...VE... TO...G...O... TO... SCH...OOL...
I...LO...VE ...Y...OU...
...I'M... THIR...STY...
I HEARD THE VOICES... BUT THEY SOUNDED STRANGE... DIFFERENT ...
MOMMY, I'M SCARED ...!
MOMMY, TALK TO ME...
BUT SHE ONLY SAID...
MOMMY, DON'T DIE!

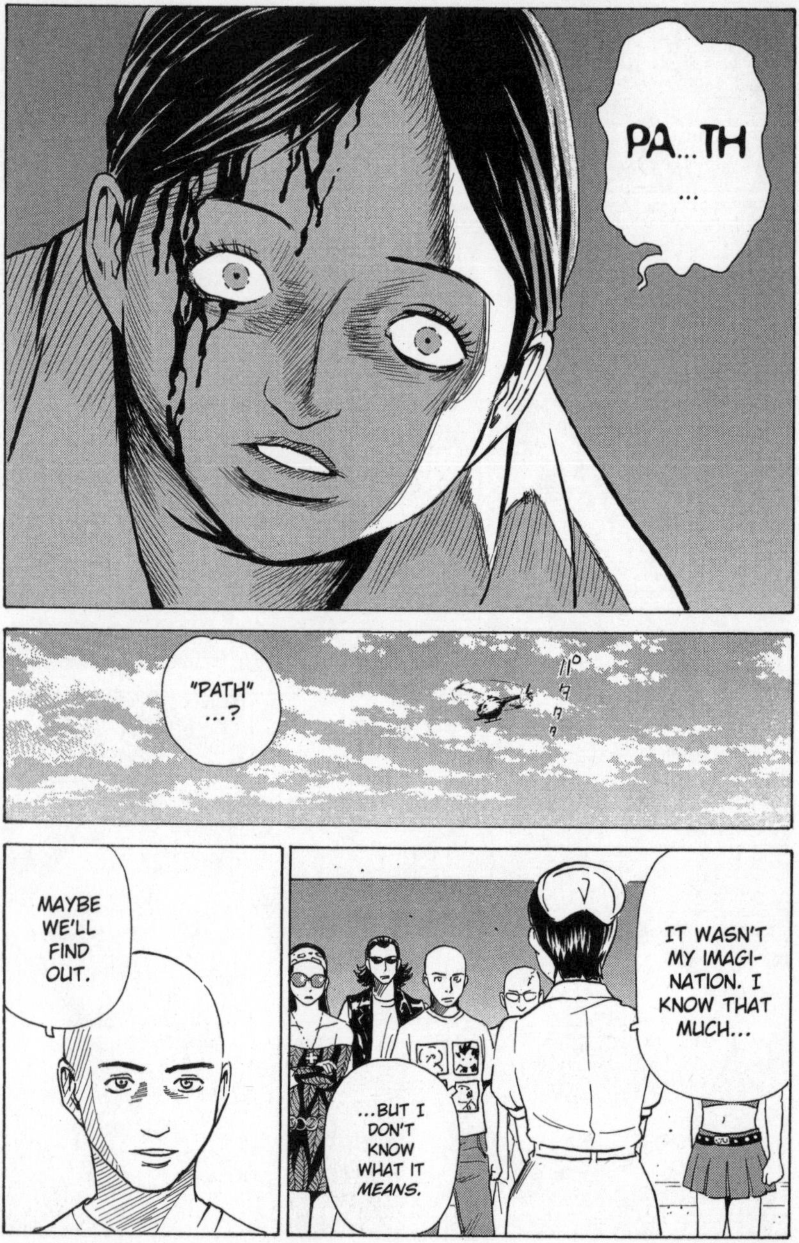
PA...TH ...
"PATH" ...?
IT WASN'T MY IMAGI-NATION. I KNOW THAT MUCH...
...BUT I DON'T KNOW WHAT IT *MEANS.*
MAYBE WE'LL FIND OUT.

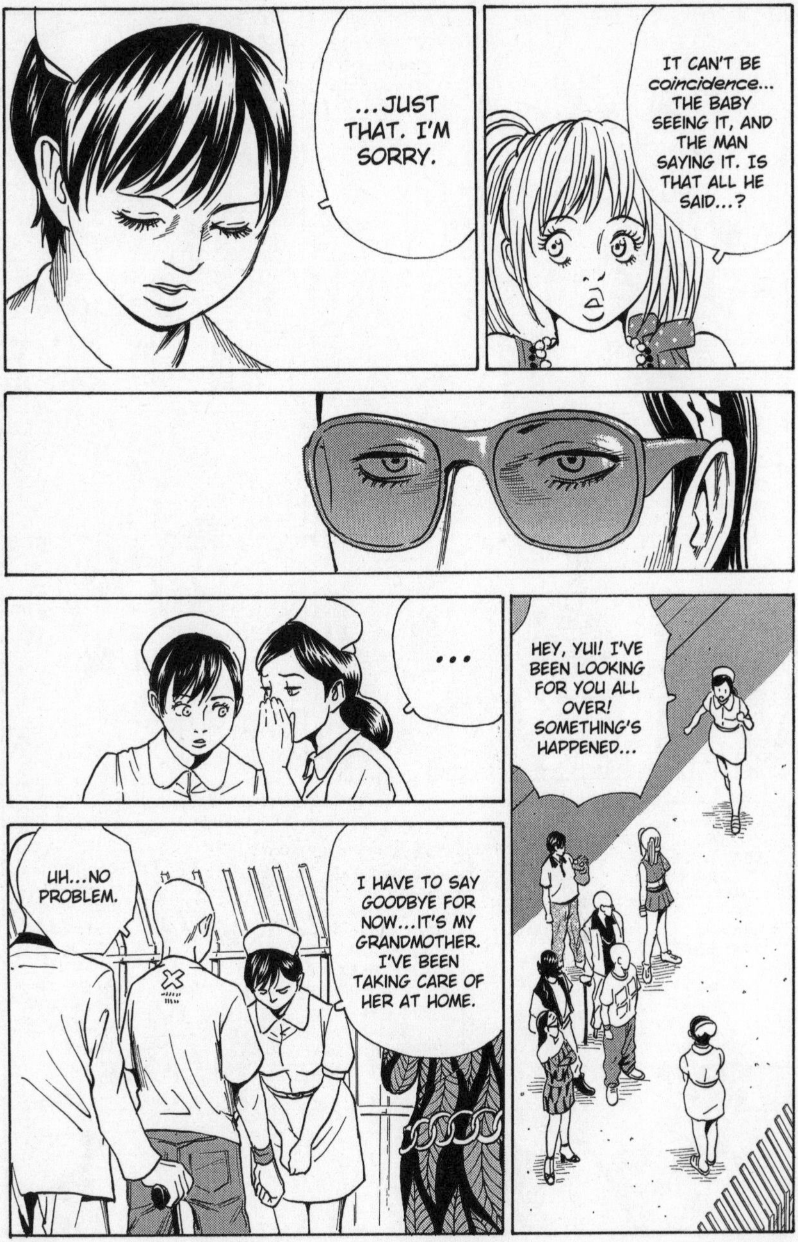
IT CAN'T BE *coincidence*... THE BABY SEEING IT, AND THE MAN SAYING IT. IS THAT ALL HE SAID...?
...JUST THAT. I'M SORRY.
HEY, YUI! I'VE BEEN LOOKING FOR YOU ALL OVER! SOMETHING'S HAPPENED...
...
I HAVE TO SAY GOODBYE FOR NOW...IT'S MY GRANDMOTHER. I'VE BEEN TAKING CARE OF HER AT HOME.
UH...NO PROBLEM.

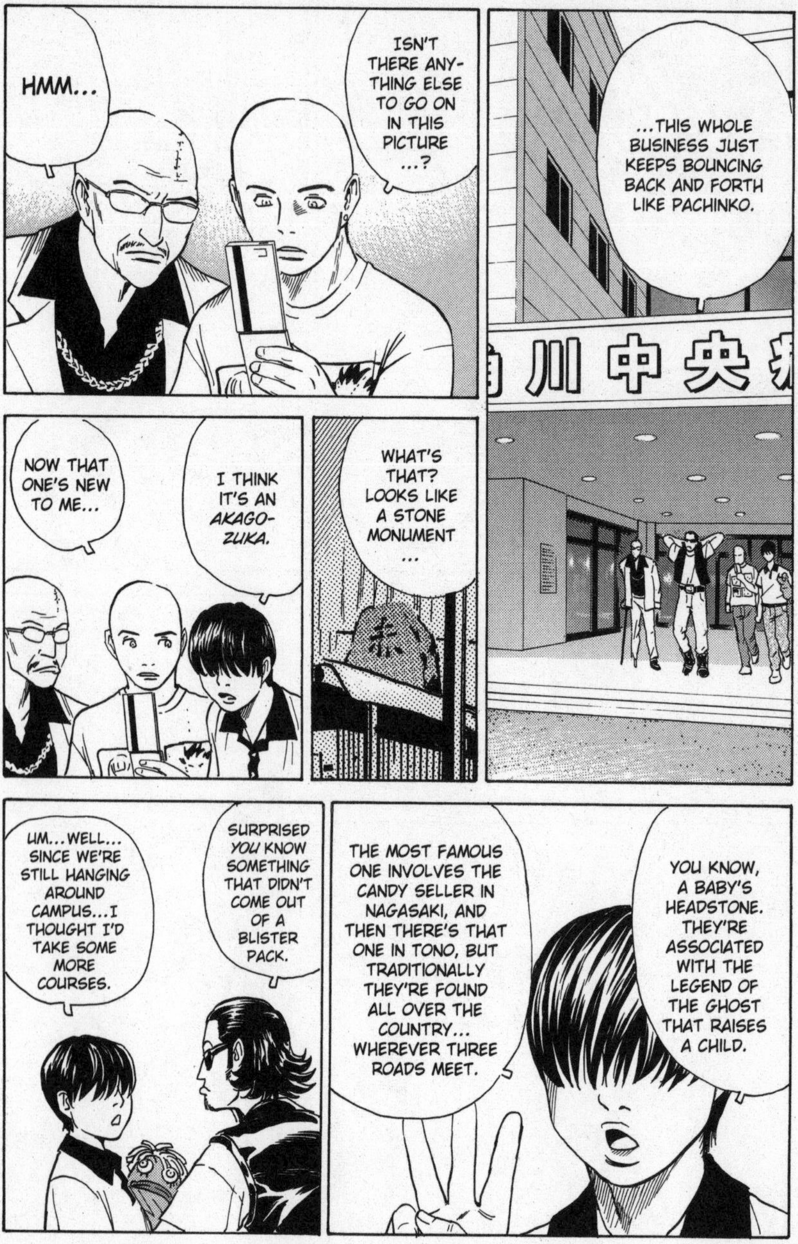
...THIS WHOLE BUSINESS JUST KEEPS BOUNCING BACK AND FORTH LIKE PACHINKO.
ISN'T THERE ANYTHING ELSE TO GO ON IN THIS PICTURE ...?
HMM...
WHAT'S THAT? LOOKS LIKE A STONE MONUMENT ...
I THINK IT'S AN *AKAGO-ZUKA*.
NOW THAT ONE'S NEW TO ME...
YOU KNOW, A BABY'S HEADSTONE. THEY'RE ASSOCIATED WITH THE LEGEND OF THE GHOST THAT RAISES A CHILD.
THE MOST FAMOUS ONE INVOLVES THE CANDY SELLER IN NAGASAKI, AND THEN THERE'S THAT ONE IN TONO, BUT TRADITIONALLY THEY'RE FOUND ALL OVER THE COUNTRY... WHEREVER THREE ROADS MEET.
SURPRISED *YOU* KNOW SOMETHING THAT DIDN'T COME OUT OF A BLISTER PACK.
UM...WELL... SINCE WE'RE STILL HANGING AROUND CAMPUS...I THOUGHT I'D TAKE SOME MORE COURSES.

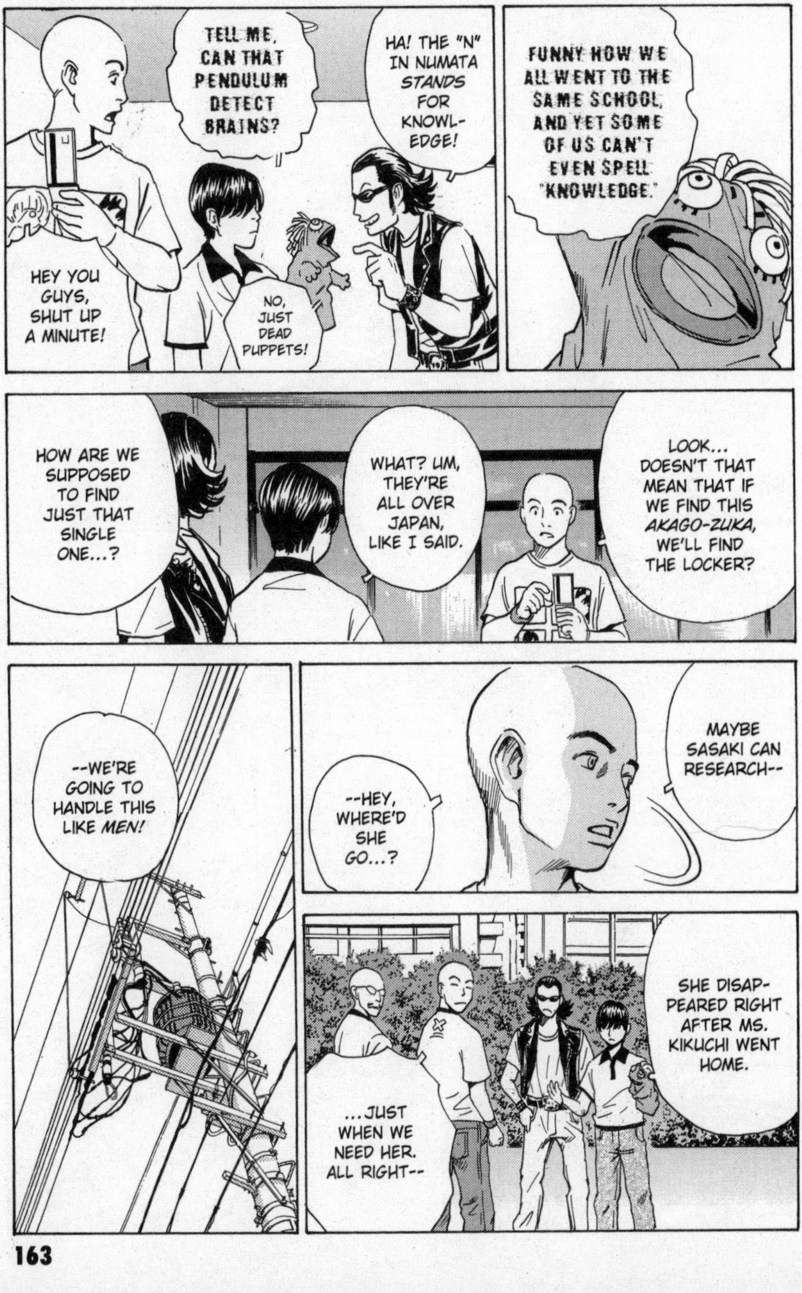
FUNNY HOW WE ALL WENT TO THE SAME SCHOOL, AND YET SOME OF US CAN'T EVEN SPELL "KNOWLEDGE."
HA! THE "N" IN NUMATA *STANDS* FOR KNOWL-EDGE!
TELL ME, CAN THAT PENDULUM DETECT BRAINS?
NO, JUST DEAD PUPPETS!
HEY YOU GUYS, SHUT UP A MINUTE!
LOOK... DOESN'T THAT MEAN THAT IF WE FIND THIS *AKAGO-ZUKA*, WE'LL FIND THE LOCKER?
WHAT? UM, THEY'RE ALL OVER JAPAN, LIKE I SAID.
HOW ARE WE SUPPOSED TO FIND JUST THAT SINGLE ONE...?
MAYBE SASAKI CAN RESEARCH--
--HEY, WHERE'D SHE GO...?
SHE DISAP-PEARED RIGHT AFTER MS. KIKUCHI WENT HOME.
...JUST WHEN WE NEED HER. ALL RIGHT--
--WE'RE GOING TO HANDLE THIS LIKE *MEN!*

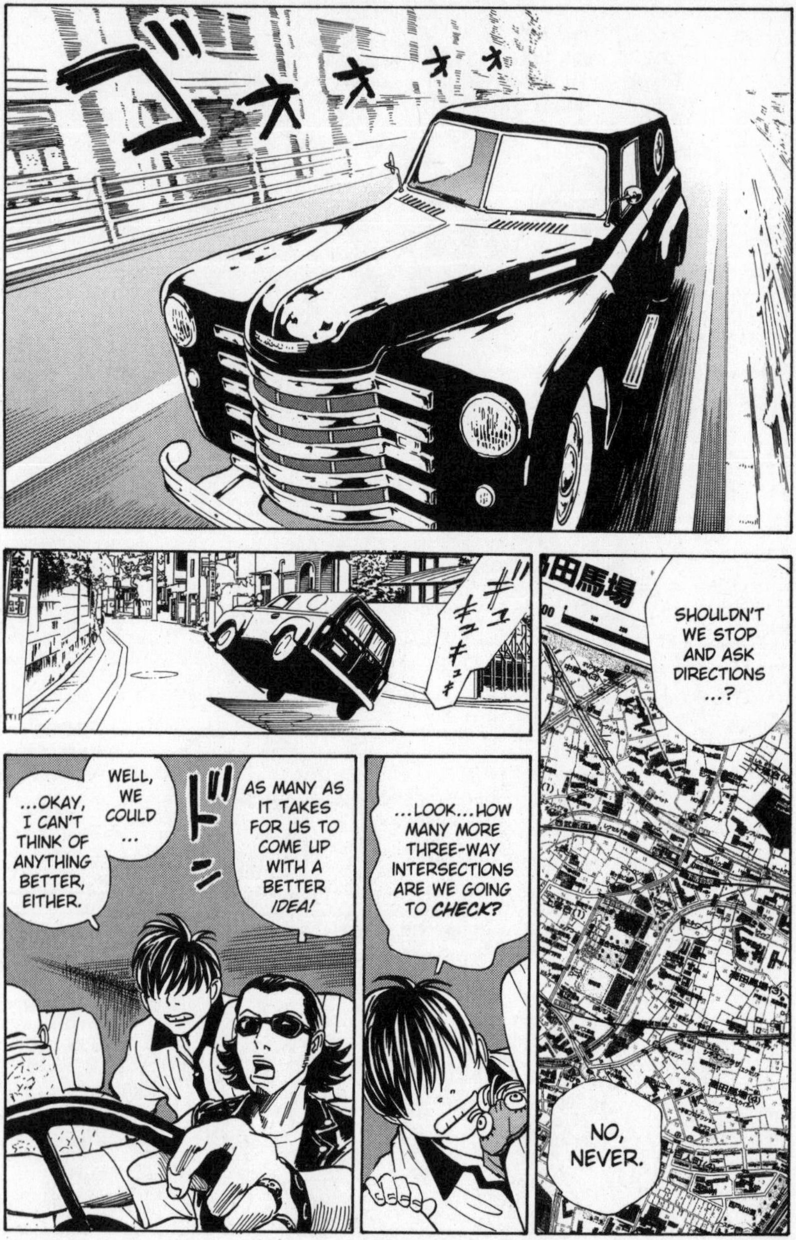
ゴオオオ
高田馬場
SHOULDN'T WE STOP AND ASK DIRECTIONS ...?
NO, NEVER.
ギュキュキュキ
...LOOK...HOW MANY MORE THREE-WAY INTERSECTIONS ARE WE GOING TO *CHECK?*
AS MANY AS IT TAKES FOR US TO COME UP WITH A BETTER *IDEA!*
ドン
WELL, WE COULD ...
...OKAY, I CAN'T THINK OF ANYTHING BETTER, EITHER.

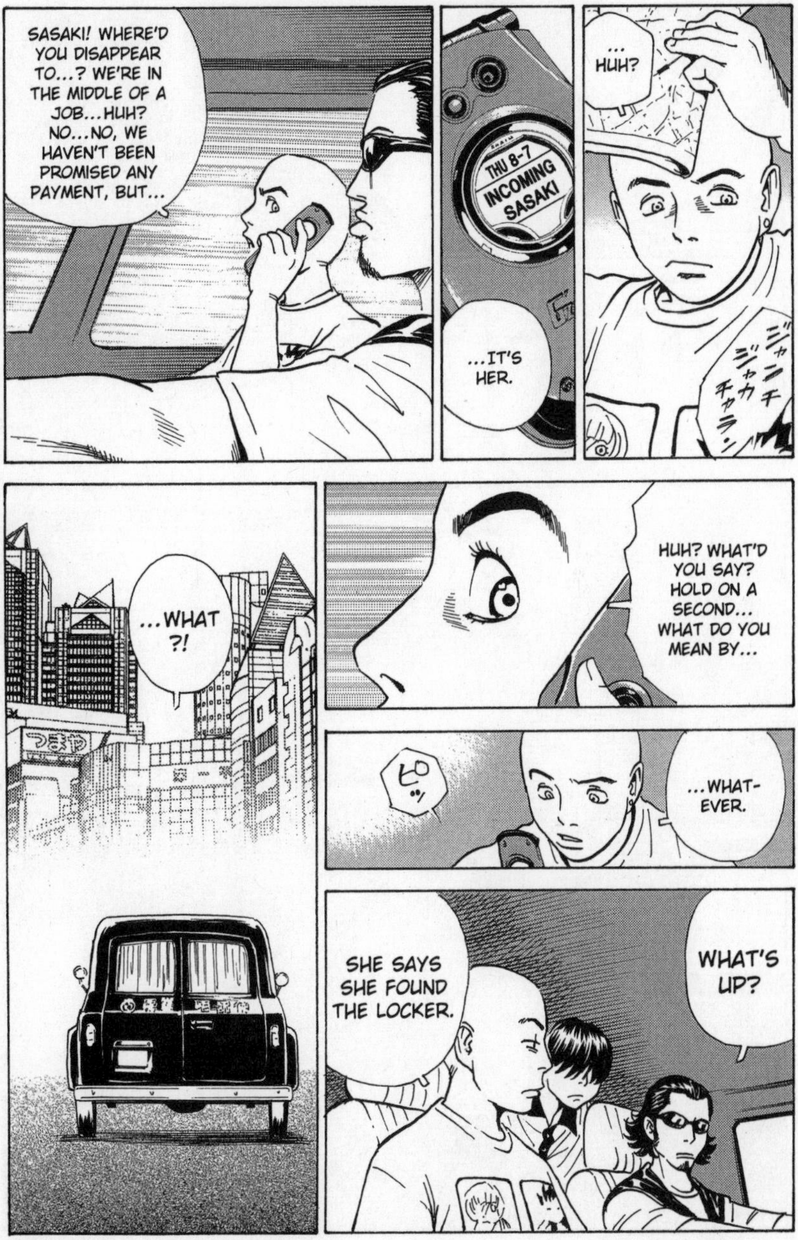
... HUH?
THU 8-7
INCOMING
SASAKI
...IT'S HER.
SASAKI! WHERE'D YOU DISAPPEAR TO...? WE'RE IN THE MIDDLE OF A JOB...HUH? NO...NO, WE HAVEN'T BEEN PROMISED ANY PAYMENT, BUT...
HUH? WHAT'D YOU SAY? HOLD ON A SECOND... WHAT DO YOU MEAN BY...
...WHAT-EVER.
ピッ
WHAT'S UP?
SHE SAYS SHE FOUND THE LOCKER.
...WHAT ?!
つまや

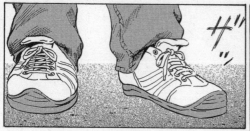

THIS IS THE ADDRESS ...

...NOW WHAT DO WE DO...?

6th delivery: princess's mirror—the end

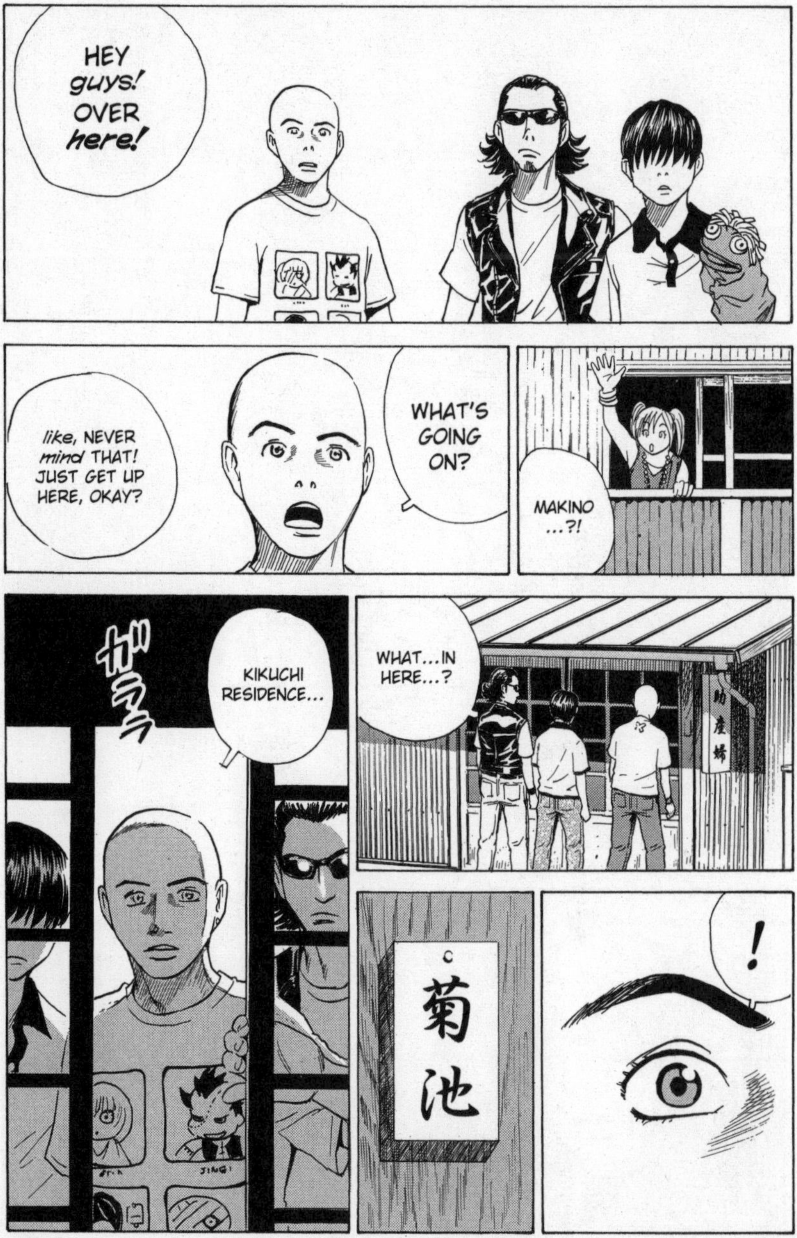
HEY guys! OVER here!
MAKINO ...?!
WHAT'S GOING ON?
like, NEVER mind THAT! JUST GET UP HERE, OKAY?
WHAT...IN HERE...?
助産婦
!
菊池
ガララ
KIKUCHI RESIDENCE...

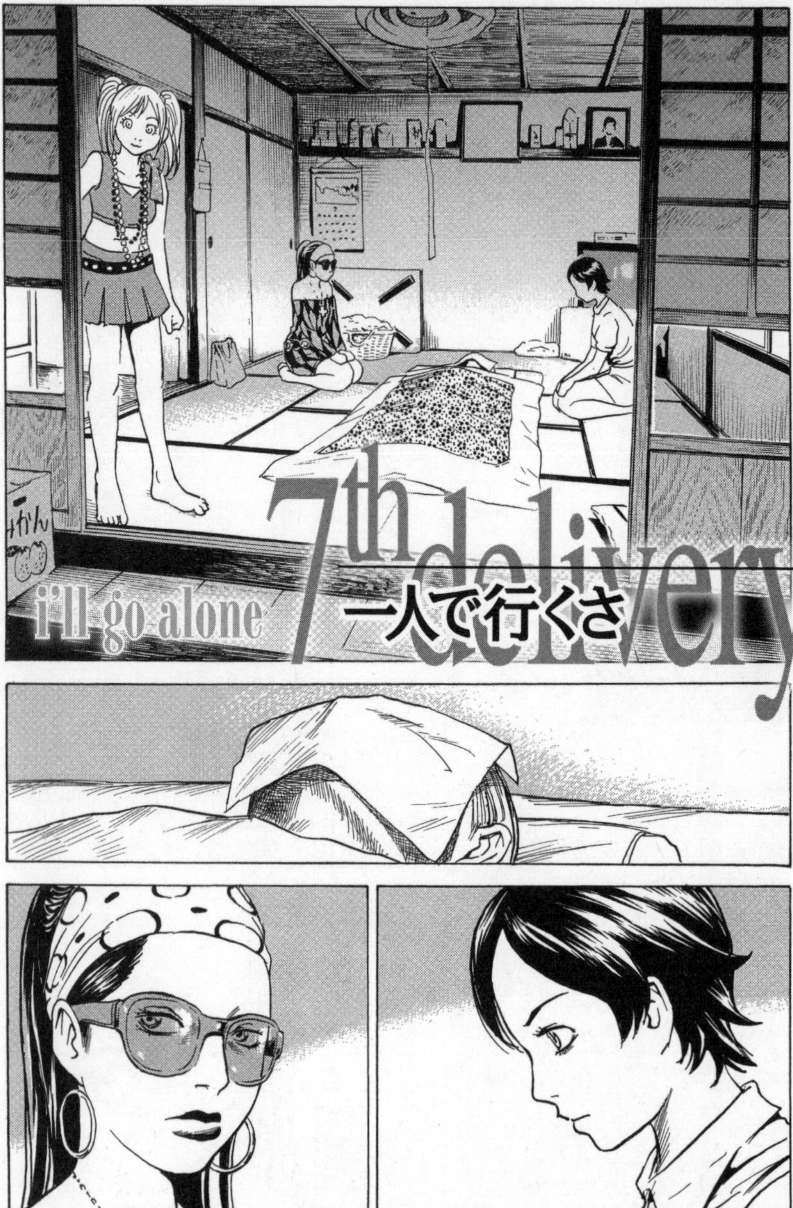

7th delivery
一人で行くさ
i'll go alone
みかん

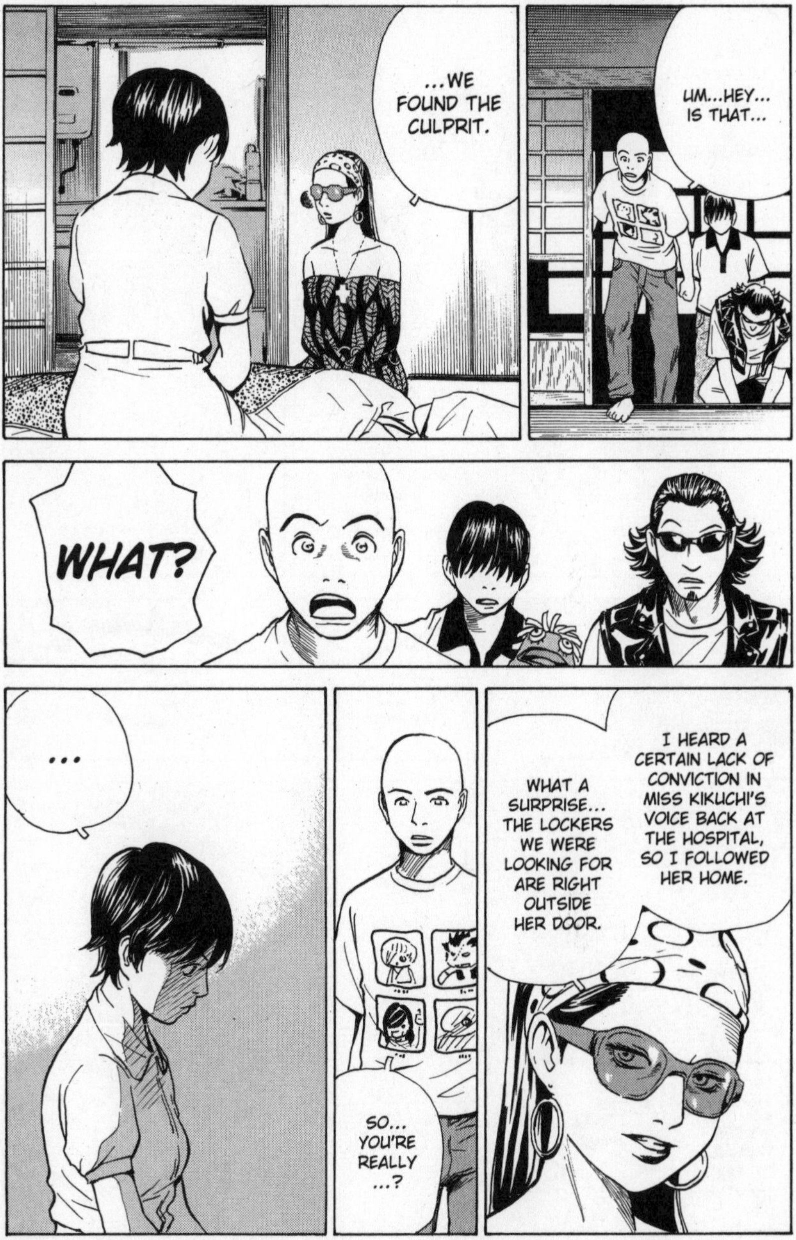
UM...HEY... IS THAT...
...WE FOUND THE CULPRIT.
WHAT?
I HEARD A CERTAIN LACK OF CONVICTION IN MISS KIKUCHI'S VOICE BACK AT THE HOSPITAL, SO I FOLLOWED HER HOME.
WHAT A SURPRISE... THE LOCKERS WE WERE LOOKING FOR ARE RIGHT OUTSIDE HER DOOR.
SO... YOU'RE REALLY ...?
...

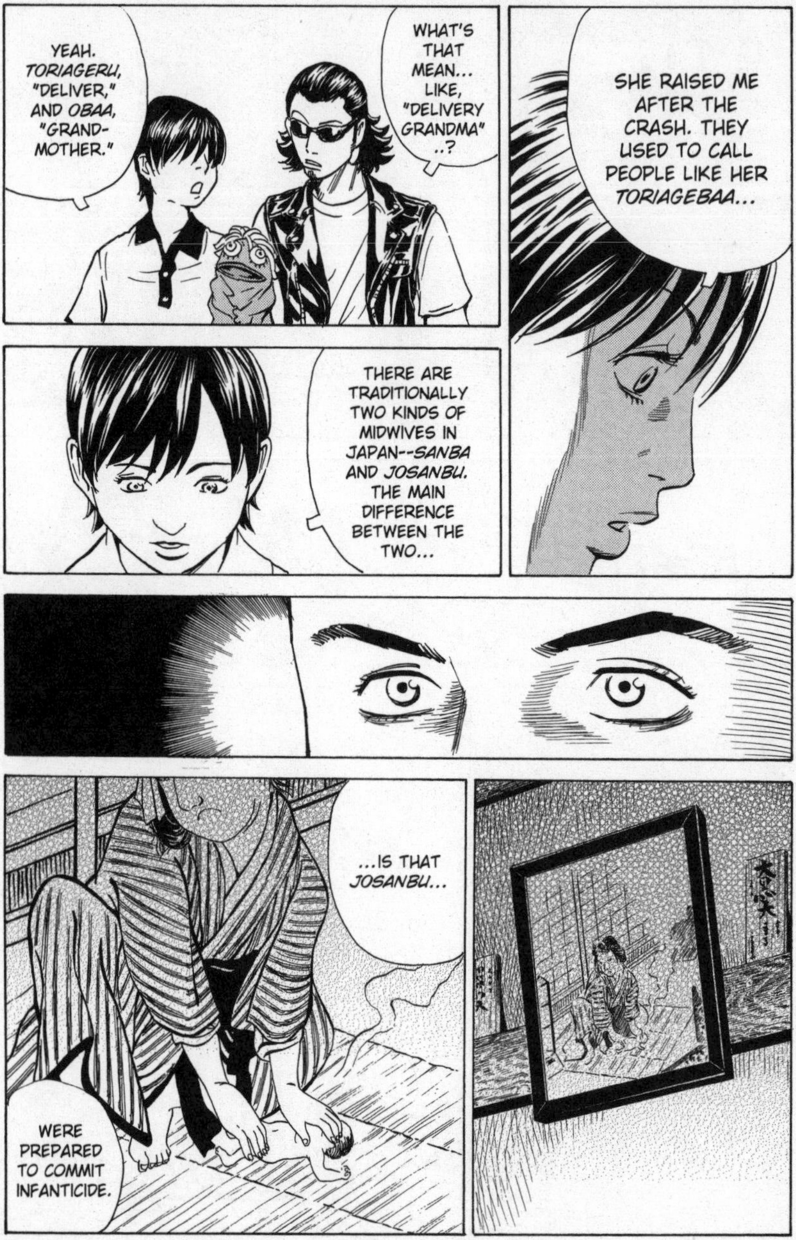
SHE RAISED ME AFTER THE CRASH. THEY USED TO CALL PEOPLE LIKE HER *TORIAGEBAA*...
WHAT'S THAT MEAN... LIKE, "DELIVERY GRANDMA" ..?
YEAH. *TORIAGERU*, "DELIVER," AND *OBAA*, "GRAND-MOTHER."
THERE ARE TRADITIONALLY TWO KINDS OF MIDWIVES IN JAPAN--*SANBA* AND *JOSANBU*. THE MAIN DIFFERENCE BETWEEN THE TWO...
...IS THAT *JOSANBU*...
WERE PREPARED TO COMMIT INFANTICIDE.

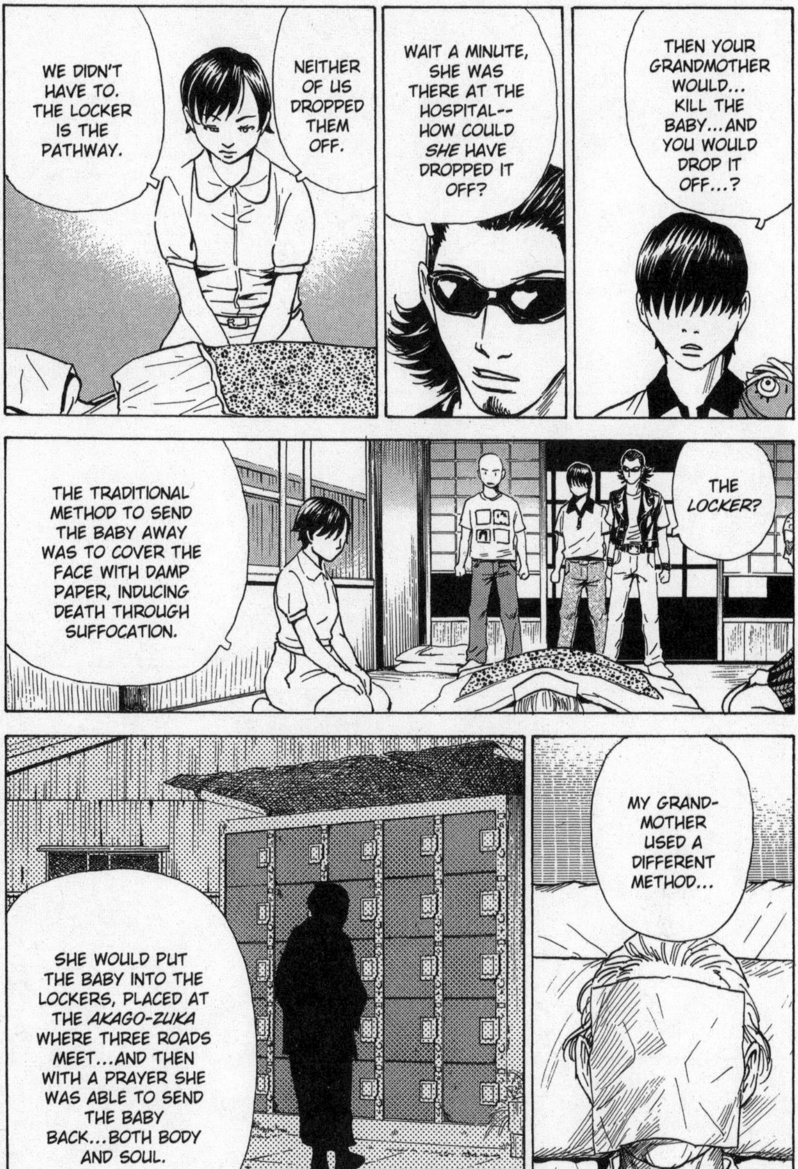
THEN YOUR GRANDMOTHER WOULD... KILL THE BABY...AND YOU WOULD DROP IT OFF...?
WAIT A MINUTE, SHE WAS THERE AT THE HOSPITAL--HOW COULD *SHE* HAVE DROPPED IT OFF?
NEITHER OF US DROPPED THEM OFF.
WE DIDN'T HAVE TO. THE LOCKER IS THE PATHWAY.
THE *LOCKER?*
THE TRADITIONAL METHOD TO SEND THE BABY AWAY WAS TO COVER THE FACE WITH DAMP PAPER, INDUCING DEATH THROUGH SUFFOCATION.
MY GRAND-MOTHER USED A DIFFERENT METHOD...
SHE WOULD PUT THE BABY INTO THE LOCKERS, PLACED AT THE *AKAGO-ZUKA* WHERE THREE ROADS MEET...AND THEN WITH A PRAYER SHE WAS ABLE TO SEND THE BABY BACK...BOTH BODY AND SOUL.

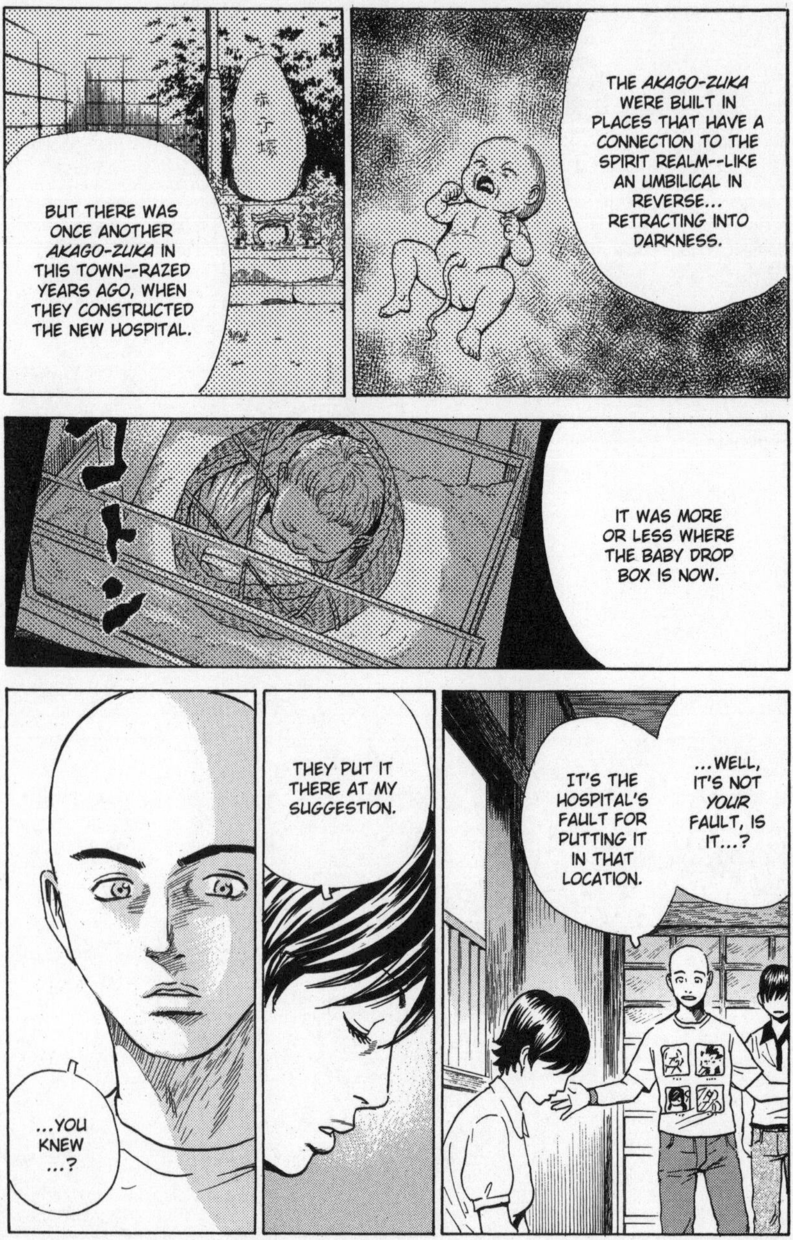

THE AKAGO-ZUKA WERE BUILT IN PLACES THAT HAVE A CONNECTION TO THE SPIRIT REALM--LIKE AN UMBILICAL IN REVERSE... RETRACTING INTO DARKNESS.
赤子塚
BUT THERE WAS ONCE ANOTHER AKAGO-ZUKA IN THIS TOWN--RAZED YEARS AGO, WHEN THEY CONSTRUCTED THE NEW HOSPITAL.
IT WAS MORE OR LESS WHERE THE BABY DROP BOX IS NOW.
ゴトン
...WELL, IT'S NOT YOUR FAULT, IS IT...?
IT'S THE HOSPITAL'S FAULT FOR PUTTING IT IN THAT LOCATION.
THEY PUT IT THERE AT MY SUGGESTION.
...YOU KNEW ...?

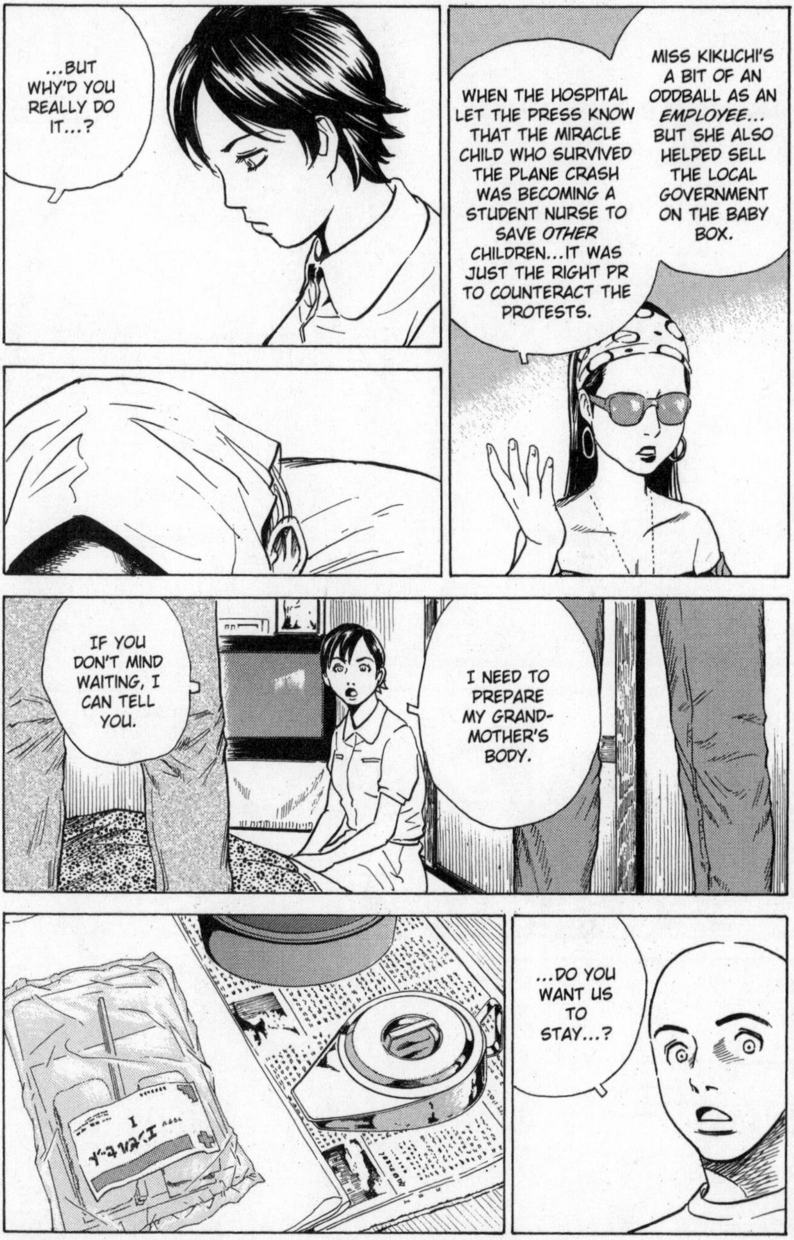
MISS KIKUCHI'S A BIT OF AN ODDBALL AS AN *EMPLOYEE*... BUT SHE ALSO HELPED SELL THE LOCAL GOVERNMENT ON THE BABY BOX.
WHEN THE HOSPITAL LET THE PRESS KNOW THAT THE MIRACLE CHILD WHO SURVIVED THE PLANE CRASH WAS BECOMING A STUDENT NURSE TO SAVE *OTHER* CHILDREN...IT WAS JUST THE RIGHT PR TO COUNTERACT THE PROTESTS.
...BUT WHY'D YOU REALLY DO IT...?
I NEED TO PREPARE MY GRAND-MOTHER'S BODY.
IF YOU DON'T MIND WAITING, I CAN TELL YOU.
...DO YOU WANT US TO STAY...?

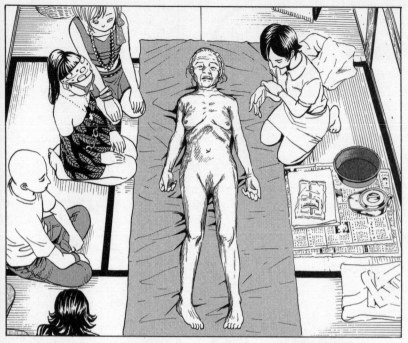

174

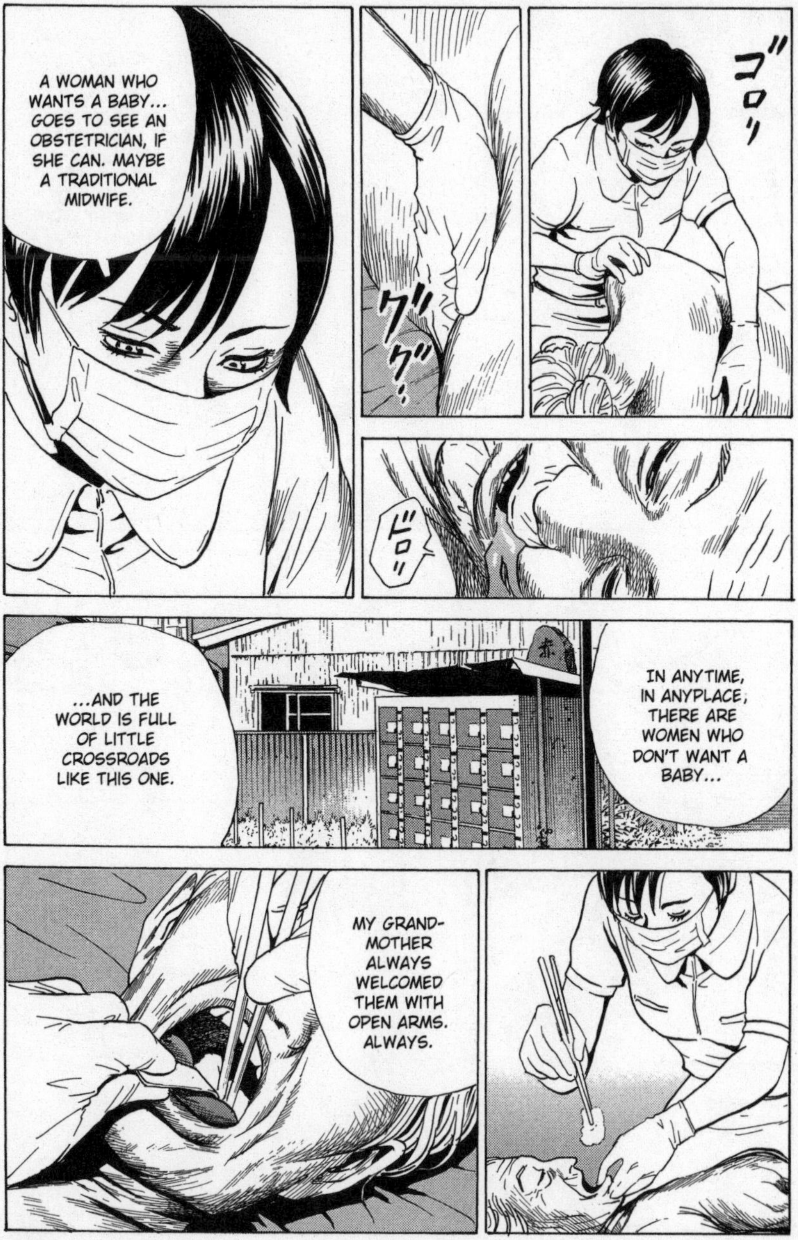
ゴロリ
グググ
ドロッ
A WOMAN WHO WANTS A BABY... GOES TO SEE AN OBSTETRICIAN, IF SHE CAN. MAYBE A TRADITIONAL MIDWIFE.
IN ANYTIME, IN ANYPLACE, THERE ARE WOMEN WHO DON'T WANT A BABY...
...AND THE WORLD IS FULL OF LITTLE CROSSROADS LIKE THIS ONE.
MY GRAND-MOTHER ALWAYS WELCOMED THEM WITH OPEN ARMS. ALWAYS.

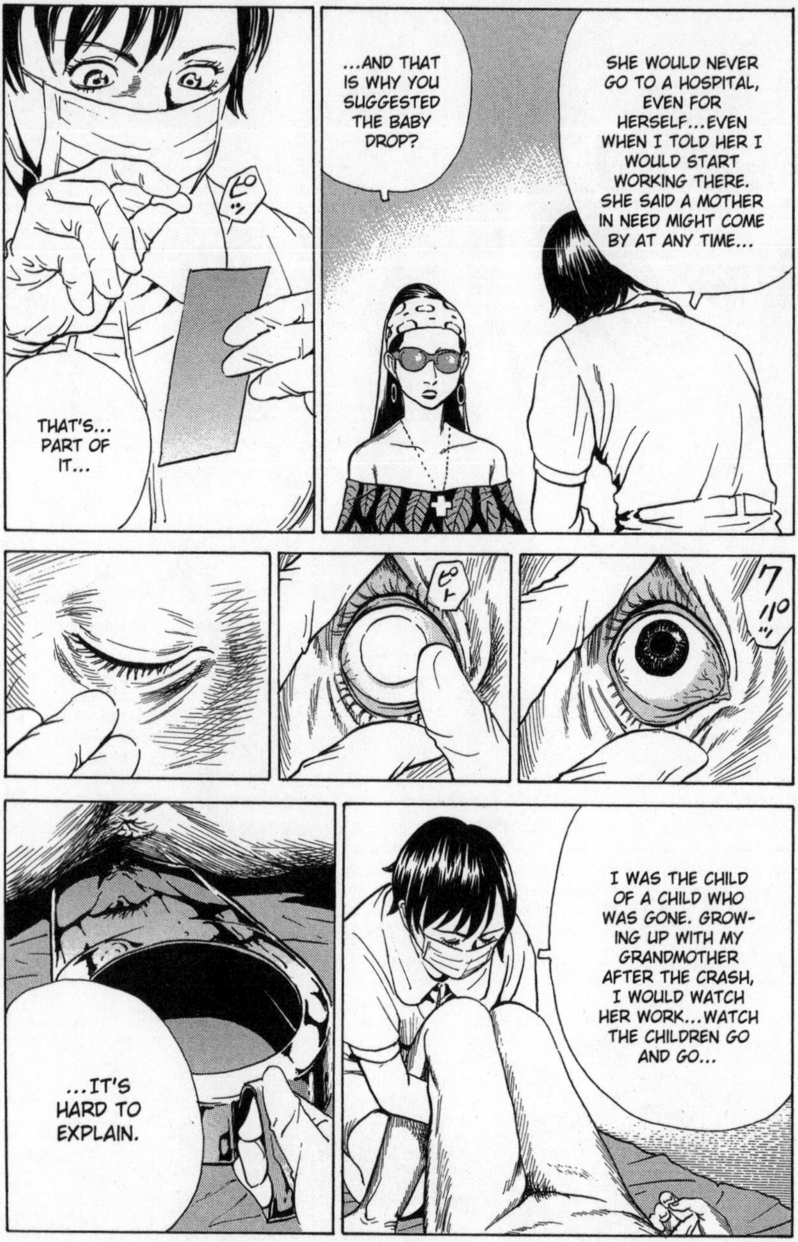
SHE WOULD NEVER GO TO A HOSPITAL, EVEN FOR HERSELF...EVEN WHEN I TOLD HER I WOULD START WORKING THERE. SHE SAID A MOTHER IN NEED MIGHT COME BY AT ANY TIME...
...AND THAT IS WHY YOU SUGGESTED THE BABY DROP?
ピッ
THAT'S... PART OF IT...
クパッ
ピト
I WAS THE CHILD OF A CHILD WHO WAS GONE. GROWING UP WITH MY GRANDMOTHER AFTER THE CRASH, I WOULD WATCH HER WORK...WATCH THE CHILDREN GO AND GO...
...IT'S HARD TO EXPLAIN.

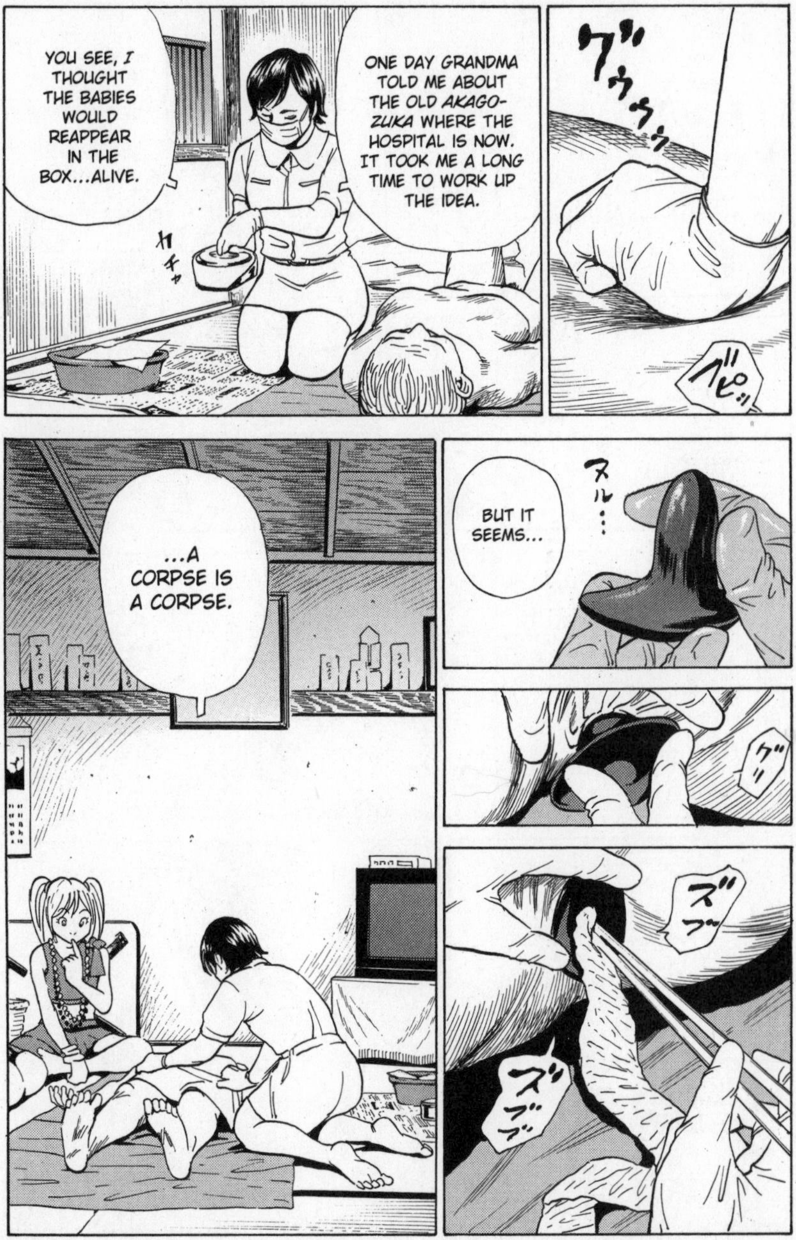
グゥゥゥ
ペピッ
ONE DAY GRANDMA TOLD ME ABOUT THE OLD *AKAGO-ZUKA* WHERE THE HOSPITAL IS NOW. IT TOOK ME A LONG TIME TO WORK UP THE IDEA.
YOU SEE, *I* THOUGHT THE BABIES WOULD REAPPEAR IN THE BOX...ALIVE.
カチャ
ヌル…
BUT IT SEEMS...
グッ
ズブ
ズブブ
...A CORPSE IS A CORPSE.

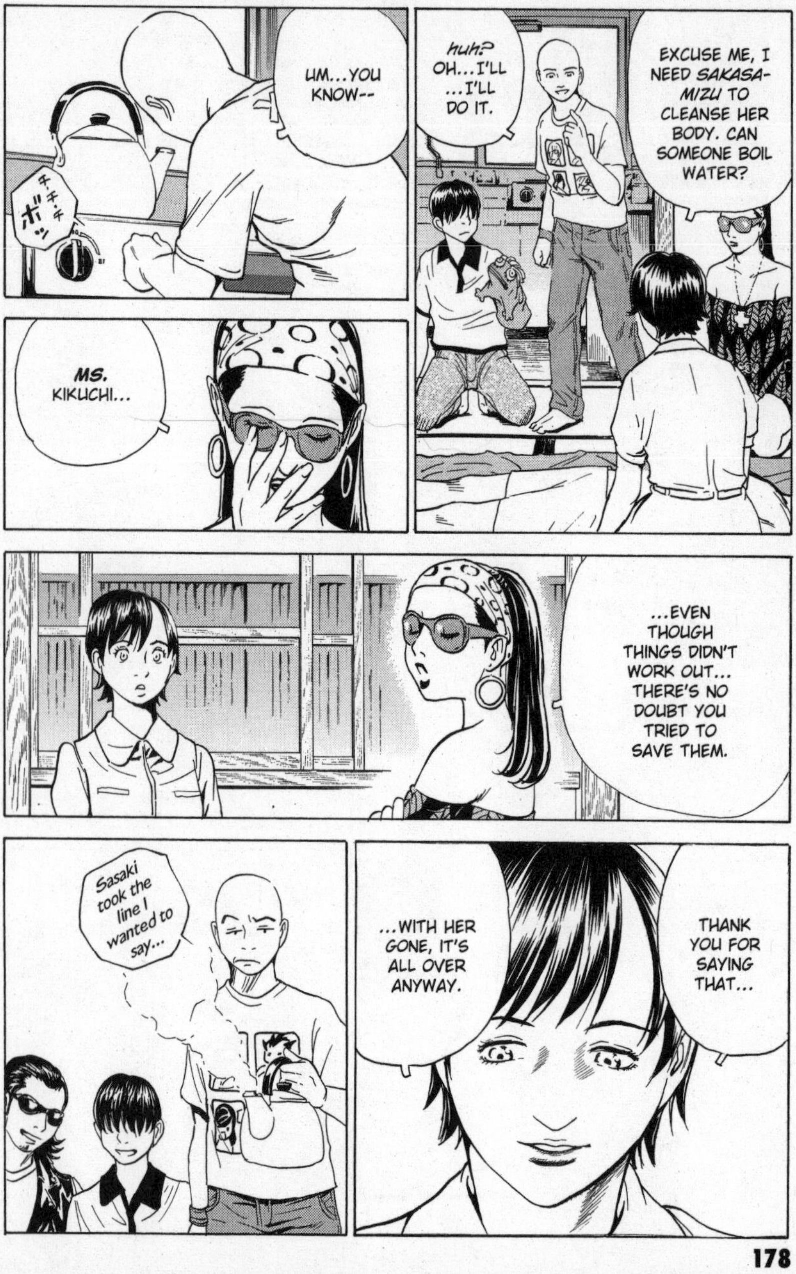
EXCUSE ME, I NEED *SAKASA-MIZU* TO CLEANSE HER BODY. CAN SOMEONE BOIL WATER?
huh? OH...I'LL ...I'LL DO IT.
UM...YOU KNOW--
チ・チ・チ
ボッ
MS. KIKUCHI...
...EVEN THOUGH THINGS DIDN'T WORK OUT... THERE'S NO DOUBT YOU TRIED TO SAVE THEM.
THANK YOU FOR SAYING THAT...
...WITH HER GONE, IT'S ALL OVER ANYWAY.
Sasaki took the line I wanted to say...

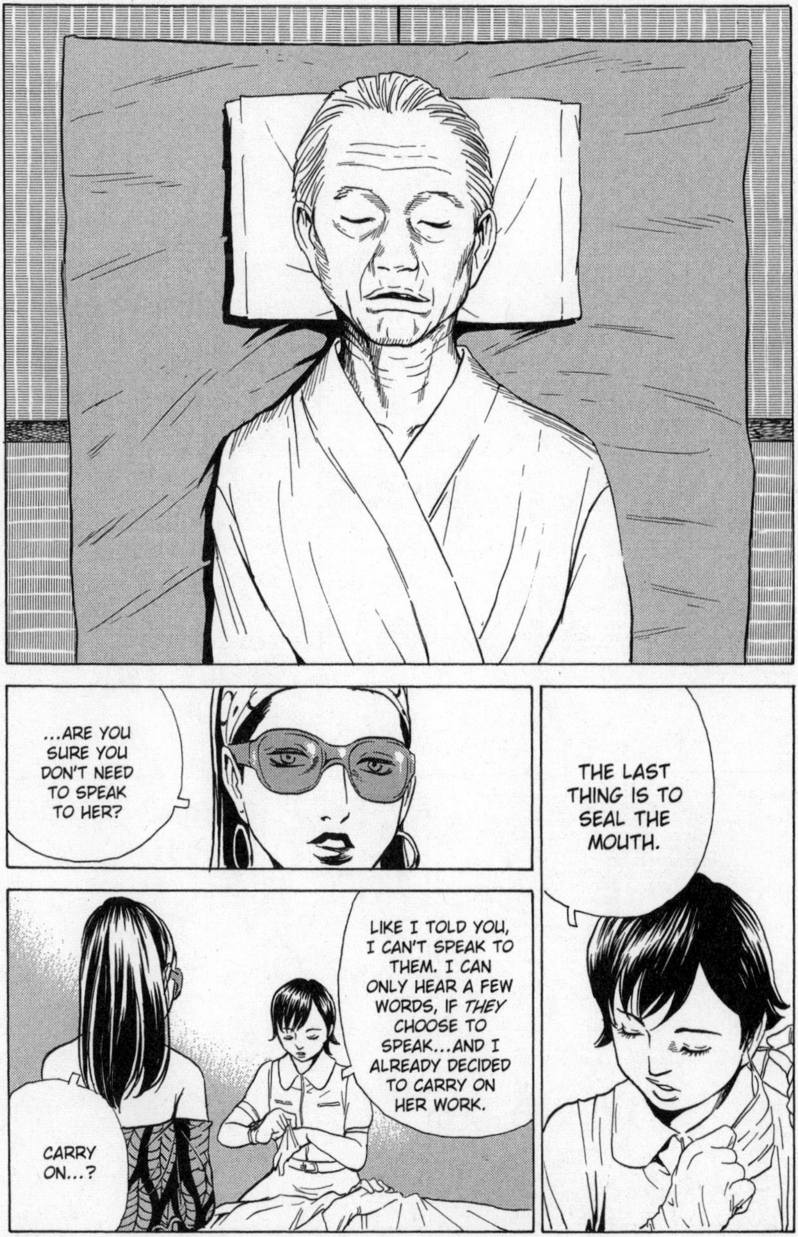
THE LAST THING IS TO SEAL THE MOUTH.
...ARE YOU SURE YOU DON'T NEED TO SPEAK TO HER?
LIKE I TOLD YOU, I CAN'T SPEAK TO THEM. I CAN ONLY HEAR A FEW WORDS, IF *THEY* CHOOSE TO SPEAK...AND I ALREADY DECIDED TO CARRY ON HER WORK.
CARRY ON...?

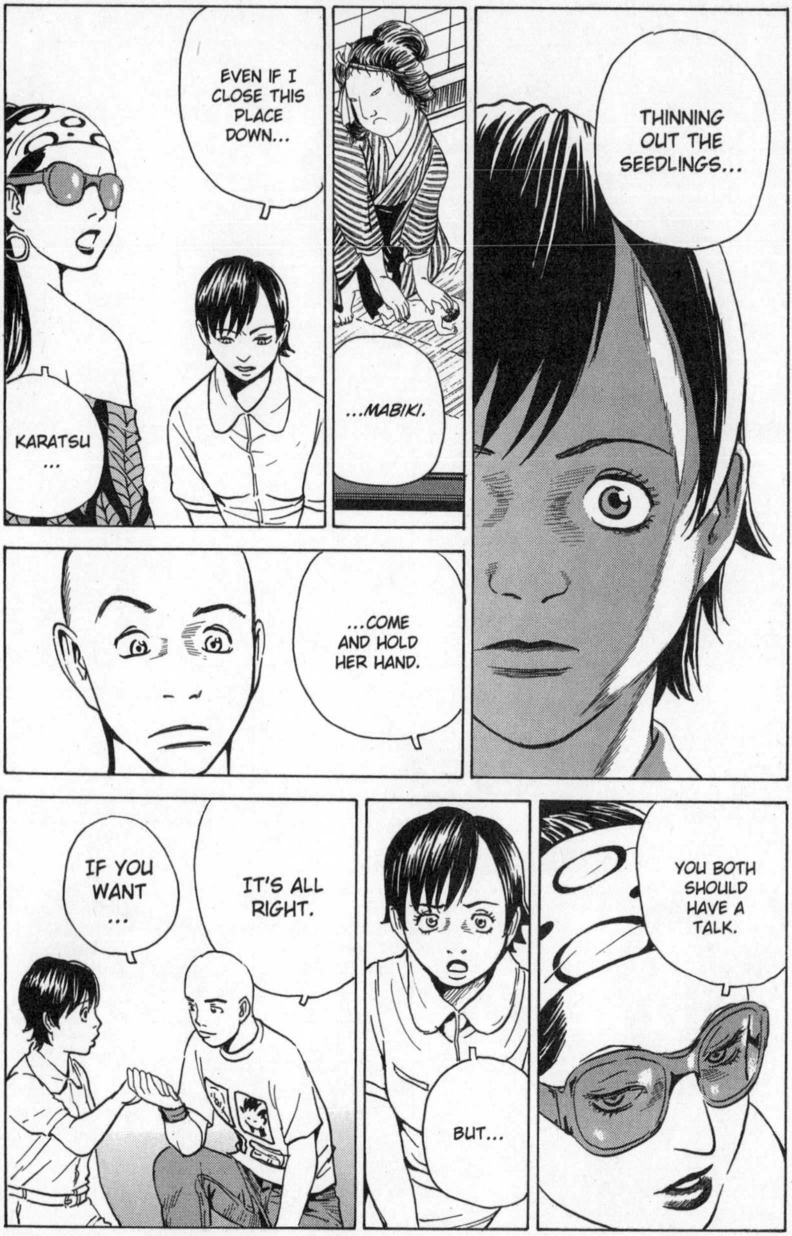
THINNING OUT THE SEEDLINGS...
...MABIKI.
EVEN IF I CLOSE THIS PLACE DOWN...
KARATSU ...
...COME AND HOLD HER HAND.
YOU BOTH SHOULD HAVE A TALK.
BUT...
IT'S ALL RIGHT.
IF YOU WANT ...

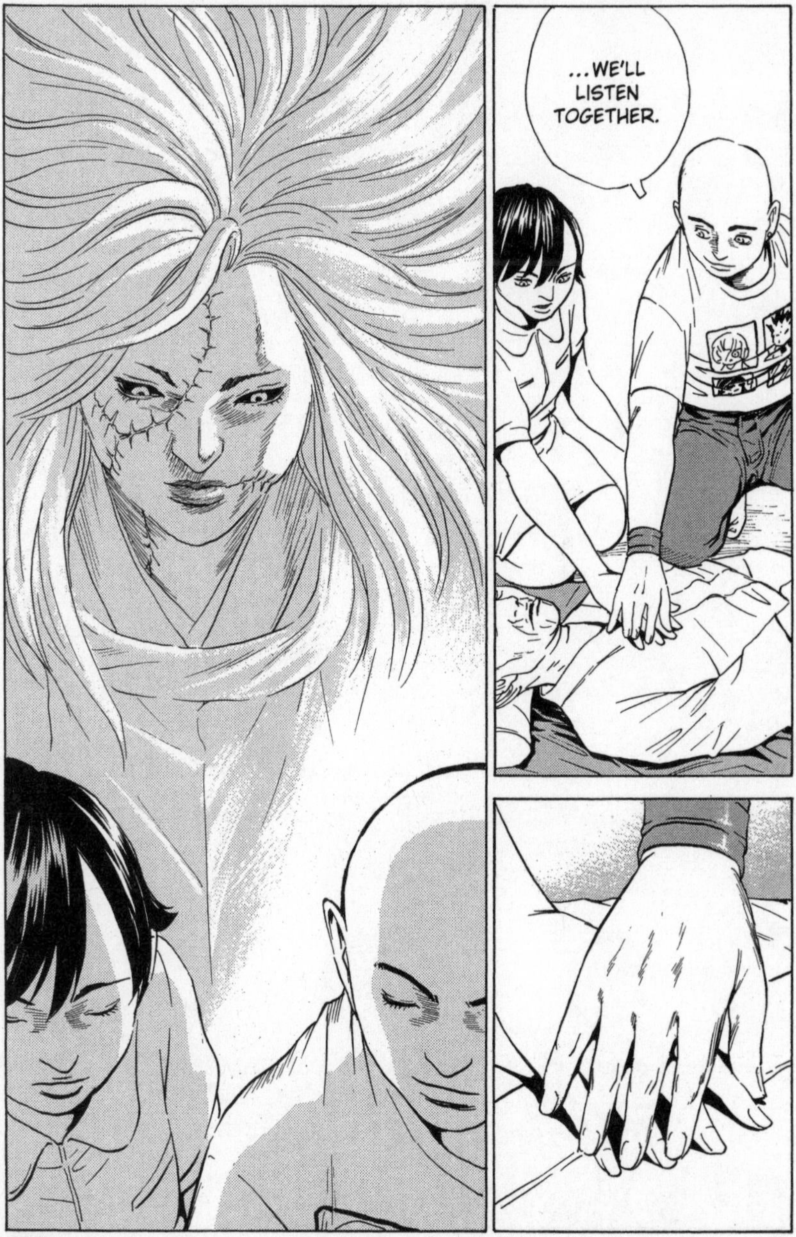
...WE'LL
LISTEN
TOGETHER.

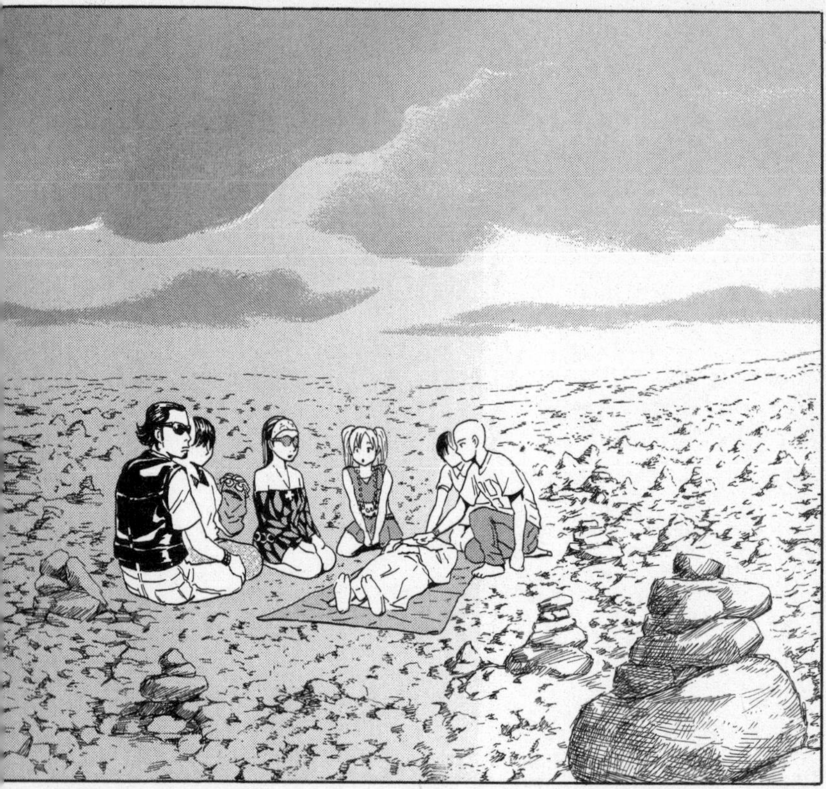

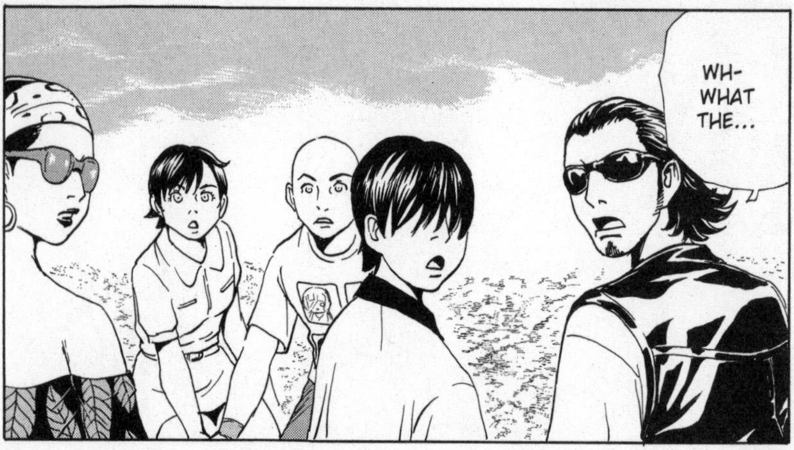
WH-
WHAT
THE...

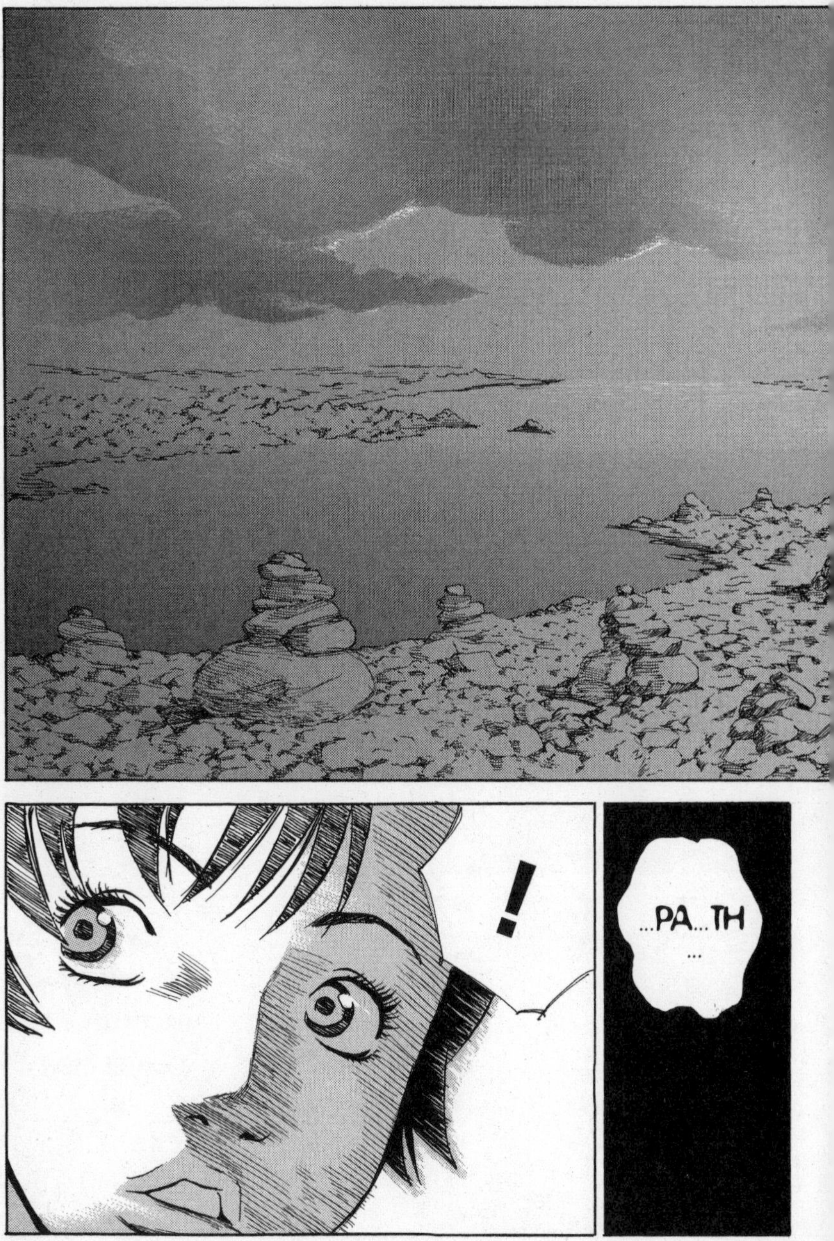
...PA...TH ...
!

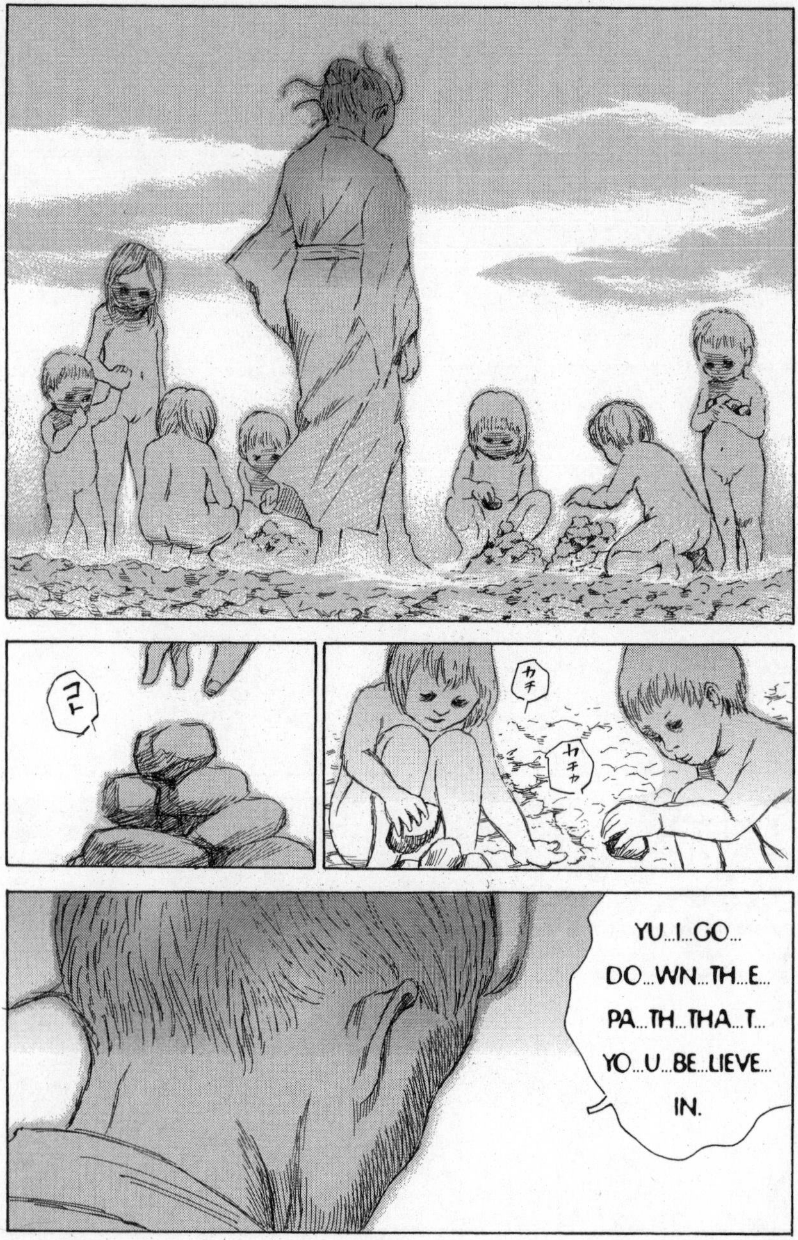
カチ
カチャ
コト
YU...I...GO... DO...WN...TH...E... PA...TH...THA...T... YO...U...BE...LIEVE... IN.

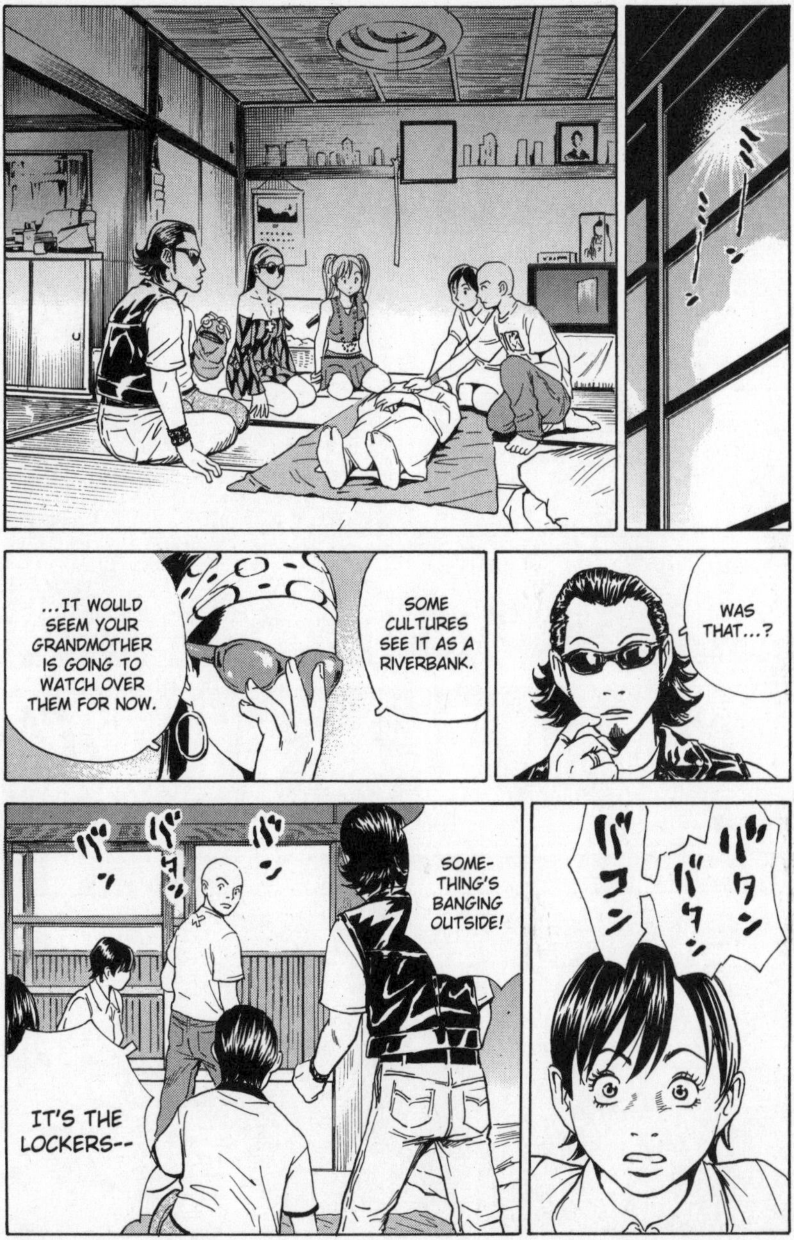
ミーン
ミーン
WAS THAT...?
SOME CULTURES SEE IT AS A RIVERBANK.
...IT WOULD SEEM YOUR GRANDMOTHER IS GOING TO WATCH OVER THEM FOR NOW.
バタン
バタン
バコン
バン
バタン
SOME-THING'S BANGING OUTSIDE!
IT'S THE LOCKERS--

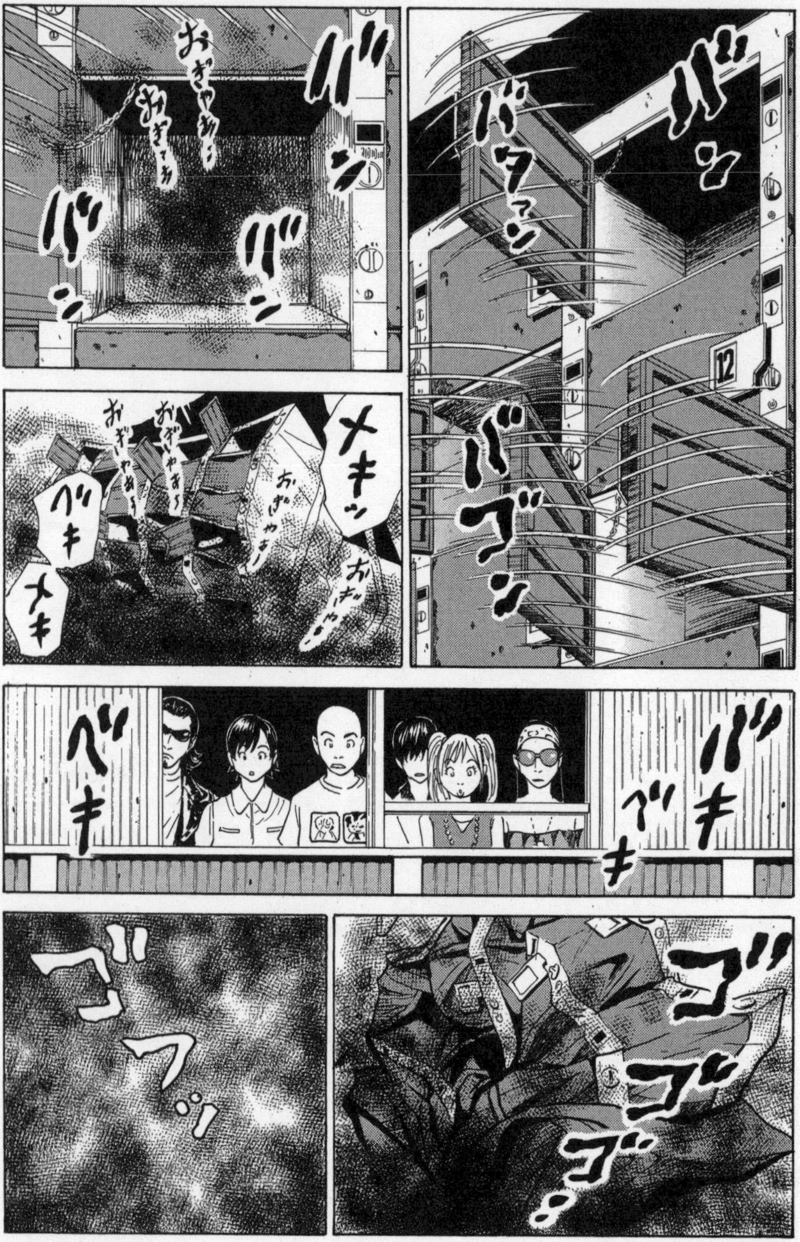
バン
バタアン
バゴン
バン
おぎゃあ〜
おぎゃあ〜
バン
バン
メキッ
おぎゃあ〜
おぎゃあ〜
おぎゃあ〜
おぎゃあ〜
ベキ
メキ
バキ
バキ
ベキ
ゴゴゴ…
ゴフッ

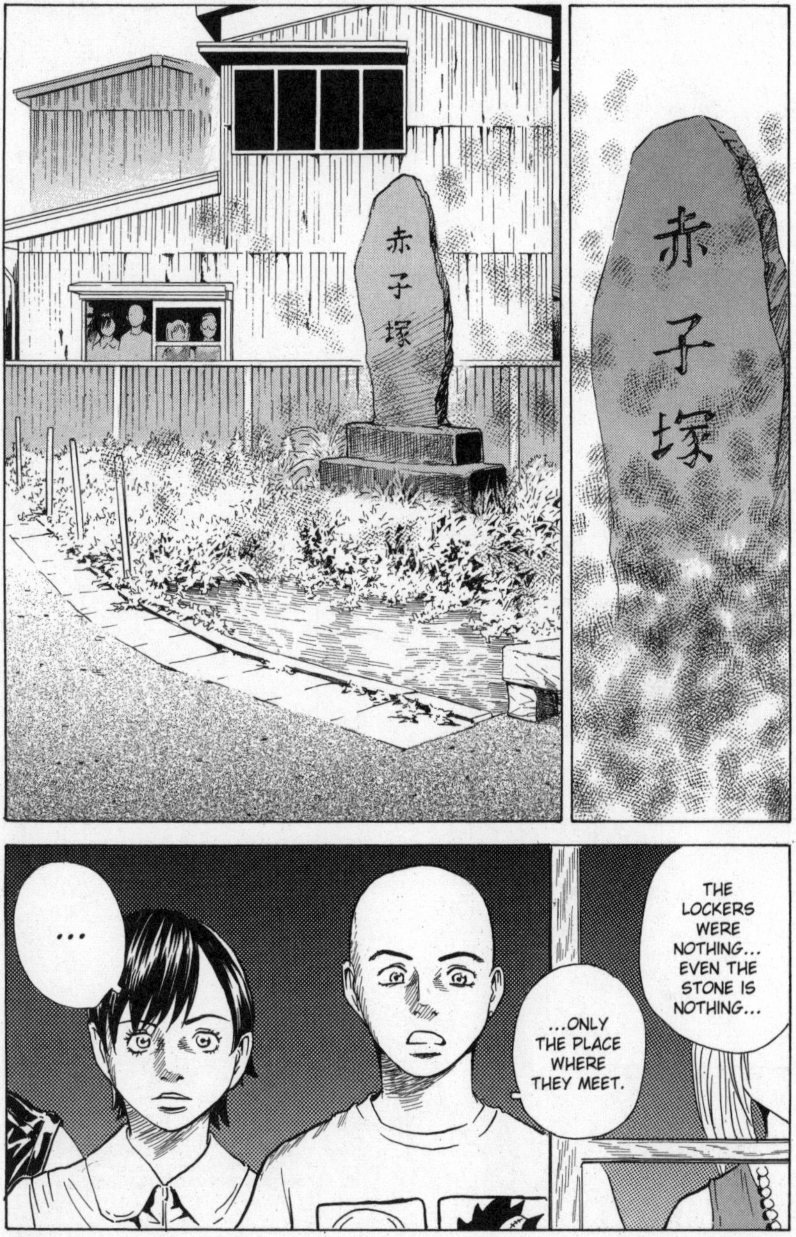
赤子塚
赤子塚
THE LOCKERS WERE NOTHING... EVEN THE STONE IS NOTHING...
...ONLY THE PLACE WHERE THEY MEET.
...

THANK YOU FOR DRIVING ME BACK.

UM...ARE YOU GOING TO BE ALL RIGHT?

...I KEEP TRYING, BUT I STILL DON'T REALLY KNOW.

HOW TO FACE DEATH, I MEAN. IT'S SOMETHING A NURSE *SHOULD* KNOW...DON'T YOU THINK...?

川中央病院

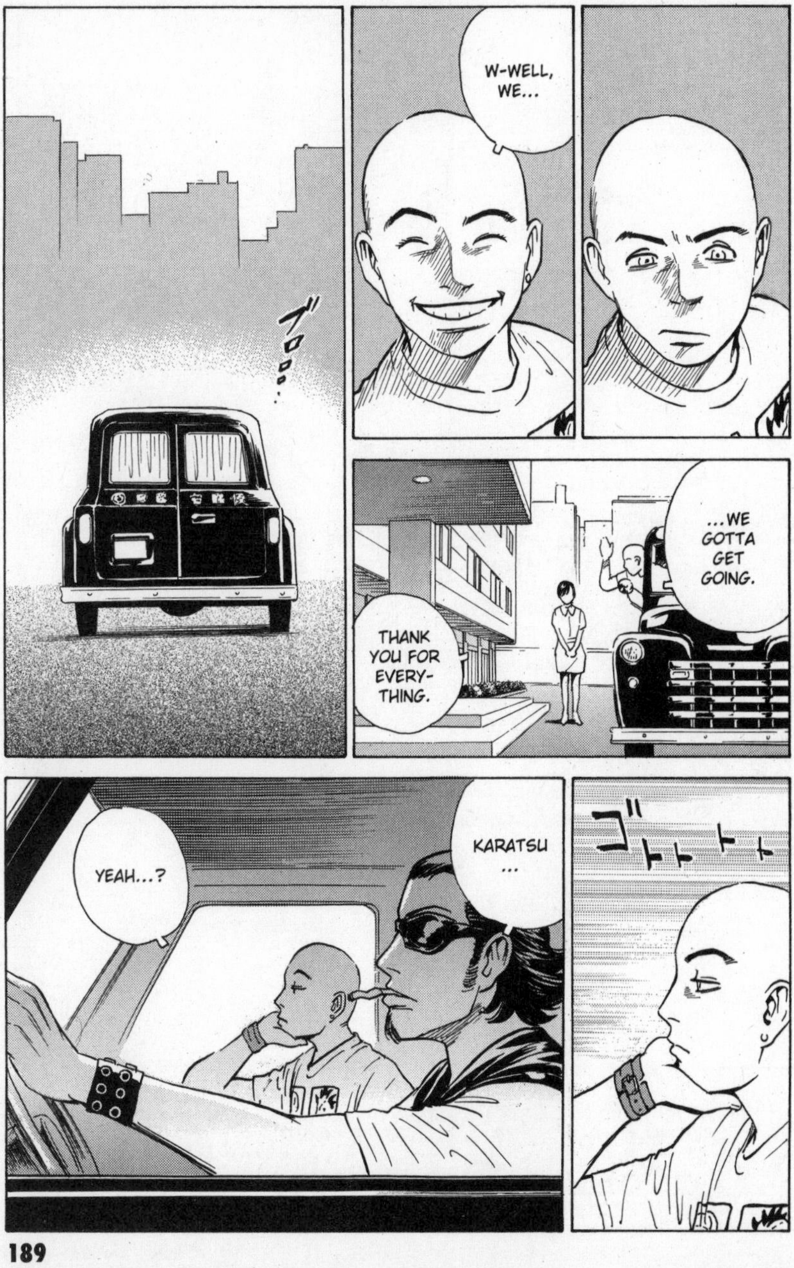
W-WELL, WE...
...WE GOTTA GET GOING.
THANK YOU FOR EVERYTHING.
ブロロロ...
ゴトトトト
KARATSU...
YEAH...?

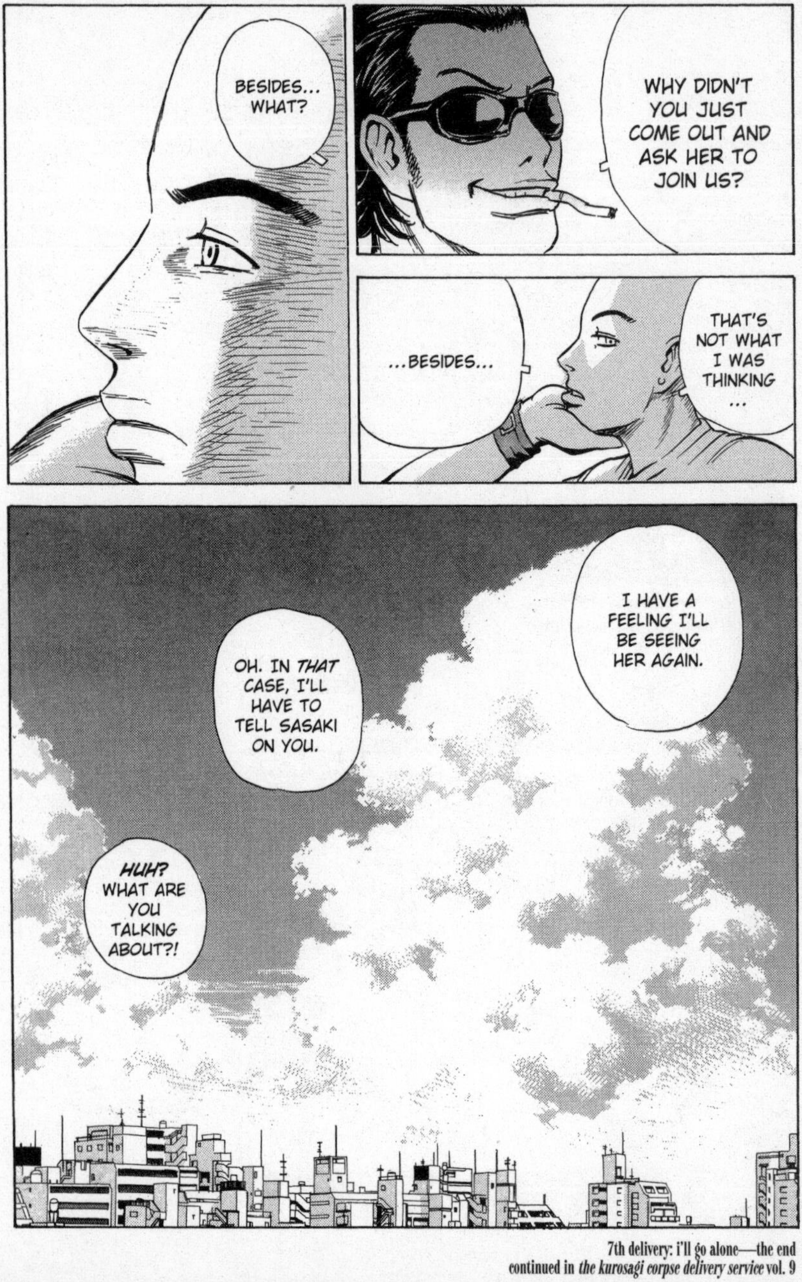
WHY DIDN'T YOU JUST COME OUT AND ASK HER TO JOIN US?
THAT'S NOT WHAT I WAS THINKING ...
...BESIDES...
BESIDES... WHAT?
I HAVE A FEELING I'LL BE SEEING HER AGAIN.
OH. IN *THAT* CASE, I'LL HAVE TO TELL SASAKI ON YOU.
HUH? WHAT ARE YOU TALKING ABOUT?!

7th delivery: i'll go alone—the end

continued in *the kurosagi corpse delivery service* vol. 9

DISJECTA MEMBRA

SOUND FX GLOSSARY AND NOTES ON KUROSAGI VOL. 8 BY TOSHIFUMI YOSHIDA
introduction and additional comments by the editor

TO INCREASE YOUR ENJOYMENT of the distinctive Japanese visual style of this manga, we've included a guide to the sound effects (or "FX") used in this manga. It is suggested the reader *not* constantly consult this glossary as they read through, but regard it as supplemental information, in the manner of footnotes, or perhaps one of those nutritional supplements, the kind that's long and difficult to swallow. If you want to imagine it being read aloud by Osaka, after the manner of her lecture to Sakaki on hemorrhoids in episode five of *Azumanga Daioh*, please go right ahead. In either Yuki Matsuoka or Kira Vincent-Davis's voice—I like them both.

Japanese, like English, did not independently invent its own writing system, but instead borrowed and modified the system used by the then-dominant cultural power in its part of the world. We still call the letters we use to write English today the "Roman" alphabet, for the simple reason that about 1,600 years ago, the earliest English speakers, living on the frontier of the Roman Empire, began to use the same letters the Romans used for their Latin language to write out English.

Around that very same time, on the other side of the planet, Japan, like England, was another example of an island civilization lying across the sea from a great empire—in this case, that of China. Likewise, the Japanese borrowed from the Chinese writing system, which then, as now, consisted of thousands of complex symbols—today in China officially referred to in the Roman alphabet as *hanzi*, but which the Japanese

pronounce as *kanji*. For example, all the Japanese characters you see on the front cover of *The Kurosagi Corpse Delivery Service*—the seven which make up the original title and the four each which make up the creators' names—are examples of kanji. Of course, all of them were hanzi first—although the Japanese did also invent some original kanji of their own, just as new hanzi have been created over the centuries as Chinese evolved.

(Note that whereas both "kanji" and "hanzi" are examples of foreign words written in Roman letters, "kanji" gives English speakers a fairly good idea of how the Japanese word is really pronounced—*khan-gee*—whereas "hanzi" does not—in Mandarin Chinese it sounds something like *n-tsuh*. The reason is fairly simple: whereas the most commonly used method of writing Japanese in Roman letters, the Hepburn system, was developed by a native English speaker, the most commonly used method of writing Chinese in Roman letters, called the Pinyin system, was developed by native Mandarin speakers. In fact, Pinyin was developed to help teach Mandarin pronunciation to speakers of other Chinese dialects; unlike Hepburn, it was not intended as a learning tool for English speakers per se, and hence has no particular obligation to "make sense" to English speakers or, indeed, to users of the many other languages spelled with the Roman alphabet.)

Whereas the various dialects of Chinese are written entirely in hanzi, it is impractical to render the Japanese language entirely in them. To compare once more, English is a notoriously difficult language in which to spell properly, and this is in part because it uses an alphabet designed for another language, Latin, whose sounds are different (this is, of course, putting aside the fact the sounds of both languages experienced change over time). The challenges the Japanese faced in using the Chinese writing system for their own language were even greater, for whereas spoken English and Latin are at least from a common language family, spoken Japanese is unrelated to any of the various dialects of spoken Chinese. The complicated writing system the Japanese evolved represents an adjustment to these great differences.

When the Japanese borrowed hanzi to become kanji, what they were getting was a way to write out (remember, they already had ways to *say*) their vocabulary. Nouns, verbs, many adjectives, the names of places and people—that's what kanji are used for, the fundamental data of the written language. The practical use and processing of that "data"—its grammar and pronunciation—is another matter entirely. Because spoken Japanese neither sounds nor functions like Chinese, the first work-around tried was a system called *manyogana*, where individual kanji were picked to represent certain syllables in Japanese. A similar method is still used in Chinese today to spell out foreign names; companies and individuals often try to choose hanzi for this purpose that have an auspicious, or at least not insulting, meaning. As you will also observe in *Kurosagi* and elsewhere, the meaning behind the characters that make up a personal name are an important literary element of Japanese as well.

The commentary in Katsuya Terada's *The Monkey King* (also available from Dark Horse, and also translated by Toshifumi Yoshida) notes the importance that not only Chinese, but also Indian culture had on Japan at this time in history—particularly, through Buddhism. Just as in Western history at this time, religious communities in Asia were associated with learning, as priests and monks were more likely to be literate than other groups in society. It is believed the Northeast Indian *Siddham* script studied by Kukai (died 835 AD), founder of the Shingon sect of Japanese Buddhism, inspired him to create the solution for writing Japanese still used today. Kukai is credited with the idea of taking the manyogana and making shorthand versions of them—which are now known simply as *kana*. The improvement in efficiency was dramatic: a kanji previously used to represent a sound, that might have taken a dozen strokes to draw, was now replaced by a kana that took three or four.

Unlike the original kanji they were based on, the new kana had *only* a sound meaning. And unlike the thousands of kanji, there are only forty-six kana, which can be used to spell out any word in the Japanese language, including the many ordinarily written with kanji (Japanese keyboards work on this principle). The same set of forty-six kana is written two different ways depending on its intended use: cursive style, *hiragana*, and block style, *katakana*. Naturally, sound FX in manga are almost always written out using kana.

Kana works somewhat differently than the Roman alphabet. For example, while there are separate kana for each of the five vowels (the Japanese order is not A-E-I-O-U as in English, but A-I-U-E-O), there are, except for *n*, no separate kana for consonants (the middle *n* in the word *ninja* illustrates this exception). Instead, kana work by grouping together consonants with vowels: for example, there are five kana for sounds starting with *k*, depending on which vowel follows it—in Japanese vowel order, they go KA, KI, KU, KE, KO. The next set of kana begins with *s* sounds, so SA, SHI, SU, SE, SO, and so on. You will observe this kind of consonant-vowel pattern in the FX listings for *Kurosagi* Vol. 8 below.

Katakana are generally used for manga sound FX, but on occasion hiragana are used instead. This is commonly done when the sound is one associated with a human body, but can be a subtler aesthetic choice by the artist as well. In *Kurosagi* Vol. 8 you can see an example on 32.7, with the SA of Rei turning her head away, which in hiragana style is written さつ. Note its more cursive appearance compared to the other FX. If it had been written in katakana style, it would look like サツ.

To see how to use this glossary, take an example from page 6: "6.4 FX: KYORO KYORO—looking around sound." 6.4 means the FX is the one on page 6, in panel 4. KYORO KYORO is the sound these kana—キョロキョロ—literally stand for. After the dash comes an explanation of what the sound represents (in some cases, like this, it will be less obvious than others). Note that in cases where there are two or more different sounds in a single panel, an extra number is used to differentiate them from right to left; or, in cases where right and left are less clear, in clockwise order.

The use of kana in these FX also illustrates another aspect of written Japanese—its flexible reading order. For example, the way you're reading the pages and panels of this book in general—going from right to left, and from top to bottom—is similar to the order in which Japanese is also written in most forms of print: books, magazines, and newspapers. However, some of the FX in *Kurosagi* (and manga in general) read left to right. This kind of flexibility is also to be found on Japanese web pages, which usually also read left to right. In other

words, Japanese doesn't simply read "the other way" from English; the Japanese themselves are used to reading it in several different directions.

As might be expected, some FX "sound" short, and others "sound" long. Manga represent this in different ways. One of many instances of "short sounds" in *Kurosagi* Vol. 8 is 6.2's SU—スツ. Note the small ツ mark it has at the end, which stands for the sound "tsu"—in hiragana, such as 32.7, it looks like つ. The half-size "tsu" seen at the end of FX like this means the sound is the kind which stops or cuts off suddenly; that's why 6.2 and 32.7 are written as SU and SA, and not SUTSU and SATSU—you don't pronounce the "tsu" when used this way. Note the small "tsu" has another occasional use *inside*, rather than at the end, of a particular FX, where it indicates a doubling of the consonant sound that follows it.

There are three different ways you may see "long sounds"—where a vowel sound is extended—written out as FX. One is with an ellipsis, as in 105.4's KOTO. Another is with an extended line, as in 61.6's HOOO HO HO HO HO. Still another is by simply repeating a vowel several times, as in 70.1's GOOOOO. You will note that the HOOO in 61.6's HOOO HO HO HO HO has a "tsu" at its end, suggesting an elongated sound that's suddenly cut off; the methods may be combined within a single FX. As a visual element in manga, FX are an art rather than a science, and are used in a less rigorous fashion than kana are in standard written Japanese.

The explanation of what the sound represents may sometimes be surprising, but every culture "hears" sounds differently. Note that manga FX do not even necessarily represent literal sounds. Such "mimetic" words, which represent an imagined sound, or even a state of mind, are called *gitaigo* in Japanese. Like the onomatopoeic *giseigo* (the words used to represent literal sounds—i.e., most FX in this glossary are classed as giseigo), they are also used in colloquial speech and writing. A Japanese, for example, might say that something bounced by saying PURIN, or talk about eating by saying MUGU MUGU. It's something like describing chatter in English by saying "yadda yadda yadda" instead.

One important last note: all these spelled-out kana vowels should be pronounced as they are in Japanese: *A* as *ah*, *I* as *eee*, *U* as *ooh*, *E* as *eh*, and *O* as *oh*.

2   All of the titles are once again song names. For this volume, the songs are by the folk rock group GARO. The band was made up of three members: Mamoru "Mark" Horiuchi, Tomiaki "Tommy" Hidaka and Masumi "Vocal" Ono. With a sound sometimes compared to Crosby, Stills, Nash & Young, they had a million-selling #1 hit with 1973's *Daigakuseigai no Kissaten* (which means "A Café in a Campus Town") and were an emblem of Japanese rock for the next two years, but broke up at the end of 1975.

5.2   The *tsubo* is a traditional Japanese measure of area—still in use even though Japan is metric—equal to 3.05785 sq. meters. The translator notes that if his math is correct, 500 tsubo is only 2/5 of an acre, but bear in mind that's impressive by Japanese land prices. Come to think of it, a lot that size (17,790 sq. feet) is nothing to sneeze at in America, either. In the immortal words of Harvey Korman (peace be upon him), "Land…'Land: see *snatch.*'"

6.2   **FX: SU**—starting to step away

6.4   **FX: KYORO KYORO**—looking around sound

10.1   There are certain stations of the cross a school manga must traverse: among these are the beach episode, the hot-springs episode, and this, the first for *Kurosagi*, the campus-festival episode. The scene at the post office–owned spa resort in Vol. 6 might have counted as a hot-springs episode, but (and this is a qualification for all such episodes) it would have needed the main female and male characters present to allow full cast interaction—see *Genshiken* Vol. 8. *Campus* festivals in manga tend to be of three main types: the "culture fest," (usually an excuse to set up a themed café in one's homeroom), a track and field day, or this, the big student club sign-up. *Kurosagi*'s version is pretty mild; the master of campus-festival scenes in manga is doubtless Kosuke Fujishima in *Oh My Goddess!*, especially in those early volumes, with all the teeny- tiny signs that needed to be retouched in such detail.

12.1   The editor himself might have patronized the rough tape-trade to be found in certain off-campus anime clubs, but he had no intention of introducing these beastly practices to the ivy-covered halls (actually, only Harwood had ivy on it; that's why it was used for the dorm scenes in *Real Genius*) of Pomona College, anno MCMLXXXVII. Instead he was part of the Laissez-Faire Club at Pomona

College, whose purpose was to "smoke cigars, drink Cognac, and discuss the virtues of a free economy." The first two were a bit ahead of the curve; the cigar boom wouldn't hit for another ten years, and hip-hop hadn't yet discovered "yak"; its most lavish ads were still in *The Far Eastern Economic Review* rather than *Vibe* (not after I cut them out of the magazine, however, and pasted them to the wall, together with any coverage of Amy Yip. And I know there weren't no *Vibe* magazine in '87, but please allow me the rhetorical indulgence). As for the third, there was a feeling among some students in 1987 that the Democrats were becoming the enemies of freedom rather than the Republicans. One could respect P. J. O'Rourke, denouncing drug tests and Ollie North in his writing for *Rolling Stone*; one could have no respect whatsoever for Tipper Gore, pursuing the menace of Prince and Twisted Sister. The problem, of course, was that Republicans like P. J. O'Rourke weren't the kind gaining political power, whereas Democrats like Tipper Gore would continue to do so. In retrospect, the idea that tacking right would promote liberty wasn't the most well-considered opinion, but it was driven in part by the leisurely (as we did all things) contempt Gen-X had for the baby boomers in power. Not so much for their era, the terrible and glorious 1960s, but for their shame and resentment of it, for the pathetic spectacle of their culture war over who was on what side, that they maintained

(and still maintain) even as the country's real problems changed with the decades—bearing out once and for all, whether liberal or conservative, the charges laid against them when they were young: that their generation cared only about itself, and could not grow up.

13.5   FX: GATA—getting up out of chair

15.4   FX: KATA—opening laptop

15.7   FX: TATATA TATA—keyboard sounds

16.4   FX: BA—grabbing computer back

16.5   FX/balloon: GACHA—door opening

18.1   Even as we enjoy a few cheap laughs (for what other sort could the Kurosagi gang afford?), we do not wish to show disrespect to our esteemed comrades in the gothic-lolita community. Patrick Macias invited me to sit in on his "Japanese Schoolgirl Inferno" panel at AWA (I'm not sure why he invited *me* to sit in—I'm more *Collezioni* than *Emporio*). The panel was named for the book he wrote with coauthor Izumi Evers (the woman who created the look of *PULP* magazine) and illustrator Kazumi Nonaka—*Japanese Schoolgirl Inferno*, fun and wild, details the last forty years of Japanese school-girl fashion trends, from creation, to co-opting, to rejection, and then to reincarnation. Most importantly, it rejects the idea that fashion is necessarily superficial or something only purchased, but shows how it can be made from the ground up (sometimes, from the gutter up) to reflect a chosen meaning. Ephemeral—like all things. A major asset to the panel was an elegantly actual goth loli in the front row, who discussed what the scene was like in Atlanta, GA, and the reaction to it, often unhip, but not always unkind (one old lady told her it was wonderful that young girls were starting to dress more modestly). The *New York Times*, ever alert to breaking news, picked up on the existence of goth loli recently (admittedly, I'm counting on them more to keep an eye on things like Iraq and the financial crisis). Initial comments on the Jezebel blog in reaction to the article included such remarks as: "What are they rebelling against?" "Messed up." "Makes me uncomfortable." "All this says to me is 'I want attention.'" "There is no point at which I do not find this subculture absolutely ridiculous." In other words, the exact same comments that have been made about every youth style since cavekids started wearing those stupid deer hides, instead of respectable bearskins like their dads.

18.6 **FX: PAKU PAKU**—sound of the mouth flapping

19.3 This suggests he saw her "performance" at the fanboy's funeral in Vol. 5.

19.6 There's gotta be a name for that ponytail Nakano (*vide* Vol. 7, notes for 22.1) is sporting; only otaku have that ponytail. It goes back at least to Hino in *Otaku no Video*. Let's give it a name. *O-tail*, or *opptaku*, or maybe *otaku no suisei*. Japanese speakers are invited to weigh in on whether those last two sound clever.

20.2 Probably Asuka from *Neon Genesis Evangelion*. This is the point where I might have attempted a smart remark about his life-size figure and those awful otaku, but as I'm the awful otaku editing the fan-service-filled *Neon Genesis Evangelion: The Shinji Ikari Raising Project*, first volume out in June, it wouldn't sound quite right.

20.4 **FX: SU**—passing over a photo

23.4 **FX: SU**—touching body sound

23.5 **FX: KATA KATA KATATA**—body shaking

24.1 **FX/balloon: PIKU PIKU**—fingers twitching

24.2.1 **FX: SU**—removing hand

24.2.2 **FX/balloon: PITA**—body suddenly stopping

26.4 **FX/balloon: BUROROROROO**—car sound

27.5 **FX: GURI**—pushing on the ring for his pendulum

27.6 **FX: CHARAN**—sound of metal chain dangling

28.3 **FX: HYUN HYUN HYUN**—sound of the pendulum swinging

29.6 **FX: BAKI BAKI GASASA**—breaking branches and sliding sound

32.7 **FX: SA**—turning head away

35.2 **FX: SU**—placing hand on body

44.4 There is an actual term, *yurei buin*, "ghost club members," used for the not-uncommon practice of campus clubs inflating their membership to claim more funding from their schools. It's done through the simple expedient of getting students to sign the club register, even if they have no intention of ever attending a meeting.

45.1 This is Mori Tower, the iconic building associated with Tokyo's trendy, expensive Roppongi Hills complex. Opening in 2003, it was first sighted in *Kurosagi* on page 70 of Vol. 5, and has served to literally hang over the heads of its main cast ever since, reminding them of just how nonmaterialistic their status is. Nakano back in 14.4 even mentioned that the campus golf club was having *their* new-member party in Roppongi Hills, putting Kurosagi's basement meeting room in rather sharp contrast.

45.2.1 FX/balloon: BURORORO—engine sound

45.2.2 FX/balloon: KII—sound of brakes

45.3 FX: SHA SHA—scribbling sound

46-47 What's so wonderful about this chapter title page is that it puts me in mind of those 1970s "mystery" comics (as Howard Chaykin points out, the Comics Code wouldn't allow them to say "horror") where people were always getting married to ghosts, ghouls, and skeletons. Check out Dave Merrill and Shaindle Minuk's Stupid Comics blog for some choice examples at http://www.misterkitty.org/extras/stupidcovers/stupidcomics92.html. Well, come to think of it, this story puts me a little in mind of them, too.

48.2 Note that the two kanji that spell Kaneari's name mean "money" and "have."

49.1 FX: GURU—sound of the fridge toppling

49.5 The one vanity the editor has never been able to comprehend is designer pens. It might come from taking an early interest in cartooning

(and calligraphy, which was big in the late '70s), which taught, as Thulsa Doom would say, what is the nib, compared to the hand that wields it?

50.1.1 FX: SU—taking out towel

50.1.2 FX/balloon: HIRA—sheet of paper falling out

50.2 FX: PASA—sheet of paper landing on floor

52.2 FX/balloon: SHUUU—sound of an automatic door opening

52.3 The phenomenon of people using manga cafés (*mankissa* in Japanese, after *kissaten*, "café"—basically, private manga libraries where one pays by the hour) to spend the night is known even outside Japan, thanks to Hiroko Tabuchi's widely syndicated piece for the Associated Press in May of 2007, which also discussed its relation to those who survive on part-time work arranged by cell phone. Tabuchi mentioned a net café (they are often also manga cafés) where cubicles rented for 82 cents an hour, showing that the 700-yen all-night package here is quite realistic.

52.4 FX/balloon: GISHI—chair creaking

52.5 FX: PATA—putting down pad of paper

53.1 FX/balloon: MOGU MOGU—eating sound

53.2 FX: SHA SHA—sketching sound

54.1 The translator notes that *bijin-ga* often refers to such glamour pictures of Japan's *ukiyo-e*—the famous, frequently colorful woodblock prints that influenced the

Impressionists when Europe discovered them in the nineteenth century. However, the term can be applied to works in other media, even modern ones such as photography, as long as the subject remains a Japanese woman in traditional dress.

55.2 The traditional word for a wedding in Japanese is *kekkonshiki*, which combines three kanji by themselves pronounced *ketsu*, "union," *kon*, "marriage," and *shiki*, "ceremony" (the rules of Japanese pronunciation make the first two combine to be read *kekkon* instead of *ketsukon*). Kaneari changes this to the near-rhyming *meikonshiki* by making the first kanji *mei*, "afterlife," instead.

55.3 Note the Mumume-tan figurine, no doubt left by the fleeing Nakano.

59.2 **FX: KATA**—rattle of the picture frame

59.3 As seen in Vol. 2. In the Silver Age, there would have been a big ol' box in the panel to remind you of this, but such primitive methods have been replaced with *Disjecta Membra*.

61.6 **FX: HOOO HO HO HO HO HO**—chuckles. I'm not sure Makino is aware she's quoting *The 36th Chamber of Shaolin*, AKA *Master Killer*.

62.3 *Ema* means "horse picture," meaning that it is symbolic of the literal offering of a horse that used to be made (by those who could afford it) in exchange for a blessing at a Shinto shrine. Even today, some shrines maintain a stable for a *goshinme*, a horse kept by the priests for the gods to ride.

Excel, for whom there is no god but Il Palazzo, blasphemously stole the steed from one such temple in Vol. 1 of the *Excel Saga* manga.

62.6 Karatsu is making himself a little arch here (*get it?*); most Japanese don't stress too much about performing the rites of more than one religion—it should also be noted that, just as in America, performing the rites isn't necessarily a sign of deep personal belief, but may be done simply for tradition's sake, social obligation, or (especially with Shinto rites) having fun with friends. And just as we see here, many Japanese aren't adverse to Christian rites either, or at least, the appearance of them; some get married at places made up to look like churches, with an actor portraying a priest (as seems to be the case on page 78). There have, of course, been actual Japanese Christians for centuries (the new prime minister of Japan, Taro Aso, is Catholic), and there are also some Japanese of whatever faith who truly consider themselves "religious" in the American sense—but faith, or anything else for that matter, is rarely allowed to trump social harmony in Japan.

66.1 **FX: SU**—putting a photograph down

67.3 **FX: SU**—paintbrush touching *ema*

67.5 **FX: HYUOOOO**—sound of gusting wind

68.1 **FX: HYUUU**—sound of wind

68.4 **FX: KATA KATA GATA**—sound of the *ema* rattling. The *ema* says, by the way, "Dedication: New Bride

Kurara Gotokuji, Died 2007; New Groom Zatou Seijo, Died June 7, 2006. After Death Marriage." The 2007 date is taken from the fact this particular chapter of *Kurosagi* appeared in the June 5, 2007, issue of its current home magazine, *Comic Charge*.

70.1 **FX: GOOOOO**—sound of train pulling away

70.3.1 **FX/balloon: PI**—hanging up cell

70.3.2 **FX/balloon: KAN KO**—footstep on stairs

72.2 **FX: GUI**—tugging sound

72.4.1 **FX/black: GA DOKA**—impact sounds

72.4.2 **FX/white: BAKI BOKI**—breaking bone sounds

73.1 **FX: GO**—sound of head hitting floor

73.2 **FX/balloon: PIIPOO PIIPOO PIIPOO**—ambulance siren

74.4 As you might expect, Sasayama didn't say "Jane Doe" in the original, but *kooryo-shinahito*, "traveler deceased," a technical term for an unidentified body. Although Japan does sometimes use the name "Taro Yamada" to signify a generic Japanese (a little like the way you might use "John Smith" in America), there is no custom of assigning a standard pseudonym to the unidentified dead.

75.2 The editor doesn't even *have* a cell phone, not being what you'd call an early adopter (he *did* finally buy an iPod a few months ago— used, from his sempai, Toren Smith), but he doesn't think you can perform all these functions yet on an American cell phone. But the rest of the world has always been a bit ahead of the cell curve. I remember some years ago Hiroyuki Yamaga (most recently, coproducer of *Gurren Lagann*, and director of its recap episode) showing off his 3G phone at Fanime Con, before such things were available in the U.S. But of course, nothing would show up on its screen, as it used a Japan-only service. It felt like that scene in *Spinal Tap* where Nigel Tufnel says, "You would, though, if it were playing."

75.3 **FX: MOMI MOMI**—massaging shoulder

75.4 **FX: SU**—placing hand on body

77.1 **FX: SU**—pointing sound

77.2 **FX: SA**—lifting sheet

79.1 **FX: PA**—sound of spotlight turning on

79.2 **FX: PACHI PACHI PACHI PACHI**—clapping sounds

81.3 Not as in high school A/V, refuge of the chaste, but AV as in "adult video"—the Japan porno industry uses the English-language term.

81.5 **FX/balloon: VUU VUU VUU**— cell phone vibrating

81.6 **FX: CHA**—putting phone to ear

82.3 **FX: TA**—putting glass down

84.1 **FX: BASA**—sound of photos being dumped on table

85.2 This time, the *musakari ema* reads "New Bride Ao Sasaki, Died 2007; New Groom Yaro Nozaki, Died 2005. After Death Marriage."

85.4 **FX: KATAN**—hanging *ema*

85.5 **FX: GARA PATAN**—closing shrine door

86.1 FX: BYUUU—gust of wind

86.3 FX/balloon: KATA KATA KATA KATAN—sound of the *ema* rattling

87.1 FX/balloon: JANKA JAKA JAAN—mobile phone ringing

88.2 FX/balloon: JARI—sound of footstep in gravel

89.4 FX: KAKOKO KAKO KAKOKO—keyboard sounds

90.2 FX: BA—turning around quickly

90.6 FX/balloon: TO—back of foot hitting bookshelf

91.2 FX: GU—gripping throat sound

93.2 FX/balloons: CHAKKA CHAKKA—sound of the blinkers flashing

94.2 FX/balloon: PAAAN—gunshot

94.3 FX/balloon: TSUU TSUU TSUU TSUU—busy line sound

95.5 The term used in the original Japanese was *keizai yakuza*, "financial gangsters," a phrase that arose in the 1980s as some mobsters started getting MBAs. Exactly how many businesses in Roppongi Hills have yakuza money behind them is open to debate, and the speculation is colored by resentment and envy towards the upscale nature of the complex (in what is already one of the most expensive cities in the world). However, yakuza involvement in legitimate business (as well as their more traditional ones) is no mere manga story. A humorous and no-nonsense introduction to the realities of the yakuza is Robert Whiting's *Tokyo Underworld: The Fast Times and Hard Life of an American Gangster in Japan*. This 1999 book is sort of *Megatokyo* meets *The Godfather*, based around the true story of Nick Zapetti, a petty New York mobster who went to Roppongi and opened a pizza parlor patronized by the yakuza, styling himself "the Mafia Boss of Tokyo" and changing his name to Koizumi (!). Along the way, Whiting has a lot to say about organized crime's influence on politics and the economy in Japan—and how U.S. business and government interests haven't been above trying to make their own deals with it.

96.3 FX: CHA—readying gun sound

96.5 FX: PAAAN—gunshot

97.2 FX/balloon: TATA—running sound

97.3 FX/balloon: TA—coming to a stop

97.5.1 FX/balloons: PACHI PACHI—hitting up button

97.5.2 FX/balloon: PACHI—hitting up button

98.2 FX: GUGUGUGU—squeezing sound

98.4 FX: DARAN—arms going limp

98.5 FX/balloon: NII—smirk

100.1 FX: DOSA—Sasaki hitting floor

100.4 FX: PAKIIIN—sound of *ema* breaking

101.4 FX: DON DON DON—banging on door

102.1 FX/balloon: GACHA—door opening

102.5 FX: HYUN HYUN—sound of pendulum swinging

104.1 It seems to me that you rarely see the punched-in aspect of a bullet wound portrayed this way in American comics; there's even a suggestion of the bullet's spin. I wonder whether in *Kurosagi*'s Housui Yamazaki and *MPD-Psycho*'s Sho-u Tajima, author Eiji Otsuka found the kind of artists whose relatively clean, clinical style supports an idea Philip Simon and I sense in Otsuka's work—not simply voyeurism, but the consciousness of voyeurism. Perhaps due to his anthropologist's training, he seems to take as a given that many of us humans (including, of course, himself) are inclined to stare at and perhaps even like the lurid, the extreme, or the taboo. Rather than say "don't look," or "you shouldn't look," or "oh, what a terrible thing it is to look at this," Otsuka is interested in what might be learned if on such occasions we decided to look *at* our looking. The immediate inspiration for *MPD-Psycho*, which premiered in 1997, was not only the Aum Shinrikyo cult terrorist attacks two years before, but also the media frenzy surrounding them, which famously led *Akira*'s Katsuhiro Otomo to declare that the reporters came off as crazier than the cult—but of course, presumably, it earned ratings.

105.1 Imagine a country where someone's dead of a pistol wound, and you can immediately assume it was organized crime. Most handgun deaths here are hardly that colorful. See also the notes for Vol. 1's 51.3 for how *Kurosagi* illustrates the difference between Japan's gun culture and our own.

105.4 FX: KOTO—putting a board down on the table

106.1 FX: KOKI—cracking knuckles

106.2 FX: SU—placing hand on body

107.4 FX/balloons: PINPOON PINPOON—doorbell sound

107.5 FX/balloon: PI—pressing button

109.1 FX: KATA—putting glass down

109.2 FX: GATAN—falling down sound

109.5.1 FX: ZU ZU—being pulled down sound

109.5.2 FX/balloon: KACHI KACHI—bottles rattling

109.5.3 FX/balloon: KATA—rattling sound

109.5.4 FX/balloon: KATAN—glass falling over

110.1-2 FX: NU NUUUUU—sound of head coming through table. The ghost is wearing the *tsunokakushi*, the traditional bridal headdress of a Shinto wedding (seen earlier, of course, on several of the *ema*). Japanese tradition says it is to hide the "horns" of evil impulses held by the bride—selfishness and jealousy (often meaning "jealousness" towards the mistresses it is assumed her husband will take!). It has been claimed that the move towards Christian-style weddings (not necessarily Christian weddings; see the note for 62.6) represents a wish by some Japanese women to reject the symbolism of the *tsunokakushi*, but it's the editor's impression that it's more a decision of style than symbolism. Weddings in Japan, as they are in many places, are often an occasion for deeply traditional *gestures*, not necessarily deeply held attitudes; in particular, no one expects a marriage in 2007 Japan to be like that of 1957, or even 1987 (the country having gone through something of a quiet sexual revolution in the 1990s—the upside of its long recession being a loosening of social restrictions, as old institutions and attitudes lost respect). One of Otsuka's constant themes as a writer, though, is the *latent* power of folklore, and the idea that every society lives in both its present and past.

111.4 **FX: FU**—sound of the lights going out

112-113.1 **FX: WAAAAAA**—final scream

115.1 **FX: KATA**—picking up broken *ema*

115.3 **FX/balloon: BO**—*ema* catching fire

115.4 **FX: PACHI PACHI**—crackling fire sound

115.6 **FX: HYUOOO**—sound of the wind gusting

116.1 **FX: KATA KATA**—*ema* rattling

116.2 **FX: KATA KATA**—*ema* rattling

117.1 **FX: MIIIN MIIIN**—sound of cicadas

118.2 **FX/balloon: KII**—bike brake sound

118.3 **FX: KIII**—locker creaking closed

118.4 **FX: PATA**—locker door closing

118.6 **FX: KARARA**—sound of bike rolling

119.1 **FX: KIII**—bike brakes

119.3 Roadside coin lockers, like roadside vending machines (see notes for Vol. 2, 105.1), or ads that hang from subway ceilings without being snatched down, are all testament to Japan's lingering sense of social restraint. Of course, as Haruki Murakami wrote in *Underground*, his study of the Aum Shinrikyo terror attacks, that restraint

extended to its victims writhing poisoned beneath those very same subway ads, receiving no help from their fellow passengers—not so much out of callousness, but out of a wish to wait until a station was reached, and the matter could be dealt with by the authorities. This, incidentally, is also what enables one to enjoy the most shocking manga on a train without fear of offending others (it's not like all Japanese are into sex and violence, or manga for that matter), for what would be truly impolite would be to *notice*.

119.4.1 **FX/balloon: GOTOTO**—sound of something moving inside

119.4.2 **FX/balloon: GOSO**—sound of something shifting inside

119.7 **FX: KIII**—locker door creaking

120.1 **FX: OGYAAAA ONGYAAAA OGYAAA GYAAA GYAA**—baby wailing

120.2 **FX: OGYAA NGYAAA**—more wailing

120.3 **FX: GUGYAAA**—wailing starting to fade

121.1 **FX: GYAAA**—small waning wail

121.2 **FX: BAAAAN**—locker slamming shut

121.3 **FX: SHAAAA**—sound of bikes speeding away

121.6 *Namu amida butsu* is a traditional chant associated with Pure Land Buddhism (see notes for Vol. 7's 6.2.2), although Karatsu's *nanmaida* way back in Vol. 1's 11.4 was a variation on it. *Amida butsu* refers to the Buddha Amida, or Amitabha, whereas *namu* derives from the Sanskrit *namaste*; often translated "hail," "praise," or "amen," and a part of many longer prayers.

122-123 The editor was talking over Vol. 8 with his pal, Director of Asian Licensing Michael Gombos, when Gombos gave a discourse on the shoes in this scene. It seems these sorts of sandals—two Velcro straps over the toe and one over the ankle—are the type commonly worn by nurses and teachers in Japan. Japanese teachers do a bit more walking than American ones, as, in Japan, it's the teachers who move from class to class each period, while the students stay put in a homeroom. When teachers get to school, they take off the shoes they arrived in, and switch to these sandals in the *shokuin-shitsu*, the teachers' room. Now, what Gombos found interesting is that even though this footwear is as cheap as the 1,000 yen *oyajigutsu* that old men wear— the slip-ons with the faux patent leather and the fake gold chains— that they are, in short, as he put it, "the least boner-iffic imaginable," they nevertheless become a fetish to those lads who find themselves with strange and wonderful feelings towards a certain teacher, or, presumably, health-care professional. At this point I invoked Rule 34, but Gombos riposted this was an Internet rule. We wondered whether an appropriate corollary for reality might not be called Rule 34A, for "actual," or perhaps 34', for "prime," sort of like the E' that designates Kereellis on the back cover of this book. Gombos pointed out this might imply reality has now become the puppet of the Internet, but I said that was more a plot point for Vol. 10. Anyway, it seemed we were starting to digress a little from the shoes, so I mentioned it seemed odd, this thing about nurses wearing open-toed sandals, since wouldn't there be a hygiene issue? But Gombos pointed out this is Japan, where you're allowed to smoke in the hospital. And that pretty much put paid to all Japanese ways we might consider strange, because before we tut-tut, let us reflect that as of 2007, the average Japanese lived to 82, whereas the average American made it no further than 78.

124.1 Once again, this is the Kadokawa Central Hospital, evidently just another part of the publisher's inescapable empire.

126.6 FX: GU—grasping body

126.7 FX: GORORI—turning body over

128.2 FX: PACHI—eyes opening

128.3 FX: NYU—starting to frown

128.4 FX: GUNYU—scrunching face

129.1 FX: ONGYAAAAA GYAAA HONGYAAAAAA—wailing like a baby

130.1 FX: NGYAAA AAAA GYAAA ONGYAAA—wailing

130.3 FX: TATATATA—running off

130.5 FX: OGYAAAA OGYAAA NGYAAA—wailing

130.6 FX: PIII PIII PIII—alarm sound

131.1 FX: DADADADA—running sound

131.2 FX: GACHA—door opening

133.4 There was, of course, the incident last September in Omaha (which sounds Japanese, but it's in Nebraska) where a widower, who said he was unable to care for them any longer, left *nine* of his children at a hospital under a similar law. Although it seemed outrageous, there was a surprising amount of sympathy for the father's decision, with those supporting him saying it reflected a lack of government assistance to families, and pointing out it's not unknown for parents overwhelmed by stress to abuse or even kill their children. In the words of Bushwick Bill, "It's a fucked-up situation, I feel sorry for the families, but this song was inspired by the truth."

133.5 FX: KIII—door creaking open

134.2 Japan has a national health-care plan, but unlike those in many Western European countries, it doesn't pay for abortion (or contraception, for that matter). Many people are surprised to hear the birth-control pill was only legalized there in 1999, and condoms and the "rhythm method" remain the most common forms of contraception—which means that abortion remains a common default method of "birth control" as well.

135.4 FX: SU—placing hand on baby

136.1 FX: SU—lifting hand

137.2 "Angel Care" is the actual term used in Japanese nursing, pronounced *enzerukea* ("en-zeh-roo-keh-ah") and the procedure is in fact as shown here and in more detail later on in "7th Delivery." It should be emphasized that its intent is to make the body temporarily presentable, as opposed to embalming, which seeks to slow its decay over the longer term.

140.4 FX: CHARA—pendulum dangling

141.2 FX: KON—hitting with cane

142.3 FX: KIII—door opening

142.4 FX: GOTON—baby being dropped off

143.1 FX: PIII PIII PIII—alarm sound

143.2 FX: PIII PIII—alarm sound

143.6 FX: ZA—footsteps

150.2 FX: SU—placing hand on baby

151.1 FX: KASHA—shutter sound

152.4 FX: GOTO GOTO GOTON GO GOTO—sound of something moving around loudly

152.5 FX: DON GOTO DOKO GON— sound of pounding on the little door

153.3 FX: GAAAA—sound of the drawer being slid out

153.4 FX: MOGO GOSO MOGOGO GOSO GUMO—sound of struggling and muffled groans

154.1.1 FX/white: BARI—body bag opening up

154.1.2 FX/black: OGYAAA GYAAA AAAA OGYAAA ONGYAAAA— baby wails

154.2 FX: ONGYAAA ONGYAAA ONGYAAAA—baby wails

155.1 FX: PATATATA—sound of a distant helicopter

157.6 FX: PATATATA PATATATA— distant helicopter sound

158 This is almost certainly inspired by the infamous JAL Flight 123, which crashed into Japan's Mount Osutaka in the early evening of August 12, 1985, killing 520 people—still the deadliest single aircraft disaster in history. Four were found alive (including a mother and her eight-year-old daughter) when rescue crews landed in the remote area the next morning, although Yumi Ochiai, a flight attendant who was one of the four, later said that she could see the search helicopters during the night (its pilot had originally reported no sign of survivors) and could hear screams and moans that gradually weakened.

158.1 **FX: BATATATA**—helicopter sound

159.7 **FX: BA**—eyes opening suddenly

162.5 Yata is making reference to the legend of the *Ko Sodate Yurei*; please see the notes in Vol. 4 for 147.4 for more details.

164.1 **FX: GWOOOO**—sound of a speeding car

164.3 **FX/balloon: GYUKYUKYUO**—tires squealing

164.5 **FX: DON**—sound of the tires hitting the road

165.1 **FX/balloon: JANKA JAKA CHARAN**—ring tone

165.5 **FX/balloon: PI**—hanging up

166.1 **FX/balloon: KIII**—car braking

166.2 **FX: ZA**—footstep

167.7 **FX: GARARA**—sound of a sliding door opening

170.6 Carl Djerassi, one of the original developers of oral contraceptives in the 1950s, wrote in his 2003 memoir *This Man's Pill* that abortions in Japan can be very expensive—as much as $2,000 (in the United States, they tend to range between $300 and $1,000), and suggests lobbying by doctors eager to keep this revenue was a factor behind the great delay in birth-control pills becoming legal in Japan. By contrast, Djerassi notes, Viagra was made legal in Japan less than a year after it came on the market in the U.S. (there are stories of foreigners during those few months paying for an entire trip in Japan by bringing a Viagra prescription to sell off at $200 a pill). A *josanbu*'s "services" would presumably be much less; nor would such a traditional midwife report the "procedure," as a doctor is required to by law in Japan for an abortion.

172.3 **FX/inset: GOTON**—sound of a baby dropping into the post

175.1 **FX: GORORI**—body being rolled over

175.2 **FX: GUGU**—pressure being applied to stomach

175.3 **FX/balloon: DORORI**—fluid oozing out

175.5 Infanticide is in no way legal in Japan (abortions are permitted only through the twenty-second week of pregnancy), nor is it an act a typical Japanese woman would commit without feeling personal guilt and remorse; the story "Maternal Instinct" in Vol. 3 of Housui Yamazaki's *Mail* deals with a variation on this theme. But with the greater acceptance of abortion in general, there has been more willingness to accept "stillbirths" when the only ones in the know are the *josanbu* and the pregnant woman herself. Sasayama alludes to such attitudes in Vol. 6's 143.1. As with the mysterious "crying woman" of Volumes 5 and 6, Otsuka uses a crone (in an archetypal and not pejorative sense) to embody acts that once had a ritualistic conception, but today are often just acts.

176.2 FX/balloon: PI—peeling off sound

176.3 FX/balloon: KUPA—eyelid being spread open

176.4 FX/balloon: PITO—eye cover/ sticker being applied

177.1.1 FX: GUUUU—pressure being applied to lower abdomen

177.1.2 FX/balloon: BUPI—bowels evacuating

177.2 FX: KACHA—putting on metal cover

177.3 FX: NURU—spreading lubricant

177.4 FX/balloon: GURI—pushing in funnel-like instrument

177.5.1 FX/balloon: ZUBU—sound of cotton being pushed in

177.5.2 FX/balloon: ZUBUBU—more cotton being inserted

184.2.1 FX/balloon: KACHI—sound of stone being stacked

184.2.2 FX/balloon: KACHA—more stones

184.3 FX/balloon: KOTO—stone being placed on top

185.1 FX: MIIIN MIIIN—sound of cicadas

185.3 Kikuchi's grandmother is seen acting in the role of Jizo, the incarnation of the Buddha who took a vow to save the souls of those trapped in the realms of hell. William R. LaFleur's *Liquid Life: Abortion and Buddhism in Japan* (the title refers to *mizuko*, "water baby"; i.e., miscarriages and abortions) speaks of the folk belief that such souls end up on a deserted riverbank known as Saino-kawara in Meido, the realm of the dead. There, they play by stacking stones, an act that earns grace for their families on Earth. But at night, they are frightened by demons who come to knock down the stones. Jizo is said to wander the riverbank as a guardian, protecting the *mizuko* and praying for their eventual salvation. LaFleur notes that although this belief is comforting to women who have had such experiences, Buddhist temples make a good business of it, too, by selling personal Jizo figurines that can be decorated with children's clothing or toys; the author saw literally thousands of them lining the courtyards and walkways of a temple in Kamakura.

185.5 FX/balloon: BATAN BATAN BAKON—sound of wooden locker doors opening and slamming shut

185.6 FX: BAN BATAN BAN—slamming/ banging sounds

186.1 FX/balloon: BATAN BATAAN BAGON—sound of wooden locker doors opening and slamming shut

186.2.1 FX/balloon: BAN BAN BAN— sound of wooden locker doors opening and slamming shut

186.2.2 FX/small: OGYAA OGYAA— faint sound of a wailing baby

186.3.1 FX/small: OGYAA OGYAA OGYAA OGYAA—faint sound of a wailing baby

186.3.2 FX/balloon: MEKI—sound of wood cracking

186.3.3 FX/balloon: BEKI—sound of wood breaking

a

186.3.4 FX/balloon: MEKI—sound of wood cracking

186.4.1 FX/balloon: BAKI—sound of wood breaking

186.4.2 FX/balloon: BEKI—sound of wood breaking

186.4.3 FX/balloon: BEKI—sound of wood breaking

186.5 FX: GOGOGOGO—rumbling

186.6 FX: GOFU—small imploding sound

189.4 FX: BURORO—car sound

189.5 FX: GOTOTOTOTO—sound of car rattling

189-190 The editor can't help but wonder if the staging of the last scene is meant to be reminiscent of the end of Hayao Miyazaki's 1979 classic *Lupin III: The Castle of Cagliostro*. Numata, with his grin, goatee, and most especially, bent cigarette, seems to conjure Jigen. *Cagliostro*, made a decade before Miyazaki broke out to the wider public with *Kiki's Delivery Service* (his first box-office smash), was actually his directorial debut in film, although he had directed TV anime beforehand. It's probably the greatest pure adventure film anime has produced, comparable in speed, wit, and excitement to its near-contemporary, *Raiders of the Lost Ark* (incidentally, the Spielberg praise-quote on the Special Edition DVD for *Cagliostro* has never, to my knowledge, actually been confirmed, but is simply based on a fan rumor dating back to the early '80s that he *did* like the movie!). It is true that Miyazaki's knight-errant take on Lupin reformed the reprobate seen in the original *Lupin III* manga (published by Tokyopop), but in Miyazaki's hands, it was magic.

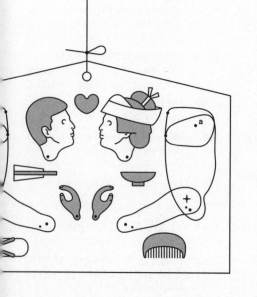

STAFF D

Embalming
［エンバーミング］：死体修復

STAFF E

Channeling
［チャネリング］：宇宙人と交信

STAFF E'

Puppet
［マペット］：宇宙人が憑依

お届け物は死体です。

黒鷺死体宅配便
the KUROSAGI corpse delivery service

story
EIJI OTSUKA

art
HOUSUI YAMAZAKI

original cover design
BUNPEI YORIFUJI

translation
TOSHIFUMI YOSHIDA

editor and english adaptation
CARL GUSTAV HORN

lettering and touch-up
IHL

DARK HORSE MANGA

contents

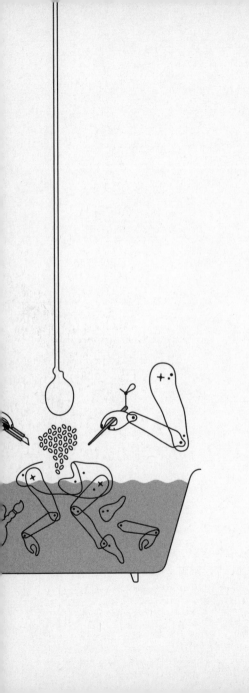

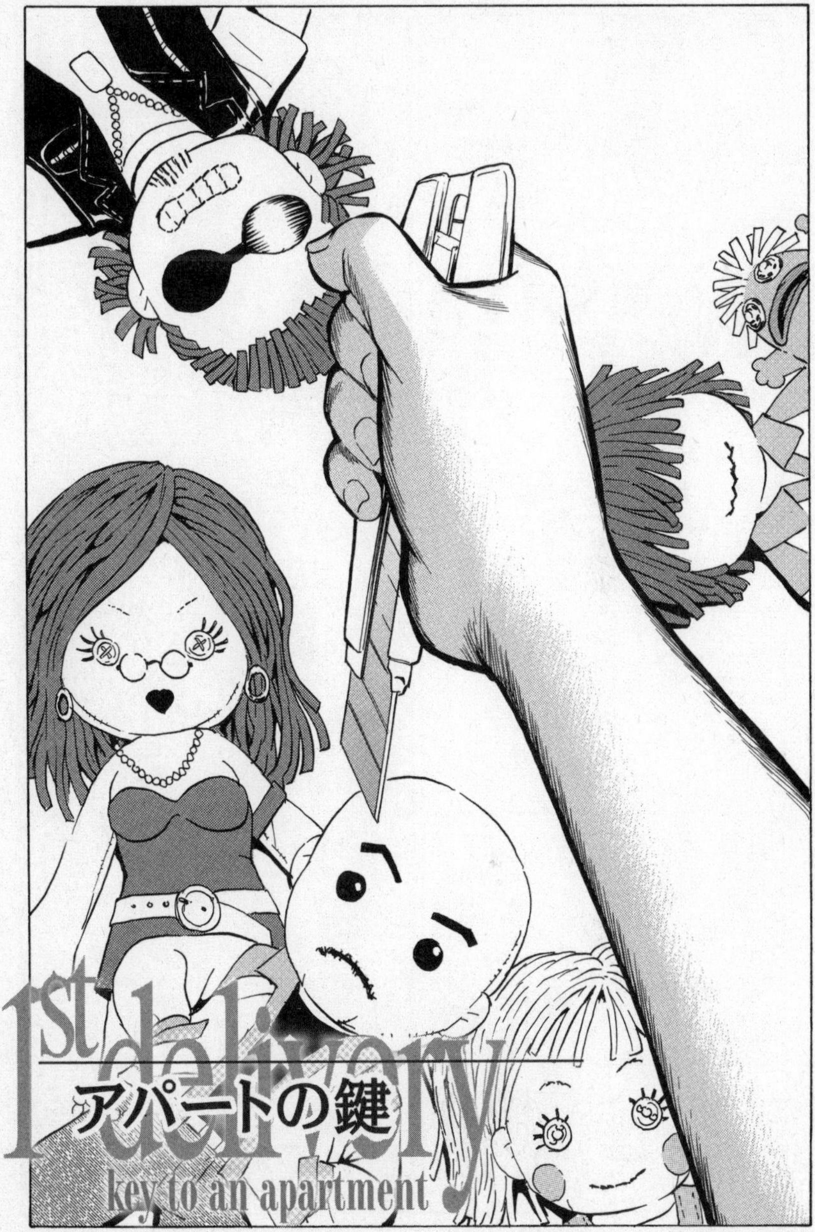
1st delivery
アパートの鍵
key to an apartment

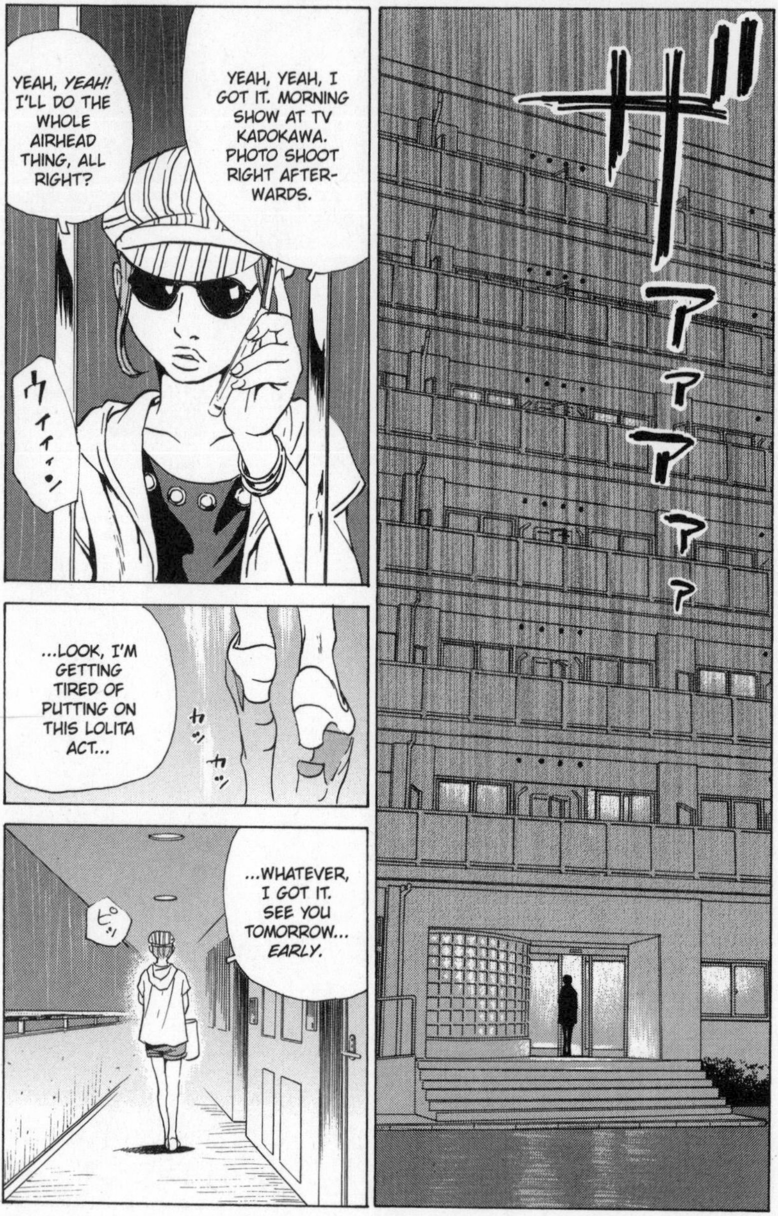
ザァァァァァ
YEAH, YEAH, I GOT IT. MORNING SHOW AT TV KADOKAWA. PHOTO SHOOT RIGHT AFTER-WARDS.
YEAH, *YEAH!* I'LL DO THE WHOLE AIRHEAD THING, ALL RIGHT?
ウィィィン
...LOOK, I'M GETTING TIRED OF PUTTING ON THIS LOLITA ACT...
カッ
カッ
...WHATEVER, I GOT IT. SEE YOU TOMORROW... *EARLY.*
ピッ

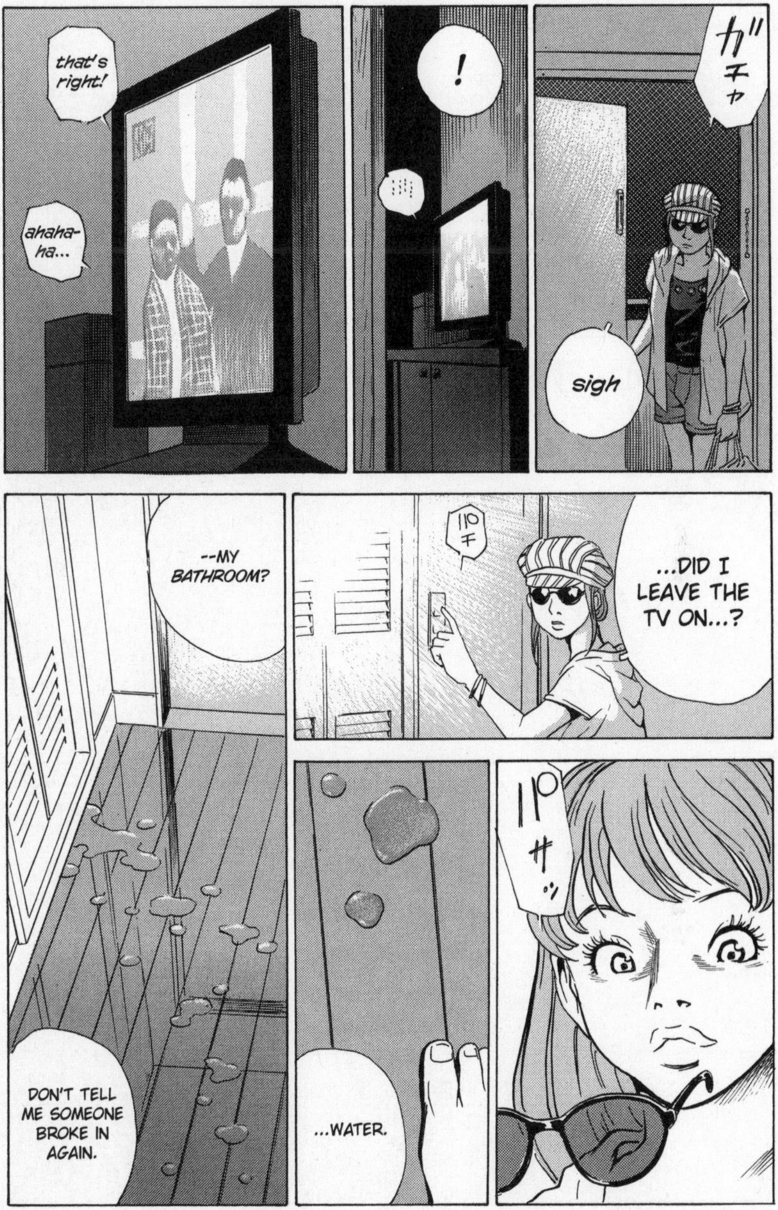
ガチャ
sigh
!
that's right!
ahahaha...
パチ
...DID I LEAVE THE TV ON...?
パサッ
...WATER.
--MY BATHROOM?
DON'T TELL ME SOMEONE BROKE IN AGAIN.

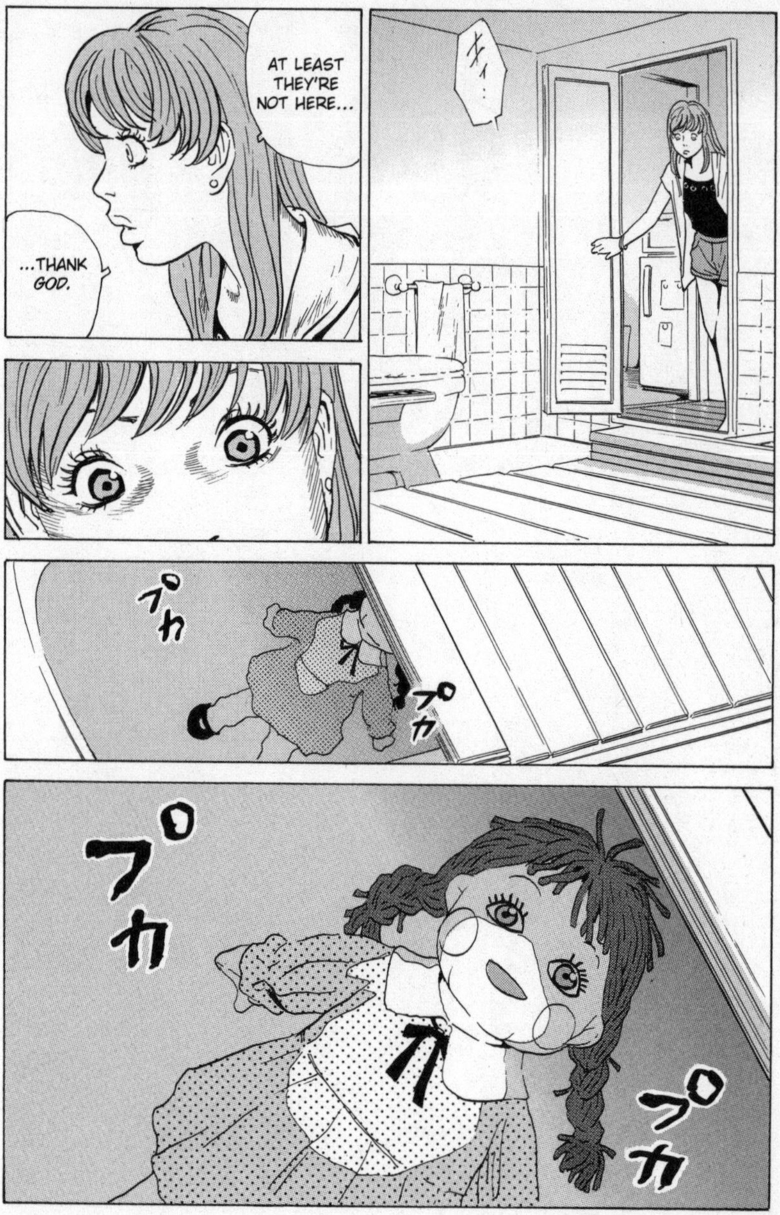
キィ…
AT LEAST THEY'RE NOT HERE...
...THANK GOD.
プカ
プカ
プカ
プカ

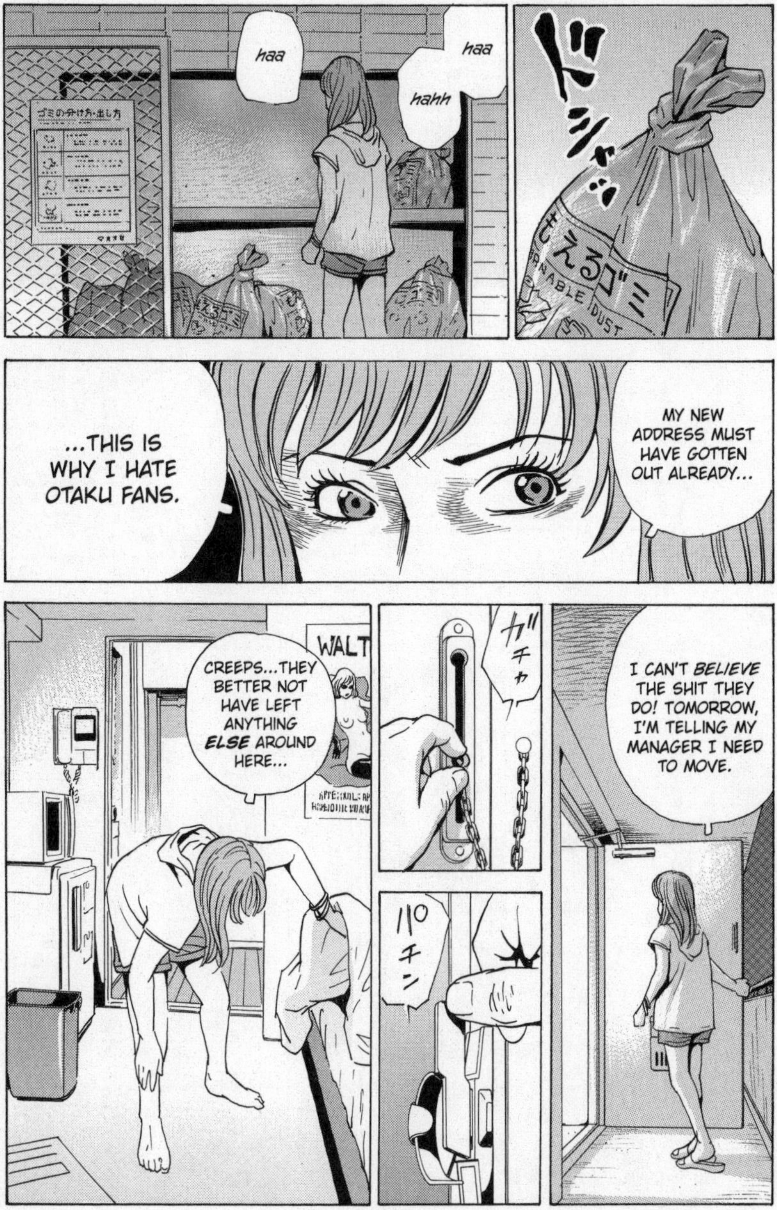

ドシャッ
ゴミの分け方・出し方
haa
haa
hahh
MY NEW ADDRESS MUST HAVE GOTTEN OUT ALREADY...
...THIS IS WHY I HATE OTAKU FANS.
I CAN'T *BELIEVE* THE SHIT THEY DO! TOMORROW, I'M TELLING MY MANAGER I NEED TO MOVE.
ガチャ
パチン
WALT
CREEPS...THEY BETTER NOT HAVE LEFT ANYTHING *ELSE* AROUND HERE...

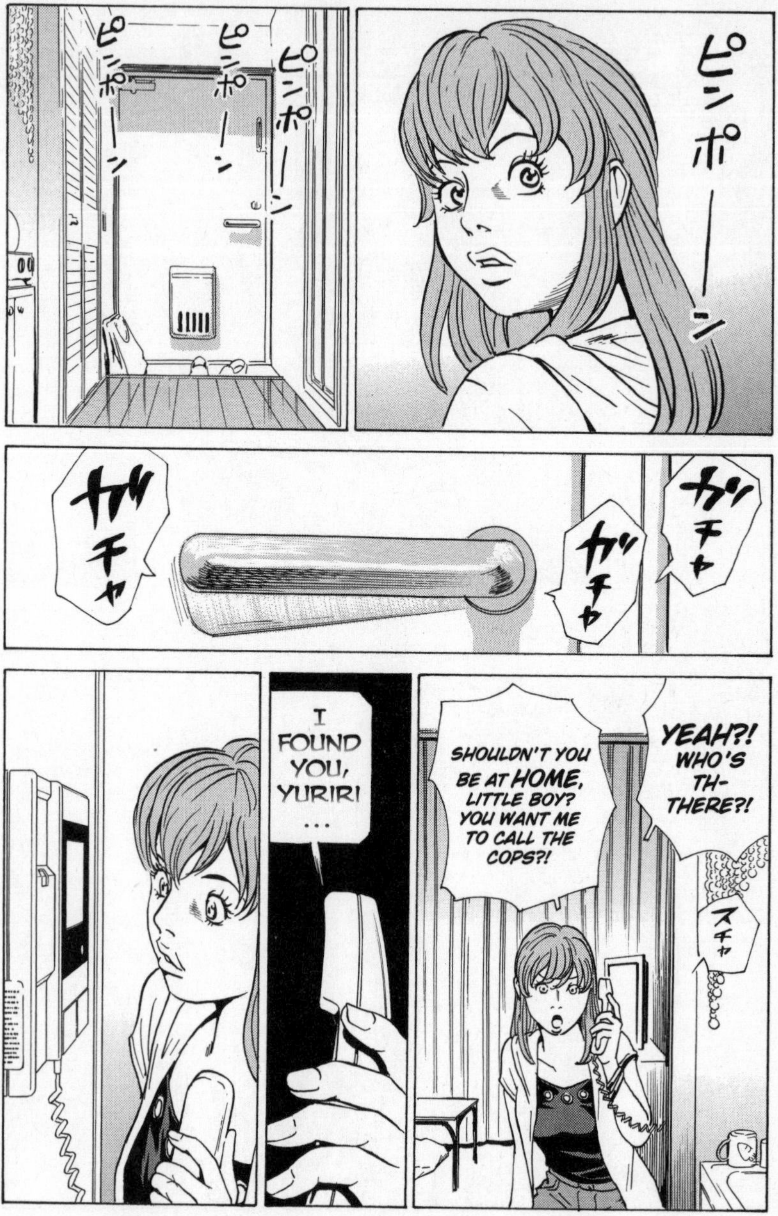

ピンポーーン
ピンポーーン
ピンポーン
ピンポーン
ガッチャ
ガッチャ
ガッチャ
YEAH?! WHO'S TH- THERE?!
SHOULDN'T YOU BE AT HOME, LITTLE BOY? YOU WANT ME TO CALL THE COPS?!
スチャ
I FOUND YOU, YURIRI ...

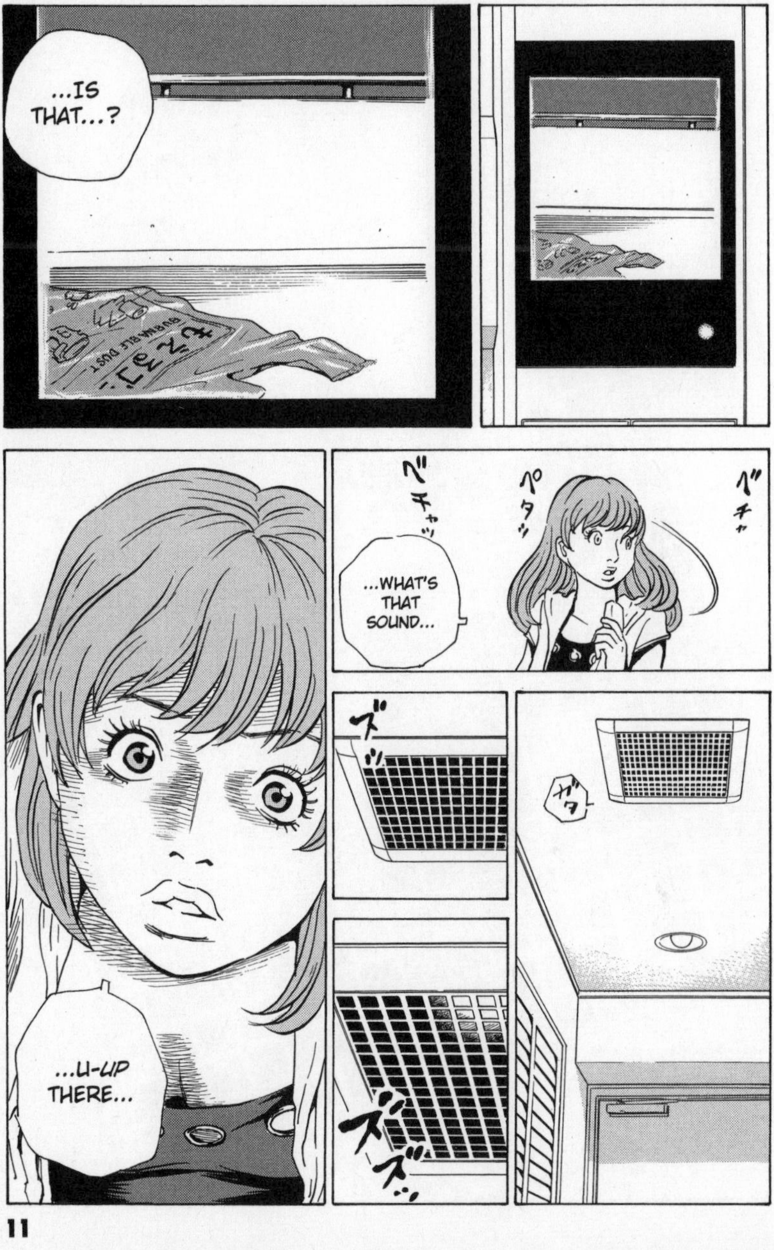
...IS THAT...?
ベチャッ
ペタッ
ベチャ
...WHAT'S THAT SOUND...
ズッ
ガタ
ズズッ
...U-UP THERE...

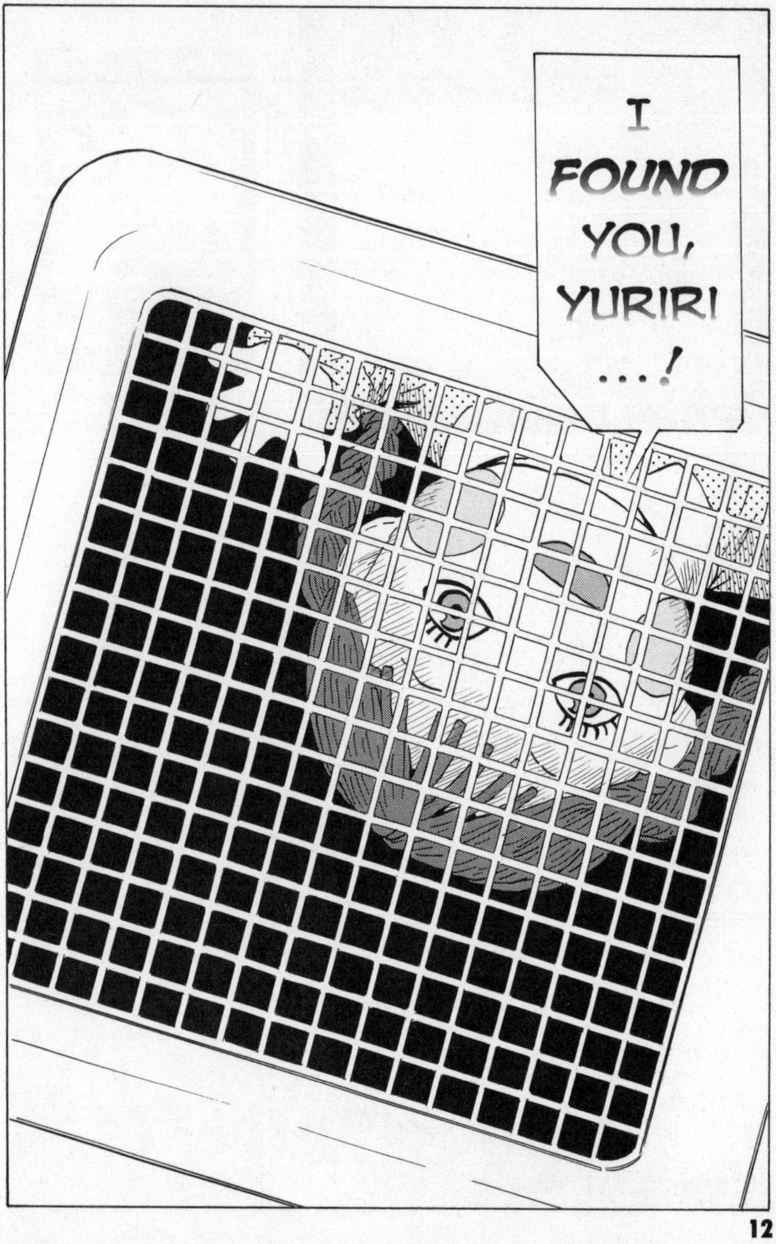
I FOUND YOU, YURIRI ...!

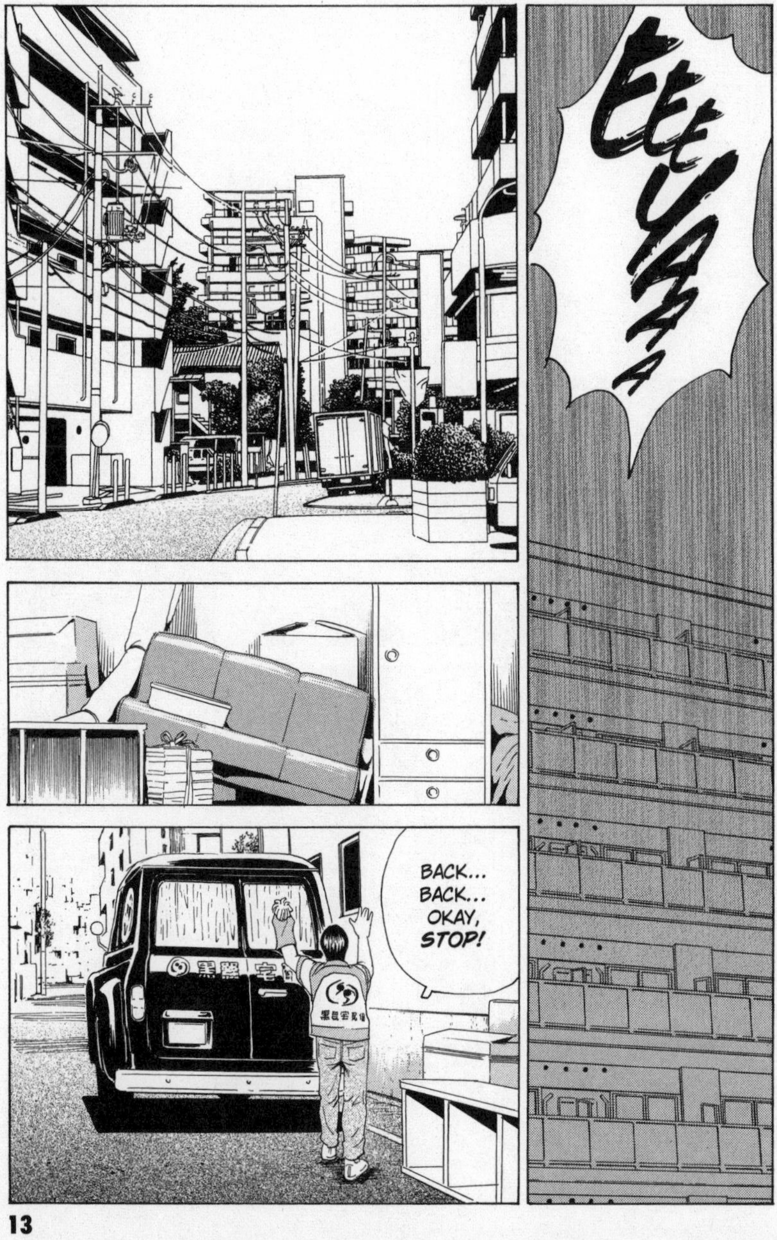
EEEYAAA
BACK... BACK... OKAY, STOP!

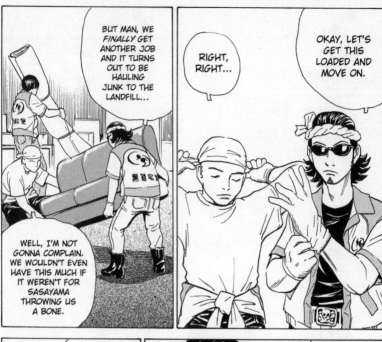

OKAY, LET'S GET THIS LOADED AND MOVE ON.
RIGHT, RIGHT...
BUT MAN, WE *FINALLY* GET ANOTHER JOB AND IT TURNS OUT TO BE HAULING JUNK TO THE LANDFILL...
WELL, I'M NOT GONNA COMPLAIN. WE WOULDN'T EVEN HAVE THIS MUCH IF IT WEREN'T FOR SASAYAMA THROWING US A BONE.
AND THIS *IS* THE ONLY WORK WE'VE HAD THIS MONTH.
YEAH, YEAH, I KNOW... SHIT.
ACTUALLY, THE CITY'S WAGES AREN'T TOO BAD. NO WONDER HE ALWAYS WANTS TO KEEP HIS BUDGET TO HIMSELF.
...WAIT. BEFORE WE HAUL IT OFF, LET ME GIVE IT A CHECK...YOU NEVER KNOW.

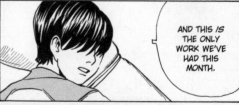

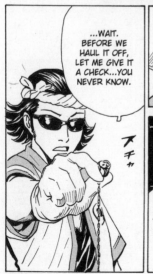

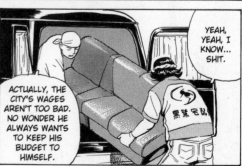

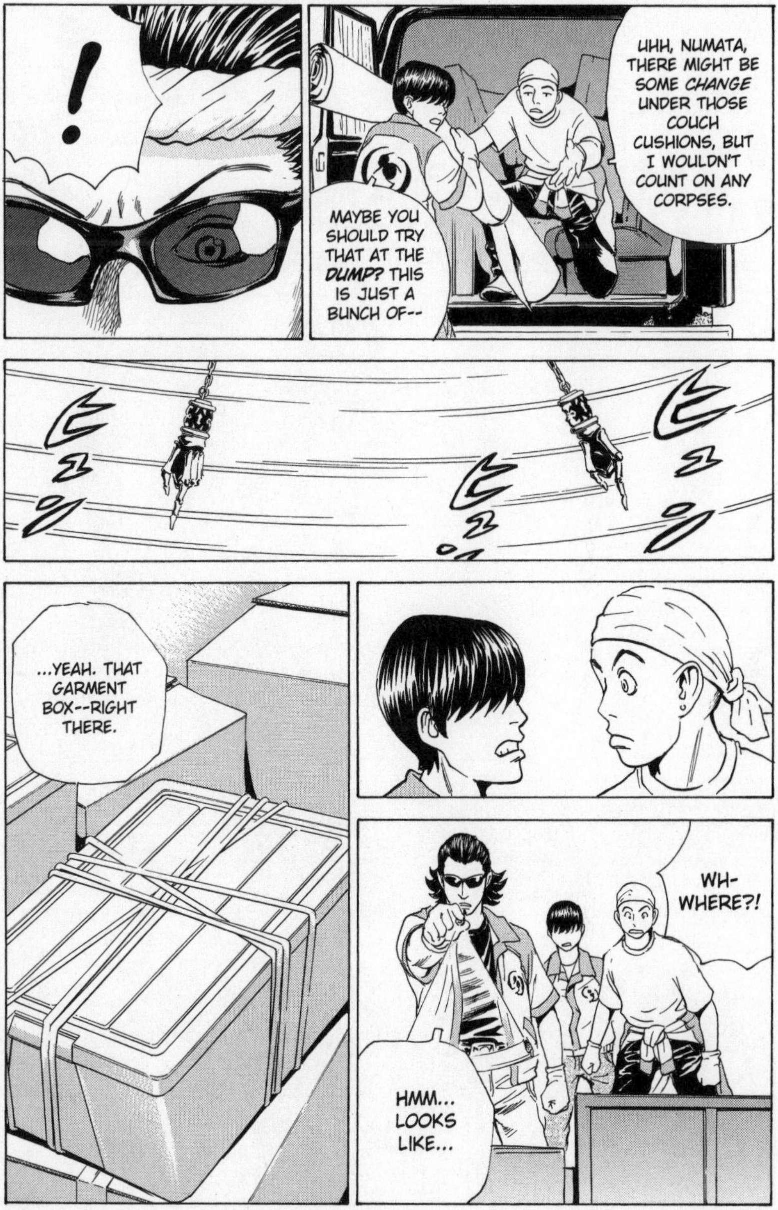
UHH, NUMATA, THERE MIGHT BE SOME *CHANGE* UNDER THOSE COUCH CUSHIONS, BUT I WOULDN'T COUNT ON ANY CORPSES.
MAYBE YOU SHOULD TRY THAT AT THE ***DUMP?*** THIS IS JUST A BUNCH OF--
!
WH- WHERE?!
HMM... LOOKS LIKE...
...YEAH. THAT GARMENT BOX--RIGHT THERE.

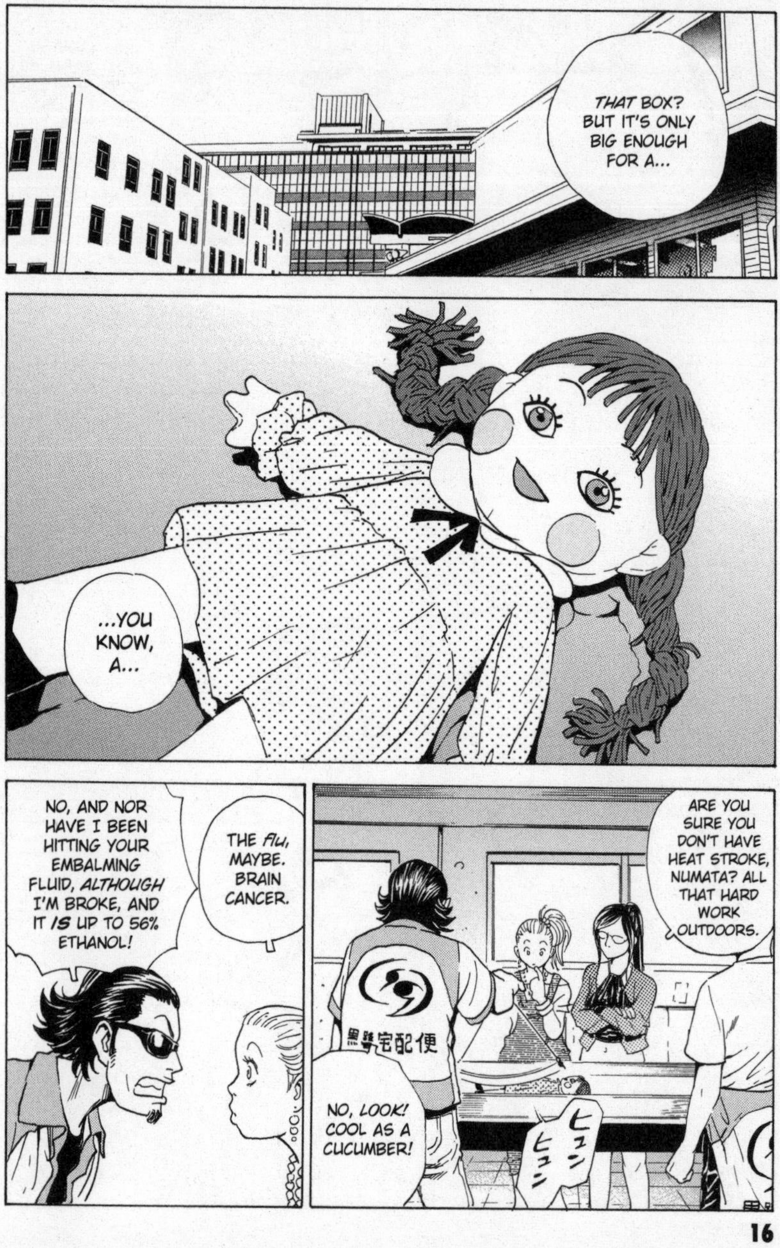
THAT BOX? BUT IT'S ONLY BIG ENOUGH FOR A...
...YOU KNOW, A...
ARE YOU SURE YOU DON'T HAVE HEAT STROKE, NUMATA? ALL THAT HARD WORK OUTDOORS.
黒鷺宅配便
NO, *LOOK!* COOL AS A CUCUMBER!
ヒュン ヒュン
THE *flu,* MAYBE. BRAIN CANCER.
NO, AND NOR HAVE I BEEN HITTING YOUR EMBALMING FLUID, *ALTHOUGH* I'M BROKE, AND IT *IS* UP TO 56% ETHANOL!

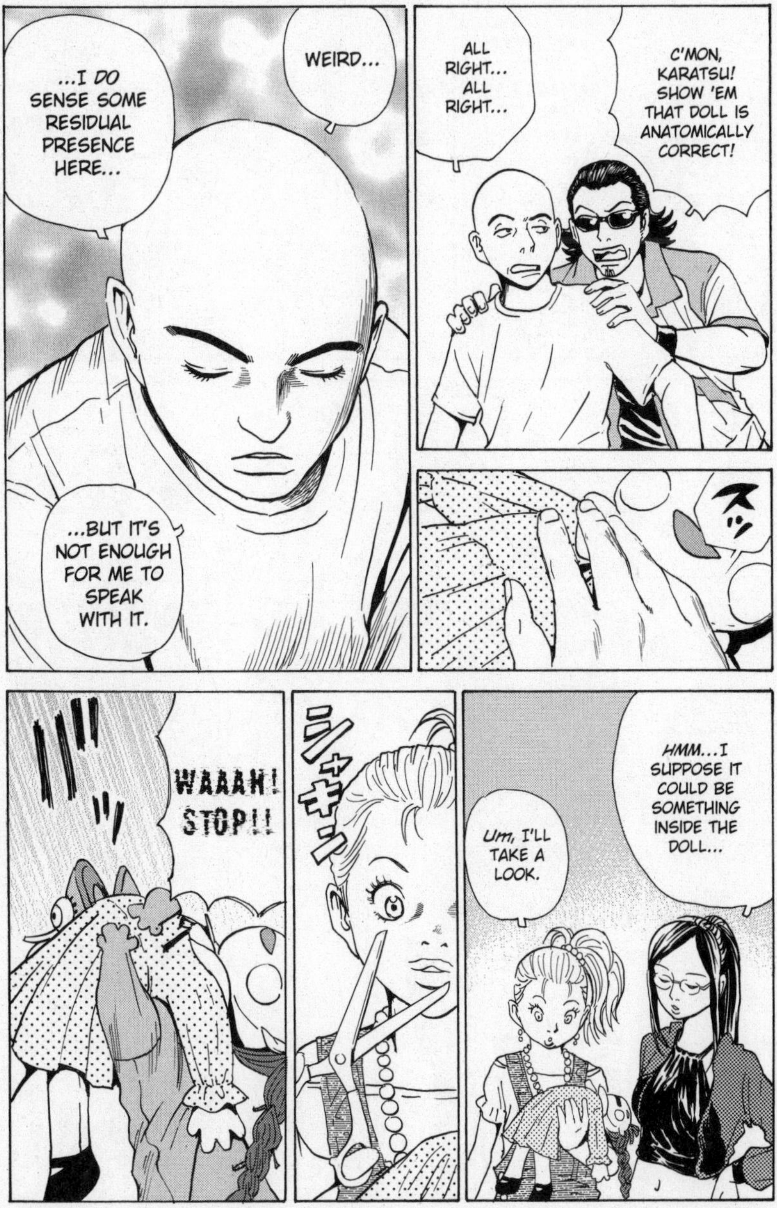
C'MON, KARATSU! SHOW 'EM THAT DOLL IS ANATOMICALLY CORRECT!
ALL RIGHT... ALL RIGHT...
スッ
WEIRD...
...I DO SENSE SOME RESIDUAL PRESENCE HERE...
...BUT IT'S NOT ENOUGH FOR ME TO SPEAK WITH IT.
HMM...I SUPPOSE IT COULD BE SOMETHING INSIDE THE DOLL...
Um, I'LL TAKE A LOOK.
シャキーン
WAAAH! STOP!!

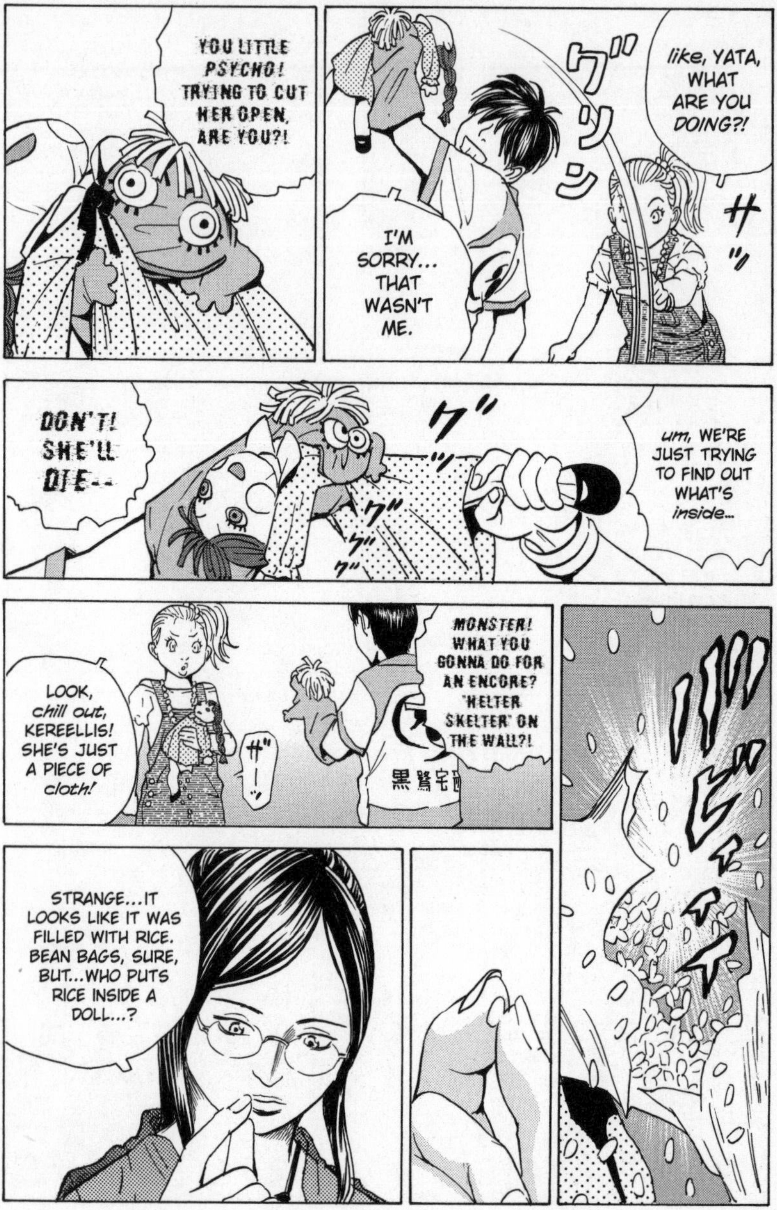
like, YATA, WHAT ARE YOU DOING?!
I'M SORRY... THAT WASN'T ME.
サッ
YOU LITTLE PSYCHO! TRYING TO CUT HER OPEN, ARE YOU?!
um, WE'RE JUST TRYING TO FIND OUT WHAT'S inside...
グッ
DON'T! SHE'LL DIE--
MONSTER! WHAT YOU GONNA DO FOR AN ENCORE? "HELTER SKELTER" ON THE WALL?!
ザーッ
LOOK, chill out, KEREELLIS! SHE'S JUST A PIECE OF cloth!
STRANGE...IT LOOKS LIKE IT WAS FILLED WITH RICE. BEAN BAGS, SURE, BUT...WHO PUTS RICE INSIDE A DOLL...?

AND *anyway*, KEREELLIS, SOMEONE HAD ALREADY POKED SOME HOLES IN IT.
LOOK. IT'S A THIN TEAR...*box* CUTTER, MAYBE.
SORRY, PAL. KARATSU CAN'T TALK TO IT, AND AS MAKINO POINTS OUT, IT'S JUST...
YOU HUMAN *BASTARDS!* I KNOW—UNLIKE THE INHABIT-ANTS OF DELTA PAVONIS IV—YOU HAVE ONLY *ONE* HEART!
AND YET, HOW CAN IT BE SO *COLD?* CLOTH MATTERS NOT! JUDGE ME BY MY CLOTH, DO YOU? *NO!* THIS GIRL HAS A *SOUL!* LET ME TALK TO HER!
...lolwut?
UH-HUH!
...REALLY ...?
I SEE, I SEE...
...HE *BETTER* NOT BE JOKING.

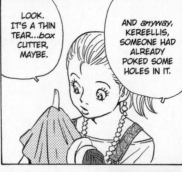

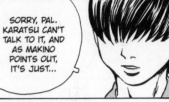

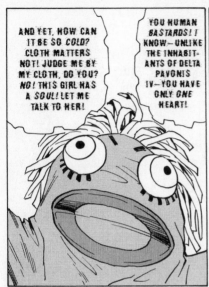

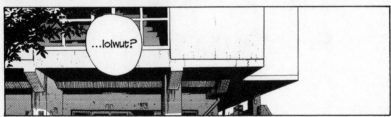

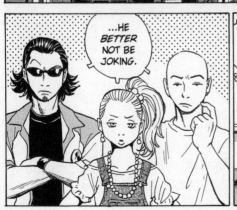

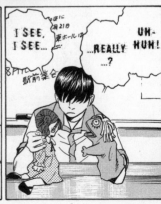

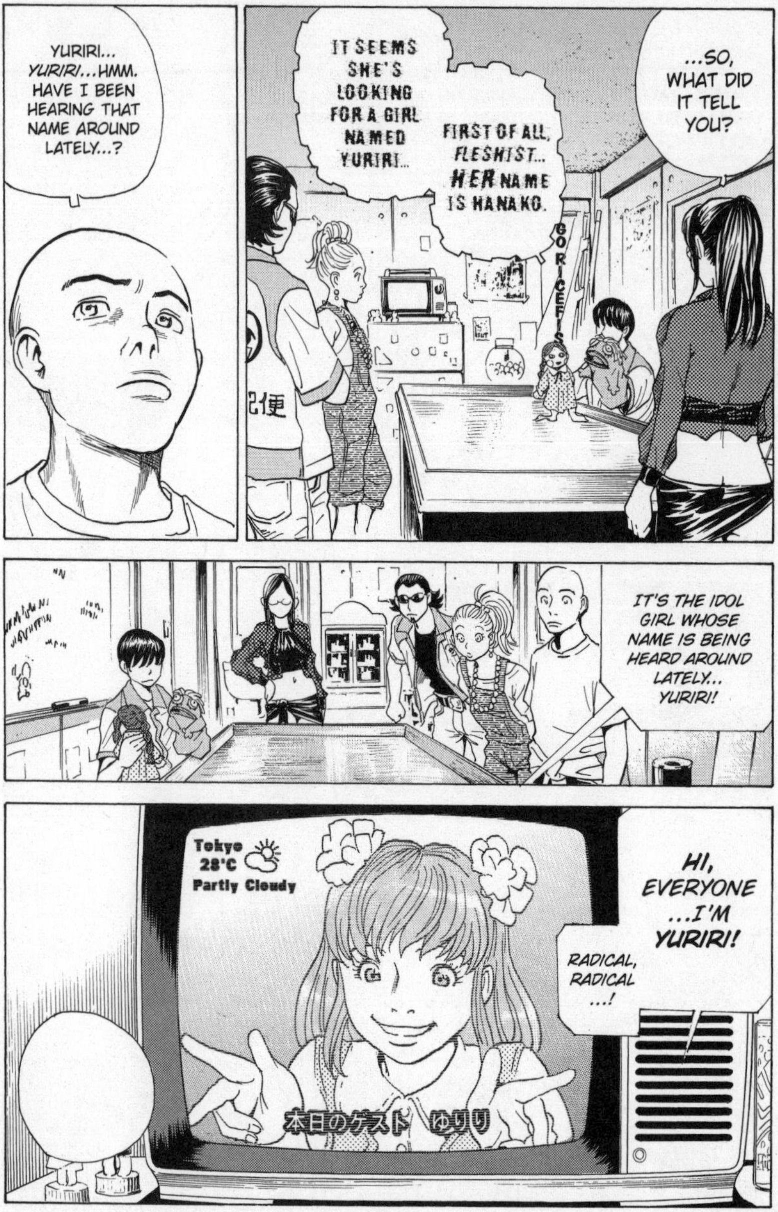
...SO, WHAT DID IT TELL YOU?
FIRST OF ALL, FLESHIST... HER NAME IS HANAKO.
IT SEEMS SHE'S LOOKING FOR A GIRL NAMED YURIRI...
GO RICEFIS
YURIRI... YURIRI...HMM. HAVE I BEEN HEARING THAT NAME AROUND LATELY...?
IT'S THE IDOL GIRL WHOSE NAME IS BEING HEARD AROUND LATELY... YURIRI!
HI, EVERYONE ...I'M YURIRI!
RADICAL, RADICAL ...!
Tokyo 28°C Partly Cloudy
本日のゲスト　ゆりり

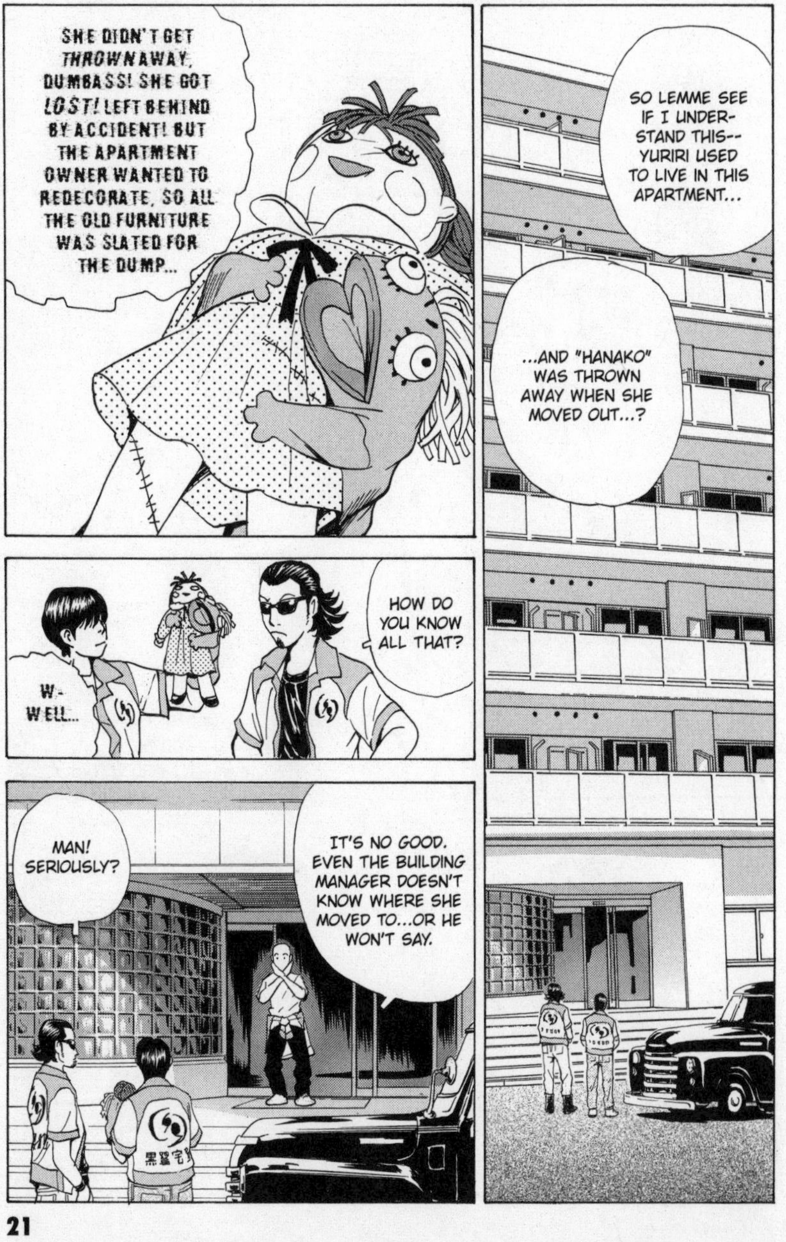
SO LEMME SEE IF I UNDERSTAND THIS-- YURIRI USED TO LIVE IN THIS APARTMENT...
...AND "HANAKO" WAS THROWN AWAY WHEN SHE MOVED OUT...?
SHE DIDN'T GET THROWN AWAY, DUMBASS! SHE GOT LOST! LEFT BEHIND BY ACCIDENT! BUT THE APARTMENT OWNER WANTED TO REDECORATE, SO ALL THE OLD FURNITURE WAS SLATED FOR THE DUMP...
HOW DO YOU KNOW ALL THAT?
W-WELL...
IT'S NO GOOD. EVEN THE BUILDING MANAGER DOESN'T KNOW WHERE SHE MOVED TO...OR HE WON'T SAY.
MAN! SERIOUSLY?

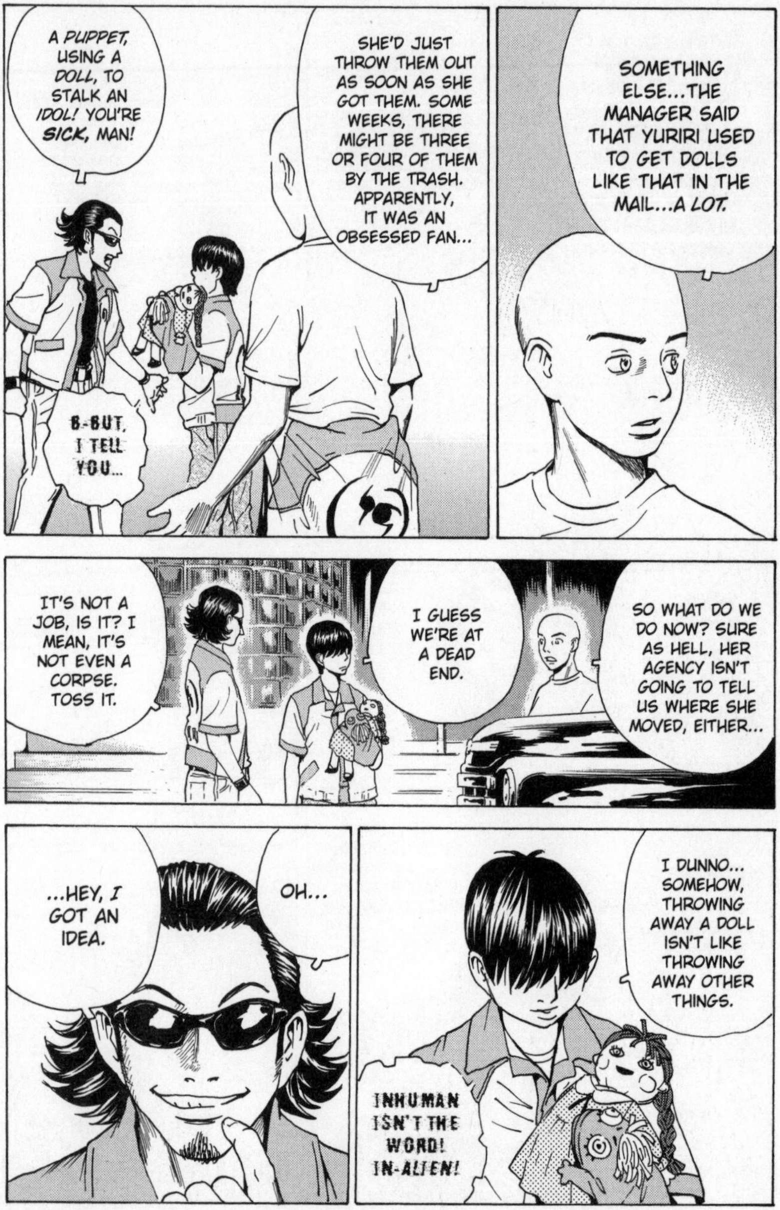
SOMETHING ELSE...THE MANAGER SAID THAT YURIRI USED TO GET DOLLS LIKE THAT IN THE MAIL...A *LOT.*
SHE'D JUST THROW THEM OUT AS SOON AS SHE GOT THEM. SOME WEEKS, THERE MIGHT BE THREE OR FOUR OF THEM BY THE TRASH. APPARENTLY, IT WAS AN OBSESSED FAN...
A *PUPPET,* USING A *DOLL,* TO STALK AN *IDOL!* YOU'RE ***SICK,*** MAN!
B-BUT, I TELL YOU...
SO WHAT DO WE DO NOW? SURE AS HELL, HER AGENCY ISN'T GOING TO TELL US WHERE SHE MOVED, EITHER...
I GUESS WE'RE AT A DEAD END.
IT'S NOT A JOB, IS IT? I MEAN, IT'S NOT EVEN A CORPSE. TOSS IT.
I DUNNO... SOMEHOW, THROWING AWAY A DOLL ISN'T LIKE THROWING AWAY OTHER THINGS.
INHUMAN ISN'T THE WORD! IN-ALIEN!
OH...
...HEY, *I* GOT AN IDEA.

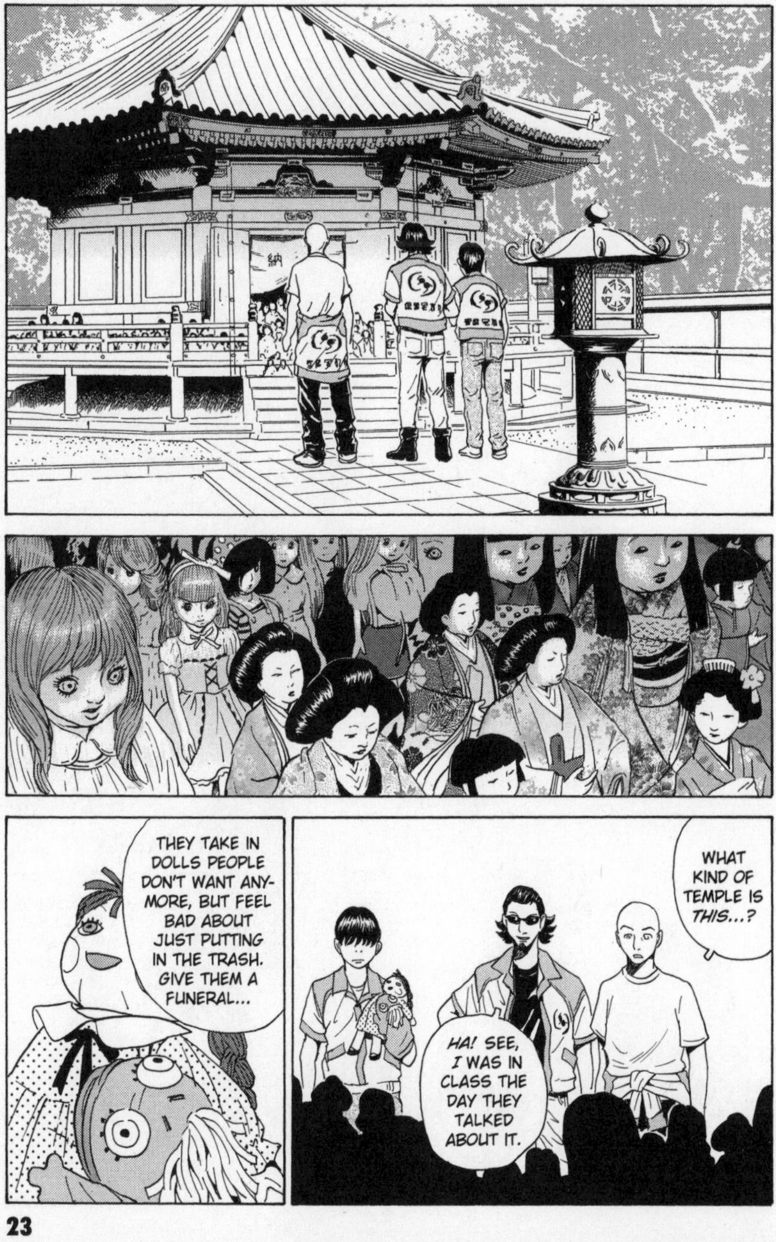
WHAT KIND OF TEMPLE IS *THIS*...?
HA! SEE, *I* WAS IN CLASS THE DAY THEY TALKED ABOUT IT.
THEY TAKE IN DOLLS PEOPLE DON'T WANT ANY-MORE, BUT FEEL BAD ABOUT JUST PUTTING IN THE TRASH. GIVE THEM A FUNERAL...

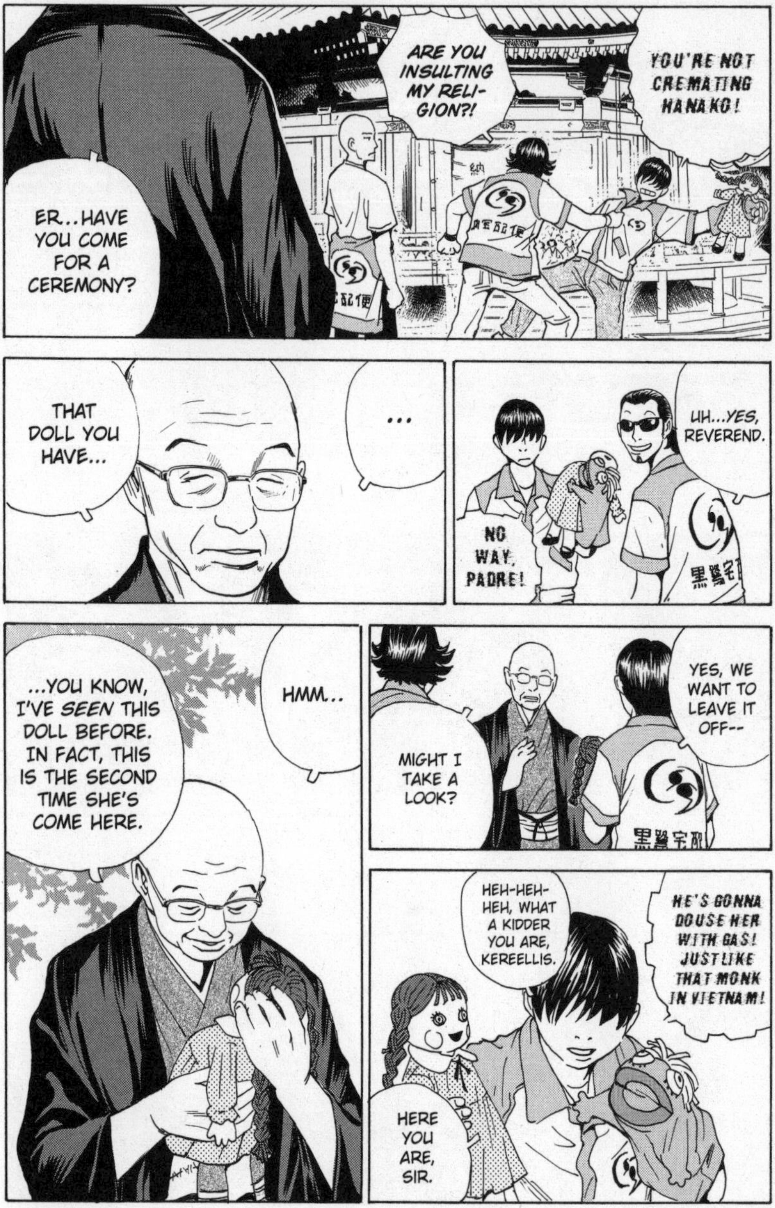
YOU'RE NOT CREMATING HANAKO!
ARE YOU INSULTING MY RELI-GION?!
ER...HAVE YOU COME FOR A CEREMONY?
UH...YES, REVEREND.
NO WAY, PADRE!
...
THAT DOLL YOU HAVE...
YES, WE WANT TO LEAVE IT OFF--
MIGHT I TAKE A LOOK?
HE'S GONNA DOUSE HER WITH GAS! JUST LIKE THAT MONK IN VIETNAM!
HEH-HEH-HEH, WHAT A KIDDER YOU ARE, KEREELLIS.
HERE YOU ARE, SIR.
HMM..
...YOU KNOW, I'VE SEEN THIS DOLL BEFORE. IN FACT, THIS IS THE SECOND TIME SHE'S COME HERE.

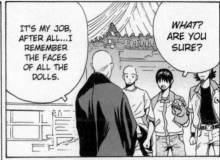

WHAT? ARE YOU SURE?
IT'S MY JOB, AFTER ALL...I REMEMBER THE FACES OF ALL THE DOLLS.
WE HAD A THEFT HERE BEFORE...AND THIS IS ONE OF THE DOLLS THAT WERE TAKEN.
...THEFT? OF DOLLS?
YES...AND NOT ONLY THAT ONE...I THINK IT WOULD BE EASIER TO SHOW YOU.
THIS WAY PLEASE, SIR.
UM... YEAH.
HERE THEY ARE...TAKE A LOOK.

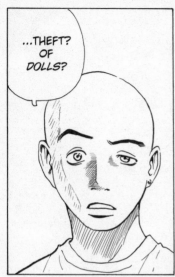

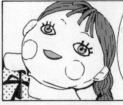

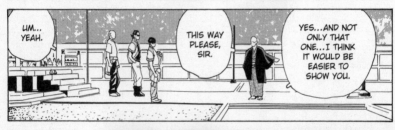

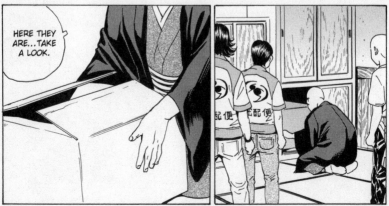

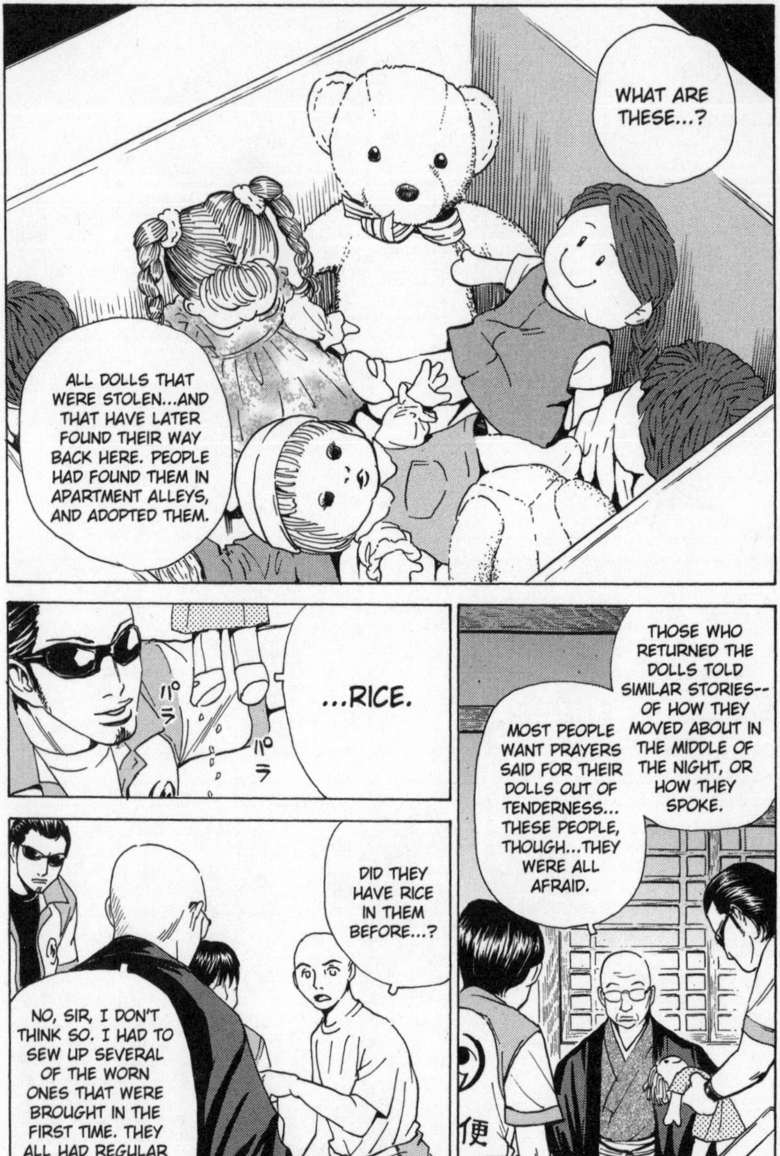
WHAT ARE THESE...?
ALL DOLLS THAT WERE STOLEN...AND THAT HAVE LATER FOUND THEIR WAY BACK HERE. PEOPLE HAD FOUND THEM IN APARTMENT ALLEYS, AND ADOPTED THEM.
THOSE WHO RETURNED THE DOLLS TOLD SIMILAR STORIES--OF HOW THEY MOVED ABOUT IN THE MIDDLE OF THE NIGHT, OR HOW THEY SPOKE.
MOST PEOPLE WANT PRAYERS SAID FOR THEIR DOLLS OUT OF TENDERNESS... THESE PEOPLE, THOUGH...THEY WERE ALL AFRAID.
便
パラ
パラ
...RICE.
DID THEY HAVE RICE IN THEM BEFORE...?
NO, SIR, I DON'T THINK SO. I HAD TO SEW UP SEVERAL OF THE WORN ONES THAT WERE BROUGHT IN THE FIRST TIME. THEY ALL HAD REGULAR STUFFING.

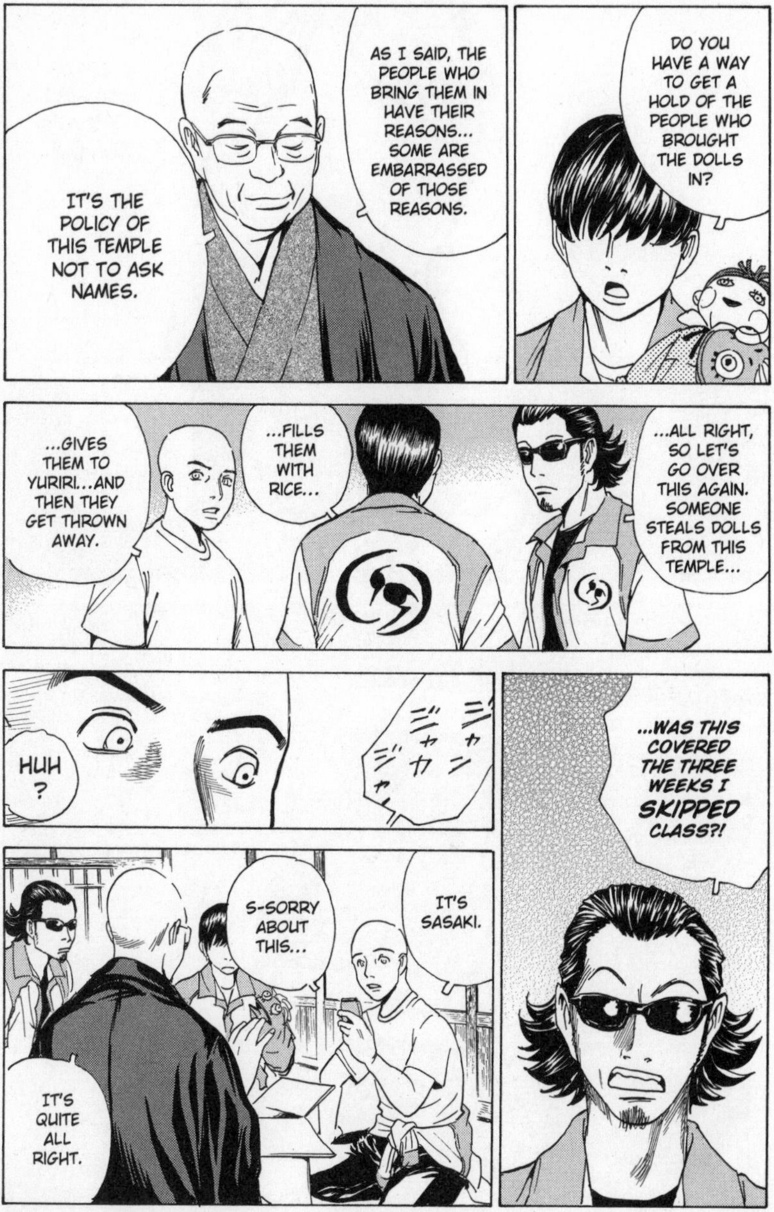
DO YOU HAVE A WAY TO GET A HOLD OF THE PEOPLE WHO BROUGHT THE DOLLS IN?
AS I SAID, THE PEOPLE WHO BRING THEM IN HAVE THEIR REASONS... SOME ARE EMBARRASSED OF THOSE REASONS.
IT'S THE POLICY OF THIS TEMPLE NOT TO ASK NAMES.
...ALL RIGHT, SO LET'S GO OVER THIS AGAIN. SOMEONE STEALS DOLLS FROM THIS TEMPLE...
...FILLS THEM WITH RICE...
...GIVES THEM TO YURIRI...AND THEN THEY GET THROWN AWAY.
...WAS THIS COVERED THE THREE WEEKS I *SKIPPED* CLASS?!
ジャンジャカジャ
HUH?
IT'S SASAKI.
S-SORRY ABOUT THIS...
IT'S QUITE ALL RIGHT.

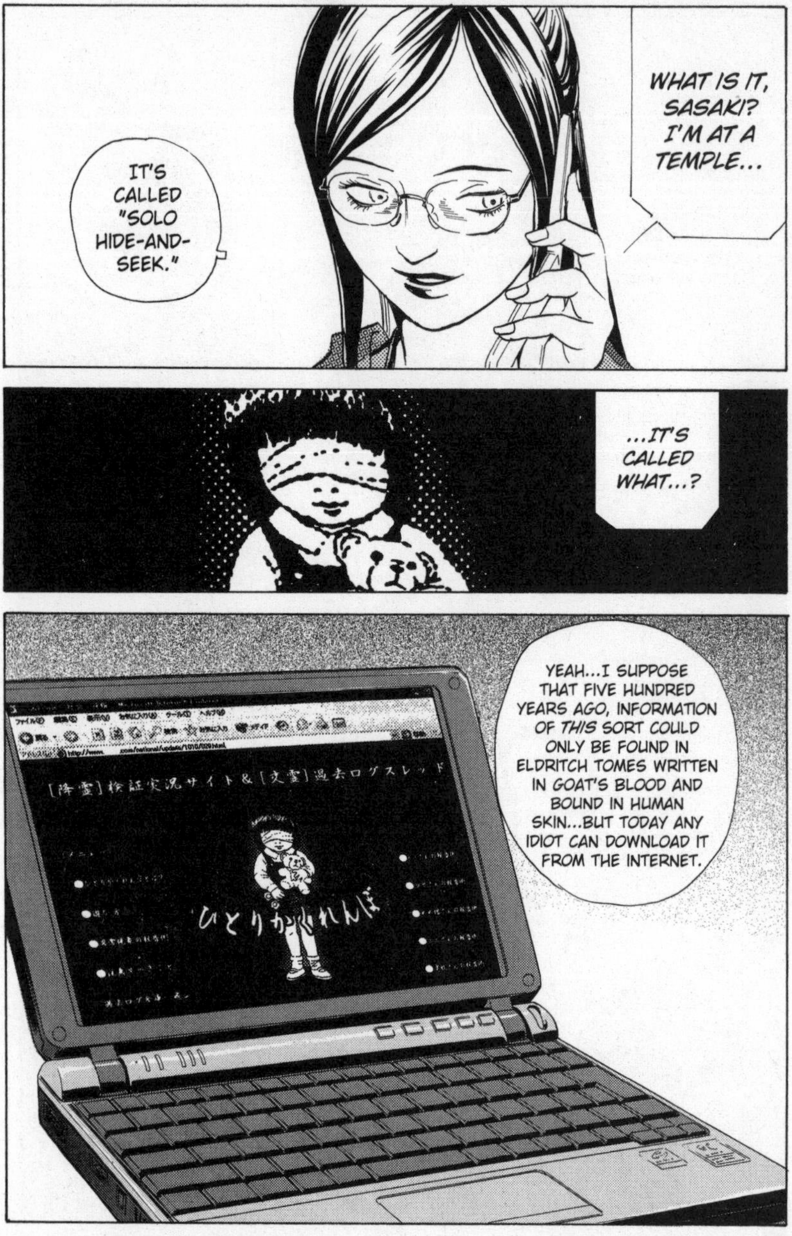
WHAT IS IT, SASAKI? I'M AT A TEMPLE...
IT'S CALLED "SOLO HIDE-AND-SEEK."
...IT'S CALLED WHAT...?
[降霊]検証実況サイト&[交霊]過去ログスレッド
YEAH...I SUPPOSE THAT FIVE HUNDRED YEARS AGO, INFORMATION OF *THIS* SORT COULD ONLY BE FOUND IN ELDRITCH TOMES WRITTEN IN GOAT'S BLOOD AND BOUND IN HUMAN SKIN...BUT TODAY ANY IDIOT CAN DOWNLOAD IT FROM THE INTERNET.

1st delivery: key to an apartment—the end

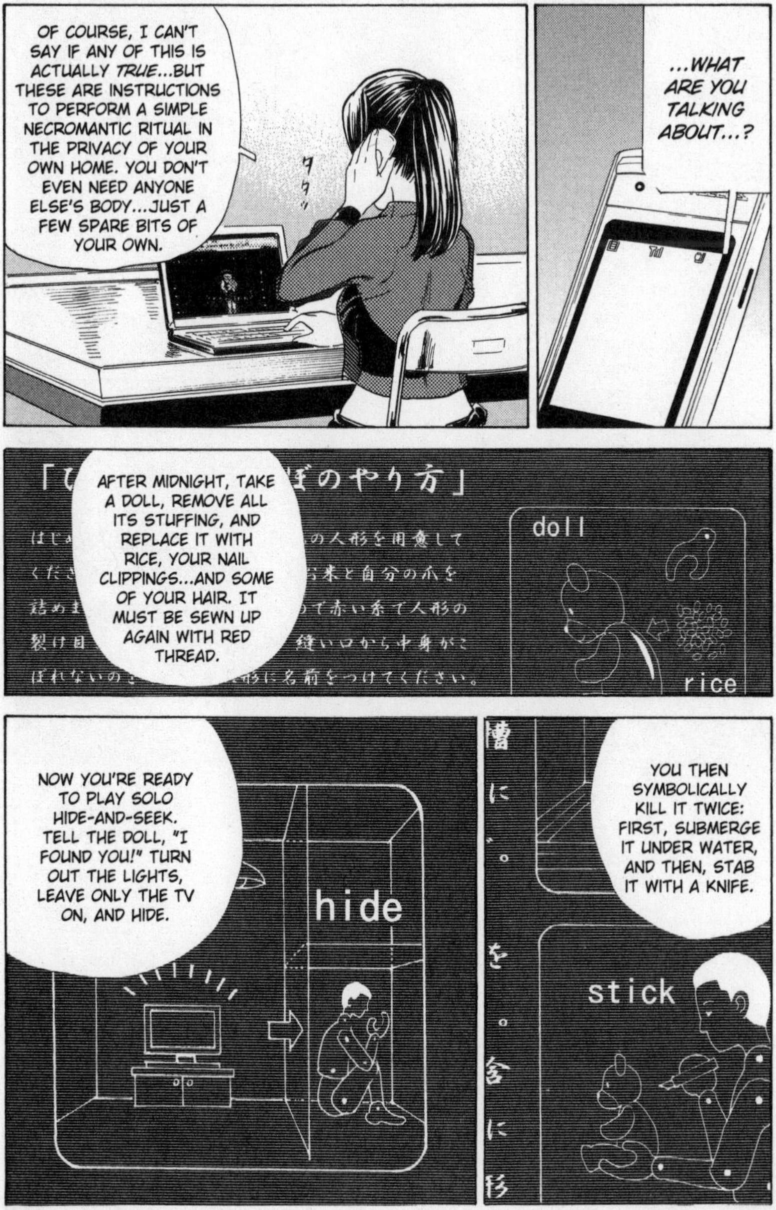
...WHAT ARE YOU TALKING ABOUT...?
OF COURSE, I CAN'T SAY IF ANY OF THIS IS ACTUALLY *TRUE*...BUT THESE ARE INSTRUCTIONS TO PERFORM A SIMPLE NECROMANTIC RITUAL IN THE PRIVACY OF YOUR OWN HOME. YOU DON'T EVEN NEED ANYONE ELSE'S BODY...JUST A FEW SPARE BITS OF YOUR OWN.
AFTER MIDNIGHT, TAKE A DOLL, REMOVE ALL ITS STUFFING, AND REPLACE IT WITH RICE, YOUR NAIL CLIPPINGS...AND SOME OF YOUR HAIR. IT MUST BE SEWN UP AGAIN WITH RED THREAD.
doll
rice
YOU THEN SYMBOLICALLY KILL IT TWICE: FIRST, SUBMERGE IT UNDER WATER, AND THEN, STAB IT WITH A KNIFE.
stick
NOW YOU'RE READY TO PLAY SOLO HIDE-AND-SEEK. TELL THE DOLL, "I FOUND YOU!" TURN OUT THE LIGHTS, LEAVE ONLY THE TV ON, AND HIDE.
hide

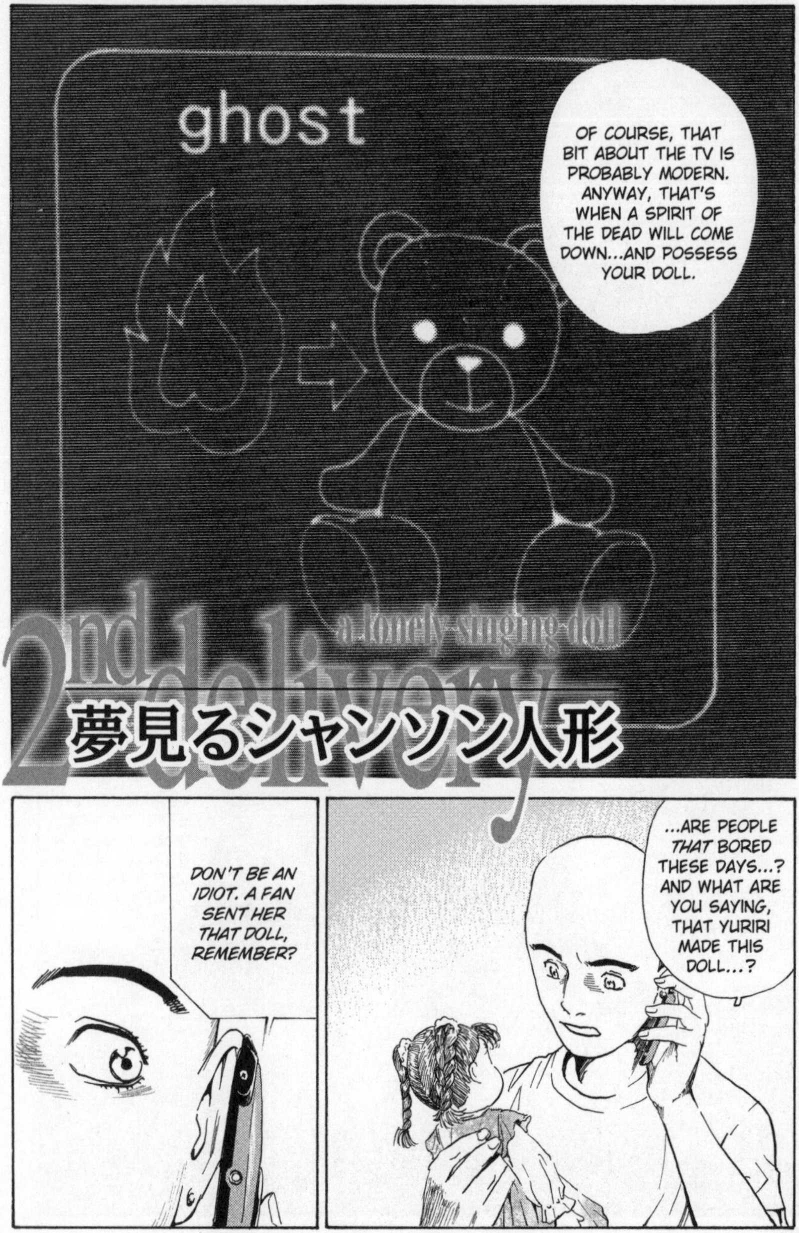
ghost
OF COURSE, THAT BIT ABOUT THE TV IS PROBABLY MODERN. ANYWAY, THAT'S WHEN A SPIRIT OF THE DEAD WILL COME DOWN...AND POSSESS YOUR DOLL.
2nd delivery
a lonely-singing-doll
夢見るシャンソン人形
...ARE PEOPLE *THAT* BORED THESE DAYS...? AND WHAT ARE YOU SAYING, THAT YURIRI MADE THIS DOLL...?
DON'T BE AN IDIOT. A FAN SENT HER THAT DOLL, REMEMBER?

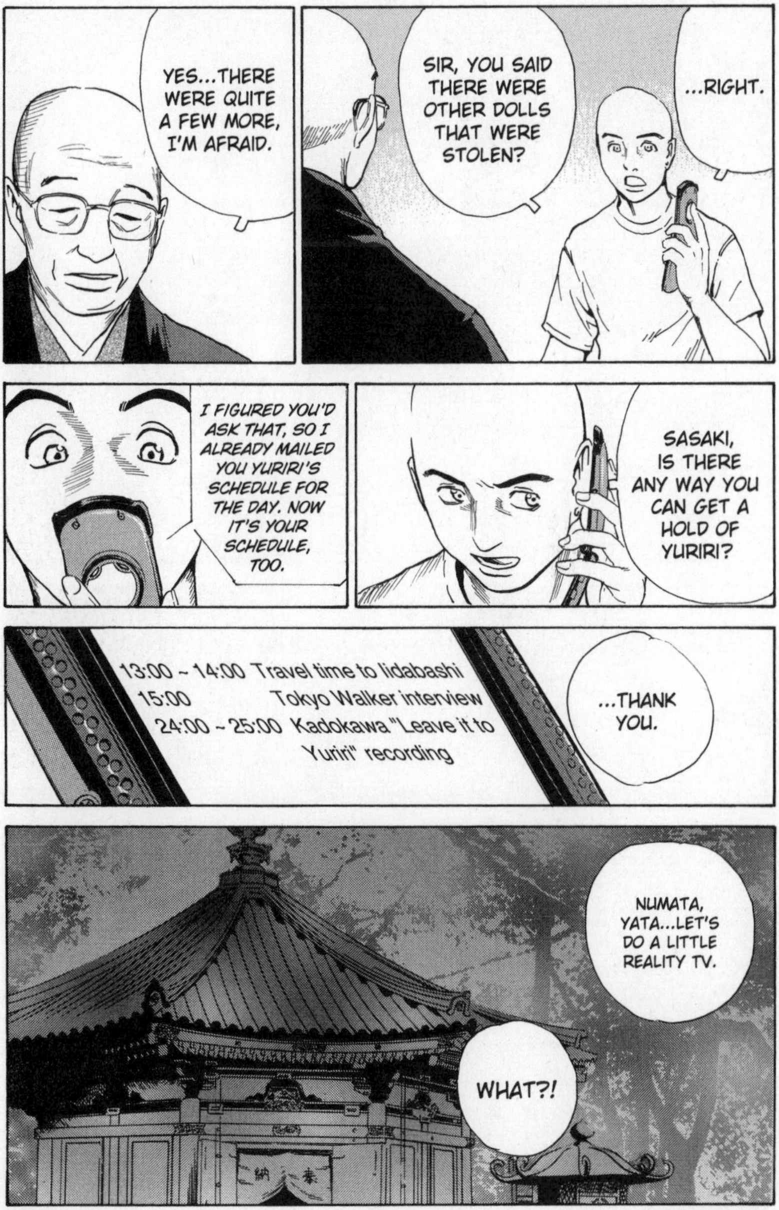
...RIGHT.
SIR, YOU SAID THERE WERE OTHER DOLLS THAT WERE STOLEN?
YES...THERE WERE QUITE A FEW MORE, I'M AFRAID.
SASAKI, IS THERE ANY WAY YOU CAN GET A HOLD OF YURIRI?
I FIGURED YOU'D ASK THAT, SO I ALREADY MAILED YOU YURIRI'S SCHEDULE FOR THE DAY. NOW IT'S YOUR SCHEDULE, TOO.
...THANK YOU.
13:00 ~ 14:00 Travel time to Iidabashi
15:00 Tokyo Walker interview
24:00 ~ 25:00 Kadokawa "Leave it to Yuriri" recording
NUMATA, YATA...LET'S DO A LITTLE REALITY TV.
WHAT?!

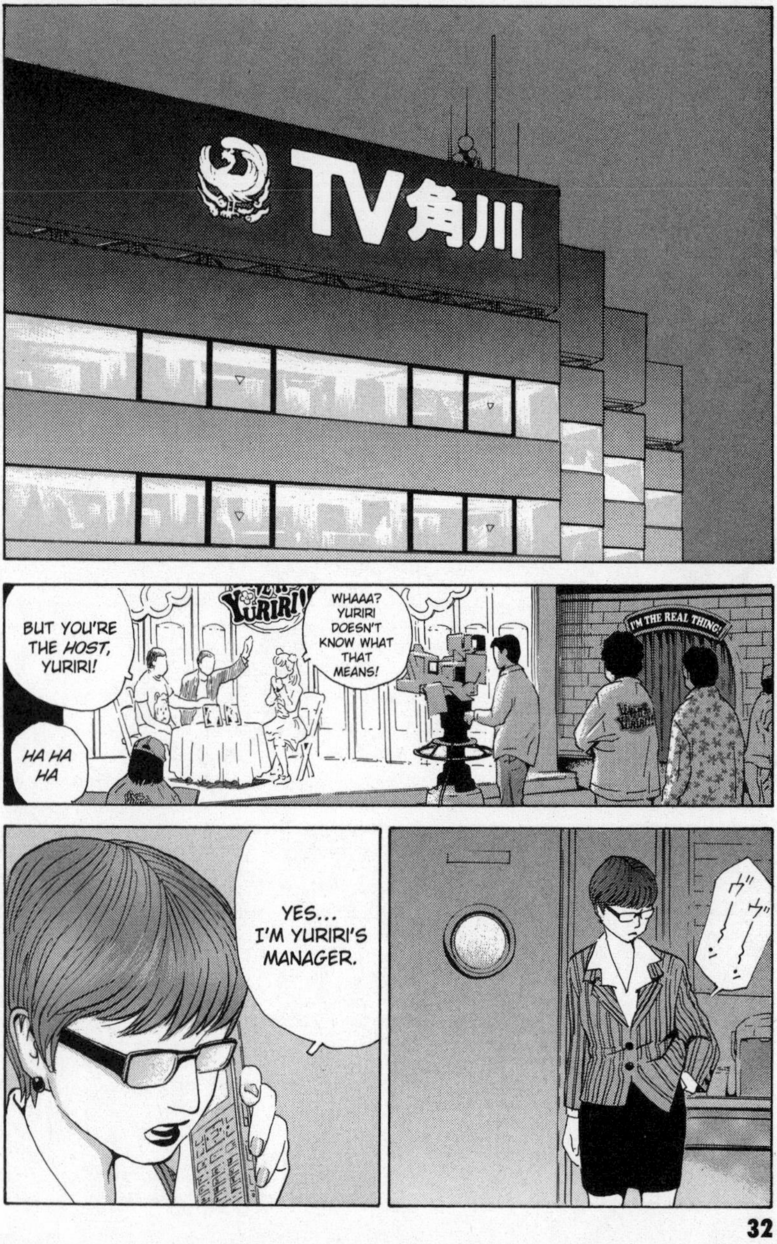
TV角川
I'M THE REAL THING!
WHAAA? YURIRI DOESN'T KNOW WHAT THAT MEANS!
BUT YOU'RE THE *HOST*, YURIRI!
HA HA HA
YES... I'M YURIRI'S MANAGER.

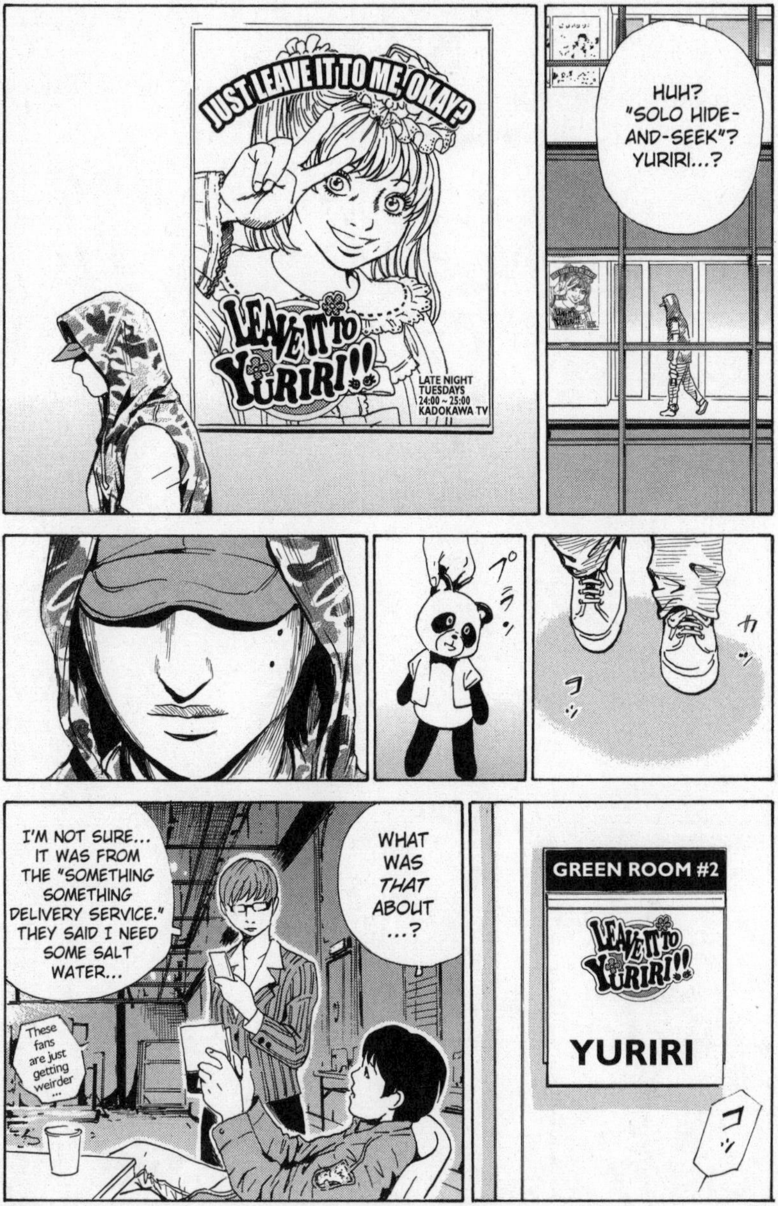
HUH? "SOLO HIDE-AND-SEEK"? YURIRI...?
JUST LEAVE IT TO ME, OKAY?
LEAVE IT TO YURIRI!!
LATE NIGHT TUESDAYS 24:00 ~ 25:00 KADOKAWA TV
カッ
コッ
プラン
GREEN ROOM #2
LEAVE IT TO YURIRI!!
YURIRI
コッ
WHAT WAS THAT ABOUT...?
I'M NOT SURE... IT WAS FROM THE "SOMETHING SOMETHING DELIVERY SERVICE." THEY SAID I NEED SOME SALT WATER...
These fans are just getting weirder...

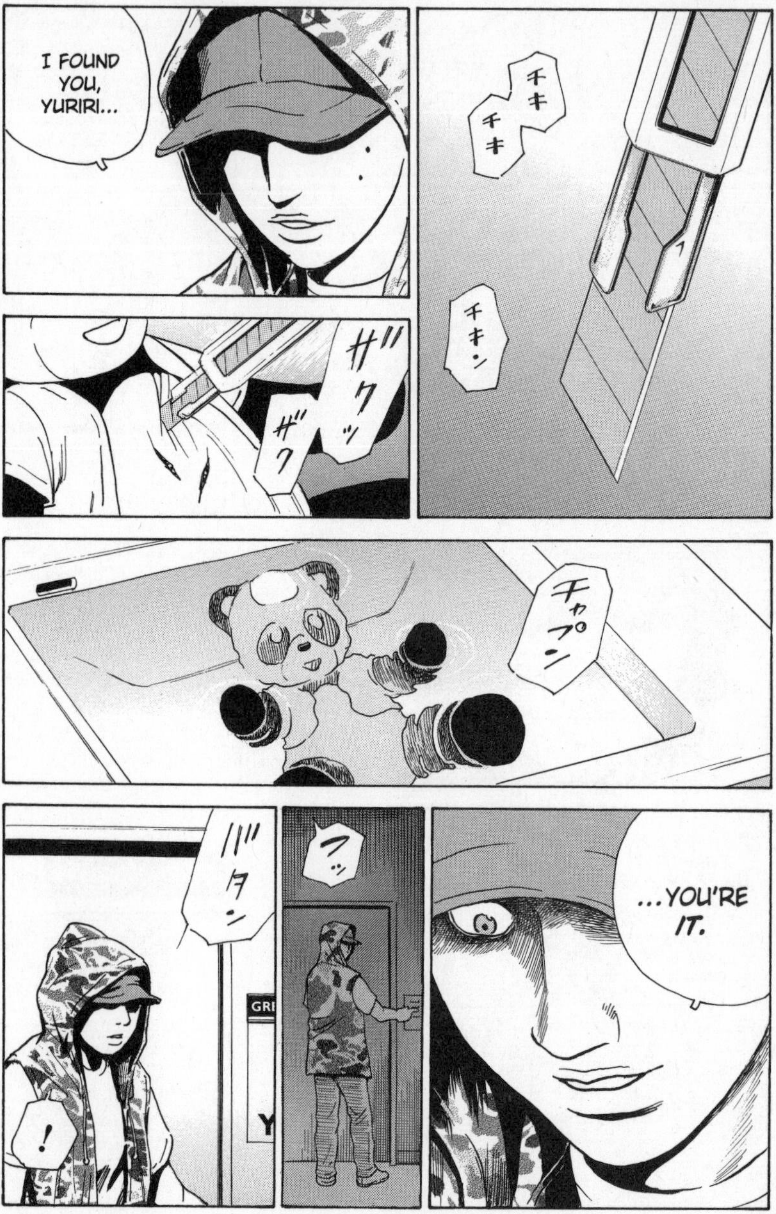
チキ
チキ
チキン
I FOUND YOU, YURIRI...
ザクッ
ザク
チャプン
...YOU'RE IT.
フッ
バタン
!

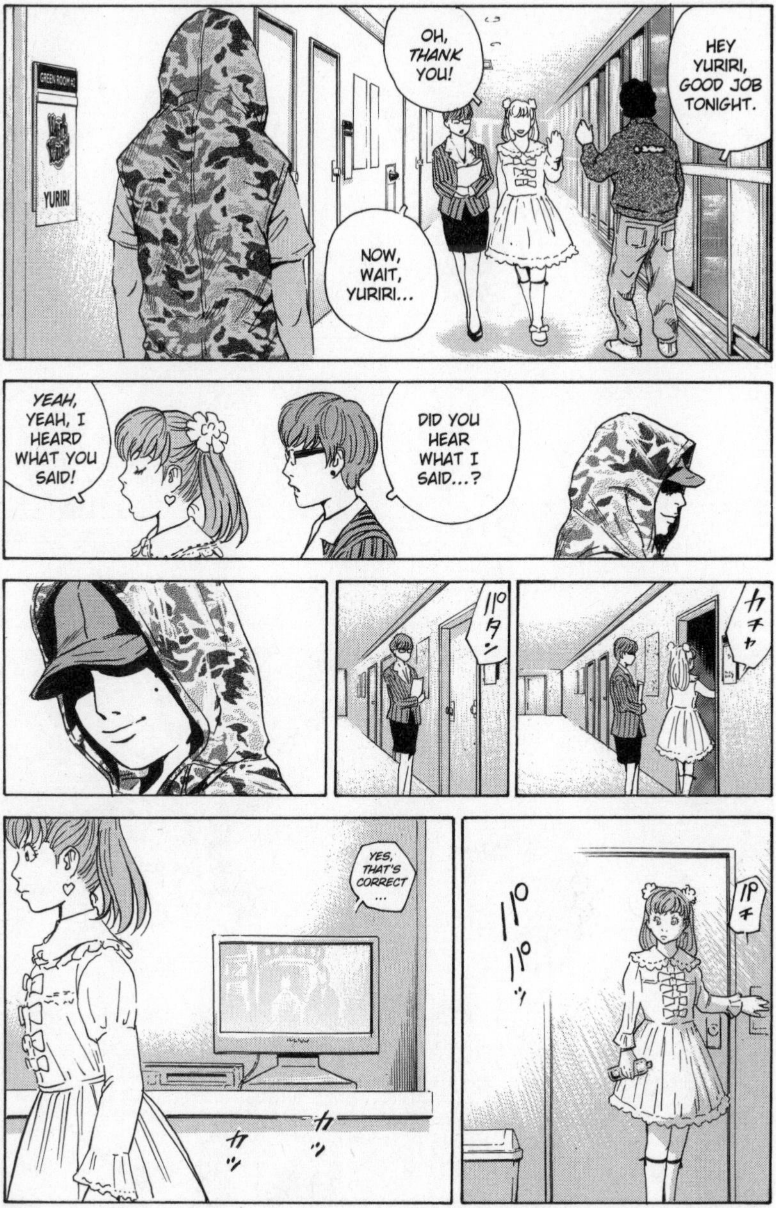
HEY YURIRI, GOOD JOB TONIGHT.
OH, *THANK* YOU!
GREEN ROOM #2
YURIRI
NOW, WAIT, YURIRI...
DID YOU HEAR WHAT I SAID...?
YEAH, YEAH, I HEARD WHAT YOU SAID!
カチャ
パタン
パチ
パパッ
YES, THAT'S CORRECT ...
カッ
カッ

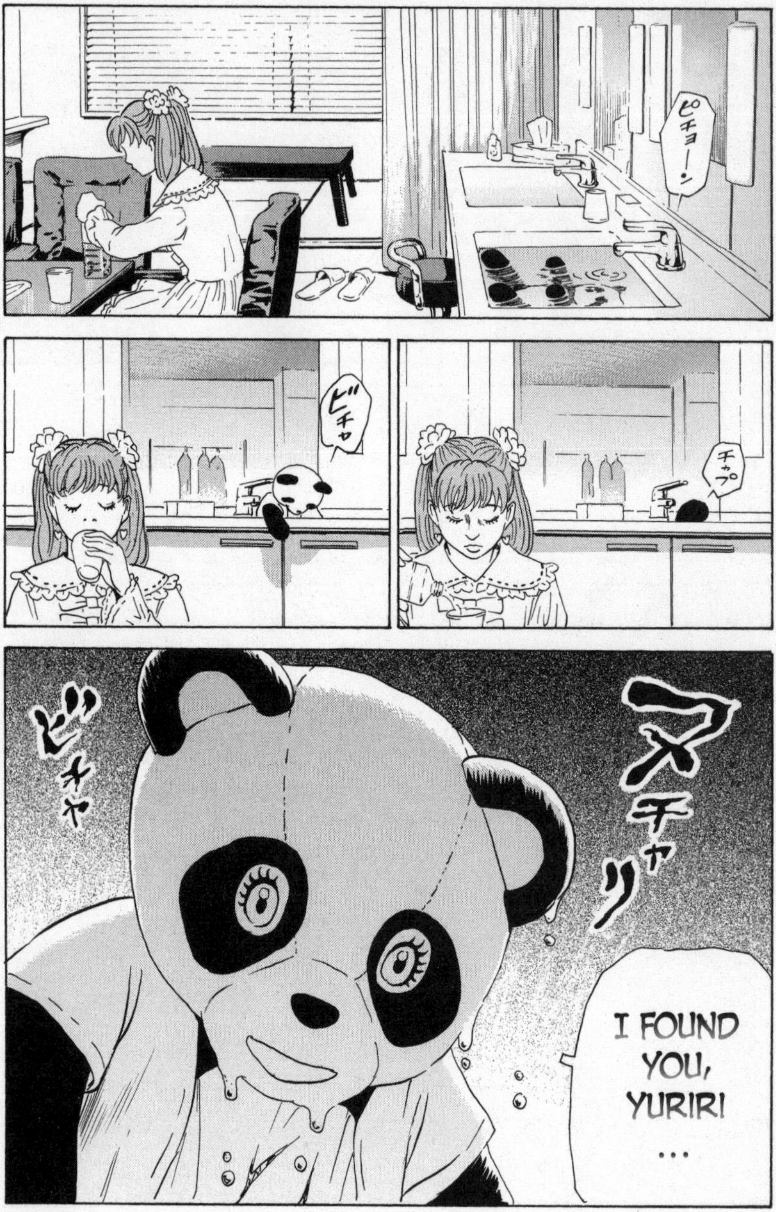
ピチョーン
チャプ
ピチャ
ヌチャリ
ピチャ
I FOUND YOU, YURIRI
...

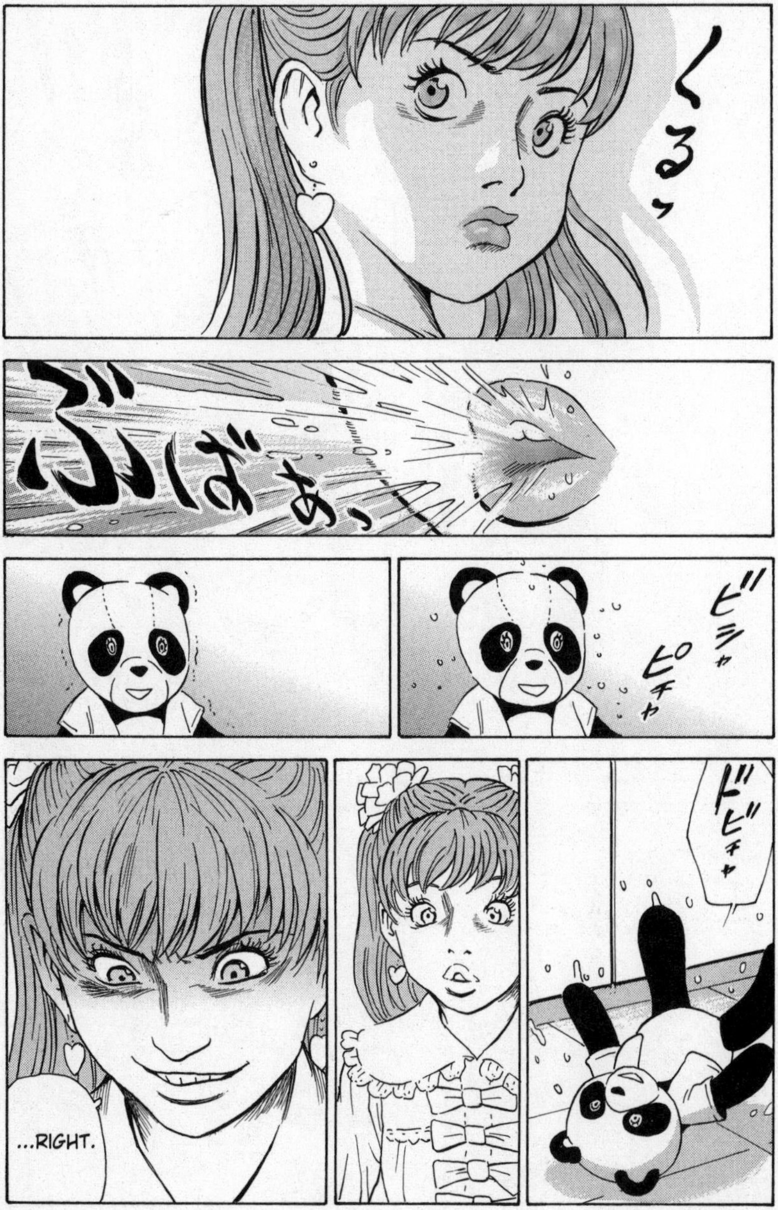

くるっ
ぶばぁっ
ビシャ
ピチャ
ドビチャ
...RIGHT.

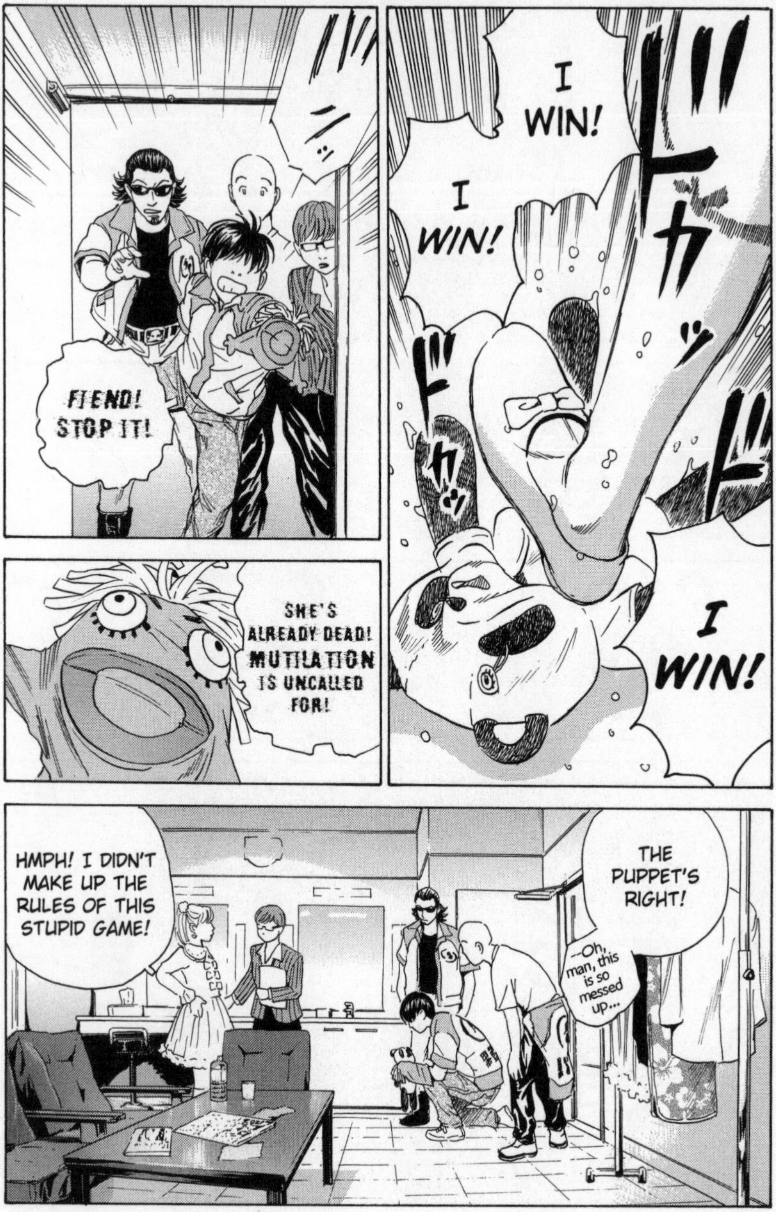
I WIN!
I WIN!
I WIN!
...
FIEND! STOP IT!
SHE'S ALREADY DEAD! MUTILATION IS UNCALLED FOR!
THE PUPPET'S RIGHT!
--Oh, man, this is so messed up...
HMPH! I DIDN'T MAKE UP THE RULES OF THIS STUPID GAME!

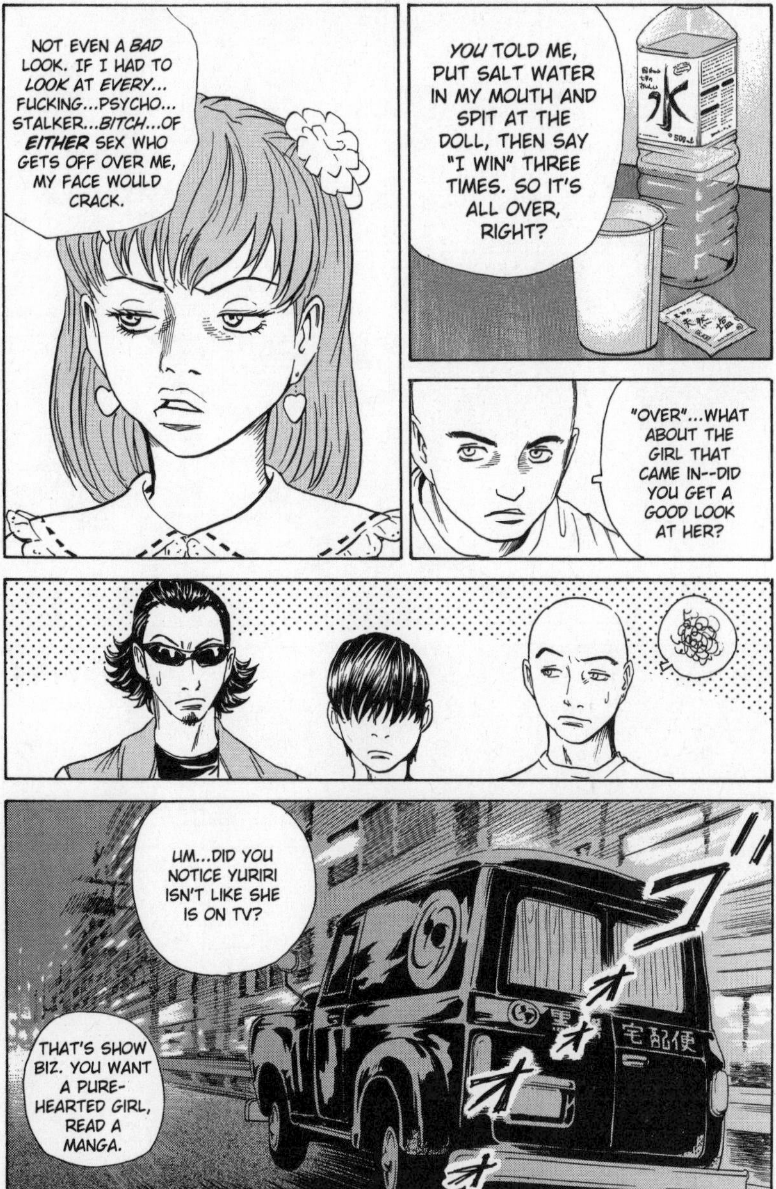

YOU TOLD ME, PUT SALT WATER IN MY MOUTH AND SPIT AT THE DOLL, THEN SAY "I WIN" THREE TIMES. SO IT'S ALL OVER, RIGHT?
水
"OVER"...WHAT ABOUT THE GIRL THAT CAME IN--DID YOU GET A GOOD LOOK AT HER?
NOT EVEN A *BAD* LOOK. IF I HAD TO *LOOK* AT *EVERY*... FUCKING...PSYCHO... STALKER...*BITCH*...OF **EITHER** SEX WHO GETS OFF OVER ME, MY FACE WOULD CRACK.
UM...DID YOU NOTICE YURIRI ISN'T LIKE SHE IS ON TV?
ゴオオオオ
宅配便
THAT'S SHOW BIZ. YOU WANT A PURE-HEARTED GIRL, READ A MANGA.

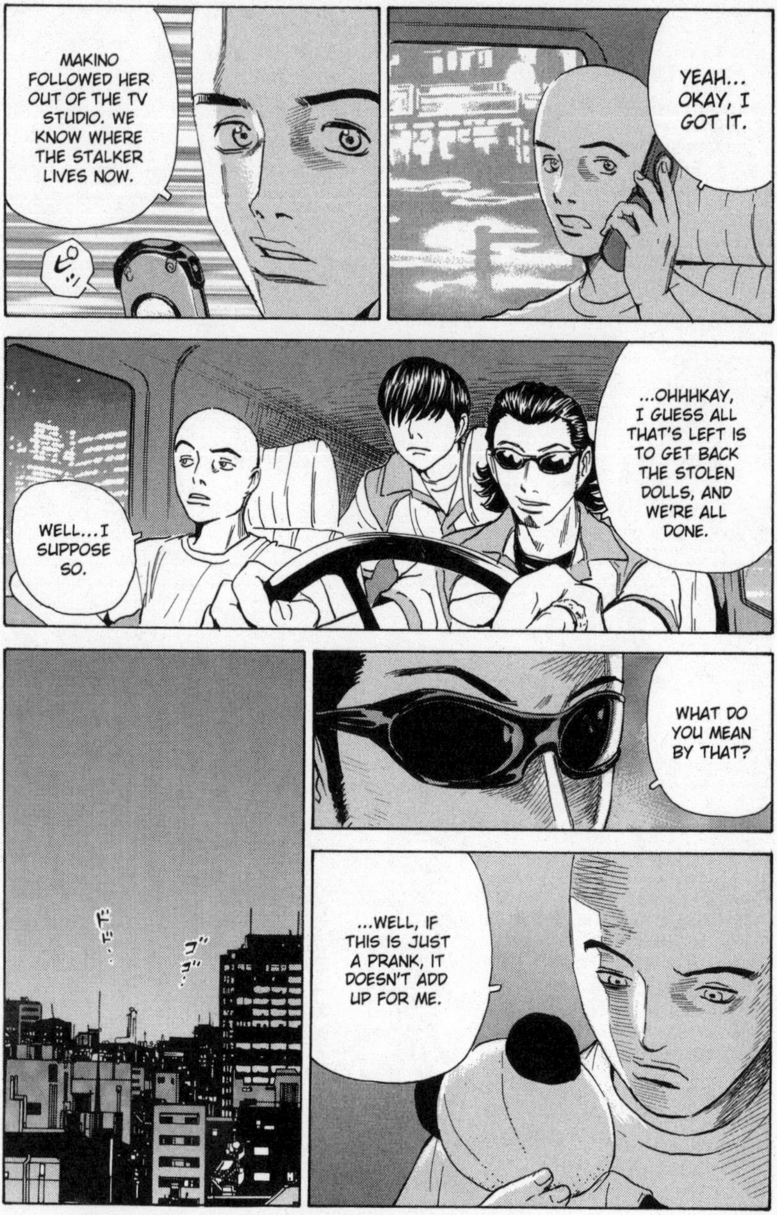
YEAH... OKAY, I GOT IT.
MAKINO FOLLOWED HER OUT OF THE TV STUDIO. WE KNOW WHERE THE STALKER LIVES NOW.
...OHHHKAY, I GUESS ALL THAT'S LEFT IS TO GET BACK THE STOLEN DOLLS, AND WE'RE ALL DONE.
WELL...I SUPPOSE SO.
WHAT DO YOU MEAN BY THAT?
...WELL, IF THIS IS JUST A PRANK, IT DOESN'T ADD UP FOR ME.

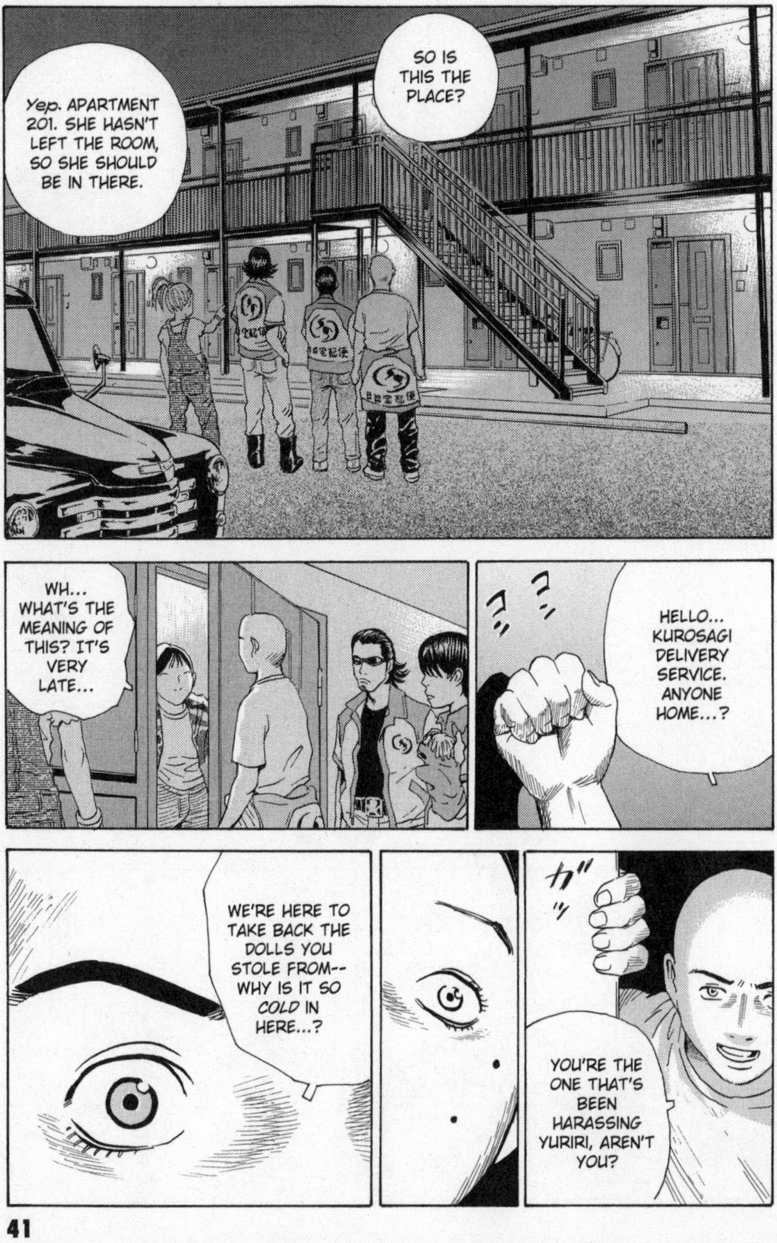
SO IS THIS THE PLACE?
Yep. APARTMENT 201. SHE HASN'T LEFT THE ROOM, SO SHE SHOULD BE IN THERE.
HELLO... KUROSAGI DELIVERY SERVICE. ANYONE HOME...?
WH... WHAT'S THE MEANING OF THIS? IT'S VERY LATE...
ガッ
YOU'RE THE ONE THAT'S BEEN HARASSING YURIRI, AREN'T YOU?
WE'RE HERE TO TAKE BACK THE DOLLS YOU STOLE FROM-- WHY IS IT SO *COLD* IN HERE...?

HE'S--
カッ
メキッ
OW!
N-NUMATA, SHE'S CRUSHING MY F- FINGERS... PULL...
HUH ?!
--he's dead..

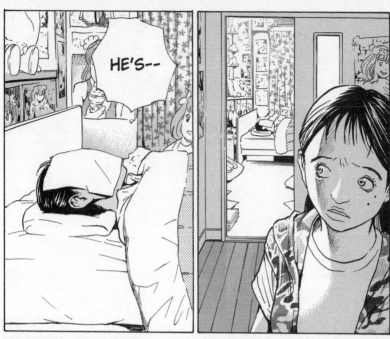

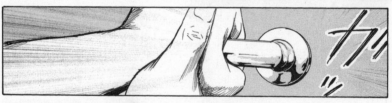

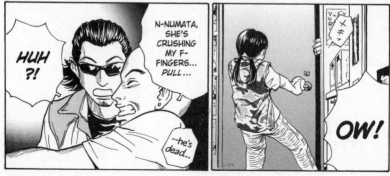

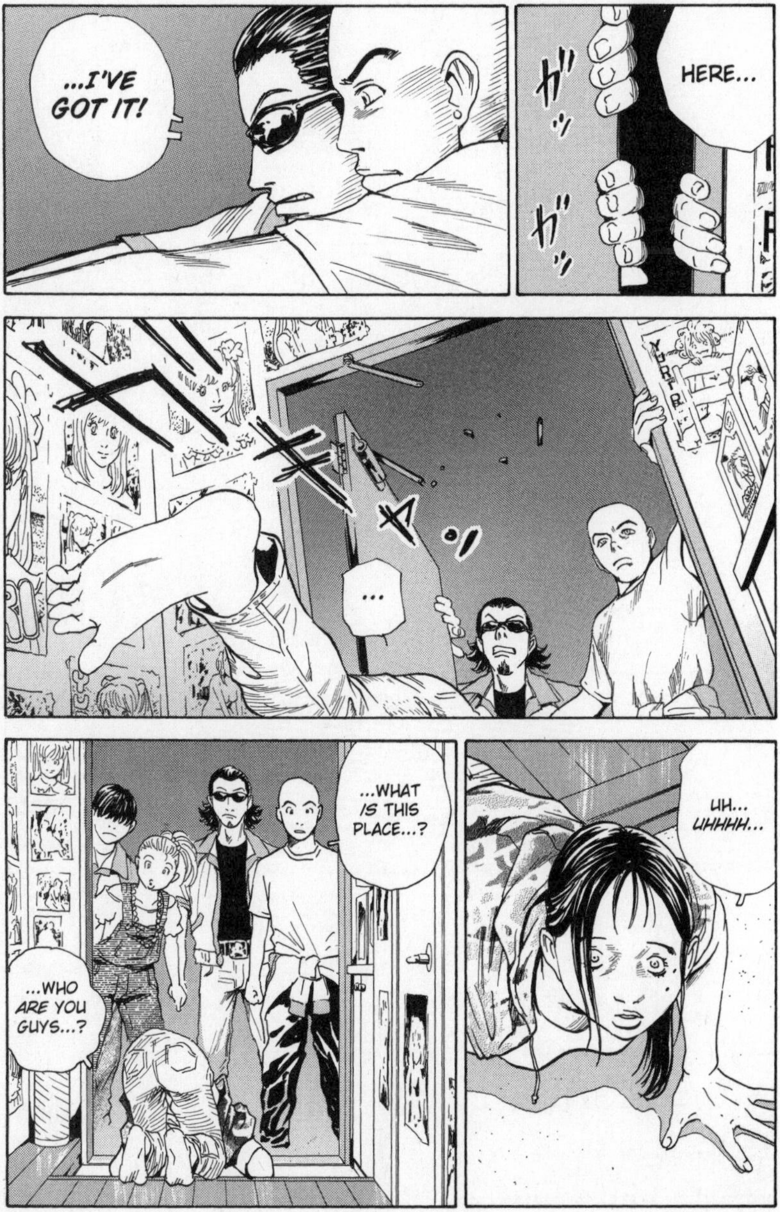
ガッ
ガッ
HERE...
...I'VE GOT IT!
...
UH... UHHHH...
...WHAT IS THIS PLACE...?
...WHO ARE YOU GUYS...?

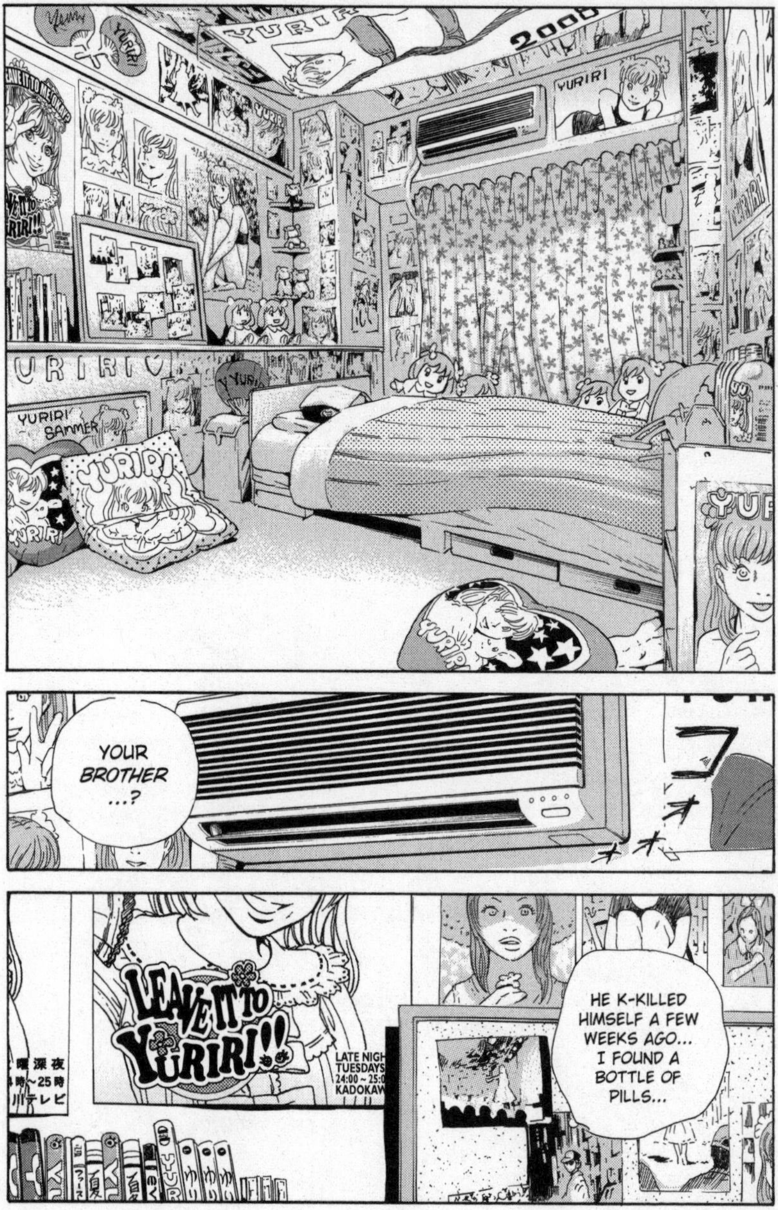
YURIRI
2008
YOUR BROTHER ...?
LEAVE IT TO YURIRI!!
HE K-KILLED HIMSELF A FEW WEEKS AGO... I FOUND A BOTTLE OF PILLS...

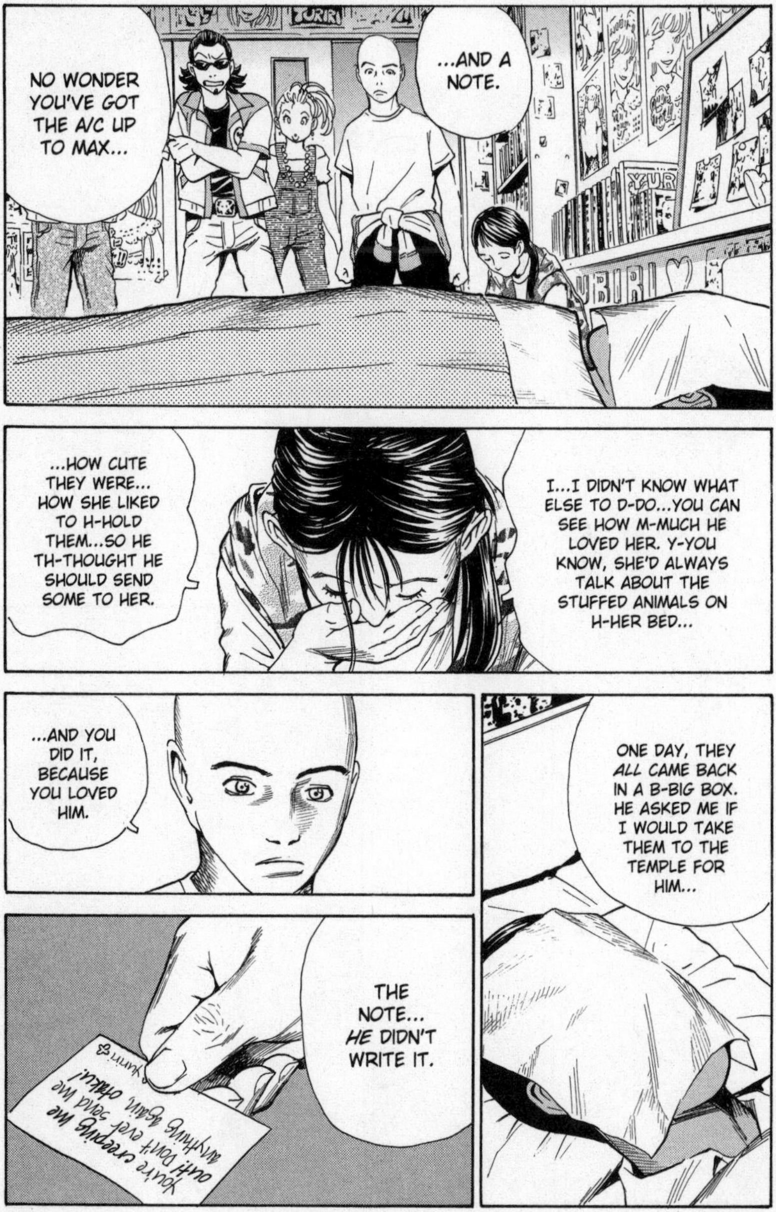

YURIRI
...AND A NOTE.
NO WONDER YOU'VE GOT THE A/C UP TO MAX...
YURIRI
I...I DIDN'T KNOW WHAT ELSE TO D-DO...YOU CAN SEE HOW M-MUCH HE LOVED HER. Y-YOU KNOW, SHE'D ALWAYS TALK ABOUT THE STUFFED ANIMALS ON H-HER BED...
...HOW CUTE THEY WERE... HOW SHE LIKED TO H-HOLD THEM...SO HE TH-THOUGHT HE SHOULD SEND SOME TO HER.
ONE DAY, THEY *ALL* CAME BACK IN A B-BIG BOX. HE ASKED ME IF I WOULD TAKE THEM TO THE TEMPLE FOR HIM...
...AND YOU DID IT, BECAUSE YOU LOVED HIM.
THE NOTE... *HE* DIDN'T WRITE IT.
You're creeping me out! Don't ever send me anything again, otaku!
Yuriri

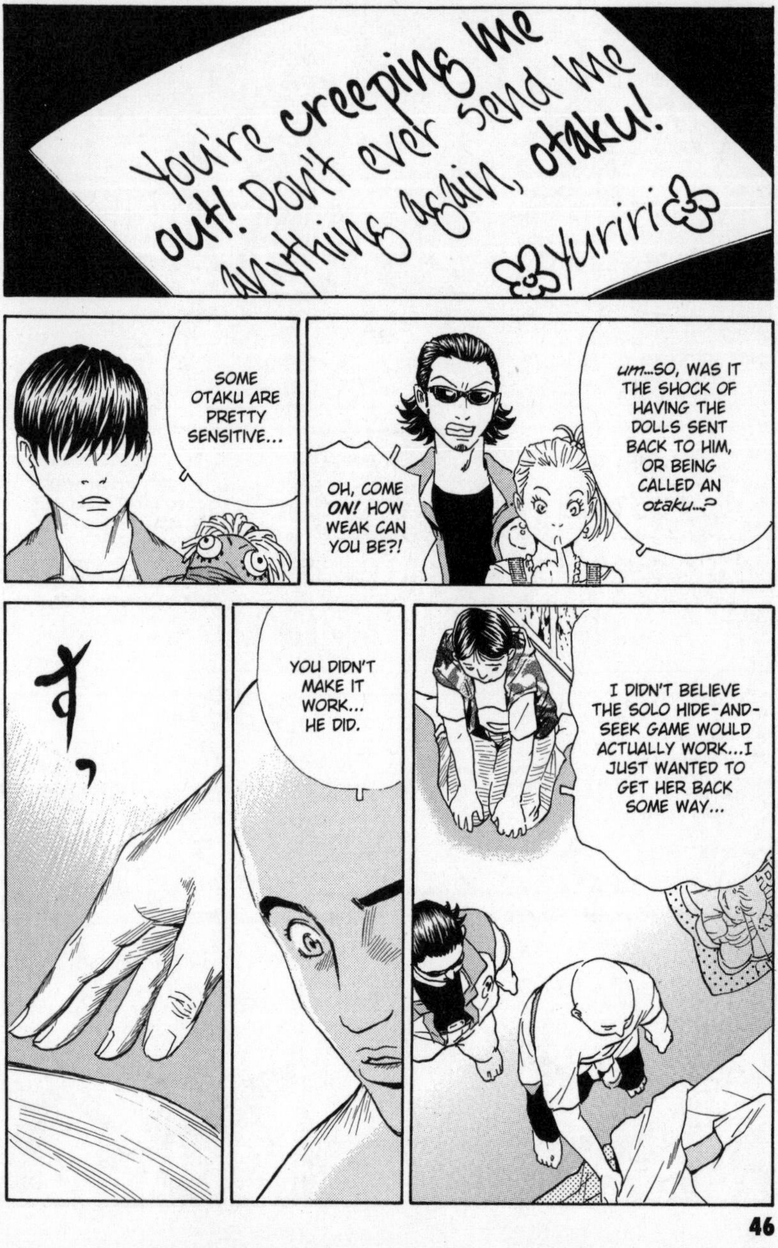
You're creeping me out! Don't ever send me anything again, otaku!
Yuriri
um...SO, WAS IT THE SHOCK OF HAVING THE DOLLS SENT BACK TO HIM, OR BEING CALLED AN otaku...?
OH, COME ON! HOW WEAK CAN YOU BE?!
SOME OTAKU ARE PRETTY SENSITIVE...
I DIDN'T BELIEVE THE SOLO HIDE-AND-SEEK GAME WOULD ACTUALLY WORK...I JUST WANTED TO GET HER BACK SOME WAY...
YOU DIDN'T MAKE IT WORK... HE DID.
す,

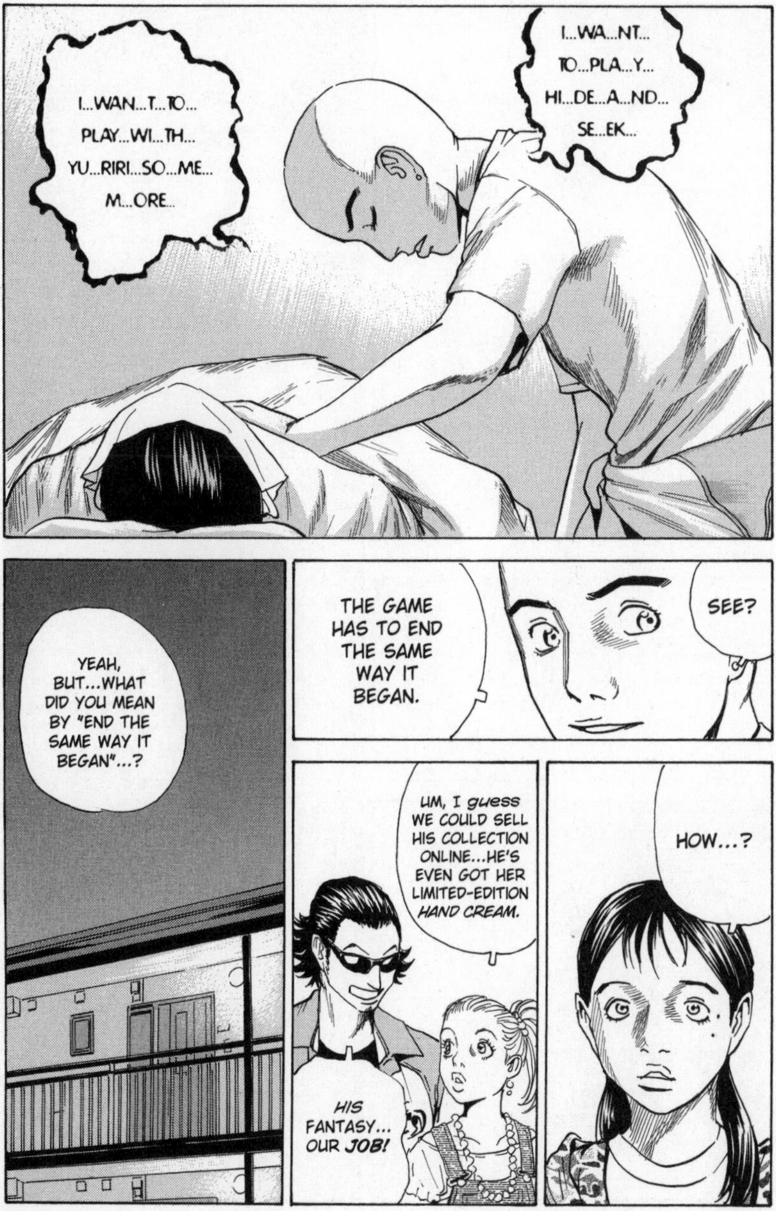
I...WA...NT... TO...PLA...Y... HI...DE...A...ND... SE...EK...
I...WAN...T...TO... PLAY...WI...TH... YU...RIRI...SO...ME... M...ORE...
SEE?
THE GAME HAS TO END THE SAME WAY IT BEGAN.
HOW...?
UM, I *guess* WE COULD SELL HIS COLLECTION ONLINE...HE'S EVEN GOT HER LIMITED-EDITION *HAND CREAM.*
HIS FANTASY... OUR ***JOB!***
YEAH, BUT...WHAT DID YOU MEAN BY "END THE SAME WAY IT BEGAN"...?

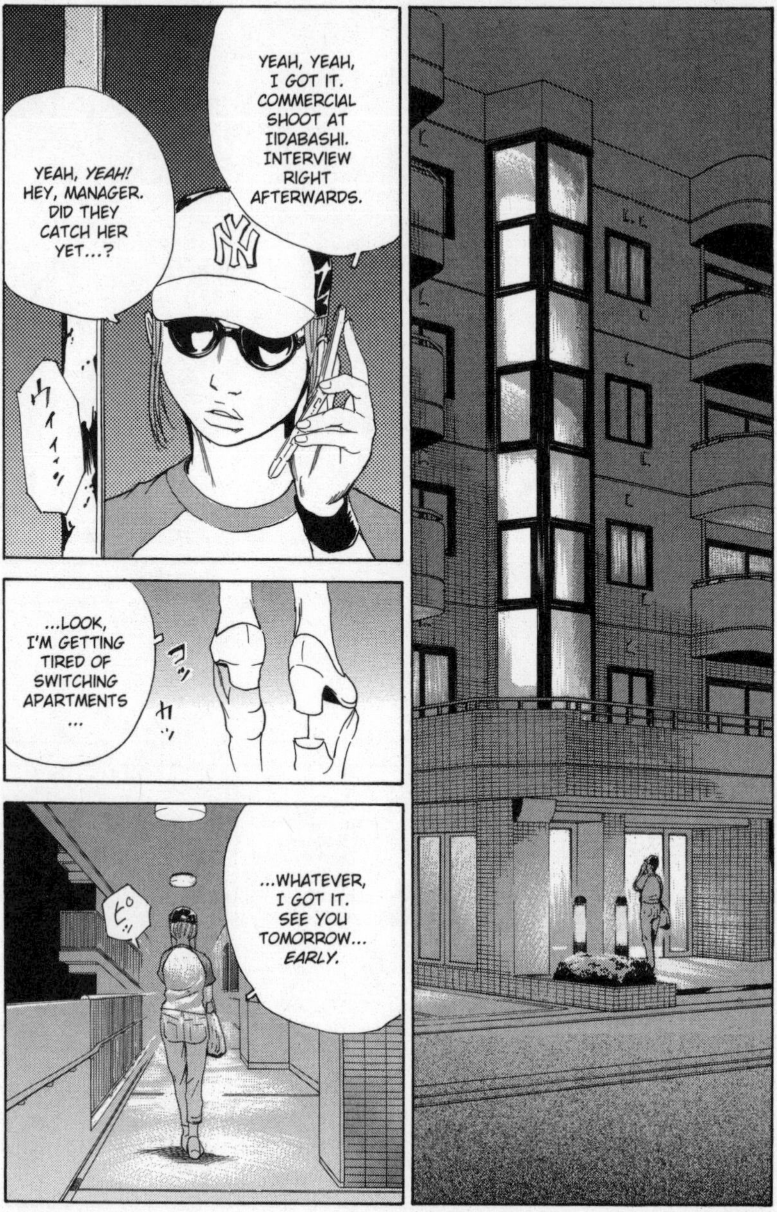
YEAH, YEAH, I GOT IT. COMMERCIAL SHOOT AT IIDABASHI. INTERVIEW RIGHT AFTERWARDS.
YEAH, *YEAH!* HEY, MANAGER. DID THEY CATCH HER YET...?
...LOOK, I'M GETTING TIRED OF SWITCHING APARTMENTS ...
...WHATEVER, I GOT IT. SEE YOU TOMORROW... *EARLY.*

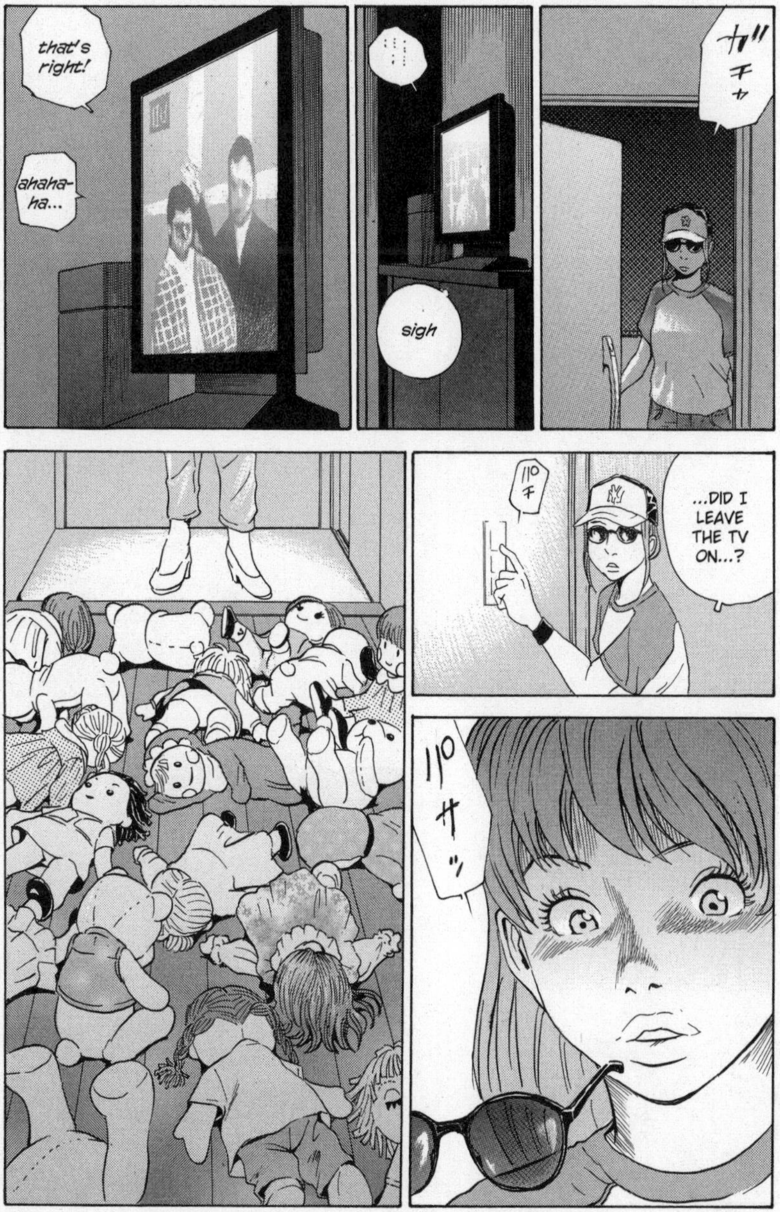
ガチャ
……
sigh
that's right!
ahahaha...
パチ
...DID I LEAVE THE TV ON...?
バサッ

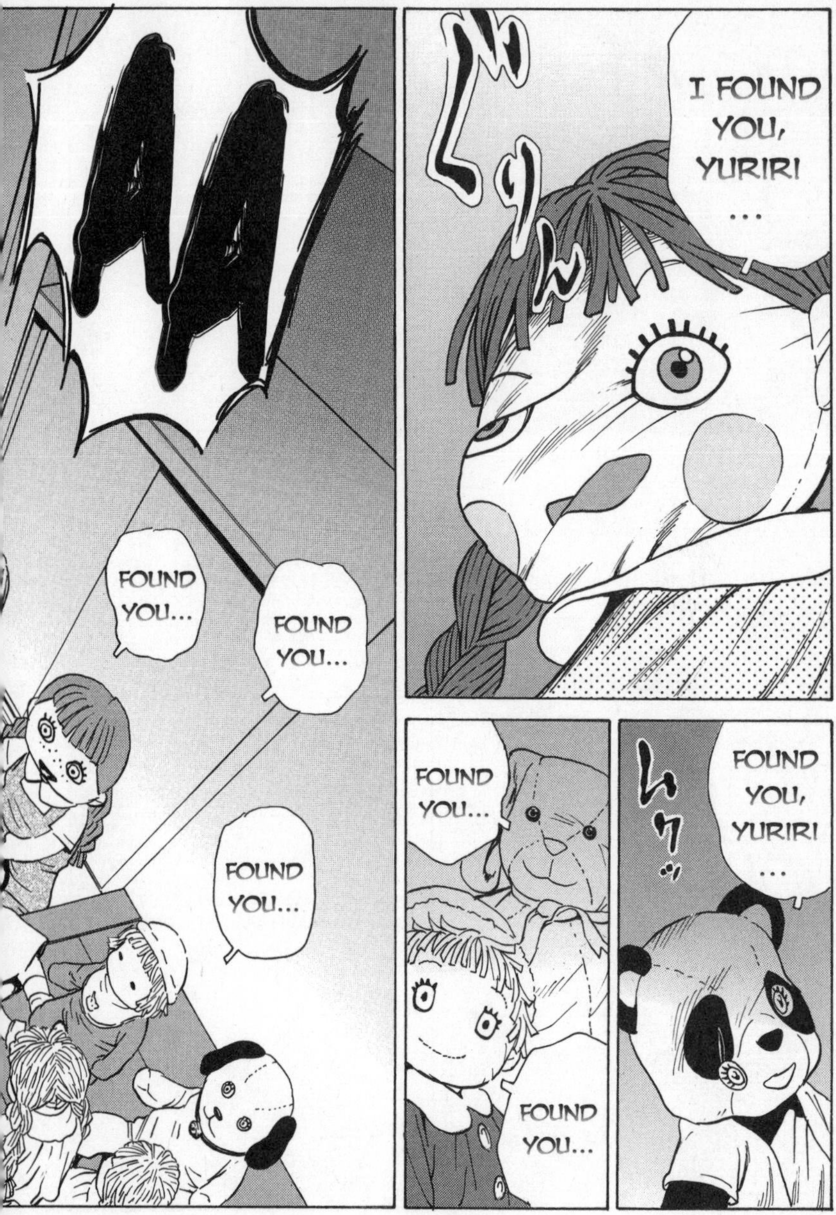
I FOUND YOU, YURIRI ...
FOUND YOU, YURIRI ...
FOUND YOU...
FOUND YOU...
FOUND YOU...
FOUND YOU...
FOUND YOU...

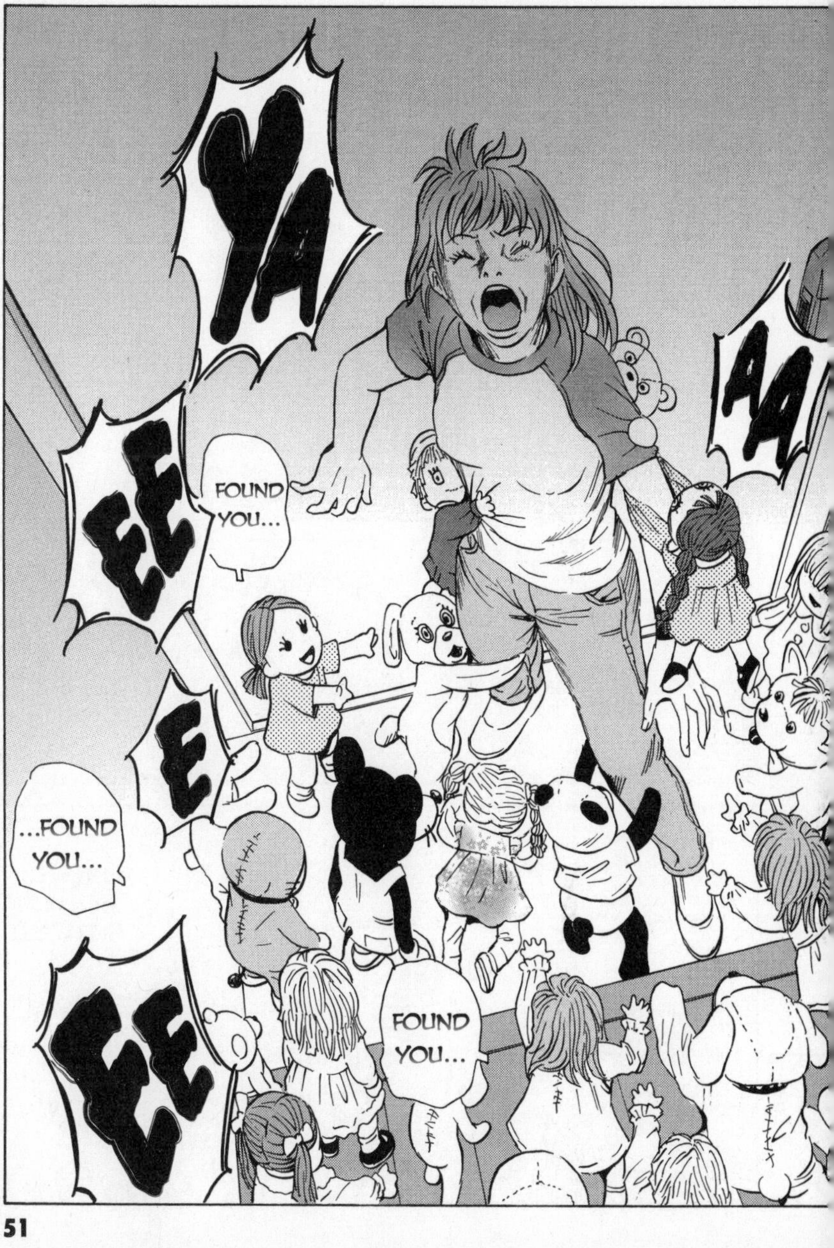
YA
AA
FOUND YOU...
EE
E
...FOUND YOU...
FOUND YOU...
EE

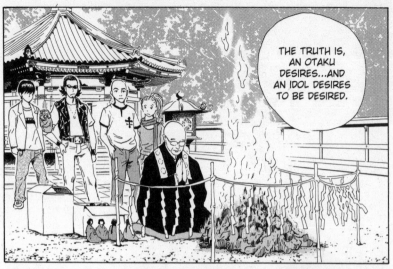

THE TRUTH IS, AN OTAKU DESIRES...AND AN IDOL DESIRES TO BE DESIRED.
...EACH SOMEHOW HAS TO BURN WITHOUT BEING CONSUMED...BUT STILL, EACH HAS TO BURN.
FAREWELL, HANAKO! FAREWELL!
YEAH, I'VE BEEN WONDERING ABOUT THAT. HANAKO'S A *GIRL'S* NAME. THE SPIRIT IN THE DOLL WAS A *DUDE!*
SOB... SOB...
WELL, IT SEEMS THAT YOU'RE SUPPOSED TO NAME THE DOLLS "HANAKO"... according to the ancient wisdom of the Net.

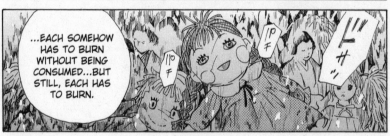

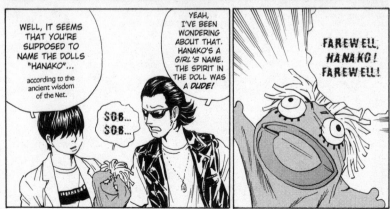

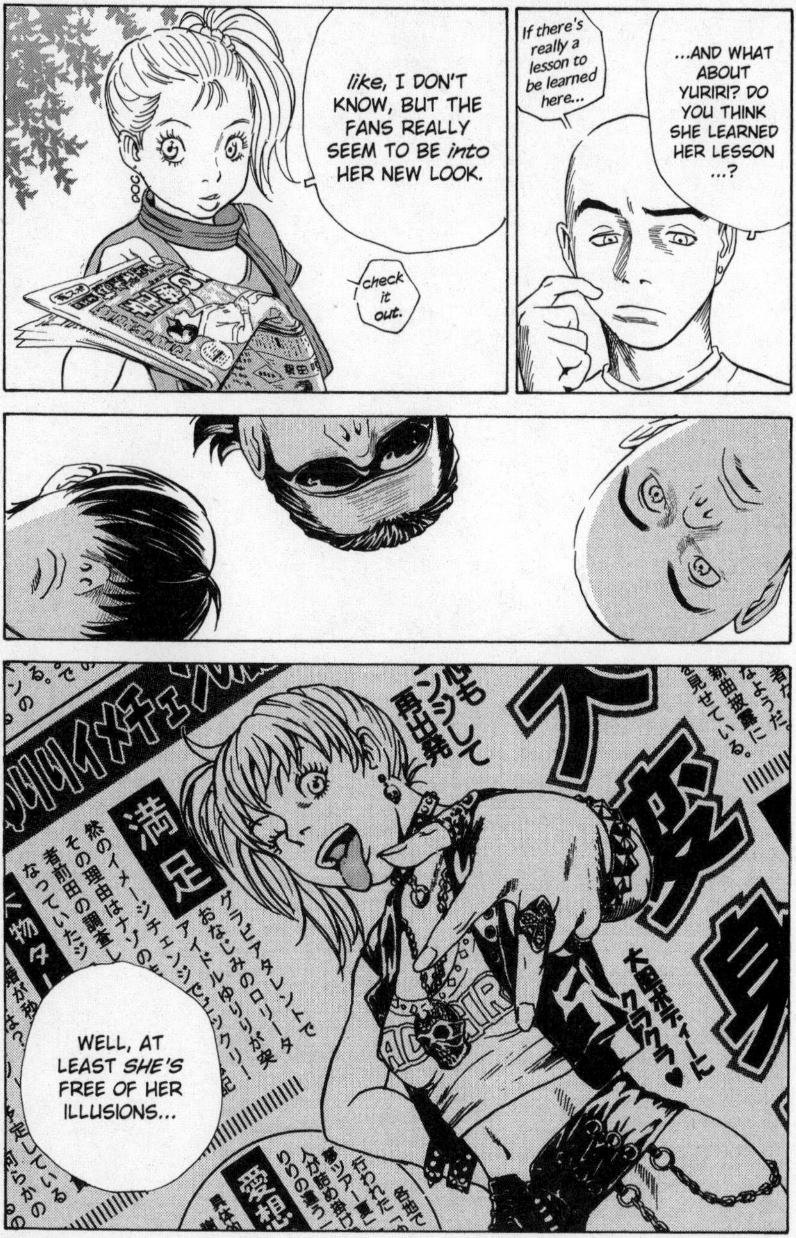
If there's really a lesson to be learned here...
...AND WHAT ABOUT YURIRI? DO YOU THINK SHE LEARNED HER LESSON ...?
like, I DON'T KNOW, BUT THE FANS REALLY SEEM TO BE *into* HER NEW LOOK.
check it out.
WELL, AT LEAST *SHE'S* FREE OF HER ILLUSIONS...

2nd delivery: a lonely singing doll—the end

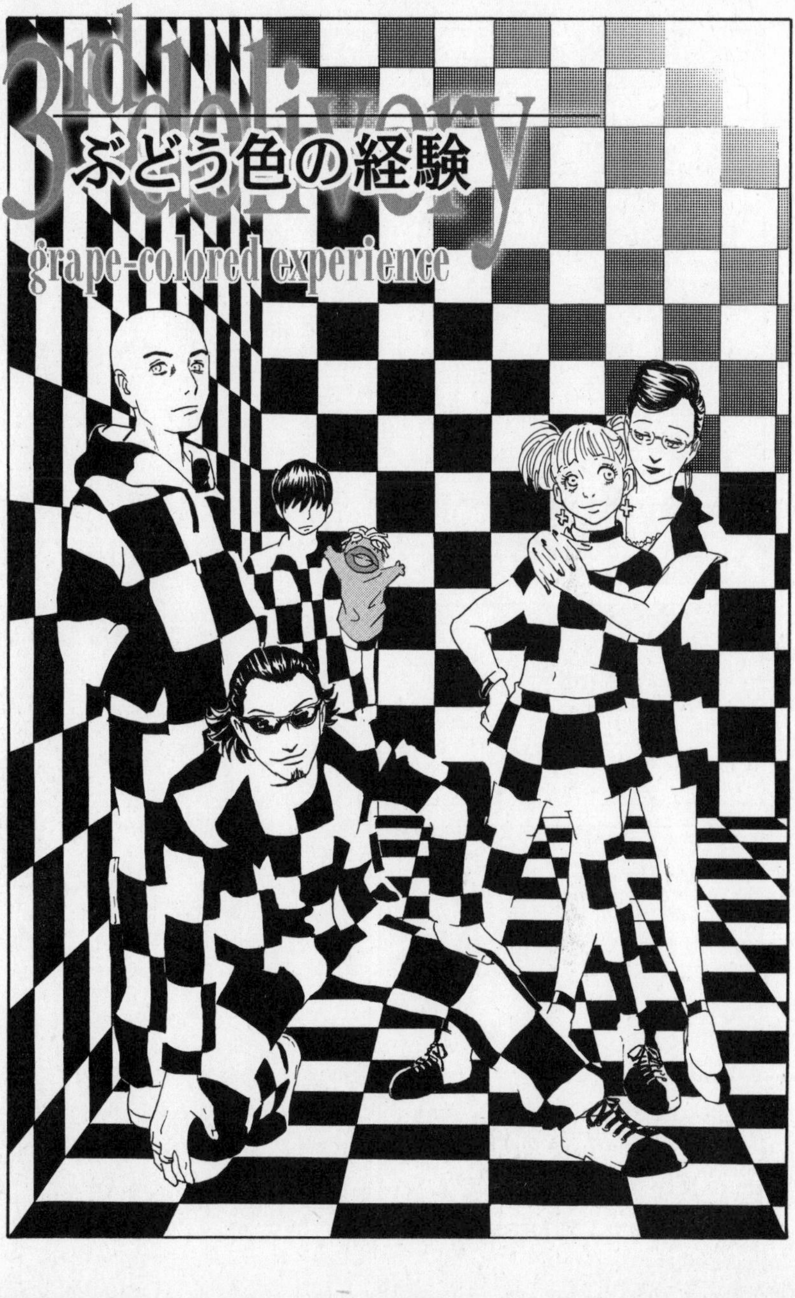
3rd delivery
ぶどう色の経験
grape-colored experience

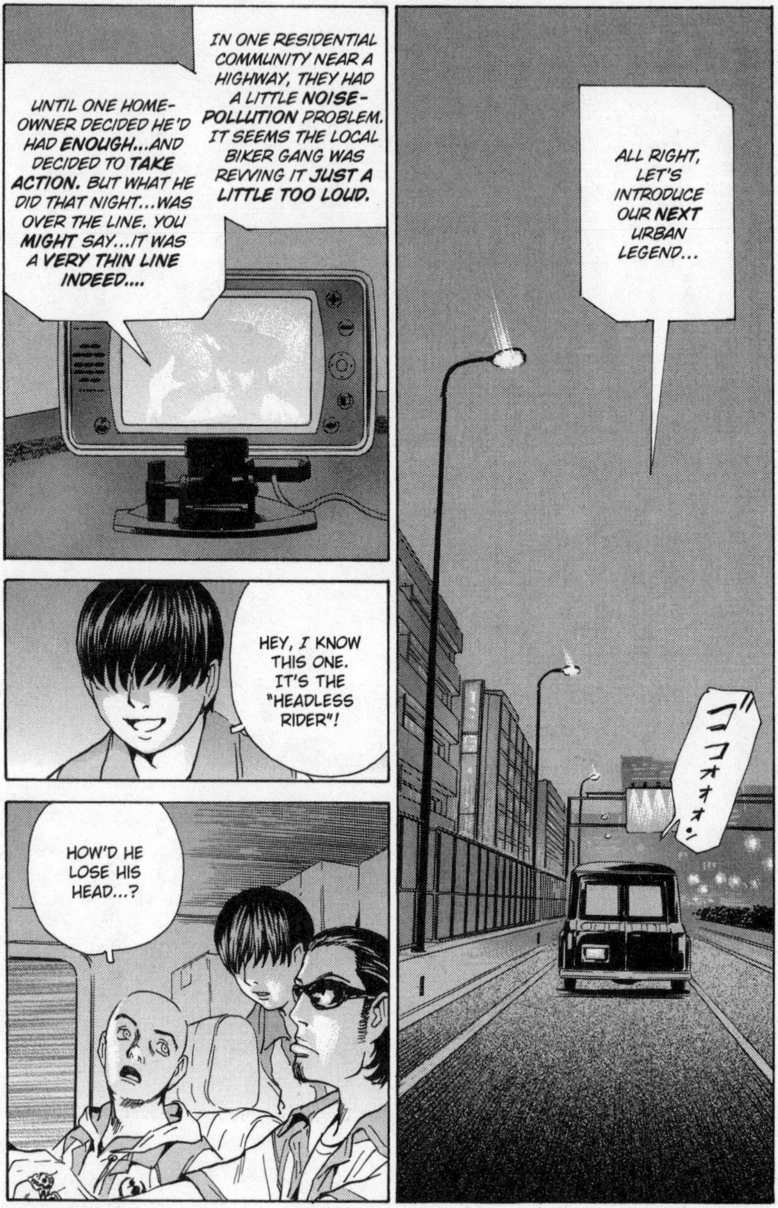
ALL RIGHT, LET'S INTRODUCE OUR **NEXT** URBAN LEGEND...
ゴゴオオオ…!
IN ONE RESIDENTIAL COMMUNITY NEAR A HIGHWAY, THEY HAD A LITTLE **NOISE-POLLUTION** PROBLEM. IT SEEMS THE LOCAL BIKER GANG WAS REVVING IT **JUST A LITTLE TOO LOUD.**
UNTIL ONE HOME-OWNER DECIDED HE'D HAD **ENOUGH...**AND DECIDED TO **TAKE ACTION.** BUT WHAT HE DID THAT NIGHT...WAS OVER THE LINE. YOU **MIGHT** SAY...IT WAS A **VERY THIN LINE INDEED....**
HEY, I KNOW THIS ONE. IT'S THE "HEADLESS RIDER"!
HOW'D HE LOSE HIS HEAD...?

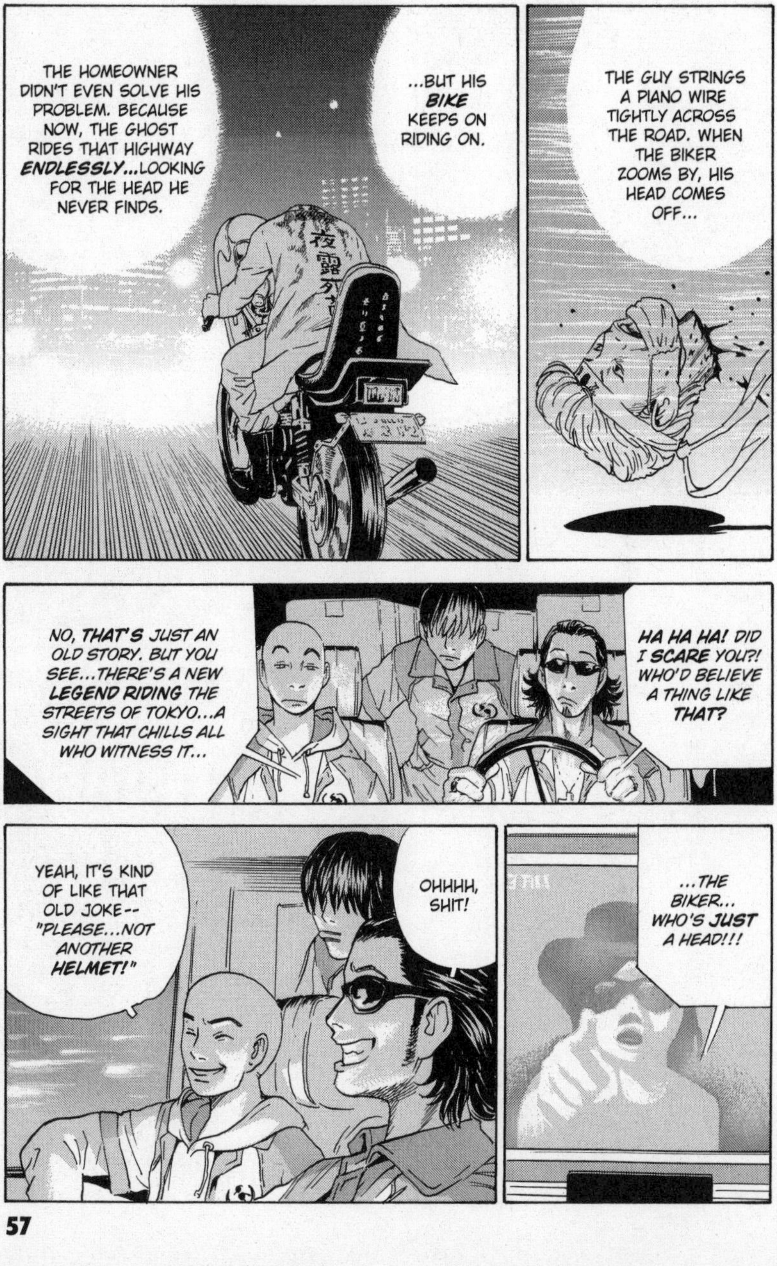
THE GUY STRINGS A PIANO WIRE TIGHTLY ACROSS THE ROAD. WHEN THE BIKER ZOOMS BY, HIS HEAD COMES OFF...
...BUT HIS **BIKE** KEEPS ON RIDING ON.
THE HOMEOWNER DIDN'T EVEN SOLVE HIS PROBLEM. BECAUSE NOW, THE GHOST RIDES THAT HIGHWAY **ENDLESSLY...**LOOKING FOR THE HEAD HE NEVER FINDS.
HA HA HA! DID I ***SCARE*** *YOU?! WHO'D BELIEVE A THING LIKE* ***THAT?***
NO, ***THAT'S*** *JUST AN OLD STORY. BUT YOU SEE...THERE'S A NEW* ***LEGEND RIDING*** *THE STREETS OF TOKYO...A SIGHT THAT CHILLS ALL WHO WITNESS IT...*
...THE BIKER... WHO'S ***JUST*** *A HEAD!!!*
OHHHH, SHIT!
YEAH, IT'S KIND OF LIKE THAT OLD JOKE-- *"PLEASE...NOT ANOTHER* ***HELMET!"***

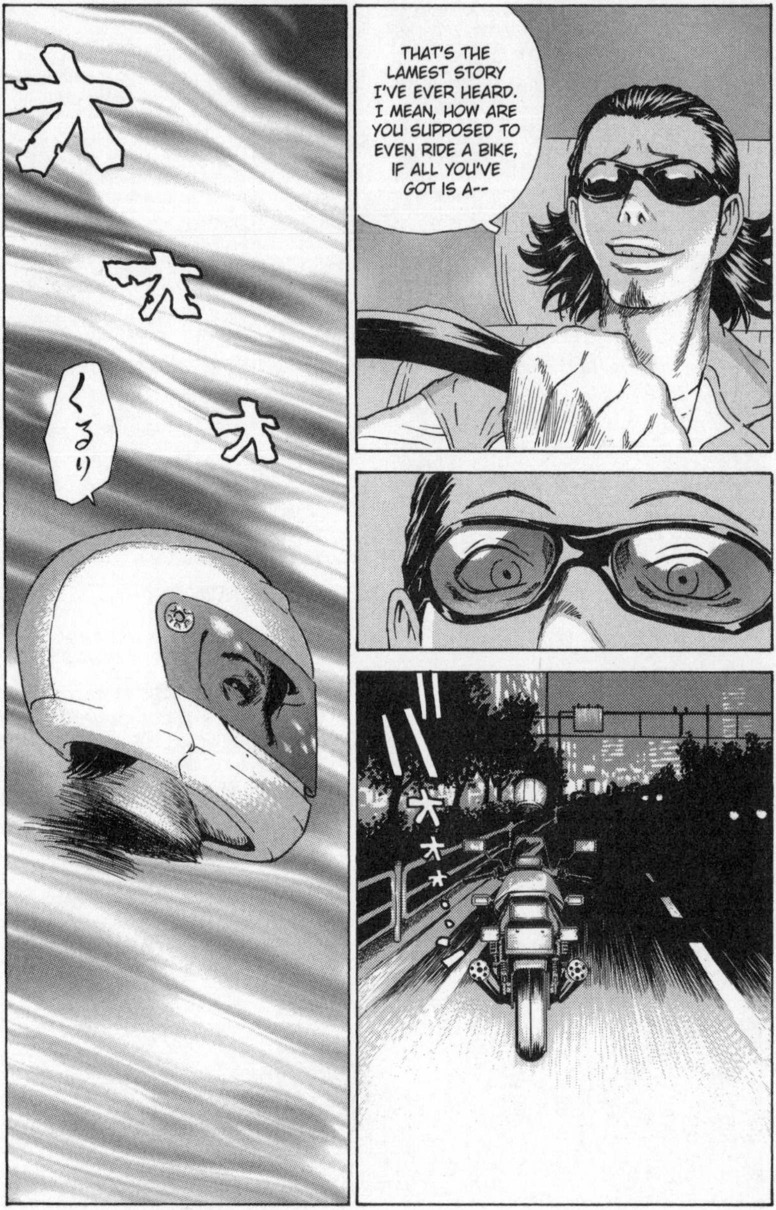
THAT'S THE LAMEST STORY I'VE EVER HEARD. I MEAN, HOW ARE YOU SUPPOSED TO EVEN RIDE A BIKE, IF ALL YOU'VE GOT IS A--
ホォォ
ホォォ
くるり

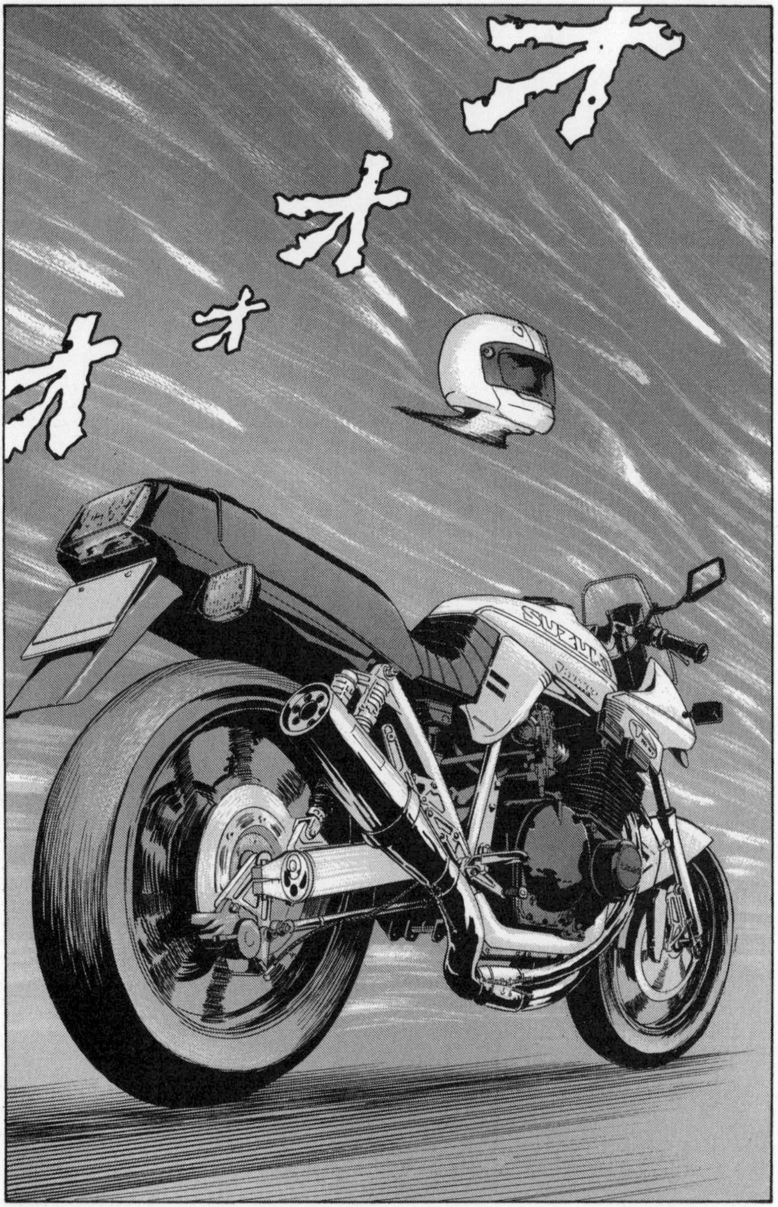
オォオオ

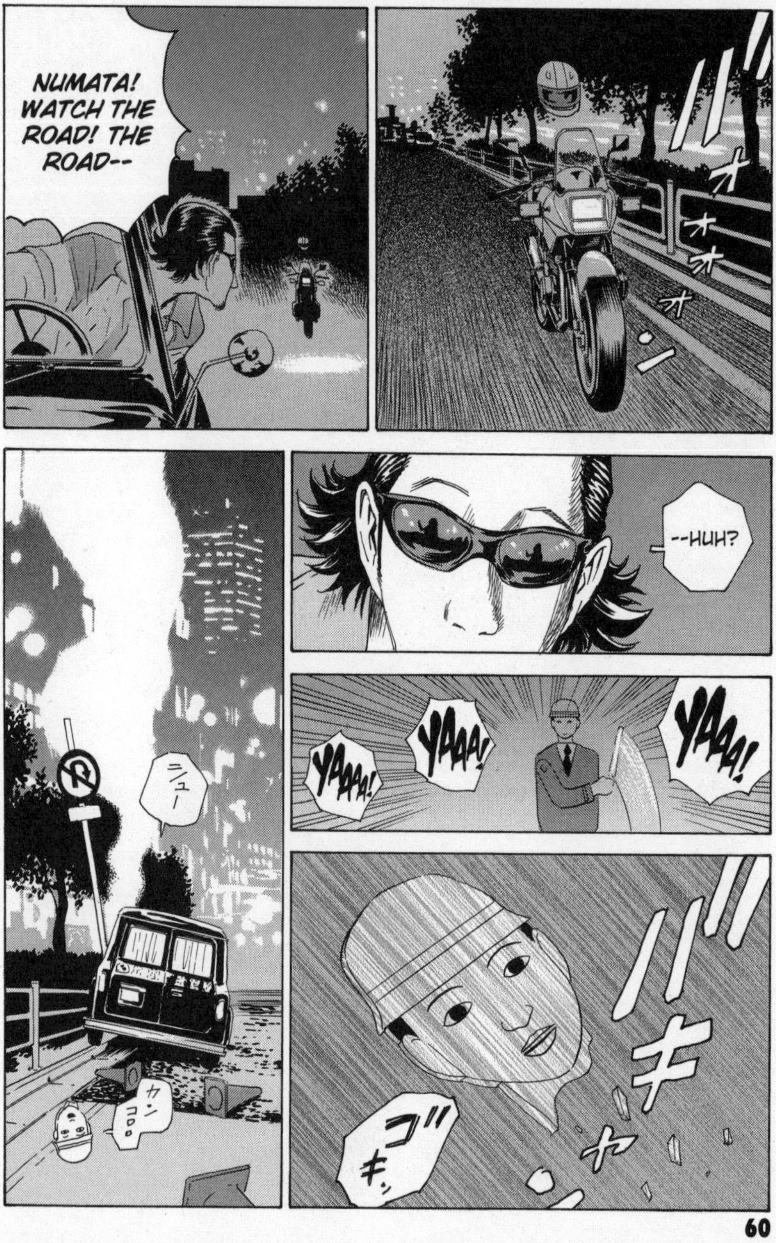

NUMATA! WATCH THE ROAD! THE ROAD--
--HUH?
YAAAA!
YAAA!
YAAAAA!
バキャ
ゴキッ
ニュー
カンコロ。

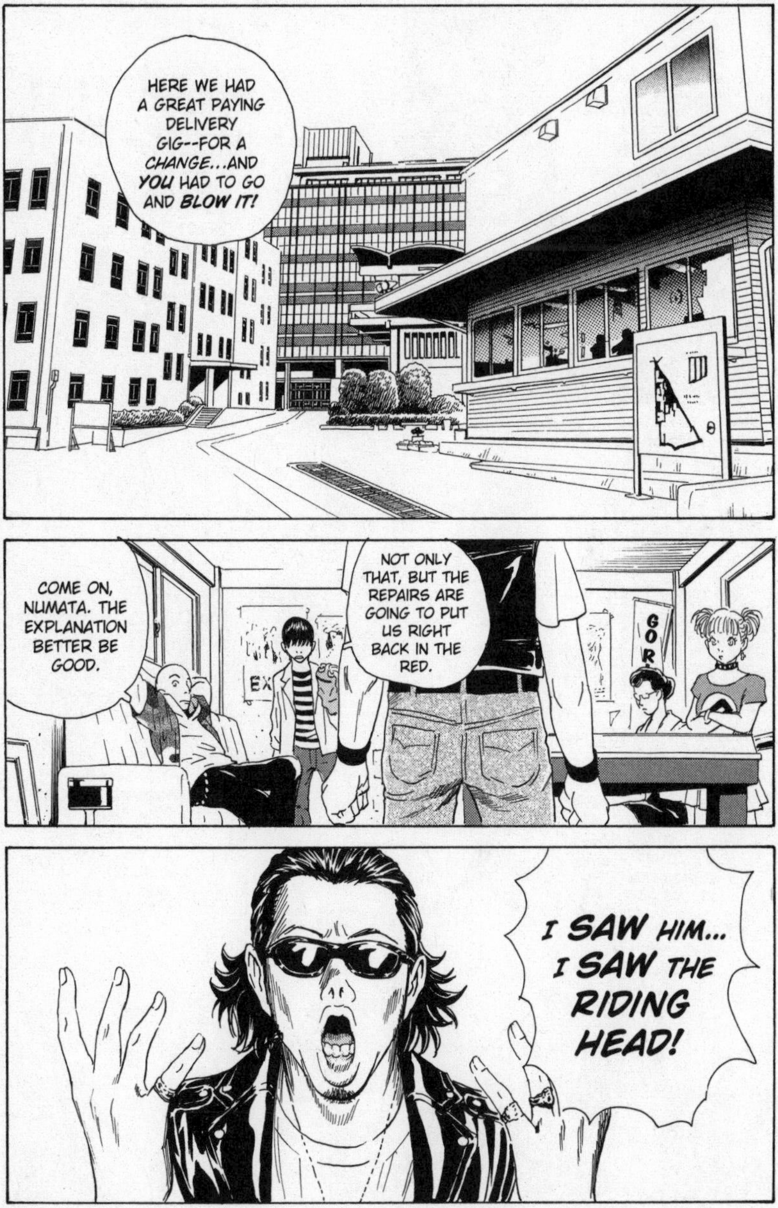
HERE WE HAD A GREAT PAYING DELIVERY GIG--FOR A CHANGE...AND YOU HAD TO GO AND BLOW IT!
NOT ONLY THAT, BUT THE REPAIRS ARE GOING TO PUT US RIGHT BACK IN THE RED.
COME ON, NUMATA. THE EXPLANATION BETTER BE GOOD.
I SAW HIM... I SAW THE RIDING HEAD!

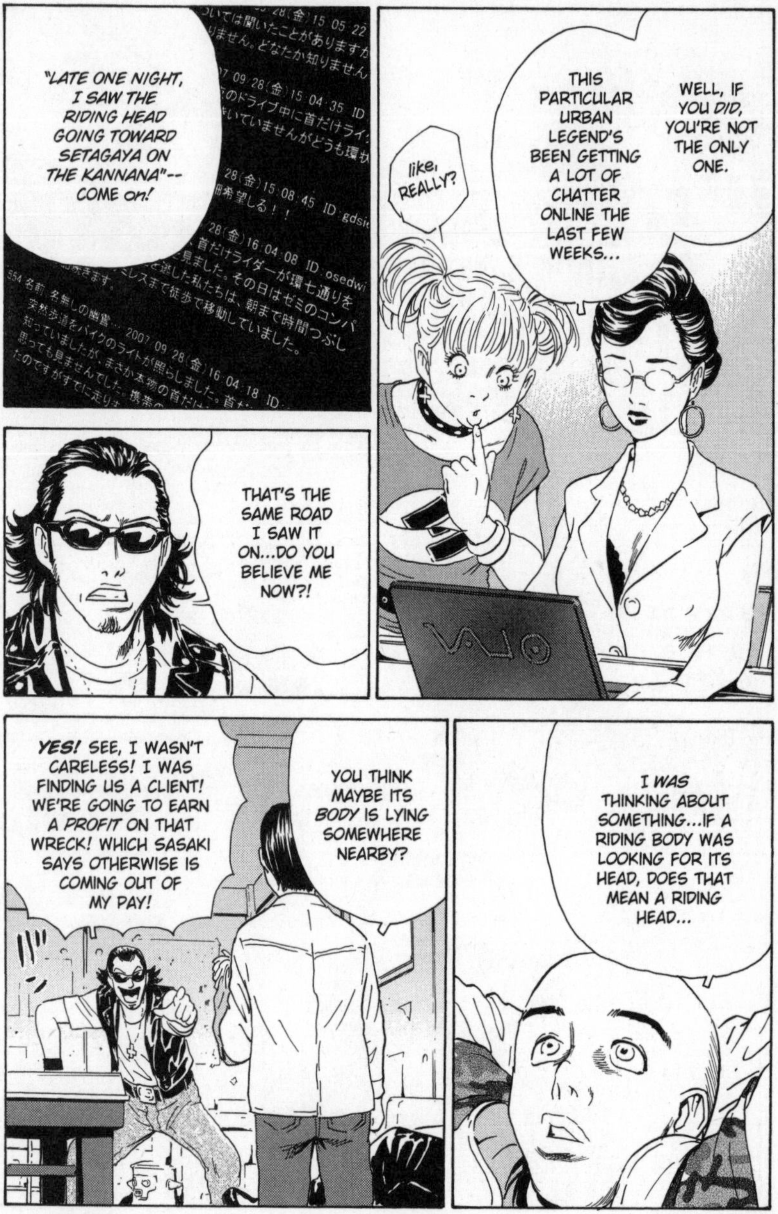
WELL, IF YOU *DID*, YOU'RE NOT THE ONLY ONE.
THIS PARTICULAR URBAN LEGEND'S BEEN GETTING A LOT OF CHATTER ONLINE THE LAST FEW WEEKS...
like, REALLY?
"LATE ONE NIGHT, I SAW THE RIDING HEAD GOING TOWARD SETAGAYA ON THE KANNANA"-- COME *on!*
THAT'S THE SAME ROAD I SAW IT ON...DO YOU BELIEVE ME NOW?!
I *WAS* THINKING ABOUT SOMETHING...IF A RIDING BODY WAS LOOKING FOR ITS HEAD, DOES THAT MEAN A RIDING HEAD...
YOU THINK MAYBE ITS *BODY* IS LYING SOMEWHERE NEARBY?
YES! SEE, I WASN'T CARELESS! I WAS FINDING US A CLIENT! WE'RE GOING TO EARN A *PROFIT* ON THAT WRECK! WHICH SASAKI SAYS OTHERWISE IS COMING OUT OF MY PAY!

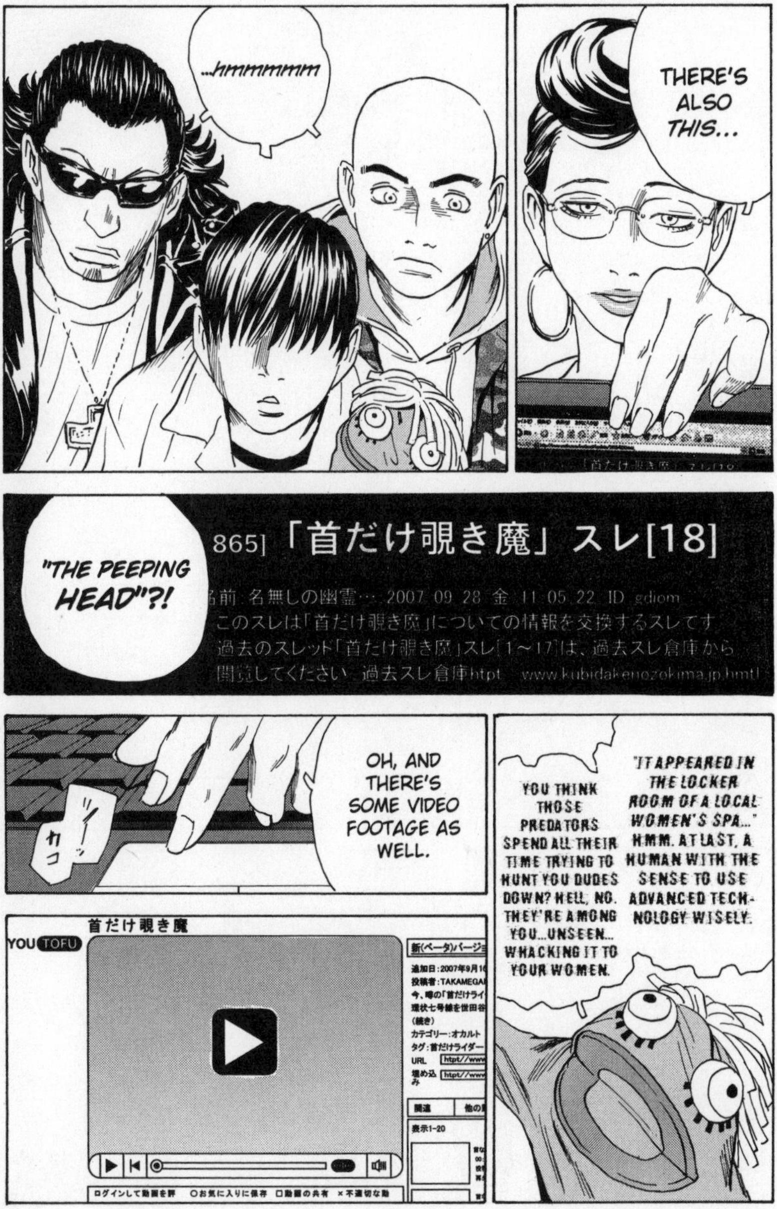
THERE'S ALSO THIS...
...hmmmmmm
865]「首だけ覗き魔」スレ[18]
名前：名無しの幽霊…：2007 09 28 金 11 05 22 ID gdiom
このスレは「首だけ覗き魔」についての情報を交換するスレです
過去のスレッド「首だけ覗き魔」スレ[1～17]は、過去スレ倉庫から
閲覧してください 過去スレ倉庫htpt www.kubidakenozokima.jp.hmtl
"THE PEEPING HEAD"?!
"IT APPEARED IN THE LOCKER ROOM OF A LOCAL WOMEN'S SPA..." HMM. AT LAST, A HUMAN WITH THE SENSE TO USE ADVANCED TECHNOLOGY WISELY.
YOU THINK THOSE PREDATORS SPEND ALL THEIR TIME TRYING TO HUNT YOU DUDES DOWN? HELL, NO. THEY'RE AMONG YOU...UNSEEN... WHACKING IT TO YOUR WOMEN.
OH, AND THERE'S SOME VIDEO FOOTAGE AS WELL.
ツーッ
カコ
首だけ覗き魔
YOU TOFU
新(ベータ)バージョ
追加日：2007年9月16
投稿者：TAKAMEGAI
今、噂の「首だけライ
環状七号線を世田谷
(続き)
カテゴリー：オカルト
タグ：首だけライダー
URL httpt//www
埋め込み httpt//www
関連 他の
表示1-20
ログインして動画を評 ○お気に入りに保存 □動画の共有 ×不適切な動

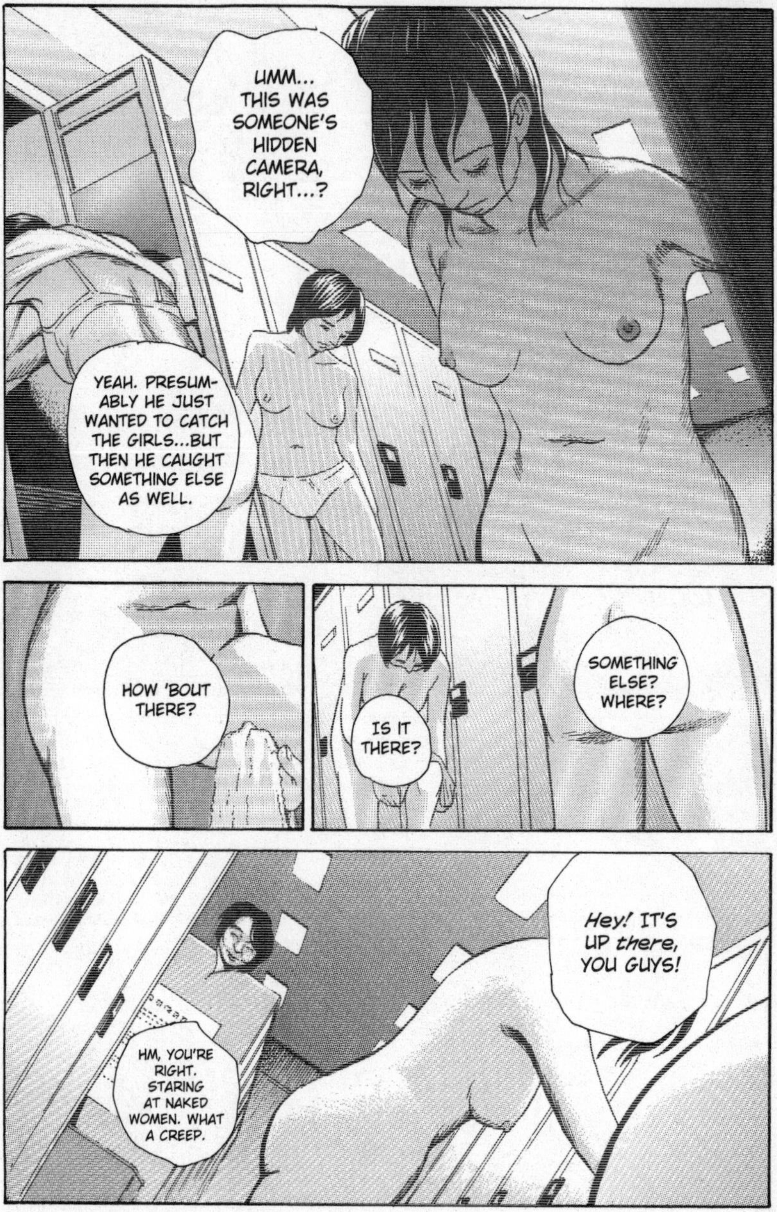
UMM... THIS WAS SOMEONE'S HIDDEN CAMERA, RIGHT...?
YEAH. PRESUM-ABLY HE JUST WANTED TO CATCH THE GIRLS...BUT THEN HE CAUGHT SOMETHING ELSE AS WELL.
SOMETHING ELSE? WHERE?
IS IT THERE?
HOW 'BOUT THERE?
Hey! IT'S UP *there*, YOU GUYS!
HM, YOU'RE RIGHT. STARING AT NAKED WOMEN. WHAT A CREEP.

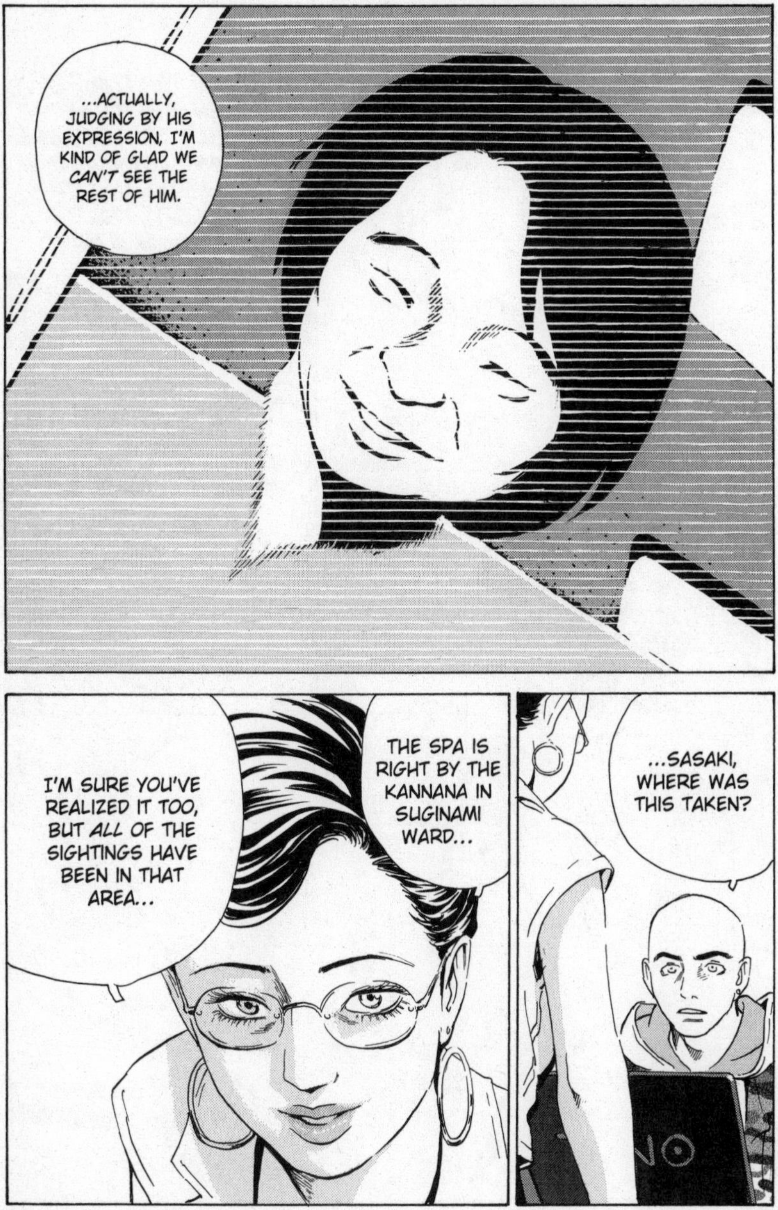
...ACTUALLY, JUDGING BY HIS EXPRESSION, I'M KIND OF GLAD WE *CAN'T* SEE THE REST OF HIM.
...SASAKI, WHERE WAS THIS TAKEN?
THE SPA IS RIGHT BY THE KANNANA IN SUGINAMI WARD...
I'M SURE YOU'VE REALIZED IT TOO, BUT *ALL* OF THE SIGHTINGS HAVE BEEN IN THAT AREA...

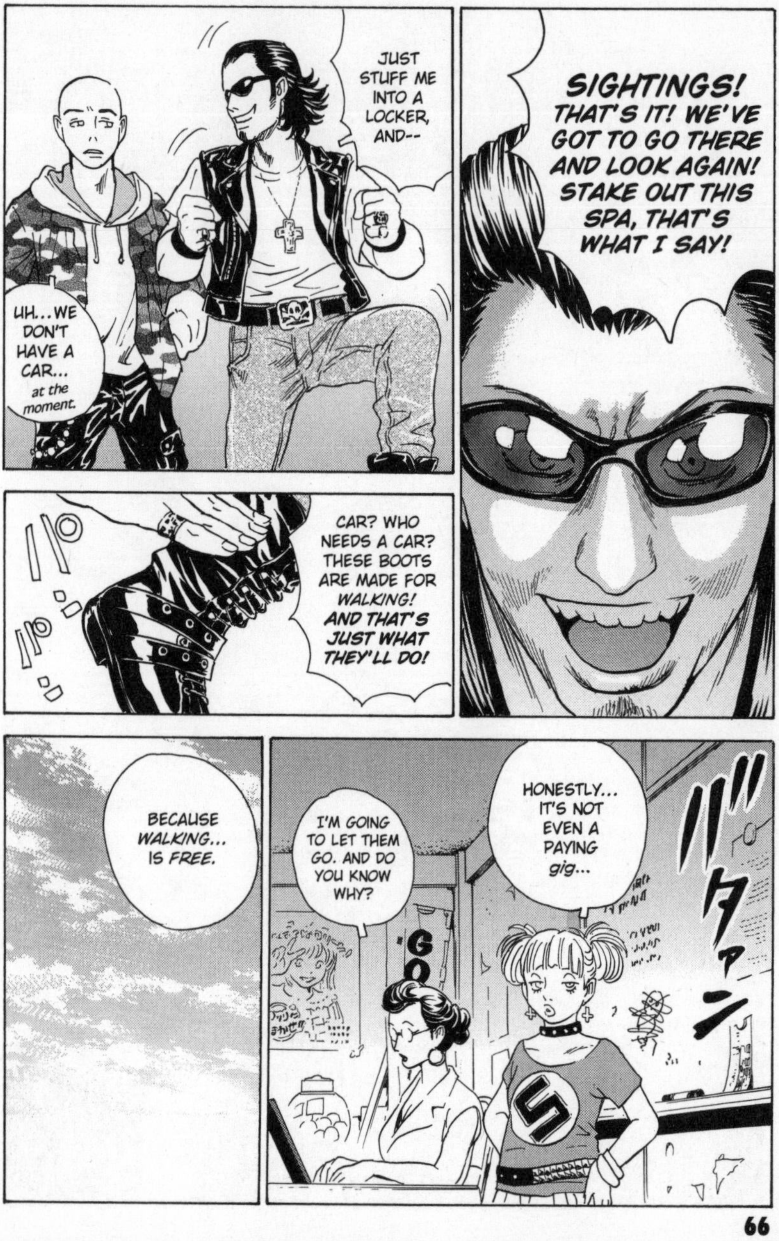
SIGHTINGS! THAT'S IT! WE'VE GOT TO GO THERE AND LOOK AGAIN! STAKE OUT THIS SPA, THAT'S WHAT I SAY!
JUST STUFF ME INTO A LOCKER, AND--
UH...WE DON'T HAVE A CAR... at the moment.
CAR? WHO NEEDS A CAR? THESE BOOTS ARE MADE FOR WALKING! AND THAT'S JUST WHAT THEY'LL DO!
HONESTLY... IT'S NOT EVEN A PAYING gig...
I'M GOING TO LET THEM GO. AND DO YOU KNOW WHY?
BECAUSE WALKING... IS FREE.

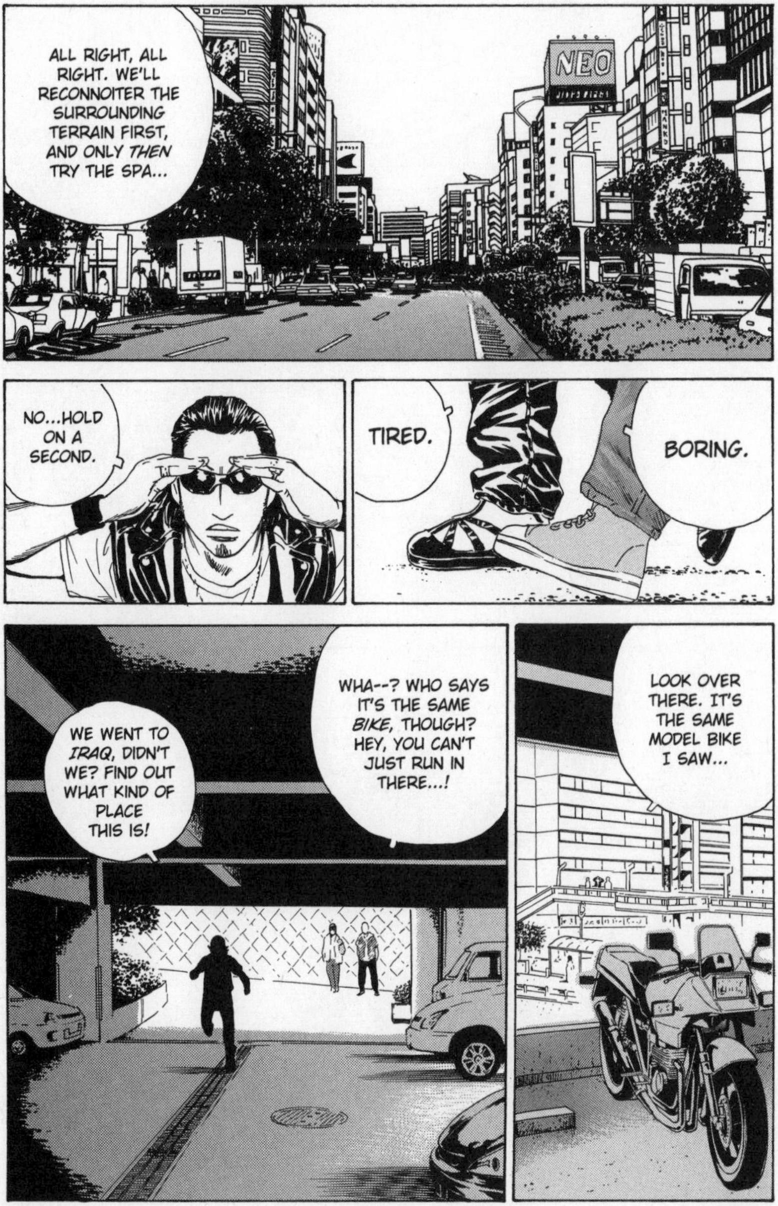
ALL RIGHT, ALL RIGHT. WE'LL RECONNOITER THE SURROUNDING TERRAIN FIRST, AND ONLY *THEN* TRY THE SPA...
NEO
BORING.
TIRED.
NO...HOLD ON A SECOND.
LOOK OVER THERE. IT'S THE SAME MODEL BIKE I SAW...
WHA--? WHO SAYS IT'S THE SAME *BIKE*, THOUGH? HEY, YOU CAN'T JUST RUN IN THERE...!
WE WENT TO *IRAQ*, DIDN'T WE? FIND OUT WHAT KIND OF PLACE THIS IS!

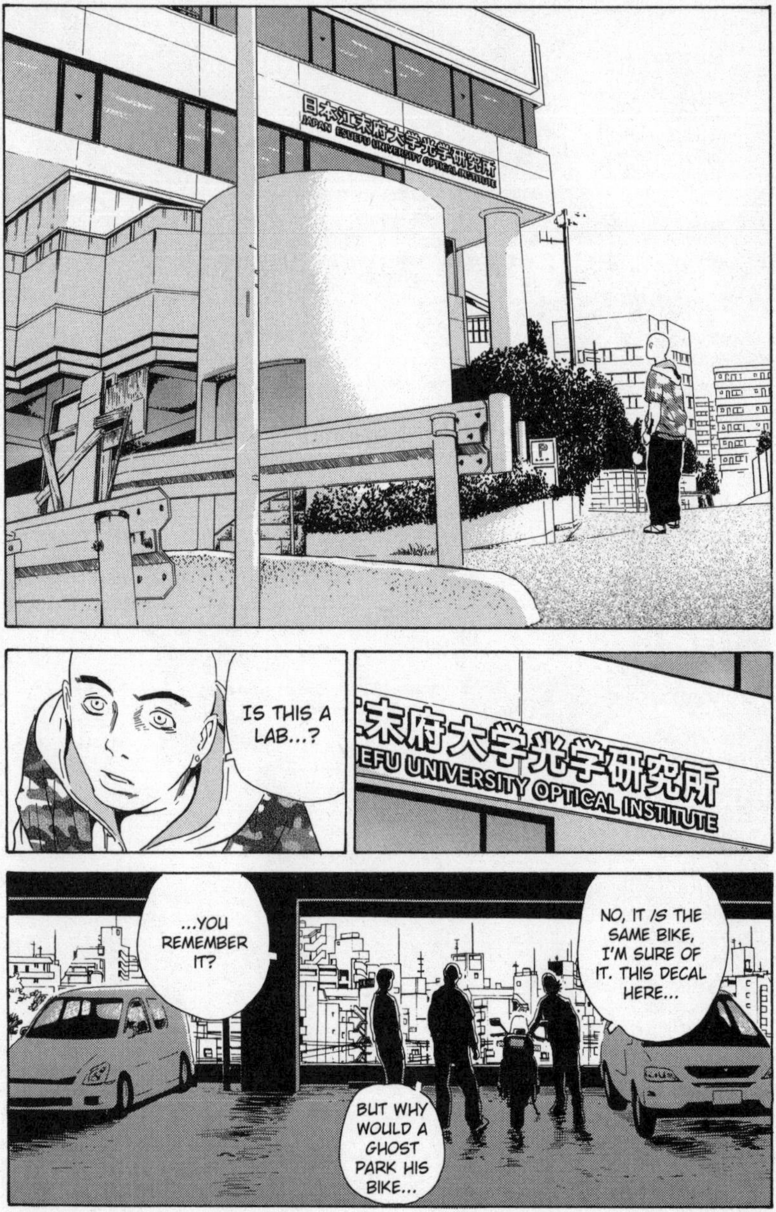
日本江末府大学光学研究所
JAPAN ESUEFU UNIVERSITY OPTICAL INSTITUTE
末府大学光学研究所
UNIVERSITY OPTICAL INSTITUTE
IS THIS A LAB...?
NO, IT *IS* THE SAME BIKE, I'M SURE OF IT. THIS DECAL HERE...
...YOU REMEMBER IT?
BUT WHY WOULD A GHOST PARK HIS BIKE...

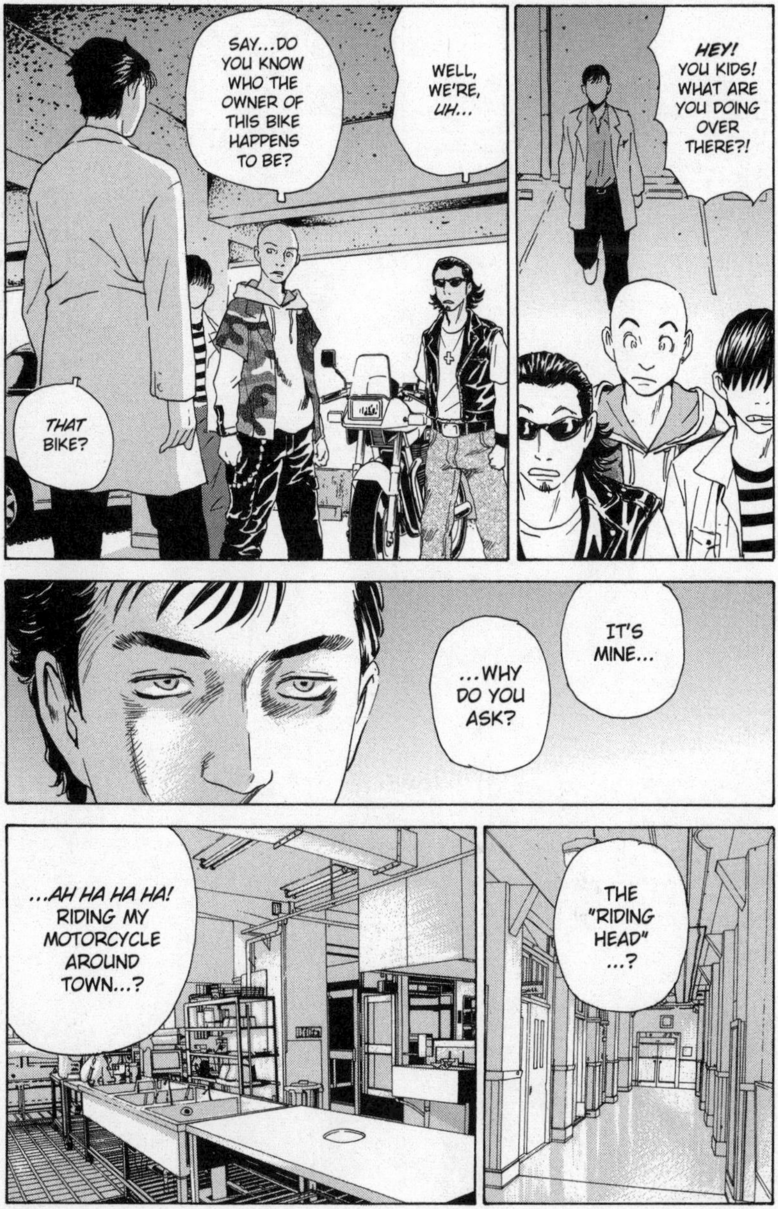
HEY! YOU KIDS! WHAT ARE YOU DOING OVER THERE?!
WELL, WE'RE, UH...
SAY...DO YOU KNOW WHO THE OWNER OF THIS BIKE HAPPENS TO BE?
THAT BIKE?
IT'S MINE...
...WHY DO YOU ASK?
THE "RIDING HEAD" ...?
...AH HA HA HA! RIDING MY MOTORCYCLE AROUND TOWN...?

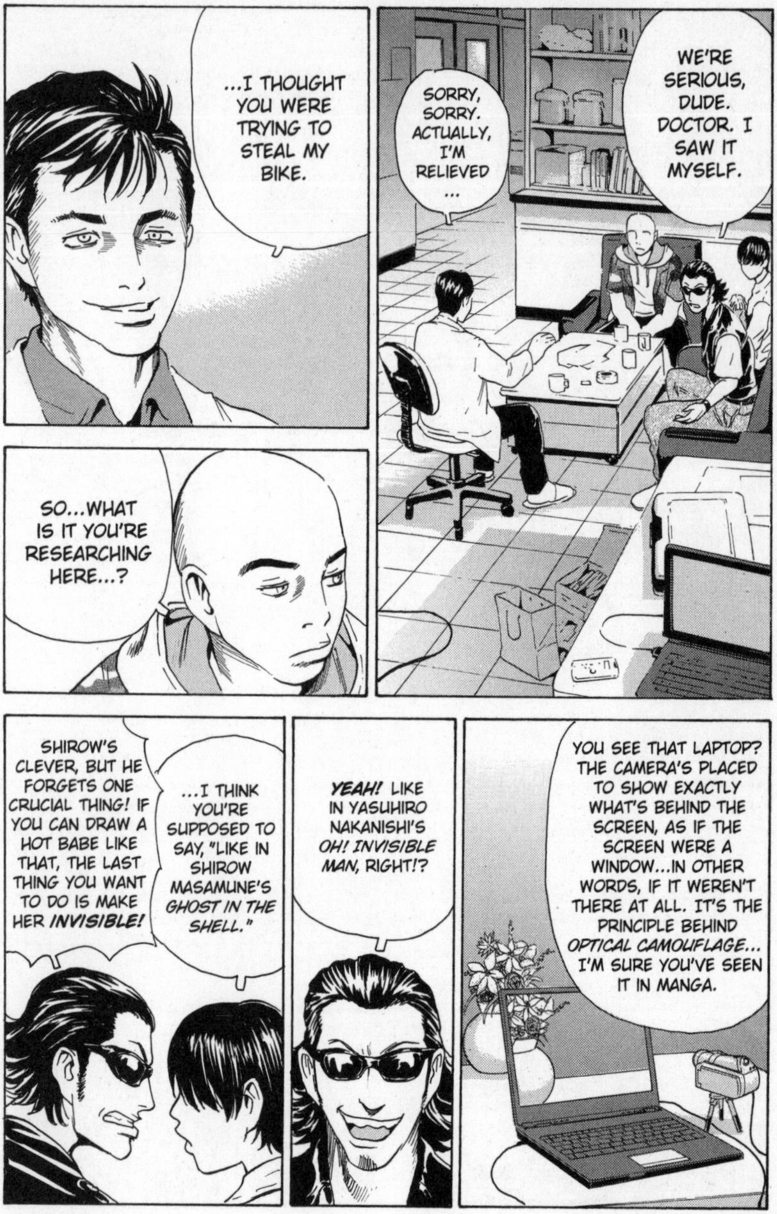
WE'RE SERIOUS, DUDE. DOCTOR. I SAW IT MYSELF.
SORRY, SORRY. ACTUALLY, I'M RELIEVED ...
...I THOUGHT YOU WERE TRYING TO STEAL MY BIKE.
SO...WHAT IS IT YOU'RE RESEARCHING HERE...?
YOU SEE THAT LAPTOP? THE CAMERA'S PLACED TO SHOW EXACTLY WHAT'S BEHIND THE SCREEN, AS IF THE SCREEN WERE A WINDOW...IN OTHER WORDS, IF IT WEREN'T THERE AT ALL. IT'S THE PRINCIPLE BEHIND *OPTICAL CAMOUFLAGE*... I'M SURE YOU'VE SEEN IT IN MANGA.
YEAH! LIKE IN YASUHIRO NAKANISHI'S *OH! INVISIBLE MAN*, RIGHT!?
...I THINK YOU'RE SUPPOSED TO SAY, "LIKE IN SHIROW MASAMUNE'S *GHOST IN THE SHELL*."
SHIROW'S CLEVER, BUT HE FORGETS ONE CRUCIAL THING! IF YOU CAN DRAW A HOT BABE LIKE THAT, THE LAST THING YOU WANT TO DO IS MAKE HER ***INVISIBLE!***

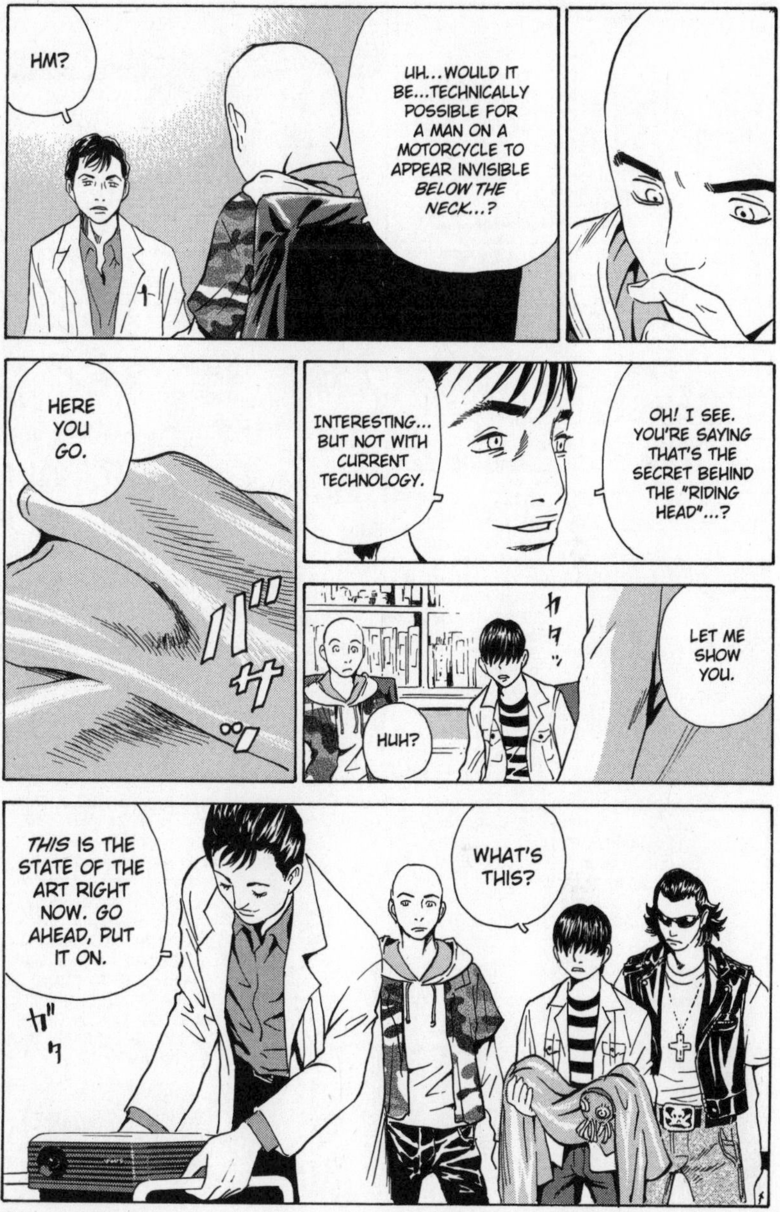
UH...WOULD IT BE...TECHNICALLY POSSIBLE FOR A MAN ON A MOTORCYCLE TO APPEAR INVISIBLE *BELOW THE NECK*...?
HM?
OH! I SEE. YOU'RE SAYING THAT'S THE SECRET BEHIND THE "RIDING HEAD"...?
INTERESTING... BUT NOT WITH CURRENT TECHNOLOGY.
LET ME SHOW YOU.
カタッ
HUH?
HERE YOU GO.
バサッ
WHAT'S THIS?
THIS IS THE STATE OF THE ART RIGHT NOW. GO AHEAD, PUT IT ON.
ガタ

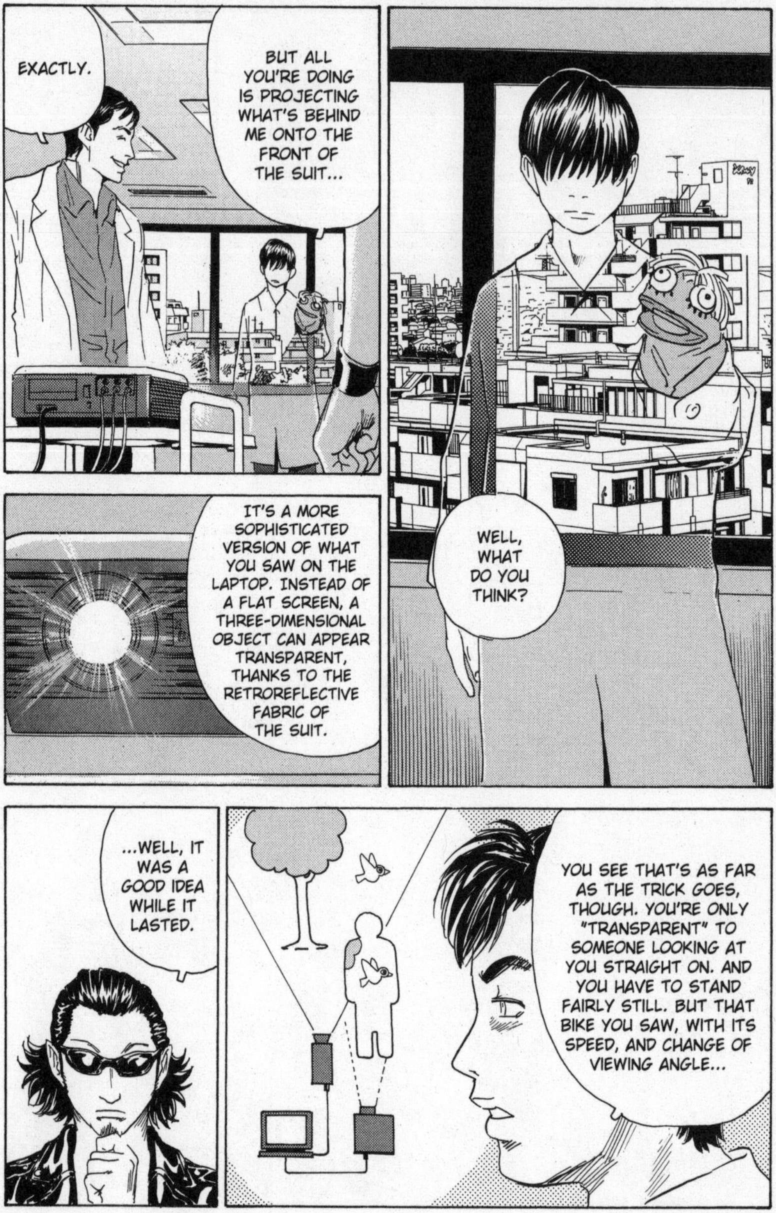
WELL, WHAT DO YOU THINK?
BUT ALL YOU'RE DOING IS PROJECTING WHAT'S BEHIND ME ONTO THE FRONT OF THE SUIT...
EXACTLY.
IT'S A MORE SOPHISTICATED VERSION OF WHAT YOU SAW ON THE LAPTOP. INSTEAD OF A FLAT SCREEN, A THREE-DIMENSIONAL OBJECT CAN APPEAR TRANSPARENT, THANKS TO THE RETROREFLECTIVE FABRIC OF THE SUIT.
YOU SEE THAT'S AS FAR AS THE TRICK GOES, THOUGH. YOU'RE ONLY "TRANSPARENT" TO SOMEONE LOOKING AT YOU STRAIGHT ON. AND YOU HAVE TO STAND FAIRLY STILL. BUT THAT BIKE YOU SAW, WITH ITS SPEED, AND CHANGE OF VIEWING ANGLE...
...WELL, IT WAS A GOOD IDEA WHILE IT LASTED.

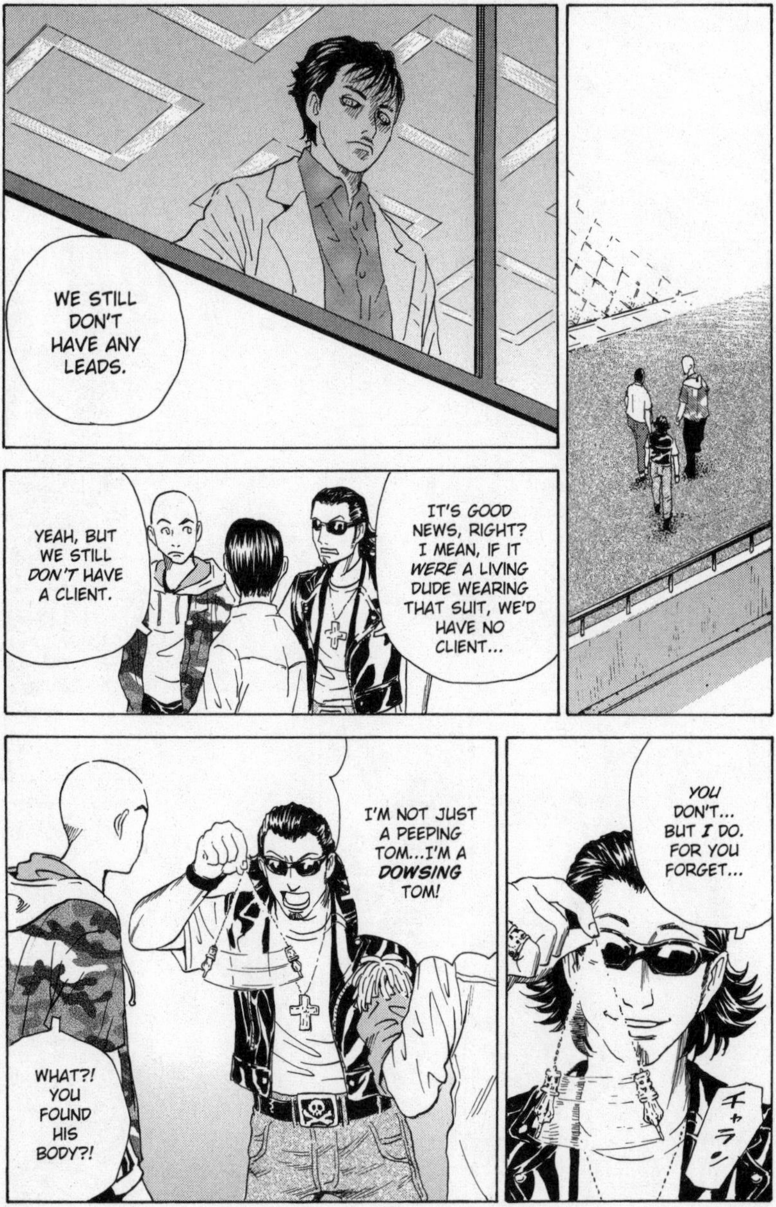
WE STILL DON'T HAVE ANY LEADS.
IT'S GOOD NEWS, RIGHT? I MEAN, IF IT *WERE* A LIVING DUDE WEARING THAT SUIT, WE'D HAVE NO CLIENT...
YEAH, BUT WE STILL *DON'T* HAVE A CLIENT.
YOU DON'T... BUT *I* DO. FOR YOU FORGET...
チャラン
I'M NOT JUST A PEEPING TOM...I'M A ***DOWSING*** TOM!
WHAT?! YOU FOUND HIS BODY?!

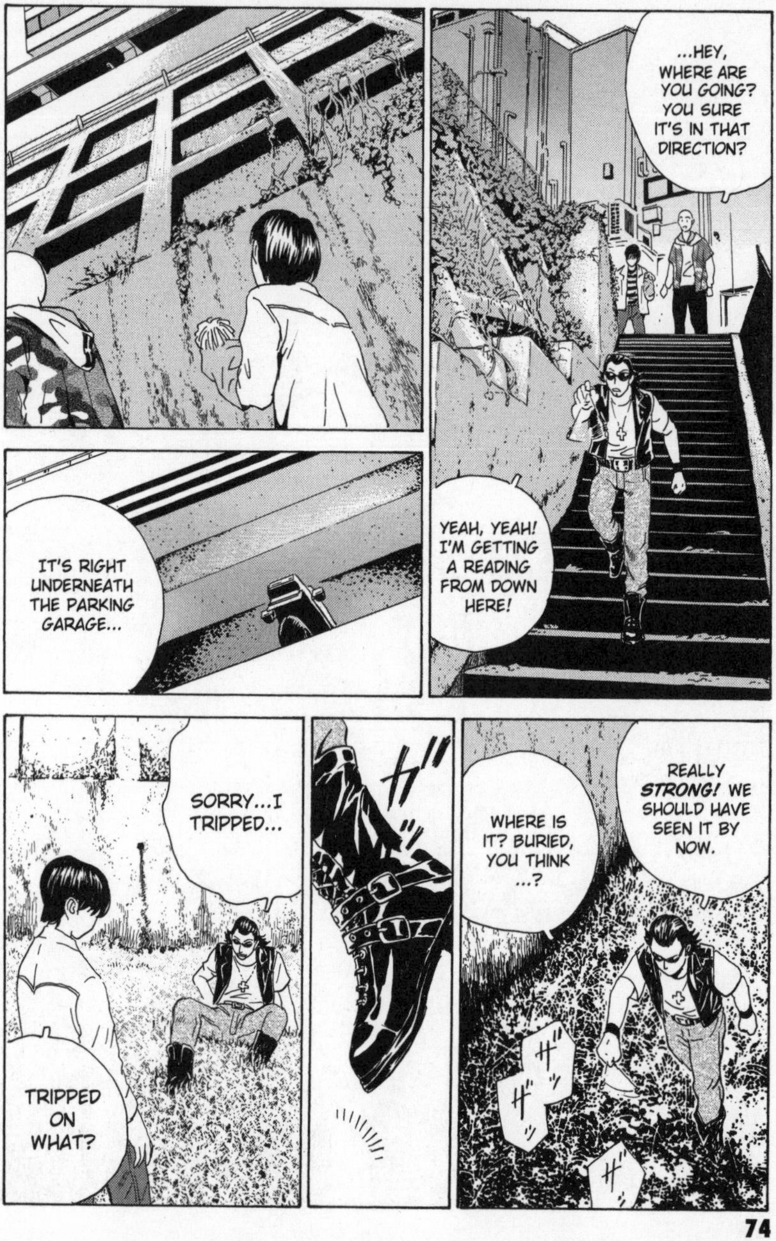
...HEY, WHERE ARE YOU GOING? YOU SURE IT'S IN THAT DIRECTION?
YEAH, YEAH! I'M GETTING A READING FROM DOWN HERE!
IT'S RIGHT UNDERNEATH THE PARKING GARAGE...
REALLY **STRONG!** WE SHOULD HAVE SEEN IT BY NOW.
WHERE IS IT? BURIED, YOU THINK ...?
ザッ
ザッ
ザ
ガッ
SORRY...I TRIPPED...
TRIPPED ON WHAT?

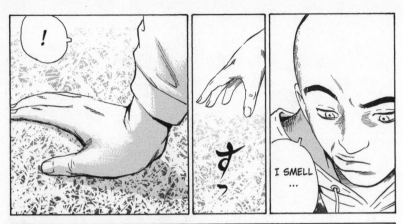

I SMELL ...

A CORPSE.

...YOU NEVER ENTIRELY GET USED TO IT.

WHAT ?!

75

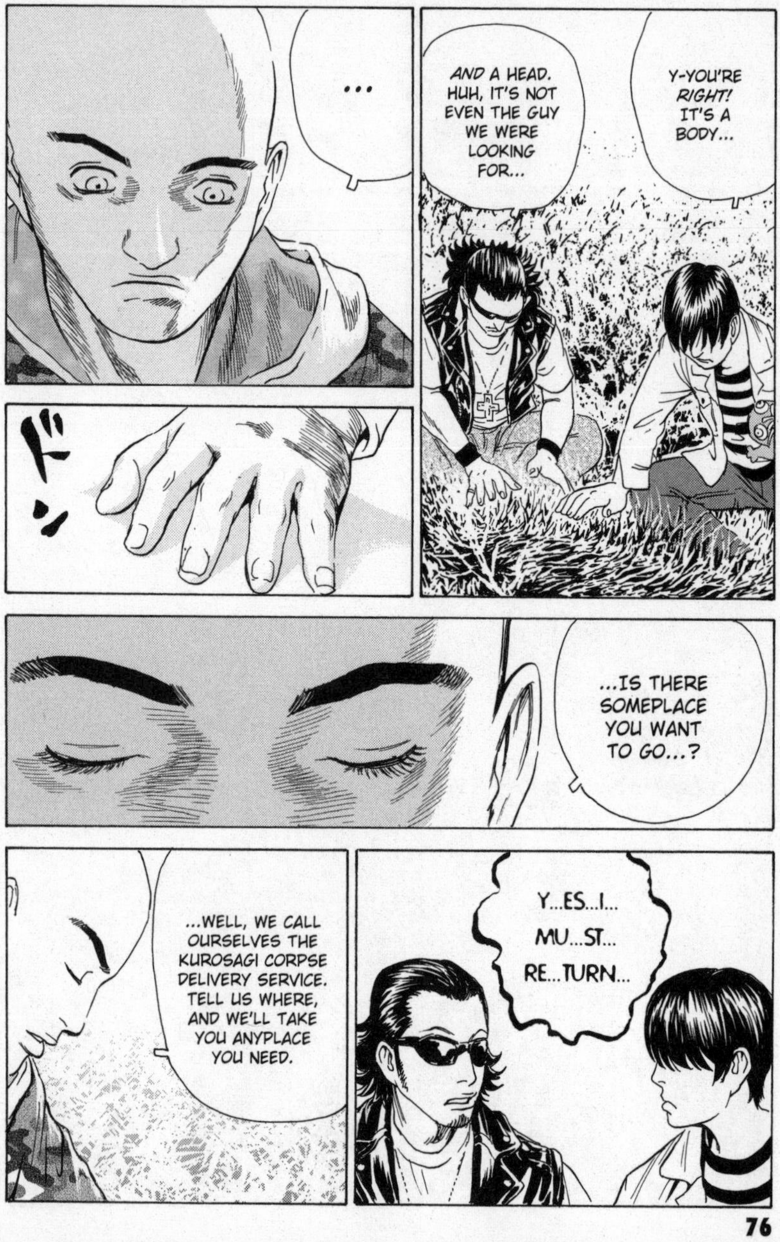
...
ドン
AND A HEAD. HUH, IT'S NOT EVEN THE GUY WE WERE LOOKING FOR...
Y-YOU'RE *RIGHT!* IT'S A BODY...
...IS THERE SOMEPLACE YOU WANT TO GO...?
...WELL, WE CALL OURSELVES THE KUROSAGI CORPSE DELIVERY SERVICE. TELL US WHERE, AND WE'LL TAKE YOU ANYPLACE YOU NEED.
Y...ES...I... MU...ST... RE...TURN...

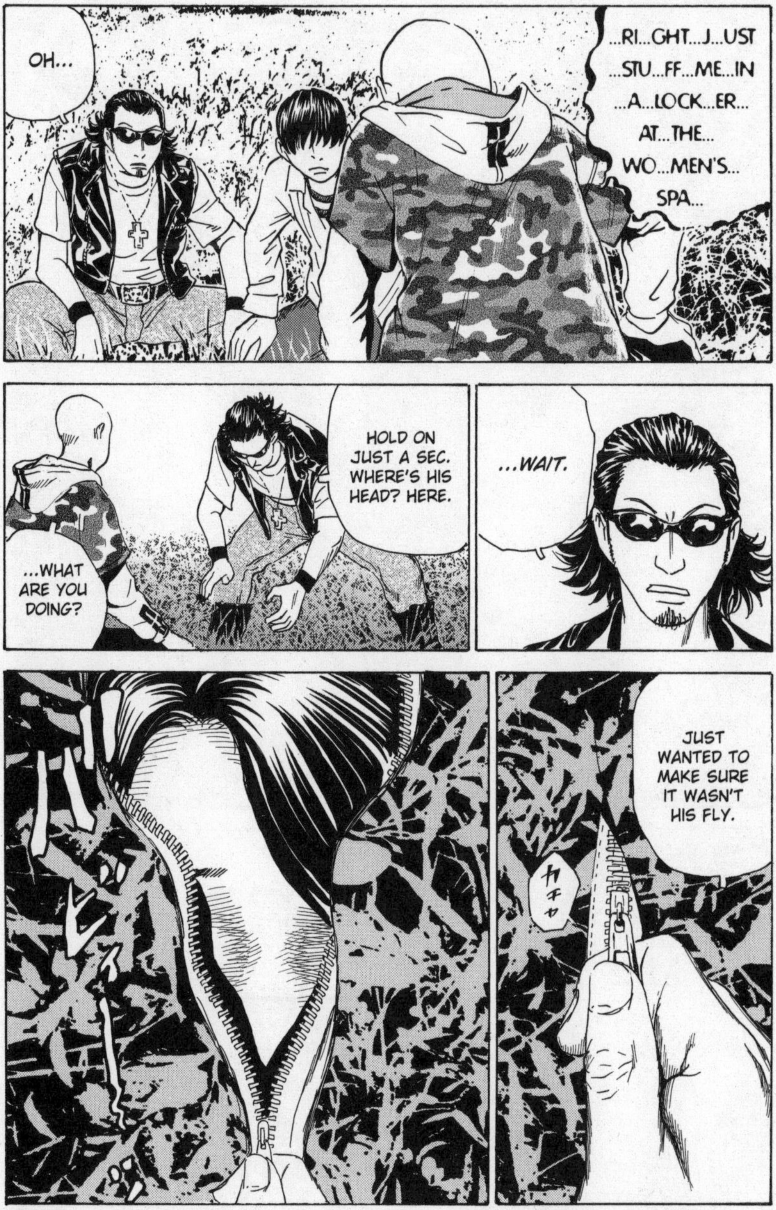
...RI...GHT...J...UST ...STU...FF...ME...IN ...A...LOCK...ER... AT...THE... WO...MEN'S... SPA...
OH...
...WAIT.
HOLD ON JUST A SEC. WHERE'S HIS HEAD? HERE.
...WHAT ARE YOU DOING?
JUST WANTED TO MAKE SURE IT WASN'T HIS FLY.
カチャ

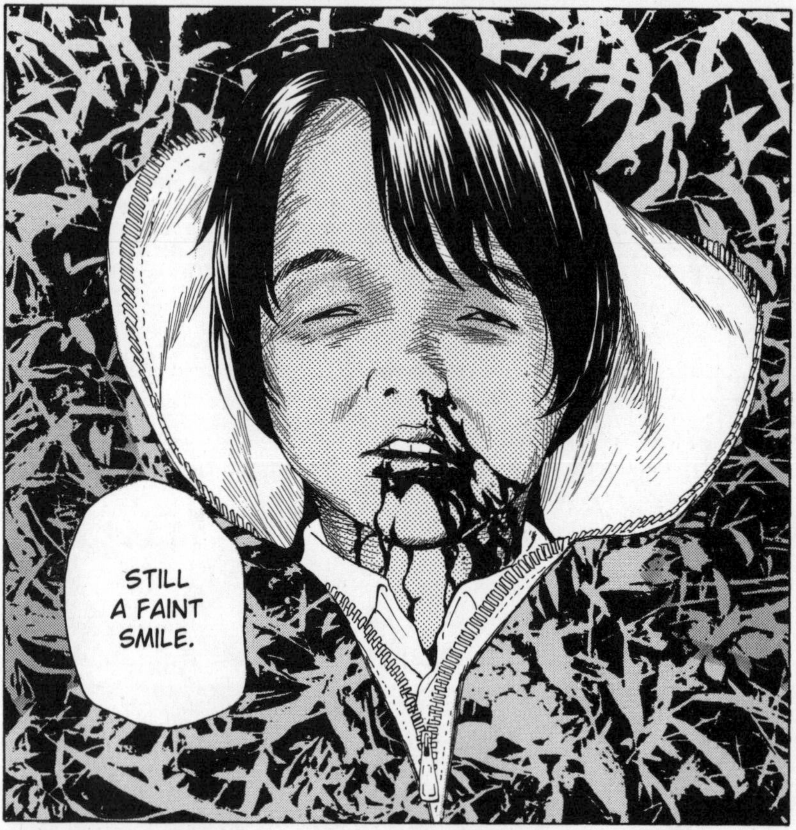
STILL A FAINT SMILE.

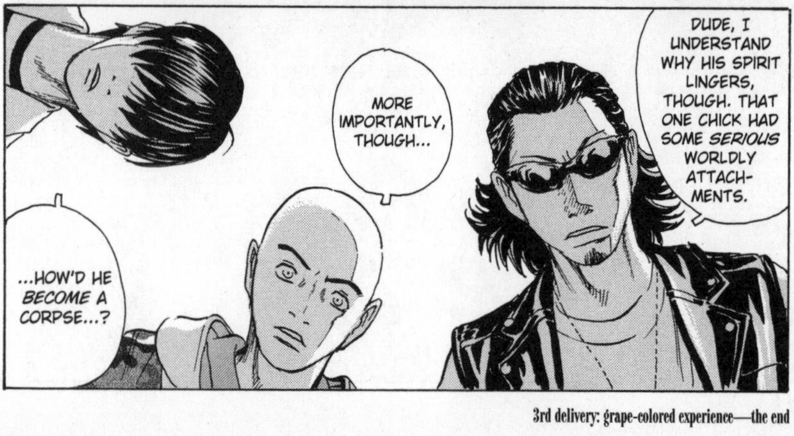
DUDE, I UNDERSTAND WHY HIS SPIRIT LINGERS, THOUGH. THAT ONE CHICK HAD SOME *SERIOUS* WORLDLY ATTACH-MENTS.
MORE IMPORTANTLY, THOUGH...
...HOW'D HE *BECOME* A CORPSE...?

3rd delivery: grape-colored experience—the end

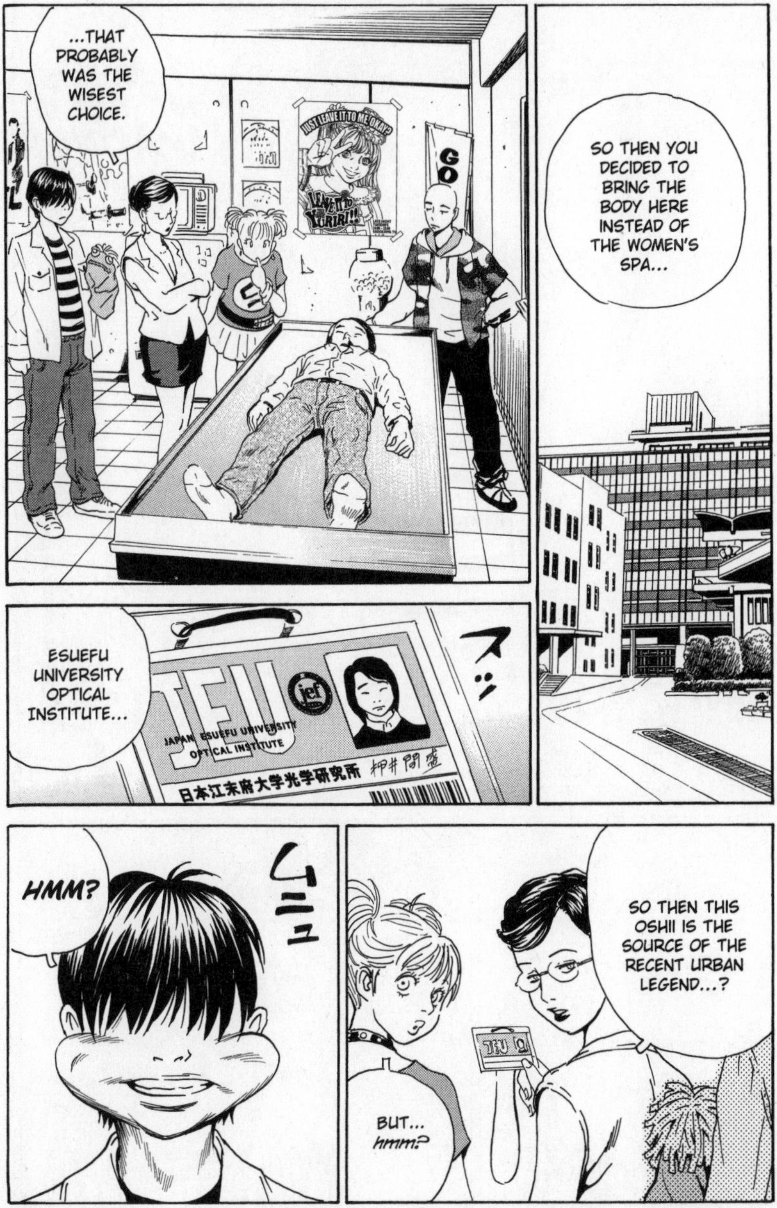

SO THEN YOU DECIDED TO BRING THE BODY HERE INSTEAD OF THE WOMEN'S SPA...
...THAT PROBABLY WAS THE WISEST CHOICE.
JUST LEAVE IT TO ME, OKAY!?
LEAVE IT TO YURIRI!!
ESUEFU UNIVERSITY OPTICAL INSTITUTE...
スッ
JEU
JAPAN ESUEFU UNIVERSITY OPTICAL INSTITUTE
日本江末府大学光学研究所
押井問盛
SO THEN THIS OSHII IS THE SOURCE OF THE RECENT URBAN LEGEND...?
BUT... *hmm?*
HMM?
ムニュ

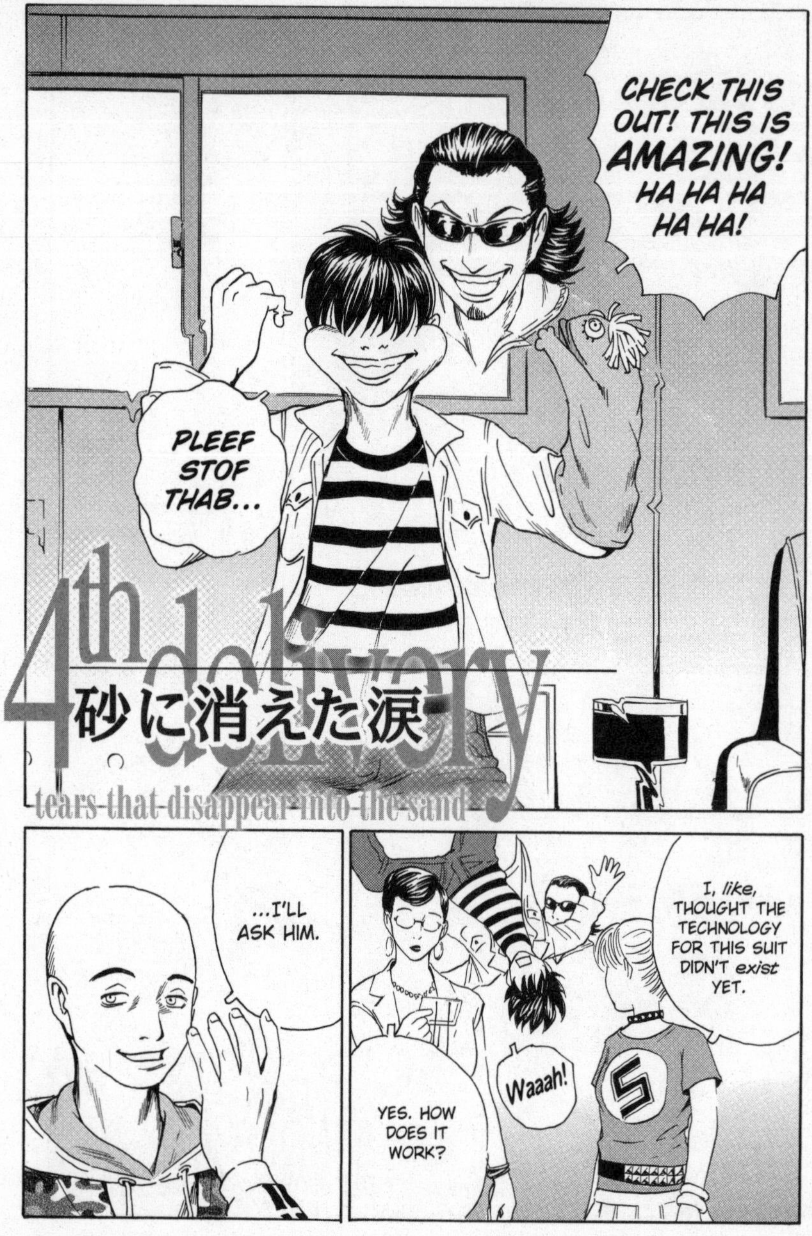
CHECK THIS OUT! THIS IS AMAZING! HA HA HA HA HA!
PLEEF STOF THAB...
4th delivery
砂に消えた涙
tears-that-disappear-into-the-sand
I, *like*, THOUGHT THE TECHNOLOGY FOR THIS SUIT DIDN'T *exist* YET.
Waaah!
YES. HOW DOES IT WORK?
...I'LL ASK HIM.

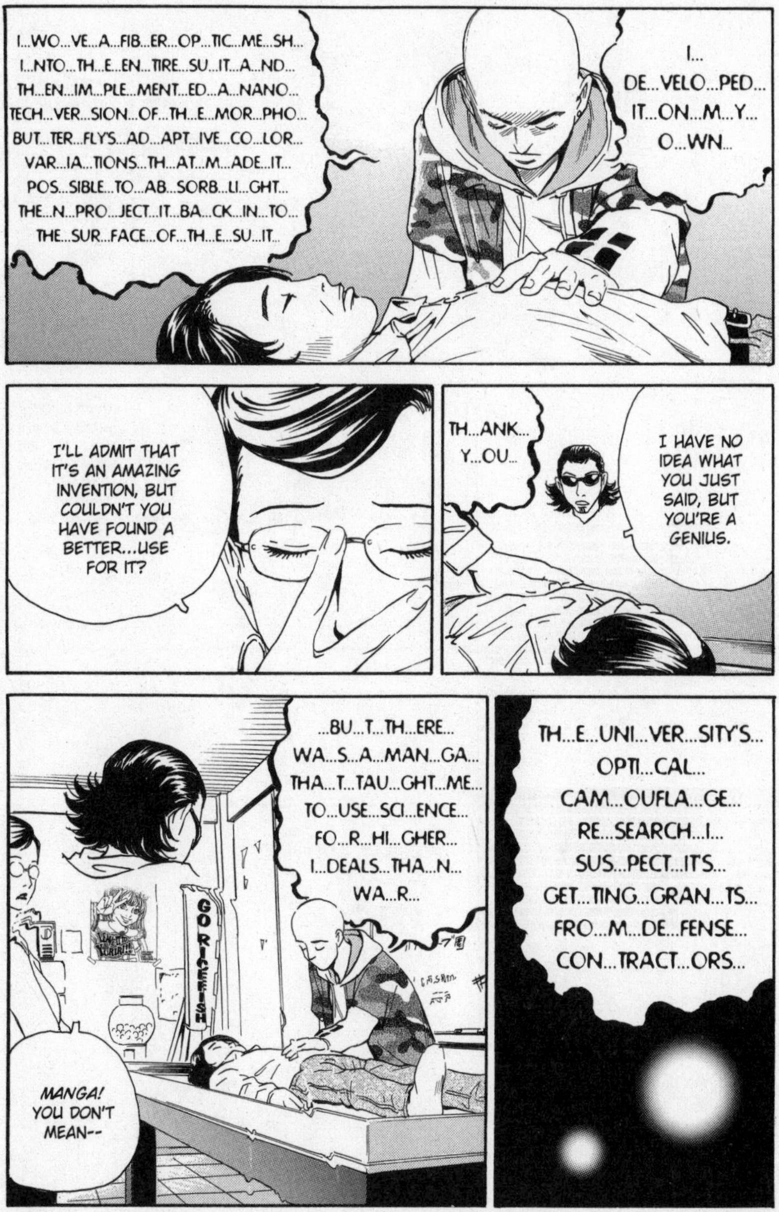

I... DE...VELO...PED... IT...ON...M...Y... O...WN...
I...WO...VE...A...FIB...ER...OP...TIC...ME...SH... I...NTO...TH...E...EN...TIRE...SU...IT...A...ND... TH...EN...IM...PLE...MENT...ED...A...NANO... TECH...VER...SION...OF...TH...E...MOR...PHO... BUT...TER...FLY'S...AD...APT...IVE...CO...LOR... VAR...IA...TIONS...TH...AT...M...ADE...IT... POS...SIBLE...TO...AB...SORB...LI...GHT... THE...N...PRO...JECT...IT...BA...CK...IN...TO... THE...SUR...FACE...OF...TH...E...SU...IT...
I HAVE NO IDEA WHAT YOU JUST SAID, BUT YOU'RE A GENIUS.
TH...ANK... Y...OU...
I'LL ADMIT THAT IT'S AN AMAZING INVENTION, BUT COULDN'T YOU HAVE FOUND A BETTER...USE FOR IT?
TH...E...UNI...VER...SITY'S... OPTI...CAL... CAM...OUFLA...GE... RE...SEARCH...I... SUS...PECT...ITS... GET...TING...GRAN...TS... FRO...M...DE...FENSE... CON...TRACT...ORS...
...BU...T...TH...ERE... WA...S...A...MAN...GA... THA...T...TAU...GHT...ME... TO...USE...SCI...ENCE... FO...R...HI...GHER... I...DEALS...THA...N... WA...R...
GO RICEFISH
MANGA! YOU DON'T MEAN--

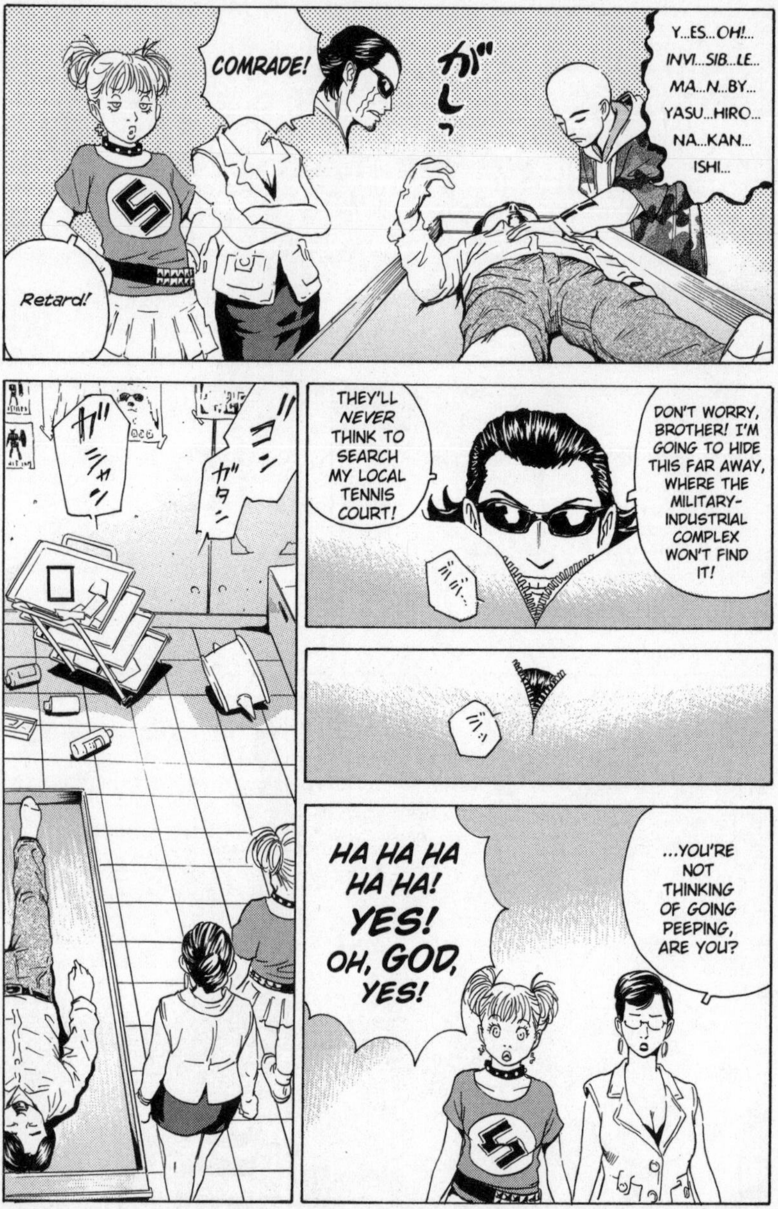

Y...ES...OH!... INVI...SIB...LE... MA...N...BY... YASU...HIRO... NA...KAN... ISHI...
がしっ
COMRADE!
Retard!
DON'T WORRY, BROTHER! I'M GOING TO HIDE THIS FAR AWAY, WHERE THE MILITARY-INDUSTRIAL COMPLEX WON'T FIND IT!
THEY'LL *NEVER* THINK TO SEARCH MY LOCAL TENNIS COURT!
ジジ…
ジッ
...YOU'RE NOT THINKING OF GOING PEEPING, ARE YOU?
HA HA HA HA HA! YES! OH, GOD, YES!
ゴン
ガタン
ガシャン

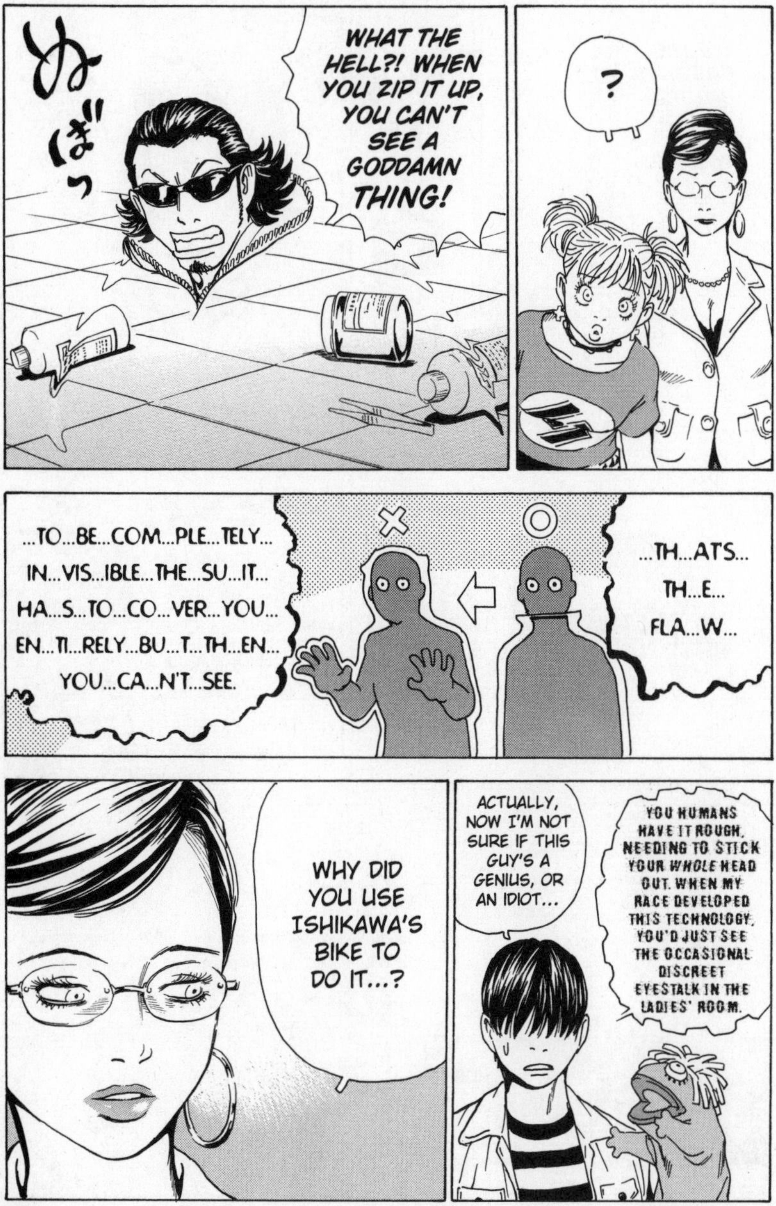
?
ぬぼっ
WHAT THE HELL?! WHEN YOU ZIP IT UP, YOU CAN'T SEE A GODDAMN THING!
...TH...AT'S... TH...E... FLA...W...
...TO...BE...COM...PLE...TELY... IN...VIS...IBLE...THE...SU...IT... HA...S...TO...CO...VER...YOU... EN...TI...RELY...BU...T...TH...EN... YOU...CA...N'T...SEE.
YOU HUMANS HAVE IT ROUGH, NEEDING TO STICK YOUR *WHOLE* HEAD OUT. WHEN MY RACE DEVELOPED THIS TECHNOLOGY, YOU'D JUST SEE THE OCCASIONAL DISCREET EYESTALK IN THE LADIES' ROOM.
ACTUALLY, NOW I'M NOT SURE IF THIS GUY'S A GENIUS, OR AN IDIOT...
WHY DID YOU USE ISHIKAWA'S BIKE TO DO IT...?

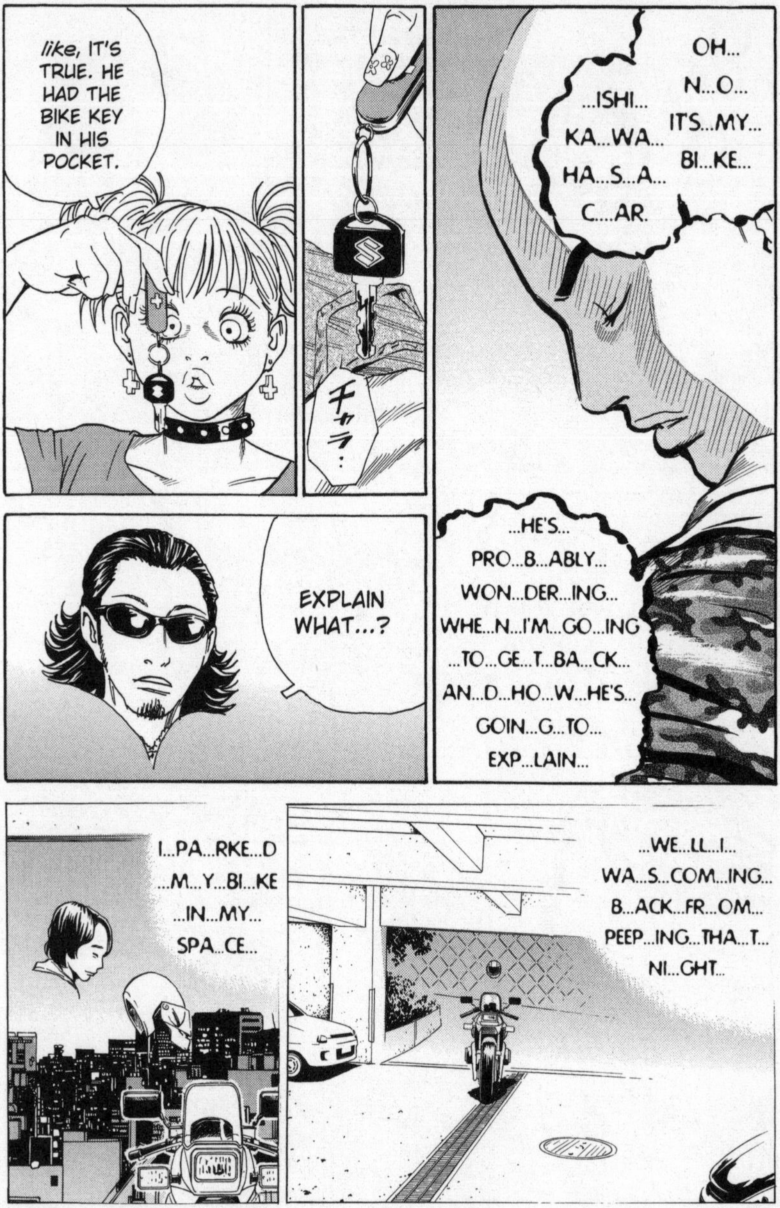
OH... N...O... ITS...MY... BI...KE...
...ISHI... KA...WA... HA...S...A... C...AR.
...HE'S... PRO...B...ABLY... WON...DER...ING... WHE...N...I'M...GO...ING ...TO...GE...T...BA...CK... AN...D...HO...W...HE'S... GOIN...G...TO... EXP...LAIN...
チャラ…
like, IT'S TRUE. HE HAD THE BIKE KEY IN HIS POCKET.
EXPLAIN WHAT...?
...WE...LL...I... WA...S...COM...ING... B...ACK...FR...OM... PEEP...ING...THA...T... NI...GHT...
I...PA...RKE...D ...M...Y...BI...KE ...IN...MY... SPA...CE...

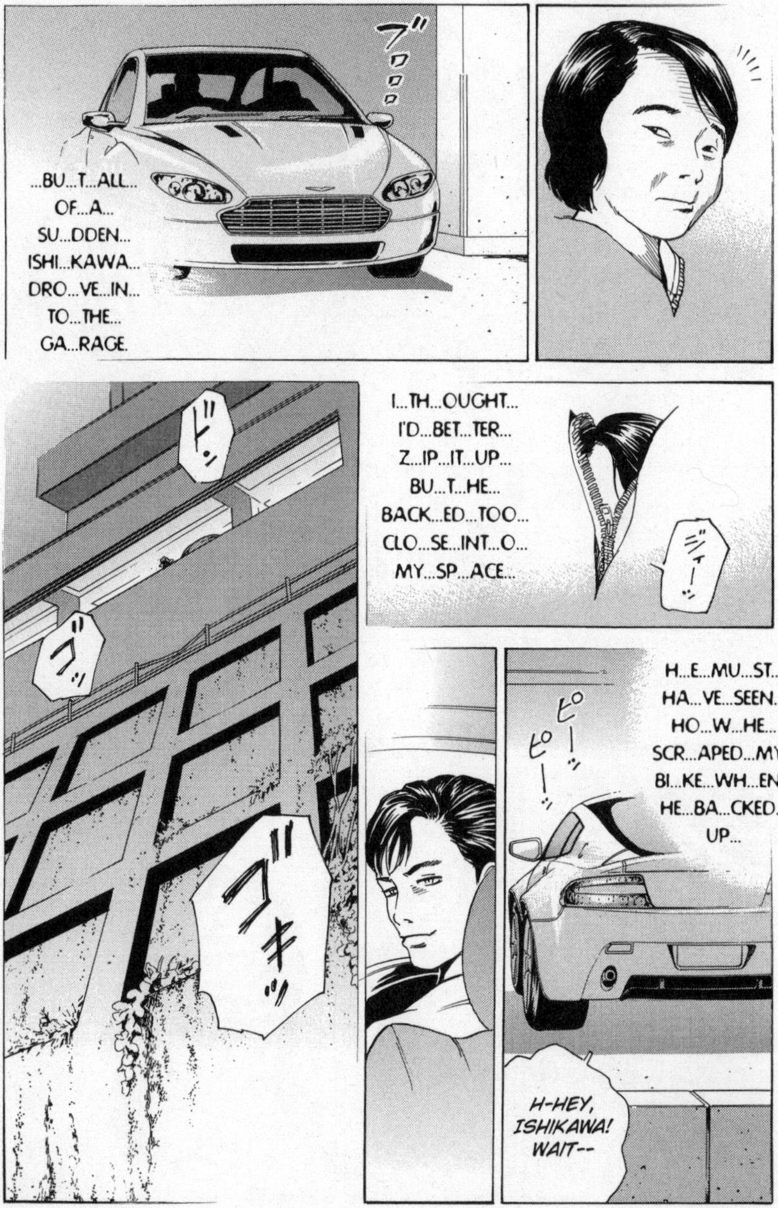
ブロロロ
...BU...T...ALL... OF...A... SU...DDEN... ISHI...KAWA... DRO...VE...IN... TO...THE... GA...RAGE.
I...TH...OUGHT... I'D...BET...TER... Z...IP...IT...UP... BU...T...HE... BACK...ED...TOO... CLO...SE...INT...O... MY...SP...ACE...
ジィー…ッ
H...E...MU...ST... HA...VE...SEEN... HO...W...HE... SCR...APED...MY... BI...KE...WH...EN... HE...BA...CKED... UP...
ピーッ
ピーッ
H-HEY, ISHIKAWA! WAIT--
ドッ
ガッ
ゴキッ

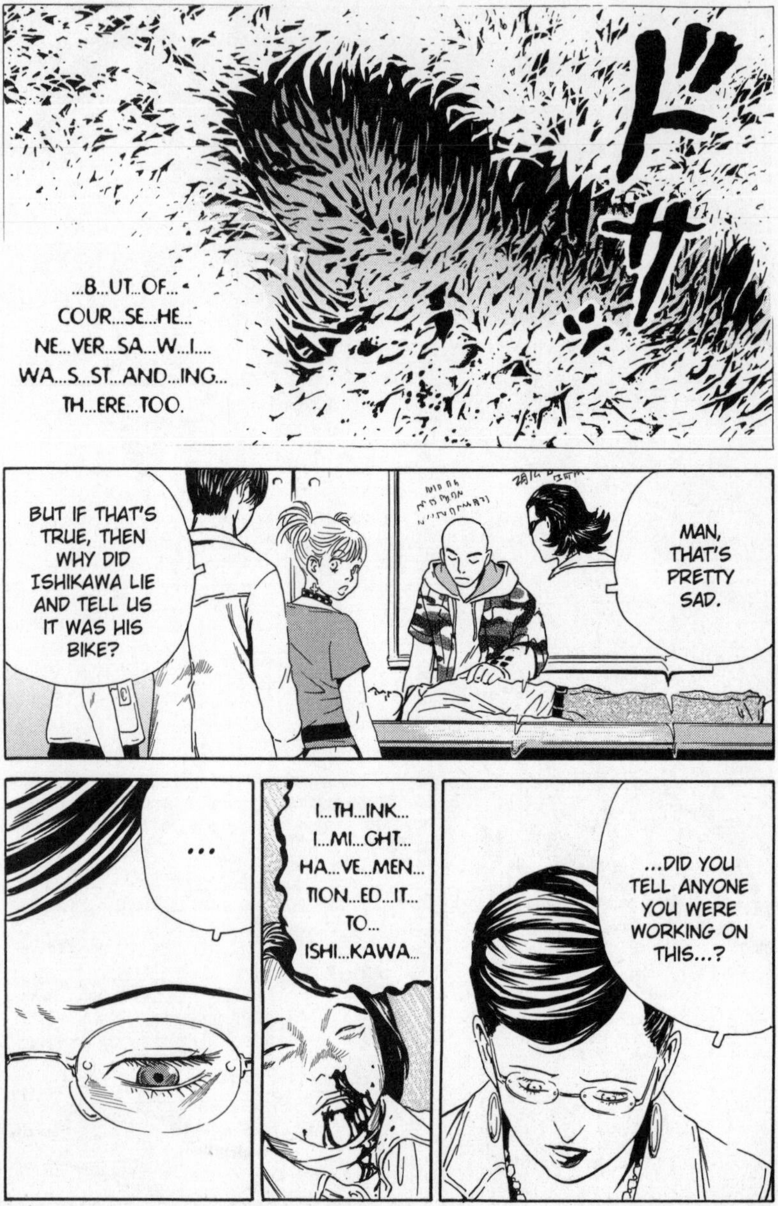
ドサッ
...B...UT...OF... COUR...SE...HE... NE...VER...SA...W...I.... WA...S...ST...AND...ING... TH...ERE...TOO.
MAN, THAT'S PRETTY SAD.
BUT IF THAT'S TRUE, THEN WHY DID ISHIKAWA LIE AND TELL US IT WAS HIS BIKE?
...DID YOU TELL ANYONE YOU WERE WORKING ON THIS...?
I...TH...INK... I...MI...GHT... HA...VE...MEN... TION...ED...IT... TO... ISHI...KAWA...
...

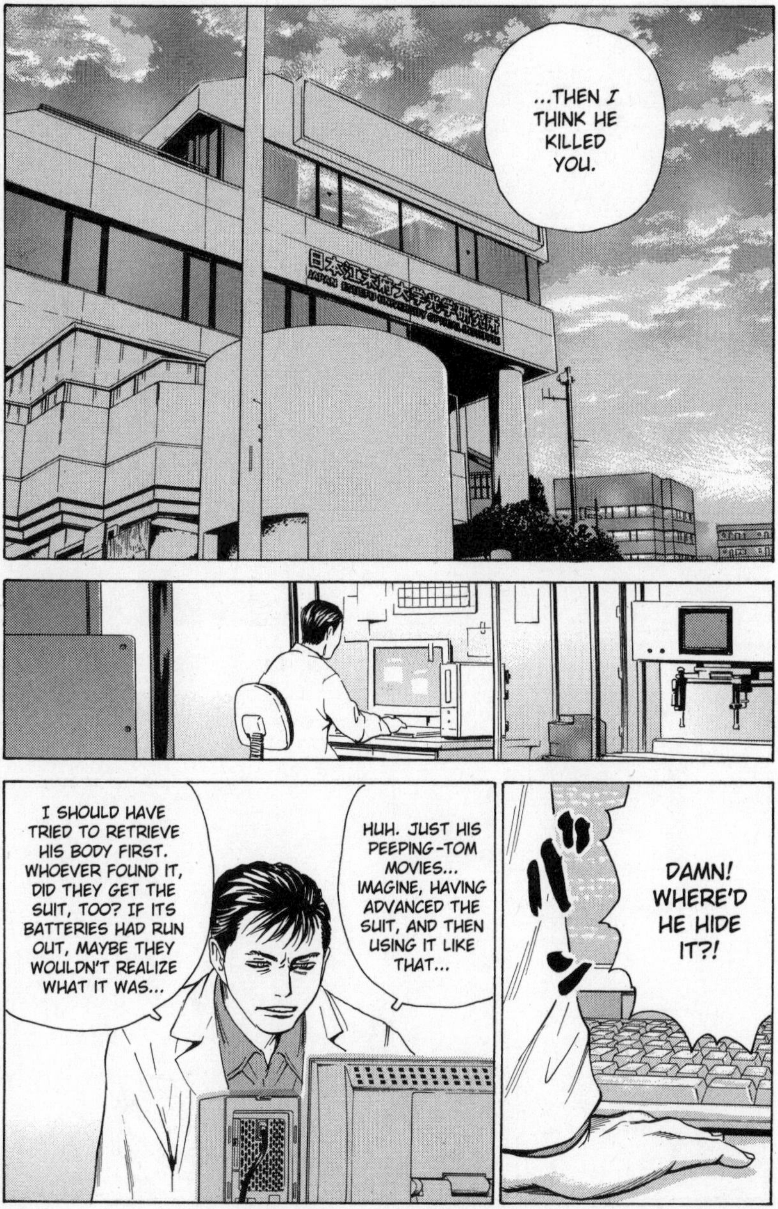
...THEN I THINK HE KILLED YOU.
DAMN! WHERE'D HE HIDE IT?!
HUH. JUST HIS PEEPING-TOM MOVIES... IMAGINE, HAVING ADVANCED THE SUIT, AND THEN USING IT LIKE THAT...
I SHOULD HAVE TRIED TO RETRIEVE HIS BODY FIRST. WHOEVER FOUND IT, DID THEY GET THE SUIT, TOO? IF ITS BATTERIES HAD RUN OUT, MAYBE THEY WOULDN'T REALIZE WHAT IT WAS...

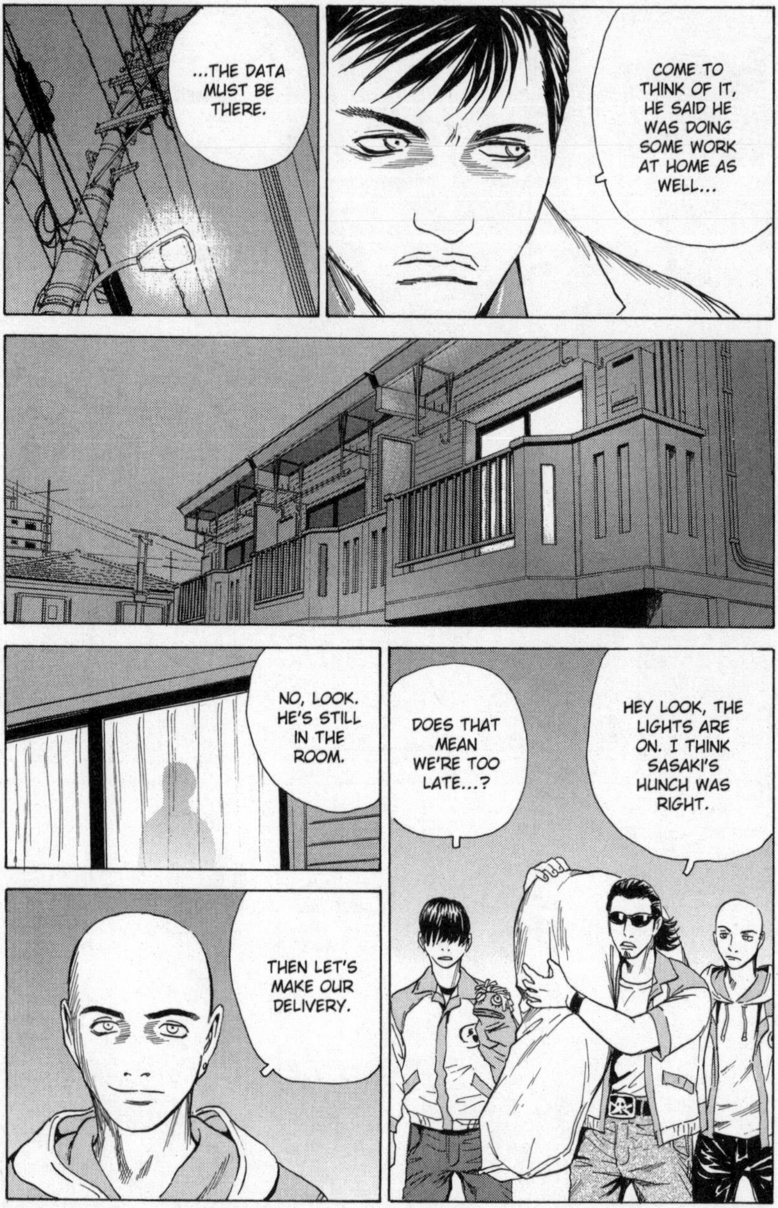
COME TO THINK OF IT, HE SAID HE WAS DOING SOME WORK AT HOME AS WELL...
...THE DATA MUST BE THERE.
HEY LOOK, THE LIGHTS ARE ON. I THINK SASAKI'S HUNCH WAS RIGHT.
DOES THAT MEAN WE'RE TOO LATE...?
NO, LOOK. HE'S STILL IN THE ROOM.
THEN LET'S MAKE OUR DELIVERY.

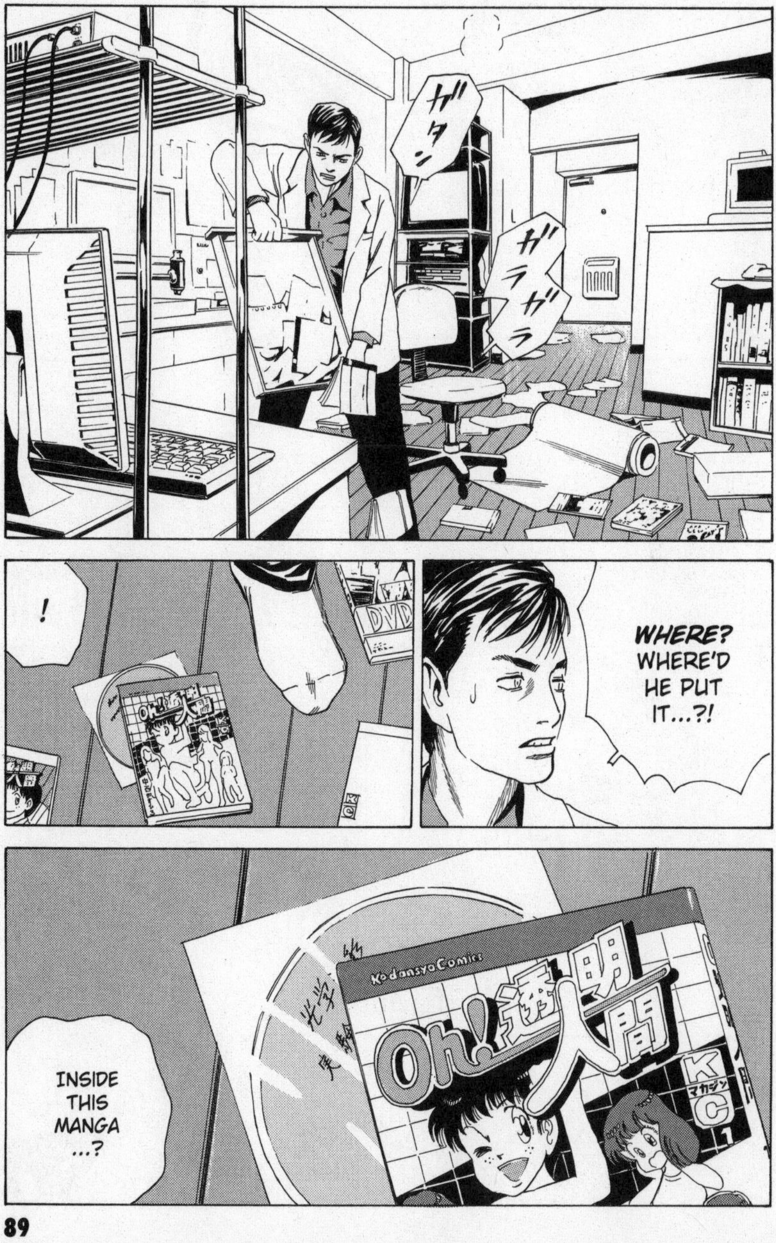
ガタン
ガラガラ
WHERE? WHERE'D HE PUT IT...?!
!
Oh!透明人間
INSIDE THIS MANGA ...?

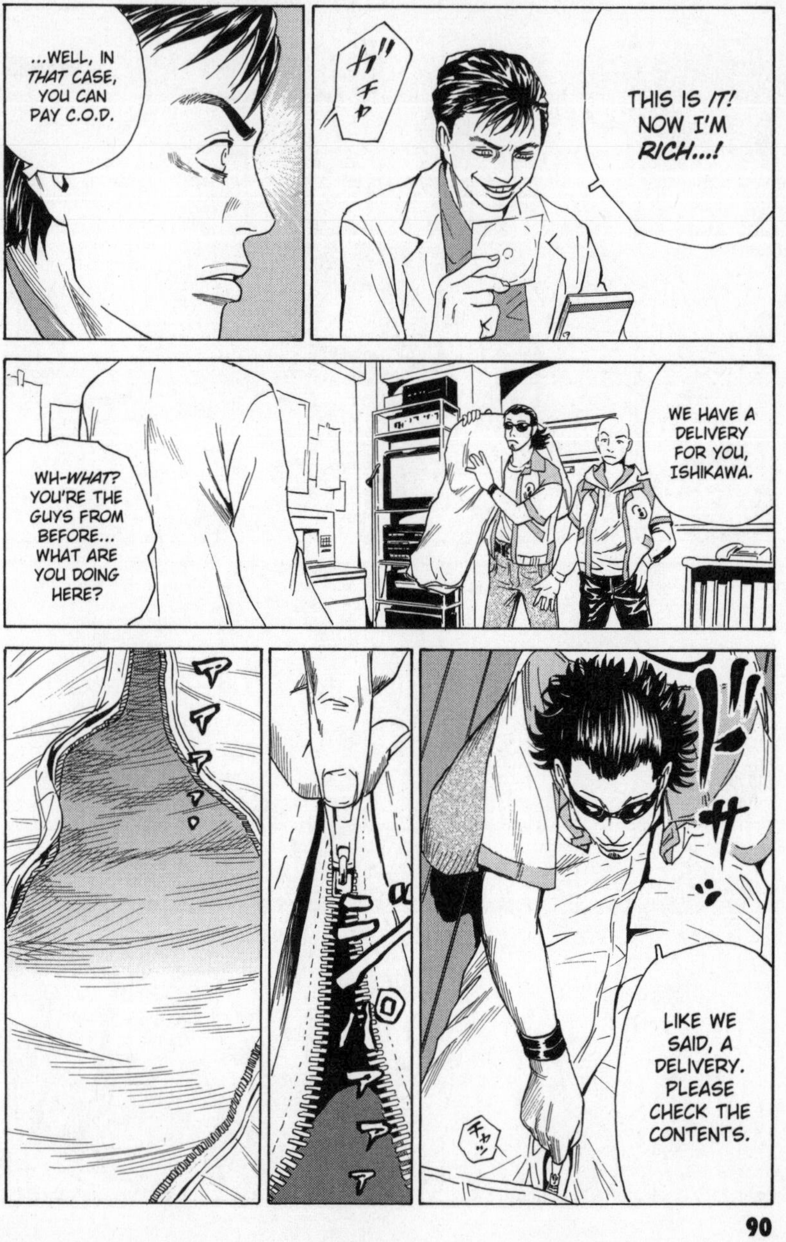

ガチャ
THIS IS IT! NOW I'M RICH...!
...WELL, IN THAT CASE, YOU CAN PAY C.O.D.
WE HAVE A DELIVERY FOR YOU, ISHIKAWA.
WH-WHAT? YOU'RE THE GUYS FROM BEFORE... WHAT ARE YOU DOING HERE?
LIKE WE SAID, A DELIVERY. PLEASE CHECK THE CONTENTS.

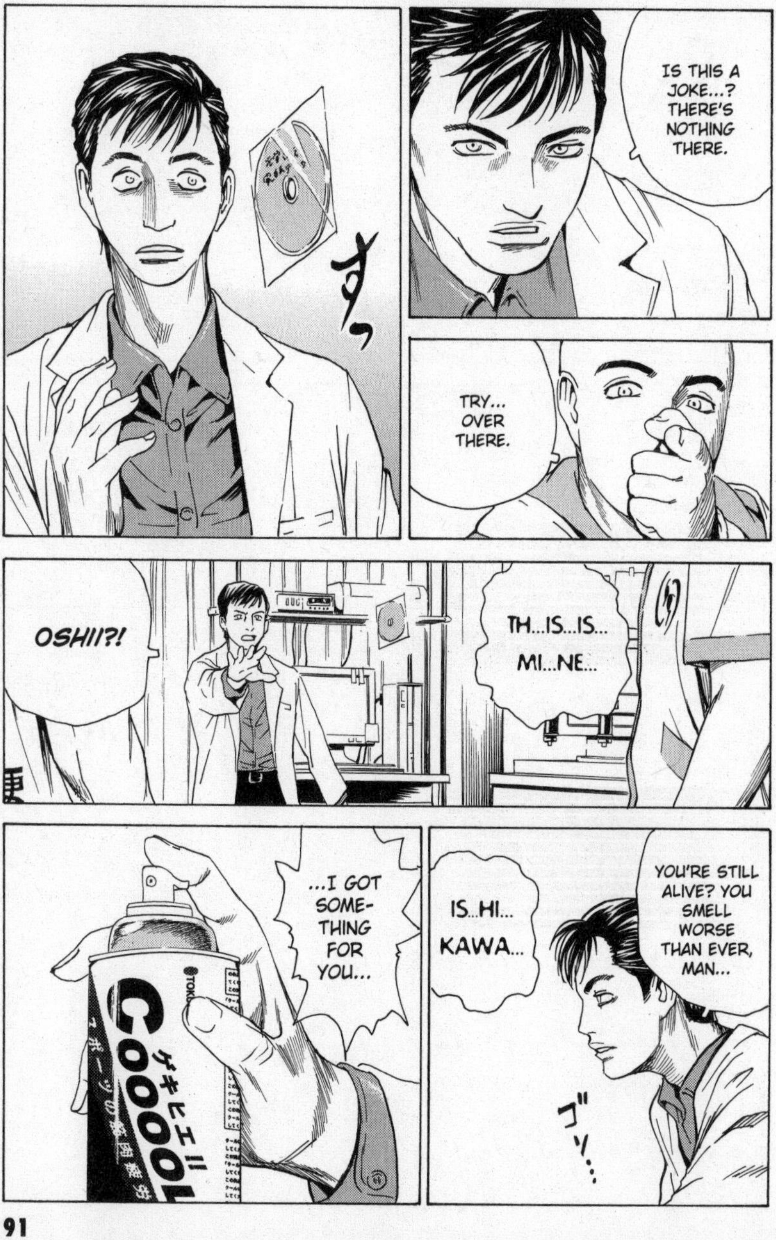
IS THIS A JOKE...? THERE'S NOTHING THERE.
TRY... OVER THERE.
すっ
TH...IS...IS... MI...NE...
OSHII?!
YOU'RE STILL ALIVE? YOU SMELL WORSE THAN EVER, MAN...
IS...HI... KAWA...
ゴソ...
...I GOT SOME-THING FOR YOU...

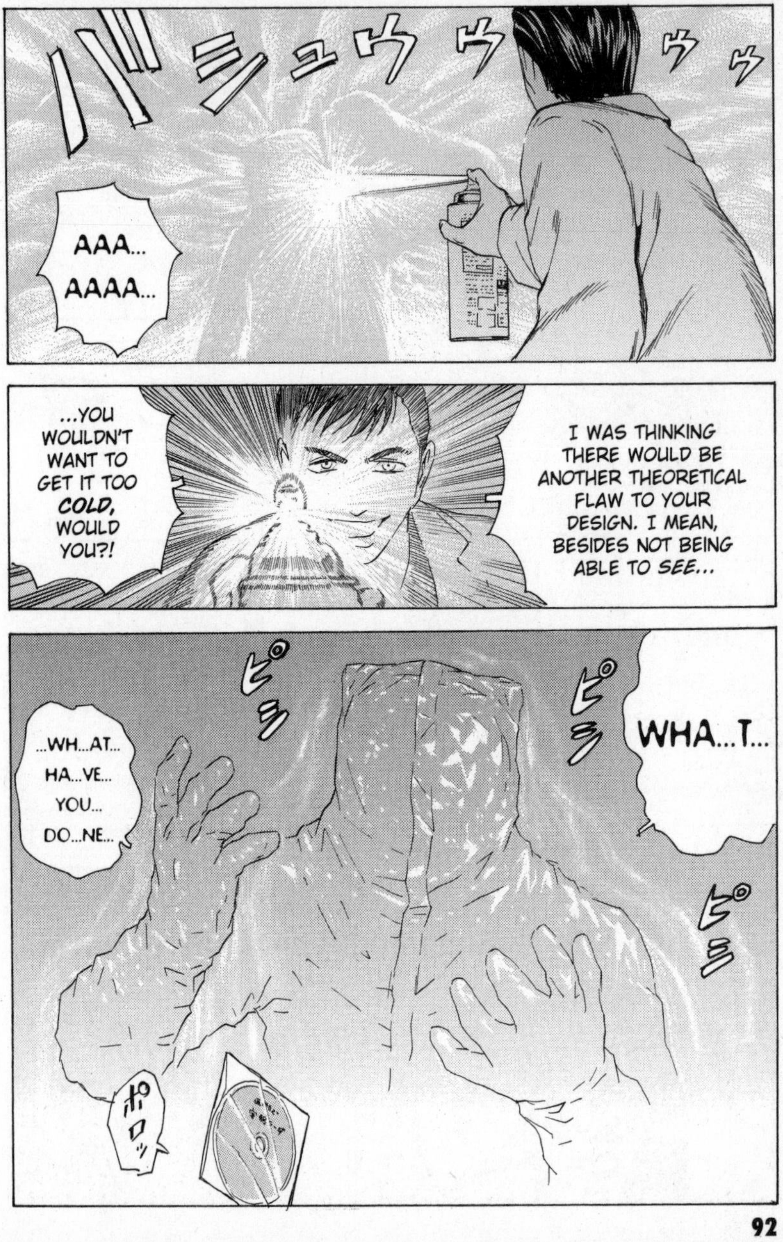
バシュウウウウ
AAA... AAAA...
I WAS THINKING THERE WOULD BE ANOTHER THEORETICAL FLAW TO YOUR DESIGN. I MEAN, BESIDES NOT BEING ABLE TO SEE...
...YOU WOULDN'T WANT TO GET IT TOO COLD, WOULD YOU?!
WHA...T...
ピシ
ピシ
...WH...AT... HA...VE... YOU... DO...NE...
ピシ
ポロッ

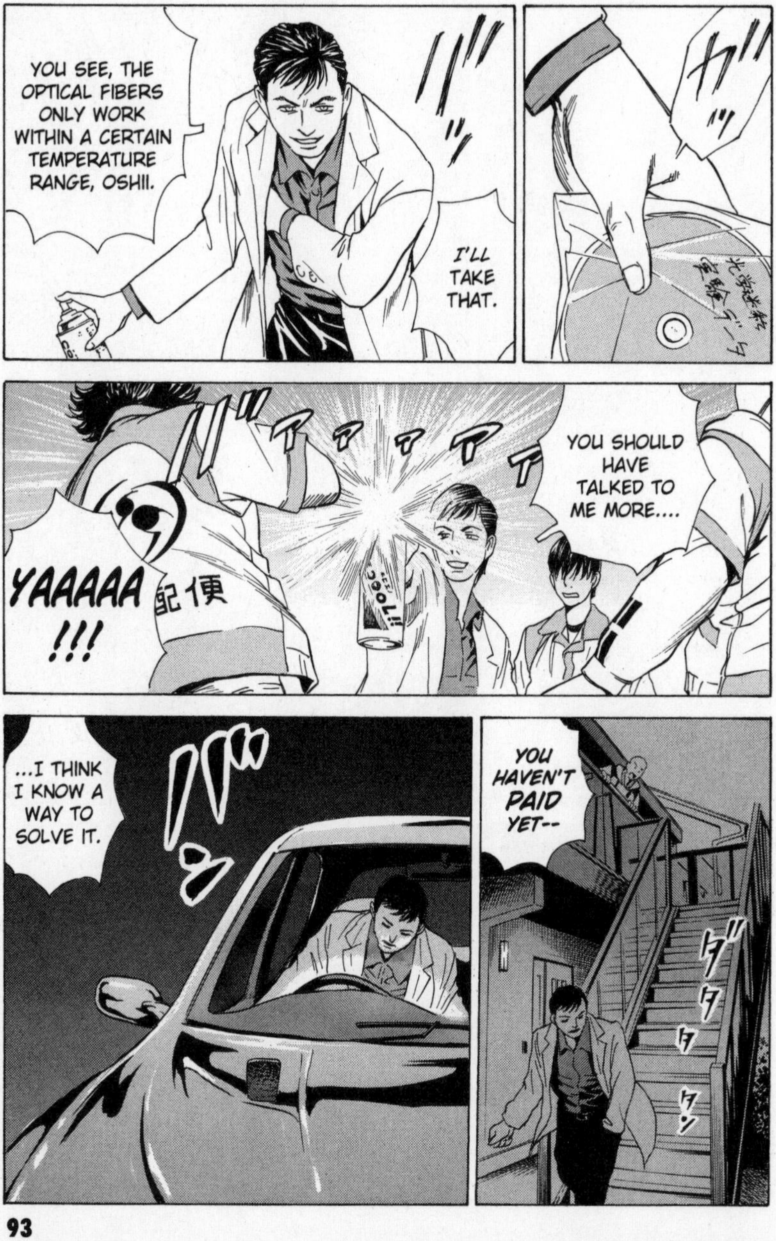
YOU SEE, THE OPTICAL FIBERS ONLY WORK WITHIN A CERTAIN TEMPERATURE RANGE, OSHII.
I'LL TAKE THAT.
YOU SHOULD HAVE TALKED TO ME MORE....
COOL!!
YAAAAA !!!
YOU HAVEN'T PAID YET--
...I THINK I KNOW A WAY TO SOLVE IT.

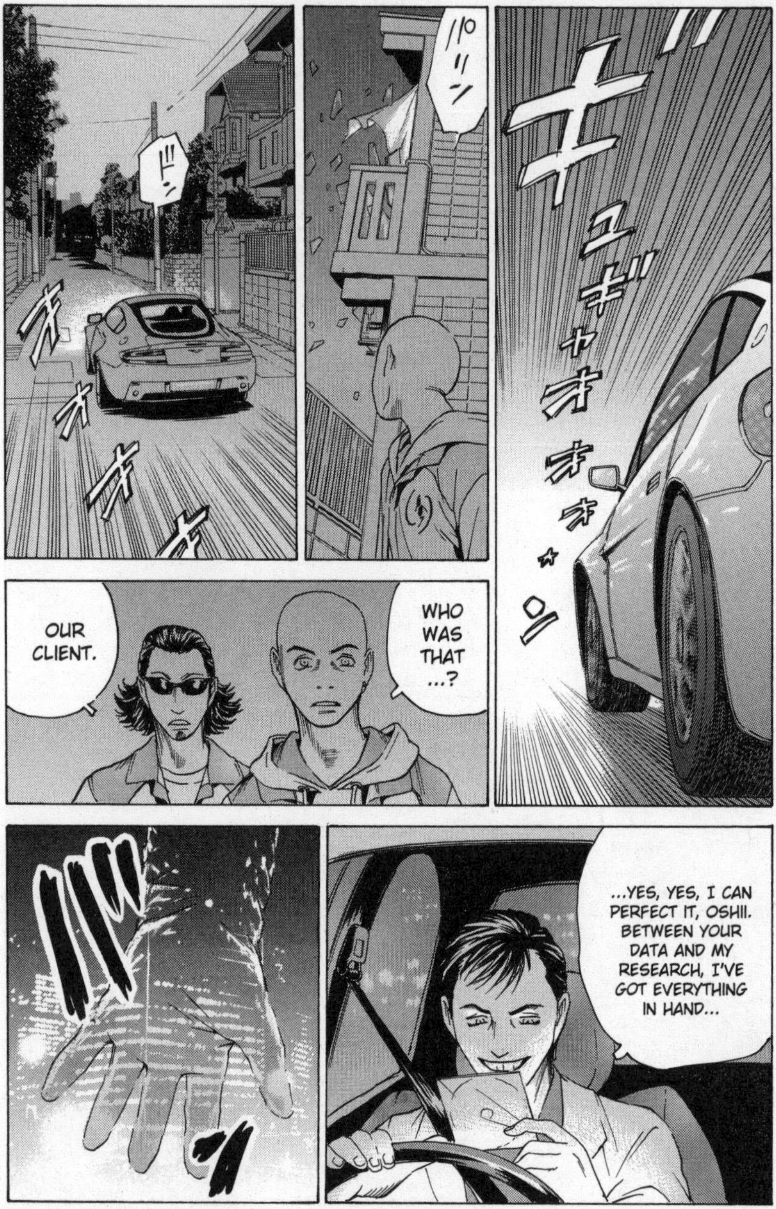

ギュギャオオォォ☆ン
パリーン
ドン
オオオオ
WHO WAS THAT ...?
OUR CLIENT.
...YES, YES, I CAN PERFECT IT, OSHII. BETWEEN YOUR DATA AND MY RESEARCH, I'VE GOT EVERYTHING IN HAND...

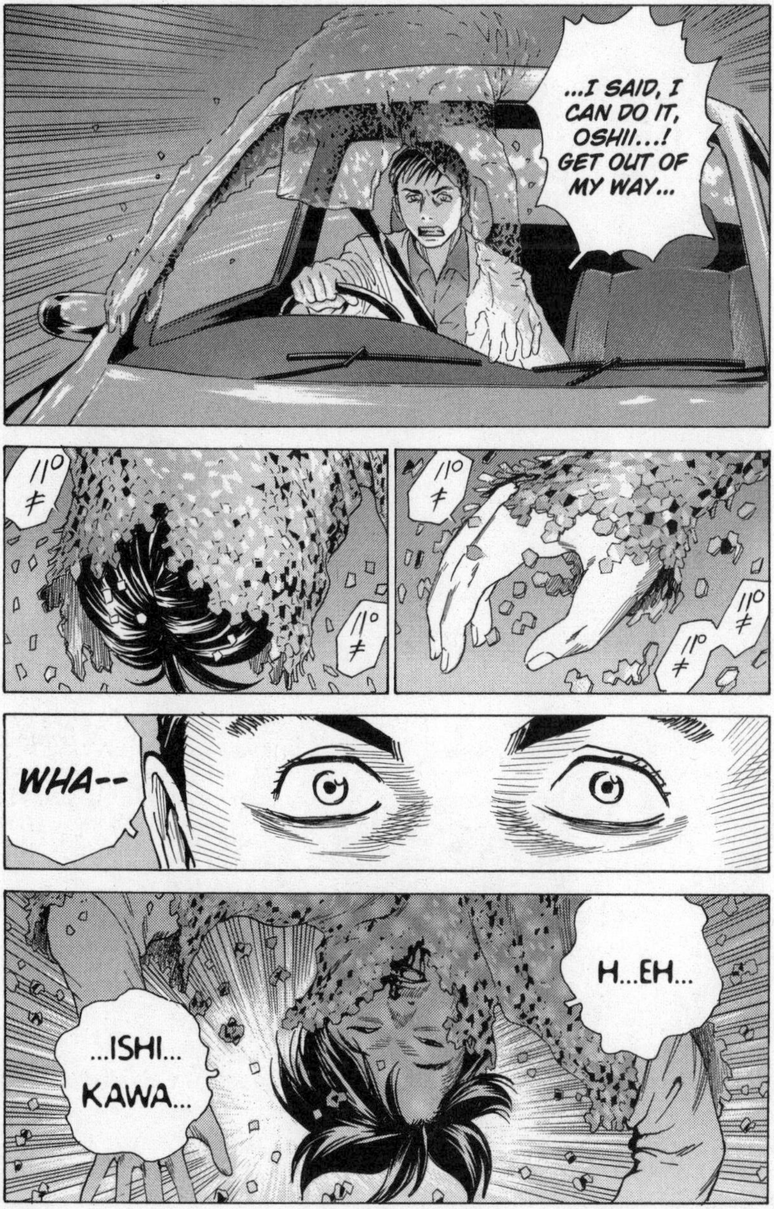
...I SAID, I CAN DO IT, OSHII...! GET OUT OF MY WAY...
パキ
パキ
パキ
パキ
WHA--
H...EH...
...ISHI... KAWA...

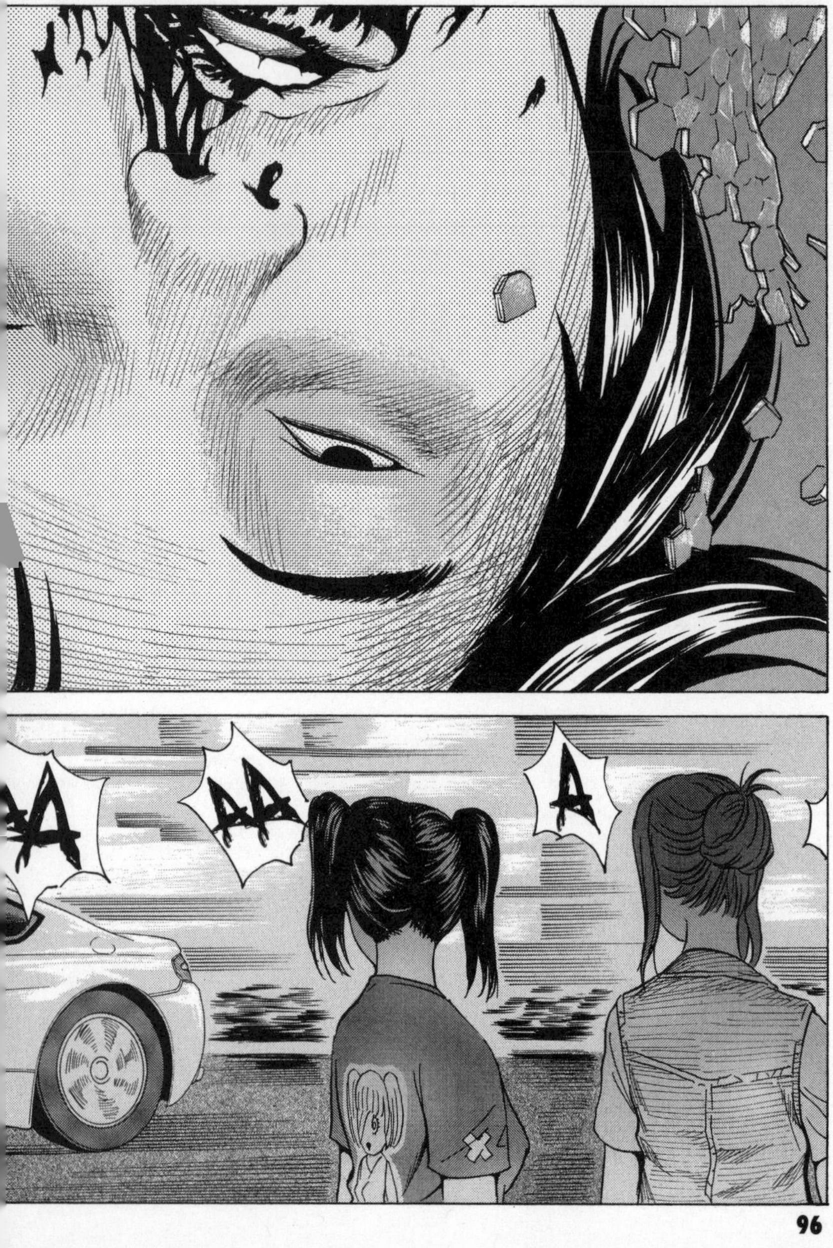
A
AA
AA

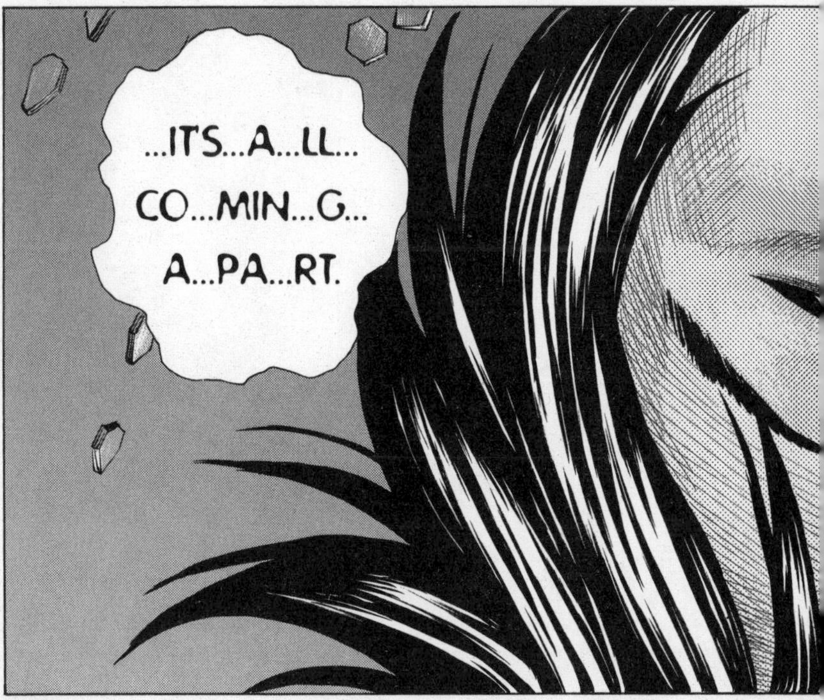

...IT'S...A...LL... CO...MIN...G... A...PA...RT.

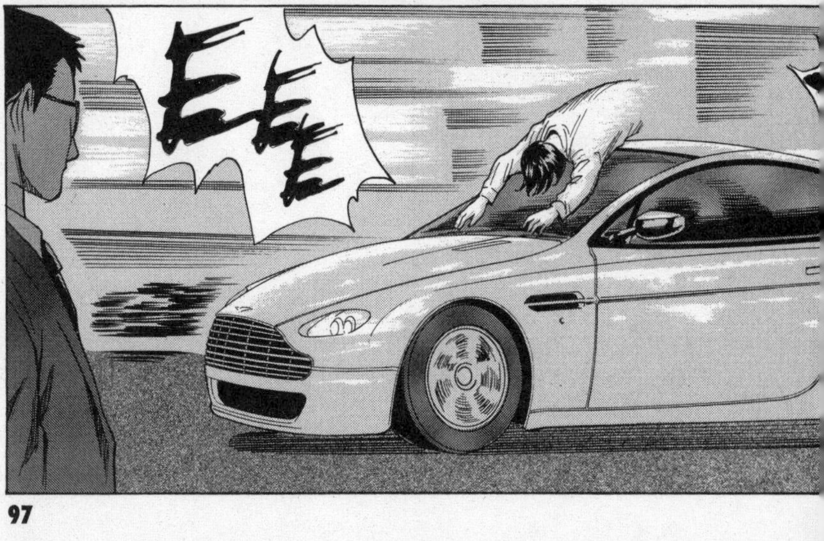

EEE

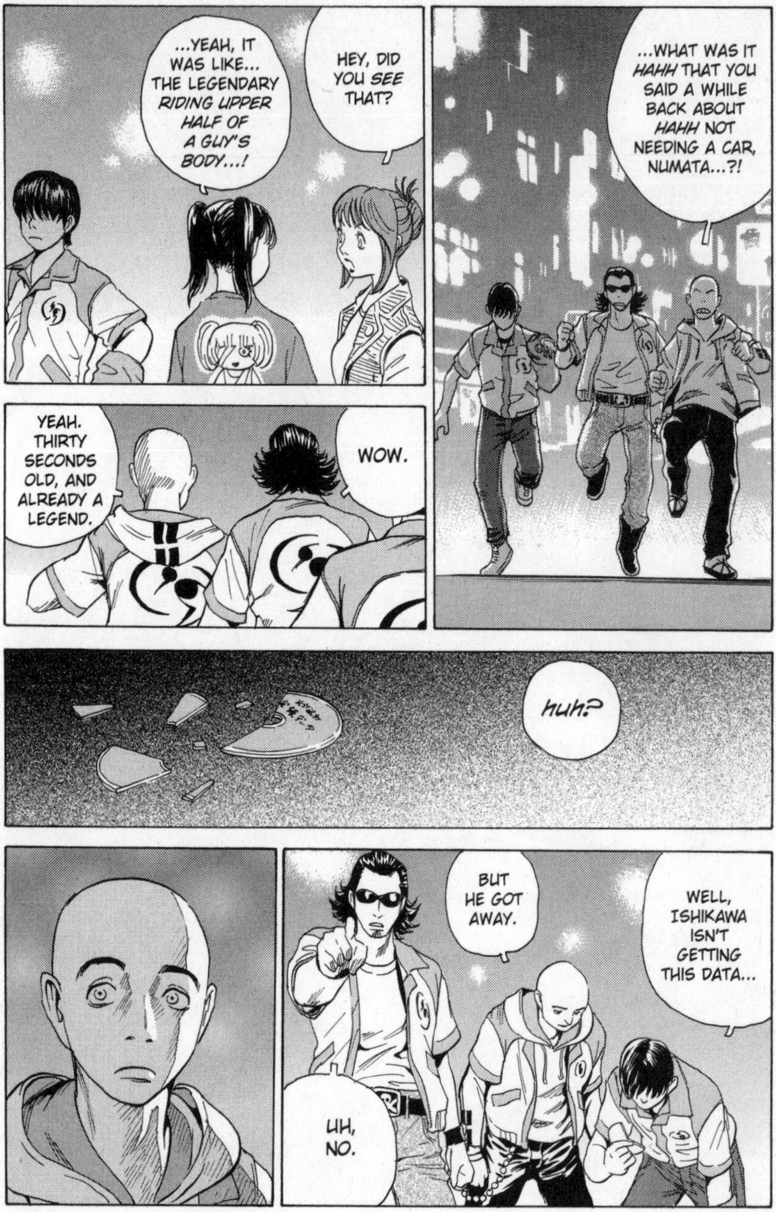
...WHAT WAS IT *HAHH* THAT YOU SAID A WHILE BACK ABOUT *HAHH* NOT NEEDING A CAR, NUMATA...?!
HEY, DID YOU *SEE* THAT?
...YEAH, IT WAS LIKE... THE LEGENDARY *RIDING UPPER* HALF OF A GUY'S BODY...!
WOW.
YEAH. THIRTY SECONDS OLD, AND ALREADY A LEGEND.
huh?
WELL, ISHIKAWA ISN'T GETTING THIS DATA...
BUT HE GOT AWAY.
UH, NO.

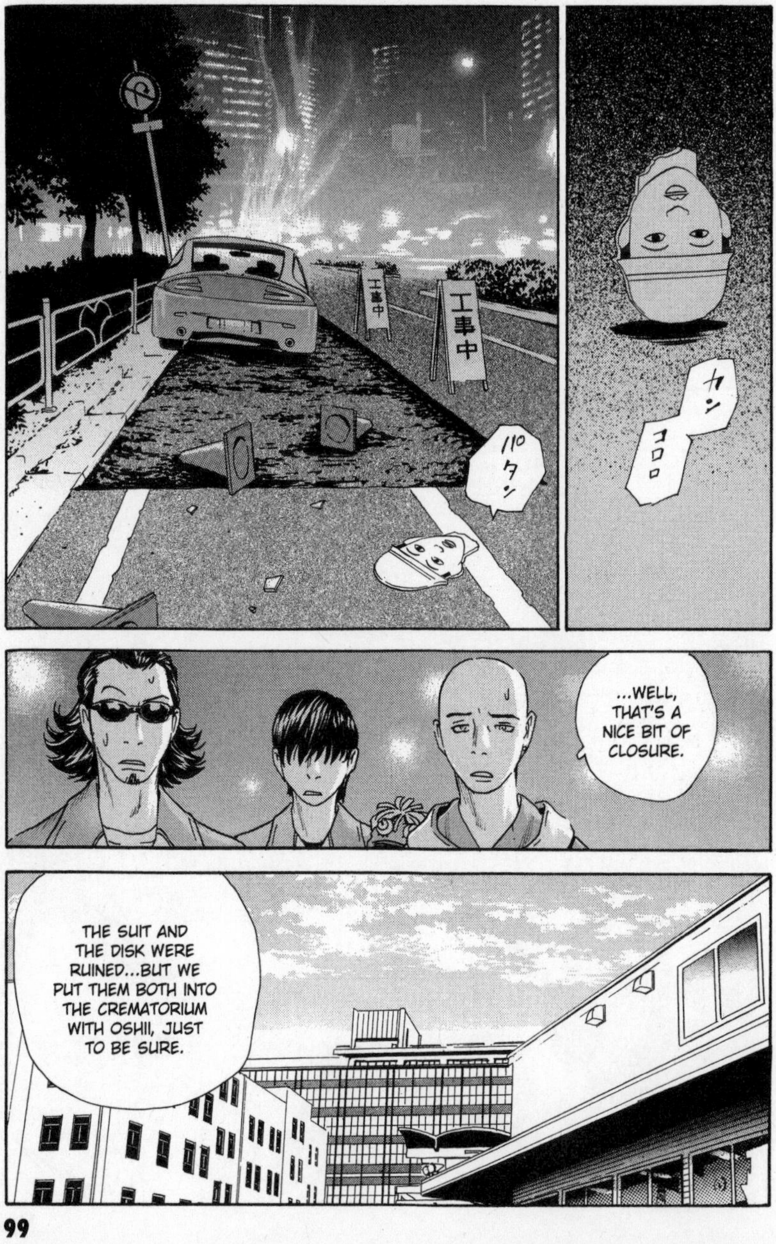
カン
コロロ
工事中
工事中
パタン
...WELL, THAT'S A NICE BIT OF CLOSURE.
THE SUIT AND THE DISK WERE RUINED...BUT WE PUT THEM BOTH INTO THE CREMATORIUM WITH OSHII, JUST TO BE SURE.

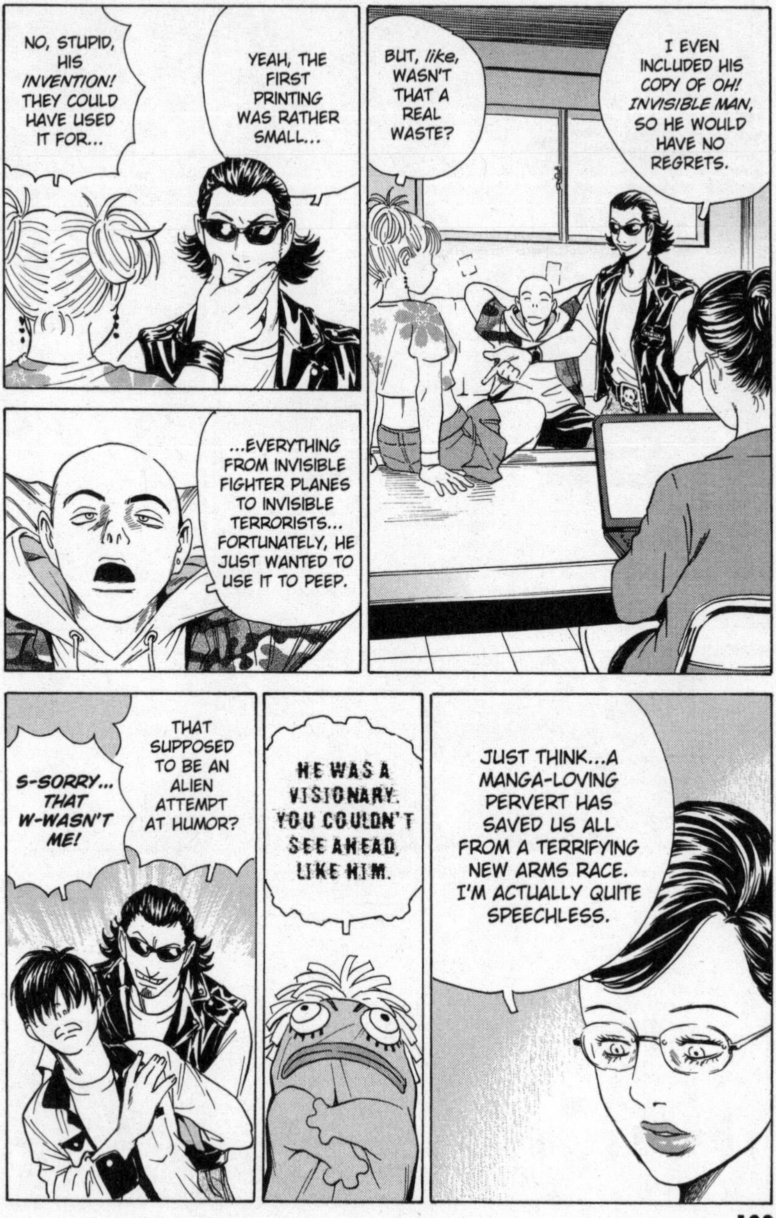
I EVEN INCLUDED HIS COPY OF OH! *INVISIBLE MAN*, SO HE WOULD HAVE NO REGRETS.
BUT, *like*, WASN'T THAT A REAL WASTE?
YEAH, THE FIRST PRINTING WAS RATHER SMALL...
NO, STUPID, HIS *INVENTION!* THEY COULD HAVE USED IT FOR...
...EVERYTHING FROM INVISIBLE FIGHTER PLANES TO INVISIBLE TERRORISTS... FORTUNATELY, HE JUST WANTED TO USE IT TO PEEP.
JUST THINK...A MANGA-LOVING PERVERT HAS SAVED US ALL FROM A TERRIFYING NEW ARMS RACE. I'M ACTUALLY QUITE SPEECHLESS.
HE WAS A VISIONARY. YOU COULDN'T SEE AHEAD, LIKE HIM.
THAT SUPPOSED TO BE AN ALIEN ATTEMPT AT HUMOR?
S-SORRY... THAT W-WASN'T ME!

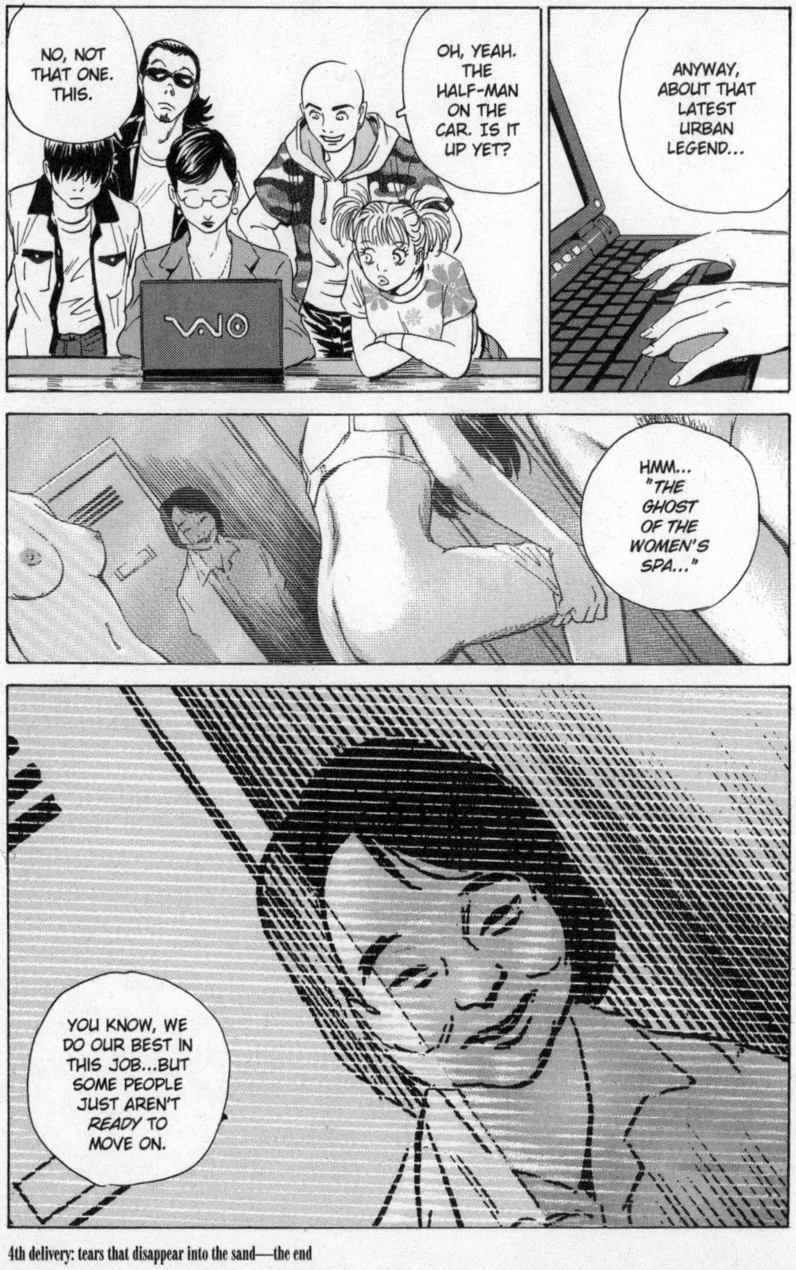
ANYWAY, ABOUT THAT LATEST URBAN LEGEND...
OH, YEAH. THE HALF-MAN ON THE CAR. IS IT UP YET?
NO, NOT THAT ONE. THIS.
VAIO
HMM... "THE GHOST OF THE WOMEN'S SPA..."
YOU KNOW, WE DO OUR BEST IN THIS JOB...BUT SOME PEOPLE JUST AREN'T *READY* TO MOVE ON.

4th delivery: tears that disappear into the sand—the end

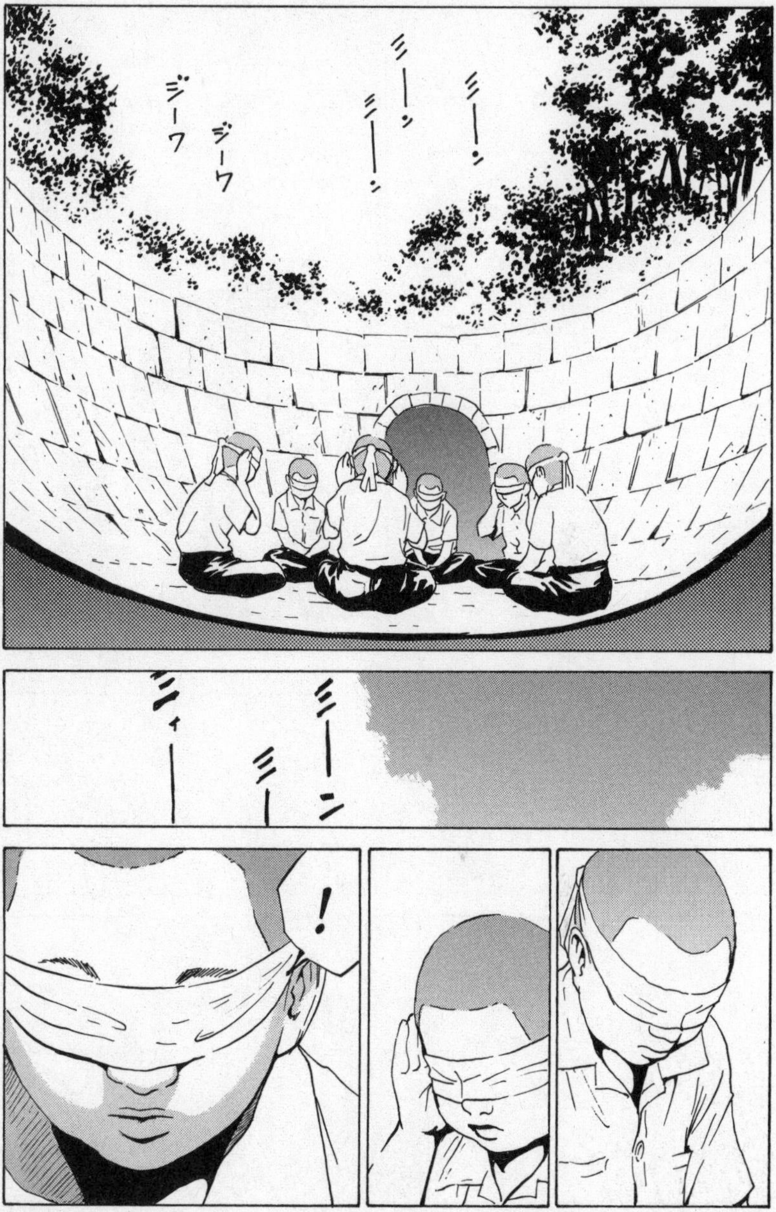
ミーン
ミーン
ミーン
ジーワ
ジーワ
ミーン
ミー
ミィー
!

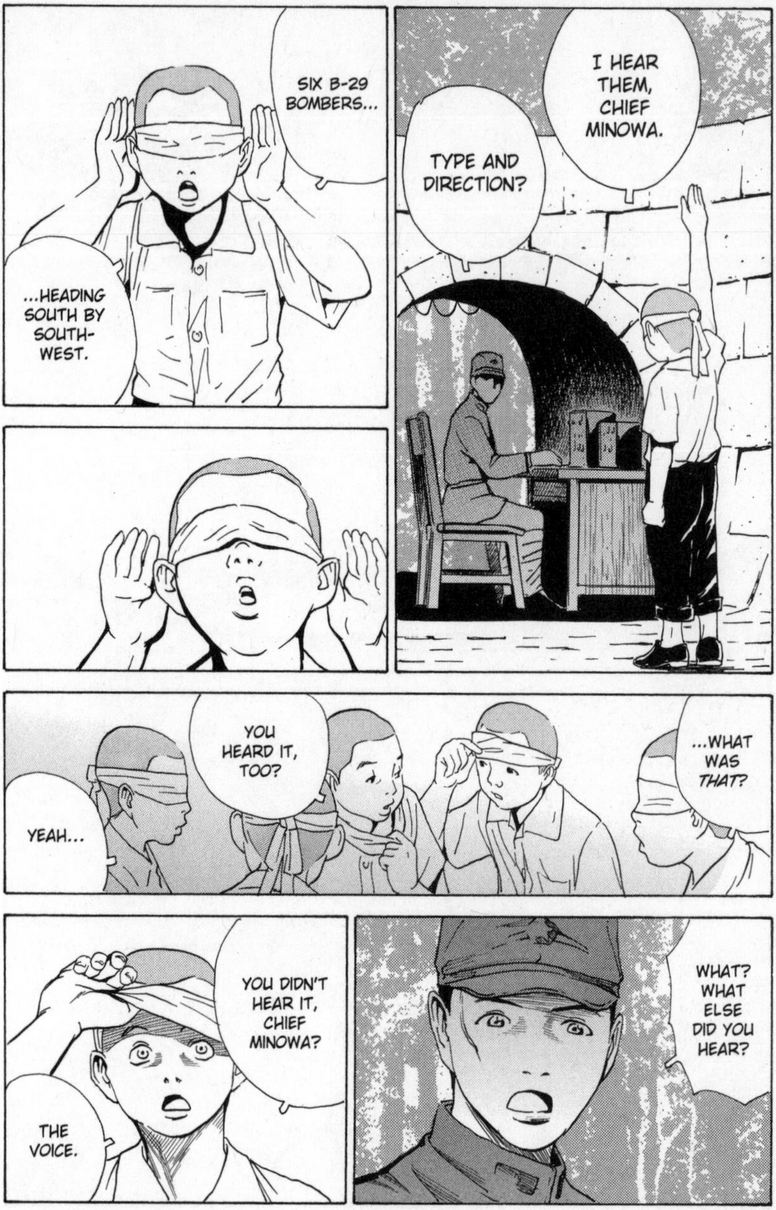
I HEAR THEM, CHIEF MINOWA.
TYPE AND DIRECTION?
SIX B-29 BOMBERS...
...HEADING SOUTH BY SOUTH-WEST.
...WHAT WAS *THAT?*
YOU HEARD IT, TOO?
YEAH...
WHAT? WHAT ELSE DID YOU HEAR?
YOU DIDN'T HEAR IT, CHIEF MINOWA?
THE VOICE.

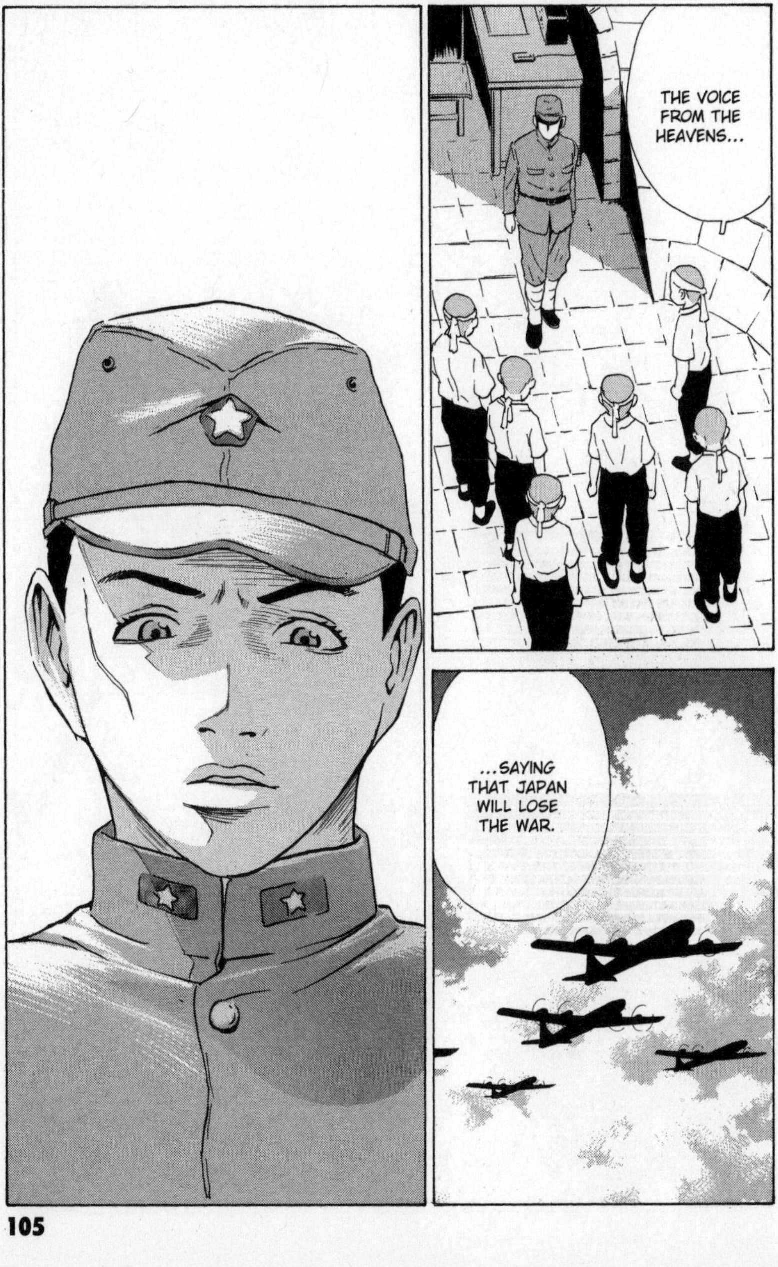
THE VOICE FROM THE HEAVENS...
...SAYING THAT JAPAN WILL LOSE THE WAR.

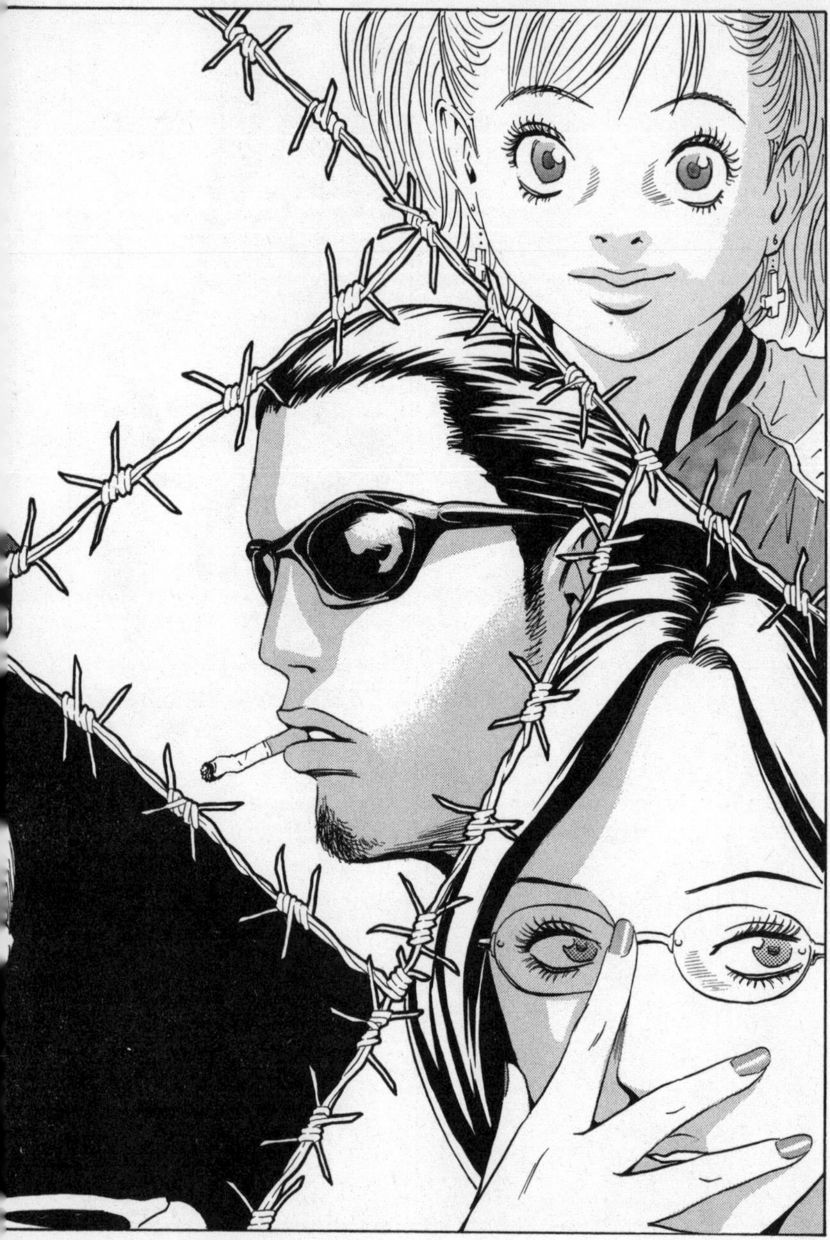

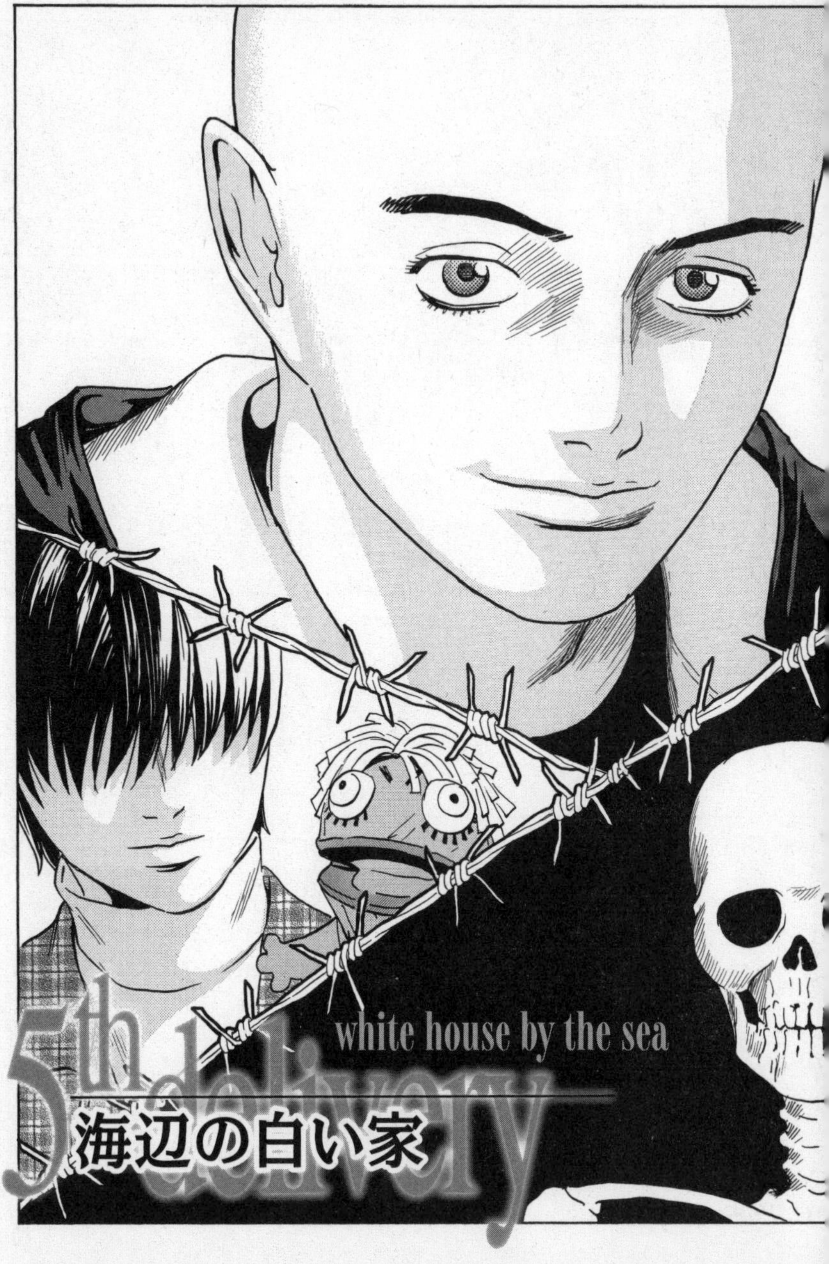
white house by the sea
5th delivery
海辺の白い家

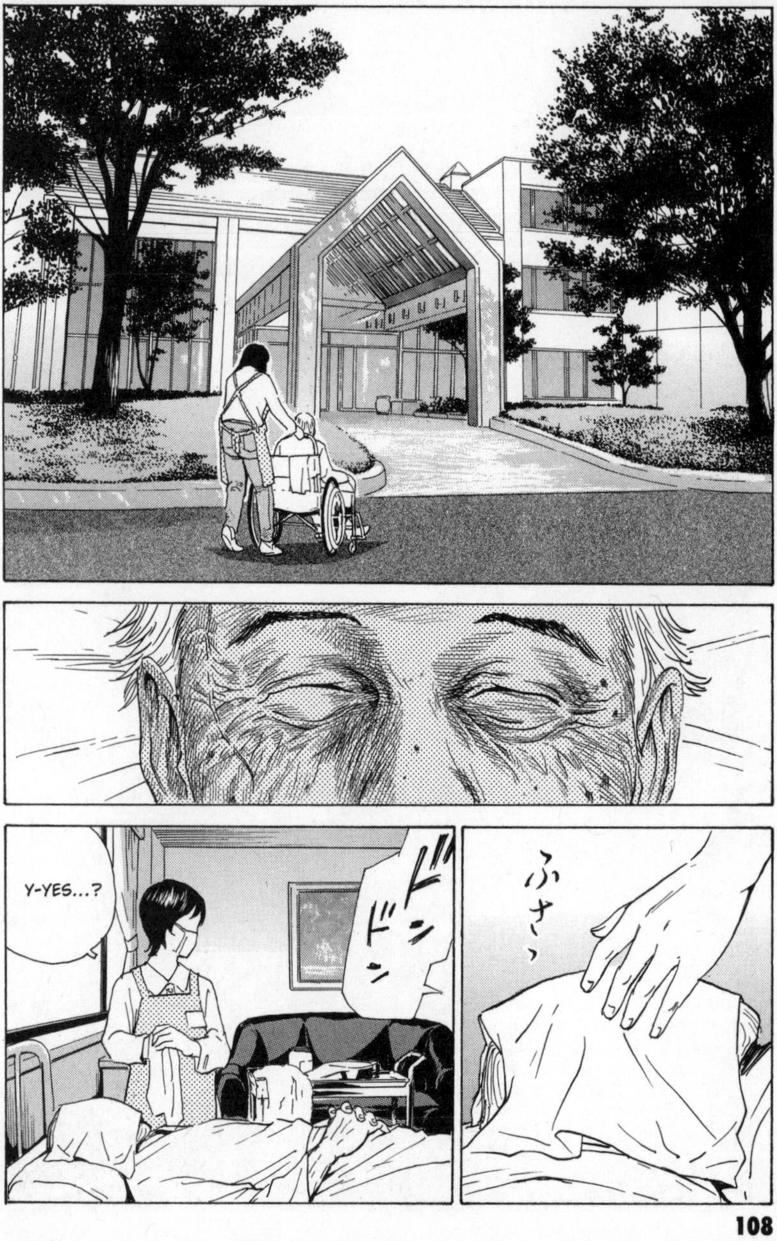
ふさっ
ドンドン
Y-YES...?

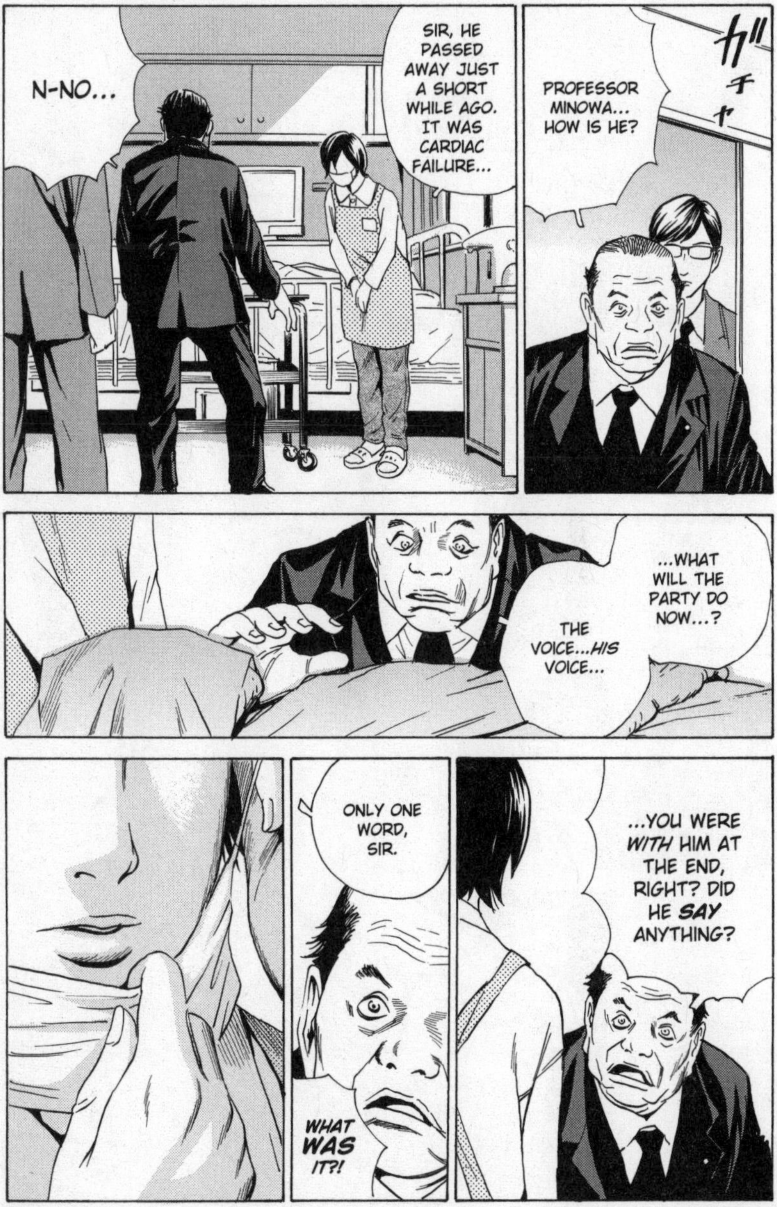
ガチャ
PROFESSOR MINOWA... HOW IS HE?
SIR, HE PASSED AWAY JUST A SHORT WHILE AGO. IT WAS CARDIAC FAILURE...
N-NO...
...WHAT WILL THE PARTY DO NOW...?
THE VOICE...*HIS* VOICE...
...YOU WERE *WITH* HIM AT THE END, RIGHT? DID HE *SAY* ANYTHING?
ONLY ONE WORD, SIR.
WHAT **WAS** *IT?!*

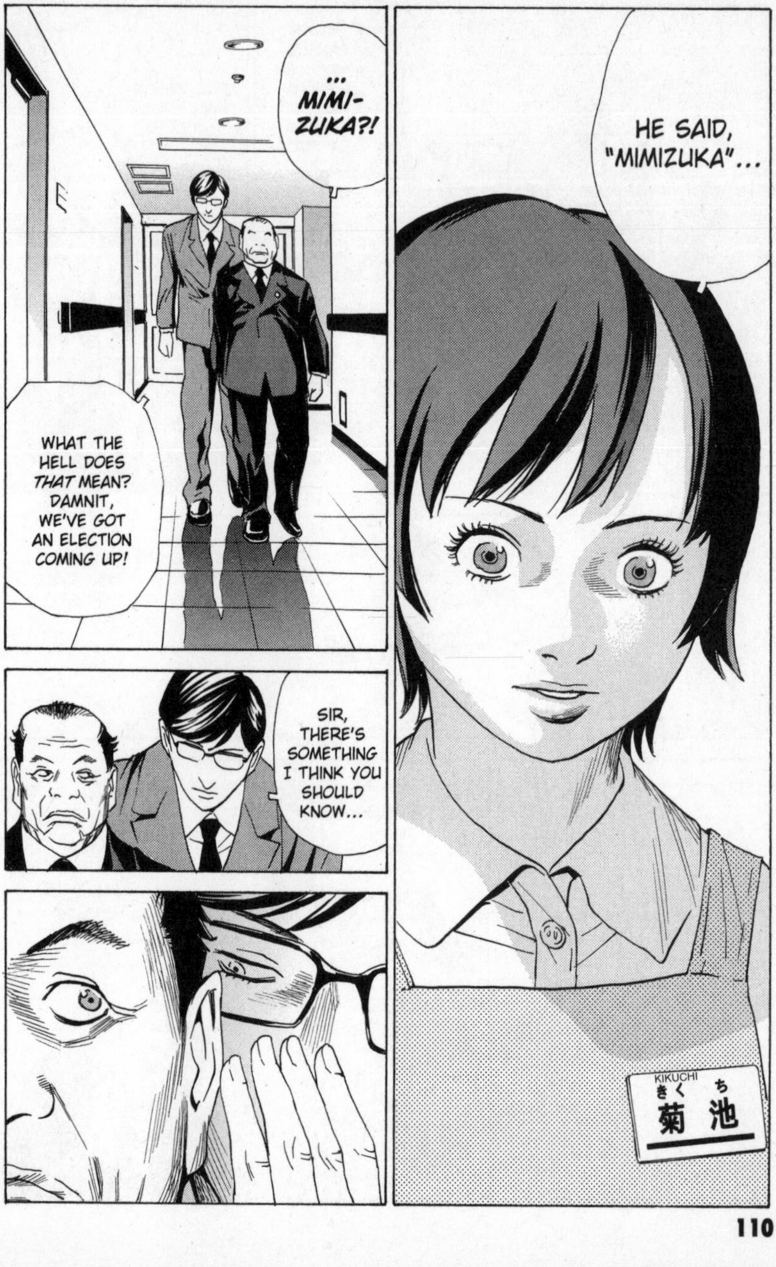
HE SAID, "MIMIZUKA"...
KIKUCHI
きくち
菊池
... MIMI-ZUKA?!
WHAT THE HELL DOES *THAT* MEAN? DAMNIT, WE'VE GOT AN ELECTION COMING UP!
SIR, THERE'S SOMETHING I THINK YOU SHOULD KNOW...

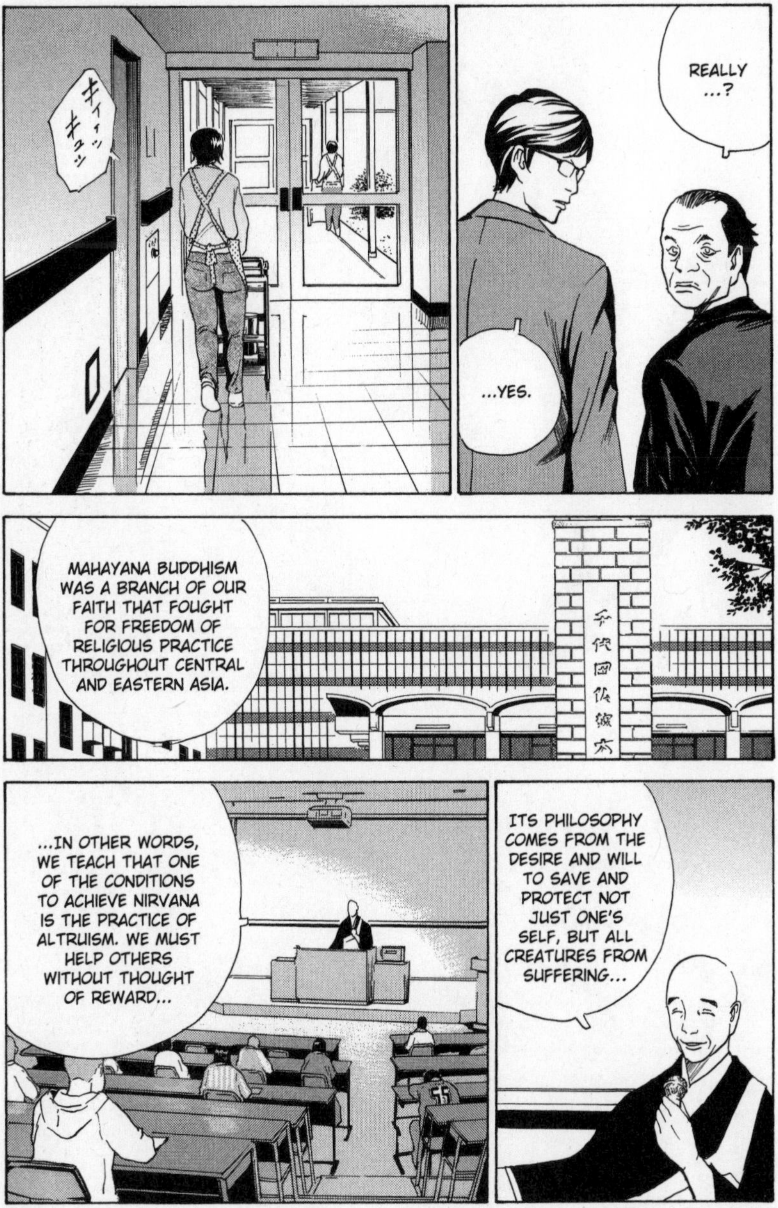
REALLY ...?
...YES.
キィッ
キュッ
MAHAYANA BUDDHISM WAS A BRANCH OF OUR FAITH THAT FOUGHT FOR FREEDOM OF RELIGIOUS PRACTICE THROUGHOUT CENTRAL AND EASTERN ASIA.
ITS PHILOSOPHY COMES FROM THE DESIRE AND WILL TO SAVE AND PROTECT NOT JUST ONE'S SELF, BUT ALL CREATURES FROM SUFFERING...
...IN OTHER WORDS, WE TEACH THAT ONE OF THE CONDITIONS TO ACHIEVE NIRVANA IS THE PRACTICE OF ALTRUISM. WE MUST HELP OTHERS WITHOUT THOUGHT OF REWARD...

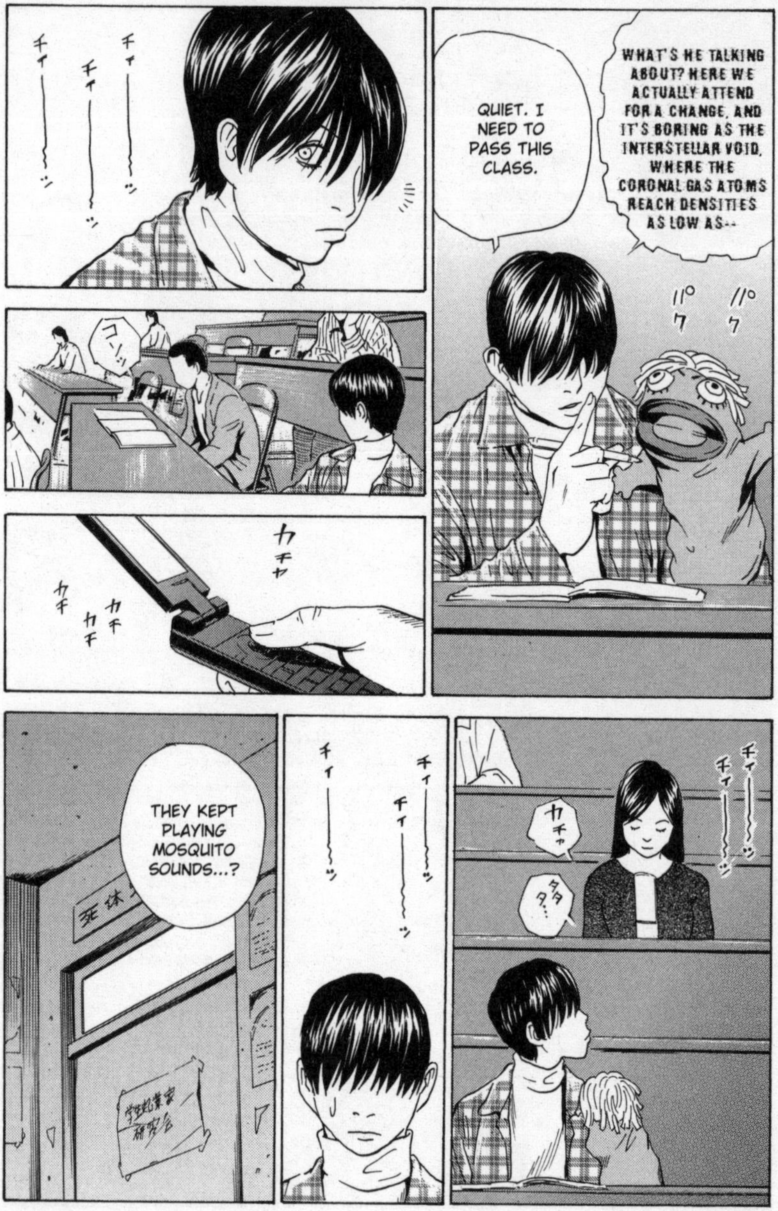
WHAT'S HE TALKING ABOUT? HERE WE ACTUALLY ATTEND FOR A CHANGE, AND IT'S BORING AS THE INTERSTELLAR VOID, WHERE THE CORONAL GAS ATOMS REACH DENSITIES AS LOW AS--
QUIET. I NEED TO PASS THIS CLASS.
パク パク
チァーーーッ
チィーーーッ
チィーーーッ
コーンッ
カチャ
カチ カチ
カチ
チィーーッ
チィーーッ
カチャ
タタタ…
チィーーッ
チィーーーッ
チィーーッ
THEY KEPT PLAYING MOSQUITO SOUNDS...?

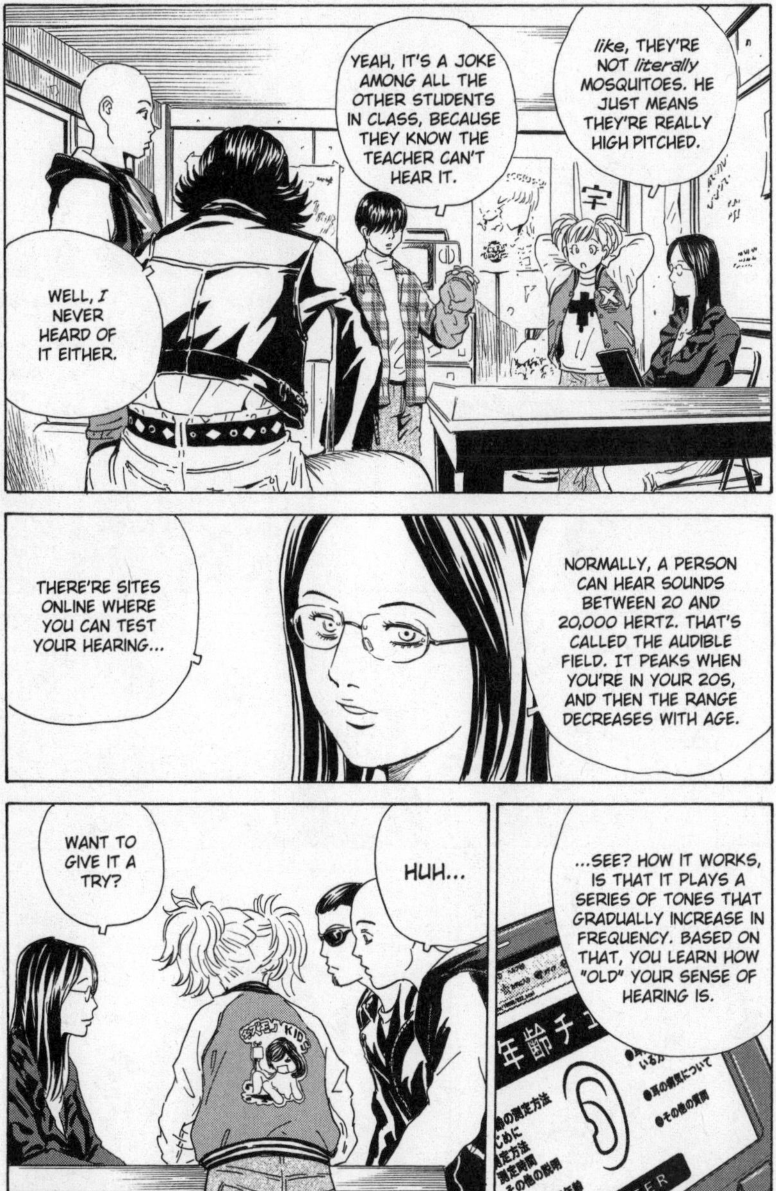
like, THEY'RE NOT *literally* MOSQUITOES. HE JUST MEANS THEY'RE REALLY HIGH PITCHED.
YEAH, IT'S A JOKE AMONG ALL THE OTHER STUDENTS IN CLASS, BECAUSE THEY KNOW THE TEACHER CAN'T HEAR IT.
WELL, *I* NEVER HEARD OF IT EITHER.
NORMALLY, A PERSON CAN HEAR SOUNDS BETWEEN 20 AND 20,000 HERTZ. THAT'S CALLED THE AUDIBLE FIELD. IT PEAKS WHEN YOU'RE IN YOUR 20S, AND THEN THE RANGE DECREASES WITH AGE.
THERE'RE SITES ONLINE WHERE YOU CAN TEST YOUR HEARING...
...SEE? HOW IT WORKS, IS THAT IT PLAYS A SERIES OF TONES THAT GRADUALLY INCREASE IN FREQUENCY. BASED ON THAT, YOU LEARN HOW "OLD" YOUR SENSE OF HEARING IS.
HUH...
WANT TO GIVE IT A TRY?

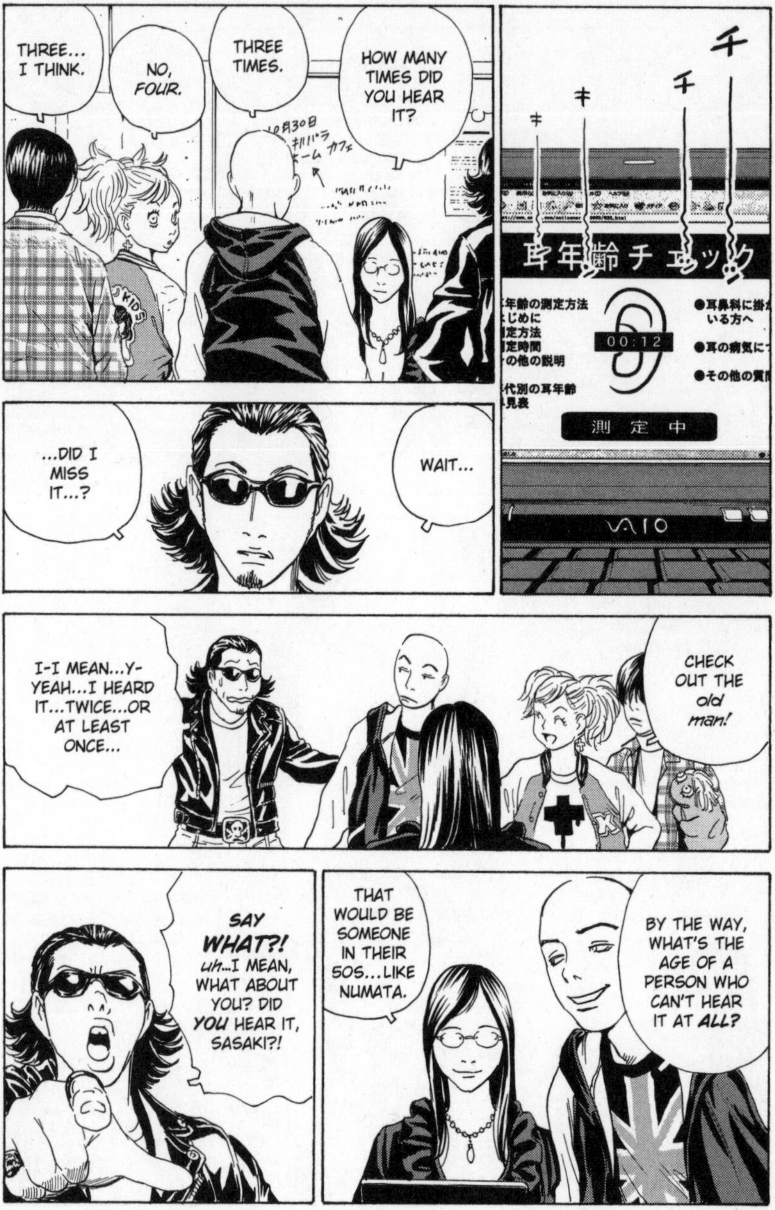

キ
キ
チ
チ
耳年齢チェック
00:12
測定中
HOW MANY TIMES DID YOU HEAR IT?
THREE TIMES.
NO, FOUR.
THREE... I THINK.
WAIT...
...DID I MISS IT...?
CHECK OUT THE *old man!*
I-I MEAN...Y-YEAH...I HEARD IT...TWICE...OR AT LEAST ONCE...
BY THE WAY, WHAT'S THE AGE OF A PERSON WHO CAN'T HEAR IT AT ***ALL?***
THAT WOULD BE SOMEONE IN THEIR 50S...LIKE NUMATA.
SAY ***WHAT?!*** *uh*...I MEAN, WHAT ABOUT YOU? DID ***YOU*** HEAR IT, SASAKI?!

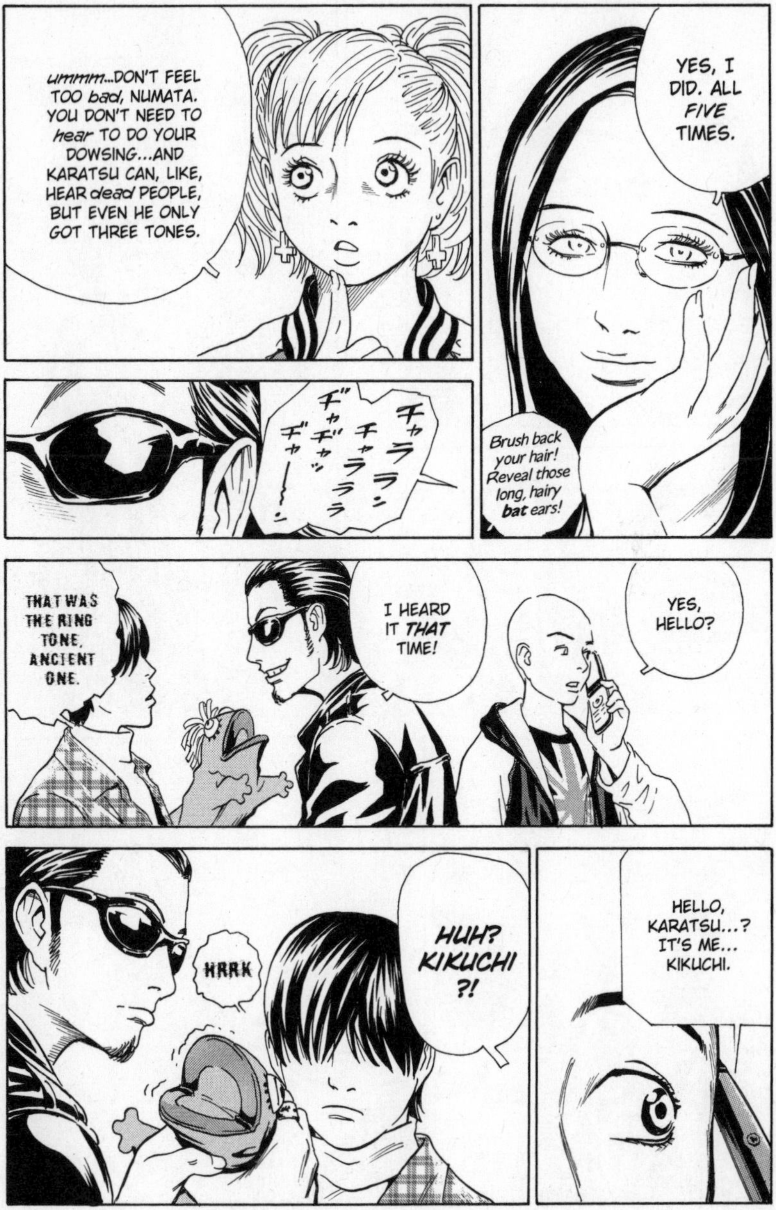
YES, I DID. ALL *FIVE* TIMES.
Brush back your hair! Reveal those long, hairy ***bat*** *ears!*
ummm...DON'T FEEL TOO *bad*, NUMATA. YOU DON'T NEED TO *hear* TO DO YOUR DOWSING...AND KARATSU CAN, LIKE, HEAR *dead* PEOPLE, BUT EVEN HE ONLY GOT THREE TONES.
チャララン
チャラララ
ヂャヂャッ
ヂャー～ン
YES, HELLO?
I HEARD IT *THAT* TIME!
THAT WAS THE RING TONE, ANCIENT ONE.
HELLO, KARATSU...? IT'S ME... KIKUCHI.
HUH? KIKUCHI?!
HRRK

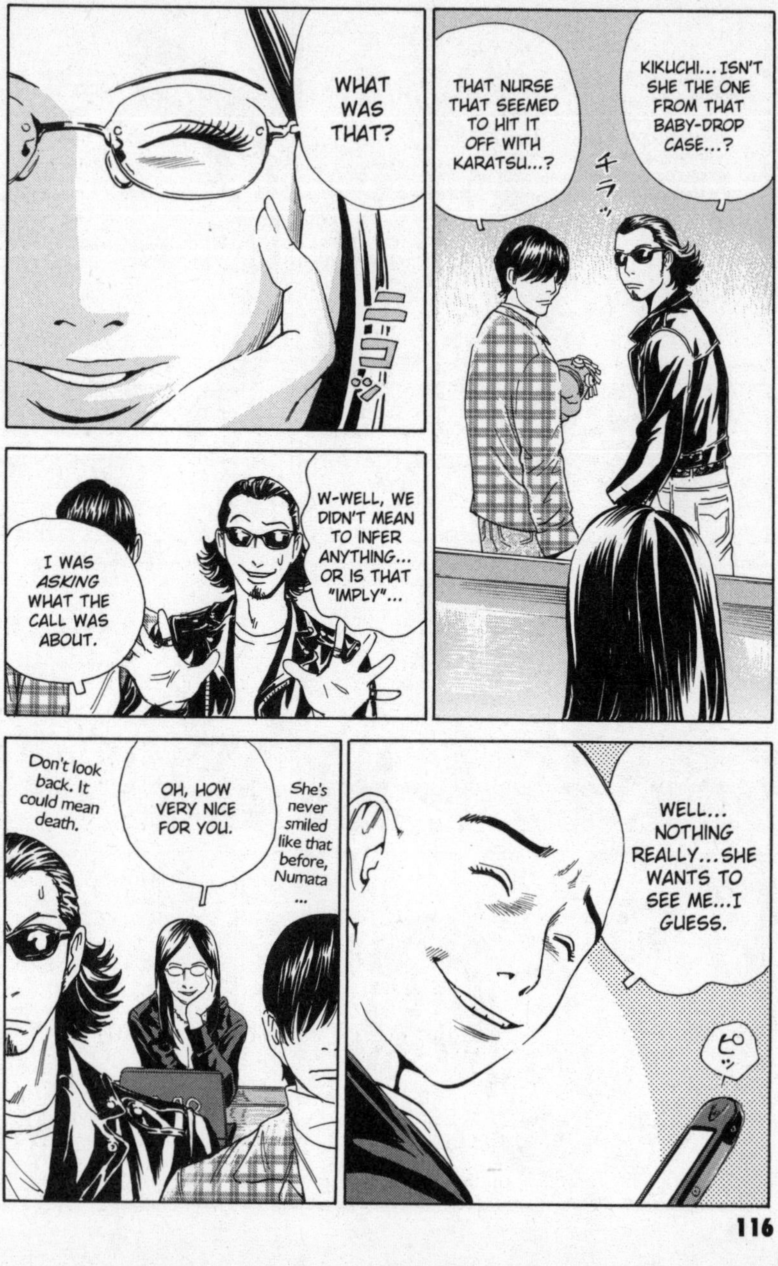
KIKUCHI... ISN'T SHE THE ONE FROM THAT BABY-DROP CASE...?
THAT NURSE THAT SEEMED TO HIT IT OFF WITH KARATSU...?
チラッ
WHAT WAS THAT?
ニコッ
W-WELL, WE DIDN'T MEAN TO INFER ANYTHING... OR IS THAT "IMPLY"...
I WAS *ASKING* WHAT THE CALL WAS ABOUT.
WELL... NOTHING REALLY... SHE WANTS TO SEE ME... I GUESS.
ピッ
She's never smiled like that before, Numata...
OH, HOW VERY NICE FOR YOU.
Don't look back. It could mean death.

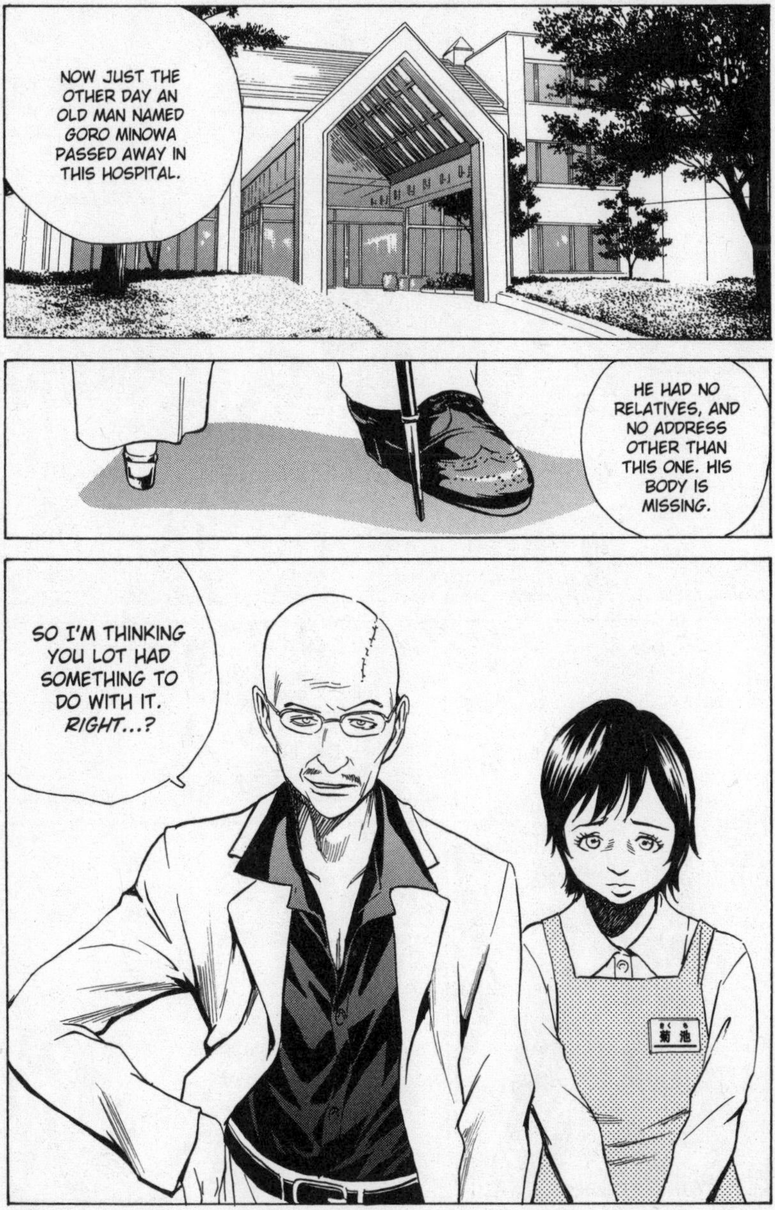
NOW JUST THE OTHER DAY AN OLD MAN NAMED GORO MINOWA PASSED AWAY IN THIS HOSPITAL.
HE HAD NO RELATIVES, AND NO ADDRESS OTHER THAN THIS ONE. HIS BODY IS MISSING.
SO I'M THINKING YOU LOT HAD SOMETHING TO DO WITH IT. *RIGHT...?*
菊池

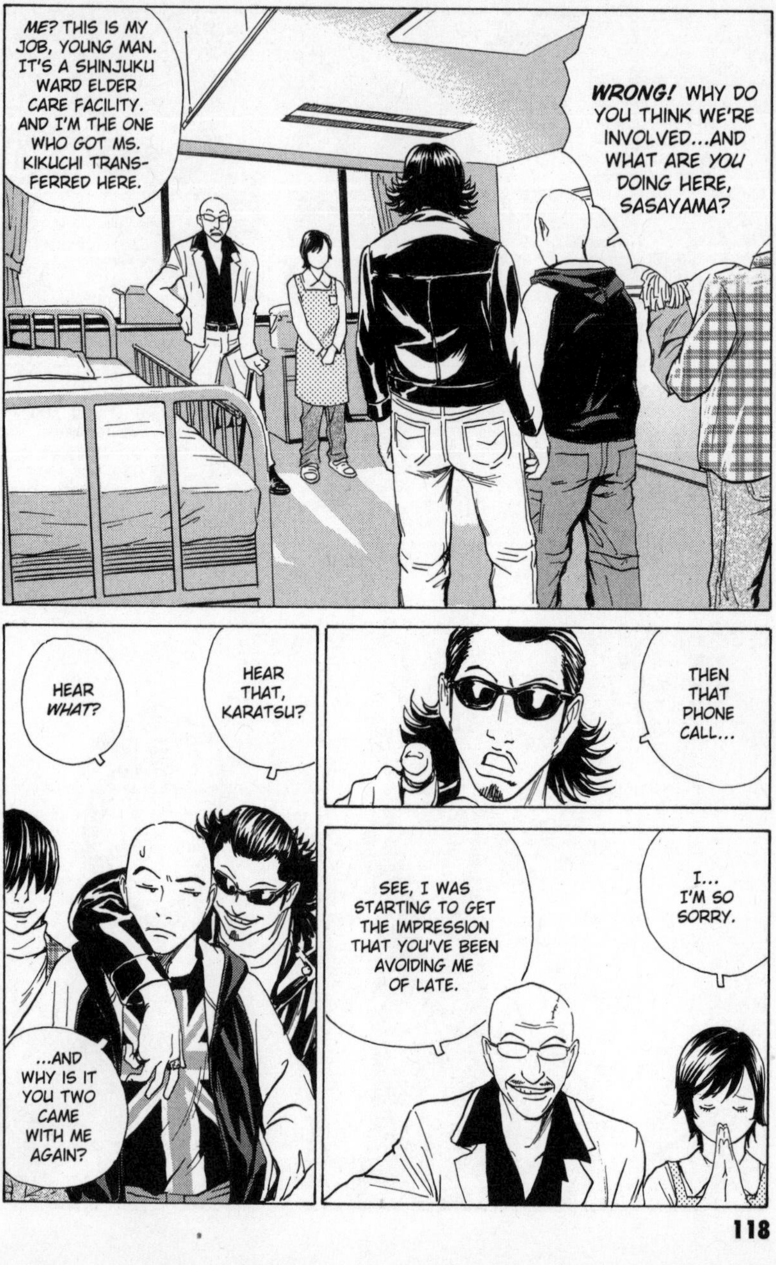

WRONG! WHY DO YOU THINK WE'RE INVOLVED...AND WHAT ARE YOU DOING HERE, SASAYAMA?
ME? THIS IS MY JOB, YOUNG MAN. IT'S A SHINJUKU WARD ELDER CARE FACILITY. AND I'M THE ONE WHO GOT MS. KIKUCHI TRANSFERRED HERE.
THEN THAT PHONE CALL...
I... I'M SO SORRY.
SEE, I WAS STARTING TO GET THE IMPRESSION THAT YOU'VE BEEN AVOIDING ME OF LATE.
HEAR THAT, KARATSU?
HEAR WHAT?
...AND WHY IS IT YOU TWO CAME WITH ME AGAIN?

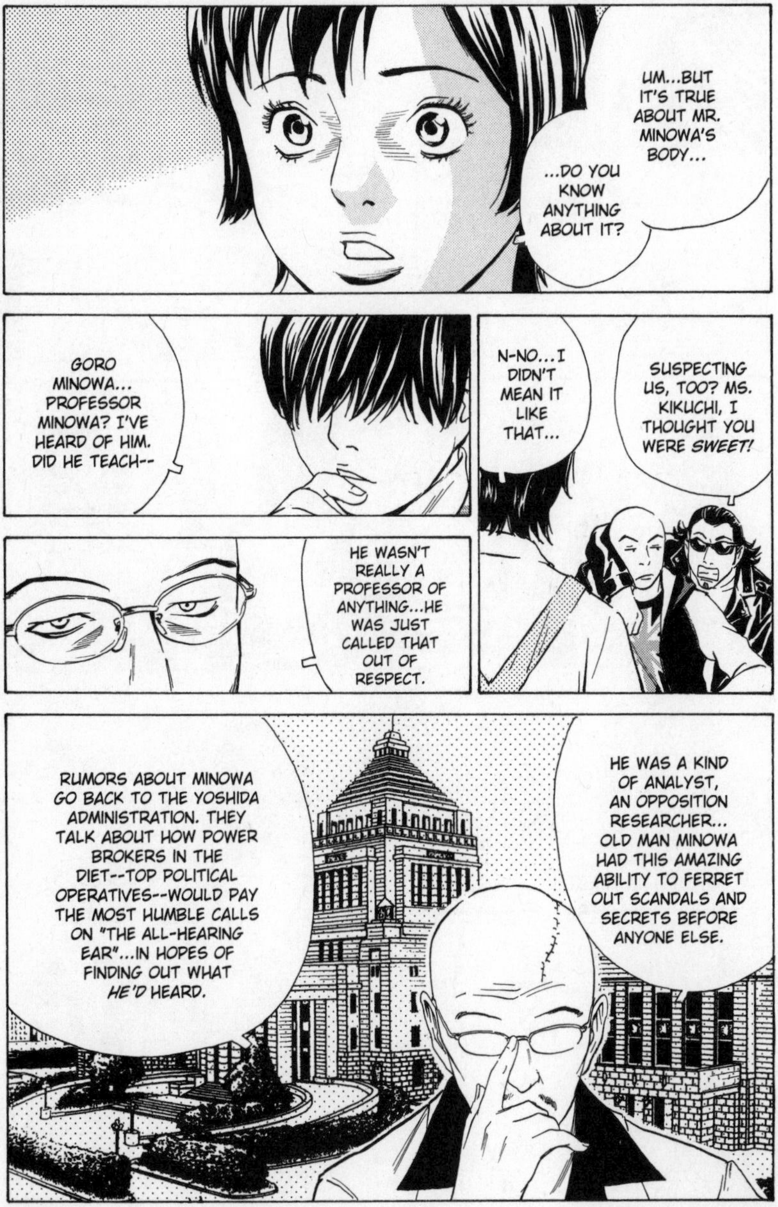
UM...BUT IT'S TRUE ABOUT MR. MINOWA'S BODY...
...DO YOU KNOW ANYTHING ABOUT IT?
SUSPECTING US, TOO? MS. KIKUCHI, I THOUGHT YOU WERE *SWEET!*
N-NO...I DIDN'T MEAN IT LIKE THAT...
GORO MINOWA... PROFESSOR MINOWA? I'VE HEARD OF HIM. DID HE TEACH--
HE WASN'T REALLY A PROFESSOR OF ANYTHING...HE WAS JUST CALLED THAT OUT OF RESPECT.
HE WAS A KIND OF ANALYST, AN OPPOSITION RESEARCHER... OLD MAN MINOWA HAD THIS AMAZING ABILITY TO FERRET OUT SCANDALS AND SECRETS BEFORE ANYONE ELSE.
RUMORS ABOUT MINOWA GO BACK TO THE YOSHIDA ADMINISTRATION. THEY TALK ABOUT HOW POWER BROKERS IN THE DIET--TOP POLITICAL OPERATIVES--WOULD PAY THE MOST HUMBLE CALLS ON "THE ALL-HEARING EAR"...IN HOPES OF FINDING OUT WHAT *HE'D* HEARD.

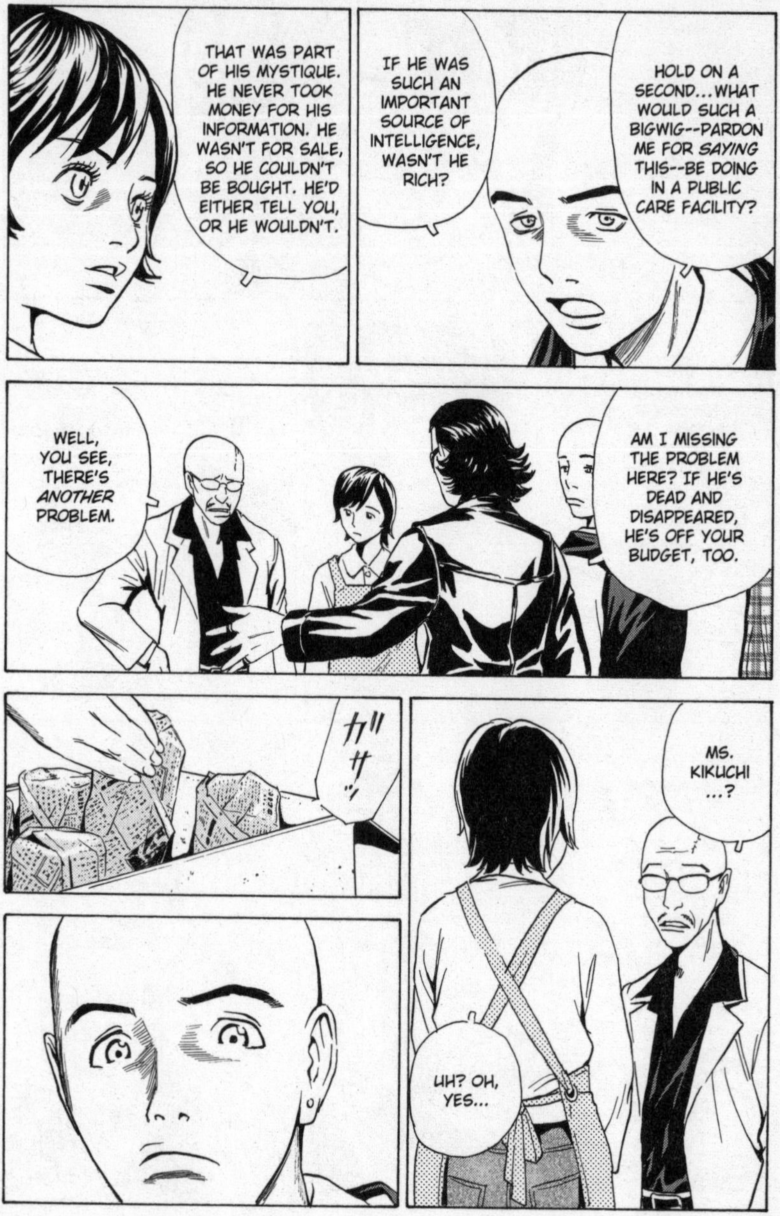
HOLD ON A SECOND...WHAT WOULD SUCH A BIGWIG--PARDON ME FOR *SAYING* THIS--BE DOING IN A PUBLIC CARE FACILITY?
IF HE WAS SUCH AN IMPORTANT SOURCE OF INTELLIGENCE, WASN'T HE RICH?
THAT WAS PART OF HIS MYSTIQUE. HE NEVER TOOK MONEY FOR HIS INFORMATION. HE WASN'T FOR SALE, SO HE COULDN'T BE BOUGHT. HE'D EITHER TELL YOU, OR HE WOULDN'T.
AM I MISSING THE PROBLEM HERE? IF HE'S DEAD AND DISAPPEARED, HE'S OFF YOUR BUDGET, TOO.
WELL, YOU SEE, THERE'S *ANOTHER* PROBLEM.
MS. KIKUCHI ...?
UH? OH, YES...
ガサッ

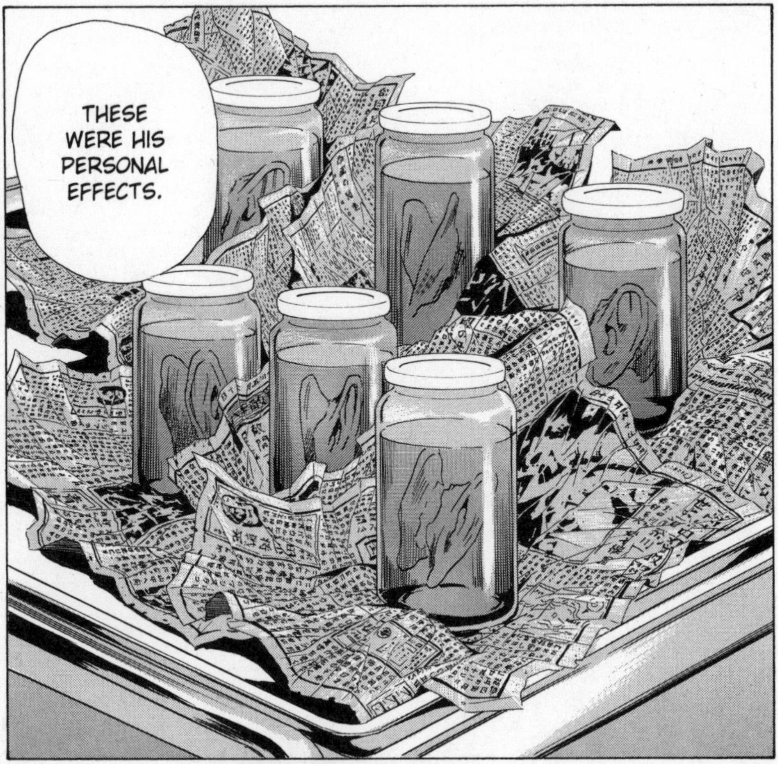
THESE WERE HIS PERSONAL EFFECTS.

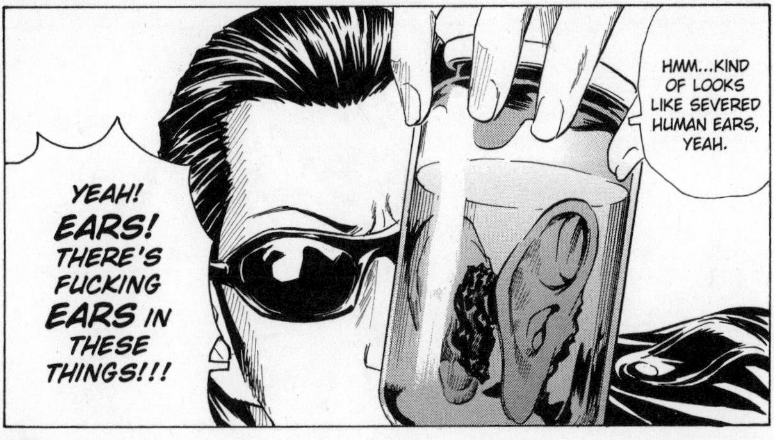
HMM...KIND OF LOOKS LIKE SEVERED HUMAN EARS, YEAH.
YEAH! EARS! THERE'S FUCKING EARS IN THESE THINGS!!!

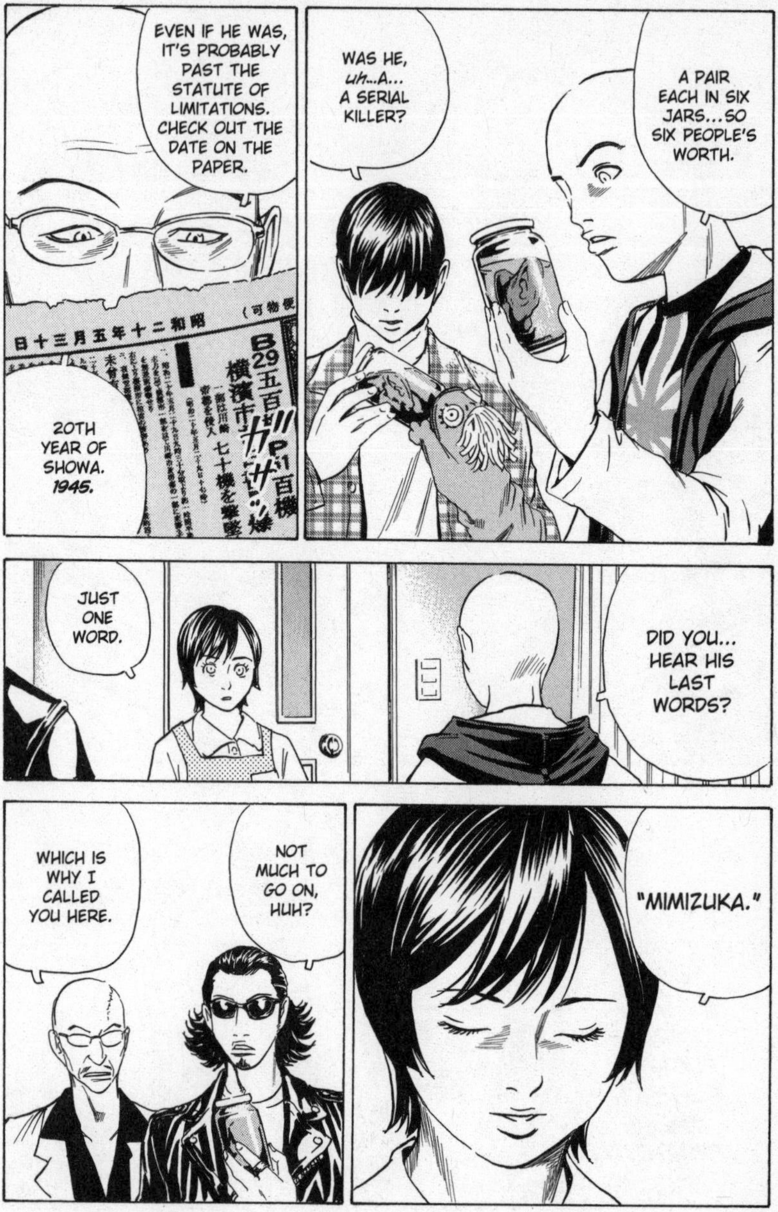
A PAIR EACH IN SIX JARS...SO SIX PEOPLE'S WORTH.
WAS HE, uh...A... A SERIAL KILLER?
EVEN IF HE WAS, IT'S PROBABLY PAST THE STATUTE OF LIMITATIONS. CHECK OUT THE DATE ON THE PAPER.
昭和二十年五月三十日
20TH YEAR OF SHOWA. 1945.
DID YOU... HEAR HIS LAST WORDS?
JUST ONE WORD.
"MIMIZUKA."
NOT MUCH TO GO ON, HUH?
WHICH IS WHY I CALLED YOU HERE.

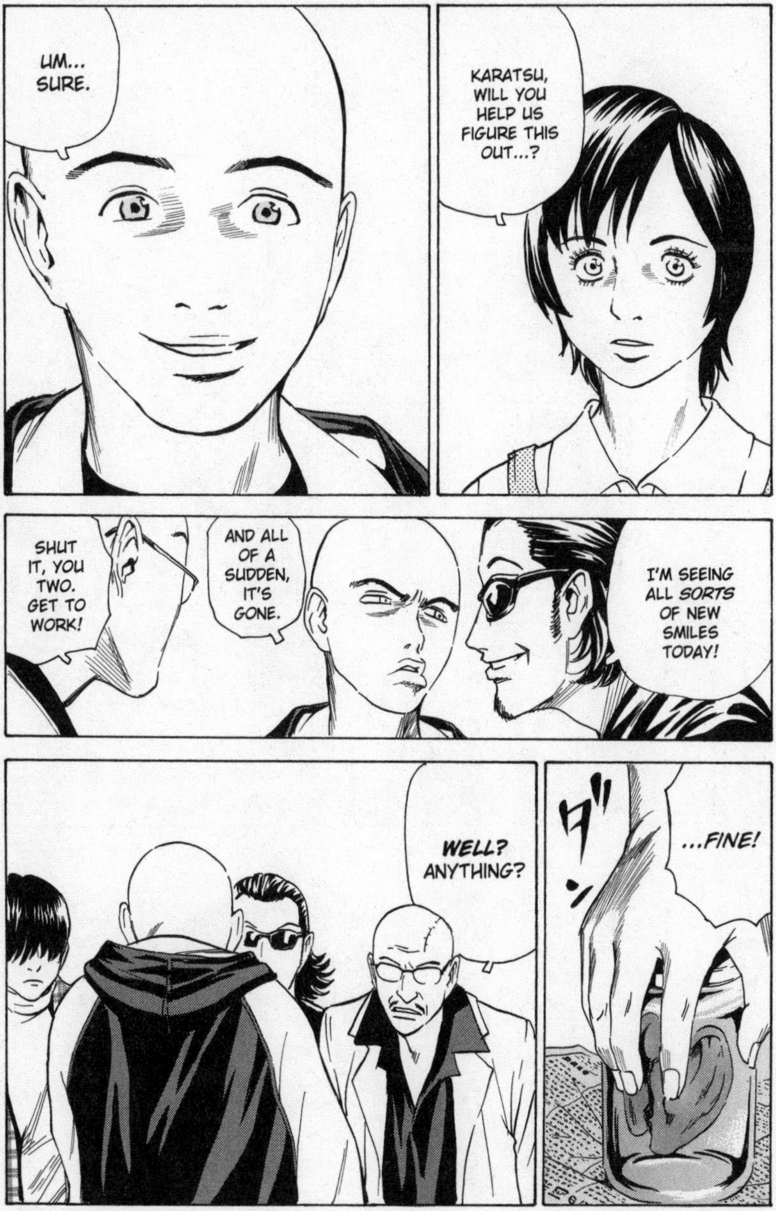
KARATSU, WILL YOU HELP US FIGURE THIS OUT...?
UM... SURE.
I'M SEEING ALL *SORTS* OF NEW SMILES TODAY!
AND ALL OF A SUDDEN, IT'S GONE.
SHUT IT, YOU TWO. GET TO WORK!
ダッ
...FINE!
WELL? ANYTHING?

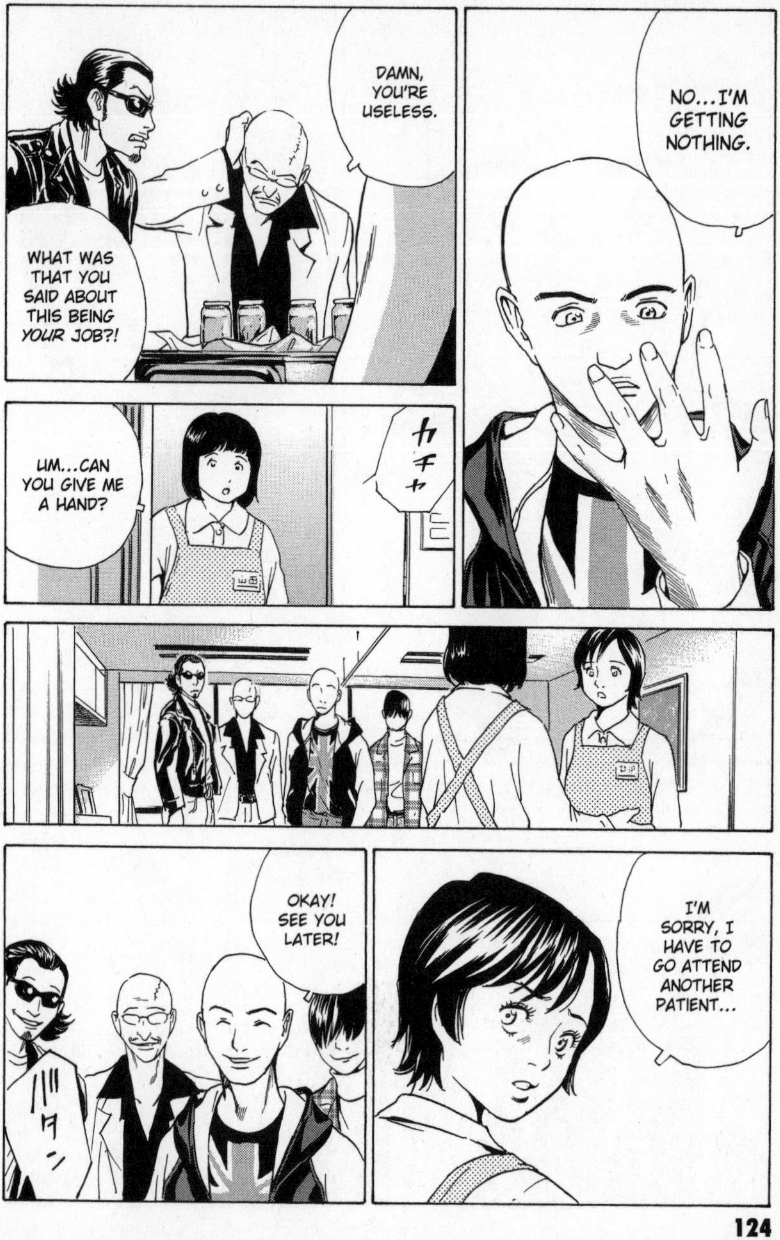
NO...I'M GETTING NOTHING.
DAMN, YOU'RE USELESS.
WHAT WAS THAT YOU SAID ABOUT THIS BEING *YOUR* JOB?!
カチャ
UM...CAN YOU GIVE ME A HAND?
I'M SORRY, I HAVE TO GO ATTEND ANOTHER PATIENT...
OKAY! SEE YOU LATER!
バタン

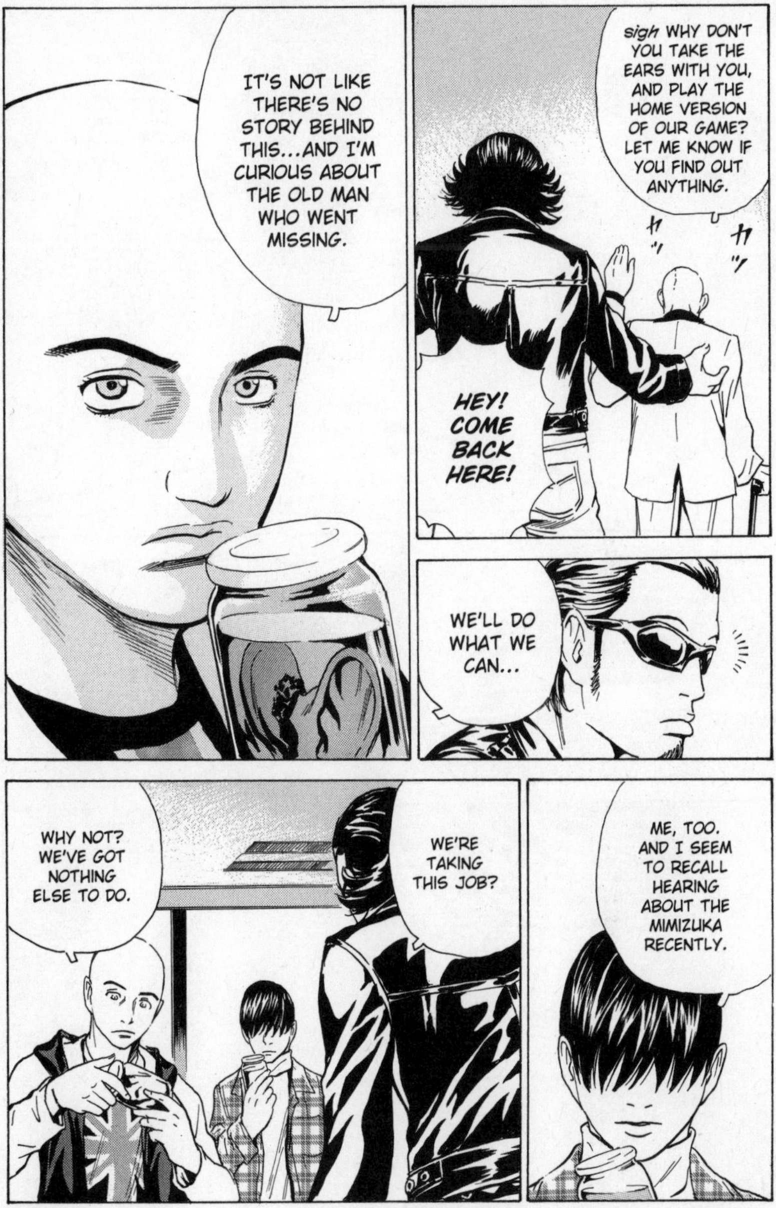

sigh WHY DON'T YOU TAKE THE EARS WITH YOU, AND PLAY THE HOME VERSION OF OUR GAME? LET ME KNOW IF YOU FIND OUT ANYTHING.
HEY! COME BACK HERE!
WE'LL DO WHAT WE CAN...
IT'S NOT LIKE THERE'S NO STORY BEHIND THIS...AND I'M CURIOUS ABOUT THE OLD MAN WHO WENT MISSING.
ME, TOO. AND I SEEM TO RECALL HEARING ABOUT THE MIMIZUKA RECENTLY.
WE'RE TAKING THIS JOB?
WHY NOT? WE'VE GOT NOTHING ELSE TO DO.

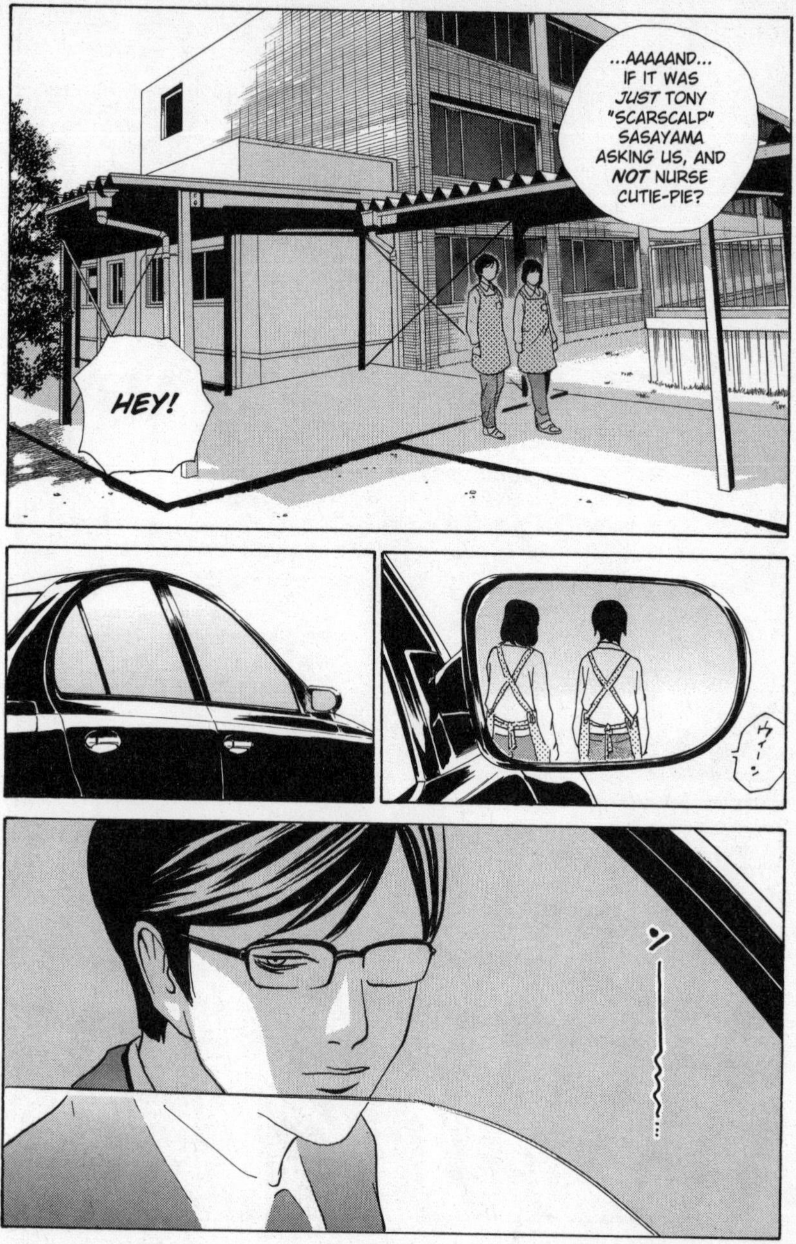
...AAAAAND... IF IT WAS JUST TONY "SCARSCALP" SASAYAMA ASKING US, AND NOT NURSE CUTIE-PIE?
HEY!
ウィーン

5th delivery: white house by the sea—the end

6th delivery
ある事情
a certain situation

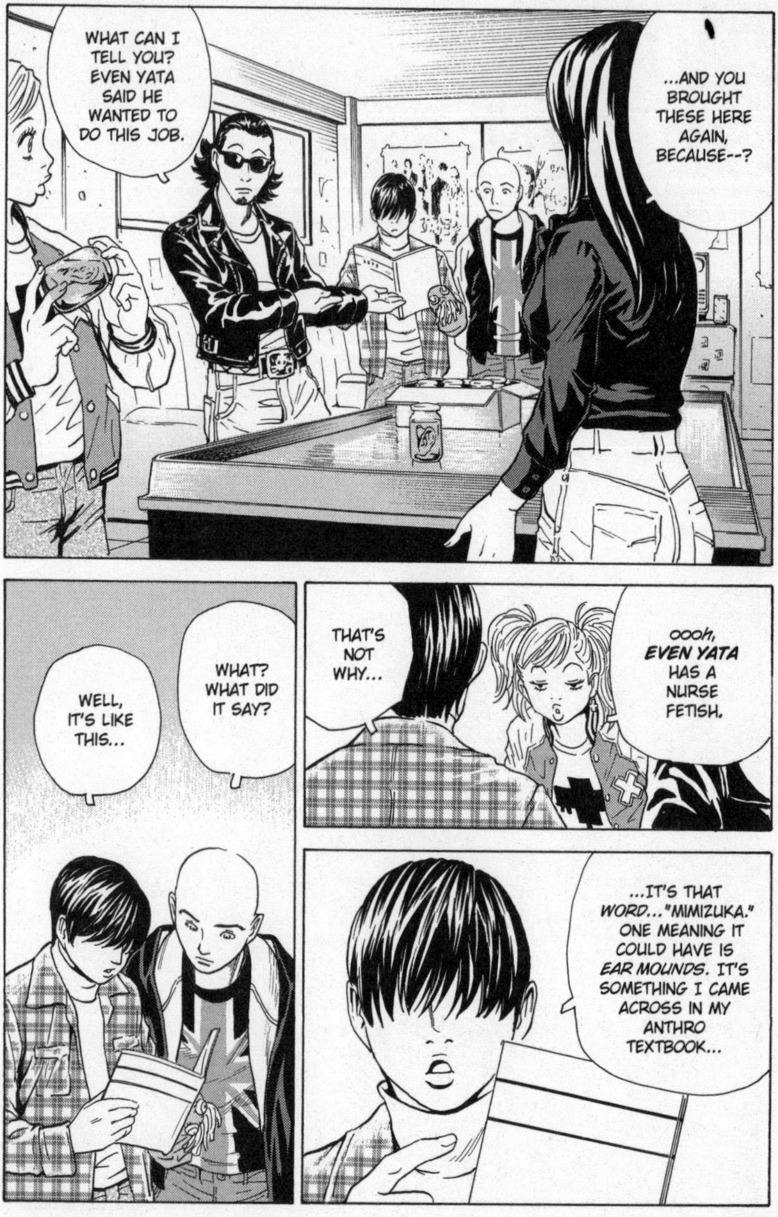
...AND YOU BROUGHT THESE HERE AGAIN, BECAUSE--?
WHAT CAN I TELL YOU? EVEN YATA SAID HE WANTED TO DO THIS JOB.
oooh, *EVEN YATA* HAS A NURSE FETISH.
THAT'S NOT WHY...
WHAT? WHAT DID IT SAY?
WELL, IT'S LIKE THIS...
...IT'S THAT *WORD*... "MIMIZUKA." ONE MEANING IT COULD HAVE IS *EAR MOUNDS*. IT'S SOMETHING I CAME ACROSS IN MY ANTHRO TEXTBOOK...

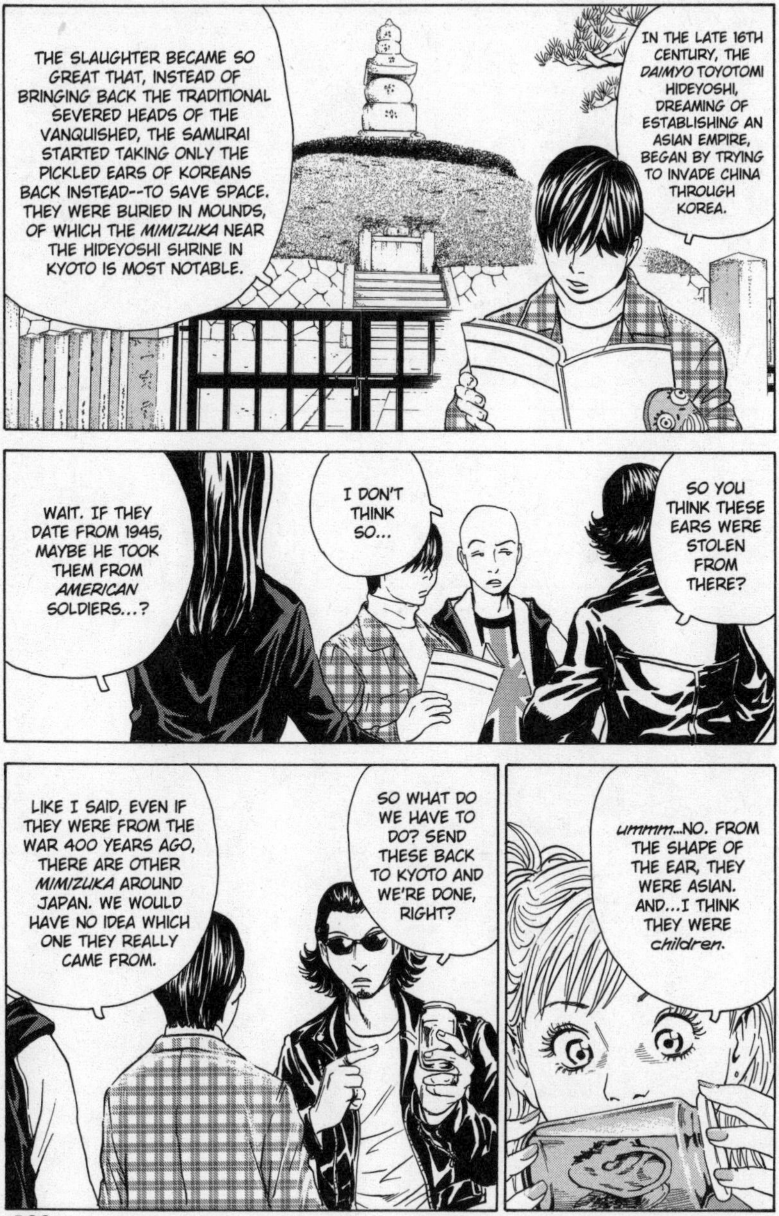
IN THE LATE 16TH CENTURY, THE DAIMYO TOYOTOMI HIDEYOSHI, DREAMING OF ESTABLISHING AN ASIAN EMPIRE, BEGAN BY TRYING TO INVADE CHINA THROUGH KOREA.
THE SLAUGHTER BECAME SO GREAT THAT, INSTEAD OF BRINGING BACK THE TRADITIONAL SEVERED HEADS OF THE VANQUISHED, THE SAMURAI STARTED TAKING ONLY THE PICKLED EARS OF KOREANS BACK INSTEAD--TO SAVE SPACE. THEY WERE BURIED IN MOUNDS, OF WHICH THE MIMIZUKA NEAR THE HIDEYOSHI SHRINE IN KYOTO IS MOST NOTABLE.
SO YOU THINK THESE EARS WERE STOLEN FROM THERE?
I DON'T THINK SO...
WAIT. IF THEY DATE FROM 1945, MAYBE HE TOOK THEM FROM AMERICAN SOLDIERS...?
ummm...NO. FROM THE SHAPE OF THE EAR, THEY WERE ASIAN. AND...I THINK THEY WERE children.
SO WHAT DO WE HAVE TO DO? SEND THESE BACK TO KYOTO AND WE'RE DONE, RIGHT?
LIKE I SAID, EVEN IF THEY WERE FROM THE WAR 400 YEARS AGO, THERE ARE OTHER MIMIZUKA AROUND JAPAN. WE WOULD HAVE NO IDEA WHICH ONE THEY REALLY CAME FROM.

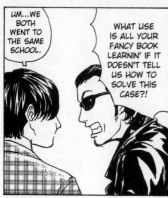

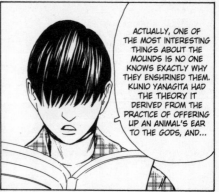

ACTUALLY, ONE OF THE MOST INTERESTING THINGS ABOUT THE MOUNDS IS NO ONE KNOWS EXACTLY WHY THEY ENSHRINED THEM. KUNIO YANAGITA HAD THE THEORY IT DERIVED FROM THE PRACTICE OF OFFERING UP AN ANIMAL'S EAR TO THE GODS, AND...
WHAT USE IS ALL YOUR FANCY BOOK LEARNIN' IF IT DOESN'T TELL US HOW TO SOLVE THIS CASE?!
UM...WE BOTH WENT TO THE SAME SCHOOL.

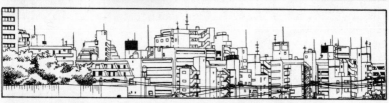

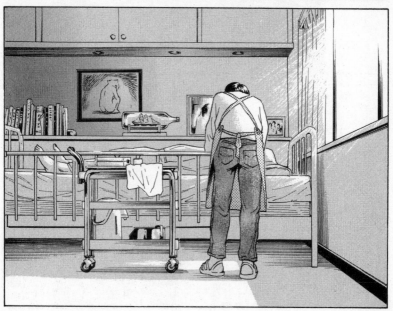

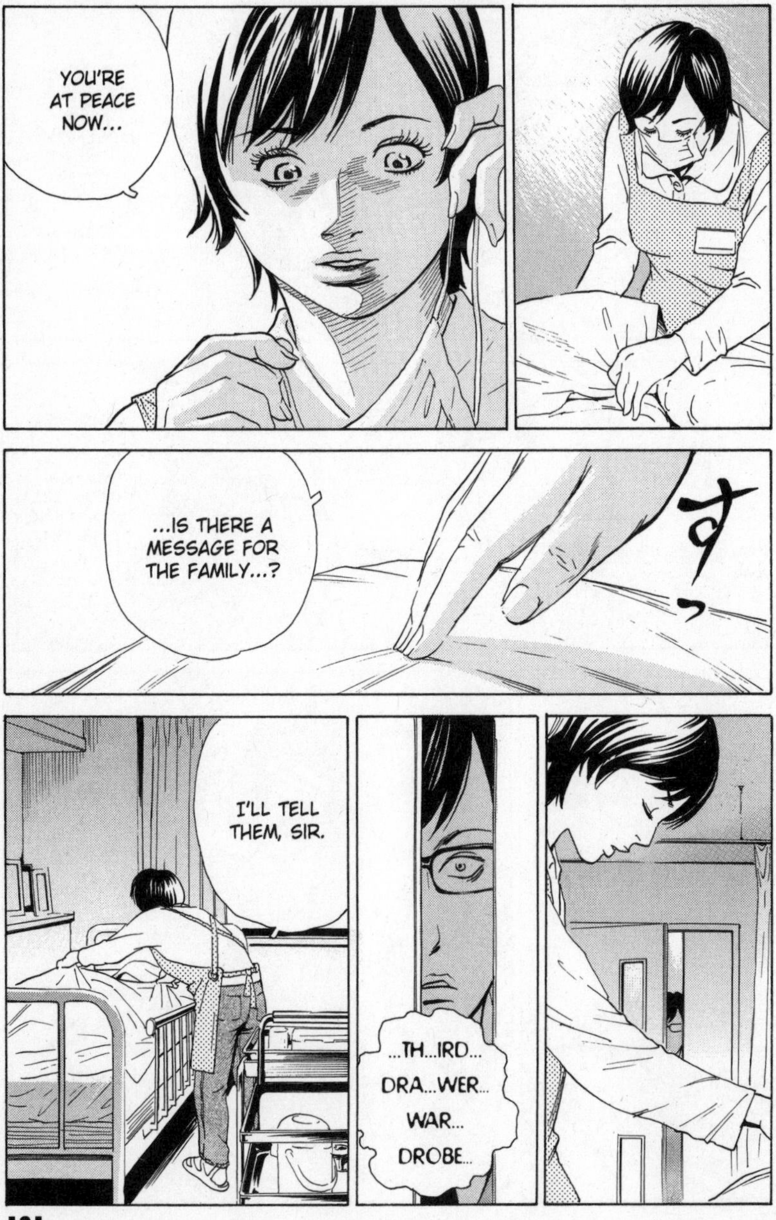
YOU'RE AT PEACE NOW...
...IS THERE A MESSAGE FOR THE FAMILY...?
すっ
...TH...IRD... DRA...WER... WAR... DROBE...
I'LL TELL THEM, SIR.

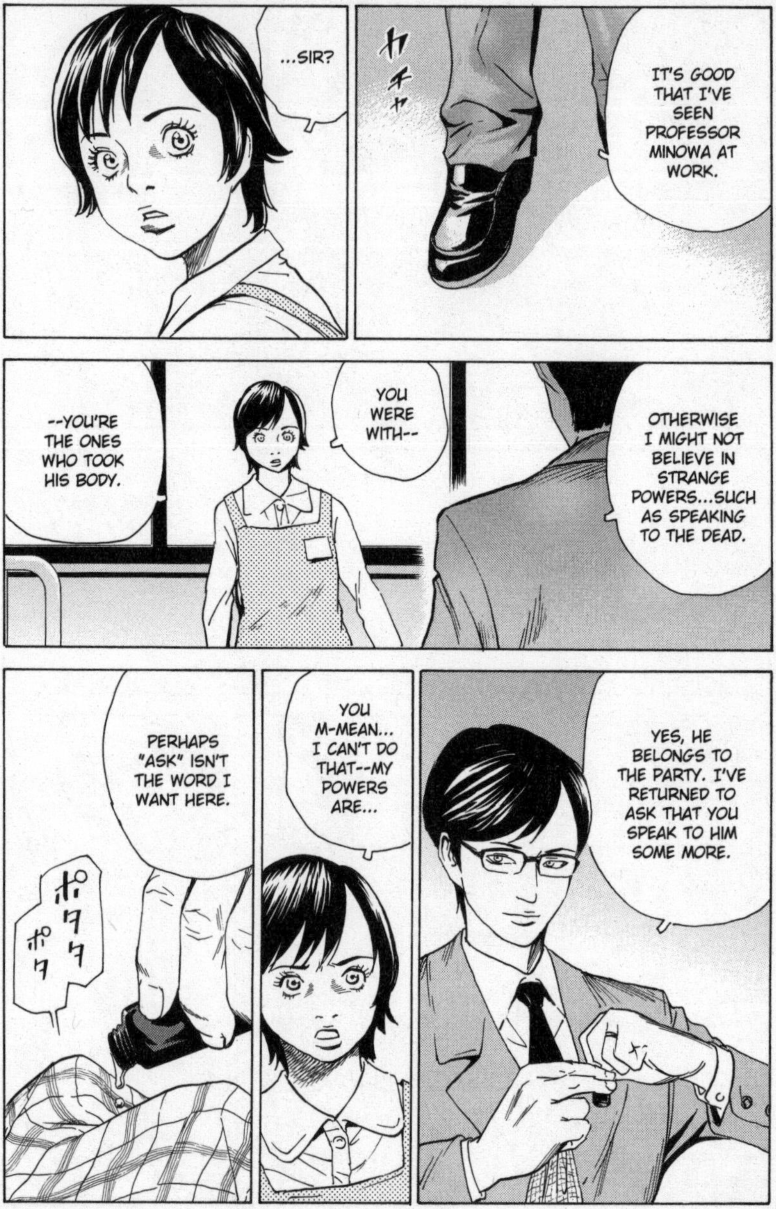
カチャ
IT'S GOOD THAT I'VE SEEN PROFESSOR MINOWA AT WORK.
...SIR?
OTHERWISE I MIGHT NOT BELIEVE IN STRANGE POWERS...SUCH AS SPEAKING TO THE DEAD.
YOU WERE WITH--
--YOU'RE THE ONES WHO TOOK HIS BODY.
YES, HE BELONGS TO THE PARTY. I'VE RETURNED TO ASK THAT YOU SPEAK TO HIM SOME MORE.
YOU M-MEAN... I CAN'T DO THAT--MY POWERS ARE...
PERHAPS "ASK" ISN'T THE WORD I WANT HERE.
ポタタ
ポタ

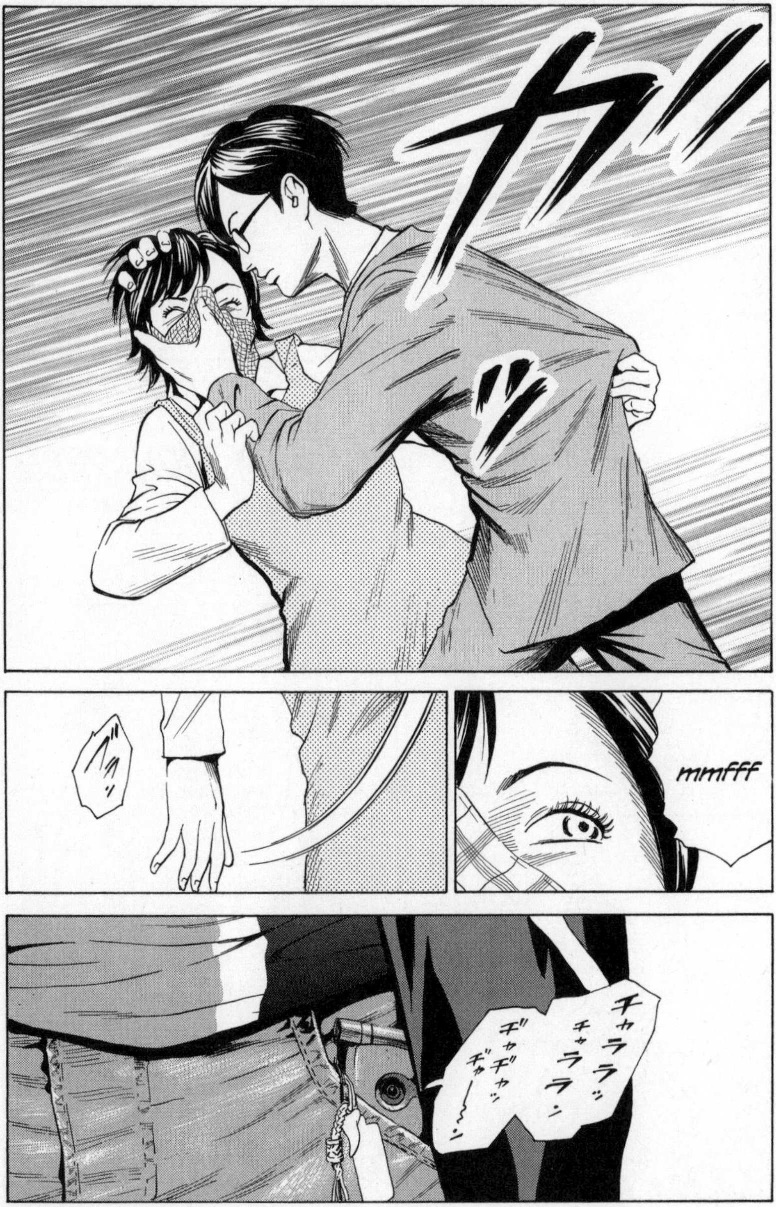
ガッ
mmfff
チャララッ
チャララ～
ギャギャッ
ギャ～～～

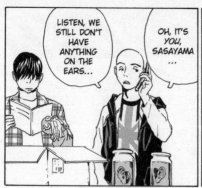

...YES, HELLO?
スチャッ
OH, IT'S *YOU*, SASAYAMA ...
LISTEN, WE STILL DON'T HAVE ANYTHING ON THE EARS...
KIDNAPPED ?!
RIGHT IN THE MIDDLE OF PREPARING A BODY.
THE SECURITY CAMERA CAUGHT IT. EITHER HE DIDN'T KNOW IT WAS THERE, OR HE DIDN'T CARE.
LOOK, I'M COMING OVER, OKAY? I'VE GOT THE FULL CLIP ON A FLASH DRIVE. WE'LL LOOK AT IT THEN.
...

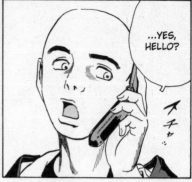

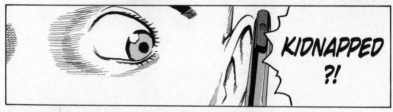

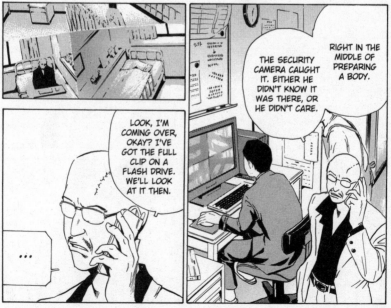

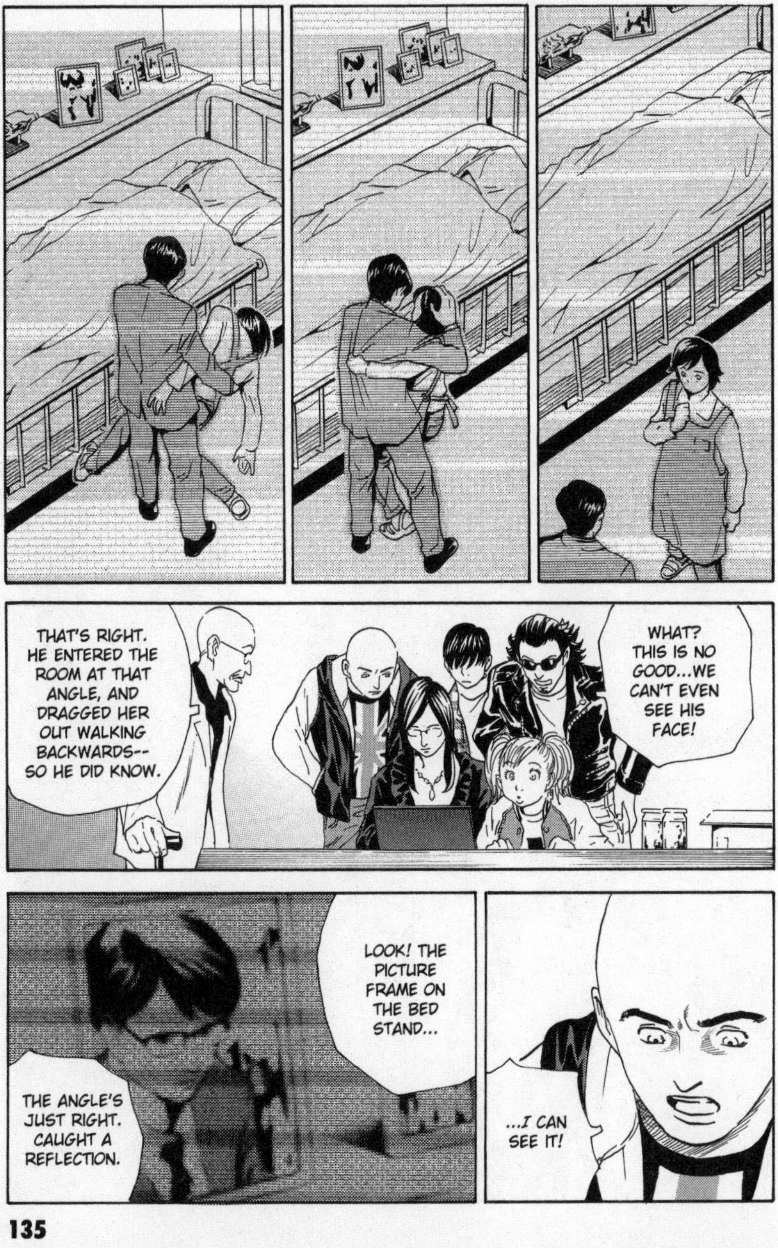
WHAT? THIS IS NO GOOD...WE CAN'T EVEN SEE HIS FACE!
THAT'S RIGHT. HE ENTERED THE ROOM AT THAT ANGLE, AND DRAGGED HER OUT WALKING BACKWARDS-- SO HE DID KNOW.
...I CAN SEE IT!
LOOK! THE PICTURE FRAME ON THE BED STAND...
THE ANGLE'S JUST RIGHT. CAUGHT A REFLECTION.

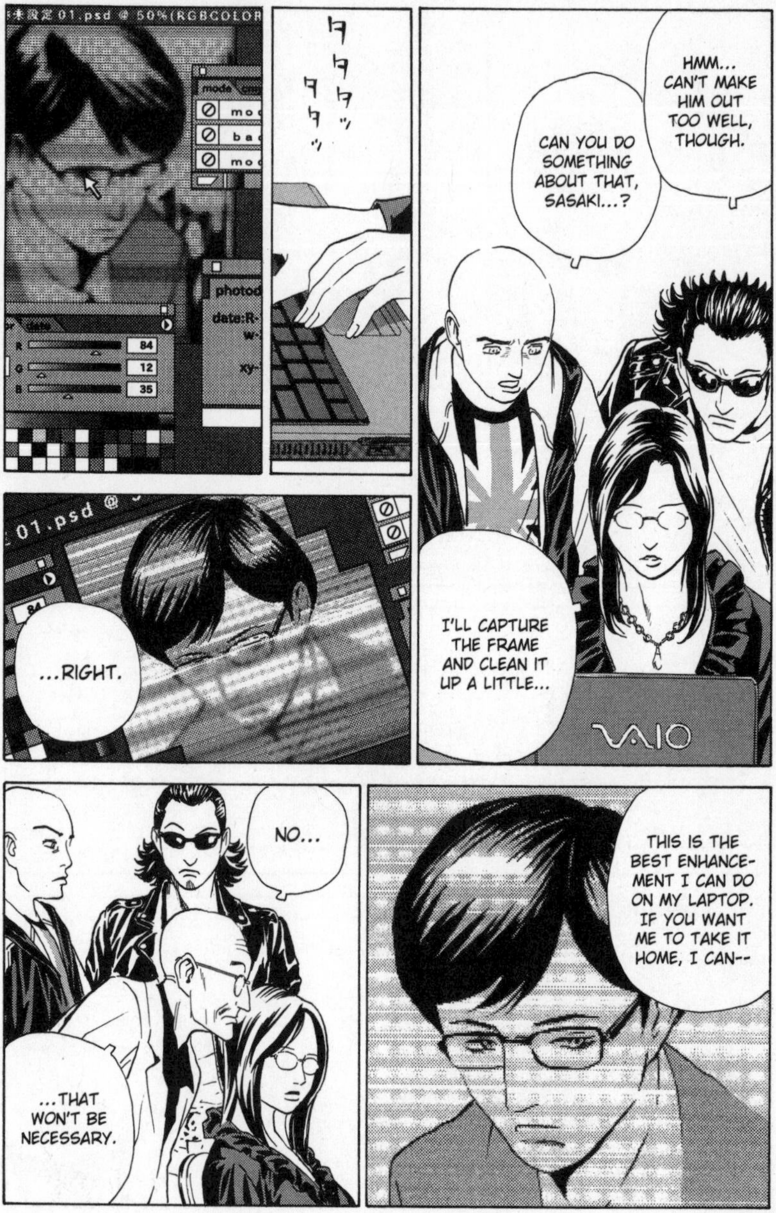
HMM... CAN'T MAKE HIM OUT TOO WELL, THOUGH.
CAN YOU DO SOMETHING ABOUT THAT, SASAKI...?
I'LL CAPTURE THE FRAME AND CLEAN IT UP A LITTLE...
タタタッ
タタッ
...RIGHT.
THIS IS THE BEST ENHANCE-MENT I CAN DO ON MY LAPTOP. IF YOU WANT ME TO TAKE IT HOME, I CAN--
NO...
...THAT WON'T BE NECESSARY.

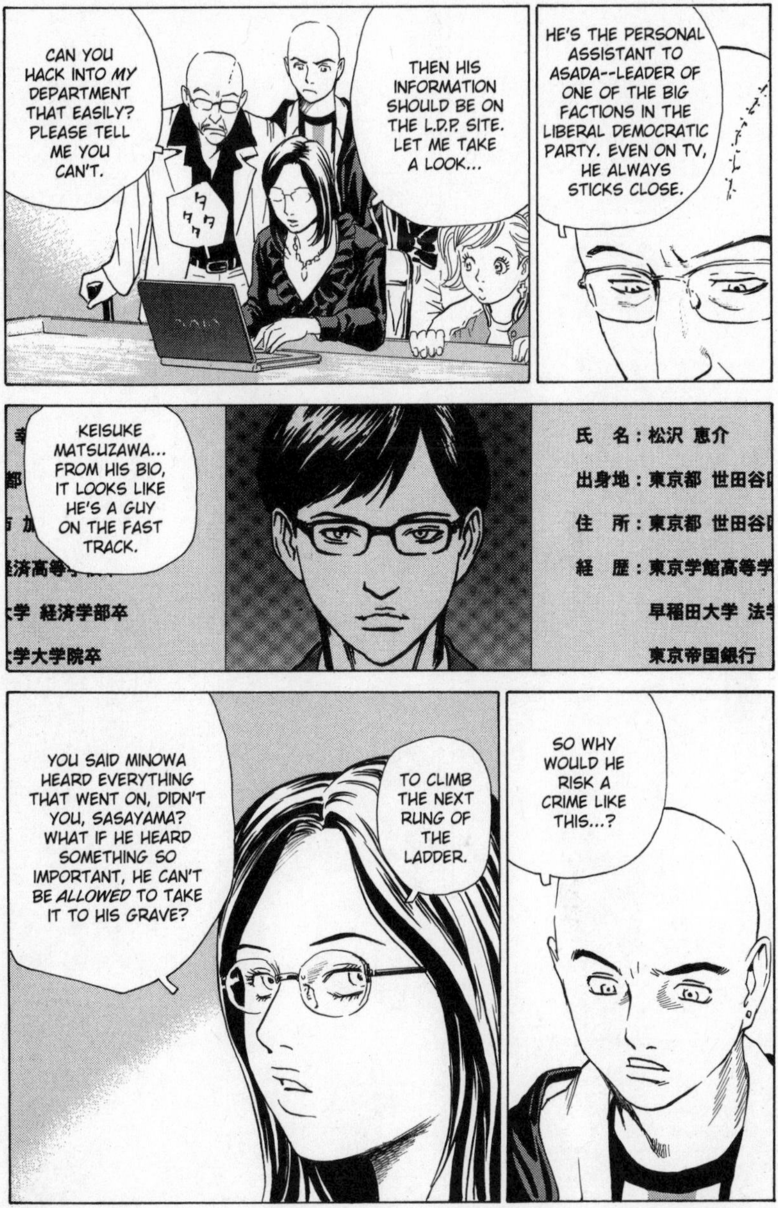

HE'S THE PERSONAL ASSISTANT TO ASADA--LEADER OF ONE OF THE BIG FACTIONS IN THE LIBERAL DEMOCRATIC PARTY. EVEN ON TV, HE ALWAYS STICKS CLOSE.
THEN HIS INFORMATION SHOULD BE ON THE L.D.P. SITE. LET ME TAKE A LOOK...
タタタタ
CAN YOU HACK INTO *MY* DEPARTMENT THAT EASILY? PLEASE TELL ME YOU CAN'T.
氏　名：松沢 恵介
出身地：東京都 世田谷
住　所：東京都 世田谷
経　歴：東京学館高等学
早稲田大学 法
東京帝国銀行
KEISUKE MATSUZAWA... FROM HIS BIO, IT LOOKS LIKE HE'S A GUY ON THE FAST TRACK.
SO WHY WOULD HE RISK A CRIME LIKE THIS...?
TO CLIMB THE NEXT RUNG OF THE LADDER.
YOU SAID MINOWA HEARD EVERYTHING THAT WENT ON, DIDN'T YOU, SASAYAMA? WHAT IF HE HEARD SOMETHING SO IMPORTANT, HE CAN'T BE *ALLOWED* TO TAKE IT TO HIS GRAVE?

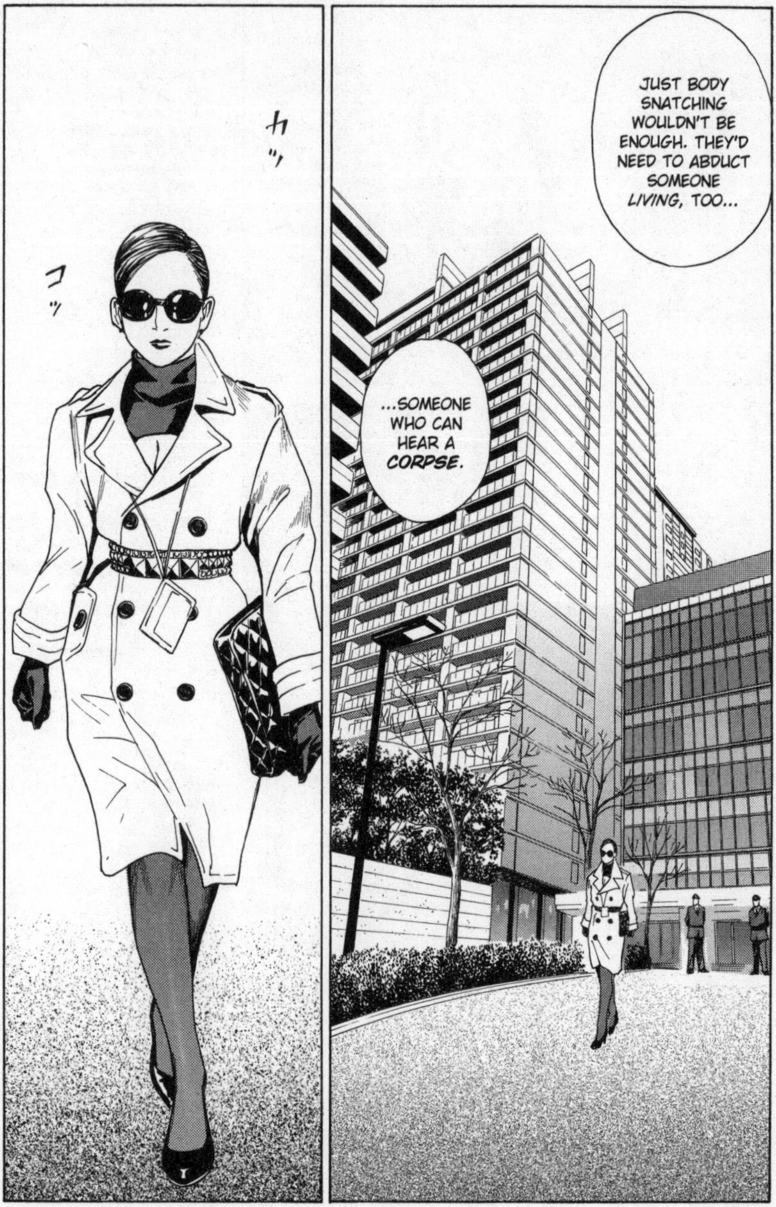
JUST BODY SNATCHING WOULDN'T BE ENOUGH. THEY'D NEED TO ABDUCT SOMEONE *LIVING*, TOO...
...SOMEONE WHO CAN HEAR A **CORPSE**.
カッ
コッ

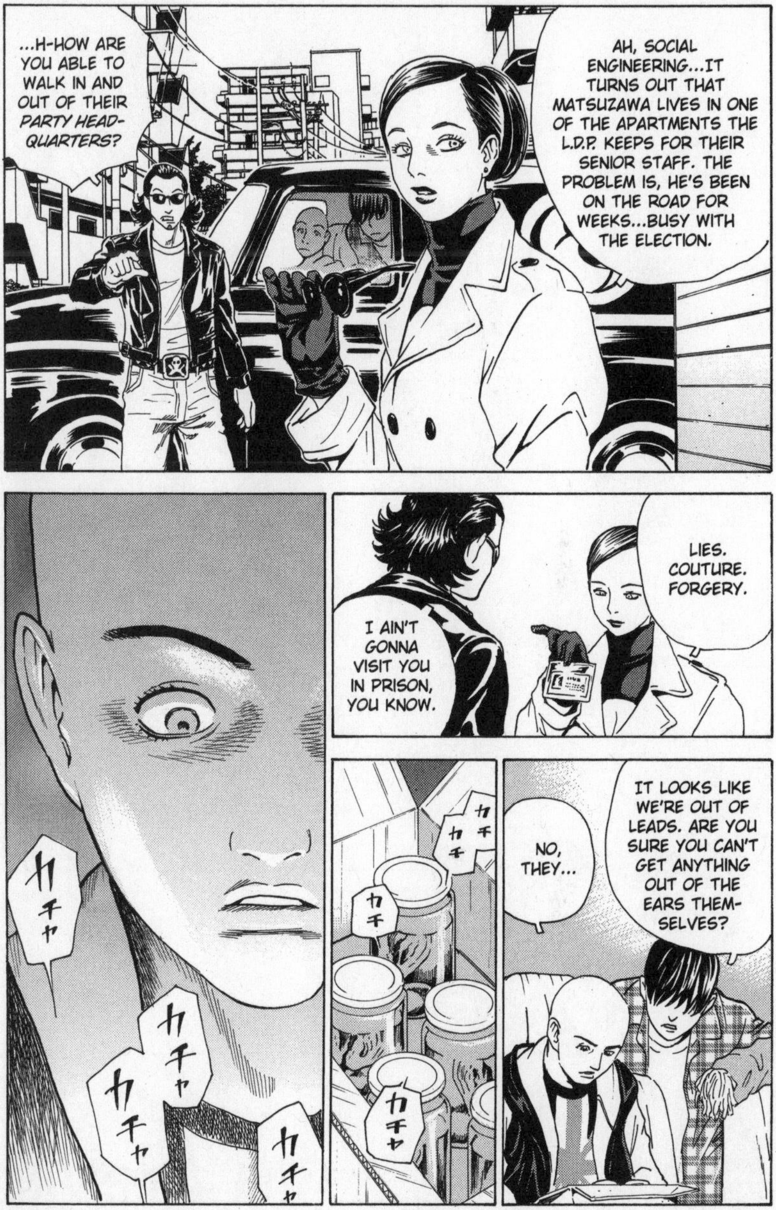
AH, SOCIAL ENGINEERING...IT TURNS OUT THAT MATSUZAWA LIVES IN ONE OF THE APARTMENTS THE L.D.P. KEEPS FOR THEIR SENIOR STAFF. THE PROBLEM IS, HE'S BEEN ON THE ROAD FOR WEEKS...BUSY WITH THE ELECTION.
...H-HOW ARE YOU ABLE TO WALK IN AND OUT OF THEIR *PARTY HEAD-QUARTERS?*
LIES. COUTURE. FORGERY.
I AIN'T GONNA VISIT YOU IN PRISON, YOU KNOW.
IT LOOKS LIKE WE'RE OUT OF LEADS. ARE YOU SURE YOU CAN'T GET ANYTHING OUT OF THE EARS THEM-SELVES?
NO, THEY...
カチ
カチ
カチ
カチャ
カチャ
カチャ
カチャ
カチャ

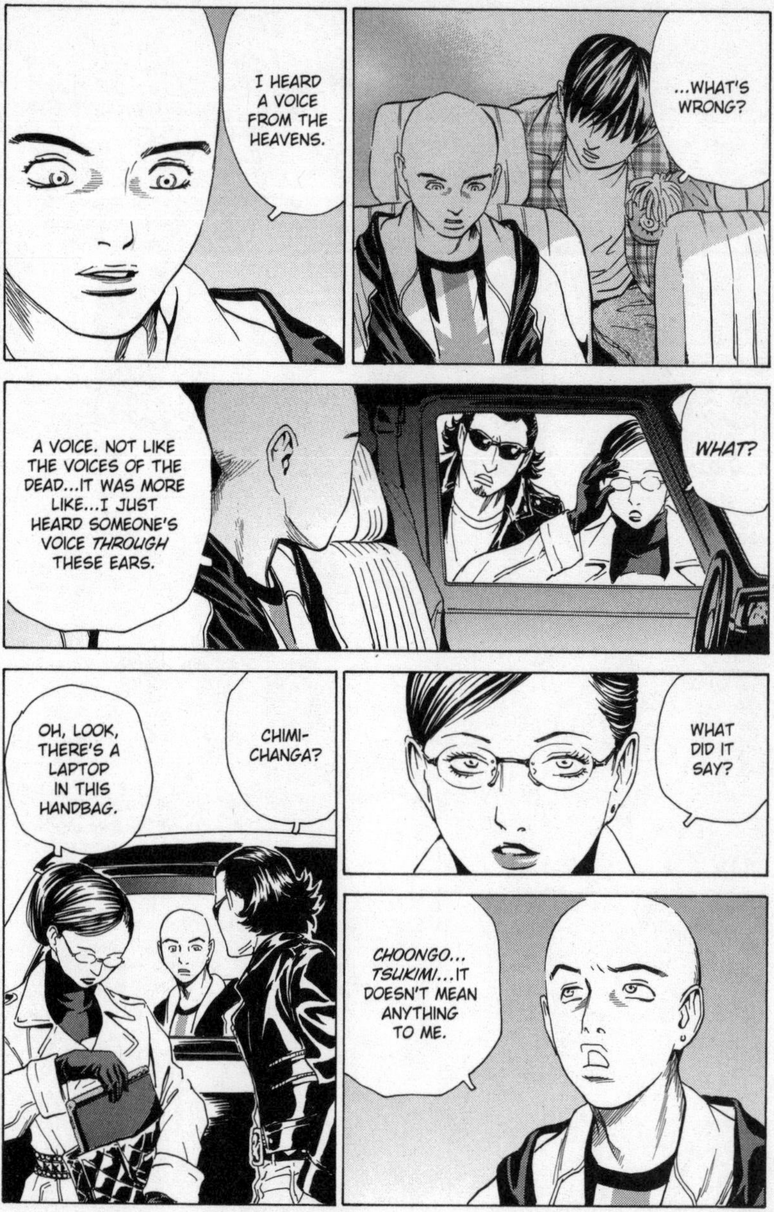
...WHAT'S WRONG?
I HEARD A VOICE FROM THE HEAVENS.
WHAT?
A VOICE. NOT LIKE THE VOICES OF THE DEAD...IT WAS MORE LIKE...I JUST HEARD SOMEONE'S VOICE *THROUGH* THESE EARS.
WHAT DID IT SAY?
CHOONGO... TSUKIMI...IT DOESN'T MEAN ANYTHING TO ME.
CHIMI-CHANGA?
OH, LOOK, THERE'S A LAPTOP IN THIS HANDBAG.

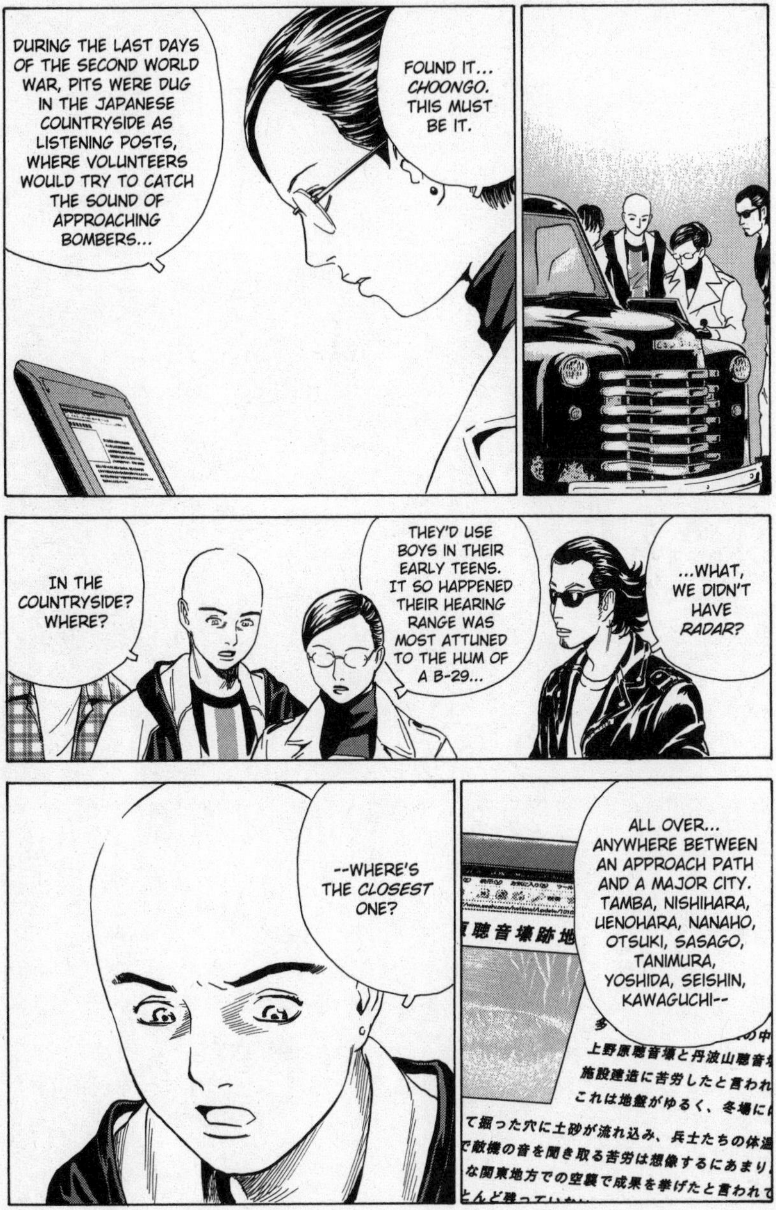
FOUND IT... *CHOONGO.* THIS MUST BE IT.
DURING THE LAST DAYS OF THE SECOND WORLD WAR, PITS WERE DUG IN THE JAPANESE COUNTRYSIDE AS LISTENING POSTS, WHERE VOLUNTEERS WOULD TRY TO CATCH THE SOUND OF APPROACHING BOMBERS...
...WHAT, WE DIDN'T HAVE *RADAR?*
THEY'D USE BOYS IN THEIR EARLY TEENS. IT SO HAPPENED THEIR HEARING RANGE WAS MOST ATTUNED TO THE HUM OF A B-29...
IN THE COUNTRYSIDE? WHERE?
ALL OVER... ANYWHERE BETWEEN AN APPROACH PATH AND A MAJOR CITY. TAMBA, NISHIHARA, UENOHARA, NANAHO, OTSUKI, SASAGO, TANIMURA, YOSHIDA, SEISHIN, KAWAGUCHI--
上野原聴音壕と丹波山聴音
施設建造に苦労したと言われ
これは地盤がゆるく、冬場に
て掘った穴に土砂が流れ込み、兵士たちの体温
で敵機の音を聞き取る苦労は想像するにあまり
な関東地方での空襲で成果を挙げたと言われて
--WHERE'S THE *CLOSEST* ONE?

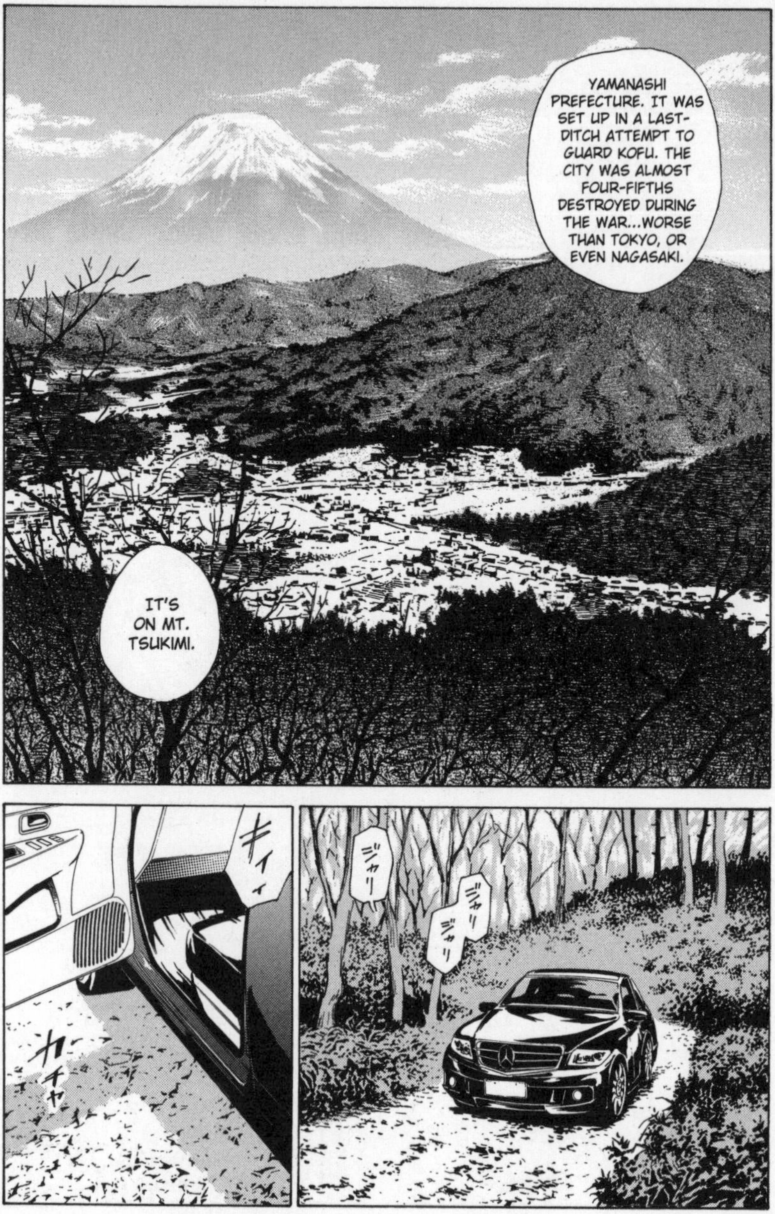
YAMANASHI PREFECTURE. IT WAS SET UP IN A LAST-DITCH ATTEMPT TO GUARD KOFU. THE CITY WAS ALMOST FOUR-FIFTHS DESTROYED DURING THE WAR...WORSE THAN TOKYO, OR EVEN NAGASAKI.
IT'S ON MT. TSUKIMI.
ジャリ
ジャリ
ジャリ
キィィ
カチャ

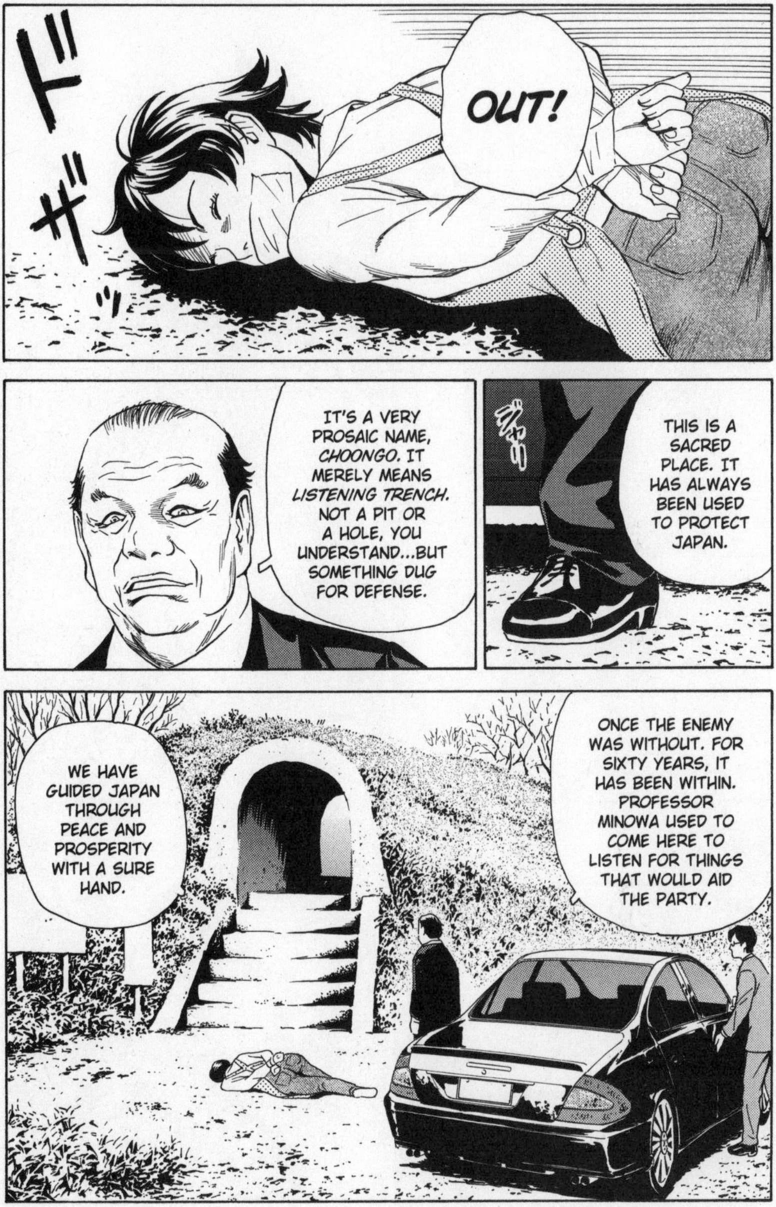
ドザッ
OUT!
THIS IS A SACRED PLACE. IT HAS ALWAYS BEEN USED TO PROTECT JAPAN.
IT'S A VERY PROSAIC NAME, *CHOONGO*. IT MERELY MEANS *LISTENING TRENCH*. NOT A PIT OR A HOLE, YOU UNDERSTAND...BUT SOMETHING DUG FOR DEFENSE.
ONCE THE ENEMY WAS WITHOUT. FOR SIXTY YEARS, IT HAS BEEN WITHIN. PROFESSOR MINOWA USED TO COME HERE TO LISTEN FOR THINGS THAT WOULD AID THE PARTY.
WE HAVE GUIDED JAPAN THROUGH PEACE AND PROSPERITY WITH A SURE HAND.

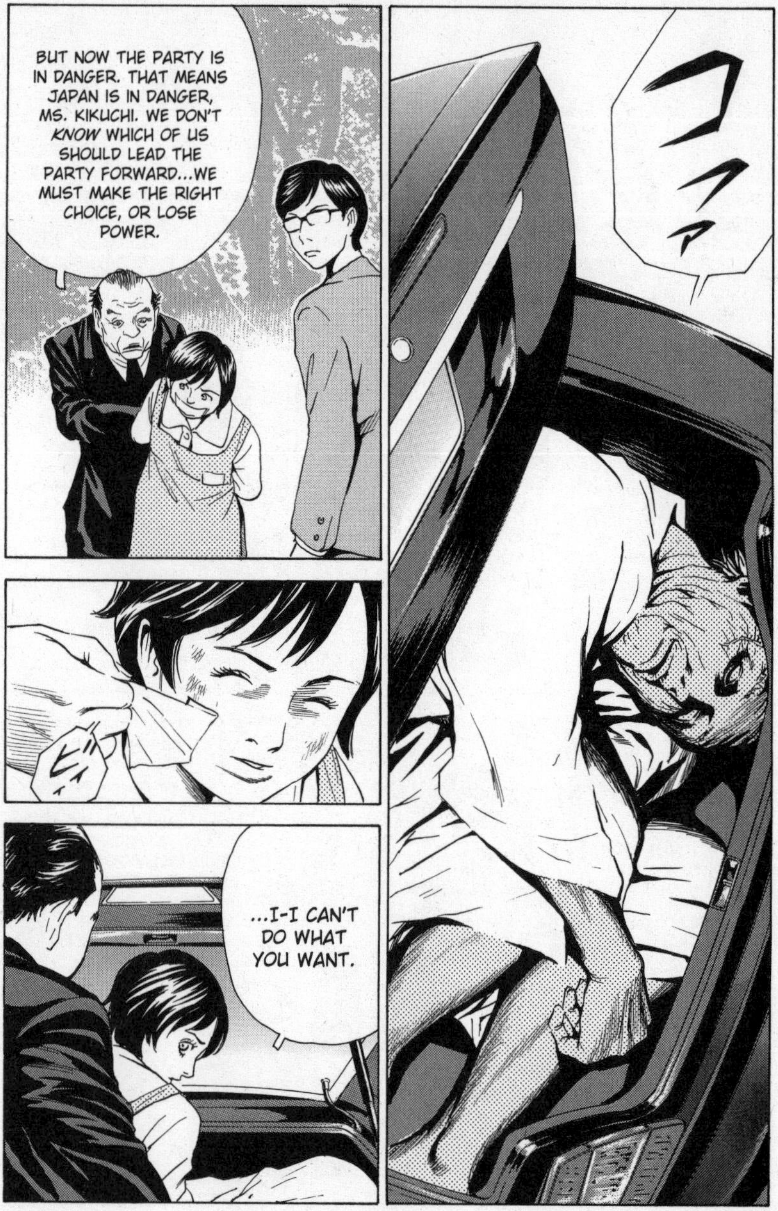
BUT NOW THE PARTY IS IN DANGER. THAT MEANS JAPAN IS IN DANGER, MS. KIKUCHI. WE DON'T *KNOW* WHICH OF US SHOULD LEAD THE PARTY FORWARD...WE MUST MAKE THE RIGHT CHOICE, OR LOSE POWER.
...I-I CAN'T DO WHAT YOU WANT.

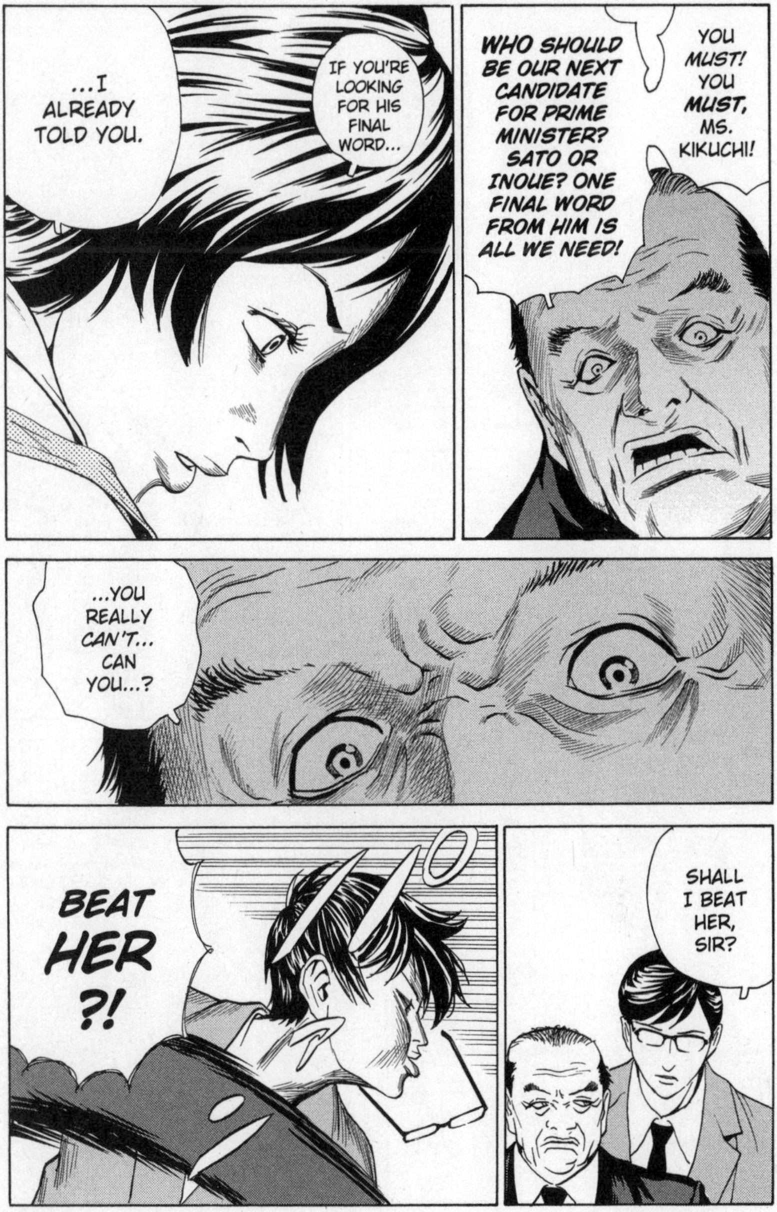
YOU MUST! YOU MUST, MS. KIKUCHI!
WHO SHOULD BE OUR NEXT CANDIDATE FOR PRIME MINISTER? SATO OR INOUE? ONE FINAL WORD FROM HIM IS ALL WE NEED!
IF YOU'RE LOOKING FOR HIS FINAL WORD...
...I ALREADY TOLD YOU.
...YOU REALLY CAN'T... CAN YOU...?
SHALL I BEAT HER, SIR?
BEAT HER ?!

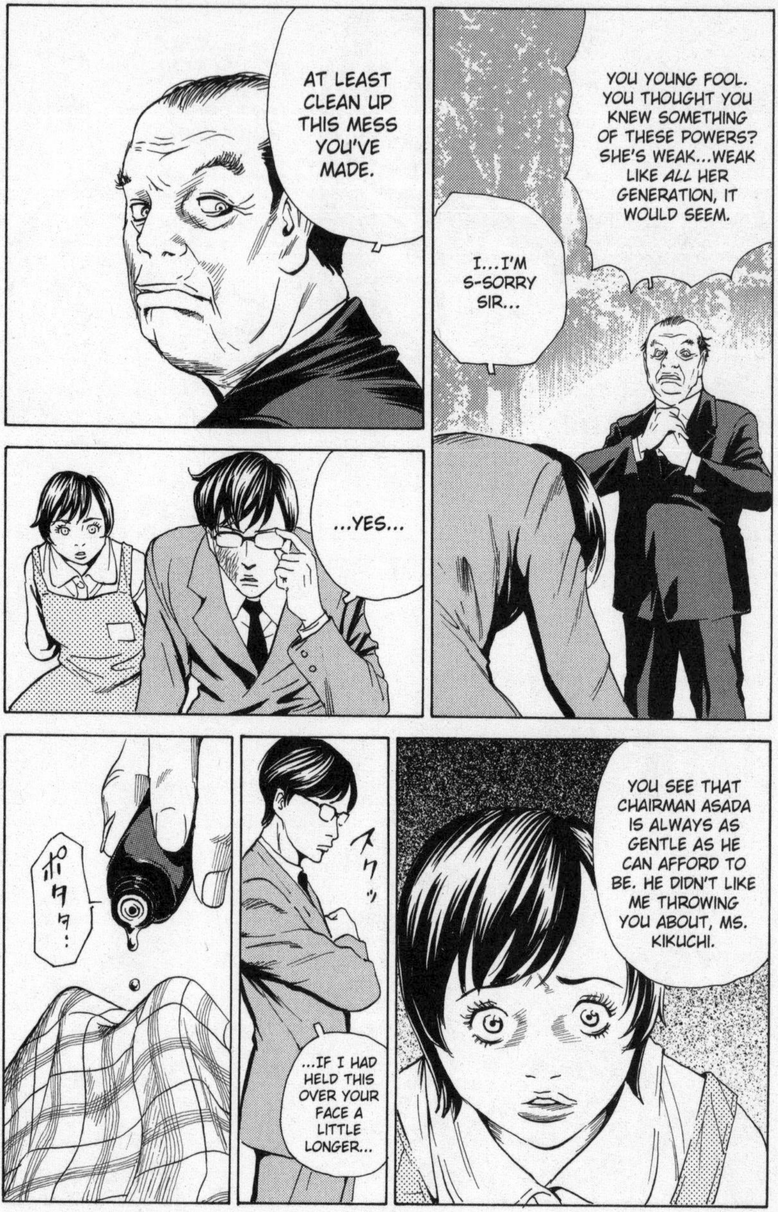
YOU YOUNG FOOL. YOU THOUGHT YOU KNEW SOMETHING OF THESE POWERS? SHE'S WEAK...WEAK LIKE *ALL* HER GENERATION, IT WOULD SEEM.
I...I'M S-SORRY SIR...
AT LEAST CLEAN UP THIS MESS YOU'VE MADE.
...YES...
YOU SEE THAT CHAIRMAN ASADA IS ALWAYS AS GENTLE AS HE CAN AFFORD TO BE. HE DIDN'T LIKE ME THROWING YOU ABOUT, MS. KIKUCHI.
スクッ
...IF I HAD HELD THIS OVER YOUR FACE A LITTLE LONGER...
ポタタ…

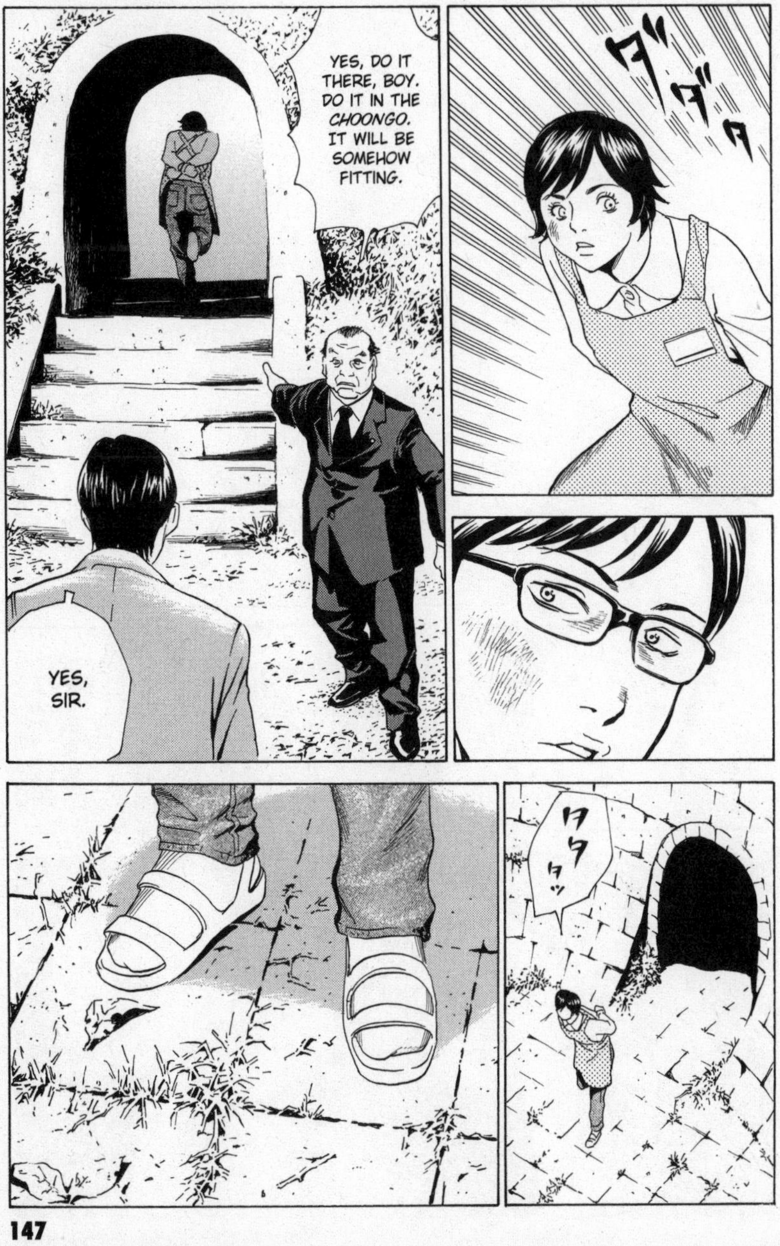
YES, DO IT THERE, BOY. DO IT IN THE *CHOONGO.* IT WILL BE SOMEHOW FITTING.
YES, SIR.

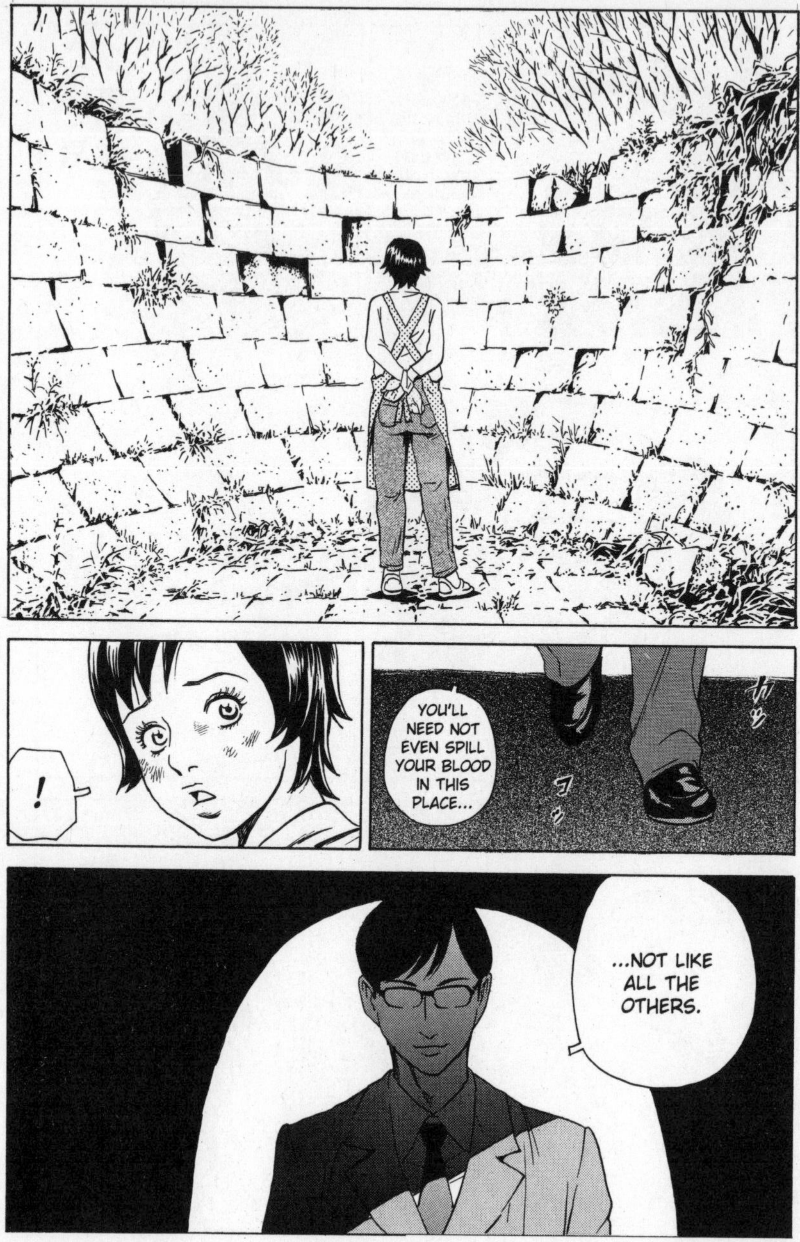
YOU'LL NEED NOT EVEN SPILL YOUR BLOOD IN THIS PLACE...
!
...NOT LIKE ALL THE OTHERS.

6th delivery: a certain situation—the end

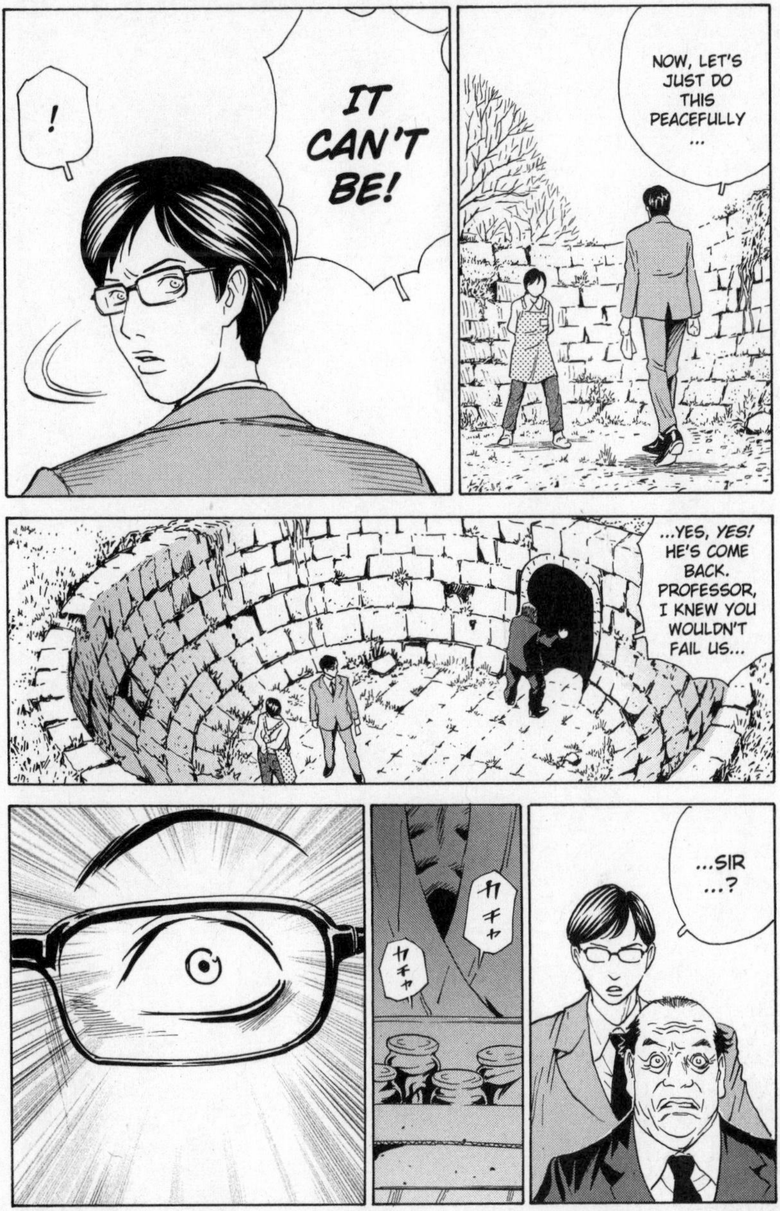
NOW, LET'S JUST DO THIS PEACEFULLY ...
IT CAN'T BE!
!
...YES, YES! HE'S COME BACK. PROFESSOR, I KNEW YOU WOULDN'T FAIL US...
...SIR ...?
カチャ
カチャ

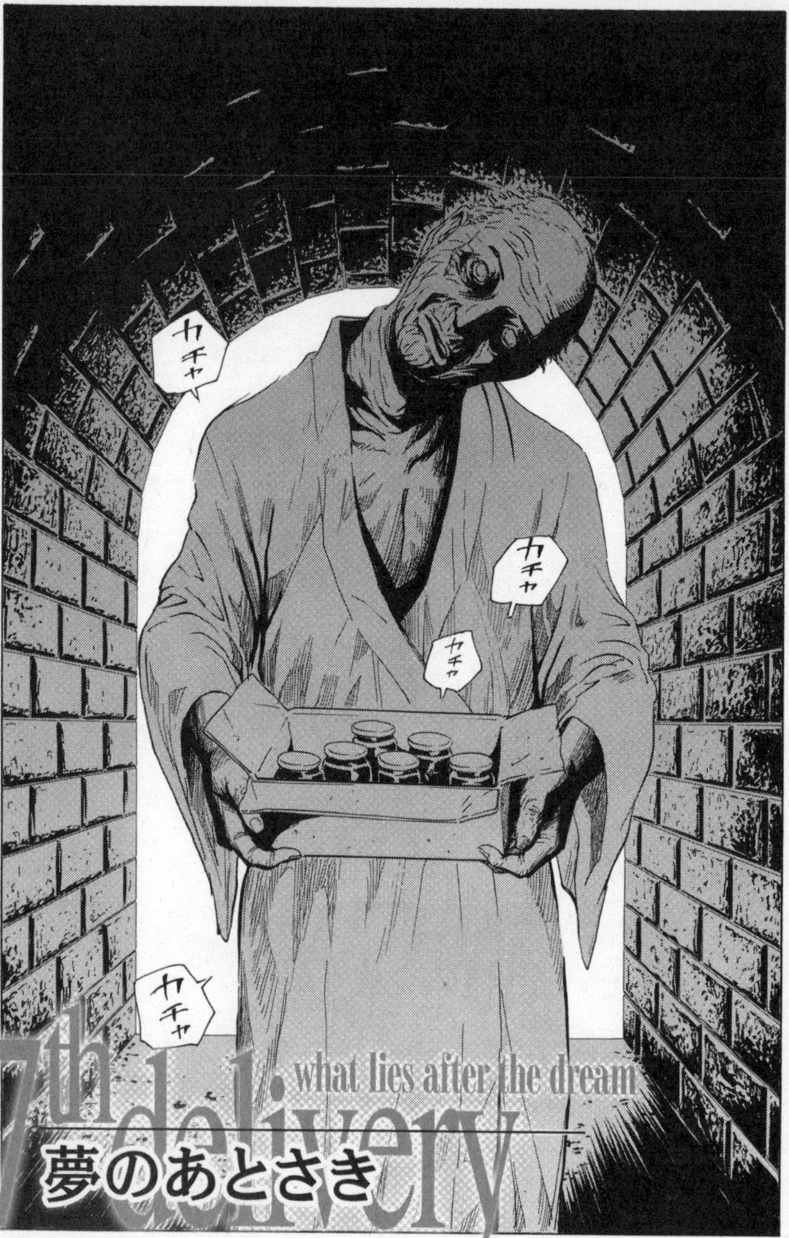
カチャ
カチャ
カチャ
カチャ

7th delivery

what lies after the dream

夢のあとさき

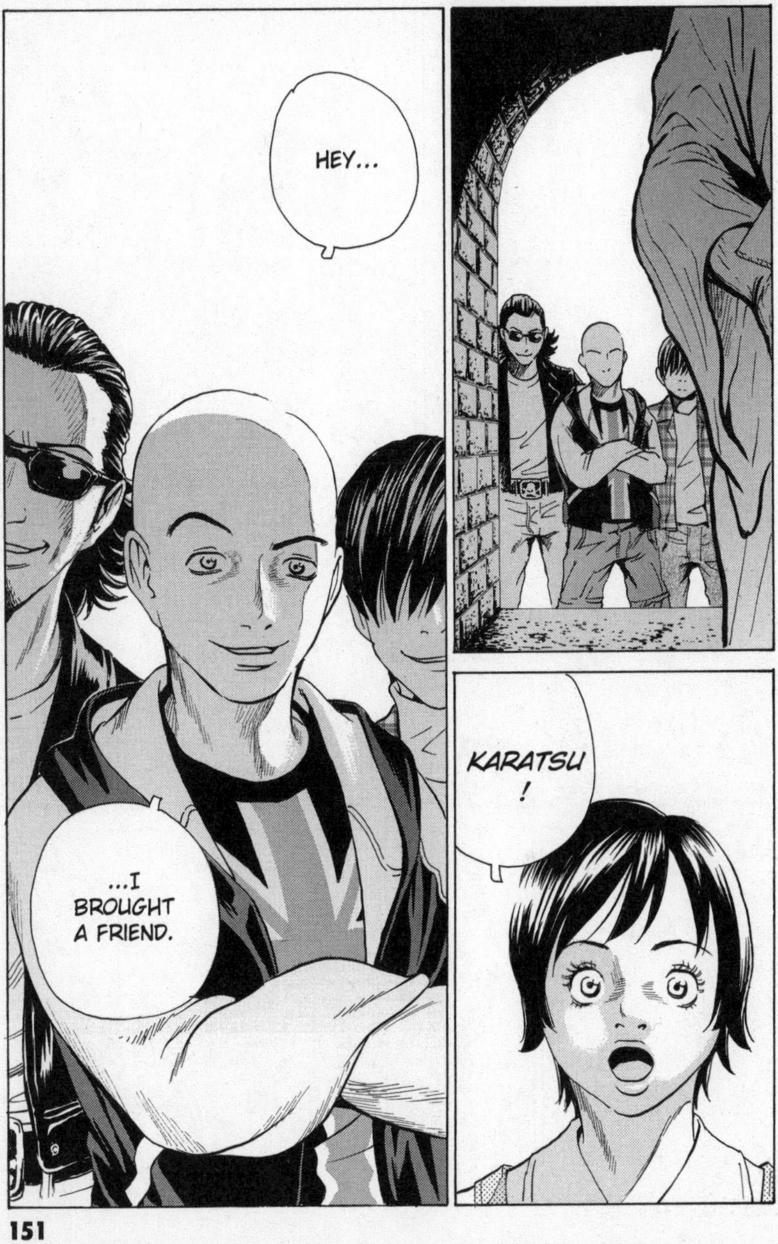
KARATSU!
HEY...
...I BROUGHT A FRIEND.

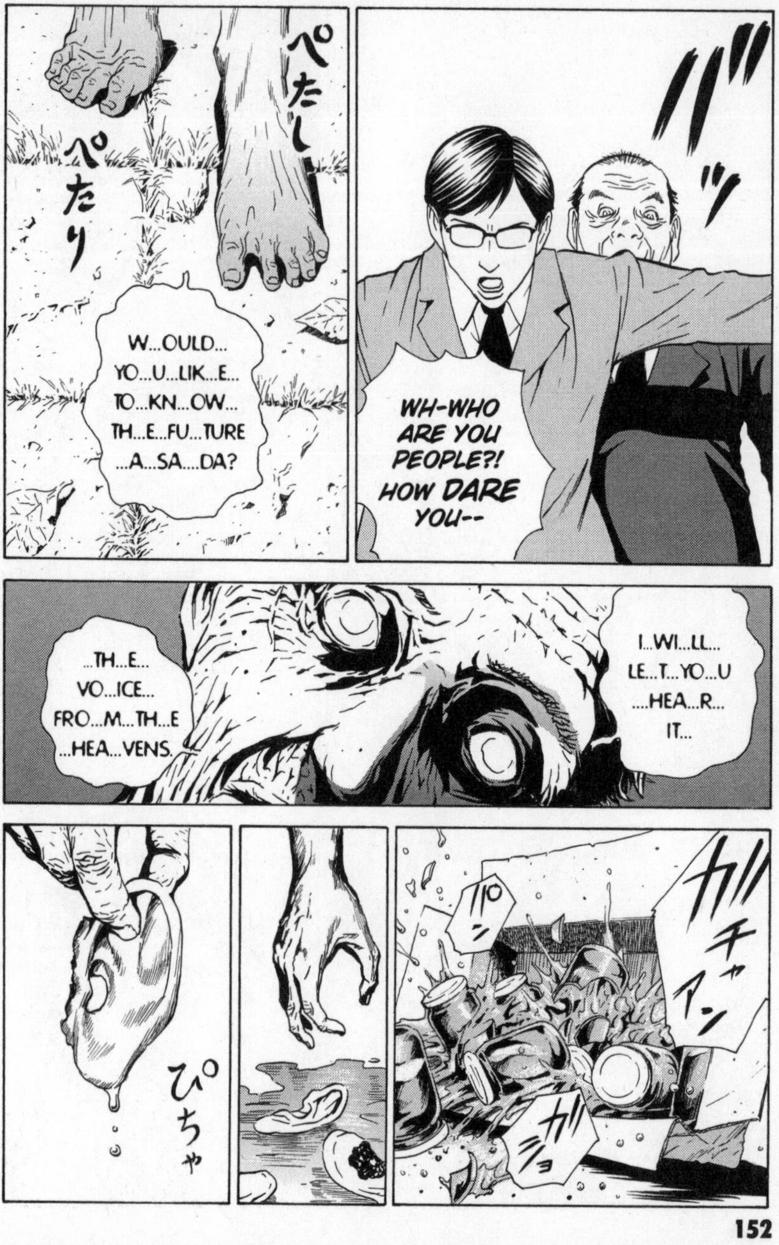
バッ
WH-WHO ARE YOU PEOPLE?! HOW DARE YOU--
ぺたし
ぺたり
W...OULD... YO...U...LIK...E... TO...KN...OW... TH...E...FU...TURE ...A...SA...DA?
I...WI...LL... LE...T...YO...U ....HEA...R... IT...
...TH...E... VO...ICE... FRO...M...TH...E ...HEA...VENS.
ガチャアン
パン
ガショ
ぴちゃ

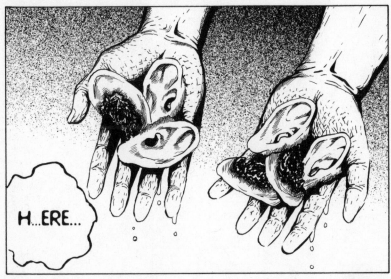

H...ERE...

LIS...TEN...

...HEAR.

I...
I...

...H...EAR...

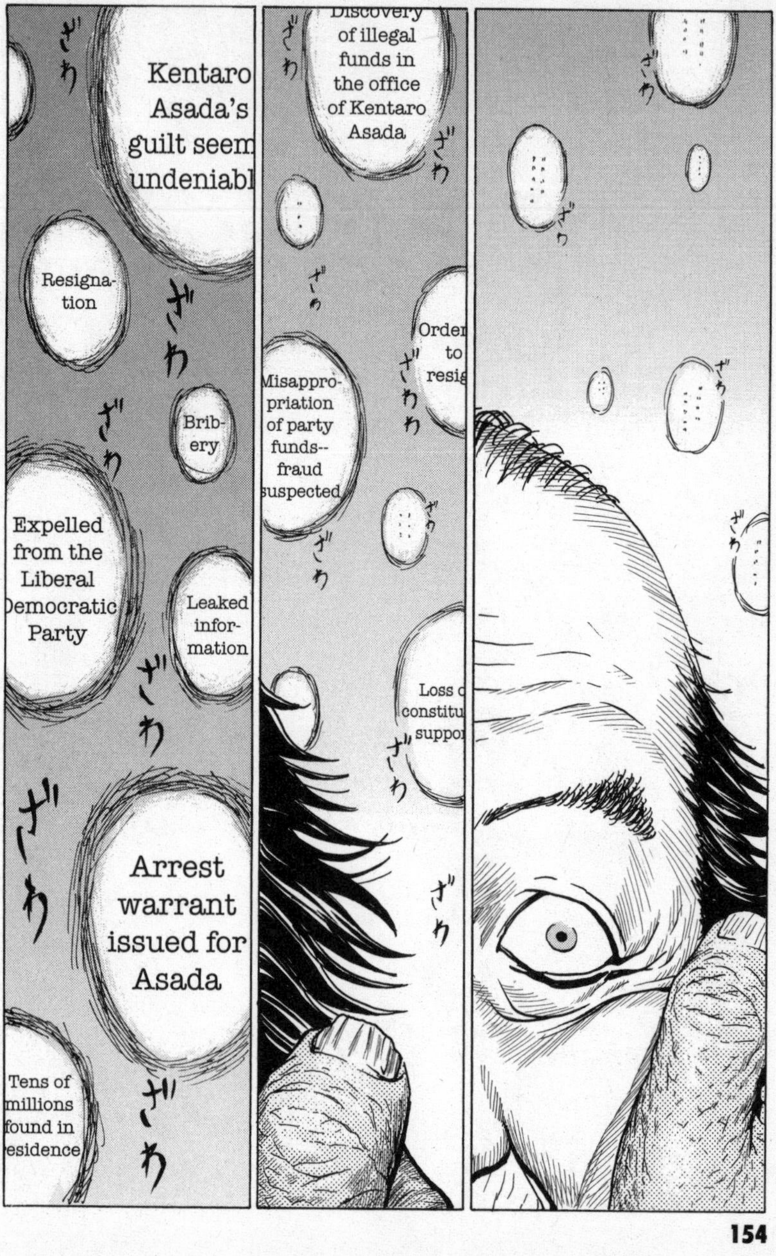
ざわ
ざわ
ざわ
ざわ
Discovery of illegal funds in the office of Kentaro Asada
ざわ
ざわ
Orde to resig
ざわわ
Misappro-priation of party funds--fraud suspected
ざわ
ざわ
Loss o constitu suppor
ざわ
ざわ
ざわ
Kentaro Asada's guilt seem undeniabl
Resigna-tion
ざわ
Brib-ery
ざわ
Expelled from the Liberal emocratic Party
Leaked infor-mation
ざわ
ざわ
Arrest warrant issued for Asada
Tens of millions found in esidence
ざわ

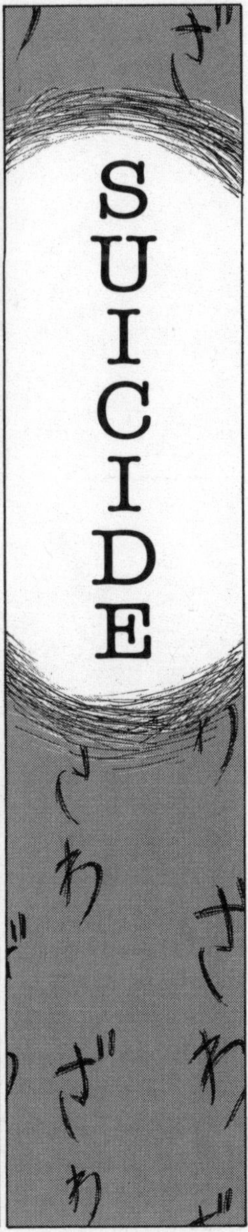
SUICIDE
ざわ
ざわ
ざわ
ざわ

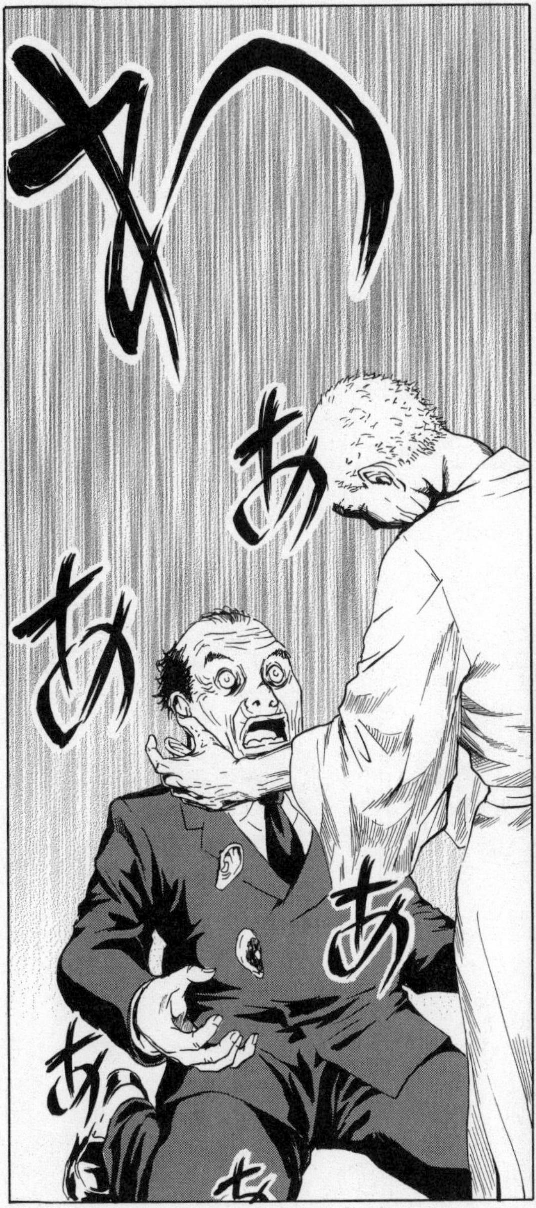
あ
あ
あ
あ

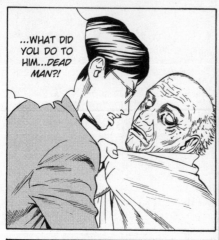

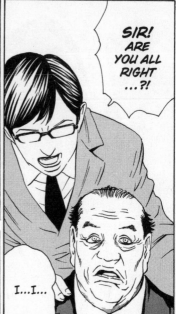

SIR! ARE YOU ALL RIGHT ...?!
I...I...
...WHAT DID YOU DO TO HIM...DEAD MAN?!
DON'T...
...DON'T BOTHER THE PROFES-SOR...
S-SIR...?
...
SIR, PLEASE WAIT FOR ME!

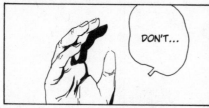

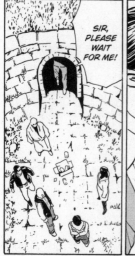

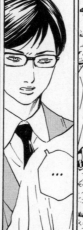

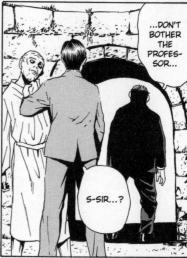

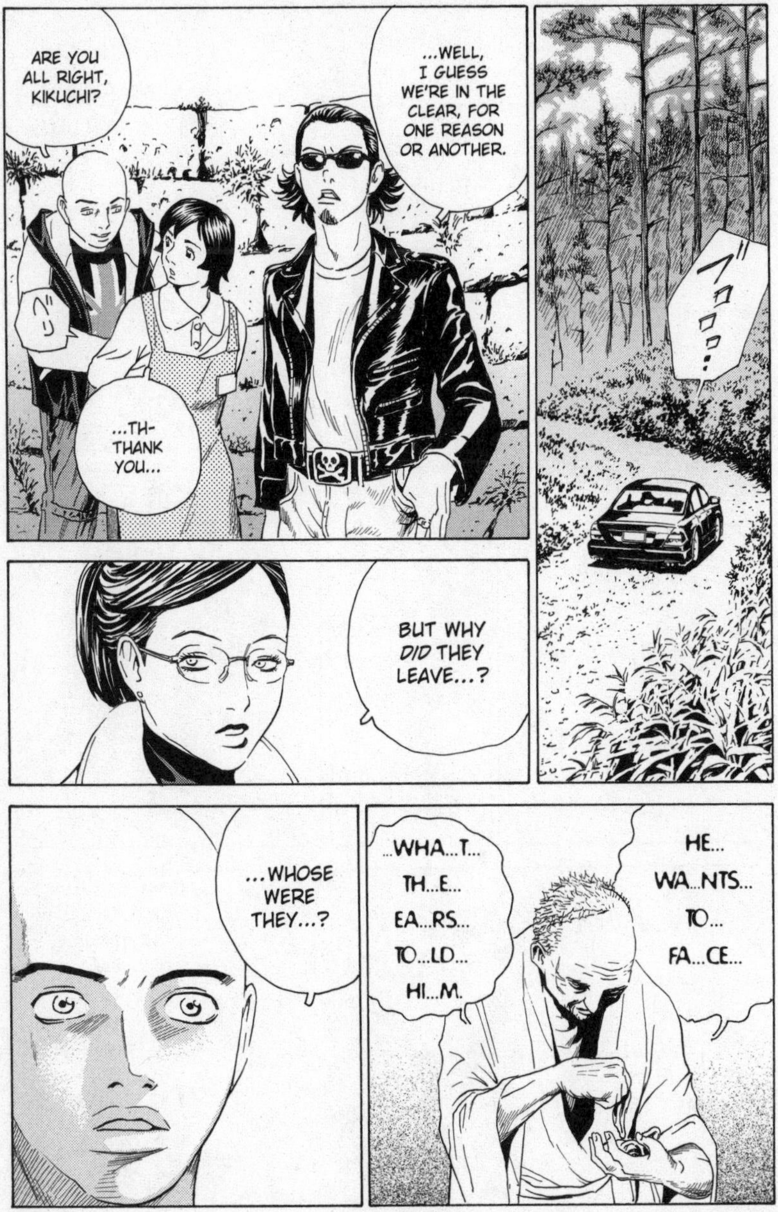
ブロロロ…
...WELL, I GUESS WE'RE IN THE CLEAR, FOR ONE REASON OR ANOTHER.
ARE YOU ALL RIGHT, KIKUCHI?
ベリ
...TH-THANK YOU...
BUT WHY *DID* THEY LEAVE...?
HE... WA...NTS... TO... FA...CE...
...WHA...T... TH...E... EA...RS... TO...LD... HI...M.
...WHOSE WERE THEY...?

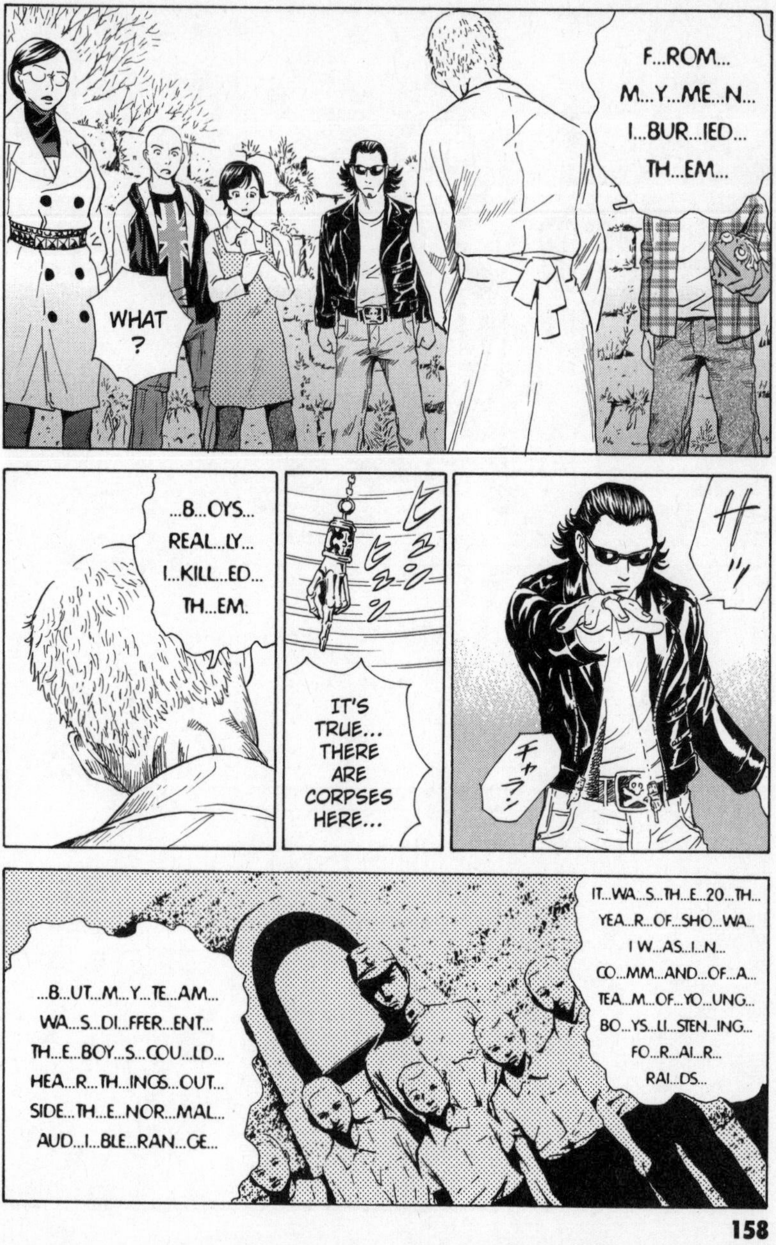
F...ROM... M...Y...ME...N... I...BUR...IED... TH...EM...
WHAT ?
ハッ
チャラ…
IT'S TRUE... THERE ARE CORPSES HERE...
...B...OYS... REAL...LY... I...KILL...ED... TH...EM.
IT...WA...S...TH...E...20...TH... YEA...R...OF...SHO...WA... I W...AS...I...N... CO...MM...AND...OF...A... TEA...M...OF...YO...UNG... BO...YS...LI...STEN...ING... FO...R...AI...R... RAI...DS...
...B...UT...M...Y...TE...AM... WA...S...DI...FFER...ENT... TH...E...BOY...S...COU...LD... HEA...R...TH...INGS...OUT... SIDE...TH...E...NOR...MAL... AUD...I...BLE...RAN...GE...

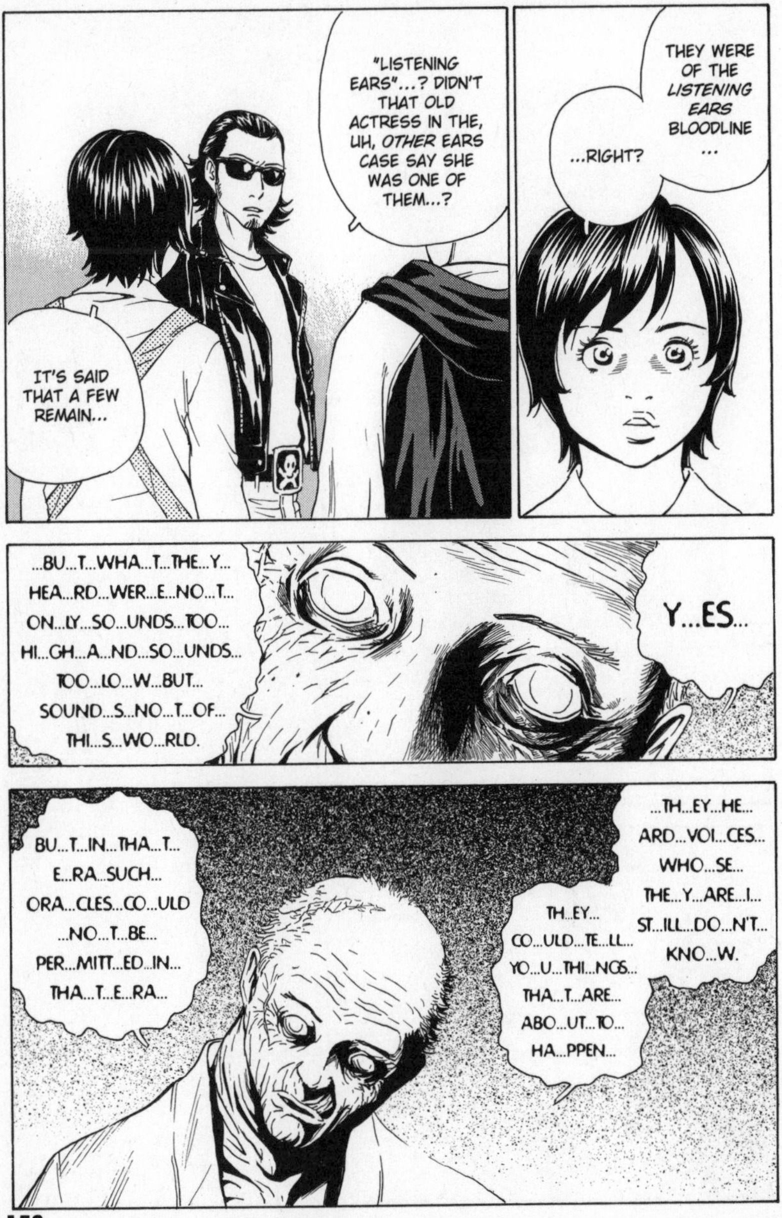
THEY WERE OF THE *LISTENING EARS* BLOODLINE ...
...RIGHT?
"LISTENING EARS"...? DIDN'T THAT OLD ACTRESS IN THE, UH, *OTHER* EARS CASE SAY SHE WAS ONE OF THEM...?
IT'S SAID THAT A FEW REMAIN...
Y...ES...
...BU...T...WHA...T...THE...Y... HEA...RD...WER...E...NO...T... ON...LY...SO...UNDS...TOO... HI...GH...A...ND...SO...UNDS... TOO...LO...W...BUT... SOUND...S...NO...T...OF... THI...S...WO...RLD.
...TH...EY...HE... ARD...VOI...CES... WHO...SE... THE...Y...ARE...I... ST...ILL...DO...N'T... KNO...W.
TH...EY... CO...ULD...TE...LL... YO...U...THI...NGS... THA...T...ARE... ABO...UT...TO... HA...PPEN...
BU...T...IN...THA...T... E...RA...SUCH... ORA...CLES...CO...ULD ...NO...T...BE... PER...MITT...ED...IN... THA...T...E...RA...

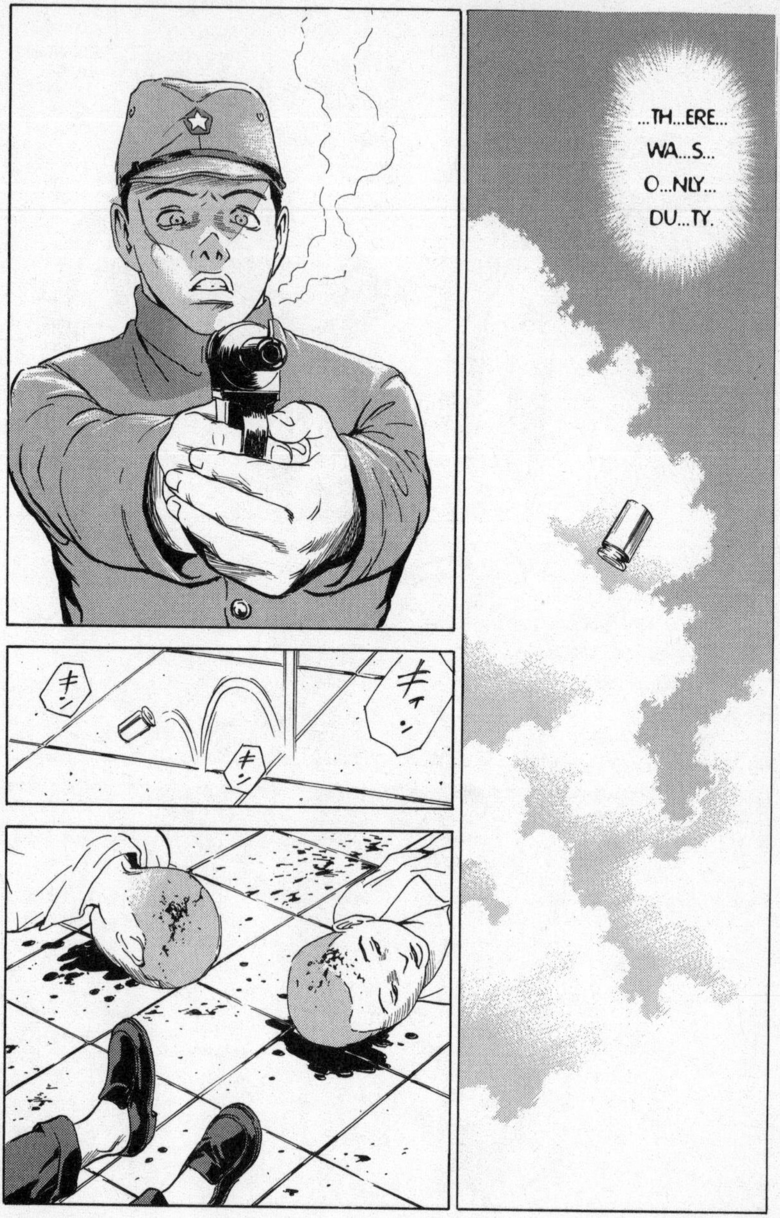
...TH...ERE...
WA...S...
O...NLY...
DU...TY.
キィ・ン
キ・ン
キ・ン

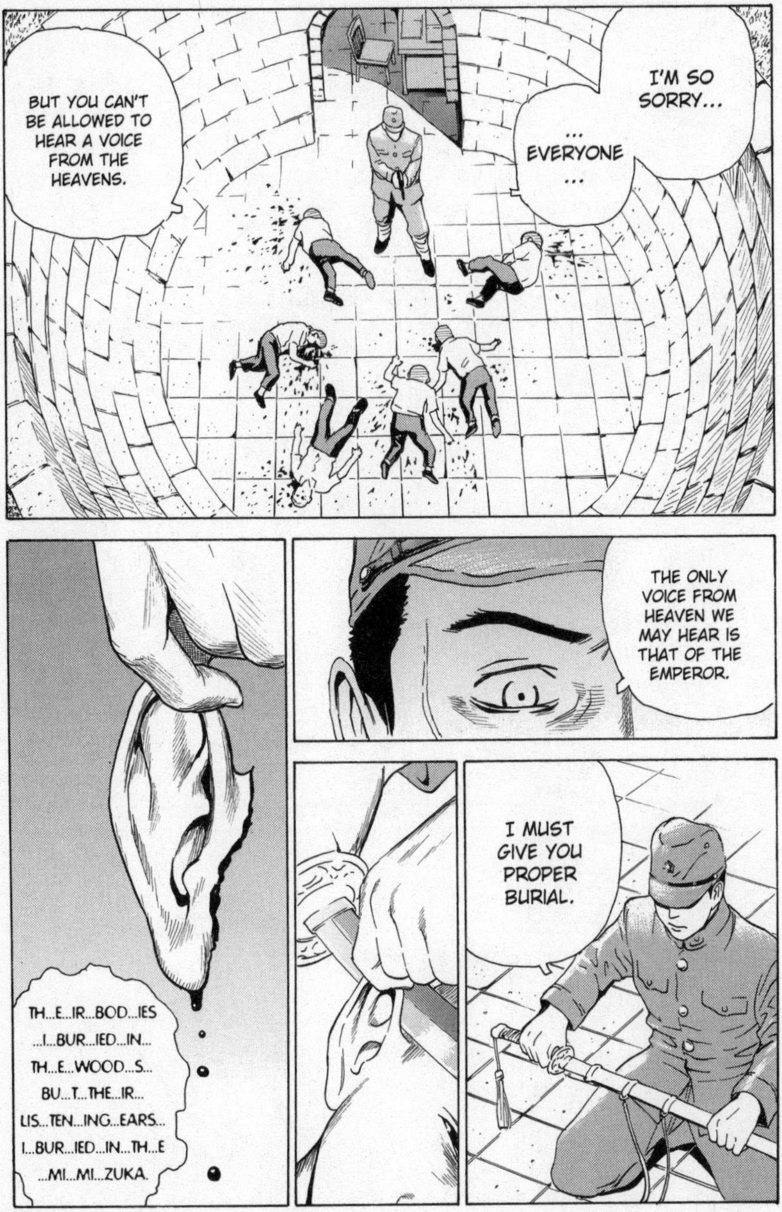
I'M SO SORRY...
... EVERYONE ...
BUT YOU CAN'T BE ALLOWED TO HEAR A VOICE FROM THE HEAVENS.
THE ONLY VOICE FROM HEAVEN WE MAY HEAR IS THAT OF THE EMPEROR.
I MUST GIVE YOU PROPER BURIAL.
TH...E...IR...BOD...IES ...I...BUR...IED...IN... TH...E...WOOD...S... BU...T...THE...IR... LIS...TEN...ING...EARS... I...BUR...IED...IN...TH...E ...MI...MI...ZUKA.

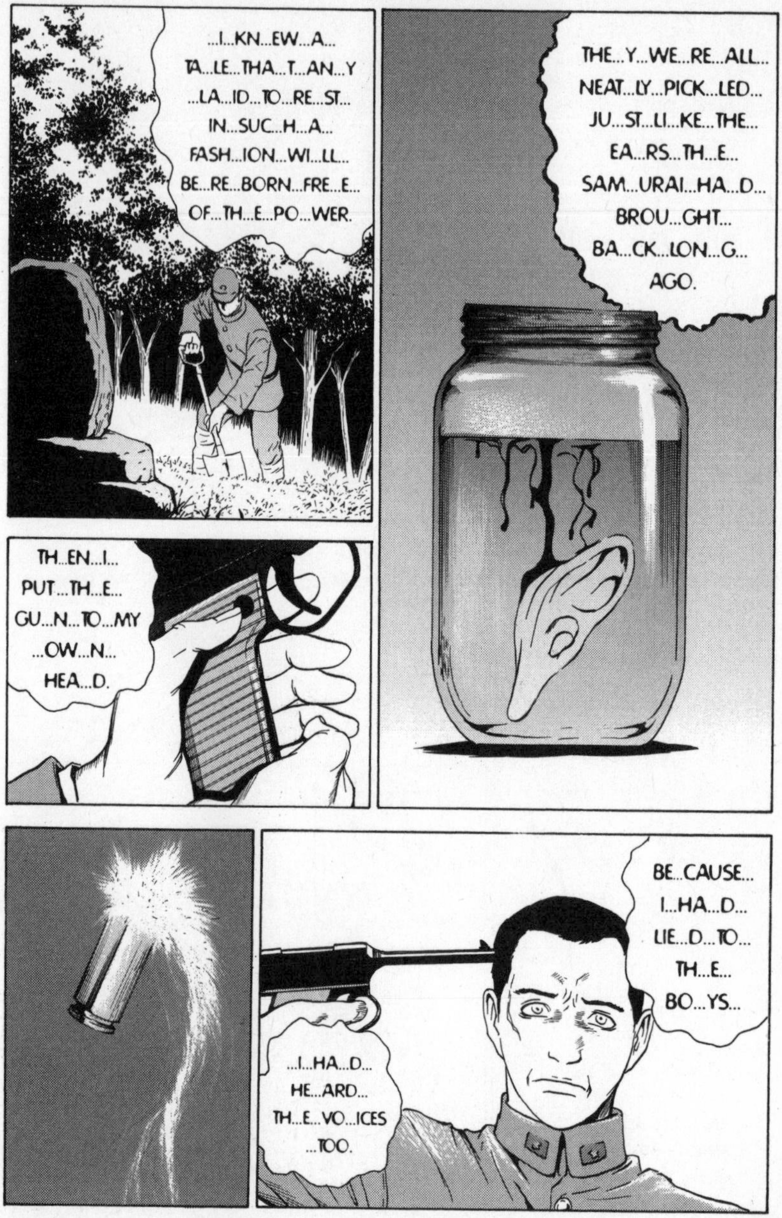
THE...Y...WE...RE...ALL... NEAT...LY...PICK...LED... JU...ST...LI...KE...THE... EA...RS...TH...E... SAM...URAI...HA...D... BROU...GHT... BA...CK...LON...G... AGO.
...I...KN...EW...A... TA...LE...THA...T...AN...Y ...LA...ID...TO...RE...ST... IN...SUC...H...A... FASH...ION...WI...LL... BE...RE...BORN...FRE...E... OF...TH...E...PO...WER.
TH...EN...I... PUT...TH...E... GU...N...TO...MY ...OW...N... HEA...D.
BE...CAUSE... I...HA...D... LIE...D...TO... TH...E... BO...YS...
...I...HA...D... HE...ARD... TH...E...VO...ICES ...TOO.

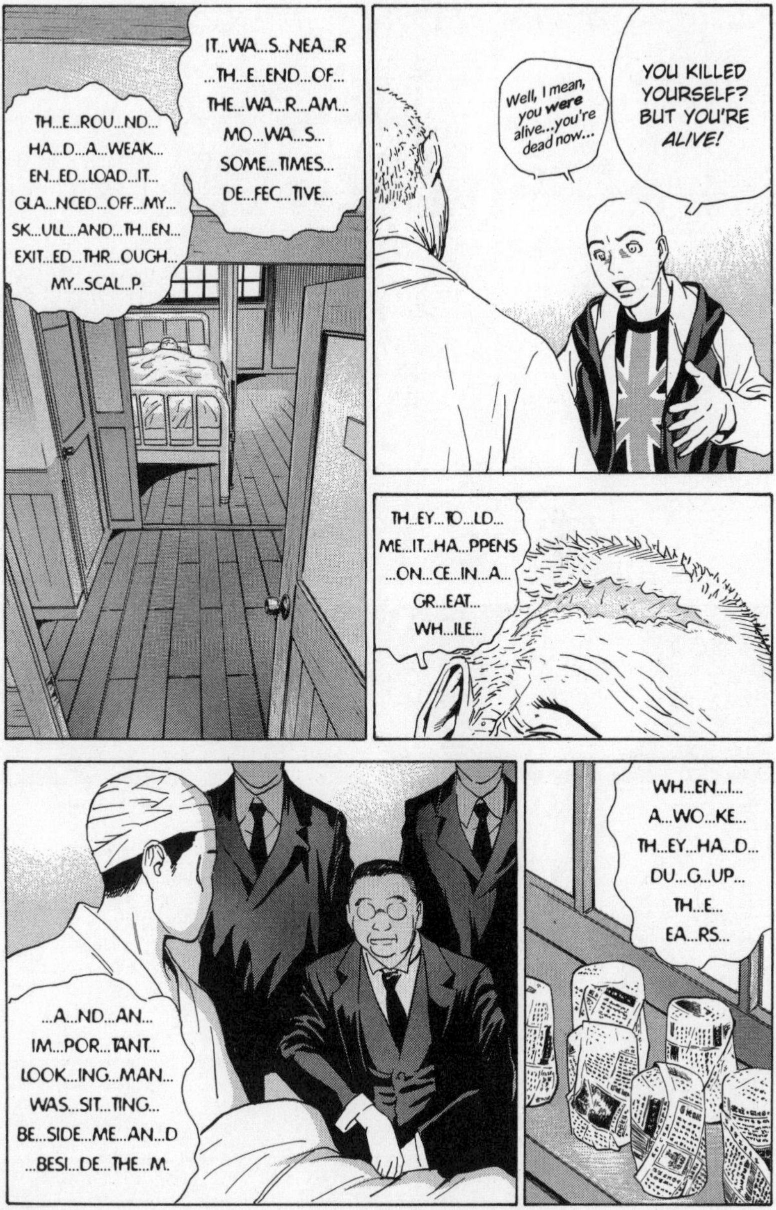
YOU KILLED YOURSELF? BUT YOU'RE *ALIVE!*
Well, I mean, you **were** alive...you're dead now...
TH...EY...TO...LD... ME...IT...HA...PPENS ...ON...CE...IN...A... GR...EAT... WH...ILE...
IT...WA...S...NEA...R ...TH...E...END...OF... THE...WA...R...AM... MO...WA...S... SOME...TIMES... DE...FEC...TIVE...
TH...E...ROU...ND... HA...D...A...WEAK... EN...ED...LOAD...IT... GLA...NCED...OFF...MY... SK...ULL...AND...TH...EN... EXIT...ED...THR...OUGH... MY...SCAL...P.
WH...EN...I... A...WO...KE... TH...EY...HA...D... DU...G...UP... TH...E... EA...RS...
...A...ND...AN... IM...POR...TANT... LOOK...ING...MAN... WAS...SIT...TING... BE...SIDE...ME...AN...D ...BESI...DE...THE...M.

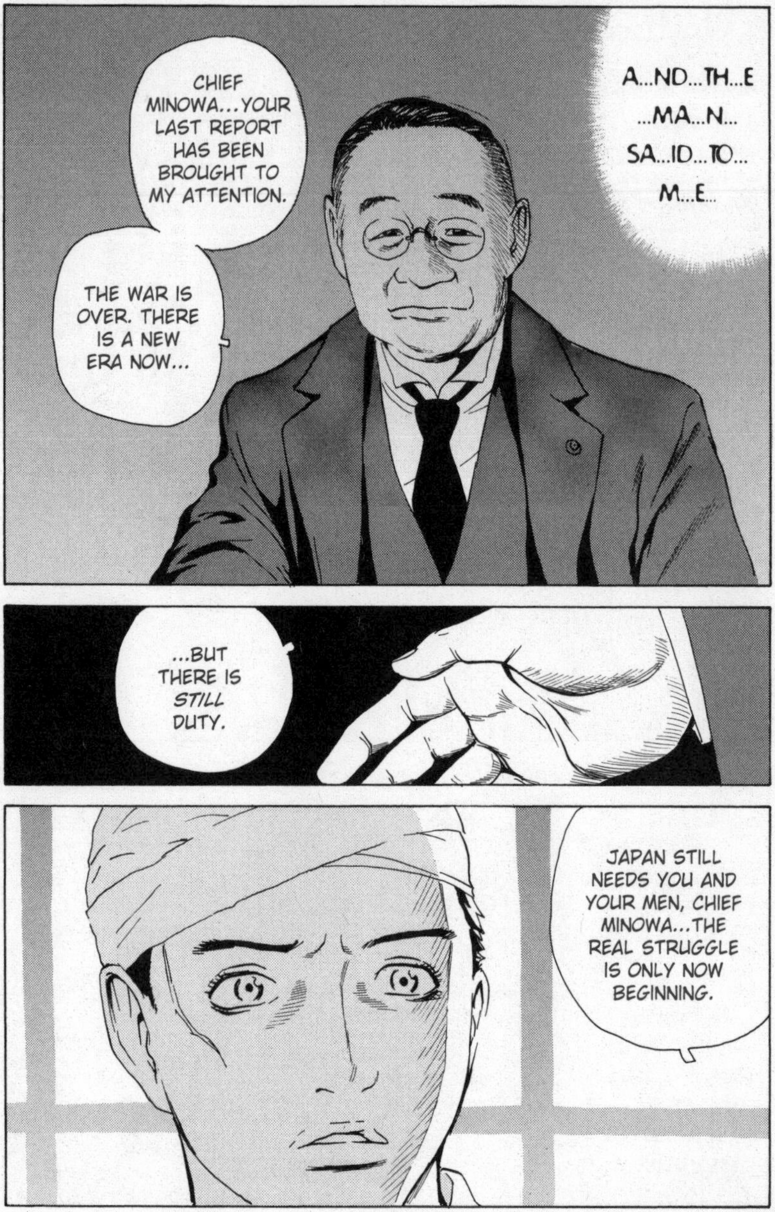
A...ND...TH...E ...MA...N... SA...ID...TO... M...E...
CHIEF MINOWA...YOUR LAST REPORT HAS BEEN BROUGHT TO MY ATTENTION.
THE WAR IS OVER. THERE IS A NEW ERA NOW...
...BUT THERE IS *STILL* DUTY.
JAPAN STILL NEEDS YOU AND YOUR MEN, CHIEF MINOWA...THE REAL STRUGGLE IS ONLY NOW BEGINNING.

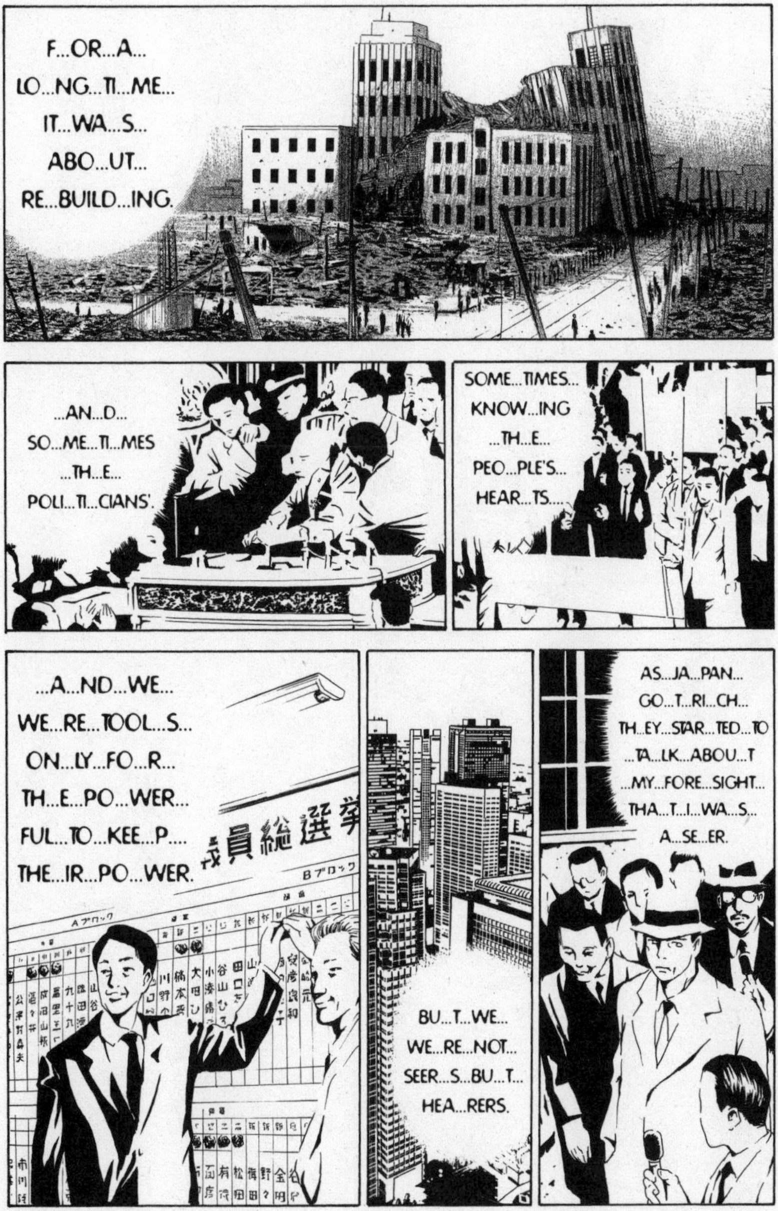
F...OR...A...
LO...NG...TI...ME...
IT...WA...S...
ABO...UT...
RE...BUILD...ING.
SOME...TIMES...
KNOW...ING
...TH...E...
PEO...PLE'S...
HEAR...TS....
...AN...D...
SO...ME...TI...MES
...TH...E...
POLI...TI...CIANS'.
AS...JA...PAN...
GO...T...RI...CH...
TH...EY...STAR...TED...TO
...TA...LK...ABOU...T
...MY...FORE...SIGHT...
THA...T...I...WA...S...
A...SE...ER.
BU...T...WE...
WE...RE...NOT...
SEER...S...BU...T...
HEA...RERS.
...A...ND...WE...
WE...RE...TOOL...S...
ON...LY...FO...R...
TH...E...PO...WER...
FUL...TO...KEE...P....
THE...IR...PO...WER.

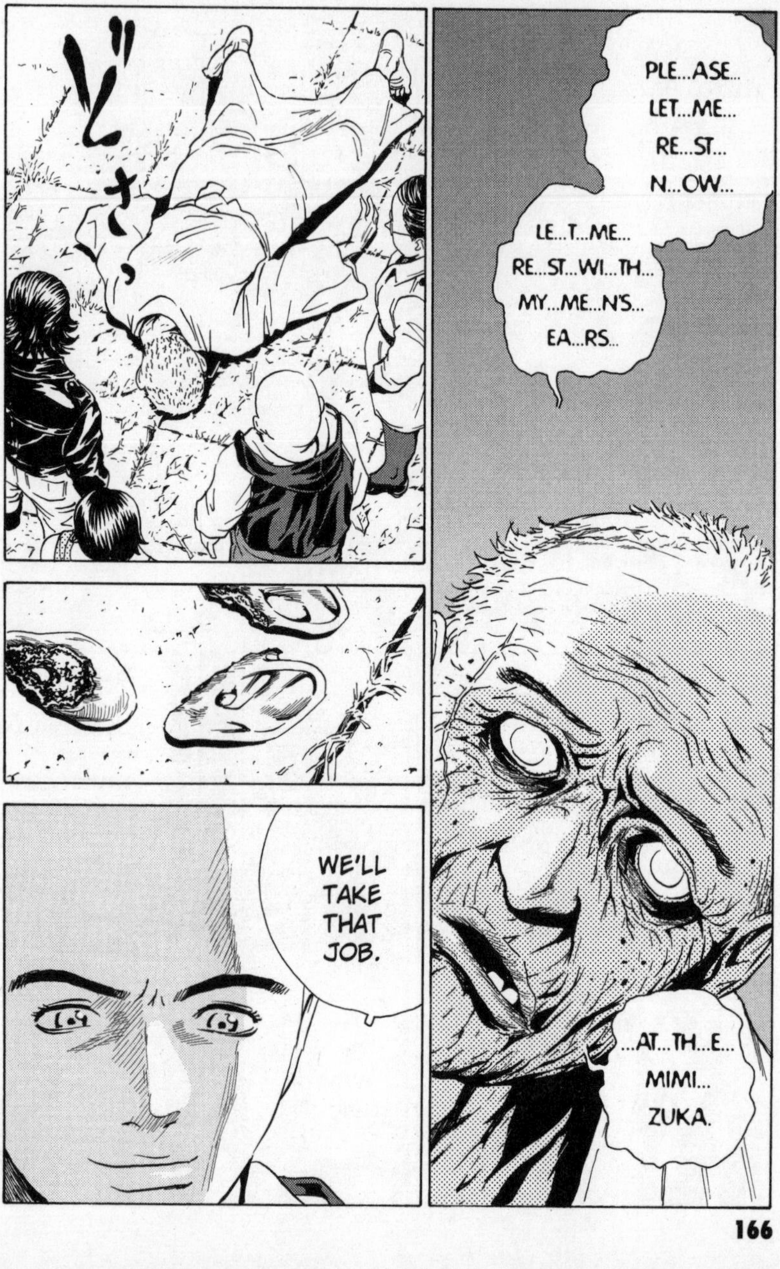
PLE...ASE... LET...ME... RE...ST... N...OW...
LE...T...ME... RE...ST...WI...TH... MY...ME...N'S... EA...RS...
...AT...TH...E... MIMI... ZUKA.
どさっ
WE'LL TAKE THAT JOB.

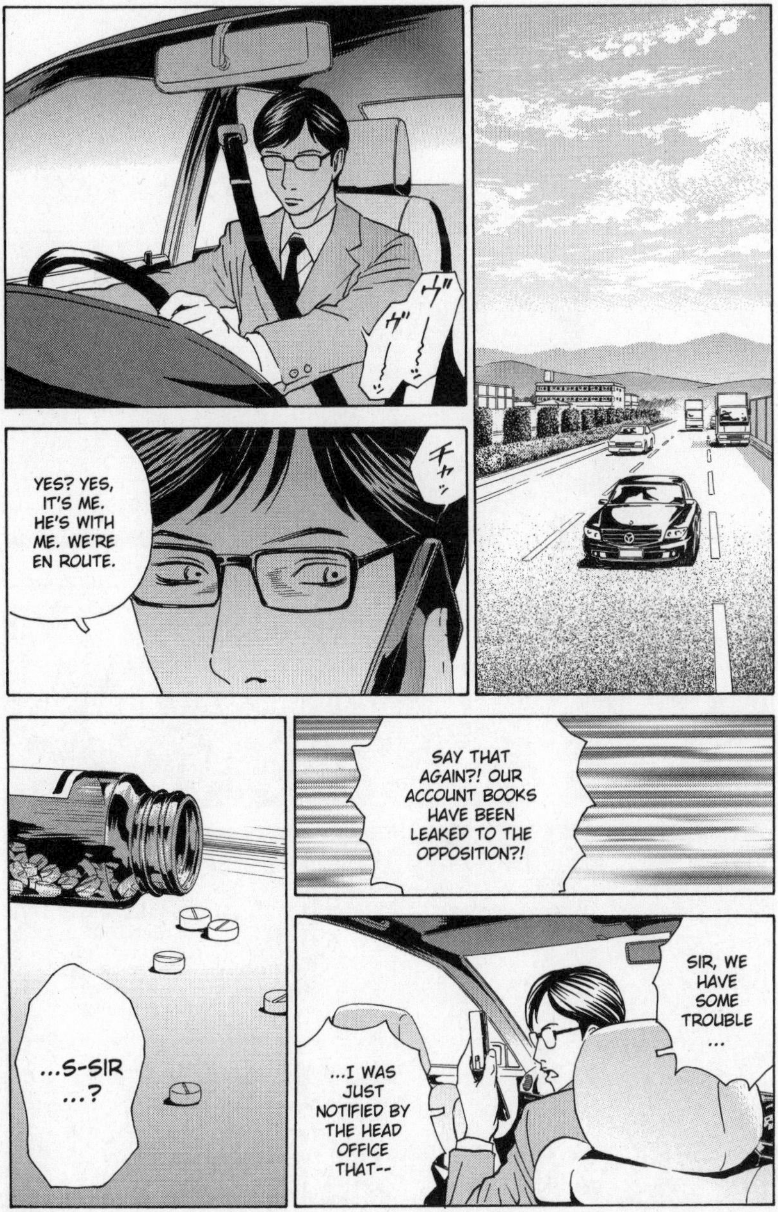
ヴヴ
チャッ
YES? YES, IT'S ME. HE'S WITH ME. WE'RE EN ROUTE.
SAY THAT AGAIN?! OUR ACCOUNT BOOKS HAVE BEEN LEAKED TO THE OPPOSITION?!
SIR, WE HAVE SOME TROUBLE ...
...I WAS JUST NOTIFIED BY THE HEAD OFFICE THAT--
...S-SIR ...?

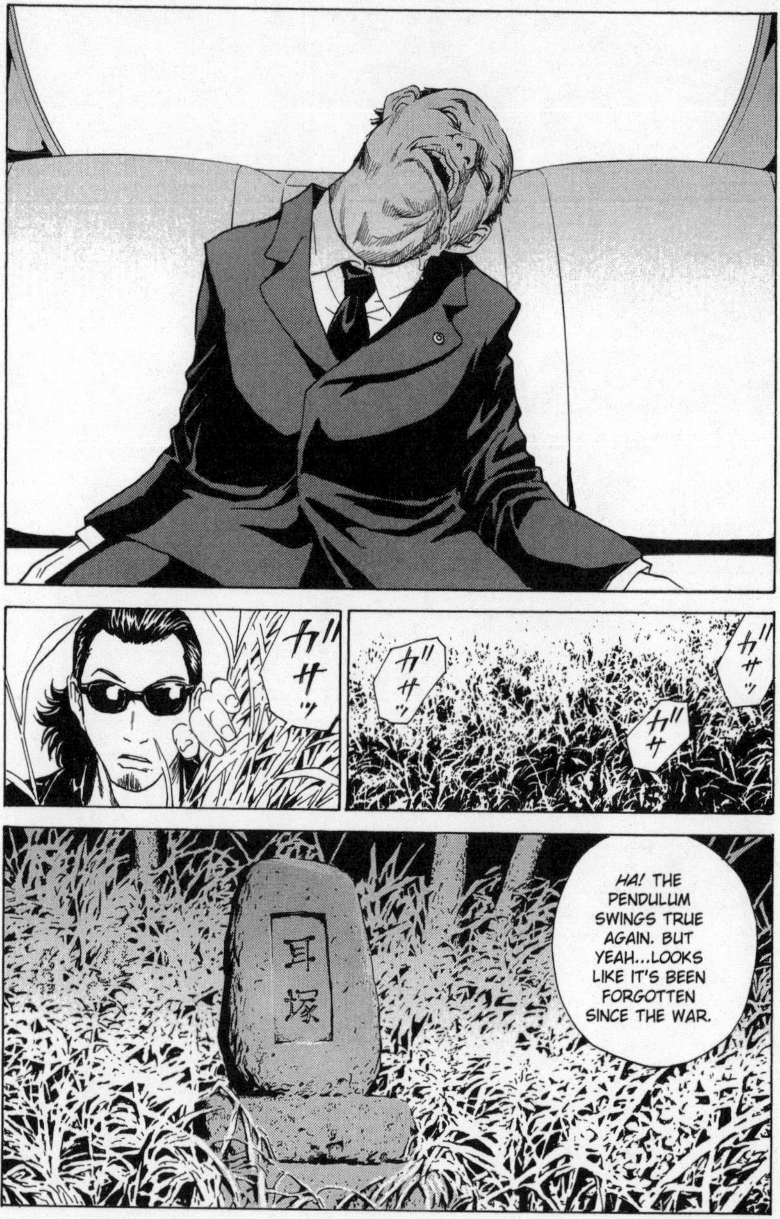
ガサッ
ガサッ
ガサ
ガサッ
HA! THE PENDULUM SWINGS TRUE AGAIN. BUT YEAH...LOOKS LIKE IT'S BEEN FORGOTTEN SINCE THE WAR.

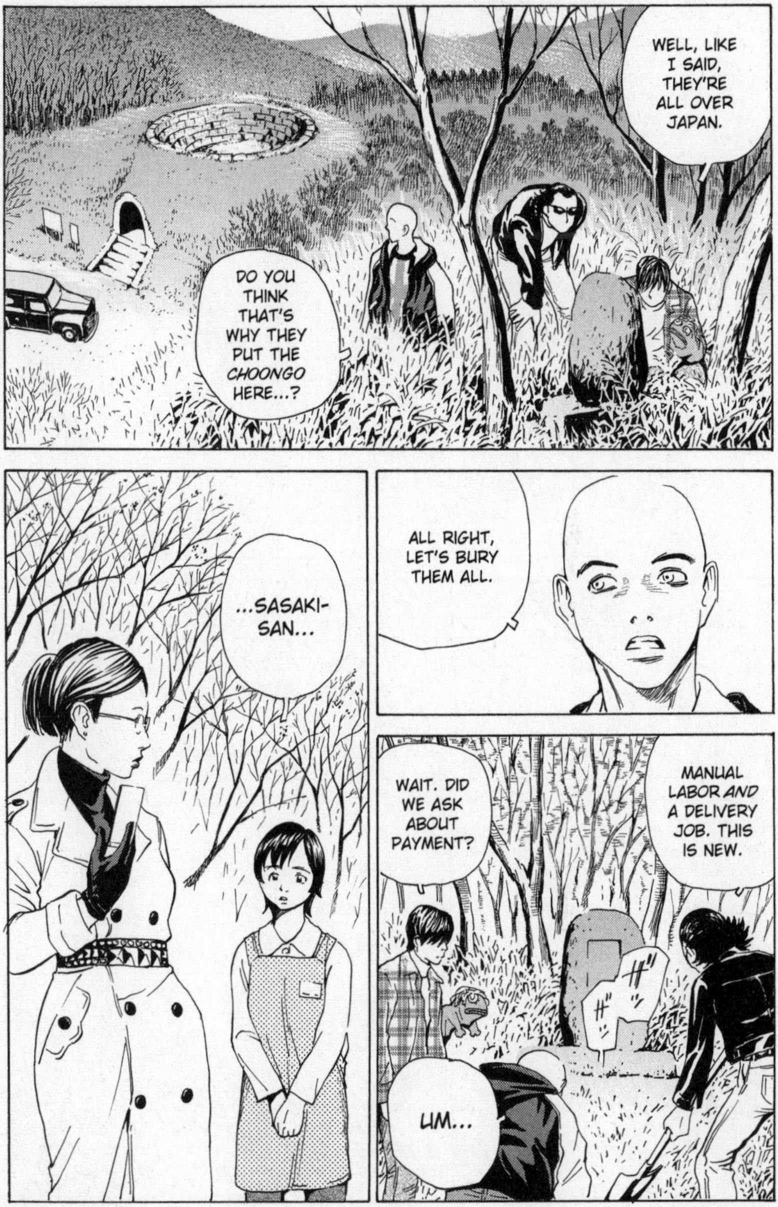
WELL, LIKE I SAID, THEY'RE ALL OVER JAPAN.
DO YOU THINK THAT'S WHY THEY PUT THE *CHOONGO* HERE...?
ALL RIGHT, LET'S BURY THEM ALL.
MANUAL LABOR *AND* A DELIVERY JOB. THIS IS NEW.
WAIT. DID WE ASK ABOUT PAYMENT?
UM...
...SASAKI-SAN...

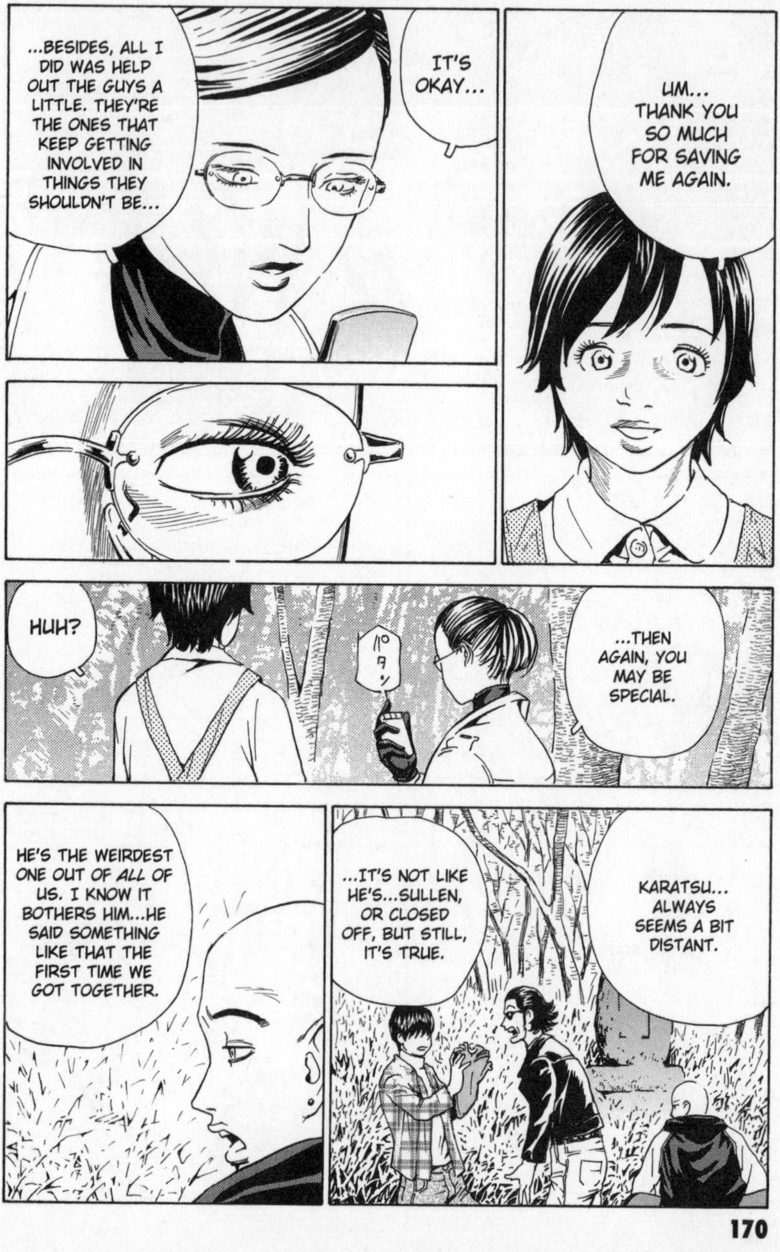
UM... THANK YOU SO MUCH FOR SAVING ME AGAIN.
IT'S OKAY...
...BESIDES, ALL I DID WAS HELP OUT THE GUYS A LITTLE. THEY'RE THE ONES THAT KEEP GETTING INVOLVED IN THINGS THEY SHOULDN'T BE...
...THEN AGAIN, YOU MAY BE SPECIAL.
パタン
HUH?
KARATSU... ALWAYS SEEMS A BIT DISTANT.
...IT'S NOT LIKE HE'S...SULLEN, OR CLOSED OFF, BUT STILL, IT'S TRUE.
HE'S THE WEIRDEST ONE OUT OF *ALL* OF US. I KNOW IT BOTHERS HIM...HE SAID SOMETHING LIKE THAT THE FIRST TIME WE GOT TOGETHER.

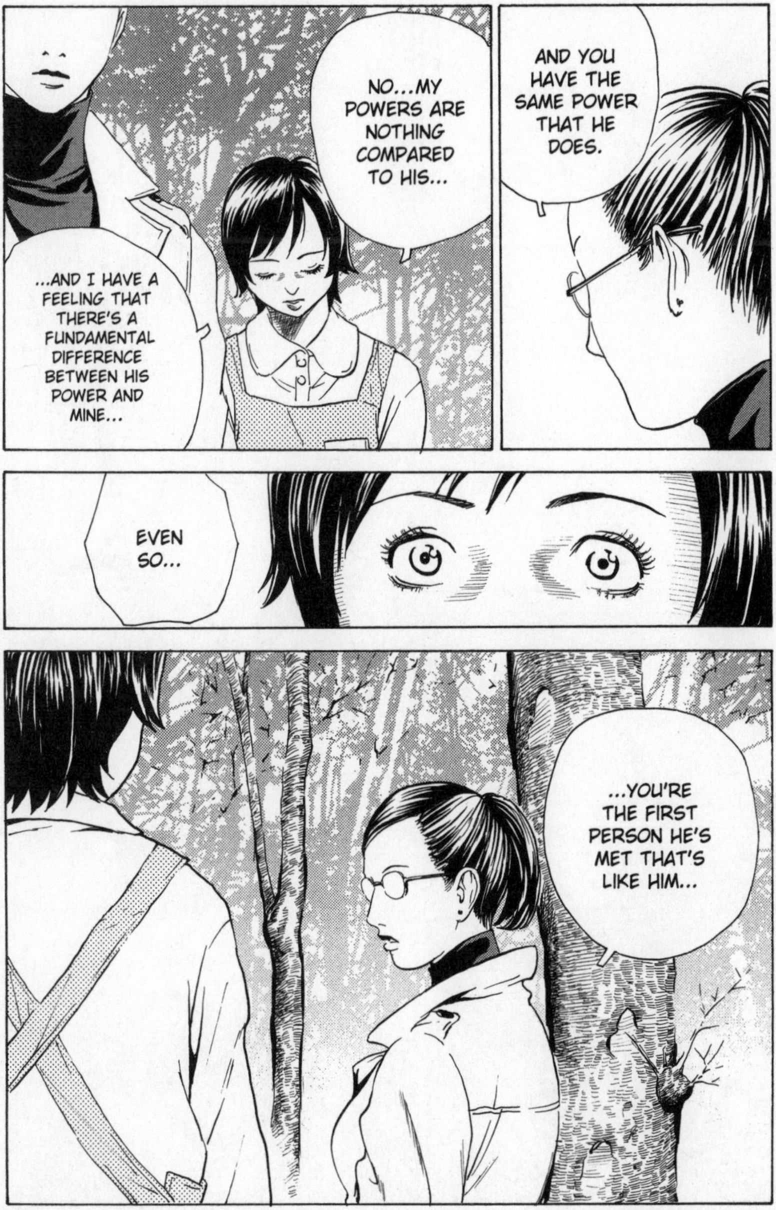
AND YOU HAVE THE SAME POWER THAT HE DOES.
NO...MY POWERS ARE NOTHING COMPARED TO HIS...
...AND I HAVE A FEELING THAT THERE'S A FUNDAMENTAL DIFFERENCE BETWEEN HIS POWER AND MINE...
EVEN SO...
...YOU'RE THE FIRST PERSON HE'S MET THAT'S LIKE HIM...

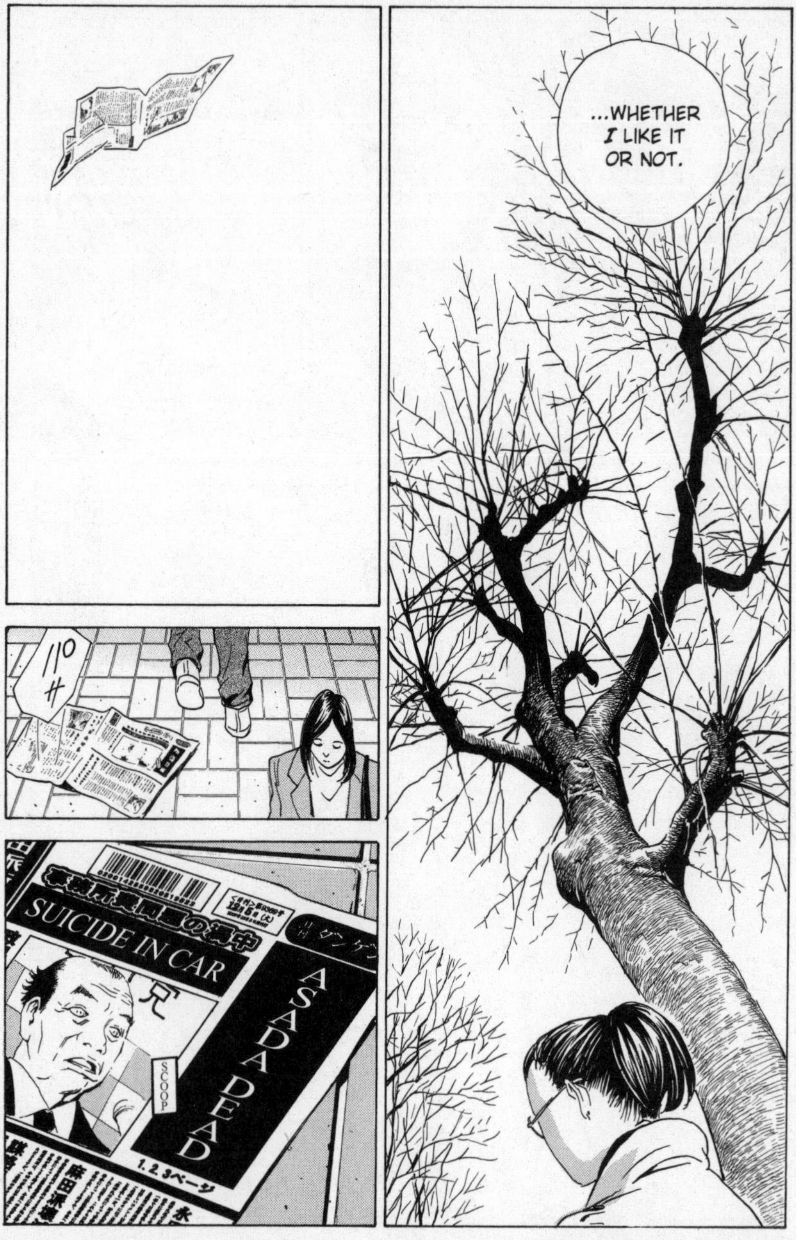
...WHETHER I LIKE IT OR NOT.
パサ
SUICIDE IN CAR
ASADA DEAD
SCOOP
1.2.3ページ

7th delivery: what lies after the dream—the end

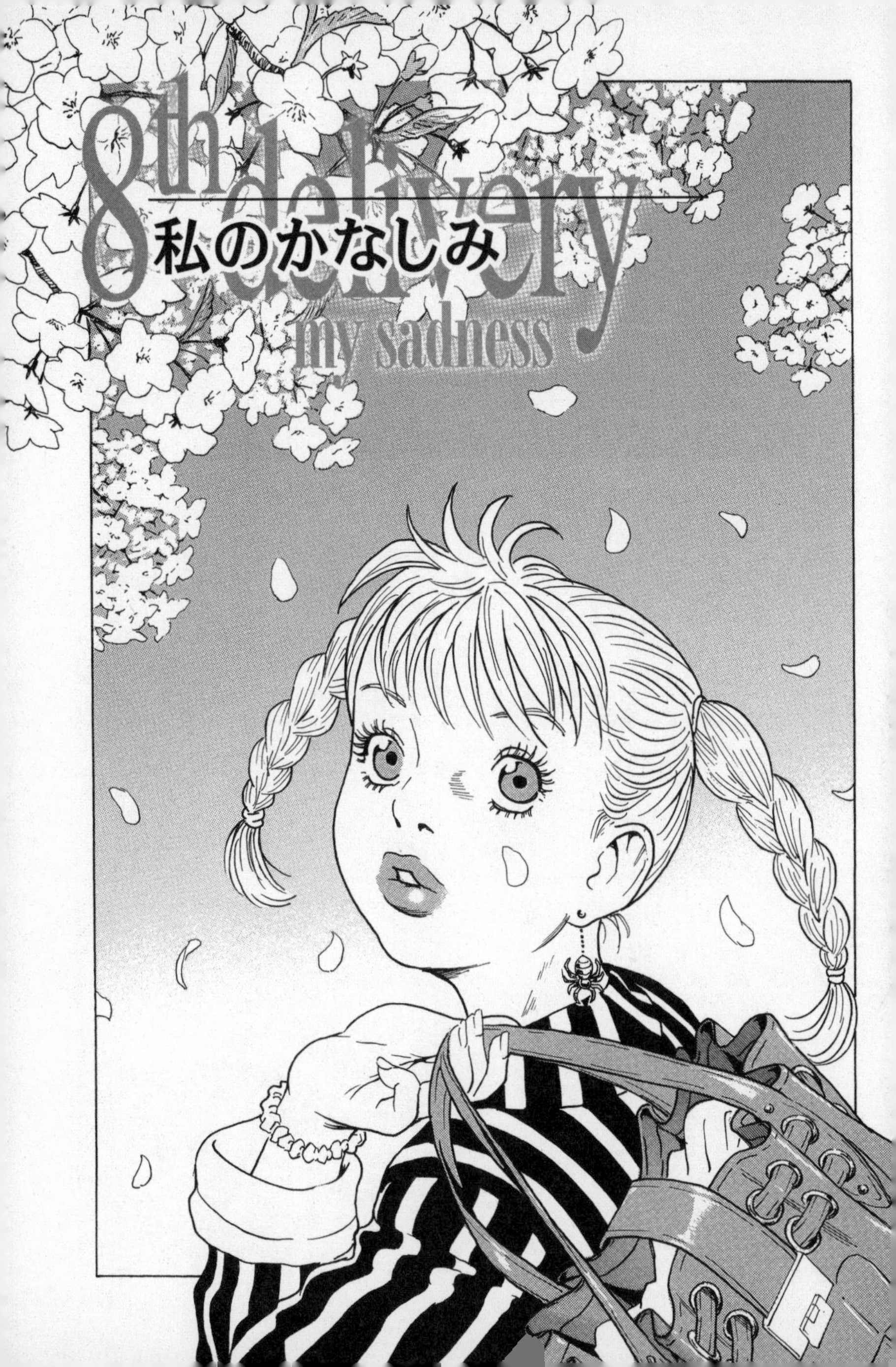
8th delivery
私のかなしみ
my sadness

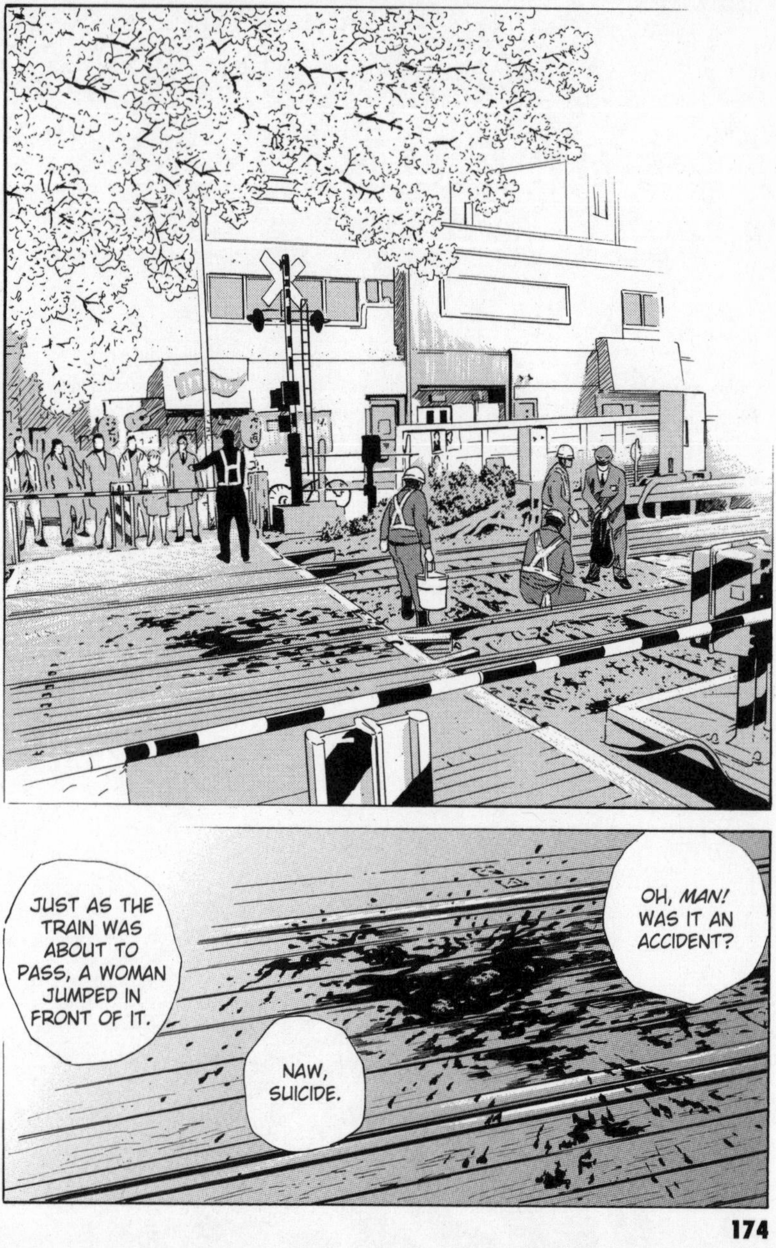
OH, *MAN!* WAS IT AN ACCIDENT?
NAW, SUICIDE.
JUST AS THE TRAIN WAS ABOUT TO PASS, A WOMAN JUMPED IN FRONT OF IT.

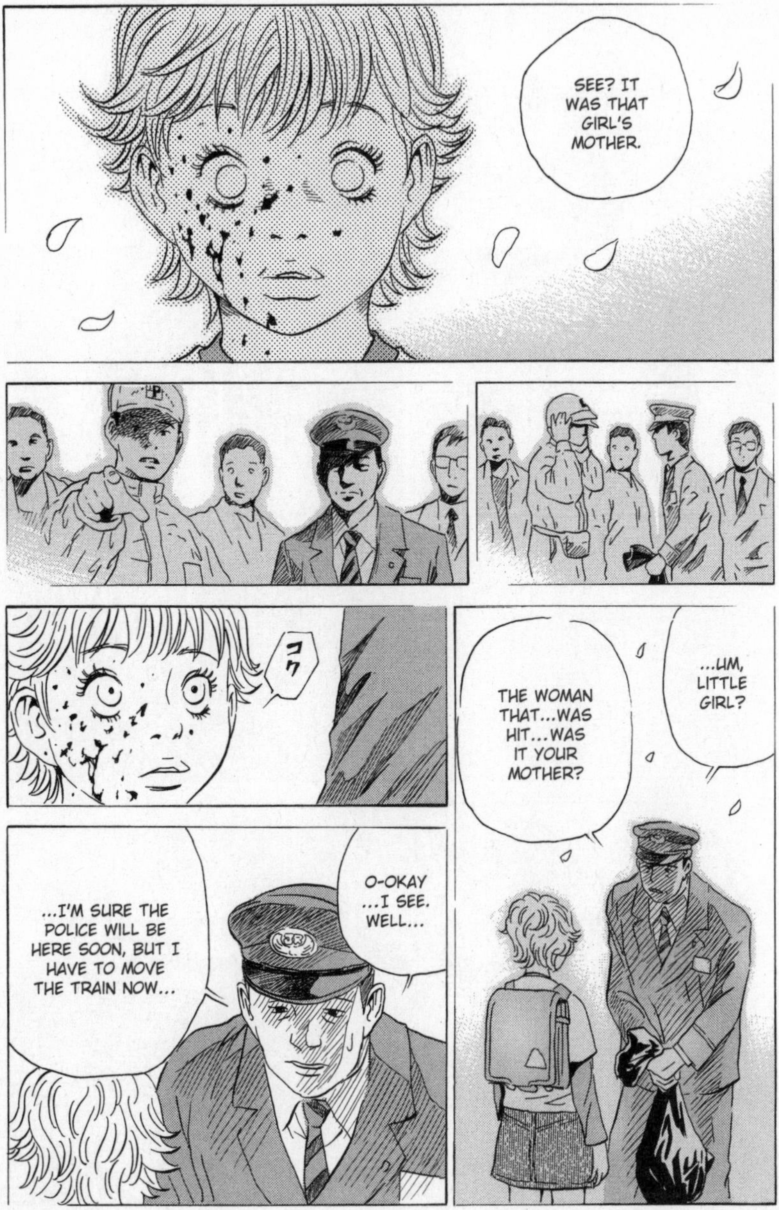
SEE? IT WAS THAT GIRL'S MOTHER.
...UM, LITTLE GIRL?
THE WOMAN THAT...WAS HIT...WAS IT YOUR MOTHER?
コク
O-OKAY ...I SEE. WELL...
...I'M SURE THE POLICE WILL BE HERE SOON, BUT I HAVE TO MOVE THE TRAIN NOW...

...huh?

WHEN THEY COME...WILL YOU PLEASE GIVE THEM THIS? IT'S FROM YOUR MOTHER...

MY *mother?* B-BUT...

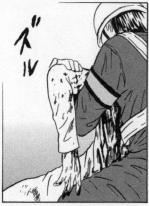

ズ
ル

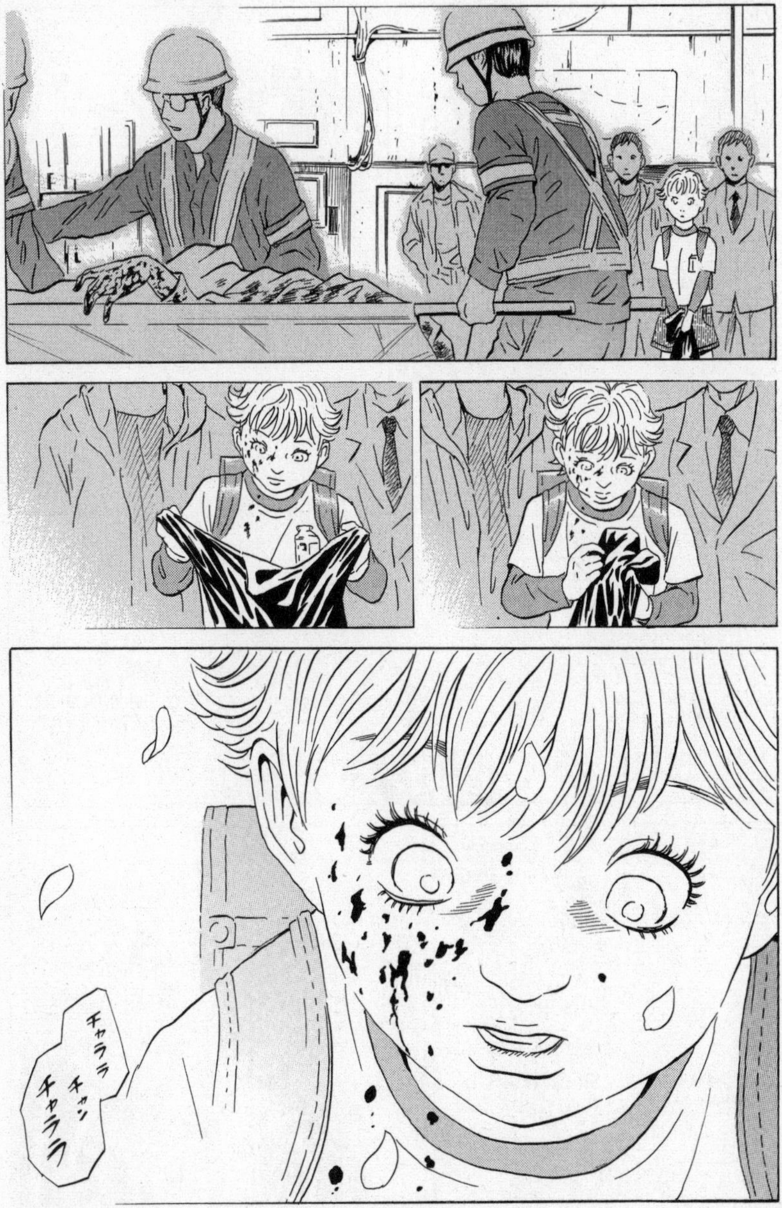
チャララ
チャン
チャララ

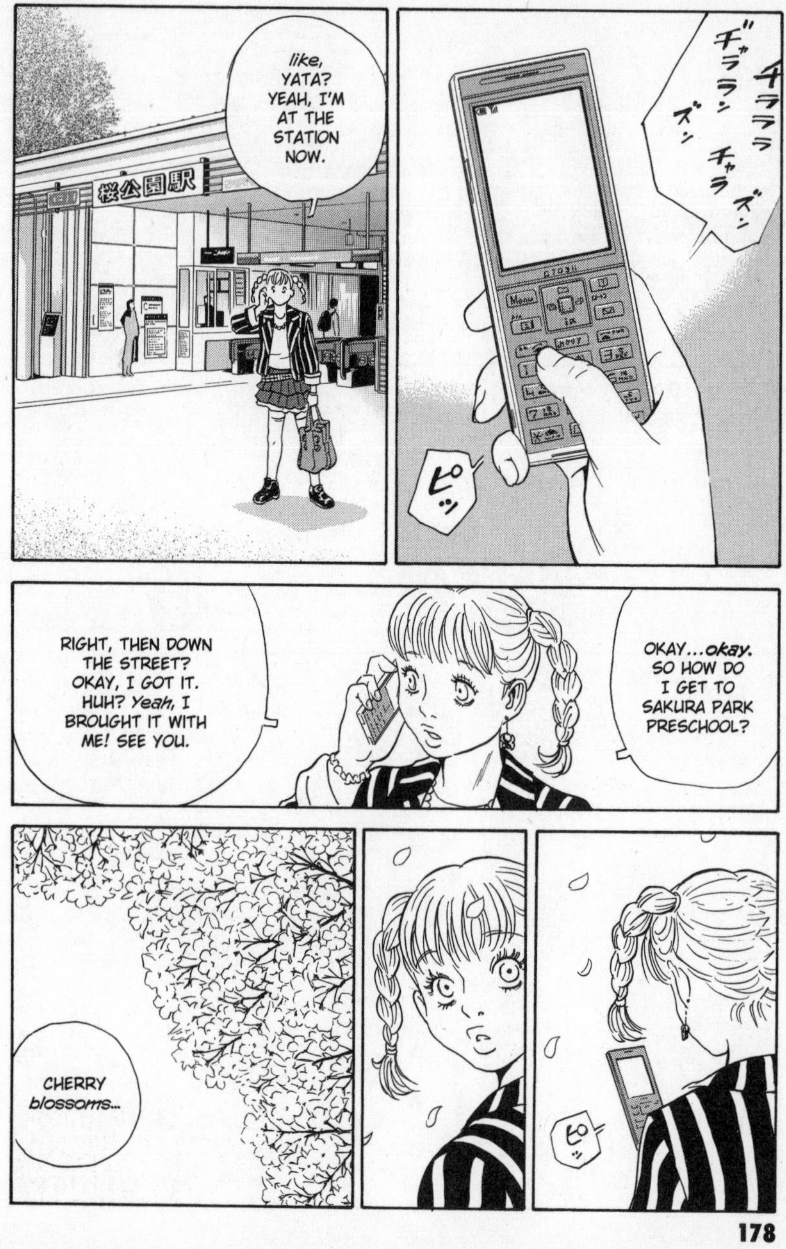
チラララ チャラ ズン ヂャララン ズン
ピッ
like, YATA? YEAH, I'M AT THE STATION NOW.
OKAY...*okay.* SO HOW DO I GET TO SAKURA PARK PRESCHOOL?
RIGHT, THEN DOWN THE STREET? OKAY, I GOT IT. HUH? *Yeah,* I BROUGHT IT WITH ME! SEE YOU.
ピッ
CHERRY *blossoms...*

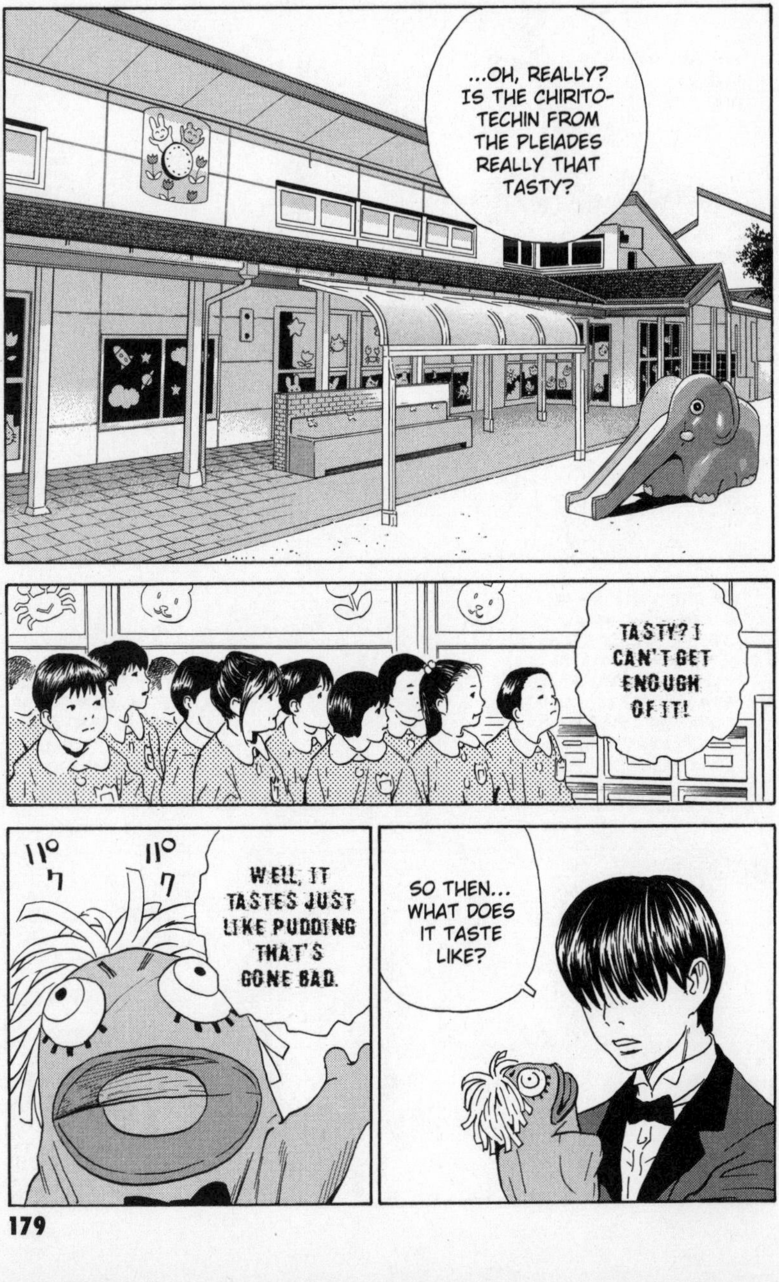
...OH, REALLY? IS THE CHIRITO-TECHIN FROM THE PLEIADES REALLY THAT TASTY?
TASTY? I CAN'T GET ENOUGH OF IT!
SO THEN... WHAT DOES IT TASTE LIKE?
WELL, IT TASTES JUST LIKE PUDDING THAT'S GONE BAD.
パク パク

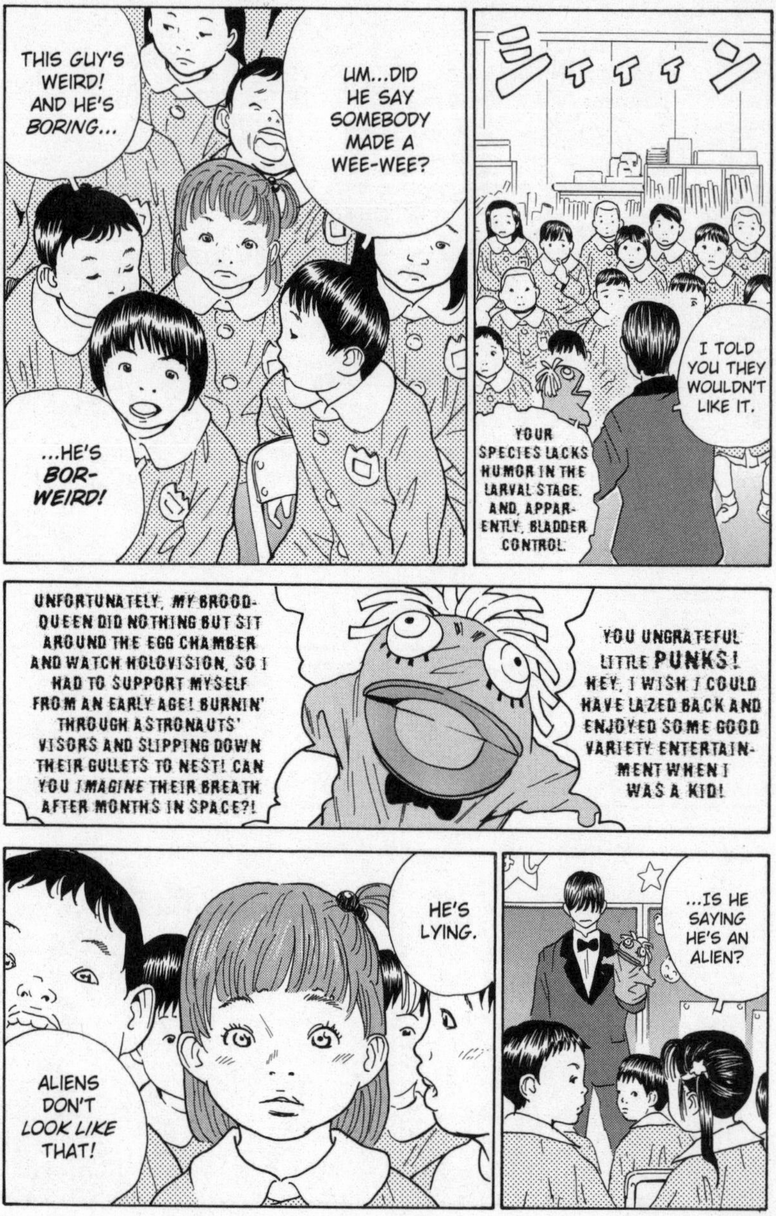
シィィィン
I TOLD YOU THEY WOULDN'T LIKE IT.
YOUR SPECIES LACKS HUMOR IN THE LARVAL STAGE. AND, APPARENTLY, BLADDER CONTROL.
UM...DID HE SAY SOMEBODY MADE A WEE-WEE?
THIS GUY'S WEIRD! AND HE'S *BORING*...
...HE'S *BOR-WEIRD!*
YOU UNGRATEFUL LITTLE **PUNKS!** HEY, I WISH *I* COULD HAVE LAZED BACK AND ENJOYED SOME GOOD VARIETY ENTERTAINMENT WHEN I WAS A KID!
UNFORTUNATELY, *MY* BROOD-QUEEN DID NOTHING BUT SIT AROUND THE EGG CHAMBER AND WATCH HOLOVISION, SO I HAD TO SUPPORT MYSELF FROM AN EARLY AGE! BURNIN' THROUGH ASTRONAUTS' VISORS AND SLIPPING DOWN THEIR GULLETS TO NEST! CAN YOU *IMAGINE* THEIR BREATH AFTER MONTHS IN SPACE?!
...IS HE SAYING HE'S AN ALIEN?
HE'S LYING.
ALIENS DON'T *LOOK LIKE* THAT!

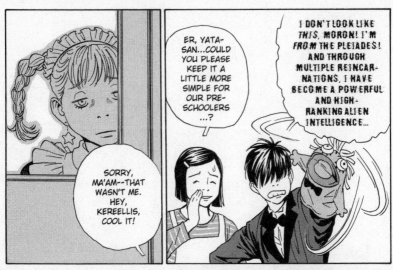

I DON'T LOOK LIKE *THIS*, MORON! I'M *FROM* THE PLEIADES! AND THROUGH MULTIPLE REINCARNATIONS, I HAVE BECOME A POWERFUL AND HIGH-RANKING ALIEN INTELLIGENCE...
ER, YATA-SAN...COULD YOU PLEASE KEEP IT A LITTLE MORE SIMPLE FOR OUR PRESCHOOLERS ...?
SORRY, MA'AM--THAT WASN'T ME. HEY, KEREELLIS, COOL IT!
YOU'RE AN ALIEN?
YOU'RE A POOPIE ALIEN!
YATA-SAN...
I SMELL POOPIE!
GEEZ, I *knew* YATA COULDN'T HANDLE THIS ON HIS OWN...
ガラッ
Okay...
Downcast heart, prickly heart...
I'll raise and round out any heart!

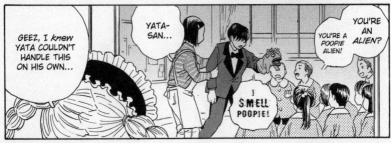

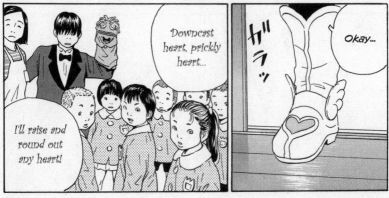

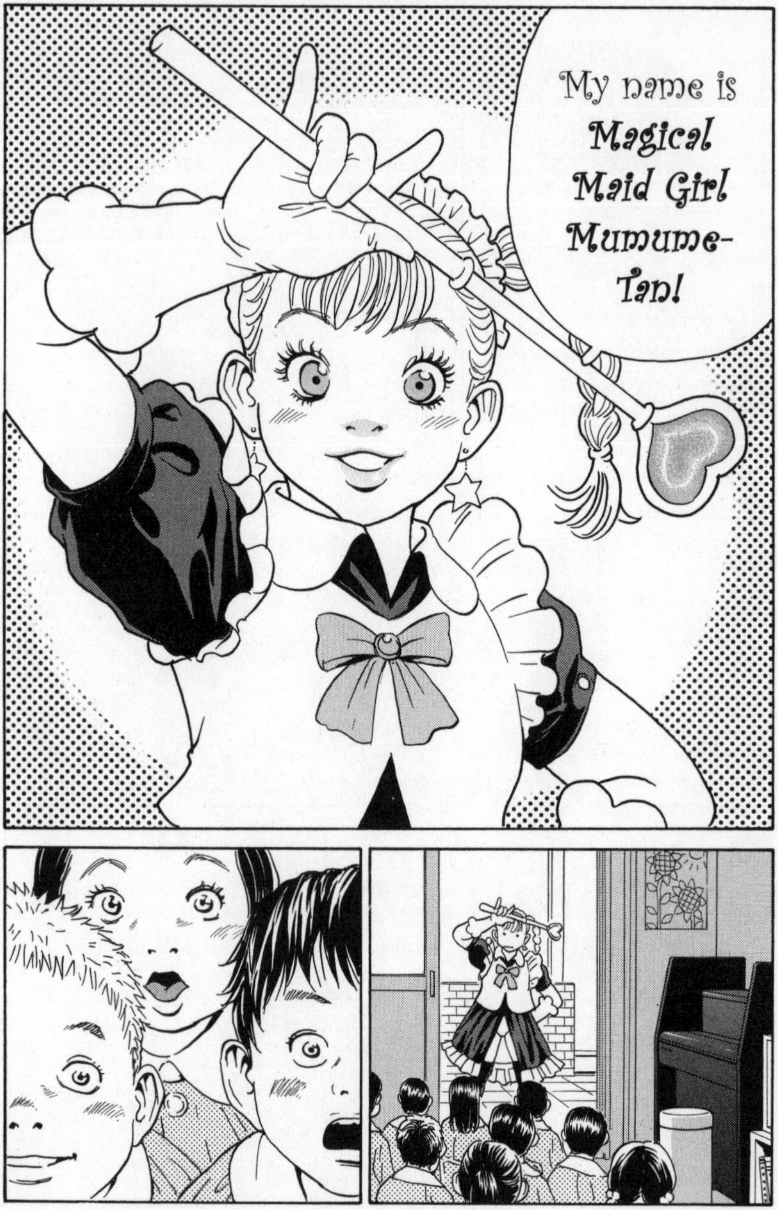
My name is Magical Maid Girl Mumume-Tan!

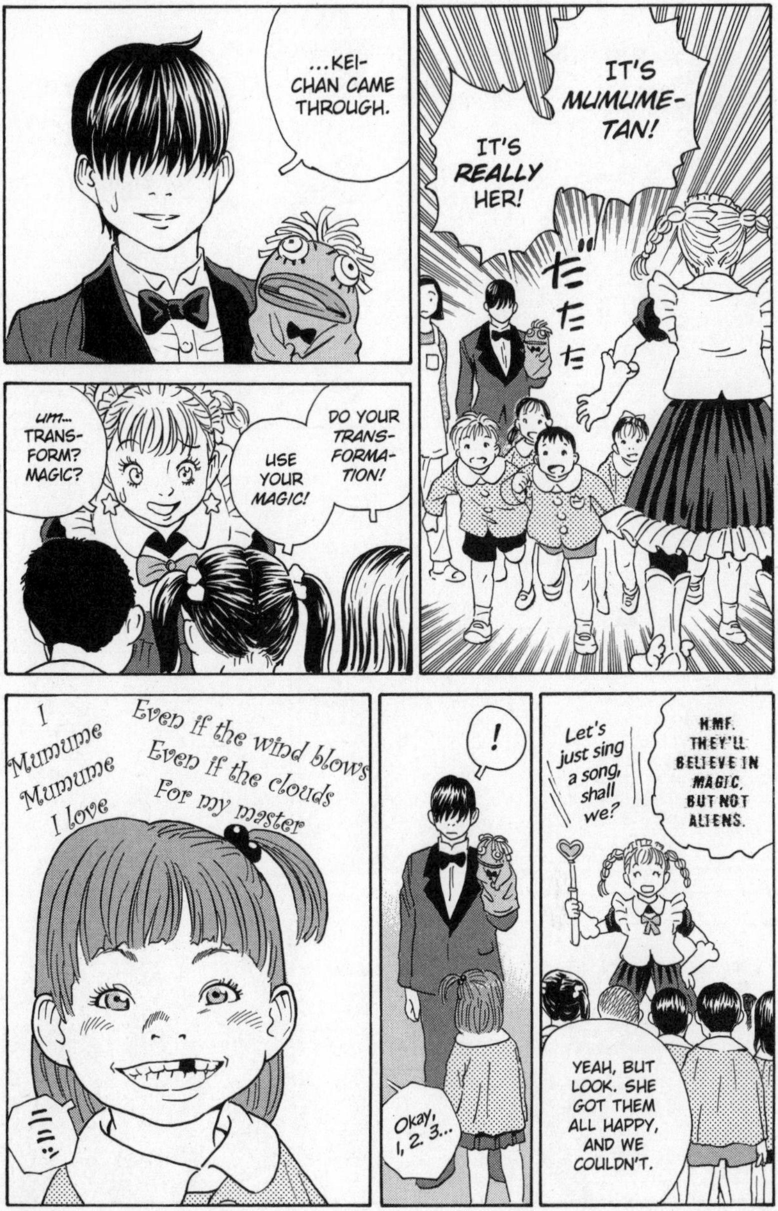
IT'S MUMUME-TAN!
IT'S REALLY HER!
だたたた
...KEI-CHAN CAME THROUGH.
DO YOUR TRANSFORMATION!
USE YOUR MAGIC!
um... TRANSFORM? MAGIC?
HMF. THEY'LL BELIEVE IN MAGIC, BUT NOT ALIENS.
Let's just sing a song, shall we?
YEAH, BUT LOOK. SHE GOT THEM ALL HAPPY, AND WE COULDN'T.
!
Okay, 1, 2. 3...
Even if the wind blows
Even if the clouds
For my master
I
Mumume
Mumume
I love

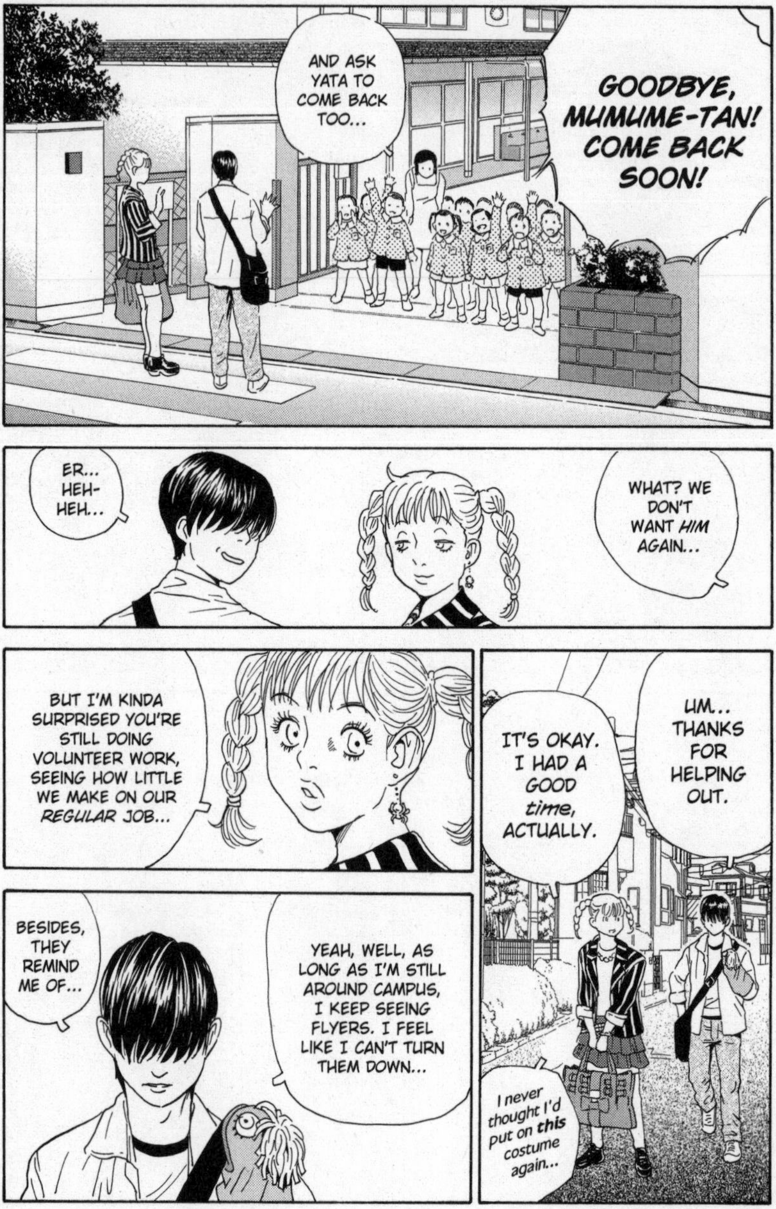
GOODBYE, MUMUME-TAN! COME BACK SOON!
AND ASK YATA TO COME BACK TOO...
WHAT? WE DON'T WANT *HIM* AGAIN...
ER... HEH-HEH...
UM... THANKS FOR HELPING OUT.
IT'S OKAY. I HAD A GOOD *time*, ACTUALLY.
I never thought I'd put on **this** costume again...
BUT I'M KINDA SURPRISED YOU'RE STILL DOING VOLUNTEER WORK, SEEING HOW LITTLE WE MAKE ON OUR *REGULAR* JOB...
YEAH, WELL, AS LONG AS I'M STILL AROUND CAMPUS, I KEEP SEEING FLYERS. I FEEL LIKE I CAN'T TURN THEM DOWN...
BESIDES, THEY REMIND ME OF...

MY HOST BODY HERE HAD A FEMALE KIN-PAIR WITH WHOM HE SHARED 50% OF HIS GENETIC SEQUENCE.

...

WELL... UM...

YEAH...?

SHE... WELL...

DID SHE PASS AWAY?

SISTER ...?

WHEN I WAS IN THE SIXTH GRADE, MY PARENTS SUDDENLY SAID WE WERE ALL GOING ON A FAMILY VACATION. IT WAS A LONG ROAD TRIP, AND MY SISTER AND I GOT BORED. WE FELL ASLEEP IN THE BACK.

WHEN I WOKE UP, THE CAR HAD STOPPED IN A DEEP WOOD...BUT EVERYONE ELSE WAS ASLEEP NOW.

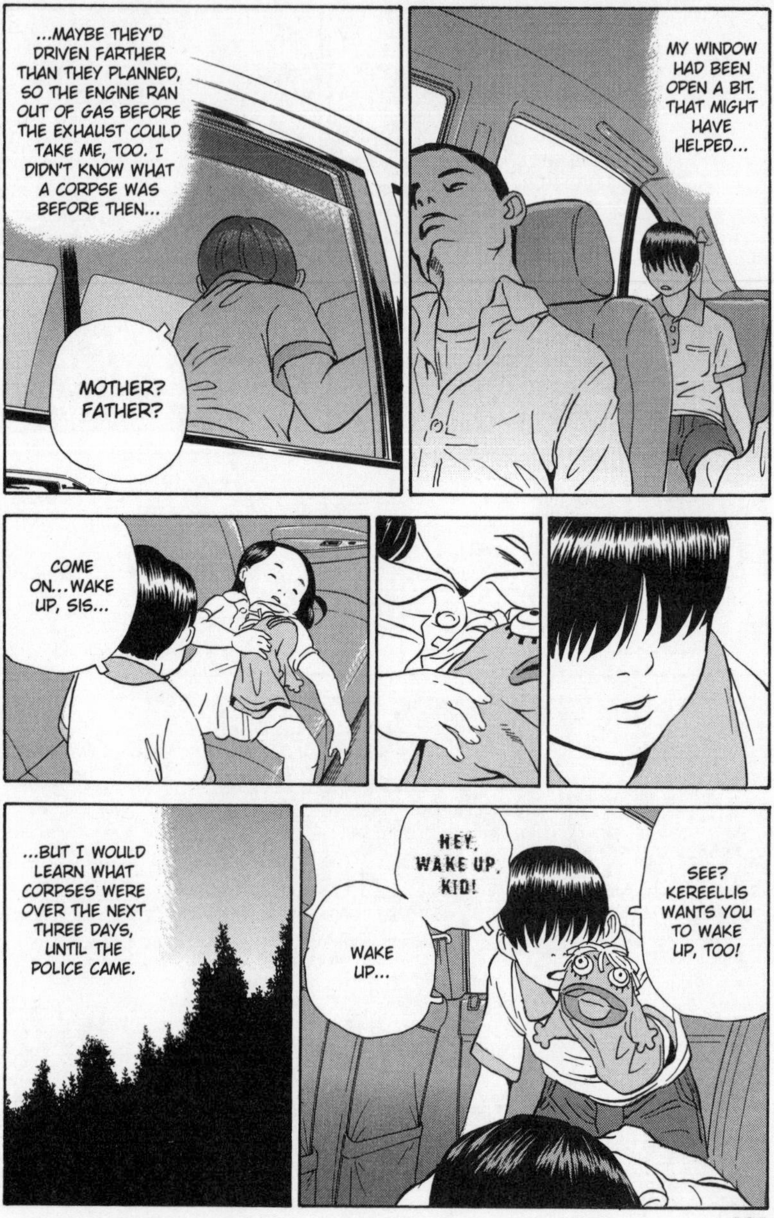
MY WINDOW HAD BEEN OPEN A BIT. THAT MIGHT HAVE HELPED...
...MAYBE THEY'D DRIVEN FARTHER THAN THEY PLANNED, SO THE ENGINE RAN OUT OF GAS BEFORE THE EXHAUST COULD TAKE ME, TOO. I DIDN'T KNOW WHAT A CORPSE WAS BEFORE THEN...
MOTHER? FATHER?
COME ON...WAKE UP, SIS...
SEE? KEREELLIS WANTS YOU TO WAKE UP, TOO!
HEY, WAKE UP, KID!
WAKE UP...
...BUT I WOULD LEARN WHAT CORPSES WERE OVER THE NEXT THREE DAYS, UNTIL THE POLICE CAME.

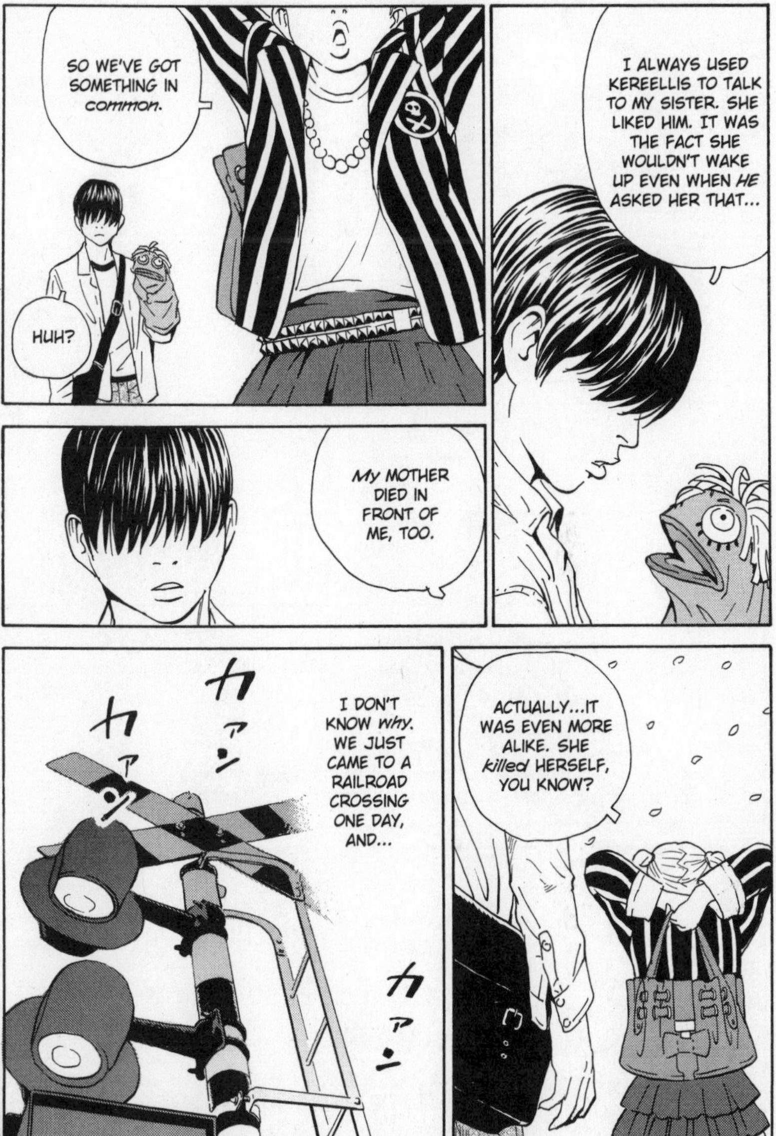

I ALWAYS USED KEREELLIS TO TALK TO MY SISTER. SHE LIKED HIM. IT WAS THE FACT SHE WOULDN'T WAKE UP EVEN WHEN *HE* ASKED HER THAT...
SO WE'VE GOT SOMETHING IN *common*.
HUH?
My MOTHER DIED IN FRONT OF ME, TOO.
ACTUALLY...IT WAS EVEN MORE ALIKE. SHE *killed* HERSELF, YOU KNOW?
カァン
カァン
I DON'T KNOW *why*. WE JUST CAME TO A RAILROAD CROSSING ONE DAY, AND...
カァン

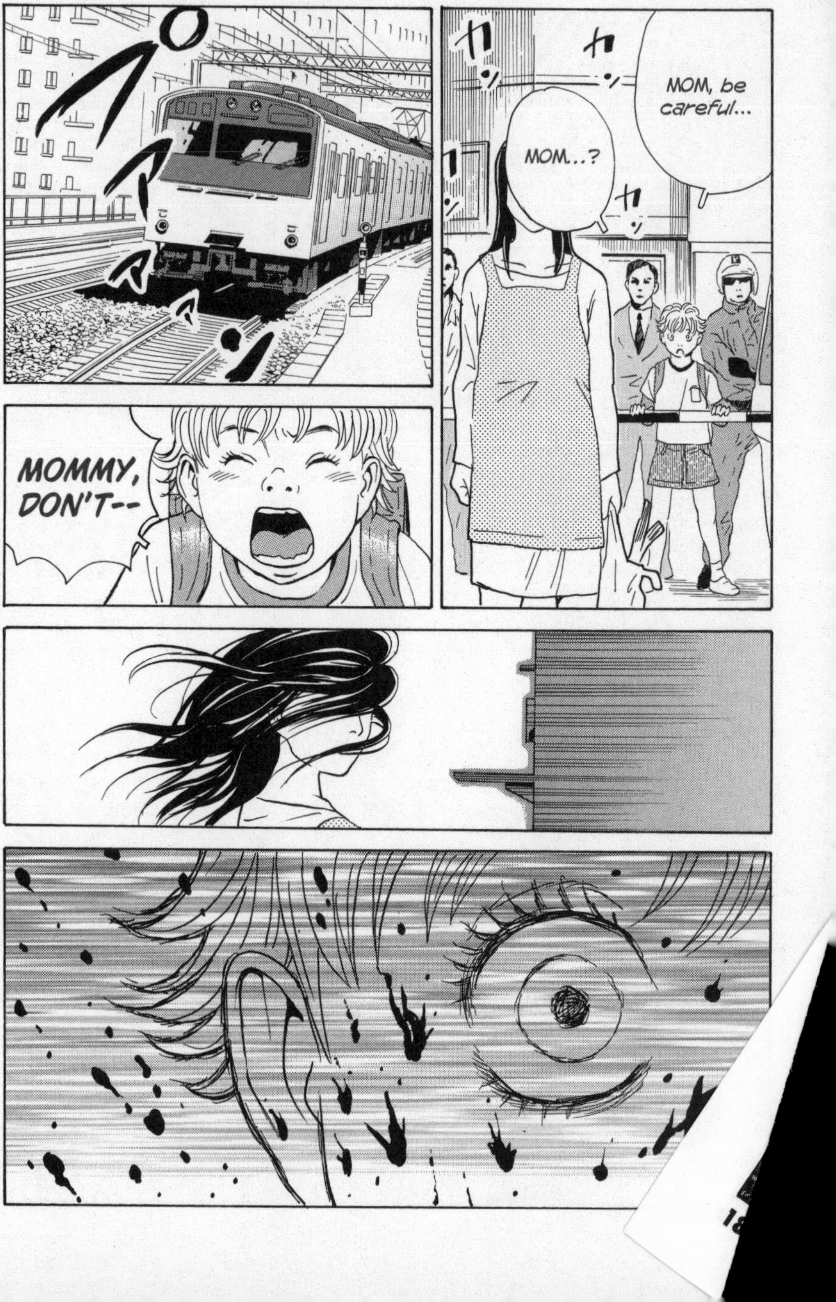
カッ
カッ
MOM, be careful...
MOM...?
カッ
カッ
MOMMY, DON'T--

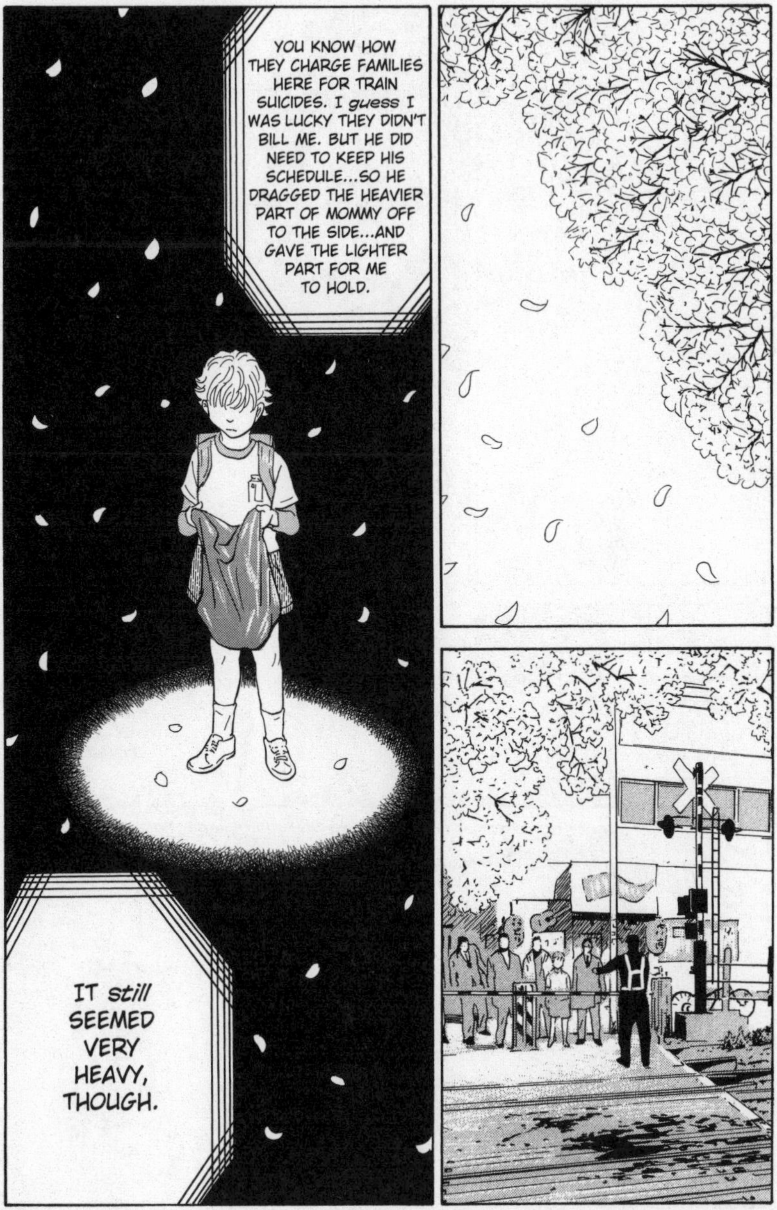
YOU KNOW HOW THEY CHARGE FAMILIES HERE FOR TRAIN SUICIDES. I *guess* I WAS LUCKY THEY DIDN'T BILL ME. BUT HE DID NEED TO KEEP HIS SCHEDULE...SO HE DRAGGED THE HEAVIER PART OF MOMMY OFF TO THE SIDE...AND GAVE THE LIGHTER PART FOR ME TO HOLD.
IT *still* SEEMED VERY HEAVY, THOUGH.

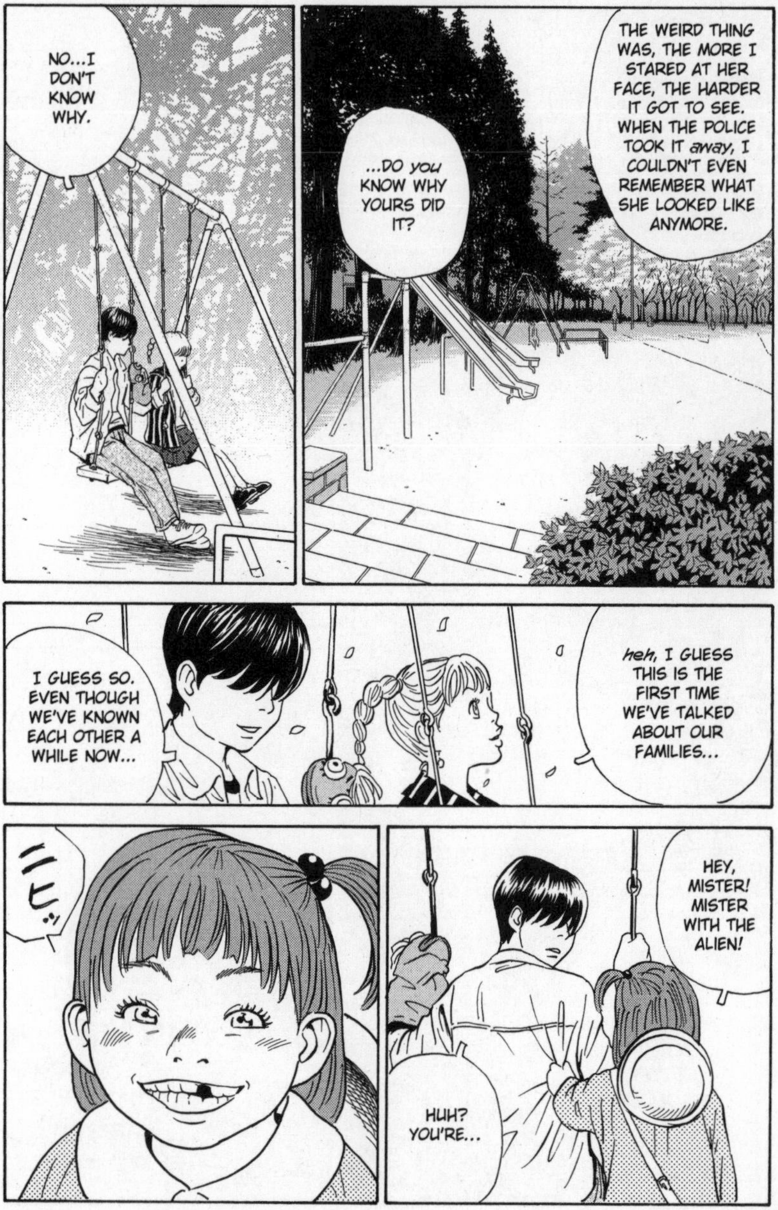
THE WEIRD THING WAS, THE MORE I STARED AT HER FACE, THE HARDER IT GOT TO SEE. WHEN THE POLICE TOOK IT *away*, I COULDN'T EVEN REMEMBER WHAT SHE LOOKED LIKE ANYMORE.
...DO *you* KNOW WHY YOURS DID IT?
NO...I DON'T KNOW WHY.
heh, I GUESS THIS IS THE FIRST TIME WE'VE TALKED ABOUT OUR FAMILIES...
I GUESS SO. EVEN THOUGH WE'VE KNOWN EACH OTHER A WHILE NOW...
HEY, MISTER! MISTER WITH THE ALIEN!
HUH? YOU'RE...
ニヒッ

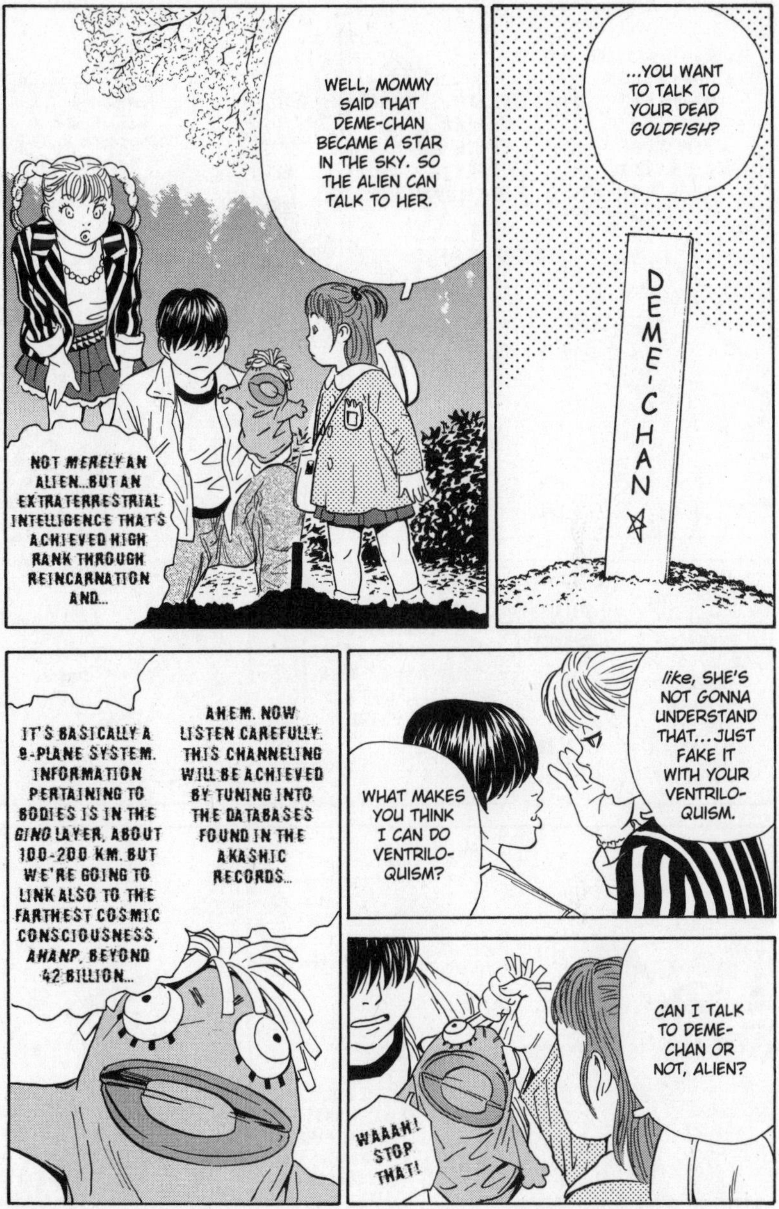
...YOU WANT TO TALK TO YOUR DEAD *GOLDFISH?*
DEME-CHAN ☆
WELL, MOMMY SAID THAT DEME-CHAN BECAME A STAR IN THE SKY. SO THE ALIEN CAN TALK TO HER.
NOT *MERELY* AN ALIEN...BUT AN EXTRATERRESTRIAL INTELLIGENCE THAT'S ACHIEVED HIGH RANK THROUGH REINCARNATION AND...
like, SHE'S NOT GONNA UNDERSTAND THAT... JUST FAKE IT WITH YOUR VENTRILOQUISM.
WHAT MAKES YOU THINK I CAN DO VENTRILOQUISM?
CAN I TALK TO DEME-CHAN OR NOT, ALIEN?
WAAAH! STOP THAT!
AHEM. NOW LISTEN CAREFULLY. THIS CHANNELING WILL BE ACHIEVED BY TUNING INTO THE DATABASES FOUND IN THE AKASHIC RECORDS...
IT'S BASICALLY A 9-PLANE SYSTEM. INFORMATION PERTAINING TO BODIES IS IN THE *GINO* LAYER, ABOUT 100-200 KM. BUT WE'RE GOING TO LINK ALSO TO THE FARTHEST COSMIC CONSCIOUSNESS, *AHANP*, BEYOND 42 BILLION...

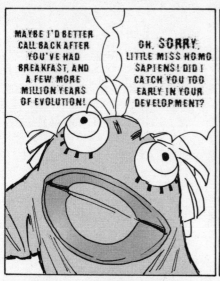

ENOUGH WITH THE NONSENSE. THE BOTTOM LINE IS YOU *can't*, RIGHT? YOU'RE USELESS.
BUT...
WHAT'S "USELESS," MUMUME-TAN?
OH, SORRY, LITTLE MISS HOMO SAPIENS! DID I CATCH YOU TOO EARLY IN YOUR DEVELOPMENT?
MAYBE I'D BETTER CALL BACK AFTER YOU'VE HAD BREAKFAST, AND A FEW MORE MILLION YEARS OF EVOLUTION!
...YOU THINK I CAN'T UNDERSTAND *this*...?
WE'LL SEE IF YOU *CAN*, OR IF YOU'RE JUST A CHIMP WITH GOOD POSTURE.
ALL RIGHT. WE'LL FORM A CIRCUIT. EVERYONE ADJUST YOUR INTERNAL FREQUENCY TO THE LOCAL LAYER...
ARE WE GONNA CALL UP THE D.J. AND MAKE *requests?*
UM, IT'S KIND OF HARD TO EXPRESS IN EARTH LANGUAGE...
ALL RIGHT, ALL RIGHT! I MEAN, *HOLD HANDS*, STUPID!
fine, I'LL DO IT...

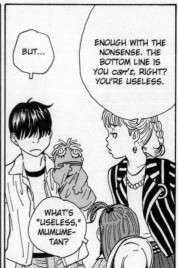

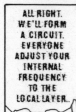

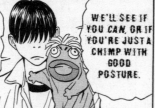

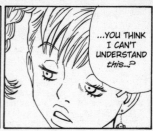

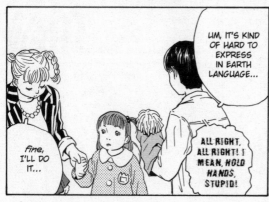

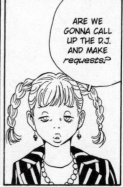

ホッ
ホッ
ホッ
OKAY... CONCENTRATE BUT DON'T THINK...FEEL THE WAVES...
Who are you— Bruce Lee?
MINDFULNESS, MAKINO! YOU TOO, LITTLE GIRL!
OKAY.
YEAH, yeah...
ざーさあ

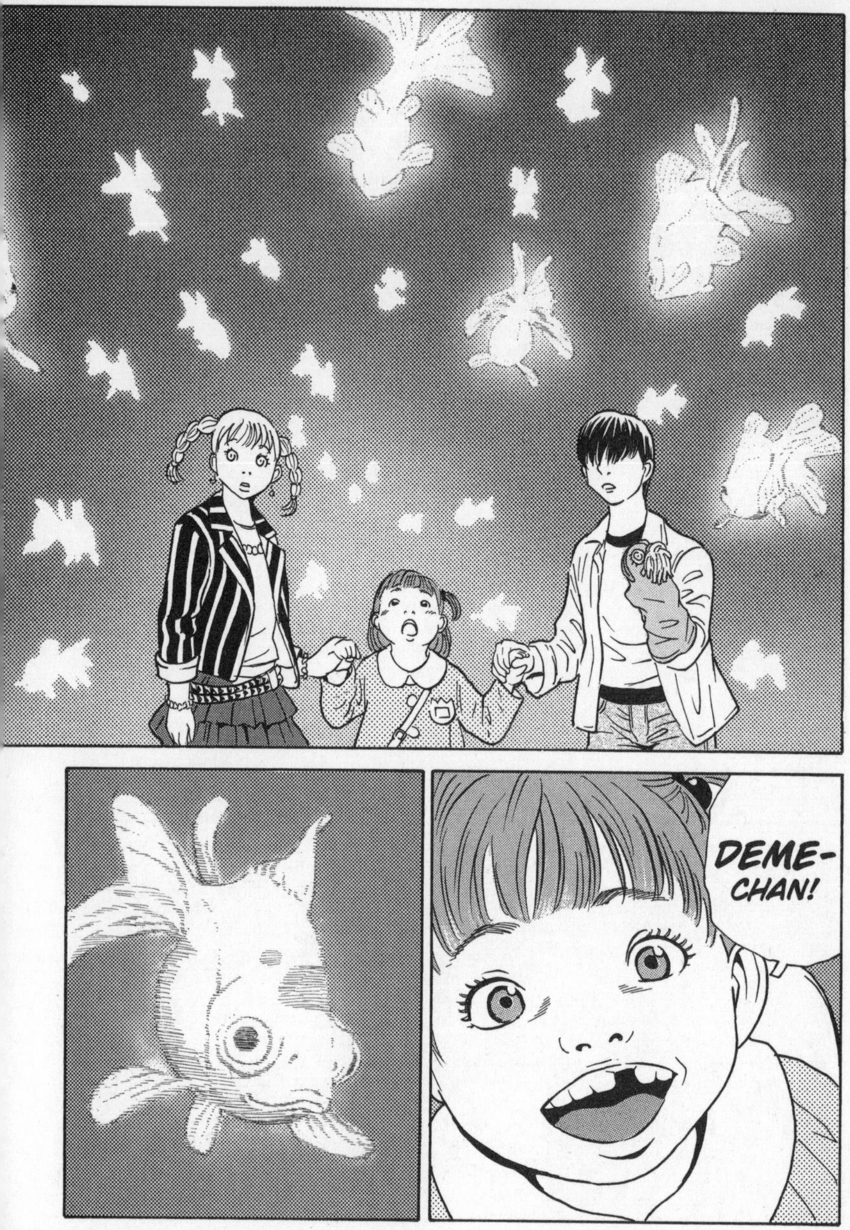
DEME-
CHAN!

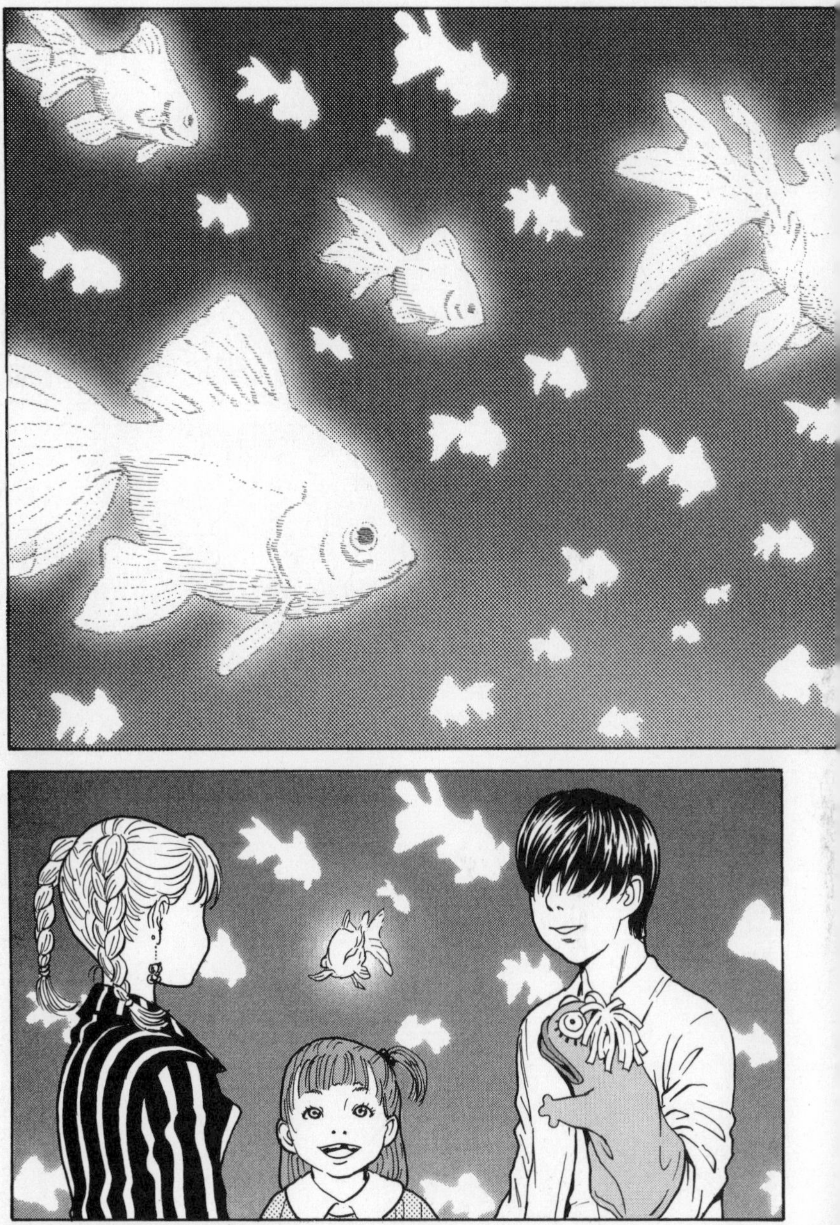

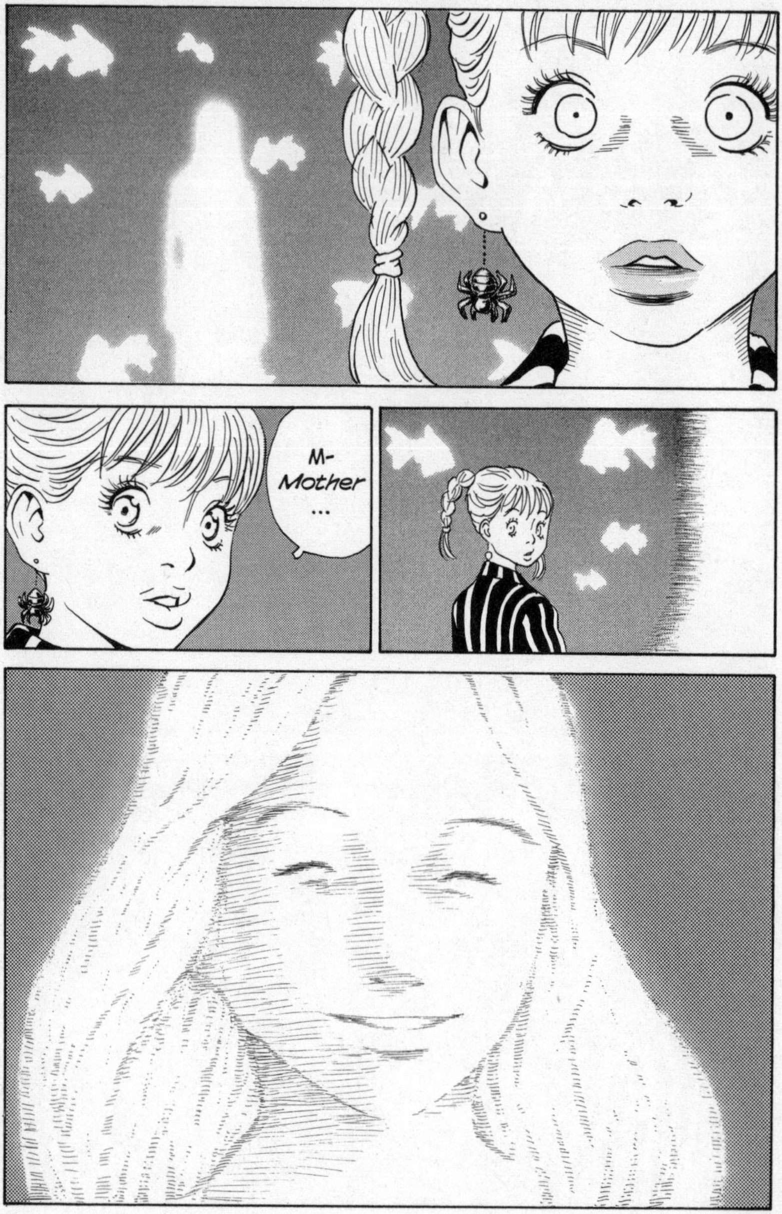
M-Mother...

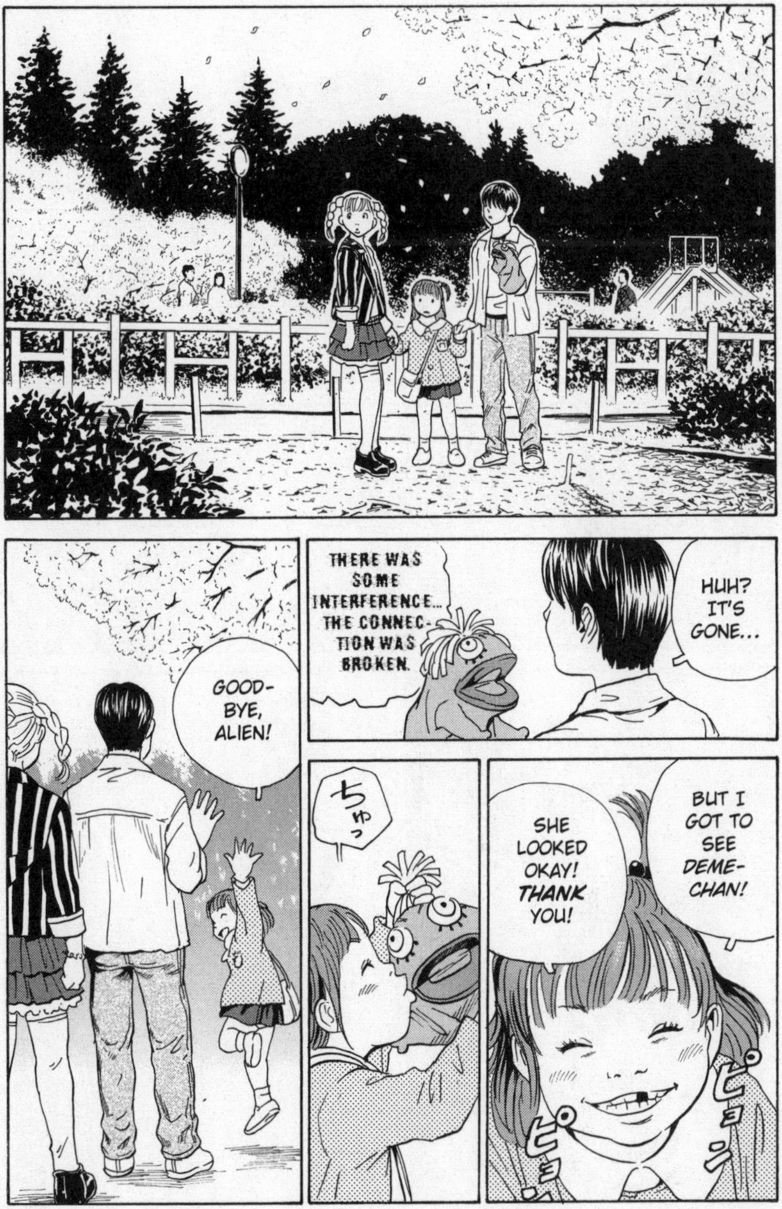
HUH? IT'S GONE...
THERE WAS SOME INTERFERENCE... THE CONNECTION WAS BROKEN.
BUT I GOT TO SEE DEME-CHAN!
SHE LOOKED OKAY! THANK YOU!
ちゅっ
GOOD-BYE, ALIEN!

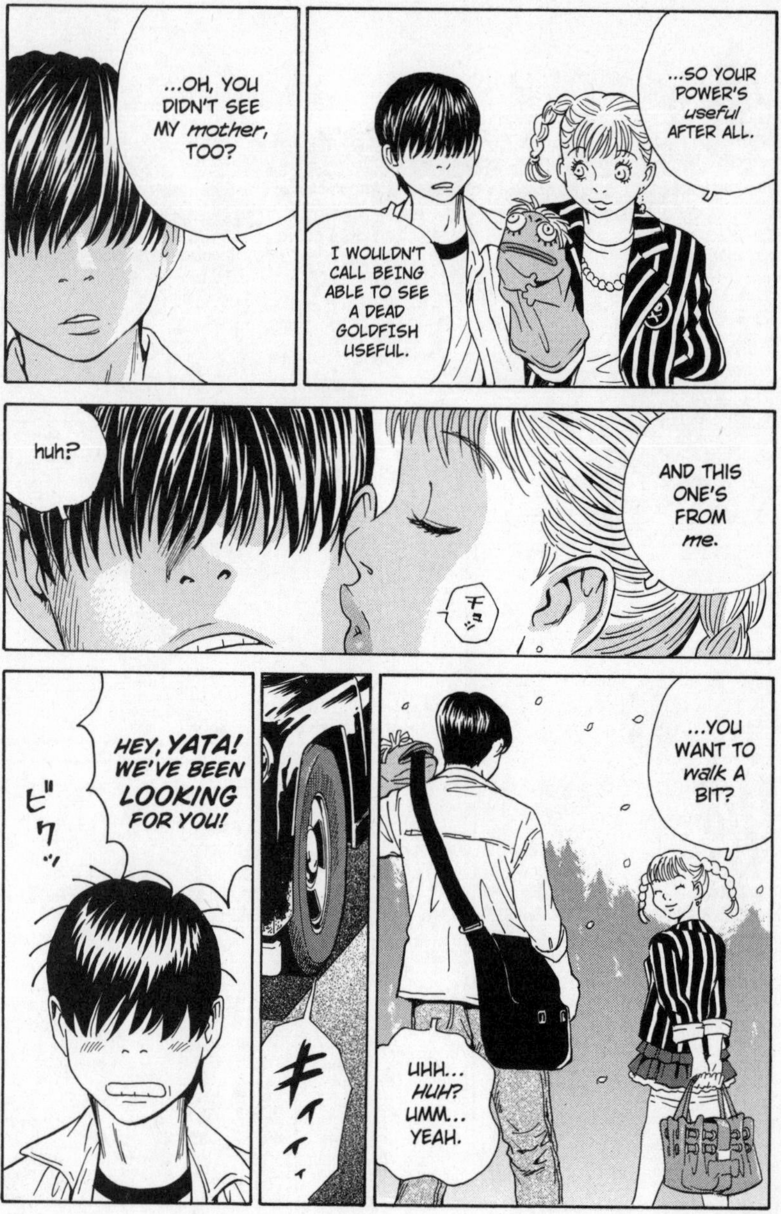
...SO YOUR POWER'S *useful* AFTER ALL.
I WOULDN'T CALL BEING ABLE TO SEE A DEAD GOLDFISH USEFUL.
...OH, YOU DIDN'T SEE MY *mother*, TOO?
AND THIS ONE'S FROM *me*.
チュッ
huh?
...YOU WANT TO *walk* A BIT?
UHH... *HUH?* UMM... YEAH.
キィィ
HEY, YATA! WE'VE BEEN LOOKING FOR YOU!
ビクッ

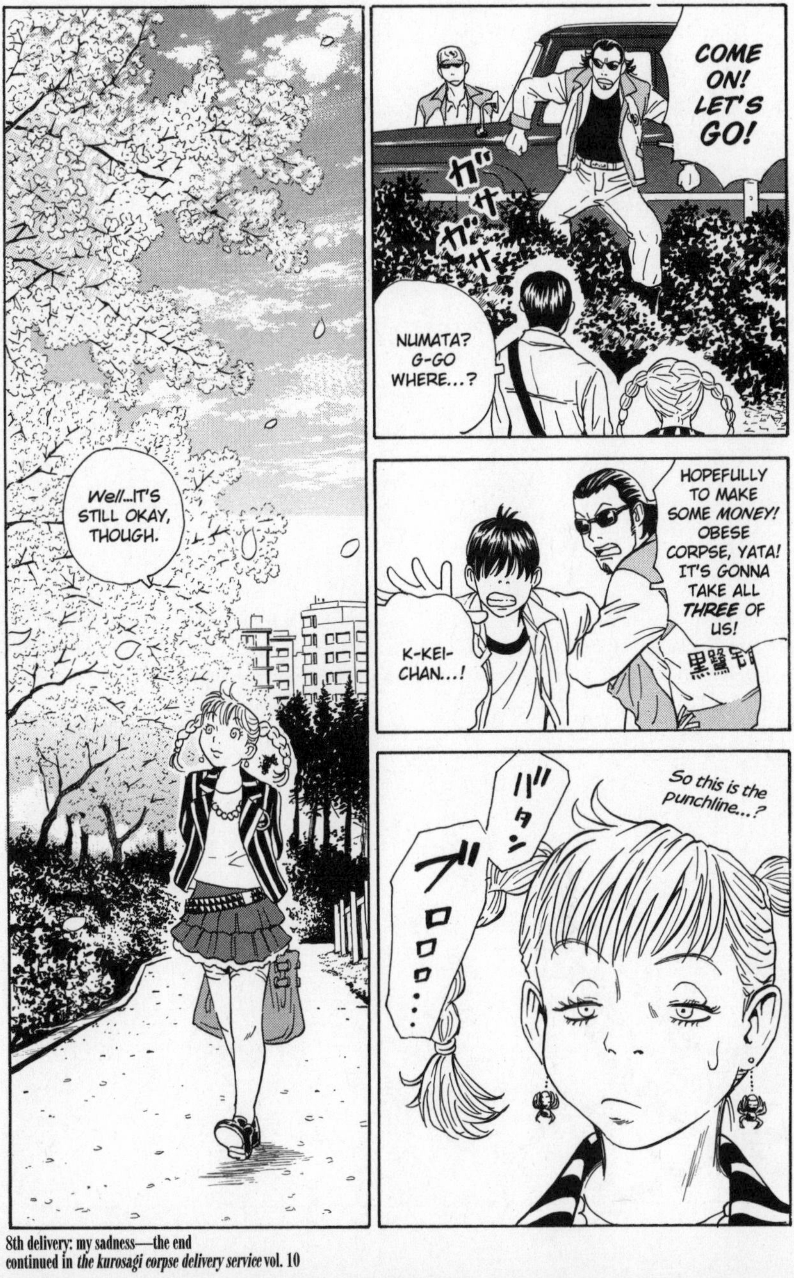
COME ON! LET'S GO!
ガサ
ガサ
NUMATA? G-GO WHERE...?
HOPEFULLY TO MAKE SOME MONEY! OBESE CORPSE, YATA! IT'S GONNA TAKE ALL THREE OF US!
K-KEI-CHAN...!
So this is the punchline...?
バタン
ブロロロ…
Well...IT'S STILL OKAY, THOUGH.

8th delivery: my sadness—the end

continued in *the kurosagi corpse delivery service* vol. 10

DISJECTA MEMBRA

SOUND FX GLOSSARY AND NOTES ON KUROSAGI VOL. 9 BY TOSHIFUMI YOSHIDA
introduction and additional comments by the editor

TO INCREASE YOUR ENJOYMENT of the distinctive Japanese visual style of this manga, we've included a guide to the sound effects (or "FX") used in this manga. It is suggested the reader *not* constantly consult this glossary as they read through, but regard it as supplemental information, in the manner of footnotes, or perhaps one of those nutritional supplements, the kind that's long and difficult to swallow. If you want to imagine it being read aloud by Osaka, after the manner of her lecture to Sakaki on hemorrhoids in episode five of *Azumanga Daioh*, please go right ahead. In either Yuki Matsuoka or Kira Vincent-Davis's voice—I like them both.

Japanese, like English, did not independently invent its own writing system, but instead borrowed and modified the system used by the then-dominant cultural power in its part of the world. We still call the letters we use to write English today the "Roman" alphabet, for the simple reason that about 1,600 years ago, the earliest English speakers, living on the frontier of the Roman Empire, began to use the same letters the Romans used for their Latin language to write out English.

Around that very same time, on the other side of the planet, Japan, like England, was another example of an island civilization lying across the sea from a great empire—in this case, that of China. Likewise, the Japanese borrowed from the Chinese writing system, which then, as now, consisted of thousands of complex symbols—today in China officially referred to in the Roman alphabet as *hanzi*, but which the Japanese pronounce as *kanji*. For example, all the Japanese characters you see on the front cover of

The Kurosagi Corpse Delivery Service—the seven which make up the original title and the four each which make up the creators' names—are examples of kanji. Of course, all of them were hanzi first—although the Japanese did also invent some original kanji of their own, just as new hanzi have been created over the centuries as Chinese evolved.

(Note that whereas both "kanji" and "hanzi" are examples of foreign words written in Roman letters, "kanji" gives English speakers a fairly good idea of how the Japanese word is really pronounced—*khan-gee*—whereas "hanzi" does not—in Mandarin Chinese it sounds something like *n-tsuh*. The reason is fairly simple: whereas the most commonly used method of writing Japanese in Roman letters, the Hepburn system, was developed by a native English speaker, the most commonly used method of writing Chinese in Roman letters, called the Pinyin system, was developed by native Mandarin speakers. In fact Pinyin was developed to help teach Mandarin pronunciation to speakers of other Chinese dialects; unlike Hepburn, it was not intended as a learning tool for English speakers per se, and hence has no particular obligation to "make sense" to English speakers or, indeed, to users of the many other languages spelled with the Roman alphabet.)

Whereas the various dialects of Chinese are written entirely in hanzi, it is impractical to render the Japanese language entirely in them. To compare once more, English is a notoriously difficult language in which to spell properly, and this is in part because it uses an alphabet designed for another language, Latin, whose sounds are different (this is, of course, putting aside the fact the sounds of both languages experienced change over time). The challenges the Japanese faced in using the Chinese writing system for their own language were even greater, for whereas spoken English and Latin are at least from a common language family, spoken Japanese is unrelated to any of the various dialects of spoken Chinese. The complicated writing system the Japanese evolved represents an adjustment to these great differences.

When the Japanese borrowed hanzi to become kanji, what they were getting was a way to write out (remember, they already had ways to *say*) their vocabulary. Nouns, verbs, many adjectives, the names of places and people—that's what kanji are used for, the fundamental data of the written language. The practical use and processing of that "data"—its grammar and pronunciation—is another matter entirely. Because spoken Japanese neither sounds nor functions like Chinese, the first work-around tried was a system called *manyogana*, where individual kanji were picked to represent certain syllables in Japanese. A similar method is still used in Chinese today to spell out foreign names; companies and individuals often try to choose hanzi for this purpose that have an auspicious, or at least not insulting, meaning. As you will also observe in *Kurosagi* and elsewhere, the meaning behind the characters that make up a personal name are an important literary element of Japanese as well.

The commentary in *Katsuya Terada's The Monkey King* (also available from Dark Horse, and also translated by Toshifumi Yoshida) notes the importance that not only Chinese, but also Indian culture had on Japan at this time in history—particularly, through Buddhism. Just as in Western history at this time, religious communities in Asia were associated with learning, as priests and monks were more likely to be literate than other groups in society. It is believed the Northeast Indian *Siddham* script studied by Kukai (died 835 AD), founder of the Shingon sect of Japanese Buddhism, inspired him to create the solution for writing Japanese still used today. Kukai is credited with the idea of taking the manyogana and making shorthand versions of them—which are now known simply as *kana*. The improvement in efficiency was dramatic: a kanji previously used to represent a sound, that might have taken a dozen strokes to draw, was now replaced by a kana that took three or four.

Unlike the original kanji they were based on, the new kana had *only* a sound meaning. And unlike the thousands of kanji, there are only 46 kana, which can be used to spell out any word in the Japanese language, including the many ordinarily written with kanji (Japanese keyboards work on this principle). The same set of 46 kana is written two different ways depending on its intended use: cursive style, *hiragana*, and block style, *katakana*. Naturally, sound FX in manga are almost always written out using kana.

Kana works somewhat differently than the Roman alphabet. For example, while there are separate kana for each of the five vowels (the Japanese order is not A-E-I-O-U as in English, but A-I-U-E-O), there are, except for *n*, no separate kana for consonants (the middle *n* in the word *ninja* illustrates this exception). Instead, kana work by grouping together consonants with vowels: for example, there are five kana for sounds starting with *k*, depending on which vowel follows it—in Japanese vowel order, they go KA, KI, KU, KE, KO. The next set of kana begins with *s* sounds, so SA, SHI, SU, SE, SO, and so on. You will observe this kind of consonant-vowel pattern in the FX listings for *Kurosagi* Vol. 9 below.

Katakana are generally used for manga sound FX, but on occasion hiragana are used instead. This is commonly done when the sound is one associated with a human body, but can be a subtler aesthetic choice by the artist as well. In *Kurosagi*

Vol. 9 you can see an example on 37.2, with the BUBAAAA of Yuriri spitting, which in hiragana style is written ぶばあつ. Note its more cursive appearance compared to the other FX. If it had been written in katakana style, it would look like ブバアツ.

To see how to use this glossary, take an example from page 6: "6.1 FX: ZAAAAAA—sound of pouring rain." 6.1 means the FX is the one on page 6, in panel 1. ZAAAAAA is the sound these kana—ザアアアアアア—literally stand for. After the dash comes an explanation of what the sound represents (in some cases, like this, it will be less obvious than others). Note that in cases where there are two or more different sounds in a single panel, an extra number is used to differentiate them from right to left; or, in cases where right and left are less clear, in clockwise order.

The use of kana in these FX also illustrates another aspect of written Japanese—its flexible reading order. For example, the way you're reading the pages and panels of this book in general—going from right to left, and from top to bottom—is similar to the order in which Japanese is also written in most forms of print: books, magazines, and newspapers. However, some of the FX in *Kurosagi* (and manga in general) read left to right. This kind of flexibility is also to be found on Japanese web pages, which usually also read left to right. In other words, Japanese doesn't simply read "the other way" from English; the Japanese themselves are used to reading it in several different directions.

As might be expected, some FX "sound" short, and others "sound" long. Manga represent this in different ways. One of many instances of "short sounds" in *Kurosagi* Vol. 9 is 7.5's PASA—パサツ. Note the small ツ mark it has at the end, which stands for the sound "tsu." In hiragana, such as 37.2, it looks like つ. The half-size "tsu" seen at the end of FX like this means the sound is the kind which stops or

cuts off suddenly; that's why 7.5 and 37.2 are written as PASA and BUBAAAA, and not PASATSU and BUBAAAATSU—you don't pronounce the "tsu" when used this way. Note the small "tsu" has another occasional use *inside*, rather than at the end, of a particular FX, where it indicates a doubling of the consonant sound that follows it.

There are three different ways you may see "long sounds"—where a vowel sound is extended—written out as FX. One is with an ellipsis, as in 91.5's GOSO. Another is with an extended line, as in 114.1's CHIII CHII KIII KII. Still another is by simply repeating a vowel several times, as in 59.1's OOOO. You will note that the CHIII CHII KIII KIIs in 114.1 each have a "tsu" at their end, suggesting an elongated sound that's suddenly cut off; the methods may be combined within a single FX. As a visual element in manga, FX are an art rather than a science, and are used in a less rigorous fashion than kana are in standard written Japanese.

The explanation of what the sound represents may sometimes be surprising, but every culture "hears" sounds differently. Note that manga FX do not even necessarily represent literal sounds. Such "mimetic" words, which represent an imagined sound, or even a state of mind, are called *gitaigo* in Japanese. Like the onomatopoeic *giseigo* (the words used to represent literal sounds—i.e., most FX in this glossary are classed as giseigo), they are also used in colloquial speech and writing. A Japanese, for example, might say that something bounced by saying PURIN, or talk about eating by saying MUGU MUGU. It's something like describing chatter in English by saying "yadda yadda yadda" instead.

One important last note: all these spelled-out kana vowels should be pronounced as they are in Japanese: *A* as *ah*, *I* as *eee*, *U* as *ooh*, *E* as *eh*, and *O* as *oh*.

2.1 The translator notes that all the chapter titles in Volume 9 are songs by Asami Kobayashi. She was active as a singer, actor, and model starting in the 1970s, until she retired in 1991. The title to the second chapter gets a little complicated. In the original Japanese, it is "Yume miru shanson ningyoo" (that's a long "ohhh" sound on the end, of course, rather than "oooh"), which literally translates to "the *chanson* doll that dreams" (*chanson* meaning *song* in French). This was a Japanese-language cover sung by France Gall of her own French-language original song, "Poupée de cire, poupée de son" ("doll of wax, doll of bran"—bran being a filling used in France for dolls; compare to the rice used in this story) that won the Eurovision Song Contest in 1965. French pop was, well, popular enough in Japan then (you'll recall that in *Masculin, féminin*, Chantal Goya mentions she's climbing the Japanese charts) to warrant the cover; Gall also recorded versions in German and Italian. Various artists have covered it in other languages. The song itself was written for Gall by *l'creep le plus extraordinaire* Serge Gainsbourg (and as a manga fan, the editor is no longer sure how he means that). The original French version has also been covered by The Arcade Fire and Belle and Sebastian. But "A Lonely Singing Doll" is used as the title here as this was the name of the English version, covered (also in 1965) by the UK singer Twinkle (whose own single "Golden Lights" you may possibly know from The Smiths' cover of it on *Louder Than Bombs*. And this is only the *first* note in "Disjecta Membra."

5   I love the fact that this is a *doll* version of Kereellis, who is, of course, in everyday life, a *puppet*.

6.1   **FX: ZAAAAAA**—sound of pouring rain

6.2   **FX/balloon: WIIIIIN**—sound of elevator rising

6.3   **FX: KA KA**—sound of heels

6.4   **FX/balloon: PI**—turning off mobile phone

7.1   **FX: GACHA**—sound of a door opening

7.4   **FX/balloon: PACHI**—light switch being flipped

7.5   **FX/balloon: PASA**—sound of hair falling down out of hat

8.1   **FX/balloon: KII**—door creaking open

8.4   **FX: PUKA PUKA**—sound of doll floating/bobbing

8.5   **FX: PUKA PUKA**—sound of doll floating/bobbing. Note the retractable cover on the bathtub, intended to keep heat in and suds out (one washes outside the tub in Japan before soaking a *clean* body—in America, we just throw a little more chlorine in the hot tub).

9.1   **FX: DOSHA**—wet thud as trash bag hits ground

9.3   She actually said *wota no fan*; that she hates the "wota" kind of fan. It's been an affectation the last few years in Japan, especially on the image forum 2chan, to spell *otaku*—normally written オタク, o-ta-ku—as ヲタク, or *wo*-ta-ku. This was possibly inspired—or perhaps reflective of—Hideaki Anno's 2006 decision to spell the new *Evangelion* movies ヱヴァンゲリヲン, which is romanized as *Wevangeliwon*. This risks making Anno sound like Kim Jong-Il in *Team America: World Police*, but you will be relieved to hear it's still *pronounced* "Evangelion," just as *wota* and *wotaku* are still pronounced "ota" and "otaku." The effect is a little like the way one might choose in English to use the old-fashioned spelling *phantasy* for *fantasy* (as used, for example, in the game *Phantasy Star*). The *we* ("weh") sound has not actually existed in Japanese for centuries (English, too, used to sound quite different centuries ago; anyone who's ever heard *The Canterbury Tales* will be reminded of the Swedish Chef from *The Muppet Show*), and by the early twentieth century the kana for *we* had simply become a redundant form of *e* ("eh"), so it was officially discarded in the orthographic reforms following WWII. The *wo* ("woh") sound does still exist in dialect, although generally speaking it has the same value as *o* ("oh"), and in fact as early as 1996 *Evangelion* was spelling its famous bishie's name *Kaworu*, even though, yeah, yeah, it's just pronounced "Kah-oh-roo." Bear it in mind when you read *Neon Genesis Evangelion: The Shinji Ikari Raising Project*, also from Dark Horse, and one of those love comedies Numata is so apprehensive towards. Even a non-otaku (are there any left?) may be familiar with this kind of usage from Clint Eastwood's much-acclaimed recent film *Letters from Iwo Jima*; the *Iwo* is pronounced "ee-oh," not "ee-woh," but seeing as how it was WWII that made the place famous, it is the old romanization of *Iwo Jima* rather than the postwar *Io Jima* that has remained in the popular mind.

9.5 **FX/balloon: GACHA**—placing door chain

9.6 **FX/balloon: PACHIN**—locking deadbolt

10.1 **FX: PINPOON**—doorbell sound

10.2 **FX: PINPOON PINPOON PINPOON**—doorbell sounds

10.3.1 **FX/balloon: GACHA**—jiggling-door-handle sound

10.3.2 **FX/balloon: GACHA**—jiggling-door-handle sound

10.3.3 **FX/balloon: GACHA**—jiggling-door-handle sound

10.4 **FX/balloon: SUCHA**—picking up phone

11.3 **FX: BECHA PATA BECHA**—sound of something moving with a wet squishing sound

11.4 **FX/balloon: GATA**—sound of grate rattling

11.5 **FX: ZU**—sound of something sliding along

11.6 **FX: ZU ZU**—sound of something sliding along

14.5 **FX: SUCHA**—taking out pendulum

15.3 **FX: HYUN HYUN**—pendulum swinging back and forth

16.3 **FX/balloon: HYUN HYUN**—pendulum swinging

17.2 **FX/balloon: SU**—touching doll

17.5 **FX: SHAKIN**—pair of scissors opening up

17.6 **FX: BA**—grabbing doll

18.1.1 **FX/black: SA**—Makino reaching for doll

18.1.2 **FX/white: GURIN**—Yata's body twisting out of the way

18.3.1 **FX/top: GU**—Makino tugging

18.3.2 **FX/bottom: GUGUGU**—puppet tugging

18.4 **FX: BABII**—doll tearing

18.5 **FX/balloon: ZAAAA**—sound of rice pouring out

20.4 Actually she said *rajikaru, rajikaru!* By spelling *raji* in katakana and *karu* in hiragana, the original dialogue makes the English word *radical* into a trendy-sounding Japanese verb, taking advantage of the fact *aru* is a verb ending (one of several in Japanese). Dark Horse Director of Asian Licensing Michael Gombos points out that something comparable is done in Japanese by turning the English *jealousy* into *jeraru*, which can then, like *rajikaru*, be conjugated as if it were a Japanese verb for "to be jealous."

24.2 This is an unusual volume of *Kurosagi*, in that we run into something we rarely see in the story (in fact, we haven't seen it in the main story since vol. 1)—actual, you know, Buddhist priests. You may wonder why he gets a square title in English like *Reverend*, instead of something more cool you might associate with a Buddhist priest, like, say, *Brother*. But a term like *Reverend* is closer to what the sociology majors call *unmarked*, meaning it's seen as a default or normal term, because Buddhism is a default or normal religion in Japan. Indeed, it's very common for Buddhist priests in America to call themselves *Reverend*; like most community religious leaders, they want to be seen as, well, a normal member of the community. Buddhism still has a somewhat exotic image in American culture (that is, outside the small percentage of Americans who are raised in it)—the words *Buddhist priest* call to mind a monk leaping into the air, or the Dalai Lama. *Reverend* calls to mind the guy who chews you out for having brought a copy of *Trinity Blood*

to the youth retreat (I heard this anecdote at Kumoricon). But, as you may have noticed by now, being a Buddhist in Japan is like being a Baptist in the South. Except for minor differences in doctrine. I'd like to see the *Kurosagi* gang run into the wacky American versions of themselves, who went to Howard Payne University.

26.3 FX: PARA PARA—sound of rice grains falling out

27.2 The doll-blessing temple portrayed here is—you guessed it—based on a real one. Setsuko Kamiya wrote in the October 15, 2006, issue of the *Japan Times* (eight months before the story appeared in *Comic Charge* magazine) about the annual prayer and burning ceremony, held September 25, at the Kiyomizu Kannondo Temple in Tokyo's Ueno Park. The ceremony apparently evolved out of the practice of parents bringing their children to the temple for a blessing and leaving behind a doll at the temple to represent the child (or so that any bad influences would fall upon the doll, not the child). As time went on, this intersected with the Japanese love for dolls and figurines (an affection shared, of course, with many other cultures); people who didn't feel right about simply discarding such dolls started leaving them there alongside the dolls representing children.

27.5 FX/balloon: JAN JYAKA JAN—ring tone

29.1 FX: TATA—sound of keys being tapped

31.5 Japan (like much of the world) uses a 24-hour clock, a system in the U.S. associated with the military. However, whereas "24:00" means midnight in Japan, Michael Gombos notes it's not uncommon for Japanese schedules to give 1 AM as "25:00," 2 AM as "26:00," etc., when events run into the early morning hours. There's an interesting philosophy here—that time should be given as a person experiences it; that if they're still up at 1 AM, the day is going into "overtime" for *them*.

32.2 To paraphrase Chris Rock, idols love to *not know* shit. But I bet you wouldn't catch Shokotan acting the fool like this.

32.3 **FX/balloon: VWOOON VWOOON**—sound of cell phone vibrating

33.3 **FX: KA KO**—sound of footsteps

33.4 **FX: PURAN**—sound of doll dangling

33.6 **FX: KO**—footstep

34.1.1 **FX/balloons: CHIKI CHIKI**—blade clicking out

34.1.2 **FX/balloon: CHIKIN**—blade clicking into place

34.3 **FX/balloons: ZAKU ZAKU**—stabbing sound

34.4 **FX/balloon: CHAPUN**—sound of doll getting submerged

34.6 **FX/balloon: FU**—sound of lights turning off

34.7 **FX/balloon: BATAN**—door being closed

35.3 **FX/balloon: KACHA**—door being opened

35.4 **FX/balloon: PATAN**—door being closed

35.6.1 **FX/balloon: PACHI**—turning on lights

35.6.2 **FX: PA PAA**—fluorescent lights turning on

36.1 **FX/balloon: PICHOON**—sound of dripping faucet

36.2 **FX/balloon: CHAPU**—sound of an arm coming out of the water

36.3 **FX/balloon: BISHA**—soggy splashing sound

36.4 **FX: NUCHARI BICHA**—wet sloshing/splashing sound

37.1 **FX: KURU**—sound of Yuriri turning her head

37.2 **FX: BUBAAA**—spraying-water sound

37.3 **FX: BISHA PICHA**—sound of spray hitting doll

37.5 **FX/balloon: DOBICHA**—sound of doll hitting floor with a wet thud

38.1 **FX: DOKA DOKA DOKA**—stomping sounds

38.2 **FX/balloon: BAN**—door being banged open

39.5 **FX: GWOOOO**—sound of the car

40.2 **FX/balloon: PI**—hanging-up sound

41.2 **FX: KON KON**—knock knock

41.4 **FX: GA**—grabbing door

42.3 **FX: GA**—grabbing doorknob

42.4 **FX/balloon: MEKI**—sound of Kuro's hand getting smashed

43.1 **FX: GA GA**—fingers grabbing edge of door

43.3 **FX: GAKYAN**—door being ripped off hinge

44.2 **FX: KWOOOO**—sound of the air conditioner

46.6 **FX: SU**—placing hand on body

48.2 **FX/balloon: WIIIIN**—sound of sliding doors opening

48.3 **FX: KO KA**—sound of heels on floor

48.4 **FX: PI**—hanging up cell phone

49.1 **FX/balloon: GACHA**—opening door

49.4 **FX/balloon: PACHI**—turning on light

49.5 **FX/balloon: PASA**—hair falling down out of cap

50-51.1 FX: GURIN—head turning

50-51.2 FX: MUKU—getting-up sound

52.2.1 FX/balloon: DOSA—sound of doll falling over in the pyre

52.2.2 FX/small: PACHI—crackling flame

52.2.3 FX/small: PACHI—crackling flame

52.4 *Hanako* literally means *flower child*, although it don't have none o' them hippie connotations to it; in fact, it's a very traditional name—too traditional, perhaps—these days just plain *Hana* would be considered more cool.

53.4 Eiji Otsuka's feelings about otaku are, shall we say, nuanced. On one hand, he depicted as lulzworthy Comiket being nerve-gassed in *MPD-Psycho* Vol. 4. On the other, he manages to suggest a little empathy with a weak and sad specimen as seen in this story. Or rather, is it not so much empathy for the departed, as a certain distaste for the attitude of Yuriri, who, after all, like many idols, prospers by making a cult of personality out of herself (as evidenced by all the merchandise in 44.1), but then gets outraged when she attracts cultists? Karatsu's attitude seems to be that anyone who wants to make their living as an idol has no business insulting their fans for sending tributes. The headlines seen here seem to suggest everyone became happier when Yuriri dropped her Lolita act in favor of a bad-girl image instead, trumpeting her "*Transformation!*" and "*Sexy and Revealing Body!*" on a new tour for her fans, with mutual affection.

55 Is it just the editor's doujin-corrupt brain, or are Makino and Sasaki making eyes at each other? 'Cause otherwise, this could be, like, an early-eighties album cover. Actually, that would make it even *more* like an early-eighties album cover. The editor thinks the best part of Berlin's "Sex (I'm a . . .)" is when Terri Nunn says "*I'm a bi!*" and John Crawford does that chuckle.

58.3 **FX: BAWOOOO**—motorcycle sound

58.4.1 FX: OOO—wind/motorcycle sound

58.4.2 FX/balloon: KURURI—sound of head turning

59.1 **FX: OOOO**—wind/motorcycle sound

60.1 **FX: BAWOOON**—motorcycle sound

60.4 Note the mechanical traffic director, designed for high-speed roads where it would be too dangerous for a human signaler to do the job (at least, when Numata's about). As mentioned way back in vol. 1's "Disjecta Membra," note for 94.2–3, Japan's construction sector is far larger and more active than Japan's actual construction needs. The reason for this, as you might guess, is to give as many people as many jobs as possible. Besides the jobs that involve actually building something or tearing it down, every construction site also creates employment for an outer ring of people (often student or part-time workers—even Keiichi Morisato did it once in *Oh My Goddess!*) whose job it is to direct foot or vehicular traffic *around* the site. About ten years ago, the editor was rounding a building under construction in Tokyo, where a bracket-shaped path of cones led the pedestrian off the sidewalk, a few feet out onto the street away from the scaffolding, and then back onto the sidewalk again. There was a person to signal you as you entered the path, another as you made the first turn, another as you made the second turn, and then finally one to wave you out. All with those little lighted wands.On an American street construction site there might be a worker checking their text messages, but that's about it (at least one builder I saw on Burnside had an *Operation: Mindcrime* sticker on his hard hat—cool, but I was disappointed when I read Gore Vidal's *Lincoln* and found out that Portland's main drag was named for such a poor general).

60.5.1 FX: BAKYAN—sign breaking

60.5.2 FX/balloon: GOKIN—sound of car hitting signpost

60.6 FX/balloon: SHUU—sound of steam escaping

62.2 These are, as you might guess, all forum postings about the Riding Head, although the name given it in Japanese is *kubi dake raidaa*, literally "Head-Only Rider." *Kubidake* can also mean "complete devotion," appropriate enough, as we shall see. *Kannana* is the understandably shortened form of the highway officially known as the *Tokyo-to keikaku douro kansen sengai rokan jodai nana-go sen*, or "Line 7 of the major bypass for the Tokyo city building plan". . . or something like that.

62.5 FX: BAN—hitting-table sound

63.3 Note that there are supposedly already seventeen pages of archived postings about the Peeping Head available at www.kubidakenozokima.jp.html (surprisingly, a nonexistent website). In panel 5, they're checking out the video on "YouTofu," a play on the definitely existing Japanese version of YouTube.

63.5 FX/balloon: TSUUU KAKO—sound of finger sliding down track pad then clicking

66.3 FX: PAN PAN—slapping feet

66.4 FX: BATAAN—slamming door. In the back are the Japanese versions of the Yuriri poster from 2nd Delivery, not to mention the "Go Ricefish!" banner from vol. 4, 1st Delivery. I like how they collect this stuff. It's kind of a pauper's version of the Batcave.

70.6 "*IIIIIII don't believe it! Thermoptic camouflage!*" Note how at that moment in the movie (or manga) they can still *see* the Major as she disappears, but nobody thinks to actually *shoot* her. To paraphrase Dr. Evil, "No, no, I'm just going to stand here and watch as she gradually becomes completely invisible."

71.4 FX: KATA—standing-up sound

71.5 FX: BASA—spreading out fabric

71.6 FX: GATA—setting up projector

72.3 This "invisibility suit" really exists as depicted (and, just as depicted, is more like appearing transparent than invisible) and was first reported in world media in February of 2003, based on a demo version developed by Susumu Tachi and his team at Tokyo University. Dr. Tachi, who looks like a proper manga scientist, has his homepage at www.star.t.u-tokyo.ac.jp/~tachi/.

73.4 FX/balloon: CHARAN—dangling sound

74.4.1 FX: ZA—footstep

74.4.2 FX: ZA—footstep

74.4.3 FX: ZA—footstep

74.5 FX: GA—tripping sound

75.2 FX: SU—reaching down

76.3 FX: DON—putting hand down on body

77.4 FX/balloon: KACHA—clatter of the zipper

77.5 FX: BABIIIII—zipper being pulled

79.3 When I first saw the Riding/Peeping Head close-up on 65.1, I did think, *Hey . . . this guy looks like **Mamoru Oshii!*** But then, there's a lot of cats who look like Mamoru Oshii—in Japan, anyway. I didn't expect it to actually *be* a reference to him (you have to look closely at his ID, but the guy's name is in fact Mamoru Oshii—the only difference from the film director being that different kanji are used to spell his first name. The kanji in *Esuefu* make it sound like the name of a (fictitious) urban prefecture, but it's a pun on *SF*, i.e., science fiction. I really want to see Oshii's latest, *The Sky Crawlers*. I'm a little concerned because, unlike most Oshii films, the protagonists are teenagers, and there's already more than enough anime where the protagonists are teenagers. It's not about putting the youth of today down. It's about a thirty-eight-year-old otaku, faithful follower of the scene since age eleven, requesting some equity. Shit, man, since they rebooted the movie series, James Bond is now supposed to be the same age as Daniel Craig—forty. If he can still do all that stuff with the help of CG, surely an anime character can do it with the help of Production I.G.

79.5 FX: MUNYU—cheeks being pulled

81.1 The morpho butterfly, native to Latin America, has ultrafine, iridescent scales whose structure has been studied for various applications, including thin-film optics, and, increasingly, photonic-crystal fibers. As for what that really means, I majored in history, so I'm inclined to echo Numata's response.

82.1 FX: GASHI—grasping-hand sound

82.2 FX/balloon: JIJI—closing-zipper sound

82.3 FX/balloon: JI—zipper closing

82.5.1 FX/balloon: GON GATAN—hitting obstacles

82.5.2 FX/balloon: GASHAN—knocking cart over

83.2 FX: NUBO—head appearing out of nowhere

84.2 FX/balloon: CHARA—dangling-key sound

85.3 FX/balloon: JIII—closing-zipper sound

85.4 FX: PIII PIII—reverse warning beeps

85.6.1 FX/top: DON—impact sound

85.6.2 FX/middle: GO—hitting wall on the way down

85.6.3 FX/bottom: GOKI—sound of a bone breaking

86.1 FX: DOSA—sound of body hitting ground

87.3 FX: BAN—hitting table

89.1.1 FX/balloon: GATAN—pulling out drawer

89.1.2 FX/balloon: GARA GARA—dumping out contents

89.4 This is vol. 1 of the original *Oh! Invisible Man* (in Japanese, *Oh! toumeiningen*), which, as you might guess from its appearance, was a 1980s manga series that ran in Kodansha's *Monthly Shonen*

Magazine (today, home of the *Pumpkin Scissors* manga) for eleven volumes. Yasuhiro Nakanishi has revived it in recent years, switching publishers to Shueisha, where the sequel *Oh! Invisible Man 21* (21, after this oh-so-wonderful-thus-far century) ran in the biweekly *Super Jump* magazine for eight volumes (home of the immortal *Golden Boy*). When you have "Oh" beginning an exclamatory phrase, Japanese seem to like placing the exclamation point immediately after the exclamation itself, instead of at the end of the phrase. Thus you will often see in manga a foreigner being shown to say in English "Oh! My God," rather than "Oh My God!" Now, to the native English reader, that makes it look like the stress is being put on the "Oh!" which sounds a little unnatural, but the issue likely doesn't occur to the person reading in Japanese. Gombos sees in this the Japanese simply applying their own usage of exclamations at the beginning of a phrase to English (the original title of the manga *Oh My Goddess!* is *Aa megami-sama*, where the *Aa* is the exclamation). As usual, it's not like it was intended for native English readers to fret over. It's kind of like how you see people writing *ninjas*, applying English usage to Japanese (where there's no special plural spellings to words; whether it's one attacking you or a hundred, it's just *ninja*).

90.1 **FX/balloon: GACHA**—door opening

90.4.1 **FX: DOSA**—putting body down

90.4.2 **FX/balloon: JI**—starting to pull zipper

90.5 **FX: JIPAAAAA**—pulling zipper down

90.6 **FX: IIII**—zipper coming to a stop

91.3 **FX: SU**—disc floating out of hand

91.5 **FX: GOSO**—rummaging in pocket

92.1 **FX: BASHUUUU**—spraying sound

92.2 Of course no one, even in Japan, would be crazy enough to make a consumer product like this. Ha, ha, just kidding—it's real, of course. You can buy it at www.strap ya-world.com/products/10932.html. "Please don't spray directly to skin. It may cause burn wounds."

92.2.1 That was uncalled for. I'm an American; now excuse me while *I* go buy something safe and sensible, like a Desert Eagle Mark XIX chambered for .50 Action Express.

92.3.1 **FX: PISHI PISHI PISHI**—sound of the suit's surface hardening

92.3.2 **FX/balloon: PORO**—dropping disc

93.1 **FX/balloon: GA**—grabbing disc

93.2 **FX: BA**—putting disc into coat

93.3 **FX: BAAAAAAA**—spraying face

93.4 **FX: DATATATATA**—running down stairs

93.5 **FX: BAN**—slamming door

94.1 **FX: GYUGYUWOON**—car speeding off

94.2 **FX/balloon: PARIN**—glass breaking

94.3.1 **FX/balloon: DON**—sound of something landing on car

94.3.2 **FX: WOOOOO**—car speeding away

94.6 **FX: BAN**—hand hitting windshield

95.2.1 **FX/balloon: PAKI PAKI**—suit starting to flake away

95.2.2 **FX/balloon: PAKI**—suit falling apart

95.3.1 **FX/balloon: PAKI**—suit falling apart

95.3.2 FX/balloon: PAKI—suit falling apart

99.1 FX/balloon: KAN KORON—sound of sign clattering on the ground

99.2 FX/balloon: PATAN—broken sign falling to a stop

102 Oh, yeah, and have you ever wondered what's up with pages like this—and page 54, and similar pages in other volumes? 99.9% of the time, a manga comes out in Japan one chapter at a time in an anthology magazine, and only later gets collected to graphic novel (or not; if it remains uncollected, it's sometimes because no one liked it the first time, and sometimes because the material was unfinished or insufficient in length for a graphic novel—Kenji Tsuruta, Yoshiyuki Sadamoto, and Hiroaki Samura have all done great stuff for magazines that remains uncollected). *Kurosagi* runs in Kadokawa's *Comic Charge* biweekly magazine (or rather, it did, until the magazine's recent cancellation, but don't panic—it was *Kurosagi*'s third home, and Kadokawa has promised to find it a fourth). But, being an anthology manga magazine, any given chapter of *Kurosagi* naturally has to be laid out in a particular issue in a way that takes into account all the other manga sharing that issue. Notice how "4th delivery" ends, and "5th delivery" begins, both on the left-side page. That was how they had to fit into their respective issues, but it means you have to add a "blank" page like 102 when you collect them to a graphic novel. Like most manga magazines (and unlike most major-publisher U.S. comic books),

only a very small percentage of *Comic Charge* consisted of ads—in a typical four-hundred-page issue there might be eight or nine interior pages (that is, not counting the outside or inside covers) of ads, and maybe five or six pages devoted to editorial matters (table of contents, reader giveaways, etc.)—meaning that it's over 95% actual manga content. You may be curious as to what the original *Kurosagi*-reader demographic was expected to buy. A survey of nine random issues of *Comic Charge* shows that for six of them, the inside-back-cover ad was taken out by a chain of circumcision clinics (recall *Even a Monkey Can Draw Manga*'s report on the great phimosis debate). In the ad, a handsome male model tries to free his head from a black turtleneck pulled up to his nose, a struggle despite the help of two attractive women who are already hanging off each shoulder. Three issues out of the nine had back-cover ads for the Merrell Jungle Moc (and a fourth had it on the inside front cover). Other ads to appear included the Nintendo DS test prep for the TOEIC (Test Of English for International Communication) twice; also twice, the DVD release of the film *Walking My Life* (original Japanese title: *Zo-no senaka*, "The Back of the Elephant"—English-subtitled trailer at www.shochikufilms.com/movie/zou.html), and ads for Suntory Bitter & Sharp beer and Black Boss coffee in a can.

103.1 FX: MEEN MEEN MEEN JEEWA JEEWA—sound of cicadas

103.2 FX: MEEN MEEN MEEN—sound of cicadas

108.3 FX: FUSA—cloth being placed over face

108.4 FX/balloon: DON DON—banging on door

109.1 FX: GACHA—door opening

111.2 FX/balloon: KII KII—sound of squeaky wheels on a cart

112.1 FX: PAKU PAKU—puppet mouth flapping

112.2 FX: CHII CHII CHII—high-pitched, mosquito-like sounds

112.3 FX/balloon: KOSO—rustling under desk

112.4 FX: KACHA KACHA KACHA KACHA—pressing keys

112.5.1 FX: CHII CHII—high-pitched sounds

112.5.2 FX/balloon: KACHA—pressing keys

112.5.3 FX/balloon: TATATA—tapping on keys

112.6 FX: CHII CHII CHIII—high-pitched sounds

113.4 Makino's jacket, bearing a cheerful youth with an IV, says "Kizumono Kids," meaning "Injured Kids." It's kind of Junko Mizuno-ish, don't you think?

114.1 FX: CHIII CHII KIII KII—sounds

115.3 FX/balloon: CHARARAN CHARARA JA JA JAAN—ring tone

116.1 FX: CHIRA—glancing back at Sasaki

116.2 FX: NIKO—smile

116.4 FX/balloon: PI—hanging up cell phone

120.5 FX/balloon: GASA—taking out a newspaper-wrapped object

122.2 FX: GASA—opening up paper

123.4 FX: DAN—slamming hand down

124.3 FX/balloon: KACHA—door opening

124.6 FX/balloon: BATAN—closing door

125.1 FX: KA KA—sound of cane on floor

126.2 FX/balloon: WIIIN—sound of motorized car mirror tracking Kikuchi

126.4 FX: NNNH—sound of power window being lowered

130.1 Folklorist Kunio Yanagita, of course, is an influence Eiji Otsuka has paid tribute to since the first volume, including making him a Sherlock Holmes–like detective in vol. 6.

131.3 FX: SU—placing hand on body

132.1 FX: KACHA—footstep

132.6 FX: POTATA POTA—sound of falling droplets

133.1 FX: GA—grabbing sound

133.3 FX/balloon: BURAN—hand going limp

133.4 FX/balloon: CHARARA CHARARAN JAJAJAAAN—ring tone

134.1 FX: SUCHA—placing phone on ear

136.2 FX: TATATA TATA—tapping at keys

137.3 The screen relates that Keisuke Matsuzawa was born and lives in the Setagaya Ward of Tokyo (remember that Sasayama works for one of Tokyo's other wards, Shinjuku), went to Gakkan High, and attended Waseda University School of Law, with a stint at Tokyo Empire Bank after graduation. Waseda is often considered to be the second- or third-best university in Japan (battling for the rank with Keio)—and Michael Gombos went there, in case you doubt you're in good hands with Dark Horse Manga.

138.2 **FX: KA KA**—sound of heels

139.4.1 FX/balloon: KACHI KACHI—jar rattling

139.4.2 FX/balloon: KACHI—jar rattling

139.4.3 FX/balloon: KACHI—jar rattling

139.5.1 FX/balloon: KACHI—jar rattling

139.5.2 FX/balloon: KACHI KACHI—jar rattling

139.5.3 FX/balloon: KACHI—jar rattling

141.3 Radar was invented in the years just before WWII, but the war (understandably) greatly accelerated its development. Martin Favorite suggests that the critical issue in Japan's case seems to be that senior officers didn't grasp its importance until late in the war, and hence Japanese radar in 1945 remained as much as three years behind America's, (which was also using its advanced radar offensively, to help guide its bombs). A dramatic illustration of this difference is in the fact that on December 7, 1941, the Japanese naval air task force approaching Pearl Harbor was actually picked up by U.S. Army radar on Oahu (but dismissed as a false alarm), yet the attackers themselves had no radar! You can see a picture of a surviving *choongo* at www.outdoor.geocities .jp/kotetsu0213/dsc02802.jpg.

142.2.1 FX/balloon: JARI JARI—sound of tires on gravel

142.2.2 FX/balloon: JARI—sound of tires on gravel

142.3 FX/balloon: KII—door creaking open

143.1 FX: DOZA—Kikuchi hitting gravel

144.1 FX: KOFAA—sound of the truck being opened

145.5 FX: PAAAN—slap

146.4 FX: SUKU—standing-up sound

146.5 FX/balloon: POTATA—sound of droplets

147.1 FX: DADADA—running sound

147.4 FX/balloon: TATATA—running sound

148.2 FX: KO KA—footsteps

149.5.1 FX/balloon: KACHA—jar rattling

149.5.2 FX/balloon: KACHA—jar rattling

150.1.1 FX/balloon: KACHA—jar rattling

150.1.2 FX/balloon: KACHA—jar rattling

150.1.3 FX/balloon: KACHA—jar rattling

150.1.4 FX/balloon: KACHA—jar rattling

152.1 FX: BA—jumping in the way

152.2 FX: PETASHI PETARI—bare footsteps

152.4.1 FX/balloon: GASHAAN—breaking glass

152.4.2 FX/balloon: PAN—popping-jar sound

152.4.3 FX/balloon: GASHO—muffled shattering sound

152.6 FX: PICHO—dripping sound

153.4.1 FX: BICHARI—wet squishing sound

153.4.2 FX: KUCHU—wet pressing sound

154.1 FX: ZAWA ZAWA ZAWA ZAWA—distant murmuring sound

154.2 FX: ZAWA ZAWA ZAWAWA ZAWA ZAWA ZAWA—murmuring sound

154.3 FX: ZAWA ZAWA ZAWA ZAWA—loud murmuring sound

155.1 FX: ZAWA ZAWA ZAWA ZAWA—loud murmuring sound

155.2 FX: WAAAAAAAAAAA—scream

157.1 FX/balloon: BURORORO—car driving away

157.2 FX/balloon: BERI—ripping duct tape off

158.2.1 FX/balloon: SA—taking out pendulum

158.2.2 FX/balloon: CHARAN—sound of dangling chain

158.3 FX: HYUN HYUN—sound of pendulum swinging

160.3 FX/balloons: KYAN KIN KIN—sound of bouncing shell casing

164.1 This is the Shigeru Yoshida referred to in 119.5. Prime minister of Japan during most of the postwar U.S. occupation (1945–52), Yoshida laid the groundwork for the basic rules of Japanese policy ever since: concentrate on domestic economic development and leave defense to the United States. In *Modern Times*, conservative historian Paul Johnson compares Yoshida's role to that of Adenauer in Germany or de Gasperi in Italy; that is, a politician who can take credit for leading a former Axis power out of devastation and on the path to peace and prosperity. This seems fair enough, but Johnson also characterizes Yoshida as "a former diplomat and thus from the background closest to Anglo-Saxon traditions of democracy and the rule of law," whereas John Dower in *Embracing Defeat* views Yoshida as believing that "the Japanese people were not capable of genuine self-government"—the two views are not necessarily contradictory. The editor, by the way, thinks that because the *actual* America is full of *both* liberal and conservative people—and that's not likely to change anytime soon—it's a good idea to try to understand America by reading both conservative and liberal *interpretations* of its history. So, if you've read Howard Zinn's *A People's History of the United States*, try Paul Johnson's *A History of the American People* (the differences in phrasing between

the two titles are themselves interesting), and vice versa. Note that the present (at least, as of March 2009—his ratings are dropping fast) prime minister of Japan, the famously manga-loving Taro Aso, is Shigeru Yoshida's maternal grandson.

166.2 FX: DOSA—corpse falling down

167.2 FX/balloon: VWOON VWOON—sound of cell phone vibrating

167.3 FX/balloon: CHA—placing phone on ear

168.2.1 FX/balloon: GASA—moving through foliage

168.2.2 FX/balloon: GASA—moving through foliage

168.2.3 FX/balloon: GASA—moving through foliage

168.3 FX/balloon: GASA—moving through foliage

169.3 FX/balloon: ZA ZA—digging sound

170.4 FX/balloon: PATAN—closing cell phone

172.3 FX/balloon: PASA—sound of newspaper landing on ground

175.5 FX/balloon: KOKU—nod

176.6 FX: ZURU—wet, dragging sound

177.4 FX/balloon: CHARARA CHAN CHARARA—ring tone

178.1.1 FX/balloon: CHIRARA JARARAN CHARA ZUN—ring tone

178.1.2 FX/balloon: PI—answering phone

178.4 FX/balloon: PI—hanging up

179.4 FX: PAKU PAKU—sound of puppet's mouth flapping

180.1 FX: SHIIIIN—sound of silence

181.4 FX: GARA—opening sliding door

183.1 FX: DADADA—kids running to Mumume-tan. A good reminder of the fact that many of the shows otaku lavish their, er, affection upon were technically directed at children; famous magical-girl series of the '90s such as *Sailor Moon* and *Cardcaptor Sakura* ran in *Nakayoshi* magazine, a shojo monthly (since 1954!) intended for readers in junior-high and elementary school. But with *Nakayoshi*'s circulation numbers having declined from 1.8 million in 1995 to 400,000 today, there is, of necessity, often more acceptance of the otaku element in marketing, with the perception that a contemporary magical-girl show such as *Futari wa Pretty Cure* (also a *Nakayoshi* title) is kept going in large part through otaku support (*vide* Kohta Hirano's plot to insert himself into the show in the back of *Hellsing* Vol. 7). The editor feels the idea that it's only otaku who sexualize this stuff is a *little* overstated; for example, it was quite possible to see a *Sailor Moon* routine at Japanese strip clubs in the mid-'90s, and they're not really an otaku thing. It's hard (*uh-huh-huh-huh*), you know, for me to properly express how much I like *Hellsing*. It's not so much conveying the intensity, as the proper tone. I'm not especially into vampires, Nazis, or the Alucard x Integra equation, so it's not like that. It's more like—in Howard Hibbett's *The Floating World in Japanese Fiction*, there's a woodcut reproduced from Ejima Kiseki's 1715 story "The Rake," where the rake, witnessing a dance at an inn, exclaims, "*It's so delightful I can hardly bear it!*" I'm that guy. By the way, in the same book, Hibbert shows a scene from Saikaku's *The Man Who Spent His Life in Love* of a man peeping on a bathing woman, suggesting not much has changed in Japanese pop culture these last three hundred years.

183.2 "Kei-chan," is it? If you'll recall, her full name is Keiko Makino.

183.6 **FX/balloon: NINI**—smirk

187.5 **FX: KAN KAN KAN**—warning bells

188.1 **FX: KAN KAN KAN KAN**—warning bells

188.2 **FX: PWAAAN**—train horn

190.5 **FX/balloon: NIHI**—smirk

191.5 The "Akashic Records" (from the Sanskrit *akasha*, "aether") refer to a supposed complete account of all human knowledge, past, present, and future, supposedly existing on another plane (also supposed to exist). The concept apparently arose in the nineteenth-century Theosophist movement and is very useful as an all-purpose plot device in fantasy and SF, sort of like orichalcum. Then again, it's possible that Kereellis is just *fucking with us*.

193.1 **FX/balloons: HO HO HO**—jogging man exhaling

193.5 **FX: ZAAA**—sound of wind through the trees

197.3 **FX: PYON PYON**—jumping up and down in happiness

197.4 **FX/balloon: CHU**—kiss

198.3 **FX/balloon: CHU**—kiss

198.5 **FX/balloon: KIIII**—sound of brakes

198.6 **FX: BIKU**—twitch of fear

199.1 **FX: GASA GASA**—tromping through bushes

199.3 **FX/balloons: BAN BURORORO**—door closing and car driving away

STAFF D

➤ **Embalming**
[エンバーミング]：死体修復

STAFF E

Channeling
[チャネリング]：宇宙人と交信

STAFF E'

Puppet
[マペット]：宇宙人が憑依

お届け物は死体です。

the KUROSAGI corpse delivery service
黒鷺死体宅配便

eiji otsuka 大塚英志 housui yamazaki 山崎峰水

publisher **MIKE RICHARDSON**
editor **CARL GUSTAV HORN**
editorial assistant **RACHEL MILLER**
omnibus edition designers **BRENNAN THOME**
and **ETHAN KIMBERLING**
original series designer **HEIDI FAINZA**
digital art technician **CHRISTINA McKENZIE**

English-language version
produced by Dark Horse Comics

THE KUROSAGI CORPSE DELIVERY SERVICE OMNIBUS EDITION BOOK THREE
© OTSUKA Eiji Jimusyo 2007, 2008 © Housui YAMAZAKI 2007, 2008. Edited by
KADOKAWA SHOTEN. First published in Japan in 2007, 2008 by KADOKAWA COR-
PORATION, Tokyo. English translation rights arranged with KADOKAWA CORPORA-
TION, Tokyo, through TOHAN CORPORATION, Tokyo. This English-language edition
© 2016 by Dark Horse Comics, Inc. All other material © 2016 by Dark Horse Comics,
Inc. Dark Horse Manga™ is a trademark of Dark Horse Comics, Inc. All rights reserved. No portion of this publication may be reproduced, in any form or by any means,
without the express written permission of Dark Horse Comics, Inc. Names, characters,
places, and incidents featured in this publication are either the product of the author's
imagination or are used fictitiously. Any resemblance to actual persons (living or dead),
events, institutions, or locales, without satiric intent, is coincidental.

Published by
Dark Horse Manga
A division of Dark Horse Comics, Inc.
10956 SE Main Street
Milwaukie, OR 97222
DarkHorse.com

To find a comics shop in your area,
call the Comic Shop Locator Service
toll-free at 1-888-266-4226

First edition: February 2016
ISBN 978-1-61655-887-1

1 3 5 7 9 10 8 6 4 2

Printed in the United States of America

Mike Richardson President and Publisher **Neil Hankerson** Executive
Vice President **Tom Weddle** Chief Financial Officer **Randy Stradley** Vice
President of Publishing **Michael Martens** Vice President of Book Trade Sales
Scott Allie Editor in Chief **Matt Parkinson** Vice President of Marketing **David
Scroggy** Vice President of Product Development **Dale LaFountain** Vice
President of Information Technology **Cara Niece** Vice President of Production
and Scheduling **Ken Lizzi** General Counsel **Davey Estrada** Editorial Director
Dave Marshall Editor in Chief **Scott Allie** Executive Senior Editor **Chris
Warner** Senior Books Editor **Cary Grazzini** Director of Print and Development
Lia Ribacchi Art Director **Mark Bernardi** Director of Digital Publishing

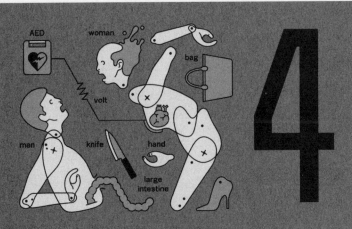

AED
woman
bag
volt
man
knife
hand
large
intestine
4

the KUROSAGI corpse delivery service
黒鷺死体宅配便
eiji otsuka 大塚英志 housui yamazaki 山崎峰水

STAFF A	STAFF B	STAFF C

Psychic	Dowsing	Hacking
[イタコ]：死体との対話	[ダウジング]：死体の捜索	[ハッキング]：情報の収集

→

OMNIBUS EDITION

The Corpse Delivery Service find they're being beaten to their clients by a bike-riding pilgrim with electrical means to reanimate the dead . . . A virtual gaming world may have players online but no longer *alive* . . . A child convicted of murdering her family is paroled to the very school where the Kurosagi crew have gotten part-time jobs! Plus five other strange stories!

M P D - P S Y C H O

多　重　人　格　探　偵

田島昭宇 ✕ 大塚英志

S H O - U   T A J I M A   ✕   E I J I   O T S U K A

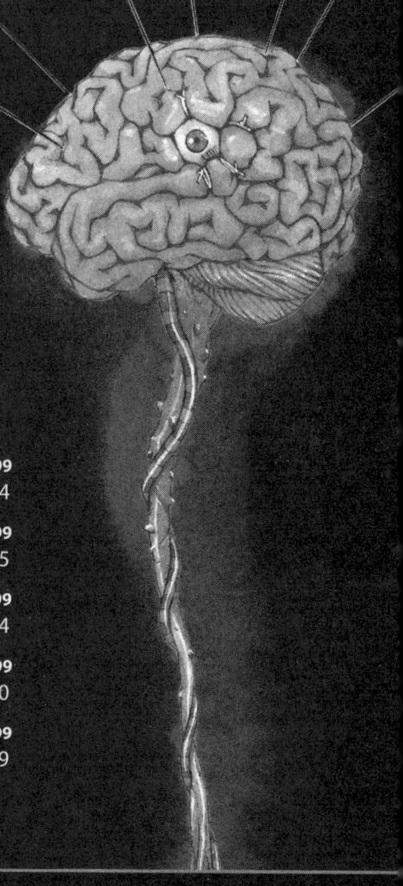

Police detective Yosuke Kobayashi's life is changed forever after a serial killer notices something "special" about him. That same killer mutilates Kobayashi's girlfriend and kick-starts a "multiple personality battle" within Kobayashi that pushes him into a complex tempest of interconnected deviants and evil forces.

Originally licensed by another U.S. publisher, *MPD-Psycho* was deemed too shocking for them to release, but Dark Horse is always prepared to give manga readers what they want and is proud to present *MPD-Psycho* uncensored, in all of its controversial and unflinchingly grotesque glory!

Volume 1 $10.99
ISBN 978-1-59307-770-9

Volume 2 $10.99
ISBN 978-1-59307-840-9

Volume 3 $10.99
ISBN 978-1-59307-858-4

Volume 4 $10.99
ISBN 978-1-59307-897-3

Volume 5 $10.99
ISBN 978-1-59307-962-8

Volume 6 $10.99
ISBN 978-1-59307-996-3

Volume 7 $12.99
ISBN 978-1-59582-202-4

Volume 8 $12.99
ISBN 978-1-59582-263-5

Volume 9 $12.99
ISBN 978-1-59582-330-4

Volume 10 $12.99
ISBN 978-1-59582-763-0

Volume 11 $12.99
ISBN 978-1-61655-386-9

DARK HORSE MANGA

DarkHorse.com

AVAILABLE AT YOUR LOCAL COMICS SHOP OR BOOKSTORE! TO FIND A COMICS SHOP IN YOUR AREA, CALL 1-888-266-4226.

For more information or to order direct visit darkhorse.com or call 1-800-862-0052 Mon.-Fri. 9 A.M. to 5 P.M. Pacific Time. *Prices and availability subject to change without notice.

MPD-PSYCHO © OTSUKA Eiji Jimusyo, SHO-U TAJIMA 1997, 1998. First published in Japan in 1997, 1998 by KADO-KAWA SHOTEN Publishing Co., Ltd., Tokyo. English translation rights arranged with KADOKAWA SHOTEN Publishing Co., Ltd., through TOHAN CORPORATION, Tokyo. (BL 7057)

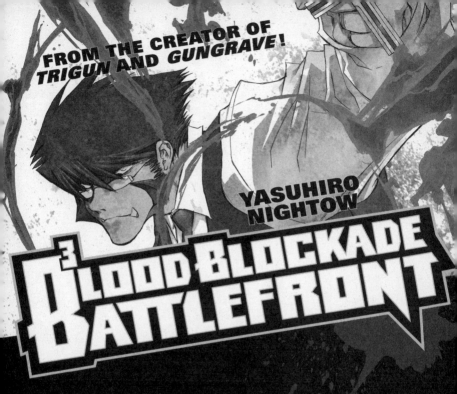

FROM THE CREATOR OF TRIGUN AND *GUNGRAVE!*

YASUHIRO NIGHTOW

³BLOOD BLOCKADE BATTLEFRONT

Three years ago, a gateway between Earth and the Beyond opened over New York City. In one terrible night, New York was destroyed and rebuilt, trapping New Yorkers and extradimensional creatures alike in an impenetrable bubble. New York is now Jerusalem's Lot, a paranormal melting pot where magic and madness dwell alongside the mundane, where human vermin gather to exploit otherworldly assets for earthly profit. Now someone is threatening to breach the bubble and release New Jerusalem's horrors, but the mysterious superagents of Libra fight to prevent the unthinkable.

Trigun creator Yasuhiro Nightow returns with *Blood Blockade Battlefront*, an action-packed supernatural science-fiction steamroller as only Nightow can conjure.

VOLUME ONE
ISBN 978-1-59582-718-0 | $12.99

VOLUME TWO
ISBN 978-1-59582-912-2 | $10.99

VOLUME THREE
ISBN 978-1-59582-913-9 | $10.99

VOLUME FOUR
ISBN 978-1-61655-223-7 | $12.99

VOLUME FIVE
ISBN 978-1-61655-224-4 | $12.99

VOLUME SIX
ISBN 978-1-61655-557-3 | $12.99

VOLUME SEVEN
ISBN 978-1-61655-568-9 | $12.99

AVAILABLE AT YOUR LOCAL COMICS SHOP OR BOOKSTORE To find a comics shop in your area, call 1-888-266-4226 For more information or to order direct: • On the web: DarkHorse.com E-mail: mailorder@darkhorse.com • Phone: 1-800-862-0052 Mon.–Fri. 9 AM to 5 PM Pacific Time.

DARK HORSE MANGA

Kekkai Sensen © Yasuhiro Nightow. All rights reserved. Original Japanese edition published by SHUEISHA, Inc., Tokyo. English translation rights in the United States and Canada arranged by SHUEISHA, Inc. (BI 7099)

DRIFTERS

KOHTA HIRANO

Heroes from Earth's history are deposited in an enchanted land where humans subjugate the nonhuman races. This wild, action-packed series features historical characters such as Joan of Arc, Hannibal, and Rasputin being used as chess pieces in a bloody, endless battle!

From Kohta Hirano, creator of the smash-hit *Hellsing*, *Drifters* is an all-out fantasy slugfest of epic proportion!

VOLUME ONE	VOLUME TWO	VOLUME THREE
978-1-59582-769-2	978-1-59582-933-7	978-1-61655-339-5

$12.99 each

**AVAILABLE AT YOUR LOCAL COMICS SHOP OR BOOKSTORE
TO FIND A COMICS SHOP IN YOUR AREA, CALL 1-888-266-4226**

For more information or to order direct: On the web: DarkHorse.com E-mail: mailorder@darkhorse.com
Phone: 1-800-862-0052 Mon.–Fri. 9 AM to 5 PM Pacific Time.

Drifters © Kouta Hirano. Originally published in Japan in 2010 by Shonen Gahosha Co., Ltd., Tokyo. English translation rights arranged with Shonen Gahosha Co., Ltd., Tokyo through Tohan Corporation, Tokyo. (BL 7092)

**DARK
HORSE
MANGA**

EDEN

It's an Endless World!

Be sure to check out *Tanpenshu*, Hiroki Endo's incredible slice-of-life short-story collections! Volumes 1 and 2 available now from Dark Horse Manga!

Volume 1
ISBN 978-1-59307-406-7

Volume 2
ISBN 978-1-59307-454-8

Volume 3
ISBN 978-1-59307-529-3

Volume 4
ISBN 978-1-59307-544-6

Volume 5
ISBN 978-1-59307-634-4

Volume 6
ISBN 978-1-59307-702-0

Volume 7
ISBN 978-1-59307-765-5

Volume 8
ISBN 978-1-59307-787-7

Volume 9
ISBN 978-1-59307-851-5

Volume 10
ISBN 978-1-59307-957-4

Volume 11
ISBN 978-1-59582-244-4

Volume 12
ISBN 978-1-59582-296-3

Volume 13
ISBN 978-1-59582-763-0

Volume 14
ISBN 978-1-61655-288-6

$12.99 each

AVAILABLE AT YOUR LOCAL COMICS SHOP OR BOOKSTORE!

To find a comics shop in your area, call 1-888-266-4226. For more information or to order direct visit DarkHorse.com or call 1-800-862-0052, Mon.– Fri. 9 A.M. to 5 P.M. Pacific Time. *Prices and availability subject to change without notice.

Eden © Hiroki Endo. First published in Japan by Kodansha Ltd., Tokyo. Publication rights for these English editions arranged through Kodansha Ltd. (BL 7041)

THE KAZUO KOIKE LIBRARY FROM DARK HORSE MANGA

LONE WOLF AND CUB OMNIBUS
Volume 1: ISBN 978-1-61655-134-6
Volume 2: ISBN 978-1-61655-135-3
Volume 3: ISBN 978-1-61655-200-8
Volume 4: ISBN 978-1-61655-392-0
Volume 5: ISBN 978-1-61655-393-7
Volume 6: ISBN 978-1-61655-394-4
Volume 7: ISBN 978-1-61655-569-6
Volume 8: ISBN 978-1-61655-584-9
Volume 9: ISBN 978-1-61655-585-6
Volume 10: ISBN 978-1-61655-806-2
$19.99 each

NEW LONE WOLF AND CUB
Volume 1: ISBN 978-1-59307-649-8
Volume 2: ISBN 978-1-61655-357-9
Volume 3: ISBN 978-1-61655-358-6
Volume 4: ISBN 978-1-61655-359-3
Volume 5: ISBN 978-1-61655-360-9
Volume 6: ISBN 978-1-61655-361-6
Volume 7: ISBN 978-1-61655-362-3
$13.99 each

SAMURAI EXECUTIONER OMNIBUS
Volume 1: ISBN 978-1-61655-319-7
Volume 2: ISBN 978-1-61655-320-3
Volume 3: ISBN 978-1-61655-531-3
Volume 4: ISBN 978-1-61655-567-2
$19.99 each

PATH OF THE ASSASSIN
Volume 1: ISBN 978-1-59307-502-6
Volume 2: ISBN 978-1-59307-503-3
Volume 3: ISBN 978-1-59307-504-0
Volume 4: ISBN 978-1-59307-505-7
Volume 5: ISBN 978-1-59307-506-4
Volume 6: ISBN 978-1-59307-507-1
Volume 7: ISBN 978-1-59307-508-8
Volume 8: ISBN 978-1-59307-509-5
Volume 9: ISBN 978-1-59307-510-1
Volume 10: ISBN 978-1-59307-511-8
Volume 11: ISBN 978-1-59307-512-5
Volume 12: ISBN 978-1-59307-513-2
Volume 13: ISBN 978-1-59307-514-9
Volume 14: ISBN 978-1-59307-515-6
Volume 15: ISBN 978-1-59307-516-3
$9.99 each

COLOR OF RAGE
ISBN 978-1-59307-900-0
$14.99

CRYING FREEMAN
Volume 1: ISBN 978-1-59307-478-4
Volume 2: ISBN 978-1-59307-488-3
Volume 3: ISBN 978-1-59307-489-0
Volume 4: ISBN 978-1-59307-498-2
Volume 5: ISBN 978-1-59307-499-9
$14.99 each

LADY SNOWBLOOD
Volume 1: ISBN 978-1-59307-385-5
Volume 2: ISBN 978-1-59307-443-2
Volume 3: ISBN 978-1-59307-458-6
Volume 4: ISBN 978-1-59307-532-3
$14.99 each

FOR MATURE READERS

AVAILABLE AT YOUR LOCAL COMICS SHOP OR BOOKSTORE! • To find a comics shop in your area, call 1-888-266-4226.
For more information or to order direct visit DarkHorse.com or call 1-800-862-0052 Mon.–Fri. 9 AM to 5 PM Pacific Time. Prices and availability subject to change without notice.

DarkHorse.com   New Lone Wolf and Cub © Kazuo KOIKE/Hideki MORI/Gosuki KOJIMA. Lone Wolf and Cub © Kazuo Koike and Goseki Kojima. Color of Rage — KARAADO © KAZUO KOIKE/SEISAKU KANO. Path of the Assassin © KAZUO
KOIKE/GOSEKI KOJIMA. Crying Freeman © by KAZUO KOIKE and RYOICHI IKEGAMI. Lady Snowblood © KAZUO KOIKE/KAZUO KAMIMURA. Samurai Executioner © Kazuo Koike and Goseki Kojima. Dark Horse Manga™ is a trademark of
Dark Horse Comics, Inc. All rights reserved. (BL 7063)